Writer's Market '74

Writer's Market '74

Edited by

Jane Koester and Rose Adkins

WRITER'S DIGEST   CINCINNATI, OHIO 45242

Library of Congress Catalog Card Number 31-20772
ISBN 0-911654-28-3

Published by
Writer's Digest, 9933 Alliance Rd., Cincinnati, Ohio 45242

Copyright © 1973 by Writer's Digest

Printed and bound in the United States of America

CONTENTS

Getting the Most from Your Writer's Market

This 45th edition of the *Writer's Market* will help you earn more from freelancing this year if you will not only use the Table of Contents, but will actually read it, like a book, a few pages at a time. You'll discover several different markets to which you can sell variations of your same research. And read the index, too. It will trigger other ideas.

A new addition to this volume is a section called "How Much Should I Charge?" aimed at the writer asked to do assignments on a freelance rather than staff basis.

To learn the editorial slant of a magazine is to learn what its readers like. To do this, try reading through categories unrelated to those that interest you. Compare Home and Garden with Theater magazines, for example. See how requirements are influenced by the differing readers? Learn to write for a magazine's readers and you'll sell your work to that magazine's editor. Study this book, and marketing trends will come clear to you.

Every listing in this book was mailed to the person or company who supplied it for verification, and all changes they made have been incorporated into the listings. A few magazine and publishing houses go out of business or move after *Writer's Market* is published, but most listings remain correct all year and can be relied on. Freelancers are reminded that, while editors switch jobs frequently, magazine requirements change more gradually because publications continue to reach the same audience for some time after an editor leaves.

A listing in this directory does not mean that *Writer's Digest* endorses the market; you must determine for yourself which ones you prefer to work with. We welcome information from you on address and editor shifts, discontinued markets, and dubious editorial business practices. Verified changes or warnings will be published in *Writer's Digest* market columns.

If a publication isn't listed, it is because (1) the publication doesn't actively solicit freelance material, (2) it doesn't pay for material, (3) it has suspended or ceased publication, (4) *Writer's Digest* has received complaints about it and it has failed to answer inquiries satisfactorily.

Each market is classified in its single best category. Priorities for classification are as follows: (1) type of market, e.g., consumer magazine, trade journal; (2) audience who reads it, e.g., women, juveniles, sportsmen; and (3) kind of material it buys, e.g., travel hints, cheesecake, regional articles. Headnotes refer you to overlapping categories which include magazines buying similar material.

All publications are copyrighted unless their listing says "Not copyrighted." Many publications that "buy all rights" will reassign rights to the author after publication; if they do, their listings indicate this. "Query first" in listings applies to nonfiction only; editors who require queries for fiction say so in their listing. Do not send fiction, poetry, fillers, etc., to an editor who doesn't specifically request that kind of material.

Listings are alphabetized on a word by word basis; for example:

A.D.
AAA Texas Division Texas Motorist
Abingdon Press
Accounting & Business Research
AFI-Atelier Films, Inc.
African Progress
All-Church Press, Inc.
Allen, George & Unwin Ltd.
Allen, J.A., & Co., Ltd.

A letter followed by a period is considered one word; a group of letters without periods (AA) are considered one word; hyphenated compounds are considered one word. Titles containing an & or the abbreviation St. are alphabetized as if the abbreviation were spelled out. Titles beginning with U.S. are also alphabetized as if spelled out.

Abbreviations used in this book are listed below. The Postal Service's two-letter state codes are used in addresses.

A30¢	30 Australian cents	MI	Michigan
b&w	black & white	MN	Minnesota
		MO	Missouri
ms(s)	manuscripts(s)	MS	Mississippi
N.A.	North American	MT	Montana
NZ	New Zealand dollars	NC	North Carolina
S.A.E.	self addressed envelope	ND	North Dakota
S.A.S.E.	self addressed stamped envelope	NE	Nebraska
		NH	New Hampshire
AK	Alaska	NJ	New Jersey
AL	Alabama	NM	New Mexico
AR	Arkansas	NV	Nevada
AZ	Arizona	NY	New York
CA	California	OH	Ohio
CO	Colorado	OK	Oklahoma
CT	Connecticut	OR	Oregon
DC	District of Columbia	PA	Pennsylvania
DE	Delaware	PR	Puerto Rico
FL	Florida	RI	Rhode Island
GA	Georgia	SC	South Carolina
HI	Hawaii	SD	South Dakota
IA	Iowa	TN	Tennessee
ID	Idaho	TX	Texas
IL	Illinois	UT	Utah
IN	Indiana	VA	Virginia
KS	Kansas	VI	Virgin Islands
KY	Kentucky	VT	Vermont
LA	Louisiana	WA	Washington
MA	Massachusetts	WI	Wisconsin
MD	Maryland	WV	West Virginia
ME	Maine	WY	Wyoming

NOTES ON FREELANCING

When a major publication like *Life* dies, or a *Saturday Review* falters under new management, writers begin to worry about the magazine business as a whole. They shouldn't. The fact is, that for every magazine which goes out of business, four or five new ones are created. The many new listings for magazines in this edition attest to the insatiable public appetite for a wide variety of subject matter. What kinds of publications are they?

Consumer Magazines. These are magazines bought on newsstands or subscribed to at home by the general public. Major ones are often called "the slicks" because they are printed on slick, smooth paper stock. Examples would be *Reader's Digest, McCall's, Playboy*, and *Sports Illustrated*. They may pay from $300 to $3,000 for an article or short story, but demand top-quality professional writing. The competition here is keen, as freelancers vie for the top money. Newcomers do break in every year, but only when they show outstanding talent.

Secondary consumer magazines include hundreds of specialized publications aimed at a limited portion of the general public which has a common interest by virtue of religious faith, a hobby, political viewpoint, membership in a fraternal organization, etc. Such publications include *St. Anthony Messenger, Workbasket, National Review, Rotarian*. In recent years, many of these have also turned to slick paper, although most do not have the high gloss of the mass-circulation magazines mentioned above. Rates at these magazines may vary from 1¢ to 10¢ per word, and although they also want professionally researched articles and well-written fiction, competitors at any one market are fewer here.

The "Little" magazines are independent journals of poetry, fiction, and commentary that are financially sponsored by men and women who seek pure literature and provocative thought. From these ranks have come some of America's greatest writers and some of its worst. These magazines include university quarterlies; the tabloid literary papers of New York, Chicago, and San Francisco; and the hundreds of multilithed "one-man reviews."

Recently there has been a proliferation of "Alternate and Radical" publications edited by communes, collectives, left- and right-wing liberals, and radical crusaders who raise their voices in opposition to the conventional or "establishment" press. Many pay only in contributor's copies, but some, like *Mother Earth News* and *Gnostica News*, offer respectable sums to writers.

Trade Journals. Sometimes called "the businesspaper press", trade journals are magazines whose editorial content is designed only for persons in a specific trade or profession. Editors are looking for freelance articles, photographs, cartoons, etc., that are allied to their fields and will help readers conduct themselves successfully in their businesses or jobs. For example, *Automotive News* is a magazine published for the manufacturers and dealers in the trade, who want information on selling or servicing cars.

Sponsored Publications. These are magazines produced by business firms, unions, associations, institutions, or specialty publishers, usually to be given away to employees, customers, or friends of the organization. They are called "internal" publications if they are written for the employees, dealers, salesmen of a company. "Externals" are produced either for stockholders or to give a good impression of the company to the general public, or to be mailed to persons influential in using the company's product.

Farm Publications. Most magazines for rural audiences are edited like technical trade journals, telling farmers and their wives how to raise crops and run their businesses successfully. But some are general interest consumer publications, like *Capper's Weekly*, which require no technical knowledge of farming but do insist that writers understand the interests of a farm audience.

These editors buy stories, articles, photographs, poems, clippings, and fillers. We'll discuss writing and marketing these individual types of material in the sections which follow, and then talk about the other active markets for writing, the book and play publishers, and television agents. Marketing greeting cards, audiovisual scripts, gags, and material for foreign publishers is discussed in the prefaces to these sections of *Writer's Market*.

WRITING AND MARKETING A SHORT STORY

This edition of the *Writer's Market* lists hundreds of markets for short stories. Studying the individual magazines is very important. Plot remains important at the smaller religious and juvenile magazines but at many quality markets you'll find some stories that are bought by editors because they illuminate an interesting character's mind or simply reemphasize in a well-written way, a closeness between two people, even though there may not be a "story" in the usual beginning-middle-end sense. However, this does not mean that editors are receptive to formless writing. The short story writer must cultivate disciplined originality —brilliance within a framework of knowledge of plot, character, style, atmosphere, and balance among them.

Always polish and repolish what you have written. A short story's effect depends on impact. No sentence you have written may meander; each sentence must contribute to the whole. And check carefully any facts in your story. Readers delight in reminding writers that, sparkling-characterization-in-your-last-story-or-no, Peking is not in Manchuria.

Finally, remember your First Commandment for Selling Writers and study the publication to which you wish to submit material. The groan of the man's magazine editor who receives stories about "A Boy and His Dog" is still heard regularly throughout the land. Writers who submit these inappropriate stories do real harm to their fellow professionals, as they encourage editors to save the time and trouble of reading unsolicited manuscripts by refusing to read unsolicited submissions at all.

To be a successful fiction writer you must have stories that cry to be told. You should be familiar with every technical aspect of your craft. Finally, you must write, write, and write.

WHERE CAN YOU SELL YOUR ARTICLES?

Opportunities for the nonfiction writer are better than ever; but, while many editors are looking hard for article ideas, their standards are high. Articles must be thoroughly researched, more smoothly written than ever before. The editor wants a point of view, an angle, an approach. He wants hard digging and thoughtful writing.

What types of articles are selling now? The simplest, and probably least helpful answer is "well-written ones." However, here are a few of the types in demand at top general interest magazines.

1. The Blockbuster. The controversial article that will make news, get talked about, sell copies.

2. The Big Name. Top magazine editors are always looking for a fresh angle on a "name"—the television or show business personality, the major political figure, the "inside" story about a person suddenly thrust into the national limelight. Personality profiles were always in demand but now they need more digging and depth.

3. Light, funny, offbeat pieces. Humor is an elusive thing and few people can agree on just what is funny, but editors continue to look for it.

4. America in the '70's. The dilemma of an affluent society vs. pockets of poverty; drug abuse; civil rights and black power; cities strangling in their own smog; upheaval in the Church; the role of the university—are all questions the reader seeks answers to ... but here too, from a "name" he respects as having unique experience with the problem and because the writer has made the discussion meaningful to the reader on his own level.

Probably the most notable change in some major magazine article styles in the last few years is the inclusion of the author's own personal reaction to the subject he's writing about. While the magazine article was always differentiated from the newspaper story because it had a particular viewpoint as opposed to (ideally) a straight presentation of facts, the magazine writer never wrote himself and his feelings into his article as much as he does now in "the new journalism."

Here are some of the article types frequently bought by special interest consumer magazines, house organs, trade journals.

1. The How-To-Do-It Article. Just about anything the reader can do, written in simple, easy-to-understand language, stressing personal satisfaction and/or possibly saving money—how to refinish furniture; how to fish for trout; how to get along with your husband; how to bridge the generation gap.

2. The Success Article. Tells how one person came to be as renowned or wealthy as he is. Trade journals use this to describe the techniques used by businessmen who have become tops in manufacturing or retailing; fraternal magazines use it to show how a Lion or Rotarian became a leader in the community; religious magazines use it to show how a person overcomes handicaps to his personal salvation.

3. The Expose. (But be sure you're on firm ground in case of a libel suit!) How a jury was bribed; inferior materials used in a public project; a shady business selling materials through fraud; conflict-of-interest involving a politician.

There are rules for writing effective nonfiction: First, you need to catch attention with the lead—it should arrest the reader in some way. It can be a quote, an anecdote, a statement of fact, or simply a mood paragraph. A lead is what makes you want to read the following article. But it must not cheat—you can't put a sex lead on a fishing story just to hook the reader. A good article has a theme and a point of view; and the ending should sum up and reinforce that point. Finally, ruthlessly eliminate all extraneous material from your article, material which doesn't support your theme.

The articles a magazine has published are not necessarily an infallible guide to what it will publish. While you are reading the October issue (put together last July), the editors may be planning to head off in an entirely different direction. However, reading a magazine is still the best guide, and it should give you a feeling for the magazine's basic approach.

HOW TO SELL AN ARTICLE

An editor can judge a short story or certain kinds of humor writing only by reading the manuscript itself. In the case of article writing, however, most freelancers save a lot of time and energy by using "the query letter" in advance of submitting the actual article.

After doing enough research to determine the selling points of his article idea to the editor, the writer drafts a letter to the editor suggesting the article and pointing up why he feels this particular magazine's readers would be interested in the idea.

Many freelancers discover that the way they start out their letter to the editor may turn out to be the first paragraph of their eventual article. It might start with a question, which the article would answer, or a provocative statement that the editor might take issue with, or an anecdote which illustrates the point the writer is going to make in the article.

Letters should be single-spaced and no longer than it takes to make your point. If you think your article idea is too complex to explain in a one-page single-spaced typed letter, you probably have an article which is too complex itself and you should be more selective about pinning down a specific point of view you want to get across.

Many freelancers who use the query letter try not to tell too much in their query letter so that there is still a certain amount of surprise and excitement left for the editor when he actually sees the article. But you can't hold back everything and you must do enough selling in the letter to convince the editor he wants to see the article.

What should you say about your own qualifications for writing the article? If you have some special background in this field, mention it. If not, but you plan to quote some experts on the subject, point that out. If you have not written for this particular editor before but have sold articles to comparable magazines he would respect, mention them. If you don't have any previous writing credits just don't mention it. Don't say "I'm just a beginner but I know I could do a good article for you."

If the editor is interested in your suggesion he will probably reply that he "will be glad to read it on speculation." This means that he does not promise to buy it but is interested enough to read it.

If you do get such a go-ahead from an editor, reply immediately indicating when he can expect the article from you. Always deliver the article by that date or before. If the editor says he is not interested in your idea, draft the letter to another editor and try your luck with someone else. (Remember that you may have to reslant your letter to the next editor to stress a slightly different angle.)

Selecting which editor to send your letter to, of course, is an important task, and it can only be done after studying the listings of magazine requirements in directories like this and in perusing back copies of magazines themselves.

WHAT ABOUT PHOTOGRAPHS?

Photographs are a powerful method of communication, and the writer who adds them to his article package is helping to guarantee sales that might otherwise be lost. Plus many editors pay extra for photos.

Top magazines require professional-quality photographs (see Rus Arnold's "Writer with a Camera" on p. 31 if you want to hit these), but you don't have to be an expert to sell photos to many secondary consumer and trade publications. Get an inexpensive 35mm or reflex camera that takes available-light photos with good contrast and learn to use it. Kodak publishes a helpful series of guides, most of them available at camera supply stores, for the new photographer. *How to Make Good Pictures* ($1.50) is a good one to start with.

Then take your camera along as you research your articles. You can photograph the person you're interviewing, or the campground you're reporting on for a travel magazine, or whatever else you're writing about, at the same time you're gathering facts. It saves you a lot of extra trips.

If you don't wish to invest in expensive darkroom equipment for developing your own photos, you have three choices open to you: (1) You can depend on the corner drugstore film service for both negative development and enlargements; (2) you can buy an inexpensive kit for developing your own negatives at home and then order enlargements from a local commercial photographer, or (3) you can have your film developed and contact printed by a commercial photo lab such as the ones Rus Arnold mentions. Custom labs charge about $1.75 for developing a roll of film and making an 8½x11″ proofsheet of your contacts. They charge about $1.75 for each 8x10 glossy enlargement.

OTHER PICTURE SOURCES

If you don't care to take your own pictures, you have these alternatives open to you: (1) you can try to interest a good local freelance photographer in working with you on speculation; if the article sells, you'd get paid for the text, he for the pictures; (2) you can advise the editor the name of a good local photographer (send some sample photographs and information about his professional background) and if the editor is interested in your article, he may assign the photographer to illustrate it; (3) you can hire your own local commercial photographer to shoot pictures to fit your specific article's needs, pay him his fee and then collect the total article package check from the editor; (4) you can assemble already existing photographs which would be helpful illustrations for your article. For example, you can usually purchase prints from local newspaper photographers for $2 to $5 each of material they have already shot which would be appropriate for your needs.

One source often untapped by writers is the library or museum, both of which offer photostat services. They will furnish, for a small fee, copies of documents' pages from old books, etc. Many public service agencies, public relations offices, industrial companies offer good quality photos free to writers. These pictures are usually connected with some commercial venture or public service project, but are well-suited for magazine and newspaper feature articles.

HOW CAN YOU PUBLISH YOUR POETRY?

The same general rules are applicable in marketing poetry as in marketing any other kind of writing: (1) check this book to see which magazines say they use poetry; (2) study samples of the magazines themselves to see the kinds of subject matter, styles, and line lengths preferred; and (3) submit neatly typed copy to an appropriate magazine and enclose a self-addressed stamped envelope.

You must be serious about writing poetry, as the pay is usually nominal. The periodicals of greatest interest to serious poets are those which have a reputation for publication of excellent poetry, such as some of the university quarterlies and other well-established literary magazines. For all publications, short poems have a better chance than those over twenty lines. The odds at these markets favor serious poetry over light verse.

A steady income from submissions to quality publications is almost impossible to come by, but there are some commercial outlets which buy material from people with a facility for verse forms. Chief of these are the greeting card publishers. Work in this field is completely anonymous, requires a high degree of expertness not only in poetic forms but in knowledge of the field and of audience preference.

Many other markets exist for poetry. Newspapers, church and other organizational organs, even trade journals, often use verse. There are, too, perennial "little" magazines appearing and disappearing on the scene. Many small publications are not copyrighted, however; so the poet should realize he may be placing his work (that he might want to re-use later) in the public domain.

You may be a competent craftsman with a flair for verse. And certainly this is nothing to be sneezed at—you can make a steady income. Becoming a poet is quite another thing, though. There are contests and competitions which give you some chance to gain prominence, but for the most part it is a long process of building a reputation through consistently good, published poetry. It is hardly worth the trouble unless poetry matters more to you than anything else in life.

WHAT KINDS OF FILLERS DO EDITORS BUY?

Depending on the amount of advertising space sold, or other considerations, a magazine editor is often faced with the problem of one or two inches of white space at the end of a column in the back of the magazine where an article or story has ended. It is to fill these brief spaces that he buys fillers. They may be thought-provoking quotations, short verse, a humorous news item or short nonfiction "featurettes."

The short "featurettes" range from 10 to 750 words. They are usually single ideas, tightly written, telling the reader how to: (1) save time, (2) increase business, (3) do something more easily, (4) improve his personality, (5) improve human relations. Your ideas can come from your own experiences as a gardener, National Guardsman, hot rodder or expectant mother—the range is infinite.

Editors also buy features for entertainment or inspiration: (1) historical anecdotes, (2) general interest items on unique people, business, community programs, (3) humor. Human interest pieces are fun to write. The lead is very important, too, since you have so little room in which to maneuver, but pruning every excess word and phrase is a vital necessity.

Regardless of the type of filler you write, these rules hold true: (1) double-space on 8½x11 paper, and put your name and address in the upper left-hand corner; (2) keep a carbon, as some editors don't return short pieces, (3) make sure photographs with practical how-to fillers are sharp and clear, or that illustrations are neat drawings from which the magazine's art department can make finished sketches.

If the editor buys clippings, these should be related to his magazine's subject matter and readership. Paste them on an 8½x11 sheet of white paper, and put your name and address in the upper left-hand corner, with title of the newspaper (or other source) and the issue date directly underneath the clipping.

WHAT IS THE BOOK MARKET?

Today's book market, like the magazine market, is predominately a nonfiction market. While a single novel, in all editions, may sell millions of copies, there are 10 times as many nonfiction titles published each year as there are novels. That means you have a better chance getting published if you have a nonfiction book idea. How to submit an outline and sample chapters or a complete manuscript, rights and royalties, and other facets of marketing books are discussed in the preface to the Book Publishers section.

A word about poetry books: Unless you are a Pulitzer Prize winning poet, or have in some other way built a name it is very difficult to place books of poetry. Why? Because publishers lose money on them since few people buy books of poetry (Rod McKuen is the exception). Most people have to build a reputation first in magazines and then only can they sometimes find a publisher. Those publishers who do publish poetry are so listed in this directory.

WHAT IS THE MARKET FOR PLAYS?

While Broadway is still the mecca for the big money producers, Off-Broadway, Off-Off-Broadway, university theaters, and many other community theaters offer a vehicle for the new playwright today.

In addition, there are markets among play publishers who print playbooks for the use of schools and other amateur groups. While the playwright will be offered a royalty agreement by most play producers, some play publishers will offer only an outright fee rather than a royalty. Experienced playwrights refuse to surrender all rights to their plays in exchange for a single payment. How much money should a playwright expect? For amateur performances of a one-act play, the rates usually are $10 for each performance. For amateur performance of a long play—$50 to $75 for the opening performance and $25 for each succeeding performance. In a professional theater, royalty agreements vary widely. It could be a flat fee of several hundred dollars for a series of performances or a percentage of box office gross of from 2% to 10%.

SELLING THE TELEVISION SCRIPT

Although a writer can sell an article to a magazine or a book manuscript to a book publisher without an agent, he cannot sell a script to a television show except through an agent. A list of literary agents appears in this edition of *Writer's Market*. Those agents which do deal especially with television scripts are so indicated.

Television agents are interested in seeing scripts submitted for shows already on the air or announced to be on the air in the coming season. They are not interested in just an idea for an existing series, or looking at a short story that a writer thinks will make a good television show. They are only interested in scripts written in teleplay form [see examples published occasionally in *Writer's Digest* magazine, or sample scripts in books such as Philip Wylie's *Writing for Television*] that show the writer has an awareness of the limitations in settings in a particular show, the peculiar idiosyncrasies of characters in a specific show, the general mood of a show. The writer who does not work directly for the producer of such a show must spend a great deal of time familiarizing himself with the material he sees on his home television screen and analyzing it for technical details.

There have been a few rare cases where a freelance writer not located in California has sold (through an agent) a script for an existing series, but to be a full-time professional television writer, you must live in California where the shows are produced and you will have a better chance of getting assignments.

Since the film business has changed so much in recent years—production is no longer centered in a few large movie companies, and "film properties" are assembled, along with casts, directors and production facilities by many different independent producers—it's not possible to keep a current list of markets in this directory for films.

Writers who have motion picture film scripts should submit them to agents, the same as for television, since producers will not look at

```
Your Legal Name                        About 0,000 words
(Your Pen Name)
Street Address
City, State, Zip Code




                    CENTER YOUR TITLE IN CAPS

                              by

                    Your Name (or Pen Name)

     Begin your story or article about halfway down the
first page, three or four spaces below the name you wish
to appear on it when published.  Indent paragraphs five
spaces, always double space your copy, and type only on
one side of the paper.  Double space between paragraphs--
do not triple space.
     Letters, telegrams, newspaper clippings, etc., when
used within the body of the text, should also be double
spaced; they must be given an extra indentation of five or
more spaces to make them stand out.
     For pica type, your margins should be 1 1/4" at the
top and on the left; about 1" on the right; and 1" on the
bottom.  For elite type, use a uniform margin of 1 1/2"
on all four sides.  Stay away from any paper, typewriting,
or ribbon that is "offcolor."
```

First Page of Manuscript

scripts directly from writers, and agents are more likely to know which of the independents might be interested. To familiarize themselves with current trends in film subject matter and the industry situation in general, writers should read copies of publications such as *Daily Variety* (6404 Sunset Blvd., Hollywood CA 90028) or *Hollywood Reporter* (6715 Sunset Blvd., Hollywood CA 90028). The Writers Guild of America West (8955 Beverly Blvd., Los Angeles CA 90048) offers a Manuscript Registration Service to writers—both Guild members and nonmembers—who want a legal date of completion for their material. Details and registration fee information available from the Guild.

DON'T FORGET THESE OTHER "BACKYARD MARKETS"

What opportunities for freelance jobs are there in your own community? Does your nearby metropolitan daily need a correspondent from your county? Does a local retail store which advertises in your paper need someone to help it prepare advertisements? Does a man who is running for political office need a writer to help prepare publicity releases, his speeches before club groups, etc.? Does a local businessman who is attending a convention of his business need help with a speech he is going to give to fellow hardware dealers? Does the local board of education want to obtain Federal funds and need help in preparing a proposal to submit to a government agency? Is your town about to celebrate its centennial and possibly interested in publishing a memorial booklet you would write? These are just some ideas to start. Taking a closer look at your own community will give you others.

PREPARING AND MAILING A MANUSCRIPT

The way your manuscript is typed tells an editor a lot about you as a writer. If it's sloppy, with uneven margins, filled-in *e*'s and *a*'s, and pages of all different lengths, he'll know you're an amateur. But if you type your material cleanly, in the established format that all professionals use, you impress him as a writer who's serious about his craft and his markets. Here's the way to prepare an article or short story for submission.

Type your name and address (and pseudonym, if you use one) in the upper left-hand corner of the page. The number of words (rounded to the nearest hundred) appears in the upper right-hand corner. Drop down a few lines and type your title, then beneath it the name (a pseudonym if you use one) you wish to appear on your published piece.

Drop down a few more lines and begin your story or article about halfway down the first page, three or four spaces below your name or pseudonym. Indent paragraphs five spaces, *always double space your copy, and type only on one side of the paper.* Double space between paragraphs—do not triple space.

john doe

2250 SUNNYSIDE LANE • ANYTOWN, N.J. 08000 • TELEPHONE (200) 560-0000

john doe

2250 SUNNYSIDE LANE • ANYTOWN, N.J. 08000

Writer's Business
Letterhead and
Envelope

Quotations from letters, telegrams, newspaper clippings, etc., when used within the body of the text, should also be double spaced; they must be given an extra indentation of five or more spaces to make them stand out.

For pica type, your margins should be 1¼″ at the top and on the left; about 1″ on the right; and 1″ on the bottom. *For elite type*, use a uniform margin of 1½″ on all four sides. Stay away from any paper, typewriting, or ribbon that is "offcolor."

If you set your margins as suggested, each line of pica type will contain about ten words, making it easy for you to compute the total in your manuscript. Every word counts, even the word "a." Or you can count the exact number of words on three (for a short script) or five (for a manuscript of fifty or more pages) pages and compute the total from that.

Each page after the first should be numbered consecutively and carry your last name in the upper left-hand corner of the page. The page number goes at the top right-hand corner. Try to type the same number of lines on each page of your manuscript—use micrometric carbon paper, which has a guide along one margin to show you how many lines you have left on the page; or make a guide along one edge of your backing sheet, letting the line numbers extend ¼″ at left or right from under the page you're typing on.

When typing a book manuscript, type your name, address, and the number of words in the work on the book's title page as described. All subsequent pages carry the author's last name in the top left corner and the page number in the top right corner. Chapter opening pages give the chapter number and title about a third of the way down the page; the text begins two or three lines below that. Number the pages of a book consecutively, not chapter by chapter.

Many writers find that it helps them sell if they invest in a simple business letterhead for queries, correspondence, and covering letters. Like a professionally typed manuscript, it makes a good impression on the editor. Usually it's best not to include "Freelance Writer," "Author," or any list of your credits on the letterhead. (Credits belong *in* your letter, if you're submitting to an editor who doesn't know you.) However, you may wish to list the *professional* writers organizations you belong to—these should be printed at the bottom of the sheet. (An example of acceptable letterhead appears on page 22.)

Mail your article or short story, the pages paperclipped (not stapled) together, in a large 9″x12″ outer envelope with stiff cardboard backing. (For manuscripts of five or fewer pages, you may fold them in thirds and mail in a regular business envelope.)

A book manuscript can be mailed in the box that your typing paper came in. Send the pages loose, without stapling or binding in any way. Clip return postage to your covering letter or to the first page of your manuscript. (First class letters cannot be enclosed with manuscripts at the Special Foreign Rate to Canada.)

Any book (it's wise to insure it) or periodical manuscript may be mailed as "Special Fourth Class Rate—Manuscript" anywhere in the United States and its possessions for 14¢ for the first pound and 7¢ for each pound or fraction thereafter. This mail is slower than First Class, and manuscripts receive fourth class handling; but the smaller expense remains a great advantage. (Some postmasters in smaller Post Offices are not familiar with this special rate, and if they question your use of it, just refer them to Postal Regulation 135.13.

Keep in mind, however, that the Post Office is not required to return your package to you if for some reason it is undeliverable at the addressee's end, unless you include the statement "Return Postage Guaranteed" on the front, and pay the postage to get it back.) If a letter is enclosed, 8¢ must be added to the Special Fourth Class rate and the envelope marked "First Class Letter Enclosed." A letter may be enclosed with a manuscript mailed under First Class rates. First class surface rates to Canada are the same as U.S. 8¢ per oz. 1 thru 12 ozs.; 13 ozs. to 16 ozs. (inclusive) $1.00. Over 1 pound consult Post Office. Air Mail rate straight 11¢ per oz. Weight limit 60 lbs.

Include a return 9x12 self-addressed envelope with return postage stuck to it; or include your inexpensively printed business reply envelope if you decide to arrange with your Post Office for a business permit. (All that's required is that you deposit funds in advance to cover reply postage, and that your reply envelope comply with postal regulations.) Do not use U.S. stamps for return postage from Canada. You must enclose International Reply Coupons as U.S. stamps are not valid for mailing in that country. (Buy Coupons at the Post Office.)

Always keep one or two carbons of any manuscript you submit, to guard against possible loss in the mails (or at the printer's, in the event your piece is accepted for publication.) To help you keep track of where your manuscript has been, type on the back of this carbon the name and address of the market you send it to, and the date. If the manuscript is returned with a rejection slip, mark the date it came back, and enter the name and address of the next market where you submit it. It's always a good idea to have the names of two or three markets where you plan to send your work next marked down already on the back of your carbon.

Some of the listings in *Writer's Market '74* include the phrase "will consider photocopied submissions." This does not mean that a number of copies of an original manuscript can be submitted simultaneously to a number of markets. It simply means that some editors are willing to consider the submission of a photocopy rather than the original ms. This permission is granted with the understanding that it is being submitted in photocopy form to only one editor at a time.

Some markets—especially religious and juvenile publishers, *will accept simultaneous submissions* because their circulations are noncompetitive. In such cases, the listings include the phrase "will consider simultaneous submissions."

HOW LONG SHOULD YOU WAIT FOR A REPLY?

The freelance writer who sends off a story or an article to a magazine usually turns to the other ideas on his desk and temporarily forgets about his submission. But one day he realizes it's been too long since he heard anything from his brainchild. He wonders if, whether he inquires about it, he'll be jeopardizing a possible sale. Are they really considering it or has the editor had an accident and it's at the bottom of a big stack of unread mail? Maybe it was lost?

Depending on the magazine's staff and the amount of mail it gets, an editor may take from 3 weeks to two months to report on submissions. A book editor may require 3 months or longer. And remember that when an editor says he reports in six weeks, that means six weeks from the time he received your manuscript. If you live on one coast and he's on the other, it may have taken a week or 10 days to reach him, so take that into consideration.

If you've had no report from a publisher by the maximum reporting time given above, just write a brief inquiry letter to the editor asking if your manuscript or article query (and give the story title or a brief description of the article) is still under consideration. It's a good idea to enclose a self-addressed stamped envelope with this letter too, to expedite a reply. (And, of course, your original submission must always include sufficient return postage.)

In the rare case where a publisher fails to report even after your inquiry, after waiting a reasonable length of time (four to six weeks) write a registered letter to the editor, advising that you are withdrawing your manuscript from that publication's consideration for resubmission elsewhere. Then retype an original copy of the manuscript and resubmit it to another market. Also, send the details to *Writer's Market* so we can follow up with the publisher in question and check against possible other complaints in our files. If the facts warrant, we will then publish appropriate notices in *Writer's Digest* magazine.

THE LAW OF COPYRIGHT

The U.S. Congress has been working for several years on a revision of existing copyright law. This may be completed in 1974 or 1975, but in the meantime Philip Wittenberg's *The Protection of Literary Property* (The Writer, Inc.) and Margaret Nicholson's *A Manual of Copyright Practice* (Oxford) are good references for writers' copyright questions.

Various pamphlets and circulars on copyright are available free from the U.S. Copyright Office, Library of Congress, Washington DC 20559. And this office will also supply information about copyright search, filing copyright, etc., on request.

Scattered throughout this book are references to the various types of rights magazine editors buy on the articles, stories, poetry, etc., they publish. Following is a list of definitions of each of these rights. Book rights are discussed in the preface to the Book Publishers.

The law of copyright in foreign countries differs from that in America. When submitting material for consideration to a foreign publication or book firm, writers should ask at that time what rights the particular firm or publication purchases.

All Rights. Some magazines, either because of the top prices they pay for material, or the fact that they have book publishing interests or foreign magazine connections, sometimes buy only "All Rights." A writer who sells an article or story or poem to a magazine under these terms, forfeits the right to use his material in its present form elsewhere himself. Some editors who buy all rights will reassign the remaining rights to the author on request after publication. If the writer thinks he may want to use his material later (perhaps in book form) then he must take care in submitting to these types of markets.

First Serial Rights. The word serial here does not mean publication in installments, but refers to the fact that libraries call periodicals "Serials" because they are published in serial or continuing fashion. First Serial Rights means the writer offers the periodical the right to be first to publish his article, story, or poem in a periodical. All other rights to the material belong to the writer. (The publisher holds these rights as trustee of the author, however, and must assign them to the author on his request by letter. The letter should identify the author, the work, the copyright and be signed.) Variations on this right are, for example, First North American Serial Rights. Some magazines use this purchasing technique to obtain the right to publish first in both America and Canada since many American magazines are circulated in Canada. If they had purchased only First U.S. Serial Rights, a Canadian magazine could come out with prior or simultaneous publication of the same material. When material is excerpted from a book which is to be published and it appears in a magazine or newspaper prior to book publication this is also called First Serial Rights.

Second Serial Rights. This gives a newspaper or magazine the opportunity to print an article, poem or story after it has already appeared in some other newspaper or magazine. The term is also used to refer to the sale of part of a book to a newspaper or magazine after the book has been published, whether or not there has been any first serial publication.

Reprint Rights. Some magazines simply refer to the type of rights they buy as reprint rights. This means they are willing to buy a story or article which has previously appeared in another publication.

Simultaneous Rights. This term covers articles and stories which are sold to publications (primarily religious magazines) which do not have overlapping circulations. A Baptist publication, for example, might buy "Simultaneous Rights" to a Christmas story which they like very much, even though they know a Presbyterian magazine may be publishing the same story in a Christmas issue. Any writer who submits to such a magazine has the responsibility of indicating to that editor, either on the first page of the manuscript itself or in a covering letter, that the manuscript is a "simultaneous submission."

Public Domain. Any material which is "published," that is, printed, mimeographed, multilithed, Xeroxed, or even typed copies which are sold or distributed to the public in a publication which has not been previously copyrighted, is placed in the public domain. That is, it is free for the public to use thereafter without infringing on the rights of the author of such material. The writer can still try to sell it elsewhere but so can anyone else. And it cannot subsequently be copyrighted in its same form. If you want to protect a poem that will be published in an uncopyrighted newspaper or literary magazine, you can get application forms from the Copyright Office for a "Contribution to a Periodical"; have the newspaper or magazine publish the copyright symbol, year, and your name with your contribution when it appears; and then on publication send 2 copies of the issue with the filled-out application form and a check for $6 to the Copyright Office.

Can you copyright before publication? According to the present copyright laws no manuscript can be copyrighted before publication except a dramatic script or musical composition. However, a writer's manuscript is protected by common law before publication.

LAW AND THE WRITER

How much freedom does the nonfiction writer have to "pick up" the ideas, facts and anecdotes of others? First, ideas and facts are not copyrightable—only the specific words and phrases used by a writer as he expounds his ideas, reports the facts, and tells his anecdotes. Rewriting in your own words is the best way to avoid most copyright problems.

But what about using directly quoted material that is copyrighted? The doctrine of "fair use" of copyrighted material as established in the courts is this: is the use reasonable and not harmful to the copyright owner's rights? There are no specific number of words, lines or notes that can be defined as fair use. Five hundred words from a long book might be "fair use" but only 25 words making up a complete poem might be copyright infringement. Apply this test to what you want to use: am I impairing the market value of the original?

The use of material from letters is another problem facing writers. The law says that although the receiver has physical possession of the letter, the thoughts and ideas expressed in it still belong to the writer of the letter. That means you need permission of the sender to quote from any letter you want to use.

Libel. You can be sued for damages if you print a false, defamatory statement which tends to injure the reputation of a living person or exposes him to public hatred, contempt or ridicule. Fiction can be dangerous too, if someone can prove you were using him as a model for an unsavory character in your story or novel. The three major lines of defense against libel are truth, privilege (for example, editorial reporting of official proceedings) and fair comment (on public matters).

Invasion of Privacy. The laws differ from state to state so if there is any doubt about a photograph you want to take or copy you want to write about a specific person, getting his permission first is the safest thing to do. The most common defenses against suits for invasion of privacy are: the person is currently a public figure or the name or picture was not used for trade or advertising purposes.

Consult an Attorney. If you have a hot article or book idea but are worried about some of the legal ramifications, the best thing to do is to consult an attorney. You'll find "Lawyers' Referral Services" listed in most Yellow Pages. This is usually the local Bar Association. For from $10 to $25 you can consult up to one hour with an attorney on your problem.

WILL AN EDITOR STEAL YOUR IDEA?

The vast majority of editors are scrupulously honest in their dealings with writers and bend over backward to respect the writer's property. When an editor likes a writer's idea well enough to want to use it, but doesn't care for the manuscript itself, he'll return the manuscript and offer to buy the idea only for a sum less than his usual rates. (He pays less because he'll have to write the idea up himself or assign it to another writer.) If the writer prefers not to sell his idea, the editor simply won't use it—although he'll probably buy a manuscript that's similar if he receives one from another writer. Sometimes a writer will submit a manuscript that resembles one the editor has already purchased, or that contains an idea the editor has already thought of, or that isn't quite as good as another writer's manuscript that arrived the same day with the same basic idea. In this situation, the editor will merely return the manuscript to the writer, with or without an explanation, and not make an offer to buy the idea. In a few rare instances, an editor will inadvertently use an idea that he's remembered from a rejected manuscript—without realizing where it came from. However, the possibility of this happening should not concern the writer, because editors take care to avoid the occurrence.

—Kirk Polking

HOW MUCH SHOULD I CHARGE?

How does the freelancer decide what to charge for various writing services? His fee depends basically on two things: (1) how much he thinks his time is worth, and (2) how much the client is willing or can afford to pay.

Since the rates paid by advertising agencies, retail stores and other firms who are consistent users of part-time freelance writers vary from city to city, the list which follows can only serve as a rough guideline. The best thing for the freelancer to do is contact other writers, or friends in business who have used part-time freelancers in his area and get some idea of what's been paid for certain kinds of jobs in the past.

Writer's Digest regularly publishes in its monthly magazine, articles on "Freelance Job Opportunities for Writers." Here are some of the jobs and the rates which have been paid to writers for them.

Advertising copywriting: $3.50 to $7.50 per hour or a "package" price which might be just $25 for a press release or small ad on up to several hundred dollars for a more complex assignment.

Associations, writing for, on miscellaneous projects: $3 to $5 per hour.

As-told-to books: author gets full advance and 50% royalties; subject gets 50% royalties.

Audio cassette scripts: $120 for 20 minutes.

Audio visual scripts: $1,000 to $1,500 advance against 5 to 10% royalties for 5 to 10 script/visual units.

Biography, writing, for a sponsor: $500 up to $3,000 plus expenses over a 4-year period.

Booklets, writing and editing: $500 to $1,000.

Book manuscript copy editing: $2 to $5 per hour.

Book manuscript rewriting: $500 to $1,000 and up.

Business films: 10% of production cost on films up to $30,000. $150 per day; $20 per hour where % of cost not applicable.

Comedy writing, for night club circuit entertainers: Gags only, $5 to $7, Routines, $100 to $300 a minute. Some new comics try to get 5-minute routines for $100 to $150; but top comics may pay $1,500 for a 5-minute bit from a top writer with credits.

Commercial reports, for business, insurance companies, credit agencies, market research firms: $1 to $2 per report.

Company newsletters, "house organs": $50 to $200, 2 to 4 pages.

Conventions, public relations for: $500 to $5,000.

Correspondent, magazine, regional: $5 per hour.

Criticism, art, music, drama, local: free tickets plus $1 to $5.

Editing, freelance book: $2 to $5 per hour.

Editing a group of religious publications: $75 to $250 per month.

Educational film strips: $1,200.

Educational films, writing: $200 for one reeler (11 minutes of film); $1,000 to $1,500 for 30 minutes.

Educational grant proposals, writing: $50 to $125 per day plus expenses.

Family histories, writing: $200 to $500.

Fiction rewriting: $150 for 10-page short story to $10,000 for complete novel rewrite, under special circumstances.

Folders, announcement, writing: $25 to $350.

Gallup Poll interviewing: $1.75 per hour.

Genealogical research, local: $3 to $5 per hour.

Ghostwriting business speeches, major markets: $500.

Ghostwriting political speeches: $10 to $20 per hour.

Government, local, public information officer: $10 per hour, to $50 to $100 per day.

History, local, lectures: $25 to $100.

House organs, writing and editing: $50 to $200, 2 to 4 pages.

Industrial and business brochures, writing: 4 pages, $120; 8 to 12 pages, $200.
Industrial films: $500 to $1,200, 10-minute reel; 5 to 12% of the production cost of films that run $750 to $1,000 per release minute.
Industrial promotion: $7.50 to $40 per hour.
Industrial slide films: 14% of gross production cost.
Journalism, high school teaching, part-time: % of regular teacher's salary.
Library public relations: $5 to $25 per hour.
Magazine stringing: $5 per hour.
New product releases, writing: $250 plus expenses.
Newspaper ads, writing, for small businesses: $10 for small 1-column ad.
Newspaper column: 80¢ per column inch to $20 per column.
Newspaper stringing: 20¢ to 50¢ per column inch.
Paperback cover copy: $40 to $75.
Pharmacy newsletters: $125 to $300.
Photo-brochures: $700 to $15,000.
Photocomposition on electric typewriter: $6 per hour, 5¢ per line on short jobs.
Political campaign writing: $200 to $250 per week; $25 per page piecework jobs.
Programmed instruction materials, writing: $1,000 to $3,000 per hour of programmed training provided. Consulting/editorial fees: $25 per hour; $200 per day, plus expenses, minimum.
Public relations: $125 per day plus expenses.
Publicity writing: $30 per hour; $100 per day.
Radio copywriting: $60 to $165 per week.
Record album cover copy: $75 to $100.
Retail business newsletters: $200 for 4 pages, writing, picture taking, layout and printing supervision.
Retainer for fund-raising writing for a foundation: $500 per month.
Retainer for publicity and PR work for an adoption agency: $200 per month.
Retainer for writing for businesses, campaign funds: usually a flat fee but the equivalent of $5 to $20 per hour.
Reviews, art, drama, music, for national magazines: $5 to $50.
School public relations: $2 to $10 per hour.
Shopping mall promotion: 15% of promotion budget for the mall.
Slide presentation for an educational institution: $1,000.
Slide film, single image photo: $75.
Sports information director, college: $120 to $700 per month.
Syndicated newspaper column, self-promoted: $2 each for weeklies; $5 to $25 per week for dailies, based on circulation.
Teaching creative writing, part-time: $15 to $25 per hour of instruction.
Teaching high school journalism, part-time: % of regular teacher's salary.
Teaching home-bound students: $5 per hour.
Technical typing: 25¢ to 35¢ per page.
Technical typing masters for reproduction: $2 per hour for rough setup then $1 to $3 per page or $4 to $5 per hour.
Technical writing: $5 to $12 per hour.
Textbook and Tradebook copy editing: $3.50 to $5 per hour. Occasionally 75¢ per page.
Translation, literary: $25 to $50 per thousand words minimum.
Travel folder: $100.
TV news film still photo: $3 to $5.
TV news story: $15 to $25.
TV filmed news and features: $15 per film clip.

If there are substantial differences in rates in your area for any of these jobs—or you'd like to add other job categories with which you have personal experience, please drop a line with the facts to Kirk Polking, Jobs for Writers, care of *Writer's Market*, 9933 Alliance Road, Cincinnati, Ohio 45242. Your comments will help other freelancers and future editions of this directory.

A book containing more detailed discussions of each of these Jobs for Writers is in preparation by *Writer's Digest*.

WRITER WITH A CAMERA
by Rus Arnold

Every nonfiction writer must have some working knowledge of what goes into providing an editor with photographs. Today the visual image is as much a part of the article as is the written word.

Much of the technology of picture-taking has been simplified or eliminated by modern cameras, leaving the photojournalist free to concentrate on the more professional area of what to photograph, how to make an effective statement.

Any camera that can produce sharp, clear photographs can be used to illustrate articles. Your choice should be the one you find easiest to use. [Before you buy a camera, make sure you can return it for a full refund if you find it difficult to handle. Usually you'll only need to shoot one roll of black and white and one of color film to tell.—Ed.] Many writers are still working with the 2¼x2¼ twin-lens reflex (Rolleiflex, etc.), once the standard, and some have the more expensive 2¼x2¼ single-lens reflex (Hasselblad, etc.). But the 35mm camera is by far the most popular with professional photojournalists, because of its smaller size, lighter weight, greater flexibility and adaptability, and its lower operating cost.

One of the many great advantages of the 35mm camera is its built-in exposure control, either manual (you set exposure by matching two needles) or automatic. There are a number of reliable 35mm automatics at low cost (Canonet, etc.). The more advanced worker prefers a single-lens reflex, which can take a variety of lenses (Pentax, Canon, Nikon, etc.) so he can eventually have wide-angle and telephoto lenses.

Once you have a camera and have mastered the simple instructions in the manual, the most important thing to learn is what to photograph. This means studying your markets. Editorial demands change; the kids-pets-cheesecake pictures that were once so salable now bring only rejection slips. They were decorative, but today's editor wants illustration, action, and relevance. And the relevance must be to that particular editor's readers.

How would you photograph a man with a fishing rod? That depends on the magazine. For *Field & Stream* it would be a fisherman wading in the rapids and fighting a prize fish. But for *Fishing Gazette* it had better be a sporting-goods dealer, placing the rod into an effective display rack, or demonstrating it to a customer.

The successful writer-with-a-camera does all his research and interviewing first, then decides what is best said in pictures, what is best said in words. (Why describe a scene when you can photograph it?) He then takes off the hat labeled "Writer" and puts on the one labeled

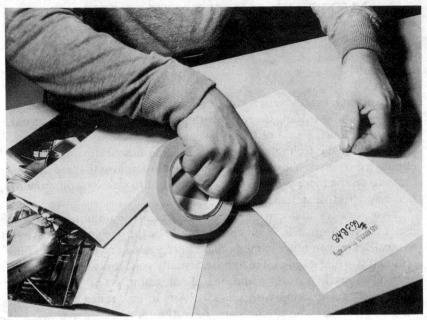

Photo © Rus Arnold

Each photograph should be separately labeled with all the information the editor may need so he can write his captions. The double-spaced caption sheet can be fastened to the bottom of the print with masking tape on the back surfaces.

"Photographer." With picture-taking, as with writing, his emphasis goes into telling the story simply, directly, clearly, rather than fancy writing or pictures-to-hang-on-a-wall. The pictures, with their captions, should reinforce, illustrate, and amplify the text, rather than repeat it.

An editor gets a first impression of your article from its appearance as it reaches his desk. Package it in a professional manner, and you get a more careful reading. The right size prints, on the right kind of paper—that's as important as double-spaced typing on white paper with adequate margins and proper headings. The prints should be 8x10, either high-gloss or on smooth stock. A very few editors will accept 5x7's, but snapshot prints and Polaroids brand you as a novice. A few markets still insist on color transparencies being 2¼x2¼ or larger, but the 35mm transparency is now almost universally accepted and—in the better markets—preferred. Color prints are not acceptable at most markets.

Each photograph should carry your name and address (rubber-stamped on the back), some identifying number (written lightly on the back in pencil, so as not to damage the photo surface itself), and should be accompanied by adequate captioning information. You do not have to write the actual caption; the editor does that, to fit his style and space. But he does want you to tell him who is in the picture, what they are doing, where it takes place, and anything else that might be pertinent. And woe be to the writer who gets the names or addresses wrong! [For a good example of caption writing, see the one above, printed as submitted.—Ed.]

Whether you hire a photographer or sell your own picture-taking services, you should be aware of the standards set up by ASMP (The Society of Photographers in Communication, 60 E. 42nd St., New York NY 10017) which are followed by most pros whether or not they are ASMP members and are agreed to by major magazine publishers. The minimum rate is $200 for a shooting day plus all necessary travel and material costs, with the photographer retaining all rights. The minimum payment for one-time publication of a photograph out of the photographer's files is $50 for black-and-white. Rates for color vary by size and the magazine's circulation.

Prints to be mailed should be protected with a sandwich of oversize corrugated boards, which can be cut from a grocery carton, with the ribs of one sheet at right-angles to the ribs of the other. Corners cut from old envelopes can be used, with tape, to hold the prints away from the edges of the cardboard.

Photo © Rus Arnold

Photo © Rus Arnold

Color transparencies should be mailed in their cardboard mounts, not in glass. Your name and address, and some picture identification, can be placed on the small mounts; the rest can be typed on a separate sheet. The transparencies, each in a transparent protective sleeve, can be hinged with tape to the top of the caption sheet.

There are, of course, journalists who accept lower rates—and others who get more, often considerably more. Whatever you find acceptable, be sure to have it clearly understood, and in writing. If you send an editor photographs not of your own making, be sure to indicate the source and terms, whether these are free pictures from a government agency or an institution, from a public relations firm or one of the people involved in the story—or pictures by some other photographer other than yourself, submitted for possible purchase. If they are free pictures, be sure you have clearance for publication in writing, and convey to the editor any requirements as to picture credits.

As a general rule, you need no permission from people who appear in photographs published as editorial matter in magazines or newspapers. The need for written permission really occurs only if the pictures are used for advertising. Some magazines, however, do require signed releases (particularly true detective, confession, and company-sponsored publications); these usually will provide the necessary blank form, to be signed by every individual whose face is recognizable. However, if a picture is to be used in such a way as to injure the subject financially, socially, or emotionally, even a signed release may be inadequate; an experienced publications attorney should be consulted before such publication.

To guarantee that an editor will use your pictures, you should consider his layout problems. Give him a choice of vertical and horizontal on every situation if possible and you help him fit the space he has. Give him a variety of situations (long shots, medium shots, close-ups) and you help the editor create a more interesting page. The pro works in terms of a series rather than individual pictures, except when he is doing a cover shot. Then he follows some set rules. If it's a newsstand magazine the prime interest should be in the upper half, where it will show on display in newsstand racks. In any case, the face or action should point to the right, to urge the reader to open the book. The picture must be the right shape for the particular publication, and there must be "waste" space in the composition in those areas where that magazine overprints its name, date, and contents.

While most of your shooting will be for articles, don't overlook the book and encyclopedia market. While studying these publications will show you many posed and stilted pictures, don't try to offer such work. These are precisely what editors are trying to avoid in their new editions. They want the same dramatic treatment that the magazines are using, and many of them are now even using series instead of single pictures.

What about processing? The beginner has enough to learn without getting involved in darkroom procedures, or risking his results. And most pros would rather be out researching or shooting or talking to editors, than working in the darkroom. So there are now custom labs that work exclusively for journalists. Typical are Modernage, 319 E. 44th St., New York 10017, and Astra, 6 E. Lake St., Chicago 60601. You can trust such labs, and rely on their guidance and advice.

If you do want your own darkroom, processing the black-and-white films calls for less investment and less room than printing, since you need perfect darkness only long enough to load the film into a daylight tank. A closet might do. A tank, a few film-reels, a good thermometer, a kitchen bell-timer, bottles, a funnel—$25 to $50 will do it. For making enlargements, however, you need more (and livable) darkroom space, an enlarger (from about $150 and up), adequate sink space, safelights, trays, print washer, print dryer. It's best to visit a few one-man darkrooms before you decide on your own.

As for color processing, even the fussy photojournalists who insist on doing their own black-and-white darkroom work, usually send the color out to a lab. But they avoid the discount houses, trusting their work only to custom labs or to the film manufacturer's facilities.

A SAMPLE MODEL'S RELEASE

> In consideration for value received, receipt whereof is acknowledged, I hereby give (name of firm or publication) the absolute right and permission to copyright and/or publish, and/or resell photographic portraits or pictures of me, or in which I may be included in whole or in part, for art, advertising, trade or any other lawful purpose whatsoever.
>
> I hereby waive any right that I may have to inspect and/or approve the finished product or the advertising copy that may be used in connection therewith, or the use to which it may be applied.
>
> I hereby release, discharge and agree to save (name of firm or publication) from any liability by virtue of any blurring, distortion, alteration, optical illusion or use in composite form, whether intentional or otherwise, that may occur or be produced in the making of said pictures, or in any processing tending towards the completion of the finished product.
>
> Date_____   Model_____
>
>   Address_____
>
>   _____
>
> Witness_____

As Rus Arnold pointed out in the preceding section, most magazines and newspapers do not require releases on photographs to be used strictly for editorial illustrations. But a model release *is* required from all recognizable persons in a picture which is to be used for advertising purposes (including photographs appearing in sponsored publications, company brochures, etc.), or which *may* be used for advertising purposes (for example, a magazine cover).

The release protects the photographer against possible suits for invasion of privacy or legal damages, since many states have laws which forbid a name, picture, or quotation from being used for commercial purposes without the subject's authorization. If the person in the photograph is a minor, the release must be signed by his parents or guardians. The "value received" varies from an established professional model's fee down to $1.00 or the subject's simple gratification in seeing his photograph published.

Get a release for an editorial photograph whenever it's convenient, to hold open the possibility of later selling it for commercial use. And never send your original model release along with a photograph—copy it, and keep the original safely in your files, where you can find it, should you need it.

CONSUMER MAGAZINES

Alternate and Radical Publications

The publications here offer writers a forum for expressing anti-establishment or minority ideas and views that wouldn't necessarily be published in the commercial or "establishment" press. Included are a number of "free press" publications that do not pay except in contributor's copies. Writers are reminded that these publications sometimes remain at one address for a limited time or prove unbusinesslike in their reporting on, or returning of, submissions. However, the writer will also find a number of well-established, well-paying markets in this list.

THE ADVOCATE, Box 74695, Los Angeles CA 90004. Editor: Dick Michaels. For homosexuals. "Complete news and feature coverage of American homosexual scene, just as a regular newspaper covers heterosexual scene. Various columns, opinion, etc." Biweekly. Circulation: 30,000. Buys all rights, or first rights if writer prefers. Pays on publication. Will send a sample copy to a writer for 50¢. Query not required, but advisable. Reports in 2 weeks. Enclose S.A.S.E. for return of submissions.
Nonfiction: News or features having to do with homosexuals. Length: 1,000 to 3,000 words. Payment is $15 to $30 usually.
Photos: 8x10 b&w glossies purchased with mss and with captions. Payment is $10 to $20.
Fillers: Newsbreaks, puzzles, clippings, jokes, and short humor pertaining to homosexuals.

ALTERNATIVES/THE MODERN UTOPIAN, P.O. Box 36604, Los Angeles CA 90036. Editor: Richard Fairfield. For "college students and professors, middle-class professionals, high-school- and college-educated persons interested in interpersonal relations, alternative life styles." Quarterly. Circulation: 5,000. Buys or acquires all rights. Occasionally uses manuscripts from freelancers. Pays on publication: a negotiated amount, in copies, and/or with a membership entitling writer to receive all materials published during the year. Will send a sample copy to a writer for $1. No query required. Reports in 1 month. Enclose S.A.S.E. for return of submissions.
Nonfiction, Photos, Fiction, and Poetry: "Emphasis is on the interpersonal, critique, and personal growth . . ." The writer should use "his own style—personalized, descriptive." Uses articles on "communal or cooperative living, unusual life styles, free schools, social change, personal growth, conscious expansion, utopian thought." Interested in how-to, personal experience, interview, inspirational, humor, expose, and photo articles; contemporary problems, religious, and humorous fiction; and brief poetry. Photos are purchased with manuscripts and captions; submit b&w glossies.

AMAZON QUARTERLY, 554 Valle Vista Ave., Oakland CA 94610. Editors: Laurel Akers and Gina Roberson. For "lesbians—all ages, races, and in all geographical locations. Mostly college educated. Feminists." Subject matter includes "anything without a heterosexual bent—not necessarily lesbian—just definitely not heterosexual." Established in 1972. Quarterly. Circulation: 2,000. Copyrighted. "All rights are reserved to the authors. Their written consent is required for reprint." Payment in contributor's copies. Uses about 20 mss per issue. Will send sample copy to writer for 80¢. Submit complete ms. Will consider photocopied submissions. "Just send in a manuscript with a stamped, self-addressed envelope and include about 2 sentences of biographical data. We only accept material written by women." Reports in 2 months. Enclose S.A.S.E. for return of submissions.
Nonfiction and Photos: "We need essays, theoretical explorations of lesbianism and reviews. We'd also like articles that attempt to show where lesbians are 'at' across the country; how different areas, cities, etc., are moving. Reviews of current lesbian

literature. Finds of old journals of lesbian interest. Articles on lesbians in 'herstory'." Length: open. "Interested in art photos with lesbian content."
Fiction: Interested in lesbian fiction. Length: open.
Poetry: "Poetry is not our particular interest, but we do accept some; not heterosexual."

ASTRAL PROJECTION, P.O. Box 4383, Albuquerque NM 87106. Editor: Skip Whitson. For "mainly young people interested in the coming earth changes and occult knowledge." Publishes "2 or 3 times a year." Established in 1968. Circulation: 25,000. Buys 3 or 4 mss a year. Payment on acceptance. ("As we are a volunteer publication we pay less than most for articles.") Will send a sample copy to writer for $1. Will consider photocopied submissions. Reports within 2 months. Enclose S.A.S.E. for return of submissions.
Nonfiction: Interested in publishing material pertaining to the "occult, metaphysical, earth changes, health foods, and living off the land."

BLACK MARIA, P.O. Box 230, River Forest IL 60305. Editorial Collective: Ms. Ippolito, Everett, and Rowley. For "mostly women, but some men. Interests lie mostly in that our audience is interested in redefining woman's position in society, the family, and herself." Established in 1971. Subject matter "must be written by women. Subjects include those pertinent to women's liberation, e.g., redefining history to include woman, life style change through role reversal in family. Any and all articles, stories, poems, etc., which are pro-woman and define her as an active, intelligent, complete human being. Case histories of self-discovery, etc. Do not have to directly relate to woman's liberation if well-written and thorough." Quarterly. Circulation: 1,000. Acquires all rights, but will reassign rights to author after publication. Also acquires second serial rights. Uses 30 mss a year. Pays on publication in contributor's copies. Will send sample copy to writer for $1. Will consider photocopied submissions, but prefers original. Submit seasonal material 3 or 4 months in advance of issue date. Returns rejected material in 2 months. Reports on material accepted for publication in 1 month. Enclose S.A.S.E. for return of submissions.
Nonfiction: Writer should use "understatement in stories or articles with a 'moral,' gutsy and to the point, pro-woman, non-rhetorical, etc., in all submissions. Clearly our focus is woman's liberation, but we prefer a more subtle approach than political rhetoric. Nothing which hits one over the head! We are not here to preach, but rather to share experiences and information, whether gained through personal insight or study in, a certain field. And although our focus and main concern is 'woman's liberation,' any article or library piece well-written and exciting can find a place in our magazine—we do not demand adherence to a particular set of beliefs, short of a positive attitude towards women's move to free themselves from the home or any position which may be restrictive to them. We would not like immediate, newsy articles about specific events. Since our magazine is quarterly, we prefer more general, nontransitory themes for articles. Topical subjects and themes *Black Maria* would like covered are the International Women's Movement, alternative living arrangements (role reversal, commune, single women, gay women, etc.), minority women's views towards women's liberation (will print articles that disagree or situations that don't work out." Buys informational, personal experiences, interviews, inspirational, historical, think, and book reviews. Seeking "book reviews on unknown women writers, books out-of-print (by or about autobiography, history, women). Meant as synopsis as well as reviewing." Length: open.
Photos: Purchases photos with or without mss and purchased on assignment. Buys 2x3 to 8x10 b&w glossy and magazine format 6x9. No color. Photo theme should be related to overall subject of magazine, "but need not be limited to photos of women. Any photography submitted by a woman will be considered."
Fiction: "Fiction hopefully would not deal with the immediate, in and of itself. Using a recent occurrence to prove a point is okay." Buys experimental, mainstream, fantasy, historical fiction. Also buys serialized novels. Length: open.
Poetry: Accepts traditional forms, free verse, avant-garde forms and light verse related to subject matter. "Poets should submit at least 3 examples of their work." Length: 4 to 75 lines.

THE BOSTON PHOENIX, 1108 Boylston St., Boston MA 02215. For the young, educated, middle class and counterculture. Weekly. Circulation: 200,000. Buys all

rights, but will reassign rights to author after publication. Buys 10 short stories, and 100 poems a year. Payment on publication. Will send free sample copy to writer on request. Query first. Will consider photocopied submissions. Reports in 4 to 6 weeks. Enclose S.A.S.E. for response to query or return of submission.
Nonfiction, Fiction, and Poetry: "Anything that's well-written to appeal to our audience. Movies, rock, books, politics. Experimental, mainstream, and humorous fiction; serialized novels. Themes open. Short stories up to 5,000 words." Pays $50 to $100. Poetry any length but usually not longer than 4 typewritten double-spaced pages. Blank verse, free verse, and avant-garde forms. Pays $10 flat rate.

BOTH SIDES NOW, 1232 Laura St., Jacksonville FL 32206. Collective editorship. An alternative newspaper for "persons involved actively or as a spectator in counter-culture movements, politics, contemporary art, music, theatre, organic living. Readership is generally college-educated and not necessarily young—many students, but also many middle-aged progressives." Monthly. Circulation: 6,000. All rights revert to author. Uses 15 to 20 mss a year. Pays in copies. Will send a sample copy to a writer for 25¢. No query required. Reports in 3 weeks. Enclose S.A.S.E. for return of submissions.
Nonfiction and Photos: Articles on "the counter-culture and radical/liberal politics in the U.S. and the world. No particular expectations in style or structure. Will consider anything well-researched and coherent. Staff does tend to favor the surprising and avant-garde. Will accept and often do publish work with viewpoints not identical to staff. We are always interested in material to apply to departments such as 'Health Foods,' 'Religion,' 'Women,' and others." Uses how-to's, personal experience articles, interviews, profiles, inspirational articles, humor, spot news, coverage of successful business operations, historical and think pieces, exposes, new product articles, photo features, travel pieces, and reviews of film, music, and literature. Brevity preferred. B&w glossies and camera-ready drawings purchased with mss.
Fiction: Humorous and historical fiction; satire, science fiction, stories dealing with contemporary problems, with "the youth culture."
Poetry and Fillers: Contemporary, avant-garde, light verse. Newsbreaks, clippings, jokes, short humor.

BREAKTHROUGH!, 2015 South Broadway, Little Rock AR 72206. Editor: Korra L. Deaver. For "anyone of any age, interested in psychic awareness." Established in 1971. Bimonthly. Not copyrighted. Payment in contributor's copies. Will send a free sample copy to writer on request. Write for editorial guidelines sheet for writers. Submit only complete ms. Will consider photocopied submissions. Reports within 2 months. Submit seasonal material 2 months in advance. Enclose S.A.S.E. for return of submissions.
Nonfiction and Poetry: "*Breakthrough!* is published primarily for the purpose of instruction. 'How-to' articles which explain how one acquires an understanding of, and personal use of such pyschic gifts as clairvoyance, precognition, astral projection, etc., are welcome. These are uncharted paths in the soul's journey through eternity, and an experience which throws light on any breakthrough in these areas will help others to achieve a similar awareness. Most magazines treat the phenomena itself by factual reporting, or interviews with known psychics. We want to instruct others in achieving a similar awareness." Uses informational, how-to, personal experience, inspirational, and think articles. Length: less than 5,000 words. Open to all forms of poetry, on themes relating to psychic awareness.

THE COOPERATOR, 17819 Roscoe Blvd., Northridge CA 91324. Editor: Louis K. Acheson, Jr. Published by the International Cooperation Council, a coordinating body of about 130 organizations who "foster the emergence of a new universal man and civilization based upon unity in diversity among all peoples." Quarterly. Circulation: 1,200 to 1,500. Not copyrighted. Uses 25 mss a year. Pays in contributor's copies. Will send free sample copy to writer on request. No query required, but "suggest writer read *The Cooperator* first if possible." Reports in 2 months. Enclose S.A.S.E. for return of submission.
Nonfiction, Fiction, Photos, Poetry, and Fillers: "General materials related to our purposes wanted. Need content and style. Top priority is 1,000-to 2,000-word articles that deal with science, art, philosophy, religion, education, human relations or other fields in search of universals." Also wants 300- to 500-word reviews of suitable

current books, films, or plays; good poetry up to 40 lines; short humor and quotes; and b&w glossy photos. Uses some fiction of 1,000 to 2,000 words. Pays in contributor's copies.

THE DIXON LINE, Box 278, Los Alamitos CA 90720. Editor: Dixon Gayer. For audience that is "politically and socially liberal and progressive; college or university educated for the most part; not the New Left, but many shades from moderate to very liberal. We are dedicated to racial equality, world peace, public education, less hypocrisy." Monthly. Circulation: 1,500. Acquires "whatever rights we can get, free. We don't need all rights." Uses 20 mss a year. Will send a sample copy to a writer for 50¢. Returns rejected material "as soon as possible." Reports acceptance by sending a copy of the publication. Enclose S.A.S.E. for return of submissions.
Nonfiction: "We are 'extremely' interested in articles about 'extreme' groups—and that term takes in everything from the KKK to the Birch Society. Also interested to some degree in New Left activities. We love good political and social satire. Good, I said." Wants personal experience, interviews, profiles, humor, spot news, good think pieces, exposes. "Articles should be relatively short (unless the piece is very outstanding). Prefer objective style similar to newspaper (either straight news or feature style). Not interested in opinion pieces except from writers of some stature or authority. Content must be documentable. Don't send poetry, short stories, or articles about subjects we don't deal with." Length: 500 to 3,000 words.

THE DRAMA REVIEW, 32 Washington Place, Room 73, New York NY 10003. Editors: Michael Kirby, Paul R. Ryan. For "theatre practitioners, students, professors, general theatre-going public." Established in 1955. Quarterly. Circulation: 15,000. Buys all rights. Buys 5 to 10 mss a year. Payment on publication. Will send sample copy to writer for $2. Query first or submit complete ms. Submit seasonal material 3 to 4 months in advance. "Each issue has a special theme. Writers should read current issue to see what is planned for next issue." Returns rejected material in 2 to 4 weeks. Reports on material accepted for publication in 3 months. Enclose S.A.S.E. for return of submissions or reply to queries.
Nonfiction and Photos: "Articles documenting contemporary and historical trends in the performing arts. Objective reporting; factual, as opposed to critical." Length: "Article should be only as long as it needs to be (no padding)." Pays 2¢ to 3¢ a word. 8x10 b&w photos purchased with or without mss. Captions required. Pays $10 to $15 per published photo.

THE DRUMMER, 4221 Germantown Ave., Philadelphia PA 19140. Editor: Al Robbins. For an educated audience between ages of 18 and 45, interested in politics, the arts, and the manifestations of current reality; interested in progressive social change. Established in 1967. Weekly. Buys first North American serial rights. Payment on publication. Will send free sample copy to writer on request. Will consider photocopied submissions. Submit only complete ms. Reports in 2 to 3 weeks. Enclose S.A.S.E. for return of submission.
Nonfiction and Photos: "Political sagas, interesting, in-depth, well-researched news stories that get the story behind the news. Subjects: environment, social change, alternative culture, social phenomena, 'hot' in-depth news; appeal to Philadelphia audience important. I encourage writers to be as creative as possible while at the same time maintaining the awareness that they're writing for a large, diversified audience." Also wants camping and/or travel stories for summer, with a countercultural emphasis. Informational, how-to, interview, humor, think articles, expose, photo, travel and spot news articles wanted. Length: 3,000 word maximum. Pays $5 to $50. Photos are purchased with or without accompanying mss, captions optional. "Good quality and contrast" b&w. Pays $5 to $10. Photo Dept. Editor: Neil Benson.
Poetry: "We publish the best work of young poets. Blank verse, free verse, and avant-garde forms. Interested in innovative forms." Pays $2 per poem.

ELYSIUM NEW LIVING, 5436 Fernwood Ave., Los Angeles CA 90027. Editor: Ed Lange. Publication of Elysium Institute. For behavioral scientists. Established in 1961. Quarterly. Circulation: 20,000. Rights purchased vary with author and material; may buy all rights. Buys about 8 mss a year. Pays on acceptance. Will send a sample copy to writer for $1. Query first. Submit seasonal material 3 months in advance. Reports in 2 weeks. Enclose S.A.S.E. for response to query or return of submission.

Nonfiction and Photos: Publishes material on "behavioral sciences, dealing with body taboos, sex education, and developing human potential. Explores alternate life styles and deals frankly with sexual subjects. Writer should use documented research. No exploitative or sensational material. Intimate, first-person approach." Buys how-to, personal experience articles, and interviews. Length: 1,500 words. Pays "up to 5¢, sometimes 10¢ per word." Photos are purchased with mss; with captions only. 8x10 b&w glossies. Pays $10. Pays $25 for 2¼x2¼ color prints.

EVERGREEN REVIEW, 53 E. 11 St., New York NY 10003. Editor: Barney Rosset. Not actively seeking freelance material at present.

GAY SUNSHINE, P.O. Box 40397, San Francisco CA 94140. Established in 1970. For "gay people of all ages throughout North America and abroad. We especially appeal to people interested in the political and literary aspects of the gay liberation movement." Bimonthly. Circulation: 8,000. Payment in contributor's copies. Query first. Reports within 4 weeks. Will send sample copy to writer for 50 cents. Will consider photocopied submissions. Enclose S.A.S.E. for reply to queries.

Nonfiction and Photos: "We are a newspaper of gay liberation, and publish interviews, personal articles, political articles and graphics. Recent literary interviews include Allen Ginsberg, John Wieners, Harold Norse. Material should relate to gay people and gay consciousness. Author should write to us first regarding style, structure, etc." Length: Maximum of 10 to 15 pages, typed double-spaced. Payment in contributor's copies or "negotiable". B&w photos purchased on assignment. Captions required. No color.

Fiction: Experimental. "Should relate to our theme." Length: "negotiable; contact us first."

Poetry and Fillers: Blank verse, free verse and avant-garde forms. Newsbreaks.

GNOSTICA NEWS, P.O. Box 3383, St. Paul MN 55165. Editor: Ronald Wright. For "general cross section" interested in occult and psychic subjects. Established in 1971. Monthly. Circulation: 10,000. Rights purchased vary with author and material. Buys 4 to 6 mss per issue. Pays on acceptance. Will send a free sample copy to a writer on request. Submit only complete ms. Will consider photocopied submissions. Submit seasonal material one month in advance. Reports in 2 weeks. Enclose S.A.S.E. for return of submissions.

Nonfiction, Photos, Fiction, Poetry, and Fillers: Publishes material on "science fiction, occult, psychology, parapsychology, astronomy, science, organic gardening and cooking, 'back to nature theme,' and ecology. We emphasize the occult more than other magazines like us, but with a scientific approach." Buys informational, how-to, personal experience, interview, profile, humor, historical, photo articles, spot news and reviews of all types. Length: 100 to 5,000 words. Payment is $1 to $50. Photos purchased with or without mss. Payment is open. Buys science fiction and fantasy. Length: 10,000 words maximum. Payment is $100. Poetry relating to occult subject matter. Payment is $10 maximum. Puzzles, clippings, jokes, short humor. Payment is $10 maximum.

GRASS ROOTS FORUM, P.O. Box 472, San Gabriel CA 91778. Editor: Henry Wilton. For "ages 14 to 70, from thinking, intelligent craftsmen, to PH.D.'s, M.D.'s, etc." Established in 1967. Monthly. Circulation: 5,000. Rights acquired are open. Uses 20 mss a year. Payment in contributor's copies. Will send a sample copy to writer for 10¢. Submit only complete ms. Will consider photocopied submissions. Reports in 2 weeks. Enclose S.A.S.E. for return of submissions.

Nonfiction, Photos, Poetry, and Fillers: Publishes material on "political, economic, social subjects; all aspects of our culture; current events. In prose or verse; from liberal perspective. Emphasis on truth, reality, justice as it would serve the underdog. We do not want erotica, trivia, falsehoods, etc. We are seeking cogent, astute observations regarding national issues, political events; activities of dissenting groups and minorities." Buys informational, interview, humor, expose articles; book and music reviews. B&w photos must be of general interest and authentic. Photos used with or without mss and on assignment. Accepts traditional, avant-garde, blank, and free verse. Buys jokes and short humor. Payment in contributor's copies.

GREEN EGG, P.O. Box 2953, St. Louis MO 63130. Editor: Tim Zell. For "intellectuals, libertarians, radical thinkers, humanists, ecology-oriented persons, science fiction fans and authors, counter-culture people, communitarians, avant-garde life style people." Established in 1967. 8 times a year. Circulation: 1,000. Copyrighted. Pays in copies; "free subscription to all contributors, whether their material is used or not." Will send a sample copy to a writer on request. No query required. "If unsolicited mss are to be used eventually, they are filed. Writers must specify if they wish notification of acceptance or return of ms." Submit seasonal material at least 3 months in advance. Reports in 1 month, "only if return or acknowledgment requested." Enclose S.A.S.E. for return of submissions.
Nonfiction, Photos, and Fiction: "Any material dealing with various aspects of the Aquarian Age; science fiction, occult, Paganism, communes, sex, magic, witchcraft, philosophy, books, ESP, erotica, vegetarianism, theology, ecology, psychology, revolution, evolution, Velikovsky, nudity, rational anarchy, experimental marriage forms, counter-culture, life styles, astrology, anthropology, etc. Orientation toward Neo-Paganism and the Aquarian age is specifically sought. No negative, 'anti-this-or-that' material, Christian fundamentalism, pro-war views, or establishment thinking. Not politically oriented." Uses how-to's, interviews and profiles of movement people, inspirational and think pieces, humor, exposes, photo features, book reviews; science fiction, historical and pagan religious short stories, and the occult. Length: 250 to 2,800 words. B&w glossies used with mss.
Fillers: Newsbreaks, book reviews. Length: 100 to 650 words.

THE LADDER, P.O. Box 5025, Washington Station, Reno NV 89503. Editor: Gene Damon. For Lesbian and women's liberation audience that is "serious, and much more concerned with reform than revolution." Subject matter includes "any and all material that pertains to the gaining of full human status for all women, including Lesbians." Bimonthly. Circulation: 3,150. Acquires one time use rights, insists on acknowledgement when material is reprinted. Pays in contributor's copies. Will send a sample copy to a writer for $1.25. Query preferred for articles and photos. Reports in 20 days. Enclose S.A.S.E. for return of submissions or reply to queries.
Nonfiction: "Any article dealing with women or Lesbians, having to do with women's rights, women's liberation, any civil rights violation that particularly affects women, biographical articles on famous women. No particular slant. Prefer clean, concise style." Length: 1,500 to 5,000 words.
Photos: "Use many, as illustrations for stories and articles." Mostly pictures of women. B&w glossies.
Fiction: "Prefer fiction connected to Lesbians in some way, but will accept relevant sensitive portraits of women, especially those that show their limitations in a male-ordered, male-run world. No limitations except no pornography. Can be either sympathetic or not, but must be well-written. Need many short-shorts. Using increasing amount of fiction with future issues." Length: 300 to 5,000 words.
Poetry: "By and about women, all and any women. Probable preference given to Lesbian themes but quality is the primary criterion. Using increasing amounts of poetry."
Fillers: Especially needs short humor. Also wants newsbreaks, clippings, jokes, and other fillers.

LOS ANGELES FREE PRESS, 6013 Hollywood Blvd., Los Angeles CA 90028. Editor: Art Kunkin. For "iconoclasts of all ages." Established in 1964. Publishes "mostly personal journalism, critical reviews of films, concerts, and plays (these are usually assigned), and book reviews." Weekly. Circulation: 95,000. Buys first North American serial rights. Buys 1,000 mss a year. Payment within two weeks of publication. Will send sample copy to a writer for 25¢. Submit only complete ms. Will consider photocopied submissions. Reports as soon as possible. Enclose S.A.S.E. for return of submissions.
Nonfiction and Photos: "We are interested in all styles except the theoretical, general essay (and sometimes we use these too). Prefer first-person approach. We like to think we are more irreverent and hence more honest than other papers of our type. We read anything for possible inclusion, even tedious 'I am the new Messiah' pieces

or police brutality pieces where the writer has finally seen the light. We'd like more first person experiences of the silent working class. We like photographs with articles. Would like pieces on commune life and 'far-out' cultural happenings." Buys informational, how-to, personal experience, interviews, profiles, humor, expose, spot news, and reviews. Length: open. Payment is usually $20 per article. Buys photos with or without mss and captions always required. Pays $5 for any size clear b&w photo.

Fiction, Poetry, and Fillers: Uses experimental and humorous fiction. Length: open. Payment is open. Seldom prints poetry, "but can be swayed by high quality poems on contemporary themes." Length: open. Payment is open.

THE LUNATIC FRINGE, P.O. Box 237, South Salem NY 10590. Editor: John H. Countermash. For "people in jail, out of jail, and other interested parties." Issues contain almost entirely poetry with some fiction and articles. Established in 1971. Quarterly. Circulation: 600. Buys simultaneous rights. Pays in contributor's copies and "some cash awards." Will send sample copy to writer for $1. Enclose S.A.S.E. for return of submission.

Nonfiction, Fiction, and Poetry: "No do-gooder types; honesty, solid, sad, happiness, love, hate, from birth to death, from heaven to hell. There are no other publications even remotely like ours." Poetry, preferably brief, but all are considered. Traditional forms, blank verse, free verse, avant-garde forms, and light verse.

MARIJUANA REVIEW, Amorphia, Box 744, Mill Valley CA 94941. Editor: Michael R. Aldrich, Ph.D. For "young (17-25), mostly marijuana smokers-students, hippies, activists; and middle-aged (25-45) professional, suburbanites, interested in marijuana." Established in 1968. Published sporadically. Circulation: 5000. Buys all rights, but will reassign them to author after publication. Payment in contributor's copies. Will send a sample copy to writer for 50¢. Query first. Will consider photocopied submissions. Submit seasonal material 3 months in advance. Reports in one month. Enclose S.A.S.E. for return of submissions.

Nonfiction, Photos, and Fiction: Publishes "anything relevant to marijuana and its legalization: research, news items, features of history and legend, pipes, recipes, etc., also stories, filmscripts and literature." Seeking material for "pro-legalization of marijuana. Mine is the only magazine in the country exclusively devoted to marijuana. Occasional issues devoted entirely to literature of marijuana; some issues almost entirely statistics and research." Uses informational, how-to, personal experience, interviews, profiles, inspirational, humor, historical, expose, nostalgia, personal opinion, travel, book and record reviews, spot news, new product, and technical articles. Regular columns that seek freelance material are: "Bust Measurements-arrest and sentencing data; Kozy Kitchen Kannabis Kuisine—cooking with marijuana; Cultural Heritage Series—unusual pipes." Length: 200 to 2,000 words. All photos should be b&w. Uses experimental, adventure, erotica, fantasy, and historical fiction as it relates to marijuana. Length: 200 to 2,000 words.

Poetry and Fillers: Avant-garde poetry accepted as it relates to subject matter. Length: 2 to 50 lines. Uses newsbreaks, puzzles ("stoned"), clippings, jokes, short humor, and "dope lore." Length: 50 to 500 words.

NATURAL LIFE STYLES, Box 1101, Felton CA 95018. Editor: Sally Freeman. For "basically (though not entirely) young; oriented toward counter culture—i.e., grow your own, make it yourself, devise your own entertainment and pleasure." Established in 1971. Bimonthly. Buys all rights, but will reassign them to author after publication. Pays on publication. Buys about 50 mss a year. Will send sample copy to writer for 50¢. Will send editorial guidelines sheet to a writer upon request. Query first; do not send unsolicited mss. Will consider photocopied submissions. "We follow the seasons, spring planting, fall harvest." Submit seasonal material 4 to 5 months in advance. Reports as soon as possible. Enclose S.A.S.E. for reply to queries.

Nonfiction, Photos, and Poetry: Seeks articles on "natural foods, homesteading/how-to, environment, consumer protection, crafts, articles concerned with the quality of living in a self-determined life style. Write about what you know, what you've done yourself. Write well—style and quality are important to us. Clarity is essential; wit and a personal style rate high with us. We are aimed more toward a youthful audience than most health food magazines, more toward a general audience than most homesteading mags, more sophisticated in terms of writing quality, more socially aware. We do not want to see 'health food nut' scare articles, recipes that nobody but the most spartan devoted masochistic health food addict could eat or 'We are a sick nation because of the food we eat' approach. We would like to see an article that is thoroughly researched and noncliche on mysticism." Length: 1000 to 6000 words. Pays $10 to $60. Purchases photos with mss. Buys poetry, but "quality essential and should relate to spirit of magazine. Will pay, but not much."

NEW EARTH TRIBE NEWS P.O. Box 264, Menomonee Falls WI 53051. Editor: Stephen P. Stavrakis. For "pacifists, ecology freaks, the kind of people who read *The Whole Earth Catalogue*. We want the publication to act as a learning/teaching tool for practical, day-to-day resistance and nonviolent change." Established in 1972. Monthly. Circulation: 500. Not copyrighted. Uses 10 to 20 mss a year. Payment on acceptance. Write for copy of guidelines for writers. Query first. Will consider photocopied submissions. Submit seasonal material 2 months in advance. Reports on material accepted in 1 to 2 months. Returns rejected material in 1 to 2 months. Enclose "enough stamps" for reply to queries.
Nonfiction and Photos: "We want to avoid the rhetoric of political consciousness in favor of humanistic/positivistic consciousness. We want to encourage self-responsibility, self-discovery, and solidarity among the people of this 'Spaceship Earth'. Some of the types of things we could use: Nonviolent 'movement' articles, Gandhian philosophy, personal accounts of resistance (such as tax resistance), personal accounts of recycling, living off the land, 'community' living experiments, and other ecological efforts; yoga articles, health and organic foods, art, etc. *Whole Earth* kinds of information for 'Access' column." Length: 750 words, maximum. Pays $5 to $20. B&w photos purchased with and without mss. "Good for photo offset; sharp, clear, etc." Pays $5 to $10.
Fiction and Poetry: Experimental, religious and fantasy. 750 words. Pays $5 to $20. Free verse, blank verse, traditional and avant-garde forms, light verse. Length: 2 to 30 lines. Pays maximum of $10.

NEW GUARD, 1221 Massachusetts Ave., N.W., Washington DC 20005. Editor: Jerry Norton. "Mostly for young people under 30 with a substantial number of college students. Virtually all are political conservatives or libertarians." Established in 1962. Monthly. Circulation: 12,000. Buys all rights. Buys 10 mss a year. Payment on publication. Will send free sample copy to writer on request. Query. Will consider photocopied submissions. Submit seasonal material 3 months in advance. Reports on material in 2 weeks. Enclose S.A.S.E. for reply to queries.
Nonfiction: Articles on economics, philosophy, foreign policy and history; book and movie reviews. Articles should have a conservative-libertarian viewpoint; youth-oriented. Length: 2,000 words maximum. "Our payments vary from contributor's copies to $100 an article, depending on quality of the article, qualifications of the author, and our financial condition. Writers should work out payment with us before publication."

NEW PRIORITIES, 156 Fifth Avenue, New York NY 10016. Editor: M. Vincent Hayes. For "the universities, government, corporate executives, lawyers, responsible activists in all professions and walks of life." Established in 1971. Quarterly. Circulation: 5,000. Buys first North American serial rights. No payment. Will send a sample copy to a writer on request for $2. Query first required. Reports in 3 weeks. Enclose S.A.S.E. for return of submissions and reply to queries.
Nonfiction: "Feature articles on the role of the citizen in shaping our nation's goals. Citizen participation in local government, citizen action on behalf of the environment and consumer protection, use of the courts to make laws more responsive to the needs of all citizens. If the writer is involved in citizen action, so much the better. He can tell what his group is doing—perhaps preventing a superhighway from bulldozing a residential neighborhood. Or he can write about such action from firsthand interviews. Not interested in causes that are too special. Would like to see articles on how the citizen can influence local government; how the citizen can use the courts to work for change; stories of activist programs that worked. It is the magazine of responsible activism—a forum for citizens who want to work for change in our society by using the mechanism provided by the constitution. No rhetoric or shouting, but responsible activism." Length: 1,500 to 3,000 words.

NOLA EXPRESS, P.O. Box 2342, New Orleans LA 70116, Editors: Darlene Fife and Robert Head. Underground tabloid. Established in 1968. Biweekly. Circulation: 10,000. Will send sample copy to writer for 35¢. Reports in 2 weeks. Enclose S.A.S.E. for return of submissions.
Nonfiction and Photos: News, interviews and photos. No fiction. Pays $15 for articles; $5 for photos.

NORTHWEST PASSAGE, Box 105, South Bellingham Station, Bellingham WA 98225. Editor: Mary Kay Becker. For "college or college age; straight middle-class." Established in 1969. Biweekly. Circulation: 6,000. Not copyrighted. Does not pay. Will send a free sample copy to writer on request. Submit only complete ms. Will consider photocopied submission "if original." Reports in one month. Enclose S.A.S.E. for return of submissions.
Nonfiction, Photos, Fiction, Poetry, and Fillers: Publishes "ecological/environmental coverage, particularly of the Northwest; local and regional news, fiction, poetry, reviews, original photography and art. New ideas relating to personal life style are always welcomed." Publishes all types of fiction, nonfiction, and poetry. Length: open. Regular columns are: Cheapos (advice on low-cost living), Food Freaks (sustenance and nourishment organically), and Molasses Jug (recipes, homemaking hints). Length: 250 to 2,500 words, nonfiction; 1,500 to 2,500 words, fiction; 1 to 450 lines, poetry. For b&w and color photos "negative (35mm or 2¼x2¼) required." Uses newsbreaks and imaginative puzzles.

OFF OUR BACKS, 1346 Connecticut Ave., N.W., Washington DC 20036. "Collective staff." For women from all over the country. Established in 1970. Monthly. Circulation: 8,000. Not copyrighted. No payment. Will send sample copy to writer for 35¢. Query first or submit complete ms. Will consider photocopied submissions. Reports "as soon as possible." Enclose S.A.S.E. for response to query or return of submission.
Nonfiction and Photos: "News, analysis, health features, women's culture, and reviews. Especially would like women to cover news relevant to women all over the country. Especially interested in conferences. Would like in-depth coverage and analysis We cover news from a feminist point of view. Informational, how-to, personal experience, humor, historical, expose, personal opinion, photo, book and film reviews, and spot news. News can be short; articles maximum 1,000 words." Interested in "any photos, b&w only."
Fiction and Poetry: Experimental, adventure, science fiction, fantasy, humorous, romance, and historical fiction. Length: no minimum, 1,000 words maximum. Will consider all kinds of poetry, no limit. Poetry Editor: Betsy Donahoe.

ONTOLOGICAL THOUGHT, P.O. Box 328, Loveland CO 80537. Editor: Robert Moore. For "readers interested in the expressions of the highest qualities of character in everyday living." Monthly. Will send sample copy upon request. Query first. Enclose S.A.S.E. for reply to queries.
Nonfiction: Each issue centers on a special theme. "We are not a market for commercial writers or for those who aspire to be writers per se. We maintain a high literary standard, but our contributors are not what you call literary people. They are people of intelligence and character, capable of offering stability and balance and a sense of direction to anyone who seeks to express these qualities in their own living. For this reason it is mandatory that potential contributors request and read a free sample copy to acquaint themselves with the unique style and tone of the journal before submitting a ms. Length: 300 to 1,500 words."

ORB, 1701 Terrace Drive West, Lake Worth FL 33460. Editor: Achille David Di Bacco. For "people of all age groups and from all walks of life who are serious explorers of occultism, religion and metaphysics." Established in 1967. Bimonthly. Buys all rights, but will reassign rights to author after publication "with our written permission". Payment in contributor's copies. "We will make occasional exceptions." Will send free sample copy to writer on request. Write for copy of guidelines for writers. Reporting time varies; "usually in 3 to 4 weeks." Enclose S.A.S.E. for return of submissions.
Nonfiction: "Dedicated to in-depth explorations into occult, religious and metaphysical philosophy. Within this framework, writers are free to deal with any as-

pect of these general areas. We are not asking for scholarly dissertations, necessarily, but neither do we want material which deals with the purely 'sensational' aspect of our subject, or meaningless double-talk." Informational, how-to, personal experience, interview, profile, inspirational, humor, historical, think pieces, personal opinion; reviews of music, books, cinema, theater. Length: open.

Fiction: Must relate to overall theme. Experimental, mystery, suspense, adventure, science fiction, fantasy, humorous, religious, historical; condensed and serialized novels. Length: open.

Poetry: Traditional forms, blank verse, free verse, avant-garde forms. Must relate to overall theme. Length: open.

ORION MAGAZINE, Lakemont GA 30552. Editor: David Anthony Kraft. For "adults who have a definite desire for awakening, illuminating experience." Bimonthly. Pays in contributor's copies. Will send a sample copy for 75 cents. Reports immediately. Enclose S.A.S.E. for return of submissions.

Nonfiction and Poetry: Study the magazine before submitting. "Good material in the mystic and metaphysical realm, particularly stuff that is not shrouded in meaningless jargon and repetition." Length: 800 to 1,500 words. Also uses brief poetry relating to metaphysics.

Fiction: "Would also like to see short fiction illustrating a philosophical or metaphysical point." Length: 800 to 1,500 words.

How To Break In: "The metaphysical market—a broad field with an extremely varied stable of magazines—presents quite a challenge to a potential author. The universal rule of slanting your material after studying a publication is an essential, particularly when trying to break into print for the first time. Avoid repetition of a well-known theory as the sole object of your article; in the same category, do not expound the obvious. Impenetrable jargon and convoluted logic form a significant portion of submissions to *Orion*; naturally, they are rejected, as are articles which, despite rhetoric, say nothing. Dogmatic compositions and simplistic accounts of inspiration have little to recommend themselves to an editor. Be especially mindful of punctuation and proper grammar, and submit material in proper manuscript form. The single essential requirement is that you have something interesting and worthwhile to say to our readers, and which is not simply reiteration of previously published articles. That is the criteria by which we will judge your work, and the criteria by which you should compose your material. The work you submit should be the kind of article you would be exceptionally impressed to read in a good magazine."

OUTLOOK, *The Libertarian Monthly,* 208A Mercer St., New York NY 10012. Editor: Gary Greenberg. For college students, young professionals, modern life styles, self-liberated people interested in politics but turned off by the established political parties. Established in 1970. Circulation: 1,000. Monthly. Buys first North American serial rights. Payment in contributor's copies, or "nominal." Will send free sample copy to writer on request. Query first or submit complete ms. Enclose S.A.S.E. for response to query or return of submission.

Nonfiction: "Articles on personal and political liberation, exposing government atrocities. Emphasis on either personal experience or factual expose; touch of humor appreciated. Free market economics articles, and articles about individual rights, alternative institutions, political trends, anarchism. Reviews considered also: rock, books, film, and theater reviews.

THE RAG, 2330 Guadalupe, Austin TX 78705. Edited by the Rag Collective. For the "University of Texas students and Austin freaks." Subject matter includes "political muckraking, poems, consumer stuff, music, and book reviews." Established in 1966. Weekly. Circulation: 8000. Member of Underground Press Syndicate (not copyrighted). No pay, "we all work for the glory, but we'll feed you if you're ever in Austin." Will send a sample copy to a writer for 25¢. Will consider photocopied submissions. "In late August we're usually looking for how-to-survive-at-the-Big-University stuff." Submit seasonal material a week in advance. "We do not report, but if accepted it would appear in a month. We also do not return mss."

Nonfiction, Photos, and Fiction: Freelancer should show "ways for an anticapitalist to survive in a capitalist society, for a woman to survive and keep her dignity in a sexist society. Our publication practices complete anarchy. No 'culture hero' pieces or other ego flights. More Naderlike assaults on uncritical consumerism." Uses informational, how-to, personal experience, interviews, humor, expose, and personal

opinion. "We often print half-page or full-page photos just because they are good photos. B&w only." Uses experimental fiction and serialized novelettes.
Poetry and Fillers: Uses traditional forms, blank verse, free verse, and avant-garde forms. Accepts newsbreaks ("man bites dog, police bite people") and "freak oriented" humor.

THE REPORTER FOR CONSCIENCE' SAKE, 550 Washington Bldg., 15th St. and New York Ave., N.W., Washington DC 20005. Editor: Rick J. Long. Established in 1940. For "conscientious objectors—mainly religious, both from World War II era and Vietnam era." Monthly. Circulation: 4,000. Not copyrighted. Payment in contributor's copies. Query first. Reports in 10 days. Will send free sample copy to writer on request. Write for copy of guidelines for writers. Will consider photocopied submissions. Enclose S.A.S.E. for reply to queries.
Nonfiction: "Articles on conscientious objection as it relates to the military and Selective Service System; news on peace activities in Washington; war objectors around the world; war tax objection; national service, amnesty; book and film reviews; junior high and high school ROTC. An attempt should be made to keep material simple enough to be of use to high school students. Personal witness stories and in-depth reports are encouraged." Length: 300 to 5,000 words. Columns open to freelance submissions include "Washington Report on Amnesty" and "War Objectors Around the World".

ROOT, 59 Holdsworth Court, Passaic NJ 07055. Editor: Ira Levine. For "people who have torn away from the Establishment method to a less chaotic but viable life style." No payment. Enclose S.A.S.E. for return of submissions.
Nonfiction, Photos, Fiction, and Poetry: "We are extremely interested in publishing articles, fiction, poetry, and photography of incarcerated men and women who otherwise might have no means of expressing themselves to the general public. This offer applies to former convicts as well." Does not want matter "falling within any portion of the political spectrum." Length: open.

SAN FRANCISCO BALL, 250 Columbus Ave., Suite 209, San Francisco CA 91406. Editor: Ed Vernon. Established in 1970. Weekly. Circulation: 65,000. Buys all rights. Payment on acceptance. Will send a sample copy to a writer for $1.00, a tear sheet free. Will send editorial guidelines sheet to a writer on request. Submit only complete ms. Will consider photocopied submissions. Reports in 1 week.
Nonfiction, Photos, and Fiction: "Humorous and graphic sexual (mostly hetero) material." Buys personal experience, interview, humor, expose, nostalgia articles. Needs material for column "Letters to Love Worn." Length: 700 to 2,000 words. Payment is 1 to approximately 2 cents a word. Photos (proofsheets or 8x10's) purchased without mss. Payment is $4 per 8x10. Humorous and erotic fiction. Length: 700 to 2,000 words. Payment is approximately 2 cents a word.

SAN FRANCISCO BAY GUARDIAN, 1070 Bryant St., San Francisco CA 94103. Editor: Bruce Brugmann. For "a young liberal to radical, well-educated audience." Established in 1966. Published every two weeks. Circulation: 25,000. Buys all rights, but will reassign them to author after publication. Buys 200 mss a year. Payment on publication. Will send a free sample copy to writer on request. Query first for nonfiction with sample of published pieces. Will consider photocopied submissions. Reports in one month. Enclose S.A.S.E.
Nonfiction and Photos: Publishes "investigative reporting, features, analysis and interpretation, how-to and consumer reviews, and stories must have a San Francisco angle." Freelance material should have a "public interest advocacy journalism approach (on the side of the little guy who gets pushed around by large institutions). More interested in hard investigative pieces. Fewer stories about isolated suffering welfare mothers and other mistreated individuals; should be put in context (with facts) of groups and classes. We would like to see articles on how to survive in the city—in San Francisco." Buys informational, how-to, interview, profile, think, historical, expose, nostalgia, photo, travel articles, and pop culture reviews. Reviews of 800 to 1,500 words pay $25; short articles of 1,500 to 2,500 words pay $25 to $50; long articles of over 2,500 words pay $50 to $75 and up. Dept. Editor: William Ristow. Photos purchased with or without mss. B&w full negative prints, on 8x10 pa-

per. Pays $10 per published photo, "sometimes $15 for specially assigned shots"; $40 to $50 for photo essay. Dept. Editor: Louis Dunn.

SCREW, Box 432, Old Chelsea Station, New York NY 10011. Editors: Jim Buckley and Al Goldstein. For a male audience, with college degrees. Interested in liberalized sex. Weekly. Circulation: 100,000. Buys all rights. Buys about 200 mss a year. Pays on publication. Will send a sample copy to a writer for $1. Submit seasonal material 2 months in advance. Reports in 6 to 8 weeks. Enclose S.A.S.E. for return of submissions.

Nonfiction and Photos: "Anything informational, irreverent, true, humorous, or political in the realm of sex. Should be cynical and at least peripherally antidoctrinaire. Lighthearted, also. We treat sexual hangups as something universal and something to be laughed up. We're looking for factual, informative articles. We need women writers." Seeks material for "My Scene" department—"sexual fantasies or actual unusual experiences." Buys how-to's, personal experience articles, interviews, profiles, inspirational articles, humor, spot news, coverage of successful business operations, historical articles, think pieces, exposes, new product articles, photo and travel features, and new methods articles. Length: 750 to 2,000 words. Pays $40 to $150. B&w glossies purchased with mss; uses "art photos." Pays $10 to $60. Nonfiction Editor: Peter Dvarackas. Photo Editor: Anthony Gambino.

Fiction: Seeks "sexual mystery fiction"; humorous, historical, confession, and contemporary problems fiction. "Fiction currently overworked by writers submitting to us." Length: 750 to 2,000 words. Pays $40 to $150. Dept. Editor: Peter Dvarackas.

Fillers: Newsbreaks, clippings. Length: 100 to 300 words. Pays $10 to $30. Dept. Editor: Anthony Gambino.

SECOND CITY, 1155 W. Webster St., Chicago IL 60614. Editor: Robbyelee Terry. An alternative press. "We consider ourselves to be the voice of the movement in Chicago." Monthly. Pays in contributor's copies. Will send a sample copy to a writer for 25¢. Enclose S.A.S.E. for return of submissions.

Nonfiction: "Marxist reportage and analyses of class struggles all over the world, although we especially need good coverage of Chicago. We are also interested in political activities on campus and specific projects of radical political organizations." Wants book reviews. "We carry many each issue; interested in books of political and/or cultural interest to our readers." Also covers art and music field, primarily Chicago.

THE SECOND WAVE, Box 344, Cambridge A., Cambridge MA 02139. Editorial collective. For "women who are involved in, or interested in, the Women's Liberation Movement." Publishes "articles, poems, stories, relevant to women and their struggle for liberation—theoretical, personal, etc." Established in 1971. Quarterly. Circulation: 5,000. Acquires all rights. Uses about 50 mss a year. Payment in contributor's copies. Will send a sample copy to a writer for $1. Will consider photocopied submissions. Enclose S.A.S.E. for return of submissions.

Nonfiction and Photos: Freelancer should use "a feminist approach, though not necessarily 'movement' perspective—e.g., we are not interested in stories telling how great it is to belong to one's man, etc. Would like to see articles on any areas of female oppression not usually dealt with in the mass or feminist media." Buys informational, personal experience, interviews, profile, humor, historical, think, photo. Length: 1,500 to 15,000 words; "although in some cases smaller or larger articles will be used: where space and quality allow." B&w photos purchased without mss and captions optional. "No smaller than 3x5—photo larger than page (7x9½) size can be cropped or reduced to size."

Fiction and Poetry: Buys experimental, mainstream, and humorous fiction. Length: 1,500 to 15,000 words. Uses all forms of verse. "We are especially seeking good poetry that deals with the experience of being a woman in America: needs, problems, struggles, feelings, consciousness. Would like poetry with a distinctly feminist (in a broad sense) slant." Length: 6 to 30 lines.

SEXUAL FREEDOM, P.O. Box 14034, San Francisco CA 94114. Editor: Stephen L.W. Greene. For a "non-homogeneous group of people interested in the rapidly developing field of sexuality; those interested in life." Established in 1967. Every two months. Circulation: 20,000. Rights purchased vary with author and material.

May buy all rights, but will reassign rights to author after publication, first North American serial rights or first serial rights. Buys about 15 mss a year. Payment on acceptance or publication. Will send sample copy to writer for $1. Write for copy of guidelines for writers. Query first or submit complete ms for nonfiction. Submit only complete ms for fiction. Will consider photocopied submissions. Submit seasonal material 2 weeks in advance. Reports on accepted material in 2 weeks. Returns rejected material "as soon as possible." Enclose S.A.S.E. for return of submission or response to query.

Nonfiction and Photos: "We cover the broad expanse of human sexuality and sensuality. Writers should have a point of view as well as supportive material in the form of data for nonfiction or description for fiction. Possible subject matter includes: new developments in research on sexuality, personal accounts of interesting incidents, women's liberation, legal aspects of sex, news stories, political comments, etc. We offer a non-sophomoric, insightful sensitive outlook on sensuality and sexuality. We're explicit, but never crude; humorous, but not cynical; appreciative, but not naive. We accept articles ranging in length from 4 to 10 pages. We look for clarity, a sense of style, and a point of view. Particularly interested in articles covering sex therapy, the working of an open marriage, political aspects of sex, works on Wilhelm Reich, developments in the field of humanistic and radical psychology, analytical descriptions of the porno movie industry." Regular columns include: News, Your Sexual Enemies (accounts of forces that inhibit a healthy sexual expression, for example, VD, political forces, etc.). Nonfiction length: 2,500 words, although longer will be considered. Pays $10 for spot articles, $25 to $100 for longer articles. B&W photos are purchased with or without accompanying mss; captions optional. Pays $10 to $30.

Fiction, Poetry and Fillers: Experimental, mainstream, adventure, erotica, science fiction, fantasy, humorous, romance, confession, religious, and historical fiction considered. Pays $10 to $100. Traditional poetry, blank verse, free verse, avant-garde forms, and light verse also purchased. Newsbreaks, puzzles, clippings, jokes and short humor.

SIPAPU, Route 1, Box 216, Winters CA 95694. Editor: Noel Peattie. For "libraries, editors and collectors interested in Third World studies, the counterculture and the underground press." Established in 1970. Semi-annually. Circulation: 500. Buys all rights, but will reassign rights to author after publication (on request). Payment on publication. Will send sample copy to writer for $1. Query. Will consider photocopied submissions. Reports on material in 3 weeks. Enclose S.A.S.E. for return of submissions.

Nonfiction: "Primarily book reviews, interviews, descriptions of special libraries and counter-culture magazines and underground papers. We are an underground 'paper' about underground 'papers'. We are interested in personalities publishing dissent, counter-culture and Third World material. Informal, clear and cool. We are not interested in blazing manifestos, but rather a concise, honest description of some phase of dissent publishing, or some library collecting in this field, that the writer knows about from the inside." Personal experience, interview, successful library operations.

STRAIGHT CREEK JOURNAL, 1450 Pennsylvania St., Denver CO 80203. Editor: Stephen Foehr. For persons who are interested in "environmental, political, social, spiritual activism, music, and the arts." Weekly. Circulation: 10,000. Not copyrighted. Established in 1972. Buys 50 to 60 mss per year. Pays on publication. Will send a sample copy to a writer on request. Write for copy of guidelines for writers. Query first for nonfiction; submit complete ms for fiction and poetry. Submit seasonal material 1 month in advance. Reports in 2 to 4 weeks. Enclose S.A.S.E. for return of submissions or reply to queries.

Nonfiction and Photos: "We are primarily concerned with human values and what effect politics, finance, etc., have on those values." Political and environmental articles; humor, human interest; "dealing with making people aware. Not overly wordy or rhetorical. Must be credulous, have facts to back up opinions and conclusions. Take approach to put the reader into the action or identify with a person or cause; set a mood." Length: 600 to 1,500 words. Pays $5 for 8x10 b&w photos with sharp contrast.

Fiction: Experimental, mystery, suspense, science fiction, fantasy, humorous. Length: 1,000 to 1,700 words. Pays $10 to $20.
Poetry: Traditional forms, blank verse, free verse, avant-garde forms; light verse. No payment.

UNDERSTANDING MAGAZINE, P.O. Box 206, Merlin OR 97532. Editor: Daniel Fry. Pays on publication. Enclose S.A.S.E. for ms return.
Nonfiction and Fillers: Articles that contribute to a better understanding among "all peoples of earth and those not of earth." This may be a social condition, a new idea, or a controversial group. Prefers objective rather than subjective material; some personal ESP experiences. Study publication. "Would like to see more material on UFO sightings, evaluations of the world in which we live." Length: 1,000 words maximum. Pays 1¢ per word. For news clippings of unusual occurrences, pays $1 per clipping.
Poetry: Must express good will and make a positive point. Length: 36 lines maximum. Pays 10¢ per line.

THE UNSPEAKABLE VISIONS OF THE INDIVIDUAL, P.O. Box 439, California PA 15419. Editors: Arthur Winfield Knight and Glee Knight. For "adults with general interest leaning toward the literary world." Established in 1971. 3 yearly. Circulation: 700. Buys all rights. Buys 30 to 50 mss a year. Will send sample copy to a writer for $2. Submit complete ms. Reports on material accepted for publication in 1 month. Returns rejected material in 1 month. Enclose S.A.S.E. for return of submissions.
Nonfiction and Photos: "Good, competent material with an individual approach. No biases or taboos toward language and experience." Informational, personal experience, interview, profile, expose, all types of reviews. Pays $1 minimum. Photos purchased with or without manuscripts. 5x7 or 8x10 b&w. Pays $1 minimum.
Fiction: Experimental and mainstream. Pays $1 minimum.
Poetry: "Competent." Pays $1 minimum.

WEATHER REPORT, P.O. Box 1221, San Marcos TX 78666. Editor: John Pfeffer. For "college students, faculty, administrators (not favorable) some townspeople of a liberal nature." Publishes material on controversial issues. Established in 1970. Biweekly. Not copyrighted. Circulation: 5,000. Does not pay. Submit only complete mss. Will consider photocopied submissions. Returns material "when wanted by the writer." Enclose S.A.S.E.
Nonfiction, Photos, and Fillers: Publishes "any style wished by writer; keep to about two pages typed double spaced." Uses informational, how-to, interviews, think, expose, photo, and spot news articles. Uses b&w photos. 5x7 preferred and captions required. Uses newsbreaks, short humor.

WITCHCRAFT DIGEST, Suite 1B, 153 West 80th St., New York NY 10024. Editor: Dr. Leo Louis Martello. For readers "from late teens to seventies, all walks of life; from farmers to pharmacologists, counter culture and establishment, college students, university and free school students." Established in 1970. Annual. Circulation: 3,000. Buys all rights, but will reassign rights to author after publication. Buys 6 to 10 ms a year. Pays on publication. Will send sample copy to writer for $1. Submit only complete ms. Will consider photocopied submissions. Submit seasonal material at least 6 months in advance. Reports "immediately." Enclose S.A.S.E. for return of submissions."
Nonfiction: "Writers must be versed in witchcraft as the old religion which worships a mother goddess and a horned god, having nothing to do with the Christian devil. Most writers fail because they don't know the truth and send in material that is theologically wrong, sensational or confused (like lumping witches and satanists together). We treat witchcraft as it really was and is: the old religion. We use other articles on the occult only if they are related to our subject. Published for those in the know, or who want to know. Articles covering the witch holy days are most wanted at this time. News of articles, radio and TV programs giving issue, month, day, etc., that show religious discrimination by calling witches 'evil, in league with devil,' etc. Those that ignorantly or deliberately link genuine witches, old religionists, with 'pop witches', satanists, etc. "Wants mss of 1,000 words or less. Pays 1¢ per word or by arrangement. Payment in contributor's copies also.

Animal Publications

The following magazines deal with pets, hunting dogs, racing and show horses, and other pleasure animals. Magazines about animals bred and raised for food are classified in Farm Publications.

ANIMAL CAVALCADE, 11926 Santa Monica Blvd., Los Angeles CA 90025. Editor: William Riddell, D.V.M. For "pet owners of all ages who want information on subjects related to the health and care of their pets." Bimonthly. Circulation: 44,300. Buys first right. Buys about 50 mss a year. Pays on publication. Will send a sample copy to a writer for 50¢. Submit seasonal material at least 3 months in advance. Returns rejected material "within 60 days." Acknowledges acceptance of material "upon publication." Enclose S.A.S.E. for return of submissions.
Nonfiction and Photos: Publishes "material on pet care, nutrition, training and research. This publication serves the veterinary profession in the same way *Today's Health* serves the practitioners of human medicine. It is sponsored by the Animal Health Foundation, a nonprofit charitable organization devoted to improving animal health through authoritatively written articles. Subject matter must be approved by a panel of veterinarians before publication. We strive for a rather subtle educational form of entertainment." Buys how-to's, interviews, profiles, humor, spot news, historical articles, personal experience articles, photo features, and articles on travel with pets. Length: 100 to 2,000 words. Pays $5 to $35. B&w glossies, color transparencies, and 35mm color purchased with mss; with captions only. "Photos must involve pets."
Fiction: Humorous, adventure, and juvenile fiction. Length: 100 to 1,000 words. Pays $5 to $25.
Fillers: Newsbreaks, puzzles, clippings, jokes, short humor. Length: 100 to 2,000 words. Pays $5 to $25.

ANIMAL KINGDOM, New York Zoological Park, Bronx NY 10460. Editor: Simon Dresner. For individuals interested in wildlife, zoos, aquariums, and members of zoological societies. Bimonthly. Buys first North American serial rights. Pays on acceptance. Reports in about three weeks. Enclose S.A.S.E. for return of submissions.
Nonfiction and Photos: Natural history articles, conservation and science topics related to natural history. No botany or poetry. Lengths: 2,000 to 3,000 words. Payment ranges from $75 to $250. Payment for photos purchased with mss is negotiated.

ANIMAL LOVERS MAGAZINE, P.O. Box 783, Arlington Heights IL 60006. Editor: Mrs. Anita Coffelt. For "pet owners who enjoy reading stories about animals, articles on care, feeding and health, wildlife articles, etc. Sincere animal lovers dedicated to welfare of all animals. Majority are adult." Established in 1969. Quarterly. Circulation: 3,000. Buys all rights, but will reassign rights to author after publication. Pays on acceptance. Will send a sample copy to a writer for 50¢. Submit only complete ms for fiction and nonfiction. Will consider photocopied submissions. Submit seasonal material 3 months in advance. Reports in 4 to 6 weeks. Enclose S.A.S.E. for return of submissions.
Nonfiction, Photos, and Fiction: "Stories and articles on all members of the animal kingdom, including birds. Majority of material related to cats, dogs, birds. Approximately one story or article per issue on a zoo animal, wildlife, or other animal (horse, hamster, etc.). Articles on preservation of endangered species; articles opposing cruelty to animals, profiles of persons performing extraordinary good deeds for animals, etc. We look for a unique story line. Readers seem to prefer a warm, touching theme ... or those with a humorous slant ... human interest qualities." Buys informational, personal experience, interview, humor articles. Length: 700 to 900 words. Payment is 1¢ a word. Sharp, clear b&w photos of any size purchased with or without accompanying mss; captions optional. "Animal subjects only—cleverly posed photos will be considered first." Payment is $2 per photo.

ANIMALS, 180 Longwood Ave., Boston MA 02115. Editor: William Mallard. Established in 1868. Monthly publication of the Massachusetts S.P.C.A. Not copyrighted. Buys one-time rights. Pays on acceptance. Will send free sample copy to a writer on request. Query first required, as no ms will be returned. Submit seasonal material 4 months in advance. Does not return mss.
Nonfiction and Photos: "Articles about animals. Taboo subjects are animal training, commercial use of animals for entertainment, domesticated wild animals and birds; animals in captivity; hunting, etc. Length: 300 to 600 words. B&w photos to accompany story, if possible. Pays 1½¢ per word and $1 and up for photos and drawings. Keep a copy of your ms and photos, as we cannot return same. Authors will be notified only if their copy is accepted and being held for use. Allow up to 4 months for use of material."

APPALOOSA NEWS, Box 403, Moscow ID 83843. Editor: Don Walker. Monthly. Established in 1946. Pays on acceptance. Not copyrighted. Circulation: 28,000. Will send free sample copy on request. Reports "as soon as possible." Enclose S.A.S.E.
Nonfiction: 3,000-word articles on Appaloosa ranches, uses of Appaloosas. Payment varies from no payment to $50, depending on nature of submission.
Photos: Color (any size) and b&w (5x7) photos of Appaloosas are purchased. Pays $5 to $15.
How To Break In: "Just get with us on an idea and *do it!*"

THE BACKSTRETCH, 19363 James Couzens Highway, Detroit MI 48235. Editor: Ruth A. LeGrove. Quarterly. Will send free sample copy to a writer on request. Enclose S.A.S.E. for return of submissions.
Nonfiction: Uses articles slanted to, and of special interest to, thoroughbred trainers and owners. Payment to be determined after examination of material.

CANADA RIDES, R.R. 1, Spruce Grove, Alberta, Canada TOE 2CO. Editor: Mary Jo Birrell. For "equine enthusiasts of all ages, horse clubs, ranchers and retired ranchers; city people who are interested in western culture." Articles and stories on "any subject in which the horse can be dominant, or at least in the background." Established in 1972. Quarterly. Circulation: 8,000. Buys all rights but will reassign rights to author after publication. Buys 20 mss a year. Payment on publication. Will send sample copy for 75¢. Query for nonfiction. Submit complete ms for poetry and fiction. "Give approximate word count on ms." Will consider photocopied submissions. Reports in 1 month. Enclose S.A.S.E. with submissions and queries.
Nonfiction and Photos: "Stories of current or past rodeo champions, western artists, special horse personalities or horse types, and old-time policemen. Anything western, historical and/or horsey such as outstanding cattle spreads, a story of an elderly artist/ex-cowboy, ghost towns, ancient, infamous crimes. Although we insist on a professional caliber of writing, the magazine is meant to be informal almost to the point of being homespun. This is one of the few Canadian horse magazines that is Canada-wide, rather than provincial. Therefore, the material should be Canadian. If we seem to be stressing 'western', it is only because of the cowboy and the horse being associated with the west. We are equally as interested in western history as long as the horse is part of it." Also interested in informational, how-to, personal experience, interviews, profiles, inspirational, humor, historical and gymkhana reviews. Length: 1,000 to 5,000 words. Pays 4¢ a word. Photos are purchased with ms. Prefers 8x10 b&w; no color. Pays $7.
Fiction and Poetry: "We don't accept much poetry or fiction, but will look at any with a western or horsey flavor." Western and historical fiction length: 1,000 to 1,500 words. Pays 4¢ a word. Poetry must relate to theme of magazine. Length: open. Pays 4¢ a word.

THE CANADIAN HORSE, 48 Belfield Rd., Rexdale, Ont., Canada. Editor: Phil Jones. For thoroughbred owners, breeders, trainers, and race track officials. Monthly. Buys all rights. Pays on publication. Will send a sample copy to a writer for $1. Enclose S.A.E. and International Reply Coupons.
Nonfiction and Photos: Factual articles on racing, breeding, training of horses, prominent horses, and racing personalities in Canada. "In historical pieces, cite as many references as possible. In articles about current horsemen, use as many quotes

as are practical." Length: to 1,000 words. Pays 3¢ a word. Buys 8x10 b&w glossies. Pays $10.

CAT FANCY, 11558 Sorrento Valley Rd., San Diego CA 92121. Editor: Leslie S. Smith. Bimonthly. Circulation: 120,000. Will send a sample copy to a writer for $1. Buys all rights and pays on publication. Submit seasonal material (spring, summer, fall, winter) 6 months in advance. Reports on submissions in 90 days. Include S.A.S.E. for return of submissions.
Nonfiction: Articles from 1,000 to 3,000 words dealing with grooming, health, care, breeding of cats; traveling with cats, etc. Pays 3¢ per printed word. Query not required. Read previous issues for style.
Photos: Purchased with mss or captions only. Professional quality. Pays from $10 for 8x10 b&w glossy, and from $50 for color transparencies 2¼ square or larger. Photo editor: Paul Jeffryes.
Fiction: Lengths, 1,500 to 4,000 words. Must be good fiction dealing with cats, but no cute stories with the cat as narrator. Pays 3¢ per printed word.
Poetry: Traditional forms, blank verse, free verse, avant-garde forms, light verse. Pays $10.

CATS MAGAZINE, P.O. Box 4106, Pittsburgh PA 15202. Editor: Jean Laux. Monthly. Buys North American serial rights only. Pays on publication. Will send free sample copy to a writer on request. Reports on submissions in one month. Enclose S.A.S.E. for return of submissions.
Nonfiction: Articles on the domestic cat in relation to society: in art, science, history, medicine; truly unusual cats; outstanding cat owners who are famous for other reasons; cat artists, photographers, authors, etc.; cat care and cat health (preferably by veterinarians—or with their byline). Length: 1,000 to 2,000 words. Pays 3¢ per word.
Photos, Poetry, and Fillers: Photos may be included with articles. Pays $5 to $10; b&w only; up to 8x10. Poetry about cats. Length: 4 to 24 lines. Pays 20¢ per line; minimum $1. Fillers on cats. Length: up to 600 words.

DOBERMAN NEWS, P.O. Box 1198. Lakeport CA 95453. Editor-Publisher: Steve S. Brown. For Doberman fanciers of "all professions, ages, interests." Bimonthly. Circulation: 2,000. Buys all rights. Pays on publication. Will send a sample copy to a writer for $1.25. "Nonstaff writers are specially instructed as to subject availability, length, etc." Query first. Time for returning rejected material "depends." Acknowledges acceptance of material immediately.
Nonfiction, Photos, Poetry, and Fillers: All material "circumvolves the dog, Doberman." Publishes "society pages, obedience, Jr. handling, technical features, kennel stories," and "foreign affairs, current events, national standings, laws (congressional actions), etc.," that relate to Dobermans. Articles can be how-to, personal experience, interviews, profiles, inspirational, humor, spot news, successful business operations (kennels), historical, think pieces, expose, new product, photo, travel, or merchandising techniques. Payment is "1¢ a published word, plus $1 a photo, by credit only usable on subscriptions, ads, for staff and freelancers." Maximum credit is $25. Length: minimum is 300 words; no maximum. Fillers can be puzzles, clippings, jokes, or short humor.

DOG FANCY, 11558 Sorrento Valley Rd., San Diego CA 92121. Senior Editor: Bruce Sessions. For dog owners. Pays on publication. "Material that absolutely cannot be used will be returned almost immediately. Reporting time on others will not be more than 90 days. We cannot assume responsibility for material sent to *Dog Fancy.* However, great care is exercised in the handling of your work. Please do not ask for special handling such as billing for return postage, etc. We simply cannot do it. Pack your work carefully." Enclose S.A.S.E. for return of submissions.
Nonfiction and Fiction: Needs articles that would appeal to dog owners: factual articles on health, grooming, care, etc., that are well-written and accurate. Fiction welcome, but avoid the "cute" story being told by a dog. Pays 3¢ a word.

DOG WORLD, 10060 West Roosevelt Road, Westchester IL 60153. For dog breeders, judges and exhibitors. Does not pay. Enclose S.A.S.E. for return of submissions.
Nonfiction: Uses articles of two typed pages or more, double-spaced with 2-inch margins. General articles on dogs. Also breed material submitted by breeders, vet-

erinarians who have actual experience in the field. June biannual is breed standards issue for all recognized AKC breeds. Deadline for this issue is April 5.

HORSE & RIDER, Covina CA 91723. Editor: Ray Rich. For "owners, breeders, and riders of Western type of horse." Buys all rights. Pays on acceptance. Will send a sample copy to a writer on request. No query required. Enclose S.A.S.E. for return of submissions.

Nonfiction and Photos: "Features on training, breeding, feeding, medical advice, general horse care and how-to articles of interest to active horsemen; historical Western articles relating to the horse world. We seldom buy features without photos." Length: 500 to 3,000 words. Pays up to $200 for features with photos; pays $75 for cover chromes; $50 for inside color per chrome.

HORSE, OF COURSE!, Temple NH 03084. Editor: R.A. Greene, DVM. "For people who like horses." Bimonthly. Established in 1972. Rights purchased vary with author and material. Buys all rights, but will reassign rights to author after publication; buys first North American serial rights or first serial rights. Payment on publication. Will send sample copy to writer for $1. Submit complete ms. Submit seasonal material 6 months in advance. Reports in 90 days. Enclose S.A.S.E.

Nonfiction and Photos: "We cater to horse interest rather than to some particular phase of it. Horses, horse farms, horse people. Hobbies, etc., related to horses; e.g., horse training. Limit subject matter to any one article. Be sure it's interesting and readable." Also interested in rider fashions, special and unusual horse uses, light, historical topics. Length: 400 to 2,000 words. Pays $5 to $25. Uses 5x7 or 8x10 b&w glossies with articles. No additional payment.

Fiction: Adventure, western, humorous, historical "on horse themes only." Pays $5 to $25.

Fillers: Jokes, short humor. Length: 400 words maximum. Pays $5.

HORSEMAN, The Magazine of Western Riding, 5314 Bingle Road, Houston TX 77018. Editor: Tex Rogers. Monthly. For owners of western or stock-type horses. Will send free sample copy to a writer on request. Buys one-time rights. Buys 60 to 70 mss a year from freelancers. Pays on acceptance. Query before submitting. Returns rejected material in 3 weeks. Enclose S.A.S.E. for reply to queries.

Nonfiction: "Articles must be 'how-to', practical pieces that will help owners show, breed or train their horses better. You've got to know horses to write this kind of article. Non-horsemen forget it!" Also interested in historical pieces, strictly about a horse or involving horses as central theme. Length: 1,000 to 5,000 words. Pays 4¢ a word for all rights, 3¢ a word for first time rights, and 1¢ a word for reprint rights.

Photos: Pays $6 for all rights to photos used with articles if negatives accompany photos. Needs good color photo picture stories on horse handling at western ranches, horse breaking and training at ranch level.

Fillers: Will use puzzles pertinent to western equine events—all breeds. Must be camera-ready.

HORSEMEN'S JOURNAL, 425 13th St., N.W., Suite 1038, Washington DC 20004. Editor and Publisher: Tony Chamblin. The monthly official membership magazine for Horsemen's Benevolent and Protective Assn. Aimed at owners, trainers and breeders of thoroughbred race horses, and racing fans. Special issues include Champions of Year, January (deadline Dec. 10); Kentucky Derby, April (deadline March 10); Keeneland, July (deadline June 10); Saratoga, August (deadline July 10); Stallion, December (deadline November 10). Buys first rights. Pays on publication. Will send a sample copy to a writer for 75¢. Query preferred. Reports in 2 to 6 weeks. Enclose S.A.S.E.

Nonfiction: Articles of 1,000 to 3,000 words; lively features or personality profiles; technical aspects of racing—stories from veterinarians, or about horse shoeing, etc. Also guest editorials and short features of about 1,500 words slanted to horsemen. Query preferred. Pays $25 and up.

Photos: Purchases photos with mss or with captions only; must be 8x10. Pays $5 per photo used.

Fillers: Material of interest to horsemen and racing fans.

HUNTING DOG MAGAZINE, P.O. Box 330, Greenfield OH 45123. Editor: George R. Quigley. "For persons interested in sporting dogs as distinguished from show dogs." Established in 1965. Monthly. Circulation: 30,000. Rights purchased vary with author and material. Payment on publication. Query first required for a major feature article. Will consider photocopied submissions. "Mss must be typed, double-spaced, one side of page and word count on front. We are leaning heavily on mss with photos." Reports in 2 weeks or less. Enclose S.A.S.E.

Nonfiction and Photos: "We carry informative articles on training, breeding, and hunting dogs. We also carry coverage on the field trials, hunts and lots of personality features. Keep in mind that a customer picking *Hunting Dog* up at the newsstand wants to read about hunting, dogs, and hunting with dogs. We do not dwell on subjects outside the dog field. We are the largest sporting dog publication in the market. In fact, we are the only book dealing solely with hunting dogs. We would like not to see training stories by writers who are not really expert in the field and writers trying to advocate training hunting dogs by show dog or utility dog methods. We do want action hunting stories, training how-to's by experts, kenneling, dog transportation, etc. Use some historical material on breeds; also we need beagle news, foxhound news, coonhound news, bird dog news for regular columns." Length: 1,000 to 2,000 words. Pays 2¢ a word. Photos purchased with mss and captions are required as a guide. Pays $5 each for 5x7 or 8x10 (only) b&w photos. Pays $50 for color cover. 35mm or 2¼x2¼ for 8½ x11 format.

NATIONAL HUMANE REVIEW (Official publication of the American Humane Association), P.O. Box 1266, Denver CO 80201. Editor: Eileen F. Schoen. Established in 1913. For children, professionals in the humane field, and others with "an interest in animals and the organized humane movement." Monthly. Circulation: 15,000. Buys first North American serial rights only. Buys 30 to 50 mss a year from freelancers. Write for copy of guidelines for writers. No query required. Submit seasonal material 4 months in advance. Reporting time varies, from "immediate or up to 3 months, depending on editor's travel schedule and magazine deadline." Enclose S.A.S.E.

Nonfiction and Fiction: "Primarily, we sell the idea of kindness, rather than a specific organization"; freelance material should "illustrate how kindness achieves more positive results than brutality." Articles can be personal experience, inspirational, or humor pieces. Do not send "articles on local humane societies, individuals who are 'one-man' humane societies, dog training from a 'how-to' approach, pet cemeteries, municipal (dog catcher) articles, editorials on animals. All of these, if used, are staff-written. No submissions on all the pets a family has." Humor, adventure, contemporary problem, and animal fiction should read like nonfiction, so it appears to be an article. Length: 1,000 to 2,000 words, prefer 2,000 words. Pay is 1½¢ a word.

Photos: Pays $5 per b&w photo. Vertical pictures of children and animals for cover. Also photo series, humorous or serious, of animals alone or with people.

How To Break In: "We are an excellent market for new writers. Nearly all our material comes from nonprofessionals. 'The Personal View of Humaneness' is a feature we plan to use at intervals. Stories heard, events witnessed, experiences lived—these are the things that shape individual awareness and give personal meaning to the humane ethic. A new writer could write something for this new series, emphasizing the personal view of humaneness."

NATIONAL STOCK DOG MAGAZINE, Rural Route 1, Butler IN 46721. Editor: E.G. Emanuel. For farmers, ranchers, stockmen, dog owners. Subject matter includes letters from readers, training information, unusual stories related to livestock working dogs and their owners. Quarterly. Not copyrighted. Returns rejected material and acknowledges acceptance "as requested by sender." Enclose S.A.S.E.

Nonfiction and Photos: "Most of our material is supplied to us, free of charge, by our readers." Length varies. Payment per word negotiable "depending on the suitability of the material." Uses sharp, b&w photos of dogs working livestock. Payment negotiable.

THE QUARTER HORSE JOURNAL, Box 9105, Amarillo TX 79105. Editor: Audie Rackley. For readers "from all walks of life. Farmers and ranchers, mostly horse owners." Established in 1948. Special issues in April—racing; May—performances; August—youth; September—Western wear; December—stallion issue. Monthly. Circulation: 58,800. Buys all rights. Buys about 24 mss a year. Payment on acceptance. Query first or submit complete ms. Submit seasonal material 2 months in advance. Enclose S.A.S.E.

Nonfiction, Photos, and Fillers: "*The Quarter Horse Journal* is owned by the American Quarter Horse Association and covers all facets of the quarter horse business. Our main purpose is the promotion of the breed and serving our membership." Publishes "current events such as race and show results. Features include outstanding breeders and their successes, personalities, and their contributions to the QH breed. Technical articles related to improvement of the breed welcomed. More technical articles with current research available." Length: 800 to 2,500 words. Pays $25 to $100. Purchases photos with mss. 4x5 or 8x10 b&w glossies. Prefers 2¼x2¼ or 4x5 color transparencies. Payment included with mss. Buys newsbreaks and puzzles (horseword).

How To Break In: "Any sincere, talented writer acquainted with the Quarter Horse breed, and who has a background of information, has a very good chance of getting his material accepted. Unfortunately, very few submit material other than those who have contributed in the past. Material must be related to the industry or tied closely to it. We are always open for suggestions and will discuss editorial matter with those interested."

THE QUARTER HORSE OF THE PACIFIC COAST, P.O. Box 4822, Sacramento CA 95825. Editor: Don Sammons. For quarter horse owners and breeders principally from West coast, though publication is distributed throughout the U.S. Publishes special issues like Racing issue, April; Stallion issue, November. Monthly. Circulation: 4,000. Buys first rights. Pays on acceptance. No query required. Submit seasonal material two months in advance of publication. Returns rejected material in 1 month. Acknowledges acceptance of material in 1 month. Enclose S.A.S.E. for return of submissions.

Nonfiction and Photos: Articles on the quarter horse in show and at work, on successful business operations. "Remember our audience is very knowledgeable on the subject." Maximum length: 1,000 words. Pays $30 to $40. Purchases b&w glossies with mss and with captions.

SOUTHEASTERN ARABIAN HORSE, 404 Wall St., P.O. Box 128, Fountain Inn SC 29644. Editor: Leonard Crotts. "Our readers (Arabian horse owners) are all ages, tending to have better than average income, education and tastes. Anything with a slant toward horses—not even necessarily Arabian as long as the writer does not try to 'sell' another breed." Established in 1972. Monthly. Circulation: 8,000 plus. Buys all rights, but will reassign rights to author after publication. Payment on publication. Write for copy of guidelines for writers. Submit complete ms. Will not consider photocopied submissions. Submit seasonal material 6 months in advance. Reports on material accepted for publication in 2 weeks. Returns rejected material "as soon as read". Enclose S.A.S.E.

Nonfiction and Photos: "We would like to see good first-person (or 'as told to') articles as well as how-to pieces; historical material, fiction, surveys of music or art when applicable. Writer must write from a high level of competency whether he knows the field or gets his material from interviews or research. We will use new, untried writers. We like writers with experience to give us something other than the old, tired grocery list writing so prevalent in animal magazines. Still, we must not get so far out that we lose our audience." Length: 2,000 words maximum. Pays $100 to $125. Pays $8 for 8x10 glossy photos accepted with mss; captions required. Proof sets desirable. Captions optional for photos submitted without mss. Color transparencies for cover use only. Payment by arrangement.

THE THOROUGHBRED RECORD P.O. Box 580, Lexington KY 40501. Editor: William Robertson. For persons interested in thoroughbred horses. Weekly. Buys all rights, but will reassign rights to author after publication. Pays on acceptance. Will send a sample copy to a writer on request. Usually reports within 2 weeks. Enclose S.A.S.E.

Nonfiction and Photos: Articles on thoroughbred racing, breeding, veterinary science, animal husbandry (horses), farm techniques (livestock), nutrition, etc. Also personalities, historical articles, editorial opinion, etc. Length: open. Payment about 3¢ a word, except for articles which require considerable research. Photos purchased with mss or on assignment. Pays $10.

TROPICAL FISH HOBBYIST, 211 West Sylvania Ave., Neptune City NJ 07753. Managing Editor: Neal Pronek. Monthly to tropical fish hobbyists, pet dealers, naturalists, biologists. Buys all rights. Pays on acceptance. Reports within a week. Enclose S.A.S.E.
Nonfiction: Writer must know what he's writing about. 750- to 1,500-word articles on breeding tropical aquarium fishes, new and unique fishes, and general articles related to the hobby (not general essay-type articles about the joys or woes of being a tropical fish keeper). Informal style. Can also use personality profiles of successful aquarium hobbyists; query first on these. Pays from 1½¢ to 3¢ per word. Study publication before submitting.
Photos: B&w glossy or color transparencies any size. $5 for b&w; $10 for color.

THE WESTERN HORSEMAN, 3850 North Nevada Ave., Colorado Springs CO 80901. Editor: Chuck King. For admirers of stock horses. Monthly. Buys first North American serial rights. Pays on acceptance. Reports in 2 to 3 weeks. Enclose S.A.S.E.
Nonfiction and Photos: Dealing with training, handling, feeding, etc., of horses; personalities in the horse world. Query Chan Bergen, Assistant Editor, before submitting. Pays 3¢ per word. Photos purchased with mss.

Art Publications

AMERICAN ARTIST, 165 W. 46th St., New York NY 10036. Editor: Susan E. Meyer. "Present needs supplied by current staff of writers."

ART NEWS, 750 Third Ave., New York NY 10017. Editor: Milton Esterow. For persons interested in art. Monthly. Circulation: 37,000. Query first. Enclose S.A.S.E.
Nonfiction: "I'm buying in-depth profiles of people in the art world—artists, curators, dealers. And investigative pieces, including some on antiques. The format is now very flexible to cover personalities, trends, a single painting, and we'll have monthly reports on the art markets. There's a real thirst for art information, and that's what we're trying to satisfy." Wants "humanized" art coverage. Length: 800 words; "some major pieces as long as 8,000 words." Pays $75 to $500.

ARTS MAGAZINE, 23 E. 26th St., New York NY 10010. Editor: Gregoire Muller. For persons interested in art, especially artists, museum officials, designers, art teachers, students, and art collectors. Established in 1926. Monthly, except July and August. Circulation: 27,000. Buys all rights. Pays on publication. Query first. Study magazine before submitting. Enclose S.A.S.E. for reply to queries.
Nonfiction and Photos: Art analysis, articles on the current art world—new discoveries, developments, old and modern art. Length: open. Payment to be negotiated. B&w glossies and color transparencies purchased to illustrate articles.

ARTS MANAGEMENT, 408 West 57th St., New York NY 10019. Editor: A.H. Reiss. For cultural institutions. Five times annually. Circulation: 6,000. Buys all rights. Pays on publication. Query first. Reports in several weeks. Enclose S.A.S.E.
Nonfiction: Short articles, 400 to 900 words, tightly written, expository, explaining how art administrators solved problems in publicity, fund raising, and general administration; actual case histories emphasizing the how-to. Also short articles on the economics and sociology of the arts and important trends in the nonprofit cultural field. Must be fact-filled, well-organized and without rhetoric. Payment is 2¢ to 4¢ per word. No photographs or pictures.

DESIGN MAGAZINE, 1100 Waterway Blvd., Indianapolis IN 46202. Editor: Edward A. Kieta. Established in 1898. For "teachers of art (elementary and secondary)." Bimonthly. Circulation: 11,500. Buys all rights. Buys 60 to 75 mss a year from freelancers. Pays on publication. Reports on material under consideration in 60 days. Enclose S.A.S.E.

Nonfiction and Photos: "We need articles showing art class projects for elementary and high school. Copy should be short with heavy emphasis on b&w photos, preferably showing kids doing the thing described with closeups of actual work. Emphasize the nitty-gritty of how-to-do it. It's not enough to tell teachers that someone's doing something new. Tell them how to adapt it." Pays $15 to $50.

METROPOLITAN MUSEUM OF ART BULLETIN, Metropolitan Museum of Art, Fifth Ave. and 82nd St., New York NY 10028. Editor: Katharine Stoddert. Quarterly. Query first. "Writers contributing must write entirely on speculation." Enclose S.A.S.E.

Nonfiction: Publishes museum news, discussion of events and exhibitions, etc. Each issue usually covers a single theme. Writers must be acknowledged experts in their fields. "Our museum experts scrutinize everything very carefully." Length: 750 words; 1,500 to 2,000 words. Pays $75 for short pieces, $150 for longer articles.

TODAY'S ART, 25 W. 45th St., New York NY 10036. Editor: Ralph Fabri. For "artists (professional and amateur), art teachers, and museums." Monthly. Circulation: 86,000. Buys first rights. Pays on publication. Query first. Enclose S.A.S.E.

Nonfiction and Photos: "Only items referring to art and art projects in public and high schools (for a special school edition) and how-to articles in all fields of art with b&w and some color illustrations. Articles should be easy to follow. Most articles we receive are not sufficiently detailed and a lot have to be rewritten to make them more informative." Length: 400 to 850 words. Pays $25 to $50.

How To Break In: "Every now and then, someone comes up with a good idea, even if no idea can be completely new, of course. But there are many technical and esthetic possibilities in art. Indeed, there's no limit to them. If a writer, young or old, is sure he has something like that, and knows how to present it in an easily comprehensible manner, we are glad to consider the article. But we don't want philosophizing about art, and we do not wish to promote unknown artists."

WESTART, P.O. Box 1396, Auburn CA 95603. Editor: Jean L. Couzens. Semi-monthly. Newspaper covering west coast art news, events, competitions, etc. Not copyrighted. Pays on publication. Reports promptly. Enclose S.A.S.E.

Nonfiction and Photos: Short features on west coast art subjects of unusual interest. No hobbies. Length: 500 to 700 words. Likes one or more accompanying photos. Pays 30¢ per column inch for both copy and photos.

Astrology and Psychic Publications

Magazines listed here regard astrology, psychic phenomena, ESP experiences, and related subjects as sciences or as objects of serious scientific research. Semireligious, occult, mysticism, and supernatural magazines are classified in the Alternate and Radical category. UFO publications will be found among the Science magazines.

AMERICAN ASTROLOGY, 2505 N. Alvernon Way, Tucson AZ 85712. Editor: Joanne S. Clancy. Monthly. Also publishes *American Astrology Digest* annually. Pays on publication. Include S.A.S.E.

Nonfiction: Articles with astrological and astronomical themes. Current affairs in particular demand. Must be good astrology and slanted to the layman.

AQUARIAN ASTROLOGY FOR ALL THE SIGNS, 355 Lexington Avenue, New York NY 10017. Editor: Anne Keffer. For "ages 15 to 30; education not a factor; interests—astrology, the occult, yoga, organic foods/macrobiotics, religion, mysticism, meditation—only peripheral in most cases because our readers are average young people concerned about their futures, their love lives, their relationships with the family, school, and work." Quarterly. Buys all rights. Pays on acceptance. Reports in 4 weeks. Enclose S.A.S.E.

Nonfiction: "Topics of general interest to young people must be treated astrolog ically; Sun Sign articles preferred. Technical astrology articles must be simple and comprehensible to average reader. Language should be plain, not hip. Dated articles must reach us 8 months prior to publication. All material must be astrologically oriented. No personal testimony. No Sun Sign articles that cover fewer than all twelve signs. No promotion of drugs, immoderate sexuality or lawlessness. No predictions of disaster." Length: 1,500 to 5,000 words. Pays 2¢ a word and up.

ASTROLOGY GUIDE, 315 Park Ave. S., New York NY 10010. Editor: Dal Lee. Bimonthly. Buys first rights. No query required. Reports in one week. Enclose S.A.S.E.
Nonfiction: Astrological articles helpful to the individual reader; not too profound. Length: 1,500 to 2,000 words. Pays 2¢ to 3¢ a word.

ASTROLOGY–YOUR DAILY HOROSCOPE, 355 Lexington Ave., New York NY 10017. Monthly. Buys all rights. Pays on acceptance. Enclose S.A.S.E.
Nonfiction: Articles on astrology, either popularized or moderately technical. Anxious to attract new writers and can promise a steady market plus a great deal of help from the editor. Knowledge of astrology is necessary. Length: 1,500 to 4,000 words. Pays 2¢ a word, or by arrangement.

BEYOND REALITY MAGAZINE, 303 W. 42 St., New York NY 10036. Editor: Harry Belil. For "university students interested in the occult, UFOs, parapsychology, ESP, etc." Established in 1971. Bimonthly. Circulation: 125,000. Buys all rights, but will reassign rights to author after publication. Payment on publication. Write for copy of guidelines for writers. Query or send complete ms. Will consider photocopied submissions. Returns rejected material in 1 month. Enclose S.A.S.E.
Nonfiction and Photos: Short articles dealing with the occult. "Should know the subject they are writing about, and include researched material." Book reviews. Length: 2,000 words. Pays $30 to $50 for articles; $10 for personal experiences. No additional payment for photos. Photo Dept. Editor: Gary Parsons.
Fillers: Newsbreaks and clippings. Length: 200 to 500 words. Pays $5 to $10.

EVERYWOMAN'S DAILY HOROSCOPE, 355 Lexington Ave., New York NY 10017. Monthly. Buys all rights. Pays on acceptance. Enclose S.A.S.E. for ms return.
Nonfiction: Articles on astrology, either popularized or moderately technical, especially slanted to women. "We are anxious to attract new writers and can promise a steady market plus a great deal of help from the editor. Knowledge of astrology is necessary." Length: 1,500 to 3,500 words. Pays 2¢ per word, or by arrangement.

FATE, Clark Publishing Co., Highland House, 500 Hyacinth Place, Highland Park IL 60035. Editor: Mary Margaret Fuller. Monthly. Buys all rights; occasionally North American serial rights only. Pays on publication. Query first. Reports on submissions in 4 to 8 weeks. Enclose S.A.S.E.
Nonfiction and Fillers: Personal psychic experiences, 300 to 500 words. New frontiers of science, and ancient civilizations, 2,000 to 3,000 words; also parapsychology, occultism, witchcraft, magic, spiritual healing miracles, flying saucers, etc. Must include complete authenticating details. Prefers interesting accounts of single events rather than roundups. Pays minimum of 3¢ per word. Fillers should be fully authenticated. Length: 100 to 300 words.
Photos: Buys good glossy photos with mss or with captions only. Pays $5 to $10.

HOROSCOPE, Dag Hammarskjold Plaza, New York NY 10017. Editor: Julia A. Wagner. Monthly. Specialized market, strictly limited to those writers who have a thorough knowledge of astrology and actual experience in this field. Buys all rights. Ms must be accompanied by one carbon copy. Reports in two months. Pays on acceptance. Enclose S.A.S.E. for return of submissions.
Nonfiction: Articles with a genuine astrological basis. Increase in teenaged readers reported. Well-written research and expository reports of studies of prominent personages acceptable; must be strictly astrological. Length about 2,500 to 3,000 words. Pays 5¢ a word.

Fillers: Short prose (100 words), fillers and anecdotes having astrological basis. Submit at least ten at a time.

HOROSCOPE GUIDE, 350 Madison Ave., Cresskill NJ 07626. Editor: Jim Hendryx. Monthly. Buys all rights. Pays on acceptance. Will consider photocopied submissions. Reports in about a month. Include S.A.S.E.
Nonfiction: Anything of good interest to the average astrology buff, preferably not so technical as to require more than basic knowledge of birth sign by reader. Lengths: 1,000 to 5,000 words. Pays 1½¢ per word. Query not desired.
Poetry: 4 to 16 lines on astrology. Pays 50¢ a line.

MOON SIGN BOOK, P. O. Box 3383, St. Paul MN 55165. Editor: R.M. Wright. For "persons from all walks of life with interests in the occult." Established in 1906. Annual. Circulation: 100,000. Rights purchased vary with author and material. Pays on publication. Query first or submit complete ms. Reports in 2 to 4 weeks. Enclose S.A.S.E.
Nonfiction and Photos: "Astrology is the primary subject, but we can use material in any field of the occult. We are a yearly publication dealing with farming, gardening, yearly forecasts for all types of activities, with informative articles on astrology. We try to be educational as well as practical." Length: 3,000 to 10,000 words. Pays 3¢ to 5¢ a word. Photos on assignment.
Poetry: Traditional forms, blank verse, free verse, avant-garde forms, light verse. Length: 100 lines maximum. Pays $5 to $25.
Fillers: Puzzles which are "occult in nature." Pays $5 to $25.
How To Break In: "The *Moon Sign Book* is a farming and gardening almanac emphasizing astronomical effects on planting, growing, harvesting and using crops to maximum advantage. Since 80% of the book is taken up with tables, we have room for only a few outside articles. Those articles should have something to do with either astrology or gardening (we are also interested in herbs, herbal remedies). Since most freelancers are not astrologers I would suggest that they concentrate on the many aspects of organic gardening or possibly how-to-do features that relate in some way to farming and gardening. Short articles on the occult phenomena (enhancing growth psychically), are also good possibilities for the beginning writer. We are continually looking for astrologers capable of writing 'Sun Sign' predictions for *Moon Sign Book*. We generally stick with one, but we find that quality depends on a variety, and would like to find a few more writers to back us up."

MYSTIQUE, 161 E. Erie St., Chicago IL 60611. Editor: Arv Miller. Established in 1972. Quarterly. Circulation: 100,000. Rights purchased vary with author and material. Buys all rights, but will reassign rights to author after publication or buys first North American serial rights. Payment on publication. Query first or submit complete ms. Reports on material accepted for publication in 2 to 3 weeks. Returns rejected material in 2 to 6 weeks. Enclose S.A.S.E.
Nonfiction and Photos: "Areas include ESP, astrology, the supernatural, witchcraft, magic, spiritualism, psychic sciences. Casual and friendly approach to subject matter desired. Stay away from heavy-handedness, clinical or scholarly style. We don't want articles that involve the hereafter or pieces that center around death, fear or superstition." Also uses book reviews on the occult and news items about current occult happenings. Length: 250 to 3,500 words. Pays $20 to $150. Purchases unusual trick photography with occult flavor. Pays $10 to $15 for b&w; $25 to $50 for color (double exposures).
Fillers: Newsbreaks and clippings on the same theme.

OCCULT, Popular Library Publishers, 355 Lexington Ave., New York NY 10017. Editor: Anne Keffer. General field of psychic phenomena. Quarterly. Buys all rights. Pays on acceptance. Do not send for sample copy. Query not required. Reports in 3 weeks. Enclose S.A.S.E. for return of submissions.
Nonfiction: "Occult: ghosts, witchcraft, hauntings, magic, spiritualism, ESP, mediums, astral projection, etc. No fiction. Subject matter is based on documented evidence or substantiated by scientific research." Length: 2,500 to 5,000 words. Payment is $75 to $150.

THE OCCULT COMMENTARY, 240 Main St., Danbury CT 06810. Editor: R.C.H. Parker. For "persons with a basic interest in all forms of psychic phenomena, occult sciences, and higher research in parapsychology, color psychology, and mind development—philosophy or Eastern religions." Bimonthly. Circulation: 60,000. Buys all rights. Buys 200 plus mss a year. Pays on publication. Will send a free sample copy to a writer on request. Query first. Submit seasonal material 3 months in advance. Reports as soon as possible. Enclose S.A.S.E.

Nonfiction, Photos, Fiction, and Fillers: "Timely articles relating to occult and metaphysical study and application in day-to-day living. Family articles, light research, humor, teenage/college level descriptions for occult areas. Want new approaches, new ideas rather than reviewing older ideas. Support ideas with research. We approach occult/metaphysical as a means to personal development rather than all encompassing answer, emphasis on use of occult sciences day to day—rather than just history or philosophical concepts. Do not want standard approach to astrology, or UFO or ghost articles unless of exceptional merit." Length: 300 to 1,500 words. Payment is $10 to $45. B&w glossy photos purchased with mss, also 35mm negatives. Payment is $5 to $100. Buys humorous, contemporary problem, and religious fiction. Length: 300 to 1,500 words. Payment is $10 to $45. Dept. Editor: Terri Bomgardner. Buys clippings, short humor, mystic/occult fillers. Payment is $2 to $5.

PROBE THE UNKNOWN, 5650 W. Washington Blvd., Los Angeles CA 90016. Editor: M. Uyehara. For those interested in documented cases of psychic phenomena. Established in 1972. Bimonthly. Circulation: 92,000. Buys all rights. "Most of our articles are written by freelance writers, but they must send an inquiry first." Payment on publication. Will send free sample copy to a writer on request. Query first. Will consider photocopied submissions. Returns rejected material in 2 to 3 weeks. Enclose S.A.S.E. for reply to queries.

Nonfiction and Photos: "Any documented cases of parapsychology, psychic phenomena, and the 'unknown' in general. The writing must be as objective as possible, and we discourage any 'sensationalism'. Must be written for the layman. Must have quotes from people involved in the subject." Investigative articles; first-hand reports. Length: 1,500 to 5,000 words. Pays 4¢ to 10¢ a word "depending on quality". 5x7 or 8x10 b&w photos purchased with mss and on assignment. Captions required. Pays $5 to $10.

Fillers: Newsbreaks, clippings. Length: 50 to 500 words. Pays 1¢ to 2¢ a word. Dept. Editor: Pat Alston.

PSYCHIC, 680 Beach St., Suite 418, San Francisco CA 94109. Editor: James Grayson Bolen. For general public interested in straightforward material on psychic phenomena. Bimonthly. Buys all rights. Pays on acceptance. Query first is mandatory. Reports in 4 to 6 weeks. Enclose S.A.S.E. for reply to queries.

Nonfiction and Photos: Documented articles and objective reports on ESP, psychic phenomena and nonoccult, related areas, as well as scientific research and data. See copy of magazine for style. Informative reporting, balance of comments on material, documentation, short bibliography for reader reference, opinions of authorities (both pro and con)—no editorializing. Lengths, 2,500 to 3,500 words. Pays $75 to $150. Photos purchased only with mss. Can be b&w glossy prints or any size transparency. Photography Editor: John Larsen.

YOUR PERSONAL ASTROLOGY MAGAZINE, 315 Park Ave., S., New York NY 10010. Editor: Dal Lee. Quarterly. Buys first rights only. Reports on submissions in one week. Enclose S.A.S.E. fo ms return.

Nonfiction: Astrological articles helpful to the individual reader; not too profound. Length: 1,500 to 2,000 words. Query not necessary. See any recent issue for kind of articles desired. Pays 2¢ to 3¢ a word.

Automotive and Motorcycle

These magazines are concerned with the maintenance, operation, performance, racing, and judging of automobiles and motorcycles. Publications that treat vehicles as a means of transportation or shelter instead of as a hobby or sport are classified in the Travel, Camping, and Trailer category. Journals for teamsters, service station operators, and auto dealers will be found in the Auto and Truck classification of the Trade Journals section.

AMA NEWS (Publication of the American Motorcycle Association), Box 141, Westerville OH 43081. Editor: John Yaw. For members of the American Motorcycle Association; their "average age is approximately 30, their average education is through high school, and their average family income is above $13,000." Publishes material oriented to the policies, programs, and activities of the AMA; material that encourages responsible and safe motorcycling. "AMA does not publish road tests and technical articles. Its main editorial themes are motorcycle-related legislation, public relations, touring, and amateur and professional competition." Monthly. "The material must be exclusive and oriented to American Motorcycle Association programs and policies." Payment on publication. Will send a free sample copy to a writer on request. No query required. Submit seasonal material 2 months in advance of publication. Enclose S.A.S.E. for return of submissions.
Nonfiction and Photos: Uses interviews, profiles, spot news, and think pieces; personal experience, historical, and travel articles. "Will accept material of any length. Longer articles will be serialized." Pays 2¢ a word. Purchases b&w glossies and color transparencies with mss.

CAR AND DRIVER, 1 Park Ave., New York NY 10016. Editor: B. Brown: Monthly. Circulation: 620,000. Buys all rights. Pays on publication. Query first. Reports in 2 months. Enclose S.A.S.E. for return of submissions.
Nonfiction: "Our need is increasing for the more sophisticated treatment of automobiles and motor racing slanted to a 20-40 age audience. We want articles on exciting, interesting cars; on personalities, past and present, in the automotive industry and automotive sports." The "inside story" new and original. Humorous articles as well. Pays $200 to $300 for articles of 1,500 to 2,000 words.
Photos: Purchased with article, b&w glossy, pays from $15.

CAR CRAFT, 8490 Sunset Blvd., Los Angeles CA 90069. Publisher: Steve Green. Reader audience: men and women, 18 to 34 years. Monthly. Pays on acceptance. Buys all rights. Query first. Reports within 10 days. Enclose S.A.S.E.
Nonfiction and Photos: Drag racing articles, 900 to 2,000 words. Pays $50 to $100 per page. Photos purchased with mss. Should be 8x10 b&w glossy or 2¼x2¼ color transparencies.

CAR REPAIR, 229 Park Ave. S., New York NY 10003. Editor: Tony Hogg. For "men interested in making fairly simple repairs on their own cars to save money. They are blue collar high school graduates." Annual. Buys all rights. Buys 3 or 4 mss a year. Pays on acceptance. Will send a sample copy to a writer on request. Query first. Submit seasonal material 6 months in advance. Reports in 2 weeks. Enclose S.A.S.E. for reply to queries.
Nonfiction and Photos: "Articles on how to repair various auto ills; factual, step-by-step exposition of how to make the repairs. Photos must be included, and they too must be of a step-by-step nature. Our emphasis is on do-it-yourself. No emphasis on fancy or weird cars, styles, souped-up engines, etc." Length: 250 to 1,500 words. Pays $25 to $200. B&w glossies and color transparencies for cover purchased with ms; with captions only.

CARS MAGAZINE GROUP: CARS, RODDER AND SUPER/STOCK, SPEED AND SUPERCAR, 1560 Broadway, New York NY 10036. Editor: Alan Root. For "auto enthusiasts, all ages, interested in high performance and racing." Monthly. Circulation: 100,000 to 200,000. Buys all rights. Buys approximately 200 mss a year. Pays on publication. Will send a sample copy to a writer for 25¢. Query first. "We accept photocopied mss from writers we have been dealing with and can trust." Reports "quickly." Enclose S.A.S.E.
Nonfiction and Photos: Buys illustrated features on high performance and racing: how-to's, interviews, and profiles. Length: open. Payment is $50 per page with b&w photos accompanying article; $75 per page with 35mm color or color transparencies accompanying mss; average feature runs $150.

CHOPPERS MAGAZINE, 16200 Ventura Blvd., Suite 213, Encino CA 91316. Editor: Chris Bunch. For "chopper owners and builders. Demographically, they're 21 to 40, oriented toward Harley-Davidson, maximum education high school level, politically disenfranchised." Monthly. Circulation: 65,000. Buys all rights "unless otherwise agreed on." Buys 12 to 15 mss a year. Payment on publication. Will send a sample copy to a writer for $1. Query required. Submit seasonal material at least 6 months in advance. Reports in 2 weeks. Enclose S.A.S.E.

Nonfiction and Photos: "We cover the entire field of customized bikes. Stories consist of photo and minor text about a particular customized bike; technical stories on how to modify visually or for performance; personal accounts from the chopper rider's point of view. For technical subjects, prefer simple, readable, step-by-step approach. For stories on individual bikes, insist on complete details (technical sheet available to prospective writer on request). New journalism or 'wolfean' prose acceptable. Less interested in pretty pictures of bikes than in hard specifics of building. Prefer facts that are of use to readers. Use black humor, hip folksiness, semi-underground style." Length: open. Pays 1¢ to 5¢ per word. Uses 5x7 b&w photos (prints or contact sheets and negatives). Pays up tp $6. 35mm, 2¼ or larger color transparencies. Pays $15 to $25 for interior color, dependent on quality; $30 to $50 for cover or centerfold. All photos must relate to theme of magazine.

How To Break In: "We are very open to over the transom material that suits our needs. We also, if the story has *any* potential whatsoever, are more than willing to work with a writer. Even if the story isn't at all usable, we'll let the writer know why we bounced the item. We're also very open to pre-manuscript contact with a writer, since our interest area and readership are so specialized. It does seem, though, that most of our writers come from within the custom field, and aren't the 'work the field' type freelancers."

THE CLASSIC CAR, P.O. Box C, Hummelstown PA 17036. Editor: William S. Jackson. For the classic car enthusiast, highly specialized in his interest. Uses writing with a "good nonfiction prose syle. More interested in clear, factual writing than a lot of 'flash.' " The publication has a "finer focus than general automotive magazines. The reader is extremely knowledgeable to begin with. Accuracy is of utmost importance." Quarterly. Circulation: 5,000. Buys first rights. Buys 6 to 10 mss a year from freelancers. Pays on publication. Will send a sample copy to a writer on request. Query first. Reports in a week to 10 days. Enclose S.A.S.E.

Nonfiction and Photos: Wants "historical articles on various makes and models of classic cars, photo articles on cars, restoration how-to articles, meet coverage, interviews, and profiles." Length: 500 to 5,000 words. Pays $25 to $100. 8x10 b&w glossy photos, 4x5 color transparencies. Preferred with captions only. Pays $1 to $5 for b&w; $5 to $25 for color.

CYCLE, One Park Ave., New York NY 10016. Editor: Cook Neilson. Monthly. Circulation: 375,000. Buys all editorial rights. Will read unsolicited mss, but queries preferred. Enclose S.A.S.E.

Nonfiction, Photos, and Fiction: Road tests are staff-written, and racing coverage is not wanted as its use is diminishing. Photos are needed with mss. Fiction will be considered if it is "brilliant." Payment is $100 to $350 for articles; $25 to $100 for photos. 35mm color is acceptable, though b&w photos are preferred.

CYCLE GUIDE GROUP: CYCLE GUIDE, CYCLE MECHANICS, CUSTOM CHOPPER, 1440 W. Walnut, Compton CA 90220. Editor: Frank Connor. For motorcycle enthusiasts interested in cycles in general, customized cycles, choppers and/or how to maintain and repair them. Monthly; quarterly; monthly. Circulation: 175,000; 45,000; 50,000. Buys all rights. Pays on publication. Query first. Enclose S.A.S.E.

Nonfiction and Photos: Articles to entertain, inform, and instruct the motorcyclist on all aspects of motorcycles and motorcycling. Stress on how-to. Buys some reports on cycling events and personal adventure pieces of cyclists; also, articles on cycle modification. For *Cycle Mechanics,* uses highly technical articles on maintenance and repair of cycles, including new developments, product analysis, and shop talk items. How-to photos should accompany features. Length and payment to be negotiated.

CYCLE NEWS GROUP: CYCLE NEWS EAST, CYCLE NEWS WEST, CYCLE NEWS CENTRAL, Box 498, Long Beach CA 90801. Publisher: Charles Clayton. For motorcycle club and competition enthusiasts. Weekly and biweekly. Buys first publication rights and reprint rights. Payment within 45 days following publication. No query necessary. Write for copy of guidelines for writers. Enclose S.A.S.E. for return of submissions.

Nonfiction and Photos: Articles on activities, history, trends and news of motorcycle sport and touring in the regional areas. Especially needs articles of interest to new "fun riders." Also interviews with cycling personalities, and motorcycle race coverage of all types—the chances of selling increase with the quality of the report. Payment for copy and race results is 50¢ a published inch, $1 for in-depth articles. Photos can be 8x10 or 5x7 glossy b&w, with complete identification written on back of photo, photographer's name, date, event. Prefers negatives with photos. Payment is 50¢ a column inch for editorial photos, and $7.50 each if photo is used in advertisement.

Fiction: Uses fiction, under 1,500 words; generally, serialized travel stories and humor. Payment is 50¢ per published inch.

CYCLE WORLD, 1499 Monrovia Ave., Newport Beach CA 92663. Editor: Ivan Wagar. For active motorcyclists, "15-45 years old. Half are road riders, half are dirt riders." Subject matter includes "road tests (staff-written), features on special bikes, customs, racers, racing events; technical and how-to features involving mechanical modifications." Monthly. Circulation: 192,000. Buys all rights. Buys 200 to 300 mss a year from freelancers. Pays on publication. Will send sample copy to a writer for 75¢. Query first. Submit seasonal material 2½ months in advance. Reports in 4 to 6 weeks. Enclose S.A.S.E.

Nonfiction and Photos: Buys informative, well-researched travel stories; technical, theory, and how-to articles; interviews, profiles, humor, spot news, historical pieces, think pieces, new product articles and satire. Also buys material for the column "Racing Review," which contains short, local racing stories with photos. Taboos include articles about "wives learning to ride, 'my first motorcycle.'" Length: 800 to 5,000 words. Pays 5¢ to 7½¢ a word. Purchases photos with mss and with captions only. Buys b&w glossies, color transparencies, 35mm color. Pays $5 to $50 for b&w.

Fiction: Needs mystery, science fiction, and humorous stories. Does not want to see racing fiction or "rhapsodic poetry." Length: 1,500 to 3,000 words. Pays 5¢ to 7½¢ a word.

DIRT CYCLE, 222 Park Ave., S., New York NY 10003. Editor: Robert Schleicher. For those whose "prime interest is in motorcycle trail riding and off-road racing." in Established in 1970. Monthly. Circulation: 95,000. Buys all rights. Buys 50 mss a year. Payment on publication. Will send free sample copy to writer on request. Query first. Will not consider photocopied submissions. Submit seasonal material 3 months in advance. Reports on submissions in 2 to 4 weeks. Enclose S.A.S.E.

Nonfiction and Photos: "Road tests. Motorcycle preparation, tuning and hop up. Off-road competition reports. Dirt-riding motorcycle custom-builts. How to ride off-road. Must be experienced riders able to converse in style riders and racers can understand. Friendly, rather than authoritative text, but completely factual. All articles must be photo-illustrated with both color and b&w." Length: 1,000 to 4,000 words. Pays $100 to $225. Pays $7 for 8x10 b&w glossy prints; $25 to $75 per magazine page for 2¼ or larger color transparencies.

DUNE BUGGIES AND HOT VWs, THE FUN CAR JOURNAL, P.O. Box 2260, 2630-C Grace Lane, Costa Mesa CA 92626. Editor/Publisher: Jim Wright. Bimonthly. Circulation: 80,000. Buys North American serial rights only. Pays on publication. Will send a sample copy to a writer on request. No query required. Reports in one month. Enclose S.A.S.E. for return of submissions.

Nonfiction and Fiction: "Articles on Volkswagens, dune buggies, and related activities: race reports, how-to articles, technical articles, travel, new car features." Will consider fiction. Length: open. Pays $45 per page.

Photos: Purchased with mss only. 8x10 b&w glossies for inside, 35mm or 2¼ color transparencies for possible cover use. Pays $10 for b&w, $55 for partial color, $75 for entire cover.

EASYRIDERS MAGAZINE, Box 2086, Seal Beach CA 90740. Editor: Lou Kimzey. For "adult men—men who own, or desire to own, expensive custom motorcycles. The individualist—a rugged guy who enjoys riding a chopper and all the good times derived from it." Bimonthly. Circulation: 100,000. Buys first rights. Buys 12 to 20 mss a year. Payment on acceptance. Will send a sample copy to a writer for 25¢. Reports in 2 to 3 weeks. Enclose S.A.S.E. for return of submissions.

Nonfiction, Poetry, and Fillers: "Masculine, candid material of interest to young men. Must be bike oriented, but can be anything of interest to a rugged young man. It is suggested that everyone read a copy before submitting—it's not *Boy's Life.* Light, easy, conversational writing style wanted, like guys would speak to each other without women being around. Gut level, friendly, man-to-man. Should be bike oriented or of interest to a guy who rides a bike. *Easyriders* is entirely different from all other motorcycle or chopper magazines in that it stresses the good times surrounding the owning of a motorcycle—it's aimed at the rider and is nontechnical, while the others are nuts and bolts. Not interested in technical motorcycle articles. We carry no articles that preach to the reader, or attempt to tell them what they should or shouldn't do." Buys personal experience, interviews, humor, expose (motorcycle oriented) articles. Length: 1,000 to 3,000 words. Payment is 5¢ to 10¢ a word, depending on length and use in magazine. "It's the subject matter and how well it's done—not length, that determines amount paid." Traditional, contemporary, avant-garde poetry, light verse. Length: open. Payment is minimum $5. Dept. Editor: Louis Bosque. Risque joke fillers, short humor. Length: open. Payment: open.

Photos: B&w glossies, 35mm color, 2¼x2¼ color transparencies (2¼x2¼ preferred) purchased with mss. "We are only interested in *exclusive* photos of exclusive bikes that have never been published in, or photographed by, a national motorcycle or chopper publication. Bikes should be approved by editorial board before going to expense of shooting. Submit sample photos—Polaroids will do. Send enough samples for editorial board to get good idea of the bike's quality, originality, workmanship, interesting features, coloring." Photo Editor: Pete Chiodo. Payment is $50 to $150 for cover, $75 to $150 for centerspread, $10 for b&w and $35 for color for "In the Wind," $25 up for arty, unusual shots, and $100 to $200 for a complete feature.

Fiction: "Gut level language okay. Any sex scenes, not to be too graphic in detail. Dope may be implied, but not graphically detailed. Must be bike oriented, but doesn't have to dwell on that fact. Only interested in hard hitting, rugged fiction." Length: 5,000 to 10,000 words. Payment is 5¢ to 10¢ a word, depending on length and use in magazine.

ENGINE, 229 Park Ave., South, New York NY 10003. Editor: Tony Hogg. For "men interested in inner workings of cars and repairs." Annual. Buys all rights. Buys 5 or 6 manuscripts per year. Will send sample copy to a writer on request. Query first. Submit seasonal or special material 6 months in advance. Reports in 2 weeks. Enclose S.A.S.E.

Nonfiction and Photos: "How-to's. Approach should be step by step; emphasis on clarity. No news on racing or souped-up autos." Length: 250 to 1,500 words. Pays $25 to $200. Photos purchased with manuscripts; with captions only. B&w glossies, color transparencies for cover.

FOUR WHEELER MAGAZINE, 11044 McCormick Street, North Hollywood CA 91603. Editor: Bill Sanders. For an audience of four-wheel-drive vehicle riders. Age bracket from 25 to 60. Some high school, some college educated readers. All are devout four wheelers, off-roaders, campers, etc. Established in 1963. Seasonal articles: winterizing in winter sports, desert runs for spring and fall, etc. Monthly. Circulation: 50,000. Rights purchased vary with author and material, but may buy all rights. Buys about 48 to 50 mss a year. Payment on publication. Will send free sample copy to writer on request. Seasonal and all material should be submitted three months prior to publication. Will consider photocopied submissions if we have proof it is not submitted elsewhere. Reports as soon as possible. Enclose S.A.S.E. for return of submissions.

Nonfiction, Photos, and Fiction: "Publish articles about four-wheeling, i.e., technical, Jeep runs, travel to remote areas, including foreign to U.S., humorous four-wheel sidebars, club competition, etc. All articles must be about four-wheeling or off-road activity. Any style is allowed—should be edited closely for spelling, etc., before submission. *Four Wheeler* is the pioneer magazine in the field, hence copied by others. We would like to see four-wheel drive club and unusual features concentrating on four-wheel-drive activities. Also competition events on the east coast." Buys informational, how-to, personal experience, interview, profile, humor, historical, nostalgia, photo, and travel, new product, and technical articles. Seeks freelance material for "Campfire Column": club activities. Length: 500 to 2,000 words. Pays $25 to $100 ($125 depending on time expended getting and writing article). Photos purchased with mss (without for "Photo of the Month"), and on assignment. Captions required. 8x10 glossies for b&w; high speed Ektachrome for color. Payment included in payment for article. Pays $10 for "Photo of the Month." "We use very little fiction, and it must relate to subject matter." Buys humorous fiction. Length: 1,000 to 2,000 words. Pays $25 to $125.

HI-PERFORMANCE CARS, Magnum/Royal Publications, Inc., 1560 Broadway, New York NY 10036. Editor: Alan Root. For "those who are interested in the technical and sport value of the automobile." Monthly. Circulation: 280,000. Buys all rights. Buys 150 mss a year. Payment on publication. Will send free sample copy to writer on request. Write for copy of editorial guidelines. Query first; "we like to see samples." Will not consider photocopied submissions. Submit seasonal material (for holidays) 4 months in advance. Reports on material within 2 weeks. Enclose S.A.S.E. for reply to queries.
Nonfiction and Photos: "We consider informative, well-constructed articles and features on drag racing, mini-cars and setups, formula V; technical how-to-do-its; personality features on racers, automotive engineers, race coverage, etc. In depth studies of technical innovations in the automobile accessory field and how to employ them. We welcome writers to submit any pertinent article that indicates a trend, discusses an important development, etc.; different points of view that are valuable and original." Length: 1,500 to 6,000 words. Pays minimum of $100. Photos purchased with ms. Captions required. Pays $40 per page for b&w with ms; at least 5x7. Color strips or 2x2 color slides; $75 per page with story. Dept. Editor: Al Kirschenbaum.
Fiction: Adventure, humor, satire, historical; related to subject matter. Length: 1,500 to 2,500 words. Pays minimum of $100. Dept. Editor: Ms. Lauren Fransen.
Fillers: Automotive puzzles, short humor and satire.

HOT ROD, 8490 Sunset Blvd., Los Angeles CA 90069. Editor: Terry Cook. For "automotive oriented young males." Monthly. Circulation: 850,000. Buys all rights. Buys about 12 mss a year from freelancers. Pays on acceptance. Enclose S.A.S.E. for return of submissions.
Nonfiction and Photos: Technical, high-performance, safety, racing, pictorial automotive themes. Length: 1,000 to 5,000 words. Pays $100 to $250 for feature articles; $300 to $500 for highly technical, well-researched articles. Photos purchased with mss. Should be 8x10 b&w glossy, color transparencies, or 2¼x2¼ color. Pays $10 to $250.

MINICYCLE MAGAZINE P.O. Box 2869, Laguna Hills CA 92653. Editor: Brick Price. For "those interested in the many aspects of minicycling. The editorial content is tailored to the mechanically minded youth market and adults with average ability." Buys first rights. Enclose S.A.S.E. for return of submissions.
Nonfiction and Photos: Needs "technically oriented how-to articles concerning minicycles and motorcycles up to 125cc. Also use-oriented articles such as travels, clubs, events, etc. Policy inclines toward off-road usage of minicycles under adult supervision with particular attention to outdoor activities." Accident material not purchased. Length: 1,500 to 3,000 words. Pays $35 per printed page including photos.

MOTOR TREND, 8490 Sunset Blvd., Los Angeles CA 90069. Managing Editor: Steve Spence. For automotive enthusiasts. Monthly. Circulation: 600,000. Buys all rights, except by negotiation. Reports in 10 days. Enclose S.A.S.E. for return of submissions.
Nonfiction: Automotive and related subjects. Emphasis on performance cars, foreign and domestic. Superior writing a must, packed with facts. Pays $100 per

printed page in magazine. Query suggested from regulars; unknowns should send mss

Photos: Buys photos with mss and captions only. Automotive subject matter. 8x10 glossies. Pays $15 to $50 each.

Fillers: Automotive newsbreaks. Length: 500 to 750 words. Pays $35 to $50 each.

MOTORCYCLIST, 8490 Sunset Blvd., Los Angeles CA 90069. Editor: Bob Greene. For "motorcycle enthusiasts of all ages—from teens to senior citizens." Monthly. Circulation: approximately 100,000. Buys all rights. Buys 20 to 50 mss a year from freelancers. Pays on acceptance. Query first. Reports "shortly after receipt." Enclose S.A.S.E. for return of submissions.

Nonfiction: "Most material is of general interest nature within motorcycling: technical, travel, event coverage, road tests, etc. Our only requirement is that material submitted show motorcycling in a favorable light." Also buys inspirational and historical articles, interviews, and profiles. Length: Up to 3,000 words. Pays $60 to $80 per published page. "Payment dependent on published space."

Photos: Purchased with mss and with captions only. Uses b&w glossies, color transparencies, and 35mm color. Payment: b&w, from $15; color, from $50.

OFF-ROAD VEHICLES AND ADVENTURE MAGAZINE, 131 South Barrington Place, Los Angeles CA 90049. Editor: Tom Madigan. For those interested in off-road vehicles. Monthly. Circulation: 175,000. Buys first rights. Buys over 30 mss a year from freelancers. Pays on publication. Will send a sample copy to a writer on request. No query required, "but we can help the writer out if we have prior knowledge of his plans." Submit seasonal material 4 months in advance of publication. Returns rejected material "immediately, if requested." Acknowledges acceptance one month prior to publication. Enclose S.A.S.E. for return of submissions.

Nonfiction and Photos: Uses articles on "4-wheel drives, dune buggies, how-to's on off-road vehicles and race and recreational use of these vehicles. Don't send buggy or vehicle test features unless you have special access to production models." The emphasis is on "sequential photos—we're heavy on photos." Buys how-to's, spot news, new product articles, travel pieces, and coverage of off-road races. Style should be "very loose writing—'buddy-buddy' talk." Length: 600 to 1,400 words, with photos. Pays $40 to $50 per page. Photos bought with captions only. B&w glossies; color transparencies. "Proofsheets and negatives are acceptable."

1001 CUSTOM & ROD IDEAS, 131 South Barrington Place, Los Angeles CA 90049. Editor: Lee Kelley. For teen hot-rodders. The writer must know "automotive field and be able to write clearly, simply," and "support the hot-rodders' viewpoints." Bimonthly. Circulation: 160,000. Buys all rights. Buys 40 to 60 mss a year from freelancers. Pays on publication. Will send a sample copy to a writer on request. No query required, "but a note or a call could save time—the subject of the article is a prime interest and varies greatly." Submit seasonal material 3 months in advance. Returns rejected material "immediately on request." Enclose S.A.S.E.

Nonfiction and Photos: Publishes "automotive hop-up, bolt-on performance, and how-to features especially geared toward street-driven rods. Individual local auto features on a neighbor's hot rod are not suggested, unless they are really great." Length: 300 to 2,000 words. Pays $40 per page. Color transparencies, and b&w glossies are purchased with mss. Will look at proofsheets and negatives.

POPULAR CYCLING, 131 South Barrington Place, Los Angeles CA 90049. Editorial Director: George Elliott. Monthly. Circulation: 100,000. Not copyrighted. Pays on publication. Query first. Enclose S.A.S.E.

Nonfiction and Photos: Motorcycles, technical, how to ride, how to race in competition; road tests; vehicles for transporting motorcycles; coverage of competition events (only the larger races throughout the country and Europe); new products covering all accessories. Must be concise and to the point. Length: 500 to 3,000 words. Payment for articles is $40 a printed page. 8x10 b&w glossies with proofsheets and negatives. Pays $10. 2¼x2¼ transparencies in proofsheet form. Pays $65 to $150.

POPULAR HOT RODDING, Argus Publishers Corp., 131 South Barrington Pl., Los Angeles CA 90049. Editor: Lee Kelley. For automotive enthusiasts. Monthly. Circulation: 276,000. Buys all rights. Pays on publication. Will send a sample copy to a writer on request. Query first. Reports on submissions "as soon as possible." Enclose S.A.S.E.
Nonfiction and Photos: Wants automotive how-to's. Length: open. Pays $50 per printed page. Purchases photos with mss, and with captions only. Uses 8x10 b&w glossies, 2¼x2¼ color transparencies.

POPULAR IMPORTED CARS, KMR Publications, 21 West 26th St., New York NY 10010. Editor: Frank W. Coggins. Bimonthly. Enclose S.A.S.E for ms return.
Nonfiction: Articles on all aspects of driving and maintaining an import in the U.S. Ideas on constructive modifications and improvements to appearance and running gear welcome. Pieces on club activities, rallying and "sedan racing" as well as some travel features with heavy accent on the vehicle used wanted. Best length about 1,200 words. Pays $75 to $150. Buys all rights; will release second or other rights on request.
Photos: Must accompany mss. 5x7 or 8x10 glossy. Color 2¼ sq. minimum size. Pays $5 to $15.

ROAD AND TRACK, 1499 Monrovia Avenue, Newport Beach CA 92663. Editor: Ron Wakefield. Buys all rights, but may be reassigned to author after publication. Query first. Reports in 6 weeks. Enclose S.A.S.E.
Nonfiction: "The editor welcomes freelance material. If the writer is not thoroughly familiar with the kind of material used in the magazine, he is wasting both his time and the magazine's time. *Road & Track* material is highly specialized and that old car story in the files has no chance of being accepted." Recent articles are "Back to Basics," a track test of 9 imported cars; "Hop Rod", a spoof on R&T's own road tests; a biography of world champion driver, Emerson Fittipaldi; competition news. Payment is minimum of 10¢ per word and often reaches twice that.
How To Break In: "One wishing to break into *Road and Track*'s pages should study its format carefully, study many issues past and recent, and submit only that work which he is sure fits into the magazine's specialized area of coverage."

ROAD RIDER, P.O. Box 678, South Laguna CA 92677. Editor: Roger Hull. For persons whose primary interest is "motorcycling—road-oriented." Established in 1970. Monthly. Circulation: 35,000. Buys all rights, but will reassign rights to author after publication. Buys about 35 mss a year. Pays on publication. Submit complete ms for nonfiction, "but query first for special event reporting, spot news, and technical articles. Would be interested in seasonal material, but query first." Submit seasonal material 6 months in advance, "unless arranged in advance." Enclose S.A.S.E.
Nonfiction and Photos: "Primarily motorcycle travel stories accenting the human element. Informal, relaxed style is preferable. We do not advise submission by non-motorcyclists—writers must be familiar with the field. We deal only with road-oriented material, no competition or dirt-riding. Accompanying photos are almost a necessity. We are not in the market for arty, contrived pieces. All product testing is staff-originated." Buys informational articles, how-to's, personal experience articles, humor, photo features, travel pieces, spot news, and technical articles. Length: "flexible; query if over 2,500 words." Pays $25 "or per agreement." B&w glossies purchased with mss; captions optional. but identification preferred. Must be "sharp, clear; no size requirements."
Poetry: Traditional forms, light verse. Must relate to motorcycling. "We rarely find poetry we can use, so when we do like one, length isn't of too much concern. Pay would average about $20 a throw. Use 3 or 4 per year."

ROD & CUSTOM, 8490 Sunset Blvd., Los Angeles CA 90069. Editor: Bud Bryan. For street rod enthusiasts. Monthly. Buys all rights. Pays on publication. Enclose S.A.S.E. for return of submissions.
Nonfiction: Articles on street rodding, with primary emphasis on home-built, early-type street rods and special interest cars which are built for recreation, not racing. Pays $50 per published page.

Photos: Purchased with mss. Should be 8x10 b&w glossies, color transparencies, 2¼x2¼. Pays $10 to $250.

STOCK CAR RACING MAGAZINE, 1420 N. Prince St., Alexandria VA 22314. Editor: Richard S. Benyo. "Audience is as varied as the sport; main portion is adult, blue- and white-collar." Established in 1966. Monthly. Circulation: 85,000. Buys all rights. Buys 50 mss a year. Payment on publication. Will send sample copy to writer for 75¢. Query first or submit complete ms. Will not consider photocopied submissions. Reports on material in 2 weeks. Enclose S.A.S.E.
Nonfiction and Photos: "Interviews and driver profiles, track features, technical articles, historical pieces. Would like to see pieces on tracks, drivers, isolated races in the vein of Tom Wolfe, Gay Talese, et al, to balance our straight pieces. Suggest writers read a current issue for style and emphasis." Length: 800 to 2,500 words. Pays $40 to $300. 8x10 b&w glossies purchased with or without accompanying ms and on assignment. Pays $15. 35mm or 2¼x2¼ color transparencies. Pays $100 to $200. Photos must relate to magazine theme.

STREET ROD, P.O. Box 2967, Portland OR 97208. Editor: Bruce Craig. For "persons interested in making street rods out of pre-1948 cars. Reader age goes from 12 years up—average, 30 years old. Education varies greatly." Established in 1971. Monthly. Circulation: 45,000. Buys all rights. Buys 120 to 150 mss a year. Pays on publication. Will send a sample copy to a writer on request. Submit complete ms. Will consider photocopied submissions. Reports in 1 month. Enclose S.A.S.E.
Nonfiction: "Articles, primarily automotive how-to's, and pictorial coverage of pre-1948 street rods. Keep articles automotive oriented. Don't use a lot of slang; no cusswords, and no emphasis on drinking. Our magazine deals strictly with the pre-1948 auto whereas others deal with all years of automobiles. We're interested in articles on metal working, such as chopping a top." Buys how-to's, personal experience articles, profiles, humor, nostalgia, coverage of successful business operations, new product articles, and technical articles. Length: "varies greatly according to the number of pictures with an article. Many articles contain very few words, but many pictures. We pay $50 per page."
Photos: Purchased with or without ms or on assignment, captions optional. For 8x10 or 5x7 b&w glossies, pays $50 a page with mss or individually. For 2¼x2¼ or larger color transparencies for cover, pay is $50 to $250, "according to visual impact."

SUPER STOCK & DRAG ILLUSTRATED, 1420 Prince St., Alexandria VA 22314. Editor: Jim McCraw. For "ages 12 to 45, high school—plus, automotive minded, affluent." Established in 1964. Subject matter is "drag racing: race coverage, technical articles, photo features, color action photography, interviews with drivers, mechanics, builders, officials." Monthly. Circulation: 125,000. Rights purchased vary with author and material, but may buy all rights, and may reassign them back to author after publication. Buys 50 to 75 mss a year. Payment on acceptance or publication—depending upon familiarity with writer. Will send a sample copy to a writer for 60¢. Query first required. Submit seasonal material 3 months in advance. Enclose S.A.S.E.
Nonfiction and Photos: "Terse inquiry letters, please, with brief description of intended subject and slant. *Super Stock* is a 'racer's friend', deals with political issues within the drag racing world. We deal in controversy on the rules of racing, etc. We do not use cartoons or humor. We would like to see some articles about women in drag racing as drivers/mechanics." Buys informational, how-to, profile, photo, and technical articles. Pays $50 per published page. Photos purchased with and without mss, on assignment, and captions required. 35mm, 2¼x2¼, 4x5 b&w negatives. 35mm, 2¼x2¼, 4x5 Kodak negatives. Prefers automobiles engaged in drag racing, on the drag strip; prefer wild action shots. Payment varies.

SUPERCYCLE, 1560 Broadway, New York NY 10036. Editor: Joe Oldham. Bimonthly. Buys all rights. Pays on publication. Reports in 2 to 4 weeks. Enclose S.A.S.E. for return of submissions.
Nonfiction: Articles of interest to motorcycle enthusiasts. All mss must include good photos, 5x7 minimum. Length: open. Pays about $30 per page for mss with photos.

Aviation Publications

The publications here aim at professional and private pilots, and at aviation enthusiasts in general. Magazines intended for the in-flight passengers of commercial airlines are grouped in a separate In-Flight category in the Sponsored Publications section. Technical aviation and space journals, and those for airport operators, aircraft dealers, or other aviation businessmen are listed under Aviation and Space in the Trade Journals.

AERO MAGAZINE, 4731 Laurel Canyon Blvd., Suite 3, North Hollywood CA 91607. Editor: Wayne Thoms. For "owners of business and pleasure aircraft." Bimonthly. Circulation: 97,000. Buys first rights. Buys about 24 mss a year from freelancers. Pays on publication. Will send a sample copy to a writer for 25¢. "Queries are recommended, and if writer is a novice or non-experienced pilot, the ms should be checked over by an experienced pilot before submission." Will accept photocopied submissions, if stated on ms that it is not being simultaneously submitted elsewhere. Returns rejected material and acknowledges acceptance of material in 2 to 4 weeks. Enclose S.A.S.E. for return of submissions.
Nonfiction: Uses "serious articles pertinent to aircraft ownership, including technical, proficient, and profitable utilization of contemporary aircraft." *Aero* is "the only publication that goes strictly to aircraft owners. It does not cover learn-to-fly, historical, nostalgia, agricultural, military, or airline subject matter." Buys how-to's, personal experience articles, interviews, profiles, think pieces, new product and successful business operation coverage, photo stories, and travel pieces. Writer "should realize that all the readers have at least a private license and elementary subjects have no interest for the readers. Reporting should be concise and straightforward." Length: to 2,500 words. Pays $35 to $50 per printed page with photos.
Photos: Purchased with ms. Uses b&w glossies, color transparencies, color prints. Pays $50 for cover; $10 to $35 for inside color.

AIR LINE PILOT, 1625 Massachusetts Avenue, N.W., Washington DC 20036. Editor: C.V. Glines. "Our main readership is composed of airline pilots who are members of the Air Line Pilots Association. Other readers include flying buffs, business aircraft pilots, stewards and stewardesses, and airline industry executives." Monthly. Circulation: 45,000. Buys all rights. Buys about 25 mss a year from freelancers. Pays on publication. Will send a free sample copy on request. Query first. Reports "as soon as decision is made." Enclose S.A.S.E. for return of submissions.
Nonfiction: Wants "articles on aircraft safety, aviation history, weather, airline pilots with interesting hobbies and sidelines, air racing, and similar subjects of interest to airline pilots. Especially interested in phase of aviation history dealing with development of airline flying. "Interested writers should ask for a copy. We keep the airline pilot in mind at all times—his interests, desires and his special brand of professionalism. While we treat some subjects lightly, we do not kid around with safety subjects." No aircraft safety articles from "amateurs who know not whereof they speak." Length: 1,000 to 2,500 words. Payment is $75 a printed page.
Photos: B&w glossies purchased with mss. Payment varies. Color transparencies and 35mm color purchased for 4 color covers. Payment is $100 up.

AIR PROGRESS, Petersen Publishing Co., 437 Madison Avenue, New York NY 10022. Editor: Richard B. Weeghman. "For pilots and aspiring pilots and people interested in all aspects of private, commercial, and military aviation." Publishes special issues "on special aviation topics like homebuilt, military, sport, and great aircraft." Monthly. Circulation: 130,000. Buys all rights or first rights. Buys "many" mss each year from freelancers. Pays on acceptance. No query required. Submit seasonal material 3 to 4 months in advance. Returns rejected material and acknowledges acceptance "quickly." Enclose S.A.S.E. for return of submissions.
Nonfiction and Photos: Buys mss on aviation subjects: how-to's, interviews, profiles, humor, historical pieces. Primary subject is private flying; also uses mss on military subjects. "Write well and interestingly." Pays minimum $100 per article or an average of $300 per article. Buys b&w glossies, color transparencies, 35mm color.

THE AOPA PILOT, 7315 Wisconsin Ave., Bethesda MD 20014. Executive Editor: Robert I. Stanfield. For plane owners, pilots, and the complete spectrum of the general aviation industry. Official magazine of the Aircraft Owners and Pilots Association. Monthly. Circulation: 175,000. Pays on acceptance. Reports promptly. For staff-prepared material contained in the magazine's "What's New" feature, information should be received 10 weeks in advance of publication date, which is normally about the first of each month. Enclose S.A.S.E. for return of submissions.

Nonfiction: Factual articles up to 2,500 words that will inform, educate and entertain flying enthusiasts ranging from the student to the seasoned professional pilot. These pieces should be generously illustrated with good quality photos, diagrams or sketches. No military or airline material. Quality and accuracy essential. "Each issue carries at least two fast-paced personality features, one on aircraft maintenance information, another on new or unusual planes or aeronautical equipment; a first-person featurette on how a pilot profited from a hair-raising flying adventure, a travel feature on interesting spots that can be visited by airplane, and an article concerning FAA or general aviation policies. Additional features on weather in relation to flying, legal aspects of aviation, flight education, pilot fitness, aviation history and aero clubs are used periodically. Short features of 100 to 300 words written around a single photograph, and strong photo features are always in demand." Payment is about 7¢ per word.

Photos: Pays $10 to $25 for each photo or sketch used. Exceptionally good cover color transparencies also purchased.

How To Break In: "Be aviation oriented and study the magazine (available at most airport pilots' lounges). And remember that our audience consists solely of pilots; thus a writer must speak the 'language' and be knowledgeable in the subject area."

AVIATION TRAVEL, P. O. Box 7070, Arlington VA 22207. Editor: Brad Bierman. For "owners of business and private aircraft; ages 30 to 50; well-educated; interested in fishing, hunting, boating, photography, golf, sightseeing, beaches, resorts, outdoor and other sports." Bimonthly. Established in 1972. Circulation: 130,000. Buys all rights. Buys about 20 to 30 mss a year. Pays on publication. Will send a sample copy to a writer for $1. Write for copy of guidelines for writers. Query first or submit complete ms for nonfiction. Will consider photocopied submissions. Submit seasonal material 3 to 4 months in advance. Reports in 2 months. Enclose S.A.S.E.

Nonfiction and Photos: "Short travel articles—where to go, what to see and do. We may feature a general area or special activity, event, or resort which must be accessible by private or business plane. The U.S.A., Canada, Mexico, and the Bahamas are preferred. Airport and flight info are helpful, but not required. The style should be light and nontechnical. Stories must be short, informational, and specific enough to be helpful to the traveler. Destinations must be emphasized, rather than flight. Dates, admission, what to take, etc., increase the value of a story. We're the only travel-oriented aviation magazine, featuring places and events accessible by general aviation. We're interested in fly-in wilderness, fishing, hunting, golfing and camping stories at specific locations. Each issue features items of particular interest during the period immediately following." Buys informational articles, how-to's, personal experience articles, interviews, humor, historical articles, photo features, travel pieces, new product articles, and technical articles. Length: 200 to 1,500 words. Pay "varies: about 5¢ per word, depending on subject and quality." Photos purchased with mss or without mss; captions required. Pays "$5 and up, depending on photo, for b&w glossies 5x7 and larger." Pays $5 and up, "depending on photo and use, for transparencies only."

Fillers: Newsbreaks, jokes, short humor.

CANADIAN AVIATION, 481 University Ave., Toronto 2, Ontario, Canada. Editor: Hugh G. Whittington. For "pilots and owners of aircraft: private, corporate and airline." Subject matter is "totally Canadian." Special issues: avionics, general aircraft buyers' guide, business and corporate aviation special annual aviation directory of Canada. Monthly. Circulation: 15,000. Buys first rights. Buys 25 to 35 mss a year from freelancers. Pays on publication. Query required. "Send a story outline first, discuss detail later." Deadline is first of month preceding month of issue. Reports "as soon as possible." Enclose S.A.E. and International Reply Coupons for return of submissions.

Nonfiction and Photos: Wants "pilot evaluations of aircraft, where-to fly stories, educational pieces, historical aviation items, etc." Articles can be how-to, personal experience, interviews, profiles, inspirational, humor, spot news, successful business operations, historical, think pieces, expose, new product, photo, travel, and merchandising techniques. Length: 500 to 3,000 words. Payment is $50 to $350. Buys b&w glossy photos and color transparencies with mss. Payment is $10 to $100.

GREAT LAKES FLYER, 654 Fourth St., N.W., Grand Rapids MI 49504. Editor: Joyce M. Warren. For "private aircraft owners, pilots (student through airline captain), flying clubs and various organizations, and those connected with or interested in the aviation industry." Established in 1967. Monthly. Circulation: 30,000. Not copyrighted. Buys 6 to 12 mss a year. Pays on publication. Will send a sample copy to a writer on request. Query first or submit complete ms. Will consider photocopied submissions. Reports in 2 months. Enclose S.A.S.E. for return of submissions.
Nonfiction and Photos: "25% of editorial content is devoted to news coverage, 50% to regular columns, and 25% to editorial features. Regular columns are devoted to pilot education, aviation medicine, antique aircraft, homebuilt aircraft, vacation spots for the flyer, and various organized aviation groups. Editorial features are done on such subjects as aircraft flight tests, governmental regulations, aviation industry problems, and individuals with special interest or appeal. We're the only regional newspaper in the Great Lakes area covering aviation events and activities." Buys informational articles, how-to's, personal experience articles, humor, nostalgia, and travel articles. Length: 1,500 to 3,000 words. Pays $10 to $20. 5x7 b&w glossies purchased with mss; captions required.

PLANE AND PILOT, Box 1136, Santa Monica CA 90406. Editor: O.N. Werner. Copyrighted. For pilots, aircraft owners, operators. Pays on publication. Will send sample copy for $1. Reports in six weeks. Enclose S.A.S.E.
Nonfiction and Photos: Must be technically correct, aimed at pilot proficiency, training, how to improve flight skills, safety. Photos must accompany mss. 1,500 to 2,000 words. Pays $100 to $200. 8x10 b&w glossy photos included in ms payment.

Black Publications

In this category are black general interest publications (including newspapers) and magazines.

Additional markets for black-oriented material will be found in other sections of this book.

BLACK AMERICA, 24 West Chelten Ave., Philadelphia PA 19144. Editor: J. Morris Anderson. General interest magazine for blacks. Bimonthly. Buys all rights. Pays on publication. Query first. Enclose S.A.S.E.
Nonfiction: Articles on fashion, social problems, community, education, and other subjects of interest to an adult black audience. Also carries home decorating and cooking features. Length: varies. Pays $25.
Fiction: Publishes 1 short story per issue relating to black life. Length: varies. Pays $25.
Poetry: Pays $15 to $25.

BLACK TIMES: Voices of the National Community, Box 10246, Palo Alto CA 94303. Editor: Eric Bakalinsky. Established in 1971. For "military personnel, blacks and nonblacks whose interest is survival with dignity; for nonblacks interested in the black experience." Monthly. Circulation: 40,000. Not copyrighted. Buys 50 mss a year. Payment in contributor's copies. Query first or submit complete ms. Reports on material in 15 days. Will send sample copy to writer for 50 cents. Will consider photocopied submissions. Enclose S.A.S.E.
Nonfiction and Photos: "Consumer education and other ordinary truths of immediate interest to blacks; celebrations of individuals and groups, their efforts and goals

in community service and survival." **Length**: 4,000 words maximum. Pays $10 to $80. Dept. Editor: Noe Jiivyn. 8x10 b&w glossy photos purchased with or without mss. Captions required. Pays $10 to $20. Photo Dept. Editor: Cee Wright.

Fiction: Experimental, mainstream, mystery, adventure, western, erotica, science fiction, fantasy, humor, romance, confession, religious, historical. Length: 4,000 words maximum. Pays $10 to $80. Dept. Editor: Frank Lee Downe.

Poetry and Fillers: Open to all forms of poetry. Length: 400 lines maximum. Pays $10 to $40. Puzzles, jokes, short humor, pithy truths. Length: 500 words maximum. Pays $10 to $25. Poetry Dept. Editor: I. Odus. Filler Dept. Editor: Shirley Grit.

BLACK WORLD, 1820 South Michigan Avenue, Chicago IL 60605. Editor: Hoyt W. Fuller. Special issues: April, drama; May, Pan-African; June, fiction; September, poetry; February, black history. Established in 1942. Monthly. Circulation: 100,000. Rights purchased vary with author and material, but may buy all rights, then reassign them to author after publication. Buys 85 mss a year. Payment on publication. Will send a free sample copy to a writer on request. Will send editorial guidelines sheet to a writer on request. Submit seasonal material 3 to 4 months in advance. Enclose S.A.S.E. for return of submissions.

Nonfiction, Fiction, and Poetry: "Articles, fiction, poems, book reviews dealing with black American, Caribbean, African experiences, with emphasis on cultural and political aspects. Emphasis is on the positive and the constructive; approach problems, issues, situations from black context, with black audience in mind." A recent article is "The Black Social Worker's Role in the Black Community" (Better). Buys informational, historical, and book and record reviews. Length: up to 3,900 words. Pays $25 to $150. Fiction should relate to subject matter. Length: up to 3,900 words. Pays $35 to $150. Buys free verse and avant-garde forms of poetry. Should relate to subject matter. Pays $10 to $35.

CORE, 200 W. 135 St., New York NY 10030. Editor: Doris Innis. Publication of the Congress of Racial Equality. Established in 1970. Bimonthly. Circulation: 20,000. Rights acquired vary with author and material. Uses about 60 freelance articles a year. "Most of our articles are donated." Will send free sample copy to writer on request. Query first. Will consider photocopied submissions. Submit seasonal material at least 2 months in advance. Reports on material within 6 months. Enclose S.A.S.E. for response to queries.

Nonfiction and Photos: "Articles about or related to the black movement, black people's oppression, projected or attempted solutions. Also profiles of Black Movement people. Interviews. Health, food, books, sports. Also interested in travel, fashion, movies or African affairs. The writer's style and emphasis is up to him. We like variety. Of course, it helps if his outlook is black nationalist, but it's not mandatory. We try to make black nationalism (a little understood concept) digestible for the common man as well as the intellectual. Most articles are donated." Length: 500 to 5,000 words. Pays $25 for b&w photos on assignment. Captions optional.

Fiction: Should relate to magazine's theme. Length: 500 to 5,000 words. "Most are donated."

Poetry and Fillers: Free verse and avant-garde forms. Should relate. Length: open. Short humor and anecdotes. Length: 500 to 1,500 words. "Most are donated."

THE CRISIS, 1790 Broadway, New York NY 10019. Editor: Henry Le Moon. Official publication of the NAACP. "Our audience includes government officials, schools and libraries, representative of the leadership group in the black community across the nation, and persons involved in the broad area of human relations." Established in 1910 by W. E. B. Du Bois. Monthly (June/July, August/September issues are combined). Circulation: 100,000. Uses 50 freelance mss a year. "Our payment to writers at this time is in contributor's copies only." Submit complete ms. Reports on material within a month. Enclose S.A.S.E. for return of submissions.

Nonfiction: "Articles dealing with civil rights and general welfare of Negroes and other minorities." Informational, interview, profile, historical, think pieces, exposes. Length: 3,000 words maximum.

Fiction: Short stories with a racial theme.

Poetry: Traditional forms, blank verse and free verse. Should relate to magazine's theme. Length: 40 lines maximum.

EBONY MAGAZINE, 820 S. Michigan Ave., Chicago IL 60605. Editor: John H. Johnson. Address mss to Charles L. Sanders, Managing Editor. For black readers of the U.S., Africa, and the Caribbean. Monthly. Circulation: 1,300,000. Buys all rights. Buys about 20 mss a year from freelancers. Pays on publication. Query first. Submit seasonal material 2 months in advance. Reports in 1 to 2 weeks. Enclose S.A.S.E. for return of submissions.

Nonfiction: Achievement and human interest stories about, or of concern to, black readers. Photo essays, interviews, think pieces, profiles, humor, inspirational and historical pieces are bought. Length: 2,500 words minimum. Pays $150 and up.

Photos: Purchased with mss, and with captions only. Buys 8x10 glossies, color transparencies, 35mm color. Submit negatives and contacts when possible. Photo stories. Pays $150 and up.

ESSENCE, 102 E. 30th St., New York NY 10016. Editor-in-Chief: Marcia Gillespie. For black women, ages 18 to 34. Monthly. Circulation: 200,000. Buys North American serial rights. Pays after publication. Will send a sample copy to a writer for 70¢. Query first for nonfiction. Will consider photocopied submissions. Reports in 4 to 6 weeks. Enclose S.A.S.E. for return of submissions.

Nonfiction: General articles of interest to black women; in-depth articles. Possible subjects include consumer affairs, shopping guides, child care, careers, politics and politicians, the arts, entertainment-personality pieces, and other black interest pieces. Length: varies. Pays $150 to $400.

Photos: Purchased with or without mss. Black themes. Payment varies.

Fiction: High quality stories with black themes. Some short-shorts. Recent titles include "A Gift for Mama," "Honor Among Thieves." Length: maximum 3,000 words. Pays $150 to $300. Dept. Editor: Sharyn Skeeter.

Poetry: No limitations on subject matter. Must be high quality. Length: 65 lines maximum. Pays $25 to $50.

How To Break In: "My guidelines to freelancers are brief. All manuscripts must be typed and double spaced, with the wordage no longer than 3,500. The usual article lengths for us fall between 1,500 and 3,000 words. First time *Essence* authors must submit on speculation, and it takes 4 to 6 weeks for my editors to read and evaluate. Subjects that I am most interested in are as follows: lifestyles, family health, day care, education, women's health, money savers, budgets, people pieces that go beyond facades, new trends, politics, sex, and religion."

JET, 820 S. Michigan Ave., Chicago IL 60605. Editor: John H. Johnson. For black readers interested in current news and trends. Weekly. Circulation: 500,000. Study magazine before submitting. Enclose S.A.S.E. for return of submissions.

Nonfiction and Photos: Articles on topics of current, timely interest to black readers. News items and features: religion, education, African affairs, civil rights, politics, entertainment. Buys informational articles, interviews, profiles, spot news, photo pieces, and personal experience articles. Length: varies. Payment to be negotiated.

SEPIA, 75 East Wacker Drive, Chicago IL 60601. Editor: Ben Burns. For "black readers of all age groups and interests." Monthly. Circulation: 100,000. Buys all rights. Buys about 75 mss a year from freelancers. Pays on acceptance. Will send a sample copy to a writer for 60¢. Will consider photocopied submissions. Submit seasonal material 3 months in advance. Reports in 1 week. Enclose S.A.S.E.

Nonfiction and Photos: "We are in the market for well-written, provocative factual articles on the role of black Americans in all phases of American life. We look for a good writing style, no different from any popularly written publication. We are constantly in need of articles with current news value, but strictly projected for future publication. In this respect, we specifically look for queries on events that will be in the news when our magazine reaches its readers. Articles may be on interesting personalities, entertainers, sports figures, human interest or controversial topics. We will consider any subject if it has good reader appeal for a black audience. It cannot be overemphasized that contributors should study recent issues for general content and style." Buys interviews, profiles, historical articles, exposes, coverage of successful business operations, photo essays. Length: 1,500 to 3,000 words. Pays $75 to $200. Photos are purchased with mss. B&w glossies, color transparencies.

Business and Finance Publications

In this listing are national and regional publications (including newspapers) of general interest to businessmen. Those in the National grouping cover national business trends, and include some material on the general theory and practice of business and financial management. Those in the Regional grouping report on the business climate of specific regions.

Magazines that use material on national business trends and the general theory and practice of business and financial management, but which have a technical, professional slant, are classified in the Trade Journals section, under the Business Management, Finance, Industrial Management, or Management and Supervision categories.

National

BARRON'S NATIONAL BUSINESS AND FINANCIAL WEEKLY, 22 Cortlandt St., New York NY 10007. Editor: Robert M. Bleiberg. For business and investment people. Weekly. Will send free sample copy to a writer on request. Buys all rights. Pays on publication. Enclose S.A.S.E. for ms return.
Nonfiction: Articles about various industries with investment point of view; shorter articles on particular companies, their past performance and future prospects as related to industry trends for "News and Views" column. Length: 2,000 words or more. Pays $200 to $500 for articles; $100 and up for "News and Views" material. Articles considered on speculation only.

BLACK BUSINESS DIGEST, 3133 N. Broad St., Philadelphia PA 19132. Editor: Vincent A. Capozzi. For "the academic world and the educated layman, both black and white. We are heavily subscribed to by institutions of higher learning." Monthly. Pays on acceptance. Submit complete ms for nonfiction. Will consider photocopied submissions. Reports in 6 weeks. Enclose S.A.S.E.
Nonfiction: "We are a magazine concerned with minority economics. Articles range from black manufacturing through to politics insofar as the political scene affects minority economics. Occasionally articles on travel, the medical profession, and community development groups are accepted. Avoid the usual magazine formula story and opinionated pieces which cannot be substantiated. Facts and figures are required to back up contentions. Both black and white authors are represented. Our theme is 'black and white economic cooperation.' Do not send articles which go overboard in condemning white racism; pieces which, while making various charges, have not an authoritative document to back up the contentions." Recent articles include "Black Women Marketing Executives" (Moragne), profiles of five black women in marketing; "Just What Has OMBE Done for Minority Women?" (Peterson), a review of the activities at the Office of Minority Business Enterprise. Length: 750 to 2,500 words. Payment negotiable.

BLACK ENTERPRISE, 295 Madison Ave., New York NY 10017. Editor: Pat Patterson. For black men and women interested in succeeding in the business world. Monthly. Circulation: 125,000. Buys all rights. Pays on publication. Query first. Study magazine before submitting. Enclose S.A.S.E. for return of submissions.
Nonfiction: Basically a how-to magazine: how a black person can break into and get ahead in business in the U.S. Publishes factual articles and slightly technical articles on economic developments, business trends and how-to, career opportunities in business; primarily informational and analytical, with a positive approach toward the free enterprise system. Length: varies. Payment to be negotiated according to the nature of the article.

BOARDROOM REPORTS, 11 W. 42 Street, New York NY 10036. Editor: Martin Edelston. For "high level business executives and their advisors." Biweekly. Circulation: 15,000. Buys all rights. Buys about 75 mss a year. Pays on publication. Will send a sample copy to a writer on request. Query first. Submit seasonal material at least 2 months in advance and newsletter items 3 weeks in advance. Reports in 3 weeks. Enclose S.A.S.E.

Nonfiction: "This periodical combines many newsletters in a single publication. The newsletters cover each of 37 major facets of a business operation, from accounting and computers through transportation and warehousing. The purpose is to keep the nation's decisionmakers fully informed on the entire range of executive responsibilities in the shortest possible time. We buy useful information for business leaders; articles that will help business plan ahead, articles that will help executives perform more effectively. Information should be useful, high level, and tightly written." Buys how-to's, interviews, and think pieces. Length: 750 to 1,500 words. Pays $150 per printed page. Newsletter items, about 80 words, $10.

BUSINESS WEEK, (incorporating *Generation*), 330 W. 42nd St., New York NY 10036. Does not solicit freelance material.

THE EXCHANGE MAGAZINE, published by the New York Stock Exchange, 11 Wall St., New York, NY 10005. Editor: Edward Kulkosky. For present and potential investors. Monthly. Pays on acceptance. Query first. Enclose S.A.S.E.
Nonfiction: "Articles must have current interest. Investors must be able to relate indirectly and directly. We do profiles of industries, also timely pieces on trends in business, investment, finance, economics and government." Pays up to $350 for standard pieces up to 1,800 words.

EXECUTIVES WEALTH REPORT, c/o Institute for Business Planning, 14 Plaza Rd., Greenvale NY 11548. Editor: Burton DeFren. For business executives. Buys all rights. Pays on publication. Mss should be double spaced with 50 character lines. Reports in 1 week. Enclose S.A.S.E. for return of submissions.
Nonfiction: "Wants articles on building personal and corporate wealth. New or little known, practical ways of making money, saving money, and cutting taxes; written in an interesting, straightforward style." Length: 1,000 to 1,200 words. Payment is 8¢ to 12¢ a word.

FINANCE, 5 E. 75th St., New York NY 10021. Managing Editor: J. Richard Elliott. For bankers, brokers, corporate financial officers, and insurance officials. Monthly. Will send a sample copy to a writer on request. Query first. Study the publication carefully before submitting. Enclose S.A.S.E. for reply to queries.
Nonfiction and Photos: Prefers a lively, human interest style; "tell the story in terms of the people involved. We are using more international articles and pieces on economics, and would like to encourage writers in those areas." Encourages statistical material. No academic pieces, historical articles, or industry profiles. Length: 1,200 to 2,000 words. Pays $200 minimum. Photos purchased with mss.

FORBES, 60 Fifth Ave., New York NY 10011. "We do not buy freelance material."

FORTUNE, 1271 Ave. of the Americas, New York NY 10020. Staff-written.

IMPETUS, 481 University Ave., Toronto, Ont., Canada. Editor: Ann Rhodes. For senior business executives and professionals. Established in 1970. Monthly. Circulation: 167,000. Rights purchased vary with author and material. May buy all rights or first North American serial rights. Buys approximately 20 mss a year. Payment on acceptance. Will send free sample copy to writer on request. Query essential. Will not consider photocopied submissions. Submit seasonal material 9 to 12 months in advance. Reporting time varies on mss accepted for publication. Returns rejected material in 1 month. Enclose S.A.S.E. for reply to queries.
Nonfiction and Photos: General interest articles for senior level business executives and professionals. Length: 1,000 to 2,750 words. 8x10 b&w photos and color transparencies. Pays 5¢ to 10¢ a word; $15 to $50 for b&w photos; $25 to $75 for color.

MONEY, Time-Life Building, Rockefeller Center, New York NY 10020. Managing Editor: William Simon Rukeyser. "For the middle to upper middle income, sophisticated, well-educated reader. We picture our readers as neither insiders or idiots." Established in 1972. Monthly. Query first; all material purchased on assignment. Enclose S.A.S.E. for reply to queries.
Nonfiction: Material on personal economics. "We deal with careers, investments, spending, how people handle their money. We cover taxation, tax shelters, savings,

insurance—everything involving money." Length: 2,000 to 3,000 words. Payment varies.

WALL STREET REPORTS, 54 Wall St., New York NY 10005. Editor: Richard A. Holman. For persons interested in stocks and the stock market. Established in 1967. Monthly. Circulation: over 35,000. Query first. Study magazine before submitting. Enclose S.A.S.E. for reply to queries.
Nonfiction: Buys articles from market experts which will better inform investors and persons interested in investments. Length and payment to be negotiated.

Regional

ALASKA CONSTRUCTION AND OIL, 109 W. Mercer St., Seattle WA 98119. Editor: Martin H. Loken. For "management in Alaska's fields of construction, oil development, timber, mining, transportation." Special issue: Annual Forecast and Review (January). Monthly. Circulation: about 8,000. Buys first rights. Buys 35 to 40 mss a year. Pays on publication. Query first. Reports in 2 months. Enclose S.A.S.E. for reply to queries.
Nonfiction and Photos: "Anything related to the development of the state of Alaska—except tourism and fisheries." Writer should "get 'inside' the subject. We're not interested in puff, editorial elevation of our advertisers, etc. No newspaper style." Buys how-to's, interviews, profiles, photo essays, coverage of successful business operations. Length: 500 to 2,000 words. Pays $1 a column inch. Photos purchased with mss. Color transparencies, b&w glossies. Pays $10 for b&w, $50 for color.

AUSTIN, P.O. Box 1967, Austin TX 78767. Editor: George Seagert. For central Texas residents, primarily businessmen. Monthly. Not copyrighted. Query first. Pays on acceptance. Reports in about two weeks. Enclose S.A.S.E.
Nonfiction: Articles 800 to 1,200 words about the Austin/central Texas area business, historical, civic, art and community endeavors. Payment negotiable; averages 2¢ per word. Query first.
Photos: Purchased with mss or with captions only. Pays $5 to $20.
Fiction: About 1,000 words, used infrequently. Query first.

BUSINESS WEST, P.O. Box 536, Oakland CA 94604. For "businessmen of all types, above average in income and education, who are interested in promising stocks and companies." Monthly. Buys all rights. Buys a varying number of mss a year. Pays on publication. Will send a sample copy to a writer for $1.00. No query required. Submit seasonal material 2 months in advance. Reports in 2 to 4 weeks. Enclose S.A.S.E. for return of submissions.
Nonfiction and Photos: Wants "articles describing various west coast companies and their operations." Length: 1,500 to 5,000 words. Payment is $10 to $50. B&w glossy photos purchased with mss.

CANADIAN BUSINESS MAGAZINE, 1080 Beaver Hall Hill, Montreal 1, Quebec, Canada. Editor: Robin Schiele. Monthly. Reports on submissions in 8 weeks. Buys first Canadian serial rights only. Query first. Pays on acceptance. Enclose S.A.E. and International Reply Coupons with queries and submissions.
Nonfiction: Articles of interest to Canadian businessmen dealing with trade, technology, management, science, finance and government action as it affects private business in Canada. Length: 1,000 to 2,500 words. Pays $150.

COMMERCE, 130 S. Michigan Ave., Chicago IL 60603. Editor: Gordon A. Moon II. "Most of our material is staff-written."

FLORIDA TREND MAGAZINE, Box 2350, Tampa FL 33601. Editor: Don Teverbaugh. For business, industrial and financial executives with Florida interests. Monthly. Circulation: 34,000. Not copyrighted. Pays on publication. Will send a sample copy to a writer on request. Query first. Reports immediately. Enclose S.A.S.E. for reply to queries.
Nonfiction: Articles on successful people or ventures with emphasis on how it was done, in the state of Florida only. Also items relating to general Florida news and

financial news. Length: 500 to 2,000 words. Always query first. Pays $1 per inch for shorts, $50 and up for profiles, $100 to $300 for major research stories.
Photos: "Top dollar for photos to illustrate major stories or events in Florida and also for picture stories."

FORT WORTH, 700 Throckmorton, Fort Worth TX 76102. Editor: Barbara Winkle. For "top executives of area companies as well as other Chamber of Commerces across the United States." Established in 1923. Monthly. Circulation: 4,500. Buys all rights. Buys about 10 to 12 mss a year. Payment on acceptance. Will send free sample copy to a writer on request. Will send editorial guideline sheet to a writer on request. Submit seasonal material 2 months in advance. Reporting time varies. Enclose S.A.S.E. for return of submissions.
Nonfiction, Photos, Fiction, and Fillers: "Feature type stories of interest to the businessman." Approach should be "a business angle with emphasis on Fort Worth." Buys historical, think pieces, photo articles and book reviews. Length: 300 to 1,000 words. Pays $10 to $50. Photos are purchased with or without mss and captions are required. Pays $50 maximum for picture story. Specifications: b&w, 5x7 or 8x10. No color. Pays $10 to $50 for 300- to 1,000-word fiction. Pays $10 to $50 for 300- to 1,000-word humor fillers.

THE HILLSDALE REPORT, Public Relations Division, Hillsdale College, Hillsdale MI 49242. Editor: Beth A. Herbener. For "people in middle management positions, active in community affairs and volunteer work. How-to articles for businessmen, as well as more substansive material about free market economy, management theory, and principles which underlie the free society." Established in 1962. 10 times per year. Circulation: 5,000. Rights purchased vary with author and material. Buys 10 mss a year. Payment on publication. Will send free sample copy to writer on request. Query first. Will consider photocopied submissions. Reports on material accepted for publication in 2 weeks. Returns rejected material in 2 weeks. Enclose S.A.S.E. for reply to queries.
Nonfiction: Informational, how-to, think pieces, successful business operations. "Emphasizes traditional values concerning free market economics and the moral and political values which underlie the free society. Writers should keep this in mind." Length: 4,000 words maximum. Pays $150 per ms.

HOUSTON BUSINESS JOURNAL, 5314 Bingle Road, Houston TX 77018. Editor: Mike Weingart. For "businessmen, investors, management; 25 to 60 years old, generally college graduates." Weekly. Circulation: 10,000. Buys all rights. Buys about 100 mss per year. Pays on publication. Will send a sample copy to a writer on request. Query first. Submit seasonal material 1 month in advance. Reports in 2 weeks. Enclose S.A.S.E. for reply to queries.
Nonfiction: "Exclusively about business and it must have specific applications or examples about Houston business. Everything is localized. We publish some special issues, generally to coincide with a meeting or convention, such as a special section on the American Bankers Association convention, or the National Homebuilders Association convention." Buys how-to's, personal experience articles, interviews, profiles, coverage of successful business operations, think pieces, and articles on merchandising techniques. Length: 300 to 1,500 words. Pays $1.50 per column inch.
How To Break In: "Probably the best way for someone to sell us copy is anytime a Houston-based company is doing something of business news significance in their hometown. It might be a meeting before a group of local analysts or it might be the opening of a major facility. We have a correspondent in London who keeps up with the list of Houston-based companies and whenever one of them is in the news there, she goes ahead with an interview with the top executives. She sends us the story, we publish it, and she gets paid."

INDIANA MAGAZINE, 1100 Waterway Blvd., Indianapolis IN 46202. Editor: Phyllis L. Thom. For "the business executive (presidents, vice presidents, managers, purchasing agents) in Indiana." Established in 1955. Monthly. Circulation: 8,500. Rights purchased vary with author and material, but may buy first or second serial rights. Buys 12 to 15 mss a year. Payment on publication. Will send a sample copy to

a writer for 25¢. Query first required. Submit seasonal material 2 months in advance. Reports in 1 month. Enclose S.A.S.E. for reply to queries.
Nonfiction: "Business oriented features of interest to Indiana businessmen. One-half of the magazine contains articles of general business interest, and one-half features a specific segment of business and industry each month such as construction in Indiana." Buys think, successful business operations, and merchandising technique articles. Length: 500 words. Pays $25 to $75. Dept. Editor: E.A. Kieta.

INVESTOR, WISCONSIN'S BUSINESS MAGAZINE, 611 N. Broadway, Milwaukee WI 53202. Editor: Don Adams. For Wisconsin business and professional persons. Established in 1970. Monthly. Circulation: over 15,000. Buys all rights but will reassign rights to author after publication. Buys 30 to 50 mss a year. Payment on publication. Will send free sample to writer on request. Write for copy of guidelines for writers. Query first. Will consider photocopied submissions. Reports on material in 1 month.
Nonfiction and Photos: Articles on "Wisconsin business and public affairs, interpretations and analyses of state news items or national news items as they relate to Wisconsin and Wisconsin business." Length: 1,200 to 3,500 words. Pays $35 to $400. B&w (8x10) photos purchased with ms or on assignment. Captions optional. Pays $25 to $60 for color transparencies.

KENTUCKY BUSINESS, 300 West York St., Louisville KY 40203. Editor: Ernest E. Sears, Jr. For executives of Kentucky business and industry. Kentucky-related news and features on business. Monthly. Circulation: 5,000 plus. Usually buys North American serial rights only; author can specify in most cases. Pays on acceptance. Will send a sample copy to a writer on request. Primarily staff-prepared, so query is desirable. Subjects planned 6 months in advance for the monthly major feature on some phase of Kentucky business and industry, are announced in January and June. Reports in one month. Enclose S.A.S.E. for reply to queries.
Nonfiction and Photos: Feature material on phases of Kentucky business and industry only; emphasis on new business personnel, accomplishments, labor-management relations. Factual, with documentation where appropriate. Length; 1,000 to 1,600 words. Payment by arrangement; maximum, $250. Photos seldom purchased except from Kentucky photographers. 8x10 b&w glossies. Payment by arrangement; photographer should specify price where convenient.

MICHIGAN BANKING & BUSINESS NEWS (formerly *The Michigan Tradesman*), 1886 Osage Drive, Okemos MI 48864. Editor: J.H. O'Neil. For bank and business executives in the state, plus the state legislature. Established in 1883. Monthly. Circulation: 5,000. Not copyrighted. Pays on acceptance. Will send free sample copy to a writer on request. Submit complete ms. Will consider photocopied submissions. Reports in 1 week. Enclose S.A.S.E. for return of submissions.
Nonfiction and Photos: "Require only features on banking or business activities, preferably in Michigan. Marketing or merchandising innovations among banks. Would consider banking features dealing with a topic from another state. Banking features must be both interesting and informative. In business features, readability is keyword. Business features must deal with Michigan." Length: 1,000 to 1,200 words. Pays 5¢ to 15¢ a word. 8x10 b&w glossy photos purchased with mss. Captions required. Pays $5 to $10.

NEW ENGLANDER MAGAZINE, 3 Arlington St., Boston MA 02116. Editor: Bradford W. Ketchum, Jr. Monthly for "top and operating business and industrial leaders throughout New England." Will send free sample copy to a writer on request. Prompt reports on submissions. Buys all rights. Pays on publication. Enclose S.A.S.E. with all mss and queries.
Nonfiction and Photos: All articles must have New England business angle and interest. Will consider either ideas or finished articles. Payment varies. Glossy photos purchased with mss or with captions only.

NEW JERSEY BUSINESS, 50 Park Pl., Newark NJ 07101. Director of Publishing: Howard C. Dolainski. Issued monthly. Edited for business and industry executives

of New Jersey. Payment on acceptance. Reports in two weeks. Buys all rights. "However, if occasion arises, we can accommodate an author by first rights only." Include S.A.S.E. for return.
Nonfiction: Wants general business stories of New Jersey, not specific companies, of approximately 600 to 1,000 words. Pays flat fee of $50 and up.

THIS IS WEST TEXAS, P.O. Box 1561, Abilene TX 79604. Editor: J.L. Martin, Jr. For "top business executives of the western 60% of Texas." Established in 1918. Bimonthly. Circulation: 3,700. Buys all rights. Buys 12 mss a year. Pays on acceptance. Will send a sample copy to a writer for $1. Submit only complete ms. Will not consider photocopied submissions. Reports in 60 days. Enclose S.A.S.E.
Nonfiction and Photos: Publishes "historical, humorous, and factual stories related to west Texas." Length: 4,500 to 5,000 words. Payment is $25. B&w glossy photos purchased with accompanying mss. No extra pay for photos.

VOICE OF BUSINESS, Chamber of Commerce of Hawaii, Dillingham Bldg., 735 Bishop St., Honolulu HI 96813. Editor: Doris Huddleston. Query first. Reports in 2 weeks. Enclose S.A.S.E.
Nonfiction: Short feature articles about business, commerce, industry, and economics as well as regulation or legislation thereof. Must be related to the state of Hawaii. Length: 50 to 500 words. Pays 2¢ to 3¢ per word.

Confession Publications

DAUNTLESS BOOKS GROUP: SECRETS, REVEALING ROMANCES, CONFIDENTIAL CONFESSIONS, DARING ROMANCES, EXCITING CONFESSIONS, SECRET ROMANCES, 1120 Avenue of the Americas, New York NY 10036. Editorial Director: Jean Sharbel. *Secrets* and *Revealing Romances*, monthlies, are major magazines here; others are bimonthlies. Reports in 2 weeks. Buys all rights. Pays on acceptance. Enclose S.A.S.E. for ms return.
Fiction: Confession stories written in a strongly dramatic, sincere, emotional style with fresh plot complication. First-person stories about marriage and courtship must be plausible, realistic and interesting. Stories written from feminine viewpoint preferred, but man's viewpoint stories may be used occasionally. Sex used, but not lurid or thrown in just for the sake of sensationalism. Length: short-shorts from 2,000 to 3,000 words; shorts from 3,500 to 7,500 words and novelettes up to 8,500 words. *Secrets* and *Revealing Romances* pay 3¢ to 4¢ per word; bimonthlies pay 3¢ a word.

INTIMATE STORY, 295 Madison Ave., New York NY 10017. Editor: Ellen Davidson. Monthly. Buys all rights. Buys 10 to 12 mss a month. Reports in 4 weeks. Enclose S.A.S.E. for return of submissions.
Fiction: Uses first-person stories on courtship and marriage, teen love affairs, and exciting current situations dealing with social problems and their emotional effects. Man-women relations stressed, and all stories must have the feeling of real happenings. Most any problem commonly encountered in life can be used. In all cases the reader must be able to identify with the protagonist, so no matter how many mistakes the protagonist may make, she must engender deep sympathy. "The heroine need not suffer earthshaking, abject guilt, and endings need not involve a moral lesson. The story should be written around the situation-climax-resolution formula. The reader should be able to see that the protagonist has learned something about life and about herself. The heroine must face up to something, and she must be a better person for it. I also use stories from man/boy's point of view, but never more than one per issue." Length: 2,000 to 6,000 words. Pays 3¢ a word.
How To Break In: "Any young writer can break into the magazine I edit by writing a story that I find acceptable. But I use fiction only, rarely buy anything under 2,000 words. Of course, I'd love something at 1,500 words, but that's almost the toughest length of all to pull off. Every manuscript submitted is read. Out of the 10 to 12 manuscripts a month that I buy, at least one or two will be from 'unknown' writers;

sometimes it will be their very first sale. Some of these 'new' writers go on to be regulars in the magazine, others don't seem to be able to make it again."

KMR ROMANCE GROUP: MY LOVE SECRET CONFESSION, UNCENSORED CONFESSIONS, REAL ROMANCES, REAL STORY,

21 W. 26th St., New York, NY 10010. Editor: Ardis Sandel. *Real Story*: monthly; *Real Romances*: monthly; others bimonthly. The first two publications are aimed mainly toward the teenage audience, married and unmarried; *Real Romances* seeks out the young married's problem story (also the girl on her first job in the big city); *Real Story* tries for the older (18 to 45) woman's story. Reports on submissions in 4 to 6 weeks. Buys all rights. Buys about 400 mss a year. Payment on publication. Enclose S.A.S.E.

Nonfiction: Articles dealing with sexual problems of interest to both married women and single girls. Length: up to 2,000 words. Pays up to $75.

Fiction: First-person confession stories; no racial stories. *My Love Secret Confession* and *Uncensored Confessions* want fiction about the modern teenager facing real (no matter how unusual) situations and problems. Prefers a "slice of life" story, especially one dealing with teenage sex problems. Emphasizes good characterization, developing real people. *Real Romances* uses stories about the problems of young marrieds in modern-day society, city and small town. Stories where the protagonist helps him or herself. Also stories of young women on their own for the first time in a city; courtship stories. *Real Story* also prefers a "slice of life" story rather than the lengthy saga, and the editor reports the problem with most beginners' mss here is that the subject matter is too usual, without a different twist or angle to make the story usable. All four publications use lengths from short-shorts up to 7,500 words. Pays up to $150 depending on length

MODERN ROMANCES,

1 Dag Hammarskjold Plaza, New York NY 10017. Editor: Rita Brenig. Managing Editor: David Sutton. Monthly for "blue collar class women." Buys all rights. Pays on acceptance. Reports on submissions within six weeks or less, and rejects are accompanied by an individual criticism designed to help writers in preparing future submissions. Enclose S.A.S.E.

Fiction: First-person confession stories, 5,000 to 7,500 words. Feminine narrator preferred, but masculine not taboo; in either case, narrator should be someone a reader will like and root for. Because of the need for reader identification, avoid glamorous backgrounds with which these high-school educated readers are unfamiliar. A sense of reality is important. Pays 5¢ a word.

How To Break In: "The way for a newcomer to make a sale to *Modern Romances* is to write a story. *All* our stories are carefully read—and we do buy from newcomers if the stories warrant it. It's a good idea for a new writer to read several issues of our magazine before trying to write for us. The second advisable thing for a talented—but somewhat inexperienced—writer to do is to start out by writing about people, situations, and backgrounds that are totally familiar to him or her. Of course, these situations, characters, backgrounds, should also be of the type that our blue-collar women readers are familiar with. This is probably some of the oldest advice in the world."

MY ROMANCE GROUP: MY ROMANCE, INTIMATE SECRETS, INTIMATE ROMANCES, TRUE SECRETS, SECRET STORY, MY CONFESSION,

Magazine Management, 575 Madison Ave., New York, NY 10022. Editorial Director: Cara Sherman. For "women between the ages of 16 and 30." Bimonthly, except for *True Secrets* and *My Romance*, which are monthly. Circulation: 170,000 average per issue. Buys all rights. Buys about 150 mss a year. Payment on acceptance. Will send editorial guidelines sheet to a writer on request. Reports in 4 to 6 weeks. Enclose S.A.S.E. for return of submissions.

Nonfiction: "Though we do not purchase much nonfiction, if the subject is of interest, relevance, and handled appropriately for our readership, we will consider nonfiction for publication." Length: 3,000 to 5,000 words. Pays $125 to $150.

Fiction: "We look for tender love stories, touching baby stories, and stories dealing with identifiable marital problems, particularly sexual. To a lesser degree, we are interested in realistic teen stories, male-narrated stories, and tales with supernatural overtones. Stories should be written in the first person, preferably female. They should deal with a romantic or emotional problem that is identifiable and realistically portrays how the narrator copes with her conflict and resolves it. Using a conversational tone, the story is an open, honest confession of her distress, how it affects those close to her, how she works it out. We reject stories based on hackneyed themes and outdated attitudes. In our contemporary society, stories condemning premarital sexual experience, abortion, those that preach chastity, etc., are unsuitable for our needs." Length: 1,500 to 6,000 words. Pays $75 to $150.

PERSONAL ROMANCES 295 Madison Ave., New York NY 10017. Editor: Johanna Roman Smith. Monthly. Buys all rights. Pays on acceptance. Reports on submissions in 4 to 6 weeks. Enclose S.A.S.E. for return of submissions.
Fiction: First-person stories told in strong up-to-date terms by young marrieds, singles, and teens revealing their emotional, sexual, and family conflicts and their search to resolve personal problems. Blue collar, white collar group identification. Length: 1,500 to 6,000 words. Top pay is up to $175.

REAL CONFESSIONS, MODERN LOVE CONFESSIONS, 315 Park Ave., South, New York NY 10010. Editor: Ruth Beck. Monthly for women from teens on. "As a rule, love, marriage, courtship problems, loneliness, attractiveness, children's problems are main concerns of our readership." Buys all rights. Pays prevailing rates on acceptance. Will not consider photocopied submissions. Will send sample copy for 25¢. Reports in 8 weeks. Enclose S.A.S.E. for return of submissions.
Fiction: "First-person stories, usually told by female narrator, dealing with themes of love and marriage—although almost any dramatic, human experience has potential for a good story for us. We prefer upbeat stories, with original themes and plots. Credibility of plot is important, and background material must be accurate (medical, technical allusions, etc.). Give us a story that has a 'real life' ring, with the emphasis on action and emotion, rather than narration; simple, colloquial style of narration. Language and sentence structure should be simple and direct. We cannot settle for the 'same old story,' no matter how well it is written. We must have new approaches, new ideas, fresh plots." Length: 4,000 to 8,000 words. Also uses short-short stories. Length: 2,000 words.

TRUE CONFESSIONS, 205 E. 42nd St., New York NY 10017. Editor: Florence J. Moriarty. Monthly. Buys all rights. Pays on acceptance. Reports on submissions in 12 weeks. Enclose S.A.S.E. for return of submissions.
Nonfiction and Fillers: Limited market for fresh, well-written, solid features dealing with love and marriage problems. Length: 1,000 to 2,500 words. Child-care features covering problems of infancy to toddler stage. Length: 500 to 1,200 words. Query Helen Vincent, Managing Editor, with outline on features. Must have fresh slant, interest-holding development of material. Pays 5¢ per word for features, but rate varies according to merit. Buys brief, provocative fillers that are suitable to the format.
Fiction: Strongly realistic, emotional, exciting, woman-oriented first-person stories about average people who make highly interesting reading. "We are after the unusual that is also believable. Our greatest need is for stories in the 5,000 to 7,500-word class. All stories must be based on themes and problem situations that relate and are of interest to young women. Special attention should be given the handling of a story's lead. It must be provocative, immediately stirring up reader interest for the story that is about to unfold. The characters should come through as real people, not puppets who are manipulated by the writer to 'make the story come out right.' " No abnormal sex or strictly sex-situation stories wanted. Pays 5¢ per word. Uses novelettes, about 18,000 words. For a story to command this length, it must have adequate plot complication and strong drama. Uses one book-length novelette an issue; pays flat rate of $800.

TRUE LOVE GROUP: TRUE LOVE, TRUE EXPERIENCE, 205 E. 42nd St., New York NY 10017. Editor: Bruce Elliott. Appeals principally to women in their mid-twenties. Monthly. Buys all rights. Pays on acceptance. Will send a sample copy to a writer for 50¢. Enclose S.A.S.E. for return of submissions.
Fiction: Good stories told in first person; family life, love, courtship, health; about teenagers, old-agers, babies, romantic couples—humor, whimsy, suspense. "In short, it is the story that counts and pays. Do not send the hackneyed sin stories about pregnancy-before-marriage, the illegitimate child born of a single meeting,

the overdone back street." Length: 4,000 to 8,000 words for regular stories; 2,000 to 4,000 words for "minis" and "brief encounters." Pays 3¢ per word.

TRUE STORY, 205 E. 42nd St., New York NY 10017. Editor: Sue Hilliard. Buys all rights. Pays on acceptance. Reports in six weeks. Christmas material should be submitted in August. Enclose S.A.S.E. for return of submissions.
Nonfiction: Usually by assignment. Length: 2,500 to 3,500 words. Also uses filler articles of interest to young wives and mothers. Length: 1,500 to 2,500 words. Pays $25 to $100.
Fiction: "First-person stories, woman or man-narrated, relating to modern problems of love, courtship, marriage, in-law troubles, infidelity, children, aimed primarily toward blue collar audience. Mixed marriage stories considered, racial and religious. Topical timely themes as often mirrored in headlines." Pays 5¢ per printed word.

Consumer Service and Business Opportunity Publications

Magazines in this classification are edited for individuals who don't necessarily have a lot of money, but who want maximum return on what they do have—either in goods purchased or in earnings from investment in a small business of their own. Publications for business executives are listed under Business and Finance. Those on how to run specific businesses are classified in Trade, Technical, and Professional Journals.

BUSINESS OPPORTUNITIES JOURNAL, 1328 Garnet Ave., San Diego CA 92109. Editor: Hal D. Steward. "Our readers are those persons actively involved in buying and selling real estate, those who are active investors in the stock market, and those who deal in buying and selling business opportunities." Established in 1970. Monthly. Circulation: 48,000. Buys first serial rights. Buys 20 mss a year. Payment on acceptance. Will send free sample copy to writer on request. Query first. Reports on material within a week. Enclose S.A.S.E. for reply to queries.
Nonfiction and Photos: "In-depth reports on the economies of states and major regions; financial success stories; articles on how to make money in real estate and in investments; features on investment opportunities in foreign countries, and some articles on public affairs. Looking for articles on real estate and investment opportunities in the U.S. and Canada. The articles should be slanted toward those who are actively involved in the world of making money." Length: 750 to 2,000 words. Pays minimum of $25. 5x7 or 8x10 b&w photos purchased with mss. Captions required.

CONSUMER GUIDE, 7954 N. Karlov, Skokie IL 60076. Editor: Lawrence Teeman. For a "general consumer readership." Established in 1967. Frequency varies; "we publish issues to coincide with the introduction of new products." Circulation: 200,000. Buys all rights. Pays on publication. Will send a sample copy to a writer on request. Write for copy of guidelines for writers. Query first. Will not consider photocopied submissions. Reports in 1 month. Enclose S.A.S.E. for reply to queries.
Nonfiction and Photos: "All our editorial is bought from freelancers who are qualified in specific product areas. The writer, therefore, must have a strong background of experience in the product areas discussed. He must be able to test actual products for first-hand recommendations and critical appraisal. All our issues are specials— we publish full issues on autos, bicycles, home appliances, guns, fishing and hunting equipment, stereo and hi-fi equipment, etc. We specialize in complete reviews of everything available from leading manufacturers. Our major competition is *Consumer Reports,* but we present much wider coverage to complete product areas." Length: 3,000 to 4,000 words. Pays $150 to $300. "8x10 b&w photos must accompany mss"; captions required. Pays $100 for color photos.

CONSUMER REPORTS, 256 Washington St., Mt. Vernon NY 10050. Staff-written.

CONSUMERS' RESEARCH MAGAZINE (formerly *Consumer Bulletin*), Washington NJ 07882. Editor: F.J. Schlink. Monthly. Limited amount of freelance material used. Query first. Enclose S.A.S.E.

Nonfiction and Photos: Articles of practical interest to ultimate consumers concerned with tests and expert judgment of goods and services which they buy. Must be accurate and careful statements, well-supported by chemical, engineering, scientific, medical, or other expert or professional knowledge of subject. Pays approximately 2¢ per word. Buys b&w glossies with mss only. Payment negotiated.

FDA CONSUMER, 5600 Fishers Lane, Rockville MD 20852. Editor: Wayne L. Pines. For "all consumers of products regulated by the Food and Drug Administration." A Federal Government publication. Established in 1967. Monthly. December/January and July/August issues combined. Circulation: 16,000. Not copyrighted. "All purchases automatically become part of public domain." Buys 8 to 10 freelance mss a year, by contract only. Payment on acceptance. "Actual payment processed by General Services Administration acting upon notice by editor that terms of contract have been fulfilled." Query first. "We cannot be responsible for any work by writer not agreed upon by prior contract." Enclose S.A.S.E. for reply to query.

Nonfiction and Photos: "Articles of an educational nature concerning purchase and use of FDA regulated products and specific FDA programs and actions to protect the consumer's health and pocketbook. Authoritative and official agency viewpoints emanating from agency policy and actions in administrating the Food, Drug and Cosmetic Act and a number of other statutes. All articles subject to clearance by the appropriate FDA experts as well as the editor. The magazine speaks for the Federal Government only. Articles based on facts and FDA policy only. We cannot consider any unsolicited material. All articles based on prior arrangement by contract. The nature and subject matter and clearances required are so exacting that it is difficult to get an article produced by a writer working outside the Washington DC metropolitan area." Length: average, 2,000 words. Pays $400. B&w photos are purchased on assignment only. Currently have blanket contract with Black Star organizations for assigned work.

THE FRANKLIN LETTER, P.O. Box 95, Demarest NJ 07627. Editor: Mark Godwin. For "opportunity seekers and others interested in starting a business of their own." Established in 1971. Monthly. Buys all rights. Pays on publication. Will send a sample copy to a writer for $1. Query first. Will not consider photocopied submissions, but will buy news clippings that fit in with its editorial requirements. Enclose S.A.S.E.

Nonfiction: "This is a newsletter on how to make money full-time or part-time. We publish case histories of successful people, mail order information, financing hints for individuals and small businesses, capital sources, etc. Especially interested in little known tips, insider's secrets, and other types of information not generally known to the general public. Our audience is composed of ambitious, aggressive people interested in making money. Many run their own business, so all material must be practical, workable, and preferably based on successful experience. If material is authenticated with a news clipping, so much the better. All material is heavily edited or rewritten to suit our particular style. All we need are the bare facts; writing style is unimportant." Buys how-to's, success stories, merchandising techniques, etc. Length: as short as possible. Pays a minimum of $10.

INCOME OPPORTUNITIES, 229 Park Ave. S., New York NY 10017. Editor: Joseph V. Daffron. Managing Editor: Robert E. Starrett. For persons "30 to 70, interested in owning an independent business, franchise; selling, mail order." Publishes Sales and Small Business Directory (February) and Directory of Money-Making Ideas (October). Monthly. Circulation: 130,000. Buys all rights. Buys 100 to 150 mss per year. Pays on acceptance. Will send a sample copy to a writer for $1. Query first. Submit seasonal or special material 6 months in advance. Reports in 1 week. Enclose S.A.S.E. for return of submissions.

Nonfiction and Photos: "Semi-inspirational mss on selling; successful business stories; descriptions of franchises. The writing should be factual, clear, and interesting." Buys how-to's, personal experience articles, interviews, inspirational articles, and coverage of successful business operations. Length: 500 to 2,000 words.

Pays $25 to $250. B&w glossies and color transparencies for cover purchased with mss; with captions only.

Fillers: "Especially coverage of successful business operations." Length: 65 lines long by 65 characters per line, or 65 lines long by 35 characters. Pays $25 to $75.

MEDIA & CONSUMER, P.O. Box 850, Norwalk CT 06852. Editor: Francis Pollock. For "consumer writers and editors, print and broadcast; advertising, marketing, public relations and business leaders; consumer affairs officials in government; educators and students; and concerned consumers." Established in 1972. Monthly. Circulation: 1,000. Buys all rights. Payment on publication. Will send sample copy to writer for $1.50. Query first. Submit seasonal material 2 months in advance. Enclose S.A.S.E. for reply to query.

Nonfiction: "Original investigative articles on consumer affairs coverage and pressure interfering with such coverage. Seeing one or two issues should best convey our approach, i.e., that of a journalism review working for more and better coverage of consumer affairs." Informational, how-to, personal experience, interviews, expose and book reviews. Length: 500 to 2,500 words. Pays $50 to $200. Photos purchased on assignment.

MONEYTREE NEWSLETTER, 417 Water St., Task Bldg., Kerrville TX 78028. Editor: R.J. Wilson. Pays on acceptance. Send large S.A.S.E. for sample copy. Enclose S.A.S.E. for return of submissions.

Fillers: "Items dealing with money. How to invest it, make it grow rapidly, how to get big savings—these have the best chance of acceptance. Popular articles in these areas included 'How to Purchase a New Car for $125 Over Cost' and sources of low-cost or interest-free loans available to anyone no matter where they live. Our readers want to get rich, or if wealthy already, stay rich." Also uses capsule articles on "health, self-help, vocational training, practical science, money-making opportunities, etc. Also capsulized write-ups about free publications, product samples, items of value, etc. And wants condensed summaries of consumer aids and important protective actions by FTC, FDA, Agriculture Dept., HEW, etc. All submissions must be documented by author." Length: 10 to 60 words. Payment is $5.

SMALL BUSINESS DIGEST, G.P.O. Box 972, New York NY 10001. Editor: A. Costar. For mail order opportunity seekers. Quarterly. Circulation: 17,600. Not copyrighted. Pays on acceptance. Will send a sample copy to a writer for $1.00. Reports in 1 week. Enclose S.A.S.E. for return of submissions.

Nonfiction: Uses articles on mail order opportunities, sources of supply, and honest ideas or plans for earning money at home, by mail, etc.

Detective and Crime Publications

The magazines below are markets for nonfiction accounts of true crimes. Markets for criminal fiction (mysteries) are listed in Fiction magazines.

CONFIDENTIAL DETECTIVE, CRIME DETECTIVE CASES, 235 Park Avenue, South, New York NY 10003. Editor: B.R. Ampolsk. Bimonthly. Buys all rights. Pays on acceptance. Query preferred. Include S.A.S.E. for return of submissions.

Nonfiction and Photos: True crime stories. Material must be documented with newsclips. Length: 2,500 to 5,000 words. Pays up to $125 per story. Photos purchased with mss or captions only. Pays up to $15 each.

CROOK'S MAGAZINE, 17241 Hatteras St., Encino CA 91316. Editor: Rollo Bretwick. For "detective story readers who want to identify with the successful criminal rather than the cop; crooks, or any rebellious, adventurous person." Quarterly. Buys first rights. Buys 60 to 80 mss per year. Pays on publication. Reports in 2 to 3 weeks. Enclose S.A.S.E. for return of submissions.

Nonfiction and Fiction: "The crook must get away with it in all stories—crime pays. The catharsis at the end is the success of the crime, not the capture of the criminal.

Otherwise, it must be a good suspenseful yarn. For once the cops will be the enemies and crooks the heroes, and the crooks will get away with the crime. There should not be stories treating child molestation, rape, etc. The crimes will be mostly robberies, swindles, cons, etc." Buys how-to articles, personal experience pieces, interviews, profiles, humor, coverage of successful crooked business operations, historical and think pieces, and exposes. For fiction, buys mystery, science fiction, humorous stories, historical fiction, and detective and crime stories. Length: nonfiction, 3,000 words maximum; fiction, 10,000 words maximum. Pays 3¢ to 5¢ a word.

Poetry: Light verse. Pays 5¢ a word minimum.

Fillers: Jokes, short humor. Pays 5¢ a word minimum.

DETECTIVE FILES GROUP: DETECTIVE FILES, HEADQUARTERS DETECTIVE, DETECTIVE CASES, DETECTIVE DRAGNET, Globe Communications Corp., 1440 St. Catherine St. W., Montreal 107, Quebec, Canada. Editor: Dominick Merle. Bimonthly. Enclose S.A.E. and International Reply Coupons.
Nonfiction and Photos: "We're looking for current, sensational crimes detailing police investigation and culminating in an arrest. Rarely use anything short of murder. No open-and-shut cases; no unsolved crimes. Main market is U.S. Send either queries or completed mss and photos. There is steady income here for those who deliver." Length: 2,500 to 5,000 words. Pays $100 to $200.

FRONT PAGE DETECTIVE, INSIDE DETECTIVE, 1 Dag Hammarskjold Plaza, New York NY 10017. Editor: James W. Bowser. Monthly. Buys North American serial rights only. Pays on acceptance. Will consider photocopied submissions. Reports on submissions in 10 days. Enclose S.A.S.E. for return of submissions.
Nonfiction: Articles on current crime; must have plenty of drama, action, good police deduction. Lengths: 3,500 to 4,500 words. Pays $200 to $300. Prefers query; however, if querying on current crime, be prepared to deliver ms fast. Good available photos can help sell a ms.
Photos: Purchased with mss or with captions only. Must have crime theme. 8x10 or 5x7 glossies preferred. No color. Pays $10 to $20 for singles; $100 to $125 for photo series. Requires model releases if posed.

MASTER DETECTIVE, 235 Park Avenue South, New York NY 10003. Editor: Albert P. Govoni. For crime buffs, armchair detectives. Established in 1929. Monthly. Circulation: 125,000. Buys all rights. Buys about 125 mss a year. Payment on acceptance. Will send a sample copy to a writer for 50¢. Will send editorial guidelines sheet to a writer on request. Query first required; "we will guide." Reports in 1 week. Enclose S.A.S.E. for reply to queries.
Nonfiction and Photos: Subject matter is "crime only. No shorts." Length: 5,000 to 6,000 words. Pays a flat $200. Address to Managing Editor. Photos purchased with or without mss. Wants quality and drama in 8x10 b&w glossies. Pays $12.50.
How To Break In: "This is not a market for the amateur. We buy short pieces only rarely. Most shorts which appear in the magazine are staffwritten. We are always interested in competent new writers, but we prefer them to be experienced newspapermen who have a basic understanding of the legal problems inherent in our material, and how to cope with same in their copy. Ideally, the new writer should be a reporter or desk man who has worked on the local case he's trying to sell us, a man with established contacts and rapport with the law enforcement people involved. How does he sell us his first story? A query is a must, and it should be brief but comprehensive and explicit, incorporating these points: Locale of crime, date, names of victim and suspect, current status of case (has suspect been indicted, bound over for trial, trial date set or pending), amount of detective work required for solution of case; also we want to know about the art situation: are photos available, and how many? Writer should enclose his phone number. If we're interested, we'll very likely call him and discuss his story, suggesting guidelines for treatment. We are always ready to work hard to develop a promising writer, and many of our most reliable veterans began with us exactly as outlined above. Some have gone on to write several books."

OFFICIAL DETECTIVE STORIES, 235 Park Avenue South, New York NY 10003. Managing Editor: Edward Gibbons. Monthly. Buys all rights. Pays on acceptance. Query mandatory. Reports in one week. Enclose S.A.S.E.

Nonfiction and Photos: True, current stories of crime detection, Length: 5,000 to 6,000 words. Study magazine to see exactly what is wanted. Pays $200. Photos purchased to illustrate stories. Prefers 8x10 glossies, professionally finished. Needs complete caption information and identification for all photos. Pays $7.50 per print used.

OFFICIAL POLICE DETECTIVE, TRUE CRIME DETECTIVE, DETECTIVE WORLD, BEST TRUE FACT DETECTIVE, 5202 Casa Blanca Rd., Scottsdale AZ 85253. Editor: Tommy Kay. For "devotees of the 'true crime' detective story." Established in 1945. Quarterly. Circulation: 40,000 to 95,000. Buys all rights, but will reassign rights to author after publication. Buys 50 to 100 mss a year. Payment on acceptance (checks mailed within 30 days of acceptance). Will send sample copy to writer for 50¢. Query first for nonfiction. Send complete ms for fillers. Will not consider photocopied submissions. Submit seasonal material 5 months in advance. Reports on material accepted for publication in 4 weeks. Returns rejected material in 4 to 6 weeks. Enclose S.A.S.E. for reply to queries or return of submissions.
Nonfiction and Photos: "True stories on crime, especially murders. Lean to sexually motivated crimes. Format generally moves from discovery of body down trail of investigation to eventual solution and trial. Please read copies of current issues before submitting. Short articles on crime humor, kudos to lawmen for solving cases; crime and legal informational pieces, and those on victims of crimes." Regular columns include "Above and Beyond the Call of Duty" (tributes to lawmen) and "The Clue" (special clues used to break cases). Length: 800 to 3,500 words. Pays $15 to $75. 5x7 or 8x10 b&w glossies purchased with mss. Captions required. Uses 2x2 (or larger) color transparencies for cover. Payment to be negotiated. "Top of $75."
Fillers: Crime crossword puzzles, clippings for "Legal Laffs," jokes, short humor on crime. Length: 100 to 1,500 words. Pays $5 to $15.

STARTLING DETECTIVE, TRUE POLICE CASES, 1440 St. Catherine St. West, Montreal, Que., Canada. Editor: Dominick A. Merle. Bimonthly. Buys all rights. Pays on acceptance. Reports in one week. Enclose S.A.E. and International Reply Coupons for return of submissions.
Nonfiction: "We are constantly in need of current crime cases; we seek those accounts which cover the very latest murder, kidnapping, bank robbery, etc. We find that the best approach in the writing of fact-detective stories is the unfolding of the action in chronological sequence: the finding of the body, the arrival of the police at the scene, their search for clues, the questioning of witnesses, the running down of suspects—and ending with some clever deduction which leads to the apprehension of the chief suspect. The best stories are those in which the culprit's identity is not known to the police for more than 24 hours; this allows for the running down of false clues and suspects. When the killer's identity is known immediately, there is, of course, no possibility for suspense, mystery or detective work. These are what we call 'open-and-shut' cases and should be avoided. We do not seek straight articles on crime subjects." Send query or completed ms and photos. Length: 3,000 to 7,000 words. Pays $100 to $200; more for "blockbusters."
Photos: Purchased with mss; 8x10 preferred. Pays $7.50 to $15.
How To Break In: "First, read a few issues of the magazines to become familiar with the style. Second, when you spot a mysterious murder in your area, clip all newspaper accounts, talk to detectives after an arrest is made, to gather more details; talk to anyone else who might have some information to offer. Third, query me about the story or write it on speculation. Stay away from unsolved cases or 'oldies.' I'm also more receptive to cases which have not attracted national exposure. I'm constantly seeking more stories and new writers and there could be a good market here for those who deliver."

TRUE DETECTIVE, 235 Park Avenue South, New York NY 10003. Editor: A.P. Govoni. Managing Editor: Edward Gibbons. Monthly for armchair detectives, both male and female. Will send sample copy for 50¢. Reports in one week. Buys all rights. Pays on acceptance. No fiction or poetry. Enclose S.A.S.E. for ms return.
Nonfiction: Accurate, timely stories of true crimes, preferably murder, with photos of principals, etc. Must be written with strong characterization, motivation, detective work, suspense. Published upon indictment, also stories after trial. Police image must be good. Query mandatory. Length: 5,000-6,000 words. Pays $200.

Education Publications

Magazines in this listing approach the subject of education with the interests of parents and the general public in mind. Journals for professional educators and teachers are included under Education in the Trade Journals section.

AMERICAN EDUCATION, U.S. Office of Education, 400 Maryland Ave., S.W., Washington DC 20202. Editor: Leroy V. Goodman. For educators and lay readers with a special interest in the field of education. Monthly except combined January-February. August-September issues. Not copyrighted. Pays on publication. Query before submitting material. Reports in 2 weeks. Enclose S.A.S.E. for reply to queries.
Nonfiction: "Articles that describe specific federally supported programs and projects of proven effectiveness and include helpful information on how they may serve as models for other schools or school districts." Brisk, bright writing desired; full of facts, people, and anecdotes. Length: 2,500 words average. Payment varies with circumstances; average is $250.

CANADIAN RED CROSS SOCIETY RESOURCE PACKAGE, 95 Wellesley St., East Toronto MYH 1HC, Ontario, Canada. Editor: Carol Kelly. For teachers and high school groups. Quarterly. Circulation: 30,000. Buys first rights. Payment on acceptance. Query first. Acknowledges material in 1 or 2 days. Enclose S.A.E. and Canadian postage for response to queries.
Nonfiction and Photos: Educational materials for elementary and high school levels. Material oriented to Red Cross principles and philosophy, health and safety; human understanding and service to others. Pays 2¢ to 5¢ per word; $3 to $10 for b&w photos accompanying mss. Captions required.

CAREER EDUCATION NEWS, 230 W. Monroe St., Chicago IL 60606. Contact: Elaine Katz, Director of McGraw-Hill's Educational Publications and Innovative Communications. Semimonthly.
Nonfiction: Information about earliest education levels to adult continuing education in the U.S.; educational equipment, programs, etc. All articles about career awareness and skills.

CHANGE MAGAZINE, NBW Tower, New Rochelle NY 10801. Editor-in-Chief: George W. Bonham. For "academic intellectuals, primarily leading faculty, college, and university presidents, professional people, and others concerned with higher education in America." Monthly. Circulation: 35,000. Buys all rights. Buys about 150 mss per year. Pays on publication. Will send a sample copy to a writer on request. Query first. Reports in 1 month. Enclose S.A.S.E.
Nonfiction: "As the leading publication in higher education, our magazine uses highly sophisticated, in-depth writing with high intellectual content. Two-thirds of the magazine consists of major articles, all assigned. In-depth reports, which comprise about one-fourth of the magazine, are on events, profiles, academic, social, and cultural problems. The remainder are assigned regular columns." Length: 3,000 to 8,000 words. Pays $100 to $550 for major article.

FOREWORD, 145 E. 69th St., New York NY 10021. Editor: R. Ames Crozier. For today's undergraduate college student. "Offers an authoritative 'informational clearinghouse in print' by reporting what new changes affecting student life are taking place, and how our readers can act on them. As its name implies, *Foreword* is a magazine that prefaces tomorrow so that students can move ahead today." Established in 1971. Monthly, September through May. Circulation: 400,000. Buys all rights but will reassign rights to author after publication. Payment on acceptance. Will send sample copy to a writer for 75¢. Write for copy of guidelines for writers. Query first on articles longer than 1,000 words. "Shorter pieces (tips, notes, ideas, etc.) can be sent directly." Will consider photocopied submissions. "All submissions must arrive 2 months in advance of issue date." No issues appear during the summer. Reports on material in 1 month. Enclose S.A.S.E. for return of submissions or reply to queries.

Nonfiction: "Each month, a 12- to 16-page center section is presented on a single timely topic of future concern, in brief guideline fashion, so that those interested can investigate it fully on their own. Two main student interest groups have sustained prominence on today's undergraduate campus that must be fully considered when writing for us. The largest group consists of those attending college for its more traditional benefits—a good job and a secure future. The second, finding college's conventional motivations less than stimulating, follows the current wave of 'new naturalism'. But regardless of chosen life styles or ambitions, all our readers do share common concerns. Our objective is to answer those concerns. Additionally, we will publish 1 monthly feature-length article (query preferred but not necessary) and are looking for freelance writers qualified to review current events, books, film, music and science on a continuing basis for our regular monthly columns. If interested, please send detailed background profile and writing samples." 2,000 to 5,000 words. Pays $500 to $1,500 for lengthy articles; $50 to $200 for those shorter.

P.T.A. MAGAZINE, 700 North Rush St., Chicago IL 60611. Editor: Donald Mahoney. Art Director: Grazyna Girdvainis. For "more than 8 million PTA members throughout America." Monthly. Buys all rights. Pays on publication. "The editor would prefer to see a finished ms, but he will respond to queries if the writer encloses samples of his previous work." Enclose S.A.S.E.
Nonfiction: "Articles of interest to parents with children in 3 specific age categories: preschool, elementary school, and secondary school. Emphasis will be on reports with substantive information dealing with the problems parents face as parents and with problems their children face as children, whether the young people are in the preschool, elementary, or secondary school age bracket. A contributor's style should be popular, no matter how serious his subject matter may be. He should talk directly to the parents with whom he wishes to communicate. Articles on new trends in education, psychology, drug abuse, health care, the changing mores of our times, any subject of interest to parents, teachers, and students are solicited." Length: average 1,800 words. Payment open.
Photos: "Photo stories with or without a message."
Fiction and Poetry: "Quality fiction and poetry only. Contributors to literary reviews invited to submit. Payment in fee and copies."

Fiction Publications

The following popular magazines are unusual today because they carry little or no nonfiction. They are grouped together here (except for the Confessions, which have their own classification) for the benefit of the fiction specialist who might otherwise overlook them. Additional markets for these and other kinds of fiction will be found in nearly every category of this book.

Fantasy

FANTASTIC STORIES, 69-62 230 St., Bayside Station, Flushing NY 11364. Editor: Ted White. 15-to 30-years of age audience. Established in 1952. Every 2 months. Circulation: 25,000. Buys first world serial rights. Buys 100 mss a year. Pays on publication. Will send sample copy to a writer for 65¢. Submit complete ms. Will consider photocopied submissions. Reports "as soon as possible." Enclose S.A.S.E. for return of submissions.
Fiction: Fantasy. Length: open. Pays 1¢ to 3¢ a word.

WEIRDBOOK, P.O. Box 35, Amherst Branch, Buffalo NY 14226. Editor: W. Paul Ganley. For fantasy and supernatural fans. Published once or twice a year. Buys North American serial rights. Pays on publication. Will send a sample copy to a writer for 50¢. Reports in 1 to 6 weeks. Enclose S.A.S.E. for return of submissions.
Fiction and Poetry: Interested in weird tales and poems along the lines of Lovecraft, Poe, Dunsany, and C.A. Smith. "Be familiar with the subject of weird tales in the

tradition of the old magazine *Weird Tales.* If you don't normally read such material, you won't be able to write it." Length: to 10,000 words; also uses short-shorts. Pays a minimum of $1 per printed page. No length requirements for poetry.

General Interest

FICTION, 193 Beacon St., Boston MA 02116. Editor: Vincent McCaffrey. For "young (18 to 30) in college or college graduates for whom reading is a primary interest, as well as politics, products and services oriented toward a free and individualistic life style." Established in 1972. Bimonthly. Circulation: 1,000. Buys first North American serial rights. Will send free sample copy to writer on request. Write for copy of guidelines for writers. Submit complete ms. Will consider photocopied submissions, if clean and clear. "Each year we will have a special poetry issue, as well as a special children's issue." Submit seasonal material 2 months in advance. Enclose S.A.S.E. for return of submissions.
Fiction, Nonfiction and Photos: "Short stories, sketches, serializations, reviews of fiction, drama or screenplays, and authors. Mysteries, westerns, romances, satire, humor, science fiction. In fact, any genre. Quality and craftsmanship, artistic style and originality are first requirements. Looking for prose that emphasizes theme, plot and characterization. Art for art's sake. Fiction is an art form and is treated as such. We do not edit material received. *Fiction* is a gallery for artists of the written word. Our dominant theme is the individual. None of the typical *Playboy, Redbook* or *McCall's* type stories." Length: open. Pays $10 to $20 for nonfiction; $10 to $30 for fiction. Pays $5 for b&w photos purchased with or without accompanying mss.
Poetry and Fillers: Traditional forms, blank verse, free verse, avant-garde poetry, light verse. Length: open. Pays $5 to $30. Jokes and short humor (as short as possible). Pays $5 to $10. All must relate to fiction or fictional subjects.

GREEN'S MAGAZINE (Fiction for the Family), Box 313, Detroit MI 48231. Editor: David Green. For a "general audience, with stories aimed at all age and interest levels." Established in 1972. Quarterly. Circulation: 5,000. Buys first North American rights, and will reassign rights to author after publication. Buys 40 mss a year. Payment on publication. Will send sample copy to writer for $1. Submit complete ms. Reports on material in 6 weeks. Enclose S.A.S.E. for return of submissions.
Fiction: "For family-type reading. One children's story per quarterly issue. Others range from sci-fi to 'women's' and adventure. Humor welcome. Study several issues. Quality and communication and penetrating characterization are requisites (plus freshness and vitality)." Length: 1,000 to 3,500 words. Pays $10 to $25.
Poetry: Themes open. Length: 40 lines maximum. Pays $3.

THIS ISSUE, Box 15247, Emory University Sta., Atlanta GA 30333. Editor: Mel McKee. For "a general audience." Monthly. Buys all rights. Pays on publication. Will send a copy to a writer for $1.25. Reports in 1 month. Enclose S.A.S.E. for return of submissions.
Fiction: Wants all kinds of fiction: children's stories, science fiction, romance, mystery, quality. Wants to appeal to a broad audience, reaching the university and the home. Therefore, more restrictions on taste than material aimed just to an academic market. Length open: uses short-shorts of under 2,000 words as well as longer stories. Pays $25 minimum. "Various creative contests and publishing opportunities for the winners found in each issue."
Poetry and Nonfiction: "All kinds. Would like to see more humorous poems." Pays $5 minimum. Department Editor: H.E. Francis. Also uses essays.

Mystery

ALFRED HITCHCOCK'S MYSTERY MAGAZINE, 784 U.S. 1, Suite 6, North Palm Beach FL 33408. Editor: Ernest M. Hutter. General audience. Established in 1956. Monthly. Buys first North American serial rights and all foreign serial rights. Payment on acceptance. Submit only complete ms. "All mss must be typewritten, double-spaced on plain white bond paper (never onion skin, carbons or photocopies) and accompanied by a self-addressed stamped envelope. Your name and address should appear in the top left-hand corner of the title page." Reports promptly.

Fiction: "Mystery and suspense short fiction (new stories only; no reprints or true crime). As this is a mystery-suspense-crime fiction magazine, subject matter should definitely fit into this category. Originality, good writing and plotting, and plausibility will determine acceptance or rejection. Any gross sensationalism is taboo, such as bloody violence, racial strife, profanity, perversion or explicit sex. It will benefit a writer to study a copy of the magazine thoroughly before submitting any material." Length: 1,000 to 10,000 words. Pays 5¢ per word.

How To Break In: "New writers usually do best in the shorter lengths, where there generally aren't as many characters and plot complications to juggle."

ELLERY QUEEN'S MYSTERY MAGAZINE, 229 Park Avenue, South, New York NY 10003. Editor: Ellery Queen. Address mss to Eleanor Sullivan, Managing Editor. Monthly. Circulation: 273,000. Buys first rights. "Authors retain all subsidiary and supplementary rights, including radio and TV. We are also looking for fine reprints providing the author owns and controls the reprint rights." Buys about 160 mss a year. Pays on acceptance. "It is not necessary to query us as to subject matter or to write asking for permission to submit the story." Will consider photocopied submissions, but prefers original. "Do not ask for criticism of stories; we receive too many submissions to make this possible." Returns rejected material and acknowledges acceptance of material "usually within 1 month." Enclose S.A.S.E.

Fiction: "We publish every type of mystery: the suspense story, the psychological study, the deductive puzzle—the gamut of crime and detection, from the realistic (including the 'policeman's lot' and stories of police procedure) to the more imaginative (including 'locked rooms' and 'impossible crimes'). We need tougher stories for our Black Mask section—but we do not want sex, sadism, or sensationalism-for-the-sake-of-sensationalism. We especially are interested in 'first stories'—by authors never before in print." There are "three criteria: quality of writing, originality of plot, and craftsmanship. The most practical way to find out what *EQMM* wants is to read *EQMM.*" Also wants detective and crime short stories with sports backgrounds—baseball, football, golf, auto racing—whatever sport the writer is familiar with. "We do not want fact-detective cases or true stories; this is a fiction magazine." Length: 1,500 to 6,000 words. Pays 3¢ to 8¢ per word for original stories.

How To Break In: "We are quite well known for publishing first short stories; that is, the first published fiction of many writers, in our Department of First Stories. We often publish more than one first story per issue."

MIKE SHAYNE MYSTERY MAGAZINE, 8230 Beverly Blvd., Los Angeles CA 90048. Editor: Cylvia Kleinman. Monthly. Buys magazine serial rights only. Pays on acceptance. Reports in 3 weeks. Enclose S.A.S.E. for return of submissions.

Fiction: Strong, fast-moving stories. Length: 1,000 to 6,000 words. Pays 1¢ a word and up.

How To Break In: "A new, sincere writer breaks into MSMM by studying the type of material we use. He should know pace of story, type of mystery we use. Best to send very short material to start, as the new author doesn't handle novelette lengths convincingly."

Science Fiction and Speculative Fiction

AMAZING STORIES, 69-62 230 St., Bayside, Flushing NY 11364. Editor: Ted White. For 15- to 30-year age group. Established in 1926. Every 2 months. Circulation: 30,000. Buys first world serial rights. Buys 100 mss a year. Pays on publication. Will send sample copy for 65. Submit complete ms. Will consider photocopied material. Reports "as soon as possible." Enclose S.A.S.E. for return of submissions.

Fiction: Science fiction only. Length: open. Pays 1¢ to 3¢ a word.

ANALOG SCIENCE FICTION & SCIENCE FACT, 420 Lexington Ave., New York NY 10017. Editor: Ben Bova. For general technical-minded audience. Monthly. Buys all English serial rights. Pays on acceptance. Reports within 3 to 4 weeks. Enclose S.A.S.E. for return of submissions.

Nonfiction and Photos: Needs illustrated technical articles. Length: 5,000 words. Pays 5¢ a word. Buys photos with mss only. Pays $5 each.

Fiction: Stories of the future told for adults interested in science and technology; central theme usually interaction of strong characters with science or technology-based problems. Length: 3,000 to 60,000 words. Serials only on consultation with Editor. Pays 3¢ to 4¢ a word for novelettes and novels, 5¢ a word for shorts under 7,500 words.

ETERNITY SF, PO Box 193, Sandy Springs SC 29677. Editor: Stephen Gregg. Established in 1972. Quarterly. Buys first North American serial and second serial rights. Buys about 40 mss a year. Payment on acceptance. Will send a sample copy to a writer for $1. Query first for nonfiction and book reviews. Will consider photocopied submissions. Reports in 1 to 2 weeks. Enclose S.A.S.E.
Nonfiction, Fiction, and Poetry: Subject matter consists of "science fiction and fantasy; both traditional and 'new wave.' We think we are more open to new writers, new ideas, and experimentation. There are absolutely no taboos. However, we prefer not to see attempts at humor in nonfiction submitted." Buys interview, profile, personal opinion, and book reviews. Length: 3,000 words maximum. Pays ½¢ a word. Buys experimental, science fiction, and fantasy fiction. Length: up to 15,000 words; up to 40,000 words for 2-part serial. Pays 1¢ a word. Buys traditional and avant-garde forms and free and light verse. Pays 10¢ a line.

FANTASY AND SCIENCE FICTION, 347 E. 53rd St., New York NY 10022. Editor: Edward L. Ferman. Buys first North American serial rights and first foreign rights; also option on first anthology rights. Uses some reprints. Enclose S.A.S.E. for return of submissions.
Fiction: Wants quality science fiction. Especially needs well-plotted science fiction with good, strong characters and action. Classifications from absolute fantasy to strict science fiction; story types from pulp to slick to quality to experimental. Length: 400 to 15,000 words. Pays 2¢ a word for originals, 1¢ a word for reprints.
Poetry: Science fiction or fantasy poetry, short verse (preferably light). Length: up to about 30 lines. Pays $10 and up.

GALAXY MAGAZINE, 235 E. 45th St., New York NY 10017. Editor: Ejler Jakobsson. Bimonthly. Pays on acceptance. Enclose S.A.S.E. for return of submissions.
Fiction: Wants quality science fiction stories. Length: to 60,000 words. Pays 2¢ to 3¢ a word.

VERTEX, 8060 Melrose Ave., Los Angeles CA 90046. Editor: Don Pfeil. For "the intelligent, above average science fiction/science fact reader." Established in 1972. Bimonthly. Buys all rights but will reassign rights to author after publication or buys first North American serial rights. "Depending on author 'name', payment is on acceptance or prior to publication." Will send sample copy to writer for $1. Write for copy of guidelines for writers (S.A.S.E. must be enclosed). Query first. "Read issues before submitting." Will not consider photocopied submissions. Reports on material in 6 to 8 weeks. Enclose S.A.S.E. for reply to queries.
Fiction: "Top quality science fiction; no spooky stuff, no fantasy, no sex unless rele²vant. We aim for good writing appealing to the high IQ reader and written by same." Length: 2,000 words up to novelette length. Pays $125 to $500.
Nonfiction and Photos: "Articles should emphasize extrapolated current social, environmental, or science developments which may constitute our future." Length: 3,000 to 7,000 words. Payment ranges from $125 to $250. Photos purchased on assignment.

IF—WORLDS OF SCIENCE FICTION, 235 E. 45th St., New York NY 10017. Editor: Ejler Jakobsson. Bimonthly. Pays on acceptance. Enclose S.A.S.E. for return of submissions.
Fiction: Wants believable science fiction stories. Read magazine before submitting. Length: to 20,000 words. Pays 2¢ to 3¢ a word.

Western

WESTERN FICTION, P.O. Box 1302, Springfield IL 62705. Editor: George O. Dillon. For "Wild West buffs of all ages." Established in 1969. Monthly. Circulation:

125,000. Rights purchased vary with author and material; buys all rights (but will reassign rights to author after publication), first North American serial rights, or first serial rights. Buys 36 to 80 mss a year. Pays on publication. Write for copy of guidelines for writers. Query first "with lead page digest, description of characters, biography and photo of author" or submit complete ms. Will consider photocopied submissions. Submit seasonal material 3 to 4 months in advance. Reports in 4 to 6 months. Enclose S.A.S.E. for return of submissions.
Nonfiction and Fiction: "Wild West only. We look for believability, locale, proper usage of Wild West terms, etc." Length: 2,000 to 6,000 words. Pays 1¢ to 1½¢ a word.

ZANE GREY WESTERN MAGAZINE, 8230 Beverly Blvd., Los Angeles CA 90048. Editor: Cylvia Kleinman. Monthly. Buys magazine serial rights only. Pays on acceptance. Reports within 3 weeks. Enclose S.A.S.E. for return of submissions.
Fiction: Wants stories with authentic, realistic western background and characterization. Length: 5,000 words maximum. Pays minimum of 1¢ a word.

Food and Drink Publications

Magazines classified here aim at individuals who are interested in and appreciate fine wines and fine foods. Journals aimed at food processors, manufacturers, and retailers will be found in the Trade Journals.

BON APPETIT, 4700 Belleview, Kansas City MO 64112. Editor: M. Frank Jones. For persons interested in food preparation and service. Established in 1956. Bimonthly. Circulation: over 265,000. Buys all rights. Pays on publication. Study magazine before submitting. Enclose S.A.S.E. for return of submissions.
Nonfiction: Feature articles on cooking, including recipes and preparation. Emphasis is on entertainment. Purchases some travel articles, which must detail the foods (including preparation and service) native to the region visited. Also carries articles on wines, including vintage studies and the like. Length and payment to be negotiated.

CALIFORNIA COOKBOOK BULLETIN, 555 Buena Vista W. 405, San Francisco CA 94117. Editor: R. David Herndon. For "affluent middle class and upper class, high and low income who like wine, fine music, travel, language, books." Established in 1972. Monthly. Circulation: 12,000. Buys all rights and simultaneous rights. Buys "unlimited number" of mss a year. Payment on publication. Will send sample copy to writer for $1. Write for copy of guidelines for writers. Query. Will consider photocopied submissions. Submit seasonal food articles 2 months in advance of every holiday. Reports on material in 30 days. Enclose S.A.S.E. for reply to queries.
Nonfiction and Photos: "Gourmet secrets, recipes, special interest exclusives, features, food decoration, table arrangements, color and texture, gourmet accessories; how to do it the gourmet way at the beach, park, festival, etc." Informational, how-to, personal experience, interview, profile, historical, think pieces, nostalgia, spot news, new product. Should be "easy to read, general interest, with outstanding, crisp flair. Not throwaway material." Length: 250 to 1,000 words. Pays 5¢ to 12¢ per word. 8x10 b&w glossies and color. Pays $5 for b&w; $10 for color. Captions optional.
Poetry and Fillers: Traditional forms, blank verse, free verse, light verse. Pays 5¢ to 12¢ per word. Length: open. Newsbreaks, clippings, jokes, short humor. Length: open. Pays 5¢ to 12¢ per word.

EPICURE, 383 Madison Ave., New York NY 10017. Editor: Zack Hanle. For people interested in food and drink, travel and entertaining. Established in 1973. Bimonthly. Rights purchased vary with author and material. Usually buys all rights. Payment on acceptance. Query first. Enclose S.A.S.E for response to query or return of submission.

Nonfiction: Articles about food, wine, travel, and home entertaining. Food articles may contain recipes. "A lively style, with wit and warmth, along with firm knowledge of the subject, will help writers sell to us." Length: 1,500 to 3,000 words.

GOOD FOOD, Radnor PA 19088. Contact: Mary Blake. Articles about "new ways to delight your family at mealtimes, how to save time in the kitchen, and how to save money when food shopping. Nutrition, gourmet secrets, new appliances, new products and techniques." Published monthly. No freelance. Assignments only.

GOURMET, 777 Third Ave., New York NY 10017. Managing Editor: Miss Gail Zweigenthale. For moneyed, educated, traveled, food-wise men and women. Monthly. Purchases copyright, but grants book reprint rights with credit. Pays on acceptance. Suggests a study of several issues to understand type of material required. Reports within 2 months. Enclose S.A.S.E.
Nonfiction: Uses articles on subjects related to food and wine—travel, adventure, reminiscence, fishing and hunting experiences. Prefers personal experiences to researched material. Recipes included as necessary. Not interested in nutrition, dieting, penny-saving, or bizarre foods, or in interviews with chefs or food experts, or in reports of food contests, festivals, or wine tastings. Buys recipes only as part of an article with interesting material to introduce them and make them appealing. "Gourmet Holidays" written by staff contributors only. The same is true for material including specific hotel or restaurant recommendations. Sophisticated, light, nontechnical. Length: 2,500 to 3,000 words. Current needs include American regional pieces (no restaurants) and European material.
Poetry and Verse: Light, sophisticated with food or drink slant.

GUSTO INTERNATIONAL, 360 Lexington Ave., New York NY 10017. Editor: Sylvia Linden. For people who are interested in how to shop, prepare, cook and serve international foods. Established in 1972. Quarterly. Circulation: 100,000. Buys all rights. Buys 30 mss a year. Payment on publication. Submit seasonal material 4 months in advance. Will consider photocopied submissions. Reports within 4 weeks. Enclose S.A.S.E. for return of submissions.
Nonfiction and Photos: "Our stories and articles are short, maximum 1,500 words, completely food oriented, with recipes and photos included. We are aiming at a male audience, and therefore prefer articles directed to or written by men. Humorous, light articles, well researched, without humor being strained. *Gusto* is a food magazine written for both women and men keenly interested in serving food in the home." Personal experience, interview, profile, humor, historical, nostalgia and personal opinion articles. Length: 500 to 1,500 words, including recipes or how-to. Pays $50 to $150. Photos are purchased with accompanying mss; captions required.

THE PURPLE THUMB, Winepress Publishing Co., P.O. Box 423, Van Nuys CA 91408. Editor: Edward S. Sullivan. For "amateur wine and beer makers, wine connoisseurs, and others interested in the making, history, and traditions of wine and beer." Bimonthly. Circulation: 5,000. Pays on publication. Will send free sample copy to a writer on request. Query first. Reports in 30 days. Enclose S.A.S.E.
Nonfiction: "Authoritative, informative articles on wine and beer, ranging from technical data on making wine and beer at home, to gourmet recipes, reviews of domestic and foreign wines and wineries. To a sophisticated audience—no faking it; generalized, inspirational type writing not wanted." How-to, personal experience, interviews, profiles, successful business operations, historical, photo articles. Length: "Up to 2,500 words, shorter lengths preferred." Payment is $15 to $50.
Photos: Purchased with mss and with captions only. B&w glossies. Payment is $5 for first North American rights.

VINTAGE MAGAZINE, 245 E. 25th St., New York NY 10014. Editor/Publisher: Philip Seldon. For a "broad-based audience of wine drinkers, ranging from the wealthy and sophisticated expert to the novice with a desire to become interested in wine. These are middle income families and above; generally college-educated." Monthly. Circulation: 100,000. Buys all rights. Pays on publication. Will send a sample copy to a writer for $1. Submit seasonal material 2 months in advance. Reports in 3 months. Enclose S.A.S.E. for return of submissions.

Nonfiction: "Subject matter includes features on wine mainly written by wine experts, although travel pieces and human interest stories can be written by nonexperts. All editorial material should have a wide emphasis. There is no other publication treating this subject matter in depth for the consumer. Do not send compilations from wine books. Stress gourmet interests." Length: 900 to 3,000 words. Pays $100 to $200; "more for big names."

Photos: Purchased with mss; with captions only. B&w glossies, color transparencies, 35mm color. Rate of payment "open."

Fiction: Mystery, humorous, adventure related to subject matter of *Vintage*. Length: to 2,000 words. Pays $100 to $200; "more for big names."

Poetry and Fillers: Contemporary poetry. Puzzles, jokes, short humor.

WINE NOW, 575 West End Ave., New York NY 10024. Editor: Richard Figiel. For "wine drinkers of all ages, sizes, colors, levels of education, etc. We are geared to the average wine drinker rather than the connoisseur. Mostly informational material relating to different wines and aspects of the culture of wine, winemaking, wine enjoying." Established in 1972. Every 2 months. Circulation: 450,000. Not copyrighted. Acquires all rights, but will reassign rights to author after publication. Payment on acceptance. Will send free sample copy to a writer on request. Query first. Will consider photocopied submissions. Submit seasonal material at least 4 months in advance. Reports in 6 weeks. Enclose S.A.S.E. for reply to queries.

Nonfiction and Photos: Informational, how-to, personal experience, humor, historical, personal opinion, travel. Wine tips for beginners. Dieting with wine. Cheese and wine. "Articles must be lively and entertaining as well as instructive. No dissertations on the 1959 vintage in Médoc, please. Basically, just an openminded, unsnobbish approach. We want to encourage people to explore different wines, learn about them, know what to look for in them. Others write to connoisseurs and the serious wine people. We write to the people just getting into wine and those more casual and less monied." Length: 1,000 to 3,000 words. Pays $25 to $150. $5 for b&w glossy photos purchased with ms. Captions required. $10 for 35mm and 8x10 color transparency purchased with ms. Photo Dept. Editor: Kathleen Toman.

Poetry and Fillers: "Must relate somehow to wine." Traditional, blank verse, free verse, avant-garde and light verse. Length: 100 lines maximum. Pays $10 to $50. Puzzles (any type), jokes, short humor. Length: "Something to fill one-half to 1 page." Pays $10 to $50.

WINE WORLD, 7555 Woodley Ave., Van Nuys CA 91406. Editor: Roy Brady. For "people who enjoy wine and would like to learn more about the subject: its history, traditions, romance, technology, and types. Market studies indicate our readers to be in the middle to high income group with a college education." Established in 1971. Bimonthly. Circulation: over 50,000. Usually buys first North American serial rights. Buys over 20 mss a year. Pays on publication. Write for copy of guidelines for writers. Query first. Submit seasonal material at least 3 months in advance. Reports in 3 to 4 weeks. Enclose S.A.S.E. for return of submissions.

Nonfiction and Photos: "Articles with photos on viticulture, history, romance, tradition, just about anything of interest to the wine lover. Use a reportorial approach. We usually use first-person accounts. Articles must be authoritative, informative, and entertaining. We do not write only for the expert, but for the person who would like to learn more about wine. Our style is simple and straightforward. We have sufficient coverage of California wines. We'd like to see Bordeaux, Burgundy, and the rest of the European scene." Buys informational articles, how-to's, interviews, profiles, humor, historical pieces, think pieces, exposes, nostalgia, photo features, travel articles, and coverage of new products, technical items, and successful business operations. Length: 800 to 3,000 words. Pays $25 to $200. Captioned photos purchased with mss. Pays $5 to $15 for 8x10 single weight b&w glossies, $15 to $30 for 2¼ square color transparencies.

WINES AND VINES, 703 Market St., San Francisco CA 94103. Editor: Philip Hiaring. For "winery executives, wholesalers, retailers, wine hobbyists, vineyardists, suppliers to the wine trade and to the grape-growing field." Special issues include brandy issue (January), vineyard issue (February), statistics issue (April), champagne issue (June), marketing issue (September), directory issue (December). Monthly. Circulation: 5,500. Buys first North American serial rights and simultaneous rights. Buys 4 or 5 mss a year. Pays on acceptance. Will send a sample copy to a writer on request. Query preferred. Reports in 2 weeks. Enclose S.A.S.E.

Nonfiction and Photos: "Articles on technical matters or relating to general industry problems: grape growing, wine production, distribution, and marketing. Interested in interviews and spot news. I prefer not to see material that would obviously come across my desk from large wine companies or importers." Length: 1,000 to 2,500 words. Pays $25 to $50. 4x5 or 8x10 b&w glossies purchased with mss; captions required. Pays $5 to $10.

General Interest Publications

Publications classified here are edited for national, general audiences and carry articles on any subject of interest to a broad spectrum of people. Other markets for general interest material will be found in the Black, Men's, Newspaper and Sunday Supplements, Regional, and Women's classifications in the Consumer section; and in the Sponsored Publications section.

THE ATLANTIC MONTHLY, 8 Arlington St., Boston MA 02116. Editor in Chief: Robert Manning. For a professional, academic audience. Monthly. Circulation: 325,000. Buys first North American serial rights. Pays on acceptance. Will send a sample copy to a writer for $1. Reports in 2 weeks to several months. Enclose S.A.S.E. for return of submissions.

Nonfiction: "We prefer not to formulate specifications about the desired content of *The Atlantic* and suggest that would-be contributors examine back issues to form their own judgment of what is suitable." Length: 2,000 to 5,000 words. Rates vary from $100 per magazine page base rate. Author should include summary of his qualifications for treating subject.

Fiction: Short stories by unestablished writers, published as Atlantic "Firsts" are a steady feature. Two prizes of $750 and $250 are awarded annually to the best of these when a sufficient number of stories are published. Candidates should so label their submissions and list their previous publications, if any, as authors whose stories have appeared in magazines of national circulation are not considered eligible. Will also consider stories by established writers in lengths ranging from 2,700 to 7,500 words. Payment depends on length, but also on quality and author.

Poetry: Uses three to five poems an issue. These must be of high literary distinction in both light and serious poetry. Interested in young poets. Base rate for poetry is $2 per line.

CARTE BLANCHE MAGAZINE, 3460 Wilshire Blvd., Los Angeles CA 90010. Editor: J. Walter Flynn. "The magazine is geared to a family audience and professional businessmen and women with reference to travel, dining, and entertainment." Established in 1964. General subject matter consists of travel, dining, entertainment oriented material. No fiction, short stories, fillers, puzzles. Bimonthly. Circulation: 450,000. Buys all rights. Buys about 16 to 18 mss a year. Payment on acceptance. Will send free sample copy to a writer on request. Will send editorial guidelines sheet to a writer on request. Query first. Reports as soon as possible. Will consider photocopied submissions. Enclose S.A.S.E. for return of submissions.

Nonfiction and Photos: "We seek no particular style except the personal approach for travel, dining, and entertainment oriented articles. Almost everything submitted to us and the other magazines in our field are overworked and have been published before. What would we prefer? Good ideas!" Length: 1,500 to 1,800 words. Pays approximately $100 for every 600 words. Photos purchased with or without mss, captions optional. Color only. 35mm, 2¼x2¼, and 4x5 transparencies.

How To Break In: "Writers should read our magazine to be familiar with our style and presentation. We do not care whether or not a writer is well known, established, young or old. If they understand our audience and format, and can write an interesting story, we will consider it for publication."

CHANGING TIMES, The Kiplinger Magazine, 1729 H St., N.W., Washington DC 20006. Editor: Robert W. Harvey. For general, adult audience interested in personal finance, family money management and personal advancement. Established in 1947. Monthly. Circulation: 1,500,000. Buys fillers only. Buys all rights. Pays on acceptance. Reports in 30 days. Enclose S.A.S.E. for return of submissions.

Fillers: "Original topical quips and epigrams for our monthly humor feature, 'Notes on These Changing Times.' All other material is staff-written." Pays $5.

How To Break In: "Don't waste your postage or our time by sending article queries or manuscripts to *Changing Times.* It is a staff written magazine. The only thing we buy is original topical quips and epigrams for our monthly humor feature."

COUNTRY CLUBBER, 4303 Memorial Dr., Suite A, Decatur GA 30032. Editor: E. J. Green. For "members of country clubs interested in recreation, entertaining and elegant living." Established in 1972. Monthly. Circulation: 22,000. Buys all rights but will reassign rights to author after 60 days. Buys 60 to 100 mss a year. Payment on publication. Submit complete ms. Submit seasonal material (Valentine's Day, Thanksgiving, Christmas, Fourth of July, New Year's) 3 months in advance. Reports on material accepted for publication within 60 days. Returns rejected material in 30 days. Will send sample copy to writer for 75 cents. Enclose S.A.S.E. for return of submissions.

Nonfiction and Photos: Articles on golf, tennis, swimming, boating, good foods, gourmet cooking, travel, entertaining, gardening (slant to the South), business (personalities or great firms). "Keep in mind that our readers are all club members and try to give emphasis to that fact. They are sophisticated with above average wealth and wide interests." Length: 1,000 to 2,000 words. Pays 5¢ to 7¢ a word. 5x7 or 8x10 b&w glossy prints. Pays $5 per print. Color prints or transparencies. Pays $10.

Fillers: Jokes, short humor. Length: 15 lines maximum. Pays 5¢ to 7¢ a word.

GOOD READING, Henry F. Henrichs Publications, Litchfield IL 62056. Editor: Mrs. Monta Crane. Monthly. Not copyrighted. Buys 50 to 75 mss a year. Pays on acceptance. Will send a sample copy to a writer for 25¢. No query required. Submit seasonal material 4 months in advance. Reports in 1 to 2 months. Enclose S.A.S.E. for return of submissions.

Nonfiction and Photos: Articles on "current or factual subjects, slanted to readers in the busy, modern world, and articles based on incidents related to business, personal experiences that reveal the elements of success in human relationships. All material must be clean and wholesome and acceptable to all ages. Material should be uplifting, not degrading in any way." Length: 1,000 words maximum; "preferably shorter." Pays $5 to $30. B&w glossies purchased with mss "occasionally."

GRIT, 208 W. 3rd St., Williamsport PA 17701. Editor: Terry L. Ziegler. For "residents of all ages in small-town and rural America." Weekly. Circulation: 1,300,000. Buys one-time rights. Buys "more than 1,000 mss a year." Pays on acceptance. Will send a sample copy to a writer on request. No query required. Submit seasonal material 3 to 4 months in advance. Reports in 2 to 6 weeks. Enclose S.A.S.E.

Nonfiction: Human interest, inspirational, historical articles. "*Grit* is interested in receiving stories on small towns recovering from adversity; small towns which can be examples for other communities in the projects they have accomplished; small town celebrations, anniversaries, etc.; stories of particular interest to men—adventure, hunting, fishing, the outdoors, etc.; patriotic stories which have an immediate tie-in with a date; inspiring stories of personal courage and devotion and stories about individuals or groups who are making an important contribution to their community, neighbors, or American way of life. Stories about outstanding personalities (adults and teenagers). Also, concise stories about people of special interest (the grandson of Buffalo Bill, or the minister who is also a sheriff)." Also buys material for " 'Odd, Strange, and Curious,' a feature which focuses on the extremely unusual in photographs and copy." Wants "nothing promoting alcoholic beverages, narcotics, immoral behavior, unpatriotic action. We prefer the emphasis to be on people, even when the subject is places or things. Can use occasional well-illustrated articles of 1,500 to 3,000 words if subject and treatment warrant. For us, these are extra-length features." Length: 300 to 800 words. Pays minimum of 2¢ a word. Feature Editor: Kenneth D. Loss.

Fiction: "For children up to 12. Prefer adventure, humor, mystery, holiday, nature, historical, and animal stories. However, we receive many more animal stories than we need and often not as many of the other type as we'd like." Length: 600 to 750 words. Pays 2¢ a word. Department Editor: Richard A. Frank.

Photos: Purchased with mss, $5 per b&w glossy; with captions only, $7.50 per b&w glossy; 35mm color, $25 per slide; color transparencies, $25; color transparencies with caption only, $30.

Poetry: Buys traditional poetry and light verse. Length: 4 to 32 lines. Pays $3 per poem.

Fillers: Puzzles. Pays 2¢ a word minimum.

HARPER'S MAGAZINE, 2 Park Ave., Room 1809. New York NY 10016. Editor: Robert Shnayerson. For well-educated, socially concerned, widely read men and women and college students who are active in community and political affairs. Monthly. Circulation: 325,000. Buys first North American serial rights only. Buys approximately 12 non-agented, non-commissioned, non-book-excerpted mss a year. Pays on acceptance. Will send a sample copy to a writer for $1. Will look only at material submitted through agents or which is the result of a query. Reports in 2 to 3 weeks. Enclose S.A.S.E. with all queries and submissions.

Nonfiction: "For writers working with agents or who will query first only, our requirements are: Public affairs, literary, international and local reporting, humor." Also buys exposes, think pieces, and profiles. Length: 1,500 to 8,000 words. Pays $200 to $1,500.

Photos: Occasionally purchased with mss. Others by assignment. Pays $35 to $400. Department Editor: Sheila Berger.

Fiction: On contemporary life and its problems. Also buys humorous stories. Length: 1,000 to 5,000 words. Pays $300 to $500.

Poetry: 60 lines and under. Pays $2 per line.

How To Break In: "Personal, impassioned essays are published in our 'Commentary' department. Length should be 200 to 1,000 words. Token payment only."

HOLIDAY, 1100 Waterway Blvd., Indianapolis IN 46202. Managing Editor: Sandi Servaas. For a "mature audience, travel and leisure oriented." Pays on publication. Write for copy of guidelines for writers. Query first. "Will consider photocopied submissions." Enclose S.A.S.E. for reply to queries.

Nonfiction: Articles "on a wide range of subjects related to travel; regions, communities, resorts, in all parts of the world—but particularly in the United States, Canada, Mexico, the Caribbean, Europe, and Mediterranean areas. Also wanted are articles about unusual trips, as well as remote but unusual places; short articles on travel, recreational activities; golfing, boating, fishing, hunting, camping, hiking; service articles concerning travel facilities and accessories. All article ideas should first be submitted in summary form—not to exceed 300 words. The writer should state his qualifications and include information on illustrative material." Finished article length: 1,000 to 2,000 words. Payment ranges from $50 for filler material to $1,000 for feature articles.

Photos: "Unusual and technically perfect pictures, both color transparencies and b&w, on subjects related to the article needs." Editor wants "a descriptive summary of what you have" before photos are submitted.

How To Break In: "The only suggestion I'd have is in the category of 1 to 2-pagers. We now subscribe to the philosophy that if you have one six-pager, then you'd also better have six one-pagers (for maximum reader interest). So we're big on short, punchy pieces. Subjects have included, and will include Holiday Hearing Aid (information on the best upcoming concerts of the year all over the U.S.), Holiday Spec Sheet (an overview of the best bets in sports events this fall), Holiday Go Betweens (suggestions for gifts to take to European friends) and the like. In most cases, the emphasis is on research rather than style, although we'll reject anything that is not really light and clever. These things are something like *Esquire's* and *Playboy's* one-pagers, except that there really is a point to them and also a lot of information. I must tell you, however, that many of these are prepared by the staff since it's easy to send out research letters from here—and also we have a lot of ideas for quickies. But we will consider quickie queries from people—and they'll have to prepare them on speculation. I can think of one guy who asked if he could do something lyrical on sandcastles since he'd built so many. I told him no, but that we'd like a one-pager quickie on exactly how to build sandcastles, which beaches of the world were best for sandcastle building, etc. A very unusual but travel-angled article idea."

HORIZON, 1221 Avenue of the Americas, New York NY 10020. Quarterly. Copyrighted. Circulation: 124,000. Pays on acceptance. Reports in two weeks. Include

S.A.S.E. for ms return.
Nonfiction· History, the arts, archaeology, letters, biography. Length: 3,000 to 5,000 words. Payment: depends on material.

INTELLECTUAL DIGEST, 110 E. 59th St., New York NY 10022. Editor: Martin Goldman. "We assign a limited number of original articles to scholars, artists, and freelancers." Examples of recent original articles are "What Dylan Did" (Hedgepeth); "Energy Series" (Shepherd); "I Experience a Kind of Charity" (Murphy/ Brodie); "Frames: The Quality of Preminger" (Haskell).

LIBERTY, THEN AND NOW, Liberty Library Corp., 250 W. 57 St., New York NY 10019. Editor: James Palmer. Buys all rights.
Nonfiction and Fiction: Material that "makes it *Liberty, Then and Now.*" Pays $100 to $500.

MACLEAN'S, 481 University Ave., Toronto, Ont., Canada M5W 1A7. Editor: Peter C. Newman. For general interest audience. Monthly. Buys first rights. Pays on acceptance. "Query with 200- or 300-word outline before sending any material." Submit seasonal material 4 months in advance. Reports in 2 weeks. Enclose S.A.E. and International Reply Coupons.
Nonfiction: "Audience is Canadian and for this reason most of our articles are on Canadian subjects. We want articles on people, places, politics, business, science, medicine, education, entertainment, adventure, sport, social problems and many other things. We don't want articles that are superficial, poorly researched, badly organized, biased, exaggerated or too breathless." Recent articles are "Reflections on a Fall From Grace" (Trudeau) and "Interview With Simone de Beauvoir." Length: 2,000 to 5,000 words; 3,500 words preferred. Pays $400 minimum; "$1,000 some cases."
Photos: Interested primarily in Canadian subjects. Buys b&w glossies, color transparencies, 35mm color. Pays "$125 per page or per day, whichever is greater." Director of Graphics: Ralph Tibbles.

MIDNIGHT, Globe Newspapers, 1440 St. Catherine St. W., Montreal 107, Quebec, Canada. Weekly. Buys first North American rights. Pays on acceptance. Query preferred, but will consider unsolicited material. Reports in 3 days. Enclose International Reply Coupons for return of submissions or reply to query.
Nonfiction: Interested in photos and research for tabloid stories with accent on heavy human interest, good fortune, misfortune, medical expose, exposes of nationally known products and services, medical-scientific phenomena; offbeat personalities, animal, offbeat actions and situations. The newspapers themselves are best editorial guide. Stories must be factual and no older than six months. "All feature submissions must have strong photos." Pays $75 minimum, $200 maximum for topnotch frontpager. Articles Editor: Joan Thomas.
Photos: Will buy news photos with supporting newspaper clips or other research. Action and drama are main criteria. Exceptional photos warrant exceptional rates.

MODERN PEOPLE, 3550 North Lombard Street, Franklin Park IL 60131. Editor: Thor Christopher. "For men and women of all ages and walks of life who are interested in the world around them." Established in 1972. Circulation: 300,000. Weekly. Buys full rights, except in cases of special negotiation. Buys 2,000 mss a year. Payment on acceptance. Will send a free sample copy to a writer on request. Will send editorial guidelines sheet to a writer on request. Queries accepted, but not required. Reports in 2 weeks. Enclose S.A.S.E. for return of submissions.
Nonfiction: Subject matter consists of "general interest, personalities, self-help, human interest, consumer protection. Writer should be brief, concise, and shouldn't waste words. Articles should point out the good side of life and people. Features should take a positive attitude even on a negative subject. Our publication differs from others in that we have a fresh look and style in weekly national newspaper format. We don't just merely tell our readers something. We experience it with them. We would like to see features on famous personalities (not necessarily Hollywood personalities) who have interesting lives." Buys informational, personal experience, how-to, interview, profile, inspirational, humor, historical, think pieces, expose, nostalgia, personal opinion, photo, travel, reviews, spot news, successful

business operations, new product, merchandising techniques, technical articles, making and saving money, consumer protection and ecology, ESP, the occult, hypnotism, physical and emotional health, TV and movie personalities, sports, humor and nostalgia. "We're always looking for the 'big story'; significant or highly interesting stories that have not run elsewhere. Avoid topics previously 'done to death' by the news media". Length: 250 to 1,000 words, "limited to 800 words and shorter, if possible." Pays 3¢ a word and up depending on depth of article. Address to Editor.

Photos: "Prefer articles to be photo-illustrated wherever possible; usually with good, clear action photos rather than just mug shots. Should be b&w prints (color accepted, if necessary) with enough contrast for good reproduction. Prefer 5x7 or larger. Contact sheets accepted for picture selection only. Unbought photos returned. Also buy one-or-two-shot photostats with brief caption." Pays minimum of $5 per accepted photo; will negotiate for exceptional photo stories.

Fillers: Buys humorous, offbeat and human interest shorts and unusual news shorts. Length: 50 to 250 words. Also puzzles and tests of similar length. Pays minimum of 3¢ a word.

NATIONAL ENQUIRER, Lantana, FL 33460. Editor: Nat Chrzan. For "mainly mature adults—education range is broad—the type of person you see at supermarket checkouts. That's where most of our 3 million copies are sold each week." Subject matter consists of "human interest, offbeat, occult, self-help subject matter aimed at a mass audience and written in a straightforward style. The criteria is—'Will it interest at least 50% of the nation?' " Weekly. Circulation: 3,000,000. Rights purchased vary with author and material. Buys 2,000 mss a year. Payment on completion of assignment to meet the editorial standards of the articles editor. "We do not accept unsolicited mss and all spec material will be returned unread. Query first with a 1-or 2-paragraph note." Will consider photocopied submissions. Enclose S.A.S.E. for reply to queries.

Nonfiction, Photos, and Fillers: Approach should include "plenty of documented facts and good, clearly understood writing. Generally we are looking for a positive, happy, 'life is okay' approach. Most stories are based on personal interviews with experts, etc., with extensive use of quotes. We like articles on how the average person can find happiness and peace of mind in a world where he is bombarded with depressing news." Buys informational, how-to, personal experience, interview, inspirational, think, expose, photo articles. Length: 1,000 to 2,000 words. Pays $125 minimum with no top limit for first class material. Address to Executive Editor. Photos purchased with or without mss, on assignment, and captions required. Good tonal range 8x10 b&w glossy. Pays "around $125" depending on news value. No color. Dept. Editor: Ted Mutch. Buys 5- or 6- paragraph general interest shorts.

NATIONAL GEOGRAPHIC MAGAZINE, 17th and M Streets, N.W., Washington DC 20036. Editor: Gilbert M. Grosvenor. For members of the National Geographic Society. Monthly. Circulation: 8,000,000. Buys first publication rights with warranty to use the material in National Geographic Society copyrighted publications. Buys 30 to 40 mss a year. Pays on acceptance. Will send a sample copy to a writer for $1. Query first. Writers should study several recent issues of *National Geographic* and send for leaflets "Writing for National Geographic" and "National Geographic Photo Requirements." Returns rejected material and acknowledges acceptance of material in 3 to 4 weeks. Enclose S.A.S.E. for return of submissions.

Nonfiction and Photos: "First-person narratives, making it easy for the reader to share the author's experience and observations. Writing should include plenty of human-interest incident, authentic direct quotation, and a bit of humor where appropriate. Accuracy is fundamental. Contemporary problems such as those of pollution and ecology are treated on a factual basis. The magazine is especially seeking short American place pieces with a strong regional 'people' flavor. Examples that have recently appeared are 'The People of Cumberland Gap' and 'Appalachia: Mountain Voices, Mountain Days.' The use of many clear, sharp color photographs in all articles makes lengthy word descriptions unnecessary. Historical background, in most cases, should be kept to the minimum needed for understanding the present." Length: 8,000 words maximum for major articles. Shorts of 2,000 to 4,000 words "are always needed." Pays from $1,500 to $3,500 for acceptable articles; from $250 per page for color transparencies. One- or 2-page synopsis of article idea should be submitted to James Cerruti, Senior Assistant Editor. Photographers are advised to submit a generous selection of photographs with brief, descriptive captions to Mary G. Smith, Assistant Editor.

THE NATIONAL INFORMER, 3550 N. Lombard, Franklin Park IL 60131. Editor: Jack Steele. For "the sophisticated, mature adult, who likes to be informed on topics he usually doesn't find in the daily papers." Weekly. Circulation: 500,000. Buys all rights. Buys about 600 mss a year. Pays on acceptance. Will send a sample copy to a writer for 25¢. Reports in about 3 weeks. Enclose S.A.S.E. for return of submissions.
Nonfiction and Photos: "Our readers like human interest, self-help, and do-it-yourself types of features, particularly if these are sex-oriented. Also, our readers like to be shocked by sex expose features. We're looking for shocking features that expose and titillate. The writer should keep his article fast-paced, informative, and exciting without losing track of his main theme. We don't like slow, plodding features that inform but don't entertain. Our stories need to do both. We do not buy consumer articles or stories with settings in foreign countries." Recent representative articles include "How to Have the Perfect Sex Partner" and "Housewife Witches Exist!" Length: 600 to 1,200 words. Pays 2¢ per word. B&w glossies purchased with mss. Pays $5 to $100. Department Editor: Norton Newcomb.

THE NATIONAL INSIDER, 2713 N. Pulaski Rd., Chicago IL 60639. Weekly. Newspaper. Established in 1962. Query first. Rights purchased vary with author and material but include all rights; all rights, but will reassign rights to author after publication, first North American rights and simultaneous rights. Enclose S.A.S.E. for reply to query.
Nonfiction and Photos: "Ideally, half of the material we buy for each issue is sex-oriented and the other half is simply well-rounded, in-depth reporting on people of significant note. The sex stories we buy can range from incredible Hollywood scandals to self-help articles and recent developments in sex information (such as surveys, new sex life styles, marriage, birth control, sex and race). An example of the nonsex celebrity story we buy would be the story of Fernand Legros, the first man Clifford Irving wrote a hoax about. Some of the other areas of interest we have are funny hard luck stories, bloodless crime stories, and sensational exclusives. For example, *Insider* was the first publication to give the story of children who have died of old age. We pay $75 to $300; more 'for exceptional blockbusters.' " 8x10 b&w glossy prints with sharp definition for letterpress printing purchased with mss and as photostats with cutlines that are complete. "Payment on photos depends entirely on the accompanying ms or the unusual nature of the photo."

THE NATIONAL NEWS EXTRA (formerly *The National News Exploiter*), 2715 N. Pulaski Rd., Chicago IL 60639. Editor: Robert J. Sorren. Established in 1969. Weekly. Rights purchased vary with author and material, but include all rights; all rights but will reassign rights to author after publication, first North American rights, and simultaneous rights. Buys approximately 500 mss a year. Payment on acceptance. Will send sample copy to writer on request. Query first, "but we do review material on speculation." Will not consider photocopied submissions. Submit seasonal materials (for all national holidays) 2 months in advance. Reports on material in 2 weeks. Enclose S.A.S.E. for return of submissions or reply to query.
Nonfiction and Photos: "We buy three types of celebrity stories: 1) insulting starlets (women in entertainment who brag about the awful way they treat men). 2) Tough-talking males (men in entertainment who are surly). 3) Nonsex celebrity scandals. We also buy first-person accounts of hair-raising experiences, blood and gore murders fully illustrated with on the scene photos, bizarre crimes, unsolved murders, senseless crime, on the scene disaster photospreads, stories of the ugly ducklings, ironic stories, quirks of nature (Siamese twins, etc.), suicides, law and order stories. We need straight reporting with all the facts necessary to support the story and photographs to illustrate the copy." Length: 3,000 words maximum. Pays $75 to $300. Photos purchased with mss and as photospots with complete cutlines. 8x10 b&w. Payment varies.

NATIONAL POLICE GAZETTE, 520 Fifth Ave., New York NY 10036. Editor: Nat K. Perlow. For persons "between the ages of 20 and 65." Established in 1845.

Monthly. Circulation: 200,000. Buys all rights. Buys about 200 mss a year. Pays on publication. Submit seasonal material 3 months in advance. Reports in 1 month. Enclose S.A.S.E. for return of submissions.

Nonfiction: "Primary interests are sports, general interest articles, latest medical breakthroughs, and profiles of people in the news. Also interested in success stories. We have a keen interest in all features concerning consumer frauds, sports, crime, adventure. We adhere to a hard-hitting formula, being brash instead of subtle. Articles should be anecdotal and written in a light, breezy style." Wants "more sport personality stories based on interviews rather than rehashes from newspaper clips." Buys how-to's, interviews, profiles, inspirational and photo articles, humor, spot news, exposes, new product coverage. Length: 1,000 to 1,500 words. Pays $50 to $150 (5¢ to 10¢ a word).

THE NATIONAL TATTLER, 2717 N. Pulaski Rd., Chicago IL 60639. Editor: Robert J. Sorren. For a predominantly female audience. Established in 1964. Weekly. Circulation: over 1,000,000. Rights purchased vary with author and material, but include all rights; all rights but will reassign rights to author after publication, first North American rights, and simultaneous rights. Buys approximately 1,000 mss a year. Payment on acceptance. Will send free sample copy to writer on request. Write for copy of editorial guidelines. Query first, "but we do review material on speculation." Will not consider photocopied submissions. Submit seasonal material 2 months in advance of holiday. Reports on material in 2 weeks. Enclose S.A.S.E. for return of submissions or reply to query.

Nonfiction and Photos: "We buy 30 types of nonfiction stories. They are stories of unexplained phenomenon that are well-documented, young achiever stories, expert advice on the safety of children, celebrity stories (exposes to offbeat information), human interest volunteer stories, self-help pieces, inspirational stories about handicapped people overcoming the odds of their disabilities, unique photospot stories with complete cutlines, stories that prove success and/or money isn't (aren't) everything, antidrug stories, government waste and exposes, medical breakthrough pieces (generally involving the trials of the patient), stories that prove crime doesn't pay (but absolutely bizarre and without blood and gore), antirat race stories, consumerism-ecology pieces, stories that deal with women breaking through previously 'men only' job classifications, anticommunist stories, stories about events generally not recorded in history, progress isn't everything stories, faith-healing investigations, antiradical women's lib stories, rags to riches stories, stories that concern people who go from bad to good, stories involving mistaken identity, the reunion of long lost relatives, statistical stories, and mechanical device stories, in which people refuse to let some artifact of the industrial age vanish. Straight reporting with all the facts necessary to support the story and photographs to illustrate the copy." Length: 3,000 words maximum. Pays $50 to $1,000 and "more for exceptional blockbusters." Photos (8x10 b&w glossy prints) purchased with accompanying ms and as photospots with cutlines that are complete. "Payment for photos depends entirely on the accompanying ms or the unusual nature of the photo."

THE NEW YORKER, 25 W. 43rd St., New York NY 10036. Editor: William Shawn. Weekly. Reports in two weeks. Pays on acceptance. Enclose S.A.S.E. for return of submissions.

Nonfiction, Fiction, and Fillers: Single factual pieces run from 3,000 to 10,000 words. Long fact pieces are usually staff-written. So is "Talk of the Town," although ideas for this department are bought. Pays good rates. Uses fiction, both serious and light, from 1,000 to 6,000 words. About 90 percent of the fillers come from contributors with or without taglines (extra pay if the tagline is used).

PAGEANT, 205 E. 42nd St., New York NY 10017. Editor: Nat K. Perlow. For "primarily young marrieds." Monthly. Circulation: over 300,000. Buys all rights. Buys about 150 mss a year. Pays on acceptance. Query first. Will read only 1-page queries which include a brief outline of article; does not read unsolicited mss. Enclose S.A.S.E. for response to query.

READER'S DIGEST, Pleasantville NY 10570. Monthly. "Items intended for a particular feature should be directed to the editor in charge of that feature, although the contribution may later be referred to another section of the magazine as seeming more suitable. Manuscripts cannot be acknowledged, and will be returned—usually within eight or ten weeks—only when return postage accompanies them."

Nonfiction: "*Reader's Digest* is especially interested in receiving the following sorts of material: First Person Articles. An article for this series must be a previously unpublished narrative of an unusual personal experience. It may be dramatic, inspirational or humorous, but it must have a quality of narrative and interest comparable to stories published in this series. Contributions must be typewritten, preferably double-spaced, no longer than 2,500 words. It is requested that documents or photographs not be sent. Payment rate on acceptance: $3,000. Base rate for general articles is $2,000 for first sale. Address to: First Person Editor."

Fillers: "Life in These United States contributions must be true, unpublished stories from one's own experience, revelatory of adult human nature, and providing appealing or humorous sidelights on the American scene." Maximum length: 300 words. Payment rate on publication: $100. Address to: Life in U.S. Editor. Humor in Uniform: "True and unpublished stories based on experiences in the armed forces." Address: Humor in Uniform Editor. Maximum length: 300 words. Payment rate on publication: $100. Toward More Picturesque Speech: "The first contributor of each item used in this department is paid $25. Contributions should be dated, and the sources must be given." Address: Picturesque Speech Editor. "Current issues carry notes about requirements in the following departments: Personal Glimpses, Laughter, The Best Medicine, Campus Comedy and other brief items. Poetry is not solicited."

REALITES MAGAZINE, 551 Fifth Ave., New York NY 10017. For a well-educated readership interested in culture and the fine things in life. Monthly. Circulation: over 100,000. Buys all rights. Pays on publication. Query first. Address managing editor. Enclose S.A.S.E.

Nonfiction: Articles on the past, present, and future of the world's arts, culture, politics, entertainment; articles on travel and fine foods. Length and payment to be negotiated.

SATURDAY EVENING POST, 1100 Waterway Blvd., Indianapolis IN 46202. Editor: Fred Birmingham. For family readership. Bimonthly. Rights purchased vary with author and material. Query first or submit complete ms. Payment on acceptance. Enclose S.A.S.E. for return of submissions or reply to queries.

Nonfiction, Fiction, Poetry and Fillers: Wants articles, short stories (300 to 2,500 words), and short poems about the affirmative things in life. Short, humorous fillers also needed. Pays from $10 to $1,250, "depending on quality or assignment."

SATURDAY NIGHT, 52 St. Claire Ave. East, Toronto, Ont., Canada. Editor: Robert Fulford. For business and professional people. Monthly. Pays on publication. Reports in three weeks. Buys first North American serial rights. Query essential. Include S.A.E. and International Reply Coupons.

Nonfiction: Uses articles about Canadian politics, literature and the arts, travel and business. 2,500 words for features; other articles, 1,200 words. Pays $100 minimum.

SIGNATURE—The Diners' Club Magazine, 260 Madison Ave., New York NY 10016. Managing Editor: Ken Gouldthorpe. For Diners' Club members—"businessmen, urban, affluent, traveled, and young." Monthly. Circulation: 800,000. Buys first rights. Buys approximately 75 mss a year. Pays on acceptance. Write for copy of guidelines for writers. Query first. Submit seasonal material, including seasonal sports subjects, at least 3 months in advance. Returns rejected material in 2 weeks. Enclose S.A.S.E. for reply to queries.

Nonfiction: "Articles aimed at the immediate areas of interest of our readers—in travel, social issues, personalities, sports, entertainment, food and drink, business, humor. *Signature* runs 5 to 8 nonfiction articles an issue, all by freelancers." Subjects covered in past issues of *Signature* include profiles of film producer, David Wolper, and automobile executive, John De Lorean. Articles on implications of dropping birth rate; the urban transportation crush; a tour of western saloons. The editors want "no personalized essays, even for humor articles." Length: 2,500 words minimum. Pays minimum $500; "higher rates depend on importance of subject, ability of writer, whether he has worked for us in the past, etc." Articles Editor: Jack Eppinger.

Photos: "Picture stories or support are usually assigned to photographers we have worked with in the past. We rarely ask a writer to handle the photography also. But if he has photos of his subject we will consider them for use."

SUNSHINE MAGAZINE, Henry F. Henrichs Publications, Inc., Litchfield IL 62056. Editor: Mrs. Monta Crane. For "persons of all ages with varied interests." Monthly. Not copyrighted. Buys 50 to 75 mss a year. Pays on acceptance. Will send a sample copy to a writer for 25¢. No query required. Submit seasonal material 4 months in advance. Reports in 1 to 2 months. Enclose S.A.S.E. for return of submissions.

Nonfiction: "We accept some short articles, but they must be especially interesting or inspirational. *Sunshine Magazine* is not a religious publication, and purely religious material is rarely used. We receive far too much material on the subjects of retirement, adjustment to old age. We use nothing with a sexual emphasis." Pays $5 to $30.

Fiction: "Fiction stories must be wholesome, well-written, with clearly defined plots. There should be a purpose for each story, but any moral or lesson should be well-concealed in the plot development. Avoid trite plots that do not hold the reader's interest. A surprising climax is most desirable. Material should be uplifting, not degrading in any way." Length: 1,000 to 1,400 words. Pays $5 to $30.

SWINGERS WORLD, 8060 Melrose Ave., Los Angeles CA 90046. Editors: Don Pfeil and Elaine Stanton. For "swingers and would-be swingers." Established in 1972. Subject matter must be "swinger oriented." Bimonthly. Buys first North American serial rights. Buys 50 mss a year. Payment on publication. Will send a sample copy to a writer for $1.50. Will send editorial guidelines sheet to a writer on request (enclose S.A.S.E.). Query first required. Reports in 2 weeks. Enclose S.A.S.E. for reply to queries.

Nonfiction: "Articles must be pro-swinger. Slick." Length: approximately 2,500 words. Pays about $100.

TOWN AND COUNTRY, 717 Fifth Ave., New York NY 10022. Managing Editor: Jean Barkhorn. For upper-income Americans. Monthly. Not a large market for freelancers. Always query first. Enclose S.A.S.E.

Nonfiction: "We're always trying to find ideas that can be developed into good articles that will make appealing cover lines." Wants provocative and controversial pieces. Length: 1,500 to 2,000 words. Pays $300. Department Editor: Frank Zachary. Also buys shorter pieces for which pay varies. Department Editor: Richard Kagan.

WORLD, 488 Madison Ave., New York NY 10022. Editor: Norman Cousins. Biweekly. Query first to Peter Young, Managing Editor. Enclose S.A.S.E.

Nonfiction: "*World* attempts to do more than report on books, plays, movies, music, and the arts in just the United States alone. We attempt to review and report on cultural events on a world scale—'cultural' being defined in its broadest sense. Our dominant editorial concern, then, is the proper care of the human habitat—protecting it against war, world environmental poisoning, overcrowding, or any of the things that indignify and humiliate human beings." Contributors should analyze the basic ideas the editors are focusing on (such as environment and the world scene) and offer material related to those ideas. Pays "roughly $200 a magazine page."

Health Publications

ACCENT ON LIVING, P.O. Box 726, Bloomington IL 61701. Editor: Raymond C. Cheever. Issued quarterly to handicapped people and specialists in rehabilitation. Buys first publication rights. Pays on publication. Will send sample copy for 75¢. Query preferred. Will consider photocopied submissions, provided they are not simultaneously submitted elsewhere. Reports in 2 weeks. Enclose S.A.S.E. with queries and submissions.

Nonfiction: Articles, 200 to 750 words, about seriously disabled people who have overcome great obstacles and are pursuing regular vocational goals. Especially interested in new technical aids, assistive devices, bathroom and toilet aids and appliances, clothes and aids for dressing and undressing, aids for eating and drinking, as would be helpful to individuals with limited physical mobility. Intelligent discussion articles concerning the public image of and acceptance or non-acceptance of physically disabled in normal living situations. Pays up to $50 for good articles accompanied by photos.

Photos: Purchased with mss. Also photos of newly developed assistive devices enabling persons with disabilities to perform the routines of normal daily living. Pays $5 to $10.

THE ANSWER PREVENTIVE MEDICINE, 11808 Western Ave., Stanton CA 90680. Medical Editor: H. Rudolf Alsleben, M.D. For "persons of all ages concerned with health, ecology, nutrition, etc. They are of all professions, and all income groups are represented." Monthly. Circulation: 50,000. Buys first rights. Pays on publication; "we have paid for some pieces on acceptance, and we might handle more this way." Will send a sample copy to a writer for 75¢. Submit seasonal material at least 3 months in advance. Reports in 3 weeks. Enclose S.A.S.E. for return of submissions.

Nonfiction and Photos: "The objective of this publication is to bring to the public, as well as the professional communities, a viewpoint—both physical and spiritual—of life, compatible with our modern times. We will explore with literary freedom the worlds of health, nutrition, and medicine. It is our intent to present a sense of urgency. The attackers against life are gaining in momentum and power. We who hold any ammo against such attackers must begin a tremendous counter-attack. We need profiles of medics, research, citizens who solved or prevented health problems; nutrition articles by known authorities, etc. Ours is the only publication by a physician in the prevention field for patient and physician alike. Also, we try to write largely from case history research and experience, not general information. Writers must study our publication. Articles must be documented or must be written by a doctor. We have to watch all claims and must see proof; we need meaty articles." Buys personal experience articles, interviews, profiles, coverage of successful business operations, think pieces, exposes of food and drugs, etc., possibly new product articles, and travel articles "if the article has something to do with health." Length: 1,500 words maximum. Pay "varies with quality and importance. Most short articles bring about $35. Each is judged on its merit, though. We have paid about $75 for an article with weight behind it. We'd also go higher on a celebrity feature—someone on organic foods, a medical expert, etc." B&w glossies purchased with mss. Pays $20 "and up."

Fillers: Newsbreaks, clippings. Length: "short." Pays $10 minimum.

CONFIDENTIAL HEALTH, 3550 N. Lombard St., Franklin Park IL 60131. Editor: Dennis Parker. Monthly. Buys full rights, except in cases of special negotiation. Pays on acceptance. Queries accepted, but not required. Reports in two weeks. Enclose S.A.S.E. for return of submissions.

Nonfiction and Photos: New developments in health field, medical advances, offbeat health features, physical fitness and exercise, preventive medicine, psychological self-help, health foods (pro or con), and little known sports. 1,000 words maximum. Pays 2¢ a word and up, depending on research required. Buys b&w photos, illustrating articles. Pays $5 or negotiable.

EXCEPTIONAL PARENT, P.O. Box 101, Back Bay Annex, Boston MA 02117. Editors: Dr. Stanley Klein, Dr. Lewis Klebanoff, Dr. Maxwell Schleifer. For "the parents of children with mental, intellectual, emotional, and physical disabilities, and the professionals and para-professionals who treat these children." Monthly. Circulation: 6,000. Buys all rights. Buys about 20 mss per year. Pays on publication. Will send a sample copy to a writer for $2. No query required. Reports in 4 months. Enclose S.A.S.E. for return of submissions.

Nonfiction and Photos: "The general intent of the magazine is to provide practical guidance for the parents of disabled children. We print articles covering every conceivable subject within this area, including legal issues, tax info, recreation programs, parent groups, etc. This is a consumer publication within a very specialized market. That we provide practical guidance cannot be stressed too strongly. Articles should be jargon-free. Articles within special areas are checked by an advisory board in the medical and allied professions. There is no other magazine of this type. It is unique in that it is aimed at the parents, and is for them, not about them. We are dealing in a very sensitive area. What's more, our readership is sensitized, understandably, to a marked degree." Buys how-to's, personal experience articles, profiles, new product articles. Length: 800 to 3,000 words. Pays 5¢ a word. Photos accompanied by signed releases are purchased with mss "if the photos are acceptable."

FAMILY HEALTH, 1271 Ave. of the Americas, New York NY 10020. Managing Editor: Mrs. Sylvie Reice. Monthly. Circulation: 1,000,000. Send single-page query first. Will consider photocopied submissions. "Address queries to the Editors." Reports "promptly." Enclose S.A.S.E.
Nonfiction: Articles on medicine, child raising, family relationships, emotional health, beauty, medical costs, physical fitness, food and nutrition. "Emphasis on new scientific advances or new approaches to good health and well-being; no historical reviews or broad surveys of standard topics. Human interest health stories desirable as well as stories about celebrities and their health problems. Articles must be authoritative but lively, high level of writing required. Uses brief items with medical angle." Length: 1,500 to 2,500 words. Pay for major articles is $500 to $1,000; features, $100 to $500.

FITNESS (formerly *Fitness for Living*), 33 East Minor St., Emmaus PA 18049. Editor: John Haberern. For men and women, 25 to 55 years of age. Bimonthly. Circulation: 80,000. Buys all rights. Pays on acceptance. Reports in 2 to 3 weeks. Enclose S.A.S.E. for return of submissions.
Nonfiction and Photos: Articles should be typed, triple-spaced, from 1,200 to 2,000 words, ranging from exercise to reports on what are the best foods for fitness. Must show that personal fitness programs can be enjoyable. Also information on how to get people moving on an exercise program. Pays 4¢ to 5¢ a word. Query essential. Photos purchased with mss. 5x7 or 8x10 glossy, pays $5 to $15.

HEALTH, American Osteopathic Assn., 212 E. Ohio St., Chicago IL 60611. Editor: George W. Northup, D.O. For "readers with at least a high school education." Issued 10 times a year. Buys first rights only. Pays on acceptance. Will send free sample copy on request. Query first, including writer's qualifications. Reports in six weeks. Enclose S.A.S.E.
Nonfiction and Photos: Articles of 1,500 to 2,000 words on medicine and health. Should be factual. Slant to the lay reader interested in his own health and that of his family. Almost never buys personal experience articles. Material must be accurate and "thoroughly researched." Style should be "comprehensive, authoritative." Address Mary Anne Klein, Assistant Editor. Pays 4¢ per word. Buys photos with mss only. 8x10 glossies preferred. No color. Pays $5 per photo used.

HEALTH FOODS & NUTRITION NEWS, 10 W. 56th St., New York NY 10019. Editor: Wendy Lyon. For "every thinking consumer" and for those already interested in health foods. Query first. Enclose S.A.S.E.
Nonfiction: Interested in articles on nutrition and foods and in related subjects, such as ecology. Slant "toward the young, the 'in' crowd."

LIFE AND HEALTH, 6856 Eastern Ave., N.W., Washington DC 20012. Editor: M. G. Hardinge, M.D., Managing Editor: Don Hawley. Established in 1884. Monthly. Circulation: 130,000. Buys all rights. Buys 100 to 180 mss a year. Payment on acceptance. Will send editorial guidelines sheet to a writer on request. Submit seasonal health articles 6 months in advance. Reports on material in 5 to 10 weeks. Enclose S.A.S.E.
Nonfiction, Photos, Poetry, and Fillers: General subject matter consists of "short, concise articles that simply and clearly present a concept in the field of health. Emphasis on prevention; faddism avoided." Approach should be a "simple, interesting

style for laymen. Readability important, Medical jargon avoided. Material should be reliable and include latest findings. We are perhaps more conservative than other magazines in our field. Not seeking sensationalism." Buys informational, interview, some humor. Regular columns that seek freelance material are "Youth Corner" and "Your Wonderful Body." Length: up to 2,000 words. Pays $50 to $150. Purchases photos with mss. 5x7 or larger b&w glossies. Pays $7.50. Color photos usually by staff. Pays $75. Buys some health related poetry. Pays 50¢ per line. "Can use some in-depth briefs on structure or function such as fingernails, hair, salivary digestion, shivering, etc." Pays $10 to $20.

LISTEN MAGAZINE, 6840 Eastern Ave., N.W., Washington D.C. 20012. Editor: Francis A. Soper. Monthly. Pays on acceptance. Buys all rights. Query first. Reports in about 3 weeks. Enclose S.A.S.E.
Nonfiction: Specializes in preventative angle, presenting positive alternatives to various drug dependencies. Uses articles from 500 to 1,500 words; popularized medical, legal, and educational articles on alcohol and narcotics problems; mental health; occasional outdoor or inspirational articles. Especially interested in youth-slanted articles or personality interviews encouraging nonalcoholic and nondrug ways of life. Pays 2¢ to 4¢ a word.
Photos: Buys photos, especially pix illustrating submitted mss. Pays $5 to $10 for singles. Payment for photo series and illustrated articles depend on number of pix, quality, and subject matter. Uses no color.
Fiction and Poetry: Seldom uses fiction except when based directly on an actual experience relating to the alcohol or narcotics problem or some phase of it. Not over 2,500 words. Also pays 2¢ to 4¢ a word for fiction. Uses occasional poetry. Short poems preferred—inspirational, nature, or seasonal.
How To Break In: "We encourage manuscripts from teenage writers in the form of personal experiences or convictions in our subject area."

SWEET 'N LOW, 363 Seventh Ave., New York NY 10001. Editor: June Mintz. For persons concerned about weight control. Established in 1972. Monthly. Circulation: 250,000. Query first; do not send complete ms. Buys all rights, but will reassign rights to author after publication. Buys 10 to 15 mss a year. Pays on publication. Will send free sample copy to writer on request. Enclose S.A.S.E.
Nonfiction: "We cover cosmetics, skin care, and beauty with our staff. From freelance writers, we buy articles on health, diet, and general well-being—mostly aimed at women. Informational, personal experience, and humor." Length: 1,000 to 2,500 words. Pays $50 to $150.

TIME OF YOUR LIFE, 2360 S. Garfield Ave., Monterey Park CA 91754. Editor: Fred Rifkin. For "members of Weight Watchers of Los Angeles County, Kern County, Santa Barbara County, and Antelope Valley. They range in age from the very young to the very old; varying education, interests etc.; all are or were overweight." Monthly. Circulation: over 75,000. Buys first rights. Pays on publication. Will send a sample copy to a writer on request. No query required. Submit seasonal material at least 3 months in advance. Reports in 2 months. Enclose S.A.S.E. for return of submissions.
Nonfiction, Photos, and Fiction: "Articles should be of a general nature, interesting to a wide variety of people. Subjects are related to housewives' interests with emphasis on personal problems about weight, hobbies, and sports. Articles relating to weight problems are given priority. Fiction is fine, again with a preference for 'weighty' stories. We'll give preference to stories about Weight Watchers, stories where weight works for or against a person, etc. Ours is the only magazine published by a franchise of Weight Watchers International. We treat each other in a very personal fashion." Buys personal experience articles, profiles, interviews, humor, inspirational articles, photo features. Buys humorous stories, and stories concerned with contemporary problems. Length: 400 to 2,500 words. Pays $12.50 to $25. Captioned b&w glossies purchased with mss. Pays $7.50.

TODAY'S HEALTH, 535 N. Dearborn St., Chicago IL 60610. Editor: David A. Sendler. For "average young American parents, high school age youngsters, adults with high school education." Monthly. Circulation: 610,000. Buys all rights. Pays on acceptance. Will send a sample copy to a writer on request. Query first. "No un-solicited mss." Enclose S.A.S.E.

Nonfiction and Photos: "Looks for family angle wherever possible and covers such subject areas as nutrition, recreation, child development, ecology and other health-related community problems, latest developments in the treatment of diseases. Also looks for fresh insights on improving the ways people interact, health angles on major news events and personalities, and well-documented pieces crusading for better, healthier living. Prefers upbeat approach to stories. Medical articles must be scientifically accurate. Photo stories usually assigned." Buys only one-time rights for photos. Length: 2,500 to 3,000 words. Pays $500 to $1,000. Pays $50 minimum for b&w and $150 for color photos.

How To Break In: "We would first be attracted to a compelling story suggestion; one that we'd ask the writer to build into a substantial outline. We'd get some notion of the writer's style and organizational skills from the outline, and we might also request writing samples to get further insight into the writer's strengths and weaknesses. We do run a short regular feature, '*Today's Health* News,' and contributors would certainly be encouraged to approach us with newsy items turned out with a touch of wit or poignance or some other special quality."

WEIGHT WATCHERS MAGAZINE, 635 Madison Ave., New York NY 10022. Feature Editor: Edythe Tomkinson. Monthly. Circulation: 750,000. Buys first North American serial rights. Will send a sample copy to a writer for 75c. Query not required. Enclose S.A.S.E. for return of submissions.

Nonfiction, Photos, Fiction, and Fillers: Food, beauty, and fashion are staff-written. Medical articles, household tips wanted. No dieting or exercise stories. Length: about 3,000 words. Also needs short fiction. Length: to 2,500 words, preferably shorter. Payment varies according to merit of article, length, and author's experience; usually $225 to $275, higher for experienced writers. Photographer credit given for photos. Uses newsbreaks, jokes, and short humor fillers.

History Publications

ALASKA JOURNAL, 422 Calhoun Avenue, Juneau AK 99801. Editor: R. N. De Armond. For "people interested in Alaska and primarily in its history and arts, including painting and other graphic arts, sculpture, ceramics, pottery." Established in 1971. Quarterly. Circulation: 4000. Buys first North American serial rights. Buys 25 mss a year. Payment on publication. Will send sample copy to a writer for $1. Query first required. Will consider photocopied submissions, "if adequately clear." Reports in 1 month. Enclose S.A.S.E. for reply to queries.

Nonfiction and Photos: General subject matter consists of "scholarly articles on general history of Alaska and Yukon Territory, Canada; articles on arts and artists of the same area. Historical articles should be documented. Most articles require illustrations. Articles on the arts must be illustrated or arrangements made for illustrations, black and white, or color. We would like to see some short articles, to 2000 words, on American period of Alaska's history." Length: 200 to 7,500 words. Pays 1¢ to 5¢ a word. Photos purchased with mss and captions are required. Pays $5 to $10 for 5x7 or 8x10 b&w glossies. Pays to $25 for 35mm Kodachrome color transparencies.

AMERICAN HERITAGE, 1221 Avenue of the Americas, New York NY 10020. Editor: Oliver O. Jensen. Established in 1954. Bimonthly. Circulation: 210,000. Buys all rights. Buys about 20 mss a year. Pays on acceptance. Before submitting, "check our five- and ten-year indexes to see whether we have already treated the subject." Query first. Submit seasonal material 8 months in advance. Returns rejected material in 1 month. Acknowledges acceptance of material in 2 months. Enclose S.A.S.E. for reply to queries.

Nonfiction: Wants "historical articles intended for intelligent lay readers rather than professional historians." Emphasis is on authenticity, accuracy, and verve.

Style should stress "readability and accuracy." Length: 4,000 to 5,000 words. Pays $350 to $750. Articles Editor: E.M. Halliday.
Fillers: "We occasionally buy shorts and fillers that deal with American history."
How To Break In: "Our needs are such that the criteria for a young, promising writer are unfortunately no different than those for an old hand. Nevertheless, we have over the years published quite a few 'firsts' from young writers whose historical knowledge, research methods, and writing skills meet our standards from the start. Everything depends on the quality of the material. We don't really care whether the author is twenty and unknown, or eighty and famous."

AMERICAN HISTORICAL REVIEW, 400 A St., S.E., Washington DC 20003. Editor: R.K. Webb. Issued five times a year for professional historians and others interested in a serious approach to history. Reports within two months. Enclose S.A.S.E.
Nonfiction: Articles on scholarly historical subject matter. Preferred length for articles is 6,000 to 10,000 words, including footnotes. Query not necessary.

AMERICAN HISTORY ILLUSTRATED, CIVIL WAR TIMES ILLUSTRATED, Box 1831, Harrisburg PA 17105. Editor: Robert H. Fowler. Aimed at general public with an interest in sound, well-researched history. Monthly except March and September. Buys all rights. Pays on acceptance. Will send a sample copy of either for $1. Write for copy of guidelines for writers. Query preferred. Suggestions to freelancers: "Do not bind ms or put it in a folder or such. Simply paperclip it. We prefer a ribbon copy, not a carbon or xerox. No multiple submissions, please. It is best to consult several back issues before submitting any material, in order to see what we have already covered and to get an idea of our editorial preferences. Please include a reading list of materials used in preparing the article." Reports within two weeks. Enclose S.A.S.E. for reply to queries.
Nonfiction: U.S. history, pre-historic to the 1950's, biography, military, social, cultural, political, etc. Also the U.S. in relation to the rest of the world, as in World Wars I and II, diplomacy, The Civil War; military, biography, technological, social, diplomatic, political, etc. Style should be readable and entertaining, but not glib or casual. Slant generally up to the author. Taboos: footnotes, shallow research, extensive quotation. 2,500 to 6,000 words. Pays $50 to $200.
Photos: Buys only occasionally with mss; 8x10 glossies preferred. Does welcome suggestions for illustrations. Address to Frederic Ray, Art Director.

THE AMERICAN WEST, 599 College Ave., Palo Alto CA 94306. Editor: Donald E. Bower. For "many old and young people interested in the history of the West and in modern-day observations about the West." Bimonthly. Circulation: 30,000. Buys all rights. Buys approximately 30 mss a year. Pays on acceptance. Will send a sample copy to "an accredited writer" on request. Write for copy of guidelines for writers. Query first. Will consider photocopied submissions. Reports in 3 to 4 weeks. Enclose S.A.S.E. with queries and submissions.
Nonfiction: "Articles about the West, wilderness, personalities of the old and new West. Our magazine is closest in idea to *American Heritage*, but deals primarily with the West." Prefers historical pieces "with graphics if at all possible." Wants articles that are "well-researched, in-depth, written with a flair. They should cover the subject, but not be too pedantic or studious. Also use articles on natural history, archaeology, conservation and the environment. No militant articles. Too many pieces are scantily researched, reminiscences of some long-lost relative, etc. A bibliography listing major sources should be included as an appendix to the article." Length: 2,500 to 4,000 words. Pays $75 to $300. For "Collector's Choice" feature, buys "short, 1,000-word portraits of noteworthy men, places, happenings of the West." Pays $75.
Photos: Purchased with ms. "We prefer captioned photos to be sent with submitted mss. Often seek photos ourselves. B&w or color. Prefer 4x5 transparencies." Also buys photo studies of "scenic wonders of the West." Pays $10 to $50 per transparency.
How To Break In: "Best bet for us would be our 'Collector's Choice', 1,000 word article with a rare or unusual photo or piece of art. Another possibility is our Book Review Section."

ARCHAEOLOGY, 260 West Broadway, New York NY 10013. Editor: Phyllis Pollak Katz. Published by the Archaeological Institute of America. For professional and amateur archaeologists. Quarterly. Pays on publication. Will send a sample copy to a writer for $2.50. Query preferred. Enclose S.A.S.E.

Nonfiction and Photos: Archaeological subjects written by trained archaeologists. Length: 7 or 8 printed pages, with photos. Pays $6 per printed page. Photos must accompany mss. No extra payment.

ART AND ARCHAEOLOGY NEWSLETTER, 243 East 39th Street, New York NY 10016. Editor: Otto F. Reiss. For "educated middle class, including many teachers; students and young people interested in archaeology as a career; some professional archaeologists of renown." Established in 1962. Quarterly. Circulation: 1,000. Buys first North American serial rights and second serial rights. Payment on acceptance. Will send a sample copy to a writer for 80¢ in 8¢ stamps. Query first. Will consider photocopied submissions. Reports in 10 days to 4 weeks. Enclose S.A.S.E. for reply to queries.

Nonfiction and Photos: General subject matter consists of "archaeology; ancient history; ancient technology and sciences; manners and mores in antiquity. Travel stories of people who have visited ancient sites that lie off the tourist and sightseeing bus circuit. Stories by people who dropped in on archaeological excavations in progress. Illustrated with b&w photographs." Approach should be "brief, condensed, yet with telling detail—newsmagazine style. We are less pedantic; more lively and readable." Buys archaeological articles, with emphasis on lands surrounding the Mediterranean. Length: 800 to 2,500 words. Pays $15 to $30. Purchases photos with or without mss, or on assignment; captions required. Accepts b&w glossies only.

DETROIT IN PERSPECTIVE: A JOURNAL OF REGIONAL HISTORY, Detroit Historical Museum, 5401 Woodward Ave., Detroit MI 48202. Editor: W. Sprague Holden. For members of the Detroit Historical Society and nonmember subscribers interested in regional history. Material is strictly limited to articles about the past of Detroit and southeastern Michigan and about persons and events which influenced the city and area. Established in 1972. Three issues a year: Autumn, Winter, Spring. Circulation: 2,000 to 3,000. Buys all rights but will reassign rights to author after publication. Buys 15 to 20 mss a year. Payment on publication, or earlier. Will send sample copy to a writer for $2.50. Submit complete ms. Will consider photocopied submissions but originals, typed double-spaced, are preferred. Reports on material accepted for publication in 1 month. Enclose S.A.S.E.

Nonfiction and Photos: "We seek carefully researched, well-documented articles on the Detroit region's past told in a lively, nonacademic style. We eschew with equal vigor the dull and heavily academic and the hyped-up overly 'popular.' Stories strong in human interest." Historical only. No fiction. Length: 2,500 to 5,000 words, "but we aren't rigid about it." Pays up to $100. 5x7 or 8x10 b&w photos and other b&w illustrations highly desirable, and are purchased with manuscript.

FIRESIDE CHATS, P.O. Box 172, Hyde Park NY 12538. Editor: Gustav Detjen, Jr. Official publication of the Franklin D. Roosevelt Philatelic Society of Hyde Park, NY. For "stamp collectors of all age, both sexes, various professions and crafts, who are primarily interested in Roosevelt stamps and other material relating to Franklin D. Roosevelt, Mrs. Roosevelt, and the Roosevelt era." Established in 1966. Monthly. Circulation: 600. Not copyrighted. Pays on publication. Will send a sample copy to a writer for 50¢. Submit seasonal material 3 months in advance. Reports in 2 weeks. Enclose S.A.S.E. for return of submissions.

Nonfiction and Photos: Historical articles which refer to FDR. Writer should have a "constructive attitude toward FDR. We are not interested in any derogatory material." Articles of philatelic and historic interest. Length: 250 to 500 words. Pays $5 to $30. B&w photos purchased with mss.

FRONTIER TIMES, P.O. Box 3338, 1012 Edgecliff Terrace, Austin TX 78764. Editor: Pat Wagner. Established in 1957. Bimonthly. Circulation: 150,000. Buys first American serial rights. Payment on acceptance. Query first. Reports within 4 to 6 weeks. Enclose S.A.S.E.

Nonfiction and Photos: "We use material (factual) about the West concerning events which took place between 1830 and 1910. Our geographical area covers the 17 western states, although we sometimes run Canadian, Alaskan and Mexican stories if the 'feel' is right. The material must be documented, and we do not like fiction based on fact, a lot of dialog that cannot be substantiated. First-person accounts based on memory solely are not encouraged. We are not looking for the dry textbook approach, but we do insist that the material be researched and accurate. We like an author to use the amount of words that it takes to tell his story without padding." Length: 750 to 4,000 words. Payment 2¢ a word. "Photographs submitted with mss are returned after publication." Uses color for cover only—$75 for one-time reproduction rights. The transparency is returned after publication.

JOURNAL OF AMERICAN HISTORY, Indiana University, Ballantine, Bloomington IN 47401. Editor: Martin Ridge. Buys all rights. Pays on publication. No query required. Reports in 8 to 10 weeks. Enclose S.A.S.E.
Nonfiction: Scholarly articles on American history. Length: 900 words. Pays 1¼¢ per word.

MANKIND, The Magazine of Popular History, 8060 Melrose Ave., Los Angeles CA 90046. Editor: Alvaro Cordona-Hine. Primarily college graduate reader audience. Bimonthly. Buys North American serial rights only. Buys about 50 mss a year. Pays on publication. Will send sample copy for $1.25. Enclose S.A.S.E.
Nonfiction: "Queries are preferred and should be extensive enough so the editors may determine where the article is going. We have found that most of the over-the-transom submissions are poorly researched for this market. Assignments are given only to writers who have sold here before or have a reputation in the field of historical writing. We are looking for articles on any aspect of history that can be rendered meaningful and alive and which lends itself to illustration. We would like to emphasize high quality writing together with accurateness and a fresh approach to history. We do not wish to see superficiality, survey generalizations or material of a shocking nature. We see far too many articles on the Civil War and most other aspects of American history." Prefers 5,000 words or less, but occasionally uses longer pieces; on occasion two-parters of 8,000 to 10,000 words. Pays $100 to $500 for articles.
Photos: Purchased with mss. Pays $35 per page for b&w. Pays $75 per page for color.
How To Break In: "There are no special departments for the beginner who wants to break in, save 'Guest Column' which runs, usually to 2,000 words and takes current events and compares them to similar happenings in the past. Check the magazine. A new writer can break in only by submitting an article impossible to turn down. This not only means finding something original in history but treating it our way. Our way is to present material accurately and excitingly. Dry accounts filled with dates, the usual doctorate dissertation, is out, but so are gushy and romanticized accounts. Best way is to read the magazine and submit queries. Warning: we are really overstocked. That is not just a rejection ploy."

MONTANA, The Magazine of Western History, Montana Historical Society, 225 No. Roberts, Helena MT 59601. Editor: Mrs. Vivian Paladin. Quarterly. Circulation: 14,000. Prefers to buy first rights. Pays on acceptance. Will send a sample copy to a writer on request. Write for copy of guidelines for writers. Query first. Reports in 1 month. Enclose S.A.S.E. for reply to queries.
Nonfiction and Photos: "Interested in authentic articles on the history of the American and Canadian West which show original research on significant facets of history rather than the rewriting of standard incidents generally available in print. Evidence of research must accompany articles, either in the form of footnoting or bibliography. Strict historical accuracy is a must for us: we cannot use fictional material, however authentic the background may be. Unless it is very skillfully and authentically employed; contrived dialog is not acceptable." Length: 3,500 to 5,500 words with rare photographs if possible. Photos (b&w) purchased with ms. Pays $40 to $100, "depending on length and quality."

OLD WEST, P.O. Box 3338, Austin TX 78764. Editor: Pat Wagner. Quarterly. Pays on acceptance. Query first. Reports within 4 to 6 weeks. Enclose S.A.S.E.
Nonfiction and Photos: Principal interest here is in well-illustrated (with old

photos) historical documentaries—Western life from 1850 to 1910. These can deal with ghost towns, ranch life, lost mines, all facets of western life during that period. Accuracy and readability essential. List of sources must be provided with manuscript. No modern western material. Length: 1,500 to 4,000 words preferred. Pays minimum 2¢ a word. "Photographs are returned after publication."

POPULAR ARCHAEOLOGY, Box 18365, Wichita KS 67218. Editor: Dan Vap. For all age ranges; all extremely interested in archaeology. "Designed to become the missing link between the professional, the student and the layman of all degrees ... from armchair to digger." Established in 1972. Biweekly. Circulation: 5,000. Buys all rights but will reassign rights to author after publication. Buys first North American serial rights and second serial (reprint) rights. Buys 50 to 100 mss a year. Payment on publication. Will send sample copy to writer for 50¢. Submit only complete ms. Submit seasonal material 1 month in advance. Enclose S.A.S.E. for return of submissions.
Nonfiction and Photos: "Nontechnical language. Facts must be correctly stated, but we do cover all theories." Personal experience, interview, historical, travel, book reviews. 250 to 2,000 words. Pays 4¢ a word. 5x7 or 8x10 b&w photos purchased with or without ms. Captions required. Pays $5.
Fiction: Historical, archaeological. Length: 250 to 2,000 words. Pays 4¢ a word.

SEA CLASSICS, 7950 Deering Ave., Canoga Park CA 91304. Editor: Jim Scheetz. For persons "who enjoy in-depth accounts of ships and events at sea." Bimonthly. Circulation: 55,000. Buys first rights. Buys 30 mss a year. Pays on publication. Will send a sample copy and editorial guidelines sheet to a published writer on request. Reports in 3 weeks. Enclose S.A.S.E. for return of submissions.
Nonfiction: "Historical articles dealing with men and ships at sea—from the stately liners to the deadly torpedo boats. Articles should show research and a thorough knowledge of the subject, with new data or fresh approach. A good collection of photographs must support the article. Emphasis is being placed on the liners, research vessels, lumber boats, ice breakers—anything related to the lore of the sea. We recently even included an article on ships appearing on stamps from around the world." Length: 1,000 to 3,500 words. Payment to $150, "depending mostly on photo collection."
Photos: "Photographic content is much more important and is usually the determining factor as to whether or not we can use the article." (Photos emphasize ships as products of the shipbuilder's art, and seldom show people or crews.) B&w and color photos purchased with mss; with captions. "No copyrighted photos or any photos to which rights are held can be accepted unless author has a release."
Fillers: Museum and reunion news items for "Shore Log." Payment with copies when requested.

THE TENNESSEE VALLEY HISTORICAL REVIEW, P.O. Box 3013, Nashville TN 37219. Editor: James A. Crutchfield. Address mss to Mrs. Patt Lockhart. For "all ages interested in our heritage." Established in 1972. Quarterly. Buys all rights, but will reassign rights to author after publication. Payment on publication. Will send sample copy to a writer for $1. Query first. Will consider photocopied submissions. Submit seasonal material 3 months in advance. Enclose S.A.S.E. for reply to queries.
Nonfiction and Photos: Freelancers should "tell their historical story in an interesting way. We have articles on Tennessee and would like to see subjects from North and South Carolina, Virginia, Georgia, Florida, Alabama, Arkansas, Mississippi and Kentucky." Length: 4,000 words maximum. Pays minimum of $25. Photos are purchased with accompanying mss.

TRUE WEST, P.O. Box 3338, Austin TX 78764. Editor: Pat Wagner. Established in 1953. Bimonthly. Circulation: 175,000. Buys first North American serial rights. Pays on acceptance. Query first. Enclose S.A.S.E.
Nonfiction and Photos: "Factual accounts regarding people, places, and events of the frontier West, 1850 to 1910. We publish no poetry. Sources are required. If firsthand account, reminiscences must be accurate as to dates and events. Memory only is too vulnerable to error. We do not publish articles with purely local appeal, such

as the history of a county, a geneological study, or subjects more suitable for text-books or scholarly journals. We strive for accounts with an element of action, suspense, heroics, and humor. The better known outlaws, Indians, lawmen, explorers have been done to death. As a rule of thumb almost any subject that can be researched in the large public library has received excessive coverage. The untold stories, we feel, are to be found in court records, old diaries, family records, small towns, old newspapers (if reliable), privately published books and pamphlets, and interviews with alert old people." Preferred length: 750 to 4,000 words. Pays 2¢ a word. Buys color cover photos; minimum size, 5x7. Pays $75. "We usually buy mss and accompanying photos as a package. All photos are returned after publication."
How To Break In: "You will note that our word limit is 750 to 4,000 at present. We use articles from 750 to 1,000 in our short features section ('Wild Old Days'). This section would be a good point to attack for the beginner for several reasons, the principal one being that it will steer him away from broad subjects that have been written about, both in magazines and book form, until there is little new to add. Few publishers repeat an oft-told tale with which its readers are already familiar. A second advantage a limited word length offers is the writer's being forced to select a high spot. If writing about a person or a town it would be difficult to condense the history from beginning to end of either into 750 words. Yet the most exciting thing that happened to either might well be told in an article of such length and be more impressive over all than a chronological coverage of three or four thousand words. In short, we believe it would help a beginner to seek out the overlooked stories of the West—about some colorful incident, place or person deserving of mention in frontier history."

VIRGINIA CAVALCADE, Virginia State Library, Richmond VA 23219. Managing Editor: Kent Druyvesteyn. Quarterly. Reports on submissions in three months. Buys all rights. Pays on acceptance. Query first with outline or abstract.
Nonfiction and Photos: Articles related to Virginia history only; must reflect author's intensive original research into special subject. No articles on genealogy. Footnotes and bibliography required, but not published; all direct quotes must be footnoted in ms. In general, it is more satisfactory to develop a small area of history in detail than to attempt comprehensive coverage. Articles should be suitable for illustration. Material should contain well-rounded development of historical personalities and events. Articles should not deal with living persons. "We do not consider articles which contain fanciful passages of literary contrivances; material is geared to the reader who is so familiar with his facts that no embellishment is necessary to make subject interesting. We want good basic writing." Length: 2,500 to 3,000 words. Pays flat rate of $100. Photos used with mss. B&w, any size; color, 4x5 transparencies preferred. No color prints.

VIRGINIA MAGAZINE OF HISTORY AND BIOGRAPHY, Virginia Historical Society, P.O. Box 7311, Richmond VA 23221. Editor: William M.E. Rachal. Quarterly for serious students of Virginia history. Usually buys all rights. Pays on publication. Reports in one month. Enclose S.A.S.E. for return of submissions.
Nonfiction: Carefully researched and documented articles on Virginia history, and well-edited source material relating to Virginia. Must be dignified, lucid, scholarly. Length: 1,500 to 15,000 words. Appropriate illustrations are used. Pays $2 per page.

THE WESTERN PRODUCER, Second Ave. N., Saskatoon, Sask., Canada. Editor: T.R. Melville-Ness. For "mainly rural, farm-ranch oriented" audience. Circulated in 4 western Canadian provinces. Weekly. Newspaper. Circulation: 150,000. Buys first rights. Pays on acceptance. Reports in 1 month. Enclose S.A.E. and International Reply Coupons for return of submissions.
Nonfiction: Publishes authentic, pioneering western Canadiana, history, memoirs, real experiences. Preferred length not over 2,500 words for short features, longer for serials. Payment varies from 1¢ to 5¢ per word, depending on need and quality.
Photos: Good pioneering photos, Canadian scenic, or seasonal photos accepted. Uses color pix features in addition to b&w. Color transparencies (2¼x2¼) of good quality, all subjects. Pays $5 to $35, depending on use.
Fiction: Based on western situations (not shooting stories), humorous and otherwise, light love stories. Payment varies from 1¢ to 5¢ a word.

Hobby and Craft Publications

Magazines classified here are for collectors, do-it-yourselfers, and craft hobbyists. Publications for electronics and radio hobbyists will be found in the Science classification.

ACQUIRE, Acquire Publishing Co., 170 Fifth Ave., New York NY 10010. Editor: Robert Campbell Rowe. For "collectors of limited objects produced, mostly, in the postwar era—porcelain, medallic arts, plates, esoterica." Established in 1973. Bimonthly. Circulation: 50,000. Buys all rights, but will reassign rights to author after publiction. Buys 50 mss a year. Payment on acceptance. Will send sample copy to writer for $1. Query first. Will consider photocopied submissions. Reports on material in 2 weeks. Enclose S.A.S.E. for reply to queries.
Nonfiction and Photos: "News articles on trends, specific events in the area of contemporary collectibles; profiles and interviews. Tight, fact-filled, newsy." Interested in discoveries of collectibles; informational, how-to, personal experience, humor, expose, nostalgia, personal opinion, travel, all types of reviews; spot news, successful business operations, new product, merchandising techniques, technical. Length: 250 to 5,000 words. Dept. Editor: J. Bowles. Pays $35 to $250. B&w photos purchased with or without mss or on assignment. Captions required. Pays $10 to $100.

AMERICANA, 1221 Avenue of the Americas, New York NY 10020. Editor: Peter Andrews. For "a very well-educated, mature audience, interested in American history, especially such things as architecture, design, crafts, travel, etc." Established in 1973. Bimonthly. Circulation: 250,000. Buys all rights. Payment on acceptance. Will send sample copy to writer on request. Query first. Reports on material in 3 weeks. Enclose S.A.S.E. for reply to queries.
Nonfiction: "Materials of the broadest range of American creation from gardens to cut glass; from collecting Revere silver to automobile hood ornaments. We are interested in anything Americans have created. Our special approach is that, although we are interested in the creative American past, we are a contemporary magazine. The ideal reaction to any story is that the reader will want to and be able to do something about it now; to go to that place, prepare that meal, collect that object, now." Length: 1,000 to 2,000 words. Pays $200 to $300.

AMERICAN AIRCRAFT MODELER, 733 15th St., N.W., Washington DC 20005. Editor: C. Sweeney, Jr. For "the well-read, experienced modeler." Established in 1932. Monthly. Circulation: 133,000. Buys all rights. Buys 150 mss a year. Payment on publication. Will send free sample copy to writer on request. Write for copy of guidelines for writers. Query first. Will consider photocopied submissions. Reports on material in 2 months. Enclose S.A.S.E. for reply to queries.
Nonfiction and Photos: "Technique" articles on model airplanes, boats and cars. All for the experienced modeler. All phases of airplane modeling. Informational, how-to, personal experience, humor, historical, think pieces, new products. Length: 5 to 10 double-spaced pages. Pays $75 to $400. 5x7 b&w glossies and color transparencies purchased with or without mss, or on assignment. Captions required.

AMERICAN COLLECTOR, 13920 Mt. McClellan Blvd., Reno NV 89506. Editor: John F. Maloney. For "collectors, antique buffs and investors; middle-aged, well-educated, affluent." Established in 1970. Monthly. Circulation: 45,000. Buys all rights, but can reassign rights to author after publication. Buys 110 mss a year. Payment on publication. Write for copy of editorial guidelines. Query first or submit complete ms. Will consider photocopied submissions. Reports in 2 weeks. Enclose S.A.S.E.
Nonfiction and Photos: "Articles about collecting or collections with emphasis on how-to, prices, investment potential but also including background history and overall significance of the collector's item. Feature articles with more research than human interest; e.g., how to collect snuff bottles; the rising value of George III silver. All articles slanted toward collectors must be interesting yet must be informative, with up-to-date info on prices, availability, trends, etc. Can be an examination of a single collection with insight into collector's motivations. Each article must be significant and relevant; no fillers; no 'the joys of collecting' type of stories. No cov-

erage of minor auctions. Current interest is in 'the new collectibles': Art Deco, '50s stuff, pinball machines, offbeat collections, comic books, beer cans, etc." Length: 500 to 2,000 words. Pays $1 per published inch. B&w negatives or prints purchased with ms. Captions required. Pays $5. 35mm color transparencies or slides. Pays $10.

THE ANTIQUE TRADER, P.O. Box 1050, Dubuque IA 52001. Publisher: Ed Babker. For "the antiques trade, antique dealers and collectors all across the country." Buys all rights. "We invite authoritative and well-researched articles on all types of antiques and collector's items." Enclose S.A.S.E. for return of submissions.
Nonfiction and Photos: "Each article should have a liberal number of b&w photos and be double-spaced, typewritten on one side of a sheet. When we buy an article it is for publication in *The Antique Trader Weekly* and for possible reprinting at a later date in one other Babka Publishing Co. publication. In the event that it is reprinted, a fee of 40% of the original fee will be paid the author. We reserve the right to edit any ms to fit our editorial requirements. We also solicit news items, pictures of collections of antiques or collector's items, short notes of interest to the antiques hobby, pictures of antique shows, flea markets, etc. We will also run a short write-up on any new shop opening. For this type of news, we do not pay the submitter, we print these as a service to the antiques hobby as a whole, and we invite individuals to send us this type of news with this spirit in mind. We will pay anywhere from $5 to $30 for articles, depending on the length, the quality of the writing and the quality of the photos. Longer, more in-depth articles with good sharp photos, naturally are worth more to us. We also welcome features which are accompanied by a good color transparency or negative. These may be considered for use as a cover story. Payment on such cover stories ranges from $30 to $50."

THE ANTIQUES JOURNAL, Box 88128, Dunwoody GA 30338. Editor: John Mebane. For "antique collectors and dealers." Monthly. Circulation: 100,000. Buys all rights. Buys about 100 mss a year. Pays on publication. Will send a sample copy to a writer for 75¢. Query preferred. Submit seasonal material at least 6 months in advance. Returns rejected material in 3 weeks. Acknowledges acceptance of material in 3 weeks. Enclose S.A.S.E. for return of submissions or reply to queries.
Nonfiction: "Factual articles dealing with antiques and collectible objects." Writer should do "sound research on single categories of antiques, with emphasis on the newer collectible objects." Does not want "descriptions of historic homes or museums displaying antiques." Also occasionally uses interviews. Length: 750 to 2,500 words. Pays $25 to $70. Purchases b&w glossy photos with mss.

BOAT BUILDER, 229 Park Ave., South, New York NY 10003. Editor: Marie DiGioia. For "people interested in building their own boats." 3 times a year. Circulation: 50,000. Buys all rights. Buys 6 to 7 mss a year. Pays on acceptance. Reports in 4 weeks. Enclose S.A.S.E. for return of submissions.
Nonfiction and Photos: Needs articles that are "step-by-step exposition of how to build different boats, in clear, semitechnical language." New product articles come from manufacturers. Length: 250 to 1,500 words. Payment is $25 to $300. B&w glossy photos with captions are purchased with manuscripts.

BOTTLES AND RELICS/COLLECTOR'S WORLD, Drawer L, Conroe TX 77301. Editor: Donald L. Osborne. Monthly. Buys first North American serial rights. Buys 100 mss a year. Payment on acceptance. Will send sample copy to writer for 25¢. Write for copy of guidelines for writers. Query first or submit complete ms. Reports on material in 4 weeks. Enclose S.A.S.E.
Nonfiction: Treasure hunting articles on old things wanted by collectors; bottles, relics, antiques, primitives, etc. What collectors are buying; how to find, restore, evaluate and sell them. Lost or missing art treasures, antiques, rare items, etc. Treatment should be objective and informational. Length: 1,500 to 2,000 words. Pays $25 to $40 (average $35).
Fillers: On topics above. Length: 300 to 500 words. Pays $5 to $15.

CAR MODEL MAGAZINE, 1309 East McDowell Rd., Phoenix AZ 85006. Executive Editor: Edward K. Dorris. For hobby group, mostly 8 to 25 age group, racing group, with varied interests and education. Established in 1961. Monthly. Rights purchased vary with author and material. Buys 50 mss a year. Write for copy of

editorial guidelines. Query first. Reports in 4 weeks. Enclose S.A.S.E.
Nonfiction and Photos: "Hobby magazine for model building, racing, collecting.
Regular columns cover penpals, racing reports, club reports, special feature model
building or racing articles." Buys how-to articles. Length varies. Pays $25 per
printed page. Buys photos with mss. Captions are required. Uses b&w only. Pays
$10 to $15 per printed page.

CRAFT HORIZONS, 16 E. 52nd St., New York NY 10022. Editor-in-Chief: Rose
Slivka. Bimonthly. Circulation: 33,000. Published by American Crafts Council for
professional craftsmen, artists, teachers, architects, designers, decorators, collectors,
connoisseurs and the consumer public. Will send a free sample copy to a writer
upon request. Reports as soon as possible. Pays on publication. Enclose S.A.S.E.
Nonfiction and Photos: 1,000-word articles and accompanying photos on the subject of creative work in ceramics, weaving, stitchery, jewelry, metalwork, woodwork,
etc. Discussions of the technology, the materials and the ideas of artists throughout
the world working in the above media. Pays $75 to $100 per article. Query required.
Accompanying photos should be 8x10 b&w glossies. Pays $7.50 per b&w glossy.

CREATIVE CRAFTS MAGAZINE, P.O. Box 700, Newton NJ 07860. Editor: Sybil
C. Harp. For adult craft hobbyists, teachers, therapists, mature youngsters. 8 times a
year. Buys all rights. Pays on publication. Will send a sample copy to a writer for
60¢. No query required. Enclose S.A.S.E. for return of submissions.
Nonfiction: "Most articles accepted are written by knowledgeable craftsmen. How-
to articles must be clearly written with complete sources of materials given. We are
looking for fresh ideas and new approaches to traditional crafts." Pays $30 to $50
per published page. Articles should be accompanied by photos of finished product,
plus those necessary to illustrate how-to procedure.
Photos: With mss. Should be sharp, b&w glossy. Color transparencies are also used.

CUT & SEW, c/o EnterMedia, Inc., 524 E. William St., Ann Arbor MI 48108. Executive Editor/Publisher: Arthur J. Harger. Editor/Publisher: Kazia Sulikowski. For
"women and men who sew, crewel, knit, crochet and do specialty handcraft work
with fabrics and vinyls." Established in 1970. Monthly. Circulation: 1,750,000.
Buys all rights. Buys 20 to 40 mss a year. Payment on publication. Will send a free
sample copy to a writer on request. Query first. Submit seasonal material two
months in advance. Reports within 3 weeks. Enclose S.A.S.E. for reply to queries.
Nonfiction, Photos, and Poetry: Publishes "self-help articles, new applications for
materials, new materials, new techniques, patterns, wall fabric applications." Freelancer should use "very straightforward 'middle American' prose. We are the only
service publication in the field. We are distributed free via courtesy circulation and
we are distributed locally and regionally by independent businessmen-dealers."
Buys informational, how-to, expose, photo, reviews of fabric design, spot news, new
product, and technical articles. A regular column called "A Stitch in Time Saves
Nine" seeks freelance material on innovations in fabric and plastic sewing, etc.
Length: 500 to 2,000 words. Pays $75 to $200. Purchases photos with mss and on
assignment; captions required. Pays $15 and up for b&w only. Also "buys a photo
every month of best design we find handicrafted on fabric—pay $50 for this." Buys
free and light verse, 2 each issue. Length: 10 to 40 lines. Pays $50 per published
poem.
Fillers: Buys knitting puzzles and short humor about sewing. Length: 25 words and
up. Must query for puzzles. Pays $10 for published item, $50 for puzzle.

DECORATING AND CRAFT IDEAS MADE EASY, P.O. Box 2327, Ft. Worth TX
76101. Editor: Leon Parkman. For "women who wish to make things to decorate
their homes." 12 times a year. Circulation: 600,000. Buys first rights. Pays on publication. Will send a sample copy to a writer on request. Submit seasonal material at
least 3 months in advance. Reports in 30 days. Enclose S.A.S.E.
Nonfiction: "Articles on how to make things with materials readily available at local
arts and crafts shops. The article must tell how a project is used to decorate the home
and contain step-by-step instructions." Length: approximately 2,000 words.
Photos: Purchased with mss; with captions only. Color transparencies, 35mm color.
"All photos must be sharp." Payment and rights bought are by arrangement. Department Editor: Fredrica Daugherty.

Fillers: "Might consider decorating tips, etc." Payment by arrangement. Department Editor: Fredrica Daugherty.

EARLY AMERICAN LIFE, P.O. Box 1831, Harrisburg PA 17105. Editor: Robert G. Miner. For "anyone interested in the warmth and beauty of early America. They enjoy social history, antiques, reproductions, etc." Established in 1970. Bimonthly. Circulation: 100,000. Buys all rights. Buys 50 mss a year. Payment on acceptance. Will send a free sample copy to writer on request. Write for copy of guidelines for writers. Query first. Will consider photocopied submissions. Unsolicited seasonal material should be submitted 4 months in advance; 3 months in advance on assignment. Reports in 1 month. Enclose S.A.S.E. for reply to queries.
Nonfiction and Photos: "Articles on early (1600-1850) architecture; decorating, furniture, arts, crafts, trades, craft projects, travel to historic sites (our 'Living History' series) and how Americans of the period lived and worked. We try to tell our readers 'how it was' and how they can achieve early American style today. We do not do history as such (famous people, battles, etc.) but try to recapture the feeling and design of the period. We then try to relate all subjects to today's needs." Length: 750 to 4,000 words. Pays $10 to $125. Photos purchased with or without mss. Pays minimum of $5 for high contrast b&w photos; minimum of $25 for color.

EMBROIDERER'S JOURNAL, 220 Fifth Ave., New York NY 10001. Editor: Juliette Hamelecourt. For "embroiderers and sewers." Established in 1972. Bimonthly. Circulation: 15,000. Buys all rights, but will reassign rights to author after publication. Buys about 50 mss a year. Will send a sample copy to a writer on request. Write for copy of guidelines for writers. Query first. Reports in 6 to 8 weeks. Enclose S.A.S.E. for reply to queries.
Nonfiction: "How-to articles. The writer must have a know-how of embroidery stitchery. Interested in patterns." Buys how-to and photo articles. Length: 1,500 words. Pays $25.
Photos: "Good, sharp b&w glossies and color transparencies." Payment variable. Dept. Editor: M. O'Reilly.

FAMILY HANDYMAN, 235 E. 45th St., New York NY 10017. Editor: Morton Waters. Enclose S.A.S.E. for return of submissions.
Nonfiction and Photos: Step-by-step articles, up to 1,000 words, in nontechnical language, with b&w photos, on home improvement, repair and maintenance for do-it-yourselfers. Pays $40 to $100 on acceptance.
Fillers: Shorts, 100 to 300 words, with or without photos and rough drawings as needed, on expert tips or shortcuts for do-it-yourselfers. Pays $5 to $15 on acceptance.

FLEA MARKET QUARTERLY, Box 243, Bend OR 97701. Editor: Annette O'Connell. For "active adults, many retired, who spend their leisure time traveling, building various collections and who enjoy the give and take of flea market bargaining." Established in 1973. Quarterly. Circulation: 5,000. Buys all rights. Payment on acceptance. Will send sample copy to writer for $1. Query first. Reports on material in 2 weeks. Enclose S.A.S.E. for response to query.
Nonfiction and Photos: "We want articles that will inspire collectors to visit flea markets or to become flea market dealers. Articles that show how certain collectors have enhanced their collection through flea market activity. Any collector article should have a flea market slant. Some suggested titles: 'My Experience As a Flea Market Dealer,' 'The Unbelievable Find' or 'Take Your Family on a Flea Market Outing!' Also want interviews with exceptionally successful flea market dealers and/or operators." Informational, nostalgia, personal experience, merchandising techniques. Length: 1,500 words maximum. Pays $30 to $50 for collector features; $5 to $20 for short items. Pays $3 for photos not accompanied by mss.

FLYING MODELS, P.O. Box 700, Newton NJ 07860. Editor: Don McGovern. For "adult minded model aviation hobbyists including mature youngsters. Radio control, free flight, controline, static, R/C boats and cars." Established in 1927. Monthly. Circulation: 35,000. Buys all rights. Buys 96 to 120 mss a year. Payment on acceptance. Will send writer a sample copy for 60c. Submit seasonal material six

months in advance. Reports as soon as possible. Enclose S.A.S.E. for return of submissions.
Nonfiction: Publishes "nonfiction. Heavy how-to model airplane features written by the person who designed the craft, and they have to be good. Glossy photos a must. Scale drawings (usually 4X) accurately rendered. Some aviation historic features slanted to model airplane interest. Also technical flight articles, etc., for model plane use. All articles and features are written by model aviation hobbyists familiar with the magazine and its style and needs. 'Outsiders' don't have the technical know-how to write for us. Strong how-to, major show coverage, and product tests."

GEMS AND MINERALS, P.O. Box 687, Mentone CA 92359. Editor: Don MacLachlan. Monthly for the amateur gem cutter, jewelry maker, mineral collector, and rockhounds. Buys first N.A. serial rights. Pays on publication. Reports within a month. Query first. Enclose S.A.S.E.
Nonfiction and Photos: Material must have how-to slant. No personality stories. Field trips to mineral or gem collecting localities used; must be accurate and give details so they can be found. Four to eight typed pages plus illustrations preferred, but do not limit if subject is important. Frequently good articles are serialized if too long for one issue. Pays 50c per inch for text and pix as published.

HANDWEAVER AND CRAFTSMAN MAGAZINE, 220 Fifth Ave., New York NY 10001. Publisher: Patric Donahue. For professionals and amateurs. Bimonthly. Circulation: 18,000. Buys first rights. Buys about 60 mss a year from freelancers. Pays on publication. Will send a sample copy to a writer on request. No query required. Submit seasonal material at least 2 months in advance. Enclose S.A.S.E. for return of submissions.
Nonfiction: Articles on "handweaving and embroidery—from a technical or specific standpoint. Readers are very knowledgeable and want useful, technical information. Also interested in spinning, design, anthropological and historical approaches; exhibits. Avoid typical hyped-up approach used in ladies' craft magazine." Does not want "macramé or fad craft articles." Length: 500 to 1,500 words. Pays $25.
Photos: Purchased with mss "usually, but this is flexible." B&w glossies. Payment negotiable.

HOME WORKSHOP, 229 Park Ave., South, New York NY 10003. Editor: Marie DiGioia. For "people, usually men, interested in building furniture, etc." Annual. Circulation: 50,000. Buys all rights. Buys 1 or 2 mss a year. Pays on acceptance. Query first. Submit seasonal material 6 months in advance. Reports in 4 weeks. Enclose S.A.S.E. for reply to queries.
Nonfiction and Photos: Uses "how-to articles on building projects, written in factual, step-by-step style." New product features come from manufacturers. Length: 250 to 1,500 words. Pays $25 to $200. B&w glossy photos are purchased with mss, and with captions only. Color transparencies are bought for the cover.

LADY'S CIRCLE HOMECRAFTS (formerly *Lady's Circle Arts & Crafts*), 21 W. 26 St., New York NY 10010. Editor: Lydia Peraza. For "women, teens, children and men interested in all sorts of crafts to make as hobby, school and community projects and also as extra income." Established in 1971. Quarterly. Circulation: 200,000. Buys all rights. Buys 30 to 40 mss a year. Payment on publication. Will send a free sample copy to writer on request. Query first. Submit seasonal material 3 months in advance. Enclose S.A.S.E. for reply to queries.
Nonfiction and Photos: "All types of crafts such as plastic casting, doll furniture, working with driftwood, dry flowers, macrame, soap making, candles, and all types of do-it-yourself crafts that do not require expensive or heavy tools. We buy ideas as well as completed mss. Easy to follow, very clear instructions are a must for all articles. Pottery, wood carving, all types of crafts using trash can candidates like coffee tins, lids, etc., boutique gifts; anything that has good extra income earning possibilities. We do not need anything like making paper flowers, felt slippers, beaded jewelry and other childish projects. Would like to see articles on how to sell crafts." Pays $50 per ms or idea to $200, depending on length and subject. Pays $10 per 8x10 b&w glossy when purchased without ms. Pays $25 for color (2¼ square) when purchased without ms. "We prefer finished shot in color and 'how-to' instructions in black and white."

LAPIDARY JOURNAL, P.O. Box 80937, San Diego, CA 92108. Editor: Pansy D. Kraus. For "all ages interested in the lapidary hobby." Established in 1947. Monthly. Circulation: 58,000. Rights purchased vary with author and material. Buys all rights, or first serial rights. Payment on publication. Will send free sample copy to writer on request. Will send editorial guidelines to a writer on request. Query first. Will consider photocopied submissions. Enclose S.A.S.E. for reply to queries

Nonfiction and Photos: Publishes "articles pertaining to gem cutting, gem collecting and jewelry making for the hobbyist." Buys informational, how-to, personal experience, historical, travel, and technical articles. Pays 1c a word. Buys good contrast b&w photos. Contact editor for color. Payment varies according to size.

McCALL'S NEEDLEWORK AND CRAFTS MAGAZINE, 230 Park Ave., New York NY 10017. Managing Editor: Eleanor Spencer. Issued semiannually. All rights bought. Payment varies. Strictly how-to. Enclose S.A.S.E. for return of submissions.

Nonfiction: Accepts the made-up items accompanied by the directions, diagrams, and charts for making them. Directions must be step-by-step.

MAKE IT WITH LEATHER (formerly *The Craftsman*), P.O. Box 1386, Fort Worth TX 76101. Editor: Earl F. Warren. Buys all rights. Bimonthly. Established in 1965. Circulation: 180,000. Buys 60 mss a year. Payment on publication. Will send free sample copy to writer on request. Write for copy of guidelines for writers. Reports on material in 6 to 8 weeks. Enclose S.A.S.E. for return of submissions.

Nonfiction and Photos: "How-to-do-it leathercraft stories illustrated with cutting patterns, carving patterns. First-person approach even though article may be ghosted. Story can be for professional or novice. Strong on details; logical progression on steps; easy to follow how-to-do-it." Length: 2,000 words maximum. Payment starts at $15 to $20 plus $5 to $10 per illustration. "Most articles judged on merit and may range to '$200 plus' per ms. Depends on project and work involved by author." 5x7, or larger, b&w photos of reproduction quality purchased with mss. Captions required. Pays $5 minimum. Color of professional quality is used. Ektachrome slides or sheet film stock. Negs needed with all print film stock. Pays $8.50 minimum. All photos are used to illustrate project on step-by-step basis, and also finished item.

Fillers: "Tips and Hints." Short practical hints for doing leathercraft or protecting tools, new ways of doing things, etc. Length: 100 words maximum. Pays $5 minimum.

MILITARY COLLECTORS NEWS, P.O. Box 7582, Tulsa OK 74105. Editor: Jack Britton. For "military collectors of all ages and education." Monthly. Circulation: 3,200. Buys all rights. Buys about 24 mss a year. Pays on publication. Will send a sample copy to a writer on request. Submit seasonal material 2 months in advance. Reports in 1 week. Enclose S.A.S.E. for return of submissions.

Nonfiction and Photos: "Military history and identification of military items—medals, insignia, uniforms, daggers, swords, aircraft, etc. World War I and II—all periods (Civil War, Korea, Vietnam war, and all earlier periods)." Wants articles on "how to identify fakes, personal experience war articles, interviews with military personnel, spot news of gun shows, exposes of fakes and reproductions, and war photos." Length: 500 to 2,000 words. Pays $1 to $10. Photos purchased with mss; with captions only. Buys b&w glossies, color prints. "Photos of WW II and earlier; insignia, medals, weapons; men in uniform; personalities." Pays $1 to $3.

Fillers: Buys military clippings, jokes, and short humor. Length: "1 page or less." Pays $1 to $2.

MODEL AIRPLANE NEWS, White Plains Plaza, One N. Broadway, White Plains NY 10601. Editor: Arthur F. Schroeder. Monthly. Circulation: 100,000. Buys all rights. Pays on publication. Will send free sample copy on request. Reports as soon as possible. Include S.A.S.E. for return of submissions.

Nonfiction: "This is a good market for freelancers who have a knowledge of model plane building. Uses articles dealing with model airplanes in all phases, as well as material on general aviation if it has a tie-in with model airplanes. Text should be illustrated with photographs and drawings, for which extra is paid. Query sug-

gested." 1,500 to 2,000 words. Pays $50 to $300.
Photos: 5x7 glossy b&w with ms or caption only.

MODEL RAILROADER, 1027 N. 7th St., Milwaukee WI 53233. Editor: Linn H. Westcott. For adult hobbyists interested in scale model railroading. Monthly. Buys rights "exclusive in model railroad and rail fan field." Query first. Study publication before submitting material. Reports on submissions within four weeks. Enclose S.A.S.E. for reply to queries.
Nonfiction: Wants construction articles on specific model railroad projects (structures, cars, locomotives, scenery, benchwork, etc.). Also photo stories showing model railroads. First-hand knowledge of subject almost always necessary for acceptable slant. Pays base rate of $28 first page, $21 additional pages. (Page is typically 960 words plus 30 sq. in. of illustration, both getting same rate for area.)
Photos: Buys photos with detailed descriptive captions only. Pays $5 and up, depending on size and location. Color: double b&w rate. Full color cover: $60.

THE NEWSPAPER COLLECTOR'S GAZETTE, 2164 E. Broadmor, Tempe AZ 85282. Publisher: Barbara Stuhlmuller. Bimonthly offset publication for newspaper collectors, historians, journalists. Pays on acceptance. Reports within a week. Buys no rights. Will send a sample copy to a writer for $1. Query first. Enclose S.A.S.E.
Nonfiction and Photos: History of journalism and printing or newspaper collecting as a hobby. Articles on the American press before 1900. Bibliography essential. Uses newspaper style with headline. "Writers should be advised that articles which consist of a compilation of the delightful contents of an early newspaper are not acceptable. Our readers already know the joys, or they wouldn't be newspaper collectors. What we seek is 'the news behind the news, newspaper, or newsman,' researched and not easily available elsewhere." Length: maximum 2,500 words. Pays 1¢ a word; $15 maximum for article. Buys 4x5 b&w glossies with mss.

NUMISMATIC SCRAPBOOK MAGAZINE, P.O. Box 150, Sidney OH 45365. Editor: Russell Rulau. For "coin collectors, mostly specialists in U.S. coins or related numismatic items such as medals, tokens, and paper money. Mostly middle income or high middle income brackets." Monthly. Circulation: 10,500. Buys first rights. Buys 10 mss a year. Pays on publication. Query first. Returns rejected material in 2 weeks. Acknowledges acceptance of material in 4 weeks. Enclose S.A.S.E. for reply to queries.
Nonfiction and Photos: "Articles on U.S. coins or related subjects, especially those based on original research or personal experience." Buys personal experience and historical pieces. Length: 250 to 4,000 words. Pays 2c per published word with additional allowance for art. Photos purchased with mss. B&w glossies.

THE OLD BOTTLE MAGAZINE, Box 243, Bend OR 97701. Editor: Shirley Asher. For collectors of old bottles, insulators, relics. Monthly. Circulation: 14,000. Buys all rights. Buys 35 mss a year. Pays on acceptance. Will send a sample copy to a writer on request. No query required. Reports in 1 month. Enclose S.A.S.E. for return of submissions.
Nonfiction, Photos, and Fillers: "We are soliciting factual accounts on specific old bottles, canning jars, insulators and relics." Stories of a general nature on these subjects not wanted. "Interviews of collectors are usually not suitable when written by non-collectors. A knowledge of the subject is imperative. Would highly recommend potential contributors study an issue before making submissions. Articles that tie certain old bottles to a historical background are desired." Length: 250 to 2,500 words. Pays $10 to $50 for article with illustrations. Photos purchased with mss. B&w glossies. Pays $3. Clippings. Pays $5.

1001 FASHION AND NEEDLECRAFT IDEAS, 149 Fifth Ave., New York NY 10003. Editor: Shirley Howard. For home sewers and needlecrafters. Semiannual. Buys all rights. Pays on publication. Query first. Enclose S.A.S.E.
Nonfiction: Interested in articles about items that can be made by sewing, knitting, and crafts. Publishes knitting instructions, directions for hand-crafted items. Length and payment to be negotiated.

THE PHILATELIC REPORTER AND DIGEST, Erbe Publishers, 230 Tyrone Circle, Baltimore MD 21212. Editor: Theodore H. Erbe. For "stamp collectors or investors—would be composite American type a bit conservative—collecting stamps from 1 to 50 years." Established in 1959. Monthly. Circulation: 1,250. Buys all rights, but will reassign them to author after publication. Buys 60 to 70 mss a year. Payment on publication in contributor's copies where much rewriting is needed. Will send a sample copy to a writer for 65¢. Query advised. Reports in 2 weeks. Enclose S.A.S.E.

Nonfiction: Publishes "articles and features that deal with stamp collecting of a certain country, geographical area of a given topic featured on the stamp (animals, birds, flowers, and so on), and with some copy on investment and marketing of stamps and related material." Freelancer "should know stamps if dealing with a regular-type feature; or he should have a strong philatelic tie-in if the material is of general, but related value (i.e., —economic conditions as they affect stamp markets). The *Reporter* stresses the 'business' of stamps more than other stamp publications which are aimed more clearly at stamp collecting in general. Readership audience more advanced than most stamp magazines. Yet still is general and not highly specialized stamp periodical. Not interested in articles on new issues of stamps, reprints of publicity handouts by stamp-issuing bureaus, odds-and-ends of random commentary. Need more strange, fascinating countries or topical stamp copy—short— boiled down to interesting heart of the idea—not too wordy or verbose." Regular columns that seek freelance material are: lead article, Odds and Ends, Adventures with Stamps, Cinderella Comments, The Market, The Specialist, Worth Watching, and Crystal Ball. Payment varies with feature. "Some copy so poorly done we cannot pay for it as it requires too much reworking. Good scripts requiring little editing bring 1¢ to 2¢ a word and up for repeats. Length: varies with feature, runs from 150 to 1,200 words."

Poetry and Fillers: Short verse on stamp collecting might be of interest. Looking for philatelic greeting card humorous ideas: friendship, get-well, birthday—but must deal with stamps in some way. Newsbreaks, such as philatelic misquotes are also considered.

POPULAR CERAMICS, 6011 Santa Monica Blvd., Los Angeles CA 90038. Editor: Bill Geisler. For "hobby ceramists of all ages, studio owners, teachers, etc." Monthly. Circulation: 51,790. Buys few mss. Pays on publication. Will send a sample copy to a writer on request. Submit seasonal material 6 months in advance of publication. Reports in 1 week. Enclose S.A.S.E. for return of submissions.

Nonfiction and Photos: "How-to articles on ceramics, human interest stories related to ceramics, technical stories on ceramics. We really do not encourage freelance writers." Length: 800 to 1,000 words. Payment to be negotiated. Photos purchased with mss. B&w glossies, color transparencies.

POPULAR CRAFTS, 7950 Deering Ave., Canoga Park CA 91304. Editor: Sherrill Kushner. For "anyone who is interested in crafts; beginners and advanced. Articles are geared to the entire family." Established in 1972. Monthly. Rights purchased vary with author and material. Circulation: 91,000. Buys approximately 60 mss a year. Pays 30 to 60 days after publication. Will send a sample copy to a writer on request. Write for copy of guidelines for writers. Submit complete ms. Will consider photocopied submissions. Seeks material for holiday projects. Submit seasonal material 4 months in advance of issue date. Reports in 1 week to 2 months. Enclose S.A.S.E. for return of submissions.

Nonfiction and Photos: "70% of the magazine is how-to craft stories. 30% is informative reading material relating to a particular area of crafts, such as Hollywood hobbies, organic gardening. All how-to stories must contain a 3- to 8-paragraph introduction, instructions for making the project (instructions must be complete and easily understood), and suggestions for use. While most of the projects we publish are for women, we run complete projects in 'Just for the Guys' and age-level crafts in 'Just for the Kids.' Holiday projects, such as Halloween, Christmas, Valentine's, are always needed." Buys how-to's, personal opinion articles, and new product articles. Length: 200 to 1,500 words. Pays $15 to $175. Photos purchased with mss or on assignment; captions preferred. Uses 8x10 b&w glossies or contacts and negatives and 2¼x2¼ color transparencies.

POPULAR HANDICRAFTS & HOBBIES, P.O. Box 428, Seabrook NH 03874. Editor: Barbara Pedersen. For "women interested in handicrafts—things to make and do. Also interested in hobbies, particularly those with spare-time earning potential." Established in 1965. Bimonthly. Circulation: 100,000. Buys all rights. Buys about 50 mss a year. Pays on acceptance. Will send a sample copy to a writer for 50¢. Enclose S.A.S.E. for return of submissions.

Nonfiction and Photos: How-to and informational articles about crafts and hobbies of interest to the audience. Length: 2,500 words maximum. Pays 2¢ to 5¢ a word. 2¼x2¼ minimum b&w and color photos purchased with or without mss.

POPULAR NEEDLEWORK, P.O. Box 428, Seabrook NH 03874. Editor: Phyllis Tarbuck. For a "needlework" audience. Established in 1965. Bimonthly. Circulation: 100,000. Buys all rights. Buys 35 mss a year. Will send a free sample copy to a writer on request. Submit seasonal material 5 months in advance. Enclose S.A.S.E. for return of submissions.

Nonfiction and Photos: Publishes articles on "patterns, sewing projects, and short cuts." Buys informational, how-to, and personal experience articles. Length: up to 2,500 words. Photos purchased with mss. Both color and b&w have a 2¼x2¼ minimum size requirement. Pays $50 for cover photo.

POSTAL BELL, P.O. Box 2730, Santa Clara CA 95051. Editor: William H. McConnell. For "stamp collectors, whose ages and interests vary widely." Established in 1939. Bimonthly. Circulation: 300. Copyright applied for. "Since this publication is nonprofit, we may pay for an unusual article; most, however, are submitted without pay." Query first. Will consider photocopied submissions. Submit seasonal material 6 to 8 weeks in advance of issue date. Reports in 3 weeks. Enclose S.A.S.E. for reply to queries.

Nonfiction: "Most of the items are stories related to stamps and the nation issuing them. Generally, they relate to the people and culture of Japan. If there is a technical write-up concerning stamp issues, this type of article is always welcome." Length: 500 words. Pays about $10 "if the article is a special one."

QUILTER'S NEWSLETTER, Box 394, Wheatridge CO 80033. Editor: Bonnie Leman. For "women of all ages with one common interest—quilts and quiltmaking." Monthly. Circulation: 20,000. Buys first rights. Buys about 15 to 20 mss a year. Pays on acceptance. Will send a sample copy to a writer for 50c. No query required. "Articles about specific quilt shows are bought 2 to 3 months in advance." Reports in 2 weeks. Enclose S.A.S.E. for return of submissions.

Nonfiction and Photos: "We will consider any material dealing with quiltmaking, collecting, or pattern collecting. Famous quilts, new quilt ideas, quilts with an interesting history, museum quilts, anecdotes or cartoons about quilts, poems or fillers about the same; human interest stories about quilters. No rehashes of old quilt books. No history of quilting in general." Buys how-to's, personal experience articles, interviews, profiles, humor, and coverage of successful quilting business operations. Seeks freelance material for departments "Quilt Quiz (Just for Fun)" and "Old Fashioned Quilting," which carries interesting information about an old quilt or pattern. Length: 500 to 600 words maximum. Pays 1¢ a word minimum; "2¢ or more to a writer we wish to encourage." B&w glossies purchased with mss. Pays $1 for "ordinary snapshots, $5 for larger glossies."

Poetry: Traditional, light verse, sentimental. "Subject matter should be quilts or quilters." Length: open. Pays $2 minimum.

Fillers: Puzzles, clippings, "unusual quilt facts or information." Length: open. Pays $1 minimum.

RAILROAD MODEL CRAFTSMAN, P.O. Box 700, Newton NJ 07860. Managing Editor: Tony Koester. For "adult model railroad hobbyists, above average, including mature youngsters. All gauges, scales, plus collecting, railfanning." Established in 1933. Monthly. Circulation: 72,000. Buys all rights. Buys 180 to 240 mss a year. Payment on acceptance. Will send a sample copy to a writer for 60c. Will send editorial guidelines sheet on request. Reports as soon as possible. Submit seasonal material six months in advance. Enclose S.A.S.E. for return of submissions.

Nonfiction and Photos: "Nonfiction. How-to model railroad features written by persons who did the work. They have to be good. Glossy photos a must. Drawings where required must be to scale, accurately and completely rendered. Some railroad prototype features if of interest to modelers and with modelers' slant. All of our features and articles are written by active model railroaders familiar with the magazine and its requirements, 'Outsiders' don't have the technical know-how to write for us. We're superior, of course! Nonmodel railroad writers invariably write up some local hobbyist as 'Joe Doaks has a railroad empire in his basement made all by himself,' treating him as some kind of nut. We do not want the cartoon of little men tying the little girl to model railroad track. We do want topnotch how-to model railroading articles." Pay varies. Purchases photos with and without mss. Captions required. Buys sharp 8x10 glossies and 35mm transparencies. Payment varies.

RAILROAD MODELER, 7950 Deering Ave., Canoga Park CA 91304. Editor: Denis Dunning. For those interested in model railroading activities. Established in 1971. Monthly. Circulation: 75,000. Buys first North American serial rights. Buys 50 mss a year. Payment on publication. Will send free sample copy to a writer on request. Write for copy of guidelines for writers. Query first. Will not consider photocopied submissions. Submit seasonal material 4 months in advance. Returns rejected material in 1 month. Enclose S.A.S.E. for reply to queries.
Nonfiction and Photos: Articles on "all areas of model railroading, building individual models, complete layouts, new ways of producing models; also the prototypes as they relate to the model field. Must have firsthand knowledge of model railroading. Large stress is made on photo features, preferably in color." Informational, how-to, historical, technical. Length: 1,000 to 4,000 words. Pays $25 to $100. 5x7 or larger b&w photos purchased with ms. Pays minimum of $10 for any size color transparency.

R/C MODELER MAGAZINE, P.O. Box 487, Sierra Madre CA 91024. Editor: Don Dewey. For adult male radio control model aircraft and boating enthusiasts; sport and competitive. Monthly. Buys first international printing rights plus commercial reproduction of full-size plans. Pays on publication. Will send free sample copy to writer on request. Reports in 2 weeks. Enclose S.A.S.E. for return of submissions.
Nonfiction and Photos: Model aircraft (R/C) construction and "how-to" articles, slanted to average age 36 male. Highly specialized and technical. Good electronic how-to articles also purchased if applicable to radio control. To 5,000 words. Pays $50 to $300. Photos purchased with ms.

RELICS, P.O. Box 3338, Austin TX 78764. Editor: Robert Stout. Bimonthly to collectors of Americana. Buys N.A. serial rights only. Will send sample copy for 35¢. Pays on acceptance. Query appreciated. Reports in 4 to 6 weeks. Enclose S.A.S.E. for reply to queries.
Nonfiction and Photos: General subject matter includes collectibles such as bottles, wire, or any item having to do with life and times of yesterday. Also pieces pertaining to personal collections if specific information is given, such as current value, how to judge, where to find, how to preserve. Articles must contain useful hints for the collector. Subject preferably American in origin. 2,500 words is tops. Pays 2¢ per word. No mss considered unless accompanied by photos or drawings of item. Photos and drawings are returned after publication.

ROCKHOUND, P.O. Box 328, Conroe TX 77301. Editor: John H. Latham. For "gem and mineral hobbyists." Bimonthly. Circulation: 20,000. Buys serial rights. Buys about 80 mss a year. Pays on acceptance. Will send a sample copy to a writer. Reports in 1 month. Enclose S.A.S.E. for return of submissions.
Nonfiction and Photos: "We want field-trip type articles. The subtitle of our magazine is 'Where and How to Find Gems and Minerals,' which defines exactly what we are after. Articles should detail where to go and how to get there, what is found after you get there, digging fee if any, description of local conditions." Buys how-to's, coverage of successful business operations ("mines that admit rockhounds"), travel "to collect specimens." Length: 250 to 3,000 words. Pays 2¢ a word. B&w glossies, color transparencies, 35mm color, and color prints purchased with mss; with captions only. Pays $5 for b&w photo, $10 for color, $15 for color transparencies (2¼x2¼) for cover.

SCOTT'S MONTHLY JOURNAL, 10102 F Street, Omaha NE 68127. Editor: William W. Wylie. For stamp collectors. Monthly. Circulation: 28,500. Buys all rights. Pays on publication. Will send a sample copy to a writer for 75¢. Query first. Reports at once. Enclose S.A.S.E.

Nonfiction and Photos: Articles are done on assignment. Lengths, to 1,200 words. Pays $10 per published page. Writer should be informed stamp collector. Photos purchased to illustrate mss.

THE SPINNING WHEEL, Everybodys Press, Inc., Hanover PA 17331. Editor: A. Christian Revi. For antique collectors and dealers. 10 times a year. Pays on publication. Buys exclusive rights unless author wishes some reservations. Enclose S.A.S.E. for return of submissions.
Nonfiction: Authentic, well-researched material on antiques in any and all collecting areas; home decorating ideas with antiques. Prefers combined scholar-student-amateur appeal. No first-person or family history. Prefers draft or outline first. Requires bibliography with each ms. Quality illustrations. Length: 500 to 1,500 words. Pays minimum $1 per published inch, including pictures.
Photos: Photos and professional line drawings accepted. Photos should be top quality b&w, no smaller than 5x7. If of individual items shown in groups, each should be separated for mechanical expediency. Avoid fancy groupings.

SPORTS PLANES, P.O. Box 1136, Santa Monica CA 90406. Editor: D. N. Werner. For "sport, antique, homebuilt and race plane enthusiasts." Established in 1969. Monthly. Circulation: 35,000. Buys all rights. Buys 75 to 100 mss a year. Payment on acceptance. Will send free sample copy to writer on request. Query first or submit complete ms. Will consider photocopied submissions. Submit seasonal material 3 months in advance. Reports on material within 2 months. Enclose S.A.S.E. for return of submissions or reply to queries.
Nonfiction and Photos: "Articles about sport, antique, homebuilt and race planes. How-to pieces on building homebuilts, restoring old planes. Emphasis should always be on the plane. Currently looking for new plans for homebuilts." Informational, how-to and photo. Length: 1,000 to 3,000 words. Pays $50 to $250. B&w photos and color purchased with mss. 8x10 or proofsheets for b&w. 35mm or 2¼ slides for color.
Fillers: Newsbreaks. Length: 250 to 1,000 words. Pays $25 to $50.

STRATEGY & TACTICS, 44 E. 23rd St., New York, NY 10010. Editor: James F. Dunnigan. Bimonthly. Circulation: 22,000. Buys all rights. Buys "one or two" ms a year. Pays on publication. Will send a sample copy to a writer for $4. Query first. Enclose S.A.S.E.
Nonfiction: "Analytic history, primarily military. Stress a modular, analytic, technical approach. The magazine carries a game, in which conflict situations are created so that you are in a position to make the vital decisions and, in the game at least, change the way things are or will be. The magazine contains 1 feature article on the same subject as the game, as well as other feature articles of the same length on different subjects. Also included are game and book reviews, commentary on existing games, and discussions of subscribers' questions on the gaming field." Length: 2,500 to 10,000 words. Pays "10¢ per column inch (50 words) currently about $6 per page with illustrations."

TEXTILE CRAFTS, P.O. Box 3216, Los Angeles CA 90028. For "people who are interested in handcraft textile work: weaving, crocheting, macrame, spinning, dyeing, etc. Serious textile people." Established in 1969. Quarterly. Circulation: 1,200. Buys all rights. Buys 20 mss a year. Payment on publication. Will send free sample copy to writer on request. Query. Immediate reports on material. Enclose S.A.S.E. for reply to queries.
Nonfiction: "How-to articles, book reviews, calendars of events, shows, personality reviews." Informational, interviews, new product, technical. Length: open. Pays 1¢ per word.

TREASURE WORLD, P.O. Box 217, Conroe TX 77301. Editor: John H. Latham. For treasure-hunting buffs. Buys all serial rights. Pays on acceptance. Reports on submissions in four weeks. Enclose S.A.S.E. for return of submissions.
Nonfiction, Photos, and Fillers: Factual articles on lost mines and buried or sunken treasures. Pays 2¢ per word and up. Photos: $5 for each picture used to illustrate story. Fillers: 100- to 300-word material for "Treasure Nuggets" department. Pays $12.50.

TRI-STATE TRADER, P.O. Box 90, 27 N. Jefferson St., Knightstown IN 46148. Editor: R. Thomas Mayhill. Aimed at audience of hobbyists, antique buffs, collectors, etc., especially for Lower Great Lakes and Ohio Valley. Weekly tabloid. Circulation: 23,584. Rights negotiable. Will send free sample copy on request. Reports in two weeks. Enclose S.A.S.E.

Nonfiction and Photos: Articles about hobbies, antiques, places of historical interest, general collections and genealogy relating to central states of Indiana, Ohio, Kentucky, Tennessee, Michigan, Illinois, Wisconsin, western Pennsylvania and West Virginia. "Show sources of factual information." Length: 500 to 1,200 words preferred. Pays 25¢ per column inch, less for reprints. "Bonus for exceptional copy." Will negotiate on special items and pays extra for sharp b&w photos, which may be 2, 4, or 6 inches wide.

Fillers: Reprints of factual and interesting historical material about same central states as above. Must give original source.

TRUE TREASURE, P.O. Drawer 1, Conroe TX 77301. Editor: John H. Latham. Aimed at an audience of treasure hunters and collectors interested in the exploration of lost mines and buried or sunken treasure. Bimonthly. Circulation: 90,000. Buys North American serial rights only. Pays on acceptance. Will send free sample copy on request. Ms should be double-spaced and accompanied by a letter verifying that facts in article submitted are true. Reports in four weeks. Enclose S.A.S.E. for return of submissions.

Nonfiction and Photos: Articles of 150 to 3,500 words in length and dealing with lost mines and buried or sunken treasure. Stories must be documented and should be accompanied by photos if possible. No query required. Pays 2¢ per word. Photos purchased with mss at $5 per picture used. Must pertain to accompanying article. No specifications; Polaroid O.K.

Fillers: "Treasure Nuggets" of 100 to 250 words pay $12.50.

WOMEN'S CIRCLE, P.O. Box 428, Seabrook NH 03874. Editor: Marjorie Pearl. Monthly. Buys all rights. Pays on publication. Will send a sample copy to a writer for 35¢. No query required. Reports in 1 to 2 months. Enclose S.A.S.E. for return of submissions.

Nonfiction: "Articles on hobbies, handicrafts, needlework, and collections of interest to women. Not interested in religion or politics." Length: 700 to 1,000 words. Pays approximately 3¢ a word for mss "accompanied by either finished art, good photos, or items which can be photographed."

Photos: Color transparencies for cover.

THE WORKBASKET, 4251 Pennsylvania, Kansas City MO 64111. Editor: Mary Ida Sullivan, Issued monthly. Pays on acceptance. Query first. Reports within six weeks. Include S.A.S.E. with all queries and submissions.

Nonfiction: Uses articles, 400 to 500 words, which explain how a person or a family has benefited, financially or otherwise, by sewing, needlecraft, etc. Interested in step-by-step directions for making project. Also has a how-to short-stuff section which uses material on hobbies, ideas for pin-money and the like. These are limited to 250 words or under and bring a flat sum of $2. Pays 2c a word for articles, plus $3 to $5 for accompanying art.

Photos: 5x7 or 8x10 pix with mss.

WORKBENCH, 4251 Pennsylvania, Kansas City MO 64111. Editor: Jay W. Hedden. Bimonthly. Queries not necessary. Write for copy of guidelines for writers. All rights purchased, after publication of story all but first magazine rights returned to author on request. Reports within ten days. Enclose S.A.S.E. for return of submissions.

Nonfiction and Photos: Articles of interest to the do-it-yourselfer, anything from building furniture to remodeling a home. "Word length and style not important. All articles rewritten to fit a particular space and meet *Workbench* slant. No subject limitations as long as in our field; no taboos except common sense, and no mention of liquor." Must have drawings with accurate dimensions. Prefers photos, uses several per page. Buys stories as package; photos, drawings and copy. "Rates run from $20 to $50 per published page with writers new to us. Those who prove they can consistently produce good material get $75 per page and up. More for assigned articles. Please read several recent issues, as scope of articles varies considerably." Buys 4x5

color transparencies for cover which also illustrate the lead story. Pays $100 to $150.
Fillers: Need shop tips, consisting of copy and photo or drawing. Pays $5 to $10.

WORLD COINS, P.O. Box 150, Sidney OH 45365. Editor: Russell Rulau. Published monthly for coin collectors. Buys first rights. Query first. Pays on publication. Will send free sample copy on request. Reports in 4 weeks. Enclose S.A.S.E.
Nonfiction and Photos: Short numismatic articles, from 400 to 2,000 words, with one to three illustrations on any coin, paper money or token subject based on original research. No material on U.S. coins, etc., accepted. Factual data only, including personal experience. Also buys longer numismatic articles, catalogs, depth studies, etc., of any length and with any number of illustrations, but only if based on original research by the author or author's source reference. Especially interested in medieval period of coinage circa 800 to 1450 AD. Pays 2¢ per published word, plus allowances for art. "Size and style and rate of payment for photos submitted with mss vary with type of art and difficulty of reproducing."

Home and Garden Publications

THE AMERICAN HOME, 641 Lexington Ave., New York NY 10022. Editor: Fred R. Smith. For young homemakers. Monthly. Will not consider unsolicited manuscripts, but will review query letters from professional writers. Reports immediately. Enclose S.A.S.E.
Nonfiction: Writers may query, but no unsolicited mss will be read. Editorial focus is on subjects dealing with the home and homemaking: decorating, building and remodeling, food, kitchens, gardening, home crafts. Before and after experience accomplishments are of interest. Subjects should interest both men and women. Believability, depth of information, and authenticity are a must. The editors want copy and ideas which will add pleasure to homemaking. Length: 300 to 3,000 words. Payment depends on quantity and quality. Address mss to the Editorial Department or to the department for which it is intended.
Photos: All photography done on commission only.

APARTMENT LIVING, P.O. Box 18387, Wichita KS 67218. Editor: Daniel J. Vap. For "all ages—average 35 years. Average income; $12,000. Majority live in garden apartments. Family apartments. Not swingle singles." Established in 1970. Quarterly. Circulation: 25,000. Rights purchased vary with author and material, but may buy all rights, may reassign them to author after publication, or may buy first North American serial rights. Buys 12 to 24 mss a year. Payment on publication. Will send sample copy to a writer for 50¢. Will send editorial guidelines sheet to a writer on request. Submit seasonal material 2 months in advance. Reports in 2 to 4 weeks. Enclose S.A.S.E. for return of submissions.
Nonfiction, Photos, and Fiction: General subject matter consists of "four basic areas; decorating, to-do's, and cooking." Seasonal articles on to-do's and travel—all seasons. "No 'homey touch.' Clear, factual, modern. Example: If one submits a story on leather crafting the reader should get a feel for the hobby . . . and know where and how to proceed with it if it interests him. Garden apartment emphasis. Inexpensive decorating and travel ideas. No personal experiences in apartments nor people talking about noisy neighbors. Considering a serialized novel . . . and other use of fiction." Buys informational, how-to, travel, and new product articles. Length: 750 to 1500 words. Pays 6¢ a word. Also has regular columns in cooking and household hints. Length: 250 words maximum. Photos purchased with mss and captions are required. 8x10 b&w glossies. Pays $10.

BETTER HOMES AND GARDENS, 1716 Locust St., Des Moines IA 50336. Editor: James A. Autry. For "middle-and-up income, homeowning and community-concerned families." Monthly. Circulation: 21,000,000. Buys all rights. Pays on acceptance. Query preferred. Submit seasonal material 1 year in advance. Mss should

be directed to the department where the story line is strongest. Enclose S.A.S.E.
Nonfiction: "Freelance material is used in areas of travel, health, cars, money management, and home entertainment. Reading the magazine will give the writer the best idea of our style. We do not deal with political subjects or areas not connected with the home, community and family." Pays top rates based on estimated length of published article. Length: 250 to 1,000 words.
Photos: Shot under the direction of the editors. Purchased with mss.
How To Break In: "Follow and study the magazine, to see what we do and how we do it. There are no secrets, after all; it's all there on the printed page. Having studied several issues, the writer should come up with one or several ideas that interest him, and hopefully us. We consider freelance contributions in the areas of health, education, cars, money matters, home entertainment, and travel. The next step is to write a good query letter. It needn't be more than a page in length (for each idea), and should include a good stab at a title, a specific angle, and a couple of paragraphs devoted to the main points of the article. This method is not guaranteed to produce a sale, of course; there is no magic formula. But it's still the best way I know to have an idea considered."

FLOWER AND GARDEN MAGAZINE, 4251 Pennsylvania, Kansas City MO 64111. Editor-in-Chief: Rachel Snyder. For knowledgeable home gardeners. Monthly. Picture magazine. Circulation: 600,000. Buys first rights. Pays on acceptance. Will send a sample copy to a writer on request. Write for copy of guidelines for writers. Query first. Reports in 6 weeks. Enclose S.A.S.E. for reply to queries.
Nonfiction: Interested in illustrated articles on how-to-do certain types of gardening, descriptive articles about individual plants. Flower arranging, landscape design, house plants, patio gardening are other aspects covered. "The approach we stress is practical (how-to-do-it, what-to-do-it-with). We try to stress plain talk, clarity, economy of words. We are published in 3 editions: Northern, Southern, Western. Some editorial matter is purchased just for single edition use. Most, however, is used in all editions, so it should be tailored for a national audience. Material for a specific edition should be slanted to that audience only." Length: 1,000 to 1,200 words. Pays 3 to 4½¢ a word.
Photos: Buys photos submitted with mss or with captions only. Pays up to $12.50 for 5x7 or 8x10 b&w's, depending on quality, suitability. Also buys color transparencies, 35mm and larger. Pays $20 to $125 for these, depending on size and use.

HOME LIFESTYLES, 363 Seventh Ave., New York NY 10001. Editor: Mel Shapiro. Established in 1967. 9 times a year. Circulation: 438,000. Buys all rights but will reassign rights to author after publication. Buys 20 to 40 mss a year. Payment on publication. Will send sample copy to writer for 50¢. Query first or submit complete ms. Will not consider photocopied submissions. Reports on material in 3 to 4 weeks. Enclose S.A.S.E. for return of submissions or reply to queries.
Nonfiction and Photos: Shelter material; family-oriented articles; gardening, maintenance, building, decorating. "Approach should be practical." Length: 500 to 2,000 words. Pays $50 to $100. 8x10 b&w photos purchased with mss.

HORTICULTURE, 300 Massachusetts Ave., Boston MA 02115. Editor: Edwin F. Steffek. Published by the Massachusetts Horticulture Society. Monthly. Pays after publication. Query first. Reports in 6 weeks. Enclose S.A.S.E. for reply to query.
Nonfiction and Photos: Uses authentic articles from 500 to 1,000 words on plants and gardens, indoors and out, based on actual experience. Study publication. Pays 2¢ to 3¢ per word, more for special features. Photos: Color must be accurate tones, transparencies only, preferably not Ektachromes "and accurately identified."

HOUSE AND GARDEN, 420 Lexington Ave., New York NY 10017. Editor-in-Chief: Mary Jane Pool. For homeowners and renters in middle and upper income brackets. Monthly. Circulation: 1,300,000. Buys all rights. Pays on acceptance. Will not send sample copy. "Study magazine before submitting." Reports immediately. Enclose S.A.S.E. for return of submissions.
Nonfiction and Photos: Subjects of interest to "families concerned with their homes. Nothing for young marrieds specifically." Anything to do with the house or gardens and affiliated subjects such as music, art, books, cooking, etc. Length: about 1,500 words. Payment varies. Jerome H. Denner, Asst. Editor, is department editor. Photos purchased with mss only.

HOUSE BEAUTIFUL, 717 Fifth Ave., New York NY 10022. Editor-in-Chief: Wallace Guenther. Monthly. Circulation: 850,000. Buys all rights. Pays on publication. Query first. Reports in 1 month. Enclose S.A.S.E. for reply to queries. **Nonfiction:** Occasionally buys articles of 1,000 to 2,000 words in fields of entertaining, remodeling, art, music, personal life style. Most travel, gardening and decorating material is staff-prepared, but submissions in these areas will be considered. Also buys shorter articles for "Insight," news/feature section on any subject related to the home and personal environment. All stories should be focused on a specific subject related to living today; might also be a personal experience story. Pays $150 to $450. Submit general stories to Linda B. Downs, Senior Editor; "Insight" stories to John H. Ingersoll, Senior Editor.

LEISURE HOME LIVING & LAND INVESTMENT, 13 Evergreen Rd., Hampton NH 03842. Editor: Richard M. Livingstone. For "middle-aged active people with above-average education and income. Their interests are in leisure living in vacation homes." Established in 1970. Annual. Circulation: 30,000. Rights purchased vary with author and material; usually buys all rights. Buys about 5 mss a year. Pays on publication. Will send a sample copy to a writer for $2. Submit complete ms. Will consider photocopied submissions. Reports in 1 month. Enclose S.A.S.E. **Nonfiction:** "Articles dealing with all aspects of vacation or second home field. These are homes of unusual design and vacation home communities. Material must deal with the northeast area." Buys informational, how-to, and photo articles. Length: 1,000 to 2,000 words. Pays "$25 up." **Photos:** Purchased with or without mss; captions required. Pays $5 each.

NATURAL GARDENING, 235 E. 45th Street, New York NY 10017. Editor: William L. Meachem. 9 times a year. Circulation: 450,000. No free sample copies available. Reports on submissions in 6 weeks. Buys all rights. Pays on acceptance. Enclose S.A.S.E. **Nonfiction and Photos:** Anything on the natural gardening concept, especially do-it-yourself and how-to articles. Interesting authoritative articles written from the viewpoint of the beginning as well as the experienced gardener. Length: 800 words or less. Pays 5c per word or more. Photos purchased with mss and with captions only; must be garden subject. 8x10 b&w, 4x5 color accepted. Payment varies.

ORGANIC GARDENING AND FARMING, Organic Park, Emmaus PA 18049. Monthly. Buys first publishing rights for "*Organic Gardening and Farming* and the right to reuse in other Rodale Press publications with agreed additional payment." Pays on publication. Write M.C. Goldman, Managing Editor, for free sample copy and copy of guidelines for writers. Will consider photocopied submissions. Acknowledges submissions on receipt. Enclose S.A.S.E. for return of submissions. **Nonfiction:** Uses factual, informative and interesting articles based on the organic (natural) concept of agriculture—that is, the use of natural fertilizer, ground rock, mineral fertilizer, biological insect control, etc., and avoidance of chemicals, poisons, etc. Mulching, composting, garden and farm techniques, livestock, house plants, improving varieties, nutritional aspects, landscaping, soil building, home garden, fruit, vegetable, shrubs, flower growing. Also "Homecraft" section on practical do-it-yourself projects for gardening, "back-to-the-land" ideas for home craft make-it-yourself projects, ecological living ideas, environmental action, etc." Length: 1,000 to 2,000 words. Pays $45 to $150. **Photos:** Photo stories, photos with mss, and single related photos. Enlargements (4x5 or larger preferable), b&w glossy prints. Also color transparencies (4x5) for cover use. Pays $5 to $15 each for b&w photos showing gardening activities, procedures; very specific, highly functional. Pays $50 to $100 for color covers; 4x5 preferred, but will accept 2¼ square. No 35mm. **Fillers:** Garden, how-to ideas, build-it-yourself, etc. Food preparation for recipes page. Length: about 200 to 400 words. Pays $15 to $35.

THE PLACE WHERE YOU LIVE, 336 Mountain Rd., Union City NJ 07087. Editor: James Blanchard. For "home handymen and women living in own home; age 35 to 45, about average income." Established in 1972. Monthly. Circulation: 12,000.

Buys all rights. Buys 60 mss a year. Payment on publication. Will send free sample copy to a writer on request. Will send editorial guidelines sheet to a writer on request. Query first required. Will consider photocopied submissions. Reports in 2 weeks. Enclose S.A.S.E. for reply to queries.
Nonfiction and Photos: "This is a monthly hardback magazine that shows how to improve the home and what is available on the market as far as better products and unusual products are concerned. Articles we seek are of two kinds: (1) do-it-yourself at the hammer and saw level and (2) interesting new and unusual products for the home, i.e., pre-assembled circular staircase. Photographs required. Our theme is that one should 'do-it-yourself' not to save money, but to acquire a better home than is possible using contractors. We do not want articles about commonplace products available in any general supply store." Buys informational, how-to, photo, and new product articles. Length: 1,200 to 1,800 words. Pays $50 to $100. Purchases photos with mss. Captions are required. Pays $5 to $10 for 8x10 b&w and $25 to $50 for 2¼x2¼ color transparencies.

POOL 'N PATIO, 3923 W. 6th St., Los Angeles CA 90020. Editor: Fay Coupe. Issued twice yearly, in April and June, to residential owners of swimming pools. Reports on submissions at once. Buys all rights. Pays on publication. Include S.A.S.E. with submissions.
Nonfiction and Photos: Articles on how to make pool maintenance easier; technical articles on equipment, unusual use of pools, or unusual pools; human interest or glamour stories on pool owners. Pays 3¢ to 5¢ per word. Length: 500 to 1,500 words. Photos purchased with mss. Payment varies.

POOL NEWS, 3923 W. 6, Los Angeles CA 90080. Editor: Fay Coupe. For pool owners. Established in 1961. Twice a year. Circulation: 150,000. Buys all rights but will reassign rights to author after publication. Buys 300 mss a year. Payment on acceptance. Query first or submit complete ms. Will consider photocopied submissions. Returns rejected material immediately. Reports on material accepted for publication in 1 month. Enclose S.A.S.E. for reply to queries or return of submissions.
Nonfiction and Photos: Stories on the care of pools or ideas for pools. Pays 5¢ a word. B&w photos purchased with mss. Captions required.

TODAY'S HOMES, 229 Park Ave., S., New York NY 10003. Editor: John Lauderdale. For "people who are planning to build their own home, from initial selection of plans to final construction." Quarterly. Circulation: 60,000. Buys all rights. Buys 15 to 20 mss a year. Query first. Will not consider photocopied submissions. Submit seasonal material 3 to 4 months in advance. Reports immediately. Enclose S.A.S.E. for reply to queries.
Nonfiction and Photos: "Articles on planning and designing kitchens and bathrooms; general landscaping; how to select building materials; financial trends applicable to future homeowners (mortgages, insurance, etc.). All articles are slanted to help the layman better understand what is available so that he can more intelligently talk with contractors and get the most for his money. All articles are 'meat and potatoes' stories. Lots of facts translated so that a person outside the building field can understand what would normally be too technical." Length: 2,000 to 3,000 words. Pays $100 to $200. 8x10 b&w glossies purchased with mss. Captions required.

YARD AND FRUIT, Box 1651, Nashville TN 37202. Publisher: Charles D. Cook. For the homeowner who is interested in using flowers, vegetables and fruit and nut trees to turn his yard, no matter how small or how urban, into a beautiful and productive homestead. Bimonthly. Pays on publication. Query first. Enclose S.A.S.E.
Nonfiction: Interested in publishing articles on the how-to's of gardening, landscaping, fruit raising and lawn care. "We would like articles aimed at the gardener with limited space, at the beginning gardener, and at the gardener who wants to grow some of his own food. We are especially interested in personal experience articles. We would like gardeners to tell us their own stories, to give us their advice and hints, and to share the pleasures and fulfillments their gardening provides them." Length: 3,500 words maximum. "Payment for a 2,000-word article begins at $40."
Photos: Pays $15 for b&w glossies; $50 minimum for color transparencies for cover.

Humor Publications

These are magazines that specialize in humor. Other publications that use humor can be found in nearly every category in this book. Some of these have special needs for major humor pieces; some use humor as fillers; many others are simply interested in material that meets their ordinary fiction or nonfiction requirements but has a humorous slant. Check under both Fiction and Nonfiction bold headings to find those markets whose editors have specifically mentioned their needs for humor.

CAPITOL COMEDY, Suite 7D, 220 Madison Ave., New York, NY 10016. Editor: L. Schwartz. Biweekly. Buys United States rights. Pays on acceptance. Write for copy of sample gags. "Submit unlimited number of gags on 8½x11 paper, with separation between each gag." Reports in 1 week. Enclose S.A.S.E. for return of submissions.
Fillers: "This humor newsletter, satirizing national politics, is interested in one-liners and short jokes on national politics and prominent politicians." Pays $5 each.

MAD MAGAZINE, 485 Madison Ave., New York NY 10022. Editor: Al Feldstein. Work almost exclusively with a group of professional steady contributors. Enclose S.A.S.E.
Nonfiction: *"Mad* deals with that which is most familiar to the most people . . . the so-called American scene and well-known international incidents and personages. Satirical article format." Very few unsolicited pieces have been accepted, but they were of exceptional quality. Be sure you are familiar with the magazine before you submit anything.

NATIONAL LAMPOON, 635 Madison Avenue, New York NY 10022. For "college educated, 18 to 35." Established in 1970. Monthly. Circulation: 600,0000. Buys first North American serial rights. Buys approximately 10 unsolicited mss a year. Payment on acceptance. Will consider photocopied submissions. Reports in 3 weeks. Enclose S.A.S.E. for return of submissions.
Nonfiction and Fiction: "Humorous and satirical articles in a number of formats. Some familiarity with the magazine is necessary to gain an idea of the approach we take. Our publication is adult in nature. We do not want to see trite and overused formats, like the interview; unoriginal attempts at broad political satire; subjects of diminishing interest and concern, like uncurbed dogs or rude cab drivers." Length: 3,500 words maximum. Pays 10¢ a word. Buys humorous fiction.

ORBEN'S CURRENT COMEDY, ORBEN COMEDY FILLERS, 67-00 192nd St., Apt. 1507, Flushing NY 11365. Editor: Robert Orben. For "speakers, toastmasters, businessmen, public relations people, communications professionals." Biweekly, monthly. Buys all rights. Pays at the end of the month for material used in issues published that month. "Material should be typed and submitted on standard size paper. Please leave 3 spaces between each item. Unused material will be returned to the writer within a few days if S.A.S.E. is enclosed. If you do not want the material returned, you should hear from us within 7 weeks if any items have been accepted. We do not send rejection slips. Please do not send us any material that has been sent to other publications. If S.A.S.E. is not enclosed, all material will be destroyed after being considered except for items purchased."
Fillers: "We are looking for funny, performable one-liners, short jokes, and stories that are related to happenings in the news, fads, trends, and topical subjects. The accent is on comedy, not wit. The ultimate criteria is, 'Will this line get a laugh if performed in public?' Material should be written in a conversational style and, if the joke permits it, the inclusion of dialogue is a plus. We are particularly interested in material that can be used by speakers and toastmasters: lines for beginning a speech, ending a speech, acknowledging an introduction, specific occasions, anything that would be of use to a person making a speech. We can use lines to be used at sales meetings, presentations, conventions, seminars, and conferences. Short, sharp comment on business trends, fads, and events is also desirable. Please do not send us material that's primarily written to be read rather than spoken. We have

little use for definitions, epigrams, puns, etc. The submissions must be original. If material is sent to us that we find to be copied or rewritten from some other source, we will no longer consider material from the contributor." Pays $2.

WILSON'S WESTERN HUMOR, P.O. Box 71, Casper WY 82601. Publisher: J. Wilson. Quarterly. Buys all rights. Pays on acceptance for jokes; pays "within 30 days" for short stories. Reports in 4 weeks. "Material not returned unless S.A.S.E. enclosed."
Fiction: "Well-plotted and humorous short stories. Characterization important. Easy reader identification. O. Henry style most acceptable." Length: maximum 2,000 words. Pays $50 to $100.
Fillers: Jokes. "Must be new, fresh, and original. Must be humorous. No canned material. Interested in western, black, American Indian, Mexican American, and Yiddish material." Pays 10¢ a word.

Juvenile Publications

This section of Writer's Market *includes publications for children ages 2 to 12. Magazines for young people 12 to 25 appear in a separate Teen and Young Adult category.*

Most of the following publications are produced by religious groups, and wherever possible, the specific denomination is given. For the writer with a story or article slanted to a specific age group, the sub-index which follows is a quick reference to markets for his story in that age group.

Those editors who are willing to receive simultaneous submissions are indicated. (This is the technique of mailing the same story at the same time to a number of low-paying religious markets of nonoverlapping circulation. In each case, the writer, when making a simultaneous submission, should so advise the editor.) The few mass circulation, nondenominational publications included in this section which have good pay rates are not interested in simultaneous submissions and should not be approached with this technique. Magazines which pay good rates expect, and deserve, the exclusive use of material.

Writers will also note in some of the listings that editors will buy "second rights" to stories. This refers to a story which has been previously published in a magazine and to which the writer has already sold "first rights." Payment is usually less for the re-use of a story than for first-time publication.

Juvenile Publications Classified by Age

Two- to Five-Year-Olds—*Children's Playmate, Children's Service Programs, The Friend, Happy Times, Highlights for Children, Humpty Dumpty's Magazine, The Kindergartner, My Weekly Reader, Nursery Days, One/Two, Our Little Friend, Story Friends, Summer Weekly Reader, Wonder Time*

Six- to Eight-Year-Olds—*Annals of the Holy Childhood, The Brownie Reader, Child Life, Children's Day, Children's Digest, Children's Playmate, Children's Service Programs, Crusader, Explore, The Friend, Fun for Middlers, Highlights for Children, Humpty Dumpty's Magazine, Jack and Jill, Merry-Go-Round, More, My Weekly Reader, On the Move, One/Two, Primary Treasure, Quest, Ranger Rick's Nature Magazine, Roadrunner, Story Friends, Summer Weekly Reader, Vacation Fun, Video-Presse, Wonder Time*

Nine- to Twelve-Year-Olds—*Adventure, American Red Cross Youth News, Annals of the Holy Childhood, Child Life, Children's Day, Children's Digest, Children's Service Programs, Climb, Crusader, Five/Six, The Friend, The Good Deeder, Highlights for Children, Jack and Jill, Jet Cadet, Junior American Modeler, Junior Discoveries, Junior Life, Junior Trails, My Pleasure, My Weekly Reader, News Explorer, News*

Time, On the Line, On the Move, Quest, Ranger Rick's Nature Magazine, Summer Weekly Reader, Summertime, Three/Four, Trails, Vacation Fun, Video-Presse, Wee Wisdom, Whenever Whatever, Young Judaean, Young Musicians, Young World.

ADVENTURE, 127 Ninth Ave., N., Nashville TN 37234. Editor: W. Mark Moore. Established in 1970. Issued monthly in weekly parts for boys and girls in first and second grade. Circulation: 206,000. Reports on submissions in three months. Buys all rights. Pays on acceptance. Not interested in simultaneous submissions. Enclose S.A.S.E. for return of submissions.

Nonfiction: Articles, up to 900 words, about children's experiences, adventure, nature, travel, biography, hobbies, how-to, science, history, pets. Other themes are home, school, nature, love and understanding, God, seasonal, animals, places and events. Contains Bible-related activities for children to do. Would like to see articles on ecology. Especially needs color photo stories, with low word count. Pays 2½¢ per word. Query not necessary. Seasonal deadlines 12 months in advance; emphasis on Christmas, Easter, Thanksgiving, patriotic subjects. Articles should show why their subjects are significant to the reader.

Fiction: Stories, 900 to 1,200 words; mystery, adventure, heroes, science, missions, everyday experiences of boys and girls in this and other lands. Fiction should picture children as they are today. (They don't sit at nailed-down desks and most of them don't live on farms). Pays 2½¢ per word.

Photos: Color transparencies or photos purchased with articles. Captions required. Rate of payment varies with quality.

Poetry: To 24 lines; nature, religious experiences, child experiences, humor. Pays $3 to $10.

AMERICAN RED CROSS YOUTH NEWS, American National Red Cross, 18th and E Sts., N.W., Washington DC 20006. Editor: Mary Ellen Hughes. For "elementary school children, mainly grades 4 to 6, ages 9 to 12." Established in 1919. Seven times a year, October through May, excluding January. Circulation: 258,000. Buys first publication rights, serially and otherwise, in English and any other language or medium, including Braille and Acoustical recording for blind or handicapped children. Right to republish for Red Cross purposes any time, in any language and in any such media. Buys about 25 mss a year. Payment on acceptance. Will send free sample copy to a writer on request. Will send editorial guidelines sheet to a writer on request. Query first for all material. Submit seasonal material 6 months in advance. Reports in 4 to 6 weeks. Enclose S.A.S.E. for reply to queries.

Nonfiction: General subject matter consists of short stories emphasizing service, the positive side of life for children and about children, also now desire more humorous, innovative treatment of seasonal, traditional topics. Short plays, more games that teach, science experiments, more ways to involve children. Good nonfiction on contemporary topics needed regularly. Since publication is that of Red Cross, also emphasize health, well-being, service, international friendship among children. Length: 1000 to 1500 words. Payment varies, but averages $100 to $125.

Photos, Fiction, and Fillers: Photos purchased with mss, and on assignment. 8x10 b&w glossies. Payment varies. Buys mystery, suspense, adventure, western, science fiction, fantasy, humorous, and historical fiction. Length: 1,000 to 1,500 words. Payment varies with mss, but averages $50 to $125. Buys puzzles (riddles, connect the dots, find the features in the picture, games to play), jokes, and short humor. Payment varies.

ANNALS OF THE HOLY CHILDHOOD, N.S.P.O. Box 6758, Pittsburgh PA 15212. Editor: Fred J. McCool; Managing Editor: Thomas F. Haas. For "Catholic elementary school children, grades 1 through 8." Established in 1904. Published monthly, October through May. Circulation: 300,000. Not copyrighted. Buys 16 mss a year. Pays on acceptance. Will send a sample copy to a writer on request. Write for copy of guidelines for writers. No query required. Submit seasonal material 4 months in advance. Reports in 2 weeks. Enclose S.A.S.E. for return of submissions.

Nonfiction and Fiction: "Prime subject matter deals with foreign missions conducted by Catholic priests and sisters for children. We also publish stories with a moral, projects for the lower grades, and puzzles. Stories or articles should be geared to the age interest, have a moral, and add to the child's knowledge. Our major thrust is the missions, though, and factual information about this is supplied by missionaries in the field." Buys inspirational articles, humorous articles and stories, and adventure, religious, and juvenile fiction. Length: 600 to 000 words. Pays $25 to $50

THE BROWNIE READER, 1100 Waterway Blvd., Indianapolis IN 46202. Managing Editor: Susan L. Holibaugh. "For Brownie Girl Scouts who are in the 7 to 9 age bracket. We think of Brownies as being imaginative and creative, as most children are, and as young people striving to learn more about the world around them which relates directly to the life they lead." Seasonal issues involve special scouting holidays: Juliette Low's birthday, Thinking Day, Girl Scout Birthday. 9 issues a year. Buys all rights. Pays after publication. Will consider photocopied submissions. Submit seasonal material 6 months in advance. Returns rejected material in 8 to 10 weeks. Acknowledges acceptance of material in 6 to 8 weeks. Enclose S.A.S.E. for return of submissions.
Nonfiction: Articles on "nature, science, how-to-make projects, people in other lands—stressing the children of the land, articles on health and safety, places of interest. The writer should be reminded that the *Brownie Reader* is to be used by the Brownie as an extension of her Brownie troop, but it is also to be used to make the Brownie want to try, to do, and to discover all by herself. Also, it is wise to remember that Brownies come not only from the suburbs, but from urban areas also, and are of many races and creeds." Buys how-to's and think pieces. Length: 50 to 800 words. Pays approximately 3¢ a word.
Photos: "Only photos of Brownie Girl Scouts or girls of that age level." B&w glossies. Buys all rights "unless otherwise specified by author at time of submission." Pays "approximately $3 per photo."
Fiction: "Fiction should be light. It does not have to pertain to Girl Scouting but can be a general type of children's story. Also there should be a moral but should not moralize." Juvenile and humor stories. Length: 300 to 800 words. Pays approximately 3c a word.
Poetry: Buys light verse. Length: open. Payment: open.

CHILD LIFE, 1100 Waterway Blvd., Indianapolis IN 46202. Editor: E. Catherine Cummins. For children of ages 7 to 11. 10 times a year. Buys all rights unless otherwise specified by author at time of submission. Pays after publication. Submit seasonal material 8 months in advance. Simultaneous submissions not accepted. Will send sample copy for 50¢. Write for copy of guidelines for writers. Reports in 8 to 10 weeks. Enclose S.A.S.E. for return of submissions.
Nonfiction: Present-day science, nature, general information, words, international stories. Little-known anecdotes about famous people, events or accomplishments in which identity is withheld until the end. Length: 1,000 words maximum. Pays about 3¢ per word.
Photos: B&w glossy 8x10 preferred. Buys photos submitted with mss to illustrate articles. Pays about $2.50 per photo.
Fiction and Drama: From 600 words for beginner stories to 1,200 for older children. Uses some 2-part serials, about 2,400 words in length. Should be written in realistic, nonmoralizing, nonacademic style. Likes humor or suspense in fiction. No talking, inanimate objects. Pays about 3¢ per word. Also very short, lively plays that can be produced in living room or classroom with minimum of simple props and small casts.
Poetry: Needs range from four-line couplets to long poems. Pays minimum of $5.
Fillers: Puzzles, mazes, tricks and games. Make-its should use materials readily available at home or school and involve a minimum of adult guidance. Explanatory sketches and/or a sample of the finished project should be included if practical.

CHILDREN'S DAY, Fawcett Publications, 1515 Broadway, New York NY 10036. Editor: James Wyckoff. For children ages 6 to 14. Annual. Buys all rights. Buys 20 mss a year. Pays on acceptance. Query first. Reports "fairly soon." Enclose S.A.S.E. for reply to queries.
Nonfiction: Wants "top quality material on anything of interest. Treat the reader in a respectful way—not condescending." Length: 5,000 words maximum. Payment is open.

CHILDREN'S DIGEST, 52 Vanderbilt Ave., New York NY 10017. Managing Editor: Elizabeth R. Mattheos. Monthly except June and August, for children ages

seven to 12. Buys reprint rights. Pays on publication. Reports in three weeks. Enclose S.A.S.E. for return of submissions.
Nonfiction and Fiction: Accepts only reprint material.

CHILDREN'S PLAYMATE, 1100 Waterway Blvd., Indianapolis IN 46202. Editor: Beth Wood Thomas. For "bright, appreciative children, ages 3 to 8." 10 times a year. Circulation: 250,000. Buys all rights unless otherwise specified at time of submission. Pays after publication. Will send sample copy for 50¢. Write for copy of guidelines for writers. No query. "We do not consider resumes and outlines. Reading the whole ms is the only way to give fair consideration. The editors cannot criticize, offer suggestions, or review unsolicited material that is not accepted." Submit seasonal material 8 months in advance. Simultaneous submissions not accepted. Reports in 8 to 10 weeks. Enclose S.A.S.E. for return of submissions.
Fiction: Short stories, not over 600 words for beginner readers. No inanimate, talking objects. Humorous stories, unusual plots. Vocabulary suitable for ages 3 to 8. Pays about 3c per word.
Nonfiction: Beginning science, not more than 600 words. Pays about 3¢ per word.
Poetry: Length: 4 lines minimum. Pays about 25¢ a line; minimum of $5.
Fillers: Puzzles, dot-to-dots, color-ins, mazes, tricks, games, guessing games, and brain teasers. "Attention to special holidays and events is sometimes helpful." No fixed rate.

CHILDREN'S SERVICE PROGRAMS, Concordia Publishing House, 3558 S. Jefferson Ave., St. Louis MO 63118. Issued annually by The Lutheran Church—Missouri Synod, for children, aged three through eighth grade. Receipt of children's worship scripts will be acknowledged immediately, but acceptance or rejection may require up to a year. All mss must be typed, double-spaced on 8½x11 paper. S.A.S.E. must be enclosed for ms return. Write for details.
Nonfiction: Four 16-page Christmas worship service programs for congregational use published yearly. Every script should present a worship service emphasizing the Biblical message of the Gospel through which God shares His love and in which His people rejoice. Christmas plays or services requiring elaborate staging or costumes will not be accepted. Pays $100, but buys few mss.

CLIMB, Warner Press, 1200 E. Fifth St., Anderson IN 46011. Editor: William A. White. For "ten-year-old boys and girls from across the U.S.A. and Canada." Publishes material "dealing with Christian living and example." Weekly. Circulation: 22,000. Not copyrighted. Buys 225 mss a year. Pays on publication. Will send a sample copy to a writer on request. Write for copy of guidelines for writers. No query required. Will consider photocopied submissions. Submit seasonal material 4 to 5 months in advance. Reports in 2 weeks. Enclose S.A.S.E. for return of submissions.
Nonfiction and Photos: "These stories might deal with current situations of 10- and 11-year-olds who have done something about a problem in their community; current Christian laymen and how they see their job as a Christian; current Christian athletes;" etc. Writer should use a 10-year-old's vocabulary and "lots of dialog." Buys how-to's, interviews, profiles, think pieces, travel pieces, humor, historical articles, and personal experience nonfiction. Length: 250 to 1,000 words. Pays $7.50 per 1,000 words. B&w glossy photos purchased with mss. Pays $5 to $25; one-time use.
Fiction: "Should challenge and guide readers in the meaning of living a winsome, Christian life." Stories of adventure; also, religious, contemporary problem stories. Length: 800 to 1,200 words. Pays $7.50 per 1,000 words.
Poetry: Prefers "readers' poems." Length: 4 to 20 lines. Pays 20c per line or $2 per poem.
Fillers: Buys puzzles, clippings, jokes, short humor.

CRUSADER, 1548 Poplar Ave., Memphis TN 38104. Editor: Lee Hollaway. For boys ages 6 through 11, who are part of a boys' program in Southern Baptist Churches called Royal Ambassadors. General interest articles. Established in 1970. Monthly. Circulation: 100,000. Rights purchased vary with author and material. May buy first North American serial rights, first serial rights, second serial (reprint) rights, simultaneous rights. Buys 50 to 100 mss a year. Payment on acceptance. Will send free copy to writer on request. Write for copy of guidelines for writers. Will consider photocopied submissions. Submit seasonal material 8 to 10 months in advance. Submit material to Chuck Frevele, Manuscript Editor. Reports in 2 weeks to a month. Enclose S.A.S.E.

Nonfiction and Photos: "Articles of general interest to the age group. Articles should often aid the child's interest in the world around him. Subjects we'd like to see covered are: God's love and concern for all men; pages, squires, and knights of the Middle Ages; Spanish-speaking people in the U.S.; juveniles in trouble with the law." Informational, how-to (simple), humor, historical (limited), photo, and travel articles. Length: maximum 1,000 words. Pays minimum $5, no maximum. Photos are purchased with or without manuscripts, and on assignment. Captions optional. Prefers 5x7 b&w or larger glossy. Pays $5 to $15 per photo. "Nonfiction photo stories involving boys as well as self-explanatory photos without copy involving boys."

Fiction and Fillers: 2 or 3 short stories each year are purchased. Mainstream, mystery, adventure, humorous, and religious fiction. Length: no minimum, maximum 1,000 words. Pays 2½¢ a word. Prefers simple puzzles involving drawing.

DISCOVERY, 999 College Ave., Winona Lake IN 46590. Editor: Vera Bethel. For "fourth, fifth, and sixth graders who attend Sunday school." Weekly. Circulation: 14,000. Not copyrighted, "but with masthead notice that all material is property of the author and is not to be used." Pays on acceptance. Buys 300 mss a year. Will send a sample copy to a writer on request. Submit only complete mss. "We do not read tearsheets. Typed mss only." Accepts simultaneous submissions. Submit seasonal material 3 months in advance. "Especially need seasonal material, no matter when." Reports on material in 1 month. Enclose S.A.S.E. for return of submissions.

Nonfiction and Photos: How-to, personal experience, hobby articles. School and home activities. Informational, historical, and photo articles. Length: 200 to 1,000 words. Pays 2¢ a word. Photos purchased with mss. B&w glossies. Pays $3.50 to $10.

Fiction: All types, but with a Christian philosophy. Fiction should have a lot of action, and have some sort of religious background. Length: 1,000 to 2,000 words. Pays 2¢ a word.

Poetry: Nature poetry. Traditional forms; blank, free, and light verse. Length: 8 to 16 lines. Pays 25¢ a line, $2 minimum.

EXPLORE, Box 179, St. Louis MO 63166. Editor: Rosalie Logan. For "6- and 7-year-olds in Christian Churches (Disciple of Christ) and Church schools." Established in 1969. Weekly. Circulation: 25,000. Not copyrighted. Buys 200 mss a year. Payment on acceptance. Will send a sample copy to a writer for 25¢. Will send editorial guidelines sheet to a writer on request. Submit seasonal material 6 months in advance. Reports in 30 days. Enclose S.A.S.E. for return of submissions.

Nonfiction, Photos, Fiction, and Poetry: General subject matter consists of "children of first and second grade school age in believable real life situations." Length: 600 words maximum. Pays 1¢ a word. Buys b&w photos with mss sometimes. Captions optional. Buys religious stories. Length: 600 words maximum. Pays 1¢ a word. Buys traditional forms, blank and free verse. Length: 12 lines maximum. Pays 25¢ a line.

FIVE/SIX, 201 8th Ave., S., Nashville TN 37203. Editor: Miss Martha Wagner. Published monthly in weekly format for children in grades five and six in United Methodist Church schools. Will send free sample copy to a writer on request. Buys all rights. Pays on acceptance. Submit double-spaced copy, 48-character line count. Reports on submissions within three months. Enclose S.A.S.E.

Nonfiction and Photos: Most articles requested by editor from writers. Subject matter relates to or correlates with church school curriculum and interests of children in grades 5 and 6. Should not be overly moralistic or didactic. May provide information to enrich cultural understanding in religion and in relationships with other people. Length: 400 to 1250 words. Pays 3¢ to 4¢ per word. Photos purchased with mss. B&w glossies; color transparencies. Pays $1 to $25.

Fiction, Poetry, and Fillers: Modern day life, problems. Unusual historical stories; church history. No slang, references to drinking, or smoking. Might-have-happened Biblical stories. Length: about 1,250 words. Also well-written biography, not composed from encyclopedias, 900 to 1,000 words. Pays 3¢ to 4¢ a word. Poetry to 20 lines. Pays $1 per line. Puzzles. Pays $5.

THE FRIEND, 50 East North Temple, Salt Lake City UT 84150. Managing Editor: Lucile C. Reading. For children from age 4 to 12. Special issues: Christmas, Easter, foreign countries. Established in 1970. Monthly. Circulation: 150,000. Buys first rights. Payment on acceptance. Will send free sample copy to writer on request. Write for copy of guidelines for writers. Submit only complete ms. Submit seasonal material 6 months in advance. Enclose S.A.S.E. for return of submissions.

Nonfiction: Current subjects, science, nature, pets, things to make and do. Length: 1,000 words maximum. Pays 3¢ a word and up.

Fiction: Stories for holidays; stories about other countries, children in them. Wholesome and optimistic; high motive, plot, and action. Character-building stories preferred. Stories for young children should not exceed 500 words. Length: 1,000 words maximum. Pays 3¢ a word and up.

Poetry: Serious or humorous; holiday poetry. Any form. Good poetry, with child appeal. Pays 25¢ a line and up.

FUN FOR MIDDLERS, American Baptist Board of Educational Ministries. Valley Forge PA 19481. Editor: Gracie McCay. Monthly for children 8 to 9 years. Pays on acceptance. Enclose S.A.S.E. for return of submissions.

Nonfiction: Articles on current issues, interesting subjects. Reports of noteworthy activities of boys and girls. Pays up to 2c per word.

Fiction: Maximum 1,000 words. Biographies of people making significant use of their lives.

Poetry: 12 lines maximum.

Fillers: How-to-do-it projects, puzzles.

THE GOOD DEEDER, Your Story Hour, Berrien Springs MI 49103. Editor: Roselyn Edwards. For boys and girls, ages 10 to 15. Circulation: approximately 10,000. Not copyrighted. "We welcome second rights mss." Pays "within a month of acceptance. Reports during the first week of each month on mss received since last report." Submit seasonal material 3 months in advance. Enclose S.A.S.E.

Nonfiction: "Any subject of interest to children 10 to 15. Morals must be woven into article, not tacked on. Currently overstocked on nonfiction." Length: 750 words, 1,000 words, and 1,500 words. Pays 1¢ a word.

Photos: B&w glossies. 8x10 for cover; any size for inside use. "Payment varies with quality of pictures." Pays $7.50 for cover photo.

Fiction: "Health, temperance, adventure, attitudes to parents, holiday stories. No serials. All stories should be character-building." Length: 750 words, 1,000 words, and 1,500 words. Pays 1¢ a word.

HAPPY TIMES, Concordia Publishing House, 3558 South Jefferson Ave., St. Louis MO 63118. Editor: Mrs. Jean Schneider. For children ages 2 to 5. Established in 1964. Monthly. Circulation: 150,000. Rights purchased vary with author and material. May buy all rights. Buys about 20 mss a year. Payment on publication. Will send free sample copy to writer on request. Write for copy of guidelines for writers. Submit only complete ms. Submit seasonal material at least 6 months in advance. Reports in 6 months. Enclose S.A.S.E.

Nonfiction and Photos: Emphasize a fun angle rather than directly instructional angle. Illustrations should accompany articles. Pays $3 to $7.50 per double-spaced page. Photos are purchased with and without mss. No b&w accepted. Transparencies only purchased. Pays $15 to $30.

Fiction, Poetry and Fillers: Religious stories and stories showing good deeds, honesty, etc. Fantasy also. Open on theme. Pays $3 to $7.50 per double-spaced page. All types of poetry. Open on theme. No length limits. Pays $3 per page. Fingerplays, action, games, and papercraft. Pays $3 for filler material.

HIGHLIGHTS FOR CHILDREN, 803 Church St., Honesdale PA 18431. Editors: Walter B. Barbe and Caroline C. Myers. For children 2 to 12. 11 times a year. Circulation: approximately 1,000,000. Buys all rights. Pays on acceptance. Write for copy of guidelines for writers. No query. Submit complete ms only. Will consider photocopied submissions. Reports in 2 months. Enclose S.A.S.E.

Nonfiction: "Most factual features, including history and science, are written on assignment by persons with rich background and mastery in their respective fields. But contributions always welcomed from new writers, especially science teachers, engineers, scientists, historians, etc., who can interpret to children useful, interesting, and authentic facts, but not of the bizarre or 'Ripley' type; also writers who have lived abroad and can interpret well the ways of life, especially of children in other countries, and who don't leave the impression that our ways are always the best. Sports material, biographies, articles about sports of interest to children. Direct, simple style, interesting content, without word embellishment; not rewritten from encyclopedias. State background and qualifications for writing factual articles submitted. Include references or sources of information with first submission. Length: 1,000 words maximum. Pays minimum $50. Also buys original party plans for children 7 to 12, clearly described in 600 to 800 words, including pencil drawings or sample of items to be illustrated. Also, novel but tested ideas in arts and crafts, with clear directions, easily illustrated, preferably with made-up models. Projects must require only salvage material or inexpensive, easy-to-obtain material. Especially desirable if easy enough for early primary grades and appropriate to special seasons and days. Also, fingerplays with lots of action, easy for very young children to grasp and parents to dramatize, step-by-step, with hands and fingers. Avoid wordiness. Pays minimum $30 for party plans; $10 for arts and crafts ideas; $25 for fingerplays."

Fiction: Unusual, wholesome stories appealing to both girls and boys. Vivid, full of action and word-pictures, easy to illustrate. Seeks stories that the child 8 to 12 will eagerly read, and the child 2 to 6 will like to hear when read to him. "We print no stories just to be read aloud; they must serve a two-fold purpose. We encourage authors not to hold themselves to controlled word lists. Especially need humorous stories, but also need winter stories; urban stories; horse stories; and especially some mystery stories void of violence; and stories introducing characters from different ethnic groups; holiday stories devoid of Santa Claus and the Easter Bunny. Avoid suggestion of material reward for upward striving. Moral teaching should be subtle. The main character should preferably overcome difficulties and frustrations through his own efforts. The story should leave a good moral and emotional residue. War, crime, and violence are taboo. Some fanciful stories wanted." Length: 400 to 1,000 words. Pays minimum 5¢ a word.

Fillers: "Some puzzles, but none that require that the child write in the book."

How To Break In: "We are pleased that many authors of children's literature report that their first published work was in the pages of *Highlights*. It is not our policy to consider fiction on the strength of the reputation of the author. We judge each submission on its own merits. With factual material, however, we do prefer either authorities in their fields or people with first-hand experience. In this manner we can avoid the encyclopedic-type article which merely restates information readily available elsewhere. A beginning writer should first become familiar with the type of material which *Highlights* publishes. We are most eager for the easy-type story for very young readers, but realize that this is probably the most difficult kind of writing. The talking animal kind of story is greatly overworked. A beginning writer should be encouraged to develop first an idea for a story which must involve only a small number of characters and likely a single-incident plot. The story must contain a problem or a dilemma which is clearly understood and presented early. It is then clearly resolved at the end of the story. Description should be held to a minimum. Dialogue is a requirement for it is a means by which children can identify with the characters in the story."

HUMPTY DUMPTY'S MAGAZINE, 52 Vanderbilt Ave., New York NY 10017. Editor: Ruth Craig. Monthly October through May; bimonthly for June-July and August-September. For children three to eight. Buys all rights. Pays on acceptance. Will send requirements sheet on request. Reports in three weeks. Enclose S.A.S.E.

Fiction: Read-aloud stories: listening vocabulary level applies, not easy-reader level. 900 words maximum. See: "A Terrible Day in Emerald Valley," May, 1973. Tell-me story: one per issue. Fully developed story, can be more complex with interpolations on part of teller and listener to be considered. 1,000 word maximum. Occasionally, a 300-word playlet, to be read and/or played; simple props and plot, small cast. See: "Noisy Noises," March, 1973. Stories considerably below maximum lengths given consideration. Subjects can be fantasy, whimsy, humor, realism, original folk tales. Avoid cliches of the animated inanimate object (for example, Sammy Sidewalk); the all too common exceptional animal (for example, The Puppy Who Couldn't Bark). Pays minimum $50.

Poetry: Pays $10 for 4 to 12 lines which will appeal to very young children.

JACK AND JILL, 1100 Waterway Blvd., Indianapolis IN 46202. Editor: William Wagner. For children 5 to 12. 10 times a year. Buys all rights. Pays on publication. Write for copy of guidelines for writers. Submit seasonal material 8 months in advance. Reports in 6 to 8 weeks. Enclose S.A.S.E. for return of submissions.
Nonfiction and Photos: "*Jack and Jill's* primary purpose is to encourage children to read for pleasure. The editors are actively interested in material that will inform and instruct the young reader and challenge his intelligence, but it must first of all be enjoyable reading. Submissions should appeal to both boys and girls." Current needs are for "short factual articles concerned with nature, science, and other aspects of the child's world. Longer, more detailed features: 'My Father (or My Mother) Is a . . .'; first-person stories of life in other countries; some historical and biographical articles." Articles should be accompanied by good 35mm color transparencies, when possible. Pays about 3¢ a word. Pays $2.50 for each b&w photo.
Fiction: "May include, but is not limited to, realistic stories, fantasy, adventure—set in the past, present, or future. All stories need plot structure, action, and incident. Humor is highly desirable." Length: 500 to 1,500 words, short stories; 1,500 words per installment, serials of 2 or 3 parts.
Fillers and Drama: "Short plays, puzzles (including varied kinds of word and crossword puzzles), riddles, jokes, songs, poems, games, science projects, and creative construction projects. Instructions for activities should be clearly and simply written and accompanied by models or diagram sketches."

JET CADET, 8121 Hamilton Ave., Cincinnati OH 45231. Editor: Dana Eynon. For children 8 to 11 years old in Christian Sunday schools. Weekly. Not copyrighted. Pays on acceptance. Will send a sample copy to a writer on request. Submit seasonal material 6 to 8 months in advance. Reports in 4 to 6 weeks. Enclose S.A.S.E. for return of submissions.
Nonfiction: Articles on hobbies and handicrafts (preferably illustrated), famous people, seasonal subjects, etc. Taboos are liquor, tobacco, murder, guns, swearing, slang, movies, and dancing. Length: 400 to 500 words. Pays up to 1½¢ a word.
Fiction: Short stories of heroism, adventure, travel, mystery, animals, biography. True or possible plots stressing clean, wholesome, Christian character-building ideals, but not preachy. Make prayer, church attendance, Christian living a natural part of the story. Length: 900 to 1,200 words; 2,000 words complete length for 2-part stories. Pays up to 1½¢ per word.
Fillers: Bible puzzles and quizzes. Pays up to 1½¢ a word.

JUNIOR AMERICAN MODELER, 733 Fifteenth Street, N.W., Washington DC 20005. Editor: William Winter. Established in 1971. Circulation: 27,000. For "the beginner novice modeler." Buys all rights. Pays on publication. Suggest query first. Enclose S.A.S.E.
Nonfiction: "Construction and how-to-do-it on boats, cars, planes, rockets, and plastics. Do not want to see non-modeling or complicated material. 5 to 10 double-spaced pages. Pays $50 to $150."

JUNIOR DISCOVERIES, 6401 The Paseo, Kansas City MO 64131. Editor: Maureen H. Box. For boys and girls 9 to 11. Weekly. Buys first and some second rights. No query required. "No comments can be made on rejected material." Enclose S.A.S.E. for return of submissions.
Nonfiction: Articles on nature, travel, history, crafts, science, Christian faith, biography of Christian leaders, Bible manners and customs, home craft ideas. Should be informal, spicy, and aimed at fourth and fifth grade vocabulary. Sharp photos and artwork help sell features. Length: 400 to 800 words. Pays 2¢ a word.
Photos: Sometimes buys pix submitted with mss. Buys them with captions only if subject has appeal. Send quality photos, 5x7 or larger.
Fiction: Stories with Christian emphasis on high ideals, wholesome social relationships and activities, right choices, Sabbath observance, church loyalty, goodwill, and missions. Informal style. Length: 1,000 to 1,250 words. "Or serials of 2 to 4 parts, average 1,250 words per installment." Pays 2¢ a word.
Poetry: Nature and Christian thoughts or prayers, 4 to 16 lines. Pays 50c for each 4 lines.

JUNIOR LIFE, P.O. Box 850, Joplin MO 64801. Editor: Mrs. Marthel Wilson. For Sunday school pupils, age 9 through 11. General religious subject matter. Quarterly in weekly parts. Circulation: 5,000. Buys simultaneous rights. Buys 25 mss a year. Quarterly pay periods. Will send free sample copy to writer on request. Write for copy of editorial guidelines. Submit complete ms. Will consider photocopied submissions. Submit seasonal material 9 months in advance. Reports on material accepted for publication in 2 months. Returns rejected material in 1 month. Enclose S.A.S.E. for return of submissions.
Nonfiction: "We use only material which takes the fundamental Christian point of view. Missionary stories are being overworked. Prefer stories about children in a contemporary American setting." Informational, personal experience, interview, inspirational, historical, think pieces, nostalgia. Length: 1,500 words maximum. Pays ¼¢ a word.
Fiction: Religious only. Length: 1,500 words. Pays ¼¢ a word.
Poetry: Light verse. Length: open. Pays $1 per poem.
Fillers: Religious fillers and items on personal experience. Length: 1 paragraph to 500 words. Pays ¼¢ a word.

JUNIOR TRAILS, 1445 Boonville Ave., Springfield MO 65802. Editor: Jewell Ready. Weekly Sunday school take home paper published monthly for 4th, 5th, and 6th graders. Established in 1919. Circulation: 112,000. Not copyrighted. Buys 110 to 125 mss a year. Pays on acceptance. Will send free sample copy to writer on request. Write for copy of guidelines for writers. Submit only complete mss. Will consider photocopied submissions. Submit seasonal material 9 to 10 months in advance. Reports in 3 weeks. Enclose S.A.S.E. for return of submissions.
Nonfiction: Biographical sketches of Christian people who have made contributions in the arts and sciences. Length: 500 to 1,000 words. Pays 1¢ per word.
Fiction: Fiction with believable plots and strong spiritual emphasis. Fiction should present likable main characters working out their problems according to Bible principles. Length: 1,000 to 1,500 words. Pays 1¢ per word.
Photos: With ms or with captions only. Size unimportant as long as subject matter and clarity of photo are excellent; must be suitable for offset printing. Pays $5 per photo used.

KIDSTUFF MAGAZINE, P.O. Box 833, Rochester NY 14603. Editor: George G. Adler. For children ages 6 to 12; their parents and teachers. "Material sought for all national holidays." Establsihed 1973. Published 11 months out of the year. Circulation: 75,000. Rights purchased vary with author and material. Buys all rights. Buys 50 to 100 mss a year. Payment on acceptance. Will send free sample copy to writer on request. Write for copy of guidelines for writers. Will consider photocopied submissions. Submit seasonal material 3 months in advance. Reports in 1 month. Enclose S.A.S.E. with queries and submissions.
Nonfiction and Photos: "We publish articles of interest to parents and teachers on subjects generally having to do with children; education, health care, things to do on a rainy day, crafts, etc. Emphasis on material for children should be high interest material, craft ideas that can be done in the home, historical literature. Emphasis on material for grownups should be informational, and balanced point of view. We believe *Kidstuff* serves as a showcase for the creative talents of kids themselves, combined with articles of interest to those who deal with children on a regular basis. Innovations in elementary teaching. Sex education; role of private school; perceptual handicapped, etc." Regular column titled "Either Here or There," a travel photo essay for kids. Reviews of current books on education, child raising, etc. Length: 300 to 1,500 words. Pays $25 to $100, sometimes more. 35mm slides are purchased with or without mss. Captions optional. Pays $5 to $10 per slide.
Fiction, Poetry, and Fillers: "We publish children's poems and stories." Length for fiction: 500 words minimum, no maximum. Pays $25 to $100. Poetry written by children only. Word puzzles are purchased for $10 to $25.

THE KINDERGARTNER, 201 8th Ave., S., Nashville TN 37202. Editor: Arba O. Herr. A United Methodist publication. For children, ages 4 and 5. Weekly. Circulation: 350,000. Buys all rights. Buys approximately 200 mss a year. Pays on acceptance. Will send a sample copy to a writer on request. No query required. Submit seasonal material "approximately one month prior to the holiday." Reports in 1 to 3 weeks. Enclose S.A.S.E. for return of submissions.

Nonfiction and Photos: Something to make or do. Length: 8 to 12 lines, or 100 words. Pays 4¢ per word. Photo stories on childlife subjects—home, family, church, seasonal, and Biblical. Photos paid through art department; storyline paid for by publishing house. Pays $7.50 to $10 "depending on size, quality, etc."

Fiction and Poetry: Stories should be about 300 words in length. Should give the child religious concepts through day-by-day experiences with his family, friends, and workers in the community. The paper relates closely to the curriculum materials and covers several broad areas of Christian concern: the child's relationship to the church fellowship; God's plan for family experience; God's plan for the world of nature; God's plan for persons to depend on one another. Pays 4¢ per word. Seasonal poetry; 4 to 6 lines. Pays 50¢ to $1 per line.

LET'S FIND OUT, Scholastic Magazines, Inc., 50 W. 44th St., New York NY 10036. Manuscript Editor: Mrs. Norma Ainsworth. For "kindergarten uses. Stories are related to the theme presented for the entire issue." Address all submissions to Mrs. Ainsworth. Enclose S.A.S.E. for return of submissions.

Nonfiction: "Uses material written by staff. There is also a column written by a professional consultant." Pays $75.

MERRY-GO-ROUND, Scholastic Magazines, Inc., 50 W. 44th St., New York NY 10036. Editor of Manuscript Department: Mrs. Norma Ainsworth. Summer magazine, weekly, 9 issues, late June through August, for first and second-grade children. Buys all rights or North American serial rights. Will send sample copy on request. Enclose S.A.S.E. with each ms. Send only one ms at a time for consideration. Be sure to keep a carbon copy in your file. Do not re-submit the same ms unless revision is specifically requested. Material for the coming summer is chosen by February.

Fiction: Stories of about 300 words, early second grade vocabulary; stories of about 400 words written to upper second grade vocabulary. Must have child-appeal, style, and real plot. Easy-to-read stories and read-to stories. Since each issue is prepared around a theme and stories must relate to this theme, they are usually done on assignment. Authors may submit samples at these levels and lengths, however. Pays $75 to $100.

Photos: Purchased with mss.

MORE, 127 Ninth Ave. North, Nashville TN 37234. Editor: W. Mark Moore. For Baptist Sunday School workers; children. Established 1970. Monthly. Circulation: 140,000. Buys all rights. Buys 1,000 to 1,500 mss a year. Payment on acceptance. Will send free sample copy to writer on request. Write for copy of guidelines for writers. Submit only complete ms. Will not consider photocopied submissions. Reports in 4 months. Enclose S.A.S.E. for return of submissions.

Nonfiction: Themes: home, school, nature, love and understanding, God, seasonal, animals, places and events. Length: up to 500 words. Pays 2½¢ per word.

Fiction: Everyday experiences of children. Length: 250 to 500 words. Pays 2½¢ per word.

Photos: Purchased with accompanying mss, captions required. 4-color transparencies or photos. Payment varies.

Poetry and Fillers: Open theme. 4 to 24 lines. Pays $3 to $10. Puzzles, fill-in blanks, Who Am I?, etc. Pays $3 to $6.25.

MY DEVOTIONS, Concordia Publishing House, 3558 S. Jefferson Ave., St. Louis MO 63118. Buys little freelance material. Write for guidelines, enclosing 16¢ postage.

MY PLEASURE, Union Gospel Press, Box 6059, Cleveland OH 44101. Editor and Executive Vice President: T.T. Musselman, Jr. For ages 9 through 12. "Study sample of our publications first; absolutely necessary to have evangelical viewpoint." Buys exclusive rights only. Enclose S.A.S.E. for return of submissions.

Fiction: "Publishes fundamental Christian fiction. We are typical evangelical Sunday school publication." Length: 825 to 1225 words. Pays 2c a word.

MY WEEKLY READER K-3, 245 Long Hill Rd., Middletown CT 06457. Managing Editor: Constance Unsworth. For children in kindergarten through grade 3; ages 5 to 9." Weekly, September through May. Circulation: "7 million in 4 editions." Buys all rights. Buys 40 to 50 mss a year. Pays on acceptance. Will send a sample copy to a writer on request. Write for copy of guidelines for writers. Will not consider photocopied submissions. "Submit at any time other than the month of July." Reports in 2 weeks. Enclose S.A.S.E. for return of submissions.
Poetry: "Poems that will appeal to young children. Subjects include children, animals, people, the real world children know, fantasy, humor, surprise. The writer must know the interests of children, use language in interesting and surprising ways, involve interesting rhythms, include obvious sensory images, and use repetition judiciously. We're highly selective. Our poems are used by teachers in classroom situations where poetry is often used to motivate or supplement curriculum ideas as well as entertain. No sing-song rhymes; no violence of any kind; do not talk down to children. Interested in seasonal themes (but prefer the unusual to the standard; for example, something other than falling leaves, snowmen, flowers); poems with obvious city settings, poems that deal with a child's personal feelings, poems about the body and senses." Length: "generally prefer short poems of 8 to 20 lines." Pays $10 to $50.

NEWS EXPLORER, Scholastic Magazines, Inc., 50 W. 44th St., New York NY 10036. Editor of Manuscript Department: Mrs. Norma Ainsworth. Issued weekly during school year for fourth grade children about nine or 10 years of age. Buys all rights. Pays on acceptance. Will send free sample copy on request. Send only one ms at a time for consideration. Be sure to keep a carbon copy in your file. Do not resubmit the same ms unless a revision is specifically requested. Enclose S.A.S.E. with each ms.
Fiction: Humor, classroom setting, boys and girls of today, or of other times, mystery, hobbies, legends, other peoples, adventure, pets. Stories must be well plotted and within the vocabulary range of the average fourth grader. 900 to 1,000 words. Pays minimum $75.

NEWSTIME, Scholastic Magazines, Inc., 50 W. 44th St., New York, NY 10036. Editor of Manuscript Department: Mrs. Norma Ainsworth. Weekly for fifth and sixth grade children of 11 and 12 years. Buys all rights. Pays on acceptance. Include S.A.S.E. for ms return.
Fiction: Stories of 1,000 to 1,300 words, short-shorts of about 600 words, well-plotted and narrated with incident; humor, classroom setting, sports, mystery, family life, folklore, other peoples, adventure, pets, wildlife, nature. Stories to provoke thought and understanding of values and differing points of view (no violence, war, dating, obvious moralizing or involved psychological problems). Pays $100 for longer stories, $50 for short ones. If stories directed to *NewsTime* are found unsuitable because of length or age level, they will be considered for *News Trails, News Explorer,* and the summer magazines.

NURSERY DAYS, 201 8th Ave. S., Nashville TN 37202. Editor: Miss Evelyn M. Andre. Published weekly for two- and three-year-olds. Will send free sample copy to a writer on request. Enclose S.A.S.E. for return of submissions.
Nonfiction and Photos: Should cover things of interest to children—church, family, nature, friends, God. Must have religious significance. Deadline 18 months in advance of publication. Photos purchased with mss; prefers 8x10.
Fiction: Short stories relating to child's personal experiences (religious significance on his own age level), 300 words maximum. Pays up to 4¢ a word.
Poetry: 4-8 lines. Pays up to $1 a line.
How To Break In: "Submit materials as specified, only a few at a time, after studying publication."

ON THE LINE, 610 Walnut Street, Scottdale PA 15683. Editor: Helen Alderfer. For children 10 to 14. Weekly. Buys first rights. Pays on acceptance. Will send a sample copy to a writer on request. Write for copy of guidelines for writers. Reports in 2 weeks. Enclose S.A.S.E. for return of submissions.
Nonfiction and Photos: Designed to increase the child's interest in Christianity, his understanding of the Bible, his identification with the church; human interest

sketches of noteworthy children; nature and hobbies. Length: 800 to 1,250 words. Pays up to 2¢ per word; less for simultaneous and second rights. Photos purchased with mss. With captions only. 8x10 semiglossy prints; no color. Especially interested in human interest shots involving youngsters over 9, animals, picture stories. Pays $5 to $10 per photo.

Fiction: Wholesome stories that help readers discover and develop their full potential as persons; that help them take their place beside other peoples of the world as true neighbors; that present the Biblical message in a contemporary, meaningful way; that help children grow in appreciation of the fine arts, especially those that enrich their understanding of Christianity; that sense problem areas of children and provide sympathetic help. Serials to five parts. Pays up to 2¢ per word; 1½¢ per word for simultaneous submissions; 1¢ per word for second rights mss.

Poetry and Fillers: Semi-humorous verse with an unexpected twist often used. Wants some nature verse. Length: 4 to 24 lines. Pays $3 to $10. Occasional quizzes and puzzles are used. Pays $3 to $10.

How To Break In: "The best approach to break into print—query on article ideas and short features, send stories and quizzes and poetry for approval."

ON THE MOVE, Canadian Red Cross Society, 95 Wellesley St. E., Toronto 5, Ont., Canada. Editor: Mrs. R.J. Frewin. For children, from kindergarten to 9th grade. 9 times a year. Circulation: 35,000. Buys first rights. Buys 40 mss a year. Pays on acceptance. Query required. Story outline preferred. Submit seasonal material 4 to 6 months in advance. Returns rejected material and acknowledges acceptance of material in "1 or 2 days." Enclose S.A.E. and Canadian postage for reply to queries.

Nonfiction: "Our material should be oriented to Red Cross principles and philosophy—i.e., stories for 'amusement or entertainment only' do not appeal to us." How-to's, humor, historical pieces, think pieces, photo essays. "Biographies of humanitarian figures." Must be "fresh, imaginative, and educationally sound." Length: 500 to 1,000 words. Pays 2¢ to 5¢ a word.

Photos: Purchased with mss; with captions only. B&w glossies. Pays $3 to $10.

ONE/TWO, 201 Eighth Ave., S., Nashville TN 37202. Editor: Jean Buchanan. For "first and second grade children who are just learning to read. Established in 1964. Weekly. Circulation: 300,000. Buys all rights. Buys around 200 mss a year. Will send free sample copy to writer on request. Write for copy of guidelines for writers. Submit complete ms. Will not consider photocopied submissions. Submit seasonal (all holidays) material 12 months in advance. Reports on material in about 1 month. Enclose S.A.S.E. for return of submissions.

Nonfiction and Photos: "We try to direct our paper toward helping to fullfill the child's personal needs at this stage of his development, for example, need for security, for help with standards of behavior." How-to, inspirational, humor, think pieces. Length: 50 to 500 words. Pays 3¢ per word. Pays minimum of $10 for b&w; $25 for color, but this varies. "Pictures of first and second grade children doing things with family." Purchased with or without ms, and on assignment. Captions appreciated. Photo Editor: Wilson Estes.

Fiction: Humorous, religious. Length: 50 to 500 words. Pays 3¢ per word.

Poetry and Fillers: Should relate to theme. Traditional forms. Poetry length: 4 to 12 lines. Pays 50¢ per line. Puzzles for young children; jokes, games, mazes, riddles, connect the dots. Length: 50 to 100 words. Pays 3¢ per word plus another amount for art.

OUR LITTLE FRIEND, PRIMARY TREASURE, Pacific Press Publishing Association, 1350 Villa St., Mountain View CA 94040. Editor: Louis Schutter. Published weekly for youngsters of the Seventh-Day Adventist church. *Our Little Friend* is for children ages 2 to 6; *Primary Treasure,* 7 to 9. Query on serial-length stories. Will accept simultaneous submissions. "We do not purchase material during June, July, and August." Enclose S.A.S.E. for return of submissions or reply to queries.

Nonfiction and Fiction: All stories must be based on fact, written in story form. True to life, character-building stories; written from viewpoint of child and giving emphasis to lessons of life needed for Christian living. Nature or science articles, but no fantasy; science must be very simple. All material should be educational or informative and stress moral attitude and religious principle. Honesty, truthfulness, courtesy, health and temperance, along with stories of heroism, adventure, nature and safety are included in the overall planning of the editorial program. *Our Little Friend* uses stories from 700 to 1,500 words. *Primary Treasure*, 900 to 1,500 words. Fictionalized Bible stories are not used. Minimum payment of 1¢ a word; sliding scale according to quality.

Photos, Poetry, and Fillers: 8x10 glossies for cover. Juvenile poetry; up to 12 lines. Puzzles.

QUEST, Box 179, St. Louis MO 63166. Editor: Miss Lee Miller. For children in grades 3 to 6. Weekly. Not copyrighted. Pays on acceptance. Sample copies are sent to writer for 25¢. Write for copy of guidelines for writers before submitting material. Enclose S.A.S.E.

Nonfiction: "Articles on travel, biographies, science or general informational interest. Include sources." Length: 600 word maximum. Pays up to 2¢ per word.

Fiction: "Uses short stories to which children can relate. Avoid preaching and moralizing." Length: 800 to 1,000 words. Pays up to 2¢ a word.

Poetry: "Limited market." Length: 16 lines maximum. Pays 25¢ per line.

Fillers: "Puzzles, illustrated if possible." Pay varies. Limited market.

RANGER RICK'S NATURE MAGAZINE, 1518 Walnut St., Philadelphia PA 19102. Editorial Director: Trudy D. Farrand. For "children from ages 4 to 12, with the greatest concentration in the 7 to 12 age bracket." Monthly, except June and September. Buys all rights, but will reassign rights to author after publication. Pays on acceptance or on publication, depending on material. "Anything written with a specific month in mind should be in our hands at least 5 months before that issue date." Enclose S.A.S.E. for return of submissions.

Nonfiction and Photos: "Articles may be written on any phase of nature, conservation, environmental problems, or natural science. Do not try to humanize wildlife in features. We limit the attributing of human qualities to animals in our regular feature, 'Ranger Rick and His Friends.' The publisher, National Wildlife Federation, discourages wildlife pets because of the possible hazards involved to small children. Therefore, pets of this kind should not be mentioned in your copy." Length: 750 words. Pays $200. "If photographs are included with your copy, they are paid for separately, depending on how they are used. However, it is not necessary that illustration accompany material."

Fillers: Games, puzzles, quizzes. Pays $10.

ROADRUNNER, American Baptist Board of Education and Publication, Valley Forge PA 19481. Editor: Nina M. Booth. A weekly periodical for children 6 to 7 years of age. Enclose S.A.S.E. for ms return.

Nonfiction: Biographies and articles in simple vocabulary, from 200 to 500 words. Pays up to 2¢ per word.

Fiction: Stories of 200 to 500 words in simple vocabulary. Pays up to 2¢ per word.

Poetry: Maximum 12 lines.

Fillers: Puzzles, how-to-do-it projects.

STORY FRIENDS, Mennonite Publishing House, Scottdale PA 15683. Editor: Mrs. Alice Hershberger. For children 4 to 8. Weekly. Not copyrighted. Pays on acceptance. Will send a sample copy to a writer on request. Submit seasonal material 6 months in advance. Enclose S.A.S.E. for return of submissions.

Nonfiction: Activity features, photo picture stories of children's everyday experiences, missionary picture stories, nature features, etc., geared to child's understanding. Pays up to 2¢ per word.

Fiction: Application of Biblical principles on a child's level of understanding. Length: 300 to 900 words. Pays up to 2¢ per word.

Poetry: Length: 3 to 12 lines. Pays $1 to $4.

Fillers: Puzzles for 4- to 8-year-old children.

SUMMER WEEKLY READER, 245 Long Hill Rd., Middletown CT 06457. Managing Editor: Robert Shapley. Fiction Editor: Mrs. Jacqueline M. Holbrook. For "children in kindergarten through grade 6; ages 6 to 12." Weekly for 9 weeks each summer. Circulation: 4,300,000 in 6 editions: *SWR Surprise* (for 5- and 6-year-olds), *SWR A* (for children who have completed grade 1), *SWR B* (for 7-year-olds), *SWR C* (for 8- and 9-year-olds), *SWR D* (for 9- and 10-year-olds), *Senior SWR* (for 11- and 12-year-olds). Buys all rights. Buys 40 to 54 mss a year. Pays on acceptance. Will send a sample copy to a writer on request. Write for copy of guidelines for writers for detailed data on each edition. Prefers original copies. "Submit material from January to July for the upcoming summer. Mss rejected are returned immediately. Others are held for consideration; the length of time the ms is held depends on when it is submitted. Authors are warned of delay in acceptance or final rejection of their mss." Enclose S.A.S.E. for return of submissions.

Fiction: Stories "with high interest topics, such as mysteries, adventure stories, amusing animal stories, human interest, high drama, suspense. The writer must know the interests of children at various age and grade levels and be familiar with readability and vocabulary control. The story content must be of value and hopefully add to the child's background of knowledge. It must meet our high standards grammatically, philosophically, and structurally. We're especially interested in human interest stories—suspenseful, intriguing, involving relationships within urban, as well as suburban, settings. We need stories dealing with current problems faced by children of today, with characters with whom readers may identify. At the primary level, we need more 'people' stories and 'machine' stories, and fewer animal stories. No tried-and-true themes: the animal who didn't know who he was, the animal or person who discovers happiness in being himself, pointless or inane mss. We avoid violence of all kinds." Length: "varies according to story and edition in which it will appear; we have limited space." Pays $40 to $90.

SUMMERTIME, Scholastic Magazines, Inc., 50 W. 44th St., New York NY 10036. Editor of Manuscript Department: Mrs. Norma Ainsworth. Summer magazine issued weekly for fifth and sixth grade children ages 11 and 12. Pays on acceptance. Buys all rights. Will send free sample copy on request. Enclose S.A.S.E. for return of submissions.

Fiction: Well-plotted and narrated with incident; humor, classroom setting, sports, mystery, family life, folklore, other peoples, adventure, pets, wildlife, nature. Stories to provoke thought and understanding of values and differing points of view (no violence, war, dating, obvious moralizing or involved psychological problems). Prefers mystery-type serials for longer stories. Length: 500 to 2,000 words. Pays $50 for short stories; $100 for longer ones.

THREE/FOUR, 201 Eighth Ave., S., Nashville TN 37203. Editor: Betty M. Buerki. Publication of The United Methodist Church. For children in grades 3 and 4. Monthly in weekly parts. Buys all rights. Pays on acceptance. Will send a sample copy to a writer on request. Deadlines are 18 months prior to publication date. Reports in 1 month. Enclose S.A.S.E. for return of submissions.

Nonfiction and Photos: Desires articles about science, nature, animals, customs in other countries, and other subjects of interest to readers. Length: approximately 500 words. Pays 4¢ a word. Photos usually purchased with manuscripts only. Uses photo features. Prefers 8x10 glossies. Also uses transparencies.

Fiction: Historical stories should be true to their setting. Stories which make a point about values should not sound moralistic. Also accepts stories written just for fun. Length: 500 to 1,000 words. Writers must know children. Fictionalized Bible stories must be based upon careful research. Pays 4¢ a word.

Poetry: Accepts light verse or religious verse. Pays 50¢ to $1 per line.

Fillers: Puzzles, quizzes, and matching games.

TRAILS, Pioneer Girls, Box 788, Wheaton IL 60187. Editor: Carole M. Sherman. For girls in grades 2 to 6. 10 times a year. Buys first rights; sometimes all rights. Pays on acceptance. Will send a sample copy and writers' packet for 50¢. Query first. Reports in 6 weeks. Enclose S.A.S.E. for reply to queries.

Nonfiction and Photos: Address to Article Editor. Inspirational articles should indicate practical relevance of Christianity to problems facing age group. Other nonfiction articles range from humorous to informative. "Payment based on content and length, usually $35 to $50." Buys b&w glossies. Usually included in ms price.

Fiction: Address to Fiction Editor. 1,000 to 2,500 words. Should be timely and honest. Stories need not have strong spiritual emphasis but should be in keeping with

Christian point of view. At least one story used every month "Payment based on content and length."
Fillers: Uses puzzles, games, etc.

VACATION FUN, Scholastic Magazines, Inc., 50 W. 44th St., New York NY 10036. Editor of Manuscript Department: Mrs. Norma Ainsworth. Summer magazine for third and fourth graders, ages 8 to 10. Buys all rights. Pays on acceptance. Will send free sample copy on request. Enclose S.A.S.E. with all submissions, and keep a carbon copy for file. Same requirements as *News Trails* and *News Explorer*.
Fiction: Summer themes. 800 to 1,000 words. Pays from $75.

VIDEO-PRESSE, 3965 est, boul. Henri-Bourassa, Montreal 459, Que., Canada. Editor: Pierre Guimar. For "French Canadian boys and girls of 8 to 15." Monthly. Circulation: 75,000. Buys all rights. Buys 20 to 30 mss a year. Pays on publication. Will send a sample copy to a writer on request. Reports in 2 weeks. Enclose S.A.S.E. for return of submissions.
Nonfiction: "Material with a French Canadian background. The articles have to be written in French, and must appeal to children aged 8 to 15." Buys how-to's, personal experience articles, interviews, profiles, humor, historical articles, photo features, travel pieces. Length: 1,500 to 3,000 words. Pays 3¢ a word.
Photos: B&w glossies, color transparencies; with captions only. Pays $5.
Fillers: Puzzles, jokes, short humor.

WEE WISDOM, Unity Village MO 64063. Editor: Jim Leftwich. Character-building monthly magazine for boys and girls. Designed to help child develop positive self-image and strength to function successfully in tomorrow's world. Free sample copy, editorial policy on request. Buys first North American serial rights only. Pays on acceptance. Enclose S.A.S.E. for return of submissions.
Nonfiction: Entertaining science articles or projects, activities to foster creativity. Pays 2¢ per word minimum.
Fiction: Short and lively stories, education for living without moralizing. "Although entertaining enough to hold the interest of the older child, they should be readable by the third grader. Character-building ideals should be emphasized without preaching. Language should be universal, avoiding the Sunday school image." Length: 500 to 1,200 words. Pays 2¢ per word minimum.
Poetry: Limited. Pays 50¢ per line. Prefers short, seasonal or humorous poems. Also buys rhymed prose for "read alouds" and pays $15 up.
Fillers: Pays $3 up for puzzles and games.

WHENEVER WHATEVER, American Baptist Board of Educational Ministries, Valley Forge PA 19481. Editor: Gracie McCay. A monthly magazine for children 10 to 11 years of age. Enclose S.A.S.E. for return of submissions.
Nonfiction: Biographies of people making significant use of their lives. Articles on current issues, interesting subjects. Reports of noteworthy activities of boys and girls. Pays up to 2¢ a word on acceptance.
Fiction: Must "provide enjoyment and at the same time stimulate thought, provoke action, and present models of behavior and thought" so children "may discover for themselves the best use of their lives, as a gift of God." Length: 1,500 words maximum.
Poetry: Suitable to format.
Fillers: How-to projects, puzzles, jokes, riddles, cartoons.

WONDER TIME, 6401 Paseo, Kansas City MO 64131. Editor: Elizabeth B. Jones. Published weekly by Church of the Nazarene for children ages 6 to 8. Will send free sample copy to a writer on request. Buys first rights. Pays on acceptance. Enclose S.A.S.E. for return of submissions.
Fiction and Poetry: Buys 500- to 750-word stories portraying Christian attitude, without being preachy. Uses stories for special days, stories teaching honesty, truthfulness, helpfulness or other important spiritual truths, and avoiding symbolism. God should be spoken of as our Father Who loves and cares for us: Jesus, as our Lord and Savior. Pays 2¢ a word on acceptance. Uses 8- 12-line verse which has seasonal or Christian emphasis. Pays 12¼¢ per line and up.

YOUNG CITIZEN, Scholastic Magazines, Inc., 50 West 44th Street, New York NY 10036. Manuscript Editor: Mrs. Norma Ainsworth. *Young Citizen* is for 5th grade children of 10 and 11, is staff-written and uses no fiction. Enclose S.A.S.E. for return of submissions.

Nonfiction and Photos: "We would be interested in timely nonfiction photojournalism that exemplifies the daily life experiences of children (including family life) the age of our readers or a year or two older; e.g., a farm child in Iowa, a child in the mountains of the western Carolinas, a Mexican-American family in the Southwest, a child in the Florida Keys. We are interested in covering a wide range of ethnic and socio-economic backgrounds. We are also interested in general news articles, not necessarily about children, that might interest our readers. We are more concerned with having two to three clear photos that tell the story and complete background information (including quotes), written in adult style, that would allow us to fashion the story at the right level for our readers. We would most likely run the articles on a single page, using no more than three photos, or, more rarely, on a double page using no more than four. For material resulting in a single page, we would pay $60; for a double page, $100."

THE YOUNG CRUSADER, 1730 Chicago Ave., Evanston IL 60201. Managing Editor: Michael Vitucci. For children 6 to 12 who are junior members of National WCTU. Monthly. Pays on acceptance. Will send a sample copy to a writer on request. Submit seasonal material 4 to 6 months in advance. Reports promptly. Enclose S.A.S.E. for return of submissions.

Nonfiction and Fiction: Uses articles on total abstinence, character building, love of animals, Christian citizenship, world friendship. Also science stories. Length: 650 to 800 words. Pays ½¢ per word.

YOUNG JUDAEAN, 817 Broadway, New York NY 10003. Editor: Barbara Gingold. For Jewish kids aged 8 to 13, and members of Young Judaean. Publication of Hadassah Zionist Youth Commission. Special issues for Jewish/Israeli holidays, or special themes which vary from year to year; for example, Hassidim Holocaust, etc. Established in 1916. Monthly. Circulation: 8,000. Rights purchased vary with author and material. Buys all rights, but will reassign rights to author after publication; buys First North American serial rights; buys first serial rights. Buys 10 to 20 mss a year. Payment in contributor's copies or small token payment. Will send sample copy to writer for 25¢. Prefers complete ms only. Will consider photocopied submissions. Submit seasonal material 3 months in advance. Reports in 2 months. Returns rejected material immediately. Enclose S.A.S.E. for return of submissions.

Nonfiction: "Articles about Jewish-American life, Jewish historical and international interest. Israel and Zionist-oriented material. Try to awaken kids' Jewish consciousness by creative approach to Jewish history and religion, ethics and culture, politics and current events." Informational (300 to 1,000 words), how-to (300 to 500 words), personal experience, interview, humor, historical, think articles, photo, travel, and reviews (book, theater, and movies). Length: 500 to 1,500 words. Pays $5 to $15. "Token payments only due to miniscule budget."

Photos: Photos purchased with accompanying mss. Captions required. 5x7 maximum. Payment included with fee for article.

Fiction: Experimental, mainstream, mystery, suspense, adventure, science fiction, fantasy, humorous, religious, and historical fiction. Length: 800 to 2,000 words. Pays $5 to $15.

Poetry and Fillers: Traditional forms, blank verse, free verse, avant-garde forms, and light verse. Poetry themes must relate to subject matter of magazine. Length: minimum 8 lines. Pays $5 to $15. Newsbreaks, puzzles (all sorts), jokes, and short humor purchased for $5.

YOUNG MUSICIANS, The Sunday School Board of the Southern Baptist Convention, 127 Ninth Ave. N., Nashville TN 37234. Editor: Jimmy R. Key. For "boys and girls, ages 9 to 11, in church choirs." Quarterly. Buys 5 or 6 mss a year. Buys all rights. Pays on acceptance. Submit seasonal material 1 year in advance. Enclose S.A.S.E. for return of submissions.

Nonfiction and Fiction: Uses "stories, articles about church music composers, hymn text writers, boys and girls in choir, music in the home, etc." Writers should study the publication before submitting. "Most materials are written on assignment to correlate with materials in *The Music Leader*." Pays "approximately 2½¢ a word."

YOUNG WORLD, 1100 Waterway Blvd., Indianapolis IN 46202. Editor: Ellen Taggart. For young people in the 10 to 14 age bracket. Monthly, except June-July and August-September. Circulation: 230,000. Buys all rights. Buys about 200 mss a year. Pays on publication. Will send a sample copy to a writer for 50¢. Write for copy of guidelines for writers. No query required, "but helpful." Submit seasonal material at least 8 months in advance. Minimum reporting time is 10 to 12 weeks. Enclose S.A.S.E.

Nonfiction and Photos: Historical, scientific, contemporary articles. "Writer should keep in mind that we're aiming toward the sophisticated youngster who is concerned with today's problems. We'd be interested in seeing articles about young people doing something; for example, a community project. Photos would be required, of course." Informational, how-to, interview, profile, humor, historical, think articles, and photo features. Length: 500 to 2,000 words. Pays 2¢ to 3¢ a word. Photos are purchased with accompanying mss; captions required. Pays $2.50 for each b&w; $5 for color.

Fiction: Adventure, mystery, humor and realism. Suspense, western, science fiction, romance (teenage), and historical fiction. Length: 1,000 to 2,500 words. Pays 2¢ to 3¢ per word.

Poetry and Fillers: Humor is desired. Traditional forms, blank verse, free verse, and light verse. Theme is open. No length limits. Pays $10 to $15. Puzzles: word, math, etc.

How To Break In: "I can suggest that the best way to break in would be to study the magazine. A writer should send for our editorial requirements sheet and look at recent issues to see how *Young World* has changed in the past year. Most of our stories and articles fall within a certain word range, and those that don't—department fillers and regular columns, etc.—are staff-written. We're always interested in news or feature items, and a new writer might have a good chance here. If he can get an interview with young people at a special event, or an interview with a sports or entertainment celebrity, and can send along photographs, we'd be more than willing to see his material. He should remember that he's competing with hundreds of writers, but he should keep in mind that we *have* published articles by writers who have never been published before. In other words, it's the material that counts, not the author's credits."

Literary and "Little" Publications

Magazines in this list publish literary criticism, literary writing, or book reviews. Many of them are quarterlies or published irregularly, and many do not pay except in contributor's copies. Nonpaying markets are included because they offer the writer a vehicle for expression that he often can't find in the commercial press. Many talented American writers found first publication in magazines like these. Writers are reminded that many "littles" remain at one address for a limited time; others are notoriously unbusinesslike in their reporting on, or returning of submissions. University-affiliated reviews are conscientious about manuscripts but some of these are also slow in replying to queries or returning submissions.

Magazines that specialize in publishing poetry or poetry criticism are found in the Poetry category. Many "little" publications that offer contributors a forum for expression of minority opinions are classified in the listing for Alternate and Radical magazines.

THE ABOVE GROUND REVIEW, P.O. Box 337, Arden NC 28704. Editor: George Roland Wood. For the "college educated, interested in fine literature." Established in 1968. Triannual. Circulation: 1,600. Rights purchased vary with author and material. Buys all rights, but will reassign them to author after publication, or buys first North American serial rights. Buys about 9 mss a year. Pays on publication. Will send a sample copy to writer for $1.50. Query first for nonfiction. Submit complete ms for poetry and fiction. Will consider photocopied submissions. Submit

seasonal material 2 months in advance. Reports in 6 weeks. Enclose S.A.S.E.
Nonfiction: "We believe our standards are more professional than those of most magazines with similar circulation." Wants "nothing political." Buys general interest articles, informational articles, interviews with writers, and reviews (literary). Length: "less than 8,000 words usually." Pays $10.
Fiction: Wants experimental, mainstream, adventure, humorous, and historical fiction. Length: maximum 8,000 words. Pays $10. Dept. Editor: James E. Wise.
Poetry: Traditional forms, blank and free verse, and avant-garde forms. Length: 1,000 lines maximum. Pays a fifth of scotch and contributor's copies for best poem each issue. Pays all other poets in contributor's copies.

AMANUENSIS, c/o English Department, P.O.T. 1215, University of Kentucky, Lexington KY 40506. Editor: Paul Stephen White. For "anyone interested in any artistic medium, but mainly literature." Established in 1971. Twice a year. Circulation: 400. Acquires first North American serial rights. No payment. Will send sample copy to writer for 75 cents. Query first. Will consider photocopied submissions. Reports on material in 1 month. Enclose S.A.S.E. for reply to queries.
Nonfiction: "We tend to be somewhat regional. However, we do try to be aware of contemporary art and put it in our rather conventional format." Humorous and think articles; nostalgia, technical and reviews of poetry and novels. Length: less than 2,000 words.
Fiction: Experimental, mystery, fantasy, humorous. Length: 2,000 words maximum.
Poetry: Traditional, blank verse, free verse, light verse and avant-garde forms. Length: open. Dept. Editor: Michale James.

AMERICAN DIALOG, 130 East 16th St., New York NY 10003. Editor: Lewis M. Moroze. For "all lovers of good and timely literature: professionals, students, writers, artists, and the general reading public." Subject matter is social commentary, reportage, and articles; also criticism of literature, art, and contemporary events. Quarterly. Circulation: 12,000. Acquires all rights. Pays in contributor's copies. Will send a sample copy to a writer for $1.25. Requires seasonal material 3 months in advance. Returns rejected material in 3 to 6 weeks. Enclose S.A.S.E. for return of submissions.
Nonfiction, Fiction, Poetry, and Fillers: "We receive mss from world-renowned authors, artists, and poets. Our purpose is to promote the Marxist view on all questions determining the future: man's dignity, his material and spiritual welfare and survival, etc.; but we are not limited to Marxist views, nor are we narrowly cultural. Exchange of themes is central to our magazine. The arts are the battleground for many conflicting ideologies. We demand professional handling of all subjects that are of vital cultural interest. Do not send hackneyed themes, pseudo-romanticism, sex to stimulate prurience, cheap sensationalism, or racially biased works." Length: 1,000 to 2,000 words. Uses historical, adventure, and contemporary problem short stories of general interest. Length: 1,000 to 2,000 words. Poetry can be contemporary or avant-garde. Length: 12 lines minimum; 50 to 100 lines maximum. Uses newsbreak fillers. Length: 250 to 500 words. Pay for all material is 3 copies of the magazine.

AMERICAN MERCURY, P.O. Box 1306, Torrance CA 90505. Business Manager and Editorial Associate: La Vonne Furr. Quarterly. Write for copy of guidelines for writers. "All mss must be typed, double-spaced, clean, ready for printer, left margin at least 1½ inches. Break up articles with periodic italicized paragraphs and/or subheads. Authors should submit biographical material to aid editor in preparing a suitable introduction." Enclose S.A.S.E. for return of submissions.
Nonfiction: *Mercury's* editorial policy is nonpartisan but generally conservative. "It will stress the positive and hopeful aspects of life and Western tradition through reliable and well-written exposes. Articles on fads, dances, narcotics, crime, entertainers are generally unwanted." Wants Americana, nature briefs, humorous comment on everyday life, politics, science, health; particular emphasis on heroic and patriotic themes; satire. "Precede book reviews with a very brief title, then describe book: Title of book in caps, by (name of author), number of pages, publisher, date of publication." Length: 1,000 words maximum for book reviews; 900 to 2,000 words for articles. "The chief requirement of articles is that they be widely interesting and of a basically constructive nature."

Poetry: Poetry is wanted so long as it is not of the "sick," bonkmilk or meaningless type. "Poetry especially must have a 'positive' and never a negative or hopeless ring to it. Profanity and obscenity are not printed. In all things, a 'victory through right principles' theme is preferred."

AMERICAN NOTES AND QUERIES, 31 Alden Rd., New Haven CT 06515. Editor and Publisher: Lee Ash. Ten times a year. no payment. Enclose S.A.S.E.
Nonfiction: Historical, artistic, literary, bibliographical, linguistic and folklore matters, scholarly book reviews and reviews of foreign reference books; items of unusual antiquarian interest.

AMERICAN QUARTERLY, Box 1, Logan Hall, University of Pennsylvania, Philadelphia PA 19174. Editor: Dr. Murray G. Murphey. For college professors, teachers, museum directors, researchers, students, college and high school libraries. Readers professionally interested in American studies. Acquires all rights. Does not pay. Reports in 3 to 6 months. Enclose S.A.S.E.for return of submissions.
Nonfiction and Photos: Scholarly, interdisciplinary articles on American studies, about twenty pages. August Summer Replacement issue contains annual review of books, articles in American Studies for the current year, dissertation listings, American Studies programs, financial aid, writings on theory of American Studies, membership directory. Occasionally uses photos.

AMERICAN REVIEW, 666 Fifth Avenue, New York NY 10019. Editor: Theodore Solotaroff. For literary and academic audience. Published 3 times a year. Buys North American serial rights only. Pays on acceptance. No query required. Reports in 6 weeks. Enclose S.A.S.E. for return of submissions.
Fiction and Poetry: Wants "first-rate fiction and poetry." Length: 4,000 to 6,000 words. Pays 6¢ a word. Poetry Editor: Richard Howard.

THE AMERICAN SCHOLAR, 1811 Q Street, N.W., Washington DC 20009. Editor: Hiram Haydn. Quarterly. Circulation: 47,000. Buys all rights. Pays on acceptance. Reports in 2 to 6 weeks. Enclose S.A.S.E. for return of submissions.
Nonfiction: Uses nontechnical treatments of science, art, religion, politics and national and foreign affairs. Length: 3,000 to 3,500 words. Pays $150.
Poetry: Uses three or four poems of highest literary quality per issue. Pays $35 to $75.

ANGEL HOUR, 388 Sunpark Place, San Jose CA 95136. Editor: Doris Spearman. Quarterly. Circulation: over 500. Will send sample copy to a writer for 25¢. No payment, but cash awards, books, records, pictures given. Subscribers' material given preference. Reports on submissions in six weeks or less. Enclose S.A.S.E.
Nonfiction and Fiction: "Anything of interest to general public which is suitable for an 'angel' publication." No holiday material. Length: 500 words maximum.
Poetry: "Any form, any subject—clean." Length: 16 lines maximum.

ANTHELION (including *N.C.P.U. Compendium*), P.O. Box 21441, Dallas TX 75211. Editor: R.W. Whitney. For "a university level readership." Bimonthly. Authors should include a brief resume and cover letter with submissions. Will send sample copy to writer for $1. Purchases all rights with return of reprint rights upon request. Pays on publication. Reports in 4 to 6 weeks. Enclose S.A.S.E.
Nonfiction and Fiction: "Devoted in alternate months to the fields of literature, social and cultural comment, and philosophy. January and July issues are devoted to literary articles and stories. Presently, we are in need of short articles dealing with the 'new' issues of our society. Interviews, reviews and like articles are used to augment our basic copy. We stress that all copy must be verifiable and logical. We seek the new writer with new insights into our modern world. Our pay for articles varies from contributor's copies up to 5¢ a word." Length: 2,500 words maximum.

ANTIOCH REVIEW, P.O. Box 148, Yellow Springs OH 45387. Editor: Lawrence Grauman, Jr. For general, literary and academic audience. Quarterly. Buys all rights. Pays on publication. Reports in 4 to 6 weeks. Enclose S.A.S.E.
Nonfiction: Relevant articles in the humanities and social sciences, politics, economics, literature and all areas of broad intellectual concern. Somewhat scholarly, but never pedantic in style, eschewing all professional jargon. Lively, distinctive prose insisted upon. Length: 2,000 to 8,000 words. Also review-articles in the huma-

nities and social sciences, including several books on a common theme, although conventional book reviews have been dropped. Length: up to 5,000 words. Pays $8 per published page.

Fiction: No limitations on style or content, though tends to print stories of contemporary significance with social or psychological implications. Length: 2,000 to 8,000 words. Pays $8 per published page.

Poetry: Prints poetry regularly, usually 10 to 20 lines. Study publication. In addition to other poems, each issue features one poet, devoting considerable space to show depth and range. Pays "$10 per page for single poems."

ARION, Department of University Professors, Boston University, 270 Bay State Rd., Boston MA 02215. Editors-in-Chief: William Arrowsmith and D. S. Carne-Ross. "Journal of humanities and classics for persons interested in literature of the classical periods of Greece and Rome." Established in 1962. Quarterly. Circulation: 1,000. Acquires all rights, but will reassign rights to author after publication. Will send a sample copy to a writer for $1.75. Query first or submit complete ms. Will consider photocopied submissions. Reports in 6 weeks. Enclose S.A.S.E.

Nonfiction: Uses "articles on classical literature; reviews, translations, imaginative criticism. We're as interested in creative translation as criticism. Length: 10 to 40 pages."

ARIZONA QUARTERLY, University of Arizona, Tucson AZ 85721. Editor: Albert F. Gegenheimer. For a university-type audience. Quarterly. Payment is in copies and a one-year subscription to the magazine. There are annual awards for the best poem of the year, the best article of the year, the best story of the year and the best book review of the year. Reports in 3 to 4 weeks except during summer. Enclose S.A.S.E. for return of submissions.

Nonfiction: "Always interested in articles dealing with the Southwest, but open to articles on any topic of general interest."

Fiction: "Quality" fiction. Southwestern interest preferred, but not essential. Length: normally not over 3,000 words.

Poetry: Uses four or five poems per issue on any serious subject. Prefers short poems; up to 30 lines can be used most readily. The author must have something to say and be equipped to say it.

THE ARK RIVER REVIEW, 440 N. Yale, Wichita KS 67208. Editors: Jonathan Katz, A. G. Sobin, Arthur Vogelsang. For "those with an interest in the leading edge of poetry and fiction." Established in 1971. Quarterly. Circulation: 600 to 1,000. Buys first North American serial rights and second serial (reprint) rights. Payment on publication and in contributor's copies. Will send sample copy to writer for $1. Will consider photocopied submissions "only if note attached affirms the ms is not being submitted elsewhere." Reports on material within 1 month. Enclose S.A.S.E. for return of submissions.

Fiction and Poetry: "We work with three editors for poetry and fiction, but with a system that does not require a concensus. Thus we hope to be open to a very wide range of material. We would, however, always prefer to take a chance on publishing something that seems really new, rather than taking something highly competent but conventional. Advise writers read an issue or two before submitting." Experimental and erotic (with redeeming graces) fiction. Length: open. Pays $3 per published page; minimum of $20 per story. Dept. Editor: Arthur Vogelsang. Free verse and avant-garde forms of poetry. Length: open. Pays 20c a line; minimum payment of $5 per poem. Dept. Editor: A. G. Sobin.

THE ARLINGTON QUARTERLY, Box 366, University Sta., Arlington TX 76010. Editor: Maurice I. Carlson. Quarterly. Circulation: 1,000. Token payment upon publication. Will send sample copy for $1.50. "Our editorial test in all categories of material is excellence in writing." Reports within 60 days. Enclose S.A.S.E. for return of submissions.

Nonfiction: Literary and scholarly essays. No restrictions as to subject matter. Mechanics of scholarly articles should conform to *MLA Style Sheet*. Not over 12 double-spaced, typewritten pages in length. Address to James Moffett.

Fiction: No restrictions as to subject matter or style. Stories of up to 12 double-spaced, typewritten pages preferred. Uses short-shorts or vignettes under 2,000 words. Address to Billi Wilemon.

Poetry: No restrictions. Any reasonable length considered. Address to Don Swadley.

ART AND LITERARY DIGEST, Madoc-Tweed Art Centre, Tweed, Ontario, Canada. Editor: Roy Cadwell. "Our readers are mostly former students of the Art Centre." Established in 1967. Quarterly. Circulation: 2,000. Not copyrighted. Payment on publication. Will send sample copy to writer for 50¢. Submit complete ms. Reports on material within 30 days. Enclose S.A.S.E. for return of submissions.
Nonfiction: Educational, how-to-do articles, inspirational, humorous, travel and personal uplift material. "Good writing is essential with integrity and knowledge. Slant toward students, alumni and others interested in art, music, writing and poetry. We do not need offbeat articles. As a house organ, we try to influence our readers to do better. Would like to receive more personal experience articles and 'I was there' type of travel articles." Length: 500 words. Pays 1¢ per word.
Fiction and Poetry: Humorous fiction. Length: 500 words. Pays 1¢ a word. Free verse, blank verse, traditional and avant-garde forms. Length: usually 12 lines, but no limit. Pays $1.
Fillers: Clippings and short humor. Length: less than 500 words. Pays 1¢ per word.

ARTS IN SOCIETY, University Extension, The University of Wisconsin, 610 Langdon St., Madison WI 53706. Editor: Edward L. Kamarck. Audience is library patrons, educators, arts administrators, and members of the general public interested in the arts. Circulation: 5,000. Buys all rights. Pays on publication. Sample copies sent to those writers who indicate that they have something to contribute to the particular focus of upcoming issues. Query first. Reports within six weeks. Enclose S.A.S.E.
Nonfiction, Photos, and Fiction: In general, four areas are dealt with: teaching and learning the arts; aesthetics and philosophy; social analysis; and significant examples of creative expression in a media which may be served by the printing process. Length: 1,500 to 3,000 words. Pays honorarium. B&w glossy photos used with captions. Buys fiction "only if illustrative of particular focus of the issue." Pays modest honorarium.

AUTHOR/POET, P.O. Box 1024, Birmingham AL 35201. Editor: Betty McCollum. For amateur poets and authors. 5 times a year. Enclose S.A.S.E. for return of submissions.
Nonfiction, Fiction, Poetry, and Fillers: "Pays $2 for each editorial, article, and short-short story used. Pays $2 and $3 for poems in each issue. For special Christmas Issue, pays $2, $3, and $5 for best Christmas poems. Pays $1 for each patriotic saying used." $100 cash prize contest for subscribers.

BALL STATE UNIVERSITY FORUM, Ball State University, Muncie IN 47306. Editors: Merrill Rippy and Frances Mayhew Rippy. For "educated readers interested in nontechnical studies of humanities, fine arts, sciences, social sciences, history, and education." Acquires all rights, "but author may always reprint at his own request without charge, so long as prior publication in *Forum* is acknowledged." Pays in 10 contributor's copies. Will send a sample copy to a writer on request. Contributors should accompany their entries with a two-sentence description of their academic background or position, their other publications, and their special competence to write on their subject. Contributors submitting multiple copies cut one month from reading time: poems, 7 copies; short stories, 9 copies; plays, 9 copies; articles, 2 copies. Special issues planned on American literature, British literature, education. Reports in 3 to 4 months. Enclose S.A.S.E. for return of submissions.
Nonfiction: Articles that are reasonably original, polished and of general interest. Length: 50 to 3,000 words.
Fiction and Drama: Short stories, one-act plays. Length: 50 to 2,000 words.
Poetry: Uses 5 to 30 poems per issue. Length: 5 to 200 lines.

BEYOND BAROQUE, 1639 Washington Blvd., Venice CA 90291. Editors: George Drury Smith and James Krusoe. Semi-annually. Acquires first rights. Query not required. Pays in contributor's copies. Reports in four to eight weeks. Enclose S.A.S.E. for return of submissions.
Nonfiction: Avant-garde, exploratory in subject matter and style. Will use one or

two articles in each issue on literary, synesthetic scene. Length: 5,000 words maximum.
Fiction: Must be highly original, exploratory in subject matter and style. Length: up to 7,500 words.
Poetry: Looking for re-evaluation of language.

BLACK CREATION, 10 Washington Place, New York NY 10003. Editor: Fred Beauford. For "nonwhites and blacks, high school graduates and over, 18 to 35 years old." Quarterly. Circulation: 10,000. Acquires first rights. Pays in copies. Will send sample copy to writer on request. Reports in 1 to 2 months. Enclose S.A.S.E. for return of submissions.
Nonfiction and Photos: "An outlet for new black writers." Seeks "anything related to the black arts." Regular columns on dance, fine arts, films, and theatre. Buys interviews, profiles. Length: open. Buys photo features and "creative" 8x11 b&w prints.
Fiction: Humorous, historical, adventure, and contemporary problems stories. Length: 1,500 to 4,000 words.
Poetry: Length: 2 to 50 lines.

BLACK SCHOLAR, P.O. Box 908, Sausalito CA 94965. Editor: Robert Chrisman. Monthly, except July and August. Query first. Enclose S.A.S.E.
Nonfiction: "This is the first journal of black studies and research. It provides a forum for black thought and black experience." Payment made in copies of the magazine. Nonblack authors by publisher's request only.

BLACK SWAMP REVIEW, Business and Fiction: 730 Union, 33A, Bangor ME 04401; Poetry: English Dept., Ellis Hall, Ohio University, Athens, OH 45701. For literary audience. Established in 1969. Published 3 times a year: April, August, and December. Circulation: 500. Acquires all rights, but will reassign them to author after publication. Buys over 50 mss a year. Payment in contributor's copies and a small fee for translations. Will send a sample copy to a writer for 50¢. Reports in 2 to 4 weeks. Enclose S.A.S.E. for return of submissions.
Fiction: Publishes short stories. "Quality is the main criteria, not any special theme—especially interested in the use of language and tone in fiction. Also interested in obtaining translations of modern fiction—any language. We are primarily a fiction and translation magazine. One of the magazine's aims is to present contemporary foreign fiction for American readers. Please, no more domestic tragedies, melodramas, homosexual and 'uncle' stories." Seeking "successful attempts in utilizing language and tone in fiction as a main consideration." Length: "no limits." Department Editor: Ronald T. Bean.
Poetry: Also looking for translations of poetry from any language. Buys traditional forms, blank verse, and avant-garde forms. Length: open. Department Editor: Horace Coleman.

BLUE CLOUD QUARTERLY, Marvin SD 57251. Editor: Brother Benet Twedten, O.S.B. Circulation: 2,178. "Copyrights are provided if the authors require them." Payment in contributor's copies. Will send free sample copy to writer on request. Enclose S.A.S.E. for return of submissions.
Nonfiction, Fiction and Poetry: Publishes creative writing and other articles by and about the American Indians.

BOOKS ABROAD, 1000 Asp, Room 214, University of Oklahoma, Norman OK 73069. Editor: Ivar Ivask. Enclose S.A.S.E. for return of submissions.
Nonfiction: Articles (maximum length 3,000 words) concerned with contemporary literature; book reviews of 200 to 300 words on new, important, original works of a literary nature in any language. All contributions in English. Payment only in offprints (25) of a major article, plus 3 complimentary copies of *Books Abroad.*

BOSTON UNIVERSITY JOURNAL, P.O. Box 357, Boston University Station, Boston MA 02115. Editor: Paul Kurt Ackermann. For libraries, universities, college educated people. Circulation: 4,000. Uses 30 mss a year. Pays in contributor's copies. Query first. Reports in 1 month. Enclose S.A.S.E.
Nonfiction, Fiction, and Poetry: "Literary criticism, poetry, scholarly articles on a

variety of subjects (must be written clearly, without jargon), a few short stories." No limitations on length.

BUCKNELL REVIEW, Bucknell University, Lewisburg PA 17837. Editor: Harry R. Garvin. For those interested in literature, arts, and sciences. Issued three times each year. Pays in copies and reprints. Reports in 2 to 4 weeks. Enclose S.A.S.E. for return of submissions.
Nonfiction: A style for scholarly readers is preferred. Length 2,500 to 6,000 words.

BULLETIN OF BIBLIOGRAPHY & MAGAZINE NOTES, 15 Southwest Park, Westwood MA 02090. Editor: Carol J. Felsenthal. For librarians, college students, college professors; anyone interested in researching various subjects and authors covered by the *Bulletin*. Established in 1897. Quarterly. Circulation: 2,400. Not copyrighted. Payment in contributor's copies. Query first. Will consider photocopied submissions. Reports in 6 weeks. Enclose S.A.S.E. for reply to queries.
Bibliographies: "We publish bibliographies on any subject although by tradition we lean more toward literary subjects. Bibliographies must conform to the MLA Style Sheet (second edition). They should not repeat bibliographic research already done and should contain a short introduction identifying the subject and informing the user of the author's rationale for inclusion or exclusion of primary or secondary material. Anyone submitting a manuscript must make certain that there is not already published a sufficient or overabundant amount of bibliographic research."

THE CALIFORNIA QUARTERLY, 310 Sproul, University of California, Davis CA 95616. Editor: Elliot Gilbert. "Addressed to an audience of educated literary and general readers interested in good writing on a variety of subjects, but will emphasize poetry and fiction." Quarterly. Payment in copies and subscriptions. Reports in 4 to 6 weeks. Enclose S.A.S.E. for return of submissions.
Nonfiction and Photos: "Original critical articles, essays, and book reviews. We have a certain bias for Western, especially California material." Length: up to 8,000 words.
Fiction: "Short. Quality; emphasis on stylistic distinction, contemporary themes, any subject." Experimental, mainstream. Length: 8,000 words. Dept. Editor: Diane Johnson.
Poetry: "Original, all types; any subject appropriate for genuine poetic expression; any length suitable to subject." Dept. Editor: Karl Shapiro.

CANADIAN FORUM, 56 Esplanade St., E., Toronto, Ont., Canada. Managing Editor: Abraham Rotstein. For professional groups, university staffs, general audience. Monthly. Payment in copies. Reports in 1 month. Enclose S.A.E. and International Reply Coupons for return of submissions.
Nonfiction: Objective, well-written, knowledgeable; on preferred subjects of original research, politics, sociology, art. No slant. Length: 2,000 words.

CANADIAN LITERATURE, c/o Publications Centre, University of British Columbia, Vancouver 8, B.C., Canada. Editor: George Woodcock. Quarterly. Circulation: 2,100. No fiction, poetry, fillers or photos. Not copyrighted. Pays on publication. Study publication. Enclose S.A.E. and International Reply coupons. Query advisable.
Nonfiction: Articles of high quality on Canadian books and writers only. Articles should be scholarly and readable. Length: 2,000 to 5,500 words. Pays $40 to $120 depending on length.

CARAVEL MAGAZINE, 315 Kneale Ave. So., Thief River Falls MN 56701. Editor: Ben Hagglund. Buys North American serial rights only. "Study requirements carefully." Reports in 1 month. Enclose S.A.S.E. for return of submissions.
Nonfiction: Articles appropriate to format. Study publication. Length: 1,000 words. Payment is $5 per 1,000 words.
Poetry: Uses verse that dramatizes people and places, and shows the richness of the world's cultures. Poet must show empathy for cultures and peoples other than our familiar ones; plus ability to express such empathy in capable, workmanlike poetry. Payment of 5¢ per line.

CARLETON MISCELLANY, Carleton College, Northfield MN 55057. Editor: Wayne Carver. Aimed mainly at those few academics "who are still alive. But who can, also, still read." Twice yearly. Circulation: 1,000. Buys North American serial rights. Pays on publication. Will send sample copy for $1.50. Suggests that writers "buy or find a recent copy of the magazine and see what we do—or try to guess what we think we're doing." Reports in 4 to 6 weeks. Enclose S.A.S.E. for return of submissions.

Nonfiction: More interested in an informal, lively tone than in specific subject matter. No taboos, but inclines toward letting the undergraduate and underground papers and magazines have the pornography, "since they think they invented it." Pays $8 per page.

Fiction: Length: 7,500 words and under, but doesn't usually run short shorts or vignettes. Pays $8 per page.

Poetry: No length limit, "but we think poems over a hundred lines presume a lot."

THE CAROLINA QUARTERLY, P.O. Box 1117, Chapel Hill NC 27514. Editor: Bruce M. Firestone. Issued three times annually. Reprint rights revert to author. Pays on publication. Reports in 8 weeks. Enclose S.A.S.E. for return of submissions. "Manuscripts should be marked 'Fiction' or 'Poetry' on envelope."

Fiction: Quality, primary emphasis on stylistic achievement, character development, interesting point of view. A market for both the beginner and the professional. "Primarily interested in capable young writers in control of their material. Almost everything we publish comes to us unsolicited through the mails." Payment is $5 a printed page.

Poetry: Poems must be original and mature in use of language with original subjects. Popular, conventional verse not wanted. Pays $5.

THE CASTALIAN, P. O. Box 75182, Los Angeles CA 90075. Editors: Jeff Wiggenbach and Wendy McElroy. For "those interested in the rational and systematic study of literature for its own sake, whether they are professionals in literature or intelligent lay readers." Established in 1973. Quarterly. Copyrighted. Buys first North American serial rights. Pays on acceptance. Will send free sample copy to writer on request. Will consider photocopied submissions. Reports on submissions within 2 months. Enclose S.A.S.E. for return of submissions.

Nonfiction: "Other than occasional book reviews, we buy only critical articles on literature. Literary criticism. Both theoretical and practical, should reflect a concern with the work of art and how it does what it does. We are not interested in intellectual history, biography and moral philosophy disguised as literary. We are interested only in literature, not in the lives of writers or the social milieu in which they wrote or the philosophical respectability of their ideas." Length: open. Pays $10 for reviews; $25 for critical articles.

Fiction: Experimental, mainstream, mystery, suspense, adventure, western, erotica, science fiction, fantasy, humorous, romance, religious, historical and serialized novels. Length: open. Pays $25.

Poetry: Traditional forms, blank verse, free verse and avant garde. Pays $10. Length: 150 lines maximum. Poetry Editor: Wendy McElroy.

CHELSEA, P.O. Box 5880, Grand Central Station, New York NY 10011. Editor: Sonia Raiziss. Payment in copies. Enclose S.A.S.E. for return of submissions.

Nonfiction, Fiction, and Poetry: Uses "some articles and occasional American or foreign fiction. Accent on style in poetry."

CHICAGO REVIEW, c/o The University of Chicago, Chicago, IL 60637. Editor: Alexander Besher. Quarterly. "Audience is international, self-renewing; people who like art and ideas." Circulation: 3,000. Copyright transferred to author on request after publication. Uses 60 to 100 mss a year. Pays in contributor's copies. "Queries rarely answered." Will not consider photocopied submissions. Reports in 2 weeks to 3 months. Enclose S.A.S.E. for return of submissions.

Nonfiction, Photos, Fiction, Poetry: "We publish original material: fiction, poetry, essays, journalism including interviews, reviews, drawings and photos. Tastes are eclectic, both 'conservative' and 'experimental'. One foot in the academy and one foot on the street. We like to 'discover' serious writers, and want writing to be coherent, alive, and accomplished in some way. Good writing will be alive years from now. The form it takes is up to the writer. Book length mss considered." Managing Editor: Douglas Unger. Nonfiction Editor: Richard Hack. Poetry Editor: Curt Matthews.

CHICAGO SUN-TIMES SHOWCASE, 401 N. Wabash Ave., Chicago IL 60611. Editor: Herman Kogan. For general newspaper reader interested in "serious and lively arts, books, literary matters." Circulation: 750,000. Buys all rights. Buys 20 mss a year. Pays on publication. Will send a sample copy to a writer for postage. Query first. Reports in 10 days. Enclose S.A.S.E.

Nonfiction and Photos: Essays, informal pieces, reminiscences, interviews, profiles of actors, directors and other theater and movie people, authors, publishers, editors, etc. "We welcome serious and humorous material, but serious material should not be stuffy or synthetically erudite; humor should avoid giddiness, flightiness, corn. Especially want material of high quality from younger writers as well as established writers. Welcome good exponents of the New Journalism." Editor requires that all material be "articulate, interesting—I detest the trite, the shopworn, the routine, the over-written." Length: 500 to 1,500 words. Payment is 5¢ to 10¢ a word. "Book reviews are assigned, but prospective reviewer's queries welcomed, with samples." Some photos purchased with mss for $5 to $25.

CIMARRON REVIEW, Oklahoma State University, Stillwater OK 74074. Editor: Clinton Keeler. Quarterly. Acquires all rights. Pays in copies. Enclose S.A.S.E. for return of submissions.

Nonfiction: Thoughtful commentary on the contemporary world. Graceful, lucid writing. No taboos. Editor: James E. Kirby.

Fiction: No adolescent adjustment problems. Good fiction only. Editor: Jeanne Adams Wray.

THE COLORADO QUARTERLY, Hellems 134, University of Colorado, Boulder CO 80302. Editor: Paul Carter. Reports in 2 to 3 weeks. Enclose S.A.S.E. for return of submissions.

Nonfiction: Articles on a wide range of subjects that concern themselves with regional, national and educational matters, written by specialists, in a nontechnical, nonacademic style. Length: 4,000 to 6,000 words.

Fiction: With plots and believable characters. No esoteric or experimental writing. Length: 3,000 to 5,000 words.

CONFRONTATION, c/o M. Tucker, English Dept., Long Island University, Brooklyn NY 11201. Editor: M. Tucker. For general audience. Published semiannually. Buys North American serial rights only. Pays on publication. Query preferred. Enclose S.A.S.E. for reply to query or return of submissions.

Nonfiction and Photos: Essays. Length: 2,000 words. Photos purchased with mss.

Fiction: Uses stories of 2,000 to 3,000 words and short stories or vignettes under 2,000 words.

Poetry: Uses all types.

THE CONNECTICUT CRITIC (formerly *New England Review*), P.O. Box 127, Cheshire CT 06410. Editor: John DeStefano. For the "well-educated, general reader interested in current literature and opinion." Established in 1968. Monthly. Circulation: 1,500. Payment in contributor's copies. Will send sample copy to writer for 60¢. Enclose S.A.S.E. for return of submissions.

Nonfiction: Wants "articles that will interest, educate and entertain on a wide range of subjects. *The Connecticut Critic* is a national magazine and material should cover cultural topics since material must appeal to well-educated readers. Need criticisms of all the arts." Accepts interviews, profiles, think pieces, nostalgia, humor and literary reviews. Length: 1,500 words for humor and literary reviews; 2,000 words for other nonfiction.

Fiction: Seeking mainstream, mystery, humorous stories. "In short stories, characterization rather than plot is the important requirement." Length: 1,000 to 3,000 words.

Poetry: Open to traditional forms, blank verse, and free verse. Length: 10 to 60 lines.

CONTEMPORA, P.O. Box 673, Atlanta GA 30301. Editor: Paula G. Putney. For "a well-educated, sophisticated group of readers." Quarterly. Buys all rights. Buys 120 to 150 mss a year. Pays on publication. Will send a sample copy to a writer for $1 and postage. Submit seasonal material 4 months in advance. Reports in 5 to 6 weeks. Enclose S.A.S.E. for return of submissions.
Nonfiction and Fiction: "Most of our mss are solicited nonfiction; some fiction is also solicited. There is always a long essay on a cinema feature. Otherwise, most subjects are appropriate. A writer should study our format." Buys interviews, profiles, and fiction on contemporary problems. Pays $100 to $250.
Poetry: Traditional, contemporary, avant-garde. Pays $1 to $1.50 per line.

CONTEMPORARY LITERATURE, Dept. of English, Helen C. White Hall, University of Wisconsin, Madison WI 53706. Editor: L.S. Dembo. Quarterly. "All details should conform to those recommended by the *MLA Style Sheet*." Enclose S.A.S.E. for return of submissions.
Nonfiction: A scholarly journal which examines various aspects of contemporary literature, from generalizations on current trends and themes, to studies of a writer, his technique, and/or his work, to other specialized treatments of studies in modern literature.

CRITICISM, Wayne State University, Dept. of English, Detroit MI 48202. Editor: Alva Gay. For college and universtiy audience of humanities scholars and teachers. Quarterly. Reports in 3 months. Enclose S.A.S.E. for return of submissions.
Nonfiction: Articles on literature, music, visual arts; no particular critical "school." Style should be clear and to the point. Length: 15 to 20 typewritten pages. No payment.

CRITIQUE: STUDIES IN MODERN FICTION, Department of English, Georgia Institute of Technology, Atlanta GA 30332. Editor: James Dean Young. For college and university teachers and students. Established in 1956. Triannual. Circulation: 1,300. Acquires all rights. Pays in contributor's copies. Submit complete ms. Will consider photocopied submissions "rarely." Writers should follow the *MLA Style Sheet*. Reports in 4 to 6 months. Enclose S.A.S.E. for return of submissions.
Nonfiction: "Critical essays on writers of contemporary fiction. We prefer essays on writers who are still alive and without great reputations. We only rarely publish essays on well-known, established writers. Currently overworked are essays on the great modern writers: Conrad, James, Joyce, and Faulkner." Uses informational articles and interviews. Length: 4,000 to 8,000 words.

DAEDALUS, 7 Linden St., Harvard University, Cambridge MA 02138. Editor: Stephen R. Graubard. Published by the American Academy of Arts and Sciences. Each issue contains studies revolving around a specific theme; contributing editors who are authorities in their fields are appointed for each issue and articles are commissioned months in advance of publication.

DE KALB LITERARY ARTS JOURNAL, 555 Indian Creek, Clarkston GA 30021. Editor: Mel McKee. Quarterly. Circulation: 1,000. Acquires North American serial rights. Payment in contributor's copies. Will send a sample copy to a writer for $1. Will not consider photocopied submissions. Reports in 3 months. Enclose S.A.S.E. for return of submissions.
Nonfiction, Photos, Fiction, Drama, and Poetry: Publishes personal essays, photographs, stories, poems, one-act plays, and songs. Any subject matter. No taboos.

DECEMBER MAGAZINE, P.O. Box 274, Western Springs IL 60558. Editor: Curt Johnson. Acquires all rights. Will send sample copy to a writer for $1. Query first for interviews. Pays in 2 contributor's copies. Reports in 5 to 9 weeks. Enclose S.A.S.E. for reply to queries or return of submissions.
Nonfiction: Interviews, humorous pieces, movies and political controversies.
Fiction: Chiefly serious fiction. Length: 5,000 words maximum.

DENVER QUARTERLY, University of Denver, Denver CO 80210. Editor: Burton Feldman. For the "general audience for literate articles on culture, literature, etc." Quarterly. Circulation: 800. Buys first rights. Buys 50 to 100 mss a year. Pays on

publication. Will send a sample copy to a writer for $1. Reports in 1 month. Enclose S.A.S.E. for return of submissions.
Nonfiction, Fiction, and Poetry: "Essays, fiction, poems, book reviews. No special approach, but well-written enough and serious enough for our kind of reader." Length: Not over 8,000 to 10,000 words. Minimum payment is $5 per 350 words for prose, $10 a page ("no matter how many lines on it") for poetry.

DESCANT, Department of English, Texas Christian University, Fort Worth TX 76129. Editor: Betsy Feagan Colquitt. Quarterly. Pays in copies. Will send sample copy for 75¢. Reports in about 6 weeks. Enclose S.A.S.E. for return of submissions.
Nonfiction: Essays dealing with recent literature. Prefers articles that are without the scholarly mechanisms. Literary criticism. Length: 4,000 words maximum.
Fiction: Length: 5,000 words maximum; "usually shorter."
Poetry: No special form or subject. About one-quarter of each issue is devoted to poetry. Length: generally limited to 40 lines, but on occasion uses long poems up to 150 lines.

THE DRAGONFLY, Box 147, Idaho State University, Pocatello ID 83201. Editor: Duane Ackerson. For "poets and editors; people interested in new directions in literature." Established in 1969. Quarterly. Circulation: 400 to 500. Acquires all rights, but will reassign rights to author after publication. All contributions are from freelance writers. Payment in contributor's copies. Will send sample copy to writer for $1. Submit complete ms. Will not consider photocopied submissions. Submit seasonal material at least 6 months in advance. Reports on material in 2 months. Enclose S.A.S.E. for return of submissions.
Nonfiction and Poetry: "An eclectic magazine, open to material from traditional to experimental, both in subject matter and form. Have devoted, or will devote, issues or pamphlets to such things as prose poetry, one-line poems, ecology poetry, science fiction poetry, sequence poems. Submissions of 3 to 5 poems preferred. Interested in fables, satire, criticisms of poetry. Mainly looking for literary quality, exuberance, humor; poetry with a sense of fantasy. Generally looking for reviews of poetry books and good general essays on trends in poetry. The best advice would be to look at the magazine." Length: 100 to 3,000 words for nonfiction; no limitations for poetry.
Fiction: Experimental, science fiction, fantasy. "Prefer very short fiction; 100 to 1,000 words."

EL PALACIO, P.O. Box 2087, Santa Fe NM 87501. Editor: Carl E. Rosnek. Published quarterly by the Museum of New Mexico for laymen and professionals interested in the arts, anthropology, and the history of southwestern U.S. Circulation: 2,000. Rights determined "by contract." Pays on publication. Will send sample copy for $1.50. Query preferred. Reports in three to four weeks. Enclose S.A.S.E.
Nonfiction and Photos: Scholarly works about the arts, anthropology, and the history of southwestern U.S. Length: 1,000 to 2,500 words. Payment is $25. Also uses b&w glossy photos on these subjects.

EL VIENTO, 348 7th Street, Huntington WV 25701. Editor: William Lloyd Griffin. Semiannual. Pays in contributor's copies. Will consider photocopied submissions. Reports in 6 weeks. Enclose S.A.S.E. for return of submissions.
Fiction, Nonfiction, Poetry, and Drama: "We use fiction, nonfiction, poetry, and one-act plays. No taboos except low quality material." Length: 500 to 3,000 words for fiction and nonfiction.

THE ELLERY QUEEN REVIEW, 82 E. Eighth St., Oneida Castle NY 13421. Editor: Rev. Robert E. Washer. For "mystery/suspense readers of Ellery Queen specifically; all ages." Established in 1968. Published irregularly. Circulation: 200 to 300. Acquires all rights, but will reassign them to author after publication; may acquire first serial rights. Does not pay. Query first for material other than nonfiction. Will consider photocopied submissions. Reports in 2 months. Enclose S.A.S.E
Nonfiction: "Reviews in general on all media's use of this genre—reactions to Ellery Queen in particular. No special style—maintain standards of literary 'common sense.' Publishing is done at home—mimeographed; strictly a vocational interest." Seeking "more critical and scholarly material within field." Length: open.

EPOCH, A Magazine of Contemporary Literature, 245 Goldwin Smith Hall, Cornell University, Ithaca NY 14850. 3 times yearly. Payment in copies. Reports in 2 months or more. Enclose S.A.S.E. for return of submissions.
Fiction: "Quality. Would like to see more stories which combine a fresh honest transcription of human experience with power or meaningfulness, but are not adverse to experimental forms." Length: 1,500 to 5,000 words.
Poetry: Approximately 30 to 40 pages each issue devoted to poetry.

L'ESPRIT CREATEUR, Box 222, Lawrence KS 66044. Editor: John D. Erickson. For readers interested in the critical study of French literature. Quarterly. Buys no rights. Pays in contributor's copies. Not necessary to query as long as article is intended for a particular issue; each issue lists coming subjects. Manuscripts should be submitted in duplicate with a self-addressed stamped envelope enclosed. Articles should be typed on standard size paper and double-spaced, including footnotes and verse. The general format to be used is that set forth in the *MLA Style Sheet.* Reports usually within 3 months.
Nonfiction: "*L'Esprit Createur* is devoted to the study of French literature; works falling within a literary movement or mode. We invite critical studies, of whatever methodological persuasion, that observe the primacy of the literary text. We are interested only secondarily in the consideration of extra-literary phenomena and in the history of literature. In addition to traditional methods, we look with interest on the new critical methods practiced in France. Aside from articles submitted for issue topics, we invite interviews of contemporary French authors and critics. This feature will appear whenever we have enough material. Length: to 4,000 words. Book reviews are welcome for consideration. They must treat works dealing with the criticism of French literature, but need not conform to the issue topic. Review length: to 700 words. Exceptions should be queried."

EVENT, Douglas College, P.O. Box 2503, New Westminster, B.C., Canada. Editor: David Evanier. Triannual. Acquires first rights. Pays in copies. No query required. Reports in 6 weeks. Enclose S.A.E. and International Reply Coupons for return of submissions.
Fiction, Poetry, and Drama: "*Event* is committed to publishing the most outstanding writing it can find—short stories, novellas, parts of novels, poetry, and plays. We will publish any style, any mode or form, if it has intensity, excellence, and clarity. Traditional or avant-garde. Our only criteria is excellence." Length: open.

THE EXPATRIATE REVIEW, P.O. Box D, Staten Island NY 10301. Editors: Roger W. Gaess and Wyatt E. F. James, New York. Edward Roditi, Paris. Subject matter is "an examination of the creative American expatriate, especially that expatriate who seeks to fulfill himself through literary activity." Acquires first rights. Pays in contributor's copies or a nominal fee. Reports within 2 to 6 weeks. Enclose S.A.S.E. for return of submissions.
Nonfiction, Fiction, and Poetry: "We are not only concerned with those deficiencies of the American cultural climate which force many artistic people to adopt for various indefinite periods of time a new home of more conducive artistic environment, but also the plight of such an expatriate. We in addition seek to mitigate the difficulties of expatriation for the creative American through informative articles which deal with the implications of, as well as the conditions leading to, such a course of action. The editors recognize that the state of affairs in America today has in essence created a new type of American expatriate—that individual committed to artistic fulfillment who leaves not for the capitals of Europe or the lucid valleys of the Far East, but for the American Underground." Interested in quality poetry, short fiction and nonfiction, and queries for book reviews "that are of relevance to the expatriate experience. Prefer some sort of expatriate background to all submissions."

EXTENSIONS, P.O. Box 383, Cathedral Station, New York NY 10025. Editors: S. Zavrian and J. Neugroschel. Published irregularly. Circulation: 4,000. Rights will revert back to authors upon request. Payment of two copies on publication. Will send a sample copy for $1. Reports in 2 months. Enclose S.A.S.E. for return of submissions.
Nonfiction, Fiction, Poetry, and Drama: Uses poetry, plays, essays, short stories,

graphics, concrete poetry, etc. "as long as material has a fresh approach and/or is an expression of new form. Length irrelevant. Writers are urged to examine magazine before submitting."

FICTION, 513 East 13th St., New York NY 10009. Editor: Mark Jay Mirsky. For persons who normally do not read fiction and for those who have stopped reading it and need an inexpensive, creative source of fiction. 3 times a year. Does not pay. Query first. Enclose S.A.S.E.
Fiction: Freelancers might have a chance with a story here, but the editor states he has a large inventory. "It's quality fiction here, the kind you see in quarterlies." Length: "nothing longer than 3,000 words."

FICTION INTERNATIONAL, Department of English, St. Lawrence University, Canton NY 13617. Editor: Joe David Bellamy. For "readers interested in the best writing by talented writers working in new forms or working in old forms in especially fruitful new ways; readers interested in contemporary literary developments and possibilities." Semiannual. Circulation: 5,000. Buys all rights (will reassign rights to author after publication), first North American serial rights, first serial rights. Buys 12 fiction, 4 interview, 40 poetry mss a year. Pays on publication. Will send sample copy to a writer for $1.00. Query first or submit complete ms for interviews; submit only complete ms for fiction, poetry, reviews. Prefers not to see photocopied submissions. Reports in 1 to 2 months. Enclose S.A.S.E. for reply to queries or return of submissions.
Nonfiction and Photos: "Regularly use interviews with well-known fiction writers." Length: 1,000 to 10,000 words. "Also use book reviews of new fiction, though these are usually assigned." Length: 600 to 1,200 words. Pays $5 to $25, sometimes more. Photos accompanying interviews purchased to illustrate interviews. 8x10 b&w glossies. Payment varies.
Fiction: "Almost no taboos or preconceptions but highly selective. Not an easy market for unsophisticated writers. Especially receptive to innovative forms or rich personal styles. Easily bored by nineteenth-century narratives or predictable, plotridden fictions. Originality and the ability to create living characters are highly desirable qualities." Portions of novels acceptable if reasonably self-contained. Length: no length limitations for fiction but "rarely use short-shorts or mss over 30 pages." Payment is $5 to $150, sometimes higher.

THE FIDDLEHEAD, Dept. of English, U.N.B., Fredericton, N.B., Canada. Editor: Robert Gibbs. Quarterly. Circulation: 750. Not copyrighted. Reports in 4 weeks. Enclose S.A.E. and International Reply Coupons for return of submissions.
Fiction: High-quality; Canadian preferred. Study publication. Pays $5 per published page.
Poetry: Integrity, originality and craftsmanship sought. Pays $5 per published page.

FLORIDA QUARTERLY, 330 J.W. Reitz Union, University of Florida, Gainesville FL 32601. Editor: Marie Speed. 3 times a year. Circulation: 1,300. Acquires all rights. Does not pay. Will send sample copy for $1.25. Reports in 6 weeks. Enclose S.A.S.E. for return of submissions.
Nonfiction: Critical, nonpolitical, literary essays, including contemporary subjects. Length: 20,000 words.
Fiction: Contemporary; nothing is unacceptable. Length: 15,000 words. Also uses short-shorts or vignettes under 2,000 words.
Poetry: Any subject matter, style, or length.

THE FLORIDA REVIEW, Dept. of English, Florida Technological University, P.O. Box 25000, Orlando FL 32816. Editor: Laurence Wyatt. For "college-educated audience." Established in 1972. Semiannual. Circulation: 5,000. Acquires all rights (will reassign rights to author after publication). Uses 20 to 30 mss a year. Will send a sample copy to a writer for $1. Submit only complete mss. Will consider photocopied submissions, but no carbons. Reports in 6 to 8 weeks. Enclose S.A.S.E. for return of submissions.
Nonfiction: "Some nonfiction bought if it is thought-provoking and exhibits outstanding ability." Personal experience, humor, historical, expose, nostalgia articles. Length: up to 3,500 words. Payment is $5 to $15.

Fiction and Poetry: Needs "good fiction and verse; we look for originality and significance, fresh ideas." Experimental, mainstream fiction. Length: 500 to 3,500 words. Payment is $5 to $15, "occasionally more if piece merits." Traditional verse forms, blank verse, free verse. No length limitations. Payment is $5 to $15.

FOLKLORE FORUM, 504 N. Fess, Bloomington IN 47401. For "folklorists, graduate students in the humanities and social sciences." Quarterly. Circulation: 300. Not copyrighted. Will send a sample copy to a writer for $1. Query first. Will consider photocopied submissions. Reports in 3 months. Enclose S.A.S.E.
Nonfiction: "Articles, monographs, bibliographies on all types of folkloristic phenomena. The emphasis is on theory. We are a communication link for folklorists and are open to varied viewpoints. Special series issues concentrate on various topics, such as Africa, music, etc." Seeks freelance material for departments on "popular culture and folklore theory." Uses historical articles and book reviews. Length: 500 to 10,000 words.

FORUM, University of Houston, Cullen Blvd., Houston TX 77004. Editor: William Lee Pryor. Primarily for a sophisticated audience; most of the contributors are university professors. Quarterly. Acquires all rights, but will reassign rights to author after publication. Pays in contributor's copies. "A query letter is a welcome courtesy, although we do not specifically request one." Enclose S.A.S.E.
Nonfiction: "We feature articles in the humanities, fine arts, and the sciences, but we also welcome those bearing on business and technology. Specialized interests involving highly technical or special vocabularies are usually not within our range, however. For articles, we stress the scholarly approach and originality. We recommend use of the Chicago *Manual of Style*. An informal style is not objectionable, but research, if any, should be accurate, thorough, and carefully documented. Our format differs from those publications of a similar orientation in that we attempt to combine scholarship with an appealing, aesthetic setting. We are very much interested in good articles on music, dance, architecture, sculpture, etc., not only for our regular issues, but also for special numbers like recent ones featuring French culture and Renaissance." Length: open.
Photos: "Customarily we have an art section in the magazine devoted to photos of paintings, drawing, sculpture, architecture, etc. Also, we try to illustrate articles, poems, and short stories with photos."
Fiction: "We are open on story themes, and we stress originality. Up to now we have not found it possible to publish condensed or serialized novels."

FOUR QUARTERS, La Salle College, Olney Ave. at 20th St., Philadelphia PA 19141. Editor: John J. Keenan. For college educated audience with literary interest. Quarterly. Circulation: 700. Buys all rights; grants permission to reprint on request. Buys 10 to 12 short stories, 30 to 40 poems, 4 articles a year. Pays on publication. Will send a sample copy to a writer for 50¢. Reports in 4 to 6 weeks. Enclose S.A.S.E.
Nonfiction: "Lively critical articles on particular authors or specific works. Think pieces on history, politics, the arts. Prefer footnotes incorporated. Style must be literate, lively, free of jargon and pedantry." Length: 1,500 to 5,000 words. Payment is up to $25.
Fiction: "Character-centered stories of high literary quality. No slicks or formula stories. I'm tired of first-person stories in which the narrator is not really a character but merely a disembodied voice." Length: 2,000 to 6,000 words. Pays up to $25.
Poetry: "Quality poetry from 8 to 32 lines. Some shorter ones used for filler without payment." Payment is up to $5.

FRAGMENTS, 54 W. 88 St., New York NY 10024. Editor: N. Greenberg. Established in 1967. Circulation: 400. Rights acquired vary with author and material. Uses 4 freelance essays and some poetry every year. Payment in contributor's copies. Will send sample copy to writer for 25¢. "All departments have a bias toward natural science/natural history." Submit complete ms. Enclose S.A.S.E. for return of submissions.
Nonfiction and Photos: "Interdisciplinary material especially related to natural sciences, and the role of insights in natural science in creative writing." Informational, personal experience, interview, historical, think pieces. Length: 400 to 2,000 words. Uses 5x7 b&w photos. Captions optional.

Fiction: Experimental, fantasy, historical. Length: 400 to 2,000 words.
Poetry: Blank verse, free verse, avant-garde forms, haiku. Length: 40 lines.

FREE LANCE MAGAZINE, 6005 Grand Ave., Cleveland OH 44104. Editors: Russell Atkins, Casper Jordan and J. Stefanski. For writers and college students and teachers. Emphasis is "largely avant-garde, on modern literary techniques and ideas, should be experimental." Semiannual. Established in 1950. Circulation: 500 to 1,000. Acquires first rights. Pays in copies. Will not consider photocopied submissions. Reports irregularly. Enclose S.A.S.E. for return of submissions.
Nonfiction: Uses philosophical, analytical, theoretical, or psychological reviews. "Avant-garde, extreme experimentation, and, occasionally, more traditional work. No special themes or subjects, as long as they are handled with some elegance, style, and technique. The approach should be an experimental emphasis on technique, a mixture of originality and eclecticism. No more mss about 'life' and its 'everyday' problems."
Fiction: Experimental, fantasy. Length: 5,000 words maximum.
Poetry: Avant-garde forms. Length: open.

THE GAR (incorporating Illuminations), Box 4793, Austin TX 78765. Editor: Hal Wylie. For students and older professional people. Established in 1971. Bimonthly. Payment in contributor's copies. Some prizes awarded. Circulation: 2,500. Copyrighted when necessary for literary materials. Query first. Will consider photocopied submissions. Reports on material in 4 months. Enclose S.A.S.E.
Nonfiction and Photos: Informational, personal experience, interview, profile, humor, historical, think pieces, expose, nostalgia, personal opinion. Reviews of books, records and the arts. "A lot of political material on local or regional matters; some ecology; occasional general articles and essays. Slightly left of center." Length: 300 to 10,000 words. $20 prize awarded annually. Photos used with or without ms.
Fiction: Experimental, mainstream, erotica, science fiction, fantasy, humorous. $10 prize awarded annually.
Poetry: Traditional forms, free verse, avant-garde forms, light verse. $10 prize awarded annually.

GOLDEN ATOM PUBLICATIONS, P.O. Box 1101, Rochester NY 14603. Editors: Larry and Duverne Farsace. For science fiction writers, editors, fans, and poets. Annual. Circulation: about 1,000. Buys all rights. Buys 30 to 40 mss a year, "mostly poetry and a few short-shorts (only on fantasy/s.f. themes)." Pays on acceptance. Will send a sample copy to a writer for 35¢. No query required. Enclose S.A.S.E.
Nonfiction, Photos, Fiction, and Poetry: Wants "exactly what we do not find on the newsstands: traditional poetry, but science fiction or fantasy or classic themes." Likes poetry "with emphasis on cosmic beauty and meaning," similar to that anthologized by Arkham House. For articles, wants "surprising discoveries made in science fiction collecting or research. Also, articles on poetry." No modern verse. Buys personal experience articles, interviews, profiles, exposes, photo articles, science fiction and fantasy, b&w glossies, and traditional poetry. Nonfiction and fiction length: 500 to 2,000 words. Pays $4 to $12. Payment for photos by arrangement. Poetry length: 4 to 24 lines. Pays 25¢ a line.

GREEN RIVER REVIEW, P.O. Box 812, Owensboro KY 42301. Editors: Raymond Tyner and Emil Ahnell. For "poets, writers, persons interested in literature, libraries, university English departments." Semiannual. Circulation: 500. Acquires all rights. Uses 8 to 10 short stories and 60 poems a year. Pays in contributor's copies. Will send a sample copy to a writer for $1.50. Submit seasonal material 4 months in advance. Reports in 2 months. Enclose S.A.S.E.
Nonfiction: Humor, historical, think pieces. Length: 3,000 to 4,000 words.
Fiction: Mystery, science fiction, humorous, historical, adventure, confession, contemporary problems, religious, juvenile. Length: 3,000 to 4,000 words.
Poetry: All kinds, including traditional, contemporary, avant-garde, light verse.

HAIKU, 61 Macdonell, Toronto Ont., Canada. Editor: E. W. Amann. For "poets and poetry readers of any age." Established in 1967. Quarterly. Circulation: 1,000. Buys all rights, but will reassign them to author after publication. Buys about 500 mss a year. Payment on acceptance "for photos and exceptional material. Payment in contributor's copies for all others." Will send a sample copy to a writer for $1. Submit complete ms. Will consider photocopied submissions. Reports in 2 to 3 weeks. Enclose S.A.E. and International Reply Coupons for return of submissions.

Nonfiction, Poetry and Photos: "Haiku and other short poetry, prose poems, and articles related to life and poetry." Seeking a "wide variety of style and outlook." Accepts free verse, avant-garde forms, and haiku. Length: 5 to 8 lines. Payment from contributor's copies to $10 to $15 per poem. Photos purchased without mss, with or without captions. B&w photos must have "good contrast" and deal with nature, man in nature, or art photos. Pays $10 to $15 for "a good photo."

How To Break In: "We are willing to pay for exceptional photography and short-form poems with impact. This is open to anyone, newcomer or otherwise. Probably the best way of judging what our editorial preferences are is to get a sample copy of our magazine and study it carefully for the type of material we publish."

HANGING LOOSE, 231 Wyckoff St., Brooklyn NY 11217. Editors: Dick Lourie, Emmett Jarrett, Ron Schreiber, Robert Hershon, Miguel Ortiz. Quarterly. Payment in copies. Will send a sample copy to a writer for $1. Reports in 1 to 2 months. Enclose S.A.S.E. for return of submissions.

Fiction: "Good fiction." Length: "up to 12 pages."

Poetry: "Any length."

HARVARD ADVOCATE, 21 South St., Cambridge MA 02138. Editor: Rodman Paul. For "the Harvard community—an intellectual audience." Established in 1866. Quarterly. Circulation: 6,000. Rights acquired vary with author and material; may acquire all rights (but will reassign rights to author after publication) or first North American serial rights. Pays in contributor's copies. Will send a sample copy to a writer on request. Will consider photocopied submissions. Query first for nonfiction; query first or submit complete ms for reviews or essays; submit complete ms for poetry and fiction. Reports on material accepted for publication in 2 months. Returns rejected material in 3 to 4 weeks. Enclose S.A.S.E.

Nonfiction: "Book reviews, literary essays, 'new journalism,' film/art/music reviews or essays, interviews. The writer should use his own approach in writing for us. No term papers. Our publication is the oldest and, we think, the best undergraduate college magazine in the country." Uses interviews, profiles, and reviews. Length: 500 to 5,000 words. Photos used with or without mss; captions optional. "Any subject is considered." Uses 8x10 b&w or color prints. Photo Editor: Brian Bohn.

Fiction: Experimental, mainstream, adventure, erotica, fantasy, humorous, romance. Length: 500 to 6,000 words. Dept. Editor: Annette Sanderson.

Poetry: Traditional forms, blank verse, free verse, avant-garde forms, light verse. Length: open. Dept. Editor: Mark Leib.

HEIRS MAGAZINE, 657 Mission St., San Francisco CA 94105. Editors: Alfred Garcia, Robert Spence, Thomas Walsh. Published irregularly. Established in 1968. Circulation: 1,000. Uses 60 to 100 mss a year. Payment in contributor's copies. Buys all rights. Will send sample copy to writer for $1, plus postage. Write for copy of guidelines for writers. Query first. Will consider photocopied submissions. Reports on material in 6 to 10 weeks. Enclose S.A.S.E. for reply to queries.

Nonfiction and Photos: "Articles about writers and artists, their life and influence, as well as their craft, desired. Material on the theater, cinema, dance, music; both in the United States and other parts of the world—the new directions they are taking, etc. State of art and literature (cultural growth) in Africa, Asia and Latin America. Reviews of art, films, books, plays. Articles on styles, movements and interpretations of the arts and cultures of people. Quality and originality essential. Submissions should have background or biographical notes about the writer. We accept art photos with or without mss. Need information about the photographer as well as the subject." Length: open. Dept. Editors: Jerry Harris, Robert Spence.

Fiction: Experimental, mainstream, science fiction, fantasy, parts of novels. "Translations wanted of folklore and mythology not published in English before. We print mss in any language, translated or untranslated." Length: open. Dept. Editor: John Lozynsky.

Poetry: Traditional forms, blank verse, free verse, translations, avant-garde forms, light verse. Dept. Editor: Thomas R. Walsh.

HOOSIER CHALLENGER MAGAZINE, 8365 Wicklow Ave., Cincinnati OH 45236. Editor: Claire Emerson. For pro, amateur, and beginner. Quarterly. No payment, but competition for prizes and awards. Enclose S.A.S.E. for response to queries and return of submissions.
Nonfiction and Photos: Wants intelligent, interesting, unusual articles. "Interested in factual sightings of flying saucers." The "Journey Into the Unknown" department publishes items "dealing with true spiritual experiences." Length: 350 words maximum. B&w photos may accompany mss.
Fiction: "Deliver us from 'over-sex' and profanity in fiction!" Uses short-shorts; any type, but must be in good taste, original, creative. Length: up to 1,000 words.
Poetry: Publishes poetry; open to any "types" including satirical verse. Length: 16 lines or less; very few longer ones considered.
Fillers: Epigrams.

THE HUDSON REVIEW, 65 E. 55th St., New York NY 10022. Managing Editor: Irene Skolnick. Quarterly. Buys first North American serial rights. Pays on publication. Reports in 6 to 8 weeks. Enclose S.A.S.E. for return of submissions.
Nonfiction, Fiction, and Poetry: Uses "quality fiction up to 10,000 words, articles up to 8,000 words; translations, reviews and poetry." Pays 2½¢ a word for prose and half rate for translations, and 75¢ to $1 a line for poetry.

THE HUMANIST, 923 Kensington Ave., Buffalo NY 14215. Editor: Paul Kurtz. Bimonthly. Published for the American Humanist Association and the American Ethical Union. "Address mss to Professor Paul Kurtz, Editor, *The Humanist*, State University of New York at Buffalo, 4244 Ridge Lea Rd., Amherst NY 14226. Articles published are usually by invitation. Unsolicited mss are, however, carefully considered. All mss should be accompanied by 3 additional copies. A contribution not accepted will not be returned unless S.A.S.E. is enclosed."
Nonfiction: "*The Humanist* attempts to serve as a bridge between theoretical philosophical discussions and the practical applications of humanism to ethical and social problems. Ethical humanism sees man as a product of this world—of evolution and human history and acknowledges no supernatural purposes. Humanism accepts ethical responsibility for human life, emphasizing human interdependence."

INFINITY REVIEW, P.O. Box 412, South Point OH 45680. Editor: James R. Pack. For "highly literate individuals either directly or indirectly involved in creative writing, including the collegiate." Established in 1969. Quarterly. Circulation: 500. Acquires all rights, but will reassign rights to author after publication. Uses approximately 75 mss a year. Payment in contributor's copies and occasional special awards. "If our editorial staff judges a specific work to be of extraordinary superiority, $10 will be given as a prize; a simple gift for excellence." Will send sample copy to writer on request. Write for copy of guidelines for writers. Submit complete ms. Will consider photocopied submissions. Reports on material accepted for publication within 4 weeks. Returns rejected material immediately. Enclose S.A.S.E. for return of submissions.
Nonfiction: Publishes material that "reflects a romantic attitude toward existence; that is, a response to nature, a celebration of the spirit, a belief in integrity, volition and personal values." Approach should be one of "objectivity and sensitivity to the real condition of man." Interested in "examples of extraordinary human ability and antideterminism; criticism which postulates the necessity of romanticism for human survival." Literary reviews. Length: open. Dept. Editor: Robert Wylie Plymale.
Fiction: Traditional, mainstream, mystery, suspense, adventure, erotica, science fiction, fantasy, humorous, historical; sketches; serialized novels. Length: open. Dept. Editor: James R. Pack.
Poetry: Traditional forms, blank verse, free verse, avant-garde forms, experimental. Length: open. Dept. Editor: Ronald Edmond Houchin.

INTER-AMERICAN REVIEW OF BIBLIOGRAPHY, Organization of American States, Washington DC 20006. Editor: Armando Correia Pacheco. For specialists and institutions interested in the culture and bibliography related to the Americas. Quarterly. Pays on acceptance. Query first. Enclose S.A.S.E.
Nonfiction: Articles, review articles, book reviews, current bibliography in 21 sub-

ject fields, notes and news related to the Americas with particular emphasis on the humanities. Pays $50 to $75.

INTERCHANGE, 38 E. 76 St., New York NY 10021. Editor: Marshall Hayes. For "intellectuals, mostly centered in the universities in the U.S., Canada and Britain. A scholarly review of books." Established in 1972. Quarterly. Circulation: 5,000. Acquires all rights. Payment in contributor's copies. Query first. Will consider photocopied submissions. Reports on material accepted in 4 weeks. Returns rejected material in 4 weeks. Enclose S.A.S.E. for reply to queries.
Nonfiction: "Essay reviews and brief reviews. Also studies of individual writers. Provides a forum where intellectuals in all fields can come together to discuss books in a civilized prose free of the jargon of any one discipline." Length: 2,500 to 6,000 words for essay reviews; 1,000 to 2,400 words for brief reviews.

THE INTERCOLLEGIATE REVIEW, 14 S. Bryn Mawr Ave., Bryn Mawr PA 19010. Editor: Robert A. Schadler. For "undergraduates, graduate students and professors. Interested generally in traditional scholarship examining the social and normative presuppositions of a free society." Established in 1965. Quarterly. Circulation: 40,000. Buys all rights. Buys 15 mss a year. Payment on publication. Will send free sample copy to writer on request. Query first. Reports on material in 2 months. Enclose S.A.S.E. for reply to queries.
Nonfiction: "Essays and articles in the social sciences and humanities, ranging from literary criticism to economics, philosophy to international relations, history, etc. Mss should be typewritten and follow a generally accepted format. Emphasis is on original, thought-provoking scholarship in support of traditional norms, free market economics and western culture. Articles should not be technical or over-specialized." Think articles. Academic reviews. Length: 2,000 to 6,000 words. Pays $50 to $200.

JANUS, 314 Bayview Ave., Seaside Park NJ 08752. Editor: Pat Jasin. For "new playwrights, producers, fans of theatre, students, scholars, theatre groups, agents." Semiannual. Circulation: 3,000. Acquires first rights. Buys 8 to 10 plays a year. Pays in contributor's copies. Will send sample copy to writer for $1.50. Reports in 6 to 10 weeks. Enclose S.A.S.E. for return of submissions.
Nonfiction and Photos: "Articles should deal with new theatre ideas . . . what is happening in reference to playwrights especially. Look for profiles on notable theatre people. If writing an article, writer should gear toward the new playwright. New markets, agent requirements, etc." Publishes personal experience, interviews, profiles, spot news, and expose. Length: 500 to 5,000 words. Payment in 2 to 25 copies. B&w glossies purchased with mss. "Prefer any photos with plays that have been produced." Pays in 2 to 10 copies.
Drama: "Must first consider plays by International New Playwrights Association members, but we do consider plays we receive from nonmembers. No stipulation on subject matter, etc. Look for playwright aiming for professional stage quality." Length: "prefer one-acts running about 5 to 47 pages, but will consider good full-lengths."

JEOPARDY, Viking Union, Western Washington State College, Bellingham WA 98225. Editor changes annually. Primarily for students of Western Washington State College; "however, subscriptions nationally as well as Canada and England (libraries, individuals, established writers)." Annually. Circulation: 2,000 to 4,000. Acquires all rights but will reassign rights to author after publication. Uses 20 to 200 mss a year. Payment in contributor's copies. Will send sample copy to writer for $1 "as copies last." Query. Will consider photocopied submissions. Reports on material annually in January or February. Enclose S.A.S.E. for reply to queries.
Nonfiction and Photos: "General subject and theme vary annually. Any qualtiy writing with aesthetic motives superseding commercial interests." Personal experience, interview, profile, think pieces. Length: 1,000 words. Queries advised on photo assignments. Captions optional. Payment in copies.
Fiction: Experimental, mainstream, fantasy. Length: 1,000 to 3,000 words.
Poetry: Traditional forms, blank verse, free verse, avant-garde forms. Themes vary. Length: open.

JESTURE MAGAZINE, Box 85, Thomas More College, Covington KY 41017. Editor: Darryl R. Price. For a serious "library audience." Established in 1965. 3 times a year. Circulation: 1,000. Buys all rights but rights revert to author upon request. Payment in contributor's copies. Will send free sample copy to writer on request. Write for copy of guidelines for writers. Query first for nonfiction; submit complete ms for fiction and poetry. Reports on material accepted for publication in 4 weeks. Returns rejected material as soon as possible. Enclose S.A.S.E.
Fiction, Nonfiction and Poetry: Short prose, experimental fiction; traditional and avant-garde forms of poetry, blank verse and free verse. Payment in copies.

JOHNSONIAN NEWS LETTER, 610 Philosophy Hall, Columbia University, New York NY 10027. Co-editors: James L. Clifford and John H. Middendorf. For scholars, book collectors and all those interested in 18th century English literature. 4 times a year. No payment. Reports immediately. Enclose S.A.S.E. for return of submissions.
Nonfiction: Interested in news items, queries, short comments, etc., having to do with 18th century English literature. Must be written in simple style. Length: maximum 500 words.
Poetry: Sometimes uses poetry which imitates that of the 18th century.

THE JOURNAL OF AESTHETICS AND ART CRITICISM, Temple University, Philadelphia PA 19122. Editor: John Fisher. Published by the American Society for Aesthetics. Quarterly. No payment. Enclose S.A.S.E. for return of submissions.
Nonfiction: Uses articles and book reviews on theories of the arts, including the visual arts, music, literature, and the theater, from a philosophic, scientific or historical standpoint.

JOURNAL OF MODERN LITERATURE, Temple University, Philadelphia PA 19122. Editor: Maurice Beebe. General subject matter: literary history of the past hundred years—American, British, and world literature in translation. 5 times a year. Buys all rights. Pays on publication. Will send a free sample copy on request. Enclose S.A.S.E. for return of submissions.
Nonfiction and Photos: Scholarly articles clearly based on research in social or biographical background, ms revisions, or textual analysis. Except in special numbers, the editors try to avoid top-of-the-head "readings" of individual works of literature. Length: "varies, from notes to full-length monographs." Pays about $100 for full-length articles. Photos purchased with mss.

JOURNAL OF POPULAR CULTURE, University Hall, Bowling Green University, Bowling Green OH 43403. Editor: Ray B. Browne. For academic, media, advertising, general readership. Established in 1967. Quarterly. Circulation: 2,000. Acquires all rights but will reassign rights to author after publication. Uses 100 mss a year. Will send free sample copy to writer on request. Query first or submit complete ms. WIll consider photocopied submissions. Reports on material in a few weeks. Enclose S.A.S.E. for reply to query or return of submissions.
Nonfiction and Photos: "Critical essays on media, books, poetry, advertising, etc." Informational, interview, historical, think pieces, nostalgia, reviews of books, movies, television. Length: 5,000 words maximum. Payment in contributor's copies (25 reprints). Uses b&w glossies.
Poetry: Avant-garde forms, light verse, popular culture subjects. Length: 100 lines.

JOURNAL OF THE FOLKLORE INSTITUTE, 504 N. Fess St., Indiana University, Bloomington IN 47401. General Editor: Richard M. Dorson. For professional (museum and university) folklorists, anthropologists, ethnologists. Acquires all rights. Pays in 25 reprints. Query first. Reports in 6 to 10 weeks. Enclose S.A.S.E. for reply to queries.
Nonfiction: Oral traditions such as legends, ballads, tales, etc. Collections of these are not published without commentary. Articles usually have a strong theoretical basis. Most accepted articles are written by professional scholars. Length: 3,000 to 8,000 words.

JOURNAL 31, P.O. Box 2109, San Francisco CA 94126. Editor: David Plumb. For "those who are interested in contemporary trends within the context of literature, art, social political thought, psychology, and drama of any age group." Established in 1972. Quarterly. Circulation: 500. Rights remain with author. Buys 100 to 200 mss a year "depending on volume of good material." Payment in contributor's copies. Will send sample copy to writer for $1. Query first for nonfiction only. Reports in "4 weeks or sooner." Enclose S.A.S.E. for reply to queries or return of submissions.

Nonfiction and Fiction: "Present trends in art: experimental or kitsch. The impact of, D.H. Lawrence in modern psychology. Contemporary South American literature. Tightly written articles and stories with feeling. Order within chaos; good hook and the equipment to make a good story; the ability to carry a metaphor; smooth flowing cadence. We endeavor to present a good cross-section of modern work within a format that does not overwhelm the reader. Trend is toward appreciation as opposed to patronization." Uses profiles. Length: 3,000 to 10,000 words. Uses science fiction, humorous, and contemporary problem material. Length: 2,500 to 3,000 words.

Photos: B&w glossies with captions only.

Fillers: "Short, fictional pieces with contemporary punch." Length: 50 to 150 words.

JUDAICA BIBLIOGRAPHY AND NEWS, 135 W. 26 St., New York NY 10001. Editor: Paul Stone. For students, adults, professionals, laymen, Jewish, non-Jewish, teachers, housewives, clubmen and women; community leaders. Established in 1970. Bimonthly. Circulation: 25,000. Will send free sample copy to writer on request. (Enclose self-addressed envelope and 16¢ postage.) Enclose S.A.S.E. for return of submissions.

Nonfiction: "Link between book publishers and the consumers of books. Dedicated to the tradition of interpreting, enlightening and teaching the history, culture and heritage of the Jewish people through books." Length: 500 words maximum. Pays $10 to $25.

JUNCTION, Room 237-C, La Guardia Hall, Brooklyn College, Brooklyn NY 11210. Editor: William Sanders. For graduate English students and faculty. Established in 1972. Semi-annually. Circulation: 1,000. Buys all rights but will reassign rights to author after publication. Payment in contributor's copies. If available, will send free sample copy to writer on request. Query. Will consider photocopied submissions. Reports on material in 1 month. Enclose S.A.S.E. for return of submission.

Nonfiction: Literary criticism, especially English and American. Interview, profile, book reviews. Length: 3,000 words maximum. Dept. Editor: Howard Portnoy.

Fiction: Experimental, mainstream. Length: open. Dept. Editor: Marshall Scott Grossman.

Poetry: Traditional forms, free verse, avant-garde. Length: open. Dept. Editor: Matthew Robert Sanders.

Fillers: Satire, parody. Length: open. Dept. Editor: Veronica Kelly.

KANSAS QUARTERLY, Dept. of English, Kansas State University, Manhattan KS 66502. Editors: Harold W. Schneider and Ben Nyberg. For "adults, mostly academics, and people interested in literature, midwestern history, and art." Established in 1968. Quarterly. Circulation: 1,100. Acquires all rights, but will reassign them to author after publication. Pays in contributor's copies. Will send a sample copy to a writer for $2. Query first for nonfiction. "Follow *MLA Style Sheet* and write for a sophisticated audience." Reports in about 2 to 3 months. Enclose S.A.S.E. for return of submissions or reply to queries.

Nonfiction, Photos, Fiction, and Poetry: Accepts poetry, short stories; art, history and literary criticism on special topics. "We emphasize the history, culture, and life style of the Mid-Plains region. We do not want children's literature, 'slick' material, or special interest material not in keeping with our special numbers." Accepts historical articles on "special topics only." Photos should have captions; 4x6 b&w preferred. Accepts experimental and mainstream fiction. Length: 250 to 10,000 words. Accepts traditional and avant-garde forms of poetry, blank verse, and free verse. Poetry themes open.

KARAMU, English Department, Eastern Illinois University, Charleston IL 61920. Editor: Allen Neff. For literate, university-educated audience. Established in 1967.

Annually. Circulation: 300. Acquires first North American serial rights. Uses 25 mss a year. Payment in 2 contributor's copies. Will send sample copy to writer for $1. Submit complete ms. Reports on material in 5 months. Enclose S.A.S.E. for return of submissions.

Nonfiction: Articles on contemporary literature. Length: open.

Fiction: Experimental, mainstream. Length: 2,000 to 8,000 words. Dept. Editor: Gordon Jackson.

Poetry: Traditional forms, free verse, avant-garde. "Quality with visual perception or with fresh language." Length: 3 to 80 lines, "but we do publish longer poems." Dept. Editor: Ms. Carol Elder.

THE LAKE SUPERIOR REVIEW, Box 724, Ironwood MI 49938. Editor: Cynthia Willoughby. For all those who appreciate good literature and art. Triannual. Circulation: 1,000. Acquires first North American serial rights. Pays in contributor's copies. Will send a sample copy to a writer for $1. Reports in 4 weeks. Enclose S.A.S.E. for return of submissions.

Nonfiction: "Occasionally we use short, pointed articles dealing with contemporary controversial issues." Length: "open, but prefer prose under 2,500 words."

Fiction: "Subject matter open. We like naturalistic themes and style." Length: "seldom use anything over 3,000 words."

Poetry: "We use any good poetry but prefer short, experimental poems. We appreciate rich, unique use of language."

LEGEND, 39213 Gloucester, Westland MI 48185. Editor: Bonnie E. Parker. For teenagers to senior citizens. Poetry, traditional and contemporary, rhymed and unrhymed, book reviews, essays and critiques of poetry. Established in 1972. Quarterly. Acquires all rights, but will reassign rights to author after publication. Payment in contributor's copies. Will send sample copy to a writer for $1. Write for copy of guidelines for writers. Submit complete ms. Will consider photocopied submissions "if print is clear." Name and address must appear on every page of ms. Submit material 4 months in advance of issue date (January, April, July and October). Reports on material accepted for publication on receipt. Returns rejected material in 1 to 3 weeks. Enclose S.A.S.E. for return of submissions.

Nonfiction: "We would like to see any topical subject, if it is well-written and well thought out, able to present the theme to an extremely varied group of readers. All we ask is that the writer-poet have something to say and an excitement to communicate to our readers, among whom are many of today's best writers." Informational, how-to, personal experience, think, spot news, book reviews, short essays, personal reactions to poetry. Length: open. Payment: 1 copy. Prizes up to $15.

Poetry: Traditional forms, blank verse, free verse, avant-garde and honest, hard-hitting poetry. Length: open. Payment: 1 contributor's copy. Prizes up to $15.

LETTERS, Box 175, Princeton, NJ 08540. Publisher: G.F. Bush. For "general interest readers." Established in 1972. Buys all rights. Buys at least 15 mss a year. Pays on acceptance. Will send a sample copy to a writer on request. Query first or submit complete ms. Will consider photocopied submissions. Submit seasonal material 5 months in advance of issue date. Reports in 1 month. Enclose S.A.S.E. for return of submissions or reply to queries.

Nonfiction and Photos: Letters on "any subject within moral standards. Quality writing of any style, whether classic or avant-garde; no pornography. Our subject matter is unique in format, old in demand." Length: 100 to 500 words. Pays 1¢ to 10¢ a word. Dept. Editor: Helma Nash. Photos purchased with mss; captions required. Uses minimum 5x8 b&w glossies or "good quality" color. Payment "negotiated."

Poetry: "All forms. No length limit."

LIFEFORCE (formerly *Harrison Midmonthly Review*), 213 Indian Lane, Media PA 19063. Editors: Gordon and Steve Harrison. Published monthly by the Pacific Life Centre. Established in 1972. Will send sample copy to writer for 25¢. Enclose S.A.S.E. for return of submissions.

Nonfiction: "We are especially interested in material relevant to the people of this world, who are saying yes to life through their lives and actions. Material on any form of repression in any part of the world is sought. Articles on emerging life styles, alternate communications, radical education, hobos, artists, revolutionaries, and visionaries are always needed. Interviews with men and women and children and sages who are struggling in the manner of Dan Berrigan. Joan Baez and Bill Clark would be very desirable. We're not rich; payment varies."

Fiction and Poetry: "Of the continuing struggle to further life in all of its forms in this universe."

THE LITERARY REVIEW, Fairleigh Dickinson University, Rutherford NJ 07070. Editor: Charles Angoff. Quarterly. Pays in copies. Reports in about 3 months. Enclose S.A.S.E. for return of submissions.

Nonfiction, Fiction, and Poetry: Contemporary writing in the field of belles lettres both in the U.S. and abroad. Seeks to encourage literary excellence, and is hospitable both to established writers and young writers of promise. Stresses creative rather than critical writing. No length restrictions.

LITERARY SKETCHES, P.O. Box 711, 707 Monumental St., Williamsburg VA 23185. Editor: Mary Lewis B. Chapman. For discriminating, literary-minded readers. Monthly. Buys first North American rights. Pays on acceptance. Reports in one month. Enclose S.A.S.E. for return of submissions.

Nonfiction: Uses biographical details of writers, unusual, little-known facts on writers' lives and/or works. Style should be easy, chatty—not high flown or verbose. Wants length to be no more than 750 words on average-interest article—1,000 at most on articles of great interest. Human stories should be "calculated to interest readers in picking up more of the writer's works—the sort of article that makes you feel—'I want to find out more about whomever the article discusses.' We are also interested in interviews of current authors. A feature entitled Clips and Quotes uses already published short pieces, quotes from diaries, journals, biographies, showing some feature of a writer's life and thought." Pays ½¢ per word.

THE LITTLE MAGAZINE, P.O. Box 207, Cathedral Sta., New York NY 10025. Editor: David G. Hartwell. Quarterly. Circulation: 1,500. Payment of two contributor's copies. Acquires all rights, but will reassign rights to author upon request. Will send a sample copy to a writer for $1. Query first for reviews. Submissions should be typed (no carbons, but clear photocopies acceptable). More than one poem or story may be submitted, "but not a boxful, please." Reports in 1 to 8 weeks. Enclose S.A.S.E. for return of submissions or reply to queries.

Nonfiction: Interviews; offbeat and iconoclastic articles on literary subjects and personalities; reviews of magazines and small presses. Length: 2,000 to 4,000 words for articles; 1,000 words for reviews.

Fiction: Stories of any type. Especially interested in comic and new approaches. Length: maximum 6,000 words.

Poetry: All types except light verse. No length limitations.

THE LITTLE REVIEW, P.O. Box 2321, Huntington WV 25724. Editor: John McKernan. Biannual. Circulation: 1,000. No payment. Will send a sample copy to a writer for $1.25. Reports in 1 month. Enclose S.A.S.E. for return of submissions.

Fiction and Poetry: Uses "creative fiction and poetry."

LONG ISLAND REVIEW, Box 10, Cambria Heights NY 11411. Editors: Stephen Sossaman and Edward Faranda. For those "interested in contemporary literature and criticism." Established in 1973. Published 3 times a year. Circulation: 300. Acquires first rights and second serial (reprint rights). Uses 60 mss a year. Payment in contributor's copies. Will send sample copy to writer for $1. Submit complete ms. Will consider photocopied submissions. Reports on material within 3 weeks. Enclose S.A.S.E. for return of submissions.

Nonfiction: Criticism, literary reviews. "Anything well-crafted and intelligent." Length: open.

Fiction: Experimental, mainstream. Length: under 2,500 words.

Poetry: Traditional forms, blank verse, free verse, avant-garde for ms. "Avoid mawkish sentiment." Length: open.

MACABRE, 26 Fowler St., New Haven CT 06515. Editor: Joseph Payne Brennan. For "a limited audience interested in macabre fantasy." Established in 1957. Irregular frequency. Circulation: 500. Acquires all rights. Uses 20 to 30 mss a year. Payment in copies. Will send a sample copy to a writer for 75¢. Submit only complete ms. Will not consider photocopied submissions. Reports in 2 to 3 weeks. Enclose S.A.S.E. for return of submissions.
Nonfiction and Fiction: "We use only fiction and articles in the horror/supernatural field. "Weird, eerie, supernatural material. Strong emphasis on mood and atmosphere. Short-shorts about various aspects of the supernatural. We use no science fiction or general crime material." Uses personal experience articles and suspense and fantasy fiction. Length: 500 to 1,500 words.
Poetry: Traditional forms, blank verse, free verse; related to subject matter. No light verse. Length: 20 lines maximum.

THE MALAHAT REVIEW, University of Victoria, P.O. Box 1700, Victoria, B.C., Canada. Editor: Robin Skelton. For "scholars, writers, poets, artists, university students and teachers, and anyone interested in modern writing, criticism, and art." Established in 1967. Quarterly. Circulation: 800. Buys first publication rights. Buys about 70 mss a year. Pays on acceptance. Will send sample copy for $1.50. Submit complete ms. Will consider photocopied submissions. For articles and stories, include number of words. Put name on every page. Reports within six weeks. Enclose S.A.E. and International Reply Coupons for return of submissions.
Nonfiction: Articles, book reviews never previously published in English. Emphasizes previously unpublished translations. Length: 6,000 words. Pays $10 minimum.
Photos: "Usually commissioned."
Fiction: Stories never previously published in English. Length: under 2,000 words for vignettes; 3,300 words for stories. Pays $10 minimum.
Poetry: "Modern poetry, previously unpublished translations of poetry." Buys blank verse, free verse, traditional forms, light verse, avant-garde forms, and all other kinds of poetry. Pays $10 minimum.

MARGINS, 2912 N. Hackett, Milwaukee WI 53211. Editors: Tom Montag and Dave Buege. For librarians, bookstore operators and the general reading public who are interested in little magazines and small press books." Established in 1972. Bimonthly. Circulation: 700. Acquires first North American serial rights. Payment in contributor's copies. Will send sample copy to writer for 60 cents. Query first. Reports on queries in 2 weeks. Enclose S.A.S.E. for answer to queries.
Nonfiction: "We publish reviews of little magazines and small press books, essays on poets being published in the small press, articles on events and processes relevant to little magazines and small press books. Writer should be fully informed about little magazines and small presses in this country; pieces should be concise, insightful and to the point. We are not interested in the usual literary article, do not want to see essays on poets who are popular or poets who have books out solely from commercial presses. We do not want to see poetry or fiction." Interviews with small press poets, editors and publishers. Length: open. Short reviews (100 to 200 words) of little magazines or small press books for "In the Margins."

MARK TWAIN JOURNAL, Kirkwood MO 63122. Editor: Cyril Clemens. For those interested in American and English literature. Semiannual. Pays on acceptance. "Queries welcome." Reports in 2 weeks. Enclose S.A.S.E. for reply to queries.
Nonfiction and Poetry: Critical and biographical articles dealing with Mark Twain and other American, English, and foreign authors. Payment "by arrangement." Uses some poetry.

THE MASSACHUSETTS REVIEW, Memorial Hall, University of Massachusetts, Amherst MA 01002. Editors: Jules Chametsky, Robert Tucker. Quarterly. Buys first North American rights. Pays on publication. Reports promptly. Enclose S.A.S.E. for return of submissions.
Nonfiction: Articles on literary criticism, public affairs, art, philosophy, music, dance. Average length: 6,500 words. Pays $50.
Fiction: Short stories or chapters from novels when suitable for independent publication. Pays $50.

MERLIN'S MAGIC, 318 81st St., Brooklyn NY 11209. Editor: Merlin F. Teed. Bimonthly. Publication on mimeographed sheets; not copyrighted. Payment in contributor's copy. Reports in 10 days to 2 weeks. Enclose S.A.S.E. for return of submissions.
Nonfiction: Articles on pertinent subjects of the day, editorials on writing, book reviews.
Fiction: Short-shorts.
Poetry: Prefers 20 lines or less, but will consider longer poems.

MICHIGAN QUARTERLY REVIEW, 3032 Rackham Bldg., University of Michigan, Ann Arbor MI 48104. Editor: Radcliffe Squires. Quarterly. Circulation: 2,000. Buys all rights. Payment on acceptance. Reports in 2 weeks. Enclose S.A.S.E. for return of submissions.
Nonfiction: "The magazine will have a much more definitely literary bias under my editorship. But we are still open to general articles. We especially welcome serious literary criticism." Length: 2,000 to 5,000 words. Payment is 2¢ a word (occasionally $200 to $300).
Fiction: "No restrictions on subject matter or language. Experimental fiction welcomed." Length: 2,000 to 5,000 words. Payment is 2¢ a word (occasionally $200 to $300).
Poetry: "No restrictions." Payment is 50¢ to $1 a line.

THE MIDWEST QUARTERLY, Kansas State College, Pittsburg KS 66762. Editor: Rebecca Patterson. For academic audience, including professors, graduate students, and librarians. Publishes Special Summer Literary issue. Quarterly. Circulation: 1,000. Acquires all rights. Uses 24 articles and 48 poems a year. Pays in contributor's copies. Will send a free sample copy to a writer on request. No query required. Submit material for special summer issue at least 6 months in advance. Reports in 3 months. Enclose S.A.S.E. for return of submissions.
Nonfiction: "Scholarly but unspecialized articles on contemporary thought in political science, history, sociology, literature, and the like. We avoid extreme specialization or heavy documentation and lean toward the readable and thought-provoking." Use MLA style, but without footnotes. Length: 2,000 to 5,000 words.
Poetry: Contemporary, "rarely more than 50 lines." Dept. Editor: Michael Heffernan.

MISSISSIPPI QUARTERLY, The Journal of Southern Culture, Mississippi State University, Mississippi State MS 39762. (Editorial Box 5272; Business Box 23.) Editor: Peyton W. Williams, Jr. For scholars, students, laymen. Quarterly. Circulation: 700. Buys no rights. Fees from sale of any reprint rights shared with authors. Will send free sample copy to writer on request. Follow *MLA Style Sheet.* Inquire about special theme issues. Summer issues devoted to William Faulkner. Reports in 6 weeks to 3 months. Enclose S.A.S.E. for return of submissions.
Nonfiction: Documented articles concerning the humanities and social sciences, with Southern American subjects only; book reviews on Southern subjects; notes, queries, documents (including letters), bibliography. Length: 4,000 words preferred.

MISSISSIPPI REVIEW, Southern Station, Box 37, Hattiesburg MS 39401. Editor: Gordon Weaver. For the "college educated" and "libraries." Established in 1972. Triannual. Circulation: 350 to 500. Acquires all rights, but will reassign them to author after publication. Payment on publication. Will send a sample copy to a writer for $1.75. "No queries necessary." Will consider photocopied submissions. Reports on rejected material in 1 to 2 weeks. Reports on accepted material in 1 to 2 months. Enclose S.A.S.E. for return of submissions.
Fiction: "We try to emulate the best in the field." Accepts experimental, mainstream, fantasy, and humorous fiction. Pays $3 per printed page. Length: 500 to 5,000 words.
Poetry: Open to traditional forms, blank verse, free verse, and avant-garde forms. Unrestricted to themes. Pays $5. Length: 2 to 500 lines.

MIXER: FIRELANDS FINE ARTS REVIEW, Firelands Campus, Huron OH 44839. Editor: Joel D. Rudinger. For a general educated audience. Established in

1972. Annually (March 1 is issue deadline). Circulation: 1,000. Acquires all rights, but will reassign rights to author after publication upon request. Uses about 50 mss a year. Payment in copies and cash awards. Will send a sample copy for $1.25. Submit complete mss. Will consider photocopied submissions. Reports in 4 to 6 weeks. Enclose S.A.S.E. for return of submissions and reply to correspondence.

Nonfiction: Essays for a general adult audience in nontechnical language on the media, pop culture, folklore, the fine arts; serious or satiric. Length: 3,000 words maximum.

Fiction: Traditional and experimental short stories of quality. Length: 4,000 words maximum. Will also accept short prose sketches with insight and sensitivity to the human condition. Special interest in science fiction, the supernatural, character pieces, humor, sophisticated satire.

Poetry: Strong in imagery and sound awareness. Prefer the concrete to the abstract. Will consider quality, nonsentimental poem sequences; also prose poems. Theme and length: open. Poet's comments on his own submissions also of interest and may be used with accepted submissions.

Photos: B&w's. Still life, portrait, abstract, traditional or experimental. Fresh and new insight into subject a must.

MODERN FICTION STUDIES, Dept. of English, Purdue University, Lafayette IN 47907. Editors: William T. Stafford, Margaret Church. Aimed at academic readers. Quarterly. No payment. Reports in 2 to 4 months. Enclose S.A.S.E. for return of submissions.

Nonfiction: Interested in critical or scholarly articles on American, British, and Continental fiction since 1880. Length: notes, 500 to 2,500 words; articles, 3,000 to 7,000 words.

THE MONARCHIST, 2 Wedgewood Crescent, Ottawa, Ontario, Canada K1B 4B4. Editor: J. Lee Potter. Official Publication of the Monarchist League of Canada. "The League is organized to defend the constitutional monarchy and the parliamentary system of government in Canada." Quarterly. Circulation: 5,000. Not copyrighted. Pays in contributor's copies. Will send a free sample copy to a writer on request. Reports in 2 weeks. Enclose S.A.E. and International Reply Coupons for return of submissions.

Nonfiction: "General and specific articles on monarchy in all its forms but with special reference to the monarchy in Canada and its historical development and relation to the people of Canada. A positive approach to the institution of monarchy is essential. Its relationship to constitutional parliamentary government should be emphasized. No articles on republicanism. A realistic, well-researched approach to the modern relevance of monarchy is better than syrupy sentimentalism." Wants personal experience, interviews, profiles, inspirational, historical, and think pieces along the lines of the above. Length: 500 to 1,000 words.

Poetry: Traditional and contemporary. Length: 10 to 25 lines.

Fillers: Wants newsbreaks and clippings that are "short, meaty items."

MONUMENT IN CANTOS AND ESSAYS, Route 10, Columbia MO 65201. Editor: Victor Myers. For "readers of contemporary poetry." Established in 1968. Published annually. Circulation: 300. Acquires first serial rights. Payment in 2 contributor's copies. $25 prize awarded annually from works accepted for publication. Will send sample copy to writer for 12 cents. Submit complete ms. Will not consider photocopied submissions. Reports on mss accepted for publication in 3 months. Returns rejected material immediately, "with comments." Enclose S.A.S.E. for return of submissions.

Nonfiction and Photos: "Work of literary excellence; subjects unlimited. Prefer nature, the human experience, significant human philosophy. "I seek metaphorical, symbolic photography, preferably no larger than 5½x8½ inches."

Fiction: Short stories, novel segments which can stand on their own; experimental, mainstream, erotica (only of very high quality). "No limitation beyond serious craftsmanship, excellence and newness of expression." Length: 5,000 words maximum.

Poetry: Traditional forms ("only of overwhelming excellence"), blank verse, free verse, avant-garde forms. "Interested in the inner experience of man in our times, subtle renderings of images from nature." Length: open.

MYSTERY READER'S NEWSLETTER, P.O. Box 113, Melrose MA 02176. Editor: Mrs. Lianne Carlin. For devotees and collectors of mystery, suspense, and detective fiction. Quarterly. Not copyrighted. Pays on publication. Query first. Reports in 2 weeks. Enclose S.A.S.E. with queries and submissions.
Nonfiction and Photos: Any aspect of the mystery and detective fields, including interviews with authors, scholarly essays about the subject, discussions of fictional sleuths, etc. Length: maximum 1,500 words. Pays ½¢ a word. Photos purchased with mss.
Fillers: Buys puzzles and clippings. Pays $1.

NATTY BUMPO REVIEW, 175 W. Jackson, Suite 414, Chicago IL 60604. Editors: Jeffrey Swanson, Norman Hane. For teachers and educators. Publishes material "pertaining to early American life and literature, especially referring to James Fenimore Cooper, the American Indian (Eastern tribes and Westo Confederacy), and pioneer life as literary subjects. Not interested in works on Western Indians, cowboys, life on the range, etc." Quarterly. Buys all rights for articles; buys second rights for jokes and fillers. Pays on publication. No query needed. Reports in 30 days. Enclose S.A.S.E. for return of submissions.
Nonfiction: "Almost all nonfiction is solicited and specifically on Cooper." Payment: "the maximum would probably be about $25."
Photos: B&w glossies. Payment is $10.
Fiction: Humorous and serious; prefers humorous. Subject matter: American literature, the Indian in American literature, Cooper, etc. Length: maximum 500 words. Pays $5 to $25.
Poetry: "Light verse only on eastern American Indian subjects or Cooper." Length: 20 lines. Payment is $10.
Fillers: "Jokes, items of interest, as indicated above." Length: 150 words. Payment is $10.

THE NEW ENGLAND QUARTERLY, Hubbard Hall, Brunswick ME 04011. Editor: Herbert Brown. For historians and scholars. Established in 1928. Quarterly. Does not pay. Usually reports in 4 weeks. Enclose S.A.S.E. for return of submissions.
Nonfiction: Wants scholarly articles on New England life and letters. Length: "essays should be limited to 25 pages, including documentation."

NEW ORLEANS REVIEW, Loyola University, New Orleans LA 70118. Editor: Forrest Ingram. For "anyone interested in keeping posted culturally." Established in 1968. Quarterly. Circulation: 1,000. Buys all rights, but will reassign them to author after publication. Buys about 100 mss a year. Pays on publication. Will send a sample copy to a writer for $1.50. Write for a copy of guidelines for writers. Will consider photocopied submissions. Enclose S.A.S.E. for return of submissions.
Nonfiction: "Articles on literary, political, scientific subjects and figures. Reviews of books recently published. Be informative without being overly technical." Interested in material on "ecology, new and old politics, literary movements." Length: 5,000 words average. Pays $50 minimum.
Photos: B&w glossies. Payment is $10 minimum.
Fiction: "High-quality fiction, serious or humorous." Pays $50 minimum.
Poetry: "Highest quality poetry." Pays $10 minimum.

THE NEW YORK TIMES BOOK REVIEW, 229 West 43rd St., New York NY 10036. Editor: John Leonard. Weekly.
Nonfiction: "Occasional book reviews and essays. Almost all reviewing is done on an assignment basis."

NORTH AMERICAN MENTOR MAGAZINE, 1730 Lincoln Ave., Fennimore WI 53809. Editor: John Westburg. For "amateur and experimental writers, students, teachers, professors, housewives, members of writers' clubs and societies, farmers, professional men and women, etc." Quarterly. Rights acquired vary with author and material; may acquire all rights. Payment in contributor's copies. Will send a sample copy to a writer for $1. Will consider photocopied submissions. Reports in 6 days to 6 months. Enclose S.A.S.E. for return of submissions.
Nonfiction: "Desire writing to be in reasonably good taste, traditional is preferable

to the vulgar, but emphasis should be on creativity or scholarship. I know of no other of the small magazine genre that is like this one. We make no claim to being avant-garde, but have been accused of being a rear guard periodical, for we try to follow the general traditions of western civilization (whatever that might be). Would be interested in readable articles on anthropology, archeology, American Indians, black or white Africa. Do not want vulgarity or overworked sensationalism. No stuff on riots, protests, drugs, obscenity, or treason. We do not want to discourage a writer's experimental efforts. Let the writer send what he thinks best in his best style." Length: "maximum about 5,000 words."

Photos: "Please make inquiry about photographs in advance. We like to use them if they can be reproduced on multilith offset masters."

Fiction: Accepts experimental, mainstream, science fiction, fantasy, and historical stories. Length: up to 5,000 words.

Poetry: Accepts traditional, blank and free verse, avant-garde and light verse. "Poetry from minority cultures." Length: "up to around 1,500 lines."

THE NORTH AMERICAN REVIEW, University of Northern Iowa, Cedar Falls IA 50613. Editor: Robley Wilson, Jr. Quarterly. Circulation: 2,700. Buys all rights for nonfiction and North American serial rights for fiction and poetry. Pays on publication. Will send sample copy for $1. Query first. Familiarity with magazine helpful. Reports in 6 to 8 weeks. Enclose S.A.S.E. for reply to queries.

Nonfiction: No restrictions, but most nonfiction is commissioned by magazine. Rate of payment arranged.

Photos: Purchased with ms or separately. No restrictions except good taste in subject matter. B&w prints. Payment arranged.

Fiction: No restrictions; highest quality only. Length: open. Pays minimum $10 per page.

Poetry: No restrictions; highest quality only. Length: open. Pays 50¢ per line minimum. Dept. Editor: Peter Cooley.

NORTHWEST REVIEW, University of Oregon, Eugene OR 97403. Triannual. Buys first North American serial rights only. Pays on acceptance. Reports in 1 to 3 months. Enclose S.A.S.E. for return of submissions.

Nonfiction: "Generally by invitation. Reviews, primarily those of first books or those of special interest or less chance of wide circulation, and usually solicited."

Fiction: "Interested only in highest quality stories. Will consider novellas." Dept. Editor: Patricia Brooks.

Poetry: "Highest quality only. Any length considered." Dept. Editor: James A. Heynen.

OCCIDENT, Eshleman Hall, Berkeley CA 94720. Editor: David Reid. Literary magazine of the University of California. Annual. Circulation: 3,200. Acquires all rights but will reassign rights to author after publication. Will send a sample copy to a writer for $1.00. Pays in contributor's copies. Reports in 1 to 2 months. Enclose S.A.S.E. for return of submissions.

Nonfiction and Photos: "Reviews and reportage of literary distinction." B&w glossy photos.

Fiction and Poetry: "Practiced quality of whatever approach taken is desired."

THE OHIO REVIEW, A Journal of the Humanities, 346 Ellis Hall, Ohio University, Athens OH 45701. Editor: Wayne Dodd. For "the general, educated (but non-specialized) reader." Established in 1959. Triannual. Circulation: 900. Rights acquired vary with author and material. May acquire all rights or first North American serial rights. Payment in contributor's copies and "some cash payments ($25 to $100) for articles." Will send a sample copy to writer for $2. Submit complete ms only. Will not consider photocopied submissions. Reports in 6 to 8 weeks. Enclose S.A.S.E. for return of submissions.

Nonfiction: Buys think articles only. "Quality essays of several humanistic interests that cross disciplinary lines or view their subjects against a broad intellectual background."

OPEN CELL, P.O. Box 52, Berkeley CA 94701. Editor: Milton Lowenthal. For "intellectuals, writers, students." Established in 1969. Bimonthly. Circulation: 1,000.

Buys all rights but will reassign rights to author after publication. Payment in contributor's copies. Will send free sample copy to writer on request. Write for copy of guidelines for writers. Submit complete ms. Will consider photocopied submissions. Reports on ms accepted for publication in 2 to 3 months. Returns rejected material in 2 months. Enclose S.A.S.E. for return of submissions.

Nonfiction and Photos: "We represent the new generation and require an intelligent approach to the modern world. We don't like jargon. Fresh words and fresh thoughts required." Think articles, personal opinion, photo, travel, reviews of books of intellectual interest. Length: maximum of 10 double-spaced pages. Captions are optional for b&w photos. Dept. Editor: Jennifer McDowell.

Fiction and Poetry: Experimental, mainstream, fantasy and humorous fiction. Length: 10 double-spaced pages, or 6 poems. Dept. Editor: Norman Davies. Free verse and avant-garde forms of poetry. Dept. Editor: Daniel Marlin.

OPINION MAGAZINE, P.O. Box 688, Evanston IL 60204. Editor: James E. Kurtz. For a "cross-section of professional people, teachers, people who are aware of events sociologically. Alert people. Age would be between 25 and 55." Established in 1957. Monthly. Acquires all rights. Uses 24 mss a year. Payment in contributor's copies. Will send a sample copy to writer for 25¢. Query first or submit complete ms for nonfiction. "We prefer not to consider photocopied submissions." Reports in 1 to 3 weeks. Enclose S.A.S.E. for return of submissions or reply to queries.

Nonfiction and Photos: Publishes "thought-provoking essays and articles on social problems, philosophy, and theology. Current events, articles that demand attention. Controversial. Writers should believe what they write. They should write plainly—big words do not impress us here. We don't edit mss; we publish them fully and cooperate with the writer in distribution, publicity, etc." Informational, personal experience, inspirational, historical, think, personal opinion. Length: 3,000 words maximum. Dept. Editor: Sue Meyer. Photos used without ms; captions optional. Buys b&w 5x7 or 8x10.

Fiction: Mainstream fiction. Dept. Editor: Sue Meyer.

Poetry: Traditional, free verse, and avant-garde. Dept. Editor: Sue Meyer.

Fillers: "Inspirational."

OVERFLOW ARTS (formerly *Overflow Writer*), 135 W. Liberty, South Lyon MI 48178. Editor: Pam Kelly. For university associates, students, faculty, graduates, freelance writers. "We have done well in furthering the careers of our submitters—referrals, recommendations, etc." Annual. Circulation: 2,000. Buys second serial (reprint) right. Pays in contributor's copies. Will send a sample copy to a writer for $1. No query required. Before submitting material, writers should "examine a past copy, deciding then whether we would be likely to accept their material." Reports "to those accepted. Others notified on no set schedule." Enclose S.A.S.E. for return of submissions.

Nonfiction: Personal experience, interviews, profiles, inspirational, humor, historical, think pieces. Wants humorous, satirical material for regular department of 10 Best or 10 Worst lists. No specific points of view; if extreme, it must be well done. Length: to 2,000 words.

Photos: Would use if interesting. B&w glossies, no color.

Fiction and Drama: Well-written and organized short stories and plays. Humor, if intelligent. Science fiction and historical fiction. No "sadistic/sex—love stories."

Poetry: Traditional, contemporary, avant-garde, light verse. No protest poems. Looking for new writers.

OYEZ MAGAZINE, Roosevelt University, 430 S. Michigan, Chicago IL 60605. Editor: Charles Finister. For "anyone interested in poetry/fiction/graphics, generally 18 to 40, mostly college." Semiannual. Not copyrighted. Pays in contributor's copy. Will send a sample copy to a writer for 75¢. No query required. Reports in 1 to 2 months. Enclose S.A.S.E. for return of submissions.

Nonfiction: Interviews, profiles, humor.

Photos: B&w glossies.

Fiction and Poetry: "Any subject matter." Length for fiction: maximum 2,000 words.

THE PARIS REVIEW, 17 Rue de Tournon, Paris 6, France. New York Office. 45-39 171 Place, Flushing NY 11358. Editor: George A. Plimpton. Quarterly. Buys all rights. Pays on publication. Address submissions to proper department. Enclose S.A.S.E. for return of submissions.
Fiction: Study publication. No length limit. Pays up to $150. Fiction submissions may be submitted to either office.
Poetry: Study publication. Pays 35¢ a line up to 100 lines; flat rate thereafter. Poetry mss must be submitted to Tom Clark at the Flushing office.

PARTISAN REVIEW, Rutgers University, New Brunswick NJ 08903. Editor: William Phillips. Buys first rights. Reports in "3 months plus." Enclose S.A.S.E.
Nonfiction: Buys essays and reviews. Pays 1½¢ a word.
Fiction: Short stories. Pays 1½¢ a word.
Poetry: A recent selection was from *Absences* by James Tate. Pays 40¢ a line.

THE PENNY DREADFUL, c/o The Department of English, Bowling Green State University, Bowling Green OH 43403. Editors: R. P. Bergstrom, Dara Wier. Established in 1972. Triquarterly. Circulation: 1,000. "All rights returned to author after publication." Pays in contributor's copies. Will send a sample copy to a writer for 25¢. Reports in 2 weeks. Enclose S.A.S.E. for return of submissions.
Nonfiction, Fiction, and Poetry: *The Penny Dreadful* has a tabloid format. The editors encourage submission of poems, fiction, one-act plays, book reviews and critical essays. Material from the local community will be considered as well. Book reviews, interviews, critical essays. No particular themes are prerequisites. We assume that if the word is good enough it can stand by itself. Length: 500 to 3,500 words for fiction and nonfiction; 2 to 120 lines for poetry.

THE PERIODICAL, 483 Harrington Drive, Ft. Belvoir VA 22060. Editor: Mark H. Magnussen. For members of the Council on Abandoned Military Posts and library users. Established in 1967. Quarterly. Circulation: 1,100. Buys first North American serial rights. Buys 10 to 15 mss a year. Payment on publication. Will send sample copy to writer for 50¢. Query first or submit complete ms. Will consider photocopied submissions. "May occasionally solicit material for a special issue on a particular subject; e.g., coastal fortifications. Material for these would be needed 60 days before publication." Reports on material in 4 weeks. Enclose S.A.S.E.
Nonfiction and Photos: "Factual articles related to American military posts; their history, construction, location or restoration. Prefer work of a scholarly nature with footnotes. Other subjects related to (e.g., the art of fortification) will be considered." Informational, personal experience, historical, travel, technical. Length: 300 to 5,000 words. Pays ⅓¢ per word. Photos suitable for reproduction are purchased with accompanying mss.

THE PERSONALIST, School of Philosophy, University of Southern California, Los Angeles CA 90007. Editor: John Hospers. Quarterly. No honorarium. Follow the *MLA Style Sheet.* Put footnotes at end of article. Reports in approximately eight weeks. Enclose S.A.S.E. for return of submissions.
Nonfiction: Uses critical articles pertaining to philosophy.

PERSPECTIVE: A Magazine of Modern Literature, Washington University P.O. Box 1122, St. Louis MO 63130. Editors: Jarvis Thurston and Mona Van Duyn. For literary intellectuals. Quarterly. Acquires all rights. Will reassign copyright to author upon request. No payment. Annual prize of $150 for best story and $150 for best poem. Will send sample copy for $1. Reports in one to two months. Enclose S.A.S.E. for return of submissions.
Nonfiction: Especially interested in literary criticism of contemporary poets, particularly the very modern. Length: up to 8,000 words.
Fiction: Serious, quality. The editors admire the stories of K.A. Porter, S. Bellow, W.H. Gass, Leonard Michaels. Length: up to 10,000 words.
Poetry: Uses quality poetry intended for an audience familiar with Wallace Stevens, Elizabeth Bishop, J. Merrill. No restriction on length.

PERSPECTIVES, English Department, West Virginia University, Morgantown WV 26506. Editor: Arthur C. Buck. "A page of literature, philosophy, and educa-

tion." Appears occasionally. Circulation: 100,000. Buys first rights. Pays on publication. No sample copies available. Reports in 1 month. Enclose S.A.S.E.
Nonfiction: "Essays on literary criticism, philosophy, higher education, and linguistics. Especially interested in essays on the creative process or experience and essays on the future of poetry. Interesting, informal style desired." Pays "75¢ per inch of type, which usually averages about 2¼¢ a word."
Poetry: "Used occasionally, as space permits. Poems are occasionally analyzed." Length: 40 lines maximum. No payment.
Fillers: "Short humor related to philosophy, literature, linguistics, education." No payment.
How To Break In: "Sincerity is of the utmost importance, in prose as well as in poetry. Affectation of style or vocabulary is immediately noticeable. Humility is also important. I have received letters from writers who say that I could not possibly overlook the merit of their work, or that their poems or essays are beyond comparison. In general, their work is atrocious. To me, sincerity and humility are worthy traits of a beginning writer."

PHI SIGMA IOTA NEWS LETTER, PHI SIGMA IOTA NEWS NOTES, 416 Woodside Ave., Ripon WI 54971. Editor: Dr. Daniel L. Delakas. For "undergraduates and graduates; professors and cultural services, embassy personnel, ages 18 to 75. Those who are interested in the culture of 5 Romance language countries in Europe and South America plus Latin." Subject matter consists of "Romance languages, linguistics, literature criticism and biography." Established in 1922. Biannual. Circulation: 3,000 to 5,000. Payment is in form of competition for yearly scholarships of $1,000 and $500. To compete for scholarship, must be "bona fide member of a chapter of Phi Sigma Iota." Deadlines are October 15 and April 15. Reports in 6 months. Enclose S.A.S.E. for return of submissions.
Nonfiction: Profiles, humor, historical, nostalgia, personal opinion, travel articles; literary reviews. Length: 400 to 600 words.

THE PHOENIX, West Whately, R.F.D. Haydenville, MA 01039. American Editor: James Cooney. For "all those concerned with reconciliations and healings of Earth's inherent tragedies." Quarterly. Circulation: 3,400. Acquires all rights. Pays in contributor's copies. "Each contributor receives 12 copies of the issue his or her contribution appears in, plus a year's honorary subscription." Will send a sample copy to a writer for $1.50. Will consider photocopied submissions. Reports in 3 to 4 weeks. Enclose S.A.S.E. for return of submissions.
Nonfiction: "Essays, interviews, historical articles." Length: "no restrictions."
Fiction: "Experimental, mainstream, religious, historical stories; serialized novels. All forms of serious literature." Length: "no restrictions."
Poetry: Traditional forms, blank verse, avant-garde forms. Length: open.
Photos: Diaries and woodcuts.

PRAIRIE SCHOONER, Andrews Hall, University of Nebraska, Lincoln NE 68508. Editor: Bernice Slote. Quarterly. Payment is in copies of the magazine, offprints, and prizes. Reports usually in a month. Enclose S.A.S.E.
Nonfiction: Uses two or three articles per issue. Subjects of general interest. Seldom prints extremely academic articles. Length: 5,000 words maximum.
Fiction: Uses several stories per issue.
Poetry: Uses 20 to 30 poems in each issue of the magazine. These may be on any subject, in any style. Occasional long poems are used, but the preference is for the shorter length. High quality necessary.

PRISM INTERNATIONAL, Creative Writing Department, University of British Columbia, Vancouver, B.C., Canada. Editor: Michael Bullock. For a literate audience, "interested in serious quality writing of an experimental nature and in excellent traditional kinds." 3 times a year. Circulation: 1,000. Not copyrighted. Buys 200 mss a year. Pays on publication. Will send a sample copy to a writer for $1.75. No query required. Reporting time: "we aim for 45 days." Enclose S.A.E. and International Reply Coupons for return of submissions.
Nonfiction, Photos, Fiction, Poetry, and Drama: Buys "all forms of creative writing—stories, poems, literary essays, short plays—which reach an international standard of excellence, either in the original English or in English translation. Quality is the single criterion for acceptance. Outstanding fiction, short plays, and literary es-

says are in greater demand than poetry, which we normally have in abundance. We advise would-be contributors to read our journal before submitting. We publish many poems but are almost always overstocked." Also does not want reviews or articles other than "literary essays (personal experience, profiles, travel) that have a high level of accomplishment." Length: open. Buys b&w glossy photos "for cover and occasional art photos inside." Payment is "$5 per magazine page, with copy of the magazine, for all types of material."

PSYCHOLOGICAL PERSPECTIVES, 595 E. Colorado Blvd., Suite 503, Pasadena CA 91101. Editor: William O. Walcott. Biannual. Reprint rights remain with author. Payment in copies. Enclose S.A.S.E. for return of submissions.
Nonfiction: "Articles in a psychological framework." Length: 5,000 to 7,000 words.
Fiction: Psychological insights preferred. Length: 5,000 to 7,000 words. Dept. Editor: Albert Kreinheder, 11665 W. Olympic Blvd., Los Angeles CA 90064.
Poetry: Criteria of excellence, clarity, beauty, profundity. Should clearly communicate an experience, with attention to freshness of image and phrase. Length: 40 lines maximum. Dept. Editor: J'nan Sellery, Dept. of Humanities and Social Sciences, Harvey Mudd College, Claremont CA 91711.

PYRAMID, Hellric Publications, 32 Waverley St., Belmont MA 02178. Editor: Ottone M. Riccio. For "the literary community in general and students of poetry, fiction, and the humanities in particular. Designed to appeal to high school, college, university, libraries and to late teenage, young adult and mature readers." Quarterly. Circulation: 500. Buys all rights, but will reassign them to author after publication. Pays on publication. "Query not necessary, but helpful." Will not consider photocopied submissions. Not interested in reprinting unsolicited material. Publishes some anthologies and memorial volumes and regular series of Chapbooks, but query first. Reports in 2 to 5 weeks. "Submissions without S.A.S.E. will be destroyed."
Nonfiction: Any subject; no slants or taboos. Especially interested in reviews of books of poetry. Length up to 3,000 words. Pays $3 to $20 a page plus copies and free subscription.
Fiction: Any subject, but prefers experimental in style. No taboos. Length: up to 3,000 words. Pays $3 to $20 a page plus copies and free subscription.
Poetry: Would like to see more experimental poetry. No subject or length restrictions. Pays $3 to $20 a page plus copies and free subscription.

QUARRY, Box 1061, Kingston, Ont., Canada. Editor: W.J. Barnes. For audience ages 15 to 60, "interested in creative literature, especially Canadian." Quarterly. Circulation: 600. Not copyrighted. Uses 150 to 200 mss a year. Pays on publication. Will send a sample copy to a writer for $1. Reports in 1 to 3 months. Enclose S.A.E. and International Reply Coupons for return of submissions.
Fiction, Poetry, and Drama: "Poems, short stories, occasional short plays. Especially interested in Canadian writers of quality, but also in promising new Canadian (or other) talent." Does not want social protest, "unless literary quality is especially good." Payment is $10 a page for fiction, and $10 a poem.

QUARTET, 1119 Neal Pickett Dr., College Station TX 77840. Editor: Richard Hauer Costa. For literate, urban, collegiate audience. Quarterly. Circulation: 1,000. Buys first rights only. Reprint rights revert to author provided *Quartet* receives credit line. Buys 100 mss a year. Will send a sample copy to a writer for $1. Study recent issues (available at larger colleges, libraries, etc.) before submitting ms. Reports in 6 weeks. Enclose S.A.S.E. for return of submissions.
Fiction: Any subject matter, however controversial, provided language is in good taste. Stress the integrity of the individual. Editors occasionally send criticism. Length: "Up to 6,000 words if quality is exceptional; most comfortable with fiction under 3,500 words but not 500-word anecdotes."
Poetry: Any subject, however controversial, provided language is in good taste. No light verse. Length: up to 28 lines.

QUEEN'S QUARTERLY, Queen's University, Kingston, Ont., Canada. Editor: J.K. McSweeney. For well-informed readers both within and beyond Canada. Established in 1893. Quarterly. Pays on publication. "Follow the *MLA Style Sheet* in preparing articles." Deadlines: Spring (January 2); Summer (April 1); Autumn (July 1); Winter (October 1). Reports in 3 weeks. Enclose S.A.E. and International Reply Coupons for return of submissions.

Nonfiction: Articles on literary, social, political, economic, educational and other subjects. "Articles must be well considered and show some distinction of presentation, and should be addressed to the intelligent and well-informed general reader, not to the specialist." Length: about 3,000 words. Pays $3 per printed page.

Fiction: Short stories. Priority to Canadian authors. Length: 2,000 to 4,000 words.

Poetry: "Shorter poems preferred. Priority to Canadian poets."

RELIGION AND SOCIETY, 1415 N. Second St., Stillwater MN 55082. Editor: Angus MacDonald. For "social conservatives and religious liberals—all ages. Superior education." Bimonthly. Circulation: 3,000. Acquires all rights. No payment. Will send free sample copy to a writer on request. Reports "immediately." Enclose S.A.S.E. for return of submissions.

Nonfiction: Scholarly but not pedantic articles on religion and/or society for intelligent and concerned American and foreign audience. Must analyze and evaluate current problems in terms of West European intellectual heritage. Editorial viewpoint is classical liberalism. Length: 5,000 words maximum.

THE REMINGTON REVIEW, 505 Westfield Ave., Elizabeth NJ 07208. Editors: Joseph A. Barbato and Dean Maskevich. Issued twice yearly. All rights revert to author upon publication. Reports on material in 2 to 3 months. Payment in contributor's copies. Enclose S.A.S.E. for return of material. "We are looking for quality material only. While we will consider any school or style, we tend to be wary of extremely experimental work. We are very interested in new writers."

Fiction: Length: 1,500 to 10,000 words. Dept. Editor: Joseph A. Barbato.

Poetry: Length: "Should not exceed 100 lines." Dept. Editor: Dean Maskevich.

RENASCENCE, Essays on Values in Literature, Marquette University, Milwaukee WI 53233. Editor: Dr. John D. McCabe. For English and modern language teachers, writers, critics, libraries, deans of colleges, bishops, convents, doctors, lawyers, journalists, and college students. Quarterly. Acquires all rights. Payment in copies. Enclose S.A.S.E. for return of submissions.

Nonfiction: Scholarly and critical articles on literary works of the nineteenth century and, especially, of the twentieth century. Primarily devoted to the study of values in literature. Often invites papers on special topics through announcements in its issues. Length: 2,500 to 5,000 words.

REVISTA/REVIEW INTERAMERICANA, P.O. Box 1293, Hato Rey, Puerto Rico 00919. Editor: John Zebrowski. For "mostly college graduates and people with higher degrees." Established in 1971. Quarterly. Circulation: 2,000. Acquires all rights, "but will pay 50% of money received if reprinted or quoted." Uses 65 to 75 mss a year. Payment in reprints (50) mailed to author's list. Will send a sample copy to a writer on request. Query first or submit complete ms. Will consider photocopied submissions. Submit seasonal material at least 3 months in advance. Reports in 3 months. Enclose S.A.S.E. for return of submissions or reply to queries.

Nonfiction: "Articles on the level of educated laymen; bilingual. Also book reviews. Multi-disciplinary with preference to Puerto Rican and Caribbean and Latin American themes. Interested in material on ecology and environmental management; modern Puerto Rico; urbanization of Puerto Rico; twentieth anniversary of the Commonwealth." Length: maximum 10,000 words.

Photos: B&w glossies, 4x5 minimum. Captions optional. Color; 35mm.

Fiction: "Bilingual; Spanish or English." Uses experimental, fantasy, humorous, and historical fiction.

Poetry: "Bilingual; Spanish or English." Uses traditional forms, blank verse, free verse, and avant-garde forms.

RIVERSIDE QUARTERLY, Box 40, University Station, Regina, Sask., Canada. Editor: Leland Sapiro. For "the literate reader with an interest in science fiction and fantasy." General subject matter: "Critical articles on all brands of science fiction and fantasy." Quarterly. Circulation: 1,400. All rights released to authors. Accepts "a dozen or so freelance mss per year." Pays in contributor's copies. Will send a

sample copy to a writer for 60¢. No query required. Reports in 10 days. For return of submissions, enclose S.A.E. with unattached U.S. stamps, "no stamped envelopes (which are useless in Canada) or postal coupons."
Nonfiction: "Literary rather than journalistic writing is desired. No special slant and no taboos. We use critical essays or reviews of books, magazines, movies, etc."
Fiction: Science fiction or fantasy. "Fiction writers should study several copies of the magazine before sending in mss. Do not send the cliche plot about the difficulty of a human being finding happiness, value, meaning, etc., in a mechanized world." Length: "under 3,500 preferred, but longer items considered."
Poetry: "Didactic and moralizing verse should be avoided." Dept. Editor: David Lurde, 1179 Central, Dunkirk NY 14048.

ROANOKE REVIEW, Roanoke College, Salem VA 24153. Editor: Robert Walter. Semiannual. Circulation: 200. Payment in two copies. Additional copies to accepted authors at reduced rate. Will send a sample copy to writer for 75¢. For both fiction and poetry, only restriction is quality. However, query first for exceptionally long works. Reports on submissions in 4 to 6 weeks. Enclose S.A.S.E. for return of submissions or reply to queries.
Fiction: "Only consideration is quality, such as is seen in the work of writers like George Garrett, John Hawkes, Jesse Hill Ford." Length: 2,000 to 5,000 words.
Poetry: High quality. No length restrictions. Traditional and comtemporary. "Translations considered."

ROMANCE PHILOLOGY, 2321 Dwinelle Hall, University of California, Berkeley CA 94720. Editor: Yakov Malkiel. For "graduate students, faculty members." Established in 1947. Quarterly. Circulation: about 1,200. Acquires all rights. Accepts 10 to 15 mss a year. Payment in offprints. Write for copy of guidelines for writers. Reports in 2 to 4 weeks. Enclose S.A.S.E. for return of submissions.
Nonfiction: "Articles, notes, essay reviews, book reviews, and the like. Subjects are general linguistics, theory of literature, historical grammar; dialectology, textual criticism applied to older Romance materials. We publish contributions in English and in French, German, Italian, Spanish, and Portuguese."

RUSSIAN LITERATURE TRIQUARTERLY, 2901 Heatherway, Ann Arbor MI 48014. Editors: Carl R. and Ellendea Proffer. For "readers of material related to Russian literature and art; students, teachers, Russian emigres." Established in 1971. 3 times a year. Circulation: 1,500. Acquires all rights. Uses 40 mss a year. "Most material is printed with payment in copies. When payment is made, the maximum is $200. Some poetry and photographs paid for; depends on name of writer." Will send sample copy for $5. Query first or submit complete ms. Will consider photocopied submissions. Reports on material in 3 weeks. Enclose S.A.S.E. for return of submission or reply to queries.
Nonfiction and Photos: Translations of Russian criticism, bibliographies, parodies, texts and documents from English literature. Critical articles. All in English. Informational, personal experience, interview, historical, reviews. Pays maximum of $10 for b&w glossies or negatives. "Only requirement is relation of some kind to Russian art, literature."
Fiction and Poetry: Translations only. Pays established poets $1 a line.

SCIMITAR AND SONG, Box 151, Edgewater MD 21037. Editor: Dr. Jean Sterling. Quarterly. Acquires first rights. Pays in copies. Will send a sample copy to a writer for $2. Query first "for articles." Submit seasonal material "as soon as possible in advance." Reports in 2 to 3 weeks. Enclose S.A.S.E. for return of submissions.
Nonfiction and Fiction: Inspirational and historical articles, humor, travel pieces. Fiction desired includes mystery, science fiction, adventure, historical, humorous, contemporary problems, religious, and juvenile. Length is determined by type and content of article or story.
Poetry: Traditional, contemporary, avant-garde, light verse. "No restriction on length. Annual cash prizes and trophies for best published poems."
Fillers: Puzzles, short humor on poets, writers, or poetry. Length: 50 words maximum.

SECOND COMING, P.O. Box 31246, San Francisco CA 94131. Editor: A.D. Winans. Established in 1972. Triannual. Circulation: 1,000. Pays in contributor's copies. "A token fee of $5 is paid for reviews and interviews." Will send sample copy to writer for $1. Acquires all rights but permissions to reprint by author freely given. Reports in 2 to 6 weeks. Enclose S.A.S.E. for return of submissions.

Nonfiction, Photos, Fiction, and Poetry: "We are interested in printing the best poetry and fiction available. Also interested in photography and reviews as well as an occasional interview of an interesting literary personality. No word length or style restriction, although somewhat prejudiced toward avant-garde and what was once termed 'meat poetry.'"

SEWANEE REVIEW, University of the South, Sewanee TN 37375. Editor: George Core. For audience of "variable ages and locations, mostly college-educated and with interest in literature." Quarterly. Circulation: 3,900. Buys all rights, but will reassign rights to author after publication. Pays on publication. Will send a sample copy to a writer for $2.15, current issue; $3.15, back issues. Returns rejected material in 2 months. Enclose S.A.S.E. for return of submissions.

Nonfiction and Fiction: "Short fiction, essays on literary or related themes, critical reviews (books and reviewers selected by the editors themselves)." Payment is $12 a printed page maximum.

Poetry: Traditional, contemporary, light verse. Varied subjects. Payment is "maximum 60¢ a line, although this may vary."

THE SHAKESPEARE NEWSLETTER, University of Illinois at Chicago Circle, Chicago IL 60680. Editor: Louis Marder. For Shakespeare scholars, teachers and enthusiasts. "Scholarly yet popular newsletter." Bimonthly. Circulation: 1,750. Not copyrighted. Payment in copies. Will send a sample copy to a writer for 50¢. Query first. Enclose S.A.S.E.

Nonfiction: Articles of interest and importance on criticism, biography, stage history and practice, language and all miscellaneous aspects of Shakespeare. Writer must be aware of previous scholarship on the subject. Conclusions must be valid; thesis must be original. Length: 800 to 1,500 words.

Poetry: Short poetry related to Shakespeare—critical, interpretive, parody, etc. Should be thought-provoking. Does not want poems praising Shakespeare.

THE SHAW REVIEW, S234 Burrows Bldg., University Park PA 16802. Editor: Stanley Weintraub. For academic, theatrical and lay readers interested in GBS, his work and his world. Issued 3 times a year (January, May and September). Magazine retains copyright unless author applies for one himself. "Follow *MLA Style Sheet*." Reports in 6 weeks. Enclose S.A.S.E. for return of submissions.

Nonfiction: The subject of articles should be George Bernard Shaw and his milieu—its personalities, works, relevance to his age and ours. Length: under 5,000 words preferred. Payment in 10 contributor's copies.

THE SMALL POND, 10 Overland Dr., Stratford CT 06497. Editor: Napoleon St. Cyr. 3 times a year. Circulation: 400. Acquires first rights. Pays in copies. Submit 3 to 6 poems, 1 to 2 stories at a time. Will send sample copy for $1. Reports on submissions in 15 days (longer in summer). Enclose S.A.S.E. for return of submissions.

Nonfiction: No subject restrictions, but should be relevant and authoritative. Length: 2,500 words maximum.

Fiction: Subject and style open. Length: 2,500 words maximum.

Poetry: Subject and style open. No haikus, unless a set of 3 to 6 of unusual quality are submitted. Favors a limit of 10 poems per submission. Will consider unknown poets, the only criteria being quality. "No sewing circle stuff." Length: "generally limited to 100 lines."

SMALL PRESS REVIEW, 5218 Scottwood Rd., Paradise CA 95969. Editor: Len Fulton. For "people interested in small presses and magazines, current trends and data; many libraries." Irregular frequency. Circulation: 2,500. "All rights belong to author, but we do copyright the magazine." Accepts about 12 mss a year. Pays on publication. Will send a sample copy to a writer for $1. "Query if you're unsure." Reports in 1 to 2 months. Enclose S.A.S.E. for return of submissions or reply to queries.

Nonfiction and Photos. "News, reviews, photos, articles on small magazines and presses and underground papers. Get the facts and know your mind well enough to build your opinion into the article." Uses how-to's, personal experience articles, interviews, profiles, spot news, historical articles, think pieces, photo pieces, and coverage of merchandising techniques. Length: 100 to 3,000 words. Pays 1¢ to 2¢ a word, "or on arrangement." Uses b&w glossy photos.

THE SMITH, 5 Beekman St., New York NY 10038. Editor: Harry Smith. 8 times yearly. Special issues include many issues of all poetry, one issue of all reviews and a special issue for award plays. Pays on acceptance. Buys North American serial rights. Will send sample copy to writer for $1. Query first for articles, but not for fiction and poetry. Don't enclose explanatory letters unless absolutely necessary. Reports in 6 weeks. Enclose S.A.S.E. for return of submissions or reply to queries.
Nonfiction and Photos: No taboos. Length: 5,000 words or less. Payment is "modest," by arrangement. Dept. Editor: Sidney Bernard. Occasionally purchases photos with mss. Payment is $5.
Fiction: No taboos. Publishes long stories and novellas as well as short-shorts and vignettes of under 2,000 words. Modest payment, by arrangement. Dept. Editor: Raphael Taliaferro.
Poetry: No taboos. Has published poems as long as 52 pages. Pays $5 per short poem.

SOME FRIENDS, 2931 Tanglewood, Tyler TX 75701. Editor: Terry J. Cooper. Established in 1972. Quarterly. Circulation: 1,500. Acquires second serial rights. Payment in copies. Will send a sample copy to a writer for 50¢. Submit complete ms. Will consider photocopied submissions. Submit seasonal material at least 1 month in advance. Reports in 5 weeks. Enclose S.A.S.E for return of submissions.
Nonfiction: "Any subject matter that would be interesting to our readers—interviews with hermits, desert rats, etc. No particular approach—just interesting material. Perhaps coverage of interesting discoveries of out-of-the-way archaeological finds. No set length requirements."
Photos: "No specifications." Captions optional.
Fiction: Adventure, western, experimental, fantasy, and humorous. "No minimum or maximum length." Dept. Editor: Lugene Tucker.
Poetry: Traditional forms, light verse, blank verse, free verse, avant-garde forms. "Open on poetry themes. Any length."
Fillers: Jokes, short humor.

SOUNDINGS, Box 6309, Sta. B, Nashville TN 37203. Editor: Sallie TeSelle. For students, teachers, clergymen, professionals. "*Soundings* is devoted to interdisciplinary studies—a conversation among scholars but dedicated to a rapprochement between learning and the basic humane concerns of our day." Quarterly. Circulation: 2,000. Acquires all rights. Uses 45 to 55 mss a year. Pays in contributor's copies. Will send a sample copy to a writer for $2.50. Reports in 2 months. Enclose S.A.S.E. for return of submissions.
Nonfiction: "In-depth essays on any subject, written with boldness but professional competence. Articles written from within a discipline but intelligible to those working in another discipline, pertinent to issues of contemporary interest. We have many religious and philosophical writers and are eager to review mss from the natural and social sciences, mathematics, and the professions."

SOUTH AND WEST, 2601 S. Phoenix, Ft. Smith AR 72901. Editor: Sue Abbot Boyd. Quarterly. Acquires North American serial rights only. Pays in contributor's copies. Will send sample copy to a writer for $1. Reports in 2 weeks. Enclose S.A.S.E. for return of submissions.
Nonfiction: Book reviews, scholarly articles on poetry. Length: open.
Fiction: Will use a timely or experimental short story. Can be on "any subject treated with good taste except 'I Love God' themes. We will even consider imaginative God themes, if a new dimension is offered that relates to humanity, the arts, culture, and education." Length: to 2,000 words.
Poetry: "The purpose of the magazine is to encourage new poets as well as give voice to those already established. Emphasis is on modern poetry, expression of new and young thought. This does not, however, mean prejudice against traditional po-

etry. All types of poems receive equal consideration. We prefer work that is individualistic, that reflects the personality of the writer. No subject is taboo that is handled in good taste. We prefer freshness to merely skillful execution of form. Poetry preferably not exceeding 37 lines, but will not reject a good long poem."

SOUTH ATLANTIC QUARTERLY, Box 6697, College Station, Durham NC 27708. Editor: Oliver W. Ferguson. For the academic profession. Quarterly. Proceeds of sale of rights to reprint divided with author. Reports in 6 weeks. Enclose S.A.S.E. for return of submissions.
Nonfiction: Articles on current affairs, literature, history and historiography, art, education, essays on most anything, economics, etc.—a general magazine. No taboos. Length: 2,000 to 5,000 words.

SOUTH DAKOTA REVIEW, Box 111, University Exchange, Vermillion SD 57069. Editor: John R. Milton. For a university audience. Quarterly. Acquires North American serial rights and reprint rights. Pays in contributor's copies. Will send sample copy to a writer for 50¢. Reports on submissions in 1 to 4 weeks. Enclose S.A.S.E. for return of submissions.
Nonfiction: Mainly Western American literature and history; especially critical studies of western writers. Occasional book reviews; especially western books. Contents must be reasonably scholarly, but style should be informal. Accepts anything on literature, history, culture, if it is well-written. Length: up to 7,500 words (at times has used longer).
Fiction: Western setting preferred (Great Plains and Rockies). Receptive to almost any style and approach. Prefers craftsmanship to emotional excitement. Length: up to 7,500 words (has used longer at times).
Poetry: Prefers poetry which is disciplined and controlled. Any length.

SOUTHERN FOLKLORE QUARTERLY, Anderson Hall, University of Florida, Gainesville FL 32601. Editor: Roger M. Thompson. For folklorists, musicians, literary scholars, etc. Quarterly. Reports in 3 months. Enclose S.A.S.E. for return of submissions.
Nonfiction: Folklore material with emphasis upon its collection, preservation, utilization. No payment.

THE SOUTHERN REVIEW, Drawer D, University Station, Baton Rouge LA 70803. Editors: Donald E. Stanford and Lewis P. Simpson. For academic, professional, literary, intellectual audience. Quarterly. Circulation: 3,000. Buys first rights. Pays on publication. Will send sample copy to writer for $1.50. No queries. Reports in 2 to 3 months. Enclose S.A.S.E. for return of submissions.
Nonfiction: Essays; careful attention to craftsmanship and technique and to seriousness of subject matter. "Willing to publish experimental writing if it has a valid artistic purpose. Avoid extremism and sensationalism. Essays exhibit thoughtful and sometimes severe awareness of the necessity of literary standards in our time." Emphasis on contemporary literature, especially Southern culture and history. Minimum number of footnotes. Length: 4,000 to 10,000 words. Pays 3¢ per word minimum.
Fiction: Short stories, with emphasis on modern literature and of lasting literary merit. Length: 4,000 to 8,000 words. Pays 3¢ per word minimum.
Poetry: Pays $20 minimum per page.

SOUTHWEST REVIEW, Southern Methodist University, Dallas TX 75222. Editor: Margaret L. Hartley. For college graduates. Quarterly. Buys all rights. "Our permission or copyright assignment must be obtained for reprint." Will send a free sample copy to a writer on request. Query first. Reports in 3 months. Enclose S.A.S.E.
Nonfiction: Articles may be historical, scholarly, regional, literary criticism, national and international problems, etc. "Material should be scholarly and at the same time interesting to the general reader, neither popularized or journalistic on the one hand nor overpedantic on the other." Length: "3,000 to 5,000 words. Occasionally up to 7,000." Payment is ½¢ a word.
Fiction: "No limitations on subject matter except too strongly regional subjects of a region not our own (e.g., New England stories depending much on background).

Excellent writing required, but of various styles. Prefer characterization emphasis to plot and action." Length: 3,000 to 5,000 words. Payment is ½¢ a word.
Poetry: Uses about 6 to 8 poems per issue. Any subject that is appropriate for genuine poetic treatment is good here. Looks for poetry rather than verse. Asks that the poet convey genuine insights into human life and emotion through appropriate and skillful poetic expression, but does not favor one specific form over another. "Because of the name of the university, much devotional verse is received, which is not wanted." Length: 4 to 75 lines, but needs more poems under 18 lines than longer ones. Pays $5 per poem.

SPAFASWAP, 1070 N. Ahern Dr., La Puente CA 91746. Editor: Lois J. Long. 6 times a year. Circulation: 200 plus. Not copyrighted. Uses 100 mss a year. Payment in contributor's copies. Will send sample copy to writer for 35¢. Query first or submit complete ms. Reports on material in 2 weeks. Enclose S.A.S.E. for return of submissions or reply to queries.
Poetry and Fiction: Traditional forms, free verse and light verse. Length: 24 lines maximum. Short fiction "with old-fashioned, down-to-earth" approach. Length: 200 to 250 words maximum.

SPECTRUM, University of Massachusetts, Student Union, R.S.O. 102, Amherst MA 01002. Editor: Ed Meek III. For "college-educated persons, ages 18 to 26." Established in 1966. Semiannual. Circulation: 30,000. Acquires all rights, but will reassign rights to author after publication. Pays in contributor's copies. Will send a sample copy to a writer for $1. Will consider photocopied submissions. "Issues dates are Jan. and May. Deadlines are Dec. 1 and April 15." Enclose S.A.S.E. for return of submissions.
Nonfiction: "No structure specified." Uses personal experience articles, interviews, inspirational articles, humor, historical articles, personal opinion articles, photo pieces, and book reviews. Length: 7,500 words.
Fiction: Experimental, mystery, suspense, adventure, erotica, science fiction, fantasy, humorous, and condensed novels. Length: 7,500 words. Dept. Editor: Richard Abaid.
Poetry: Traditional forms, blank verse, free verse, avant-garde forms, and light verse.

THE SQUEAK, 474 Beck Rd., Jonesville MD 49250. Editor: Gil Schaerer. 6 times a year. Circulation: 500. Pays in copies. Enclose S.A.S.E. for return of submissions.
Nonfiction: Social information, interviews, criticism. "Religion, politics, and sex from a liberal point of view."

STAR WEST, P.O. Box 731, Sausalito CA 94965. Editor: Leon Spiro. For "multilingual university linguists and students." Semiannual. Circulation: 5,000. "We obtain reprints for our authors and poets in South and Central American newspapers, and release copyright immediately upon request of foreign editor's air mail and cable." Payment in contributor's copies. Will send a sample copy to a writer on request. No query required. Mss should be typewritten on IBM selectric. "Single-spaced, no errors, ready for camera." Reports in 2 to 4 weeks. Enclose S.A.S.E. for return of submissions.
Nonfiction, Photos, and Fiction: Publishes in 9 languages. Approach should be "dynamic only. Current events, international impact." Inspirational, humor, spot news, think pieces, exposes, photo essays. Fiction may be humorous, adventure, contemporary problems, religious. Length: 500 words maximum. B&w glossy photos, "mainly of authors and poets." Photo Editor: Raymond Suen.
Poetry: Traditional, contemporary, avant-garde, light verse, surrealism. Length: 30 lines maximum.

STONECLOUD, Associated Students, University of Southern California, Los Angeles CA 90007. Editors: Dan Ilves, Autumn Stanley, Nick Warner. For "college and high school students, professors; professional as well as nonprofessional of all educational backgrounds." Uses "anything creative." Established in 1972. "Biannually, or at least annually." Circulation: 5,000. Copyright pending. Will send sample copy to a writer for $1.25. Submit complete ms. Will consider photocopied submissions. Enclose S.A.S.E. for return of submissions.

Nonfiction and Photos: "Anything to do with art creativity, human development, and toward the broader expansion of knowledge and understanding. Any structure, positive outlook, constructive, any style. Emphasis is to appeal to those not well-read in the particular subject as well as be interesting to professionals in the field." Personal experience, interview, profile, inspirational, humor, think and personal opinion. Maximum length: 7,000 words. Payment in copies. B&w photos, no larger than 8½x11. Payment in copies.

Fiction: Experimental, mystery, suspense, adventure, erotica, science fiction, fantasy, humorous, romance. Length: 7,000 words maximum. Payment in copies.

Poetry and Fillers: Traditional forms, blank verse, free verse, avant-garde. Maximum length: 500 words. Payment in copies. Clippings. Payment: 1 copy of the magazine.

STORIES FROM THE HILLS, Morris Harvey College, Charleston WV 25304. Editors: William Plumley and Barbara Yeager. Annual. High quality paperback (gloss) anthology. Acquires all rights. "Payment is in prizes, $25 to $100." Submit stories September through December, accompanied by brief vita. Reports in 6 weeks. Enclose S.A.S.E. for return of submissions.

Fiction: Wants stories that emphasize character and "reflect the myths, scenes, characters, and legends of the hills. The theme may be positive or critical. We like the hills, even with its problems. We hope that your submissions might reflect the same."

SUNDAY CLOTHES, A Magazine of the Fine Arts, 51 Sherman St., Deadwood SD 57732. Editors: Daniel Lusk, L. M. H. Lusk. For well-educated and culturally interested audience. Special summer issue features art from the South Dakota region. Established in 1972. Quarterly. Circulation: almost 2,000. Acquires all rights but will reassign rights to author after publication. Uses about 75 mss a year. Payment in 3 copies and 1-year subscription. Will send sample copy for $1.10. Submit complete ms. Will consider photocopied submissions. Submit seasonal material 3 to 4 months in advance. Reports on material in 3 weeks. Enclose S.A.S.E. for return of submissions.

Nonfiction and Photos: "We want both well-known and unknown writers. Articles by or about artists and writers; interviews, book reviews." Length: up to 6,000 words. 8x10 b&w glossy or matte photos.

Fiction: Experimental, mainstream, fantasy, western, humorous, condensed novels, serialized novels. Length: not over 8,000 words. Dept. Editor: L.M.H. Lusk.

Poetry: Traditional forms, short verse, free verse, avant-garde forms and light verse. Length: open. Dept. Editor: Daniel Lusk. All payment in 3 contributor's copies and 1-year subscription.

SUNSTONE REVIEW, P.O. Box 2321, Sante Fe NM 87501. Editor: Jody Ellis. For "poets, photographers, and people of all ages interested in good poetry." Established in 1971. Quarterly. Circulation: 300. Payment in contributor's copies. Will send a sample copy to writer for $1.50. Reports in 4 weeks. Enclose S.A.S.E. for return of submissions.

Photos, Fiction, and Poetry: Desires humor in all material. Requires "just excellent poetry. Clean cut (magazine) in appearance—not cluttered." B&w photos only. "Any good short piece of fiction acceptable." Accepts traditional forms, blank verse, free verse, avant-garde forms and light verse. Themes are open for poetry.

SYLLABUS, P.O. Box 205, Sunderland MA 01375. Editor: Dario Politella. For "all those interested in campus publications." Quarterly. Circulation: 2,000. Not copyrighted. Payment in "copies, credit, and intercessionary prayers." Will send a sample copy to a writer on request. No query required. Reports "immediately." Enclose S.A.S.E. for return of submissions.

Nonfiction and Photos: "Case history materials on the publishing problems and techniques for producing student publications. Editorial, legal, ethical, financial, and mechanical tips and cases also included." Style should be "clear, concise, crisp reportage. No taboos." Length: 800 to 1,000 words. "Longer pieces considered, depending on subject matter." Accepts b&w glossies "to illustrate how-to pieces."

Fiction: "None as such, unless clever satire on topical subject related to campus press."

Fillers: Newsbreaks, clippings, jokes, short humor. "On campus press subjects." Length: 150 words.

THE TAMARACK REVIEW, Box 159, Station K., Toronto 12, Ont., Canada. Editor: Robert Weaver; Managing Editor: John Robert Colombo. Quarterly. Material mainly Canadian. Buys North American serial rights only. Pays on publication. Reports on submissions in two months. Enclose S.A.E. and International Reply Coupons for return of submissions.
Nonfiction: Critical essays, reviews of various arts. Length: up to 4,000 words. Pays $8 to $10 per page.
Fiction: Top literary quality. Length: 2,000 to 7,000 words. Pays $10 per page.
Poetry: Serious top quality poetry, usually by Canadians. Pays $10 a page.

THE TEXAS QUARTERLY, Box 7517, University Station, Austin TX 78712. Editor: Harry H. Ransom. For a general audience; usually college and above. Established in 1958. Quarterly. Circulation: 2,000. Buys first serial rights. Buys 30 to 50 mss a year. Payment in 2 contributor's copies and 50 reprints. Will send sample copy to writer for $1.50. Submit complete ms. Submit seasonal material 4 months in advance. Reports on material in 1 month. Enclose S.A.S.E. for return of submissions.
Nonfiction: Informational, personal experience, profile, inspirational, humor, historical, think pieces, travel. Length: 6,000 words maximum.
Fiction: Experimental, mystery, suspense, adventure, humorous, historical. Length: 6,000 words maximum.
Poetry: Traditional, blank verse, free verse, avant-garde forms, light verse. Length: 4 lines minimum.

TEXAS TRAVELER, 2205AA Echols St., Bryan TX 77801. Editor: Josephine Payne. For "poets, writers, hobbyists, people in general." Bimonthly. Circulation: 200. Not copyrighted. Payment: 1 copy of issue in which work appears. Will send a sample copy to a writer for 35¢. Reports in 1 to 3 weeks. Enclose S.A.S.E. for return of submissions.
Nonfiction, Fiction, and Poetry: "We like light stuff, positive thinking, not heavy gloom and doom. Prefer nonreligious subjects. Definitely no recipes, patterns. Taboo—filthy language or coarse subjects." Length: up to 500 words; poetry, up to 16 lines.
Fillers: Newsbreaks, puzzles, clippings, jokes, short humor, short public service items. Length: under 200 words.

THOUGHT, Fordham University, 441 E. Fordham Road, Bronx NY 10458. Editor: Rev. Joseph E. O'Neill, S.J., Ph.D. Quarterly. Acquires all rights. Payment in copies. Reports within a month. Enclose S.A.S.E. for return of submissions.
Nonfiction: Uses competent articles in the field of science, literature, history, sociology, education, philosophy, and religion, written in a way to appeal to the well-educated general reader. Not interested in very technical or "popular" material. 5,000 to 11,000 words in length.
Poetry: "Occasionally uses a page or two."

TRANSATLANTIC REVIEW, Box 3348, Grand Central P.O., New York NY 10017. Editor: Joseph F. McCrindle. For American and English audience. Quarterly. Circulation: 3,000. Copyright assigned to author on publication at request. Pays on acceptance "as arranged." Will send a sample copy to a writer for $1. Reports in 4 weeks—"sometimes longer with volume." Enclose S.A.S.E. for return of submissions.
Fiction and Poetry: Short stories; experimental, mainstream, adventure, erotica, science fiction, fantasy, humor. Length: 4,500 words maximum. Pays $20 to $40. Traditional forms of poetry; blank verse, free verse, avant-garde forms. Lengths: 2 typewritten pages maximum. Pays $10 to $30. Poetry Editor: B.S. Johnson.
Nonfiction: Limited to interviews with theatrical and film writers and directors.

TRANSPACIFIC, Antioch College, Yellow Springs OH 45387. Editor: Nicholas Crome. For "persons interested in new writing—both American and foreign." Quarterly. Circulation: 1,000. "Rights released to author for the asking." Uses 100 mss a

year. Pays in contributor's copies "plus a small author's payment." Will send a sample copy to a writer for $1. No query required, but editor suggests, "Read the magazine—so you know what sort of publication it is." Reports usually in 1 to 2 weeks. Enclose S.A.S.E. for return of submissions.
Nonfiction, Photos, Fiction, and Poetry: "Poetry and fiction in English, and English translations. Occasionally literary essays. Emphasis on translations (20% to 40% usually)." B&w glossy photos.

TRI-QUARTERLY, University Hall, 101 Northwestern University, Evanston IL 60201. Editor: Charles Newman. 3 times yearly. For an intellectual and literary audience. "Our format is extremely eclectic. The tone and intentions of each issue may vary." Reports on unsolicited mss within eight weeks; solicited mss immediately. Pays on publication. Study publication before submitting mss; enclose S.A.S.E. for ms return.
Fiction and Photos: No length limits. "We are not committed to the short story as the only publishable form of fiction. Frequently excerpts from longer works tell us more about an author and his work." Study publication. Payment at $10 per page if possible. Occasionally uses photos.

TWIGS, College Box 2, Pikeville College, Pikeville KY 41501. Editor: Dr. Leonard Roberts. For "writers, college students, and university teachers." Bimonthly. Circulation: 400. Acquires first rights. Accepts 100 or more mss a year. Payment is in contributor's copies and awards (4 awards of $25.) Will send a sample copy to a writer for $1.50. Reports in 3 to 6 weeks. Enclose S.A.S.E. for return of submissions.
Nonfiction, Fiction, and Poetry: Seeks "innovative, poignant, perceptive writing. It is an experimental magazine." For nonfiction, accepts personal experience, (in Appalachia if lived and felt), think pieces, criticism on writers and literary subjects. Length: 1,500 to 3,000 words. For fiction, accepts humorous, historical, adventure, and juvenile stories. Length: 1,000 to 2,500 words. For poetry, accepts traditional, contemporary, avant-garde, and light verse. Length: 4 to 30 lines.

UNICORN: A Miscellaneous Journal, 1153 E. 26 St., Brooklyn NY 11210. Editor: Karen S. Rockow. Established in 1967. Mainly for college and graduate school students and faculty. "Well-educated and sophisticated. Not jaded." Published 3 times a year. Circulation: 500. Acquires all rights, but will reassign rights to author after publication. Uses 15 to 20 freelance mss a year. Pays an honorarium only for nonfiction. Submit complete ms. Reports in 2 to 4 weeks. Will send sample copy to writer for $1. Will consider photocopied submissions. Enclose S.A.S.E. for return of submissions.
Nonfiction and Photos: "*Unicorn* is a community of writers and readers brought together to share their favorite books and topics. Primarily, we publish essays. These range from personal essays to graceful, scholarly papers directed at a general audience. Areas of greatest interest are folklore, popular culture (especially fantasy literature, detective fiction, children's books) and medieval studies, but we will consider mss on any subject. Scholarly and semischolarly papers may include footnotes (use MLA form). The supporting scholarship must be rigorous, but avoid 'intellectualese'. We are looking for crisp, honest prose and stand committed against pretentiousness. We pay $5 honorarium for each article and essay accepted." B&w glossies, any size. Payment in cost of film plus extra roll and offprints.
Fiction: Satire, short stories. Fantasy, detective fiction. Experimental, mainstream, science fiction, humorous fiction. Length: 2,500 words maximum. Payment in copies plus offprints. Dept. Editor: Stuart Silverman.
Poetry: Traditional forms, blank verse, free verse, avant-garde forms, light verse and "concrete" poetry. Length: 1 line to 1 single-spaced page. Payment in copies plus offprints. Dept. Editor: Stuart Silverman.
Fillers: Puzzles of any type. Payment in copies plus offprints.

UNIVERSITY OF WINDSOR REVIEW, Windsor, Ontario, Canada. Editor: Eugene McNamara. For "the literate layman, the old common reader." Established in 1965. Biannual. Circulation: 200 plus. Acquires first North American serial rights. Accepts 50 mss a year. Pays in contributor's copies. Will send a sample copy to writer for $1.25 plus postage. Follow MLA style sheet. Reports in 4 to 6 weeks. Enclose S.A.E. and International Reply Coupons for return of submissions.

Nonfiction and Photos: "We publish articles on literature, history, social science, etc. I think we reflect competently the Canadian intellectual scene, and are equally receptive to contributions from outside the country; I think we are good and are trying to get better. We are receiving too many poems, too many short stories. Everybody in the world is writing them. Too many articles on literature itself. Not enough in the other areas: history, etc." Seeks informational articles. Length: about 6,000 words. For photos please inquire to Evelyn McLean.
Fiction: Publishes mainstream prose with open attitude toward themes. Length: 2,000 to 6,000 words. Dept. Editor: Alastair MacLeod.
Poetry: Accepts traditional forms, blank verse, free verse, and avant-garde forms. No epics. Dept. Editor: John Ditsky.

UNIVERSITY REVIEW, 2929 Broadway, New York NY 10025. Editors: Robert Friedman and Jonah Raskin. Established in 1969. For college and university students. Monthly. Circulation: 235,000. Rights purchased vary with author and material. Buys all rights, but will reassign rights to author after publication or buys first complete ms. Reports in 2 to 3 weeks. Will send sample copy to writer for 50¢. Will consider photocopied submissions. Enclose S.A.S.E. for return of submissions.
Nonfiction and Photos: Political and cultural articles. Nonacademic approach. Film, book and music reviews. Informational, personal experience, interview, profile, humor, historical, think pieces, expose, personal opinion. Length: 500 to 3,500 words. Pays $10 to $75. Dept. Editor: Robert Friedman. 8x10 b&w photos purchased with or without accompanying mss. Captions required. Pays $10 to $30. Photo Dept. Editor: Minton Brooks.

VAGABOND, P.O. Box 2114, Redwood City CA 94064. Editor: John Bennett. For "libraries, poets, writers, sensitive and free spirits, minority groups, people of all ages, varied education and an interest in life . . ." Established in 1965. Quarterly. Circulation: 500. Acquires all rights, but will reassign them to author after publication. Uses about 80 mss a year. Payment in contributor's copies. Will send a sample copy for 75¢. Query first for nonfiction. Reports in 1 to 2 weeks. Enclose S.A.S.E.
Nonfiction, Fiction, and Poetry: "I would prefer not to see work that was written with a market in mind. I would like to see material that deals with life and death and all their accoutrements . . . joy, laughter, love and hate." Accepts interviews. Length: not more than 5,000 words.
Fiction: Publishes genuine experimental, suspense, adventure, erotica, fantasy, humorous fiction. Length: 5,000 words maximum.

VALLEY VIEWS, P.O. Box 39096, Solon OH 44139. Editor: Nelson P. Bard. Family-oriented. Quarterly. Circulation: 5,000. Acquires no rights unless commissioned and paid for, in which case buys all rights. No query required. "*Valley Views* was established as a showcase for new writers and poets, for amateur photographers, cartoonists, and artists. Mss and artwork are solicited from college or art school students, as well as gifted adults, on a nonpaying basis. Unused materials will be promptly returned, but artists should not send canvases without writing first." Will send a sample copy to a writer. Reports in 6 weeks. Enclose S.A.S.E. for return of submissions.
Nonfiction and Photos: Wide latitude; generally light and entertaining for family and waiting room readership. Will use travel articles and first-person stories on a number of subjects. Also wants general information articles, "how-to-do-it" articles and personal articles written in the style of newspaper columnists. Does not want slanted articles on racial subjects nor soap box articles for or against political points of view. Nothing ribald. Length: 3,000 words maximum. Wants color print photos, 5x7 or smaller, but can use slides or transparencies.
Fiction and Poetry: Family type stories with a humorous slant; character portraits. No hippie or mod stories about dope addicts, etc.; no "shock effect" language. Uses short-shorts. Length for fiction: 3,000 words maximum. Length for poetry: open.

VERDURE PUBLICATIONS, 9010 Tobias, #261, Panorama City CA 91402. Editor: Lyn Hickey. Quarterly. Editorial policy is "dedicated to building the image of

U.S.A. and her people, in an era when it has become fashionable to tear down customs and traditions and sneer at anything wholesome as 'corny'." Does not pay. Acquires all rights; "will release to writer on request." Study publication. Enclose S.A.S.E. for return of submissions.

Nonfiction, Fiction, Poetry, and Fillers: Patriotism, nostalgia, family life, humor, personal experience; inspirational, seasonal, self-help material. In each issue there is one article about customs or traditions of another country. Length: 3,000 words maximum; prefers short pieces. No sensationalism or obscenity, and "nothing that tears down our society." Poetry fills approximately one-third of magazine's space. No obscure poetry. Uses short humor and anecdotes.

VILTIS, (Hope), P.O. Box 1226, Denver CO 80201. Editor: V.F. Beliajus. Six issues per year. Does not pay. Query first. Study publication before submitting ms. Enclose S.A.S.E. for reply to queries.
Nonfiction: Uses articles on folklore, legends, customs and nationality backgrounds. Folkish (not too erudite) but informative. Can be any length. Everything must be based on custom.

THE VIRGINIA QUARTERLY REVIEW, 1 West Range, Charlottesville VA 22903. Editor: Charlotte Kohler. Quarterly. Pays on publication. Reports on submissions in 2 weeks. Enclose S.A.S.E. for return of submissions.
Nonfiction: Articles on current problems, economic, historical; literary essays. Length: 3,000 to 6,000 words. Pays $5 for a page of 350 words.
Fiction: Good short stories, conventional or experimental. Length: 2,000 to 7,000 words. Pays $5 for a page of 350 words.
Poetry: Generally publishes ten pages of poetry in each issue. No length or subject restrictions. Pays 50¢ per line.

WALT WHITMAN REVIEW, Business Office: Wayne State University Press, Detroit MI 48202. Editorial Office: William White, Director, American Studies Program, Wayne State University, Detroit, Michigan 48202. Editors: William White and Charles E. Feinberg. For specialists in American literature. Quarterly. Payment in contributor's copies. Wayne State University Press and author share all rights. Reports within a few days. Enclose S.A.S.E. for return of submissions.
Nonfiction: All articles and book reviews, notes and queries should deal with Walt Whitman and his writings. Length: 500 to 6,000 words.

WASCANA REVIEW, English Department, University of Saskatchewan, Regina Campus, Regina, Sask., Canada. Editor: H.C. Dillow. Published semiannually. Reports in 6 to 8 weeks. Buys all rights. Pays on publication. Enclose S.A.E. and International Reply Coupons.
Nonfiction: Literary criticism of scholarly standard; knowledgeable articles on the theatre, the visual arts and music. Reviews of current books. Art reviews, national and international, but query is necessary if there are prints. Pays $3 per page for criticism articles. Art reviews by arrangement with Editor. Length: 2,000 to 6,000 words.
Fiction: "Quality" fiction with an honest, meaningful grasp of human experience. Form is open. Pays $3 per page. Length: 2,000 to 6,000 words.
Poetry: Poetry of high artistic merit: integrity, originality and craftsmanship. Pays $10 per page. Length: 4 to 100 lines.

WESTERN HUMANITIES REVIEW, University of Utah, Salt Lake City UT 84112. Editor: Jack Garlington. For the academic or educated lay audience. Quarterly. Acquires North American serial rights. Reports on submissions in six weeks. Enclose S.A.S.E. for return of submissions.
Nonfiction: Authoritative, readable, sophisticated articles on literature, art, philosophy, current events, history, religion, anything in the humanities. Length: about 3,500 words. Interdisciplinary articles encouraged. Departments on film and books. Pays $100 for articles; $25 for reviews.
Fiction: Stories up to 4,000 words. Pays $100.
Poetry: Seeks freshness and humor, along with significance. No length limits. Pays $35.

WESTERN WORLD REVIEW, P.O. Box 2714, Culver City CA 90230. Editor: Robert E. Sagehorn. "An independent review and opinion journal." Quarterly. Circulation: under 1,000. Acquires first rights. Pays in contributor's copies. "Information to writers on request." Query not required, but recommended. Reports in 2 weeks. Enclose S.A.S.E.
Nonfiction: "Politics—economics-philosophy—any good nonfiction of general interest." Length: open.

WORKS: A QUARTERLY OF WRITING, 56 E. 13 St., New York NY 10003. Editor: Lee Hatfield. For those "interested in contemporary literature of the highest quality." Established in 1967. Quarterly. Circulation: 2,500. Buys first North American serial rights. Buys 75 to 100 mss a year. Payment on publication. Will send sample copy to writer for $1.50. Submit complete ms. Will consider photocopied submissions. Reports on material accepted for publication in 4 to 8 weeks. Enclose S.A.S.E. for return of submissions.
Fiction and Poetry: "Fiction and poetry of outstanding merit. No restrictions of subject matter or theme, but work must measure up to our high critical standards." Experimental, mainstream. Traditional and avant-garde forms of poetry; free verse. Payment: "No set restrictions. Our contributors know that we pay as much as our funds permit."

THE YALE REVIEW, 1902A Yale Station, New Haven CT 06520. Editor: J.E. Palmer. Managing Editor: Mary Price. Pays on publication. Enclose S.A.S.E.
Nonfiction: Authoritative discussions of politics, economics, and the arts.
Fiction: Buys quality fiction. Length: 3,000 to 5,000 words.

ZEITGEIST, General Delivery, Saugatuck MI 49453. Editor: Gary Groat. Circulation: 800. Acquires all rights. No payment, but royalties paid on books published by single authors. Reports on submissions usually in one month. Enclose S.A.S.E. for return of submissions.
Nonfiction: "Good critical essays in any style on the relationship of present literary and cultural trends to the university communities. No scholarly essays, critical reviews, etc. Occasional familiar essay." Length: up to 2,000 words.
Photos: With captions only. Experimental, art oriented, any subject. B&w only.
Fiction: "Any subject, any style, slanted toward college students and faculty interest; no taboos; prefer experimental work rather than the standard stuff." Length: up to 3,000 words. Primarily uses short-shorts.
Poetry: "Nonmoralistic, nonreligious, nonhumorous, generally free verse or blank verse. No other taboos." Length: up to 400 lines.

Men's Publications

ACTION FOR MEN, TRUE ACTION, Magazine Management Co., 625 Madison Ave., New York NY 10022. Editorial Director: George Glassgold. For "blue collar men." Bimonthlies. Pays on acceptance. Always query first, "best to query the editor with a sharply pointed, easily digested paragraph or two. You must study the magazine." Enclose S.A.S.E. for reply to query.
Nonfiction: "Some special categories: combat pieces—profiles of great and heroic figures, either world-famed or little known. Emphasis should be on the unusual and the out-of-the-ordinary stunt. Americans are preferred; occasionally foreigners. Scoundrels, hoaxers—men who have pulled off great swindles, impersonations. Epic disasters—emphasis here is on careful, economical, often heartbreaking description rather than jazzed-up treatments. Behind-the-news pieces—emphasis on adventure, but with an inside flavor, set against one of the trouble spots of the world. Consumer-oriented articles—auto, home repair, loans, taxes." Buys exposes, self-help. Length: 3,000 to 5,000 words. Payment is up to $500.
Fiction: Emphasis here is on fact-adventure stories, contemporary, usually featuring Americans in exotic backgrounds. Writing style should be lean, clean, convincing, fast-moving, anecdotal, with racehorse movement and skillful, believable char-

acterization; any man-appeal subject—adventure, crime, World War II, profiles. All story backgrounds should be carefully researched. Preference in adventure material is for "stories," told in scenes and incidents, rather than "factual narratives. No Western fiction, no detective, who-dunit fiction, but heavy on large capers—espionage, hijacking, armed robbery—most 'action' subjects." Length: usually 3,000 to 7,000 words. Booklength, between 15,000 and 20,000 words. Payment is up to $500. Other male-interest fiction considered. Man and woman, thrown together by chance—who have one big, romantic involvement, then pass along their separate way. Length: 3,000 to 5,000 words. Payment is up to $500.

ADAM, Publishers Service Inc., 8060 Melrose Ave., Los Angeles CA 90046. Editor: Don Pfeil. For the young adult male. General subject: "Human sexuality in contemporary society." Monthly. Circulation: 500,000. Buys first North American serial rights. Pays on publication. Will send a sample copy to a writer for $1. Write for guidelines for writers. Query first on articles. Reports in 3 to 6 weeks. Enclose S.A.S.E. for reply to query.

Nonfiction and Fiction: Sex oriented articles. Articles and stories must be sophisticated sex and erotic in concept. Prefer slant toward the hip young swinger with more avant-garde taste. Length 1,500 to 3,000 words. Pays $100 to $200.

Photos: All submissions must contain model release including parent's signature if under 21; fact sheet giving information about the model, place or activity being photographed, including all information of help in writing a photo story.

ARGOSY, 205 E. 42nd St., New York NY 10017. Editor: Gil Paust. For the "adult male, with at least high school education, interested in outdoors, nature, adventure, exploration, camping, hunting, fishing, travel, history, automobiles, sports." Monthly. Circulation: 1,400,000. Rights bought "depends on individual arrangements." Buys 100 mss a year. Query first. Reports in 1 month. Payment in 3 weeks. Enclose S.A.S.E. for reply to query.

Nonfiction: Articles of personal adventure—humor, offbeat and exotic travel, treasure hunts, unusual outdoor stories—everything of interest to the active, intelligent male except overly sexy material. Must be documented and authentic. "We like to feel that the author was actually on the scene. We don't need anything on the movies or for our regular columns." Length: 2,500 to 3,000 words. Pays $500 to $3,000.

Photos: Major areas for photo stories are outdoor adventure, leisure, and recreation. "Before submitting, photographers should thumb through back issues of *Argosy* to see the type of stories we run." Send color transparencies as well as black and white contact sheets. Pays $100 a page for b&w, $150 for color, and from $500 to $750 for a cover. "But we will pay much more for exceptional material." Photographer is responsible for identifying and explaining his photos. Send pictures; queries cannot describe photos fully. Expenses, if any, must be arranged specifically for each assignment. Picture Editor: Bernie White.

Fiction: Needs good fiction material, 4,000 to 5,000 words, novelettes of 12,000 to 16,000 words and novel condensations of 25,000 words by top fiction authors. Fiction should also emphasize the smart male slant and deal with outdoor subjects: Man against nature, animals, the sea, mysteries, war—everything except boy-girl romances. Prices vary from an average $600 for novelettes, $1,000 and up for novels. Fiction Editor: Bruce Cassiday.

How To Break In: "To break into the pages of *Argosy* for the first time, a new writer would first have to submit a story idea that we like. It could be just two or three paragraphs. And he would also have to include the possibility of good photos. If he's a photographer himself, this would be to his credit. Then, if his story idea is accepted, we would ask him to do the piece on speculation, obviously because we have no idea of how well he can write since, as a beginner, he will have no samples of published stories. In *Argosy* there is no such thing as a small sale; we run only full-length features, no shorts."

BLUEBOOK, MAN'S ILLUSTRATED, 235 Park Ave., S., New York NY 10003. Editor: B.R. Ampolsk. Bimonthly. For "a men's adventure audience." Buys all serial rights. Pays on acceptance. Enclose S.A.S.E. for return of submissions.

Nonfiction and Photos: Wants true war and adventure stories, heavy on personality development and authentic background. Provocative expose articles. Articles on exotic vacation spots. Pays $100 to $300. Photos with caption material bought at rate of $12.50 each.

CAVALCADE GROUP: CAVALCADE, NIGHT & DAY, CLIMAX, CANDID, SQUIRE, MEN'S CHALLENGE, 7950 Deering Ave., Canoga Park CA 91304. For a male audience, ages 20 to 45. Fiction and articles of interest to men. Established in 1967. Monthly. Circulation: 100,000. Buys all rights, but will reassign rights to author after publication. Buys over 100 mss a year. Payment on publication. Will send a copy for $1. Will consider photocopied submissions. Reports in "about a month." Enclose S.A.S.E. for return of submissions.
Nonfiction: Articles that interest a man 20 to 45 years of age who is looking for light entertainment. Informational, personal experience, humor, think, expose, and travel articles. Length: 2,500 to 3,500 words. Pays $50 to $150, including photos.
Fiction: Experimental, mystery, suspense, adventure, western, erotica, science fiction, fantasy, and humorous fiction. Length: 2,500 to 3,500 words. Pays $50 to $75.
Photos: Purchased with accompanying mss only. Captions required. 8x10 preferred. Pays $5 cach for b&w. Pays $25 for color transparencies.

CAVALIER, 236 East 46th Street, New York NY 10017. Editor: Douglas Allen. For "young males, 18 to 29, 80% college graduates, affluent, intelligent, interested in current events, ecology, sports, adventure, travel, clothing, good fiction." Monthly. Circulation: 250,000. Buys first and second rights. Buys 35 to 40 mss a year. Pays on publication or before. See past issues for general approach to take. Query first except on fiction. Submit seasonal material at least 3 months in advance. Reports in 3 weeks. Enclose S.A.S.E. for return of submissions or reply to query.
Nonfiction and Photos: Personal experience, interviews, humor, historical, think pieces, expose, new product. "Frank—open to dealing with controversial issues." Does not want material on Women's Lib, water sports, hunting, homosexuality, or travel, "unless it's something spectacular or special." Length: 2,800 to 3,500 words. Payment to $300. Photos purchased with mss or with captions. "No cheesecake. Query first. Information on request."
Fiction: Mystery, science fiction, humorous, adventure, contemporary problems. Length: 3,000 to 4,000 words. Payment to $300, "higher for special." Dept. Editor: Mr. Maurice DeWalt.

DEBONAIR, MAN'S PLEASURE, ALL MAN, MAN'S DELIGHT, 13510 Ventura Blvd., Sherman Oaks CA 91403. Editor: Charles E. Fritch. Predominantly male audience "ages 21 and up." Monthly. Buys first North American serial rights. Buy 240 mss a year. Payment on publication. Will consider photocopied mss if they are "not submitted elsewhere as well." Reports in 3 to 4 weeks. Enclose S.A.S.E. for return of submissions.
Nonfiction and Fiction: Sophisticated fiction and nonfiction. "Slant, please, after reading several issues. We try for freshness. Our articles, fiction, and our girls are not ordinary. Cute, a bit naughty. Strong narrative hook on beginning, a middle, and an end. Don't begin in a bar or cocktail lounge. No lez or homo yarns." Buys informational, how-to, humor, think articles. Buys mainstream, erotica, science fiction, fantasy, mystery, and humorous fiction. Length: 500 to 3,500 words. Pays 3¢ per word up to 1,000 words, 2¢ per word thereafter

DUDE, GENT, NUGGET, 236 E. 46th St., New York NY 10017. Editor: Bruce Arthur. "For men 21 to ?; adventure and sex are their interests." Male oriented subject matter. Every 2 months. Circulation: *Dude* 75,000; *Gent* 100,000; *Nugget* 75,000. Buys first North American serial rights. Buys about 100 mss a year. Pays on publication. Will send sample copy to a writer for $1. Submit complete ms. Reports on material in 6 to 8 weeks. Returns rejected material in 1 month. Enclose S.A.S.E. for return of submissions.
Nonfiction & Photos: "Articles which are male oriented; primarily concerning sex or adventure." Informational, how-to, personal experience, interview, humor, historical, expose, personal opinion and travel. Length: 1,500 to 4,000 words. Pays $100 to $125. Photos purchased with mss.
Fiction: Adventure, erotica, science fiction, humorous. Length: 1,500 to 3,500 words. Pays $100.

ESQUIRE, 488 Madison Ave., New York NY 10022. Editor: Don Erickson. Monthly. Usually buys all rights. Payment on acceptance. Query first. Reports in 3 weeks. Include S.A.S.E. for return of submissions or reply to query.

Nonfiction: Articles vary in length, but usually average 4,000 words and rarely run longer than 5,000 words. Articles should be slanted for sophisticated, intelligent readers; however, not highbrow in the restrictive sense. Wide range of subject matter. Rates run roughly between $350 and $1,250, depending on length, quality, etc. Expenses are sometimes allowed, depending on the assignment.
Photos: Art Director Richard Weigand accepts both contacts and 11x14 b&w matte prints. Uses 35mm and larger Ektachrome and Kodachrome color transparencies. Buys all rights. Payment depends on how photo is used, but rates are roughly $25 for single b&w; $100 to $150 for b&w full page; $150 to $200 for full color page. Guarantee on acceptance. Prefers to be queried. Gives assignments and pays some expenses.
Fiction: Gordon Lish, Fiction Editor; Julie Schwartz, Assistant Fiction Editor. Unsolicited material should be sent to the latter. "Literary excellence only criterion." Payment: $350 to $1,500. Average about 1,000 to 6,000 words.

FLING, 161 E. Erie St., Chicago IL 60611. Editor-Publisher: Arv Miller. Bimonthly. Male audience—21-30 years old. Reports on submissions in one week. Buys first rights (additional payment if reprinted in Fling Festival annual). Pays on acceptance. Enclose S.A.S.E. for reply to query or ms return.
Nonfiction: Send written query to Editor on all article ideas. Subject matter must be directed to adult, male readership. Topics currently needed are: personality profiles from show business (living or dead); male success stories; off beat, social-scientific-sexual fads; controversial national issues, and in-depth political analysis of youth-oriented interests. Articles should be carefully documented and sparked with accurate quotes. Length: 3,500 to 5,000 words. Pays $125 to $300. For the Fling Report, a regular feature, uses a first-hand investigation of a new sexual phenomenon currently gaining attention in this country. This is not an expose type of piece. It is straight reporting, with one exception: author is involved with the people and events in his report. (Detailed outline is supplied to author upon assignment.) Length: 20 typewritten pages. Pays $150 and up, depending on editing and rewriting necessary. Robert Livingston, Department Editor.
Photos: Magazine buys photo-stories and glamour pinup sets. Enclose S.A.S.E. with each submission. Send b&w contact sheets, plus 2¼x2¼ or 35mm color transparencies. OK'd contacts are returned for 8x10 glossy enlargements. Buys first or second rights, with additional payment for reprint use. Study magazine carefully before submitting material. Brief fact sheet on subject or model should be enclosed. Pays $100 to $250 for first rights b&w and color; $75 to $150 for second rights b&w and color. Special photo assignments are sometimes given to freelance photographers upon written query to Editor. Expenses are paid when situation warrants.
Fiction: Short story needs are very specific. Each issue publishes two types of fiction, completely different from each other. Lead fiction is a serious story, examining "the offbeat and far-out relationships between a man and a woman." Prefers this type to be a combination of fantasy (in the John Collier tradition) backed-up with a great deal of sharp, contemporary dialogue. "The characters should be neurotic within the framework of today's modern society. There must also be a strong element of eroticism, but no clinical or detailed descriptions. Endings should be simple and logical conclusions, rather than trick or gimmicked up." Length: 3,000 to 4,000 words. Payment is $125 to $250, depending on length, importance and editing required. Other fiction should fall into the area of humor or satire. Style must be upbeat, not morbid or ponderous. Some element of sex is necessary, but must be presented within a "happy, fun-type context." Stories should be generally amusing, directed to an adult male audience. Dialogue extremely important. Should be "hip" in the sense of language in current use today. 2,000 to 3,000 words. Pays $100 to $150, depending on length, importance, and editing required. Do not submit science fiction, westerns, mysteries, period pieces, ribald classics, plotless vignettes, stories involving children, animals or ghosts.

FOR MEN ONLY, Magazine Management Co., 625 Madison Ave., New York NY 10022. Editorial Director: Ivan Prashker. Completely freelance. Buys all rights. Pays on acceptance. Reports in 2 weeks. Enclose S.A.S.E.
Nonfiction: Emphasis here is on fact-adventure stories, contemporary, usually featuring Americans in exotic backgrounds. Writing style should be lean, clean, convincing, with racehorse movement and skillful, believable characterization. Length

is usually 3,000 to 7,000 words. Pays from $275 to $400. Book-length material runs between 15,000 and 20,000 words. All story backgrounds should be carefully researched. Preference in adventure material is for stories told in scenes and incidents, rather than factual narrative. Some special categories: combat pieces, profiles of great and heroic living figures, either world-famed or little known. Emphasis should be on the unusual and the out-of-the-ordinary stunt. Bigger-Than-Life Personalities; the main need is for profiles of contemporary people, preferably Americans, occasionally foreigners. Scoundrels, hoaxers, men who have pulled off great swindles, impersonations. Epic disasters; emphasis here is on careful, economical, often heartbreaking description rather than jazzed-up treatments. Behind the News pieces; emphasis on adventure, but with an inside flavor, set against one of the trouble spots of the world. Query editor first with brief paragraph or two.
Fiction: Same rates as nonfiction. 3,000 to 4,000 words. No westerns. Adventure settings; tough cops in tight spots, treasure hunters grappling with angry tribesmen, hunters tackling giant anaconda with bow and arrow, and a few involvements with sexy women thrown in carefully but not too explicitly.

GALLERY, 936 N. Michigan, Chicago IL 60611. Editor: Don L. Pierce, Jr. For male audience, college educated, young executives, interested in rock contemporary life styles, hiking, skiing, sports, film and business. Seasonal sports issues. Established in 1972. Monthly. Circulation: 1½ million. Rights purchased vary with author and material. Payment usually on publication, but on acceptance in certain cases. Write for copy of guidelines for writers. Will consider photocopied submissions. Submit seasonal material 2 months in advance. Reports in 2 to 4 weeks. Enclose S.A.S.E. for return of submissions.
Nonfiction and Fiction: Photo essays on sports, life styles, clothes; travel, food and sports articles; personality profiles and interviews; flying; music, movie, and book reviews; articles on contemporary social and cultural topics of interest to younger men. Especially likes informative articles with hard information in them that can be broken down for easy assimilation by the reader; for example, an article on camping, a short section on the equipment required. Uses less conventional approaches in both an artistic and structural manner. A more contemporary writing style is desirable. Particularly wants articles written about rock, women and their place in the 70's, young businessmen; new products, trends and techniques. Length: open. Pays $600 to $1,000. Also buys fiction for $750 to $1,200. Length: 2,000 to 10,000 words. Theme: open. Fiction Editor: Carol Nielson.
Photos: Purchased on assignment. No b&w. 2¼x2¾ or 35mm color for features; 8x10 for gate and cover. Pays $250 page for features and $500 for cover. Pays $3,000 for gatefold.

GENESIS, 120 E. 56th St., New York NY 10022. Stephen Saunders, Executive Editor. Address all material to Pat Button. Established in 1973. Monthly. Buys first North American serial rights. Prefers complete mss. Enclose S.A.S.E.
Nonfiction, Fiction, and Poetry: Social comment, adventure, and some sports articles. Sports must be written on a one-to-one basis. Features on autos, fashion and food. Some poetry is planned.

GENTLEMEN'S QUARTERLY, 488 Madison Ave., New York NY 10022. Editor: Jack Haber. Eight times yearly. Reports on submissions in 1 to 3 weeks. Buys N.A. serial rights and foreign syndication rights only. Must enclose S.A.S.E. for reply to query. Unsolicited mss returned unread; will accept queries only.
Nonfiction: For men in the upper income bracket. Leisure, travel, sports, food and drink, art. Material must appeal to thought and cultivated interests.

KNIGHT, Publishers Service Inc., 8060 Melrose Ave., Los Angeles CA 90046. Editor: Jared Rutter. For male adults. Monthly. Buys all rights, but author may ask for and receive all rights other than first North American serial rights after publication. Pays on publication. Query first on articles. Enclose S.A.S.E.
Nonfiction: "Broad variety of subjects of interest to male adults. Sophisticated sexual slant preferred. Profiles of contemporary personalities; reports on new life styles; latest trends in erotic films, art, theater; photojournalism coverage of current social movements. Interested in articles in the subjective 'new journalism' style, as well as carefully researched reportage, but all must be erotically oriented. No interest in true adventure pieces or how-to-do-it material." Length: 2,500 to 4,000

words. Pays $50 to $150, based on quality and editorial needs.

Photos: All photo submissions must contain the following: 1) An acceptable release (containing the model's name and signature) for all models used. If the model is under 21 years old (18 if married), the signature of a parent or guardian is required. A sample model release is available on request. 2) A stamped, self-addressed envelope. 3) A fact sheet giving information about the model. 4) Place or activity being photographed. Include all information that may be of help in writing an interesting text for photo story. Sample fact sheet available on request. Uses b&w photo stories for personality profiles; photo stories covering events, places, or unusual activities, plus special material, such as erotic art, nude theater, etc. Photos bring $15 each when used to illustrate a story. Purchased separately at time issue goes to press. If submitting an entire layout, an effort should be made to capture a model in the midst of various activities; clothed and unclothed shots should be intermingled; interesting settings and backgrounds are essential. "Keep in mind that the model will become a personality if used in the magazine and emphasis should be as much on who she is as what her body looks like. Natural, real girls with whom men can easily identify are most desirable."

Fiction: Always interested in stories of male-female relationships in situations of conflict, crisis, adventure or humorous confusion. "Science fiction and fantasy settings are acceptable. Emphasis must be on erotic realism. Offbeat and controversial themes acceptable. Does not buy jokes or humorous fillers. Length: 2,500 to 4,000 words. Pays $50 to $150, based on quality and editorial needs."

MALE, 575 Madison Ave., New York NY 10022. Editor: Carl Sifakis. Issued monthly. Pays on acceptance. Enclose S.A.S.E. for reply to query.

Nonfiction: Powerful, dramatic, heroic, true adventures set in exotic backgrounds. Hard-hitting articles, exposes, personality pieces of contemporary interest, with strong male appeal. 5,000 to 7,000 words. Pays $250 to $600.

Fiction: Few male appeal stories up to 5,000 words. Query first.

Fillers: Pays $5 for short gags.

MALE CALL, 6 East 43rd St., New York NY 10017. Editor: William H. Lieberson. For the young male overseas in the military. Monthly. Circulation: 400,000. Buys all rights. Pays on acceptance. Will send a sample copy to a writer on request. No query required. Submit seasonal material at least 6 months in advance. Reports very slow. Enclose S.A.S.E. for return of submissions.

Nonfiction: "Anything of interest to males—sports, autos, adventure, etc. We are an entertainment publication and we like the articles to be written in a style that flows easily." Prefers material with military tie-in. Departments seeking material include "R and Recreations," "True Adventure," "Man at His Best," "Sound Off Column." The last uses anecdotes, poems, and sayings. Also buys photo articles. Length: 400 to 500 words or less. Pays $50 to $75.

Photos: Purchased with mss. B&w glossies, color transparencies, 35mm color. Pays $5 to $10 for b&w; "payment for color depends on use."

MAN TO MAN, MR., SIR, 21 W. 26th St., New York NY 10010. Editor: Everett Meyers. 10 times a year. Pays on publication or before. Enclose S.A.S.E.

Nonfiction: Sharply angled articles that reflect contemporary trends in such subjects as travel, music, sex, new art forms, unusual entertainment, sports, and other activities of interest to men. Length: 2,000 to 5,000 words. Pays $100 and up. Typical payment for article with one or two good b&w photos, $150.

Fiction: "Strong, imaginative stories in modern mood that include man-woman relationships; no one stereotype is demanded. Taboos are against hackneyed plotting and dull writing rather than particular themes or points of view. No rewriting is done in this market, so the original must be mature and professional in execution, as well as fresh in concept." Length: 1,500 to 5,000 words.

Fillers: Jokes for male audience. Pays $5.

MAN'S MAGAZINE, 919 Third Ave., New York NY 10022. Editorial Director: Phil Hirsch. Monthly. Queries or finished manuscripts. Pays on acceptance. Reports in 1 to 4 weeks. Buys all rights. Enclose S.A.S.E.

Nonfiction: Want authentic material presented in a terse, dramatic manner. Contributors should read at least two issues of the magazine before submitting anything. Stress on realistic dialogue, excitingly re-created scenes and vivid prose. Major need is for the big story that lends itself to coverline and lead treatment. Many of these lead stories are culled from the front pages of the nation's newspapers and given dramatic elaboration. They may be written with or without first-person bylines. There is also a need for authentic, carefully written historicals, expose, crime, personality, military. Medical articles must lend themselves to anecdotal adventure treatment. Service pieces should be geared specifically to men. Emphasis is on good plot structure, careful personality development, adventure factor. Payment for 3,500 to 6,000 words ranges from $200 to $500.

MAN'S WORLD, 575 Madison Ave., New York NY 10022. Editor: Michael Minick. For ages "20 to 35, blue collar, high school grads with some college." Bimonthly. Circulation: 125,000. Buys all rights. Payment on acceptance. Always query first. Reporting time varies. Enclose S.A.S.E. for reply to queries.
Nonfiction and Fiction: Freelancers "should be familiar with all Magazine Management publications [*Action For Men, True Action, For Men Only, Stag*]. Sensationalistic." Buys how-to's, interviews, and exposes. Length: 3,500 to 4,000 words. Pays $350. Buys adventure and erotic fiction. Length: 3,500 to 4,000 words. Pays $350. Buys condensed novels. Pays $650.

THE MEN'S DIGEST, RASCAL, BEST FOR MEN, 21 W. 26th St. N.Y. NY 10010. Editor: William Scott. *Men's Digest* and *Rascal* monthly, *Best for Men* quarterly. Reports in 4 weeks. Buys all rights. Pays on acceptance. Enclose S.A.S.E.
Nonfiction: Prefers articles with photos, on timely subjects of interest to active, virile male. Contributors especially encouraged to write on subjects currently in the public consciousness. Pays $10 to $100. Query preferred, but not required. Study magazines for style before submitting.
Fiction: "Crime, drama, horror and science fiction are all fine. The writer should remember that there is no substitute for the well-plotted, fast-moving story, which we always seek, especially if it keeps the reader guessing to the end. Sex interest is preferred, but not absolutely vital. Length has ranged from 800 to 3,000 words; 2,500 is ideal. Pays from $20 to $100 depending on length, quality, number of sales to us and established name as an author."

OUI, Playboy Enterprises, Inc., The Playboy Building, 919 Michigan Ave., Chicago IL 60611. Co-editors: Jean-Louis Ginibre and John Carroll; Managing Editor: R. C. Anderson; Articles Editor: John Lombardi. For "the relatively sophisticated man in his mid-20's." Monthly. Enclose S.A.S.E. for return of submissions.
Nonfiction and Fiction: Published by Playboy Enterprises for a group of men younger than the average *Playboy* reader, the magazine will publish "articles, short stories, satire, and humor"; emphasis on concise, contemporary articles and on the global interests of the audience. Pays $500 to $1,200.

PENTHOUSE, 909 Third Ave., New York NY 10022. Editor: James Goode. For male audience; upper income bracket, college educated. Established in 1969. Monthly. Circulation: 3,000,000. Rights purchased vary with author and material. Buys 60 to 70 mss a year. Payment on acceptance. Query first. Will consider photocopied submissions. Reports in 1 month. Enclose S.A.S.E. for response to query.
Nonfiction: Articles on general themes, but not sport or family orientated; money, sex, politics, health, crime, etc. No first person. Male viewpoint only. Length: open. Pays 10¢ a word and up. Nonfiction Editor: Eric Protter.
Fiction: Fiction with some sex content. Experimental, mainstream; mystery, suspense and adventure with erotic flavor; erotica, and science fiction. Length: 3,000 to 8,000 words. Pays $400 and up. Fiction Editor: Gay Bryant.
Photos: Purchased without mss and on assignment. "Nude girl sets." Send for spec sheet. Photo Editor: Joe Brooks.

PIMIENTA MAGAZINE, 1515 N.W. 7th St., Miami FL 33125. Editor: W. Allan Sandler. Audience is "Spanish, male, ages 19 to 50." Monthly. Circulation: 70,000.

Copyrighted. Buys about 50 mss a year. Pays on publication. Will send a sample copy to a writer for 50¢. No query required. "Stories may be submitted in English. We will translate." Reports in 1 month. Enclose S.A.S.E. for return of submissions.
Nonfiction, Photos, and Fiction: "Male interest, spicy stories, and adventure." Buys exposes, photo essays, adventure and confession stories. For a regular column, seeks "questions and answers on sex problems." Length: 2,500 to 5,000 words. Pays $25 to $100. Buys b&w glossies. Pays $20.

PIX, Publishers Service Inc., 8060 Melrose Ave., Los Angeles CA 90046. Editor: David Hine. Bimonthly. Requirements similar to *Adam* but wants hard-hitting fiction with strong sexual slant, ribald humor, articles on erotica, etc. Pays straight 3¢ per word.

PLAYBOY, 919 N. Michigan, Chicago IL 60611. Editor-Publisher: Hugh M. Hefner; Exec. Editor: Arthur Kretchmer; Managing Editor: Sheldon Wax. Monthly. Reports in 2 weeks. Buys first rights and others. Enclose S.A.S.E. with mss and queries.
Nonfiction: "Articles should be carefully researched and written with wit and insight; a lucid style is important. Little true adventure or how-to material. Check magazine for subject matter. Pieces on outstanding contemporary men, sports, politics, sociology, business and finance, games, all areas of interest to the urban male." A query is advisable here. Length is about 4,000 to 6,000 words. Pays $3,000 for lead article; $2,000 regular. The Playboy interviews run between 8,000 and 15,000 words. The freelancer outlines the questions, conducts and edits the interview, and writes the introduction. For an example of what is wanted, see "Playboy Interview: Germaine Greer." Pays $2,000. Runs an interview 11 times a year, a panel discussion once a year. The panel discussion is a conversation of seven to ten people speaking on a subject of topical interest. 8,000 to 12,000 words. Pays $4,000. Has a movie reviewer, record reviewer, theater critic, book reviewers, food and drink columnist; not looking for material in these areas. The price for each purchase of short-short material will be equal to one-half the price of a standard-length, non-lead piece, with a maximum purchase price of $1,500. Also pays $50 to $250 for idea. Pays more for idea with research which is assigned to a staff writer. If a commissioned article does not meet standards, will pay a turn-down price of $400.
Photos: Mark Kauffman, Photography Editor, suggests that all photographers interested in contributing make a thorough study of the photography currently appearing in the magazine. Generally all photography is done on assignment. While much of this is assigned to *Playboy's* staff photographers, approximately 40% of the photography is done by freelancers and *Playboy* is in constant search of creative new talent. Qualified freelancers are encouraged to submit samples of their work and ideas. All assignments made on an all rights basis with payments scaled from $600 per color page; $300 per b&w page; cover, $850. Playmate photography for entire project: $6,000. Assignments and submissions handled by Associate Editors Gary Cole and Hollis Wayne, Chicago; Marilyn Grabowski, Los Angeles. Assignments made on a minimum guarantee basis. Film, processing, and other expenses necessitated by assignment honored.
Fiction: Both light and serious fiction. Entertainment pieces are clever, smoothly written stories. Serious fiction must come up to the best contemporary standards in substance, idea, and style. Both, however, should be designed to appeal to the educated, well-informed male reader. General types include comedy, mystery, fantasy, horror, science fiction, adventure, social-realism, "problem," and psychological stories. One special requirement for science fiction is that it deal—in fresh and original ways—with human dilemmas more than technological problems. Fiction on controversial topics is welcome; the only taboo is against formless sketches and excessively subjective writing. *Playboy* has serialized novels by Ian Fleming, Vladimir Nabokov, Graham Greene, Michael Crichton, and Irwin Shaw. Other fiction contributors include Saul Bellow, John Cheever, Bernard Malamud, and P.G. Wodehouse. Fiction lengths are from 2,000 to 10,000 words; occasionally short-shorts of 1,000 to 1,500 words are used. Pays $3,000 for lead story; $2,000 regular; $1,000 short-short. Rates rise for additional acceptances. Rate for Ribald Classics is $400. Unsolicited mss must be accompanied by stamped, self-addressed envelope. Robie Macauley, Fiction Editor.
Fillers: Party Jokes are always welcome. Pays $50 each. Also interesting items for

Playboy After Hours, front section (best check it carefully before submission). The After Hours, front section, pays anywhere from $50 for a two-line typographical error to $350 for an original lead item. Subject matter should be humorous, ironic. Prefers lengths of 20 to 500 words. Ideas for Playboy Potpourri pays $75. Query first.

RAMPAGE, 3550 N. Lombard St., Franklin Park IL 60131. Editor: Jack Tyger. For sophisticated, cosmopolitan adults. Weekly. Circulation: 300,000. Buys all rights. Buys 600 mss a year. Pays on acceptance. Will send a sample copy to a writer for 25¢. Enclose S.A.S.E. for return of submissions.
Nonfiction and Photos: "Our audience consists of sophisticated, cosmopolitan adult readers who enjoy reading witty, humorous and satirical sex-oriented articles. Our readers also prefer reading shocking expose features. See 'The Six Ways Smart Men End Lousy Love Affairs.' We're always in the market for features on current trends in sex. These features should have a strong humorous or satirical slant. Example: 'Girls Have Sex with Plastic Dummy.' Humorous first-person confession stories are also in order. See: 'Anti-Sex Machines Are Out to Get You!' Writer should know how to put humor, wit and satire to good use in his features. Features must be entertaining. Rather than treating readers as groups of buyers, we try to reach each and every reader on an individual basis." Length: 600 to 1,200 words. Payment is up to 2¢ a word. B&w glossy photos purchased with mss. Payment is $5 to $100.

ROGUE, Ro-Top, Inc., 95 Madison Ave., New York NY 10016. Editor: Christopher Watson. Monthly. Study the magazine before submitting material. Reports in 4 weeks. Buys first North American serial rights. Pays on publication. Enclose S.A.S.E.
Nonfiction: Material ranges from straight reportage, particularly coverage of sexually oriented newsworthy events, to hard-hitting satire. Themes should be keyed to the young, sophisticated male market, but not too urbane. If the article is of the reportage type, photographs should accompany the ms. Serious subjects of a sexual nature excellent if erotic! Payment starts at $50. Best length is from 1,500 to 2,500 words.
Photos: Contacts preferred to enlargements. Color material should be 2¼x2¼ reversal. Buys first time and second time rights. Picture stories needed badly. "In the past they've ranged from a pic essay on a bachelor going around the world, to the Copenhagen Pornography Fair, to nude hippie demonstrations. Color section is strictly girl-boy, girl-alone, girl-girl oriented. Models should look sexy, bare, sophisticated, modern, young, friendly, pubic hair OK, clothes taboo." Rates are from $100 up for color, accompanied by b&w.
Fiction: Runs the gamut from the gutsy and sexy to the pleasantly sexy. Reader identification important. "Love-sex stories with the recognition factor for readers is where it's at." Up-to-date erotic description OK. Stay off trodden paths. Payment is similar to nonfiction.

SAGA, 333 Johnson Ave., Brooklyn NY 11206. Editor: Martin M. Singer. Monthly for men ages 17 and up. No fiction or poetry. Reports on submissions within 3 to 4 weeks. Buys all rights, but will release on request. Pays on acceptance. Address all material to Editor. Enclose S.A.S.E. for reply to query.
Nonfiction: "Articles, first-person adventure, exploration reports—anything of interest to the no-nonsense man. Emphasis has been shifted from the historical subject to the present-day happening, and narrative skill is demanded. Subjects of interest to male audience: war, politics, adventure, hunting, sports, legitimate expose (topical nature), in-depth reports on personalities, travel, crime, treasure (no rehashes, please; current or new information on established trove); science (current developments, but written for laymen). No sex; no repeats of World War II battles or engagements except mss with fresh and previously unrevealed information. This is a reader's magazine, not a glancer's. Most articles and stories turn on an epic battle of some kind: treasure hunting, man against nature, man against society, man vs. himself, etc. Stresses the 'male triumphant' theme whenever possible. Wants to tell men where to look for buried treasure, how some guy crossed an ocean on a raft, etc. Does not want historical articles on Spanish-American war heroes, etc., or Civil War heros. World War II is about the most remote history accepted. Editors ask you to query first. Length: 4,000 to 5,000 words. Pays $300 minimum; increase $10 per

purchase until permanent plateau of $350; bonus factor thereafter."
Photos: Purchased with mss or captions only. Also buys picture stories. Color very important here. Will look at 35mm; prefers 2¼x2¼. B&w and color. Prefers to see contact sheets, then order 8x10's. Payment varies depending on set and quality; $350 minimum for picture stories; $150 minimum for cover in color; 4x5 or larger transparencies. Needs b&w or color action stories for men.

SCORE, 351 W. 54 St., New York NY 10019. Editor: Tom Carroll. For "matured males with varied interests." Monthly. Buys all rights, but will reassign rights to author after publication. Buys 60 to 65 mss a year. Payment on publication. Will send free sample copy to writer on request. Query frist or submit complete ms. Submit seasonal material at least 2 months in advance. Reports on material in 6 weeks. Enclose S.A.S.E. for return of submissions or reply to query.
Nonfiction: Sexually oriented material on today's theme. Humor, expose, travel. Length: 3,000 to 4,000 words. Pays minimum of $100.
Fiction: Mysteries, science fiction (sexually oriented). Length: 3,000 to 4,000 words. Pays minimum of $75.

STAG MAGAZINE, 575 Madison Ave., New York NY 10022. Editorial Director: Noah Sarlat. Issued monthly. Reports in 2 weeks. Buys all rights. Pays on acceptance. Enclose S.A.S.E. for reply to queries.
Nonfiction: Uses fast, suspenseful, dramatic, true stories. Also uses articles on personalities and crime which run up to 5,000 words. Wants any articles of interest to men. Pays up to $500. Query first.
Photos: B&w: singles, illustrations, series. Up to $25 for each article illustration; up to $50 per page for series. Color for covers only.
Fiction: Off-trail fiction bolstered by tense atmosphere and strong sex angle is acceptable, though hero-villain plot is not necessary. 3,000 to 5,000 words. The editor suggests that the inexperienced writer stick to the well-plotted story. These pay up to $300.

SWANK, c/o Magnum/Royal Publications, 1560 Broadway, New York NY 10036. Editor: Howard Winters. For "college to middle age, bachelor-oriented males with a taste for good wines, good foods, and even better girls." Accepts seasonal material, but must be sent 2 or 3 months in advance. Monthly. Circulation: over 150,000. Buys first North American serial rights. Payment on publication. Will send a sample copy to writer free on request. Reports in around 2 months. Query first for nonfiction. Enclose S.A.S.E. for reply to queries or return of submissions.
Nonfiction and Fiction: Freelancer should have an "easy, free-moving style, not pedantic; a sense of humor doesn't hurt unless it's at the direct expense of the article or story. We'd prefer to see more articles than fiction. Would like to see articles of varied interest, including politics, sex, fast cars, faster women, sports, racing (auto, horses, etc.)." Length: 2,000 to 2,500 words. Pays $125 to $250. Fiction length: 1,500 to 2,000 words. Pays $100.

THE SWINGER, GEM, 303 W. 42 St., New York NY 10036. Editor: Will Martin. For young men. Bimonthlies. Buys all rights or first rights. Buys 85 mss a year. Pays on publication or on assignment of a script to a specific issue. Reports "as soon as we can—depending upon the volume of unsolicited material we receive." Enclose S.A.S.E. for return of submissions.
Nonfiction and Fiction: "Articles and fiction with sex-related themes, mainly. Treated straight or satirical or farcical." Length: 500 to 1,500 words. Payment is $25 to $50.
Photos: B&w glossies. "No specified price."

TOPPER, Captain Publications, 95 Madison Ave., New York NY 10016. Editor: Christopher Watson. Issued bimonthly. Reports in 4 weeks. Buys first North American rights. Pays on publication. Enclose S.A.S.E.
Nonfiction and Fiction: Always in the market for man-woman-sex oriented theme, but only if the latter are significant. Only taboo is that of bad taste, and they do not shy away from controversy of a legitimate nature. "Both fiction and nonfiction should have similar erotic effect; erotic, but not pornographic." Length: 1,500 to 2,500 words. Payment is $50 to $100.

TRUE, Fawcett Publications, One Astor Plaza, 1515 Broadway, New York NY 10036. Editor: Clair Conley. For an adventurous male audience. Buys all rights, but will reassign "remaining rights" to author upon request 90 days after publication. Send queries and unsolicited mss to Articles Editor. Enclose S.A.S.E. for reply to queries or return of submissions.
Nonfiction: Wants interviews. Outdoor pieces should offer something truly unusual, like William Humphrey writing about a bone fishing trip. Personal adventure is always of interest. Less emphasis on expose pieces. "I'm particularly open to writers outside New York." Also needs short features for "Behind the Wheel," "Man and His Health," "Man and His Money," and "Traveling Man," which are regular departments. Length for articles: about 3,000 to 5,000 words. Length for shorter features: around 1,100 words. Payment for articles is $1000. Pays $400 for shorter features.

Military Publications

The magazines below include technical and semitechnical journals for military commanders, personnel, and planners; magazines for military families; and publications for civilians interested in Armed Forces activities. All require submissions emphasizing military subjects or aspects of military life. Servicemen's magazines with non-military emphasis are classified elsewhere by their subject matter. Other magazines buying similar material, but without the military slant, will be found in the Men's, Women's, Retirement, Travel, and General Interest categories.

AIR UNIVERSITY REVIEW, United States Air Force, Air University, Maxwell Air Force Base AL 36112. Editor: Eldon W. Downs, Colonel, USAF. "For Air Force officers and top-level civilians." Professional military journal. Circulation: 18,500 in English. Not copyrighted. Query first. Buys no mss, but gives cash awards on publication. Reports in 6 weeks. Enclose S.A.S.E. for reply to queries.
Nonfiction and Photos: "To stimulate professional thought concerning aerospace doctrines, strategy, policies, plans, programs, concepts, tactics, and related techniques. Footnotes when necessary only. Prefer that the author be the expert. Book reviews are solicited. Not a publicity journal. Narrative style. Also wants articles in Spanish and Portuguese for books of readings entitled *Selections From Air University Review*. Photos desired as a supplement to articles, but not necessary. B&w glossies only." Length: 2,500 to 4,000 words. Pays in cash awards up to $100 ("unless written by Federal personnel on duty time").

AIRMAN, SAFOIIC (AIRMAN), STOP B-15, Bolling AFB DC 20332. Editor: Capt. John T. Correll. Official magazine of the U.S. Air Force. Does not pays.

ARMED FORCES JOURNAL, 1710 Connecticut Ave., N.W., Washington DC 20009. Editor: Benjamin F. Schemmer. For "senior career officers of the U.S. military, defense industry, Congressmen and government officials interested in defense matters, international military and defense industry." Established in 1863. Monthly. Circulation: 28,000. Buys all rights. Buys 15 to 20 mss a year. Pays on publication. Will send a free sample copy to writer on request. Query first. Will consider photocopied submissions. Reports in 2 to 4 weeks. Enclose S.A.S.E. for reply to queries.
Nonfiction and Photos: Publishes "national and international defense issues: weapons programs, research, personnel programs, international relations (with emphasis on defense aspect). Also profiles on retired military personnel. We do not want broad overviews of a general subject; more interested in detailed analysis of a specific program or situation. Our readers are decision makers in defense matters—hence, subject should not be treated too simplistically. Be provocative. We are not afraid to take issue with our own constituency when an independent voice needs to

be heard." Buys informational, profile, think articles. Length: 1,000 to 3,000 words. Pays up to 10¢ per word; $25 to $250 per article. 8x10 b&w glossies or color transparencies purchased with or without mss; captions required. Pays $5 for b&w, $50 for color.

How To Break In: "The writer should read our magazine and send us an article he thinks our readers would be excited to find in *Armed Forces Journal!*"

ARMY, 1529 18th St., N.W., Washington DC 20036. Editor: L. James Binder. For "active and retired military, mostly Army Reservists, civilians, industry employees. We have a broader audience than most military journals, which makes it necessary for us to walk a fine line between being too technical and oversimplifying." Monthly. Circulation: 95,000. Buys all rights. Buys 250 mss a year. Pays on publication. Will send a free sample copy to a writer on request. No query required. Reports in 1 month. Enclose S.A.S.E. for return of submissions.

Nonfiction and Photos: Wants articles up to 5,000 words relating to military affairs, history, art and science, representing the interests of the entire Army. Especially interested in articles having application to current military problems. "Freelance writer should be factual and if subject is outside of his area of expertise, use recognized authorities or sources in attribution. We also like a liberal sprinkling of actual examples to back up main points. Prefer not to see mss about obscure military actions which have no special significance—also mss which merely recount what is already in the history books." Will consider how-to, personal experience, interviews, profiles, inspirational, humor, historical, think pieces, new product, photo articles. Length: 150 to 4,500 words. Payment is 7¢ to 10¢ a word. Photos purchased with mss. B&w glossies, color transparencies, 35mm color. Payment "varies but liberal." Prefers well-illustrated articles and how well this is carried out may often be the deciding factor as to acceptance or rejection.

Fiction: Rarely uses fiction, and then only when it points out a military lesson in tactics, organization or the like. Pays 5¢ to 10¢ per word.

Fillers: "True humorous or interesting accounts of military life." Length: 100 to 500 words. Payment is $5 to $25.

GRUNT, Grunt Publications, Inc., P.O. Box 8717, Tamuning, Guam 96911. Editor: Raymond White. For military audience of all services. Monthly in 2 editions (European and Pacific). Send Pacific material to Grunt Publications, Inc., 58 Pak Tak St., 9th Floor, Kai It Bldg., Kowloon, Hong Kong. Send European material to 117/119 Mannheimerstrasse, 675 Kaiserlautern, Germany. Buys first rights. Buys 30 to 40 mss a year. Payment upon publication. Will send free sample copy to writer on request. Write for copy of guidelines for writers. Queries desired, but not essential. Enclose S.A.S.E. for reply to queries or return of submissions.

Nonfiction and Photos: "Interested in material in the following subject areas: military humor and satirization, self-improvement, exposes, interesting places and activities for military men to enjoy; how to enjoy life or benefit during active duty." Length: 1,000 to 2,000 words. Pays from $20 to $200 (including photos) depending on value of piece and work involved. "Individual photos that lend themselves to humorous captions are also considered." Pays $5 to $10 each, depending on use.

Fiction: Used "when of good, action-packed nature or along a humorous or satirical vein." Length: 1,000 to 2,000 words. Pays minumum of 2¢ per word.

Poetry and Fillers: Light, humorous, witty and satirical poems and fillers with a definite military slant. Pays $5 minimum.

INFANTRY, Box 2005, Fort Benning GA 31905. Editor: Col. Edward M. Bradford. For "company grade (lieutenants and captains) officers of the infantry. Over 90% of our readers are military." Established in 1921. Published every two months. Circulation: 13,500. Buys about 100 mss a year. Pays on publication. Will send a free sample copy to a writer upon request. Will send editorial guidelines sheet to a writer on request. Query desirable. Reports in two weeks. Enclose S.A.S.E. for reply to queries.

Nonfiction, Photos, and Fillers: Publishes articles on the "organization, weapons, tactics, and equipment of the infantry. Other topics of interest to the infantrymen and combat leaders." Infantry or infantry-related. Military organization, weapons, equipment, tactics, techniques, history, leadership. Length: 2,000 to 5,000 words; will consider longer pieces. Pays $15 to $100. Payment based on originality, quality of writing, evidence of research, illustrations furnished. Photos purchased with mss;

preferably 8x10 glossy photos. Fillers. Length: 100 to 500 words. Short humor, human interest. Pays $10 to $25.

LEATHERNECK, P.O. Box 1918, Quantico VA 22134. Managing Editor: Ronald D. Lyons. Enclose S.A.S.E. for reply to queries.
Nonfiction and Photos: Interested in articles covering present-day Marine activities. Photos are mandatory. Please query first. Not interested in former Marines in politics, sports, etc. *Leatherneck's* slant today is toward the young Marine. Large percentage of subscribers are parents and dependents of enlisted Marines, consequently material used must be impeccable in taste. Pay $150 up. Length: 2,000 to 3,000 words.
Fiction: "Have temporarily discontinued 'plot' fiction but we are definitely interested in humor pieces with which today's Marine can identify himself."
Poetry: Poems with Marine themes. Pays $10 each.
How To Break In: "Like most publications, we're interested in young writers. And, if their writing is good, we smile when we sign the check. More than one beginner has 'broken in' with us, and we've watched them go on to bigger and better things. That's happiness. Unhappiness is when we receive manuscripts from young freelancers—and older ones too—who have not done their homework. In *Writer's Market '73, Leatherneck* is listed as being 'interested in articles covering present-day Marine activities.' The manuscripts come in, and our rejection slips go out. On many of them we pen a note: 'We are sorry to be returning your manuscript, but *Leatherneck* is a magazine published for Marines. Perhaps one of the other service publications would like to see your story about the Navy, Army, Air Force, etc.' Yes, there are opportunities for young freelancers at *Leatherneck*. But they must remember that we are specialized. Our main interest is United States Marines, their problems, their interest and their accomplishments. If a young freelancer thinks he can write professionally about the Marine Corps, without having served in it, he is more than welcome to step up to our firing line. If he can't hit the target, his manuscript will be given a 'Maggie's Drawers' and returned. If he comes anywhere near the 'bull's-eye,' he will be encouraged. Our poetry column (Gyrene Gyngles) is a good opportunity for 'recruits' in the writing field to break in with us. Occasionally we buy short human interest items concerning Marines and their acts of heroism. And, of course, we're always interested in humor pieces, in good taste. You may have seen the Marine Corps' latest recruiting slogan: 'The Marines are looking for a few good men!' We go along with that. *Leatherneck* is looking for a few good freelancers."

MARINE CORPS GAZETTE, Marine Corps Association, Box 1775, MCB, Quantico VA 22134. Editor: Col. Bevan G. Cass, U.S.M.C. (Ret.). May issue is aviation oriented. November issue is historically oriented. Monthly. Circulation: 25,000. Buys all rights. Buys 140 to 160 mss a year. Pays on publication. Will send free sample copy on request. "Will send writer's guide on request." Submit seasonal or special material at least 2 months in advance. Query first. Reports in 30 to 60 days. Enclose S.A.S.E. for reply to queries.
Nonfiction: Uses articles up to 5,000 words pertaining to the military profession. Keep copy military, not political. Wants practical articles on military subjects, especially amphibious warfare, close air support and helicopter-borne assault. Also uses any practical article on artillery, communications, leadership, etc. Particularly wanted are articles on relationship of military to civilian government, in-depth coverage of problem areas of the world, Russian and Chinese military strategy and tactics. Also historical articles about Marines are always needed for the November issue, the anniversary of the Marine Corps. Otherwise historical articles not wanted unless they have a strong application to present day military problems. All offerings are passed on by an editorial board as well as by the editor. Does not want "Sunday supplement" or "gee whiz" material. Pays 3¢ to 6¢ per word.
Photos: Purchased with mss. Pays $5 each. 4x5 glossies preferred.

MILITARY LIFE, 6 E. 43rd St., New York NY 10017. Editor: William H. Lieberson. Issued monthly for young military families. Buys all rights. Pays on acceptance. Will send free sample copy to a writer on request. Reports are slow (material has to be checked for clearance since it goes into official papers). Enclose S.A.S.E. for return of submissions.

Nonfiction: "Looking for articles of about 500 words that will appeal to the military family. They should be general enough so that they will interest all three services. Also, articles that appeal to the military wife. As a rule, these women are young with small children." Also uses sports articles. Query not necessary. Average article pays $75.

Photos: Purchased with mss; prefers captions but not necessary. Must be of interest to young married service readers. Wants b&w glossies and four-color transparencies. Payment varies.

Fiction: Short humorous military anecdotes. Pays $5 to non-servicemen, $25 bond for servicemen.

Fillers: Occasionally uses short-shorts. Length: 500 to 750 words. Pays $75.

MILITARY LIVING AND CONSUMER GUIDE, 2300 South 9th St., Suite 504, Arlington VA 22204. Editor: Ann Crawford. For military personnel and their families. Monthly. Circulation: 20,000. Buys first serial rights. Pays on publication. Will send a sample copy to a writer for 25¢ in coin or stamp. Enclose S.A.S.E. for return of submissions.

Nonfiction and Photos: "Articles on military life and personalities of interest to military families all over the world. We would especially like recreational features in the Washington DC area. We specialize in passing along morale boosting information about the local area, with emphasis on the military family—travel pieces about surrounding area, recreation information, etc. We do not want to see depressing pieces, pieces without the military family in mind, personal petty complaints. Especially looking for humor about military life and the military family. Prefer 700 words or less, but will consider more for an exceptional feature. We also prefer a finished article rather than a query." Payment is 1¢ to 1½¢ a word. Photos purchased with mss. 8x10 b&w glossies. Payment is $5 for original photos by author.

Fillers: Short humor, verse "with military orientation only." Payment is $2.

MILITARY LIVING AND CONSUMER GUIDE'S CONFIDENTIAL REPORT, 2300 S. 9th St., Suite 504, Arlington VA 22204. Publisher: Mrs. Ann Crawford. For "military consumers worldwide." Bimonthly. Will send sample issue for 25¢. Enclose S.A.S.E. for return of submissions.

Nonfiction: "We use information on little-known military facilities and privileges, discounts around the world, travel information, specialized consumer information of direct interest to the military family and retirees, information affecting the health, welfare, and happiness of military families. We will consider bad news, but the emphasis is on information to boost family service morale. Items must be short and concise. Stringers wanted around the world. Payment is on an honorarium basis-1¢ to 1½¢ a word."

MILITARY REVIEW, U.S. Army Command and General Staff College, Fort Leavenworth KS 66027. Editor: Col. O.W. Martin, Jr. Professional military journal. Monthly. Total circulation: 21,200 in English, Spanish and Portuguese language editions. Not copyrighted. Pays on publication. Will send free sample copy to a writer on request. Query preferred. Reports on submissions in 1 week. Enclose S.A.S.E. for reply to queries.

Nonfiction: "Prefers the concise and the direct, expressed in the active voice; precision and clarity of expression to flowery prose; the specific to the general. Wants articles on any subject related to military affairs that is of current interest and significance. Articles dealing with national defense policy, strategy, tactics at the division and higher levels of command, military organization, foreign military and strategic affairs, military history, leadership and professional development. Cite all references." Length: 2,000 to 4,000 words. Payment varies up to $150.

Photos: Purchased with mss; b&w, 8x10 glossy. Payment varies.

NATIONAL GUARDSMAN, 1 Massachusetts Ave., N.W., Washington DC 20001. Editor: Allan G. Crist. For officers and enlisted men of the Army and Air National Guard who will devote a great deal of their own time to serious military training but do not wish to make the Service their lifetime, fulltime career. Monthly except August. Circulation: 70,000. Rights negotiable. Buys 10 to 12 mss a year. Pays on publication. Query with outline rather than submit completed ms. Reports "usually, within days." Enclose S.A.S.E. "No poems or short stories—ever!"

Nonfiction and Photos. Military policy, strategy, training, equipment, logistics, personnel policies: tactics, combat lessons learned as they pertain to the Army and Air Force (including Army National Guard and Air National Guard). No history. Material must be strictly accurate from a technical standpoint. Writer must have military knowledge. "It helps if he knows enough about Guard or other reserve forces to orient his piece toward the Guardman's frame of reference. Style should be easy to read, serious but not pedantic." Does not want " 'exposes' of every real and fancied shortcoming of the military services." Length: 2,000 to 3,000 words. Payment is 3¢ a word and up, depending on originality, amount of research involved, etc. B&w glossy photos occasionally purchased with mss. Payment is $5 to $10.

Fillers: "Military anecdotes (but not timeworn jokes)." Length: 50 to 200 words. Payment is $10.

OFF DUTY, 69 Eschersheimer Landstr., 6 Frankfurt/Main, W. Germany. Editorial Director: Thomas C. Lucey. For "U.S. military in Europe and the Pacific. Varies from young bachelor G.I.'s to over-30 and over-40 career men and their wives." Monthly in 2 editions: European and Pacific. Circulation: 175,000. Buys first rights. Buys 125 to 150 mss a year. Pays on publication. Will send a sample copy on request. Query first. Send Pacific material to Jim Shaw, *Off Duty*, P.O. Box 2139, Bangkok, Thailand. Submit seasonal queries 5 to 6 months in advance. Reports in 1 month. Enclose S.A.E. and International Reply Coupons for reply to queries.

Nonfiction: "Travel, shopping, art of living, bargains, good values in Europe or Pacific." Approach should be "practical, specific, anecdotal. Stress what to buy, why; stress where to go, how, why. This is not a dream book." Also uses articles on "travel, folklore, handicrafts, shopping, participation sports, hunting and fishing, and the like." Would prefer not to see "puff copy, newspaper-style travel copy, amateur writing." Length: 600 to 3,000 words; "mostly 1,800 to 2,000 words." Pays 3¢ to 10¢ a word.

Photos: Purchased with ms; with captions only. B&w glossies. Pays $18; inside color, $35. Color covers negotiated.

PARAMETERS: THE JOURNAL OF THE U.S. ARMY WAR COLLEGE, U.S. Army War College, Carlisle Barracks PA 17013. Editor: Colonel Paul Goodman, U.S. Army. For predominantly military audience, "age 35 years and up, well educated (large percentage of advanced academic degrees), interested in strategy, national defense, management." Biannual. Circulation: 5,000. Not copyrighted. Permission to reprint articles from the journal must be obtained from the Commandant of the U.S. Army War College. Pays on publication. No query required. Reports in 1 month. Enclose S.A.S.E. for return of submissions.

Nonfiction and Photos: "The purpose of *Parameters* is to provide a forum for the expression of mature professional thought on matters of broad military strategy, national defense policy, top military management, and other subjects of significant and current military interest. Further, it is designed to serve as a vehicle for continuing the education, and thus the professional development, of War College graduates and other senior military officers and civilians concerned with military affairs." Wants historical and photo articles as well as think pieces. "Military implications should be stressed whenever possible." Length: 2,000 to 4,000 words. Photos purchased with mss. B&w glossies. "Basis for payment: $5 per printed page or fraction thereof (to include half-tones, artwork, charts, graphs, maps, etc.) not to exceed $50 per article."

THE RETIRED OFFICER MAGAZINE, 1625 Eye St., N.W., Washington DC 20006. Editor: Colonel Minter L. Wilson, Jr., USA-Ret. For "officers of the 7 uniformed services and their families." Established in 1945. Monthly. Circulation: 175,000. Rights purchased vary with author and material. May buy all rights or first serial rights. Will send free sample copy to writer on request. Submit complete ms. Will consider photocopied submissions "if clean and fresh." Submit seasonal material (holiday stories in which the Armed Services are depicted) at least 3 months in advance. Reports on material accepted for publication within 6 weeks. Returns rejected material in 4 weeks. Enclose S.A.S.E. for return of submissions.

Nonfiction and Photos: History, humor, cultural, second-career opportunities and current affairs. "Currently topical subjects with particular contextual slant to the military; historical events of military significance; features pertinent to a retired military officer's milieu (second career, caveats in the business world; wives' adjusting, leisure, fascinating hobbies). True military experiences (short) are also useful. Because our audience is derived from all services, we tend to use articles less technical than a single-service publication might publish." Length: 1,000 to 2,500 words. Pays $25 to $250. 8x10 b&w photos (normal halftone). Pays $5. Color photos must be suitable for color separation. Pays $25 if reproduced in color; otherwise, same as b&w. Dept. Editor: Carol F. Rose.

SEA POWER, 818 Eighteenth St., N.W., Washington DC 20006. Editor: James D. Hessman. Issued monthly by the Navy League of the U.S. for naval personnel and civilians interested in naval and defense matters. Buys all rights. Pays on publication. Will send free sample copy to a writer on request. Reports in 1 to 6 months. Enclose S.A.S.E. for reply to queries.
Nonfiction and Photos: Articles on sea power in general, and the U.S. Navy, the U.S. Marine Corps, merchant marine and naval services and other navies of the world in particular. Should illustrate and expound the importance of the seas and sea power to the U.S. and its allies. Wants timely, clear, nontechnical, lively writing. 500 to 1,500 words. Pays $40 to $200, depending upon length and research involved. Query before submitting finished manuscript. Purchases 8x10 glossy photos with mss.

SOLDIERS Cameron Station, Alexandria VA 22314. Editor: Col. Edward M. Bradford. The U.S. Army's official magazine. Monthly. Circulation: 250,000. Will send free sample copy and writer guidelines on request. Pays in contributor's copies.

U.S. NAVAL INSTITUTE PROCEEDINGS, U.S. Naval Academy, Annapolis MD 21402. Publisher: Cdr. R.T.E. Bowler, Jr., USN (Ret.); Editor: Cdr. R.P. Brewer, USN (Ret.). Monthly for professional Navy audience. Circulation: over 70,000. Reports on submissions in 4 to 6 weeks. Buys all rights. Pays on acceptance. Enclose S.A.S.E. for return of submissions.
Nonfiction and Photos: Professional Navy, maritime, Marine Corps subjects. Length: 1,500 to 6,000 words. Pays 4¢ to 6¢ per word as voted by Board of Control. No query necessary. Photos purchased with mss; pays $2 each.
Fillers: Anecdotes with naval or maritime slant. Pays $10.

Miscellaneous Publications

AFRICAN PROGRESS, 114 E. 32nd St., New York NY 10016. Editor: Mr. J. Akpan. For "businessmen, diplomats, universities, students, and the general public." Established in 1970. Monthly. Circulation: 180,000. Buys all rights, but will reassign rights to author after publication. Buys 50 to 100 mss a year. Pays on publication. Write for copy of guidelines for writers. Submit complete ms. Will consider photocopied submissions. Submit seasonal material at least 2 months in advance of issue date. Reports in 1 month. Enclose S.A.S.E. for return of submissions.
Nonfiction: Articles on "economic, historical, cultural, and other aspects of life in Africa, the Caribbean and African-American relations. *African Progress* presents Africa as it is, not as a 'dark continent.' Our writers must be independent in their points of view. No Tarzan-type articles. We'd like to see articles on African-American relations, the growing black global awareness, developing nations of Africa, African fashions, cultural heritage, etc." Buys informational articles, interviews, profiles, historical articles, travel articles. Length: 1,000 to 4,000 words. Pays $50 to $200, "depending on length and quality."
Photos: Purchased without mss; "b&w, any size, not larger than 8x10." Pays $10 minimum. Contact Editor-in-Chief for photo submissions.

THE AMERICAN ATHEIST MAGAZINE, P.O. Box 2117, Austin TX 78767. Editor: Richard F. O'Hair. For "generally business and professional persons of high level of education, many in education field, media communications." Quarterly. Circulation: 35,000. Buys all rights. Buys 1 or 2 dozen mss a year. Pays on publication. Will send a sample copy to a writer on request. Reports "immediately." Enclose S.A.S.E. for return of submissions.

Nonfiction and Photos: Publishes analyses "of religion's history, dogma, creeds, gimmicks; historical or contemporary. Religion's impact on our culture as it can be scientifically diagnosed. The personalities and writings of atheists, historically, need to be reviewed. We advocate free thinking, which means that a writer should write in a way which befits himself and the subject matter: no special form is required or desired." Taboos include "emotion-laden work and work couched in such existential terms as to be undecipherable." Buys profiles, humor, historical articles, think pieces, exposes, photo essays. Length and payment variable. Uses b&w glossies. Payment varics.

Fiction: Humorous, historical, juvenile, contemporary problems. Length and payment variable.

Poetry: Traditional, avant-garde, light verse. Length and payment variable. Department Editor: Cynthis Merritt.

Fillers: Newsbreaks, clippings, jokes, short humor. Length and payment variable.

AMERICAN-SCANDINAVIAN REVIEW, 127 East 73rd St., New York NY 10021. Editor: Erik J. Friis. For Americans interested in Scandinavia. Established in 1913. Quarterly. Circulation: 6,000. Buys all publication rights. Buys 6 mss a year. Pays on acceptance. Will send a sample copy to a writer for $2. Reports in 2 weeks. Enclose S.A.S.E. for return of submissions.

Nonfiction and Photos: Wants articles about any phase of life and culture in Scandinavia, written in a popular fashion, but at the same time being scholarly and authoritative. Base articles on thorough research. Length: 2,500 words. Pays $75 maximum. Some photos purchased.

Fiction and Poetry: "Stories are usually written by Scandinavian authors, but stories by Americans, if they have a Scandinavian or Scandinavian-American locale, may be used." Short stories preferred. Pays $75. Buys some poetry; theme open.

CHANGES, P.O. Box 631 Cooper Station, New York NY 10003. Editor: Susan Graham. Established in 1969. Monthly. Circulation: 100,000. Payment 2 weeks after publication. Will send sample copy to writer for 75¢. Submit seasonal material 1 month in advance. Enclose S.A.S.E. for return of submissions.

Nonfiction and Photos: "Interviews with writers, musicians, dancers, etc.; book reviews, music reviews, jazz coverage, art, dance, theatre, film and music festivals; personalities involved with change in our society; paraphysics and the psychic world." Profiles, humor, think pieces, exposes, nostalgia, personal opinion. Length: open. Pays $15 for reviews; $25 for interviews and major articles. Photos purchased with or without mss or on assignment. Pays $5.

Poetry: Traditional forms, blank verse, free verse, avant-garde forms, light verse. Pays $10.

COLUMBIA PICTORIAL (formerly *Kamloops Bulletin*), Box 184, Kamloops, B.C., Canada. Editor: Thelma Carleton. Aimed at general adult reading public. Established in 1972. Monthly. Circulation: 10,000. Buys all rights but will reassign rights to author after publication. Pays on acceptance. Will send sample copy to writer for 50¢. Write for copy of guidelines for writers. Submit complete ms. Will not consider photocopied submissions. Submit seasonal material 3 months in advance. Reports on material accepted for publication in 2 weeks. Returns rejected material in 1 week. Enclose S.A.E. and International Reply Coupons.

Nonfiction and Fillers: "Tourist and travel articles about interesting tourist spots telling why one should travel hundreds of miles to see it. Stories on the advertisers, their products and services. Sample: Tips on buying a stereo component system or 'he teaches them to read mathematics'. No controversial subjects; we don't fight battles or carry on crusades. What we want to get away from is heavy stuff. We have a pawnbroker who advertises, so we did a story on pawnbroking from an entertaining angle. We don't want the 'this is how dogs are mistreated at the animal shelter' sort of thing. If you are going to write about dogcatchers, come up with something happy and entertaining. For out-of-area writers, items of general interest: old inns of England, the tallest things in the world, mini items (will be buying a great deal of these) such as short, humorous pieces, jokes, crossword puzzles, how-to and inspirational items. Interviews must be reported accurately. Only in certain issues such as Halloween do we use children's material. A very limited supply of special material for Christmas, Easter and so on, but would welcome something that had merit." Also uses informational articles and profiles, personal experience, historical, nostalgia. Length: 500 to 2,500 words. Pays 1¢ a word; $1 for jokes and single paragraph items. Minimum payment: $1.

Photos: Purchased with or without accompanying ms; captions are required. 5x4 b&w; no color. Pays $1 to $5. "If you have an interesting baby photo and can pencil in a thought which matches the expression on the baby's face that will bring a chuckle and good humor, send it."

EIRE-IRELAND, Box 5026, College of St. Thomas, St. Paul MN 55105. Editor: Dr. Eoin McKiernan. For intelligent readers with high interest in Ireland. Quarterly. Circulation: 4,100. Buys first rights. Buys 40 to 50 mss a year. Pays on publication. Will send a sample copy to a writer for $1. "Query us on subject." Reports in 6 weeks. Enclose S.A.S.E. for reply to queries.

Nonfiction: "Nonfiction of a critical or informative nature concerning any aspect of the Irish experience anywhere in the world: art, literature, history, music, language, etc. Though serious, scholarly or semischolarly, the articles should have an attractive style. We are not interested in sentimentality; no 'St. Patrick's Day' type of writing." Length: 2,000 to 5,000 words. Payment is $25 to $60 an article, depending on length.

EXPEDITION, The Magazine of Archaeology/Anthropology, The University Museum of the University of Pennsylvania, 33rd and Spruce Sts., Philadelphia PA 19104. Editor: Erle Leichty. For "an educated, world-traveled audience; not professional specialists, but persons sophisticated in archaeology and anthropology." Quarterly. Query first. Enclose S.A.S.E. for reply to queries.

Nonfiction and Photos: "Content should be significant, writing should be clear and forceful; good photos are essential. Though the author need not be an academician, scientific accuracy is a must. Ethnography, folk life, primate behavior, ancient art are welcome." Length: about 4,000 words. Pays $100.

GRAFICA, 705 N. Windsor Blvd., Hollywood CA 90038. Editor: Armando del Moral. For Spanish-speaking audience. Bimonthly. Circulation: 12,000. Buys first rights. Buys 30 mss a year. Pays on acceptance. Will send a free sample copy to a writer on request. Query first. "All material MUST BE SUBMITTED IN SPANISH. We are getting many in English which we have to return." Reports in 10 days. Enclose S.A.S.E. for return of submissions.

Nonfiction and Photos: Reportorial, interview-type articles of interest to general family audience and to individual members of the family, oriented toward Hispanic and Mexican American persons, their problems and progress in the world of today. Length: 2 to 12 pages. Payment is 1¢ a word. Photos purchased with mss or with captions. B&w only. Pays $2 per photo.

Fiction: Would like some good tear-jerkers in Spanish. Maximum length: 12 pages. Pays 1¢ per word.

INSECT WORLD DIGEST, P.O. Box 428, Latham NY 12110. Editor: Dr. Ross H. Arnett, Jr. For students, teachers (advanced high school, college, university), amateur and professional entomologists; nature, conservation and ecology groups. Nontechnical articles on insects. Established in 1973. Every 2 months. Circulation: 3,000. Buys first North American serial rights. Buys "36 or more mss" a year. Payment on acceptance. Will send sample copy to a writer for $1. Write for copy of editorial guidelines for writers. Query first. Will consider photocopied submissions. Submit seasonal material 6 months in advance. Reports on material accepted for publication in 2 months. Returns rejected material in 2 months. Enclose S.A.S.E.

Nonfiction and Photos: "Nontechnical articles on insects, spiders and related organisms; pesticides, study techniques. Popular writing about current research or how to get interested in insect study as a hobby. Do not emphasize danger or weird; spectacular only if spectacular to a professional. Each issue has at least 1 article on insects in relation to environment. Informational, how-to, interview, short humor, historical, think, expose, travel, new product; personal experience if it's right touch, say, collecting experiences in remote areas, etc." Length: up to 3,500 words, except for special feature articles. Pays 2¢ per word. Photos purchased with or without accompanying ms. Captions usually required. 5x7 glossy or larger. 35mm transparencies; larger preferred. Pays minimum of $10. Transparency returned after use.

JOURNAL OF GRAPHOANALYSIS, 325 W. Jackson Blvd., Chicago IL 60606. Editor: V. Peter Ferrara. For audience interested in self-improvement. Monthly. Buys all rights. Pays on acceptance. Reports on submissions in 1 month. Enclose S.A.S.E. for return of submissions.
Nonfiction: Self-improvement material helpful for ambitious, alert, mature people. Applied psychology and personality studies, techniques of effective living, etc.; all written from intellectual approach by qualified writers in psychology, counseling and teaching, preferably with degrees. Length: 2,000 words. Pays about 5¢ a word.
Fillers: Any type, pertinent to self-improvement theme. Payment varies.

KNIFE DIGEST, P.O. Box 843, Little River Station, Miami FL 33138. Editor: William L. Cassidy. For outdoorsmen, writers, collectors. Established in 1972. Published annually. Circulation: 100,000. Rights purchased vary with author and material. Buys all rights, but will reassign rights to author after publication. Buys first serial rights or second serial (reprint) rights. Buys maximum of 180 mss a year. Payment on publication. Will send sample copy for $5. Write for copy of guidelines for writers, enclosing S.A.S.E. Submit complete ms, but query on photos. Will not consider photocopied submissions. Reports on material in 2 weeks. Enclose S.A.S.E. for return of submissions or reply to queries.
Nonfiction and Photos: "Historical and technical articles on swords, daggers, dirks, hunting knives, pocket knives, foreign edged weapons, bayonets, manufacturing techniques, early manufacturers, custom knifemaking, how-to, history and oddities are used. Be factual, tight and include history whenever possible, since we are directed to the interests of technically and historically minded cutlery enthusiasts." Especially interested in New England manufacturers, English and German cutlery and American cutlery renaissance. Minimum length: 1,500 words. Pays average of 5 cents per word. Dept. Editor: William Cassidy. Photos, old prints and illustrations. Pays $5 to $10 for 8x10 b&w photos. 2½x2½ color transparencies on assignment only.
Fiction: "Rarely published, and then only if it is strictly confined to knife legend or lore and clearly identified as such."
Fillers: Newsbreaks and clippings. Length: 500 words minimum. Pays 3 cents per word.

ORPHANS' MESSENGER & ADVOCATE OF THE BLIND, P.O. Box 288, Jersey City NJ 07303. Editor: Sister Eleanor Quin, C.S.J. Published by St. Joseph's Home as a fund-raising magazine for the blind and orphans. Established in 1901. Quarterly. Circulation: 90,000. Buys all rights but will reassign rights to author after publication. Buys 30 mss a year. Will send free sample copy to a writer on request. Write for copy of guidelines for writers. Query first. Submit seasonal material 4 months in advance. Enclose S.A.S.E. for reply to queries.
Nonfiction: Contemporary stories and articles for family type magazine. Some religious themes and humorous material. Personal experience, inspirational. Length: 1,500 words maximum. Pays 1¢ per word.
Poetry and Fillers: Poetry length: maximum of 16 lines. Pays 1¢ per word. Jokes and short humor.

PARK AVENUE SOCIAL REVIEW, 250 Park Ave., New York NY 10017. Editor: Marion L. Damroth. "All material is written by staff writers."

PASSENGER TRAIN JOURNAL, 29 E. Broad St., Hopewell NJ 08525. Managing Editor: Otto Janssen. Established in 1966. For "people who are seriously interested in the maintenance of modern rail passenger service; not 'buffs'." Quarterly. Circulation: 5,200. Not copyrighted. Buys 2 or 3 freelance mss an issue. Payment on publication. Query first or submit complete ms. Reports on material in 2 to 3 weeks. Will consider photocopied submissions. Enclose S.A.S.E. for return of submissions or reply to queries.

Nonfiction and Photos: "All our articles are devoted to modern rail passenger service, here and abroad. Must be studious, carefully researched. Any article starting 'Shades of Casey Jones' is summarily rejected. We have nothing to do with freight or nostalgia about steam trains. Prefer not to see anything about model railroading, tourist railroads or personality pieces. Nothing but good, thoroughly researched articles about rail passenger service anywhere in the world, from Albania to Zaire." Length: "No limit within reason. Payment ranges from $5 for short, routine pieces to $50 to $75 for good features." 8x10 b&w glossies purchased with or without mss or on assignment. Captions required. Pays $5 for nonassignment photos. No color is used.

PERSIMMON HILL, c/o National Cowboy Hall of Fame, 1700 N.E. 63rd St., Oklahoma City OK 73111. Managing Editor: Dean Krakel. For historians, artists, ranchers, art gallery and school library patrons, junior and senior high school students. Established in 1970. Quarterly. Circulation: 3,700 subscribers; 3,000 direct sales. Buys all rights. Buys 6 mss a year. Payment on publication. Will send sample copy to writer for $1.50. Write for copy of guidelines for writers. Query preferred. Will consider photocopied submissions. Reports on material in 1 month. Enclose S.A.S.E. for reply to queries.

Nonfiction and Photos: "Historical and contemporary articles on famous western figures connected with pioneering the American West; or biographies of such people; stories of famous ranches and early manufacturers. Only thoroughly researched and historically authentic material is considered. The article may have a humorous approach to a subject. We like first-person narratives of original and authentic accounts as contrasted with the typical academic thesis." Length: 1,500 words minimum. Pays $50. "Photos submitted with or without manuscripts are subject to approval."

PHYSICIAN'S WORLD, 400 Madison Ave., New York NY 10017. Editor: Samuel Burger. For physicians. Established in 1973. Monthly. Circulation: 170,000. Buys first North American serial rights and Latin American rights. Buys 125 mss a year. Payment on acceptance. Will send sample copy to writer for $1. Query first. Submit seasonal material 3 months in advance. Reports in 2 weeks. Enclose S.A.S.E. for response to query or return of submission.

Nonfiction and Photos: "Articles on society, life styles, science, research, sports, travel. Articles should include the medical aspects of the subject, if possible. We emphasize the contemporary, the changing scene. We are also interested in theme ideas for issues. Regular columns or departments include items on films, records, and books." Length: columns, 1,200 to 1,500 words; other articles, 2,200 to 2,500 words. Pays $300 to $600. 8x10 b&w glossy prints are purchased with mss. Captions required. Pays $25. 35mm or 2x2 color photos purchased for $50. Pays $250 for cover photos.

PRACTICAL KNOWLEDGE, 325 W. Jackson Blvd., Chicago IL 60606. Editor: V. Peter Ferrara. Bimonthly. A self-advancement magazine for active and involved men and women. Pays on acceptance. Reports in 2 to 3 weeks. Enclose S.A.S.E. for return of submissions.

Nonfiction and Photos: Uses success stories of famous people, past or present; applied psychology; articles on mental hygiene and personality by qualified writers with proper degrees to make subject matter authoritative. Also human interest stories with an optimistic tone. Up to 5,000 words. Photographs and drawings are used when helpful. Pays a base pate of 5¢ a word; $3 each$for illustrations.

RAIL CLASSICS, 7950 Deering Ave., Canoga Park CA 91304. Editor: Denis Dunning. Adult male readership with an interest in railroading, both historical and modern day. Established in 1972. Bimonthly. Circulation: 50,000. Buys first North American serial rights. Buys 100 mss a year. Pays on publication. Will send free sample copy to a writer on request. Write for copy of editorial guidelines for writers. Query first or submit complete ms. Will not consider photocopied submissions.

Submit seasonal material 4 months in advance. Reports on material in 1 month. Enclose S.A.S.E. for return of submissions.

Nonfiction and Photos: "Photo features and all aspects of the railroading industry, from a railfan standpoint. Must be well-researched and give full account of the particular subject. Light photo essays are also used, but on a limited basis. All articles should cover a specific subject, whether historical or contemporary theme. We do not use general features." Informational, historical. Length: 1,000 to 10,000 words. Pays $25 to $200. Dept. Editor: Denis Dunning. B&w photos, at least 5x7, purchased with ms. Pays minimum of $10 for any size color transparency. Dept. Editor: Stuart Diaux.

RAILROAD MAGAZINE, 420 Lexington, New York NY 10017. Editor: Freeman Hubbard. For railroad men and rail fans. Monthly. Buys all rights or first rights. Pays on publication, sometimes well after. Will send a sample copy to a writer "only if the writer convinces the editor he has had experience in railroad writing. We never buy fiction, fillers, poems, photos, or clippings." Query first. Reports in 2 weeks. Enclose S.A.S.E. for reply to queries.

Nonfiction: Articles on steam, diesel, or electric locomotives; dramatic or nostalgic fact articles on any phase of railroading in the U.S. or Canada, past or present. Articles should have railroad "color," well-developed anecdotes, and technical information. Wants only writers who are railroad employees, past or present, or who specialize in rail lore. Pays 5¢ a word.

RELAX MAGAZINE, 136-138 Montezuma St., Prescott AZ 86301. Editor: Dock Voelkel. Monthly. For medical doctors in the U.S., to afford entertaining reading and suggestions for leisure-time activities for doctors and their families. Query first. Pays on publication. Enclose S.A.S.E.

Nonfiction and Fiction: Interested in building up an inventory of travel, hobby, outdoors and recreation-oriented articles. "Stories should not be medically oriented. Include names and photos of doctors who may be involved in your story." Light, personal, anecdotal approach. Length: 1,500 to 2,500 words, depending on subject. Pays $250 to $300, including photos. B&w acceptable, although color is preferred.

THE ROSICRUCIAN DIGEST, AMORC, Rosicrucian Park, San Jose CA 95114. Editor: Gerald A. Bailey. Address mss to Editorial Department. Monthly. Buys first rights and the right to reprint. Pays on acceptance. Will send free copy to a writer on request. Write for a copy of guidelines for writers. Queries accepted but not required. No fiction or poetry. Reports in 3 to 4 weeks. Enclose S.A.S.E. for reply to queries or return of submissions.

Nonfiction, Photos, and Fillers: Philosophical and inspirational subjects, art, music, science, education, biographies, historical sketches. Humanitarian, generally uplifting and helpful outlook. Should appeal to worldwide circulation. Nothing of controversial, religious or political nature used. Pays 2¢ per word. Uses some photos and fillers.

RUNDSCHAU, An American German Review, 339 Walnut St., Philadelphia PA 19106. For "students studying German and related fields, in high school and colleges across the United States (15 to 20 years old), and teachers interested in the German language and area studies. They are interested in things related to German, Germany, and German speaking Europe." Seeks material for special issues on Octoberfest, Christmas in Germany, and Fasching (February). Monthly. Circulation: 119,000. Buys all rights. Buys 45 to 50 mss a year. Pays on acceptance. Will send a free sample copy to writer on request. Query first for all material, "two paragraphs only." Submit seasonal material two to three months in advance. Reports in 4 weeks. Enclose S.A.S.E. for reply to queries.

Nonfiction and Photos: "We cover everything from drugs to Duerer. We present a wide spectrum of articles including: political events, education, ecology, personality interviews, art, sports, literature, traditions, industry, women's lib, mass-media, urban crisis, popular music and any other topic appealing to youth. We specialize in the contemporary items, not yet found in history books, with a hearty sprinkling of cultural pieces." Length: 500 to 2,000 words. Pays 5¢ a word. Photos are purchased with or without mss. 8x10 b&w glossies of sharp contrast. Captions optional. Pays $5 to $25.

Fillers: Buys German crossword puzzles, jokes and short humor in German. Length: 200 to 500 words. Pays $5 to $25.

SINGLE LIFE, 225 Kearny St., Suite 501, San Francisco CA 94108 and 6515 Sunset Blvd., Suite 202, Los Angeles CA 90024. For singles in California. Judy Rae Beal, Associate Editor. Established in 1970. Monthly. Copyrighted. Buys all rights but will reassign rights to author after publication. Payment on publication. Submit complete ms. Seasonal material must be submitted 4 months in advance. Enclose S.A.S.E. for return of submissions.

Nonfiction and Photos: "Content of publication is light with humor important. All articles must have a positive approach to being single. No 'hate' or 'swinger' type articles will be considered. Interviews with prominent single persons; light humor, general travel articles, sports and think pieces." Length: 600 to 1,000 words, but prefers lengths of 750 to 1,000 words. Pays 2¢ a word; $5 per accompanying photo. "Signed release for everyone who can be identified must accompany all photos."

Fiction: "Fiction considered if slanted to the single viewpoint."

Poetry: Pays $1 a line for light verse ("no heavy poetry").

SMITHSONIAN MAGAZINE, 900 Jefferson Drive, Washington DC 20560. Editor: Edward K. Thompson. For "associate members of the Smithsonian Institute, 87% with college education." Monthly. Circulation: 400,000. "Our material is automatically copyrighted. In the case of selling off second rights *Smithsonian* keeps half, gives the rest to photographer or writer. Payment for each article to be negotiated depending on our needs and the article's length and excellence." Pays "first half on assignment or tentative acceptance, remainder on acceptance." Will send a free sample copy to writer. Query first. Submit seasonal material 3 months in advance. Reports "as soon as possible." Enclose S.A.S.E. for reply to queries.

Nonfiction: "Our mandate from the Smithsonian Institute says we are to be interested in the same things which now interest or should interest the Institution: folk and fine arts, history, natural sciences, hard sciences, etc." Length and payment "to be negotiated."

Photos: Purchased with or without ms and on assignment. Captions required. Pays "$200 a color page, $125 b&w."

SUCCESS UNLIMITED, The Arcade Bldg., 6355 Broadway, Chicago IL 60660. Executive Editor: Arlene Canaday. Monthly. Buys all rights or second serial (reprint) rights. Pays on acceptance for articles, on publication for photos. Will send free sample copy, requirements sheet, and reader profile on request. Query first preferred. Reports in 3 to 4 weeks on mss, 2 weeks on queries. Enclose S.A.S.E. for reply to queries or return of submissions.

Nonfiction and Photos: "We are looking for articles that will inspire the reader to become a better person in his personal life and his occupation. 'How-to' pieces should help the reader improve himself, such as 'How to Win A Promotion,' or 'How to Develop a Winning Personality,' personality pieces about well-known individuals in the entertainment, sports and business fields, that exemplify success through perseverance and hard work, are regularly featured in our pages. We are interested in what motivated these men and women to attain greatness and look for those success principles that our reader can employ in his daily life and career. Such material, however, should be original and authentic and minus the encyclopedia style. Interested in investment ideas with the emphasis on the unusual rather than just stocks and bonds. Articles dealing with health and nutrition have recently been added. Use about 6 health and investment articles per year." Photos purchased with mss, especially with personality pieces. Will help sell the article. Pays $7.50 each.

SYNTHESIS MAGAZINE, P.O. Box 157, Manhattan Beach CA 90266. Editor: Thomas M. Grahm. For "inventors, entrepreneurs, and businessmen interested in all aspects of invention from a business standpoint." Bimonthly. Circulation: 5,000. Buys all rights or "first rights only." Buys about 20 mss a year. Pays on publication. Will send a sample copy to a writer on request. Query first. Submit unsolicited seasonal material 4 months in advance; submit solicited seasonal material 2 months in advance. Reports in 2 weeks. Enclose S.A.S.E. for reply to queries or return of submissions.

Nonfiction and Photos: "*Synthesis* deals with the current world of invention. Along with news of developments in law, technology, finance, and patents, it includes a steady stream of practical information for the working inventor. It pinpoints new needs and discusses the methods of developing, protecting, marketing, and manufacturing inventions which respond to such needs. 20% is news, 60% theme articles on aspects of inventions, 20% miscellaneous related topics. The emphasis is on facts, sources, dates, etc., as well as authoritative 'point of view' [point of view of inventor, entrepreneur, or businessman] articles." Buys how-to's, personal experience articles, interviews, profiles, coverage of successful business operations, historical and think pieces, exposes, new product articles, and pieces on merchandising techniques, also pieces on patent law and cases in U.S. and other countries. Length: open. Pays 2¢ a word. B&w glossies purchased with mss. Pays $10 to $50.

TATTOO, P.O. Box 1397, Smyrna GA 30080. Publisher: Scott Goldenrod. Established in 1972. For "everyone interested in the subject of tattooing." Quarterly. Buys all rights, but will reassign rights to author after publication. Buys 10 to 25 mss a year. Payment on acceptance. Query first or submit complete ms. Returns rejected material immediately. Reports on accepted material in a few weeks. Will consider photocopied submissions if legible. Will send sample copy to writer for $2.50. Enclose S.A.S.E. for return of submissions or reply to queries.
Nonfiction and Photos: "We publish anything related to tattooing. We are especially interested in profiles of artists and articles about clients, life styles, etc., but are not limited to those areas. The writer can do his own thing. If it's dull, we won't use it. If it's really good, we'll pay him more than our base rate." Length: open. Pays 5¢ a word minimum. Pays $10 minimum for photos.

VIEWS & REVIEWS, A Quarterly Magazine of the Reproduced Arts, 633 W. Wisconsin Ave., Suite 1700, Milwaukee WI 53203. Editor: Ruth Tuska. Established in 1968. For "a general audience: children, grandpas, frustrated executives, nice people, real people, out-and-out and, sometimes, down-and-out kooks. They like to read about the reproduced arts and the people who make them. And they like facts." Quarterly. Circulation: 7,000. Rights purchased vary with author and material. May buy all rights, but will reassign rights to author after publication or first North American serial rights, or first serial rights or second serial (reprint) rights. Payment on publication. Query first. Reports on material accepted for publication in 6 months. Returns rejected material in 1 week. Will send sample copy to writer for $1.50. Enclose S.A.S.E. for reply to queries.
Nonfiction and Photos: "Personality studies on performers and business people in the arts. Career studies. Articles on the production of individual works (reviews). Well-written articles on the reproduced arts that take unusual slants. We are always ready to be mavericks—provided that we can be quality mavericks. Accuracy is of paramount importance. No golden, fuzzy memories, nostalgics, or publish or perish Ph.D.'s about bubble gum wrappers and their social significance. Nor do we write about things we'd rather forget. Write well about the things you love and be accurate as they deserve and you'll be just right." Length: open. "We pay from $10 to $250 per article." 8x10 b&w photos purchased with ms. Captions optional.

WEEKDAY, 20 N. Wacker Dr., Chicago IL 60606. For the average man. Buys all rights. Enclose S.A.S.E. for return of submissions.
Nonfiction and Photos: Uses articles slanted toward the average man, with the purpose of increasing his understanding of the business world and helping him be more successful in it. Also uses articles on "How to Get Along With Other People," and articles on meeting everyday problems in real estate, home maintenance, money management, etc. Length: approximately 1,000 words or less. Pays $20 to $50 for these. Uses b&w human interest photos.

WORLD SHOPPING, Wm. H. Wise & Co., Inc., 336 Mountain Rd., Union City NJ 07087. Editor: Harry Kickey. For Americans that enjoy shopping abroad by mail. Monthly. Buys all rights. Enclose S.A.S.E. for return of submissions.
Nonfiction and Photos: "Each month we run at least four feature articles which describe a foreign store or product that can be bought abroad by mail. Recent titles include 'The Look of Pewter' (a story on pewter from Malaysia), and 'World Shopping Visits Carnaby Street' (a report on current fashion trends in London). Each article is about 1,000 to 1,500 words long though some are shorter if illustrations

(which must accompany text) are plentiful. Copy must be lively and at the same time contain specific price and postal information plus the address of the store concerned. We pay at least $50 for every article accepted. Photos purchased with mss."

Music and Sound Reproduction Equipment Publications

BLUEGRASS UNLIMITED, P.O. Box 111, Burke VA 22015. Editor: Peter V. Kuykendall. For fans of bluegrass music; musicians, etc. Established in 1966. Monthly. Circulation: 8,500. Buys all rights "but will negotiate for author's use if need arises." Buys 5 to 15 mss a year. Payment on publication. Will send free sample copy to writer on request. Query first or submit complete ms. Will consider photocopied submissions. Reports on material within 30 days. Enclose S.A.S.E.
Nonfiction and Photos: "Artists' profiles, instrument articles and reviews on related books, records, etc. No specific approach, but must make good reading with informational approach. We do not take many 'fan' style articles." Informational, how-to, personal experience, interview, profile, humor, historical, think pieces, nostalgia, personal opinion, photo, travel, spot news, successful business operations, new product, merchandising techniques, technical. Length: 500 to 5,000 words. Pays 1¢ to 1½¢ per word. B&w glossies. Usually pays $20 for cover; $10 per page for inside.
Fiction and Fillers: Experimental, mainstream, mystery, adventure, humorous, historical. Length: 500 to 5,000 words. Pays 1¢ to 1½¢ per word. Puzzles and short humor. Length: open. Pays 1¢ to 1½¢ per word.

DOWN BEAT, 222 West Adams St., Chicago IL 60606. For "musicians, student musicians and music fans; median age 22.2, college grads and students, high school students interested in jazz and popular music." Established in 1934. Published every two weeks except monthly June, September and January. Circulation: 91,000. Buys first serial rights. Buys 20 to 25 mss a year. Payment on publication. Will consider photocopied mss. Reports in 4 to 6 weeks, "but not responsible for any unsolicited material submitted." Submit seasonal material 2 to 3 months in advance. Enclose S.A.S.E. for return of submissions.
Nonfiction and Photos: "We print articles, interviews, reviews, etc. dealing with jazz and popular music and closely related subjects. No fiction or poetry wanted. Writers must be knowledgeable in required subject area. Clear, straightforward prose style and accurate, factual reporting. *Down Beat* differs from other consumer music publications in its emphasis on jazz." Accepts informational, personal experience, interviews, profiles, historical, nostalgia, personal opinion, and spot news. Length: 500 to 2,500 words. Pays $35 to $100. Dept. Editor: Dan Morgenstern. Buys 8x10 b&w glossy prints for $10 to $25. No color. "Generally, we accept photos for our files and pay on publication only."
Fillers: Buys newsbreaks and puzzles (crossword; quiz with music themes only).
How To Break In: "A short feature or, better yet, a record or performance review would be the best way to 'break in.' "

FLAG, F. P. B. Enterprises, 310 Evesham Rd., Glendora NJ 08029. Editor: Frank P. Bartucci. For "musical and entertainment oriented patrons; country, jazz, commercial music fans from 18 to 65 age group. Music articles, stories, poems, satire on the complete music scene; radio, TV, records and music at large." Established in 1971. Monthly. Circulation: 43,000. Buys simultaneous rights. Pays on publication. Will send free samply copy to a writer on request. Submit complete ms. Will consider photocopied submissions. Reports on material accepted for publication in 2 months. Returns rejected material in 1 month. Enclose S.A.S.E. for return of submissions.
Nonfiction: "Statistical works on the record industry in relation to recording artists vs. Billboard, Cashbox arbitrary chart positions. Interview, humor, historical, think,

nostalgia, expose, personal opinion." Length: 1,000 to 3,000 words. Dept. Editor: Jean Curtiss
Photos: Purchased with or without accompanying ms. 5x7 or 8x10 b&w; captions optional. Pays $1 each.
Fillers: Puzzles (country and musical); clippings, jokes, short humor. 25 to 200 words. Pays ½¢ a word or $1.50 per puzzle. Dept. Editor: Jean Curtiss.

GUITAR PLAYER MAGAZINE, 348 N. Santa Cruz Ave., Los Gatos CA 95030. Editor: Jim Crockett. For persons "interested in guitars and guitarists." 12 times a year. Circulation: 75,000. Buys all rights. Buys 30 to 35 mss a year. Pays on acceptance. Will send a sample copy to a writer on request. Query first. Returns rejected material in 1 week. Acknowledges acceptance in 1 week. Enclose S.A.S.E. for reply to queries.
Nonfiction and Photos: Publishes "wide variety of articles pertaining to guitars and guitarists: interviews, guitar craftsmen profiles, how-to features—anything amateur and professional guitarists would find fascinating and/or helpful. On interviews with 'name' performers, be as technical as possible regarding strings, guitars, techniques, etc. We're not a pop culture magazine, but a music magazine." Also buys features on such subjects as a "guitar museum, the role of the guitar in elementary education, personal reminiscences of past greats, technical gadgets and how to work them, analysis of flamenco, etc." Length: open. Pays $25 to $75. Photos purchased with mss. B&w glossies. Pays $15 to $25. Buys 35mm color slides. Pays $50. Buys all rights.
Poetry: "Pertaining to guitar, guitarists, guitar music. Can be humorous." Wants contemporary and avant-garde poetry. Length: open. Payment in copies.
How to Break In: "Read and understand the magazine. Determine the audience and its needs. Then send a brief query saying what the story would cover and in how much detail. I'll reply immediately if we've already done it, if we're working on it, if it's not for us, if I'd like to see it. If 'yes,' I'll describe what I'd like to see in the piece and when I'd want it. Simple as all that."

HARMONICA HAPPENINGS, Box 3006, Detroit MI 48231. Editor: Alex Fogel. For "harmonica enthusiasts." Quarterly. Circulation: 1,000. Buys all rights. Pays on publication. Will send a sample copy to a writer on request. Query first. Submit seasonal material 1 month in advance. Returns rejected material in 1 month. Acknowledges acceptance of material in 1 month. Enclose S.A.S.E. for reply to queries.
Poetry: Light verse. Slanted to the harmonica player. Length: 8 lines. Pays $10. Currently overstocked on verse. Pays on publication only.

HI-FI STEREO BUYERS' GUIDE, Davis Publications, 229 Park Ave. South, New York NY 10003. Editor-in-chief: Julian M. Martin. For buyers of hi-fi equipment. Monthly. Pays on acceptance. Query first. Prefers to receive synopsis of proposed article stating proposed title, a statement on why the "buyer" would be interested in reading this story, a boiled-down version of what will be in the article (in one paragraph), description of art to be supplied with story. One synopsis per sheet of paper. Only authors with published high-fidelity articles can be considered. Reports in 2 weeks. Enclose S.A.S.E. for reply to queries.
Nonfiction: Pays $100 to $250 per article.

HIGH FIDELITY, The Publishing House, State Road, Great Barrington MA 01230. Editor: Leonard Marcus. For well-educated, young, affluent readers, interested in home recording and playback systems (all disc and tape formats) and the program material to play on them. Special issues: March and August, tape; June, speakers; September, new recordings; October, new equipment; December, year's best recordings. Established in 1951. Monthly. Circulation: 260,000. Buys all rights. Buys 12 mss a year. Payment on acceptance. Will consider photocopied submissions, "if they are legible." Submit seasonal material 5 months in advance. Reports in 1 month. Enclose S.A.S.E. for return of submissions.
Nonfiction: "Material for feature articles is divided between audio equipment and music makers. Audio equipment articles should be backed up with as many technical specifications as possible and appropriate and readily understandable to the lay reader. Music articles should be slanted toward the musician's recording career or recordings of his works or to increase the reader's understanding of music. Articles

are sophisticated, detailed, and thoroughly backgrounded." Informational, how-to, interview, profile, humor, historical, nostalgia, and technical articles. Regular columns include: Speaking of Records, interviews with noted music and recording personalities about their work and favorite recordings; Behind the Scenes, reports of in-progress recording sessions here and abroad. Length: 1,000 to 3,000 words. Pays $150 to $300.
Photos: Purchased with accompanying manuscripts. Captions required. 8x10 b&w glossy payment included in ms payment. Color rarely used; inquire first.

HIGH FIDELITY/MUSICAL AMERICA, The Publishing House, State Road, Great Barrington MA 01230. Editor-In-Chief: Leonard Marcus. Monthly. Pays on publication. Enclose S.A.S.E. for return of submissions.
Nonfiction and Photos: Articles, musical and audio, are generally prepared by acknowledged writers and authorities in the field, but does use freelance material. Length: 3,000 words maximum. Payment by arrangement. New b&w photos of musical personalities, events, etc.

INTERNATIONAL MUSICIAN, 200 Mt. Pleasant Ave., Newark NJ 07104. Editor: Stanley Ballard. For professional musicians. Monthly. Not copyrighted. Pays on acceptance. Will send a sample copy to a writer on request. Query first. Reports in 1 month. Enclose S.A.S.E. for reply to queries.
Nonfiction: Articles on prominent instrumental musicians (classical, jazz, rock, or country). Particularly interested in styles of Leonard Feather, Nat Hentoff, Martin Williams, John Wilson, etc. Length: 2,000 words. Payment to be negotiated.

MODERN KEYBOARD REVIEW, 436 Via Media, Palos Verdes Estates CA 90274. Editor: Bill Irwin. For "fans, students, and teachers of modern, contemporary, popular keyboard music (piano and organ)." 6 times a year. Will send a sample copy to a writer on request. "Study publication. Query before submitting finished mss." Reports in 4 weeks. Enclose S.A.S.E. for reply to queries.
Nonfiction and Photos: "Articles about the contemporary, popular keyboard music world. Can be educational (technical), humorous, keyboard personality interview, 'how to play,' 'Careers in Music.' Most material contributed." Payment by arrangement. Photos purchased with mss. Photo features desired.
Fillers: Quizzes, puzzles, cartoons. Payment by arrangement.

MUSIC CITY NEWS, 1314 Pine St., Nashville TN 37203. Editor: R. J. Woltering. For "country music fans." Established in 1963. Monthly. Circulation: 25,000. Buys all rights. Buys 50 mss a year. Pays on publication. Query first. Reports in 30 to 90 days. Enclose S.A.S.E. for reply to queries.
Nonfiction and Photos: Publishes "features on country music artists and sometimes on country music events." Length: 200 to 1,500 words. Pays $10 to $50. Photos purchased with mss and captions required. B&w only. Pays $5.

ON & OFF CAMPUS, c/o EnterMedia Inc., 524 E. William St., Ann Arbor MI 48107. Executive Editor and Executive Publisher: Arthur J. Harger; Editor and Publisher: Robert J. Roth; Managing Editor: Stacy Root. For "college students and faculty." Established in 1971. Published every two weeks. Circulation: 2,000,000. Buys all rights. Buys 75 to 150 mss a year. Pays on publication. Will send a free sample copy to writer on request. Query first. Submit seasonal material six weeks in advance. Enclose S.A.S.E. for reply to queries.
Nonfiction and Photos: Material emphasis is on "campus musical concerts, FM stereo programming and films. We seek new approaches—exposes on concerts and campus film groups—business, LP record albums, films. Seek new technical articles, new ideas for equipment and mediums. A very unique publication—regionalized to colleges and concerts and FM." Buys informational, interviews, profiles, historical, expose, nostalgia, technical, new product, and reviews (music, concerts). Length: 500 to 2,000 words. Pays $150 to $500. Buys b&w and color photos. Pays $50 and up, b&w; pays $100 and up, color.

ROCK MAGAZINE, 166 Lexington Ave., New York NY 10016. Editor: Michele Hush. For "those of college age, often college students whose interests are mainly music (jazz, blues, folk, etc.) and other 'youth culture' subjects." Established in

1969. Bimonthly. Circulation: 118,000. Rights purchased vary with author and material. Buys approximately 350 to 400 mss a year on assignment; no more than 20 on speculation." Payment made approximately 2 to 3 weeks after publication. Will send free sample copy to writer on request. Write for copy of guidelines for writers. Query first for interview and personality pieces; query or submit complete ms for conceptual or idea-oriented stories. Reports on material within 1 month. Enclose S.A.S.E. for return of submissions or reply to queries.

Nonfiction and Photos: "Mainly rock-oriented pieces, either interviews or conceptual pieces, dealing with some phase of music and recording. The more original and unusual the approach, the better. We have no set literary style and encourage writers to develop a distinctive (but intelligible) style of their own. We do, however, prefer a somewhat skeptical or humorous viewpoint, where appropriate. And we have added a new 16-page audio and musical equipment section, and are in the market for writers knowledgeable on the technical aspects but able to relate information on the level of the average consumer." Also uses reviews of records, films and books. Length: 500 to 3,000 words, depending on type of article. Pays $15 to $45. B&w photos, "sharp, bright shots, particularly candids of known musicians." Pays $15; $7.50 for re-use.

ROLLING STONE, 625 Third St., San Francisco CA 94107. Editor: Jann S. Wenner. "Seldom accept freelance material. All our work is assigned or done by our staff."

STEREO, State Road, Great Barrington, MA 01230. Editor: Norman Eisenberg. For "those interested in quality sound reproduction in the home, including hobbyist in audio, semi-technically minded consumers, music lovers, first time hi-fi buyers, owners of existing stereo systems. Strong college/under 30 readership though not confined to this group." Established in 1960. Quarterly. Circulation: 100,000. Buys all rights, but will reassign them to author after publication in special cases only. Buys about 30 feature article mss a year, others on assignment only. Payment on acceptance. Will send a free sample copy to writer on request. Query first for nonfiction and personalized narrative. Will consider photocopied submissions. Reports in 1 to 2 weeks. Enclose S.A.S.E.

Nonfiction: Articles on hi-fi, stereo, music recordings; behind-the-scenes at studios; surveys of musical forms as related to available recordings; improvement hints for stereo systems; how-it-works pieces; new major developments and trends in audio equipment; interesting installations (pix very desirable here); how-to-buy pieces; current cultural trends related to music and audio. "We like to maintain a pretty free-wheeling approach; we edit for clarity of meaning but we do not want every piece to read as if it were written by the same author. Primary requirements here are accuracy of information, basic interest, and some degree of *au courant* relevancy. Compared to our competition, we tend to be somewhat less 'parochial' in our attitude and treatment. We like to think we have fewer hangups or sacred cows in our subject matter, both technical and musical. We enjoy kidding about our subjects. Our editorial approach may be characterized as irreverent but relevant. For us, the whole 'hi fi thing' is a blend of the technical and the musical, plus a certain indefinable ingredient that humanizes it all. We would like to see articles on the changing scene in pop music; the new movie music; developments in quadriphonic or four-channel sound; the problems of getting one's hi-fi equipment properly serviced or repaired; experiments with equipment, getting it to sound better." Buys informational, how-to, personal experience, think, personal opinion, photo, and technical articles. Length: 200 to over 3000 words. Pays average 10¢ a word.

Photos and Fillers: "Photos of hi-fi installations are always welcome, but they must be first-rate as photos. Poor lighting and poor focus seem to mar the efforts of most amateurs attempting to shoot indoor scenes. Use and payment vary, according to our specific needs at the time."

STEREO REVIEW, One Park Ave., New York NY 10016. Editor: William Anderson. Special issues include March (tape recording) and August (loudspeakers). Monthly. Usually buys all rights, but the matter is subject to individual agreement. Pays on acceptance. Query first. Reports in 2 to 3 weeks. Enclose S.A.S.E. for reply to queries.

Nonfiction and Photos: Articles on high fidelity (general aspects of component systems); music (compositions, composers, musicological and sociological aspects); humor (general, regarding equipment, music, etc.). Length: 2,500 to 3,200 words. Pays 5¢ to 10¢ a word.

Nature, Conservation, and Ecology Publications

The magazines classified here are "pure" nature, conservation, and ecology publications—that is, they exist to further the study and preservation of nature and do not publish recreational or travel articles except as they relate to conservation or nature. Other markets for this kind of material will be found in the Regional; Sport and Outdoor; and Travel, Camping, and Trailer categories, although the magazines listed there require that nature or conservation articles be slanted to their specialized subject matter and audience.

AUDUBON, 950 Third Avenue, New York NY 10022. "Not soliciting freelance material; practically all articles done on assignment only."

ENVIRONMENT, 438 N. Skinker Blvd., St. Louis MO 63130. Editor: Sheldon Novick. Aimed at a general and academic audience. Published 10 times yearly. Circulation: 30,000. Buys all rights. Payment on acceptance. Will send a free sample copy to a writer on request. Acceptance of articles by authors without scientific background or science writing experience is rare. Reports in 1 month. Enclose S.A.S.E. for reply to queries.
Nonfiction: Articles containing technical information which is not otherwise widely available on conservation and environmental pollution. 3,000 to 5,000 words. Query required. Pays $100. Address queries to Julian McCaull, Dept. Editor.
Photos: Purchased with captions only. 8x11 b&w glossies. Query required. Pays $10 to $25. Address queries to Tina Rehg, Dept. Editor.

ENVIRONMENTAL QUALITY MAGAZINE, 10658 Burbank Blvd., North Hollywood CA 91601. Editor: Richard Cramer. For ages 20 to 45 with a college education, and active in political, social, environmental, and consumer affairs. Established in 1970. Monthly. Circulation: 125,000. Rights purchased vary with material and author. Buys 100 mss a year. Pays on publication. Will send a sample copy to writer for $1. Query first. Seeks seasonal material on snowmobiling in winter months and back-packing in the summer. Submit seasonal material 5 months in advance. Reports in 2 weeks. Enclose S.A.S.E. for reply to queries.
Nonfiction and Photos: Publishes "articles discussing our physical environment, primarily air, water, wildlife, energy, noise, food additives, abortion, etc. Approach to editorial is discussion and alternatives or solutions to a problem. We offer readers names, addresses, and organizations of who cares and who doesn't about the environment. Do not want to see 'how we did it in . . .' and no personal experiences on how to fight City Hall." Buys informational, profiles, think, expose, nostalgia articles. Regular column seeking copy is called "Vanishing Point"—endangered species of the month. Length: 2,000 to 3,500 words. Payment is negotiable, depending on topic and style. Buys photos with and without mss. Captions optional. Buys b&w prints and color transparencies.
Fiction: Seeks experimental and science fiction. Length: 1,500 to 2,500 words. Payment is negotiable.

FORESTS & PEOPLE, P.O. Drawer 5067, Alexandria LA 71301. Editor: John Maddocks. For "southerners, directly or indirectly associated with forestry or concerned with the growth of forests and wildlife conservation." Established in 1950. Quarterly. Circulation: 10,000. Buys one-time use and reproduction rights. Buys 8 to 10 mss a year. Payment on publication. Will send free sample copy to writer on request. Query first; "light features need not be queried." Submit seasonal material 2 to 3 months in advance. Reports in 1 month. Enclose S.A.S.E. for reply to queries or return of submissions.

Nonfiction and Photos: "Forestry articles, outdoor recreation, southern history; unusual use of wood; wildlife. Light touch is desired. Writer should query if approaching technical subject." How-to, personal experience. humor, historical, nostalgia, travel. Length: 1,500 to 2,000 words; 200 to 300 words with photo essay. Pays $25 to $50. B&w glossy prints purchased with or without mss. Captions required.

Fiction and Poetry: Forestry-related science fiction or humorous fiction. Pays $25 to $50. Traditional forms of poetry or light verse.

FRONTIERS, A Magazine of Natural History, Academy of Natural Sciences, 19th and the Parkway, Philadelphia PA 19103. Editor: Nancy Steele. Published four times per year. Circulation: 4,500. Buys first North American serial rights only. Pays on acceptance. Reports on submissions in 2 weeks. Enclose S.A.S.E. for return of submissions.

Nonfiction: Articles on science and nature, written for high school and adult laymen, but scientifically accurate. Length: 1,000 to 2,000 words. Pays $30 to $90. Articles with b&w photos usually given preference. Accuracy, originality, and neatness all weigh heavily. Will send a sample copy to writer for $1. Query not necessary.

Photos: Purchased with mss. 8x10 b&w preferred.

LIMNOS, 3750 Nixon Road, Ann Arbor MI 48105. Editor: Jacques LesStrang. For "professional people, concerned with ecological problems of Great Lakes for recreational or conservation purposes. Ages 25 to 50, probably mostly college grads." Established in 1968. Quarterly. Circulation: 10,000. Buys first and second serial rights. Buys 30 to 40 mss a year. Payment on publication. Will send a sample copy to writer for $1. Query first for nonfiction. Submit seasonal material 4 to 6 months in advance. Reports in 3 weeks. Enclose S.A.S.E. for reply to queries or return of submissions.

Nonfiction, Photos, Poetry, and Fillers: A freelancer must "know what he is talking about. Our magazine is unique in its field." Would not like to see "Lake Erie problems, save-the-animals, save-the-trees type of Sierra Club conservation material." Buys informational, personal experience, interview, profile, historical, think, spot news, and technical articles. Length: 100 to 5,000 words. Purchases photos with or without mss, on assignment, and captions are optional. Buys 8x10 b&w and 4x5 color. Pays $5 to $25 for b&w and $25 to $100 for color. Poetry is open as to style, but theme should relate to Great Lakes. Pays $5 and up. Filler material of a serious or humorous nature relating to, respectively, water resources and the environment. Length: 50 to 500 words. Pays from $5 to $50, depending on length and use.

THE LIVING WILDERNESS, 729 15th St., N.W., Washington DC 20005. Editor: Richard C. Olson. Not actively soliciting freelance submissions, "but will consider queries."

NATIONAL PARKS & CONSERVATION MAGAZINE, 1701 18th St., N.W., Washington DC 20009. Editor: Eugenia Horstman Connally (Miss). Issued monthly for high-education level out-of-doors audience. Buys first American rights. Payment on acceptance. Query first. Enclose S.A.S.E. for reply to queries.

Nonfiction: Articles about environmental problems—population explosion, pollution, endangered wildlife, vanishing wilderness and open space, mismanaged natural resources; programs to alleviate them. Also articles about national parks and other important preservations, stressing either threats confronting them or their particularly significant features: floral, faunal, geological or historical. A 1,500- to 2,000- word illustrated article brings $50 to $100.

Photos: Expects captioned photos to be submitted with mss. Prefers 8x10 b&w glossies or 4x5 color transparencies. For photos submitted without an article, pays $5 to $50 for b&w, $10 to $75 for color.

NATIONAL WILDLIFE, INTERNATIONAL WILDLIFE, 534 N. Broadway, Milwaukee WI 53202. Editor: John Strohm. For persons interested in natural history, outdoor adventure and the environment. Bimonthlies. Buys all rights; usually buys one-time rights for photos. Pays on acceptance. Query first; reports sometimes slow. Enclose S.A.S.E. for reply to queries.

Nonfiction: Now assigning most articles but still buying occasional material on any phase of environment or outdoor recreation based on related projects. "Dedicated to the wise use of our world resources. Articles should discuss 'gee whiz' facts about nature, dangers to our natural resources, methods of preserving these resources; pieces extolling the natural beauty of our country." Length: 1,500 to 2,000 words. Payment starts at $50 per page as printed.

Photos: Mostly by assignment, but buying some good color and b&w, either to illustrate articles or for photo features, covers, etc. Needs more good single photos for "Favorite Photo" full-page use, but must be interesting or unusual enough to stand alone. Prefers 8x10 b&w prints; any size color transparency. Payment varies, averages $15 to $50 for b&w; $25 to $150 for color.

NATURAL HISTORY, 79th and Central Park West, New York NY 10024. Editor: Alan Ternes. For "well-educated, ecologically aware audience. Includes many professional people, scientists, scholars." Monthly. Circulation: 300,000. Buys first rights. Buys 20 mss a year. Pays on publication. Will send a sample copy to a writer for $1. Submit seasonal material 6 months in advance. Enclose S.A.S.E. for reply to queries or return of submissions.

Nonfiction: Uses all types of scientific articles except chemistry and physics—emphasis is on the biological sciences. Prefers professional scientists as authors. "Writer should have a deep knowledge of his subject. Then submit original ideas either in query or by ms. Should be able to supply high-quality illustrations." Length: 2,000 to 4,000 words. Payment is "$200 to $600, plus additional payment for photos used."

Photos: Uses black and white 8x10 glossy photographs; pays up to $50 per page. Some color is used; pays $75 for inside and up to $100 for cover. Buys one-time use rights.

NATURE CANADA 46 Elgin St., Ottawa, Ontario, Canada. Editor: Ted Mosquin. For "adults and high school students; interests—nature, conservation, environmental destruction." Quarterly. Circulation: 7,000. Buys all rights, but will reassign them to author after publication. Buys about 25 mss a year. Payment on publication. Reports in "1 day to 2 months." Submit seasonal material 3 months in advance. Enclose S.A.S.E. for return of submissions.

Nonfiction, Photos, and Fillers: "We publish material related to nature and environment, wildlife, land use, government policies, citizen's action, etc." Freelancer should write "material for the general public. We have more emphasis on Canadian news and on the national scene. We would not like to see material that is poorly researched or does not have a nature theme. Seeking specific stories on specific animals and species—Canadian with good photos." Buys informational, how-to, historical, think articles. Buys 8½x10 b&w photos and positive color transparencies with mss. Payment is negotiable.

OUTDOOR WORLD, 24198 Bluemound Road, Waukesha WI 53186. Editor: Robert L. Polley. For "individuals interested in and active in outdoor activities, most having above average education and who are thoughtful and reflective about the country's natural environment." Bimonthly. Circulation: 50,000. Buys first rights. Buys 30 mss a year. Will send a free sample copy to a writer on request. Will send editorial guidelines upon request. "Payment on publication. Prefer query first, and it is also preferable with us to get the query accompanied by photography if the individual has already been there." Submit seasonal material 7 months in advance. Reports in 4 to 6 weeks. Enclose S.A.S.E. for reply to queries or return of submissions.

Nonfiction: "*OW* is devoted to making Americans aware of the beauty to be found in nature and the many satisfactions to be derived therefrom. Majority of articles cover activities that can be enjoyed by entire family, such as camping, hiking, sailboating, canoeing, photography, horseback riding, skiing, observations of plant and wildlife. The articles must be literate, flowing in a natural readable manner. We like personal experiences and observations, pieces on rare and/or interesting plant-life geologic phenomena. The author should express his own thoughts about what he has seen or done to give perspective. *OW* is more visual than other outdoor magazines, has more warmth and understanding of people and the natural environment, gives more of a feeling of intimacy with the subjects covered, more of a deeply poetic and literate approach (not overdone)." How-to, personal experience, think pieces, photo and travel articles. No hunting or fishing articles. Poetry rarely used. No fillers. Length: 1,500 to 2,000 words. Payment is $100 to $150. Dept. Editor: D'Arlyn Marks. Also wants material for regular department, "Outdoor Focus." "Experiences of photographers, particularly with helpful suggestions or unusual how-to-do-it information."

Photos: Some b&w glossies purchased with mss. Payment is $15 to $25. Color transparencies and, occasionally, 35mm color purchased for covers. Payment is $35 to $100 each, depending upon number and size used. Individual cover photos, when purchased separately from inside material, $125. "We purchase one-time rights (preferably first rights) but request that we be permitted to re-use photographs in any of our publications (or promotions thereof) upon payment of an amount that is not more than 60 percent of original payment. We also request that photographer not allow photo to be used by any other publisher for a period of either 18 months after acceptance or one year after we publish it, whichever comes first."

PACIFIC DISCOVERY, California Academy of Sciences, Golden Gate Park, San Francisco CA 94118. Editor: Bruce Finson. For "people with a strong interest in natural science." Buys 20 to 25 mss a year. 6 times a year. Will send free sample copy to a writer on request. No fiction, hunting, or pet stories; no poetry. Reports on submissions within sixty days. Buys North American serial rights only. Pays on publication. Accepted manuscripts are usually published within sixty days. Enclose S.A.S.E. for reply to queries.

Nonfiction: Subjects include natural history of plants and animals, conservation, geology, astronomy, and relations between man and nature, especially in and around the Pacific Basin. Occasional articles on history of natural science, exploration, anthropology, and archaeology. Types of articles include profiles of individual species or related groups of animals or plants, narratives of scientific expeditions, reports on new biological discoveries, and explanatory articles on aspects of natural history. Overstocked with material on latest developments in ecology education. "We combine sophisticated treatment of science journals with the lively presentation of popular journals. Write in your own personal style; we do not edit to conformity. Don't talk down to the readers; they are quite knowledgeable." Length: 1,000 to 3,000 words. Query first. Pays 5¢ per word. B&w photos must accompany all mss—12 or more per article.

Photos: Should have both scientific and aesthetic interest. Must be captioned in a few sentences, and photographers credited. Some photo stories used, with longer captions and/or brief text. Query desired on all material. Pays $10 and up per photo.

SNOWY EGRET, 205 S. Ninth St., Williamsburg KY 40769. Editor: Humphrey A. Olsen. For "persons at least high school age interested in literary, artistic, and historical natural history." Semiannual. Circulation: less than 500. Buys 30 to 40 mss a year. No query required. Pays on publication. Buys N.A. serial rights. Usually reports within a month. Will send sample copy for 50¢. Enclose S.A.S.E. with submissions.

Nonfiction: Subject matter limited to material related to natural history, especially literary, artistic, philosophical, and historical aspects. Criticism, book reviews, essays, biographies. Pays $2 per printed page.

Fiction: "We are interested in considering stories or self-contained portions of novels. All fiction must be natural history or man and nature. The scope is broad enough to include such stories as Hemingway's 'Big Two-Hearted River' and Warren's 'Blackberry Winter.'" Length: maximum 10,000 words. Payment is $2 a printed page. Send mss to Dr. William T. Hamilton, 220 E. College Ave., Westerville OH 43081.

Poetry: No length limits. Pays $4 per printed page, minimum of $2. Send poems and poetry books for review to Alan L. Seaburg, 17 Usher Rd., W. Medford MA 02155.

Newspapers and Sunday Supplements

Most of these markets require submissions to be about persons, places, and things in their specific circulation areas. However, some large city and national newspapers that welcome general interest material from nonlocal writers are also included in this list. Newspapers with specialized subject matter or audiences, like The Wall Street Journal *are classified with magazines treating the same subject matter or audience. These markets include publications in the following states: Alabama* (Alabama Sunday Magazine); *Arizona* (Arizona Magazine); *California* (California Living, Los Angeles Times Home Magazine, Peninsula Living, Sacramento Union Weekender, San Deigo Union, Southland Sunday Magazine); *Colorado* (Contemporary Magazine, Empire Magazine); *District of Columbia* (Washington); *Florida* (Florida Times Journal Magazine, Miami Herald Tropic Magazine, St. Petersburg Times Floridian, Sentinel Star Florida Magazine); *Georgia* (Atlanta Journal and Constitution Magazine); *Illinois* (Chicago Sun-Times Midwest Magazine, Chicago Tribune Magazine); *Indiana* (Michiana, The Republic); *Iowa* (Des Moines Sunday Register Picture Magazine); *Kentucky* (Courier Journal and Times Magazine, The Voice-Jeffersonian); *Louisiana* (Dixie Roto, Sunday Advocate Magazine); *Massachusetts* (Christian Science Monitor, Feature Parade Magazine); *Michigan* (Detroit Magazine, Fenton Independent); *Minnesota* (Capital Magazine, Picture Magazine); *Montana* (Billings Gazette); *Nevada* (The Nevadan); *New Jersey* (Hunterdon County Democrat, South Jersey Living); *New York* (Coloroto Magazine, Family Weekly, New York Times, Parade); *Ohio* (Blade Sunday Magazine, Columbus Dispatch Sunday Magazine, Dayton Leisure); *Oregon* (Emerald Empire Magazine, Northwest Magazine); *Pennsylvania* (Butler Eagle, Philadelphia Evening and Sunday Bulletin, Today); *Rhode Island* (Rhode Islander); *South Dakota* (Sioux Falls Argus-Leader); *Texas* (Texas Magazine); *Virginia* (Newport News Daily Press Tidewater's New Dominion Magazine); *Washington* (Panorama Magazine, Seattle Times Sunday Magazine, Sunday Magazine of the Spokesman-Review, Tahoman); *West Virginia* (Panorama); *Wisconsin* (Insight, Rural Gravure, Writer's Viewpoint). *Canada* (Canadian Star Weekly, Impetus, The Islander, Weekend Magazine).*

A few editors report that some correspondents in their area are attracted to small feature items but let big news stories from their communities slip through their fingers. Freelancers, on the other hand, report that some busy newspaper editors return their submissions without even a rejection slip—or in a few cases, fail to return it at all, even when it's accompanied by a self-addressed envelope. (Since newspaper editors receive many submissions from public relations firms and other individuals who do not expect return of their material, they sometimes automatically toss material they're not interested in publishing. That means a retyping job for the freelancer. It also means you should be wary of sending photographs which are your only copies.)

ALABAMA SUNDAY MAGAZINE, P.O. Box 950, Montgomery AL 36102. Editor: Vivian Cannon. For "a general reading public." Established in 1965. Weekly. Circulation: 80,000. Buys Alabama rights only. Payment on publication. Will send sample copy in S.A.S.E. Submit seasonal material 2 months in advance. Reports in 2 weeks. Enclose S.A.S.E. for return of submissions.
Nonfiction, Photos, and Poetry: "Articles must center around people and places in Alabama or people from Alabama, how-to or general feature material concerning holidays or events. Poems are used, but no fiction material is accepted. Material should be written with Alabama readers in mind. We have more success with local or Alabama freelancers. We do use general interest or how-to type features." Buys informational, how-to, humor, historical, nostalgia, photo, and successful business operations in Alabama or Alabama people elsewhere. Length: 300 to 1,500 words. Pays $10. Photos purchased with or without mss. Captions are required. Wants clear and contrastive b&w snapshots. Pays $3. Uses color transparencies. Pays $25. Uses traditional forms of poetry. Length: 12 to 20 lines. No pay.

ARIZONA MAGAZINE, Arizona Republic, 120 F. Van Buren St., Phoenix AZ 85004. Weekly with the Sunday Republic. Editor: Bud DeWald. Query first. Enclose S.A.S.E.

Nonfiction: All articles must be Arizona-oriented, must be about something within state boundaries, or about an Arizonan doing something interesting outside state. Length: 250 to 4,000 words. Pays $40 to $175.

Photos: Purchased with ms or with captions only. 8x10 b&w; 35mm, 2¼x2¼, 4x5 or 8x10 color.

THE ATLANTA JOURNAL AND CONSTITUTION MAGAZINE, P.O. Box 4689, Atlanta GA 30302. Editor: Andrew Sparks. Query first, including short outline of material. Enclose S.A.S.E.

Nonfiction: "Most of our stories are staff-written and almost all of them have some local angle." Articles with strong Southern slant, Georgian or Southern background. Best to study magazine. Length: 2,000 words maximum. Rate of payment varies with importance of article.

THE BILLINGS GAZETTE, Billings MT 59101. Sunday Editor: Kathryn Wright. Weekly. Buys first rights. Pays on publication. Enclose S.A.S.E. with mss and queries.

Nonfiction and Photos: Features stories and photos about circulation area—northern Wyoming and eastern and central Montana—or people from it and now someplace else doing interesting things. Length: 1,000 words plus photos. Pays 20¢ per inch; $3 to $4 each for action photos.

THE BLADE SUNDAY MAGAZINE, The Blade, Toledo OH 43660. Editor: Mike Tressler. For general audience. Circulation: over 200,000. Buys first serial rights. Buys 50 to 60 mss a year. Payment on publication. Query or submit complete ms. Will consider photocopied submissions. Reports in 1 to 3 weeks. Enclose S.A.S.E. for reply to query or return of submissions.

Nonfiction: "General interest articles; personality, life style, leisure, unusual happenings, adventure. Real stories about real people. Emphasis on local (Toledo, northwestern Ohio, southeastern Michigan). Use magazine-style writing; untold stories; quoted dialog and comment." Informational, personal experience, interview, profile, historical, think articles, expose, nostalgia, and photo articles. Regular column, "Glimpse," is an entirely local single-page feature. Length: 800 to 2,500 words. Pays $20 to $65.

Photos: Purchased with or without accompanying mss, or occasionally on assignment. Captions required. 8x10 b&w glossies, sharp and unusual. Pays $5 to $7.50. Color slides or 8x10 photos. Pays $10 to $15.

BUTLER EAGLE, P.O. Box 271, Butler PA 16001. Editor: John L. Wise. Enclose S.A.S.E.

Nonfiction and Photos: Features on local personalities. Length: 500 words. Pays $10 to $20 per article. Photos may be included with article. Pays $5 to $10.

CALIFORNIA LIVING MAGAZINE, Los Angeles Herald Examiner, 1111 South Broadway, Los Angeles CA 90054. "All stories and photographs are staff assigned."

THE CANADIAN STAR WEEKLY, The Simpson Tower, 401 Bay St., Toronto 1, Ontario, Canada. Editor: Michael Hanlon. Buys North American serial rights. Pays on acceptance. Include S.A.E. and International Reply Coupons for reply to queries or return of mss.

Nonfiction: Looking for articles of interest to Canadians from coast to coast, preferably on Canadian subjects, written in a lively and informative manner with plenty of human interest. Effective use of anecdotes quite frequently provides this human interest; therefore, use an anecdotal approach to the subject. Articles submitted may cover a wide range of topics—human affairs, religion, science, politics, personalities, humor and sport, hobbies, cookery and fashion. Looking for good literary quality. Strongly recommend an outline letter, of 200 to 300 words, staking out the extent and burden of the article. A green light on the basis of such an outline does not constitute a commitment, but it does mean that they are interested in getting an

article on this topic. Length: 1,000 to 2,500 words. Pays up to $250 for short pieces and payment for a full-length article starts at $300. Alan Walker, Managing Editor.
Fiction: "We are using a novel a week, sometimes a one-shot, 'condensed,' and sometimes a two-parter. We are looking for strongly plotted stories, with plenty of action and color, and they should appeal to both men and women readers. We can use mystery, crime, suspense, westerns, adventure, human interest, as well as good romances if available. A good length for us is at least around 50,000 words, and we prefer original manuscripts. We work about 4 to 6 months ahead from the time we buy a novel to the time we use it. Our rates are $800 to $1,000. We can also use books, as long as they are just out, and have not previously been serialized." Gwen Cowley, Fiction Editor.

CAPITAL MAGAZINE, St. Paul Sunday Pioneer Press, 55 E. Fourth St., St. Paul MN 55101. Editor: R.J.R. Johnson. Weekly. Buys first rights. "Largely staff produced, but buys about 50 freelance pieces a year." Pays on acceptance. Reports in 2 to 6 weeks. Enclose S.A.S.E. for return of submissions.
Nonfiction and Photos: "Emphasis on North Central region in people, places, events articles. Emphasis on matters of current interest; stories that 'say something.' Uses both picture stories (heavy on art) and longer pieces with 1 or 2 illustrations. Both must be top quality. Story length 50 to 1,500 words depending on material. Rates vary from $25 to $100 or more, depending on overall value of story to *Capital*: interest in the article, quality of writing and photos, with color or not, etc. Continuing need for short items, complete on 1 page or less, with 1 or 2 pictures, 50 to 200 words."
How to Break In: "Read our editorial requirements very carefully and study what is being done in the best Sunday magazines available in your area."

CHICAGO SUN-TIMES' MIDWEST MAGAZINE, 401 N. Wabash, Chicago IL 60611. Editor: Richard Takeuchi. Reports on submissions in 2 weeks. Buys first rights. Pays on publication. Enclose S.A.S.E. with mss and queries.
Nonfiction: General interest articles, preferably topical, focusing on Chicago or Chicago area. Queries from writers must give a brief story outline with supporting photo possibilities. Timeliness is essential for the development of all stories. "No articles on hobbies; no straight narratives." Length: 750 to 2,500 words. Pays $50 to $300.
Photos: Purchased as package with manuscripts. Full color and b&w (8x10).

CHICAGO TRIBUNE MAGAZINE, 435 N. Michigan Ave., Chicago IL 60611. Editor: John Fink. Not soliciting freelance material. "We have a large oversupply of mss, most of which have come from writers working on assignment. Most of these writers are local writers with whom we have personal contact."
How to Break In: "Send a query letter; have a willingness to work hard, on speculation, for a while, and to take suggestions."

THE CHRISTIAN SCIENCE MONITOR, 1 Norway St., Boston MA 02115. Editor: John Hughes. International newspaper issued daily except Sundays and holidays. Special issues: travel, 2 winter vacation and 2 international travel, 2 summer vacation, 1 autumn vacation, and 1 cruise section. February and September: fashion; May and October: food. Established in 1908. Circulation: 189,000. Buys all rights. Buys about 3,700 mss a year. Payment on acceptance or publication, "depending on department." Submit only complete ms. Submit seasonal material 1 to 2 months in advance. Reports within 2 weeks. Enclose S.A.S.E. for return of submissions.
Nonfiction: "In-depth news analysis, features, and essays. Style should be bright, but not cute, concise but thoroughly researched. Try to humanize news or feature writing so the reader identifies with it. Avoid sensationalism, crime and disaster. Accent construction, solution-oriented treatment of subjects. Can use news-in-the-making stories not found elsewhere if subject has sufficient impact on current history (600 to 1,500 words). Feature pages as follows: People, Places, Things page uses colorful human interest material not exceeding 800 words, and humorous anecdotes. Home Forum page buys essays of 400 to 1,200 words; education, arts, real estate, travel, women, fashion, furnishings, consumer, environment, and science-technology pages will consider articles not usually more than 800 words ap-

propriate to respective subjects." Pays from $20 to $200. Informational, how-to, personal experience, interview, profile, humor, photo, travel, and successful business operations articles. Areas covered in travel issues include: Swiss, N.E., British, Canadian, Hawaiian, and Caribbean. Features Editor: Robert C. Cowen.

Photos: Purchased with or without mss. Captions required. Pays $10 to $50 depending upon size and where used in paper. Photo Editor: John Young.

Poetry and Fillers: Home Forum uses poetry. Wide variety of subjects and treatment; traditional forms, blank and free verse, avant-garde forms, light verse, and others. No length restriction. Pays $20 to $75. Crossword puzzles also wanted. Poetry and Filler Dept. Editor: Robert C. Cowen.

COLOROTO MAGAZINE, New York Daily News, 220 E. 42 St., New York NY 10017. Editor: Richard C. Lemon. For general audience. Weekly. Circulation: over 3 million. Buys first serial rights. Buys about 40 mss a year. Payment on acceptance. Will send free sample copy to a writer on request. Query first. Submit seasonal material 2 months in advance. Will consider photocopied submissions. Reports in 4 weeks. Enclose S.A.S.E. for reply to queries.

Nonfiction, Photos, Poetry, and Fillers: "Interested in all sorts of articles: most interested in human interest stories, articles about people (famous or unknown); least interested in essays and discussion pieces. Continuing need for New York City area subjects. Freelancer should use his own approach to material. Entertainment pieces seem to be over-abundant. We use a number, but they are mostly staff-written." Buys informational, personal experience, interview, profile, humor, nostalgia, and photo articles. Length: 100 to 3000 words. Pays $50 to $750. Photos purchased with or without mss. Captions are required. Specifications for b&w glossies or jumbo contacts: 8x10. Pays $25 for single, $150 for complete picture story. Color specifications: 2½, 4x5 or 35mm transparency. Pays from $35 for single, $200 for set. Buys light verse only. Buys puzzles.

How to Break In: "The best way is to try a feature of 1,500 to 2,000 words—with a query first, if in doubt about the suitability of the subject."

COLUMBUS DISPATCH SUNDAY MAGAZINE, 34 South Third St., Columbus OH 43216. Editor: Robert K. Waldron. Buys first time rights. Payment after publication. Enclose S.A.S.E.

Nonfiction and Photos: Strong Ohio angle is essential in all material. Buys singles, photo series, and illustrated articles. Length: 1,000 to 1,500 words. Pays minimum of 2¢ per word. B&w photos only. Pays $3 per photos. "Pay is flexible, depending on how good the piece is, how much effort has apparently been put into it, etc."

CONTEMPORARY MAGAZINE, Sunday supplement to the Denver Post, 650 15th St., Denver CO 80201. Editor: Lois Cress. For "young adults to senior citizens (both sexes), aware of today's world." Weekly. Buys first rights. Buys 10 to 20 mss a year. Pays on publication. Will send a free sample copy to a writer on request. No query required. "We are being very selective and use a very limited amount of freelance material." Submit seasonal material 3 months in advance. Reporting time varies. Enclose S.A.S.E. for return of submissions.

Nonfiction: How-to, personal experience, inspirational, humor, historical. "Most in-depth stories on medical, psychological and sociological subjects are staff-written. Topical articles are welcome. Humor articles must be refreshing, well-written. We're especially interested in the local tie-in, general interest." Length: 500 to 1,500 words. Payment is $25 to $75.

COURIER-JOURNAL AND TIMES MAGAZINE, 525 W. Broadway, Louisville KY 40202. Editor: Geoffrey Vincent. Not soliciting freelance material.

DAYTON LEISURE, Dayton Daily News, Fourth and Ludlow Sts., Dayton OH 45401. Editor: Jack M. Osler. Sunday supplement. Enclose S.A.S.E.

Nonfiction and Photos: Magazine focuses on leisure time activities in Ohio—particularly southwestern Ohio—that are interesting and unusual. Emphasis is on photos supplemented by stories. Up to 1,000 words. Photos should be glossy. "The Daily News will evaluate articles on their own merits. Likewise with photos. Average payment per article: $25." Payments vary depending on quality of writing.

How to Break In: "I suggest a writer send in a short feature in finished form along with illustrations, such as photos. Another way is for the writer to send in a brief query, outlining his story suggestion."

DES MOINES SUNDAY REGISTER PICTURE MAGAZINE, Des Moines Register, 715 Locust St., Des Moines IA 50309. Editor: Joan Bunke. For mass newspaper audience, metropolitan and rural. Established in 1950. Weekly. Circulation: 500,000. Buys first serial rights. Buys 30 to 50 mss a year. Payment on publication. Query first preferred. Submit seasonal material 6 to 8 weeks in advance. Enclose S.A.S.E. for reply to queries.
Nonfiction: "Articles heavily concentrated on Iowa, about what's going on in Iowa; how to survive in the modern world. General interest material. Anything interesting in Iowa, or interesting elsewhere with some kind of tie to Iowans." Length: 2,000 words maximum. Pays minimum $50, "higher according to quality of story and what it does for readers." Photos purchased with or without mss. Captions required. Prefers 8x10 b&w glossies. Pays $10 minimum. 35mm or larger transparencies. Pays $50 minimum for cover; $20 to $25 for inside use.

DETROIT MAGAZINE, The Detroit Free Press, 321 W. Lafayette Blvd., Detroit MI 48231. Editor: Patrick Strickler. Weekly. Circulation: 750,000. Rights purchased vary with author and material. Usually buys first-time rights only. Buys 50 freelance mss a year. Payment follows acceptance by 2 to 6 weeks. Will send free sample copy to writer on request. Query first. Will not consider photocopied submissions. Reports on material accepted for publication in 2 to 4 weeks. Returns rejected material immediately. Enclose S.A.S.E. for response to queries.
Nonfiction and Photos: "Magazine journalism concerning life in the Detroit metropolitan area and life in Michigan. Content must be filled with good, new, bright, interesting facts; anecdotal and descriptive color; upbeat, intelligent and unpredictable." Personal experience, interview, profile, humor, historical, think pieces, expose, spot news. Length: open. Payment ranges from $50 to $125, sometimes higher. B&w photos purchased on assignment or with accompanying mss. Prefers contact sheets and negatives. Captions required. Pays $25 per print used. Uses some color. Pays $125 for color cover.

DIXIE ROTO, The Times-Picayune's Magazine, 3800 Howard Ave., New Orleans LA 71040. Editor: Terence P. Smith. For general newspaper readership. Special Mardi Gras, Home Improvements, Bridal issues. Weekly. Buys first rights. Pays on publication. "I insist on queries. Freelance material must have strong local angle. We do not usually accept contributions from outside our Louisiana-Mississippi circulation area." Submit seasonal or special material 2 months in advance. Enclose S.A.S.E. for reply to queries.
Nonfiction and Photos: Uses feature articles with strong Louisiana-Mississippi identification and dramatic photo support. Interested in working with young, local writers. The column "Deep in Dixie" uses true historical anecdotes, footnoted as to sources, with an element of a plot and regional interest. Story payment is $20 to $75. B&w glossy photos, color transparencies, and color prints purchased with mss. Payment is $5 for b&w, $25 for color when reproduced in color, and $5 when reproduced in b&w.

EMERALD EMPIRE MAGAZINE, Eugene Register-Guard, Box 1232, Eugene OR 97401. Sunday Magazine Editor: David R. Emery. Buys first rights. Enclose S.A.S.E.
Nonfiction and Photos: "Need dramatic stories of Oregon and bordering areas, with emphasis on people. Length: 500 to 1500 words. Highly desirable that story be illustrated with good quality available light photos, supplemented by color photos, if possible. Supplemental sheet for editor required giving documentation on sources, reference materials, etc." Pays $30 per magazine page. $35 for color used on cover. All color transparencies returned after use.

EMPIRE MAGAZINE, The Denver Post, P.O. Box 1709, Denver CO 80201. Editor: Bill Hosokawa. Reports in a week. Buys first rights. Pays on acceptance for nonfiction; on publication for photos. Enclose S.A.S.E. for reply to queries or return of submissions.
Nonfiction: Material with strong regional interest, preferably with illustrations,

both b&w and color. Feature articles should deal with a setting inside the area of Colorado, Wyoming, New Mexico, Montana, Kansas, Nebraska, Oklahoma, northern Texas. Writing should be on a high level, informal, and full of good humor. Subject may be unusual personalities, true adventure, crime. Wants solid material that represents determined digging about exciting things, problems or situations in the region; must have strong regional peg. Also, articles in lighter vein. Length: 3,000 words maximum. Pays 4¢ to 5¢ per word.
Photos: Purchased with ms (see above), b&w singles, series, and picture stories of 500 words with 5 to 8 photos. Query. Uses color transparencies: pays $50 for covers, $100 for double spread, $25 for singles inside. Requires model release.

FAMILY WEEKLY, 641 Lexington Ave., New York NY 10022. Editor-in-Chief: Mort Persky. Managing Editor: Reynolds Dodson. No longer accepting unsolicited mss, but will consider queries. Enclose S.A.S.E. for reply to queries.

FEATURE PARADE MAGAZINE, Worcester Sunday Telegram, 20 Franklin St., Worcester MA 01613. Sunday supplement. Pays on acceptance. Enclose S.A.S.E. No fiction, poetry, or historical pieces.
Nonfiction and Photos: Illustrated feature articles of approximately five or six double-spaced pages. Must have strong central New England angle. Pays $35 to $100. Photos bought with mss or separately as photo essays or single photos that can stand by themselves as humorous, dramatic, arty, etc. B&w or color transparencies.

FENTON INDEPENDENT, 125 S. Leroy St., Fenton MI 48430. Editor: Robert G. Silbar. Weekly. Newspaper, not a magazine supplement. Buys all rights. Query first. Enclose S.A.S.E. for reply to queries.
Nonfiction and Photos: News stories, features, photos of local interest. Wants local material on local people, not generalized articles. Appreciates opinion articles on local topics. All material must have local flavor. Pays 25¢ per column inch.

THE FLORIDA TIMES JOURNAL MAGAZINE, 1 Riverside Ave., Jacksonville FL 32201. Editor: Charles Brock. Weekly. Circulation: 225,000. Buys 50 mss a year. Not copyrighted. Either rejects in 3 days, or holds ms for consideration. Pays on publication. Enclose S.A.S.E. with mss and queries.
Nonfiction and Photos: "Story should be grounded in our circulation area (Florida, South Georgia), but material involving Floridians elsewhere may be acceptable. Lean strongest toward human interest." Personal experience, interviews, profiles, photo-story, historical (query required on historical). "Through his enthusiasm, writer should indicate his interest, emotional involvement with the subject. Try to avoid the cliche, whether in word, photograph, or subject. No essay type material ('How I Bridged the Generation Gap'). We like stories that grow out of the solid ground of deep spade work." Payment is $35 to $75.

HUNTERDON COUNTY DEMOCRAT, 8 Court St., Flemington NJ 08822. Editor: Edward J. Mack. Weekly. Circulation: 20,000. Buys few mss. "Our market is localized for the county." Not copyrighted. Enclose S.A.S.E. for return of submissions.
Nonfiction and Photos: 700-word maximum on articles; 8x10 glossies or to column size. Address all material to the editor. "We need a better relationship developed between the county areas we cover and the state and national nature of most submitted articles. If this were 'built into stories' better, we'd use more. In other words, 'How does this affect us?' " Special editions: Real Estate Supplement, May 10; Annual Progress, January 15; Annual Automotive Issue, September 15; Home and Garden Section, March 15. Pays 20¢ to 50¢ per column inch.

IMPETUS, *The Financial Post,* 481 University Avenue, Toronto, Ontario, Canada. Managing Editor: Neville Nankivell. For the senior businessman. Published 10 times yearly. Circulation: 145,000. Buys first Canadian rights. Query "strongly recommended."
Nonfiction: "General topics but geared specifically to senior Canadian executives and professionals. Very limited freelance market." Length and payment dependent on subject and quality.

INSIGHT, The Milwaukee Journal, Journal Square, Milwaukee WI 53201. Editor: Mike Moore. Sunday magazine. Circulation: 550,000. Reports within 4 weeks. Buys one time rights. Pays on publication. Query preferred. Enclose S.A.S.E. for reply to queries.
Nonfiction and Photos: Emphasis on circulation area of Wisconsin and upper Michigan. Length: 2,000 words maximum. Pays $50 to $150 per article. Photos purchased with mss and with captions. Same subject matter as articles. Payment arranged with author or photographer.

THE ISLANDER, The Daily Colonist's Sunday Magazine, Victoria Press Ltd., Victoria, BC, Canada. Editor: Alec Merriman. Buys first magazine rights. Enclose S.A.E. and International Reply Coupons with mss and queries.
Nonfiction: Main interest is in Vancouver Island and British Columbia topics. Particularly interested in travel, development of the Canadian Pacific Northwest, adventure, historical characters who contributed to the settlement and expansion of industry and commerce in the Canadian West. Length: 500 to 2,000 words. Rates vary: $20 to $30 per 1,000 words. Likes photos with articles. Triple-space typing. Half-sheet size folios. No sentence or paragraph to be carried over to another folio sheet. This is because each story is set by a bank of computer operators.
Photos: Purchased with ms. B&w only. Pays $3 to $5 each.

LOS ANGELES TIMES HOME MAGAZINE, Times Mirror Square, Los Angeles CA 90053. Editor: James W. Toland. Issued every Sunday. Buys first North American serial rights. Pays on publication. Reports usually in one week. Query first. Enclose S.A.S.E.
Nonfiction: Articles devoted to the home and its environment. Solutions to problems and articles of family interest. No hobby features and only top-flight "how-to-do-it" material. Payment varies.
Photos: Prefers to originate own photography but exception would be made for residential architecture, and here photos must be high-quality 4x5 color transparencies or 8x10 glossy b&w prints. Originals only.

MIAMI HERALD TROPIC MAGAZINE, 1 Herald Plaza, Miami FL 33101. Editor: John W. Parkyn. For the population of south Florida. Established in 1967. Weekly. Circulation: 500,000. Rights purchased vary with author and material. Usually buys first Florida rights. Buys 100 mss a year. Payment on publication. Will send free sample copy to writer on request. Query first or submit complete ms. Will consider photocopied submission. Reports in 4 to 6 weeks, "frequently much less." Enclose S.A.S.E for reply to queries or return of submissions.
Nonfiction: "Well-written, informative and entertaining articles, preferably with some kind of south Florida tie-in. Articles reflecting the genuine interests of people living in our area." Interview, profile, travel, and successful business operations articles also considered. Length: 1,000 to 3,000 words. Pays $50 to $300.
Photos: Purchased with or without accompanying mss. B&w glossies or color transparencies. Pays $50 to $250, depending on quality and number of photos used.

MICHIANA, The South Bend Tribune's Magazine—Sunday supplement, Colfax at Lafayette, South Bend IN 46626. Editor: Tom Philipson. For "general cross-section of newspaper subscribers." Special travel sections, spring and fall. Weekly. Circulation: 125,000. Buys first rights. Buys 150 to 200 mss a year. Pays on publication. No query required. Submit seasonal or special material "at least 30 days in advance; better luck with 40 days or more." Reporting time varies. "We read material within 2 days of receipt. If it has possibilities, we may hold it for two months or more; otherwise it is returned immediately, providing S.A.S.E. is enclosed."
Nonfiction and Photos: "Items of general and unusual interest, written in good, clear, simple sentences with logical approach to subject. We like historical material in particular; also some religious material if unusual." Humor, think pieces, travel, photo articles with brief texts. "We avoid all freelance material that supports movements of a political nature. We do not like first-person stories, but use them on occasion. We can use some offbeat stuff if it isn't too far out." Length: 800 to 3,000 words. Payment is $40 to $50 minimum, with increases as deemed suitable. All mss must be accompanied by illustrations or b&w photos or 35mm or larger color transparencies.

THE NEVADAN, Review-Journal, Box 70, Las Vegas NV 89101. Sunday Supplement Editor: William Vincent. Sunday edition. Enclose S.A.S.E. with mss and queries.
Nonfiction and Photos: Nevada setting or strong state tie required. Length: 500 to 1,800 words plus two or three photos. Pays $25 per article; from $2 to $5 per photo.

THE NEW YORK TIMES, 229 W. 43 St., New York NY 10036. Enclose S.A.S.E. for reply to queries or return of mss.
Nonfiction: *The New York Times Magazine* appears in *The New York Times* on Sunday. "It is a news magazine. We define news in its broadest sense: background of national and international news developments, science, education, family life, social trends and problems, arts and entertainment, personalities, sports, the changing American scene. Freelance contributions are invited. Articles must be timely. They must be based on specific news items, forthcoming events, significant anniversaries, or they must reflect trends. We welcome humor, but here too we insist on news 'pegs.' We do not publish fiction nor do we solicit verse. Our full-length articles usually run to 3,500 words, and for these we pay $750 on acceptance. Our shorter pieces run from 1,000 to 2,000 words at a rate of $75 per column. (There are roughly 400 words in a column.)" The *Arts and Leisure Section* of *The New York Times* appears on Sunday. Wants "interviews with people in the arts; reporting on the current arts scene; reviews of new plays, movies, TV shows, etc.; humorous or satiric spoofs of current trends in the arts scene." Length: 800 to 2,000 words. Pays $125 to $200, depending on length. Editor, Arts and Leisure Section: Seymour Peck.
Photos: *The New York Times Magazine* wants photos that will suit its definition of news. Uses color and b&w; but likes b&w 8x10 enlargements on any type paper. Buys one-time rights. Query for photos. Rates on acceptance: $35 per picture; $300 per cover.

NEWPORT NEWS DAILY PRESS, INC., TIDEWATER'S NEW DOMINION MAGAZINE SECTION, 7505 Warwick Blvd., Newport News VA 23607. Sunday supplement. General Manager: Robert B. Smith. Magazine Editor: Howard Goshorn. Buys first publication rights only. No fiction or poetry. Sample copy of magazine sent on request. Payment on publication. Query first. Enclose S.A.S.E.
Nonfiction and Photos: Uses occasional feature, travel, or state-interest articles of 500 to 1,000 words, accompanied by glossy print photos. Rates of payment vary. Query first.

NORTHWEST MAGAZINE, The Sunday Oregonian, 1320 S.W. Broadway, Portland OR 97210. Editor: Joseph R. Bianco. For Pacific Northwest general newspaper audience. Weekly. Circulation: 402,000. Pays on publication. Reports in 2 weeks. Enclose S.A.S.E. for return of submissions.
Nonfiction and Photos: "Wildlife, some history, current social topics, travel, profiles. No hunting stories." Length: 2,000 words. Payment is $35 a magazine page (about 1,500 words). B&w photos purchased with mss. Payment is $10 a photo published.

PANORAMA MAGAZINE, *The Everett Herald,* Grand and California Aves., Everett WA 98201. Editor: Jeanne Metzger. Majority of readers are in Snohomish County, directly north of Seattle. Established in 1973. Weekly. Circulation: 50,000. Buys all rights, but will reassign rights to author after publication. Buys an average of 24 mss a year. Payment on publication "unless mss is to be held for some time." To obtain a sample copy, we "prefer writer address our circulation department." Query first or submit complete ms, but it's "best to make individual contact with editor or write query letter on material to be submitted." Will consider photocopied submissions. Reports within 1 month. Enclose S.A.S.E. with queries and submissions.
Nonfiction: "We like good picture features, good personal experience pieces, interviews with interesting people, and articles about happenings in the Northwest. In our population area we don't just stay on Northwest subjects. We'll look at anything that's well-written and has good picture art. We don't really like freelance travel material unless it's offbeat and would be someplace our people might visit."

Length: 600 to 1,800 words. Pays $20 to $25 a tabloid page, with pictures.
Photos: Photos are purchased with or without mss, or on assignment. 5x7 or 8x10 b&w glossies, "good quality." Pays $5 to $10. 35mm and larger transparencies, "must be good bright color." Pays $15 to $20 for cover photo.

PANORAMA, The Morgantown Dominion Post, Greer Bldg., Morgantown WV 26506. Sunday supplement issued weekly. Editor: Susan Conte. "We have much more material from our regular sources than we can justifiably handle at the present time."

PARADE, The Sunday Newspaper Magazine, 733 Third Ave., New York NY 10017. Weekly. Circulation: over 17 million. Buys first North American serial rights. Pays on acceptance. Query first. Enclose S.A.S.E. for reply to queries and return of submissions.
Nonfiction: "Interested in features that will inform, educate or entertain a mass circulation domestic audience. Exclusive, news-related articles and photos are required. Subjects may include: well-known personalities, sports, religion, education, community activities, family relations, science and medicine. Articles should be current, factual, authoritative." Length: about 1,500 words. Pays up to $1,000.
Photos: "Photos should have visual impact and be well composed with action-stopping qualities. For the most part, color is used on cover. Transparencies of any size are accepted. Either b&w 8x10 enlargements or contact sheets may be submitted. Accurate caption material must accompany all photos."

PENINSULA LIVING, P.O. Box 5188, Redwood City CA 94063. Editor: J. A. Gallagher. For newspaper subscribers on San Francisco Peninsula; among the nation's best educated, most affluent. Regional material exclusively. Special issue: January, travel. Established in 1954. Weekly. Circulation: 105,000. Not copyrighted. Acquires first serial rights. Buys 20 to 30 mss a year. Payment on 10th of month following publication. Will send sample copy to writer for 20¢. Query first. Will not consider photocopied submission. Submit special issue material 2 months in advance. Reports in 2 to 3 weeks. Enclose S.A.S.E. for reply to query and return of submission.
Nonfiction: "Anything we think would be of interest to our readers. Regional material exclusively. Fresh approach, narrative style desired. Regional travel, occasional personality features." Informational, how-to, personal experience, interview, profile, humor, historical, and travel. Length: 500 to 1,500 words. Pays 2¢ to 3¢ per word.
Photos: Purchased with accompanying mss; captions required. 8x10 b&w glossies. Payment with article payment; add about $5 per print used.

THE PHILADELPHIA EVENING AND SUNDAY BULLETIN, 30th and Market Sts., Philadelphia PA 19101. Executive Editor: William B. Dickinson. "Using only a limited amount of freelance copy, primarily travel." Query first. Enclose S.A.S.E.

PICTURE MAGAZINE, Minneapolis Sunday Tribune, 425 Portland Ave., Minneapolis MN 55415. Editor: Catherine Watson. Buys first rights. Enclose S.A.S.E. for ms return.
Nonfiction and Photos: "Uses photographic essays and documentaries, with emphasis on social commentary and meaningful communication about people and events in the Midwest, especially Minnesota. Payment varies on editor's use of submitted material, with most nonprofessional features bringing around $100. Color work should be in transparencies. Prefer strong, striking photographic approach to story. No snapshots."

THE REPUBLIC, 333 2nd (P.O. Box 10), Columbus IN 47201. Editor: Stu Huffman. For south-central Indiana newspaper readers. Established in 1872. Daily. Circulation: 20,000. Not copyrighted. Acquires first serial rights. Uses 100 to 150 mss a year. Payment on publication. Will send free sample copy to writer on request. Query first or submit complete ms. Will consider photocopied submissions. "Seasonal material sought annually for each season and each holiday. Should arrive 2 weeks in advance." Reports on material in 1 week. Enclose S.A.S.E. for return of submissions or reply to queries.

Nonfiction and Photos: "Saturday 'Week Ender' section open to freelance submissions of local and regional interest. Like to find freelance articles about our area to provide readers with information they are not likely to see elsewhere." Coverage desired on "Bible belt reaction to women's rights; new programs in education; efforts by small communities to attract tourists, stories about those attractions, and stories on architectural features in small towns. Length: 500 to 1,500 words. Pays $5 to $50. Photos purchased with accompanying mss, without mss or on assignment. "8x10, but will accept other sizes or negs." Pays $3 to $25. Color transparencies, 35mm to 4x5. Pays $10 to $50. Captions required, with names and addresses.
Poetry: Traditional forms, blank verse, free verse, avant-garde forms, light verse. Length: 4 to 60 lines. No payment. Dept. Editor: Marjorie Sea.

RHODE ISLANDER, The Providence Journal, 75 Fountain St., Providence RI 02902. Editor: Ted Holmberg. Sunday supplement. Circulation: 210,000. Buys all rights. Pays on publication. Will send free sample copy on request. Reports in 2 weeks. Special issues on furniture and brides. Enclose S.A.S.E. with all submissions.
Nonfiction and Photos: Articles with Rhode Island interest or angle. 500 to 1,500 words. Pays $35 minimum. Photos purchased with mss.

RURAL GRAVURE, 2564 Branch Street, Middleton WI 53562. Editor: J. C. Curren. For "rural—hometown Midwestern residents," Monthly. Circulation: 650,000. Buys 25 mss a year. Pays on publication. Will send a free sample copy to a writer on request. No query required. Submit seasonal material 6 months in advance. Reports "immediately." Enclose S.A.S.E. for return of submissions.
Nonfiction: Wants human interest stories and interviews "from Midwest only." Does not want agricultural articles. Length: 1,000 to 3,000 words. Pays $50 to $150.
Photos: B&w glossies purchased with captions only. Pays $15 to $150.

SACRAMENTO UNION WEEKENDER, 301 Capitol Mall, Sacramento CA 95812. Editor: Jackie Peterson. Weekly. Buys "one-time" rights. Buys about 100 mss a year. Query first. Enclose S.A.S.E. for reply to queries.
Nonfiction and Photos: Interested in offbeat, unusual, one-time-only items of travel, leisure, or general interest. Sometimes buys personality profiles or a first-person piece. "Readership surveys have indicated that people want nitty-gritty facts, how-to-get-there, prices, where to stay, where to eat. We're including much more of this kind of information in our recreation and travel stories than ever before. The availability of illustration often dictates my choice. I go back time after time to the few good writers who regularly submit stories to me." Length: "we cannot absorb stories much over 1,200 words." Pays $35 to $50.

ST. PETERSBURG TIMES, THE FLORIDIAN (Sunday supplement), Box 1121, St. Petersburg FL 33731. Editor: Scott DeGarmo. Art Director: Alan Urban. Buys first rights. Will send free sample copy to writer on request. Enclose S.A.S.E. for return of submissions.
Nonfiction and Photos: "Major magazine articles must have a solid Florida orientation, but reflect an awareness of national trends. Timely stories on politics, nature, entertainment, personalities. Must be high quality writing with depth, sophistication and sparkle." Length: 2,000 to 3,000 words. Pays $150 to $200, more for exceptional material. "Short articles, first rate science and medical articles that have a Florida slant or would be of special interest to the many retirees among our readership." Length: 800 to 1,000 words. Pays $50 to $100, "more for exceptional material." No "trivial historical pieces, general once-over-lightly pieces, mood pieces, local color history, personal anecdotes, domestic drama."

THE SAN DIEGO UNION, 940 Third Ave., San Diego CA 92112. Sunday Editor: Beverly Beyette. Pays on publication. Reports in 3 weeks. Enclose S.A.S.E. with mss and queries.
Nonfiction and Photos: Historical material about Southern California, New Mexico, Arizona, Nevada. Accuracy and accompanying photos, maps or illustrations essential. Length: 700 to 1,000 words. Pays $25 to $35. Photos purchased with ms.

SEATTLE TIMES SUNDAY MAGAZINE, P.O. Box 70, Seattle WA 98111. Editor: Richard Johnston. Payment on publication. Submit complete ms. Reports in 3

weeks. Enclose S.A.S.E. for return of submissions.
Nonfiction: Uses articles with good illustrations. Wants Pacific Northwest subjects only. Pays $35 for a single page article, if art is provided.
Photos: For *Seattle Times Sunday Pictorial*, buys photos of Pacific Northwest subjects only. Pays $5 minimum. Photo Editor: Herb Belanger.

SENTINEL STAR FLORIDA MAGAZINE, Box 2833, Orlando FL 32802. Editor: Bill Dunn. For a Sunday supplement audience. Weekly. Circulation: 200,000. Buys first rights. Pays on publication. Will send a free sample copy to a writer on request. "Queries are not necessary but suggested for extremely popular subjects. Best bet: follow the news." Replies in 2 to 3 weeks. Enclose S.A.S.E. for reply to queries or return of mss.
Nonfiction: "Features about any Florida subjects only. Arts, business, consumerism, education, environment, history, life styles, nostalgia, politics, science and sports." Length: 1,000 to 3,000 words. Pays $35 to $150. "Also topical comment, humor, satire." Length: 500 to 700 words. Pays $20 to $50.
Photos: B&w glossies and color transparencies sometimes purchased with mss.

SIOUX FALLS ARGUS-LEADER, 200 S. Minnesota Ave., Sioux Falls SD 57102. Executive Editor: Anson Yeager. Buys first publication rights. Payment is made on the first of each month. Query first. Enclose S.A.S.E. for reply to queries and return of submissions.
Nonfiction and Photos: Uses occasional feature stories on South Dakota subjects. Length: 500 words maximum. Pays 22¢ a column inch. Uses photo layouts related to South Dakota.

SOUTH JERSEY LIVING, 1900 Atlantic Ave., Atlantic City NJ 08404. Editor: Paul Learn. For general newspaper audience in South Jersey region. Special issues: all major holidays; also any material pertaining to Miss America Pageant. Established in 1964. Weekly. Circulation: 70,000. Buys all rights, but will reassign rights to author after publication. Buys about 200 mss a year. Payment on publication. Will send free sample copy to writer on request. Write for copy of guidelines for writers. Will consider photocopied submissions. Submit seasonal material 1 month in advance. Reports in 3 months. "If no answer within 3 months, writer should consider material rejected." Enclose S.A.S.E. for return of submissions.
Nonfiction: "Articles, profiles, interviews dealing only with South Jersey. Topics run gamut, within limit of family readership: sports, South Jersey history, hobbies, culture, music, paintings. Emphasis is on hotel and resort industries, seashore. Third-person only. No first-person. Want direct quotes, punchlines, emotional highpointing when possible. Especially interested in articles on the following subjects: legalized gambling, lotteries, legalized 'numbers'; ideas to build up seashore resort business." Informational, humor, nostalgia, new product, and technical articles also wanted. Length: 1,000 to 1,500 words. Pays $20 per magazine page for first page; $10 for each succeeding magazine page.
Photos: Purchased with or without accompanying mss. South Jersey angle. Captions required. 8½x11 b&w. Pays $10 for cover; $5 for inside use.

SOUTHLAND SUNDAY MAGAZINE, Sunday Independent Press-Telegram, Sixth and Pine, Long Beach CA 90844. Editor: James M. Leavy. Circulation: 144,000. Will send sample copy to a writer on request. Pays on acceptance. Enclose S.A.S.E. with mss and queries.
Nonfiction and Photos: Illustrated articles, chiefly on California subjects, some articles of broad general appeal. Length: 1,000 to 3,000 words. Pays up to $150 (average of about 5¢ per word). Color transparencies and 4x5 or larger glossy photos are purchased with mss.

SUNDAY ADVOCATE MAGAZINE, Box 588, Baton Rouge LA 70821. Editor: Charles H. Lindsay. Buys no rights. Enclose S.A.S.E. for return of submissions.
Nonfiction and Photos: Well-illustrated short articles; must have local, area or Louisiana angle, in that order of preference. Photos purchased with mss. Rates vary.

SUNDAY MAGAZINE OF THE SPOKESMAN REVIEW, The Spokesman Re view, Spokane WA 99210. Editor: Jack F. Johnson. Readership in eastern Washington, northern Idaho and western Montana. Reports on submissions in one week. Buys one-time rights. Pays on acceptance. Query required. Enclose S.A.S.E. for reply to queries.
Nonfiction: Subject matter of particular interest to Northwest, 1,200 to 2,000 words with photos. Pays $50 and up.
Photos: B&w and color photos (all sizes) purchased with mss or with captions only. 4x5 color transparenices also purchased for cover use, particularly of Northwest subjects. Pays up to $25 for cover; up to $75 for color pictorial feature.

TAHOMAN, Tacoma News Tribune, 711 St. Helens Ave., Tacoma WA 98401. Magazine Editor: Roland Lund. Sunday supplement. Pays on publication. Enclose S.A.S.E. for return of submissions.
Nonfiction and Photos: Articles and photos about Pacific Northwest, particularly the Puget Sound area. Historical, biographical, recreational stories. Pays $25 per printed tabloid page, whether pictures, text or both. Also occasionally buys a color picture for $25. Northwest subjects only.

TEXAS MAGAZINE, Houston Chronicle, 512 Travis, Houston TX 77002. Editor: Jack Rickman. For "newspaper readers." Established in 1945. Weekly. Circulation: 350,000. Buys all rights, but will reassign rights to author after publication. Buys under 10 mss a year. Payment on publication. Will consider photocopied submissions. Submit seasonal material 2 months in advance. Reports in 2 weeks. Enclose S.A.S.E. for return of submissions.
Nonfiction and Photos: Publishes nonfiction features. Buys personal experience articles. Length: 1,500 to 2,000 words. Pays $100 to $200. Buys 8x10 b&w glossies and 35mm color photos. Purchased with mss. Captions are required.

TODAY, The Philadelphia Inquirer Magazine, 400 North Broad St., Philadelphia PA 19130. Editor: Howard A. Coffin. "Because we are a metropolitan Sunday newspaper supplement, our readership is largely urban, and we aim for sophisticated or offbeat articles geared to the city. The local writer has the best chance." Circulation: 875,000. Buys first rights only. Buys 125 to 150 mss a year. Pays on publication. "Include phone number with submissions." Submit seasonal material 3 to 4 months in advance. Reports in 3 to 4 weeks. Enclose S.A.S.E. for return of submissions.
Nonfiction and Photos: "We want humor, youth-oriented articles, the offbeat, solid informative articles on how to cope with contemporary problems. We like the sophisticated approach—that is, a touch of *New York* magazine. We like stories that give nuggets of information, including dollar figures where appropriate. We like stories that help the reader as well as entertain. We do not want, or use, poetry or short stories or personal memoirs." Length: 300 to 3,000 words. Payment is $100 to $200. Pays $25 to $100 for photos, "but the emphasis is local. We use very little free-lance."

THE VOICE-JEFFERSONIAN, Chenoweth Sq., St. Matthews KY 40207. Editor: Bruce B. VanDusen. For middle and upper income suburban audience. Family readership, but no taboos. Weekly. Address all inquiries to the editor. Enclose S.A.S.E. for reply to queries.
Nonfiction and Photos: News and Features departments. 300 to 1,500 words on local (East Jefferson County) subjects. 5x7 b&w glossies. Pays 25¢ to 50¢ per inch; $3.50 to $10 for photos.

WASHINGTON, 225 Virginia Ave., S.E., Washington DC 20003. Editor: Peter T. Maiken. Present format established in 1970. Sunday magazine of *The Sunday Star and The Washington Daily News*. Circulation: 325,000. Rights purchased vary with author and material. Buys all rights, but will reassign rights to author after publication or buys first North American serial rights, first serial rights, second serial (reprint) rights or simultaneous rights. Buys 100 mss a year "and numerous short items". Payment on acceptance. Query first. Will consider photocopied submissions. Submit seasonal material 2 months in advance. Returns rejected material in 1 week. Will send free sample copy to writer on request. Enclose S.A.S.E. for reply to queries.

Nonfiction and Photos: "Original stories of general journalistic interest, and of a local nature. We try to reach all segments of a general readership and look for a more universal appeal in the choice of a subject. We place strong emphasis on visual elements, especially photography. Write a brief query, explaining approach and scope and point of view; telling what the writer hopes to accomplish." Length: 3,000 words maximum. Pays 5¢ a word minimum. *Notebook* column uses short items of recreational, entertainment, service or general informative interest, all local. Pays $150 page rate for color photos purchased on assignment. Art Director: John Heinly.

WEEKEND MAGAZINE, 231 St. James St. West, Montreal, PQ Canada. Editor: Frank Lowe. Weekly section of 22 newspapers. Circulation: 1,600,000. Buys 100 mss a year. Pays on acceptance. Query before submitting material. Enclose S.A.E. and International Reply Coupons with mss and queries.
Nonfiction: "Brief articles and photo features on Canadian subjects of general interest and general subjects that will interest Canadian newspaper readers." Length: maximum 2,500 words. Payment varies, but averages $400.
Photos: With ms or with captions only, including 35mm color; buys transparencies in preference to flat color. Managing Editor: Paul Rush.

WRITER'S VIEWPOINT, 1125 Valley Rd., Menasha WI 54952. Editor: Dorothy Dalton. This is a one-page section of *View,* Sunday magazine section of the *Appleton Post-Crescent.* Circulation: over 50,000. Not copyrighted. Buys about 300 mss a year. Payment on publication. Submit complete ms. Prefers originals, not photocopies. Submit seasonal material 2 to 3 months in advance. Reports in 6 to 8 weeks. Enclose S.A.S.E. for return of submissions.
Nonfiction: Articles in a humorous vein on current topics are used. Also nostalgia, if handled lightly. Length: 400 words, or 600 to 800 words. Pays $10.
Poetry: Serious poetry is used in the column "Poetry View". Unrhymed lyrics preferred. No religious poetry. Length: 20 lines maximum. Light verse. Length: 4 to 8 lines. Pays $3 per poem.

Photography Publications

CAMERA 35, 132 West 31st Street, New York NY 10001. Editor: Jim Hughes. "A very special magazine within a vertical field, directed at thinking photographers." Published 10 times a year. Buys one-time rights. Pays on publication. Enclose S.A.S.E. for return of submissions.
Photos: "Photography published in form of portfolios and essays. No taboos for either words or pictures, as long as they fit our needs. To determine needs, study at least 3 recent issues. Good literate writing mandatory. Pays $200 per mini portfolio (2 to 3 pages), $500 per maxi portfolio or essay (4 to 12 pages) b&w or color. Covers, $150. Up to $400 for technical how-to features."

FREELANCE PHOTOGRAPHY, FREELANCE PHOTO NEWS, 4 East State Street, Doylestown PA 18901. Acting Editor: William Cameron. For "amateur and professional photographers, all ages and with various educational backgrounds." Established in 1972 and 1968, respectively. Monthly (FP); Every two months (FPN). Circulation: over 25,000. Rights purchased vary with author and material, but may buy all rights. Buys "hundreds" of mss a year. Payment on acceptance or publication. Will send free sample copy to a writer on request. Will send editorial guidelines sheet to a writer on request. Query first. "If photographs are to accompany the article, they should be clearly marked with the photographer's name and address, necessary captions or pertinent information must be also clearly available, and if identifiable persons appear in any photo, the proper model release must be attached. Used photos, stories, etc. will not be returned after use unless specifically requested." Reports in two weeks. Enclose S.A.S.E. for reply to queries.
Nonfiction: Interested in articles in the following categories: "A how-to approach

toward taking photos or a unique device designed to aid in certain picture situ ations. It could be with regard to cameras, lighting, studio setup, backdrops, model handling, etc. Included in this could be new darkroom techniques or new innovations which would make use of a darkroom more efficient. Aside from the equipment and supporting areas of how-to, an article could be designed from experiences such as 'Promotion sells photos,' 'Linking your camera to a business,' 'A hobby becomes a profitable business,' etc. Unusual experiences which one may have had with a camera or other equipment. Personalities. We'd like to hear about any unique or special happenings by well-known personalities and their involvement in photography. These may be of political figures, TV and movie stars, etc. and their use of cameras and related equipment. Human interest stories. We are interested in stories which illustrate people with unusual or unique job situations and their use of cameras and related equipment. Travel stories. We are not interested in general travel items. They must be geared to a person or group of people and their experience with photography. Articles which inform the reader of how-to or what-to photograph when visiting ... (city or country) are encouraged and acceptable. Humorous articles are welcome and should be short. These could be of any item which relates to photography, on the lighter side." Also interested in "almost any idea which is photography related." Buys informational, how-to, personal experience, interview, profile, inspirational, humor, think, expose, personal opinion, photo, travel, spot news, successful business operations, new product, merchandising technique, and technical articles. Length. 300 to 3,000 words. Pays $5 to $50.

Photos: " 'The Photo Gallery' is a section of selected photographs submitted by our members and readers at large for display on a space available basis in each issue. Individual photos or a series of photos with captions are considered. Credit line will be given. No payment is made usually for photos appearing in this section. 'Photo Story' is devoted to a series of photographs which would be self-explanatory and contain captions only. A short explanatory paragraph may accompany the series." Photos purchased with and without mss. Captions required. Buys 5x7, but prefers 8x10 b&w glossies. Pays $5 and up.

Fillers: Buys newsbreaks, photo related puzzles, clippings.

MODERN PHOTOGRAPHY, 1 Astor Place, New York NY 10003. Editor: Julia Scully. Monthly. Read by photographers, about half of whom have their own darkrooms. Buys one-time rights. Pays on acceptance. Study copy of magazine before submitting and send in outline before writing script. Enclose S.A.S.E. for return of submissions.

Nonfiction: Uses articles on specialized photo techniques; other types of articles are staff-written. Pays $60 per page for text and photographs. Uses either contacts or enlargements; the latter should be 8x10 or 11x14 semi-gloss prints.

Photos: B&w 8x10 or larger prints on glossy dried matte. Uses any type transparency material for color submissions, but they must be 35mm and up in size. $35 minimum for b&w; $100 minimum for color. Please query here before submitting anything.

Fillers: Has a department buying photo kinks and gadget ideas.

THE NEWSLETTER (formerly *High Country Photographer*), P.O. Box 1961, Harlingen TX 78550. Editor: Jeffrey D. Clack. For professional and amateur photographers. "We are very personal, almost like a family together." Established in 1972. Circulation: 200 "plus." Buys all rights, but will reassign rights to author after publication. Pays on publication. Will send free copy to a writer on request. Query first on submissions, "may save time later, but not necessary." Does not accept photocopied submissions. Reports on acceptance or rejection "immediately." Enclose S.A.S.E. for reply to queries or return of mss.

Nonfiction and Photos: Wants how-to articles on photography, writing, production, marketing tips, informational and technical articles, personal experience, emphasis on successful business operation, humor, think, photo and spot news. Materials should "look sharp, think sharp." Length: up to 3,000 words. Pays $25 maximum. Photos should be b&w, 5x7 or 8x10, "must be top rate." Pays $2 and up. No color photos.

Fiction: Interested in experimental, science fiction, fantasy and humorous pieces. **Length:** 5,000 words maximum. Pays $25, "occasionally higher."

PHOTOGRAPHIC MAGAZINE, 8490 Sunset Blvd., Los Angeles CA 90069. Editor: Paul R. Farber. For "the amateur, and the advance beginner in photography, both still and motion picture—all ages." Monthly. Circulation: 150,000. Buys first rights. Payment on publication. Query first. Reports in 2 weeks. Enclose S.A.S.E. for reply to queries.
Nonfiction and Photos: "Basically seeking how-to type of article dealing with photography in all areas. Writer should be an authority on his subject and article should be well illustrated with photographs. We seek information that is generally disregarded by other publications in the field—in other words, we cater to the amateur photographer—in picture taking and beginner darkroom." Buys how-to, personal experience, interviews, new product, photos, and travel articles. No restrictions on length, but "must complete subject." Pays $60 per printed page. Pays $35 per black and white, $50 for each color print used.

POPULAR PHOTOGRAPHY, 1 Park Ave., New York NY 10016. Editor: Kenneth Poli. "Mostly for hobby photographers; about 90% are men." Also publishes 6 annuals or one-shots. Monthly. Circulation: 578,000. Buys 75 to 90 mss a year, "mostly from technical types already known to us." Pays on acceptance. Query first. Submit seasonal material 4 months in advance. Reports in 3 to 4 weeks. Enclose S.A.S.E. for reply to queries.
Nonfiction: This magazine is mainly interested in instructional articles on photography that will help photographers improve their work. This includes all aspects of photography, from camera use through darkroom procedures. Utter familiarity with the subject is a prerequisite to acceptance here. It is best to submit article ideas in outline form since features are set up to fit the magazine's visual policies. "Style should be very readable but with plenty of factual data when a technique story is involved. We're not quite as 'hardware' oriented as some magazines; we give more space to cultural and aesthetic aspects of the hobby." Buys how-to's, interviews, profiles, historical articles, new product coverage, photo essays. Length: 500 to 2,000 words. Pays $25 to $400.
Photos: Interested in seeing b&w prints of any type finish that are 8x10 or larger. Also uses any size color transparency. Buys one-time rights except when assigned, then all-time. Pays $25 and up per b&w shot; $50 and up per color shot; $250 for cover. Articles accompanied by pictures are usually bought as a package. Gives few assignments.
Fillers: Uses featurettes that run from 1 to 2 columns to 1 pagers and "Photo Tips," which are short how-to-do-its, illustrated by a single picture. Featurette length should be from 500 to 1,000 words; for the "Photo Tips," less than 100 words or whatever is necessary to give all pertinent information. Pays $25 to $75 for featurettes, depending on use; $10 for illustrated "Photo Tips."

Poetry Publications

This category includes publications that exist to discuss and publish poetry, and a few newspapers, and other special media using poetry are also included. Many magazines in the Literary and Little category are also interested in poetry submissions, and various other poetry markets are scattered through the Consumer Magazines.

Many of the markets that follow pay in contributor's copies, prizes or some form of remuneration other than money. We have included such markets because there are limited commercial outlets for poetry and these at least offer the poet a chance of publication.

AB INTRA, c/o Hellric Publications, 32 Waverly St., Belmont MA 02178. Editor: Dolores Stewart. For "young adults (college, university, high school) and mature readers interested in current poetry. No restrictions on subject matter or theme." Established in 1972. Quarterly ("more or less"). Circulation: over 500. Acquires all rights. Uses 200 mss a year. Will send sample copy to a writer for 75¢. Submit complete ms. Will not consider photocopied submissions. Reports on material accepted

for publication in 3 weeks. Returns rejected material in 1 week. Enclose S.A.S.E.
Poetry: "Striving to present more poetry that springs from the writer's 'emotional apparatus' though controlled by his intellect to sufficient degree. We're anxious for any poem that really works. Some favoring of experimental/avant-garde, but all kinds welcome." Traditional, free verse, blank verse, avant-garde (especially) and prose poems. Length: not over 600 lines. Payment: 5 copies plus 4-issue subscription.

AESOP'S FEAST MAGAZINE, 540 S. Gaylord, Denver CO 80209. Editor: Michael Walton. For poets, students, "and a small readership in the general public." Annual. Buys first rights. Buys 50 to 75 mss a year. Pays on publication. Will send a sample copy to a writer for 25¢. No query required. Reports in 1 month. Enclose S.A.S.E. for return of submissions.
Nonfiction: "Letters relating to poetry." Length: open. Payment is $5 a page minimum.
Poetry: Traditional, contemporary, avant-garde. "We recommend no special approach: all styles, subjects, and outlooks are acceptable if the quality of the poetry is unusually high. We would prefer not seeing sentimental light verse or children's verse, and we avoid grafitti, polemics, and editorializing." Length: open. Pays minimum $1 for 10 lines or less; 10¢ a line for poems longer than 10 lines.

ALL THIS AND MORE, P.O. Box 957, Jonesboro AR 72401. Editor: Richard Murray. For "readers between ages 18 to 40; high school to Ph.D. education; well-informed. Poems; some criticism and analysis of poetry." Established in 1973. Quarterly. Circulation, about 1,500. Not copyrighted. Uses 20 mss per issue. Will send writer a sample copy for $1.25. Will not consider photocopied submissions. Submit complete ms. Will not consider photocopied submissions. Submit seasonal material 2 months in advance. Reports in 1 month. Enclose S.A.S.E. for return of submissions.
Poetry: "We hope to publish high-quality poetry from freelance writers. No special approach. Only requirement is that poetry be good." Traditional and avant-garde forms, blank verse, free verse. 60 lines maximum. "All payment presently in copies."
Nonfiction: Personal experience, interview, profile, personal opinion, poetry reviews. Length: "No limit; just stick to subject." Pays maximum of $10 or minumum of 2 copies of the magazine.

THE ARCHER, P.O. Box 9488, North Hollywood CA 91609. Editor: Elinor Henry Brown. For poets of all ages. Quarterly. Established in 1951. Circulation: 500. Returns all needed rights to author after publication. Payment is one contributor's copy. Will send sample copy for 50¢. Reports on submissions as soon as possible. Include full name, address and zip code with only one poem on each sheet of 8½x11 size sheet of paper. Enclose S.A.S.E. for return of submissions and reply to queries.
Poetry: Wants poetry with human interest, empathy, active imagery, unity and sincerity. Prefers brevity and "modern, natural speech. Particularly appreciate couplets and three-line poems. No dangling 'little words' at end of free verse lines." Prefers under 11 lines and rarely uses over 30 lines.
Fillers: Uses only one- or two-line epigrams.

BACHAET, P.O. Box 1405, Municipal Plaza, Bloomfield NJ 07003. Editor: Geoffrey Jay Palefsky. Issued six times yearly. Reports in one month. S.A.S.E. must accompany submissions.
Poetry: Particularly interested in unpublished poets. Poetry in any form welcomed. Should not exceed 16 lines. Not interested in "smut material." No payment; no free copies. No query necessary.

BARDIC ECHOES, 1036 Emerald Ave., N.E., Grand Rapids MI 49503. Editor: Clarence L. Weaver. Issued quarterly. Publication is not copyrighted. Enclose S.A.S.E. "Limit submissions to no more than 5 poems. Material on hand will fill three future issues."
Poetry: Poetry may be on any subject, varied style, line length up to 40 (one full page). Payment in contributor's copy. Reports within 2 months. Sample copy (back issue) will be sent for 25¢.

THE BELOIT POETRY JOURNAL, P.O. Box 2, Beloit WI 53511. Editorial Board: Robert H. Glauber, David M. Stocking, Marion Kingston Stocking. Quarterly. Circulation: 1,100. Acquires first serial rights. Accepts approximately 60 mss a year. Payment in 3 contributor's copies. Will send a sample copy to a writer for 50¢. No query required. Reports in 4 months. Enclose S.A.S.E. for return of submissions.
Poetry: Uses all types of poetry from the most experimental to the most conservative (with emphasis in each case on quality) and is always on the lookout for interesting new talent. No restrictions as to length or form. One unusual feature is the policy of devoting occasional issues to one long poem or to a special chapbook on one theme.

BEST POETS OF THE TWENTIETH CENTURY, Drawer J, Babylon NY 11702. Editor: B. Winston Paramount. For "poets and enthusiasts who are primarily teachers, librarians, college students and professionals." Established in 1972. Quarterly. Circulation: 500 to 1,000. Buys first North American serial rights. Buys 600 mss a year. Payment on publication. Will send sample copy to writer for $3.95. Write for copy of guidelines for writers, enclosing stamped, addressed envelope. Submit complete ms. Will consider photocopied submissions. Reports on material in 1 week. Enclose S.A.S.E. for return of submissions.
Poetry: "We look for poets who are serious about the artistic techniques, and also sincerely aesthetic. Skillful rhyme and meter as well as patterns and free verse, traditional and blank verse. Above all—sincerity, not just contrived phrases. Themes are people, places, nature, philosophy. We are quite concerned with message, purpose, imagery and symbols that are not 'contrived', but 'good metaphors'. We shun prose shaped like a poem, and poems not shaped as poems but as scattered words." Length: 3 to 16 lines. "Maximum of 3 poems as one submission." Pays 50 cents to $1 per poem. Cash prizes.

BITTERROOT, 5229 Blythebourne Station, P.O. Box 51, Brooklyn NY 11219. Editor: Menke Katz. Quarterly. Payment in 1 contributor's copy. Enclose S.A.S.E. for return of submissions.
Poetry: "We need good poetry of all kinds."

BROADSIDE SERIES, 12651 Old Mill Place, Detroit MI 48238. Editor: Dudley Randall. For young blacks. Monthly. Circulation: 500. Buys first rights. Buys 12 mss a year. Pays on publication. Will send a sample copy to a writer for 50¢. Slow reports on submissions. Enclose S.A.S.E. for return of submissions.
Poetry: All black experience, all styles; no taboos except ineptness. Length: one page. Mss should be typed and double-spaced. Poems must be of high literary merit as each monthly issue usually contains only one poem. Pays $10 per poem.

CAFETERIA, 3692 Alexia Pl., San Diego CA 92116. Editor: Gordon B. Preston. For "graduate students in creative writing." Established in 1970. Biannually. Circulation: 500. Will send sample copy to writer on request. Submit complete poetry ms. Reports on submissions in 1 month. Enclose S.A.S.E. for return of material.
Poetry: Poetry on any theme. Length and type open. "We offer a $50 prize for best poem in the issue. No other payment."

CARDINAL POETRY QUARTERLY, 10418 West Drummond Pl., Melrose Park IL 60164. Editor: Eda Casciani. Quarterly. Pays in 1 contributor's copy. Reports on submissions in 2 to 3 weeks. Enclose S.A.S.E. for return of submissions.
Nonfiction: Feature essays on poetry, views of the poet, etc.; 350 words maximum length.
Poetry: Traditional, free verse, mixed verse, experimental and modern. Length: up to 30 lines.

CORDUROY, 406 Highland Ave., Newark NJ 07104. Editor: Richard Immersi. For "anyone interested in truly modern and experimental poetry." Established in 1968. Biannually. Circulation: 250. Acquires all rights, but will reassign rights to author after publication. Payment made in contributor's copies. Will send sample copy to writer for 50 cents. Will consider photocopied submissions. Reports on ma-

terial in 2 weeks. Enclose S.A.S.E. for return of submissions.
Nonfiction and Poetry: "We are looking for poems which are genuine emotional statements, rather than intellectual exercises. Honesty and being in touch with one's subject are the main criteria." Theme: open. Free verse or avant-garde forms. Also uses short prose pieces limited to 6 pages.

COYOTE'S JOURNAL, 983 Wisconsin, San Francisco CA 94107. Editor: James Koller. Irregular. Circulation: 1,000. Acquires first serial rights. Payment in contributor's copies. No free sample copies available. Query necessary unless familiar with journal. Study publication before submitting material. Reports in 1 to 4 weeks. Enclose S.A.S.E.
Nonfiction and Poetry: "Our journal is mostly poetry. We use material on ethnology, anthropology, and Indian tales."
Photos: All photos are assigned, but queries are taken note of.
Fiction: Should be "experimental work generally by poets or others interested in differentiating themselves and their knowledge from the general knowledge." No length limit.

CRAZY HORSE, Southwest Minnesota State College, Marshall MN 56258. Editor: Philip Dacey. Quarterly. Circulation: 500. Acquires North American serial rights. Payment in contributor's copies. Will send a sample copy to a writer for 50¢. Query first for nonfiction. Reports in 2 weeks. Enclose S.A.S.E.
Nonfiction: Reviews and interviews.
Poetry: "Any subject and style; no taboos. Interested in quality modern poetry." Length: open.

CREATIVE MOMENT, Poetry Eastwest Publications, P.O. Box 391, Sumter SC 29150. Editor: Dr. Syed Amanuddin. For "creative writers, poets, and those who are interested in the international scene in contemporary poetry." Established in 1972. Biannual. Circulation: 500. Acquires first serial rights. Payment in contributor's copy. Will send a sample copy to a writer for $1. Query first for articles and reviews. Will not consider photocopied submissions. Reports in 6 to 8 months. Enclose S.A.S.E.
Nonfiction: "Short articles by and about poets and reviews of poetry books published by noncommercial presses." Interested in articles "on Commonwealth poetry in England, African poetry, Canadian poetry." Length: maximum 2,500 words.
Poetry: Length: 30 lines maximum.

CREATIVE REVIEW, 1718 S. Garrison, Carthage MO 64836. Editor: Glen Coffield. Issued quarterly to amateur and professional poets. Payment is in contributor's copy. Reports on submissions in one day to three months. Include self-addressed, stamped envelope for return of submissions.
Poetry: No long poems. Publishes poetry and light verse. Specializes in poems on creative method.

CYCLOFLAME, 212 West First St., San Angelo TX 76901. Editor: Vernon Payne. Annual. Single or sample copy, $4. Copyrighted. Payment on acceptance. Buys first rights. Reports in one month. Enclose S.A.S.E. for return of submissions.
Poetry: 24 lines or less. Submit no more than three poems on varying subjects, only in December, since nonmembers of Avalon are accepted only once a year for the spring issue. "As organ of the Avalon Poets, this journal is voice for the most serious and profound, timely-timeless, spontaneous poetry of this explosive age. Let the light verse be rare. Avoid both contrived obscurity and spelled-out 'statement poems.' Egotism, exhibitionism, pseudo-love, and the sermonistic work will be rejected." Pays $1 per poem.

DRAGONFLY: A QUARTERLY OF HAIKU HIGHLIGHTS (formerly *Haiku Highlights*), 4102 N.E. 130th Place, Portland OR 97230. Editor: Lorraine Ellis Harr. Established in 1965. Quarterly. Circulation: approximately 500. Will reassign rights to author after publication. No payment, but numerous contests and awards. Will send sample copy to writer for 75 cents. Write for copy of guidelines for writers, enclosing S.A.S.E. Reports on material within 30 days. Enclose S.A.S.E. for return of submissions.

Nonfiction and Poetry: Haiku poetry in the classical, traditional style. Related short articles (300 words) and poetic forms. "We publish a crosscut of all haiku in the English language as it is being written by today's haiku poets. No long viewpoint articles. Must know haiku. No 5-7-5 English language poetry or pretty pictures."

DRIFTWOOD EAST, 95 Carter Ave., Pawtucket RI 02861. For all ages. Quarterly. Circulation: 300. No payment other than occasional prizes. Will send a sample copy to writer for 50¢. Query first for poetry. Reports in 2 to 4 weeks. Enclose S.A.S.E
Poetry: Accepts traditional forms, blank, free, and light verse. Length: 2 to 20 lines. Keep it clean.

DRYAD, P.O. Box 1656, Washington DC 20013. Editors: Merrill T. Leffler, Neil Lehrman. Quarterly. Copyrighted. Will send sample copy for 75¢. Reports in one month. Does not pay. Enclose S.A.S.E. for return of submissions.
Nonfiction: Uses reviews of small press poetry publishers.
Poetry: No line restrictions, no taboos, no rhyme for its own sake.

ENCORE, 1121 Major Ave., N.W., Albuquerque NM 87107. Editor: Alice Briley. For "anyone interested in poetry from young people in high school to many retired people. Good poetry on any theme." Established in 1966. Quarterly. Circulation: 600. Acquires all rights but will reassign rights to author after publication. Uses 240 mss a year. Will send sample copy to a writer for 25¢. Submit complete ms. Will consider photocopied submissions "provided the author is free to assign rights to *Encore.* Will require assurance if poem is accepted." Submit seasonal material 6 to 9 months in advance. Reports on material within a month. Enclose S.A.S.E. for return of submissions.
Nonfiction, Poetry and Photos: "Particularly like poetry which illustrates the magazine's theme that poetry is a performing art. Fresh approach greatly desired. Poetry by students as well as established poets." Traditional forms, blank verse, free verse, avant-garde and light verse. Some articles on related subjects. Profiles of poets, poetry reviews, technical verse writing. Length: open, but "very long articles rarely used." Prefer no larger than 5x8 b&w glossy photos with good contrast. Pays in contributor's copies.

EPOS, Crescent City FL 32012. Editor: Evelyn Thorne. Published by Rollins College. Reports within 1 week. "Sorry, no free sample copies. Single copy, $1." Payment in contributor's copies. Enclose S.A.S.E. for return of submissions.

ESSENCE, 26 Fowler St., New Haven CT 06515. Editor: Joseph Payne Brennan. Published irregularly. Reports in two weeks. Pays in contributor's copies only. Verses submitted without stamped, self-addressed envelope are destroyed.
Poetry: "Verse only, preferably short. Poetry, if we can get it. We'd like to see some genuine poetry which conveys emotion to the reader—not mere descriptive pieces or chopped-up 'picturesque speech' prose. Material should be submitted only when it has attained reasonable competence and polish." Length: 30 lines maximum.

GHOST DANCE, Dept. of Am. Thought and Language, Michigan State University, East Lansing MI 48823. Editor: Hugh Fox. For "mostly younger poets, specialists in avant-garde literature." Established in 1968. Quarterly. Circulation: 3,000. Payment in contributor's copies. Will send a sample copy to a writer for 75¢. Reports in one day. Will consider photocopied submissions. Enclose S.A.S.E. for return of submissions.
Poetry: "Completely original poetry. We have nothing to do with traditional forms and/or ideas. We represent a complete break from all previous poetic traditions. It's tomorrow's sensibility today. We even avoid repeating ourselves. We want to avoid all 'bags,' 'schools,' 'pigeon-holes,' and 'traditions.' We want the new W. C. Williamses, new Pounds, Eliots, Rimbauds, Hart Cranes, etc." Uses "concrete, sound poetry." No limitations. Dept. Editors: N. W. Werner and P. Ferlazzo.

HAPPINESS HOLDING TANK, P.O. Box 227, Okemos MI 48864. Editor: Albert Drake. For "poets of various ages, interests; other editors; students." Established in

1970. Triannually. Circulation: 300 500. All rights revert to author automatically. Payment in contributor's copies. Will send a sample copy to a writer for $1. Reports in a week. Enclose S.A.S.E. for return of submissions.

Nonfiction and Poetry: Publishes "poems of various kinds, somewhat eclectic—looking for 'excellence.' Essays and articles on modern poetry. Emphasis on younger but unestablished poets: their work to date. Emphasis on information of various kinds—to make magazine useful. Interested in printing methods of all kinds." Buys informational, how-to, and poetry book reviews. Uses all forms of poetry except light verse. Now doing chapbooks and poetry posters.

THE HARTFORD COURANT, 285 Broad St., Hartford CT 06115. Poetry Editor: Malcolm L. Johnson. Weekly. Circulation: 181,000. Not copyrighted. Uses "about 200 pieces a year." Will consider photocopied submissions. Reports in 2 to 6 weeks. Enclose S.A.S.E. for return of submissions.

Poetry: Weekly poetry column "strives for work of some literary merit. Excessively prosey works are shunned, as are sing-songy styles. Would like to receive more well-done humorous verse. No requirements as to subject matter, except that publication of the poetry in a family newspaper tends to eliminate graphically erotic poetry or any other sort that depends on the use of four-letter words." Length: Not more than 50 lines; 3 lines minimum. "No payment; we send several tearsheets."

HIRAM POETRY REVIEW, P.O. Box 162, Hiram OH 44234. Editor: Hale Chatfield. "Readers well educated concerning the goals and techniques of contemporary poetry. The largest portion of our subscribers consists of college and university libraries. Our main 'commercial' outlets are avant-garde bookstores." Semiannual. Acquires all rights, but will reassign them to author upon written request. Payment in copies and a year's subscription. Reports in 1 month. Enclose S.A.S.E. for return of submissions.

Poetry: "We seek to discover new talents: all poetry we publish is sent to us without specific invitation." Modern poetry. "We are vehemently opposed to dabbling and sentimentalizing. No light verse, although we'd consider comic poetry from those who know the difference." Length: open.

How To Break In: "Send 3 or 4 of your best poems. Do not make the fatal assumption that editors of 'little magazines' are less demanding than the editors of the paying 'slicks' and are consequently a last resort. Dogeared mss tell a sad story. Do not send carbons, xerox or 'ditto' copies. That is, send fresh and neatly typed 'originals' only."

HYACINTHS AND BISCUITS, P.O. Box 392, Brea CA 92621. Editor: Jane R. Card. Published sporadically. Circulation: 8,000. Buys North American serial rights and North American anthology rights. Pays on acceptance. Will send a sample copy to a writer for $1. Reports in 4 weeks. Enclose S.A.S.E. for return of submissions.

Nonfiction: Brief biographies of American poets. Not over 200 words. No query required. Pays $2 to $10. Local color, 200-word anecdotes or descriptions.

Poetry: Should have style, rhythm, and interesting subject background. Subjects should be related to life and all its aspects—love, marriage, friendship, children, war and peace, cities and towns, people. Philosophical approach rather than specific religious approach. Not interested in any kind of "hate" literature. Lengths vary. Pays $2 to $10.

Fillers: Regional humor. Pays $2. Limericks. Pays $1 to $5.

IDEALS, 11315 Watertown Plank Rd., Milwaukee WI 53201. Editor: Maryjane Hooper Tonn. Managing Editor: Lorraine Obst. Payment for poems or articles made at time of publication ($10 and a copy of the issue). Buys one time rights. Will send sample copy to writer on request. Reports in 2 weeks. Enclose return postage.

Nonfiction, Poetry and Photos: "*Ideals* are books containing clean, wholesome, old-fashioned American ideals, homey philosophy and general inspirational, patriotic, religious, seasonal, family, childhood or nostalgic material. Poems and articles submitted will be carefully reviewed, and such material that we believe will lend itself to use in *Ideals* will be retained in our permanent review files. Such material is carefully reviewed during the preparation of each new book. We cannot definitely guarantee that we will feature the poems or articles which we retain, but we shall make a sincere effort to do so. We assume the privilege of editing retained material where necessary. If, for any reason, you do not want us to enter your material into our review files, kindly advise us when submitting it so that we can promptly return it to you. Please do not send us your original poems or articles. Send only copies. We cannot return your submitted material after it has been entered into our review files. B&w photos should be sharp, clear 8x10 glossies. We pay $10 minimum when purchased for immediate use. We prefer 4x5 or 8x10 color transparencies, for which pay is $10 minimum. 35mm transparencies are accepted, provided they are mounted on a sheet of acetate in groups of at least 20 so they may be easily reviewed."

INLAND WRITERS MAGAZINE, 1051 Western Ave., Colton CA 92324. Editor: Ed Rimbaugh. For "anyone interested in good, sensitive and universally appreciated writing (poetry)." Established in 1972. Quarterly. Circulation: 100. Rights acquired vary with author and material. Usually acquires all rights, but will reassign rights to author after publication. Payment in contributor's copies. Will send sample copy to writer for $1. Query first or submit complete ms. Will consider photocopied submissions. Reports on material in 2 to 3 weeks. Enclose S.A.S.E. for reply to queries or return of submissions.
Poetry: "Good, well-written poetry, not too avant-garde, academic, metaphysical or political. 'Universal' themes most desired. A writer should not write anything 'special' for us, but submit his best, most sensitive work, be it 'light' or more profound. Nothing blatantly commercial or topical." Traditional forms, blank verse and free verse. Length: 3 to 36 lines.

INTERNATIONAL POETRY REVIEW, 1060 North Saint Andrews Place, Hollywood CA 90038. Editor: Dr. Henry Picola. For "grammar school students through college, and college professors." Established in 1961. Circulation: 5,000. Buys all rights, may reprint with permission only. Buys 5 mss a year. Payment on publication for articles. Will send a sample copy to a writer for $1. "Poets are advised to study our needs through market listings and guides." Query first. Submit seasonal material at least two months in advance. Reports in 1 month. Enclose S.A.S.E. for reply to queries.
Nonfiction and Photos: Publishes "interesting biographies of deceased and living poets. Articles giving new information; additional information not found in old history books. Emphasis on the paternal influence. What kind of work he pursued during his lifetime or what is he doing now. Good or bad traits of character." Length: not more than 1,800 words. Buys how-to, interview, humor, and photo articles. Has a free verse column and also a column for children to 12 years of age. Photos purchased with or without mss. Small remuneration for 5x7 b&w photos.
Poetry: "Some poets are under the delusion that poetry has to be obscure. Not enough poetry on current events. Most poets are living in the 18th century." Prints all forms of verse with occasional prizes as pay. "We pay $1 to $10 for sonnets."

JEAN'S JOURNAL, 274 Arlington Ave., Brooklyn NY 11208. Editor: Dolores Maria Goldstein. Bimonthly. Circulation: 400. Sample copy 35¢. Reports on submissions in 2 to 6 weeks. One poem per page complete with full name and address; no more than 5 submissions at one time. Enclose S.A.S.E. for return.
Nonfiction and Fiction: Articles on pertinent subjects of the day, editorials on writing, book reviews. Short stories. Length: 1,500 words maximum.
Poetry: "All types. Length: no restrictions. Payment in cash prize awards and book awards."
Fillers: Short humor.

LEMMING, 3551 42nd St., San Diego CA 92105. Editor: Rex Burwell. For "all ages though most appealing to younger readers." Established in 1970. Quarterly. Circulation: 200. Acquires all rights, but will reassign rights to author after publication. Payment in contributor's copies. Will send sample copy to writer for 50¢. Submit complete ms. Reports on material accepted for publication in 2 months. Returns rejected material in 1 week. Enclose S.A.S.E. for return of submissions.
Poetry: Free verse; imagistic. Length and theme: open.

THE LYRIC, Bremo Bluff VA 23022. Editor: Ruby Altizer Roberts and John Nixon, Jr. Payment in contributor's copies and opportunity to compete for annual cash prizes. Reports at once. Enclose S.A.S.E. for return of submissions.
Poetry: "We use poems having meter and/or rhyme; traditional type, not more than 36 lines. Prefer lyrical; we look for fresh images and vitality."

MAGAZINE, c/o Interim Books, Box 35, New York NY 10014. Editor: Kirby Congdon. General subject matter: literary, avant-garde, underground poetry. Published "about once every 2 years. Each issue has its own need and covers some idea which we feel everyone else has overlooked. That is why we are irregularly scheduled." Circulation: 500. Not copyrighted. Will send a sample copy to a writer for $2. Include covering note with new mss. "We prefer to approach poets, rather than rely on the so-called 'submission' and 'rejection-acceptance' system, but we are always interested in what other people are doing." Payment in contributor's copies. Reports in approximately 2 weeks. Enclose S.A.S.E.
Nonfiction: Interviews, profiles, historical and think pieces. "We would like to get into these areas, but so far we have only used the work of friends who do not require compensation."
Poetry: Contemporary and avant-garde. "Poetry that balances idea with emotion—an easy rule but a difficult achievement." Length: open, "but epics or book mss are an unwelcome burden."
How To Break In: "Write well! If the poet considers poetry and his own work more seriously than anything else, he will begin to write well. About 3 pages of typescript of poetry are best. Hobbyists, 'Sunday poets' platitudinists and chimers should try elsewhere. Write well! We have printed one illiterate genius, but others must spell correctly, know the grammar they use, proofread their own mss before sending them; be aware of every major 19th and 20th century English and American poet. In short, know your medium better than anyone else. We don't teach techniques; we print poems."

MAINLINE, P.O. Box 61, Sandwich PO, Windsor, Ontario, Canada. Editors: D. Farmiloe, E. McNamara, and R. Hornsey. For "poets and lovers of poetry." Established in 1968. Triannual. Circulation: 500. Buys first North American rights. Buys 60 mss a year. Payment in contributor's copies. Will send a sample copy to a writer for 75¢. Reports in 1 month. Enclose S.A.S.E. for return of submissions.
Poetry: "Author should be himself. We make no taboos except a bias for the wow-gut-thud reaction. No board of directors to answer to—free to be cranky and subjective. Avoid confessional, exquisite anguish poems. No epics." Accepts traditional forms, free verse and avant-garde forms. Dept. Editors: McNamara and Farmiloe.

MAJOR POETS, Box 52, Tremont IL 61568. Editor: Mary Marks. For "persons of all ages who love poetry." Quarterly. Pays on acceptance. Buys first rights. Poems remain property of author. Query first "if it is a long work, stating type and background." Submit seasonal material 6 months in advance of issue date. Reports in 2 months. Enclose S.A.S.E. for reply to queries.
Poetry: "*Major Poets* coincides somewhat with the 4 seasons; nature poems, or other work dealing with the 4 seasons, are acceptable. Poetry of all styles is accepted. Taboos include sexual abnormalities, four-letter words, consistent swearing. The works of persons who break rules of good grammar, punctuation, etc., are not acceptable. We try to heighten technique and quality, and whenever possible suggest that the poet take a positive view when tackling the subject. No pornography, please. We frown on 'arranged prose.' Interested in poems on patriotic days, holidays, peace, how to achieve peace, nature, family themes, vacations, important public buildings, love, important historical events and how they influence us now, inspirational things if not syrupy, anything which is uplifting." Buys traditional forms, blank verse, free verse, avant-garde forms, humorous light verse, and sonnets. Length: "under 20 lines, if possible; longer if extra good." Pays $1 "to whatever in case of longer work. Averages about 10¢ a line, or $20 for 200 lines, but this has to be excellent and especially appealing."

MELE, c/o Stefan Baciu, Department of European Languages, 1890 East West Rd., Moore 470, University of Hawaii, Honolulu HI 96822. Not academic publication. Quarterly. Will send sample copy to a writer on request for $1. Reports on sub-

mission in 3 to 6 weeks. Enclose S.A.S.E.
Poetry: Poems in any language. High quality only. Length: No limit. Payment in contributor's copies.
How To Break In: "Talent! Talent! Talent!"

MIDWEST POETRY REVIEW, Aaron Bowman Enterprises, 1517 Joy St., Granite City IL 62040. Editor: Jonella Clements Bowman. Established in 1973. Published annually in February. Circulation: 2,000. Not copyrighted. Uses 200 poems a year. No payment except prize of $50 for "best poem". Will send sample copy to writer for $5. Submit complete ms; only one poem considered at a time. Reports on material in 2 weeks. Enclose S.A.S.E. for return of submissions.
Poetry: "Subjects open. Form open. Topic and form should complement. Sensitivity, theme and technique should work to create a meaningful poem. We like subjects dealing with love and life; humor, irony, satire and well-done patriotic poems are welcome." Length: 20 lines maximum.

MODERN HAIKU, 414 N. Orange Dr., Los Angeles CA 90036. Editor: Mrs. Kay Titus Mormino. Triannual. Circulation: 600. Will send sample copy for $1.35. Reports in three to four weeks. Acquires North American serial rights only. Nonpaying, but books and cash prizes (one $15 and two $5) are awarded each issue. Deadlines are Dec. 1, April 1 and August 1. Each poem, etc., should be on separate piece of paper with complete name and address in upper left. Enclose self-addressed envelope large enough to hold returned ms without refolding. Fasten adequate postage to return envelope with paper clip. Study copy of magazine before submitting.
Nonfiction: Articles on reading, writing or understanding haiku, senryu and art. Reviews of books of or about haiku. 350 words.
Photos: Occasionally accepted if appropriate to accompanying haiku. Clear b&w 3x5. Address to Kay Titus Mormino, Editor.
Poetry: Haiku and senryu only. "We are not interested in epigrams and other forms of prose written in three lines of 5/7/5 syllables." See copy of magazine before submitting. Submit student haiku to Willene Nusbaum, Editorial Assistant, Bern KS 66408.

MODERN IMAGES, 1400 N. Jefferson, El Dorado AR 71730. Editor: Roy Douglass Burrow. Quarterly. Circulation: 100. Acquires all rights. Will send a sample copy to a writer for $1.50. Reports in 1 week. Enclose S.A.S.E. for return of submissions.
Poetry: "Emphasis on free verse and modern poetry." Length: open. No payment.

MUSTANG REVIEW, 212 So. Broadway, Denver CO 80209. Publisher: Karl Edd. Published twice yearly. Circulation: 400. Acquires first rights. Accepts 80 to 100 mss a year. Payment in copies. Will send a sample copy to a writer for 50¢. Enclose S.A.S.E.
Poetry: Emphasis on regional grassroots poetry of the Imagist type. Length: prefers 14 to 20 lines.

NEW: AMERICAN AND CANADIAN POETRY, R.D. 3, Trumansburg NY 14886. Editor: John Gill. Three times yearly. Poets retain rights. Payment in contributor's copies. Reports on submissions in 1 to 2 months. Enclose S.A.S.E. for return of submissions.
Nonfiction: Poetic criticism only for nonfiction.
Poetry: Poetry, no taboos.

NEW COLLAGE MAGAZINE, P.O. Box 1898, Sarasota FL 33578. Editor: A. McA. Miller. Established in 1969. Triquarterly. Circulation: 3,000. Acquires all rights, but will reassign rights to author after publication. Payment in contributor's copies or by special prior arrangement. Will send sample copy to writer for $1. Reports on material in 3 weeks. Enclose S.A.S.E. for return of submissions.
Poetry: "We like tight, expressive ones that body forth, not merely discuss. No tic-toc effusions about everyday sentiments. Poems we accept tend to be more in the line of Yeats than in Williams, although we are open to anything that sustains clear imagery and a strong tone." Length: No minimum. "Maximum: say, 6 typed pages."

NEW ORLANDO POETRY ANTHOLOGY, 39 Bedford Street, New York NY 10014. For "lovers of poetry in general: university and public library patrons; students, collectors." Established in 1958. Publishes eclectic poetry. Annual. Circulation: 3,000. Acquires all rights, and first and second serial rights. Payment on publication in 4 contributor's copies and cash awards for "our contest winners." Will send sample copy to a writer for $3. Seeks special material. "Our last anthology honored Marianne Moore and Langston Hughes." Reports in 6 weeks. Enclose S.A.S.E. for return of submissions.
Poetry: "There is no limit on any themes whether controversial or what's defined as 'pure poetry.' We are opposed to smut but accept erotic poetry provided it's crystallized into poetry. Unlike most anthologies, our aim is to discover new poets and include their work of merit even if they never appeared before. We hope for poetry that will be read for decades or more." Traditional forms, blank verse, free verse, avant-garde forms and experimental poetry. Length: 16 to 250 lines. Payment: "4 copies of the anthology, maximum of 6 copies; cash as well for poems of high quality."

THE NEW SALT CREEK READER, 1720½ C. St., Lincoln NE 68502. Editor: Ted Kooser. For "people interested in modern poetry." Established in 1967. Quarterly. Circulation: 400. Buys all rights, but will reassign rights to author after publication. Uses about 150 poems a year. Payment in contributor's copies. Will send sample copy to writer for $1. Submit complete ms. Reports on material in 1 month. Enclose S.A.S.E. for return of submissions.
Poetry: Poetry of all types. Themes open. Traditional forms, blank verse, free verse. Length: open.

NOTABLE AMERICAN POETS, Drawer 338, Babylon NY 11702. Editor: Linda Nash. For poets and poetry enthusiasts. Established in 1972. Quarterly. Circulation: 1,000 to 3,000. Buys first North American serial rights. Buys 600 mss a year. Will send sample copy to writer for $3.95. Write for copy of editorial guidelines (enclosing S.A.S.E. for this purpose). Submit complete ms. Will consider photocopied submissions. Reports on material in 2 weeks. Enclose S.A.S.E.
Poetry: "We will consider poetry by previously published poets only. All styles and subjects are welcome, provided they are in good taste, and were not published elsewhere. As these editions are to aid in further exposure of the 'lesser known' poet, we want the poet to send what he feels he'd be proud to show as representative of his best writing." Length: 3 to 16 lines. Maximum of 2 poems as one submission. Pays 50¢ to $1 per poem. Cash prizes.

OREGONIAN VERSE, c/o *Oregonian*, Portland OR 97201. Editor: Howard McKinley Corning. Poetry column in Sunday edition of newspaper. Pays $5 per printed poem, tenth of month after publication. Reports promptly. Buys first newspaper rights; rights revert to the poet after publication. Enclose S.A.S.E. for return of submissions.
Poetry: "Short lyrics of any type preferred. We seek poems of image and meaning, written out of experience, with a fresh use of language. Should be concise, understandable, and professionally written. No sentimental love poems, religious poems, or those in bad taste. Seasonal verse must reach us several weeks in advance." Length: 24 lines maximum.

ORPHIC LUTE, 3815 Mercier, Kansas City MO 64111. Editor: Viola Gardner. Biannual. Will send sample copy to a writer for $1. Reports on submissions promptly. Publication not copyrighted. Include S.A.S.E. for all mss and queries.
Poetry: Looks for "sensible poetry only; no avant-garde; must tell a tale or at least say something one might be benefited by; nothing controversial." Short poems desired. Pattern poems are given special slant. Some light verse used. No payment; prizes are awarded during the year.

PART TIME PUBLICLY, R.D. 2, Box 81, Corinth NY 12822. Editor: Martin Wasserman. Established in 1970. For "readers who enjoy experimental literature." Quarterly. Circulation: about 1,000. Rights acquired vary with author and material. Usually acquires all rights, but will reassign rights to author after publication. Uses 50 to 70 mss a year. Payment in contributor's copies. Submit complete ms. Reports

on material "one month after reading". Will send free sample copy to writer "when available." Will consider photocopied submissions. Enclose S.A.S.E. for return of submissions.
Poetry: "There are absolutely no taboos. All we ask is that the authors enjoy their creation and that they are honest with themselves, when developing their ideas and themes." Traditional forms, blank verse, free verse, avant-garde forms, light verse. Length: open.
Fiction: "We have no predetermined standards as to what makes good literature 'good'; do not favor any particular style or school. Interested in the essential quality and worth of each ms." Experimental, mystery, suspense, erotica, science fiction, fantasy, humorous. Length: 5,000 words maximum.

POEM, P.O. Box 1247 West Station, Huntsville AL 35807. Editor: Robert L. Welker. Three times yearly. Buys all rights, but will relinquish subsidiary rights upon request of author. Pays on publication. Produced by Huntsville Literary Association. Enclose S.A.S.E. for return of submissions.
Poetry: "High quality poetry regardless of type of poem. No stylistic limitation. No taboos." No restriction on line length. Pays $5 per poem.

POEMS FROM THE HILLS, Morris Harvey College, Charleston WV 25304. Editors: William Plumley and Barbara Yeager. Annual paperback anthology. Acquires all rights. "Payment is by prizes, $25 to $100." Submit poems in September and October, accompanied by a brief biography. Reports in 6 weeks. Enclose S.A.S.E. for return of submissions.
Poetry: "We want poetry (organic or traditional) that reflects the myths, scenes, characters, and legends of the hills, especially of Appalachia. The theme may be positive or critical. We like the hills, even with their problems. We hope that your submissions might reflect the same."

POET LORE, A NATIONAL QUARTERLY OF WORLD POETRY, Editorial Office, 52 Cranbury Road, Westport CT 06880. Editor-in-Chief: John Williams Andrews. Will send sample copy for $1. Payment in copies and $450 in prizes. "Write the editor for statement of conditions under which submissions may be made." No mss returned. Enclose S.A.S.E. with all correspondence.
Nonfiction: Can use essays for "Aspects of Modern Poetry" department: reviews.
Drama: English language verse plays.
Poetry: All types, all lengths; rhymed, unrhymed, metered, unmetered, conventional, experimental, punctuated or not. Criteria of excellence, clarity, beauty, profundity.

POETRY, 1228 N. Dearborn, Chicago IL 60610. Buys all rights. "Mss are usually reported on within 5 to 6 weeks, and the average time before publication is about 7 months from date of receipt." Payment on publication. Enclose S.A.S.E.
Poetry: "All 'schools' or approach 's considered for publication. The only criterion is excellence, but standard is extremely high." Pays $1 a line.

POETRY EASTWEST, P.O. Box 391, Sumter SC 29150. Editor: Syed Amanuddin. Published annually. Circulation: about 500. Copyrighted. Will send sample copy for $1. Reports in six months. Payment of one copy. Enclose S.A.S.E. with all submissions.
Poetry: Unpublished English poems and translations of contemporary poets of other languages. "We empathize with world poetry movement. We expect poets to emphasize human feeling instead of the cerebral muscle and we look for poetry that dramatizes the poetic experience in terms of fresh image and phrase. We are not interested in poems longer than 30 lines."

POETRY QUARTERLY, 204 Rome-Hilliard Rd., Columbus OH 43228. Editor: R. Lee. Established in 1970. Quarterly. Circulation: 200. Acquires first rights. All poems posted for copyright for author's protection. Uses 200 mss a year. Payment in contributor's copies. Will send sample copy for $1. Write for copy of guidelines for writers, enclosing S.A.S.E. Query first for submission details. Returns rejected material immediately. Reports on accepted material within 2 weeks. Enclose S.A.S.E.
Poetry: "Strong in depth, sincerity and emotion; simply stated but profound in

communication. Contemporary free verse in a 'love' vein. Little or no rhyme or religious poetry. We would like to see more good, humorous poetry or light verse." Length: 24 lines maximum. Payment: 1 contributor's copy.
Nonfiction and Photos: Short, poetry-related articles. Length: 500 words maximum. 4x5 b&w photos must be screened print. With or without mss. Captions optional.

POETRY VENTURE, 8245 26th Ave. N., St. Petersburg FL 33710. Editor: Marjorie Schuck. For "students and professional and amateur poets and writers." Biannual. Circulation: 750. Acquires first rights. Publishes about 100 poems a year. Payment in copies and subscriptions. Will send a sample copy to a writer on request. Submit seasonal material at least 1 month in advance. Reports in 8 to 10 weeks. Enclose S.A.S.E. for return of submissions.
Nonfiction: "We seek timely quotes on contemporary poetry. We present interpretations, quotes, comments, and analyses by leading authorities." Length: 100 to 800 words.
Poetry: "Traditional and modern. Poems must be original and unpublished. We like intelligible content: form that is either organic or traditional; diction that is fresh without depending on slang and remnants of Anglo-Saxon for verve; imagery that functions rather than decorates. We feature poetry of established and aspiring poets from all over the world. We seek poetry which we can feature; usually poetry written in a foreign language, and we then publish the original and the English translation." Length: open.

QUOIN, 1226 W. Talmage, Springfield MO 65803. Editor: Arlis M. Snyder. Quarterly. Circulation: 500. Not copyrighted. Payment in contributor's copies. Will send a sample copy to a writer for $1. No query required. Submit "to within 15 days of month of publication: January, April, July, October." Reporting time varies. Enclose S.A.S.E. for return of submissions.
Poetry: Uses poetry—any and all forms. Writing must be grammatically correct and word usage lexically accurate. Language must be modern, avoiding archaic forms. Metaphysical verse must be consistent with the concept employed. "No maudlin sentimentality." Length: open.
Nonfiction: Critical articles on poetry.

RAVEN, 2407 E. Northern Lights Blvd., Anchorage AK 99504. Editor: Thomas F. Sexton. For "the general public." Established in 1971. Quarterly. Circulation: 1,000. Buys all rights, but will reassign rights to author after publication. Payment in copies. Will send a sample copy to a writer for $1.50. Will consider photocopied submissions. Reports in 1 month. Enclose S.A.S.E. for return of submissions.
Poetry: "Poems of all lengths and styles. We lean toward unpublished poets. No romantic verse." Uses traditional forms, blank verse, free verse, avant-garde forms, and light verse.

THE RUFUS, P.O. Box 75982, Los Angeles CA 90075. Editor: Patricia Ann Bunin. For "poets and poetry enthusiasts." Established in 1972. Quarterly. Circulation: 300. Copyrighted; rights revert to author. Uses 300 to 400 mss a year. Payment in contributor's copies and cash prizes. Will send sample copy for $1.50. Write for copy of guidelines for writers. Query first for nonfiction. Submit complete ms for poetry. Will not consider photocopied submissions. Reports on material in 2 to 3 weeks. Enclose S.A.S.E. for return of submissions or reply to queries.
Nonfiction and Poetry: "Describe new approaches and trends in poetry, new outlook, that could only belong to a poet; reflect that extra dimension that separates poets from everyone else. Essays, editorials, book reviews (poetry books or instructional books on poetry)." Length: 300 to 500 words. "Poems of any style or subject matter but require very high standard of writing and originality." Traditional forms, blank and free verse, avant-garde forms, light verse, haiku. Length: open. All payment in contributor's copies and cash prizes.

SEVEN, 21½ N. Harvey, Oklahoma City OK 73102. Editor: James Neill Northe. Quarterly. Pays on acceptance. Enclose S.A.S.E.
Poetry: Uses only seven original poems an issue; one reprint in the column, Seven Times Seven. Wants clear-cut, well-wrought material, showing clarity of expres-

sion. Submissions must be free of involved expression and obtuse meaning. Universality is a "must." Personal poems for personal feelings are "out." Implication preferred to flat statement. "We are averse to single word titles; prefer classic sonnets, good ballads and rhythmic free verse." Pays $3 per poem.

THE SHORE REVIEW, 2931 South 57th Street, Milwaukee WI 53219. Editor: Ken Kwint. For general poetry audience. Quarterly. Circulation: 700. Acquires first rights. Uses 125 mss a year. Pays in contributor's copies. Will send a sample copy for $1. Reports within 2 weeks. Enclose S.A.S.E. for return of submissions.
Poetry: Accepts contemporary poetry. No taboos.

SILVER MOUNTAIN JOURNAL, P.O. Box 3281, Pueblo CO 81005. Editor: Sam T. Taylor, Jr. For general audience, "mostly for people interested in the arts." Established in 1972. Quarterly. Circulation: 300. Acquires all rights, but will reassign rights to author after publication. Payment in contributor's copies. Will send sample copy to a writer for $1. Will not consider photocopied submissions. Reports on material in 2 weeks. Enclose S.A.S.E. for return of submissions.
Poetry: "Looking for poetry with a general theme that will be of interest to people living in, or familiar with the southwest United States. Original work only. Traditional forms, blank verse, free verse, avant-garde. Would like a brief biographical sketch from each contributor (education, age, interests, etc.)"

SOUTHERN POETRY REVIEW, English Department, North Carolina State University, Raleigh NC 27607. Editor: Guy Owen. Payment in contributor's copies. Will send a sample copy to a writer for 50¢. "No mss considered during the summer months." Reports in 3 to 6 weeks. Enclose S.A.S.E. for return of submissions.
Poetry: In the modern mode, traditional or experimental. No light verse. Thirty lines or less.

THE SPARROW, 103 Waldron St., West Lafayette IN 47906. Editors: Felix and Selma Stefanile. For "a really intellectual yet not too limited audience." Semiannual. Circulation: about 800. Acquires first rights. Accepts about 80 mss a year. Payment in contributor's copies, and one $25 award per issue. Will send a sample copy to a writer for 50¢. Do not send query letters. Wide-open market for poets, either known or unknown. Not a market for novices, but editors have no criteria except talent. "We do not read Xeroxed, duplicated, or carbon-copy material. Study publication." Reports in 8 weeks. Enclose S.A.S.E. for return of submissions. "We don't return mss without S.A.S.E."
Nonfiction: High quality literary essays and criticism. "No real restrictions except those of taste. Any really well-written literary essay gets our attention." Length: "no limits if really good."
Poetry: "No restrictions save those of our personal taste. We believe that 'revolutionism' is a fad, and are really tired of sex-profanity-structural experimentation. We believe good poetry is never hard to recognize. We definitely don't care for rock lyrics." Wants "serious, good poetry."

SPRING RAIN PRESS, P.O. Box 15319, Seattle WA 98115. Editors: Karen Sollid, John Sollid. Established in 1971. For "libraries and individuals who are well-educated." Quarterly. Circulation: 400. Buys simultaneous rights. Buys 35 mss a year. Payment in contributor's copies. Query first for book length poetry mss. Submit other poetry in groups of five. Will send sample copy to writer for $1. Write for copy of guidelines for writers which will be sent if S.A.S.E. is enclosed. Will consider photocopied submission "if we are the only ones seeing it." Enclose S.A.S.E. for return of submissions or reply to queries.
Poetry: "Well-developed lyric poetry. Should be language and image oriented. We like quality poetry." Length: open.
Fiction: Experimental. Length: around 3,000 words.

TANGENT, 9075 River Styx Rd., Wadsworth OH 44281. Editor: Robert D. West. Quarterly. Will send sample copy to a writer for 50¢. Acquires first rights. Pays on

publication. Reports in 6 to 8 weeks. Enclose S.A.S.E. for return of submissions.
Poetry: Subject matter, style, length open. Payment in contributor's copy.

UT REVIEW, University of Tampa, Tampa FL 33606. Editor: Duane Locke. For the "highest quality literary poetry audience." Established in 1972. Quarterly. Circulation: 500. Buys all rights, but will reassign them to writer on request. Payment in contributor's copies. Will send a sample copy to a writer for 75¢. Will consider photocopied submissions. Reports in three weeks. Enclose S.A.S.E. for return of submissions.
Poetry: "We prefer complex, deep, intense interior type poetry. We favor the post-surreal and post-symbolist type of wild and mystic imagination—not the objectivist, the literalist, statementalist. We favor poetry that cannot be reduced to a theme, that cannot be paraphrased, that is ultimately inexplicable, and experienced as something holy. Plants and animals are usually the forces that engender and create the interior poetry that we want." Accepts avant-garde forms of poetry. Themes are open. Length: usually under 40 lines.

VOICES INTERNATIONAL, 6804 Cloverdale Dr., Little Rock AR 72209. Editors: Clovita Rice and D.H. Thompson. Quarterly. Buys North American serial rights. Payment in contributor's copy. Reports in 3 weeks. Enclose S.A.S.E. for return of submissions.
Nonfiction: Essays on writing.
Poetry: Quality poetry of all types, showing "purpose and individual expression." Special interest in original poetry with social consciousness and experimental poetry with impact. Must be "people-oriented. Especially interested in encouraging beginning poets who show promise and vitality." Special awards contests.

WEST COAST POETRY REVIEW, 1127 Codel Way, Reno NV 89503. Editors: William L. Fox, Bruce McAllister, William Ransom. "Mostly for writers; mainly poets and critics; publishing houses; other editors." Established in 1971. Quarterly. Circulation: 500. Acquires all rights, but will reassign rights to author after publication. Will send sample copy to writer for $1.50. Submit complete ms. Will not consider photocopied submissions. Reports on material in 1 week. Enclose S.A.S.E. for return of submissions.
Nonfiction and Poetry: "Contemporary poetry and criticism of same. Prefer serious to light. No special theme required. Would like to see criticisms of little press poetry books and informational articles on publishers and techniques of poems."

WISCONSIN POETRY ILLUSTRATED MAGAZINE, P.O. Box 187, Milwaukee WI 53201. Editor: A.M. Sterk. Not copyrighted. Will send sample copy to a writer for 63¢. Include S.A.S.E. with all mss and queries.
Nonfiction: Prizes given for good articles. Study publication for style and poetry preferences.
Photos: B&w only. Sizes up to 5x7. Payment in prizes.
Fillers: Uses jokes appropriate to format.
Poetry: Interested only in good poetry. Must have reader appeal and be realistic, articulate, different, vital to the times, of enduring value to readers of maturity and moral balance. No payment but makes generous prize awards. Guest poet issues available. Please study publication before submitting. Many universities have back copies. Also sold at newsstands.

THE WORMWOOD REVIEW, P.O. Box 8840, Stockton CA 95204. Editor: Marvin Malone. Quarterly. Copyrighted. Circulation: 700. Will send sample copy for $1.50. Reports in two to eight weeks. Buys all rights with rights reassigned to the author upon request. Pays in copies or cash equivalent, on publication. Each issue has a yellow-pages special devoted to the work of one author, artist, poet. Always enclose S.A.S.E.
Poetry: Modern poetry and prose-poems that communicate the temper and depth of the human scene. All styles and schools from ultra avant-garde to classical; no taboos. Especially interested in prose-poems or fables. 3 to 500 lines.

YES, Smith Pond Road, R.D. 1, Avoca NY 14809. Editors: Virginia Elson and Beverlee Hughes. Established in 1970. 3 times a year. Circulation: over 300. Reprint allowed if credit given. Accepts about 100 poems a year. Payment in contributor's copies. Will send a sample copy to a writer for $1. No query required. Reports in 2 weeks. Enclose S.A.S.E. for return of submissions.

Poetry: "We are trying to reach a wider and wider group of readers in the belief that poetry does not need to address itself to 'special schools' and that there is room for both tradition and experiment. We do not want the trite, the sentimental, the 'state poet laureate' type of poetry. In addition to introducing the work of many beginning writers, *Yes* publishes poems by and interviews with established poets."

Politics and World Affairs Publications

AMERICAN OPINION MAGAZINE, Belmont MA 02178. Managing Editor: Scott Stanley, Jr. "A conservative, anti-Communist journal of political affairs." Monthly except August. Enclose S.A.S.E.

Nonfiction: Articles on matters of political affairs of a conservative, anti-Communist nature. "We favor highly researched, definitive studies of social, economic, political and international problems which are written with verve and originality of style." Length should not exceed 4,000 words nor be less than 3,000. Pays $25 per published page.

Poetry and Verse: Pays minimum of $1 per line.

AMERICAS, Organization of American States, Washington DC 20006. Editor, English Edition: Flora L. Phelps. Official organ of Organization of American States. Audience is persons interested in inter-American relations. Editions published in English, Spanish, Portuguese. Monthly. Circulation: 100,000. Buys first publication and reprint rights. Pays on publication. Will send free sample copy on request. Query not required. Articles received only on speculation. Include cover letter with writer's background. Reports within two months. Not necessary to enclose S.A.S.E. for return of submissions.

Nonfiction: Articles of general hemisphere interest on history, art, literature, music, development, travel, etc. Taboos are religious and political themes or articles with non-international slant. Photos required. Length, about 3,000 words. Pays about $75.

ATLAS MAGAZINE, 1180 Avenue of the Americas, New York NY 10036. Publisher: John A. Millington. Buys one-time rights for reprints exclusively of foreign press articles.

Nonfiction: "Buys articles from the foreign press only, on politics, business, science, medicine, all the arts, etc." This is not a market for freelancers in the United States and Canada. Pays from $15 to $100, either to a specific foreign periodical or directly to the author whose article appeared in such periodical.

CANADA MONTH, 4920 de Maisonneuve West, Montreal 215, Que., Canada. Editor: Jack H. Doupe. For "Canadian persons age 15 and up, including all parliamentarians at the provincial and national levels, interested in preserving a social system based on individualism, private property, and the free market—all toward personal freedom." Established in 1961. Monthly. Circulation: 8,500. Rights purchased vary with author and material. Buys first and second serial rights. Payment on publication. Will send sample copy to writer for 25¢. Will consider photocopied submissions. Reports in 2 weeks. Enclose S.A.E. and International Reply Coupons for return of submissions.

Nonfiction: Publishes "backgrounds and analyses of current political events, preferably Canadian, otherwise of sufficiently wide interest to Canadians." Freelancer should use "his own unique approach to the real meaning of political events. We respect and value different treatments. We differ from other publications of the same nature in our anti-socialism and anti-communism. Also in our almost doctrinaire (though we try to avoid blinding ourselves) commitment to an individualistic, libertarian sort of conservatism, occasionally seasoned by some appearance of a

more organic or patriotic sort of conservatism. But we are always Canadian! We are not interested in subjects where the political-philosophical implications for freedom are not articulated. We would like to see topics on A) general elections in Canada or any of its provinces; B) socialist or communist victories and defeats, world-wide; C) Taiwan's future; D) pressure of technology vs. the individual." Buys informational (political, but Canadian), interviews, profiles, humor (re: politics, freedom), historical (Canadian), think, nostalgia, personal opinion (only if clever and preferably documented). Length: 500 to 1,500 words. Pays 2¢ a word.
Fillers: "Historical quotations in favor of freedom, preferably Canadian, British, French, and American, in that order." Length 50 to 250 words. Pays $1 to $5.

CURRENT HISTORY, 4225 Main St., Philadelphia PA 19127. Editor: Carol L. Thompson. Monthly. Pays on publication. Reports in one to two weeks. Query preferred. Enclose S.A.S.E.
Nonfiction: Uses articles on current events, chiefly world area studies, stressing their historical, economic, and political background, 3,500 to 4,000 words in length. Academician contributions almost exclusively. Pays an average of $100.

CURRENT WORLD AFFAIRS, P.O. Box 2238, Pasadena CA 91105, Editor: Dr Marshall Crawshan. For educators and researchers. Established in 1957. Monthly. Circulation: 5,000. Buys all rights. Buys 10 freelance mss a year. Payment on publication. Query first. Enclose S.A.S.E. for response to queries.
Nonfiction: Political and educational articles. Interview, historical, travel. Pays minimum of $10.

ENCORE, 572 Madison Ave., New York NY 10022. Editor: Ida Lewis. For "the urban black adult." Established in 1972. Monthly. Circulation: 100,000. Rights purchased vary with author and material. Buys all rights, but will reassign rights to author after publication. Buys first North American serial rights. Buys over 30 mss a year. Payment on publication. Will send free sample copy to writer on request. Query first. Enclose S.A.S.E. for reply to queries.
Nonfiction: News, political analysis, black history; personality pieces; book, movie, theatre, art and music reviews, third world outlook; black perspective. Pays $100 to $350.

FOREIGN AFFAIRS, 58 E. 68th St., New York NY 10021. Editor: William P. Bundy. For academics, businessmen (national and international), government, educational and cultural readers especially interested in international affairs of a political nature. Established in 1922. Quarterly. Circulation: 70,000. Buys all rights. Buys 45 mss a year. Payment on publication. Will send sample copy to writer for $2.50. Submit only complete ms. Will consider photocopied submissions. Reports in 2 to 4 weeks. Enclose S.A.S.E. for return of submissions.
Nonfiction: "Articles dealing with international affairs; political, educational, cultural, philosophical and social sciences. Develop an original idea in depth, with a broad basis on topical subjects. Serious, in depth, developmental articles with international appeal." Length: 2,500 to 4,000 words. Pays $250.
How To Break In: "There is no simple answer for the young writer. The best way is to send his manuscript to as many periodicals as possible. The editors at *Foreign Affairs* give unsolicited mss careful consideration."

FOREIGN POLICY, 345 E. 46th St., New York NY 10017. Quarterly. Usually buys all rights. Pays on publication. "Study recent issues of the magazine at the public library. And be sure to enclose S.A.S.E. with mss." Address mss to the editors.
Nonfiction: "*Foreign Policy* focuses on the American role in world affairs, offering constructive discussion of new directions for American foreign policy. Specific policy recommendations are sought. *Foreign Policy* deals with issues which confront policy makers today. And we hope that the discussions of these issues will affect the actions, or at least the thinking, of those who shape our foreign policy."
Length: 4,000 words maximum. Pays an honorarium.

THE FREEMAN, Irvington-on-Hudson NY 10533. Editor: Paul L. Poirot. For "fairly advanced students of liberty and the layman." Monthly. Buys all rights, including reprint rights. Buys about 44 mss a year. Pays on publication. Enclose S.A.S.E. for return of submissions.

Nonfiction: "We want nonfiction clearly analyzing and explaining various aspects of the free market, private enterprise, limited government philosophy, especially as pertains to conditions in the United States. Though a necessary part of the literature of freedom is the exposure of collectivistic cliches and fallacies, our aim is to emphasize and explain the positive case for individual responsibility and choice in a free economy. Especially important, we believe, is the methodology of freedom; self-improvement, offered to others who are interested. We try to avoid name-calling and personality clashes, and find satire of little use as an educational device. Ours is a scholarly analysis of the principle underlying a free market economy." See "Controlling Pollution" (Sennholz) and "The Anatomy of Consumerism" (Brunk), February 1973. Length: Not over 3,500 words. Payment is 5¢ a word.

THE NATION, 333 Sixth Ave., New York NY 10014. Editor: Carey McWilliams. Weekly. Query first. Enclose S.A.S.E.

Nonfiction and Poetry: "We welcome all articles dealing with the social scene, particularly if they examine it with a new point of view or expose conditions the rest of the media overlooks. Poetry is also accepted." Length and payment to be negotiated.

NATIONAL JOURNAL, 1730 M St., N.W., Washington DC 20036. Editor: John F. Burby. "Very limited need for freelance material because fulltime staff produces virtually all of our material."

NATIONAL OBSERVER, 11501 Columbia Pike, Silver Spring MD 20900. No longer in the market for freelance material.

NATIONAL REVIEW, 150 E. 35th St., New York NY 10016. Editor: Wm. F. Buckley, Jr. Issued fortnightly. Will send sample copy. Buys all rights. Pays on publication. Reports in a month. Enclose S.A.S.E.

Nonfiction: Uses articles, 1,000 to 3,500 words, on current events and the arts which would appeal to a politically conservative audience. Pays about 7½¢ a word. Inquiries about book reviews should be addressed to Mrs. Frank S. Meyer, Ohayo Mountain Road, Woodstock, NY 12498. Inquiries on movie, play, TV reviews, other cultural happenings, or travel should be addressed to Mr. C.H. Simonds, Feature Editor, 150 E. 35th St., New York, NY 10016.

Poetry: Uses only short satirical poems of a political nature. Should not run over 50 lines.

THE NEW REPUBLIC—A Weekly Journal of Opinion, 1244 Nineteenth St., N.W., Washington DC 20036. Editor: Gilbert A. Harrison. Pays on publication. Buys all rights. Enclose S.A.S.E. for return of submissions.

Nonfiction: This liberal, intellectual publication uses 500- to 2,000-word comments on public affairs and the arts. Pays 8¢ per published word.

NEWSWEEK, 444 Madison Ave., New York NY 10022. Staff-written.

THE PROGRESSIVE, 408 W. Gorham St., Madison WI 53703. Editor: Morris H. Rubin. Issued monthly. Pays on publication. Reports in two weeks. Query first. Enclose S.A.S.E. for return of submissions.

Nonfiction: Primarily interested in articles which interpret, from a liberal point of view, domestic and world affairs. Occasional lighter features. Up to 3,000 words. Pays $50 to $150 per ms.

THE REPUBLICAN NEWSPAPERS OF CALIFORNIA, P.O. Box 16148, San Diego CA 92116. Editor: W. J. Innis. "The majority of our readers are registered Republicans who are interested, first and foremost, in partisan politics. We run special issues at the time of such political events as California and national elections, inaugurals and conventions." Established in 1963. Monthly. Circulation: 100,000. Not copyrighted. "We expect to purchase a minimum of 40 mss in the next year." Payment on publication. Will send a free sample copy. Query first or submit complete ms. Will consider photocopied submissions if easily readable. Submit seasonal material 3 months in advance. Reports on material in 3 weeks. Enclose S.A.S.E. for reply to queries or return of submissions.

Nonfiction and Photos: "We concentrate on California, but also cover national politics. We are just beginning to draw on freelance sources; make sure it's in good taste. Interested in the inner workings of government, current legislation and social problems, as well as political personalities. Interviews with experts in fields relating to politics and with celebrities who are active California Republicans are especially welcome. We are a Republican newspaper, and all articles have a Republican slant unless they are strictly factual accounts of legislation or some nonpartisan subject. Although we may occasionally point to weaknesses in the party, we are aggressively pro-Republican." Informational, profile, humor, historical, think pieces, personal opinion. Preferred length: 1,000 words; 750 minimum, 1,500 maximum. Pays 5¢ per word. Mary Curtis, Editorial Coordinator. 8x10 b&w glossy photos purchased with or without mss. Pays $10. Dept. Editor: A. M. Gladfelter.

TIME, Rockefeller Center, New York NY 10020. Staff-written.

U.S. NEWS AND WORLD REPORT, 2300 N St., N.W., Washington DC 20037. Managing Editor: John H. Adams. Issued weekly to those interested primarily in news developments in national and international affairs. Payment made on publication. Buys all rights. Reports on submissions within a week or less. Query preferred. Enclose S.A.S.E.

Nonfiction: Uses only contributed material which has some special news significance or has been prepared by someone associated in the public mind with current news developments. Payment varies.

WASHINGTON MONTHLY, 1028 Connecticut Ave., N.W., Washington DC 20036. Editor: Charles Peters. For "well-educated people interested in politics and government; well-read." Monthly. Circulation: 30,000. Rights purchased depend on author and material; may buy all rights, first rights, or second rights. Buys about 40 mss a year. Pays on publication. Will send a sample copy to a writer for $1. Sometimes does special topical issues. "It's better not to send originals; photocopies are better." Reports in 1 to 4 weeks. Enclose S.A.S.E. for return of submissions.

Nonfiction and Photos: Responsible investigative or evaluative reporting about the U.S. government, business, society, the press, the presidency, Congress, environment, corporate responsibility, work in America, sex and politics, Indochina, muckraking. Length: "average 3,000 to 6,000 words." Pays 5¢ to 10¢ a word. Buys b&w glossies.

WORLD POLITICS, Corwin Hall, Princeton NJ 08540. Editors: Klaus Knorr, Cyril E. Black, Gerald Garvey, Walter F. Murphy. Issued quarterly to academic readers in social sciences. Pays on publication. Buys all rights. Reports in one to six months. Enclose S.A.S.E. for return of submissions.

Nonfiction: Uses articles based on original scholarly research on international aspects of the social sciences. Mss should be double-spaced throughout (including footnotes), and have wide margins. Footnotes should be placed at the end of article. Length: 3,000 to 5,000 words. Pays $50 per article.

WORLDVIEW, 170 E. 64th St., New York NY 10021. Managing Editor: Susan Woolfson. For "the informed and concerned reader who insists that discussion of public issues must take place within an ethical framework." Monthly. Buys all rights. Pays on publication. Query first. Study magazine before submitting. Enclose S.A.S.E. for return of submissions.

Nonfiction: Articles on public issues, religion, international affairs, world politics, and moral imperatives. "The editors believe that any analysis of our present cultural and political problems which ignores the moral dimension is at best incomplete—at worst, misleading. *Worldview* focuses on international affairs, puts the discussion in an ethical framework, and relates ethical judgment to specifically religious traditions." Length: 2,500 to 5,000 words. Payment to be negotiated.

Puzzle Publications

Only magazines devoted entirely to puzzles are included in this classification. The writer will find many additional markets for crosswords, brain teasers, acrostics, etc. by reading the Filler listings throughout the Consumer, Farm, Trade, Technical, and Professional, and Sponsored Publications sections of this book. Especially rich in puzzle markets are the Religious, Juvenile, Teen and Young Adult, and General Interest classifications within the Consumer section.

COMPLETE CROSSWORD PUZZLES, ORIGINAL CROSSWORD, 575 Madison Ave., New York NY 10022. Editorial Director: Arthur Goodman. Bimonthly. Buys all rights. Pays on acceptance. Refer to current issue available on newsstand as guide to type of material wanted. Submissions must be accompanied by self-addressed, stamped envelope for return.
Puzzles: Original adult crossword puzzles; sizes 15x15 and 13x13; medium and not hard. Same requirements for diagramless, but 15x15 irregular patterns only. "Currently overstocked."

CROSSWORD TIME, TODAY'S CROSSWORDS, CROSSWORD PLEASURE, Donajil Publications, Inc., P.O. Box 152, Whitestone NY 11357. *Crossword Pleasure* and *Crossword Time* bimonthly; *Today's Crosswords,* quarterly. Send single sample only "and inquire from publisher as to particular types of crosswords needed." Write for copy of instructions for writers. Enclose S.A.S.E.
Puzzles: Fresh, original, informative, quizzes, crossword puzzles only; for family audience. "When constructing new crosswords, make an accurate copy (not a photocopy) of our master diagram. Be sure that black squares and numbers are in exact same places. Send copy only. Hold the master for future submission. Put code number on top of your diagral copy and also on top of the first sheet of your definitions, along with your name and address. Also state type of puzzle, i.e., Easy, Medium, Stumper, etc. Submit diagram, with answers and numbers on 1 sheet, numbers, definitions, answer words on other, in that order. Keep definitions short—no double definitions. Avoid, if possible, obsolete variants and abbreviations. In 'categorical' puzzles (devoted to special subject), at least 20% of the total words must be related to subject." For fill-ins, "must be 21 squares wide, 18 squares deep. All words of one category. List words alphabetically in each group of 3-letters, 4-letters, etc. No words less than 3 letters, and no single black squares." For diacrostics, "first letters of words, reading downward, must spell out name and/or title of quotation. Quotations must be complete thoughts. Make diagrams 15 squares wide, depth as will." Check puzzles for accuracy before submitting. Pays $2.50 for quizzes, $4 to $10 each for crosswords.

EASY-TIMED CROSSWORD PUZZLES, 575 Madison Ave., New York NY 10022. Editorial Director: Arthur Goodman. Bimonthly. Buys all rights. Pays on acceptance. Query first. Enclose S.A.S.E. for reply to queries.
Puzzles: Uses only puzzles size 15x and 13x of easier variety. See current issue for guide. "Currently overstocked."

HANDY CROSSWORD PUZZLES (formerly *Tip-Top Crossword*), 575 Madison Ave., New York NY 10022. Editorial Director: Arthur Goodman. Bimonthly. Buys all rights. Pays on acceptance. Query first. Enclose S.A.S.E. for reply to query.
Puzzles: Original adult crossword puzzles; size 15x15 and 13x13; easy. Same requirements as for diagramless, but 15x15 irregular patterns only. Pays $5 for diagramless; up to $15 for crosswords. "Currently overstocked."

OFFICIAL CROSSWORDS, DELL CROSSWORDS, POCKET CROSSWORDS, DELL CROSSWORD ANNUALS, DELL CHALLENGER CROSSWORDS, DELL CROSSWORD PUZZLES, DELL PUZZLE PUBLICATIONS, 750 Third Avenue, New York NY 10017. Editor: Kathleen Rafferty. For "all ages from '8 to 80'—people whose interests are puzzles, both crosswords and variety features." Enclose S.A.S.E. for return of submissions.

Puzzles: "We publish puzzles of all kinds, but the market here is limited to those who are able to construct quality pieces which can compete with the real professionals. See our magazines. They are the best guide for our needs. We publish quality puzzles, which are well-conceived and well edited, with appeal to solvers of all ages and in about every walk of life. We are the world's leading publishers of puzzle publications and are distributed in many countries around the world in addition to the continental U.S. However, no foreign language puzzles, please! Our market for crosswords and anacrostics is very small, since long-time contributors supply most of the needs in those areas. However, we are always willing to see material of unusual quality, or with a new or original approach. Since most of our publications feature variety puzzles in addition to the usual features, we are especially interested in seeing quizzes, picture features, and new and unusual puzzle features of all kinds. Please do not send us remakes of features we are now using. We are interested only in new ideas. Kriss Krosses are an active market here. However, constructors who wish to enter this field must query us first before submitting any material whatever. Prices vary with the feature, but ours are comparable with the highest in the general puzzle field."

QUALITY CROSSWORD PUZZLES, FAVORITE CROSSWORD PUZZLES, WORD DETECTIVE, 855 S. Federal Highway, Boca Raton FL 33432. Editor: James L. Quinn. Bimonthly. Reports as soon as possible. Buys all rights. Pays for "articles or assigned material on acceptance, all other on publication." Request requirements sheet before submitting samples; enclose S.A.S.E. Submit seasonal material 6 months in advance. Enclose S.A.S.E. for return of submissions.

Puzzles: Buys only the unusual in puzzles, or topical crosswords with a high percentage of theme words, and on offbeat subjects. Avoid all trade names. Puzzles must contain whole words. All material must be typed. Pays according to size/length of submission. "The following types of puzzles are used in our magazines: straight crosswords, topical crosswords (must be 35% topical), double-you-make-it puzzles, diagramless puzzles, alphabetical puzzles, round and rounds, crostics, double plays, cryptograms, cross-additions, skeletons, word quizzes, slidograms, word chains, clapboard puzzles, crossword twins, and crossword triplets. We also use various types of 'filler' material—short puzzles to set on a fraction of a page, consisting of quizzes, brain teasers, conundrums, arithmetic games, off-trail material." For crosswords, use standard puzzle sizes: 11x11, 13x13, 15x15, 17x16, 19x19, though "special sizes and novelty shapes are welcomed." Page 1 should have diagram with numbers and answers inserted. Succeeding pages should have definition with answers: (word) 1. (Definition) Periods after numbers, no periods after definitions. Unused squares to be thoroughly blacked. For crostics, use 12x15 squares running horizontally. Page 1 should have quotation with author and source; the first letters of definition must spell out the complete title of author's work and at least the author's last name. Page 2 should have complete diagram with numbers and letters typed. Page 3 to have definitions followed by numbered spaces for answer, with answer inserted. "To avoid any charge of plagiarism or use of literary material without permission, use only subject matter within the 'public domain' when using quotations. If novelty or new type of puzzle is submitted, please give complete instructions for solving it." Pays $3 to $25.

Nonfiction: "Articles about words, history of words, people who work with words, items of interest to people who do crossword puzzles." Length: 1,500 words. Pays $50.

Regional Publications

The regional magazines below are general interest publications slanted to residents of and visitors to a particular city or region. Since they publish little material that doesn't relate to the area they cover, they represent a limited market for writers who live outside their area.

Many buy manuscripts on conservation and the natural wonders of their area; addi-

tional markets for such material will be found under the Nature, Conservation, and Ecology and Sport and Outdoor headings.

Publications that report on the business climate of a region are grouped in the regional division of the Business and Finance category. Newspaper Sunday supplements, which also buy material of general interest to area residents, are classified separately under Newspapers and Sunday Supplements. Magazines for farm audiences which buy regional general interest material are found in the local division of the General Interest Farming and Rural Life category in the Farm Publications section. Publications of state automobile clubs and tourist travel information bureaus are grouped with the Sponsored Publications. Regional magazines with specialized subject matter (for example, Kentucky Business) are classified in the category for national magazines treating that subject matter (in the case of the example, Business and Finance).

ADIRONDACK LIFE, Willsboro NY 12996. Editor: Lionel A. Atwill. For "past, present, or future residents or friends of New York State's Adirondack region." Established in 1970. Quarterly. Circulation: 32,000. Buys all rights but will reassign rights to author after publication. Buys 30 mss a year. Payment on publication. Will send free sample copy to writer on request. Write for copy of guidelines for writers. Query. Submit seasonal material 4 to 5 months in advance. ("We look for material that relates to the 4 seasons.") Reports on material in 2 to 3 weeks. Enclose S.A.S.E.
Nonfiction and Photos: "All material must have a common denominator—a connection with the Adirondack Park. We are interested in stories on artists, history, events, personalities, interesting trips, collectibles, natural and man-made phenomena, geography, wildlife, folk tales, and any other general interest features that take place in or are directly connected with the Adirondacks." Length: 1,000 to 2,500 words. Pays $25 to $125. 5x7 to 11x14 b&w double-weight glossies. Pays $10. 35mm and larger color transparencies. Pays $30 for one-time repro rights. "We will use 6 to 10 general scenic shots per issue. Must be taken within the Adirondacks and the location should be identified."

ARIZONA HIGHWAYS, 2039 W. Lewis, Phoenix AZ 85009. Editor: Joseph Stacey. Monthly. Buys one-time rights. Query first. Enclose S.A.S.E.
Nonfiction: Travel articles pertaining to Arizona and the Southwest. Length: 2,500 to 5,000 words. Payment open.
Photos: Arizona scenes or subjects pertaining to economic or historical development. No model releases required. Payment open.
Poetry: For back page of magazine. Length: 8 to 12 lines, on Southwestern subjects.

ATLANTA, 1104 Commerce Building, Atlanta GA 30303. Editor: Norman Shavin. Monthly. Circulation: over 23,000. Buys all rights. Buys about 20 mss a year. Pays on publication. Will send a sample copy to a writer for $1. Query first. "Always, but always, study the magazine first." Returns rejected material in 2 weeks. Acknowledges acceptance of material in 4 to 6 weeks. Enclose S.A.S.E.
Nonfiction and Photos: Articles, interviews. Material must be written for regional, urban, sophisticated audience. Subjects regularly featured are politics, sports, business, urban affairs, the arts, profiles, science. Humorous pieces sought. Do not send "ponderous essays, fiction, or poetry (whether ponderous or not)." Length: 750 to 3,000 words. Pays $100 to $350, depending on length and quality. Photos purchased with ms. B&w glossies, color transparencies.

THE ATLANTIC ADVOCATE, Phoenix Square, Gleaner Bldg., Fredericton, N.B., Canada. Editor: Ken Chisholm. Monthly. Circulation: 26,000. Buys North American serial rights. Pays on publication. Will send a sample copy to a writer for 50¢. Query first. Editorial deadlines 3 months before publication. Enclose S.A.E. and International Reply Coupons for reply to queries.
Nonfiction: "Matters concerning Atlantic Provinces of Canada; subjects of general interest; international stories with a connection to the Atlantic Provinces. Preferably written by Canadians." Length: 1,000 to 2,000 words. Payment by negotiation.
Fiction: Preferably Atlantic Provinces of Canada setting, but other material considered. Length: 1,500 words to 2,000 words. Payment by negotiation.
Fillers: Short humor. Payment by negotiation.

BIRMINGHAM MAGAZINE, 1914 Sixth Ave. N., Birmingham AL 35203. Editor: Donald A. Brown. Monthly. Circulation: 8,000. Will send free sample copy upon request. Aimed at civic, political, cultural, and business leaders; affluent audience. Reports in two to three weeks. Buys all rights. Pays on publication. Editorial deadlines are 45 days prior to publication. Prefers to see samples of work in advance and usually works by assignment. Query preferred. Enclose S.A.S.E.
Nonfiction: Timely, accurate and objective articles of Birmingham and environs; progress and problems. Professional, imaginative style, 1,500 to 5,000 words. Pays $75 to $200.
Photos: Purchased with mss. Subject matter, specifications, and payment rate worked out according to the particular story.

BUCKS COUNTY PANORAMA MAGAZINE, 50 E. Court St., Doylestown PA 18901. Editor: Sheila Martin. For suburban readers, "95% are residents of Bucks County." Monthly. Circulation: 5,000. Buys first rights. Buys approximately 36 mss a year. Pays on publication. Will send a sample copy to a writer on request. No seasonal material. Reports in 1 month. Enclose S.A.S.E. for return of submissions.
Nonfiction and Photos: "Only articles connected with Bucks County—historical or contemporary." Buys interviews, photo stories, historical articles. Length: 1,000 to 3,000 words. Pays $8 to $15. Photos purchased with mss. B&w glossies. Pays $2 to $5.
Fiction: Historical, must be oriented to Bucks County. Length: 1,000 to 3,000 words. Pays $8 to $15.

BUFFALO SPREE MAGAZINE, P.O. Box 38, Buffalo NY 14226. Editor: Richard G. Shotell. For "a highly literate readership." Established in 1967. Quarterly. Buys "first printing rights only." Enclose S.A.S.E. for return of submissions.
Nonfiction: "Intellectually stimulating essays exploring contemporary social, philosophical, artistic, and environmental concerns. We are not a political magazine. Matters of interest to western New York make up a significant part of what we print." Length: 3,000 words maximum. Pays about $75 "for a lead article." Dept. Editor: Gary Goss.
Fiction: "We print fiction, but it must be brilliant." Length: 3,000 words maximum. Pays $75. Dept. Editor: Gary Goss.
Poetry: "Experimental poetry interests us, provided it is of the highest quality." Dept. Editor: Nik Mistler.

THE CHICAGO GUIDE, 500 N. Michigan Ave., Chicago IL 60611. Editor: Allen H. Kelson. For an audience which is "95% from Chicago area; 90% college-trained; upper income; overriding interests in the arts, dining, good life in the city. Most are in 30 to 50 age bracket and well-read and articulate. Generally liberal inclination." Monthly. Circulation: 100,000. Buys first rights. Buys about 30 mss a year. Pays on publication. Will send a sample copy to a writer for 75¢. Query first. Submit seasonal material 3 months in advance. Reports in 2 weeks. Enclose S.A.S.E.
Nonfiction and Photos: "On themes relating to the quality of life in Chicago ... past, present, future." Writers should have "a general awareness that the readers will be concerned, influential native Chicagoans reading what the writer has to say about their city. We generally publish material too comprehensive for daily newspapers or of too specialized interest for them." Buys personal experience and think pieces, interviews, profiles, humor, spot news, historical articles, exposes. Length: 2,000 to 6,000 words. Pays $100 to $500. Photos purchased with mss. B&w glossies, color transparencies, 35mm color, color prints.

CHICAGO MAGAZINE, 110 S. Dearborn St., Chicago IL 60602. Editor: Richard Frisbie. Six times per year. Copyrighted. Will send sample copy for $1.35. Aimed at the upper-income urban Chicagoan and those interested in Chicago. Reports within a month. Buys all rights. Must query first. Pays within a reasonable time after acceptance. Enclose S.A.S.E.
Nonfiction: "Interested in almost anything bearing on life in the city: art, music, restaurants, shops, history, ethnic enclaves, planning, recreation, personalities, urban problems, commerce. Prefer contemporary and light-hearted approach. Must have

news peg or reason for bringing up a particular subject at this time. Like most magazines we assign far more articles than we buy out of the mail, but suggestions are welcome." Length: 1,500 to 3,500 words. Pays "about 10c a word depending on research involved and quality of writing."

Fiction: On rare occasions may use quality fiction of about 2,000 words, with a Chicago or generalized urban setting. Payment is open.

THE CHICAGO REPORTER, 111 S. Wabash Ave., Chicago IL 60602. Editor: John A. McDermott. "A specialized publication on racial issues serving 5,000 institutional leaders (i.e., executives, labor leaders, religious officials, local government officials, educators and community organization leaders) in metropolitan Chicago." Established in 1972. Monthly. Circulation: 5,000. Buys all rights, but will reassign rights to author after publication. Buys about 6 mss a year. Pays on publication. Will send free sample copy to writer on request. Query first. Will consider photocopied submissions. Submit seasonal material 2 months in advance. Reports in 1 month. Enclose S.A.S.E. for reply to queries.

Nonfiction: Publishes material relating to race relations in metropolitan Chicago. "More intensive and analytical coverage of this issue than any other media." Also publishes personal experience, profiles, think articles, exposes and interviews. Length: 1,200 words. Pays $100.

CINCINNATI MAGAZINE, 309 Vine St., Suite 55, Cincinnati OH 45202. Editor: Richard L. Gordon. For upper income Cincinnati area audience. Established in 1967. Monthly. Circulation: 12,500. Buys all rights. Buys 60 to 75 mss a year. Payment on publication. Will send free sample copy to writer on request. Query first. Will consider photocopied submissions. Submit seasonal or special material 1 year in advance. Reports in 1 to 4 weeks. Enclose S.A.S.E.

Nonfiction: "Articles pertinent to business, entertainment, art personalities, medicine, music, government with a Greater Cincinnati tie-in. All writers should query first. We like the local angle. If covering subjects of national depth the writer should explain how it affects Cincinnatians. We try to give each subject a local treatment, seeking opinions and comment from local people." Informational, how-to, personal experience, interview, profile, and historical articles wanted. Regular departments include: Queen City History (750 words) and Queen City Report (light, offbeat local happenings). Feature length: 1,500 to 1,700 words. Pays 6¢ a word.

How To Break In: "*Cincinnati* is a regional magazine, concerned with the greater Cincinnati area, which includes sections of Ohio, Kentucky and Indiana.

Our main need is for articles, and we always look for the local angle. Either something is happening in our territory, or else somebody from here is doing something interesting elsewhere. Occasionally we use fiction and poetry. Even here, we like the local (or regional) angle. We are to the big national magazine what the community weekly is to the big-city daily. We tell the home folks about themselves—but in what we hope is a literate and sophisticated manner. We use light, entertaining articles—but these are the easiest to get. The writer who can dig into a serious subject and treat it intelligently has a good chance with us. If it has to do with a fault in our community, we want the cards on the table—but we also insist upon telling what is being done to correct it, or could be done. We are constructive, not negative or pessimistic. We love humor and get very little of it. Here again, remember the local angle. If you have an idea you think might be good for us, please query by letter. If you go ahead and prepare a manuscript, you are probably wasting your time and ours. The query should state the general subject, the approach you propose, any special reason why an article is appropriate now. If you wish, write a lead to give us an idea about your writing style. If we give a go-ahead, don't worry about illustration. We prefer to handle this ourselves. Naturally, your suggestions are welcome, but we like to have a manuscript in hand before we consider illustration. We value good writing. If a manuscript is not up to our standards, we send it back for revision or, if time is short, we edit heavily and rewrite in the office. Some manuscripts show evidence of excellent research—but get nowhere because of careless writing. We like description and quotes and short sentences and long ones too. We like a change of pace now and then. We love a neat turn of phrase. Our graphics are good, and it is a real challenge for a word-person to match them. But please, no corn. Most of our readers are above average in education and income. Generally, they are well informed. Never write down to them. But, most of all, write like a writer—not a stringer-together of words. Make the words bounce. That's the fun part—both for the writer and the reader. We're a little home-town magazine. But a fellow who should know said recently that, among the city magazines, *Cincinnati* is the best, the most literate. True or not, we accept it as a goal. We need writers with ideas, and a real desire to write well."

COAST MAGAZINE, 291 South LaCienega, Beverly Hills CA 90211. Editor: Colman Andrews. For "young, involved Western Americans; college graduates, many of whom have done postgraduate work and are employed in professional, artistic, engineering, technical, educational or managerial work." Monthly. Circulation: 85,000. Buys first North American serial rights. Payment on publication. Will send free sample copy to writer on request. Query first preferred. Reports in 3 to 5 weeks. Enclose S.A.S.E. for reply to query or return of submission.
Nonfiction: "We are edited with the western American and particularly Californian in mind. We want to keep track of the pulse of the West; life styles, arts, politics, ecology, business, education, sports, food, fashion, and so on. Our slant is younger and more tuned in to alternative concepts and institutions. We would rather anticipate trends in art and society rather than merely report on them. We do not want articles particularly on rock music, criticism and personality portraits. Also, we are definitely avoiding fan type approaches to articles, both in popular music and the other arts." Length: 300 to 10,000 words. Pays 1½¢ to 5¢ a word.

COAST MAGAZINE, The King's Highway at 50th Ave., North, Myrtle Beach SC 29577. Managing Editor: Walter S. McDonald. For "vacationers, sportsmen, visitors." Weekly. Circulation: 15,000. Buys first rights. Buys approximately 20 mss a year. Pays on publication. Will send a sample copy to a writer for 50¢. Query first. Submit seasonal material 2 months in advance. Reports in 2 weeks. Enclose S.A.S.E.
Nonfiction: Humor, historical and travel pieces, photo essays. Writer should be "vacation-oriented" with a style that is "light and breezy." Length: 50 to 750 words. Pays 25¢ to 50¢ a column inch.
Photos: B&w glossies. Pays $3 to $10.
Fillers: Jokes, short humor. Length: 20 to 75 words. Pays 10¢ a column inch.

COLORADO MAGAZINE, 7190 W. 14th Ave., Denver CO 80215. Executive Editor: Davis Dutton. Six times a year. Circulation: 155,000. Buys all rights. Pays on acceptance. Prompt reports on queries; four weeks for mss. Enclose S.A.S.E
Nonfiction: Adventure and action articles which take place in the present day Rocky Mountain West (Colorado, Wyoming, Utah, Montana, Idaho, and New Mexico only). Articles should convey the unique flavor of experience and life in this region. Also wants historical, "adventure-of-the-West" articles; no narratives or flat accounts. Should bring the life of the old days to the present day reader and include action, quotations, anecdotes. In addition, uses outdoor features with seasonal sections on skiing, fishing, camping, hiking, hunting, snowmobiling. First person accounts which convey the unique sense of the sport in the Rocky Mountain West. Is "more and more interested in stories dealing with environmental concerns in the Rockies—timbering, pollution, preservation, wilderness, etc." Photos should accompany mss. Length: 2,500 to 3,000 words. Also uses featurettes on interesting places for tourists and natives to visit; must be off the beaten path. Length: 650 words. Include history, description, anecdotes, photos, maps. Pays 10¢ per word for articles, including photos.
Photos: Purchased with mss, as available. Also approximately 16 color scenics purchased individually for special center section each issue. Attractive views of Western mountains, lakes, streams, ranches, ghost towns, sunsets, flowers, animals, outdoor sports. 4x5 tranparencies preferred for scenic section; minimum size 2¼x2¼. Pays $60 for scenic photos, plus bonus for covers, spreads, etc.

COLUMBUS BUSINESS FORUM, Columbus Area Chamber of Commerce, P.O. Box 1527, Columbus, OH 43216. Editor: Elaine Black. "Not in the market for submissions from freelancers."

THE COMMONWEALTH, 611 E. Franklin St., Richmond VA 23219. Editor: James S. Wamsley. For "high caliber Virginia business, professional, political leaders; educated public at large." Special travel issue (June). Monthly. Circulation: 12,000. Buys all rights. Buys approximately 24 mss a year. Pays on publication. Will "usually" send a sample copy to a writer on request. Query first. Submit seasonal material 4 months in advance. Reports in 6 weeks. Enclose S.A.S.E.
Nonfiction: Any subject of feature quality with specific Virginia interest. No stock material on familiar attractions. Humor; adventure; history; modern serious subjects, geared for mature readership. "No routine articles on stock attractions of Virginia." Personal experience pieces, interviews, profiles, humor, historical and travel articles, coverage of successful business operations, think pieces, photo essays. Length: 1,200 to 3,000 words. Pays $50 to $100.
Photos: Professional quality, 8x10 glossies purchased with mss.

CONNECTICUT MAGAZINE, 2505 Main Street, Stratford CT 06497. Editor: Willard Clark. For persons of "all ages, 15 and up; upper middle class." 10 issues a year; monthly except for combined December/January and July/August. Circulation: 20,000. Buys all rights. Pays on publication. Will send free sample copy to a writer on request. Query first. Submit seasonal material at least 2 months in advance. Enclose S.A.S.E.
Nonfiction:"Any article pertaining to or about Connecticut. We are a relatively new publication, not having established a specific style." Buys historical articles, current events, articles on famous celebrities, book reviews, interviews, profiles, successful business operations, exposes, photo features, and travel articles limited to Connecticut. Also buys freelance materials for departments on Connecticut cuisine, Yankee gardens, politics, books in review, sports, environment, and car and driver. Length: 1,000 to 5,000 words. Pays $100 to $500.
Photos: May be purchased with manuscripts. Black and white glossies, color transparencies. Pays $50 to $500.
Fiction: Historical, contemporary problems. "Connecticut humor, history." Length: 1,000 to 5,000 words. Pays $100 to $500.
Fillers: Length: 1 to 3 inches. Pays $10 to $25.

CUE, 20 W. 43rd St., New York NY 10036. Editor: Stanley Newman. Weekly. Pays on publication. Query first. Enclose S.A.S.E.
Nonfiction: Uses different, offbeat articles on local subjects appealing to the sophisticated reader who lives in New York and vicinity. May use articles on truly different places or activities within the area *Cue* covers; pieces on institutions in New York City and vicinity which have remained obscure despite terrific accomplishment. No coverage of entertainment or entertainment personalities is needed. Top-notch, anecdotal, tight, incisive writing is demanded. Pays $125 to $175.

DALLAS MAGAZINE, 1507 Pacific Ave., Dallas TX 75201. Editor: Lucille Enix. "All material is assigned to Dallas writers."

DOWN EAST MAGAZINE, Camden ME 04843. Editor: Duane Doolittle. 10 times a year. Buys first serial rights. Pays on acceptance. Reports in two weeks. Enclose S.A.S.E. for return of submissions.
Nonfiction and Photos: Uses historical and comtemporary articles on Maine subjects. Usual feature length is 2,000 to 3,000 words. Pays 2¢ a word average. Buys photos submitted with manuscripts. Maine scenics. 8x10 size is preferred, but smaller size acceptable if sharp. Color photos should be 4x5 or larger. Pays $3 to $5 for black and white, $25 for color photos.
Fiction: Little fiction is used; like nonfiction, must be specifically related to the Maine scene or Maine character, historical or contemporary, never of romantic type.
Fillers: Sharply pointed humorous anecdotes, reflecting Maine character and/or way of life. Pays $5. "I Remember" items, concerning Maine events or people, $5 each with accompanying photo.

FOCUS/MIDWEST, P.O. Box 3086, St. Louis MO 63130. Editor: Charles L. Klotzer. Bimonthly for a literate and liberal audience in Illinois, Missouri, and the

Middle West. No photos or fillers. Buys all rights. Pays on publication. Query first and study publication before submitting ms. Reports on submissions in two months. Enclose S.A.S.E.

Nonfiction: Controversial articles of direct interest to residents or observers of Illinois and Missouri on social, political and related issues. No taboos. Material of cultural interest can have broader midwestern base. Length: up to 4,000 words. Payment varies.

Poetry: Only qualification is literary excellence.

GOLDEN GATE NORTH, P.O. Box 3028, Santa Rosa CA 95403. Editor: Ray Smith. For "educated, concerned people, slightly outdoorsy, most on ecology kick, most settled, with children." Quarterly. Circulation: 12,500. Buys all rights, but exceptions can be arranged. Buys 16 mss a year. Payment on publication. Will send sample copy to a writer for 75¢. Reports in 6 to 10 weeks. Enclose S.A.S.E. for return of submissions.

Nonfiction and Photos: Want "well-documented material on subjects of concern within the region. Each issue there is one article of regional interest (leaning toward ecology), one of Marin County interest, one of Sonoma County and one interview. Write as a reporter digging deeply into his subject, but get those anecdotes in." Buys interviews, profiles, expose, and travel articles. Length: lead articles, 3,000 words; others, 1,200 words. Pays about 5¢ a word. Buys photos with mss. Pays $10 for b&w glossies. Pays $15 for 35mm color transparencies and color prints.

INDIANAPOLIS MAGAZINE, 320 N. Meridian St., Indianapolis IN 46204. Editor: Craig J. Beardsley. Publication of the Indianapolis Chamber of Commerce for members and "others interested in Indianapolis." Established in 1964. Monthly. Circulation: 10,000. Not copyrighted. Buys "about 20 mss a year." Payment on acceptance. Will send free sample copy to writer on request. Write for copy of guidelines for writers. Query first. "If story is already completed, however, mail it on in." Will consider photocopied submissions. Submit seasonal material (occasional Christmas fiction) 2 months in advance. Reports on material in 2 weeks. Enclose S.A.S.E. for reply to queries or return of submissions.

Nonfiction and Photos: In-depth features of and about Indianapolis—"anything about Indianapolis in general, especially anything pertaining to the yearly 500 race." Informational, how-to, personal experience, interview, profile, humor, historical, think pieces, expose, nostalgia, personal opinion, travel, successful business operations, new product, merchandising techniques, technical. Length: 500 to 5,000 words. Pays $50 to $150. Captions are required for 8x10 b&w photos purchased with mss; captions optional for photos purchased without mss. Pays $15.

Fiction: Occasionally uses Christmas fiction. Pays $50 to $125.

Fillers: Jokes and short humor.

JACKSONVILLE MAGAZINE, P.O. Drawer 329, Jacksonville FL 32201. Editor: William M. Taylor. Managing Editor: Tom Ellis III. For "businessmen, community leaders; 25 to 65 years old; college education, golf, sport, business, community oriented interest, entertainment and books. Florida oriented." Established in 1963. Bimonthly. Circulation: 10,000. Buys all rights. Buys 20 to 25 mss a year. Payment on publication. Will send sample copy to a writer on request. Will send editorial guideline sheet to a writer on request. Query first. Submit seasonal material 3 to 6 months in advance. Reports in 3 weeks. Enclose S.A.S.E. for return of submissions.

Nonfiction and Photos: Freelancer should write articles "in-depth and well-documented; usually will look at photographs. Writing should be sculptured and keen. Although *Jacksonville Magazine* is published by the Jacksonville area Chamber of Commerce, it is a community magazine." Buys historical, think, photo, travel, successful business operations, and in a broad sense, technical articles. Length: usually 600 to 2,500 words, according to subject matter. Pays $25 per article. Purchases photos with and without mss or on assignment. Captions required. 8x10 b&w glossies. Pays $25 a set with feature (negatives required). Pays $25 a set for color (transparencies only) with feature.

KANSAS!, State Office Building, Topeka KS 66612. Editor: Frances L. Smith. "We are not purchasing freelance material."

KANSAS CITY MAGAZINE, Chamber of Commerce of Greater Kansas City, 620 TenMain Center, Kansas City MO 64108. Editor: James Morgan. Monthly. Payment on publication. Query first. Reports in 1 month. Enclose S.A.S.E.
Nonfiction:"Bright, interpretive articles on history, politics, business, education, science and the social sciences, sports, entertainment, art and music, urban affairs, contemporary life styles, personalities—primarily of the Greater Kansas City area. We would be receptive to offbeat, unusual aspects—personalities and events—of the Kansas City story." Length: 800 to 3,000 words. Pay "negotiated according to length and nature of articles."
Poetry: Must be about Kansas City. Payment negotiated.
Fillers: "Would be interested in humor, puzzles, of contemporary Kansas City slant." Payment negotiated.

LI MAGAZINE, *Newsday,* 550 Stewart Ave., Garden City NY 11530. Managing Editor: Stanley Green. For well-educated, affluent suburban readers. Established in 1972. Weekly. Circulation: 340,000. Buys all rights. Payment on publication. Query first. Enclose S.A.S.E. for reply to queries.
Nonfiction and Photos: "Stories must be about Long Island people, places or events." Length: 600 to 2,500 words. Pays $100 to $600. B&w contacts and 35mm transparencies purchased on assignment. Pays up to $100 per page for b&w; $200 per page for color, including cover. Art Director: George Delmerico.

LOS ANGELES MAGAZINE, 342 N. Rodeo Dr., Beverly Hills CA 90210. Editor: David R. Brown. Monthly. Buys first time local rights. Query first. Enclose S.A.S.E.
Nonfiction: Uses articles on how best to live (i.e., the quality of life) in the changing, growing, diverse Los Angeles urban-suburban area; ideas, people, and occasionally places. Writer must have an understanding of contemporary living and doing in Southern California; material must appeal to upper-income, better-educated group of people. Fields of interest include urban problems, pleasures and cultural opportunities, leisure and trends, candid interviews of topical interest; the arts. Length: 1,000 to 3,000 words. Also uses some satire and humor. Articles on art, theater. music, etc. Length: 900 words. Pays 5¢ per word minimum. Submit articles to Geoff Miller, Managing Editor.
Photos: Buys photographs with mss. Also for cover. B&w should be 8x10; color, 2¼x2¼. Query first on cover shots. Pays $15 to $35 for single article photos. Pays $100 minimum for color covers.

MAINE LIFE, RFD 1, Liberty ME 04949. Editor: David E. Olson. Predominantly rural audience. Monthly. Copyrighted. Circulation: 26,000. Will send sample copy for 25¢. Rights purchased vary with author and material. Pays on publication. Editorial deadlines are the 10th of each month preceding publication. Enclose S.A.S.E. for return of submissions.
Nonfiction and Fiction: Articles and stories of 400 words or more on rural or contemporary Maine life. Human interest essential. "We only pay for material of feature length that is accompanied by a minimum number of photos. All other material is published gratis."
Photos: Purchased with mss and with captions. Same subject matter as nonfiction. Payment varies.

MARYLAND MAGAZINE, 2525 Riva Road, Annapolis MD 21401. Editor: M. E. Dougherty. For the "general public: majority are native or adopted Marylanders (16% of subscribers are out of state)." Established in 1968. Quarterly. Circulation: 18,000. Buys first North American serial rights. Buys about 25 mss a year. Payment on publication. Will send free sample copy to writer on request. Will send editorial guideline sheet to writer on request. Query first. Will consider photocopied submissions. Submit seasonal material 6 months in advance. Reports in 3 to 6 weeks. Enclose S.A.S.E. for reply to queries.
Nonfiction and Photos: General subject matter includes "economics, history, human interest, social, agricultural, etc., articles that have to do with Maryland." Freelancer should use general " 'magazine feature style;' articles must be on Maryland subjects or personalities only. We do not want any stories on the Civil War." Buys

informational, profile, humor, historical, nostalgia, photo, travel, Maryland book reviews, and successful business operations articles. Length: 800 to 2,300 words. Pays 6¢ a word, "except on assigned in-depth subjects on which price is negotiable." Buys photos with or without mss or on assignment. Captions required. Pays $20 per b&w photo; prefers 8½x11 b&w but will consider any size. Pays $25 per color photo. Uses 35mm, 2¼x2¼, 4x5, or 5x7.

METRO HAMPTON ROADS MAGAZINE, P.O. Box 7088, Norfolk VA 23509. Editor: St. Leger M. Joynes, Jr. For "the educatd and affluent mass market of Hampton Roads (7 cities)." Monthly. Circulation: 20,000. Buys all rights "with exceptions." Pays on publication. Will send a sample copy to a writer on request. Query first. Editorial deadlines 60 to 90 days prior to cover date. Reports in 2 weeks. Enclose S.A.S.E. for reply to queries.
Nonfiction:"Regional material on eastern Virginia, Hampton Roads metro area. Appeal to educated audience. Depth important; must cover northside as well as southside of Roads in dealing with general subjects. Urban magazine style and content." Stresses "in-depth, fully researched and investigated articles. Not afraid of controversy. Some satire and humor also used." National, international travel articles accepted. Length: 1,000 to 3,000 words. Pays 4¢ a word, 5¢ a word "with acceptable photos."
Photos: Purchased with mss. "Directly related to editorial content." Also, cover photos: "query first." 8x10 b&w glossies; 2¼x2¼ color transparencies. Pays $10 to $30 for single article photos, $250 for covers.

MEXICAN WORLD, 2617 E. Hennepin Ave., Minneapolis MN 55314. Executive Editor: Theodore J. Neuhaus. For Americans interested in Mexico, including visitors, American residents and students. Established in 1966. Monthly. Circulation: 10,000. Not copyrighted. Buys 50 mss a year. Payment on publication. Will send free sample copy to writer on request. Submit only complete ms. Will consider photocopied submissions. Submit special event articles or Christmas articles 3 months in advance. Reports in 1 month. Enclose S.A.S.E. for return of submissions.
Nonfiction: "Travel articles on particular cities or areas of Mexico that will keep frequent visitors abreast of what's happening in Mexico as well as articles to help introduce Mexico to visitors making their first trip. We publish articles which tend to expand the American tourist's understanding of Mexico and its people. Either personal account or general feature style. We would like to publish more articles on the popular fiestas that take place in Mexico." Informational, how-to, personal experience, humor, historical, photo, or travel articles. Length: 250 to 4,000 words. Pays $5 to $50.
Photos: Purchased with or without mss; captions required. 3x5 b&w glossies with mss. Color prints if used with mss; slides if for cover use. Pays $10 for cover photos.
Poetry: "This is a new experimental department. Poetry must relate to magazine subject matter." Length: 15 lines maximum. Payment in copies only.

MINNESOTAN, 1999 Shepard Rd., St. Paul MN 55116. Editor: Don Picard. For Minnesota Federal Savings & Loan depositors. Established in 1973. Quarterly. Circulation: 70,000. Buys all rights, but will usually reassign rights to author after publication. Buys 12 mss a year. Payment on acceptance. Will send free sample copy to writer on request. Write for copy of guidelines for writers. Query first or submit complete ms. Will consider photocopied submissions if accompanied by statement that it is not a simultaneous submission to other publications. Submit seasonal material 5 months in advance. Reports on ms accepted for publication in 2 to 3 weeks. Returns rejected material in 2 weeks. Enclose S.A.S.E. for reply to queries or return of submissions.
Nonfiction and Photos: "Articles and features about different facets of the State of Minnesota, its history, and some of the people who live there or within 100 miles of the Twin Cities. No special slant required, other than good, readable copy with an attention-grabbing lead." Length: 1,000 to 2,000 words. Pays $100 to $250. Pays $25 for 8x10 b&w photos which are used occasionally (either with or without accompanying ms), but greatest need is for color transparencies. 35mm or larger. Pays $50.

NEVADA HIGHWAYS AND PARKS MAGAZINE, Carson City NV 89701. Editor: Donald L. Bowers. For travel or vacation-minded people. Quarterly. Buys

North American serial rights only. Pays on acceptance. Will send sample copy to a writer for 75¢. Query first. Reports on submissions in 3 to 4 weeks. Enclose S.A.S.E.
Nonfiction: Nevada-related articles only. Pays 5¢ to 8¢ per word.
Photos: Nevada subject matter only; scenery, tours, activities such as ranching and mining; special events such as rodeos. Photos purchased with either mss or captions only. 4x5 color preferred. Pays $10 to $25 on acceptance for b&w prints; $20 to $40 for 4x5 color transparencies.

NEVADA MAGAZINE, Carson City NV 89701. Editor: Donald L. Bowers. For readers interested in Nevada. Official state publication. Established in 1936. Quarterly. Circulation: 60,000. Buys first serial rights. Buys 20 to 25 mss a year. Payment on publication. Query first or submit complete ms. Enclose S.A.S.E. for reply to queries or return of submissions.
Nonfiction and Photos: Articles on the Nevada theme: historical, travel, scenic, art, business and industry, etc. Suggest writers study the magazine. Reviews of books on Nevada. Length: 500 to 2,500 words. Pays 5¢ to 8¢ a word. 8x10 b&w glossies on Nevada topics. 4x5 color transparencies on Nevada topics (uses some 2¼).

NEW ENGLAND GALAXY, Old Sturbridge Village, Sturbridge MA 01566. Editor: Catherine Fennelly. For members of Old Sturbridge Village, and those interested in New England. Quarterly. Buys first North American rights. Pays on publication. Reports within 2 months. Enclose S.A.S.E. for return of submissions.
Nonfiction: Wants articles on New England history, biography, social customs, etc. Length: 2,000 to 3,000 words. Pays $50 to $150.
Photos: Buys 8x10 photos submitted with mss. Pays $5 each.
Poetry: Uses only the best in poetry—excellent serious verse on New England. Pays $50.
Fillers: Buys fillers; must be source material on New England. Pays $5 each.

THE NEW ENGLAND GUIDE, Box 108, Concord NH 03301. Editor: Stephen W. Winship. Annual. Circulation: 130,000. Buys first serial rights. Buys approximately 8 mss a year. Pays on publication. Will send a sample copy for $1.08. Query first. Annual deadline is February 28th. Reports in 2 months. Enclose S.A.S.E. for reply to queries.
Nonfiction: Articles on New England history, episodes, historic people, little-known events, offbeat essays on experiences. Puffs not wanted. "We do not want Paul Revere's ride—Longfellow did the most fascinating version over 100 years ago and it still stands. Instead, a few years ago we ran a piece about the man who hung the lanterns. Query us first and we will shape the piece with anyone asked to do one for the magazine." Taboo is "humor: most people can't write it." Length: 250 to 600 words. Pays $30 to $50.
Photos: Purchased with mss; with captions only. B&w glossies, color transparencies; color prints. Model releases required. Payment: b&w, "$8 a column (up to 3 columns wide) and up depending on subject, effort involved"; color, maximum $70.

NEW HAMPSHIRE ECHOES, 6 Odd Fellows Ave., Concord NH 03301. Editor: Brenda Joziatis. For readers looking for nostalgia about their native state and those seeking informative articles about crafts, tourist attractions, and home restoration. Bimonthly. Established in 1970. Circulation: over 11,000. Rights purchased vary with author and material. Buys 50 to 70 mss a year. Payment on publication. Will send sample copy to writer for $1. Query first for nonfiction. Submit complete mss for poetry and fillers. Submit seasonal material 4 months in advance. Reports in 3 weeks. Enclose S.A.S.E. for reply to query or return of submission.
Nonfiction and Photos: "All material must be related to New Hampshire; its history, contemporary crafts, interesting people and places. Submit material that hasn't already been done to death. Don't use the editorial 'we.' I'd like to see holiday-oriented pieces." Regular departments include: "Brush Away the Cobwebs," a full-length feature on a particular category of antiques, for example, temple glass or early NH wood stoves; "Nooks and Crannies," a shopping column featuring un-

usual restaurants, gift shops, etc. Informational, personal experience, interview, profile, humor, historical, nostalgia, and travel articles. Length: 1,500 maximum words. Pays $25. 4x5 or 5x7 b&w glossy photos used with accompanying mss. Captions required. Also uses color transparencies. "Photos seldom purchased per se. Our cover shots are donated; authors supply those for use with their articles."
Poetry and Fillers: Traditional forms, blank and free verse. Must relate to subject matter of magazine. Length: 25 lines maximum. Pays in contributor's copies. Short humor up to 200 words. Pays in contributor's copies.

NEW HAMPSHIRE PROFILES, 3 Sheafe St., Portsmouth NH 03801. Editor: Peter E. Randall. For persons in all age and income brackets. Monthly. Buys first rights. Buys 40 to 50 mss a year. Pays on publication. Will send a sample copy to a writer for 75¢. Query first. "Writers should be very familiar with New Hampshire." Deadlines are 4 months prior to publication. Reports in 1 month. Enclose S.A.S.E.
Nonfiction: Nostalgic articles pertaining to New Hampshire. No sex or personal subjects. Must be professionally written with a lively, readable style and all material must be appropriate to New Hampshire. Buys historical articles and pieces on antiques. Length: approximately 2,000 words. Pays $25 to $50.
Photos: Purchased with mss or with captions only. Uses photo essay treatment of New Hampshire subjects. 8x10 b&w glossies; 2¼ square, or larger, color. Pays $5 to $10, b&w; $15 minimum, color.

NEW MEXICO MAGAZINE, 113 Washington Ave., Santa Fe NM 87501. Editor: Walter Briggs. For persons interested in "travel, outdoors, arts, history. 50% spend 5 days or more per year in New Mexico; 50% in 45 to 65 age group; upper income; 47% college graduates; 55% receive information about New Mexico from no other publications." Bimonthly. Circulation: 100,000. Buys first rights. Buys approximately 60 mss a year. Pays on acceptance. Will send a sample copy to a writer for 75¢. Query first. Submit seasonal material 12 months in advance. Reports in 1 to 2 months. Enclose S.A.S.E. for reply to queries.
Nonfiction: Subjects include history, camping, travel, hunting, fishing, backpacking, restaurants, art, and resorts, among others. All should have a New Mexico background. No political articles. Purpose is to promote travel and outdoor activities in New Mexico. "Historical articles should contain original research—no rehashing. Articles should be specific—no generalized paeans to the state." Buys how-to's, personal experience and historical pieces, interviews, profiles, humor, photo and travel articles. Length: 300 to 4,000 words. Pays $10 to $400.
Photos: Purchased with mss; captions only. "No singles—only complete photo stories." Buys portfolios of New Mexico subjects. B&w glossies, color transparencies, 35mm color. "Practically all work on assignment." Pays $7.50 to $30, b&w; $15 to $36, color; $100 to $400 per assignment. Department Editor: Richard C. Sandoval.
Poetry: Traditional, contemporary, avant-garde, light verse. Length: "no maximum, but prefer short poems." Payment in contributor's copies.

NEW NORFOLK MAGAZINE, Chamber of Commerce Bldg., 475 St. Paul's Blvd., Norfolk VA 23510. Editor: June S. Morrisette. Published by Norfolk Chamber of Commerce. Audience is "predominantly business management, top executives, professionals. Varying interests of business, civic endeavors, sports, and culture in just about that order." Special issues include Statistical Digest (July), Buyers' Guide (November), Azalea Festival Program (April), and Waterfront issue (June). Monthly. Circulation: 3,300. Buys first serial rights. Buys approximately 6 to 12 mss a year. Pays on publication. Submit seasonal material 3 months in advance. Reports in 3 weeks. Enclose S.A.S.E. for return of submissions.
Nonfiction: How-to's, personal experience articles, interviews, profiles, humor, successful business operations, local historical pieces, photo essays. "It should be something the businessman or woman needs to know, would like to know, or didn't get complete coverage of in other media." Material should be slanted "toward the local picture—what does it have to do with, how does it affect Norfolk." Length: 500 to 3,000 words. Pays 20¢ per column inch.
Photos: Purchased with mss; with captions only. B&w glossies. Pays $5 each.

NEW ORLEANS MAGAZINE, 433 Gravier St., New Orleans LA 70130. Editor: George H. Bacon. Buys first serial rights. "All material must be in editorial depart-

ment 6 weeks prior to publication." Enclose S.A.S.E. for return of submissions.
Nonfiction: "Articles about New Orleans and Louisiana." Length: 5,000 words for features, 1,500 words for departments. Pays $150 for features, $75 for departments.

NEW YORK MAGAZINE, 207 E. 32nd St., New York NY 10016. Editor: Clay Felker. For intelligent readers in the New York area. Circulation: 325,000. Buys all rights. Pays on publication. Query first. Reports in 1 month. Enclose S.A.S.E. for reply to queries.
Nonfiction: Articles with ample reportage (not essays) about genuinely new or important aspects of the New York scene. Length: 1,000 to 3,500 words. Pays $100 to $350. Send material to Judith Daniels, Managing Editor.

NORTH/NORD, 400 Laurier Ave. West, Ottawa, Ontario, Canada K1A OH4. Editor: Sharon Doyle. For a varied audience, from school children to businessmen to diplomats, Canadian and international. Special Christmas issue and issues on Soviet North; transportation in the North. Established in 1959. Bimonthly. Circulation: 6,000. Rights purchased vary with author and material. Buys first North American serial rights or second serial (reprint) rights. Buys 100 mss a year. Payment on acceptance. Will send free sample copy to writer on request. Write for copy of guidelines for writers. Submit only complete mss. Submit seasonal material 4 months in advance. Enclose S.A.S.E. for return of submissions.
Nonfiction: "Subjects must pertain to Canada north or other northern areas of the world such as Alaska or Scandinavia. Topics can include resource development (business mining, pipeline, construction and oil and gas industries); history (exploration, archaeology, fur trade); conservation (wilderness, wildlife, national parks, geology); adventure and human interest stories; the arts (folklore, sculpture, print making etc.); life in the north (housing, transportation, education, communications, health and welfare, government, entertainments); native peoples (customs, lifestyle, organizations etc.); features on outstanding personalities of the north as well as northern communities." Length: 500 to 2,500 words. Pays $50 to $150.
Photos: Purchased with or without mss. "We use mainly b&w, but sometimes color prints from slides for covers or special features." Prefer 8x10 b&w. Pays from $7.50 to $10 for single shot; $20 to $25 for "Face of the North," a photo feature profile of northern personality or community. Pays $50 to $75 for cover photo.
Fiction and Poetry: Fiction should relate to the North. Length: 500 to 2,000 words. Pays $50 to $150. Traditional forms, blank verse, free verse, avant-garde forms and light verse should relate to the North. Pays $20 to $75 for poetry.

NORTHWEST EXPERIENCE, P.O. Box 399, Moscow ID 83843. Editor: A. J. Marineau. For "professional and general public interested in travel and vacation in the Northwest. Articles on what to do in the northwestern states from a first-person approach." Established in 1972. Quarterly. Circulation: 10,000. Not copyrighted. Uses 40 mss a year. Payment on publication. Will send free sample copy to a writer on request. Query first. Will consider photocopied submissions. Reports on material in 30 days. Enclose S.A.S.E.
Nonfiction and Photos: Sports, outdoor recreation, points of interest, history, arts and crafts, etc. Informational, how-to, personal experience, interview, profile, inspirational, humor, historical, think pieces, nostalgia, personal opinion, travel and new product. "First-person style in a complete enough manner that the reader can also enjoy the activity or area if he wishes." Length: 300 to 1,200 words. Pays $10 to $50. 8x10 b&w glossies bought with or without mss. Captions required. 35mm to 4x5 color. Pays "$5 individual to $40 pic story."

ON THE SOUND, 235 E. 45 St., New York NY 10017. Published by Universal Publishing Inc. Editor: Michael Durham. Articles Editor: Keith Wheeler. For Long Island Sound area; Westchester County, Connecticut, Rhode Island, Block Island Sound, and Vineyard Sound. Buys first North American serial rights. Pays on publication. Enclose S.A.S.E. for return of submissions.
Nonfiction and Photos: "Magazine's editorial thrusts: leisure, conservation, sports, and history." Length: 1,200 to 2,500 words. Pays $100 for one-page articles; $300 for a major piece. Pays $50 a page for b&w photos; $75 a page for 4-color prints.

ORLANDO-LAND MAGAZINE, Box 2207, Orlando FL 32802. Editor: Edward L. Prizer. For "middle and upper age, middle and upper income, above average education, businessmen, investors, persons moving to Florida from other areas, affluent leisuretime readers, travelers." Established in 1946. Monthly. Circulation: 30,000. Rights purchased vary with author and material. Buys 25 mss a year. Payment on publication. Will send a sample copy to writer for 50¢. Query first. Will consider photocopied submissions. Submit seasonal material 3 months in advance. Reports in 2 to 4 weeks. Enclose S.A.S.E. for reply to queries.
Nonfiction and Photos: General subject matter concerns "articles on central Florida subjects only." Approach "should be a personal experience article, casual and informal. Much of our material is comprised of directly quoted conversations with person interviewed. Always use the 'I' approach. We want nothing outside of central Florida. Seeking highly unusual experiences in central Florida. Real true-life adventures." Buys informational, how-to, personal experience, interview, profile, humor, historical, think, nostalgia, personal opinion, photo articles. Length: 500 to 5,000 words. Pays 2¢ a word. Dept. Editor: Ann Parks Linn. Buys 5x7 and 8x10 b&w glossies. Purchased with ms and caption required. Pays $5 per photo.

OUTDOOR ARIZONA, 1230 East Camelback Road, Phoenix AZ 85014. Editor: Bob Hirsch. "Anyone who enjoys the Arizona outdoors is a potential reader. While we used to be very strong on hunting and fishing, we've now broadened our editorial scope to include non-game animals and birds, trips, Indian ruins, conservation subjects, etc. We try to keep an Arizona slant, even though we have readers in many other parts of the country." Monthly. Circulation: 25,000. Not copyrighted. Buys 35 to 40 mss a year. Pays on publication. Will send a sample copy to a writer for 50¢. "Except for short pieces, we prefer a query and will answer them the same day. We often see mss that are dog-eared and obviously being sent as a last resort. That can't help but count against the writer." Returns rejected material in 1 week. Acknowledges acceptance of material in 1 month or less. Enclose S.A.S.E. for reply to queries or return of submissions.
Nonfiction and Photos: "We need short 100 to 300 word articles on camping hints, how-to-do, unusual facts about Arizona (or Southwestern) wildlife or flora—especially with a photo or two. Most feature articles have a strong local interest and almost need to be done by someone who lives here." Payment is 1¢ to 3¢ a word. B&w glossy photos, color transparencies, and 35mm color purchased with mss. Payment is $3 to $5 for b&w, $15 to $25 for color.

OUTDOOR INDIANA, Room 612, State Office Building, Indianapolis IN 46204. Editor: Herbert R. Hill. 10 times a year. Circulation: 28,000. Copyrighted. All material must relate to Indiana. Buys first serial rights. Pays on publication. Reports on submissions in 1 to 4 weeks. Query preferred. Enclose S.A.S.E.
Nonfiction and Photos: Informative, concise, illustrative, bright articles on Indiana-related topics. Length: 1,000 to 2,000 words. Payment by arrangement. Photos of Indiana interest only; purchased with mss or with captions only. B&w photos, 8x10; color transparencies, 2¼x 2¼ or larger. Pays up to $10 to $12.50 for b&w; $25 for color; $50 for color cover.

THE OZARKS MOUNTAINEER, P.O. Box 646, Forsyth MO 65653. Editor: Clay M. Anderson. For "a diverse national audience of people with a strong interest in the Ozarks region." 11 times a year. Circulation: 22,000. Buys all rights. Buys at least 100 mss a year. Pays on publication, sometimes on acceptance. Will send a sample copy to a writer for 25¢. No query required. "Do not submit unless you have reviewed a recent issue." Submit seasonal material 2 months in advance. Reports in about 1 month. Enclose S.A.S.E. for return of submissions.
Nonfiction and Photos: "Subjects that are important to the region—tourism, retirement, arts and crafts, folklore, history, natural resources, forestry, sports, agriculture, etc. All must have a regional slant. We are flooded with nostalgia—would prefer that new writers not try to write vernacular." Profiles, historical pieces, photo and travel essays. Length: 300 to 3,000 words; prefers 500 to 1,200 words. Pays 1¢ a word minimum. Photos purchased with mss. B&w glossies, color transparencies,

35mm color. Buys first rights "and the rights to re-use by this company." Pays $1 to $5.

Poetry: Traditional, light verse. Length: prefers short poems. Payment in sample copies and/or subscription.

PACIFIC MAGAZINE, Box 1578, Newport Beach CA 92660. Editor: D. Morrison. Quarterly. Circulation: 50,000. Buys first serial rights. Buys about 50 mss a year. Pays on publication. Query first. Reports in 1 month. Enclose S.A.S.E. for reply to queries.

Nonfiction and Photos: "Subjects of interest to traveler to Hawaiian Islands basically, but also to Micronesia and other areas rimming Pacific Basin. Matter dealing with tourist-orientated items; places to see; stories relative to history, legends, etc. about the islands. No 'my week's stay at Waikiki Beach' type material." Seeks material for regular departments, "Recipes of Island Cooking" and "Art in the Pacific." Buys personal experience and travel articles, interviews, profiles, coverage of successful business operations, historical articles, photo essays. Length: 1,000 to 2,000 words. Pays 5¢ to 10¢ a word. Photos purchased with mss. Color transparencies, 35mm color. Buys exclusive rights. Pays $5 to $25.

PACIFICA MAGAZINE, 822 G Street, Arcata CA 95521. Editor: Alann B. Steen. For "persons of all ages interested in outdoor Northwestern U.S." Established in 1971. Circulation: 10,000. Buys first serial rights. Buys about 30 mss a year. Payment on publication. Will send a sample copy to a writer for 60¢. Query first. Will consider photocopied submissions. All mss must be typed and double-spaced. Submit seasonal material at least 3 months in advance. Reports in 10 to 20 days. Enclose S.A.S.E. for reply to queries.

Nonfiction, Photos, and Poetry: "We ask for one's own style of writing and keep the subject angled to the area." Buys informational, how-to, personal experience, interview, profile, humor, historical, nostalgia, personal opinion, photo and travel articles. Length: 500 to 3,000 words. Pays 3¢ to 10¢ per word, "upper limit depends on length and quality." Photos are purchased with or without mss, captions are required. Pays $5 for 5x7 to 11x14 b&w photos. Poetry themes are open; uses traditional and avant-garde forms, and light, free, and blank verse. Length: 4 to 24 lines. Payment is in the form of one contributor's copy.

PALM BEACH LIFE, 204 Brazilian Avenue, Palm Beach FL 33480. Editor: Martha Musgrove. "*Palm Beach Life* caters to society (America's oldest society journal) and reflects their interests. Readers are affluent . . . usually over 40, well-educated." Special issues on the arts (February) and yachting (November), and elegant living, home, family, etc. (September-October). Established in 1906. Monthly with combined September-October issue. Circulation: 10,400. Buys all rights, but will reassign them to author after publication. Payment on acceptance. Will send a free sample copy to a writer on request. Query first. Will consider photocopied submissions. Submit seasonal material 5 months in advance. Reports in 3 weeks. Enclose S.A.S.E. for reply to queries.

Nonfiction and Photos: Subject matter involves "articles on fashion, travel, music (arts). Especially personality sketches of those in society or those who cater to it. We feature color photos, 'but are crying for good b&w'; also emphasize life in Palm Beach itself. Parties are overdone. Trying to show 'doers' in society." Buys informational, interview, profile, humor, historical, think, photo, and travel articles. Length: 1,000 to 2,500 words. Pays $50 to $125. Purchases photos with and without mss, on assignment, and captions are required. Buys 8x10 b&w glossies at $5 each. Also buys 35mm or 2¼x2¼ transparencies and photo stories. Pay is negotiable.

PHILADELPHIA MAGAZINE, 1500 Walnut St., Philadelphia PA 19102. Editor: Alan Halpern. Monthly. Circulation: 90,000. Buys all rights. Pays on publication. Query first. Reports in 2 weeks. Enclose S.A.S.E. for reply to queries.

Nonfiction: Articles with a Philadelphia slant only. No general interest material. Fast-moving, terse style. No puff pieces. Unusual life styles, the offbeat, unknown phenomena in Philadelphia and Philadelphian profiles. Length: 1,200 to 1,800 words. Typical recent article is "The $75 Million Misunderstanding," a story about mismanagement of the local Model Cities program. Pays $50 minimum.

Photos: If topical and accompany ms. Small additional payment for use.

PHOENIX MAGAZINE, 1230 East Camelback Road, Phoenix AZ 85014. Editor: Kenneth A. Welch. For "high income professional and white-collar workers. Age: 85% between 25 and 60 years." Established in 1966. Monthly. Buys all rights. Buys about 24 mss a year. Payment on publication. Will send free sample copy to a writer on request. Query first. Reports in 4 weeks. Enclose S.A.S.E. for reply to queries. **Nonfiction:** "Items of local interest, appropriate to a 'city' magazine." Payment is negotiable, $50 and up.

REDWOOD RANCHER, P.O. Box 1418, Santa Rosa CA 95403. Editor: A.L. Santucci. Monthly. Circulation: 6,800. Pays on acceptance. Will send free sample copy to a writer on request. Submit outline of article for prior approval. Reports on submissions immediately. Enclose S.A.S.E. for reply to queries or return of submissions.
Nonfiction: Articles of interest to readers oriented to the agricultural industry. Also articles on camping, hunting, fishing, riding, care of animals, etc. Prefers tie-in to the northern California area. Length: 1,200 to 2,000 words. Pays 2¢ per word.
Photos: Buys photos with mss. Glossy b&w, suitable for reproduction. Pays $1.25 per column inch (20 ems).

ST. LOUISAN, 6306 Clayton Rd., St. Louis MO 63117. Editor: Bobbi Linkemer. For "those interested in the St. Louis area, recreation issues, etc." Established in 1969. Monthly. Circulation: 20,000. Buys all rights but will reassign rights to author after publication; buys second serial (reprint) rights. Buys 60 mss a year. Payment on publication. Will send free sample copy to writer on request. Query first or submit complete ms. Will not consider photocopied submissions. Submit seasonal material 4 months in advance. Reports on material in 2 months. Enclose S.A.S.E.
Nonfiction and Photos: "Articles on the city of St. Louis, metro area, arts, recreation media, law, education, politics, timely issues, urban problems/solutions, environment, etc., generally related to St. Louis area. Looking for informative writing of high quality, consistent in style and timely in topic." Informational, how-to, personal experience, interview, profile, humor, historical, think pieces, expose, nostalgia, personal opinion, travel. Length: 1,000 to 5,000 words. Pays $50 to $100. 8x10 b&w glossies purchased on assignment. "Shooting fee plus $10 to $20 per print used. All color on individual basis."
Fiction: Regional theme not necessary. Experimental, mainstream, mystery, science fiction, fantasy, humorous, historical. Length: 1,000 to 5,000 words. Pays $50 to $100.
Poetry: Traditional forms, blank verse, free verse, avant-garde forms. Length: open. Pays $25 to $50.
Fillers: Puzzles, short humor. Length: open. Payment "individual."

SAN DIEGO MAGAZINE, 3254 Rosecrans, San Diego CA 92110. Editor: Ed Self. "Not seeking freelance material at this time because of large backlog of material on hand."

SAN FRANCISCO MAGAZINE, 120 Green St., San Francisco CA 94111. Editor: Terry Link. For an upper income audience; many professionals. Monthly. Circulation: 30,000. Buys first serial rights. Buys 40 to 50 mss a year. Pays on publication. Query first. Reports "as soon as possible." Enclose S.A.S.E. for reply to queries.
Nonfiction and Photos: Interested in articles dealing with personalities, places and events of interest to San Francisco Bay area readers. Profiles, historicals, inside on political or social scene, or on architecture and city planning; exposes, photo and travel pieces, humor, spot news, interviews. "No more articles on the 1906 Earthquake!" Length: 1,000 to 5,000 words. Pays $15 to $250. 8x10 glossy photos purchased with mss or with caption only. Pays minimum $15.

SANDLAPPER, P.O. Box 1668, Columbia SC 29202. Editor: Delmar L. Roberts. For families. Monthly. Buys all rights. Pays on publication. Will send a sample copy to a writer for $1.50. Write for copy of guidelines for writers. Query first, including a short outline of article, writing experience, and possibilities for illustrations. If acknowledgement of mss is desired, writer should enclose a self-addressed post card. Submissions will be returned only when accompanied by S.A.S.E.
Nonfiction: Features people, places, things and events existing in, or having a con-

nection with, South Carolina. Articles used include those pertaining to travel, the arts, historical events, personalities and collections, sports activities, recipes, festivals, architectural attractions, state-oriented industries, social and civic organizations. Length: 700 to 2,500 words. "Rates of payment: $25 for a one-page article to $100 for the major article of the month."

Photos: Pays $3 to $7 for b&w, $10 to $15 for color. Color transparencies may be 4x5, 35mm, or 2¼ square. B&w may be 5x7 or 8x10. Purchased with mss only.

SOUTH CAROLINA MAGAZINE, Box 89, Columbia SC 29202. Monthly. Not copyrighted. Pays on publication. Reports in about 1 week. Will send free sample copy on request. Enclose S.A.S.E. for return of submissions.
Nonfiction and Photos: Matters of interest to South Carolinians about state history, places, people, education, art, etc. Length: 500 to 1,000 words. Pays 2¢ a word. Photos purchased with mss. Glossy prints, 8x10 or 5x7. Pays $5.

SOUTHERN CALIFORNIA GUIDE, 501 S. Fairfax Ave. (No. 204), Los Angeles CA 90036. Editor: Louis Rangno. Does not buy freelance material.

SOUTHERN LIVING, 820 Shades Creek Pkwy., Birmingham AL 35209. Editor: Gary E. McCalla. For "middle and upper-income home owning families in the South." Monthly. Circulation: 1,000,000. Buys all rights. Buys 100 to 150 mss a year. Pays on acceptance. Will send a sample copy to a writer on request. No query required. Address material to the respective editor: John Logue, Managing Editor; Caleb Pirtle III, Travel Editor; Lena Sturges, Foods Editor; Philip Morris, Building and Landscaping Editor; H.C. Thompson, Garden Editor. Submit seasonal material 1 year in advance. Enclose S.A.S.E. for return of submissions.
Nonfiction: All articles must deal with southern subjects: travel and recreation, foods and entertaining, homes and buildings, gardening and landscaping, and personalities. Also publishes features on Southerners who are making contributions to the South in "This Is Their South" (350 to 400 words with b&w photos), and in major length pieces (2,000 to 3,000 words). Pays $30 to $300; approximately 10¢ a published word.
Photos: Purchased with mss. Must be quality, first class professional work. Payment depends on quality. Pays up to $25 for b&w, $100 for color, $300 for covers.

SOUTHERN OUTDOORS MAGAZINE, 6300 Westpark Drive, Suite 430, Houston TX 77027. Editor: Charles Coffen. For residents of the southern portion of the United States. Bimonthly. "We buy first rights in our field." Payment on acceptance. Write for copy of guidelines for writers. Submit seasonal material 6 months in advance. Reports on material in 2 weeks. Enclose S.A.S.E. for return of submissions.
Nonfiction and Photos: Travel articles. "These articles need not necessarily concern themselves with hunting, fishing, camping or boating. Generally, they are aimed at the vacationer . . . things to see and do in a specific area, town or city." Length: 1,800 to 2,000 words. Pays $100 for ms with 8x10 b&w photos, $125 with color transparencies. Length for short subjects: 500 words. Pays $35 for copy and pictures. 35mm color transparencies considered for color covers. 2¼ square on up to 4x5. Pays $100.

THE STATE, P.O. Box 2169, Raleigh NC 27602. Editor: W.B. Wright. Monthly. Copyrighted. Will send a free sample copy on request. Pays on acceptance. Deadlines 1 month in advance of publication date. Enclose S.A.S.E. with submissions.
Nonfiction and Photos: "General articles about places, people, events, history, general interest in North Carolina. Also reports on business, new developments within the state. Emphasis on travel in North Carolina; (devote features regularly to resorts, travel goals, dining and stopping places)." Will use humor if related to region. Length: average of 1,000 to 1,200 words. Pays $25 average, $15 minimum. B&w photos purchased with mss. Pays average of $5; minimum of $3.

SUBURBAN NEW JERSEY LIFE, Box 40, Maplewood NJ 07040. Editor: Carlette M. Winslow. For readers with cultural interests; geared to NJ as a regional magazine. Established in 1931. Monthly, with June/July and December/January combined issues. Rights purchased vary with author and material. Buys first North

American serial rights, sometimes second serial (reprint) rights. Buys 20 to 30 mss a year. Payment on publication. Will send sample copy to writer for 65¢. Will consider photocopied submissions. Submit seasonal material 3 months in advance. Enclose S.A.S.E.

Nonfiction and Photos: "Articles about New Jersey issues, people, culture, history, where to go and what to do. Writer must know region thoroughly. We want comprehensive wrap-up articles about trends, using specific people, organizations, etc. as examples. Suburban lifestyles applicable to New Jersey." Informational, how-to, personal experience, profile, historical, think articles, and photo features. Length: 2,500 to 3,500 words. Pays $25 to $100. B&w glossies purchased with mss.

TEXAS METRO MAGAZINE, P.O. Drawer 5566, Arlington TX 76011. Editor: Dr. Dora Dougherty Strother. Executive Editor: S.D. Johnson. General audience: over half are college graduates, 90% are married, 38% are professionals, 30% are business executives, 15% own their own businesses. General subject matter includes "articles on travel, better living, and investment as it relates to north central Texas, a 10-county area that includes Dallas and Fort Worth." Monthly. Buys all rights. Pays on publication. Will send a sample copy to a writer on request. Query first. Submit seasonal material 3 months before publication. Enclose S.A.S.E.

Nonfiction: Editorial content includes home living, travel, sports, entertainment, personalities, education, culture, and business related to the general geographic area. Appropriate visuals must accompany articles, i.e. photos, graphs, illustrations. Articles must be aimed generally at a college-level intellect. Must contain facts which can be absorbed by scanning; loose enough to be readable, but meaty. Length: 200 to 1,000 words. Payment varies with the quality of writing and research. There are two sections in which freelance writers writing about Texas, Louisiana, Arkansas, Oklahoma, New Mexico, and Colorado stand a good chance of scoring regularly: The "Metro Travel" section and "Metro Living" section. *Texas Metro* invites attention to the "Recipes of the Southwest" (which includes the aforementioned states) and for which submissions are also solicited.

Photos: "Cover photographs should deal with travel, cooking, gardening, homes, and better living. Payment for cover photos starts at $25. Also will buy striking photos of regional interest which stand alone, sports or scenery, etc. Payment starts at $5."

TEXAS PARADE, P.O. Box 12037, Austin TX 78711. Editor: Kenneth E. Lively. Monthly. Circulation: 42,000. Will send a free sample copy on request. Reports in 1 month. Buys North American serial rights only. Pays on publication. Editorial deadlines are 1½ months preceding publication month. Enclose S.A.S.E. for return of submissions.

Nonfiction: Articles on travel, scenic attractions, business, history, sports and the outdoors with strong Texas slant. Length: 1,000 to 3,000 words. Pays $25 per printed page.

Photos: Purchased with mss and with captions. General Texas subject matter. 8x10 b&w. Pays $10 to $15.

TORONTO LIFE MAGAZINE, 56 The Esplanade, Toronto, 1, Canada. Editor: John Macfarlane. For "adults and late teens with one mutual interest—metropolitan Toronto and area: its pleasures and problems." Monthly. Buys first serial rights. Buys approximately 120 mss a year. Pays on acceptance. Query first. "Study our magazine." Submit seasonal material 3 to 4 months in advance. Reports in 2 weeks. Enclose S.A.S.E. for reply to queries.

Nonfiction: Concerning Toronto, "of either a service or searching nature. We are not interested in anything outside our area; it follows that writers outside our area have little chance of breaking in." Buys profiles, think pieces, exposes. Length: 500 to 2,500 words. Payment by arrangement.

TRENTON MAGAZINE, 104 North Broad Street, Trenton NJ 08608. Editor: Donna M. Amick. For "chamber members, government and education leaders and persons interested in the Trenton-Mercer County area." Established in 1924. Monthly. Circulation: 6,000. Buys all rights, but will reassign them to author after publication. Buys 20 to 25 mss a year. Payment on publication. Will send free sample copy to a writer on request. Query first. Reports in 6 weeks. Enclose S.A.S.E.

Nonfiction: Subject matter is "stories of community interest—with a business slant when possible. Also historical and historical figure pieces." Buys humor, historical, and nostalgia articles. Length: 1,000 to 5,000 words. Pays $10 to $100.

TULSA MAGAZINE, 616 S. Boston, Tulsa OK 74119. Editor: Larry Silvey. Audience is primarily medium to upper income level Tulsans. Monthly. Circulation: 6,000. Not copyrighted. Pays on publication. Will send sample copy for 25¢. Deadlines are at least 6 weeks prior to publication date, which is normally on the first Thursday of each month. Queries requested first. Reports immediately. Enclose S.A.S.E.
Nonfiction and Photos: Articles must revolve around people or how subject affects people and must have a Tulsa area slant. Style desired is informal and lively. 1,000 to 4,000 words. Payment is negotiable, $50 to $75, depending on length, research. Photos usually taken by staff or on assignment. May be purchased with mss.

VERMONT LIFE MAGAZINE, 63 Elm St., Montpelier VT 05602. Editor: Brian Vachon. Quarterly. Buys first rights. "Query is essential." Enclose S.A.S.E.
Nonfiction: Wants articles on Vermont, those which portray a typical and, if possible, unique, attractive aspect of the state or people. Style should be literate, clear and concise. Subtle humor favored. Word length averages 1,500 words. Payment averages 10¢ per word.
Photos: Buys photographs with mss and with captions only. Prefers b&w, 8x10 glossies or matte prints, except on assignment. Color submissions must be 4x5 or 35mm transparencies. Buys one-time rights, but often negotiates for re-use rights also. Rates on acceptance; b&w, $10; color, $50 inside, $100 for cover. Gives assignments but not on first trial with photographers. Query first.

VIRGINIA CARDINAL, Box 334, Vienna VA 22180. Editor: Richard H. Weller. Monthly. Pays on publication. Query first. "Because of our limited staff, unsolicited mss cannot be handled." Enclose S.A.S.E.
Nonfiction and Photos: "The main circulation of this magazine is in northern Virginia and metropolitan Washington. This area is one of the most affluent and influential in the nation. The magazine reflects the concerns and interests of its readers in the good life. Articles on travel, fashion, sports, gourmet food, books, and history are staff-written. However, freelance writers will find a ready market for feature articles with a fresh and different approach to Virginia's people, places, progress, and problems." Length: 1,500 to 2,500 words. Pays $25 per article. "Articles should be accompanied by photos whenever possible."

WASHINGTONIAN MAGAZINE, 1218 Connecticut Ave., N.W., Washington DC 20036. Editor: Laughlin Phillips. "For a well-educated, high income audience." Monthly. Circulation: 44,000. Buys first rights. Buys approximately 50 mss a year. Pays on publication. Will send a sample copy to a writer for $1. Query first. Submit seasonal material 2 months in advance. Reports in 2 weeks. Enclose S.A.S.E.
Nonfiction and Photos: "The *Washingtonian* is written for Washingtonians. The subject matter is anything we feel might interest people interested in the mind and manners of the city. The style, as Wolcott Gibbs said, should be the author's—if he is an author, and if he has a style. The only thing we ask is thoughtfulness and that no subject be treated too reverently. Audience is literate. We assume considerable sophistication about the city, and a sense of humor." Buys how-to's, personal experience, interviews, profiles, humor, coverage of successful business operations, think pieces, and exposes. Length: 1,000 to 7,000 words; average feature, 3,000 words. Pays 7¢ to 10¢ a word. Photos purchased with mss. B&w glossies, color transparencies, 35mm color. Payment is from $15 "for small spot" to $100 "for full page." Department Editor: A.P. Bornstein.
Fiction: "Must be Washington-oriented." Length: open. Pays 7¢ to 10¢ a word. Department Editor: Jack Limpert.
Poetry: "Washington-oriented." Length: open. Payment negotiable. Department Editor: Ellen Phillips.

WESTWAYS, P.O. Box 2890, Terminal Annex, Los Angeles CA 90051. Executive Editor: N.J. Kockler. Editor: Davis Dutton. For "fairly affluent, college-educated, mobile and active Southern California families. Average age of head of household

is 46; median income of family is $13,200." Monthly. Buys first rights. Buys approximately 250 mss a year. Pays on acceptance for mss; on publication for most photos. Query preferred. Submit seasonal material at least 4 to 6 months in advance. Reports in 3 to 6 weeks. Enclose S.A.S.E. Currently has large inventory of material.
Nonfiction: "Informative articles, well-researched and written in fresh, literate, honest style." This publication "covers all states west of the Rockies, including Alaska and Hawaii, western Canada and Mexico. We're willing to consider anything that interprets and illuminates the American West—past or present—for the Western American family. Employ imagination in treating subject. Avoid PR hand-out type style and format, and please know at least something about the magazine." Subjects include "travel, history, modern civic, cultural, and sociological aspects of the West; camping, fishing, natural science, humor, first-person adventure and experience, nostalgia, profiles, and occasional unusual and offbeat pieces. One article a month on foreign travel." Length: 1,000 to 3,000 words. Pays 10¢ a word and up.
Photos: Buys color and b&w photos with or without mss. Prefers 8x10 b&w glossies. Often publishes photo essays. Pays $25 minimum "for each b&w used as illustration;" $25 to $200 per transparency.
Poetry: Publishes 12 to 15 poems a year. Length: up to 24 lines; "occasionally longer." Pays $25.

WINDOW OF VERMONT, Box 215, Londonderry VT 05148. Editor: Calista Brown. For "the tourists visiting the state of Vermont and for the local residents during their recreational time. Subscribers are from around the world, of all ages and backgrounds." Established in 1970. Monthly. Circulation: 76,000. Rights purchased vary with author and material. Buys about 60 mss a year. Pays on publication. Will send a sample copy to a writer on request. Will consider photocopied submissions. Submit seasonal material at least 1 month in advance. Reports in 2 weeks. Enclose S.A.S.E. for return of submissions.
Nonfiction and Photos: "Our editorial is restricted to historical, recreational, environmental, and cultural subjects. Articles must pertain to forthcoming or timeless events, places, and people within Vermont. We want a light, informal style. Nothing heavy unless it involves the environment. Please, no snowmobile articles. We would like to see coverage of sports, festivals, concerts, museums, towns, artisans, maple sugaring, fall foliage, Christmas in New England. For the May issue, we use general summer articles. For November, we use hunting articles." Buys informational articles, personal experience articles, interviews, profiles, historical and nostalgia pieces, photo features, travel articles, and coverage of successful business operations. Length: 3 typewritten double-spaced pages maximum. Pays $20; "payment will increase with the growth of the publication." 8x10 b&w glossies purchased with mss. Pays $6.

WISCONSIN TRAILS, P.O. Box 5650, Madison WI 53705. Editor: Jill Weber Dean. For readers interested in natural beauty, history and folklore, recreation, and the arts. Established in 1960. Quarterly. Circulation: 20,000. Rights purchased vary with author and material. "We would like to buy exclusive rights in many cases." Payment on publication. Will send free sample copy to writer on request. Write for copy of guidelines for writers. "We prefer writers send queries or outlines." Will consider photocopied submissions. Submit seasonal material 1 year in advance. Reports in 1 month. Enclose S.A.S.E. for reply to query or return of submission.
Nonfiction: "Our articles focus on some aspect of Wisconsin life; an interesting site or event, a person or industry, or history and the arts. We do not use first-person essays, ecstacies about scenery, or biographies about people who were born in Wisconsin and immediately left the state. Feature articles range from 1,500 to 3,000 words. How-to, profile, historical, nostalgia, travel, and successful business operations articles." Length: 1,500 to 3,000 words. Pays $50 to $250, depending on length and quality. For "Where to Go, What to Do" section, pays $15 for 300 words and b&w photo.
Photos: Purchased without mss or on assignment. Captions optional. B&w photos usually illustrate a given article. Color is mostly scenic. B&w photo of a site, event, etc. for "Where to Go, What to Do" section. Pays $10 each for b&w on publication. Pays $50 for 35mm color.

YANKEE, Main St., Dublin NH 03444. Editor: Judson D. Hale. Monthly. Material relates to New England people, places, things. Usually buys all rights. Pays on acceptance. Will send free sample copy to a writer on request. Reports in 3 weeks. Enclose S.A.S.E. for return of submissions.

Nonfiction: About New England and/or New Englanders, past, present or future; interesting people, activities, controversies if of wide interest, especially the unusual in all events; historical, particularly if there is some present-day tie-in. Does not like colloquial style; taboos include "booze, sex, insanity, profanity, dope, etc." Length: 1,500 to 2,500 words. Illustrations help put a feature across. Pays $25 to $400, average $250 to $350, depending on quality, importance, manner of presentation, number of photos, etc.

Photos: Purchased with mss and with identifications only. Current New England seasonal scenics; also unusual old-time photos. Pays $25 on publication or $15 on acceptance for one-time rights. Color transparencies are often used with articles.

Fiction: Must be placed in New England either by specific location, general reference or simply by New England-type setting; or, if a city, then a New England city, such as Boston. Length: 1,500 to 2,500 words. Pays from $25 to $400; average $300 to $400, depending on quality, etc.

Poetry: Uses modern poetry. Study previous issues to determine type of material desired. Pays $25 per poem. Reports on poetry submissions in about three weeks.

YOSEMITE, P.O. Box 545, Yosemite National Park CA 95389. "Occasionally buys scientific material on natural history and human history of Sierra Nevada."

Religious Publications

Magazines in this category publish educational and inspirational religious material of interest to a general audience (including students, members, workers, and leaders) within a denomination or religion. Publications intended to assist lay and professional religious workers in teaching and managing church affairs are classified in Church Administration and Ministry in the Trade Journals section. Religious magazines for children and teenagers will be found in the Juvenile, and Teen and Young Adult classifications.

Many editors in this section have indicated whether or not they accept simultaneous submissions—submissions of a ms made to several magazines with noncompetitive circulation at the same time.

A.D., 475 Riverside Drive, New York NY 10027. Address mss to the Editors. Established in 1972. Published in two editions: one is for members of the Presbyterian Church; one is for members of the United Church of Christ. Circulation: 727,969. Always query first. Enclose S.A.S.E. for reply to queries.

Nonfiction and Fiction: The first half of the magazine contains articles of interest to both Presbyterian and United Church of Christ readers. Every issue carries at least one major piece on some important political or social problem. Length: varies. Payment is open. The Presbyterian half uses "platform" pieces, articles expressing individual opinion; personality pieces; and news stories that aren't merely of interest within some local parish. Length: 800 to 1,000 words (personality pieces), to 400 words (news items), and to 2,000 words (articles). Pays 2¢ a word minimum; average $80 to $100 per article. Length: 650 to 800 words. Pays minimum 2¢ a word. The United Church half uses news of national interest—articles on church life, community action, meditational, and self-help pieces. Length: Keep news brief, 1,000 to 3,000 words for articles. Pay is $25 to $100. The only fiction is an occasional story of seasonal interest, such as Christmas and Easter. Length: to 2,500 words. Payment is $25.

ALL-CHURCH PRESS, INC., P.O. Box 1159, Fort Worth TX 76101. Editor: Walter A. Winsett. Publishers of religious newspapers. Established in 1912. Weekly. Circulation: 100,000. Not copyrighted. Payment on publication. Will send free

sample copy to writer on request. Query first or submit complete ms. Will not con
sider photocopied submissions. Submit special material for Christmas and Easter 2
months in advance. Reports on material in 2 weeks. Enclose S.A.S.E. for return of
submissions.
Nonfiction and Photos: "Articles, human interest items, news features on all aspects
of Christian living, religion in general." Interview, profile, inspirational, humor,
historical, reviews of religious books. Length: 100 to 1,000 words. Pays $10 to $100;
more for special assignments. 8x10 b&w glossies purchased with or without accompanying ms. Captions not required. Pays $10 to $15.
Poetry: All forms of poetry. Length: Approximately 10 to 25 lines. Pays $10 to $25.

AMERICA, 106 W. 56th St., New York NY 10019. Editor: Donald R. Campion, S.J.
Published weekly for adult, educated, largely Roman Catholic audience. Usually
buys all rights. Pays on acceptance. Reports in two or three weeks. Enclose S.A.S.E.
for return of submissions.
Nonfiction and Poetry: Articles, 1,500 to 2,000 words on literature, current political
and social events. Pays $50 to $75. Poetry length: 10 to 30 lines. Address to Poetry
Editor.

AMERICAN REVIEW OF EASTERN ORTHODOXY, 1908 Highway 17-92, Fern
Park FL 32730. Editor: Right Reverend Gregory Adair. For "Eastern Orthodox
clergy, churches, libraries, seminaries, and members of the faith." 10 times a year.
Circulation: 3,000. Not copyrighted. Buys 2 or 3 mss a year. Pays on acceptance.
Will send a sample copy to a writer for 25¢. Reports immediately. Enclose S.A.S.E.
for return of submissions.
Nonfiction: "Articles on Eastern Orthodox thought, experience, or events. No fiction, poetry, or wild ideas—only Eastern Orthodox subject matter." Interviews, profiles, spot news, historical articles, exposes, travel, photo essays. Length: 100 to 1,000
words. Pays $5 for 100 words with photo; $40 for 1,000 words with 3 to 5 photos.
Photos: Purchased with mss or with captions only "if no story available and accompanied by 100 words of description." B&w glossies. Pays $5 each minimum "de-
pending on subject, etc."

ANNALS OF GOOD SAINT ANNE DE BEAUPRE, Basilica of St. Anne, Que.,
Canada. Editor: Rev. Jean-Claude Nadeau, C.Ss.R., for Catholic families, especially women readers. Monthly. Circulation: 75,000. Buys first North American serial rights. Buys approximately 150 mss a year. Pays on acceptance. Will send a
sample copy to a writer on request. Query first. Submit seasonal material 2 months
in advance. Reports in 3 weeks. Enclose S.A.E. and International Reply Coupons
for reply to queries.
Nonfiction: "Articles on devotion to St. Anne, major social problems of today, education, ecumenism, family, etc." Interviews, profiles, inspirational and think pieces,
humor. Roman Catholic slant. Religious articles of interest to a wide public. Read
issues of magazine before submitting. Length: 800 to 1,800 words. Pays 1½¢ to 2¢
per word.
Photos: Purchased with mss and returned after use if requested. Pays $25 to $40 for
color transparencies.
Fiction: Short stories with strong plot treated in fresh, original manner. Little or no
slang. Must not offend Catholic principles or be too goody-goody. Aimed at providing sound Catholic literature for a Catholic family magazine for readers of average
education and culture. Writers need not necessarily be Catholic. Length: 1,500 to
1,700 words.
Fillers: Short humor.

APPLIED CHRISTIANITY, 407 S. Dearborn St., Chicago IL 60605. Editor: James
M. Wall. For churchmen (lay and clerical) of all faiths. Weekly. Payment is made
on publication of material. Usually buys all rights. Will consider photocopied submissions. Enclose S.A.S.E. for return of submissions.
Nonfiction, Photos, and Poetry: "We consider articles of 2,400 words on all subjects
of public concern and controversy to which religion is related." Pays 2¢ a word.
Buys b&w glossies. Pays $15 to $35. Prefers short poems. No payment.

ASPIRE, 1400 Williams St., Denver CO 80218. Editor: Jeanne Pomranka. For teens and adults: "those who are looking for a way of life that is practical, logical, spiritual, or inspirational." Monthly. Circulation: 2,900. Buys 180 to 190 mss a year. Pays on publication. Will send a sample copy to a writer for an 8¢ stamp. Query first. Submit seasonal material 6 to 7 months in advance. Reports in 2 weeks. Enclose S.A.S.E.
Nonfiction: Uses inspirational articles that help to interpret the spiritual meaning of life. Needs are specialized, since this is the organ of the Divine Science teaching. Personal experience, inspirational, think pieces. Also seeks material for "God at Work," a department "written in the form of letters to the editor in which the writer describes how God has worked in his life or around him. 'Teen Talk' includes short articles from teenagers to help other teenagers find meaning in life." Length: 250 to 1,500 words. Pays maximum 1¢ per published word.
Fiction: "Anything that fits in with Divine Science teaching." Length: 250 to 1,000 words. Pays maximum 1¢ per published word.
Poetry: Traditional, contemporary, light verse. "We use very little poetry." Length: average 8 to 16 lines. Pays $2 to $4.

BAPTIST HERALD, 7308 Madison Street, Forest Park IL 60130. Dr. Reinhold J. Kerstan. For "any age from 15 and up, any educational background with mainly religious interests." Established in 1935. Monthly. Circulation: 12,000. Buys all rights. Payment on publication. Will send a free sample copy to a writer on request. Submit seasonal material 3 to 4 months in advance. Enclose S.A.S.E. for return of submissions.
Nonfiction and Fiction: "We want articles of general religious interest. Seeking articles that are precise, concise, and honest. We hold a rather conservative religious line." Buys personal experience, interviews, inspirational, and personal opinion articles. Regular columns that seek personality profiles material and stories of Christian living and action. Length: 700 to 2,000 words. Payment is $5 to $10. Buys religious and historical fiction. Length: 700 to 2,000 words. Pays $5 to $10.

BAPTIST LEADER, Valley Forge PA 19481. Editor: Vincie Alessi. For ministers, teachers, and pupils in church schools. Monthly. Buys first rights, or as agreed by author. Pays on acceptance. Will send free sample copy to a writer on request. Reports on submissions in one month. Enclose S.A.S.E. for ms return.
Nonfiction: Educational topics and social issues. Length: 750 to 1,500 words. Pays 1½ to 3¢ per word. Read magazine before submitting. Deadlines are seven months prior to date of issue.
Photos: Church school settings; church, worship, children's and youth activities and adult activities. Purchased with mss. B&w, 8x10; human interest and seasonal themes. Pays $5 to $10.

BAPTIST MEN'S JOURNAL, 1548 Poplar Avenue, Memphis TN 38104. Acting Editor: Steven E. Wall. For "ages 18 and up; conservative; high school education." Subject matter is "slanted toward men and missions." Monthly. Circulation: 50,000. Buys first North American serial rights. Buys 15 mss a year. Payment on acceptance. Will send free sample copy to writer on request. Will send editorial guidelines sheet to a writer on request. Will consider photocopied submissions. Reports in 2 weeks. Enclose S.A.S.E. for return of submissions.
Nonfiction, Fiction, and Photos: Buys informational articles. Length: 500 to 1,600 words. Pays 2½¢ a word. Buys humorous and religious fiction. Length: 500 to 1,600 words. Pays 2½¢ a word. Buys photos with mss and captions are required. Pays $5 to $10 for 8x10 or 5x7 b&w glossies.

BRIGADE LEADER, Box 150, Wheaton IL 60187. Editor: Daniel Jessen. For "men leading boys." Quarterly. Buys all rights. Pays on publication. Will send a sample copy to a writer on request. Write for copy of guidelines for writers. Query first. Reports in 3 to 5 weeks. Enclose S.A.S.E. for reply to queries.
Nonfiction and Fiction: Dealing with "men, boys, and Christian life." Length: 800 to 1,200 words. Pays 1¢ to 3¢ a word.

CANADIAN CHURCHMAN, 600 Jarvis St., Toronto, Ont. M4Y 2J6, Canada. Editor: Hugh B. McCullum. To general audience; adult with religio-socio emphasis.

Special youth section: Trend. Monthly. Not copyrighted. Circulation: 254,000. Anglican (Episcopalian). Will send free sample copy to writer on request. Pays on publication. Reports within 2 weeks. Include S.A.E. and International Reply Coupons.
Nonfiction: 750 to 1,200 words on religion (noninspirational) social action, morality. Social conditions, new religious trends, entertainment, some politics. Pays $35 to $250. Query suggested.
Photos: Purchased with ms for illustration. News photos with captions only. 8x10 glossy. Pays $10 and up.
Poetry: Limited to youth, by youth.

THE CATHOLIC DIGEST, P.O. Box 3090, St. Paul MN 55165. Editor: Fr. Kenneth Ryan. Monthly. Circulation: 500,000. 95% reprint. Buys Catholic magazine rights. Pays on acceptance. Query first. Deadlines 4 to 6 months prior to publication. Reports in 2 weeks. Enclose S.A.S.E. for reply to queries.
Nonfiction: Timely subjects; avoid history, lives of saints, visits to shrines, etc., unless new angle. Articles of general interest in science, health, education, travel, humor, etc., plus articles on current religious developments, parish life, and religious leader profiles. Length: 2,000 to 2,500 words. Pays $75 to $200.
Photos: Purchased with mss; strong family interest—interesting church, parish life abroad, etc. Uses one photo feature per issue. Also uses one color shot for cover each month; prefers subject with religious and timely significance. Can work from contact sheets or good selection of 8x10's. Pays $100 per photo feature.
Fillers: Regular features: "In Our Parish"; "People Are Like That"; "Hearts Are Trumps"; "Flights of Fancy"; "The Open Door" (about conversion); "Signs of the Times." Pays from $5 to $50.

CATHOLIC LIFE, 9800 Oakland Ave., Detroit MI 48211. Editor: Robert C. Bayer. For Catholic families with "interests centering on the factual missionary activities of the Catholic Church worldwide, particularly the overseas (Asia, Africa, Latin America) mission field." 10 times a year. Circulation: 15,750. Buys first rights. Buys 30 to 40 mss a year. Pays on publication. Will send a sample copy to a writer on request. No query for mission-related material; query first for non-mission-related material. Submit seasonal material 4 to 5 months in advance. Reports in 10 days. Enclose S.A.S.E. for return of submissions or reply to queries.
Nonfiction and Photos: Missionary topics relating to Burma, India, Bangladesh, Japan, Hong Kong, the Philippines, Africa, Latin America. Style should be reportorial. Figures cited should be exact. Where individuals are featured, releases should accompany the script. Illustrative photos that advance the story should also be included. Taboos: "The chaos and turmoil within the Church today and the civil rights approaches." Length: 800 to 1,400 words. Pays 2¢ per printed word; $2 for each photo used.

CATHOLIC RURAL LIFE, 3801 Grand Ave., Des Moines IA 50312. Editor: The Rev. Msgr. John Geo. Weber. Monthly. Will accept simultaneous submissions of articles, short stories. Will send free sample copy on request. Enclose S.A.S.E. for ms return.
Nonfiction and Photos: Buys an average of two articles per issue. Short articles preferred, with a Christian approach to rural topics and problems. None over 1,200 words. Material must have interesting presentation of facts or events in rural communities. B&w photos or drawings to illustrate articles welcomed. Payment varies. Buys photos with mss, but not more than two per article. Any size b&w.
Fiction: Not especially interested in fiction, but will consider that which teaches a lesson. Skits on rural life will be considered. Should not be over 15 minutes in length. Simple setting.

CHICAGO STUDIES, Box 665, Mundelein IL 60060. Editor: Rev. George J. Dyer. Published 3 times a year for a clerical readership. Buys all publication rights. Pays on acceptance. Reports in 6 weeks. Enclose S.A.S.E. for return of submissions.
Nonfiction: Uses articles concerning theology, canon law, Scripture, liturgy, philosophy; 3,000 to 6,000 words. Pays 2¢ a word.

CHILD EVANGELISM MAGAZINE, P.O. Box 1156, Grand Rapids MI 49501. Editor: The Rev. Paul W. Bennehoff. Monthly. Circulation: 30,000. Interdenominational, international and interracial Christian publication for families, parents, teachers. Usually buys one-time rights. Pays on acceptance. Will send a free sample copy to a writer upon request. Reports in two months. Enclose S.A.S.E. with all submissions.

Nonfiction: Articles by both educational leaders and homemakers should run approximately 1,200 to 1,500 words and deal with any type of family problem or activity. They should be positive in tone and include illustrative examples. Resolutions or objectives should be both spiritual and/or scriptural. For "Leaders' Notebook," uses how-to-do-it articles on programs, projects and other topics of interest to Sunday school superintendents, teachers, and leaders of other children's groups. Pays 1¢ per word for first rights; 2¢ per word for all rights, but usually buys first rights only.

Fiction: Two stories are used each month in the "Children's Section"—a junior story of 1,000 to 2,000 words and a primary story of 450 to 500 words. Both should contain action, conversation and a definite problem for the lead character to solve. They may be either on salvation or a step in Christian growth and should be evangelical in tone without being preachy. Pays 1¢ per word for first rights; 2¢ per word for all rights, with first rights only usually bought.

Poetry and Fillers: Used in the children's section, short poetry with a spiritual and scriptural basis. Short quizzes and puzzles used in the children's section. Must have a spiritual and scriptural basis. Pays 10¢ a line for poetry; average of $2 for puzzles and quizzes.

CHRISTIAN ADVENTURER, P.O. Box 850, Joplin MO 64801. Editor: Mrs. Marthel Wilson. General religious for those 13 through 19 years of age. Quarterly in weekly parts. Circulation: 5,000. Buys second serial (reprint) rights and simultaneous rights. Buys 115 mss a year. Quarterly pay periods. Will send free sample copy to writer on request. Write for copy of guidelines for writers. Submit complete ms. Will consider photocopied submissions. Submit seasonal material 9 months in advance. Reports on material accepted for publication in 2 months. Returns rejected material in 1 month. Enclose S.A.S.E. for return of submissions.

Nonfiction: "We use only material which takes the fundamental Christian point of view." Informational, personal experience, interview, inspirational, historical, think pieces, nostalgia. Length: 1,500 maximum; 1 paragraph minimum. Pays ¼¢ a word.

Fiction: Only religious. Preferred length: 1,500 words. Pays ¼¢ a word.

Poetry: Traditional forms, blank verse, light verse. Length: open. Pays $1 per poem.

Fillers: Religious puzzles and items of personal experience. Length: 1 paragraph to 500 words. Pays ¼¢ a word.

THE CHRISTIAN ATHLETE, Fellowship of Christian Athletes, 812 Traders National Bank Bldg., 1125 Grand Avenue, Kansas City MO 64106. Editor: Gary Warner. For "general audience of all ages interested in athletics, especially as it involves the perspective of the Christian faith. Large segment includes high school, college and professional athletes and coaches." Established in 1959. Monthly. Circulation: 50,000. Uses 15 to 25 mss a year. Payment on publication. Will send free sample copy and editorial guidelines to writer on request. Query helpful. Uses sport in season and profiles of athletes. Submit seasonal material four months in advance. Reports in one to two weeks. Enclose S.A.S.E. for reply to queries.

Nonfiction: Personal testimonies and profiles. Articles related to athletics and the Christian faith. Heart of magazine is personal profile of athlete or coach with spiritual perspective the center of article. Wants stories "with masculine approach; strong, fast-paced articles and profiles. Articles related to issues in athletics and society. Message and place of Jesus Christ focal point. We're one of the only magazines we know of dealing in two worlds of athletics and Christianity. Not a straight sport magazine or specifically religious publication but one which bridges both worlds. Avoid the trite 'goody-goody' articles. Want the Christian perspective included with a man's warts showing. Don't want the sickeningly sweet Sunday school pap." Uses informational, how-to (sport), personal experience, interview, profile, inspirational, humor, and think articles. Length: 200 to 2,500 words. Pay scale not set.

Photos: Photos used with mss and on assignment, captions optional. B&w 5x7 or

8x10. No set rate. "We can take an excellent sports photo showing emotion, drama, conflict, agony, defeat, joy, etc., and build free verse, Scripture verse, etc. around it." **Poetry and Fillers:** Uses free and light verse. Also uses clippings and short humor.

CHRISTIAN ECONOMICS, 7960 Crescent Ave., Buena Park CA 90620. Editor: H. Edward Rowe. For clergymen and laymen. Monthly. Copyrighted. Pays on acceptance. Will send a sample copy to a writer on request. Write for copy of guidelines for writers. No query required. Reports in 2 to 3 weeks. Enclose S.A.S.E. for return of submissions.
Nonfiction: Articles relating basic principles of Christianity to economic, political and social problems, with emphasis on constructive solutions. Nonsectarian. "We do not support or oppose legislation or candidates for public office. We emphasize contribution of Christianity to our national greatness." All articles submitted should be accompanied by a documentation sheet citing the sources of whatever vital facts, quotations, or statistics are used. Pays approximately $50 to $100 for 4 to 5 double-spaced, letter-size pages; decided on merit.

CHRISTIAN HERALD, 27 E. 39 St., New York NY 10016. Editor: Kenneth L. Wilson. For "persons who interpret the world religiously." Established in 1889. Monthly. Circulation: 300,000. Buys all rights. Buys about 40 mss a year. Payment on acceptance. Will send sample copy to writer for 60¢. Write for copy of editorial guidelines for writers. Query first. Will not consider photocopied submissions. Submit seasonal material (for Easter and Christmas) 3 months in advance. Reports on material accepted for publication in 5 to 6 weeks. Returns rejected material in 3 to 4 weeks. Enclose S.A.S.E. for reply to queries.
Nonfiction and Photos: "We like reportage, surveys of movements, problems, etc. Also first-person stories of religious or moral meaning." Informational, how-to, personal experience, interview, profile, inspirational, humor, historical, think pieces, nostalgia, personal opinion and photo. Length: 1,000 to 4,000 words. Pays minimum of $50. 5x7 or 8x10 b&w photos. Captions required. Pays $10. 4½x4½ color for cover use. Pays $100. Also looking for material for the following columns: "I Protest", "Moments With Impact", "The Beautiful People."

CHRISTIAN HERITAGE, Box 176, Hackensack NJ 07602. Editor: Rev. Stuart P. Garver. Published monthly except July and August for Protestant evangelicals with an interest in development inside the Roman Catholic Church. Buys first North American serial rights. Reports promptly as a rule; sometimes needs a month in the summer. Enclose S.A.S.E.
Nonfiction: Prefers readable, nonpedantic treatment of Church-State affairs, both historical and current. Interested in fact-filled and interpretive articles on effect of government policies on organized religion. Also in the market for true stories from lives of former clerics who have gone on to successful careers in other fields. Absolutely rejects all anti-Catholic material. Length: 2,200 to 2,500 words. Pay is $15 to $35.

THE CHRISTIAN HOME, 201 8th Avenue South, Nashville TN 37202. Editor: Mrs. Florence A. Lund. For "parents of children and youth." Established in 1939. Monthly. Circulation: 100,000. Rights purchased vary with author and material; may purchase all rights, but will reassign rights to author after publication. Also may buy first North American serial rights. Buys 100 mss a year. Payment on acceptance. Will send free sample copy to writer on request. Will send editorial guidelines to a writer on request. Query first for all material. Submit seasonal material 10 months in advance. Reports in 30 days. Enclose S.A.S.E. for reply to queries.
Nonfiction and Photos: Subject matter is general "articles acceptable to a liberal religious audience of parents." Buys informational, how-to, personal experience, inspirational, humor, think, photo, travel articles. Length: 1,500 to 1,800 words. Pays 2½¢ a word. Buys photos with and without mss. Captions optional.
Fiction: Buys fantasy, humorous, and religious fiction. Length: 2,000 to 3,000 words. Pays 2½¢ a word.
Poetry and Fillers: Buys blank, free, and light verse and avant-garde forms. Length: 3 to 16 lines. Pays 50¢ a line.

CHRISTIAN LIFE, Union Gospel Press, Box 6059, Cleveland OH 44101. "For young adults."
Nonfiction: Writers should be familiar with sound Sunday school literature. Length: 1,225 to 1,425 words. Pays 2¢ a word.

CHRISTIAN LIFE MAGAZINE, Gundersen Dr. and Schmale Rd., Wheaton IL 60187. Editor: Robert Walker. Issued monthly. Buys all rights. Reports in 2 weeks to a month. Enclose S.A.S.E.
Nonfiction and Photos: Devotional and missionary articles, features on Christian organizations, accounts of spiritual aid through Christian witness, church building and remodeling, Sunday school teaching techniques, Christian family life, current events in Christian life, and development of schools and colleges. In all articles, Jesus Christ should be exalted and not individual personalities. It is best to read the magazine first to become familiar with approach (a sample will be sent on request). Major features should be 2,500 to 3,000 words. Shorter articles on how problems were overcome or needs met in areas of Sunday school, church building and management, and family relationships are usually 1,500 to 2,000 words. Pays up to $175 for article and pix on publication. Clear, action photos with articles and news stories at $3 to $5.
Fiction: Well-plotted stories built upon significant problems faced by Christians in their life and walk with the Lord. Should be solved by overt character action. 3,000 to 3,500 words preferred.

CHRISTIAN STANDARD, 8121 Hamilton Ave., Cincinnati OH 45231. Editor: Edwin V. Hayden. A church weekly devoted to "the restoration of New Testament Christianity, its doctrines, its ordinances and its fruits." Enclose self-addressed, stamped envelope for manuscript return.
Nonfiction: Uses 1,000- to 2,000-word essays or feature articles dealing with arts and religion. Doctrinal, practical and inspirational themes. People or congregations accomplishing the unusual under ordinary circumstances. Pays $5 minimum for brief items.

CHRISTIANITY TODAY, 1014 Washington Building, Washington DC 20005. Editor: Harold Lindsell. Journal for the clergy and informed laymen. Query first. Enclose S.A.S.E. for reply.
Nonfiction: This is an extremely specialized publication. Do not submit without thoroughly studying the magazine. Most of content is staff-written or done on assignment. Material must be theologically precise, authoritative and highly readable. No biography. Uses essays written from an evangelical (Biblical) Protestant perspective on crucial contemporary issues and indicating the driving relevance of the Christian revelation to the modern scene. Length: 1,500 to 2,000 words. Pays $50 minimum.

CHRONICLE REVIEW, 2953 Bathurst St., Toronto, Ontario, Canada. Editor: Dr. Arnold Ages. For "exclusively Jewish readers with above average education." Special issues for High Holy Days, Passover issues. Established in 1897. Monthly. Circulation: 9,000. Buys 30 to 40 mss a year. Payment on publication. Will send free sample copy to writer on request. Submit seasonal material one month in advance. Will consider photocopied submissions. Reports in 2 to 4 weeks. Enclose S.A.S.E. for return of submissions.
Nonfiction: "We publish think pieces on Jewish-related themes; will also consider biographical profiles of Jewish figures. Our approach is not academic, but journalistic. We are independent of any religious or cultural groups within the larger Jewish community. We get enormous coverage of Israel-oriented articles; we would prefer North American copy. We would also like material to have a Canadian slant." Buys profiles and think articles. Length: 1,000 to 3,000 words. Pays $10 to $50.
How To Break In: "Send in a book review on speculation. I'm always on the lookout for well-written pieces of this nature. Or look at newspaper articles that appear to give promise of a good story. Then probe deeply."

CHURCH & STATE, 8120 Fenton St., Silver Spring MD 20910. Assistant Editor: Albert J. Menendez. Monthly except for a combined July/August issue. Circulation: 130,000. "Primarily staff-written, but anyone wishing to submit an article should carefully study the editorial policy and general orientation." Will send sample copy to writer on request.

Nonfiction: "Devoted exclusively to news and analysis of problems concerning religious liberty and the interaction of political and religious institutions. We are interested in studies of church-state problems in all countries of the world, and such issues as religious influences in politics and public policy, religious education in public schools, Vatican diplomacy, religious discrimination, etc. We are frankly partisan and vigorously espouse the principle of separation of church and state, full religious liberty and religiously neutral public education. Length: 800 to 1,600 words. A modest stipend will be paid for cogently written articles reflecting our basic editorial position and presenting original research."

THE CHURCH HERALD, 630 Myrtle Street, Northwest, Grand Rapids MI 49504. Editor: Louis H. Benes. For "a cross-section of church families with readership in all ages." Special issues include Youth (early January), Easter, Family (early May), Christmas. Weekly. Circulation: 76,500. Not copyrighted. Buys 50 to 60 mss a year. Pays on acceptance. Will send a sample copy to a writer on request. Write for copy of guidelines for writers. Submit seasonal material 3 months in advance. Enclose S.A.S.E. for return of submissions.

Nonfiction and Photos: Articles on "the creative use of leisure, communication between the generations, teenagers, ethics and business relations; problems in marriage, divorce, homosexuality and the Christian church, problems of ages, race relations, ecology (not generalities which have been covered many times), etc. We are also interested in in-depth interviews on religious themes with noted church or national leaders. The style should be popular as opposed to academic, somewhat anecdotal. Develop an argument well and analyze and explore it; organize material. The point of view should be Christian." Length: 500 to 2,000 words. Pays 1½¢ to 2½¢ a word. Photos purchased with mss. B&w glossies. Pays $5 to $15.

Fiction: Religious and juvenile. Length: 700 to 800 words. Pays 1½¢ to 2½¢ a word.

Poetry: Contemporary and avant-garde on Christian subjects. Length: 15 to 75 lines. No set rates of pay.

COLUMBIA, P.O. Drawer 1670, New Haven CT 06507. Editor: Elmer Von Feldt. Issued monthly. Circulation: 1,200,000. Enclose self-addressed, stamped envelope.

Nonfiction and Photos: 1,000 to 3,000 words. These should be directed to the Catholic layman and family and deal with current events, social problems, Catholic apostolic activities, education, rearing a family, literature, science, arts, sports and leisure. 8x10 b&w glossy photos required for illustration. Pays $100 to $300.

Fiction: To 3,000 words. From a thoroughly Christian viewpoint. Pays to $300.

Fillers: Up to 100 words. Payment $10. Short humor up to 1,000 words. Payment: up to $100.

COMMONWEAL, 232 Madison Ave., New York NY 10016. Editor: James O'Gara. Edited by Roman Catholic laymen. For college-educated audience. Special book and education issues. Weekly. Circulation: 30,000. Buys 75 mss a year. Pays on acceptance. Will send a sample copy to a writer on request. Query first. Submit seasonal material 1 month in advance. Reports in 3 weeks. Enclose S.A.S.E. with queries and submissions.

Nonfiction: "Articles on timely subjects: political, literary, religious." Buys think pieces. Length: 1,000 to 2,500 words. Pays 2¢ a word.

Poetry: Contemporary and avant-garde. Length: maximum 150 lines ("long poems very rarely"). Pays $7.50 to $25. Poetry Editor: John Fandel.

THE COMPANION OF ST. FRANCIS AND ST. ANTHONY, 15 Chestnut Park Rd., Toronto M4W 1W5, Ontario, Canada. Editor: Rev. Leo Linder, OFM Conv. Catholic family publication. Monthly. Circulation: 10,000. Buys first rights. Buys approximately 100 mss a year. Will pay on acceptance or publication. Will send a sample copy to a writer on request. Write for copy of guidelines for writers. Query first. Submit seasonal material 4 months in advance. Reports in 6 to 8 weeks. Enclose S.A.E. and International Reply Coupons for reply to queries.

Nonfiction: Treatment of national and international problems, modern moral and social issues welcome. Should be Christian in outlook, and slanted toward family reading. 1,200 to 1,500 words. For example, "I Do. I Do, I Do", "Symbols Get Out of Hand" and "Don't Waste Retirement". Pays 2¢ per word.

Photos: Purchased with mss, subject matter relating to article. Negatives or glossy photos, 5x7 or 8x10. Payment based on photos used and quality; approximately $2 to $3 per photo, more if suitable for use on cover.

Fiction: Easy reading and interest are primary considerations. While objectively stories should tend toward better Christian living, welcomes the use of humor and satire, and tongue-in-cheek treatment. 1,200 to 1,500 words. Pays 2¢ per word.

Poetry: "Brief, no specified policy of content."

THE CONGREGATIONALIST, 176 W. Wisconsin Avenue, Milwaukee WI 53203. Issued monthly except for July-August issue. Buys first rights. Will consider simultaneous submissions. Enclose S.A.S.E. for return of submissions.

Nonfiction: The *Congregationalist* is a specialized periodical published by the National Association of Congregational Christian Churches in the interests of the churches of that fellowship. Much of each issue is taken up by the space allotted to the various commissions and officials of the denomination, and only a small amount of room is left for freelance efforts. Most of the material is commissioned and is not paid for. Articles of general religious interest, particularly with a novel slant, are welcome. Top limit is 1,800 words, and 1,000 has a better chance of acceptance. Rate of payment varies with material. Pays on publication. Reports are on the slow side.

Poetry: Up to 20 lines bought sparingly.

CONTACT, 44 East Franklin Street, Room 302, Huntington IN 46750. Editor: Stanley Peters. Assistant Editor: Miss Lois Breiner. Publication of the Church of the United Brethren in Christ. For adult and high school youth audience. Weekly. Circulation: 7,500. Not copyrighted. Will accept material for first use, reprints, and simultaneous submissions. Pays on acceptance. Will send a sample copy to a writer on request. Write for copy of guidelines for writers. No query required. Deadlines are 8 months in advance. Reports in 6 to 10 weeks. Enclose S.A.S.E. with all requests and submissions.

Nonfiction and Photos: "Biographical sketches of noteworthy living and historical Christians, 'how-to' articles in churches and related organizations; also some on self-improvement, inspirational articles that avoid 'preachiness' and are liberally illustrated with anecdotes." Length: 1,300 to 1,500 words, "nothing longer unless strong enough content to merit division into parts of 1,200 to 1,500 words each." Pays ¾¢ per word for first-time use, ⅔¢ per word for reprints. Photos purchased with mss; subject matter appropriate to article. B&w glossies. Pays $1 each.

Fiction: Slanted to both youth and adults, or either group. Strongly plotted with a definite resolution which comes as a result of the action. Up to 1,500 words in length. Payment same as for nonfiction.

Poetry: Uses occasional short poems with real messages. Up to 30 lines in length.

Fillers: Newsbreaks and short humor of 50 to 150 words. Same payment as for nonfiction.

CROSS AND CROWN, 6851 S. Bennett Ave., Chicago IL 60649. Editor: The Very Rev. John J. McDonald, O.P. For priests, religious sisters and brothers, and the well-read laity. Buys all rights, but right to reuse the material is assigned back without charge if credit line is given to *Cross and Crown.* Pays on publication. No query required. Enclose S.A.S.E. for return of submissions.

Nonfiction: Wants articles that present a serious examination of important truths pertinent to the spiritual life, but placed in the context of today's world. Can include biographies and articles on contemporary culture, Scripture, prayer, the liturgy, Church renewal, Christian virtue, and ecumenism. No fiction, poetry, photos, cartoons or fillers. Length: 3,000 to 4,000 words. Pays 1¢ per word.

DAILY BLESSING, P.O. Box 2187, Tulsa OK 74102. Managing Editor: Billye Morris. Quarterly. Buys all rights. Pays on acceptance. Will send a sample copy to a

writer on request. Write for copy of guidelines for writers. Reports in 2 to 3 months. Enclose S.A.S.F. for return of submissions.
Nonfiction: Slanted to make faith in God relevant and meaningful and inspirational in everyday life. "A good meditation includes an illustration, a human experience, anecdote, or example which illustrates the idea presented in the Scripture passage. A good meditation should develop one idea only, with freshness and vitality. Share an experience or idea in a way that blesses the reader and leads him into a spirit of worship. Avoid poetry, controversy, death and war scenes, threadbare illustrations, and overworked themes, criticism of other groups, pious preachments, and quotations from copyrighted sources without permission to quote." Length: 50 characters to a line, 27 lines including title and Scripture verse. Make a thorough study of writers' guide and sample magazine. Write positive, uplifting material that has a fresh slant. Pays $5 to $15.
Photos: Scenic covers: 4x5 color transparencies or 35mm slides. Pays $35 to $75. Also scenic and mood b&w glossies. Pays $7.50 to $10.

DAILY MEDITATION, P.O. Box 2710, San Antonio TX 78206. Publisher: Rose Dawn; Editor: Ruth S. Paterson. Issued bimonthly. Reports within 60 days. Enclose S.A.S.E. for return of submissions.
Nonfiction: Pays ½¢ to 1¢ a word, on acceptance, for articles of 750, 1,200 and 1,650 words (please give exact word count on ms). Uses metaphysical teachings, inspirational articles (seasonal articles 6 months in advance), nonsectarian religious articles (emphasis on how to apply principles to reader's life).
Poetry: 14¢ a line for poetry along same lines as above. 16 lines maximum.

DAILY WORD, Unity Village MO 64063. Editor: M. Smock. Published by the Unity School of Christianity. A monthly manual of daily studies. Buys a limited number of short articles and poems. Writer must have an understanding of Unity teachings. Copyrighted. Reports in 2 to 3 weeks. Include S.A.S.E. for ms return.
Nonfiction and Poetry: To 1,000 words. Pays 3¢ a word and up. Poetry to 16 lines. Pays 25¢ a line and up.

DECISION MAGAZINE, 1300 Harmon Place, Minneapolis MN 55403. Editor: Dr. Sherwood E. Wirt. Conservative evangelical monthly publication. Buys first North American serial and second rights. Payment on publication. Reports within 2 months. Enclose S.A.S.E. for return of submissions.
Nonfiction: Uses little freelance material; best opportunity is in testimony area (1,600 to 2,000 words). Also uses short narrative, 400 to 750 words. "Our function is to present Christ as Savior and Lord to unbelievers and present articles on deeper Christian life for Christian readers. No tangents. Center on Christ in all material." Payment, on publication, is according to value of article; no set fee.
Verse and Poetry: Uses devotional thoughts and short poetry in "Quiet Heart" column. Also has "Editorial Feature" section which uses verse poems, free verse, brief narrative, illustration. No "preaching" or negativism. Positive, Christ-centered. Payment at discretion of editor.
Fillers: Uses fresh, quotable quips from known or unknown individuals, devotional thoughts.

THE DISCIPLE (incorporating *The Christian* and *World Call*), Box 179, St. Louis MO 63166. Published by Christian Board of Publication of the Christian Church (Disciples of Christ). For ministers and church members, both young and older adults. weekly. Circulation: 102,000. Buys first rights. Pays on publication. Payment for photos made at end of month of acceptance. Will send a sample copy to a writer on request. Write for copy of guidelines for writers. No query required. Will consider photocopied submissions. Submit seasonal material at least 3 months in advance. Reports in several weeks. Enclose S.A.S.E. for return of submissions.
Nonfiction: Articles and meditations on religious, historical, inspirational, "how-to-do-it" themes; short pieces. Length: 500 to 1,200 words. Pays $3 to $7.50. Also uses devotionals of 200 to 500 words for "A Faith to Live By" page. Pays $5.
Photos: B&w glossies, 8x10. Occasional b&w glossies, any size, used to illustrate articles. Pays $1 to $5. Pays $3 to $12 when used for covers. No color. Occasionally

runs a series, such as religious sculpture, photos of church stained glass windows, etc.

Fiction: Religious, inspirational, sports, family life or humorous, with not-too-obvious religious or ethical application. Length: 700 to 1,350 words. Pays $10.

Poetry: Uses 1 to 3 poems weekly. Length: 4 to 16 lines. Themes may be seasonal, historical-religious. One or two 4- to 8-line humorous verses used weekly in "Relax" column. Pays $1 to $5.

EMMANUEL, 194 E. 76th St., New York NY 10021. Editor: The Rev. Raymond A. Tartre, S.S.S. Issued monthly for the Catholic clergy. Rights to be arranged with author. Enclose S.A.S.E. for return of submissions.

Nonfiction: Wants articles of Catholic spirituality, mostly nontechnical; can be biographical, historical or critical. 1,500 to 3,000 words at about 3¢ per word.

ENGAGE/SOCIAL ACTION (incorporating *Engage* and *Social Action*), 100 Maryland Ave., N.E., Washington DC 20002. Editor: Allan R. Brockway. For "United Methodist and United Church of Christ clergy and lay people interested in in-depth analysis of social issues, particularly the church's role or involvement in these issues." Established in 1973. Monthly. Circulation: 9,000. Rights purchased vary with author and material. May buy all rights and reassign rights to author after publication. Buys about 30 mss a year. Will send free sample copy to writer on request. Write for copy of guidelines for writers. Query first or submit complete ms. Will consider photocopied submissions, but prefers original. Returns rejected material in 1 week. Reports on material accepted for publication in several weeks. Enclose S.A.S.E. for return of submissions or reply to queries.

Nonfiction and Photos: "This is the social action publication of the United Methodist Church and the United Church of Christ (published by the Board of Church and Society of the United Methodist Church in cooperation with the Council for Christian Social Action of the United Church of Christ). We publish articles relating to current social issues as well as church-related discussions. We do not publish highly technical articles or poetry. Our publication tries to relate social issues to the church—what the church can do, is doing; why the church should be involved. We only accept articles relating to social issues, e.g., war, draft, peace, race relations, welfare, police/community relations, labor, population problems. Reviews of books and music should focus on related subjects." Length: 2,500 words maximum. Pays $35 to $50. 8x10 b&w glossy photos purchased with or without mss. Captions required. Pays $15.

ENSIGN, 50 E. North Temple, Salt Lake City UT 84150. Editor: Doyle L. Green. Buys first publication rights for use in English and non-English version of *Ensign.* Submit seasonal material six months in advance. Enclose S.A.S.E. for return of submissions.

Fiction and Poetry: Publishes "fiction showing persons overcoming problems of life, poetry of life, family, and Christian virtues. It is really very difficult for the non-Mormon to crack our editorial requirements. Hence, the general areas in poetry and fiction are the only two where the market is open." Pays 3¢ to 5¢ a word.

THE EVANGELICAL BEACON, 1515 E. 66th St., Minneapolis MN 55423. For Evangelical and conservative Protestant audience. Issued biweekly. Buys first rights. Pays on acceptance. Will send free sample copy to a writer on request. Reports on submissions in two weeks. Enclose S.A.S.E. for return of submissions.

Nonfiction and Photos: Devotional material, articles on the church, people and their accomplishments. Length: 1,500 words. Pays 1½¢ per word. Photos purchased with captions only. Prefers 8x10's. Pays $3 and up.

EVANGELICAL FRIEND, P.O. Box 232, Newberg OR 97132. Managing Editor: Harlow Ankeny. Audience is conservative Christian families, mainly of the Friends (Quaker) church denomination. Monthly. Circulation: 10,000. Not copyrighted. Rarely pays for material. Will send sample copy on request. Reports within one month. Enclose S.A.S.E. for return of submissions.

Nonfiction: Varied articles of interest to Christian families. Write for definite article needs. Most done on assignment. Most articles donated.

Photos: With captions only. Thematic, landscapes, people, illustrations to be used

with specific articles. 8x10 glossies preferred. Negatives borrowed if small cropping desired. Pays $5 to $15 for one time use.
Fiction: Christian testimony, life, etc. 1,000 to 2,000 words. Rarely purchases.

EVENT, 422 S. Fifth St., Minneapolis MN 55415. Editor: James Solheim. For "Christian lay readers who are interested in social issues." 11 times a year. Circulation: 12,000. Buys all rights. Buys 6 to 8 freelance mss a year. Pays on publication. Will send a sample copy to a writer on request. Query first. Reports in 6 weeks. Enclose S.A.S.E.
Nonfiction: A majority of articles are solicited; very few freelance. This publication is "strictly issue-oriented: law and order, consumerism, the draft, American Indian, drugs, etc." Think pieces, photo essays. Must include "theological perspective." Length: 1,500 words. Pays $40 to $150.
Photos: "We maintain wide contacts with freelancers." B&w glossies. Buys first rights only. Pays $15 to $40.
Fiction: Religious, "controversial, people- and issue-oriented." Length: up to 1,500 words. Pays $50 to $100.

FAMILY DIGEST, Noll Plaza, Huntington IN 46750. Editor: Robert A. Willems. For "young and growing Catholic families." Monthly. Buys first rights. Buys approximately 60 mss a year. Pays on acceptance. Will send a sample copy to a writer on request. No query required, "prefer to see mss from first-time contributors." Submit seasonal material at least 6 months in advance. Reports in 1 month or less. Enclose S.A.S.E. for return of submissions.
Nonfiction: Articles on "family relationships, education, social concern, Church, community, personality profiles." Wants "good taste. Not 'preachy.' Practical articles to appeal to a multi-media sophisticated generation." How-to's, personal experience pieces, profiles, humor, historical, think pieces, photo essays, travel pieces. Length: maximum 1,000 words. Pays minimum 5¢ a word.
Photos: Purchased with mss; with captions only. B&w glossies, color transparencies, 35mm color. One-time use. Pays $10, b&w; pay varies for color.
Fillers: "Preferably concise, personal experience items in good taste." Length: 200 words maximum.

FISH INTERNATIONAL NEWSLETTER, 29 Commonwealth Ave., Boston MA 02116. Editor: Philip Deemer. Bimonthly. Buys all rights. Pays on publication. Reports in 2 to 3 weeks. Enclose S.A.S.E. for return of submissions.
Nonfiction: "Articles about projects of Fish chapters throughout the world, the Fish movement being one of an ecumenical lay ministry where people help their fellowmen in their community in emergency situations." Pays 3¢ a word.

FRANCISCAN MESSAGE, Franciscan Publishers, Pulaski, WI 54162. Editor: The Rev. Dismas Treder, O.F.M. For Roman Catholic adults: "majority are middle-aged, predominantly women, and married." Monthly. Circulation: 4,000. Buys North American serial rights. All mss upon purchase become the property of the magazine, but permission to reprint will be granted upon request. Buys 100 to 200 mss a year. Pays on acceptance. Will send a sample copy to a writer on request. No query required. Submit seasonal material 3 months in advance. Returns rejected material in 2 weeks. Acknowledges acceptance of material in 2 weeks. Enclose S.A.S.E. for return of submissions.
Nonfiction and Photos: 1,500- to 2,000-word factual and controversial articles dealing with positive solutions to everyday problems of interest to the average American Catholic; 1,000- to 2,000-word devotional articles in simple language. In-depth articles on such social questions and topics as poverty, religion, education, war, etc., and on Church renewal topics. Catholic (preferably Franciscan) viewpoint. Wants reportorial style; avoid preaching or armchair philosophy articles. Also considers article series by special arrangements with editor—for these, submit tentative sketch of series with query. Pays 1 to 2¢ per word. Photos purchased with mss; 5x7 or larger. All photos are returned to writers immediately after cuts are made.
Poetry: 8- to 24-line poems on eternal religious truths, human foibles, the beauty of nature; and occasional light verse. Pays 40 cents per line.

FREEWAY, Scripture Press, 1825 College Ave., Wheaton IL 60187. Managing Editor: Jerry B. Jenkins. For "Christian high school and college Sunday school class kids." Established in 1943. Weekly. Circulation: 160,000. Buys all rights, "but passes along reprint fees to author, when material is picked up after publication." Buys 100 mss a year. Will send free sample copy to a writer on request. Write for copy of guidelines for writers. Query first or submit complete ms. Will not consider photocopied submissions. Submit seasonal (Christmas, Easter) material 1 year in advance. Reports on material accepted for publication in 2 weeks. Returns rejected material in 1 week. Enclose S.A.S.E. for return of submissions or reply to queries.
Nonfiction and Photos: "Mostly person-centered nonfiction with photos. Subject must have had specific encounter with the person of Christ. Direct tie-in to faith in Christ. No simply religious or moral stories; subjects must be specifically Christ-centered. Christian message must be woven naturally into a good, true, dramatic, human interest story. Current interest is in the occult, Satanism, witchcraft and battles by Christians against grief, tragedy, danger, etc." Think articles on Biblical themes; reviews of Christian books. Length: 500 to 2,000 words. Pays $15 to $60. Pays $3 to $15 for 5x7 and 8x10 b&w photos.
Fiction: Same themes, lengths and rate of payment as nonfiction.
Poetry: Blank verse, free verse and light verse with Christian theme. Length: open. Pays $15 to $40.

FRIAR, Butler NJ 07405. Editor: Father Rudolf Harvey. For families. 11 times a year. Pays on acceptance. Enclose S.A.S.E. for return of submissions.
Nonfiction: Uses articles and features on current problems or events; profile of notable individuals; trends in sociology and education. Length, 1,800 to 3,000 words. Minimum payment of $15.

GOOD NEWS BROADCASTER, Box 82808, Lincoln NE 68501. Editor: Theodore H. Epp. Interdenominational magazine for adults from 17 years of age. Monthly. Circulation: 180,000. Buys first rights. Buys approximately 45 mss a year. Pays on acceptance. Will send a sample copy to a writer on request. Query preferred, but not required. Send all mss to Thomas S. Piper, Managing Editor. Submit seasonal material 6 months in advance. Reports in 1 month. Enclose S.A.S.E. for return of submissions.
Nonfiction and Photos: Articles which will help the reader learn and apply Christian Biblical principles to his life. From the writer's or the subject's own experience. "Especially looking for true, personal experience 'salvation' and 'how to live the Christian life' articles." Nothing dogmatic, or preachy, or sugary sweet, or without Biblical basis. Details or statistics should be authentic and verifiable. Style should be conservative and concise. Length: maximum 1,500 words. Pays 3¢ per word, more in special cases. Photos sometimes purchased with mss. Pays $5 to $10, b&w glossies; $25 to $35, color transparencies; $25, 35mm color.

GOSPEL CARRIER, Pentecostal Church of God of America, P.O. Box 850, Joplin MO 64801. A Sunday school take-home paper for adults. Quarterly in weekly parts. Buys one-time rights. Also buys second rights and will accept simultaneous submissions. Will send a sample copy to a writer on request. Deadlines for seasonal material are 6 months in advance. Reports in 30 to 45 days. Enclose S.A.S.E. for return of submissions.
Nonfiction: Articles of 800 to 1,200 words for the Evangelical market. Taboos are tobacco, drinking, dancing. Pays ¼¢ a word.
Fiction: Religious theme must be basic to the story. 1,000 to 1,800 words. Pays ¼¢ per word.
Fillers: Uses religious items.

GOSPEL HERALD, Scottdale PA 15683. Editor: John M. Drescher. Issued weekly (50 issues per year) for adult members of the Mennonite Church. Buys first and second rights. Enclose S.A.S.E.
Nonfiction: "Articles used are of a devotional and inspirational nature. Most articles are solicited." Length: 300 to 1,500 words. Rates up to 1½¢ per word on acceptance.
Poetry: Poetry must be of religious nature, with "feeling, imagery and good technique. Usually overstocked." Up to 10 lines.

GUIDEPOSTS MAGAZINE, 747 Third Ave. New York NY 10017. Editor: Leonard C. LeSourd. *Guideposts* is an inspirational monthly magazine for all faiths in which men and women from all walks of life tell how they overcame obstacles, rose above failures, met sorrow, learned to conquer themselves, and became more effective people through the direct application of the religious principles by which they live. Buys first rights. Enclose S.A.S.E.

Nonfiction and Fillers: Articles and features should be written in simple, anecdotal style with an emphasis on human interest. Short features up to approximately 250 words ($10 to $25) would be considered for such *Guideposts* features as: "Calendar of Holidays and Holy Days," "Fragile Moments," and other short items which appear at the end of major articles. Short mss of approximately 250 to 750 words ($25 to $50) would be considered for such features as "Quiet People" and general one-page stories. Full-length mss, 750 to 1,500 words ($50 to $100). All mss should be typed, double-spaced and accompanied by a stamped self-addressed envelope. Inspirational newspaper or magazine clippings often form the basis of articles in *Guideposts*, but it is unable to pay for material of this type and will not return clippings unless the sender specifically asks and encloses postage for return.

HOME LIFE, 127 Ninth Ave., N., Nashville TN 37234. Issued monthly. Buys all rights or North American serial rights. Pays on acceptance. Reports within 30 days. Enclose S.A.S.E. for return of submissions.

Nonfiction and Photos: Articles of 750 to 3,000 words. Needs material addressed to parents on the growth of children—emotional, intellectual, spiritual, physical. Also human interest content on the family development tasks—marriage, first child, growing children, children leaving home, empty nest. Emphasizes strongly personal experience/human interest approach. Pays 2½¢ per word. Photos purchased with mss; b&w 8x10 glossy. Pays $7.50 to $10. No model releases required.

Fiction: Short stories of interest to parent and family groups, written from a Christian viewpoint. Lengths, 750, 1,500, 2,250 or 3,000 words. Pays 2½¢ per word.

Poetry: Inspirational or family slant. 8 to 12 lines. Pays $2.50 minimum.

How To Break In: "We much prefer that a writer write about the area in which he is an expert: himself and his family. Readers much prefer to learn through the vicarious experience."

INTERACTION, 3558 S. Jefferson, St. Louis MO 63118. Co-editors: Earl Gaulke, Paul Pallmeyer; Managing Editor: Nancy Corbett. Issued monthly, except July-August bimonthly. Buys first rights. Will accept simultaneous submission of articles, short stories, and filler items. Payment on acceptance. Usually reports within 6 weeks. Enclose S.A.S.E. with all mss and queries.

Nonfiction and Photos: Accepts practical articles that are directed to church school teachers and leaders, as well as articles on various aspects of general education and pieces directed to teachers as persons. See "Beyond Pogo and Peanuts," June 1973 issue. Articles should be written in a popular, readable style. Preferred length: 1,000 to 1,500 words. Query not necessary. Pays $20 to $50 per article, depending on length and quality. Buys 5x7 or larger photographs with mss for $5 to $10 each. No color.

Fiction: Considered if it makes a point which will aid the church school teacher to gain new perspective of, or insights for, the teaching of the faith. Preferred length: 1,000 to 1,500 words. Pays $20 to $50 per short story.

Poetry: Accepts very little, publishes only occasionally. Poetry should be short, of a religious nature. Pays $5 to $15.

How To Break In: "A short feature might be the best bet or a how-to piece relating to Christian education."

INTERLIT, David C. Cook Foundation, Elgin IL 60120. Editor: Gladys J. Peterson. For people interested in missionary literature and Christian education, at the graduate level. Established in 1964. Quarterly. Circulation: 6,000. Rights purchased vary with author and material. Payment on acceptance. Will send free sample copy to a writer on request. Query first. Will consider photocopied submissions. Submit seasonal material four months in advance. Each issue is thematic. Reports in two weeks. Enclose S.A.S.E.

Nonfiction and Photos: Subject matter includes "literature, mass media, and leadership training—how to do it, this is what we did, etc. Query us before you start to write." Buys informational, how-to, personal experience, interview, profile, think, photo, spot news, and technical articles. Length: 500 to 5,000 words. Pays 2¢ to 4¢ a word. Purchases photos with mss and on assignment.

JEWISH CURRENT EVENTS, 430 Keller Avenue, Elmont NY 11003. Editor: S. Deutsch. For Jewish children and adults; distributed in Jewish schools. Biweekly. Pays on publication. No sample copies available. No query required. Reports in 1 week. Enclose S.A.S.E. for return of submissions.

Nonfiction: All current event items of Jewish content or interest; news; featurettes; short travel items (non-Israel) relating to Jewish interests or descriptions of Jewish communities or personalities; life in Jewish communities abroad; "prefer items written in news-style format." Length must be short. Pays anywhere from $10 to $300 for an item or article, depending on content, illustrations, length and relevance.

Photos: Purchased with mss. All items of Jewish content or interest. B&w snapshots only. Payment varies.

THE JEWISH DIGEST, Box 57-H, Scarsdale NY 10583. Editor: Bernard Postal. For "urban, well-educated families, interested in topics of Jewish interest." Established in 1955. Monthly. Circulation: 15,000. Buys first North American serial rights. Buys 10 to 20 mss a year. Payment on acceptance. Will send a sample copy to writer for 60¢. Holiday articles relating to Jewish holidays are of interest. Submit seasonal material six months in advance. Will consider photocopied submissions. Reports in 2 weeks. Enclose S.A.S.E. for return of submissions.

Nonfiction: Subject matter should be of "Jewish interest. Contemporary topics about and relating to Jews in the U.S. and abroad. We would like to see personal experiences, biographic sketches, impressions of the Jewish community here and abroad." Length: 2,000 words. Pays 2¢ a word with $50 maximum.

JEWISH SOCIAL STUDIES, 2929 Broadway, New York NY 10025. Editor: Dr. Sefton D. Temkin. For scholars and students "well read in religious circles." Quarterly. Circulation: 1,200. Buys all rights. Buys 16 mss a year. Pays on publication. Will send a sample copy to a writer for $4. All mss must be footnoted; include all names—first and last; submit 2 copies of mss. Submit seasonal material 2 months in advance. Returns rejected material in 3 months. Acknowledges acceptance of material in 1 week. Enclose S.A.S.E. for return of submissions.

Nonfiction: "Sociology and contemporary and historical aspects of Jewish life." Pays $5 per printed page.

THE LAMP, Graymoor, Garrison NY 10524. Editor: Charles Angell. Monthly. Buys all rights. Pays on acceptance. Will send free sample copy to a writer on request. Reports on submission in 10 days. S.A.S.E. must be enclosed.

Nonfiction and Photos: Accepts nonfiction ms designed to make grass roots ecumenism meaningful to average reader. Length: 1,500 to 2,000 words. Pays 4¢ per word and up. Occasionally buys 8x10 photos with mss. B&w only. Pay $7.50 and up.

LIBERTY, A Magazine of Religious Freedom, 6840 Eastern Ave., N.W., Washington DC 20012. Editor: Roland R. Hegstad. For "responsible citizens interested in community affairs and religious freedom"; professionals. Bimonthly. Circulation: 500,000. Buys first rights. Buys approximately 40 mss a year. Pays on acceptance. Will send a sample copy to a writer on request. No query required. Will consider photocopied submissions. Submit seasonal material 6 to 8 months in advance. Reports in 1 week. Enclose S.A.S.E. for return of submissions.

Nonfiction: "Articles of national and international interest in field of religious liberty, church-state relations. Current events affecting above areas (Sunday law problems, parochial aid problems, religious discrimination by state, etc.) Current events are most important; base articles on current events rather than essay form." Buys how-to's, personal experience and think pieces, interviews, profiles. Length: maximum 2,500 words. Pays $25, minimum; $100, maximum.

Photos: "To accompany or illustrate articles." Purchased with mss; with captions only. B&w glossies, color transparencies. Pays $7 to $25.

LIGUORIAN, Liguori MO 63057 Editor: Rev. L. G. Miller. For families with Catholic religious convictions. Monthly. Circulation: 382,422. Not copyrighted. Buys 75 mss a year. Pays on acceptance. Submit seasonal material 4 months in advance. Returns rejected material in 6 to 8 weeks. Enclose S.A.S.E.
Nonfiction and Photos: "Pastoral, practical, and personal approach to the problems and challenges of people today. No travelogue approach or unresearched ventures into controversial areas." Length: 400 to 1,800 words. Pays $35 to $85. Photos purchased with mss; b&w glossies.

THE LINK, 122 Maryland Ave., N.E., Washington DC 20002. Editor: Edward I. Swanson. For Protestant military personnel and their families; ages 17 to 30; some are unmarried. Monthly. Buys first rights. Buys approximately 200 mss a year. Pays on acceptance. Will send a sample copy to a writer on request. No query required. Will consider photocopied submissions. Submit seasonal material 9 months in advance. Reports in 4 weeks. Enclose S.A.S.E. for return of submissions.
Nonfiction: Articles on any subject but must be interesting, say something important, appeal to military personnel. Prefers religious, inspirational, factual articles. Prefers not to see "do-good articles and stories" in which the "godly person always wins (no, he doesn't)." Personal experience, travel, and think pieces; profiles. Length: 1,000 to 1,500 words. Pays $15 to $25.
Fiction: Mystery, adventure, religious contemporary problems. Length: 2,000 words. Pays $25 to $50.

THE LITTLE FLOWER MAGAZINE, P.O. Box 5280, San Antonio TX 78201. Editor: Rev. Hilary Smith. 6 times per year for Catholic audience. Circulation: 34,000. Publication not copyrighted. Pays on publication. "Most of our material is donated; be sure to specify honestly whether or not you just want to pass on an idea to someone, see yourself in print, or expect compensation. If we do pay for an article, we never pay less than 1¢ per word." Will send free sample copy to a writer on request. Write for copy of guidelines for writers. No query required. Reports on submissions in three weeks. Enclose S.A.S.E. for return of submissions.
Nonfiction: Simple, factual discussions of Christian living, prayer, social action, the thinking of important religious writers. "It is important that factual or doctrinal articles be about a very, very specific topic. We cannot use articles about religion in general. For example, we can always use articles on St. Therese of Liseux; a good article could be written by referring to a good biography, such as Ida Goerres' *The Hidden Face,* and concentrating on some specific topic, such as Therese's relation to nineteenth century attitudes toward women; her approach to meditation; her relationship to her superior. Since few of our readers are familiar with current religious literature, it is relatively easy to draw material from good works on specific passages in the Bible, on prayer, on current social questions, on the liturgy, etc." Avoid sentimentality and overly personal presentations. Length: 1,250 to 1,700 words.
Poetry: 4 to 30 lines; verse need not be religious. Compactness of thought is more important than carefully measured meter or forced rhymes.

LIVING MESSAGE, P.O. Box 820, Petrolia, Ontario, NON 1RO, Canada. Editor: Rita Baker. For "active, concerned Christians, mainly Canadian Anglican." Publication of the Anglican Church of Canada. Established in 1889. Monthly except July and August. Circulation: 18,000. Not copyrighted. Busy 20 mss a year. Payment on publication. Will send free sample copy to writer on request. Submit complete mss. Will consider photocopied submissions. Submit seasonal material 5 months in advance. Reports on material in 3 weeks. Enclose International Reply Coupons for return of submissions.
Fiction, Nonfiction and Photos: "Short stories and articles which give readers an insight into other lives, promote understanding and stimulate action in areas such as community life, concerns of elderly, handicapped, youth, work with children, Christian education, poverty, the 'Third World', etc. No sentimentality or moralizing. Readers relate to a warm, personal approach; uncluttered writing. 'Reports' or involved explanatory articles are not wanted. The lead-in must capture the reader's imagination. A feeling of love and optimism is important." Length: up to 2,000 words. Pays $5 to $25. 8x10 b&w prints (with article). Pays $5. Fiction length: 1,000 to 1,500 words. Pays $10 to $20.

LOGOS JOURNAL, 185 North Ave., Plainfield NJ 07060. Editor: Alden West. For "Evangelical Christians and those interested in New Testament Christianity. Material published generally has to do with some aspect of the evangelical-charismatic movement." Established in 1971. Every 2 months. Circulation: 100,000. Buys all rights. Buys 50 to 150 mss a year. Payment on publication. Will send free sample copy to a writer on request. Write for copy of guidelines for writers. "Queries are answered but not required for submission." Will consider photocopied submissions, "but not preferred." Reports on material accepted for publication within 90 days. Returns rejected material within 90 days. Enclose S.A.S.E. for return of submissions.

Nonfiction and Photos: "May be personal, reportive, humorous, news, or educational. Must be generally edifying to be accepted. The general scene rather than localized area (church or home). Interested in regional, national and international scene, and articles relating to encouraging a general religious revival. Animated but without excessive literary frills. Should get to the heart of the matter without sidetracking. Writer should know subject. No articles on Bible exposition or personal testimony." Informational, how-to, personal experience, interview, profile, inspirational, humor, think, expose, nostalgia, book reviews and spot news. Length: 2,500 words maximum. Pays 6 to 7¢ per word. Photos: 5x7 or 8x10 or larger. "No Polaroid or snapshots." Pays $5 to $10 per print. Purchased with or without ms. Captions required.

Fiction: Humorous. Length: 2,500 words maximum. Pays 6 to 7¢ a word.

Fillers: Newsbreaks and clippings. Length: 100 words maximum. Pays $2 to $15.

THE LOOKOUT, 8121 Hamilton Ave., Cincinnati OH 45231. Editor: Jay Sheffield. For the adult and young adult of the Sunday morning Bible school. Issued weekly. Buys first rights. Pays on acceptance. Will send free sample copy to a writer on request. Write for copy of guidelines for writers. Reports on submissions within one month. Study publication before submitting material. Enclose S.A.S.E. for return of submissions.

Nonfiction: Chiefly methods or news-type articles on phases of educational work of the local nondenominational church, or articles dealing with personal or family problems of Christian life or work. Length: 1,000 to 1,500 words. Pays $25 to $35.

Photos: Upright glossies, size 8x10. Human interest or scenic shots of exceptionally good composition for cover use. Sharp b&w contrasts. Pays $7.50 to $15.

Fiction: Short-short stories of 1,000 to 1,200 words. To be acceptable, fiction must be characterized by effective storytelling style, interesting quality—capable of catching and holding the reader's interest, and wholesomeness. Pays up to $35 for short stories.

THE LUTHERAN, 2900 Queen Lane, Philadelphia PA 19129. Editor: A. P. Stauderman. Lutheran Church in America. Semimonthly. Circulation: 535,800. Buys North American serial rights. Pays on acceptance. Will send a sample copy to a writer on request. Write for copy of guidelines for writers. Enclose S.A.S.E. for return of submissions.

Nonfiction: Popularly written material about human concerns with reference to the Christian faith. "We are especially interested in articles in 4 main fields: Christian ideology; personal religious life, social responsibilities; Church at work; human interest stories about people in whom considerable numbers of other people are likely to be interested." Write "primarily to convey information rather than opinions. Every article should be based on a reasonable amount of research or should exploit some source of information not readily available. Most readers are grateful for simplicity of style. Sentences should be straightforward, with a minimum of dependent clauses and prepositional phrases." Length: 500 to 2,000 words. Pays $75 to $150.

Photos: Buys pix submitted with mss. Good 8x10 glossy prints. Pays $10 to '20.

How To Break In: "A beginning writer could send us examples of previously published news and feature articles, or samples of unpublished work. A list of ideas for possible features for our magazine would also be useful in determining his or her potential for our editorial needs."

LUTHERAN FORUM, 155 E. 22nd St., New York NY 10010. Editors: Richard E. Koenig, Glenn C. Stone. For church leadership, clerical and lay, students. Quarterly. Buys all rights. Pays on publication. Will send sample copy for 50¢. Reports in 2 to 4 weeks. Enclose S.A.S.E.

Nonfiction: Articles, 1,000 to 3,000 words about important issues and actions in the Church and in relation to the secular scene. Query preferred. Payment varies; $10 minimum.
Photos: Purchased with mss or with captions only. Prefers 8x10 prints. Uses more vertical than horizontal format. Pays $5 minimum.

THE LUTHERAN JOURNAL, 7317 Cahill Rd., Edina MN 55435. Editor: The Rev. Armin U. Deye. For adult and young adult church members. Quarterly. Circulation: 92,000. Not copyrighted. Pays on publication. Reports in 6 weeks. Enclose S.A.S.E. for return of submissions.
Nonfiction and Photos: Religious, inspirational and human interest articles suitable for distribution through churches. Generally 1,000 to 1,500 words. Pays 1¢ per word. Photos purchased with mss.

THE LUTHERAN STANDARD, 426 S. 5th St., Minneapolis MN 55415. Editor: George H. Muedeking. For family audience. Semimonthly. Buys first rights or multiple rights. Pays on acceptance. Will send free sample copy to a writer on request. Reports on submissions in three weeks. Enclose S.A.S.E. for return of submissions.
Nonfiction and Photos: Uses human interest, inspirational articles, especially about members of the American Lutheran Church who are practicing their faith in noteworthy ways, or congregations with unusual programs. Also publishes articles that discuss current social issues and problems (crime, draft evasion, etc.,) in terms of Christian involvement and solutions. Length: 650 to 1,250 words, with pictures. Pays 2¢ and up per word. Photos used with mss.
Fiction: Tie-up with season of year, such as Christmas, often preferred. Length: Limit 1,200 words. Pays 2¢ per word.
Poetry: Uses very little poetry. The shorter the better; 20 lines. Pays $5 per poem.

LUTHERAN WOMEN, 2900 Queen Lane, Philadelphia PA 19129. Editor: LaVonne Althouse. 11 times yearly. Circulation: 53,000. Official magazine for Lutheran Church Women. Acknowledges receipt of manuscript and decides acceptance within two weeks. Prefers to see mss six months ahead of issue, at beginning of planning stage. Can consider up to three months before issue. (December issue is nearly completed by September 1). Type 70 characters to a line preferably. Buys first rights. Pays on publication. Query first. Enclose S.A.S.E.
Nonfiction: Anything of interest to mothers, young or old, professional or other working women, relating to the expression of Christian faith in daily life, community action, international concerns. Family publication standards. Length: 1,500 to 2,000 words. Some shorter pieces accepted. Pays $30 to $40.
Photos: Purchased with mss or with captions only. Family situations; religious art objects; overseas situations related to church. Should be clear, sharp, b&w. Pays $5 each.
Fiction: Not to exceed 2,000 words. Should show deepening of insight; story expressing new understanding in faith; story of human courage, self-giving, building up of community. Pays $30 to $40.
Poetry: Uses very little. "Biggest taboo for us is sentimentality. Obviously we'd be limited to family magazine type contributions regarding range of vocabulary, but we don't want almanac-type poetry." No limit on number of lines.

THE MARIAN, 4545 W. 63rd St., Chicago IL 60629. Managing Editor: A. Miciunas, MIC. Bimonthly. Buys first rights. Pays on publication. Will send free sample copy to a writer on request. Reports on submissions promptly. Enclose S.A.S.E. for return of submissions.
Nonfiction: Uses articles on religion, morals, social questions and Christian culture. Length: Maximum 1,000 words. Payment by arrangement.

MARIAN HELPERS BULLETIN, Eden Hill, Stockbridge MA 01262. Editor: Bro. Robert M. Doyle, M.I.C. For "average Catholics of varying ages with moderate religious views and general education." Established in 1947. Quarterly. Circulation: 750,000. Buys 18 to 24 mss a year. Payment on acceptance. Will send a free sample copy to a writer on request. Reports in 4 to 8 weeks. Submit seasonal material 6 months ¢in advance. Enclose S.A.S.E. for return of submissions.
Nonfiction and Photos: Subject matter is "of general interest on devotional, spiri-

tual, moral and social topics. Use a positive, practical, and optimistic approach, without being sophisticated. We would like to see articles on the Blessed Virgin Mary." Buys informational, personal experience, inspirational articles. Length: 300 to 1200 words. Pays $15 to $35. Photos are purchased with or without mss; captions are optional. Pays $5 to $10 for b&w glossies.

MARRIAGE, THE MAGAZINE FOR HUSBAND AND WIFE, St. Meinrad IN 47577. Editor: John J. McHale. Monthly. Circulation: 58,000. Buys North American serial rights only. Pays on acceptance. Will send sample copy to a writer for 10¢. Reports on submissions in two weeks. Enclose S.A.S.E. for return of submissions.
Nonfiction: Uses 4 different types of articles: (1) Informative and inspirational articles on all aspects of marriage, especially husband and wife relationship. Length: 2,000 to 2,500 words. (2) Personal essays relating dramatic or amusing incidents that point up the human side of marriage. Up to 1,500 words in length. (3) Profiles of outstanding couples or couples whose story will be of interest for some special reason, and profiles of individuals who contribute to the betterment of marriage. Length: 1,500 to 2,000 words. (4) Interviews with authorities in the fields of marriage (on current problems and new developments). Length: Up to 2,000 words. Pays 5¢ per word.
Photos: Purchased with mss. B&w glossies, color transparencies. Pays $17.50, half-page; $35, full-page. Requires model releases. Department Editor: O.E. Mansfield.

MARYKNOLL MAGAZINE, Maryknoll NY 10545. Editor: Rev. Donald J. Casey, M.M. For "Maryknoll missionaries and mission workers with major emphasis on the peoples of the developing countries." Pays on acceptance. Will send free sample copy to a writer on request. Query first before sending any material. Reports within two weeks. Enclose S.A.S.E. for reply to queries.
Nonfiction: "All articles in the magazine must apply in some way to the hopes and aspirations, the culture, the problems and challenges of peoples in Asia, Africa, and Latin America." Length: 1,000 to 1,500 words. Send an outline before submitting material. Average payment: $100.
Photos: Interested in photo stories and in individual b&w and color transparencies. Photo stories in b&w, up to $150; color, up to $200. An individual b&w pays $15, color pays $25. Transparencies returned after use. Query before sending photos.

THE MENNONITE, 600 Shaftesbury Blvd., Winnipeg, Canada R3P OM4. Editor: Larry Kehler. For a "general readership—age span—15 to 90 years; education—from grade school to Ph.D's; interests—themes dealing with the Christian response to such issues as the family, ethics, war and peace, life style, renewal, etc." Established in 1881. Weekly, except in July and August. Circulation: 16,000. Rights purchased vary with author and material. May buy first and second serial rights. Buys 100 to 125 mss a year. Payment on publication. Will send a free sample copy to writer on request. Submit seasonal material three months in advance. Reports in two months. Enclose S.A.E. and International Reply Coupons.
Nonfiction, Photos, Fiction, and Poetry: General subject matter is "articles on Bible study, social and political issues faced by Christians, creative responses to the challenges of 20th century life; some poetry on a variety of subjects; a small amount of fiction. *The Mennonite* is a publication of an historic peace church which pays special attention to ways and means of attempting to resolve conflict at various levels of life—family, community, national and international." Buys personal experience, inspirational, think, and personal opinion articles. Length: 500 to 1,500 words. Pays 1¢ to 2¢ a word. Purchases photos without mss and captions are optional. Pays $5 to $10 for 5x7 or 8x10 b&w glossies. Buys religious fiction. Length: 800 to 1,500 words. Pays 1¢ to 2¢ a word. Buys religious poems in traditional, blank, or free verse. Length: 2 to 40 lines. Pays 25¢ a line.

MENNONITE BRETHREN HERALD, 159 Henderson Hwy., Winnipeg 9, Manitoba, R2L 1L4, Canada. Editor: Harold Jantz. Family publication. Biweekly. Circulation: 8,000. Pays on publication. Not copyrighted. Will send a sample copy for 25¢. Reports within the month. Enclose S.A.E. and International Reply Coupons for return of submissions.
Nonfiction and Photos: Articles with a Christian family orientation; youth directed, Christian faith and life, current issues. 1,500 words. Pays 30¢ per column inch. Photos purchased with mss; pays $2.

MESSAGE MAGAZINE, Southern Publishing Assn., Box 59, Nashville TN 37202. Editor: W.R. Robinson. Bimonthly; global, and while appealing to all people, emphasizes interests and aspirations of people of color. Will send free sample copy to a writer on request. Buys all rights. Pays on acceptance or publication. Enclose S.A.S.E. for ms return.
Nonfiction: Material within Judeo-Christian framework of reality. Uses inspiring human interest stories about persons who exemplify faith in God and/or have achieved distinction in the face of great odds. Length: 500 to 800 words. Pays $5 to $25 or more.
Photos: Purchased with mss and with captions only. Photo stories of lasting interest, especially those depicting Negroes or persons in Afro-Asian countries. Pays $7.50 up for b&w; color transparencies up to $100.
Poetry: Quality poetry on religious and nature themes. Length: Up to 36 lines. Pays 25¢ per line.

THE MESSENGER OF THE SACRED HEART, Box 100, Station G, Toronto 8, Ont., Canada. Editor: Rev. F.J. Power, S.J. For "adult Catholics in Canada and the U.S. who are members of the Apostleship of Prayer." Monthly. Circulation: 20,000. Buys first rights. Buys about 12 mss a year. Pays on acceptance. Will send a sample copy to a writer on request. Submit seasonal material 3 months in advance. Reports in 1 month. Enclose S.A.E. and International Reply Coupons for return of submissions.
Nonfiction: "Articles on the Apostleship of Prayer and on all aspects of Christian living": current events and social problems that have a bearing on Catholic life, family life, Catholic relations with non-Catholics, personal problems, the liturgy, prayer, devotion to the Sacred Heart. Material should be written in a popular, non-pious style. Length: 1,800 to 2,000 words. Pays 2¢ a word. Department Editor: Mary Pujolas.
Fiction: Wants fiction which reflects the lives, problems, preoccupations of reading audience. "Short stories that make their point through plot and characters." Length: 1,800 to 2,000 words. Pays 2¢ a word. Department Editor: Mary Pujolas.

MIDSTREAM, 515 Park Ave., New York NY 10022. Editor: Shlomo Katz. Monthly. Circulation: 12,000. Buys first rights. Pays on acceptance. Will send a sample copy to a writer on request. Reports in 2 weeks. Enclose S.A.S.E. for return of submissions.
Nonfiction and Fiction: "Articles offering a critical interpretation of the past, searching examination of the present, and affording a medium for independent opinion and creative cultural expression. In sponsoring *Midstream*, a Zionist publication, we are committed above all to free inquiry." Buys historical and think pieces and fiction. Length and payment to be negotiated.

THE MIRACULOUS MEDAL, 475 E. Chelten Ave., Philadelphia PA 19144. Editorial Director: Rev. Donald L. Doyle, C.M. Quarterly. Buys North American serial rights. Buys articles only on special assignment. Pays on acceptance. Will send free sample copy on request. Normally reports in two days. Enclose S.A.S.E. for reply to queries.
Nonfiction: Buys articles only on special assignment.
Fiction: Should not be pious or sermon-like. Wants good general fiction—not necessarily religious, but if religion is basic to the story, the writer should be sure of his facts. Only restriction is that subject matter and treatment must not conflict with Catholic teaching and practice. Can use seasonal material, Christmas stories. Length: 2,000 words maximum. Pays 2¢ and up per word. Occasionally uses short-shorts from 750 to 1,250 words.
Poetry: Maximum of 20 lines, preferably about the Virgin Mary or at least with religious slant. Pays 50¢ a line and up.

MOODY MONTHLY, 820 North LaSalle, Chicago IL 60610. Editor: Robert Flood. For "Church-oriented Christian families, high school and college graduates, some with Bible school training, special interest in the Bible and in the Protestant, evangelical world." Monthly. Circulation: 180,000. Buys all rights. Buys 8 to 12 mss a year. Pays on acceptance. Will send a sample copy to a writer on request. Write for copy of guidelines for writers. Query first. Submit seasonal material 4 months in advance. Reports in 2 months. Enclose S.A.S.E.

Nonfiction and Fiction: Wants material which is warm, evangelical and clearly relevant to daily life of the individual Christian. Personal experience articles, devotionals (factual and anecdotal development), solid treatment of contemporary Christian problems, seasonals, and nonpromotional features on Christian organizations and aspects of Christian work; "news of the Christian world, developments in Christian education, personality sketches, Bible exposition, anecdotal material for women, 'How I Did It' stories of Christians in difficult situations." The "Teen Focus" section wants articles for teens on what Christian young people are doing, outstanding teens and teenage groups; helpful articles on young people's problems; teenage answers to current topics. "The Woman's View" department needs "warm, practical material clearly relevant to the Christian woman and her problems, either fiction or nonfiction." Length: 2,000 to 3,000 words. Pays 3¢ a word. Also uses religious fiction for teens. Length: 1,500 to 2,500 words. Pays 3¢ a word.

Photos: B&w glossies; 35mm color. Pays $15 to $50.

Fillers: Newsbreaks, inspirational anecdotes. Length: 200 to 800 words. Pays 3¢ a word.

MY JEWELS, Box 6059, Cleveland OH 44101. Editor: T. T. Musselman. For six- to eight-year-old children attending Christian Sunday schools. A publication of Union Gospel Press. Quarterly in 13 weekly parts. Buys all rights. Buys "very, very few mss; however, we do welcome inquiries from freelance writers who are interested in handling quarterly assignments." Payment on acceptance. Will send free sample copy to writer on request. Write for copy of guidelines for writers. Query first. Will not consider photocopied submissions. Submit seasonal material (for all major holidays and seasons) 10 months in advance. Reports on material in 90 days. Enclose S.A.S.E. for reply to queries.

Nonfiction and Photos: "Inspirational Bible study. Biographies of real children are welcome. Should be up-to-date and fresh. All material must have fundamental, evangelical Christian emphasis. Generally handled by assignment, but inquiries are welcome." Length: 400 words. Pays 2¢ a word. B&w photos and color slides are purchased with or without mss, but are not returned. "If the seller wishes to retain his original photographs and slides, he should have duplicates made that can be sold to Union Gospel Press. The duplicates will not be returned."

Fiction: Mainstream and religious fiction with Christian emphasis. Query first about length; usually 450 words. Pays 2¢ a word.

Poetry and Fillers: Traditional forms of poetry. Length: 25 lines. "See and Do" puzzles, mazes, dot-to-dot, riddles. Pays 2¢ a word "or at individual rate".

THE NATIONAL JEWISH MONTHLY, 1640 Rhode Island, N.W., Washington DC 20036. Editor: Charles Fenyvesi. National B'nai B'rith monthly magazine. Buys North American serial rights. Pays on publication. Enclose S.A.S.E. for return of submissions.

Nonfiction: Articles of interest to the Jewish community: economic, demographic, political, social, biographical. Length: 3,000 words maximum. Pays 10¢ per word maximum.

NEW CATHOLIC WORLD, 1865 Broadway, New York NY 10023. Managing Editor: Robert J. Heyer. For a "general audience, college educated." Bimonthly. Circulation: 17,000. Buys all rights. Pays on acceptance. Will send free sample copy to writer on request. Submit seasonal material 2 to 3 months in advance. Enclose S.A.S.E. for return of submissions.

Nonfiction, Photos, Fiction, and Poetry: Each issue is theme oriented. 1974 themes: 1) Catholic/Jewish Relations; 2) Lent 1974—Prayer, Fasting and Almsgiving; 3) Sacraments Revisited; 4) Religious Life of the Adolescent; 5) Spanish Catholics; 6) Pentecostals. Buys photo articles. General material concerning issues in religion, literature, politics, etc.; not historical or devotional articles. Also humorous and religious fiction. Length: 1,000 to 2,000 words. Pays $60 to $100. Photos purchased with mss. Pays $20 for b&w. 22 lines maximum for poetry. Pays $25 to $50.

NEW WORLD OUTLOOK, 475 Riverside Drive, New York NY 10027. Editor: Arthur J. Moore, Jr. United Methodist and United Presbyterian publication. For

Christians concerned with the major social issues and the direction of the church in mission. Monthly. Buys North American serial rights. Pays on publication. Will send a sample copy to a writer on request. Enclose S.A.S.E. for return of submissions.

Nonfiction: Articles tackling specific problems and how the church is handling or not handling these problems. Articles appropriate to the church in mission. Length: 2,000 to 2,500 words. Pays about $80 for four published pages, up to $150.

Photos: B&w glossies purchased with mss. Also photos from abroad of special interest or illustrating social conditions at home. Color covers. Pays $15 for b&w, $75 to $200 for cover; average cover payment, $100.

NORTH AMERICAN VOICE OF FATIMA, Fatima Shrine, Youngstown NY 14174. Editor: Steven M. Grancini, C.R.S.P. For Roman Catholic readership. Circulation: 19,000. Pays on acceptance. Publication not copyrighted. Will send free sample copy to a writer on request. Reports on submissions in two weeks. Enclose S.A.S.E. for return of submissions.

Nonfiction and Fiction: Length: 700 words. Pays 1¢ a word.

Photos: Purchased with mss; must have religious slant. Deadlines are the first and 15th of each month.

Fillers: Religious short humor appropriate to format; study publication. Pays 1¢ a word.

OMI MISSIONS (formerly *OMI Mission Magazine*), P.O. Box 96, San Antonio TX 78291. Editor: Rev. Cullen F. Deckert, OMI. For "people interested in the missions and the work of the Oblate Fathers in Texas, Mexico, and the Philippines." Quarterly. Circulation: 50,000. Not copyrighted. Buys very few mss a year. Payment on acceptance. Will send a free sample copy to a writer on request. Will consider photocopied submissions. Submit seasonal material four months in advance. Reports in a month. Enclose S.A.S.E. for return of submissions.

Nonfiction and Photos: "We accept stories about the Oblates in the above mentioned missions. Once in a while a very short seasonal story (Christmas or Easter) may be accepted. All material should be sent to the editor." Buys informational, interview, and photo articles. Length: 600 to 1,200 words. Pays 2¢ a word. Purchases photos with mss and captions are optional. B&w only.

OUR FAMILY, P.O. Box 249, Battleford, Sask., Canada SOM OEO. Editor: Rev. A. J. Materi, OMI. For the Catholic family. Monthly except July and August combined issue. Circulation: 6,941. "Usually buys first North American serial rights, but at times will buy all rights or only first Canadian rights. Will consider purchasing second serial or reprint rights if article is appropriate to current editorial needs." Payment on acceptance. Will send sample copy on request. Write for copy of guidelines for writers. Enclose S.A.E. with Canadian stamps, coin, or International Reply Coupons for return of submissions.

Nonfiction: Articles should be of an informative nature, written clearly and concisely in an unsophisticated, anecdotal style, with an emphasis on human interest. Especially welcome are challenging, contemporary articles on matters of concern to people as individuals and as families. Uses 5 types of articles: "challenging, contemporary articles on all aspects of marriage and parenthood; informative, anecdotal articles on socio-economic matters as they affect the family and individual members of the family; inspirational articles on the use of recreation and leisure by the family; provocative, hard-hitting articles on religion and its meaning in our lives; instructive articles on socio-political matters that affect the family." Also uses true life articles which reveal deep emotion, such as life crises, problems of adjustment, or spiritual journeys. Length: 1,000 to 3,000 words. "Occasionally will accept longer articles." Pays 1¢ to 2¢ a word; "sometimes more".

Photos: Purchased with ms as package (extra payment for photos). Should be at least 5x7 b&w glossies. Pays $3 to $10. We want photo stories and photo essays on personalities, events, and human/religious themes. Payment by arrangement.

Fiction: Stories that reflect lives, problems and preoccupations of audience. "Anything true to human nature. No sentimentality or moralizing. Stories which are hard-hitting, fast-moving, with a real, woven-in Christian message. For average family reader. Avoid stereotyped 'happy' endings." Length: 1,000 to 3,000 words. Pays 1¢ to 2¢ per word.

Poetry: "Should deal with man in search of himself, for God, for others, for love, for meaning in life, for commitment." Length: 8 to 30 lines. Pays $3 to $10, "depending on length and style."
How To Break In: "The magic formula for breaking into our magazine is 'work'. Study our guidelines; pour yourself into your writing, using your own style, creativity and imagination; and then ship your piece off to us. We judge a manuscript by its merits, not by its author."

OUR LADY OF THE SNOWS, National Shrine of Our Lady of the Snows, Belleville IL 62223. Editor: Rev. A. Burak, O.M.I. Published six times yearly for families, particularly women. Buys first-use rights. Pays on acceptance. Reports in one month. Will accept simultaneous submissions of articles, short stories, and filler items. "We are primarily interested in the short-short, inspirational, religious type of writing." Study publication before submitting. Enclose S.A.S.E. for return of submissions.
Nonfiction and Photos: Uses articles that are "religious, both moral and doctrinal, as well as devotional, but written for common folk. No pretension or 'intellectualism': simple language and style, but with something to say." 250 to 500 words. Pays $25 and up. Payment for 8x10 b&w photos submitted with manuscripts begins at $5.
Poetry: Also uses short, meaningful poetry. No payment.

OUR SUNDAY VISITOR, Noll Plaza, Huntington IN 46750. Editor: Richard B. Scheiber. For general Catholic audience. Weekly. Circulation: 400,000. Buys first rights. Buys about 300 mss a year. Pays on acceptance. Will send a sample copy to a writer on request. Query first. Submit seasonal material 2 months in advance. Reports in 1 week. Enclose S.A.S.E. for reply to queries.
Nonfiction: Uses articles on Catholic related subjects. Should explain Catholic religious beliefs in articles of human interest, articles applying Catholic principles to current problems, Catholic profiles, etc. Payment varies depending on reputation of author, quality of work and amount of research required. Length: 1,000 to 1,200 words. Minimum payment for major features is $100 and a minimum payment for shorter features is $50 to $75.
Photos: Purchased with mss; with captions only. B&w glossies, color transparencies, 35mm color. Pays $125 for cover photo story, $75 for b&w story; $25 per color photo, $10 per b&w photo.

THE PENTECOSTAL EVANGEL, 1445 Boonville Ave., Springfield MO 65802. Editor: Robert C. Cunningham. Issued weekly, mainly to members of Assemblies of God churches. Write for free sample copy. Will accept simultaneous submission of articles, short stories, and filler items. Enclose S.A.S.E.
Nonfiction and Photos: Wants devotional articles on individual's spiritual life, true stories of unusual answers to prayer, personal testimonials of conversion and other spiritual experiences, articles on home life which convey Christian teaching, seasonal material on Christmas, New Year, Easter, etc. It is important that writers be familiar with doctrinal views of Assemblies of God and with standards for membership in churches of this denomination. Pays 1¢ to 1½¢ per word. Buys b&w glossy prints (8x10). Color transparencies (no 35mm). Payment varies.
Poetry: Accepts only a small amount of poetry. Payment is 20¢ per line.
Fillers: Uses fillers if they have spiritual value; 10 to 150 words.

PENTECOSTAL TESTIMONY, 10 Overlea Blvd., Toronto 17, Ont., M4H 1A5 Canada. Editor: Earl N.O. Kulbeck. Monthly. Very little freelance material bought. Enclose S.A.E. and International Reply Coupons for reply to queries.
Nonfiction: Must be written from Canadian viewpoint. Subjects preferred are contemporary public issues, events on the church calendar (Reformation month, Christmas, Pentecost, etc.) written from conservative theological viewpoint. Query first. Pay ½¢ per word for originals, ¼¢ per word for reprints. Preferred lengths are 800 to 1,200 words.
Photos: Occasionally buys photographs with mss if they are vital to the article. Also buys b&w photos if they are related to some phase of the main topic of the particular issue. Should be 8x10 b&w prints. Payment is $6 to $10 for cover photos.

Fiction: Might use youth-slanted fiction. Same theological slant, same lengths, same payment as nonfiction. Submit fiction to Joy Hansell.
Fillers: Pays $2.50 for short poems and sonnets; but small amount of these bought. Rarely uses.

PENTECOSTAL YOUTH, P.O. Box 705, Joplin MO 64801. Editor: Aaron M. Wilson. "Primarily edited for youth ages 9 through 17, but is also read by a number of ministers also interested in youth. Leader edition offers program materials and suggestions for youth ministries. Evangelical and Christian in message and approaches." Established in 1956. Monthly. Circulation: 5,000. Buys second serial (reprint) rights and simultaneous rights. Buys 36 to 40 mss a year. Payment on acceptance. Will send free sample copy to a writer on request. Write for copy of guidelines for writers. Submit complete ms. Will consider photocopied submissions if clear copy. "We particularly need articles and fiction for seasonal issues, but interest must be centered in the age limits of the magazine." Submit seasonal material 60 days in advance. "Usually" reports on material accepted for publication in 30 days. Returns rejected material in 30 days. Enclose S.A.S.E.
Nonfiction and Photos: "Character-building articles of interest to youth." Informational, how-to, personal experience, profile, inspirational, short humor, historical, think and short travel articles. "Primarily published for young people of Pentecostal background, and we observe the usual 'holiness' taboos such as tobacco, alcohol, dancing, movies, etc. However, we are not presenting just spiritual or church items. It is intended as a general magazine for Pentecostal youth. Length varies; top is 2,500 words. Normally pays ¼¢ a word; more for special material or specific assignments." Photos purchased with mss. Pays $2 for "routine 8x10 b&w photos; $5 for feature photo. Negative color (8x10 prints preferred). Captions optional. Payment open, but with limited budget."
Fiction, Poetry and Fillers: Humorous and religious fiction. Length: "maximum 2,500, prefer 2,000". Pays ¼¢ a word. Light verse and traditional forms. Length: open. "Payment varies with length." Jokes and puzzles (youth and Bible type). Payment "can vary with material".

PRESBYTERIAN SURVEY, 341 Ponce de Leon Avenue, Northeast, Atlanta GA 30308. Editor: John Allen Templeton. For "members of the Presbyterian Church in the U.S.; average age, 49.5; upper level education, high percentage of college graduates, ministers; community leadership types; $10,000 yearly income average." Established in 1910. Monthly. Circulation: 126,000. Rights purchased vary with author and material. Buys 20 to 50 mss a year. Payment on acceptance. Will send sample copy to a writer for 50¢. Reports in usually 4 weeks. Submit seasonal material 4 months in advance. Enclose S.A.S.E. for return of submissions.
Nonfiction and Photos: Subject matter should be "church-related (Protestant) in content; depth articles with practical theological connotations." Buys inspirational, historical, think, and photo articles with a religious slant. Buys photos with or without mss, or on assignment, and captions are required. Pays $7.50 minimum for 8x10 b&w.

PURPOSE, 610 Walnut Ave., Scottdale PA 15683. Editor: David E. Hostetler. General interest Christian weekly intended to help readers find deeper satisfaction and meaning in life through the resources of the Christian faith and community. Sample copies free on request. Include S.A.S.E. for return of submissions.
Nonfiction and Photos: Articles 750 to 1,500 words, clearly written in terse, fast-moving style, dealing with anything of concern and interest to Christians as individuals, helping them achieve the ideals of the Christian faith personally and in their relationships with others at home and at work, in the church and community. Pays up to 1½¢ a word for unsolicited material; less for second rights and simultaneous submissions. Photos should be 8x10 b&w of professional quality. Pays $5 to $15.
Fiction: Short stories, 1,000 to 2,000 words. Same content and pay as nonfiction.
Poetry: 8 to 24 lines. Pays $3 to $10.

QUEEN OF ALL HEARTS, 40 S. Saxon Ave., Bay Shore NY 11706. Editor: James McMillan, S.M.M. For persons "religiously motivated; interested in Catholic Marian spirituality; all ages, apostolically inclined, interested in their spiritual welfare." Bimonthly. Circulation: about 10,000. Not copyrighted. Buys 40 to 50 mss a year. Pays on acceptance. Will send a sample copy to a writer on request. No query required. Submit seasonal material 6 months in advance. Reports in 1 month. Enclose S.A.S.E. for return of submissions.

Nonfiction and Photos: "Religious subjects on art, spirituality, theology, the apostolate, especially with a Marian theme. This is a devotional magazine." Length: 800 to 1,500 words. Pays $15 to $40. Photos purchased with mss. B&w glossies. Payment varies.

Fiction: Religious. Length: 1,000 to 1,800 words. Pays $15 to $40.

Poetry: Contemporary poetry with a Marian theme. Length: 4 to 24 lines. Payment in free subscription.

RECONSTRUCTIONIST, 15 W. 86th St., New York NY 10024. Editor: Dr. Ira Eisenstein. Monthly. Enclose S.A.S.E. for return of submissions.

Nonfiction: This is a general Jewish religious and cultural magazine publishing literary criticism, reports from Israel and other lands where Jews live, and material of educational or communal interest. Also uses interviews and features dealing with leading Jewish personalities. Preferred length is 3,000 words and payment is from $15 to $25, made on publication.

Fiction and Poetry: Uses a small amount of poetry and fiction as fillers.

REVIEW FOR RELIGIOUS, 612 Humboldt Building, 539 N. Grand Blvd., St. Louis MO 63103. Editor: R.F. Smith, S.J. Issued bimonthly for Roman Catholic religious men and women. Reports in 4 weeks. Enclose S.A.S.E. for return of submissions.

Nonfiction: Prefers 2,000- to 10,000-word articles on ascetical, liturgical and canonical matters. Pays minimum of $6 a page on publication.

Fiction: Occasionally accepts material on religious subjects.

Poetry: Also uses poetry on religious subjects. Pays 50¢ per line.

THE REVIEW OF BOOKS AND RELIGION, Box 2, Belmont VT 05730. Editor: Kendig Brubaker Cully. For "clergy, directors and coordinators of religious education, professors in religion and related fields, lay leaders of all faiths, and general readers, etc." Special articles on children's books and gift books. Monthly: "published in midmonth except December and August." Circulation: 1,500. Buys all rights. "Most articles are solicited, but some unsolicited mss are considered. Book reviewers are invited to submit their credentials for reviewing, and fields of interest. The bulk of the contents are book reviews in religion and adjacent fields, for which there is no pay. The reviewer keeps the book provided." Query first. Submit seasonal material 3 months in advance. Reports in 4 to 6 weeks. Enclose S.A.S.E. for reply to queries.

Nonfiction and Poetry: "Book-oriented articles; attractive style but serious content, dealing with deeply religious dimensions of existence." Length: not over 1,500 words. Poetry is occasionally accepted.

ST. ANTHONY MESSENGER, 1615 Republic St., Cincinnati OH 45210. Editor: Rev. Jeremy Harrington, O.F.M. For Catholic family and high school graduate readers. Monthly. Buys first North American serial rights. Pays on acceptance. Will send free sample copy to a writer on request. Write for copy of guidelines for writers. Reports on submissions within 4 weeks. Enclose S.A.S.E. for return of submissions.

Nonfiction: Uses human nature as subject matter. Modern society, family, religious, psychological and moral problems and positive suggestions for their solution. Also wants humor. Must be concrete, anecdotal, and be of human interest. No writing down, sentimentalism, or preachiness. Length: 2,500 to 3,500 words. Pays 6¢ per word minimum.

Photos: "We usually do our own work, but are in the market for picture stories on personalities, family and social work features." Uses b&w glossy, 7x10. Requires model releases. Pays $10 and up.

Fiction: Anything true to human nature. No sentimentality or moralizing. Need not be specifically religious. Usually 2,500 to 3,500 words. Also short-shorts. Pays minimum of 6¢ a word, up to $300.

How To Break In: "We receive more opinion articles than we want or can publish, so I would recommend a reporting type article that would interview experts on a topic of deep and personal concern to people or a first-person article in which the writer shares an experience with which others can identify. Alexander Solzhenitsyn says it well: 'The task of the writer is to select . . . universal themes and questions: the secrets of the human heart and conscience, the confrontation between life and death, the triumph over spiritual agony, the laws in the history of mankind that were born in the depths of time immemorial and that will cease to exist only when the sun ceases to shine.' "

SAINTS' HERALD, P.O. Box 1019, Independence MO 64051. Editor: Paul A. Wellington. Issued monthly. This is the family magazine of the Reorganized Church of Jesus Christ of Latter Day Saints. Reports in two weeks. Enclose S.A.S.E.
Nonfiction: Wants articles on current religious topics, church members and historical articles of 1,500 words. No payment for articles or fiction.
Photos: Pays up to $8 for good 8x10 pictures concerning the church. Payment for photos on acceptance.
Fiction: 1,500 words relating to current religious problems, challenges, trends.

SANDAL PRINTS, 1820 Mt. Elliott, Detroit MI 48207. Editor: Rev. Allen Gruenke, O.F.M. Capuchin. Bimonthly for friends of the Capuchins. Circulation: 10,500. Buys first rights. Pays on publication. Will send a sample copy to a writer on request. Query first. "Unsolicited mss are not welcome." Articles and photos not dealing specifically with the work of Capuchins will not be considered. Enclose S.A.S.E. for reply to queries.
Nonfiction and Photos: Factual articles dealing with Capuchin missions, home and foreign, and with missionary problems specific to an area in which Capuchins are working. Pays $25 minimum. Buys 8x10 or 5x7 pix with mss. Pays $5 per photo.

SCIENCE OF MIND MAGAZINE, 3251 W. 6th St., Los Angeles CA 90020. Editor: Willis H. Kinnear. Issued monthly. Buys all rights. Pays on publication. Will send free sample copy on request. Reports in six weeks. Enclose S.A.S.E.
Nonfiction: Wants articles on the spiritual aspects of science and philosophy; their relationship to religion; personal experiences of effectiveness of prayer in everyday living. Should be written in language of layman. Slant is toward constructive living by alignment of one's thought with the Power of God within one. Length is 1,000 to 1,800 words. Query not necessary. Payment is approximately 1½¢ per word. Submit all material to Editorial Department.
Verse and Poetry: Uses poems of four to eight lines as filler. Occasionally uses longer poems as centerspread. Rate varies from $3 to $10. Must have spiritual import; imminence of God in creation. Buys first rights.

SCOPE, 422 S. Fifth St., Minneapolis MN 55415. Editor: Miss Lily M. Gyldenvand. For women of the American Lutheran Church. Monthly. Circulation: 325,000. Buys first rights. Buys 200 to 300 mss a year. Pays on acceptance. Will send a sample copy to a writer on request. No query required. Submit seasonal material 4 to 5 months in advance. Reports in 2 to 3 weeks. Enclose S.A.S.E. for return of submissions.
Nonfiction and Photos: Wants live, pertinent articles with a current Christian slant. May recount personal experience with examples and illustrations with which the average woman can easily identify. "Anything that interests seriously concerned Christian women and relates to their lives or that of their family." How-to's, personal experience and inspirational pieces, interviews, profiles, think pieces, photo essays. Length: 700 to 1,000 words. Pays $10 to $50. Buys photos with mss and with captions only. B&w glossies. Pays $7 to $10.
Poetry: Light verse. "We use very little poetry." Length: 4 to 20 lines. Pays $5 to $15.
How To Break In: "A beginning writer could break into *Scope* with a sharp, sparkling, well-written piece that has some significance for our readers. We are especially interested in young women writers who have a point of view to share in regard to their faith or their desires for their own spiritual growth and enrichment."

THE SIGN, Union City NJ 07087. Editor: Rev. Augustine Paul Hennessy. Monthly. Buys all rights. Will send free sample copy to a writer on request. Reports in three weeks. Enclose S.A.S.E. for return of submissions.

Nonfiction and Photos: Uses material of general interest as well as religious material. Wants articles of 1,200 to 3,000 words on social problems, profiles, foreign affairs, human interest. Written in concrete, anecdotal style. Pays $75 to $300. Uses photographs submitted with articles and picture stories.
Fiction: Fiction should have general appeal as well as Catholic interest. Can run up to 3,500 words. Pays $250 to $300.
Poetry: Pays $10.
How To Break In: "I tell prospective writers to follow the lead of their own enthusiasm. This presupposes some knowledge and depth of feeling. Since *Sign* is geared to the evocation of hope, I remind them that challenges to hope come from areas of their own experience—a complicated home, a changing Church, and a shrinking world. And *Sign* is interested in this kind of material."

SIGNS OF THE TIMES, 1350 Villa, Mountain View CA 94041. Editor: Lawrence Maxwell. Seventh-Day Adventist. For religiously inclined persons of all ages and denominations. Monthly. Buys first rights only. Reports in one week to several months. Enclose S.A.S.E. for return of submissions.
Nonfiction: Uses articles of interest to religiously inclined of all denominations. Most material furnished by regular contributors, but freelance submissions carefully read. Sincerity, originality, brevity necessary. Lengths: 700 to 1,800 words.

SISTERS TODAY, St. John's Abbey, Collegeville MN 56321. Editor: Rev. Daniel Durken, O.S.B. "Primarily written and read by religious women of the Roman Catholic Church." Published monthly except July and August. Not copyrighted. Pays on publication. Will send free sample copy on request. Reports promptly. Enclose S.A.S.E.
Nonfiction: Articles, 1,500 to 3,500 words about the Christian life in general and religious life in particular. Religious renewal, community, prayer, apostolates for Sisters today, the role of religious women in today's world, liturgical and Scriptural commentaries. Pays $5 per printed page. Query first with brief description of article.

SOCIAL JUSTICE REVIEW, 3835 Westminister Place, St. Louis MO 63108. Editor: Harvey J. Johnson. Issued monthly except for combination of July-August issues. Does not buy any rights. Query first. Enclose S.A.S.E. for reply to queries.
Nonfiction: Wants scholarly articles on society's economic, religious, social, intellectual and political problems with the aim of bringing Catholic social thinking to bear upon these problems. 2,000 to 3,000 words. Pays about 1¢ a word.

SOUTHERN JEWISH WEEKLY, P.O. Box 3297. Jacksonville FL 32206. Editor: Isadore Moscovitz. For a Jewish audience. Established in 1924. General subject matter is human interest and short stories. Weekly. Circulation: 28,500. Not copyrighted. Buys 15 mss a year. Payment on acceptance. Will send a free sample copy to a writer on request. Will send editorial guidelines sheet on request. Submit seasonal material one month in advance. Reports in 10 days. Enclose S.A.S.E. for return of submissions.
Nonfiction and Photos: Approach should be specifically of "Southern Jewish interest." Length: 250 to 500 words. Pays $10 to $25. Buys b&w photos with mss.

SPIRITUAL LIFE, 2131 Lincoln Rd., N.E., Washington DC 20002. Editor: Rev. Christopher Latimer, O.C.D. "Largely Catholic, well-educated, serious readers. High percentage are priests and religious, but also some laymen. A few are non-Catholic or non-Christian." Quarterly. Circulation: 10,000. Buys first rights. Buys about 20 mss a year. Pays on acceptance. Will send a sample copy to a writer on request. Write for copy of guidelines for writers. No query required. "Brief autobiographical information (present occupation, past occupations, books and articles published, etc.) should accompany article. Follow *A Manual of Style* (University of Chicago)." Reports in 2 weeks. Enclose S.A.S.E. for return of submissions.
Nonfiction: Serious articles about man's encounter with God in the 20th century. Language of articles should be college-level. Technical terminology, if used, should be clearly explained. Material should be presented in a positive manner. Sentimental articles or those dealing with specific devotional practices not accepted. "*Spiritual Life* tries to avoid the 'popular,' sentimental approach to religion and to concentrate on a more intellectual approach. We do not want first-person accounts of

spiritual experiences (visions, revelations, etc.) nor sentimental treatments of religious devotions." Buys inspirational and think pieces. Length: 3,000 to 5,000 words. Pays $40 to $80. "Four contributor's copies are sent to author on publication of article."

STANDARD, 6401 The Paseo, Kansas City MO 64131. Editor: Robert D. Troutman. Adult story paper. Weekly. Will accept second rights and simultaneous submissions. Pays on acceptance. Write for copy of guidelines for writers. Reports in about 60 days. Enclose S.A.S.E. for return of submissions.
Fiction: "Stories should vividly portray definite Christian emphasis or character-building values, without being preachy. Setting, plot, and action should be realistic." Length: 2,000 to 3,000 words. Pays $20 per 1,000 words.

SUNDAY DIGEST, 850 N. Grove Ave., Elgin IL 60120. Editor: L. Richard Burnap. Issued weekly for Christian adults. Buys all rights. Pays on acceptance. Will send free sample copy to a writer on request. Write for editorial requirements pamphlet. Reports on submissions in 4 weeks. Enclose S.A.S.E. for return of submissions.
Nonfiction and Photos: Needs articles applying the Christian faith to personal and social problems, articles of family interest and on church subjects, personality profiles, practical self-help articles, personal experience articles and inspirational anecdotes. Length: 500 to 1,800 words. "Study our product and our editorial requirements. Have a clear purpose for every article or story—use anecdotes and dialog—support opinions with research." Pays 3¢ per word and up. Photos purchased only with mss. Pays about $10 each, depending on quality. Negatives requested (b&w). Return of prints cannot be guaranteed.
Fiction: Occasionally uses fiction that is hard-hitting, fast-moving, with a real woven-in, not "tacked on," Christian message. Length: 1,000 to 1,500 words. Pays 3¢ per word and up.
Poetry: Occasionally used if appropriate to format. Pays 5¢ per word and up.
Fillers: Anecdotes of inspirational value, jokes and short humor; must be appropriate to format and in good taste. Length: up to 500 words. Pays 5¢ per word and up.

SUNDAY SCHOOL LESSON ILLUSTRATOR (formerly *People*), 127 9th Ave., N., Nashville TN 37234. Editor: James E. Fitch. For members of Sunday School classes that use the International Sunday School Lessons and for adults seeking in-depth Biblical information. Quarterly. Circulation: 50,000. Buys all rights. Buys 25 mss a year. Payment on acceptance. Write for copy of editorial guidelines. Query first or submit complete ms. Will not consider photocopied submissions. Submit seasonal material (for Christmas and Easter) 1 year in advance. Returns rejected material in 1 month. Reports on material accepted for publication in 2 weeks. Enclose S.A.S.E. for return of submissions or reply to query.
Nonfiction and Photos: Journalistic articles and photo stories researched on Biblical subjects. Human interest stories that illustrate Biblical situations. Should be written in a contemporary, journalistic style and be based on International Sunday School Lesson outlines. Pays 2½¢ per word. B&w and color photos purchased with ms or on assignment. Captions required. Pays $7.50 to $10.
Fiction and Poetry: Limited amount of religious fiction. Traditional forms of poetry. Pays 2½¢ a word for fiction; $3 to $20 for poetry, depending on length.

THE SUNDAY SCHOOL TIMES AND GOSPEL HERALD, Union Gospel Press, Box 6059, Cleveland OH 44101. Editor: Rev. John Danilson. For Evangelical Christian families, missionaries; an international readership. Bimonthly. Buys all rights. Buys approximately 175 mss a year. Payment on acceptance. Will send free sample copy to writer on request. Write for copy of guidelines for writers. Query first or submit complete ms. Submit seasonal material (for all major holidays) 10 months in advance. Returns rejected material within a month. Reports on material accepted for publication in 90 days. Enclose S.A.S.E. for return of submissions or reply to queries.
Nonfiction and Photos: "Particularly interested in interview type articles about real

people and places, i.e., halfway houses, youth group directors, missionaries, etc. Personal experience articles also desired. Evangelical Christian emphasis should be maintained. Subject matter should be relevant to today's Christian. New, fresh topics are desired. Facts and figures must be accurate and verifiable. (List of sources should be supplied.) All articles must be Bible-based according to the King James Version." Length: 1,000 to 2,000 words. Pays 2¢ per word. B&w and color photos are purchased but not returned. Pays $3 for b&w; $5 to $10 for color slides.

Fiction: Must have strong evangelical viewpoint; Bible-based. Length: 1,000 to 2,000 words. Pays 2¢ per word.

Poetry and Fillers: Traditional forms, blank verse, free verse. Must be related to theme. Length: 25 lines. Pays 2¢ a word. Jokes and short humor. Pays 2¢ a word.

THE TEXAS METHODIST, P.O. Box 1076, Dallas TX 75221. Issued weekly for United Methodist pastors and laymen. Not copyrighted. Query first. Pays on acceptance. Enclose S.A.S.E.

Nonfiction and Photos: Uses articles of interest to United Methodists, especially stories concerning United Methodist personalities and activities. Pays 3¢ a word. Photos purchased with mss or with caption only. Pays $10.

Fillers: Crossword and acrostic puzzles.

THESE TIMES, The Southern Publishing Association, Box 59, Nashville TN 37202. Editor: Kenneth J. Holland. Issued monthly. Buys first and second serial rights. Will send a sample copy to a writer on request. Enclose S.A.S.E. for return of submissions.

Nonfiction: Wants inspirational articles on prayer, faith, love, courage, etc.; those that inspire trust in the Bible; religious liberty; total abstinence; physical and mental health. Feature articles on moral issues. Must show high spiritual standards, exaltation of Biblical principle. Slant for a conservative Christian publication. Preferred length is 500 to 3,000 words. Pays up to 10¢ a word on acceptance.

Photos: Buy pix with mss and for cover use. Cover pix paid for at the rate of $50 to $75 each. Buys first and second rights.

TODAY'S CHRISTIAN MOTHER, 8121 Hamilton Ave., Cincinnati OH 45231. Editor: Mrs. Wilma L. Shaffer. Quarterly. Payment on acceptance. Will send free sample copy to a writer on request. Reports on submissions within one month. Publication not copyrighted. Enclose S.A.S.E. for return of submissions.

Nonfiction: Devotional and inspirational articles for mother in the home. Also articles concerning the problems and pleasures of mothers of preschool children, and Christian child training. Length: 600 to 1,200 words. Also can use some handcraft and activity ideas for preschoolers. Study magazine before submitting. Pays minimum of 1½¢ per word.

TRIUMPH, 278 Broadview Avenue, Warrenton VA 22186. Editor: Michael Lawrence. For "traditional Catholics, ages 18 and up with college education." Established in 1966. Monthly. Circulation: 10,000. Buys first North American serial rights. Buys 15 mss a year. Payment on publication. Will send a sample copy to a writer for $1. Will consider photocopied submissions. Reports in 1 month. Enclose S.A.S.E. for return of submissions.

Nonfiction: General subject matter: "Theological, philosophical, political studies. Commentary on current events from an orthodox Catholic point of view. We are not political conservatives. We transcend the conservative—liberal dialectic. No 'human interest' stories. We would like to see articles on the growing attack on the family." Buys think pieces and movie and book reviews. Length: 1,000 to 3,000 words. Pays 2½¢ a word.

THE UNITED CHURCH OBSERVER, 85 St. Clair Ave. E., Toronto 7, Ont., Canada. Editor: A.C. Forrest; Associate Editor: Patricia Clarke. For families in the United Church of Canada. 12 times a year. Not copyrighted. Pays on acceptance. Will send a sample copy to a writer for 35¢. Query first. Reports in 1 month. Enclose S.A.E. and International Reply Coupons for reply to queries.

Nonfiction: Wants general interest articles on all subjects of interest to church people. No homiletics. Material must have some church connection. Also deal in international affairs. Bright, journalistic style is necessary. Preferred lengths are 1,000 to 2,500 words. Thorough knowledge of the subject, authority and topnotch writing are looked for. Pays $40 minimum.

Photos: Buys photographs with mss and occasional picture stories. Use both b&w and color; b&w should be 8x10; color, prefers 4x5 transparencies but can work from 2¼x2¼ or 35mm. Payment varies.

How to Break In: The best way to break in is with a well-written query which shows some familiarity with 1) our magazine, 2) religion, 3) Canada.

UNITED EVANGELICAL ACTION, P.O. Box 28, Wheaton IL 60187. Editor: Tom Johnston. For Evangelical leaders. Quarterly. Circulation: 12,000. Copyrighted. Pays on publication. Will send a sample copy to a writer on request. Query first. Deadlines approximately 9 months in advance. Leave 2-inch margins on all sides of mss. Reports in 1 to 4 weeks. Enclose S.A.S.E. for return of submissions.

Nonfiction: "Topics of interest to church leaders—including pastors and laymen—and topics which bring to bear matters of events, human interest, and special issues on the evangelical perspective." Recent article: "Why Congressmen Don't Listen to Christians". Length: 1,500 to 2,500 words. Pays about 2¢ a word. Department Editor: Agatha Partridge.

UNITED METHODISTS TODAY, 1661 N. Northwest Highway, Park Ridge IL 60068. Acting Editor: F. Paige Carlin. A general magazine for United Methodists. United Methodist ministers receive a special edition with an added section entitled Today's Ministry edited by the Rev. William C. Henzlik. Monthly. Circulation: 200,000. Buys all rights. Buys up to 75 mss a year. Will send free sample copy to writers on request. Write for a copy of guidelines for writers. Either queries or complete manuscripts are considered. Submit seasonal material 6 months in advance. Reports on material in 2 to 4 weeks. Enclose S.A.S.E. for reply to queries or return of submissions.

Nonfiction and Photos: "Articles that will help readers in their personal growth in the Christian faith, give them a view of denominational and ecumenical affairs, and present the contemporary world in Christian perspective. We like material written out of authors' own experience in strong narrative style backed by adequate and accurate research. Where appropriate, articles should have a United Methodist aspect. Even stories of ecumenical activities or inter-faith cooperation are helped if United Methodists are involved. We use some prayers and poetry as well as essays on personal faith." Submit mss to Manuscript Editor. Length: 750 to 2,000 words. Pays minimum of $100 for major features. "Unposed, technically perfect, action photos" are purchased with or without ms or on assignment. 5x7 or 8x10 black and white prints, 35mm or larger transparencies for color. Pays minimum of $10 for b&w, $25 for color. Submit to Picture Editor.

Poetry: Traditional forms, blank verse, free verse, light verse. "Should relate to our theme, but we're open on 4-line humorous verse." Maximum length 12 lines. Pays $10 to $15.

Fillers: Occasionally uses short church-related or family-related humor. Length: 1 paragraph. Pays $5.

How To Break In: "One way is for freelancers to take a good extension course in feature writing, or fiction, or whatever area of writing they are most interested in. The other way is to make a very conscious search for material that they like and then try to analyze why they like it. Then, of course, there is the other suggestion, and that is 'practice and self-criticism,' which is what all of us who write do all of the time."

U.S. CATHOLIC, 221 West Madison St., Chicago IL 60606. Not soliciting freelance material.

THE UPPER ROOM, 1908 Grand Avenue, Nashville TN 37203. Editor: Wilson O. Weldon. For "people of all ages and many Christian denominations who have personal daily devotions or family devotions." Established in 1935. Bimonthly. Circulation: 2,500,000. Buys all rights. Buys 365 meditations a year. Payment on publication. Will send a free sample copy to a writer on request. Will send editorial

guidelines sheet on request. Enclose S.A.S.E. for return of submissions.
Nonfiction: "Subject matter relates to the many facets of the Christian faith. We issue annually a leaflet on writing meditations for *The Upper Room*. This contains many topic areas of general and specific interest. Leaflet is free on request. No poetry. Space permits development of one major idea per page, accompanied by a meaningful illustration, prayer, and Thought for the Day. Bible text and Bible readings also included. We try to present the merits of the Gospel of Christ and give encouragement in putting the Gospel into practice in everyday life." Length: 250 words. Pays $7 for each meditation used.

THE VINEYARD, 1745 N. Cicero Ave., Chicago IL 60639. Editor: Rev. Daniel Gorham. Established in 1971. For "religious, mainly Eastern Orthodox Christians; also liberal Catholics and Anglicans who have a high interest in social affairs and the public conduct of churches; high on social action." Monthly. Circulation: 15,000. Not copyrighted. Buys 12 to 30 mss a year. Payment on acceptance. Query first. Will consider photocopied submissions. Submit seasonal material 2 months in advance. Reports on material in 2 months. Will send free sample copy to writer on request. Enclose S.A.S.E for reply to queries.
Nonfiction and Photos: "Need articles on the how and wherefore of the improvement of the Orthodox Church in particular and religion in general; also politics and social morals. How Christians can be involved in 'all' matters of interest, especially in the improvement of city and national government. We seek to push for an end to the various national churches in Orthodoxy, such as Greek, Romanian, Albanian, etc., and make it into an American church; to help it improve its outreach and help others not Orthodox understand the Orthodox and what is happening within that world. We don't knock anyone. Be positive only." Length: 100 to 500 words. Pays $15 to $50. B&w photos purchased with or without mss. Captions optional. Pays $10 to $50.

VISTA, Wesleyan Publishing House, Box 2000, Marion IN 46952. Address submissions to Editor of Sunday School Magazines. Publication of the Wesleyan Church. For adults. Weekly. Circulation: 63,000. Not copyrighted. "Along with mss for first use, we also accept simultaneous submissions, second rights, and reprint rights. It is the writer's obligation to secure clearance from the original publisher for any reprint rights." Pays on acceptance. Will send a sample copy to a writer on request. No query required. Editorial deadlines are 9 months in advance of publication. Reports in 6 weeks. Enclose S.A.S.E. for return of submissions.
Nonfiction and Poetry: Devotional, biographical, and informational articles with inspirational, religious, moral, or educational values. Favorable toward emphasis on: "New Testament standard of living as applied to our day; soul-winning (evangelism); proper Sunday observance; Christian youth in action; Christian education in the home, the church and the college; good will to others; world-wide missions; clean living, high ideals, and temperance; wholesome social relationships. Disapprove of liquor, tobacco, theaters, dancing. Mss are judged on the basis of human interest, ability to hold reader's attention, vivid characterizations, thoughtful analysis of problems, vital character message, expressive English, correct punctuation, proper diction. 'Know where you are going and get there.' " Length: 500 to 1,500 words. Pays 2¢ a word for quality material. Also uses verse expressing action, imagery of seasonal sentiment. Length: 4 to 16 lines. Pays 25¢ a line.
Photos: Purchased with mss. 5x7 or 8x11, b&w glossies; portraying action, seasonal emphasis or scenic value. Various reader age-groups should be considered. Pays $1 to $2.50 depending upon utility.
Fiction: Stories should have definite Christian emphasis and character-building values, without being preachy. Setting, plot and action should be realistic. See above (Nonfiction) for standards and taboos. Length: 2,000 to 2,500 words; also short-shorts and vignettes. Pays 2¢ a word for quality material.

THE WAR CRY, The Official Organ of the Salvation Army, 860 N. Dearborn St., Chicago IL 60610. Editor: Lt. Col. William Burrows. For "persons with evangelical Christian background; members and friends of the Salvation Army; the 'man in the street.' " Weekly. Circulation: 290,000. Buys all rights. Buys approximately 200 mss a year. Pays on acceptance. Will send a sample copy to a writer on request. No query required. Submit seasonal material for Christmas and Easter issues at any time. "Christmas and Easter issues are four-color. Rate of payment for material used in these issues is considerably higher than for weekly issue material." Reports in 1 month. Enclose S.A.S.E. for return of submissions.

Nonfiction: Inspirational and informational articles with a strong evangelical Christian slant, but not preachy. Prefers an anecdotal lead. In addition to general articles, needs articles slanted toward most of the holidays, including Mother's Day, Father's Day, Columbus Day, Washington's and Lincoln's birthdays, etc. Length: 1,000 to 1,800 words. Pays $15 to $35.

Photos: Occasionally buys pix submitted with mss, but seldom with captions only. B&w glossies. Pays $5 to $10.

Fiction: Prefers complete-in-one-issue stories. Stories should run 1,500 to 2,000 words and have a strong Christian slant. May have Salvation Army background, but this is not necessary and may be detrimental if not authentic. Can have modern or Biblical setting, but must not run contrary to Scriptural account. Principal Bible characters ordinarily should not be protagonists. Pays $30 to $40.

Poetry: Religious or nature poems. Uses very little poetry "except on Christmas and Easter themes." Length: 4 to 24 lines. Pays $2.50 to $15.

Fillers: Inspirational and informative items with a strong Christian slant. 1¢ to 2¢ per word.

THE WAY, Mennonite Publishing House, Scottdale PA 15683. Editor: Paul M. Schrock. Bimonthly evangelistic publication with contemporary style and format. Buys first and second serial rights. Payment on acceptance. Will send free sample copy to a writer on request. Reports within two weeks. Enclose S.A.S.E. for return of submissions.

Nonfiction: "Personal experience stories showing how faith in God gives meaning and purpose to people today, regardless of their circumstances. Short, fast-moving pieces, high in human interest, that present the Christian life in a manner which is credible and worth emulating." Length: 300 to 1,500 words. Pays 2¢ a word.

Poetry: "Poems that convey in a sincere, fresh way the joy of knowing God." Length: 4 to 12 lines. Usual payment is $5.

WEEKLY BIBLE READER, 8121 Hamilton Ave., Cincinnati OH 45231. Editor: Barbara Curie. Will send a free sample copy to a writer on request. Enclose S.A.S.E. for return of submissions.

Fiction and Fillers: "For children 6 to 7 years old. Uses very brief religion-oriented fiction stories, puzzles, and items, in prose or poetry, and pays from $1 to $10. Do not send Bible stories and nature items, which are staff-written."

WORLD OVER, 426 W. 58th St., New York NY 10019. Editors: Dr. Morris Epstein, Ezekiel Schloss. Buys first serial rights only. Pays on acceptance. Reports within three to four weeks. Enclose S.A.S.E. for return of submissions.

Nonfiction, Photos, and Fiction: Uses material of Jewish interest, past or present for ages 9 to 13 and up. Articles up to 1,200 words; serials of 4,800 words, usually divided into four sections. Query first. Pays 5¢ a word and up. Photos purchased with mss. Glossy. Fiction: Same requirements as nonfiction.

WORSHIP, St. John's Abbey, Collegeville MN 56321. Editor: Rev. Aelred Tegels, O.S.B. "For readers concerned with the problems of liturgical renewal. The readership is largely Roman Catholic with a growing percentage of readers from the other Christian churches." Monthly, except for July and August. Buys all rights. Pays on publication. Reports in two to three weeks. Enclose S.A.S.E. for return of submissions.

Nonfiction: "*Worship* magazine is engaged in an ongoing study of both the theoretic and the pastoral dimensions of liturgy. It examines the historical traditions of worship in their doctrinal context, the experience of worship in the various Christian churches, the finding of contemporary theology, psychology, communications, cultural anthropology, and sociology in so far as these have a bearing on public worship. Since the Second Vatican Council, *Worship* magazine has been fully ecumenical in its editorial board and policies as well as in its contributors and contents. Study a recent issue." Length: 3,000 to 5,000 words. Pays 1¢ to 2¢ a word.

Retirement Publications

DYNAMIC MATURITY, Suite 512, 1730 M Street, N.W., Washington DC 20036. Editor: John Bird. "DM is the official publication of AIM-Action for Independent Maturity. AIM members are the 50 to 65 age bracket, pre-retirees." Established in 1966. Bimonthly. Circulation: 70,000. Rights purchased vary with author and material. Buys 60 mss a year. Payment on acceptance. Will send a free sample copy to a writer on request. Submit seasonal material 4 months in advance. Reports in 1 week. Enclose S.A.S.E. for return of submissions.

Nonfiction and Photos: General subject matter is "health for middle years, pre-retirement planning, second careers, well-developed hobbies, 'people in action' with useful activities, exciting use of leisure, financial preparation for retirement. We like the 'you' approach, nonpreachy, use of lively examples. We try to slant everything toward our age group, 50 to 65. We do not want pieces about individuals long retired. Prefer not seeing poetry, 'inspirational' preachments." Buys how-to, personal experience, profile, humor, nostalgia, travel articles. Length: 1,000 to 2,500 words. Pays 10¢ a word minimum, up to $400 per article. Photos purchased with and without mss for covers. Captions required. Pays $15 minimum for professional quality b&w (5x7, 8x10). Pays $25 minimum for professional quality color photos (35mm or 2¼x2¼ transparencies).

MATURE YEARS, 201 8th Ave. South, Nashville TN 37202. Editor: Mrs. Daisy D. Warren. For retired persons, 60 years and older. Special holiday and seasonal issues. Quarterly. Circulation: 130,000. Buys all rights. Buys about 48 mss a year. Payment on acceptance. Will send sample copy to writer for 42¢. Write for copy of guidelines for writers. Query first. Submit seasonal material 1 year in advance. Reports in 1 month. Enclose S.A.S.E. for reply to query.

Nonfiction, Fiction and Photos: "Seasonal pieces, articles on hobbies, travel, retirement problems, short stories, etc. Projects directed toward needs of older adults. Examples of how older persons are helping others. Writing should be of interest to older adults. No poking fun or mushy sentimental articles. We treat retirement from religious viewpoint. How-to, humor and travel also considered." Length: 1,200 to 1,500 words. Pays $80 maximum. Photos purchased with accompanying mss, or on assignment. 8x10 b&w glossies. Payment varies.

Poetry and Fillers: "No mushy or sentimental poems. Traditional forms or blank verse." Length: 4 to 12 lines. Pays 50¢ to $1 per line. Also uses crossword puzzles.

MODERN MATURITY, 215 Long Beach Blvd., Long Beach CA 90801. Editor: Hubert Pryor. Publication of the American Association of Retired Persons. For retirees. Bimonthly. Buys all rights. Pays on acceptance. Will send a sample copy to a writer on request. Reports in 1 week. Enclose S.A.S.E. for return of submissions.

Nonfiction and Fiction: Service pieces for the retiree relating to income, hobbies, health, living; Americana, nostalgia, reminiscence, personality pieces, inspirational articles, current trends—anything of interest to the older American who wants to be "with it." "Especially can use thoughtful interviews with world figures in their older years, sensitive picture essays on how older people live, outspoken pronouncements by noted persons on matters concerning aging and/or retirement. Also in market for Christmas and other holiday material." Buys fiction occasionally. Length: 1,000 to 1,500 words, nonfiction; 1,500 words maximum, fiction. Pays $100 to $500.

Photos: "Special consideration for picture stories, photographic portfolios, etc." Pays $15 and up per photo; much more for color covers.

Fillers: Puzzles, jokes, short humor. Pays $5 and up.

How To Break In: "Writing a short feature would be the preferred way for a beginner to try for an acceptance by us. The writer must remember the need to hook the older (55 plus) reader."

NRTA JOURNAL, 215 Long Beach Blvd., Long Beach CA 90801. Editor: Hubert Pryor. Publication of the National Retired Teachers Association. For retired teachers. Bimonthly. Buys all rights. Pays on acceptance. Will send a sample copy to a writer on request. Reports in 1 week. Enclose S.A.S.E. for return of submissions.

Nonfiction and Fiction: Service pieces for the retired teacher relating to income, health, hobbies, living; Americana, nostalgia, reminiscence, personality pieces, inspirational articles, current trends. "Also in market for Christmas and other holiday material." Buys fiction occasionally. Length: 1,000 to 1,500 words for nonfiction; 1,500 words maximum for fiction. Pays $100 to $500.

Photos: "Special consideration for picture stories, photographic portfolios, etc." Pays $15 and up each; much more for color covers.

Fillers: Puzzles, jokes, short humor. Pays $5 and up.

RETIREMENT LIVING, 150 E. 58 St., New York NY 10022. Editor: Charles Monaghan. Associate Editor: Helen Alpert. "For pre-retirees (age 50 up) and retirees. Readers are alert, active, forward-looking, interested in all aspects of meaningful living in the middle and later years." Monthly. Buys all rights. Pays on acceptance. Will send a sample copy for 50¢. Write for copy of guidelines for writers (enclose S.A.S.E.). Queries not necessary, prefers to see mss. Submit seasonal and holiday material 4 months in advance. Reports in 2 weeks. "Manuscripts must be accompanied by S.A.S.E.; otherwise not returned."

Nonfiction and Photos: "We like factual personal experiences, humor, income ideas, money management, self-fulfillment; articles with a strong service value or how-to with names and sources for reader follow-up." Unusual travel stories only. Length: 1,000 to 2,000 words. Pays 7¢ a word. "We reserve all rights to edit and rewrite to suit our distinct style and space requirements. Photos must be of professional quality." Pays $10 and up.

Science Publications

Publications classified here aim at laymen interested in technical and scientific developments and discoveries, applied science, and technical or scientific hobbies. Journals for professional scientists, engineers, repairmen, etc., will be found in the Trade Journals section.

BIG COUNTRY 10-5 NEWS, P.O. Box 12181, Denver CO 80212. Editor: Rose Harper. For "ages 14 to 99, generally users of two-way radios known as Citizen Band. (Do not confuse with hams—amateur radio operators). All education levels. Interested in human beings in the same field or related fields and in the unusual aspects of CB radio (not too heavy on technical details)." Established in 1970. Monthly. Circulation: 2,500. Buys all rights, but will reassign them to author after publication. Payment on acceptance. Will send sample copy to writer for an 8¢ stamp. Will send editorial guidelines sheet to a writer on request (enclose S.A.S.E.). Reports in 1 month. Enclose S.A.S.E. for return of submissions.

Nonfiction and Photos: Publishes "material affecting users of CB radio. Possible subjects: Just how well do items in the Federal Register register with the average citizen? Who has influenced making of rules and regulations (Part 95 of FCC Rules and Regulations). List price—is this an advertising fraud? What sunlight, heat, cold (or any other such things) do to your CB rig. Articles only at present time." Freelancer should write with "short words, clear meanings, accuracy of facts. Don't fake the peculiar vocabulary, please, as it takes a CBer to do this. Emphasis on the worth of human beings to themselves, to others. We don't mind spice, but will not accept filth: *There is a great difference.* We are unique in our field and have created an opinion impact far beyond our size—something that should be cause for astonishment because we seldom feature VIP's (called Vicious Influence Peddlers in our field) but rather we feature 'you, me, the guy, the gal from everyday life' against a background of CB radio. We use 'handles,' or full legal names for people we feature. We are fair to the 'legals' and 'illegals' using CB radio; both have fair and valid points to make. We do not want to see cutesy stuff. Corn is ok, if it is interesting corn. No preaching, no moralizing. No standing on a pedestal and looking down at the reader. No articles about the Kennedys, absolutely, not unless one of them is caught using a CB radio with a valid reason. New product material accepted. Articles wanted on human rights. Legal rights denied the average citizen by our government agencies. Progress in the actual structure and use of CB radio. New developments in

electronics that are of medical benefit (the pacemakers for heart patients are an example of this)." Buys informational, how-to, personal experience, interview, profile, inspirational, humor, historical, think, expose, nostalgia, personal opinion, photo, travel (big on this), book reviews (in CB field), spot news, successful and unsuccessful business operations (why they succeeded or failed, too), merchandising techniques for dealers and salesmen, and technical, without using big words. Length: 500 to 1,000 words. Pays 1¢ a word. Regular column uses unusual photos. Purchases photos with and without mss and captions required. B&w snapshots. Pays $1. Pays $5 for collages pertaining to communications. Dept. Editor: Jim Harper.
Poetry: Regular poetry columns. "Poetry that touches the heart, no matter what subject." Accepts all forms of poetry. Length: 4 to 32 lines. Pays $1 to $3.
Fillers: Buys newsbreaks, clippings, short humor. Length: 50 words to 200 words. Pays $1.

FLYING SAUCER NEWS, THE METAPHYSICAL MAGAZINE, 359 West 45 St., New York NY 10036. Editor: James S. Rigberg. Established in 1953. Published twice yearly. Circulation: 5,000. Will send free sample copy on request. Enclose S.A.S.E. for return of submissions.
Nonfiction: Unidentified flying objects, occult, material about astronauts. "We prefer to reprint and pay a small sum to the author."

FREY SCIENTIFIC COMPANY, 465 South Diamond St., Mansfield OH 44903. Address all submissions to: The Editor. Buys all rights. Buys 50 to 75 rhymes a year. Pays "on acceptance, between October 1 and February 1. Rhymes that arrive after the latter date are held and paid for about November 1, the start of our next publication season." Enclose S.A.S.E. for return of submissions.
Poetry: "We use humorous quatrains and limericks in our annual school science materials catalog, which is sent to every high school and college in the U.S. Each rhyme—limerick, quatrain, or couplet—is matched as best as possible to the appropriate section of our catalog. Rhymes pertaining to physics are included in the physics section, biology in the biology section, chemistry in the chemistry section, earth science to earth science, etc." Interested in buying material from writers "who can combine, in a single rhyme, our requirements of proper rhyme construction, distinct scientific reference, and humor. Generally, we will waive any of the three requirements if the rhyme is strong in the other two." Pays $5 per rhyme.

HAM RADIO MAGAZINE, Greenville NH 03048. Editor: James R. Fisk. For amateur radio licensees and electronics experimenters. Special May issue: antenna. Established in 1968. Monthly. Circulation: 42,000. Buys all rights. Buys 200 mss a year. Payment on acceptance. Will send free sample copy to writer on request. Write for copy of guidelines for writers. Query helpful, but not necessary. Submit special issue material 6 months in advance. Reports in 1 month. Enclose S.A.S.E. for return of submissions or reply to queries.
Nonfiction and Photos: "Technical and home construction articles pertaining to amateur radio. Stress is placed on new development. Technical articles of interest to the radio amateur, or home construction articles pertaining to amateur radio equipment." Length: 500 to 5,000 words. Pays approximately $16 per magazine page. Sharp, clear glossy prints (4x5 to 8x10) purchased with accompanying mss.

THE INFO JOURNAL, P.O. Box 367, Arlington VA 22210. Editor: Paul J. Willis. For scientists and laymen interested in unusual facts and events. Irregular. Circulation: 2,000. Buys North American serial rights. Pays on publication. Will send a sample copy to a writer for $1. Query not required. Enclose S.A.S.E. for return of submissions.
Nonfiction and Photos: Articles as well-researched and documented as possible, with good references and bibliographies. Written in clear and intelligent English. Subject matter: the sciences and philosophy of science. Cryptoscience and Forteana. Natural phenomena of a controversial nature, such as UFO's, sea-serpents, unusual archaeological discoveries, developments in the physical and biological sciences not extensively covered in the standard scientific journals. "We are not interested in sensationalism, or material lacking any useful references. Ideas presented may be highly speculative, but good scholarship is sine qua non." Any

length considered, but prefers 2,000 to 5,000 words. Photos purchased with mss. All payment is by arrangement.

MECHANIX ILLUSTRATED, 1515 Broadway, New York NY 10036. Editor: Robert G. Beason. Recreation Editor: Bill D. Miller. Home and Shop Editor: Tom Philbin. Managing Editor: Arthur J. Maher. Special issues include boating (spring), new cars (October). Monthly. Buys all rights except for picture sets. Pays on acceptance. Write for copy of guidelines for writers. Query first. Reports promptly. Enclose S.A.S.E. for reply to queries.

Nonfiction: Uses 1,500- to 2,500-word feature articles about science, inventions, novel boats, planes, cars, recreational vehicles, weapons, health, money management, unusual occupations, usually with mechanical or scientific peg, but not too technical. Examples from the March '73 issue are: "Our New 1-2 Punch in the Sky" and "Build Our Budget Houseboat." Also uses home workshop projects, photos, kinks, etc. Pays from $100 to $500 and up for articles. Pays $75 to $100 per published page for Home and Shop.

Photos: Photos should accompany mss. Flat $400 for transparencies of interesting mechanical or scientific subjects accepted for cover; prefers 4x5, but 2¼ square is acceptable. Inside color: $300 for one page, $500 for two, $700 for three, etc. Single feature photos involving new developments, etc., in the field, b&w, $25. Home and Shop tips illustrated with one photo, $25. Captions are required. B&w picture sets, up to $350. Requires model releases.

Fillers: Pays $75 for half-page fillers.

How To Break In: "Read *MI* carefully before submitting an article or query. Get to know what we're looking for, along with the readership we're aiming at. You'll be saving us a lot of time. And you'll also be saving yourself a lot of time when it comes to rewrites, etc."

OCEANS, 125 Independence Drive, Menlo Park CA 94025. Editor: Don Greame Kelley. For the "alert, involved, and mobile. Two-thirds of our subscribers are under 45. Nearly two-thirds have family incomes over $15,000. Over a third have valid passports and they use them." Established in 1969. Bimonthly. Circulation: 20,000. Buys all rights, but will reassign them to author after publication; first North American serial rights, second serial rights, and simultaneous rights. Payment on publication. Buys 40 to 50 mss a year. Will send a free sample copy to a writer on request. Will send editorial guidelines sheet on request to writer. Query first desirable. Will consider photocopied submissions. Reports in 2 to 3 months, "because we are usually behind owing to the quantity submitted." Enclose S.A.S.E. for return of submissions.

Nonfiction and Photos: "Wants articles on the world-wide realm of salt water: marine life (biology and ecology), oceanography, man-sea history, geography, undersea exploration and study, voyages, ships, coastal areas including environmental problems, seaports and shipping, transocean aviation, islands, food-fishing and aquaculture (mariculture), peoples 'of the sea' including anthropological and archaeological materials." Freelancer should be "simple, direct, factual, very readable (avoid dullness and pedantry, make it lively and interesting but not cute, flip, or tongue-in-cheek; avoid purple prose). Careful research, good structuring, no padding. Our magazine is more serious than the common run of diving mags; less technical than *Scientific American*. We have a reputation for exceptional readability besides fine photography and other graphics. We do not want articles on scuba; adventuring, travel tend to be overworked. Prefer no sport fishing, boating, surfing, other purely sport-type matter. Diving OK if serious in purpose, unusual in results or story angle. We want articles on rarely visited islands, ports, or shores which have great intrinsic interest, but not treated in purely travelogue style. Can use more on sea birds, port cities, sea-based peoples." Buys informational, how-to (limited), personal experience, a few interviews, a few profiles, historical, photo, travel (not pure, per se) and limited technical articles. Length: 1,000 to 5,000 words. Pays 8¢ a word. Purchases photos with mss, sometimes separately. Captions required. Prefers 8x10 b&w glossy. Pays $15 to $75. Buys color transparencies, original, 35mm and up. Pays $25 to $100, by size, highest for cover.

POPULAR ELECTRONICS, (including *Electronics World*), 1 Park Ave., New York NY 10016. For "persons with an avocational interest in electronics. Median age: 33 years." Monthly. Circulation: 372,000. Buys all rights. Buys 80 to 90 mss a year. Pays on acceptance. Query first. Will consider photocopied submissions. Returns rejected material in 3 weeks. Acknowledges acceptance of material in 1 month. Enclose S.A.S.E. for reply to queries.

Nonfiction: "State-of-the-art reports, tutorial articles, short construction projects, etc. The writer must know what he's talking about and not depend on 'hand-out' literature from a few manufacturers or research laboratories. The writer must always bear in mind that the reader has some knowledge of electronics." How-to's, historical articles, think pieces, exposes, tutorials. Length: 3,000 words maximum. Pays $500 maximum.

POPULAR MECHANICS, 224 W. 57th St., New York NY 10019. Editor: Jim Liston. Executive Editor: Sheldon Gallager. Managing Editor: John Linkletter. Home and Shop Editor: Wayne Leckey. Buys all rights. Pays 1 week after acceptance. Query first. Include S.A.S.E. for reply.

Nonfiction: Exciting male interest articles with strong science, exploration and adventure emphasis. Looking for reporting on new and unusual developments. The writer should be specific about what makes it new, different, better, cheaper, etc. Lengths: 300 to 2,000 words. Pays $300 to $500 and up.

Photos: Dramatic photos are most important, and they should show people and things in action. Occasionally buys picture stories with short text block and picture captions. The photos must tell the story without much explanation. Topnotch photos are a must with Craft Section articles. Can also use remodeling of homes, rooms and outdoor structures. Pays $15 and up.

Fillers: How-to-do-it articles on craft projects and shop work well-illustrated with photos and drawings. Finished drawings suitable for publication are not necessary; rough but accurate pencil drawings are adequate for artist's copy. Pays $10 for filler items.

POPULAR SCIENCE, 355 Lexington Ave., New York NY 10017. Editor: Hubert P. Luckett. Monthly. Buys exclusive rights (one-time with wire-service photos). Reports within 2 weeks. Pays on acceptance. Enclose S.A.S.E. for reply to queries or return of submissions.

Nonfiction: This man's magazine of news and new ideas needs material on automobiles, television, hi-fi, electronics in general, boating, photography, hobbies, home workshop activity such as woodworking and metalworking, new products, new tools, stories on how things work, space, aviation, exploration, invention, leisure activities, adventure with a scientific or mechanical angle, and new developments in theoretical and applied science. Style should be crisp, lean, lively, and tightly organized. Articles must tie in with basic interest in applied science. Open market for how-to-make-it articles; illustrations are important. Query suggested for feature articles; many are staff-prepared. Good illustrations will enormously increase chances of acceptance. Gives some assignments usually on speculation with no guarantee for first time and unknown contributors; pays travel expenses and some others. Pays about $150 per printed page and up.

Photos: Prefers b&w 8x10 glossies to contacts, and occasionally uses color. Cover rates are open for negotiation. Usually pays a flat rate of $20 for other pix used, on acceptance. See nonfiction.

Fillers: Uses shortcuts and tips for homeowners, home craftsmen, car owners, mechanics and machinists.

RADIO-ELECTRONICS, 200 Park Ave. S., New York NY 10003. Editor: Larry Steckler. For electronics professionals and hobbyists. Monthly. Circulation: 157,000. Buys all rights. Pays on acceptance. Send for "Guide to Writing." Reports on submissions in 2 weeks. Enclose S.A.S.E. for return of submissions.

Nonfiction: Interesting technical stories on electronics, TV and radio, written from viewpoint of the TV service technician, serious experimenter, or layman with technical interests. Construction (how-to-build-it) articles used heavily. Unique projects bring top dollars. Cost of project limited only by what item will do. Emphasis on "how it works, and why." Much of material illustrated with schematic diagrams and pictures provided by author. Pays about $60 to $100 per magazine page.

Photos: Purchased with mss. Model releases required. Payment included in article price. 8x10 glossy.

SCIENCE AND MECHANICS, 229 Park Ave, S., New York NY 10003. Editor. Tony Hogg. For young men interested in mechanical and scientific subjects. Monthly. Circulation: 350,000. Will send sample copy to a writer for 60¢. Reports on submissions within 2 weeks. Buys all rights. Pays on acceptance. Query first. Enclose S.A.S.E. for reply to queries.
Nonfiction and Photos: Bright, easy-to-read but thoroughly researched features dealing with things rather than ideas: boats, guns, planes, etc.—the unending flow of new gadgets and inventions being developed. They should also deal with the physical sciences rather than the social sciences—rocketry, aviation, engineering, oceanography—new and unusual developments in these fields. Other type features of interest are round-up articles on inventions or products involved or needed in some new field, activity or sport. Length: Rarely over 2,000 words. Pays a minimum of $40 per printed page, including artwork. Payment goes considerably higher, depending on importance of material. Photos purchased with mss and captions.

SCIENCE DIGEST, 224 W. 57th St., New York NY 10019. Editor: Richard F. Dempewolff. Science monthly "covering news, trends and developments in all of the disciplines," for readers of all ages. Circulation: 160,000. Buys all rights. Buys 80 to 100 mss a year. Pays on acceptance. Will send a sample copy to a writer for 50¢. Query first. Submit seasonal material 3 months in advance. Returns rejected material in 2 to 4 weeks. Enclose S.A.S.E. for reply to queries.
Nonfiction: Authoritative pieces on any of the sciences. Illustrations are important, and should include diagrams wherever possible, and regular photo illustrations. Occasional social science and medical science articles. Read magazine before querying. "Emphasis on accuracy, interesting material, broad coverage across the disciplines." Buys personal experience articles "from experts only." Occasionally buys science-oriented think pieces, exposes, travel articles. Length: 1,000 to 2,000 words. Pays $50 to $350. Photos purchased with mss or with captions only. 5x7 or larger glossies. Accepts most sizes of 4-color transparencies for cover illustration.
Fillers: Newsbreaks. Department Editor: Douglas Colligau.

SCIENCE NEWS, 1719 N Street, N W., Washington DC 20036. Editor: Kendrick Frazier. "*Science News* is at present entirely staff-written."

SCIENTIFIC AMERICAN, 415 Madison Ave., New York NY 10017. Articles by professional scientists only.

73 MAGAZINE, Peterborough NH 03458. Publisher: Wayne Green. For amateur radio operators and experimenters. Monthly. Buys all rights. Pays on acceptance. Reports on submissions within a few weeks. Enclose S.A.S.E. for return of submissions.
Nonfiction and Photos: Articles on anything of interest to radio amateurs—construction projects, theory, activities, etc. Query not necessary but desirable. Pays approximately $20 per page. Photos purchased with ms as illustrations.

Social Science Publications

HUMAN BEHAVIOR, 12031 Wilshire Blvd., Los Angeles CA 90025. Editor: Marshall Lumsden. For a "college educated audience, interested in social, especially behavioral sciences, all ages." Established in 1972. Monthly. Circulation: 25,000. Buys first North American serial rights. Buys 20 mss a year. Payment on acceptance. Will send free sample copy to a writer on request. Query first. Will consider photocopied submissions. Reports in 30 to 45 days. Enclose S.A.S.E. for reply to queries.
Nonfiction and Photos: Subject matter consists of nonfiction on social sciences and profiles of prominent social scientists. Length: 1,500 to 3,500 words. Pays $200 to $600. Buys photos with or without mss. Pays $25 per b&w photo. Accepts size 5x7 and up. Pays $50 per color photo; size 35mm and up. Accepts color transparencies.

POPULAR PSYCHOLOGY, 14018 Ventura Blvd., Sherman Oaks CA 91043. Editor: Stephen West. Established in 1972. About half of our readers "are currently enrolled in school at undergraduate or graduate level; mostly in the social sciences. The rest of our market tends to be educated upper middle class business and professional people, many in education, social welfare, psychology and other social professions." Bimonthly. Circulation: 100,000. Buys all rights, "but we generally release on request for reprint, and if we sell the reprint, we share the proceeds." Buys "several dozen" mss a year. Payment on acceptance. Query first. Will send sample copy to writer for $1. Will consider photocopied submissions, but "if it is being considered elsewhere simultaneously, we'd like to know where." Enclose S.A.S.E. for reply to queries.
Nonfiction: "We write only about psychology, but we are fairly generous about what we include under that umbrella. Writer should know what he's talking about." Informational, how-to, personal experience, interview, profile, humor, historical, think pieces, book reviews, personal opinion (only from psychologists). Length: 1,000 to 6,000 words. Pays $50 to $500.

PSYCHOLOGY TODAY, 317 14th Street, Del Mar CA 92014. For social scientists and intelligent laymen concerned with society and individual behavior. Monthly. Unsolicited mss not generally accepted; query first. Each ms will be edited by staff and returned to author prior to publication for comments and approval. Author should retain a copy. Address all queries and ms to Articles Editor. Reports within 1 month. Enclose S.A.S.E. for reply to queries.
Nonfiction: All mss written by scholars in various fields. Primary purpose is to provide the nonspecialist with accurate and readable information about society and behavior. Technical and specialized vocabularies should be avoided except in cases where familiar expressions cannot serve as adequate equivalents. Technical expressions, when necessary, should be defined carefully for the nonexpert. References to technical literature should not be cited within article, but 10 to 12 general readings should be listed at end. Suggested length: 3,000 words. Payment is $500.

SEXOLOGY, 200 Park Ave., S., New York NY 10003. Editor: Ms. Thetis Powers. Monthly. Buys all rights. Pays on acceptance. Query first. Enclose S.A.S.E. for reply to queries.
Nonfiction: Uses articles on all aspects of sexual behavior, particularly from M.D.'s and Ph.D.'s, but freelance authors welcomed also. Articles "submitted on spec." Simple, popular style. Length: average is 1,800 words. Pays from $125 for most articles. Will pay higher for special articles.

SOCIETY, Rutgers University, New Brunswick NJ 08903. Editor-in-chief: Irving Louis Horowitz. Senior Editor: Howard S. Becker. For "educators, policy-makers, social scientists." Monthly. Circulation: 70,000. Buys all rights. Buys 20 mss a year. Pays on publication. Will send a free sample copy to a writer on request. Query first. Use Chicago Style Book. Submit seasonal or special material 6 months in advance. Reports in average of 3 months. Enclose S.A.S.E. for reply to queries.
Nonfiction: Social science and social policy. "Treatment is positive, non-ideological, informative—above all, based on social science data and findings." Does not want material on welfare and sexual deviance. Length: 4,000 to 10,000 words. Magazine Editor: Mary Symons Strong. Also wants material for regular Round-Up of Current Research.
Photos: B&w glossies. Photo submissions should be sent to Mike Fender, Art Director.

SWING, 1255 Prospect Ave., Hermosa Beach CA 90254. Managing Editor: Suzanne Heck. For "intelligent adults." Biweekly. Pays on publication. Query first for articles. Enclose S.A.S.E.
Nonfiction, Photos, and Fiction: "Deals with sociosexual material. Recent articles have dealt with new types of marital relationships, the problem of jealousy, female bisexuality, multilateral relationships, and other subjects of interest to a readership made up primarily of married couples. We are looking for well-written, well-researched articles, occasional pieces of fiction, and photo essays on these and similar subjects. While we have no self-imposed limitations on the subjects we will consider, we are not interested in obscenity, pornography, or material in poor taste." Length: 1,000 to 10,000 words. Pays 2¢ to 5¢ a word.

Sport and Outdoor Publications

The magazines listed here are intended for active sportsmen, sports fans, or both. They buy material on how to practice and enjoy both team and individual sports, material on conservation of streams and forests, and articles reporting on and analyzing professional sports such as baseball or football.

Users will note that several of the editors mention that they do not wish to see "Me 'n Joe" stories. These are detailed accounts of one hunting/fishing trip taken by the author and a buddy—starting with the friends' awakening at dawn and ending with their return home, "tired but happy."

For the convenience of writers who specialize in one or two areas of sport and outdoor writing, the magazines are subcategorized by the sport or subject matter they emphasize. Magazines in related categories (for example, Hunting and Fishing; Archery and Bowhunting) often buy similar material (in this case, articles on bow and arrow hunting). Consequently, writers should read through this entire Sport and Outdoor category to become familiar with the subcategories and note down the ones that contain markets for their own type of writing.

Magazines concerned with horse breeding, hunting dogs, or the use of other animals in sport are classified with the Animal magazines. Publications dealing with automobile or motorcycle racing will be found in the Automotive and Motorcycle category. Outdoor magazines that exist to further the preservation of nature, placing only secondary emphasis on preserving nature as a setting for sport, are listed in the Nature, Conservation, and Ecology category. Newspapers and Sunday supplements and Regional magazines are frequently interested in conservation or sports material with a local angle. Camping magazines are classified in the Travel, Camping, and Trailer category.

Archery and Bowhunting

ARCHERY WORLD, 534 N. Broadway, Milwaukee WI 53202. Editor: Glenn Helgeland. For "archers—average education, hunters and target archers, experts to beginners." Subject matter is the "entire scope of archery—hunting, bowfishing, indoor target, outdoor target, field." Bimonthly. Circulation: 65,000. Buys first serial rights. Buys 30 to 35 mss a year. Pays on acceptance "or as near to it as possible." Will send a free sample copy to a writer on request. Query first. Tries to report in 2 weeks. Enclose S.A.S.E. for reply to queries.
Nonfiction: "Get a free sample and study it. Try, in ms, to entertain archer or show him how to enjoy his sport more and be better at it." Wants how-to, semitechnical, and hunting adventure articles. "Looking for more good technical stories." Also uses profiles and some humor. Length: 1,000 to 2,200 words. Payment is $50 to $150.
Photos: B&w glossies purchased with mss and with captions. "Like to see proofsheets and negs with submitted stories. We make own cropping and enlargements." Color transparencies purchased for front cover only. Will look at color prints "if that's the only photo available."

BOW AND ARROW, P.O. Box HH/37249 Camino Capistrano, Capistrano Beach CA 92624. Editor: Chuck Tyler. For archery competitors and bowhunters. Bimonthly. Buys all rights, "but will relinquish all but first American serial rights on written request of author." Pays on acceptance. Will send free sample copy to a writer on request. Study magazine and query first. Reports on submissions in six weeks. Study publication. Author must have some knowledge of archery terms. Enclose S.A.S.E. for reply to queries.
Nonfiction: Articles: bowhunting, major archery tournaments, techniques used by champs, how to make your own tackle, and off-trail hunting tales. Likes a touch of humor in articles. Also uses one technical article per issue. Length: 1,500 to 2,500 words. Pays $35 to $125.

Photos: Purchased as package with mss; 5x7 minimum or submit contacts with negatives (returned to photographer). Pays $50 for cover chromes, 2¼ square, minimum.

BOWHUNTER MAGAZINE, 9715 King James Court, Fort Wayne IN 46804. Editor: M.R. James. "Readers are bowhunters of all ages, backgrounds and experience. All of our readers share two common passions . . . hunting with the bow and arrow and a love of the great outdoors." The October/November issue is a special for deer hunters. Established in 1971. Bimonthly. Circulation: over 50,000. Buys all rights, but will reassign them to the writer after publication. Buys more than 50 mss per year, "but writers must have a knowledge of bowhunting." Payment on publication. Will send a free sample copy to a writer on request. Will send a set of editorial guidelines on request. Copy deadline for special October/November issue is mid-June. "We are presently well-stocked with deer hunting material and advise a query letter." Reports in 4 weeks. Enclose S.A.S.E. for reply to queries or return of submissions.

Nonfiction, Photos and Fillers: "Our articles are written for, by and about bowhunters. Most material deals with big or small game hunting; however, some technical material on equipment and a few personality profiles are used. We demand that writers inform as well as entertain our readers. Woven into each article should be where-to-go and how-to-do-it material. Writers should anticipate readers' questions and answer them within the article (e.g., costs involved, services of guides or outfitters, season dates, equipment used, etc.). Our publication is called 'The Magazine for the Hunting Archer' with good reason; we use no target or field archery material. Conservation articles have a chance of selling if bowhunters can relate to them." Length: 250 to 3,500 words. Payment depends on "length, importance; varies with the average being in the $40 to $60 range, features, $100 and up." Photos are important and should accompany mss. B&w glossies should be 5x7 or 8x10 and "we do purchase a few at $5 to $10 each." Very little color used but payment for cover material is $50; uses either 35mm or 2¼x2¼ transparencies. Photo Editor: Steve Doucette. Buys an occasional newsbreak, tip, or short humor piece. Length: 100 to 200 words. Payment is $5 to $10.

Basketball

BASKETBALL WEEKLY, 19830 Mack Avenue, Grosse Point MI 48236. Publisher: Roger Stanton. 18 issues during season, November to April. Circulation: 30,000. Buys all rights. Pays on publication. For free sample copy, send a large S.A.S.E. Reports in 2 weeks. Also include S.A.S.E. with submissions and queries.

Nonfiction, Photos and Fillers: Current stories on teams and personalities in college and pro basketball. Length: 800 to 1,000 words. Payment is $25 to $35. 8x10 b&w glossy photos purchased with mss. Also uses newsbreaks.

Bicycling

BICYCLING, P.O. Box 3330, San Rafael CA 94901. Editor: Gail Heilman. Monthly. Buys all rights. Pays on publication. Will send a sample copy to a writer on request. Write for copy of guidelines for writers. Enclose S.A.S.E. for return of submissions.

Nonfiction: "Features unusual bicycle adventures, bike racing, family bicycle trips, vacations, surveys of technical problems, equipment review, health articles, bicycle commuting, racing, maintenance, Bikeway news, history. All articles should encourage the reader to ride a bicycle or to take a particular trip, or to adopt a new method of bicycle travel, through the presentation of facts or by capturing his fancy in the pleasure of cycling. Must be informative and authentic." Length: 1,000 to 4,000 words. Payment is 50¢ a column inch.

Photos: "B&w photos are welcome if accompanied by ms; prefer 8x10 b&w glossy. 35mm or 2¼ color transparencies for cover unaccompanied by ms may be considered for color covers. Interesting color covers are always in demand." Payment is $5 for b&w $25 for color covers.

Fiction: "May be humor, suspense, and adventure about adult bicycle travel." Length: 1,000 to 4,000 words. Payment is 50¢ a column inch.

Boating

AMERICAN BOATING, 3717 Mt. Diablo Blvd., Lafayette CA 94549. Editor: Miles Ottenheimer. For "boating enthusiasts in the 13 Western states." Established in 1971. Monthly. Circulation: 50,000. Buys first serial rights. Buys 40 mss a year. Payment on publication. Will consider photocopied submissions. Reports within 1 month. Enclose S.A.S.E. for return of submissions.
Nonfiction, Photos, and Fiction: General subject matter is "specific boating stories and general interest pieces. We are particularly interested in well-written stories and are looking for offbeat or different subjects, preferably with art. We try to cover the complete boating field as well as feature stories that appeal to all boatmen. We are interested in all types of articles." Length: up to 2,500 words. Pays $1 per published inch and more if agreed to by author and publisher. Dept. Editor: Dave Abrahamson. Buys photos with and without mss, on assignment, captions required. Pays $5 per 8x10 b&w glossy print used. Pays $10 for each color transparency used. Double for cover. Dept. Editor: Dave Clark. Fiction Editor: Dave Abrahamson.

BOATING, 1 Park Ave., New York NY 10016. For "sail and powerboat enthusiasts, informed boatmen, not beginners. Median age 43, income $16,000." Publishes special Boat Show issue in January; Annual in April (newsstand sale only). Monthly. Circulation: 210,000. Buys first periodical rights or all rights. Buys 130 mss a year. Pays on acceptance. Will send a sample copy to a writer for 75¢. Submit seasonal material 6 to 8 months in advance. Query first. Reports in 2 months. Enclose S.A.S.E. for reply to queries.
Nonfiction: Uses articles about cruises in powerboats or sailboats that offer more than usual interest; how-to-do-it pieces illustrated with good b&w photos; piloting articles, seamanship, etc.; new developments in boating; profiles of well-known boating people. The editor advises, "Don't talk down to the reader. Use little fantasy, emphasize the practical aspects of the subject." Length: 300 to 3,000 words. Payment is $25 to $350, and varies according to subject and writer's skill. Regular department "Able Seaman" uses expertise on boat operation and handling; about 1,100 to 1,500 words; pays $100 to $150 per piece.
Photos: Buys photos submitted with mss and with captions only. 8x10 preferred, b&w. Interested in photos of happenings of interest to a national boating audience. Pays $20 to $25 each. "Also buys color transparencies for both cover and interior use, 2¼x2¼ negative or larger preferred. Pays $100 to $300 for one time usage, but not for anything that has previously appeared in a boating publication." Creative Director: Bud Loader.
Fillers: Uses short items pertaining to boating that have an unusual quality of historical interest, timeliness, or instruction.
How To Break In: "I'd suggest that a writer study a couple of issues of the magazine to get a feeling of how we approach our reader editorially. Then select some topic that would be of interest to a national audience of boatmen, preferably both powerboatmen and sailors. We get more submissions than we can possibly use for sailors and sailing, relatively few of interest solely to powerboatmen. In other words, a new writer would have a better chance of selling a story to us if it were interesting to the dual audience, or to powerboatmen alone. Too many new writers aren't willing to do their homework, which involves studying the market first. They dump their ill-conceived, frequently badly presented material on a burdened editor and expect him to wade through the piece and give him a critique on how to improve it if he's willing to buy it. It's unrealistic, for the editor hasn't the time and isn't running a school in writing. From a time-invested standpoint, it would make sense for the beginning writer to try a short filler subject for us, rather than to go for the jackpot. Unless, of course, he has a great story or article that will sell itself. Acceptability of a piece for our magazine hinges at least as much on the quality of the writing as it does on the subject matter. One man will take a trip around the world and produce bilge water for a manuscript; another, like E.B. White, will row across Central Park Lake and make it a great adventure in the human experience. There's no substitute for talent."

CANADIAN SAILING, 626 Main St., Penticton, BC, Canada. Editor: Dr. David Boyd. Not copyrighted. Quarterly. Circulation: 4,000. Pays on publication. Will send free sample copy to writer on request. Reports in 2 weeks. Include S.A.E. and International Reply Coupons for return of submissions.
Nonfiction and Photos: Wants articles dealing with all forms of sailing, both racing and cruising. Technical articles on sailboat construction and design, sail cut and control, cruising areas and safety at sea, also humorous topics. Length: 2,000 words. Pays 2¢ a word. Photos: b&w, diagrams or maps illustrating articles.

LAKELAND BOATING, 412 Longshore Drive, Ann Arbor MI 48107. Editor: David R. Kitz. For "fresh water pleasure boaters (power and sail)." 10 times a year. Circulation: 25,000. Buys first serial rights. Buys 30 mss a year. Pays on publication. Will send a free sample copy to a writer on request. Query first. Special boat show issue in January; fitting-out articles needed for March or April issues. Mss must be typed and double spaced. Submit seasonal or special material at least 3 months in advance. Reports in "1 week to several months." Enclose S.A.S.E. for reply to queries.
Nonfiction and Photos: "Cruise stories and personal adventure-type articles seem to have the greatest interest. These should be entertainingly written, of course, but they must also be well-documented with names of harbors, marinas, charts and booklets available, eating places, motels, historical aspects and places of interest. Good photographs are necessary, almost without exception. How-to-do-it articles are always interesting, but they must be accompanied by drawings or photographs. Articles on sailing or racing technique or boat maintenance, if they are adequately illustrated, are always welcome. Fishing, canoeing, camping, hunting, general outdoor subjects, or historical articles are accepted very infrequently and only if they have a fresh and unusual twist. The majority of *Lakeland Boating* readers are knowledgeable boaters in both power and sail and for this reason are rarely interested in articles that are too fundamental or would normally appeal only to the beginner. We prefer 8x10 glossy b&w photos and/or color transparencies. However, smaller sizes and Polaroid prints (b&w) are acceptable if they are sharp and crisp; 35mm b&w photographs must be accompanied by the negatives; 35mm color slides are acceptable. Photographs intended for use on the cover must be a 2¼ size or larger. However, since the great majority of covers tie in with an inside feature, we rarely have an opportunity to use a photograph of general interest. Any outstanding photograph will always be considered, but it must be mid-America oriented." Length: 200 to 2,000 words. Payment is $20 to $150 for ms and photos.

POWER BOAT ANNUAL, 130 Shepard St., Lawrence MA 01843. Editor: Harland Wilbur. For "power boat buyers." Annual. Circulation: 74,000. Buys all rights. Buys about 3 mss a year. Pays on publication. Will send a sample copy to a writer on request. Query first. Submit seasonal material 3 months in advance. Reports in 2 weeks. Enclose S.A.S.E. for reply to queries.
Nonfiction and Photos: "Informative, helpful articles on how to buy boats and marine products, with lots of photos." Buys how-to's and personal experience articles. Length: 1,000 words minimum. Pays $30. B&w glossies, color transparencies, color prints purchased with mss.

POWERBOAT MAGAZINE, P.O. Box 3842, Van Nuys CA 91407. Editor: Bill Ames. For performance conscious boating enthusiasts. January, Boat show issue; March, Jet drive issue; June, Water ski issue; October, Outboard issue; November, Stern Drive issue. Monthly. Circulation: 50,000. Buys all rights or one-time N.A. serial rights. 70% freelance. Pays on publication. Will send free sample copy on request. Query first. Reports in 2 weeks. Enclose S.A.S.E. for reply to queries.
Nonfiction and Photos: Uses articles about power boats and water skiing that offer special interest to performance-minded boaters, how-to-do-it pieces with good b&w pictures, developments in boating, profiles on well-known boating and skiing individuals, competition coverage of national and major events. Length: 1,500 to 2,000 words. Pays $100 to $150 per article. Photos purchased with mss. Prefers b&w 8x10. 2¼x2¼ color transparency preferred for cover; top quality vertical 35mm considered. Pays $50 to $100 for one-time use.

RUDDER MAGAZINE, 1515 Broadway, New York NY 10036. Editor: Stuart James. For boat owners. Established in 1895. Monthly. Circulation: 125,000. Buys all rights. Buys 60 mss a year. Payment on acceptance. Query first required. Will consider photocopied submissions. Submit seasonal material 6 months in advance. Address Jeanne Hines, Asst. to the Editor. Reports in 1 to 4 weeks. Enclose S.A.S.E. for reply to queries.

Nonfiction and Photos: Subject matter consists of articles on boats and boating. "We're receiving too many personal cruise stories that do not add to the readers' knowledge." Buys informational, how-to, personal experience, humor, and new product articles. Length: 2,000 to 3,000 words. Pays $50 to $300. Photos purchased with or without mss, on assignment, and captions required. Specifications are "verticals for cover" (color). Pays $300.

Fillers: Buys fillers related to boating. Length: 500 to 1,000 words. Pays $50 to $100.

SAIL, 38 Commercial Wharf, Boston MA 02110. Editor: Murray Davis. For audience that is "strictly sailors, average age 35, better than average education." Special issues: "Cruising issues, fitting-out issues, special race issues (e.g., America's Cup), boat show issues." Monthly. Copyrighted. Acquires first North American serial rights. Buys 100 mss a year. Pays on publication. Will send a free sample copy to a writer on request. Submit seasonal or special material at least 3 months in advance. Returns rejected material in 2 weeks. Acknowledges acceptance of material in 1 month. Enclose S.A.S.E. for return of submissions.

Nonfiction: Wants "articles on sailing: technical, techniques, and feature stories." Interested in how-to, personal experience, profiles, historical, new product, and photo articles. "Generally emphasize the excitement of sail and the human, personal aspect." Length: 1,000 to 2,000 words. Payment is $50 to $300.

Photos: B&w glossies purchased with mss. Payment is $10 to $25. Color transparencies purchased. Payment is $35 to $200, $200 for covers.

SAILING MAGAZINE, 125 East Main Street, Port Washington WI 53074. Editor: William F. Scanen III. For "almost all sailors, most are between the ages of 35 and 44, most are professionals with incomes from $10,000 to $24,000 annually." Established in 1966. Monthly. Circulation: 20,000. Not copyrighted. Buys 3 or 4 mss a year. Payment on publication. Will send a sample copy to a writer for 75¢. Will send set of editorial guidelines to a writer on request. Query first required. Will consider photocopied submissions. Reports in 2 weeks. Enclose S.A.S.E. for reply to queries.

Nonfiction and Photos: "Usually stories are written in conjunction with pictures. These are usually cruising stories, say to islands or faraway places. We concentrate on telling a story mostly through pictorial material; the story is necessary in that it complements the pictures. We try to give the constant feeling of the experience of sailing." Buys informational, photo, and travel articles. Length: 800 to 1,300 words. Pays $20 maximum; depends on the story. Purchases photos with and without mss, on assignment and captions required. One-time rights purchased. Pays $10 per 8x10 b&w glossy used. Photo Editor: Mrs. Micca L. Hutchins.

SEA, P.O. Box 20227, 3468 Long Beach Blvd., Long Beach CA 90801. Editor: Harry E. Monahan. For "recreational boat owners in the 13 western states, including Alaska and Hawaii; also British Columbia. Power boats as well as sailboats, large and small. Interests include racing and cruising." Established in 1908. Monthly. Circulation: 56,000. Buys first North American serial rights. Buys 50 mss a year. Payment on publication. Will send free sample copy to writer on request. Query first or send complete ms. Will consider photocopied submissions. Submit seasonal material 6 months in advance. Reports in 90 days. Enclose S.A.S.E. for reply to queries or return of submissions.

Nonfiction and Photos: "Freelance material generally confined to cruising articles and technical or how-to features; most news items are covered by staff or regular correspondents. Cruising generally confined to Pacific Coast. Emphasis is on the regional material as against the national scope of the other major boating magazines." Personal experience, historical, nostalgia, travel. Length: 1,200 to 4,000 words. Pays $30 to $200. B&w photos 5x7 minimum. Pays $7.50 to $35; $35 to $100 for 35mm (minimum) color transparencies. Must relate to magazine theme. Photo Editor: Gene Esquivel.

SEA AND PACIFIC MOTOR BOAT, P.O. Box 20227, Long Beach CA 90801. Editor: Harry E. Monahan. For Western boat owners, power and sail, cruising and racing. Monthly. Buys first serial rights. Buys 30 mss a year. Pays on publication. Will send a free sample copy to a writer on request. Submit seasonal material 4 months in advance. Reports in 30 days. Enclose S.A.S.E. for return of submissions.
Nonfiction: "Freelance material mainly is cruising type stories, places to visit with a boat; in market for good technical articles from writers with credentials in the technical area they are writing about." Travel articles should be "within reasonable range of readership area." Length: 600 to 3,600 words. Payment is $35 to $150.
Photos: B&w glossies and 2¼x2¼ or larger color transparencies purchased with mss or with captions only. Payment is $7.50 to $100.

SMALL BOAT WORLD, 21 Charles St., Westport CT 08880. Editor: William J. Dukes. For "owners of small boats—mostly outboard power boats—some inboards." Subject matter is "boating how-to and where-to." Established in 1972. Published 10 times a year. Copyrighted. Buys all rights. Buys 1 ms per issue. Pays on publication. Will send a sample copy to a writer for 75¢. Query. Will not consider photocopied submissions. Submit material 2 months in advance. Enclose S.A.S.E.
Nonfiction and Photos: Articles on places to boat; how-to, personal experience. 8x10 b&w glossies purchased with mss. Pays $100 to $150.

YACHTING, Yachting Publishing Corp., 50 West 44th Street, New York NY 10036. Editor: William W. Robinson. For yachtsmen interested in powerboats and sailboats. Monthly. Circulation: 119,000. Buys North American serial rights only. Reports on submissions in 3 weeks. Enclose S.A.S.E. for ms return.
Nonfiction and Photos: Articles on yachting in narrative style. Length: 3,000 words maximum. Pays 6¢ per word. Article should be accompanied by 6 to 8 photos. Pays $15 each for b&w photos, "more for color when used."

Bowling and Billiards

BOWLERS JOURNAL, Suite 214, 1825 N. Lincoln Plaza, Chicago IL 60614. Editor: Mort Luby. For "bowling fans of all ages." Established in 1913. Monthly. Circulation: 17,000. Buys first North American serial rights. Buys 50 mss a year. Payment on publication. Will send free sample copy to a writer on request. Enclose S.A.S.E. for return of submissions.
Nonfiction and Photos: General subject matter is "profile of pros. Stories about tournaments, and unusual characters in bowling or billiards." Seeks "offbeat material" and does not want articles on handicapped bowlers. Buys interviews, profiles, and articles on successful business operations. Length: 1,000 to 2,000 words. Payment: $50 to $75. Buys 8x10 b&w glossies with mss. Captions required. Pays $10 to $20.

BOWLING, 5301 S. 76 St., Greendale WI 53219. Editor: Stephen K. James. Monthly. Pays on publication. Reports within 30 days. Enclose S.A.S.E. for return of submissions.
Nonfiction and Photos: This is the official publication of the American Bowling Congress. "This is a specialized field and the average writer attempting the subject of bowling should be well-informed. However, anyone is free to submit material for approval." Wants articles about unusual ABC leagues and tournaments, personalities, etc., featuring male bowlers. Length: 500 to 1,200 words. Pays 3¢ to 5¢ per word. $5 to $10 per photo.

THE WOMAN BOWLER, 5301 S. 76 St., Greendale WI 53219. Editor: Mrs. Helen Latham. For "women bowlers, ages 8 to 90; people bowling in sanctioned leagues and tournaments; news media; trade groups, manufacturers, etc." Monthly; May-June, July-August issues combined. Circulation: 117,000. Buys all rights. Buys about 25 mss a year. Pays on acceptance. Will send a sample copy to a writer on request. Query first. Submit seasonal material 2 months in advance. Reports in 1 month. Enclose S.A.S.E. for reply to queries.
Nonfiction and Photos: Articles on "women's bowling, competitive or administrative." Does not want articles on "senior citizens and handicapped bowling."

Buys interviews, profiles, spot news, historical pieces. Pays $15 to $50. Photos purchased with mss. B&w glossies. Pays $5 to $10.
Fillers: Puzzles. Pays $15 to $50.

Football

ALL SOUTH CAROLINA FOOTBALL ANNUAL, P.O. Box 3, Columbia SC 29202. Editor: Sidney L. Wise. Issued annually, August 1. Pays upon acceptance. Query first. Deadline for material each year is 10 weeks preceding publication date. Enclose S.A.S.E. for reply to queries.
Nonfiction and Photos: Material must be about S.C. high school and college football teams, players and coaches. Pays "modestly." Photos: Buys with mss and with captions only. B&w should be 5x7 or 8x10 glossies. Color should be 4x5 transparencies. Uses color on cover only.

FOOTBALL DIGEST, 1020 Church St., Evanston IL 60201. Editor: John Kuenster. Managing Editor: Michael K. Herbert. For football enthusiasts. Established in 1971. 10 times a year. Circulation: over 200,000. Query first. Study magazine before querying. Enclose S.A.S.E. for reply to queries.
Nonfiction and Photos: Articles on various aspects of professional football: profiles of players and coaches, studies of teams, current statistics, pertinent photos of players in action. Length and payment subject to negotiation.

FOOTBALL NEWS, 19830 Mack Ave., Detroit MI 48236. Editor: Roger Stanton. For college and professional football fans; "very knowledgeable." Established in 1939. Weekly during season. Circulation: 100,000. Not copyrighted. Buys 10 to 20 mss a year. Payment on publication. Will send sample copy to writer for 25¢. Query first. Reports in 4 weeks. Enclose S.A.S.E. for reply to query.
Nonfiction and Photos: "Articles on players and coaches; current and historical; personality pieces. Preference given to sportswriters. Highly informative, concise, positive approach." Interview, profile, historical, expose, and nostalgia articles. Length: 750 to 1,500 words. Pays $25 to $50. Buys football action photos with mss. Captions required. Pays $5 to $10. Photo Editor: Larry Donald.

TOUCHDOWN, P.O. Box 7747, Phoenix AZ 85011. Editor: William P. Waltner. For "predominately male (18 to 35), middle to high income, sports-minded" audience. Established in 1972. 9 issues yearly (July through January, then March and May). Circulation: 25,000. Rights purchased vary with author and material. Buys about 30 mss a year. Payment on publication. Will send sample copy to writer for $1. Query first or submit complete ms. Submit seasonal material 3 months in advance (June issue, preseason edition concerning what to look for in coming season). Reports on material in 4 weeks. Enclose S.A.S.E. for reply to queries or return of submissions.
Nonfiction and Photos: Articles concerning NFL pro football; player and team profiles; interviews with players and interesting personalities tied in with pro football. "Controversial pieces OK, but we do not care to see anything degrading the sport, its players, etc." Woman's column covers "humorous aspects of professional football. Recipes for quick, easy dishes. Must be written in the style of a woman as if they were talking face to face." Length 700 to 2,500 words. Pays $50 to $500. 8x10 b&w glossies. Pays $5 to $25 depending on rights and quality. "35mm color OK, but prefer larger format." Pays $35 and up; $150 minimum for cover.
Fiction: Mystery, suspense, adventure, humorous, serialized novels. Theme: open. Length: 700 to 2,500 words. Pays $50 to $500.
Fillers: Newsbreaks and short humor. Length: 10 to 200 words. Pays $5 to $25.

General Sports Interest

AAU NEWS, AMATEUR ATHLETE YEARBOOK, 3400 West 86th Street, Indianapolis IN 46268. Editor: Marsha F. Smelkinson. For "AAU members and others interested in amateur sports (track & field, swimming, boxing, wrestling, basketball, etc.), school and college coaches and athletic directors; members of sports press and media." Established in 1925. Monthly, plus yearbook. Circulation: 14,000. Payment varies. Will send free sample copy to a writer on request. Will consider photocopied submissions. Reports immediately. Enclose S.A.S.E. for return of submissions.

Nonfiction and Photos: General subject matter is "profiles of top amateur athletes and athletic volunteers or leaders. Reports on AAU championships, previews of coming seasons, etc." Writer should "emphasize contribution to amateur sport in USA. We would like to see features on unusual sports programs and the volunteers who do so much for the youth they help get involved in AAU activity." Buys interviews, profiles, photo, sport book reviews, and spot news articles. Seeks photos of champions as soon as completed. One or two for features; as available for post event coverage. Length: up to 1,000 words. Pays from $10 to $50. Color photos only on assignment. Pays $1 to $25.

BLACK SPORTS MAGAZINE, 386 Park Avenue South, New York NY 10016. Editor: Dick Edwards. For "blacks of intermediate age and education with an interest in the world of sport." Established in 1971. Monthly. Circulation: 250,000. Buys all rights. Buys 25 to 30 mss a year. Pays 60 days after publication. Will consider photocopied submissions. Submit seasonal material 3 months in advance. Reports in 3 to 4 weeks. Enclose S.A.S.E. for return of submissions.

Nonfiction and Photos: General subject matter deals with "personality profiles and situational analysis dealing with sports and constituent offshoots. Articles should be well structured, but not tightly structured, with well-defined transitions. The outlook should be one of a curious, informed observer, who acts and reacts within a given situation. *Black Sports* concerns itself less with accomplishments on the field of play and more with the man making the news. The game, coaches, players, and officials all come under close and continuous scrutiny. The key is honesty in observation and reporting, with an eye toward the Black perspective. Fan mail type profiles are horrendously overworked. No one, athletes included, is an angel. Though outright accusation may be stretching things a bit, a hint of what's really going on is a must. We would like to see articles on (1) the black pro official, (2) a legal unscrambling of all the legislative moves made in behalf of and in spite of organized sport's hierarchy." Buys interviews, profiles, historical, think, expose, and photo articles. Regular columns that solicit freelance material are: TCB, The Man, and Historically Speaking. Length: 1,200 to 2,500 words. Pays $50 to $100. Photos are purchased with or without mss and captions are required. Pays $25 per shot for 8x10 b&w glossies. Pays $50 for cover and $35 for inside color photos; transparencies preferred.

LAND OF ENCHANTMENT SPORTS MAGAZINE, P.O. Box 25024, Albuquerque NM 87125. Editor: Greg J. Lay. For persons interested in New Mexico sports. Established in 1970. Bimonthly. Circulation: 5,000. Buys all rights, but will usually assign rights to author after publication. Second serial (reprint) rights. Simultaneous rights. Buys 24 mss a year. Will send free sample copy to writer on request. Write for copy of guidelines for writers. "Prefer to see manuscript, but will gladly answer query." Will consider photocopied submissions. Submit seasonal (sports seasons) material 3 months in advance, "if possible." Reports within 3 weeks. Enclose S.A.S.E. for return of submissions or reply to queries.

Nonfiction and Photos: "Need articles for 12-year-old young athletes as well as 50-year-old sports fans. Sports and recreation in New Mexico; hiking, camping, hunting in New Mexico. Control of sports by participants; conservation of recreational resources in New Mexico; female athletes. In personality features, concentrate more on the person's motivation, less on statistics. Need age-group and prep sports mostly, but also interested in college or pro athletes." Informational, how-to, personal experience, interview, profile, inspirational, humor, historical, think pieces, expose (carefully), nostalgia, personal opinion, successful sports business operations, new sports products. Length open. Pays $5 to $25 for articles. 4x5 or 5x7 b&w glossies purchased with or without accompanying mss. Captions required.

Fiction: Any form related to sports or outdoor activity. Length open. Same rate of payment as for nonfiction.

Poetry: Traditional, blank verse, free verse, avant-garde, light verse. Length open. Pays $1 to $5.

Fillers: Quizzes with New Mexico angle, short humor, New Mexico sports featurettes. Length open. Pays $1 to $5.

LETTERMAN MAGAZINE, Box 804, 330 Naperville Road, Wheaton IL 60187. Editor: Paul Nyberg. Managing Editor: David Mathieu. *"Letterman* is America's only national high school sports magazine. It is the only publication written specifically for the 14- to 18-year-old male age group. Subscribers are members of interscholastic teams." Monthly. Circulation: 200,000. Buys all rights. Buys about 50 mss a year. Pays on publication. Will send a sample copy to a writer for 50¢. Query first. Submit seasonal material 2 to 3 months in advance. Reports in 1 month. Enclose S.A.S.E. for reply to queries.

Nonfiction and Photos: *"Letterman* is filled with basically 2 kinds of material: (1) feature articles on outstanding high school athletes. These articles are personality sketches and explain why a boy has achieved both as an athlete and academically, socially, etc. (2) instructional or training material to help boys develop in areas of skills and attitudes." Style should be "simple, straightforward, and never cute. *Letterman* is written for participants. And since our focus is on the high school sports scene, rather than the college and professional sports scene, there are no ready-made heroes. We have to create our own." Buys how-to's, personal experience and inspirational pieces, interviews, profiles, humor, spot news, historical articles, and coverage of new products. Length: 500 to 3,000 words. Pays 3¢ to 10¢ per word. Photos purchased with mss; with captions only. B&w glossies, color transparencies. Pays $10 to $50.

MINNESOTA SPORTS FAN, 224 W. Franklin, Minneapolis MN 55404. Editor: Robert E. Harris. For season ticket holders of Minnesota Vikings, North Star and Twins professional sports teams. Established in 1972. Monthly. Circulation: 23,000. Buys all rights but will reassign rights to author after publication. Buys 50 to 60 mss a year. Pays on acceptance. Will send free sample copy to writer on request. Query first. Will consider photocopied submissions. Enclose S.A.S.E. for reply to queries.

Nonfiction and Photos: "Mostly nonfiction articles of interest to Minnesota sports fans. Must have some Minnesota orientation or be of interest because of region or subject." Skiing, snowmobiling, how-to, interview, profile, personal opinion, reviews. Length: 1,200 words minimum. Pays $50 to $100. Photos purchased with accompanying mss. Captions required.

RX SPORTS AND TRAVEL, Rx Golf and Travel, Inc., 447 S. Main St., Hillsboro IL 62049. Editor: Harry Luecke. For physicians. Bimonthly. Circulation: 205,000. Buys all rights. Pays on acceptance. Query first. Reports on submissions within 2 weeks "when possible." Enclose S.A.S.E. for reply to queries.

Nonfiction: Articles on sports, recreation, leisure, and travel of interest to physicians. Articles on golf, tennis, hunting, fishing, boating, shooting and all other major participant sports and on travel. Style is in the *Sports Illustrated-Holiday-New Yorker* genre. Slant is toward physicians, but any mention of technical, medical or related subjects is strictly taboo. Aim is to entertain readers and inform them of places to go and things to do on vacation and during their leisure hours. Normal minimum is 2,000 words; maximum 3,000 words. Pays $100 to $350. "Freelance work solicited."

Photos: Purchased with mss; physicians participating in golf, tennis, fishing and other sports. Informal group shots, all physicians, preferred. Photos must have some action. No "family album" shots used. Photos are desirable but not necessary to support editorial. Photos submitted with mss may be b&w glossies or color transparencies; candid photos should be 8x10 b&w glossies.

SPORT, 205 East 42nd Street, New York NY 10017. Editor: Dick Schaap. Monthly. For male spectator sport enthusiasts, ages 18 to 35. Buys all rights. Payment is made on acceptance. Query preferred. Reports within 10 days. Enclose S.A.S.E. for reply to queries.

Nonfiction: "Most of our article ideas originate with the editors, therefore we need original, unusual sports ideas. It is no good to query us on a profile of an athlete; chances are, we have thought of doing him. But if you were to write us suggesting an unusual angle on the athlete, perhaps even a byline, we would definitely be inter-

ested. Our regular departments are mostly staff-written." Pays $350 to $1,000; $15 to $50 for acceptable shorts.
Photos: Generally assigned separate from mss. Pays $25 for b&w; $100 page rate for color or $25 plus $150 day rate on assignment; $500 for cover.

SPORTING NEWS, 1212 N. Lindbergh Blvd., St. Louis MO 63166. "We do not actively solicit freelance material."

SPORTS DIGEST, P.O. Box 494, North Miami FL 33161. Editor: Douglas A. Lang. For "professional and businessmen (dentists, lawyers, stockbrokers, doctors, etc.) and their families. All submissions should be suited for family reading." Established in 1971. Monthly. Circulation: 100,000. Generally buys all rights or may buy second serial rights. Buys 40 to 60 mss a year for national section. Local affiliates, however, make hundreds of purchases independently. Payment is generally on acceptance, although in some cases it is on publication. Will send free sample copy to a writer on request. Will setorial guidelines sheet on request. Submit seasonal material 3 to 3½ months in advance. Reports in 2 to 4 weeks. Enclose S.A.S.E. for return of submissions.
Nonfiction and Photos: General subject matter is "factual material (color illustrated) favorable to sports in general, amateur and professional alike. Special emphasis is placed on significant sports personalities and events." Tries to publish stories that are in their respective season. "New perspectives always are desirable. Slant may be serious or with a light touch. Illustrations are essential. *Sports Digest* differs from other national sports magazines in that it publishes two magazines in one: there is a section with stories of national and international interest wrapped around multiple local sections featuring articles on local sports figures and activities. Various local sections dwell heavily on accomplishments of youth. Taboo subjects include anything creating a negative impression about a sport or sports figure." Buys informational, personal experience when done by well-known persons, interviews, profiles, inspirational, humor, historical, nostalgia, personal opinion when done by well-known persons. Length: 1,200 to 1,800 words with 1,500 to 1,600 word range in high demand. Pays $75 to $125 per mss. Cover story slightly more. Photos purchased with mss and on assignment. Captions required. Pays $10 for 8x10 b&w. However, they are rarely used. Prefers 35mm and larger for color. Pays $25 each on assignment.

SPORTS ILLUSTRATED, Time & Life Bldg., Rockefeller Center, New York NY 10020. Outside Text Editor: Pat Ryan. Primarily staff-written, with small but steady amount of outside material. Weekly. Reports in 1 week. Pays on acceptance. Buys all rights or North American serial rights. Include S.A.S.E. for ms return.
Nonfiction: Material falls into two general categories: regional (text that runs in editorial space accompanying regional advertising pages) and long text. Runs a great deal of regional advertising and, as a result, considerable text in that section of the magazine. Regional text does not have a geographical connotation; it can be any sort of short feature (600 to 2,000 words) that has a timeless quality: humor, reminiscence, personality, but it must deal with some aspect of sport, however slight. Long text (2,000 to 5,000 words) must have same connection, however tenuous, with sports, should be major personality, personal reminiscence, knowing look into a significant aspect of a sporting subject, but long text should be written for broad appeal, so that readers without special knowledge will appreciate the piece. Wants quality writing. Pays $250 for regional pieces, $750 minimum for long text.
Photos: "Do not care to see photos until story is purchased."

SPORTS TODAY, 919 Third Ave., New York NY 10022. Managing Editor: Herb Gluck. For male sport enthusiasts. Bimonthly. Buys all rights. Pays on acceptance. Will send a sample copy to a writer for 50¢. No query required. Reports in 1 to 3 weeks. Enclose S.A.S.E. for return of submissions.
Nonfiction and Photos: Major emphasis is on the main spectator sports of baseball, basketball, football, hockey. Also covers golf, horse racing, etc. Wants dramatic material. Length: 1,500 to 2,000 words. Pays $200. Buys Kodachrome photos for front cover.

SPORTSHELF NEWS, P.O. Box 634, New Rochelle NY 10802. Editor: Irma Ganz. For "all ages interested in sports." Established in 1949. Bimonthly. Circulation: 150,000. Pays on acceptance. Query first required. Enclose S.A.S.E.
Nonfiction: Subject matter is exclusively sports. Buys how-to articles. Payment varies, "averages about $50 for 1,000 words."

SPORTSLAND MAGAZINE, 204-435 Berry St., Winnipeg, Manitoba, Canada R3J 1N6. Editor: Mel Dagg. Total sports concept. Monthly. Circulation: 10,000. Buys all rights but will reassign rights to author after publication. Buys 150 mss a year. Payment on publication. Will send free sample copy to a writer on request. Query first or submit complete ms. Will not consider photocopied submissions. Submit seasonal material 3 months in advance. Reports on material within 21 days. Enclose S.A.E. and International Reply Coupons.
Nonfiction and Photos: "All types of sporting articles on Manitoba and Northwestern Ontario only. More interested in large participating or spectator sports. Lots of action required." Informational, personal experience, travel (Manitoba and Northwestern Ontario only). Length: 1,500 to 3,000 words. Payment "scaled to $50." Pays $5 for solicited 8x10 b&w glossies. $3.50 for unsolicited. Pays $8 for unsolicited 35mm transparencies; $10 for solicited; $15 for unsolicited cover; $20 for solicited.
Fillers: Short humor, 800 to 1,200 words. Pays $10.

THE SPORTSWOMAN, P.O. Box 7771, Long Beach CA 90807. Editor: Marlene Jensen. For "women, age 16 to 46. Many teach physical education. Most are actively involved in sports and have feminist leanings." Established in 1973. Bimonthly. Circulation: 4,000. Rights purchased vary with author and material. May buy all rights; or all rights and will reassign rights to author after publication; first serial rights or second serial (reprint) rights. Buys 18 to 22 mss a year. Payment on publication. Will send sample copy to writer for 75 cents. Query first or submit complete ms. Will consider photocopied submissions. Submit seasonal material 2 months in advance. "We feature golf and tennis each issue, but other sports in their season." Reports on material in 2 weeks. Enclose S.A.S.E.
Nonfiction and Photos: "Profiles on top sportswomen. Interviews. Investigative journalism on discrimination and ways to beat it. Reports on unusual sports. Approach subject through the eyes of the sportswoman being discussed or interviewed." Length: 5 to 8 double-spaced, typewritten pages. Pays $50 to $150. B&w photos (8x10) purchased with ms. Occasionally purchased on assignment. Pays $25 for 2 to 3 pictures.

Golf

CAROLINA GOLFER, P.O. Box 3, Columbia SC 29202. Editor: Sydney L. Wise. Bimonthly. Buys first rights. Payment on publication. Will send free sample copy to a writer on request. Reports within 1 week. Enclose S.A.S.E.
Nonfiction and Photos: Articles on golf and golfers, clubs, courses, tournaments, only in the Carolinas. Stories on the various courses should be done "in the manner that would give the reader a basic idea of what each course is like." Length: 1,200 to 1,500 words. Pays according to quality of ms. Buys photos with mss. 5x7 or 8x10 b&w glossies. Color should be 4x5 transparencies. Pays $5.

FORE, 3740 Cahuenga Blvd., North Hollywood CA 91604. Editor: William E. Elder. Currently not soliciting freelance material.

GOLF CANADA, 50 Cartier St., St. Lambert, Que., Canada. Editor: Paul Dulmage. For audience that is "upper income, over 30, home owners." Subject matter is "golf. Anything of interest to golfers." Concentrates on "golf in Canada." Monthly. Circulation: 32,000. Not copyrighted. Buys 20 mss a year. Pays on publication. Will send a free sample copy to a writer on request. Query first. Submit seasonal material 3 months in advance. Reports on submissions in 2 weeks. Enclose S.A.E. and International Reply Coupons.
Nonfiction and Photos: Golf articles with a Canadian slant, written in light or humorous style. Also travel features on golf resorts, interviews, profiles, and historical

articles. Length: 250 to 2,000 words. Payment is $35 to $200. Color transparencies purchased with mss. Payment is $25 to $100.

Poetry and Fillers: Light verse, jokes and short humor. Length: 2 to 20 lines; 25 to 100 words. Payment is $2 to $10 for verse; $2 to $5 for fillers.

GOLF DIGEST, 88 Scribner Ave., Norwalk CT 06856. Editor: Nick Seitz. Monthly. Query first. Buys all rights. Pays promptly on acceptance. Reports within three weeks. Enclose S.A.S.E.

Nonfiction: Uses mainly instruction and how-to material, but also features on prominent and unusual golf personalities or events, but prefers initial query. Historical nonfiction pertaining to golf is also good. Up to 2,500 words. Pays a minimum of 20¢ a word (as edited). Illustrations (artwork or photographs) are a help.

Photos: 8x10 b&w glossies for inside use. Payment is $15 and more. Also uses color transparencies. Payment is up to $200. Preferred subjects are nationally known golfers, pro or amateur and other golf scenes.

Poetry and Fillers: Each issue contains some 25- to 50-word humorous shorts and 2-line epigrams. Payment is minimum $10. Also uses poems 8 lines or less.

GOLF GUIDE, 631 Wilshire Blvd., Santa Monica CA 90406. Editor: D.N. Werner. "For a golfing audience—fans and players of all ages." Established in 1969. Bimonthly. Circulation: 110,000. Buys first North American serial rights. Buys 200 mss a year. Payment on publication. Will send free sample copy to a writer on request. Will send editorial guidelines sheet to a writer on request. Query first. Will consider photocopied submissions. Submit seasonal material 3 months in advance. Reports in 2 weeks. Enclose S.A.S.E.

Nonfiction and Photos: General subject matter is "heavy on instructional articles aimed at the handicap golfer. Freelance material welcome, but must be expertly written and concern instruction. Articles should be based on the thoughts of authorities in the field—professionals on the tour or golf instructors. Writer should have a rather thorough knowledge of golf to be able to get the right material." Length: 1,500 to 2,000 words. Pays $50 to $300. Purchases photos with ms and on assignment. Captions optional. Pays $10 to $25 for 8x10 glossies. Pays up to $100 for 35mm color.

GOLF MAGAZINE, 235 E. 45th St., New York NY 10017. Editor: John M. Ross. For serious golfers. Monthly. Buys all rights. Pays on acceptance. Reports in three weeks. Most material done on assignment. Query first. Will send free sample copy on request. Enclose S.A.S.E.

Nonfiction: Must entertain, instruct or inform the average golfer. Will not accept such things as "My First Day on the Golf Course," or "How I Took Up Golf and Drove My Husband Insane." Length: 1,000 to 2,000 words. Pays from $250 to $500.

Fiction: Golf-oriented short stories. Pays $350 to $500.

Photos: Purchased with mss or with caption only. Pays $25 for b&w, $50 for color. Send b&w negatives & contact sheet. Send color in transparency form.

Fillers: Short humor.

INSIDE GOLF, 3100 Riverside Dr., Los Angeles CA 90027. Editor: Mike Doherty. For "golfers and fans." Quarterly. Circulation: 100,000. Buys all rights or North American serial rights. Pays on publication. Will send a free sample copy to a writer on request. Query first. Reports in 2 weeks. Enclose S.A.S.E.

Nonfiction: Wants "personality features on golf stars aimed to the knowledgeable fan." Length: open. Payment is "usually $125 to $150 if pictures are included."

Photos: Purchased with mss and with captions only. Wants "golf pro tournament coverage, golf stars facials or action, other interesting golf material." Payment is $10 for b&w, "up to $150 for color."

SENIOR GOLFER, P.O. Box 4716, Clearwater FL 33518. Editor: Charles B. Albury. Quarterly. Not copyrighted. Buys first North American serial rights only. Pays on acceptance. Will send a sample copy free on request. Query preferred. Reports in two weeks or less. Enclose S.A.S.E. with submissions and queries.

Nonfiction and Photos: Short items on senior golfers and their philosophy toward the game as well as their accomplishments both in and out of golf. Men who have contributed to the game need not be excellent players themselves. Must be angled

toward senior players, 50 and older. Length: 500 words or less. No set rate; $25 minimum. Photos purchased with mss and with captions only. Subject matter should be senior golfers. B&w glossies. No set rate of payment; $10 minimum.
Fiction: Will consider. No short-shorts or vignettes.
Poetry: Will consider humorous verse about senior golfers.
Fillers: Puzzles, jokes, short humor with golf angle and slanted to seniors. No set rate of payment; $5 minimum.

Guns

GUN WEEK, 119 East Court Street, P.O. Box 150, Sidney OH 45365. Acting Editor: J. O. Amos. For "outdoor sportsmen with a particular interest in firearms collecting, hunting and target shooting. Above average in income and education." Established in 1966. Weekly. Circulation: 36,000. Buys first North American serial rights. Buys about 35 to 40 mss a year, excluding regular column. Payment on publication, but special material paid on acceptance. Will send free sample copy to a writer on request. Will consider photocopied submissions, "if sharp and legible." Reports in 2 to 4 weeks. Enclose S.A.S.E. for return of submissions.
Nonfiction and Photos: General subject matter includes "any subject relating to lawful firearms ownership and use. Major portion is devoted to legislative activity relating to firearms ownership; reports of shooting competitions; test reports on new products; how-to articles. Original research on firearms preferred. Need factual reports on activity of sportsmen groups fighting anti-gun legislation at local or state levels, and reports on how non-shooters are being turned into shooters. Also will look at test reports, instruction articles and history pieces about small arms. *Gun Week* is the only weekly newspaper covering the shooting sports. Writer should strive for hard-hitting newspaper style. We emphasize news element, while magazines in our field stress narrative accounts of hunting trips, ballistic tests, etc. Because of our technical nature, we receive little material from freelancers. Would welcome more—if it is technically accurate and writer comes up with new slant. Promotion of shooting (any type, trap, skeet, rifle, pistol) as a wholesome family sport is approach we are looking for." Buys informational, how-to, personal experience, interview, profile, humor, historical, spot news, new product, and technical articles. Length: 300 to 1,000 words. Pays 1¢ to 1¼¢ per word with a $35 maximum. Purchases photos with mss, captions required. Pays $3 to $5 for sharp, clear, 5x7, 8x10 b&w glossies.
Fillers: Buys newsbreaks. Length: 100 to 250 words. Pays $2 to $5.

GUN WORLD, Box HH, 34249 Camino Capistrano, Capistrano Beach CA 92624. Editorial Director: Jack Lewis. For ages that "range from mid-twenties to mid-sixties; many professional types who are interested in relaxation of hunting and shooting." Established in 1960. Monthly. Circulation: 127,000. Buys all rights but will reassign them to author after publication. Buys "50 or so" mss a year. Payment on acceptance. Will send a free sample copy to a writer on request. Will not consider photocopied submissions. Submit seasonal material 4 months in advance. Reports in six weeks, perhaps longer. Enclose S.A.S.E. for return of submissions.
Nonfiction and Photos: General subject matter consists of "well-rounded articles—not by amateurs—on shooting techniques, with anecdotes; hunting stories with tips and knowledge integrated. No poems or fiction. We like broad humor in our articles, so long as it does not reflect upon firearms safety. Most arms magazine are pretty deadly and we feel shooting can be fun. Too much material aimed at pro-gun people. Most of this is staff-written and most shooters don't have to be told of their rights under the Constitution. We want articles on new development; off-track inventions, novel military uses of arms; do-it-yourself projects in this field." Buys informational, how-to, personal experience, and nostalgia articles. Pays $200 maximum. Purchases photos with mss and caption required. Wants 5x7 b&w.

GUNS AND AMMO, 8490 Sunset Blvd., Los Angeles CA 90069. Editor: George Martin. For "hunters and shooters," average 30 years old, college educated. Monthly. Circulation: 250,000. Buys all rights. Buys 100 mss a year. Pays on publication. No query required. Reports in 30 days. Enclose S.A.S.E for return of submissions.

Nonfiction: "We are especially interested in articles of a technical nature directly related to guns, reloading, target shooting, gunsmithing and associated shooting activities. Articles of a more general nature on hunting should be specifically keyed to the gun. No fiction. *Guns and Ammo* reserves the right to edit any accepted mss." Length: 2,000 to 2,500 words. Pays 5¢ and up per word.

Photos: Submit "lots of high quality photos" with all mss. "Probably more mss are rejected for poor illustrations than any other reason. Ideally, b&w photos should be submitted on 8x10-inch single-weight glossy paper. All illustrations should be completely captioned. Mss submitted without illustrations will almost certainly be rejected." Pays $5 per photo. "Limited use of four-color art; must be transparencies, preferably 4x5. 2¼x2¼ is acceptable." Pays $15.

GUNS MAGAZINE, 8150 N. Central Park Avenue, Skokie IL 60076. Editor: J. Rakusan. Monthly for firearms enthusiasts. Buys all rights. Buys 150 mss a year. Pays on publication. Will send free sample copy to a writer on request. Reports on submissions as soon as possible. Enclose S.A.S.E. for return of submissions.

Nonfiction and Photos: Informative articles about guns and shooting; reports on new or unusual guns, cartridges, or pieces of shooting equipment; how to shoot for better results at game or targets, etc. Also occasional historical or personality pieces of western, war, or collector interest. Length: up to 3,500 words. Pays $75 to $175. Study magazine before submitting ms. "Articles should be factual, technical, and easy-to-read." Pictures are a must but submit contact sheets for initial selection. "We do not buy separate b&w photos—they should be supplied with the ms. We do buy color transparencies no smaller than 2¼x2¼ for use in our color section and covers—payment for covers is $100 while inside color is $50 a published page."

HANDLOADER MAGAZINE, P. O. Box 3030, Prescott AZ 86301. Publisher: Dave Wolfe; Editor: Neal Knox. Bimonthly for gun enthusiasts who reload their ammunition. Buys first North American serial rights only. Pays on publication. Query with outline required. Reports in two weeks. Enclose S.A.S.E.

Nonfiction: Fresh, informative, knowledgeable, technical articles on handloading ammunition. Style serious and simple. Length: 1,500 to 3,000 words. Pays $75 to $150.

Photos: Purchased with mss and with captions only. 8x10 glossy preferred.

THE RIFLE MAGAZINE, P.O. Box 3030, Prescott AZ 86301. Publisher: Dave Wolfe. Editor: Neal Knox. Bimonthly. For advanced rifle enthusiasts. Pays on publication. Buys North American serial rights. "A detailed query will help, and is preferred." Reports in two weeks. Enclose S.A.S.E. with queries and submissions.

Nonfiction and Photos: Articles must be fresh and of a quality and style to enlighten rather than entertain knowledgeable gun enthusiasts. "We are interested in seeing new bylines and new ideas, but if a writer doesn't have a solid knowledge of firearms and ballistics, he's wasting his time and ours to submit." Length: 1,500 to 3,000 words. Pays $75 to $125. Photos should accompany ms. Buys ms and photos as a package.

SHOOTING TIMES, News Plaza, Peoria IL 61601. Executive Editor: Alex Bartimo. "The average *Shooting Times* reader is 29 years old. He has an above average education and income. He is probably a semiskilled or skilled or professional worker who has an avid interest in firearms and the shooting sports." Special reloading issue in February; handgun issue in March. Monthly. Circulation: 125,000. Buys all rights. Buys 85 to 90 mss a year. Pays on acceptance. Will send a free sample copy to a writer on request. Query first. Submit seasonal or special material 4 or 5 months in advance. Reports in 4 to 5 weeks. Enclose S.A.S.E.

Nonfiction and Photos: "Presents a well-balanced content ranging from nontechnical through semitechnical to technical stories covering major shooting sports activities—handguns, rifles, shotguns, cartridge reloading, muzzle loading, gunsmithing, how-to's, and hunting, with a major emphasis on handguns. Hunting stories must be 'gunny' with the firearm(s) and ammunition dominating the story and serving as the means to an end. Articles may run from 1,000 to 2,000 words and must be accompanied by 10 to 12 b&w glossies, 8x10, including 1 or 2 'lead' pictures." Payment is $150 to $200.

Horse Racing

AMERICAN TURF MONTHLY, 505 8th Avenue, New York NY 10018. Editor: Howard Rowe. For "horse racing bettors." Buys 50 to 100 mss a year. Enclose S.A.S.E. for return of submissions.
Nonfiction: General subject matter is "articles, systems and material treating horse racing." Approach should be "how to successfully wager on racing. It is the only publication in the country devoted exclusively to the horse bettor. We have a staff capable of covering every facet aside from system articles." Length: 1,500 to 3,000 words. Pays $35 minimum.

TURF AND SPORT DIGEST, 511 Oakland Avenue, Baltimore MD 21212. Editor: Les Woodcock. For "horse racing enthusiasts of all sorts. Range from very rich to the guy who shouldn't be betting the rent money. Range broad for all other categories. All people associated with the sport." Established in 1924. Monthly. Circulation: 50,000. Rights purchased vary with author and material. Buys all rights, but will reassign them to author after publication. Buys first North American serial rights. Buys about 70 mss a year. Payment on publication. Will send a sample copy to a writer for 75¢. Query required. Will consider photocopied submissions, "if legible and clear." Submit seasonal material 3 months in advance. Reports within 3 weeks. Enclose S.A.S.E. for reply to queries.
Nonfiction and Photos: Subject matter includes "personality pieces on jockeys, trainers, horses; news of tracks and industry; historical sketches; handicapping system; anything of interest in the racing world. Constructive criticism, etc. Not interested in breeding." Freelancer should "send a one or two paragraph outline of story he is proposing. I want two things: good writing—if profile, get inside the subject and don't be superficial—and solid facts and information. Emphasis on good writing. This is the only horse racing magazine covering the whole sport nationwide. Others specialize to an area or are pointed toward the breeding end of the business. There is always a receptive ear to a penetrating personality profile of someone in the news." Buys interviews; profile, historical, nostalgia articles. Length: 1,500 to 3,000 words. Pays $40 to $75. Purchases photos on assignment but is "interested in good, different exciting 4-color photos as possible cover or inside material." Payment varies. Pays $75 for color cover.
Fillers: Pays $15 for crossword puzzles.

Hunting and Fishing

ALASKA, Box 4-EEE, Anchorage AK 99509. Editor and Publisher: Bob Henning. Monthly. Buys first rights. Pays on publication. "No fiction, poetry, gags. No need to query first." Enclose S.A.S.E. for return of submissions.
Nonfiction: "Uses true first-person stories about any aspect of life in Alaska or Northwest Canada, including hunting and fishing articles, with emphasis on adventure, wildlife, and unique people. Writer must be personally well-acquainted with Alaska or the Yukon." Length: 100 to 3,000 words, "with occasional serials of up to 5,000 words," Payment is $10 to $150, "depending on length of article, and strength of photo support."
Photos: Prefers 35mm color transparencies or b&w glossies. Pays $25 for color cover, $5 to $15 for inside use.

ALASKA HUNTING AND FISHING TALES, Box 4-EEE, Anchorage AK 99509. Annually. Buys first North American serial rights. Pays on publication. Reports in 1 month. Enclose S.A.S.E. for return of submissions.
Nonfiction and Photos: True first-person hunting, fishing, or adventure stories from Alaska or adjacent Canada. "Material must have an Alaskan setting, and the general requirements in fact are the same as for *Alaska* magazine." Length: maximum 5,000 words; prefers 2,000 to 3,000 words. "Good photos are a must." Pays $25 to $100.

AMERICAN FIELD, 222 W. Adams St., Chicago IL 60606. Editor: William F. Brown. Issued weekly. Buys first publication rights. Payment varies and is made on acceptance. Editor will send sample copy on request. Reports usually within ten days. Enclose S.A.S.E. for return of submissions.

Nonfiction and Photos: Always interested in factual articles on breeding, rearing, development and training of hunting dogs, how-to-do-it material written to appeal to upland bird hunters, sporting dog owners, field trialers, etc. Also wants stories and articles about hunting trips in quest of upland game birds. Length wanted is between 1,000 and 2,500 words. Uses photos submitted with manuscripts if they are suitable and also photos submitted with captions only.

Fillers: Infrequently uses some 100- to 250-word fillers.

THE AMERICAN RIFLEMAN, 1600 Rhode Island Ave., N.W., Washington DC 20036. Editor: Ashley Halsey, Jr. Monthly. Official journal of National Rifle Association of America. Buys first North American serial rights, including publication in this magazine, or any of the official publications of the National Rifle Association. Residuary rights will be returned after publication upon request of the author. Pays on acceptance. Reports in one to four weeks. Will send free sample copy on request. Enclose S.A.S.E. for return of submissions.

Nonfiction: Factual articles on hunting, target shooting, shotgunning, conservation, firearms repairs and oddities accepted from qualified freelancers. No semifictional or "me and Joe" type of yarns, but articles should be informative and interesting. Will not consider anything that "winks" at lawbreaking, or delineates practices that are inimical to the best interests of gun ownership, shooting, or good citizenship. Articles should run from one to four magazine pages. Pays about $75 to $750 per article.

Photos: Full color transparencies for possible use on cover and inside. Photo articles that run one to two magazine pages.

CAROLINA SPORTSMAN, Box 2581, Charlotte NC 28201. Editor: Sidney L. Wise; Associate Editor: Lee Helmer. Bimonthly. Buys all rights. Pays on publication. Will send free sample copy to a writer on request. Reports on submissions in 3 to 8 weeks. Enclose S.A.S.E. for return of submissions.

Nonfiction and Photos: Sports stories in quick-moving, vivid, on-the-spot style, dealing with sports such as fishing, camping, and other outdoor activities in the Carolinas. 600 to 1,500 words. Pays 1¢ and up per word. B&w glossy photos and color transparencies purchased with mss.

Fillers: Sport topics. Length: 25 to 50 words.

FIELD AND STREAM, 383 Madison Ave., New York NY 10017. Editor: Jack Samson. Monthly. Buys all rights. Reports in 6 weeks. Query first. Enclose S.A.S.E. with submissions and queries.

Nonfiction and Photos: "This is a broad-based outdoor service magazine. Editorial content ranges from very basic how-to stories that tell either in pictures or words how an outdoor technique is done or device made. Articles of penetrating depth about national conservation, game management, resource management, and recreation development problems. Hunting, fishing, camping, backpacking, nature, outdoor, photography, equipment, wild game and fish recipes, and other activities allied to the outdoors. The 'me and Joe' story is about dead, with minor exceptions. Both where-to and how-to articles should be well-illustrated." Prefers color to b&w. Submit outline first with photos. Length, 2,500 words. Payment varies depending upon the name of the author, quality of work, importance of the article. Pays 18¢ per word and up. Usually buys photos with mss. When purchased separately, pays $150 and up for color.

Fillers: Buys "how it's done" fillers of 500 to 1,000 words. Must be unusual or helpful subjects. Payment is $200 to $250.

How To Break In: "A beginning writer would do best to write a short feature for our consideration˙

FISH AND GAME SPORTSMAN, P.O. Box 1654, Regina, Sask., Canada. Editor: Red Wilkinson. Quarterly. 90% freelance. Circulation: 12,000. Will send a free sample copy on request "if writers submit details on proposed articles, photos, etc." Reports in two to four weeks. Buys North American serial rights only. Pays on publication or maximum 3 months. Enclose S.A.E. and International Reply Coupons.

Nonfiction: Outdoor articles for fishermen, hunters, and snowmobilers, and campers relating to Alberta and Saskatchewan only. "We are most interested in the adventure type of article detailing a specific outdoor experience in our two-province coverage area. Articles should be supported with extensive accessory information of the terrain, the water, equipment used, the camps or accommodation, price and costs, suggestions, etc. We also buy how-to or informational articles, as long as they can be related to Alberta and Saskatchewan." Length: 1,500 to 2,000 words. Query required. Pays $40 to $125.

Photos: Purchased with mss. B&w, except for cover.

FISHING AND HUNTING NEWS, 1202 Harrison St., Seattle WA 98109. Managing Editor: Ken McDonald. For "active fishermen and hunters of all ages with the need to know how-when-where of local activity." Weekly. Circulation 120,000. Not copyrighted. Buys 4 to 5 mss a year. Pays on publication. Will send a free sample copy to a writer on request. Submit seasonal material 1 month in advance. Query first. Reports in 10 days. Enclose S.A.S.E. for reply to queries.

Nonfiction: Spot news reports of hunting and fishing conditions in Washington, Oregon, Idaho, Montana, California, Utah, Colorado, and Wyoming. Wants "hunting and fishing opportunity stories—prefer upcoming events." Stories must include "all facts needed for reader to participate in the activity—detailed guidelines." Length: 200 to 3,000 words. Payment is $4 a column (2¼x16). Would consider freelance material for a possible column on recreational vehicles.

Photos: Buys single pix with caption or pix with mss. Needs specific hunting and fishing conditions and catches. Pays $2.50 to $5 each. Buys either 2¼x2¼ or 4x5 transparencies for covers. Pays up to $25.

FISHING FUN, Box 24024, Speedway IN 46224. Editor: William Wood. For the fisherman and his family. "We can use a Christmas fiction piece for December/January issue." Established in 1972. Monthly, except October/November and December/January. Circulation: 20,000. Buys all rights "unless otherwise specified." Buys 100 mss a year. Payment on publication. Will send free sample copy to writer on request. Write for copy of guidelines for writers. Query first or submit complete ms. Submit Christmas material 4 months in advance. Reports in 4 weeks. Enclose S.A.S.E. for reply to query or return of submission.

Nonfiction: "All material must have a fishing tie-in. We are always open to fresh ideas, as long as they have a fishing theme. All material should be written with the average fisherman in mind, not the playboy-type who winters in Florida and summers in Bermuda. We feature down-to-earth items for average fishermen. We need more good, clean, humorous material. Also, good recipes. Conservation news, legislation affecting the fisherman, and unusual happenings in the world of fishing, anywhere in the U.S." Informational, how-to, personal experience, interview, inspirational, humor, personal opinion, photo, travel, reviews of fishing books, new product and technical articles. Length: 1,000 words maximum. Pays approximately 3¢ per word.

Photos: Purchased with or without accompanying mss. Captions required. "Single b&w photos used inside magazine if unusual in nature; if they will stand alone without supporting text." 8x10 glossies. Pays $3 each. 35mm or larger (used only on cover). Pays $40 to $50.

Fiction: "We need warm family-type Christmas stories related to fishing. We need more stories for our 'Fishy Tales' section of the magazine." Suspense, adventure and humorous fiction also wanted. Length: 1,000 to 1,500 words. Pays approximately 3¢ per word, "more if story warrants."

Poetry and Fillers: "We've used no poetry yet, but are open to ideas." Newsbreaks, fishing puzzles, jokes and short humor; recipes. Pays $5 to $10 and up for fillers.

FISHING WORLD, 51 Atlantic Ave., Floral Park NY 11001. Editor: Keith Gardner. Bimonthly. Circulation: 200,000. Buys first North American serial rights only. Pays on acceptance. Will send a free sample copy to a writer on request. Query advised. Reports "customarily within 2 weeks." Will consider photocopied submissions. Enclose S.A.S.E. with all submissions and queries.

Nonfiction and Photos: "Most of our articles range from 1,500 to 3,000 words with 2,500 words usually preferred. A good selection of action photos should accompany each submission. Subject matter can range from a hot fishing site to tackle and techniques, from tips on taking individual species to a story on one lake or an entire region, either freshwater or salt. However, how-to is definitely preferred over where-to, and a strong biological slant is best of all. Where-to articles, especially if they describe foreign fishing, should be accompanied by sidebars covering how to make reservations and arrange transportation, how to get there, where to stay. Angling methods should be developed in clear detail, with accurate and useful information about tackle and boats. Anecdotes should be pertinent and brief. Our readers are dedicated fishermen who want to improve their sport, not listen to yarnspinning. They are also family men, and if women and children took part in the experiences you are describing, don't hide that fact. Depending on article length, suitability of photographs and other factors, payment is up to $200 for feature articles accompanied by b&w and color transparencies. Color transparencies selected for cover use pay an additional $75."

THE FLYFISHER, 4500 Beach Drive Southwest, Seattle WA 98116. Editor: Steve Raymond. Official publication of the Federation of Fly Fishermen. For "a highly sophisticated audience of expert anglers." Quarterly. Circulation includes FFF members and member clubs. Usually buys all rights. Pays on acceptance for solicited material, pays on publication for unsolicited material. Subscribes to code of standards adopted by Outdoor Writers Association of America. Write for "notes to contributors." Query preferred. Reports in two to four weeks. Enclose S.A.S.E. for reply to queries.
Nonfiction, Photos, and Fiction: "Fly fishing, conservation as it relates to fly fishing, how-to pieces, articles on places, methods and persons related to fly fishing. Also historical and personality pieces." Length: 2,000 words preferred, but some flexibility. Pays up to $150 and sometimes higher. Photos purchased with mss and captions only. B&w glossies, 8x10 preferred, 5x7 acceptable. Pays $5 and up. Pays up to $100 for covers. Fiction with same general subject matter as nonfiction, plus some humor. Length: 1,500 to 2,000 words. Pays up to $100; sometimes higher.

FUR-FISH-GAME, 2878 E. Main St., Columbus OH 43209. Editor: A.R. Harding. Issued monthly. Buys all rights. Pays on acceptance. Will send sample copy for 25¢. Reports in three weeks. Include S.A.S.E. for return of submissions.
Nonfiction and Photos: "We buy articles on hunting, fishing, trapping, camping, boating, conservation, and any other subject concerning outdoor sports. We pay from $50 to $75 for feature articles that are used in the front of the magazine. These articles run from 2,000 to 3,000 words in length and must be illustrated by at least 4 good b&w 5x7 or 8x10 photos. We also buy a few short articles, 1,000 to 2,000 words, on hunting, camping, trapping, dogs and fishing to be used as fillers in the Gun Rack, Fishing, and Dog and Trapping departments. We pay $20 to $30 for these. These also must be illustrated, but regular size b&w snapshots are sufficient. (No color photos, please.) Color transparencies are used for covers on occasion, and we pay $25 for these. The minimum size for transparencies is 2¼x2¼. No poetry or cartoons, please."

GREAT LAKES SPORTSMAN, 26555 Evergreen, Suite 410, Southfield MI 48076. For "families with outdoor recreational interests proven by their purchases of major recreational equipment such as boats, snowmobiles, motor homes, trailers. Broad range of ages and educational levels. All like the outdoors and are concerned with ecology, good recreation land use, pollution." Monthly. Circulation: 160,000, "primarily in Michigan, Wisconsin, and Minnesota, but also in Illinois, Indiana, Ohio, some in Pennsylvania and some in upper New York State." Buys first rights. Buys 60 to 90 mss a year. Pays on publication. Will send a sample copy to a writer on request. Query first. Articles have "to be done in the Great Lakes states by Great Lakes residents." Submit seasonal material 6 months in advance. Reports in 20 to 40 days. Enclose S.A.S.E.
Nonfiction: "All articles should be of some service to the reader by telling him how to become more expert in his activity, where to get better results (in the Great Lakes area), how to modify or upgrade his equipment, how to get greater value for his recreation dollar. Articles should identify with a place (Great Lakes) or activity (outdoor). Articles must tell the reader something besides the fact that the writer had a great time fishing, hunting, or riding a trail bike. Tell why (equipment, place, or technique)." Buys how-to's, where-to's, personal experience and historical

coverage which is "part of location articles." Length: 500 to 3,000 words. Pays $75 to $230.

Photos:"We like to use the names and hometowns of people in the Great Lakes area who appear in the pix. Good pix are a must." B&w glossies, color transparencies, 35mm color. Purchased with mss.

ILLINOIS WILDLIFE, P.O. Box 116–13005 S. Western Ave., Blue Island IL 60406. Editor: Ace Extrom. For conservationists and sportsmen. "Tabloid newspaper utilizing newspaper format instead of magazine type articles." Monthly. Circulation: 35,000. Pays on acceptance. Will send a sample copy to a writer for 25¢. Reports in 2 weeks. Enclose S.A.S.E. for return of submissions.
Nonfiction and Photos: Want "material aimed at conserving and restoring our natural resources." How-to, humor, photo articles. Length: "Maximum 2,000 words, prefer 1,000-word articles." Payment open. B&w glossies. Prefers 5x7. Pays $3.
Fillers: Jokes, short humor. Length: 1 to 2 column inches.

MARYLAND CONSERVATIONIST, Tawes State Office Building B-3, Annapolis MD 21401. Editor: Raymond Krasnick. For "outdoorsmen, between 10 and 100 years of age." Bimonthly. Circulation: 8,000. Not copyrighted. Buys 20 to 30 mss a year. Pays on publication. Will send a free sample copy to a writer on request. Query first. Reports within 30 days. Enclose S.A.S.E. for return of submissions.
Nonfiction: "Subjects dealing strictly with the outdoor life in Maryland. Nontechnical in content and in the first or third person in style." How-to, personal experience, humor, photo, travel articles. Overstocked with material on pollution and Maryland ecology. Length: 1,000 to 1,500 words. Payment is 5¢ a word.
Photos: 8x10 b&w glossies purchased with mss. Payment is $15 a photo. $10 per b&w photo appearing in photo essay. Color transparencies and 35mm color purchased for covers. Payment is $50.

MICHIGAN OUT-OF-DOORS, 2101 Wood Street, P.O. Box 2235, Lansing MI 48911. Associate Editor: Wm. H. Gardiner. For "hunters, fishermen, campers, hikers, conservationists, and ecologists." Established in 1974. Monthly. Circulation: 130,000. Buys 25 to 50 mss a year. Payment on publication. Will send a free sample copy to a writer on request. Submit seasonal material 2 to 3 months in advance. Reports in 30 days. Enclose S.A.S.E. for return of submissions.
Nonfiction and Photos: General subject matter consists of "how-to, where-to, hunt, fish, camp, travel, ski, and snowmobile." Approach should have a Michigan or nearby slant. Buys informational, how-to, personal experience, humor, historical, think, nostalgia, photo, and travel articles. Would like photos or line art with all mss. Length: 1,500 to 2,500 words. Pays $50 to $100. Purchases photos with mss and captions required. B&w should be at least 5x7. Color should be 35mm or 2¼x2¼ transparencies. Pays $25 to $40 for color.

NORTHEAST OUTDOORS, 95 North Main St., Waterbury CT 06702. Editor: Ms. Aimee Suhie. Monthly. Circulation: 20,000. Buys all rights. Pays on publication. Will send a free sample copy to a writer upon request. "Queries are not required, but are useful for our planning and to avoid possible duplication of subject matter. If you have any questions, or wish to cover some event live and ask about it first, please feel free to call the editor." Deadlines are on the 10th of the month preceding publication. Reports in 15 to 30 days. Enclose S.A.S.E. with all submissions.
Nonfiction and Photos: *"Northeast Outdoors* is interested in articles, photos, cartoons, etc., that pertain to outdoor activities in the Northeast. Our focus is on family camping and associated activities, which change with the seasons. Although the majority of our readers are family campers, many of whom own and use recreational vehicles, we do not limit our material to camping subjects. We feel people who camp are interested in the outdoors and all the ways it is enjoyed. So we carry pieces on nature, archery, hunting, ice fishing, snowshoeing, canoeing—just to name a few. We also feel campers are concerned with the condition of the outdoors, so we often cover conservation, pollution and environmental subjects. We are always looking for well-written freelance material and good photos, either to illustrate articles or to be used alone. Both professional freelancers and amateurs are encouraged to send in their work. If you wish to submit something you think is appropriate,

please feel free to do so. We can't guarantee we'll use it, but we can promise we will consider carefully what you send us. Our pay rate is flexible, but it generally runs from $20 for short, simple articles, $30 to $40 for features without photos, and up to $60 for features accompanied by two or more photos. Features should be from 300 to 1,000 words. Premium rates are paid on the basis of quality, not length. For photos alone we pay $7.50 for each 8x10 black and white print that we use. Photo layouts bring $40. Also, we are looking for high impact, colorful 35mm or larger transparencies to use for our color cover. We pay up to $50 for these."

OUTDOOR LIFE, 355 Lexington Ave., New York NY 10017. Editor: Chet Fish. For "the dyed-in-the wool sportsman and the layman." Monthly. Buys about 220 mss a year. "We have no fixed rate of payment for editorial material but offer the top prices in our field." Pays on acceptance. Write for copy of guidelines for writers. Enclose S.A.S.E. for return of submissions.

Nonfiction: "We're looking for feature stories about the dramatic, humorous and adventurous aspects of fishing, hunting and the outdoors. We particularly like the exciting adventure story, but the story must be true. We use no fiction whatever and no poetry. We like the first-person narrative approach whenever possible, and then the next best thing—the as-told-to yarn. We like our writers to develop local atmosphere, to describe the country where they hunt and fish, the cost of doing it, the people and customs they may encounter. We like individuals in a story to be something more than just names. What does the man look like, what does he do for a living, where does he live? We use how-to-do and how-to-make-it articles of any length on fishing and hunting, woodcraft, camping, firearms, motor boats, fishing tackle and all kinds of related outdoor equipment. Here again the story with the personal-experience angle has the best chance. Some obvious titles are 'How to Handle a Boat,' 'How to Surf Cast,' 'How to Buy a Hunting Dog,' 'Cameras for Hunting and Fishing.' An important part of our editorial fare is the controversial article. The outstanding ingredient of *Outdoor Life* is its integrity. Phony writing doesn't score with us. Hunters and fishermen are extremely sensitive to the false note, and we've become hypersensitive to it. Also, we are expanding our regional news section (regional to: The Northeast; The Southwest; The Midsouth; The Midwest; The Great Lakes; and The West), hence there is a larger need for regional material." Length: 3,000 to 5,000 words. Pays "a minimum of $300 for an article around 3,200 words."

Photos: "Color transparency for cover, full of action, atmosphere, or human interest. Photos submitted with feature articles. We use both color and b&w. For color, we prefer transparencies. We can use 35mm slides, 2¼x2¼, and larger. If Kodacolor is used, we need both negatives and prints. We like 8x10 b&w but will settle for smaller if they are of good quality. For contacts, we must have the negatives as well as the contacts. For an article on experiences afield, 'candid camera' pix should not only show participants but actually illustrate the incidents described—action high spots and human-interest sidelights included. We are allergic to the conventional posed photos, particularly those of lucky angler or hunter with his fish or game, unless the latter are exceptional trophies. Photos on 'how-to-do' or 'how-to-make' should make technique crystal-clear. We like good picture stories, and we take that word 'story' seriously. We don't care for odd assortments of pictures taken at different times and having no real thread holding them together. A picture story should tell a story; it should be as well tied together as a textual story. It should have a beginning, a middle and end. It should stick to one cast of characters whenever possible. We want exclusive coverage of unusual fishing or hunting trips, some noteworthy event or new development in our field, wildlife conservation, game animals or birds, poisonous snakes, etc."

Fillers: " 'Kinks' describing emergency equipment made from odds and ends or emergency repairs are especially desirable." Also buys "two-column featurettes or the text for 'This Happened to Me,' but there's a pretty steady flow of such material."

PENNSYLVANIA ANGLER, P.O. Box 1673, Harrisburg PA 17120. Editor: J.F. Yoder. For Pennsylvania fishermen and boaters, both resident and visiting; all ages and educational levels, with water oriented recreational interests. Fishing and boating experiences in Pennsylvania. Special boating issue in July. Established in 1932. Monthly. Circulation: 45,000. Buys all rights. Buys 60 to 70 mss a year. Payment on acceptance. Will send free sample copy to writer on request. Write for copy of guidelines for writers. Query best, but not mandatory. Submit seasonal material 6 months in advance. Reports in 2 to 4 weeks. Enclose S.A.S.E. for reply to query or return of submission.

Nonfiction, Photos, and Fillers: "Fishing and boating in Pennsylvania. How-to, but more where-to articles are needed to make readers want to do the same things. New methods, new areas, new slants. Only the most unusual treatment on trout fishing will be considered. Avoid verbosity; cover one subject, one location, one style, one theme; no endless rambling. 3 to 5 pages of double-spaced copy with 5 to 10 good 8x10 b&w glossies have one foot in the winner's circle. We're the official fishing and boating magazine of the Commonwealth of Pennsylvania. Mss should not be condemnatory of officials' policy or action. We'd like to see more photo spreads. We need especially good boating mss and photos for July issue. Length: 200 to 1,500 words. Material purchased on a per page basis rather than per word or per photo. Payment from $25 to $125 for ms and photos. Good market for Pennsylvania action photos without mss. B&w photos for inside; pays $10 to $35. Covers, prefer 2¼ up; pays to $150. Filler material on related subjects also considered."

PENNSYLVANIA GAME NEWS, P.O. Box 1567, Harrisburg PA 17120. Editor: Bob Bell. Monthly. Circulation: 220,000. Buys all rights; reprint rights usually granted on request. Pays on acceptance. Will send free sample copy to a writer on request. Query preferred. Study magazine before submitting. Reports in 3 to 4 weeks. Enclose S.A.S.E. for reply to queries.

Nonfiction: For all outdoorsmen except fishermen—hunting, camping, trapping, natural history. Regular columns on guns, outdoor equipment, nature, archery, camping. No "winking" at law violators; this is Game Commission publication. Length: 2,500 words maximum except in unusual circumstances. Pays 3¢ per word minimum.

Photos: Purchased with mss and occasionally with captions only. B&w glossy, 5x7 or 8x10, professional quality. Pays $5 to $10.

SALMON TROUT STEELHEADER, P.O. Box 02112, Portland OR 97202. Editor: Frank W. Amato. For sport fishermen in Oregon, Washington, and California. Bimonthly. Buys first serial rights. Pays on publication. Will send free sample copy on request. Query first. Reports in 2 weeks. Enclose S.A.S.E.

Nonfiction and Photos: Articles on fishing for trout, salmon, and steelhead. How-to's and where-to's. Length: 1,000 to 2,500 words. B&w photos purchased with mss. Pays $10 to $50.

SALT WATER SPORTSMAN, 10 High St., Boston MA 02110. Editor: Frank Woolner. Monthly. Circulation: 85,000. Buys North American serial rights only. Pays on acceptance. Will send sample copy to a writer on request. Reports on submissions within one month. Enclose S.A.S.E. for the return of all submissions.

Nonfiction: Fact-feature articles, picture stories dealing with salt water sport fishing in North America, the Caribbean, Central America, South America and Hawaii "Writers must be well-informed. We prefer to rewrite an exceptional article by a well-informed fisherman, rather than buy a polished piece by a professional journalist who doesn't know his angling. No 'blood and thunder' adventure, or romantic reminiscences. Readers are modern, scientific anglers: they want facts and up-to-date information presented in a readable manner. If there is any slant, it is emphasis on the how-to of sport fishing. Fishing tournaments are not covered by *Salt Water Sportsman*; therefore, articles dealing with contests are unlikely to be accepted. The only exception would be a tournament which serves the public as a whole, rather than the needs of area promotion. We do not use editorial advertising. A popular lure or tackle combination should be described, rather than identified by trade name. Charter boat captains, boats, airlines, guides, etc., may be named, but promotion for the pure sake of promotion will be deleted." Length: feature material, 3,000 words; picture stories (6 to 12 story-telling photos), 500 to 1,500 words. Photos must accompany articles. Pays a minimum of 4¢ to 8¢ per word for copy, plus $3 for each photo used with an article. Pays slightly higher rates for picture stories.

Photos: Purchased with mss. Should be 8x10 enlargements on single-weight or doubleweight paper. "Sometimes we are able to illustrate an article from our own files, and there are occasions when we will arrange artwork to illustrate—but accompanying photos always help to sell a manuscript. Photos should never show a great number of dead fish, because our readers are sensitive to slaughter. Pictures should, wherever possible, tell the story of the article. Action photos showing jumping fish, anglers playing, beaching, gaffing or boating fish are always in demand." Buys color photos for cover use; transparencies in the 2¼x2¼ or larger frame sizes preferred, but will consider 35mm and Kodacolor prints. Pays $100 for one-time use of a four-color transparency for cover.

SOUTHERN ANGLER'S GUIDE, SOUTHERN HUNTER'S GUIDE, P.O. Box 2188, Hot Springs AR 71901. Editor: Don J. Fuelsch. Buys all rights. Issued annually. Query before submitting.. Include S.A.S.E. with submissions and queries.
Nonfiction: Hunting, fishing, boating, camping articles. Use articles that have been thoroughly researched. Condensed in digest style. Complete how-to-do-it rundown on tricks and techniques used in taking various species of fresh and salt water fish and game found in the southern states. Interested in new and talented writers with thorough knowledge of their subject. Not interested in first person or "Me and Joe" pieces. Length is flexible, 750 to 1,800 words preferred, although may run as high as 3,000 words. Pays 5¢ to 30¢ a word.
Photos: Buys photographs with mss or with captions only. Fishing or hunting subjects in southern setting. No Rocky Mountain backgrounds. B&w only—5x7 or 8x10 glossies preferred.

SPORTFISHING ANNUAL, Yachting Publishing Corp., Room 600, 50 W. 44th St., New York NY 10036. Editor: Frank T. Moss. "We purchase by direct assignment. No longer encourage unsolicited freelance material."

SPORTS AFIELD, 250 W. 55 St., New York NY 10019. Editor: Lamar Underwood. Monthly. Circulation: 1,450,000. Buys first North American serial rights. Pays on acceptance. Query first, or submit mss. Reports in 2 weeks. Enclose S.A.S.E.
Nonfiction and Photos: Uses informative how-to articles and dramatic personal experiences with good photographs on hunting, fishing, camping, boating and related subjects such as conservation and travel. Length: 2,500 to 3,500 words. Pays up to $600 and more "depending on length and quality." Uses 8x10 b&w glossies; 2¼x2¼ or larger color transparencies preferred but 35 mm are acceptable. No assignments. Buys one-time rights. Pays $25 and up for b&w; $50 and up for color.
Fiction: Buys an occasional fiction piece dramatizing the outdoors. Must have authentic background, provide adventure or humor. Length: 3,000 words. Pays up to $600 and more.
Fillers: Mainly how-to-do-it tips on outdoor subjects, with photographs or drawings. Length: "self-contained one or two pages." Payment depends on length. No queries necessary. Also buys short paragraph items of an unusual, newsworthy or how-to nature for the "Almanac" section. Pays $10 and up, "depending on length."
How To Break In: "Our readers are not interested so much in how the sun rises or the way the landscape looks. They want to know how to be better sportsmen—to catch a fish or shoot better."

VIRGINIA WILDLIFE, P.O. Box 11104, Richmond VA 23230. Editor: James F. McInteer, Jr. Monthly. For sportsmen, outdoor enthusiasts. Pays on acceptance. Buys first North American serial rights, second serial rights or reprint rights. Will send sample copy on request. Query first. Enclose S.A.S.E. for reply to queries.
Nonfiction: Uses factual hunting and fishing stories especially those set in Virginia. Boating and gunning with safety slant. Conservation projects. Conservation education. New ways of enjoying the outdoors. Slant should be to enjoy the outdoors and do what you can to improve it and keep it enjoyable. Material must be applicable to Virginia, sound from a scientific basis, accurate and easy to read. Length: prefers 800 to 1,500 words. Pays 1½¢ to 2¢ per word.
Photos: Buys photos with mss and with captions only. Should be 8x10 glossies. Pays $35 to $50 for 4x5 color transparencies for cover.

WESTERN OUTDOORS, 3939 Birch St., Newport Beach CA 92660. Editor: James E. Potter. Monthly. Buys first serial rights only. Payment on publication.

Query first or submit complete ms. Reports within 2 to 4 weeks. Enclose S.A.S.E. for reply to query or return of submission.

Nonfiction and Photos: "Where-to-go material on western fishing, hunting, boating, camping, travel, and allied subjects. Articles should deal with 11 continental western states as well as with Western Canada, Baja, Mexico, Hawaii and Alaska. Most material is assigned. Primary requirement is accurate, dependable information on the places not well known. Completed mss accompanied with 8x10 b&w glossy photos are recommended. Articles range from 1 to 6 pages in magazine, with payment averaging $35 per page. Photos and ms are considered a package deal."

Martial Arts

THE AMERICAN JUDOMAN, 4944 Date Avenue, Sacramento CA 95841. Editor: Philip S. Porter. "60% of our audience is below 16 years of age. The rest young adult judo athletes and about 2,000 judo club instructors." Special issues on Olympic reports and international reports on judo. Established in 1960. Bimonthly. Circulation: 30,000. Buys all rights. Buys about 15 to 25 mss a year. Payment on publication. Will send a sample copy to a writer for $1. Will consider photocopied submissions. Submit seasonal material 3 months in advance. Reports in 2 weeks. Enclose S.A.S.E. for return of submissions.

Nonfiction and Photos: General subject matter is "nonfiction technical and feature material on judo. Human interest on judo. Fiction on oriental martial arts." Approach should be "anything related to judo. Self-defense, today's youth, including humor. Ours is the only publication covering only judo. It is much more authoritative than any other martial arts magazine. Technical material must be sound. Special training or growth stories on local clubs are welcome." Buys personal experience, interview, profile, humor, nostalgia, personal opinion, travel (judo) and technical articles. No limit on length. Payment judged on review. Photos purchased with or without mss. Does not want "low quality photos or posed 'action shots.' " Captions optional. 8x10 b&w glossies. Pays $5 to $25.

Fiction: Buys adventure (martial arts) and humor stories with judo themes.

BLACK BELT MAGAZINE, 5650 West Washington Blvd., Los Angeles CA 90016. Editor: M. Uyehara. Audience consists of "94% male; 75% high school graduates; 20% professionals, 25% semiprofessionals, and 18% armed service personnel. Majority of readers are between the ages of 17 and 35." Monthly. Circulation: 45,000. Buys all rights. Payment on publication. Will send free sample copy to a writer on request. Will send editorial guidelines sheet on request. "We have a guide for interviewing personalities only, but we will be glad to send the writer a letter, giving editorial requirements." Query first. Will consider photocopied submissions. Reports in 2 weeks. Enclose S.A.S.E. for reply to queries.

Nonfiction, Photos, and Fillers: General subject matter is "martial arts (karate, judo, aikido, ju-jitsu, etc.), personality pieces, primarily, on top tournament players and instructors." Writer "should follow most recent issues for style and emphasis. We are de-emphasizing tournaments as they do not seem to hold as much interest for our readers as personality pieces." Length: 200 to 5,000 words. Payment varies according to the quantity (words and photos) and the quality of both ms and photos. Purchases photos with and without mss (without mss on a limited basis only). Captions required. Buys 5x7 and 8x10 b&w. Fillers should be 100 to 1,000 words in length. Pays $2 and up depending on length and quality.

KARATE ILLUSTRATED, 5650 W. Washington Blvd., Los Angeles CA 90016. Editor: M. Uyehara. Bimonthly. Buys all rights. "Seeking stringers and freelancers throughout U.S., Canada and Mexico. Stateside, we are interested in Southern and Midwestern writers especially." Pays on publication. Will send a free sample copy on request. Query first. Reports in 2 to 3 weeks. Enclose S.A.S.E. for reply to queries.

Nonfiction, Photos, and Fillers: Wants clear, objective, in-depth articles on personalities, tournaments, techniques and philosophies on tae-kwon-do, kung-fu and other karate-related sports. Must strike a responsive chord in karate novice or black belt. All material must be slanted to tie in with karate. Length: 1,500 to 3,000 words. Pays 3¢ to 7¢ per word. 5x7 or 8x10 glossies purchased with mss. Newsbreaks and clippings on personalities and news items are also used. Length: 100 to 1,000 words. Pays 3¢ to 7¢ per word.

OFFICIAL KARATE, Charlton Publications, Charlton Bldg., Derby CT 06418. Editor: Al Weiss. For karatemen or those interested in the martial arts. Established: 1968. Monthly. Circulation: 100,000. Rights purchased vary with author and material; generally, first publication rights. Buys 60 to 70 mss a year. Payment on publication. Will send free sample copy to writer on request. Query first or submit complete ms. Will consider photocopied submissions. Reports on material accepted for publication in 1 month. Returns rejected material within 2 weeks. Enclose S.A.S.E. for return of submissions or reply to queries.
Nonfiction and Photos: "Biographical material on leading and upcoming karateka, tournament coverage, controversial subjects on the art ('Does Karate Teach Hate?', 'Should the Government Control Karate?', etc.) We cover the 'little man' in the arts rather than devote all space to established leaders or champions; people and happenings in out-of-the-way areas along with our regular material." Informational, how-to, interview, profile, spot news. Length: 1,000 to 3,000 words. Pays $50 to $150. B&w contacts or prints. Pays $5.

Miscellaneous

GAMBLER'S WORLD, 527 Madison Ave., New York NY 10022. Editor: Lawrence Bernard. For "adults interested in all aspects of recreational gambling." Established in 1972. Bimonthly. Circulation: 300,000. Rights purchased vary with author and material. May buy all rights, but will reassign rights to author after publication or first North American serial rights, first or second serial rights or simultaneous rights. Payment on acceptance. Will send sample copy to writer for $1.25. Query first "always." Will consider photocopied submissions. Submit seasonal material 4 to 6 months in advance. Enclose S.A.S.E. for reply to queries.
Nonfiction and Photos: Articles must be knowledgeable on the gambling topic covered. Informational, how-to, personal experience, interview, profile, humor, think pieces, exposes. Length: 100 to 5,000 words. Payment depends on subject matter, quality of writing and length of article. Range: $25 to $500 plus. Photos purchased with mss or on assignment. Captions required.

GRIT AND STEEL, Drawer 280, Gaffney SC 29340. Manager: Mary M. Hodge. For audience of "only those interested in game (fighting) fowl. Ages 9 to 95; education —as a whole, high school." Monthly. Circulation: 6,000. Buys first serial rights. Buys 1 or 2 mss a year. Pays on publication. Will send a sample copy to a writer for 70c. Query first. Reports "as soon as possible." Enclose S.A.S.E. for reply to queries.
Nonfiction, Photos, Fiction, and Poetry: Uses material on game (fighting) fowl only. Does not actively solicit freelance material, and wants submissions only from writers with some knowledge of the subject. Will consider personal experience, interviews, successful business operations with game fowl, historical and photo articles, as well as fiction and poetry. Can be any length. Payment negotiated. Photos purchased with mss only.

HOCKEY ILLUSTRATED, 333 Johnson Ave., Brooklyn NY 11206. Editor: Alan Goldfarb. For young men and women interested in hockey. Established in 1960. 8 times a year. Circulation: 100,000. Buys all rights but will reassign rights to author after publication. Buys 65 mss a year. Payment on acceptance. Will send free sample copy to writer on request. Query first. Will not consider photocopied submissions. Submit seasonal material 3 months in advance. Reports immediately on material accepted for publication. Returns rejected material in 1 month. Enclose S.A.S.E. for return of submissions.
Nonfiction and Photos: Controversial hockey pieces, player profiles, in-depth interviews, humor; informational, personal experience, historical, expose, personal opinion. Length: 1,000 to 2,500 words. Pays $50 to $250. Pays $15 for 8x10 glossy b&w purchased with ms, without ms or on assignment. Captions required. Color: Pays $150 for cover; $50 to $75 for inside use for 35mm with available light. Photo Editor: David Elrich.
Fiction: Fantasy, humorous, historical. Length: 500 to 1,000 words. Pays $50 to $75.

RUNNER'S WORLD MAGAZINE, P.O. Box 366, Mountain View CA 94040. Editor: Joe Henderson. For "active runners or running coaches and avid followers of the sport." Established in 1966. Monthly. Circulation: 16,000. Buys all rights, but will reassign rights to author after publication. Buys 100 or more mss a year. Payment on publication. Will send free sample copy to writer on request. Write for copy of guidelines for writers. Query first. Will consider photocopied submissions. Submit seasonal material 1 month in advance "but assignment should be confirmed 2 to 3 months in advance." Reports on submissions within 2 days. Enclose S.A.S.E. for reply to queries.

Nonfiction and Photos: "We're looking for material with substance and value to readers. They don't buy the magazine primarily to be entertained, but rather to learn. It's more important what writers have to say than how stylishly they say it. This is an 'insider's' publication and few nonrunners write for us. The bulk of the magazine is personality and practical how-to features. Special emphasis is given to new research findings and techniques, written in simple, straightforward style." Length: 500 to 5,000 words. Pays $5 to $20 per published page in the magazine (500 to 1,000 words per page depending on illustrations). 8x10 b&w glossies purchased with or without ms, or on assignment. Pays $12.50. 35mm or 2¼x2¼ slide or larger for color cover use. Pays $40.

STRENGTH & HEALTH MAGAZINE, P.O. Box 1707, York PA 17405. Editor: Tom Holbrook. For a "sports oriented audience, mainly interested in weightlifting." Established in 1932. Monthly. Circulation: 100,000. Buys all rights, but will reassign rights to author after publication. Payment on publication. Will send free sample copy to writer on request. Submit complete ms. Will not consider photocopied submissions. Submit seasonal material (for baseball and football seasons) 3 months in advance. Reports on material within 1 week. Enclose S.A.S..E. for return of submissions.

Nonfiction and Photos: Sports (mainly weightlifting), exercise, general health and nutrition articles. International events in wrestling, cycling, gymnastics, fencing, karate; Russia vs. U.S.A. tournaments. "Need more originality." Length: 1,000 to 5,000 words. Pays $50 to $175. 5x7 b&w glossy prints purchased with or without mss. Captions required. Pays $5 to $10. Color transparencies for cover use only. Pays $50 to $100.

Fiction: "Related to theme, but open also." Length: 1,000 to 5,000 words. Pays $50 to $175.

THE WEEKEND, 1012 N. 3rd St., Suite 221, Milwaukee WI 53203. Editor: Rudy Pelecky. Established in 1961. For "outdoor oriented readers, interested in skiing, snowmobiling, cars (foreign and racing), camping, recreational vehicles." Weekly. Circulation: 10,500. Not copyrighted. Buys 250 to 300 mss a year. Payment on publication. Query first. Submit seasonal material (for annual festivals or events) 2 to 3 months in advance. Will send free sample copy to writer on request. Write for copy of guidelines for writers. Enclose S.A.S.E. for reply to queries.

Nonfiction and Photos: "Articles on outdoor theme: camping, trips to various parts of the country in campers, skiing experiences, snowmobiling, informational or human interest. Stories on major auto races or background pieces on races coming up, color stories on races. Approach should be first person 'how I did this' or in terms of easily identifiable persons and situations." Length: 200 to 500 words. Pays $10 minimum. B&w photos purchased with or without accompanying ms. Captions required. Pays $5 minimum.

Mountaineering

CLIMBING MAGAZINE, Box E, 310 Main Street, Aspen CO 81611. Editor: Joan E. Nice. For "mountaineers of the U.S. and Canada." Established in 1970. Bimonthly. Circulation: 3,000. Rights purchased vary with author and material. Buys 48 mss a year. Payment on publication. Will send free sample copy to a writer on request. Query first or submit complete ms. Will consider photocopied submissions. Reports in 2 weeks. Enclose S.A.S.E. for reply to queries or return of submissions.

Nonfiction and Photos: General subject matter concerns "technical rockclimbing,

mountaineering, and ski touring. Articles can be highly technical—our audience is select. Articles with general appeal also sought with a conservationist slant. We try to be a forum for all mountaineers. We would like to see articles on rock preservation, women in climbing, and attitudes towards mechanization of mountaineering." Buys informational, how-to, personal experience, interviews, profile, inspirational, humor, historical, think, personal opinion, photo, travel, mountaineering book reviews, spot news, new product and technical articles. "Regular column that seeks freelance material is called 'Routes and Rocks,' which consists of personal accounts of climbs." Length: 500 to 4,000 words. Pays about $4 to $45, according to length. Photos purchased with or without mss, on assignment, and captions are optional. Pays minimum of $5 per 8x10 (but accepts all sizes) b&w glossies. Pays $30 for color cover only. Prefers 10x12 transparencies. Should relate to subject matter.
Fiction: Buys experimental, mainstream, adventure, humorous, historical, condensed novels, and serialized novels. Length: 1,000 to 3,000 words. Payment varies.
Poetry: Buys traditional and avant-garde forms, and free, blank, and light verse. Pays $5 minimum.
Fillers: Buys climbing crossword puzzles, jokes, humor. Length: up to 500 words. Pays about 50¢ per 60 words.

MOUNTAIN GAZETTE, 1801 York Street, Denver CO 80206. Editor: Mike Moore. For "mountain lovers, environmentalists, skiers, hikers, climbers, and like that . . . they like to read." Monthly. Buys first North American serial rights, first and second serial rights. Buys between 30 and 50 mss a year. Payment on publication. Will send a free sample copy to a writer on request. Will send editorial guidelines sheet on request. Submit seasonal material 30 days in advance. Enclose S.A.S.E. for return of submissions.
Nonfiction, Photos, and Fiction: General subject matter is "primarily nonfiction dealing with those subjects—mountains, benign recreational use of the mountains (skiing, hiking, climbing, etc.). Personal exploits. Mountain communities (politics, sociology, architecture, land use, etc.). We like good writing—even the experimental. We like stylists. We offer a fairly open ended forum for writers who have something to say about the mountains. Avoid self-righteous writing when writing about the environment. Avoid hysterical glee when writing about skiing. Avoid, if you can, Buddhism when writing about climbing." Buys informational, how-to, personal experience, interview, profile, humor, historical, think, expose, nostalgia, personal opinion, photo, travel, and reviews. Length: no limitations; "we will give an entire issue to the right article. Payment is 75¢ a column inch for all writing." Buys photos without mss and captions are optional. Pays $5 minimum for 5x7, 8x9 prints (b&w). Buys experimental fiction.

Skiing and Snow Sports

INVITATION TO SNOWMOBILING, 1 Park Avenue, New York NY 10016. Editor: Sally Wimer. For "affluent, enthusiastic snowmobilers; urban and rural." Established in 1969. 4 times a year. Circulation: 130,000. Rights purchased vary with author and material. May buy all rights, or may buy first North American serial rights. Buys 15 assigned articles a year. Payment on acceptance. Will send a sample copy to a writer for $1.50. All material must be submitted between January and September. Reports in 1 week. Enclose S.A.S.E. for return of submissions.
Nonfiction and Photos: General subject matter consists of "articles to entertain or educate those getting involved and already involved with snowmobiles. Product tests, documented articles on controversial subjects, well-photographed adventure stories and the like. Technical information of good quality." Freelancer "should know snowmobiles, snowmobilers or special subject (camping, survival, etc.) related to snowmobiles; should be an expert in his field, and/or know snowmobiles inside-out. Uses only top-quality work; does not publish press releases or manufacturer-written articles. We don't want articles on 'My First Ride In a Snowmobile,' or safety first." Buys informational, how-to, personal experience, interview, profile, humor, historical, expose, nostalgia, photo, and technical articles. Pays $100 to $500 per mss. "We usually assign photographer on speculation if we have not used him before only if it fits current editorial format. Discourage amateurs. Photos seldom

purchased with mss." Send top quality b&w contact sheets. Pays $15 to $100 per b&w photo used. Top quality slides for color. Pays $15 to $100 depending on use.

MICHIGAN SNOWMOBILER, 207 Main St., East Jordan MI 49727. Editor: Marshall Sayles. Monthly. Will send a sample copy for 35¢. Reports in 1 week. Buys all rights. Pays on publication. Magazine does not use newspaper clippings, rewritten news stories, fillers, poetry, fiction. Highly specialized publication with several specialists contributing regularly. Suggests freelancer study the publication and query first. Enclose S.A.S.E. with all submissions and queries. Deadlines are the 15th of the month preceding the month of publication.
Nonfiction and Photos: Needs articles on snowmobile maintenance, proper use, safety and repair hints. Also what to wear in cold weather on long trips, what to eat on the trail, how to organize a snowmobile safari, a race or a successful club. Must have strong interest for snowmobile users. Writer must understand the snowmobile business: how they are used, where they are used, time of year, etc. Length: not much over 1,000 words. Pays $50 and up per printed page, depending upon value to reader. Photos purchased upon arrangement with editor.

NORTHWEST SKIER, 903 N.E. 45th St., Seattle WA 98105. Editor: Robert B. Hinz. Biweekly. Circulation: 15,000. Not copyrighted. Buys only first serial rights. Pays on publication. Will send sample copy to writer for 50¢. Reports on submissions immediately. Enclose S.A.S.E. for return of submissions.
Nonfiction: Well-written articles of interest to winter sports participants in the Pacific Northwest and Western Canada, or pieces of a general scope which would interest all of the winter sporting public. Character studies, unusual incidents, slants and perspectives. All aspects of winter sports covered in magazine; not just skiing. Must be authoritative, readable and convincingly thorough. Humor accepted. "Politics are open, along 'speaking out' lines. If you're contemplating a European trip or one to some other unusual recreation area, you might query to see what current needs are. When submitting article, consider pictures to supplement your text." Length: 250 words and up. Rate of payment open.
Photos: Purchased both with mss and with captions only. Wants strong graphics of winter sports scene. Doesn't want posed shots. 8x10 glossies, both b&w and color. Furnish separations. Rate of payment open.
Fiction: Uses very little and use depends on quality and uniqueness. Will use humorous fiction and short-shorts. Length: 250 words and up. Rate of payment open.
Poetry: Uses very little; quality and unusual point of view wanted. Rate of payment open.
Fillers: Uses newsbreaks, short humor, jokes. Rate of payment open.

POPULAR SNOWMOBILING, Box 115, Hopkins MN 55343. Editor: Edward L. O'Brien. For "ages 25 to 35 male snowmobilers." Established in 1970. Monthly during September through December only. Circulation: 104,000. Rights purchased vary with author and material, but may buy all rights and then reassign them to author after publication. Buys 36 to 42 mss a year. Will send a free sample copy to a writer on request. Will send editorial guidelines sheet to a writer on request. Will consider photocopied submissions. Submit seasonal material 2 months in advance. Query first. Reports in 1 week. Enclose S.A.S.E. for reply to queries.
Nonfiction and Photos: General subject matter consists of "how-to technique on tune-ups, outdoor on snowmobiles, trail riding, camping, and racing. We do not want to see articles on small town race coverage. We do want articles on snowmobile trips, adventures, and safety; community actions pro and con snowmobiles." Buys informational, how-to, personal experience, photo, travel, new product, and technical articles. Length: 2500 to 3000 words. Pays $40 per page flat rate. Photos purchased with or without mss, and on assignment. Captions required. Pays $10 per b&w 8x10 glossy. Pays $100 for color cover. 2¼x2¼ transparencies.
Poetry: Very little poetry, but some light verse. "Careful! Only funny or sporty or very unusual. Pays $5 to $10 maximum for full column."
Fillers: Buys short humor relating to snowmobiling. Length: 1 to 3 columns. Pays up to $40.

SKATING MAGAZINE, 178 Tremont Street, Boston MA 02111. Editor: Barbara R. Boucher. For a "family audience—generally members of clubs in the U.S. Figure

Skating Association. Majority of family heads probably attended college—the sport is very costly; therefore, most are professional people." Established in 1923. Monthly (8 times a year). Circulation: 25,000. Buys all rights. Buys an average of 25 mss a year. Payment on publication. Will send sample copy to a writer on request. Will consider photocopied submissions, "if we are aware of the circumstances behind it." Submit seasonal material 6 weeks in advance. Reports in 2 to 8 weeks. Enclose S.A.S.E. for return of submissions.

Nonfiction: General subject matter concerns the "sport of international figure skating, emphasis on national events: competitions, interviews with skating personalities, controversies in the skating world, histories, book reviews, innovations in techniques and equipment, club news, and personal experiences. Any theme that is in some way related to amateur figure skating could potentially be accepted. Approach is up to the author's discretion. Other magazines on skating internationally are generally less comprehensive in scope, more local in orientation, and only cover competitions—not other aspects of the sport. Articles on skating matches. We would like to see articles on the following topics in 1974: Innovations in skating music; politics of ice rinks; the isolation of a child's life devoted to one sport; profiles of foreign skaters." Buys informational, how-to, personal experience, interview, profiles, humor, historical, think, personal opinion, photo, travel to competition venues, reviews of skating books or amateur ice shows, and technical articles. Length: 800 to 1,500 words. Pays $25 per article.

Photos: Buys photos with or without mss, on assignment. Captions optional. Pays $5 per 8x10 or 5x7 b&w glossy used. Pays $2 to $5 for photos. Photo Editor: Bruce A. Boucher.

Fiction: Buys experimental, fantasy, humorous, and historical fiction. Should relate to skating. "Do *not* want any more short stories oriented toward the younger set with a moral about 'safety,' 'friendship,' etc." Pays $25.

Poetry: Buys all types of poetry and should relate to skating. Pays $10.

SKI, 235 East 45th St., New York NY 10017. Editor-in-Chief: John Fry. 7 times a year, September through March. Buys first-time rights in most cases. Pays on acceptance. Reports within 1 month. Enclose S.A.S.E.

Nonfiction: Prefers articles of general interest to skiers, travel, adventure, how-to, budget savers, technique, equipment, unusual people, places or events that reader can identify with. Must be authoritative, knowledgeably written, in easy, informative language and have a professional flair. Cater to middle to upper income bracket readers who are college graduates, wide travelers. Length: 1,500 to 2,000 words. Pays $100 to $250.

Fiction: Fiction is seldom used, unless it is very unusual. Pays $100 to $250.

Photos: Buys photos submitted with manuscripts and with captions only. Good action shots in color for covers. Pays minimum $150. B&w photos. Pays $25 each; minimum $150 for photo stories. (Query first on these.) Color shots. Pays $50 each; $100 per page.

SKIER, 20 Main St., Littleton NH 03561. Editor: Enzo Serafini. Monthly, October through March. Buys first serial rights. Query preferred. Consult editor for anything longer than 2,000 words. Reports in 2 weeks. Will send free sample copy to a writer on request. Enclose S.A.S.E. for reply to queries.

Nonfiction: Anything of interest to skiers—technique, new equipment, personalities, human interest, etc. Wants tightly written material. Pays about 5¢ per word on publication.

Photos: Buys photographs with mss and with captions only; uses single photos. Should be sharp b&w glossies, preferably 8x10. Pays $5 to $10 per picture.

SKIING, 1 Park Ave., New York NY 10016. Editor: Al Greenberg. 7 issues, monthly, August to February. Buys all rights. Pays on acceptance. Query first. Enclose S.A.S.E. for reply to queries.

Nonfiction: This magazine is in the market for any material of interest to skiers. Readership varies from teenagers to businessmen, and material used must appeal to and please the confirmed skier. Much of the copy is staff-prepared, but many articles and features are purchased freelance, provided the writing is fast-paced, concise, and knowledgeable. Writer must have a good working knowledge of skiing. Pays $75 to $350 depending on quality. Good humor and satire also needed.

Fillers: For Skiing Scene; light news of skiers. Length: 50 to 300 words. Pays $5 to $50.

SNO-MOBILE TIMES, 3000 France Avenue South, Minneapolis MN 55416. Editor: Jerry Hoffman. For "the snowmobile consumer, potential consumers. Outdoor oriented, ages 10 to 70." Established in 1969. Monthly from September through February. Circulation: 90,000. Rights purchased vary with author and material. Sometimes buys all rights. Buys 12 mss a year. Payment on publication. Will send a free sample copy to a writer on request. Will send editorial guidelines to a writer on request. Query first for all material other than nonfiction. Submit seasonal material 2 months in advance. Reports in 2 weeks. Enclose S.A.S.E. for reply to queries or return of submissions.
Nonfiction and Photos: General subject matter includes "racing, legislation, snowmobile travel, human interest, personality studies, personal experience. We publish in-depth articles that are truly objective." Buys interview, profile, inspirational, historical, nostalgia, photo, travel, and reviews. Length: 400 to 1,500 words. Pays $25 and up. Purchases photos with mss. Payment is open.

SNOTRACK, 534 N. Broadway, Milwaukee WI 53202. Managing Editor: Bill Vint. "The official publication of the U.S. Snowmobile Association, published for anyone who snowmobiles or is interested in snowmobiling. Their interests are mainly racing, but they have recreational interests too." 7 times a year, during winter months only. Buys first serial rights. Pays on acceptance. Query first. "Submit photos with a query, if photos exist already, or send samples of work." Submit seasonal material at least 3 months in advance. Enclose S.A.S.E. for reply to queries.
Nonfiction and Photos: "Interesting photo-article packages on all types of snowmobiling activities, how-to-do-it material, unusual or outstanding race events, rallies, trail rides, family activities, unforgettable personalities, humor; how-to, where-to, technical info on snowmobile maintenance, behind-the-scenes-at-the-races, spot news, interviews, profiles, travel articles. The approach should be concise and clear. We don't want stories without publishable photos." Length: 2,000 words maximum. Pays $50 to $250. Photos purchased with mss; with captions only. Pays $15 to $25 for b&w glossies, color transparencies, 35mm color. Pays $100 for color transparency for cover.
Fillers: Newsbreaks. Pays $5 to $10.

SNOW GOER, 1999 Shepard Rd., St. Paul MN 55116. Editor: Gene Schnaser. Monthly, September to February. Circulation: 250,000. Buys all rights. Pays on acceptance. Will send a free sample copy to a writer on request. Query preferred. Reports in 3 to 6 weeks. Enclose S.A.S.E. Also publishes *Snow Goer Racing Annual* on all aspects of snowmobile racing with deadline of June 1.
Nonfiction and Photos: Features on snowmobiling with strong secondary story angle, such as ice fishing, mountain climbing, snow camping, conservation, rescue. Also uses about 25% mechanical how-to stories, plus features relating to man out-of-doors in winter. " 'Me and Joe' articles have to be quite unique for this audience." Length: 5,000 words maximum. Pays $100 to $400. Photos purchased with mss and with captions to illustrate feature articles. 5x7 or larger b&w; 35mm color. Payment usually included in package price for feature.
Fillers: Short humor pays $25 to $50.

SNOWSPORTS, 1500 E. 79th St., Minneapolis MN 55420. Editor: Henry R. Fiola. For the snowmobile family. Established in 1970. 5 issues yearly from September to January. Circulation: 1,000,000 (September); 300,000 (October through January). Buys all rights. Buys 8 to 12 mss a year. Payment on acceptance. Query first or submit complete ms. Will consider photocopied submissions. Reports on material in 1 month. Enclose S.A.S.E. for reply to queries or return of submissions.
Nonfiction and Photos: "Editorial material should be oriented to places to go and things to do for the snowmobile family, including travel pieces on areas where families can take trail rides; camping and cooking on the trail, activities for clubs and groups of snowmobilers, tips about machine maintenance and driving. Nothing too technical." Informational, how-to, profile, humor, historical, travel. Length: 1,000 to 1,500 words. Pays $50 to $150. Photos purchased with accompanying mss. B&w glossy or matte prints; any size. Color slides, preferably 2¼ square.

THE STUDENT SKIER, Box 398, West Dover VT 05356. Editor: David H. Lyman. For "college students interested in travel, camping, the outdoors—especially skiing." Issued 5 times yearly (October, November, January, February and summer preview issue in April). Circulation: 250,000 (April, October, November); 50,000 (January, February). Buys all rights, but will reassign rights to author after publication. Buys 15 to 20 mss a year. Payment on publication. Will send free sample copy to writer on request. Write for copy of guidelines for writers. Query first. Will consider photocopied submissions. Submit summer stories by March 10. Reports on material in 2 weeks. Enclose S.A.S.E. for reply to queries.

Nonfiction and Photos: "First-person stories on living in ski towns. First-person stories on traveling to ski areas. Interesting characters found in ski country. Observations on skiing's effects on rural mountain communities. Ski area reviews are always sought as are stories on personal experiences while camping, skiing or living in rural ski towns. Personalities are welcomed as are opinion articles on various youth subjects dealing with the outdoors, sports and travel." Length: 2,500 to 3,500 words. Pays $35 to $100. In photos, "we are looking for ski action of good quality and technically perfect skiing. Also use trick and color effects on covers." 8x10 glossy. Pays $10 to $25. 35mm or larger transparency. Pays $50 to $75.

Fiction: Experimental, humorous. Themes open. "Give us a call." Length: 2,500 to 3,500 words. Pays $35 to $100.

Swimming and Diving

DIVE MAGAZINE, P.O. Box 7765, Long Beach CA 90807. Executive Editor: Mavis A. Hill. For "skin and scuba divers, seafood enthusiasts, tide pool buffs, marine scientists and institutions, etc., anyone interested in the ocean. Age 14 up. *Dive Magazine* relates to all divers, both experienced and widely traveled to novice and financially limited." Bimonthly. Circulation: 50,000. Buys first serial rights. Buys 60 to 70 mss a year. Pays on publication. Will send a free sample copy to a writer on request. Material is accepted on a tentative basis and is subject to change or rejection up to time of printing. Submit seasonal material about 4 months in advance. Reports in 2 weeks. Enclose S.A.S.E. for return of submissions.

Nonfiction, Photos, Fiction, Poetry, and Fillers: Wants "diving stories about sea life, underwater photography, spearfishing, undersea treasure and wreck diving, equipment, seafood; some fiction about diving and fresh water diving. 'Dive-In-Your-Own-Backyard' articles. Seeking technical oceanography items." Interested in personal experience, interviews, profiles, humor, successful business operations, historical, new product, photo, travel, and merchandising techniques articles; also mystery, science fiction, humorous, and adventure fiction. "Send up to about 2,000 words. Easy reading. First person good. Third person used also. Write to encourage diving and hobbies related to diving. Send high quality photos, preferably underwater photos. We use more freelance writers' photos than any other publication [in the same field]." Does not want "shark scare or diving danger stories, or do-it-yourself equipment building or repair. General 'this is what-I-saw-down-under' themes are overdone, with no particular point to the article other than how beautiful the underwater world is." Seeking freelance material for regular department "Life in the Sea." This should be "scientific discussion on some form of fresh water or sea life. Submission must include high quality color transparency to accompany copy. A good close-up, preferably." Also uses some poetry, contemporary and light verse; uses newsbreaks, clippings, jokes, and short humor as fillers. Payment for articles is $25 to $100. "Payment varies" for other material. Dept. Editor (except Photos): Mavis A. Hill. B&w glossy photos, color transparencies, and 35mm color purchased with mss only. "Payment varies." Photo Editor: Roy Brizz.

SKIN DIVER, 8490 Sunset Blvd., Los Angeles CA 90069. Editor: Jack McKenney. Circulation: 109,900. Pays on publication. Submit complete ms. Acknowledges material immediately. "Before material can be reviewed by the editors, all model releases and author's grant must be signed and filed at *Skin Diver* magazine. Manuscripts reviewed are either returned to the author or tentatively scheduled for future issue." Time for review varies. Mss considered "accepted" when published; all material held on "tentatively scheduled" basis subject to change or rejection up to time of printing. Enclose S.A.S.E. for return of submissions.

Nonfiction and Photos: Stories and articles directly related to skin diving activities, equipment or personalities. Features and articles equally divided into following categories: equipment, underwater photography, wrecks, treasure, spearfishing, shelling, undersea science, travel, boating, do-it-yourself, technique and archaeology. Length: 1,000 to 2,000 words, well illustrated by photos; b&w at ratio of 3:1 to color. Pays $35 per printed page. Photos purchased with mss; B&w 8x10 glossies; color: 35mm, 2¼x2¼, or 4x5 transparencies; do not submit color prints or negatives. All photos must be captioned; marked with name and address. Pays $35 per published page for inside photos; $100 for cover photos.

SURFBOARD, Box 2847, La Mesa CA 92041. Editor: Michael Morgan. For persons "interested in surfing and board building; ages range from 10 years old and up, with the highest concentration of readers between the ages of 14 and 18." Established in 1963. Annual. Circulation: 10,000. Buys all rights. Buys about 4 mss per year. Pays on publication. Will send a sample copy to a writer for $1. Query first. Submit material no later than 3 months before March 1. Will consider photocopied submissions. Submit seasonal material at least 2 months in advance. Reports in "up to 1 year." Enclose S.A.S.E. for reply to queries.
Nonfiction and Photos: "Articles related to surfboard building, performance of surfboard equipment in the water, safety in design and board building, new designs, innovations in plastics applicable to surfboards, historical information about surfboard building and performance, hypothetical futures of surfing and the board building industry." Would like to see articles on "how resins for foam (polyurethane) and laminating (polyester) are formulated—in lay terms." Buys informational articles, how-to's, personal experience articles, interviews, historical and photo features, coverage of successful business operations, new product and technical articles, and coverage of merchandising techniques. Length: 1,000 to 3,000 words. Pays 1¢ to 3¢ a word. B&w glossies purchased with and without mss. Pays $5 to $10. Photo Editor: Tom Morris.
Fiction: Science fiction, fantasy. Length: 1,000 to 2,500 words. Pays 2¢ to 4¢ a word.

SURFER, P.O. Box 1028, Dana Point CA 92629. Editor: Steve Pezman. For late teens and young adults. Slant is toward the contemporary, fast-moving and hip trend in the sport of surfing. Bimonthly. Buys North American serial rights only. Pays on publication. Will send free sample copy to a writer on request. Reports on submissions in 2 weeks. Enclose S.A.S.E. for ms return.
Nonfiction: "We use anything about surfing if interesting and authoritative. Must be written from an expert's viewpoint. We're looking for good comprehensive articles on any surfing spot—especially on the East Coast where the sport is now burgeoning. Surfing in faraway foreign lands also has a keen interest for our readers." Length: 1,500 to 3,000 words. Pays 2¢ to 10¢ per word.
Photos: Buys photos with mss or with captions only. Likes 8x10 glossy b&w proofsheets with negatives. Also uses expert color 35mm and 2¼ slides carefully wrapped. Pays $10 to $50; sometimes up to $100 for the slides. No color prints.
Fiction: "Looking for good plot, ideally with the surfing theme. Must have a connection with surfing, but not necessarily about surfing. Avoid death, injury in the water. No sharks, for example, unless they really have a necessary role in the story. Must be written from an expert's viewpoint." Length: 1,500 to 3,000 words. Also looking for bright short-short fiction with good plot twist. 500 words. Wants good humor. Pays 2¢ to 10¢ per word.
Fillers: See "Pipeline" column on surfing activities for an example of fillers needed. Also uses short humor and short news items about surfing around the world.

SWIMMING WORLD, 5507 Laurel Canyon Blvd., North Hollywood CA 91607. Editor: Albert Schoenfield. For "competitors (12 to 21), plus their coaches, parents, and those who are involved in the conduct of the sport." Monthly. Circulation: 21,500. Buys all rights. Buys 12 to 20 mss a year. Will send free sample copy on request. Query first. Reports in 1 to 2 months. Enclose S.A.S.E. for reply to queries.
Nonfiction: Articles of interest to competitive swimmers, divers and water poloists, their parents and coaches. Can deal with diet, body conditioning, medicine, as it applies to competitive swimming. Nutrition, stroke and diving techniques, developments in pool purification. Must be authoritative. Does not want results of competi-

tions. Length: 1,500 words maximum. Pays up to $25 on publication.
Photos: Photos purchased with mss. Does not pay extra for photos with mss. 8x10 b&w only. Also photos with captions. Pays $2 to $3.
Poetry: Uses verse about swimming.

THE WATER SKIER, 7th Street and Avenue G, S.W., Winter Haven FL 33880. Editor: Thomas C. Hardman. 7 times per year. Circulation: 10,500. Buys North American serial rights only. Buys limited amount of freelance material. Pays on acceptance. Will send free sample copy to a writer on request. Reports on submissions within 10 days. Enclose S.A.S.E. for return of submissions.
Nonfiction and Photos: Occasionally buys exceptionally offbeat, unusual text/photo feature on the sport of water skiing. Pays $25 per article.

WATERSPORT, Boat Owners Council of America, Division of OBC, 534 N. Broadway, Milwaukee WI 53202. Editor: A.W. Limburg. For "middle-class, middle-income outboard boating families who like to cruise, fish, and water ski—but also enjoy most other aspects of water sports." Circulation: 25,000. Buys first serial rights. Buys 24 mss a year. Pays on acceptance. Will send a free sample copy to writer on request. "Get a sample copy and study it before writing a word (other than the letter asking for the sample)." Then query first before submitting mss. Submit seasonal material 3 months in advance. Reports in 3 weeks on mss. "Photos take longer because usually we don't make final selection until close to deadline." Enclose S.A.S.E. for reply to queries.
Nonfiction: "Emphasize action opportunities for boatmen. Story subject should be of as much interest as possible to a broad audience—places, unique recreation ideas, photo essays. Much emphasis on good photos. We're a quarterly that avoids 'nuts-and-bolts' stories. We don't use stories about one lake or river. Seldom use personality stories." Length: 500 to 2,000 words. Payment is "$50 to $400 (for stories with photos)."
Photos: Purchased as package with mss and individually. Prefers color transparencies, but will use color prints, 35mm color, and 8x10 b&w glossies with mss. "We are using more b&w photos than previously." Payment for individual color transparencies is $35 to $100.

Tennis

TENNIS, 297 Westport Ave., Norwalk CT 06856. Publisher: Asher J. Birnbaum. For persons who play or are interested in playing racquet sports (tennis, badminton, table tennis, and the like), coaches of players, managers of country clubs and tennis facilities, and professionals. Established in 1965. Monthly. Circulation: over 70,000. Buys all rights. Pays on publication. Query first. Study magazine before submitting. Enclose S.A.S.E. for reply to queries.
Nonfiction and Photos: Authoritative articles on fitness, nutrition, conditioning, tournament information, club construction and maintenance, profiles of players, news of the sport. Columns are written by tennis experts. Length: varies. Payment to be negotiated. Photos purchased with mss.

TENNIS TIMES, 3000 France Ave. S., Minneapolis MN 55416. Editor: Bob Gillen. For "beginning, intermediate, and advanced tennis enthusiasts; amateur and professional tennis players; fans of the game and tennis playing families at all levels of skill." Established in 1972. Quarterly. Circulation: 85,000. Rights purchased vary with author and material. Buys about 25 mss a year. Pays on publication. Will send a sample copy to a writer "if he seems a serious prospect." Query first. Submit seasonal material 2 months in advance. Reports in 30 days. Enclose S.A.S.E. for reply to queries.
Nonfiction: "*Tennis Times* speaks the language of the active tennis player. Practical, entertaining, edited to attract novice and former players to actively engage in tennis as an interesting and healthful pastime. Regular features include advice for the consumer concerning equipment and accessory selection; the latest in tennis apparel and fashion; new products, instruction, tennis resorts, camps, clinics, news of gen-

eral interest to tennis players everywhere; tennis humor; book and film reviews, shopper items, and question and answer columns. Playing instruction, strategy, and tactics are emphasized through instructional feature articles and illustrated 'winning points' tips from teaching professionals throughout the world. Stress reader involvement. Writers should have a flair for sports writing. Pieces should have action and strong human interest. Writer should not assume that reader knows tennis terminology and organizations—explain all terms, places, and events mentioned in the article. Our publication has a more general, mass audience than existing tennis publications. We do not cater to the upper class 'tennis set.' We aim the book at readers who are discovering the sport. We have all the material we can use on Wimbledon, Forest Hills, movie stars playing tennis, Stan Smith, and Chris Evert. We're interested in material on inner city tennis programs and developing junior players." Seeks material for tennis humor, instructional, human interest anecdotes, travel and fashion. Length: 250 to 3,000 words. Pays $25 to $75, "or special arrangement for certain assignments." For stringers, pays "$25 an issue for contributing news bits."

Photos: Purchased with or without mss or on assignment; captions required. Uses 8x10 b&w glossy prints or contact sheets and negatives, "upon prior assignment arrangements." Uses 35mm color slides; "larger format acceptable and preferred for covers." Pays up to $25 per b&w photo, up to $60 per color photo.

Fiction: "Will consider fiction dealing with tennis, but have yet to use any." Length: 500 to 3,000 words. Pays $25 to $75, "or special arrangement."

TENNIS U.S.A., 205 E. 42nd St., New York NY 10017. Editor: F.E. Storer. Official publication of the U.S. Lawn Tennis Association for members and those interested in amateur tennis. Established in 1937. Monthly. Circulation: 45,000. Buys all rights. Pays on publication. Query first. Study magazine before submitting. Enclose S.A.S.E. for reply to queries.

Nonfiction and Photos: Features on all aspects of playing and teaching tennis; how-to approach. Also carries news on new techniques, construction and maintenance of tennis courts, rules, and championship meets. Buys informational articles, profiles, interviews, and photo features. Length and payment are to be negotiated.

WORLD TENNIS, 8100 Westglen, Houston TX 77042. Editor: Gladys M. Heldman. Query first. Enclose S.A.S.E. for reply to queries.

Nonfiction: General subject matter consists of articles that are "instructional, tournament player profiles, tournament reports, fiction, health and physical fitness as related to tennis." Payment varies.

Wrestling

WRESTLING GUIDE, THE BIG BOOK OF WRESTLING, 5202 Casa Blanca Rd., Scottsdale AZ 85253 Editor: Tommy Kay. Established in 1966. "The magazines are semimonthly, so we put out one 64-page wrestling magazine each month." Circulation: 40,000. Buys all rights, but will reassign rights to author after publication. Buys 120 mss a year. Payment made 4 months prior to publication. Will send sample copy to writer for 60¢. Write for copy of guidelines for writers. "If you've never sold to us in the past, submit complete article and sample photos. Experienced, query first." Will consider photocopied submissions. Submit seasonal material 3 months in advance. Reports on material within 4 weeks. Enclose S.A.S.E.

Nonfiction and Photos: "Profile articles or interviews with top professional stars; picture stories of 8 to 12 action photos plus captions and descriptions of where and how taken; fan club profiles—backgrounding the founding, officers and activities of wrestling fan clubs; general interest wrestling articles. Be sure to read recent issues. We stress approval of scientific wrestling styles over rowdy, illegal, blood 'n guts tactics, and we feature occasional profiles on amateur stars." Length: 800 to 3,000 words. Pays $15 to $35. 5x7 or 8x10 b&w glossies purchased with mss (occasionally without ms). Pays $3 to $5 for those purchased separately. 35mm or 2¼x2¼ color transparencies used for cover. Pays maximum of $25.

Fillers: Also seeking freelance material for "Fightin' Fotos," "Scrapbook of Action Photos" and sports crossword puzzles. Pays $10 for sports crosswords.

Teen and Young Adult Publications

The magazines below are for young people aged 12 to 26. Magazines aimed at 2- to 12-year-olds are classified in the Juvenile category.

ACCENT ON YOUTH, 201 8th Ave., S., Nashville TN 37203. Editor: Miss Margaret Barnhart. Published monthly for young teenagers. Buys North American serial rights, occasionally one-time rights. Pays on acceptance. Will send free sample copy to a writer on request. Mss must be typed, first copies. Tries to report on submissions within two months. Enclose S.A.S.E. for return of submissions.
Nonfiction: Articles on personal development, science, religion, nature, people, customs of other lands, vocations, teenage accomplishments, etc. Should evidence a Christian philosophy of life without being preachy, pious or moralistic. Query not necessary. Length: 900 to 1,200 words. Pays 3¢ per word and up. Seasonal material needed 8 months prior to holiday.
Photos: Purchased with mss or captions only. 5x7 or 8x10, first class quality.
Fiction: Stories interesting to teenage boys and girls, with Christian philosophy of life inherent in plot but not spelled out in moralisms. Length: 2,000 to 2,500 words. Pays $75 and up.
Poetry: Dealing with teenage interests. Payment varies with quality. Approximately 50¢ per line.
Fillers: Mostly puzzles. Payment varies.

ALIVE!, P.O. Box 179, St. Louis MO 63166. Editor: Darrell Faires. Monthly. Not copyrighted. A publication of the Christian Church (Disciples of Christ) for youth in junior high school. Circulation: 19,000. Pays on acceptance. Will send a sample copy to a writer for 25¢. Deadlines are at least 4 months in advance of publication date. "Youth will be strongly encouraged to be 'co-creators' of the magazine by their contribution of articles, poems, etc." Reports usually within two weeks. Enclose S.A.S.E.for return of submissions.
Nonfiction and Photos: First-person articles about outstanding youth; issues with which young teens must deal. Articles with photos about youth programs, projects and activities. 1,500 words maximum. Pays 2¢ per word. Photos should accompany articles. B&w glossies of young teens and teen activities. Pays $5 to $10.
Fiction: Should be related to real life issues of young teens. 1,500 to 2,000 words. Pays 2¢ per word.
Poetry: Personal insight, affirmation and humorous verse. 16 lines maximum. Pays 25¢ per line.
Fillers: Short humor and puzzles pay 2¢ per word or $3 to $10 per item.

AMERICAN NEWSPAPER BOY, 915 Carolina Ave., N.W., Winston-Salem NC 27101. Editor: Chas F. Moester. Buys all rights. Pays on acceptance. Will send list of requirements on request. Reports in 10 days. Include S.A.S.E.
Fiction: Uses a limited amount of short fiction, 1,500 to 2,000 words. It is preferable, but not required, that the stories be written around newspaper carrier boy characters. Before writing this type of fiction for this market, the author should consult a newspaper circulation manager and learn something of the system under which the independent "little merchant" route boys operate generally the country over. Stories featuring carrier contests, prize awards, etc., are not acceptable. Humor and mystery are good. Stories are bought with the understanding that *American Newspaper Boy* has the privilege of reprinting and supplying the material to other newspaper boy publications in the U.S., and such permission should accompany all mss submitted. Pays $15 and up for stories.

ART AND MAN, 50 West 44th Street, New York NY 10036. Editor of Ms Dept.: Mrs. Norma Ainsworth. For "grades 7 through 12." Buys all rights. Pays on acceptance. Uses only staff-written text. Enclose S.A.S.E. for return of submissions.
Photos: "Photographs by outside photographers are extensively used for magazine illustrations, slides, filmstrips, etc. Most of these photographs are of works of art, and fees paid depend on the nature of the work, and the purpose for which it is used."

AWARE, American Baptist Convention, Valley Forge PA 19481. Editor: John Carroll. For "high school youth between the ages of 14 and 19." Special issues for Christmas, Easter, and summer. Monthly. Buys all rights, first North American serial rights, second serial rights, and simultaneous rights. Payment on acceptance. Will send editorial guidelines sheet to a writer on request. Submit seasonal material 5 to 6 months in advance. Enclose S.A.S.E. for return of submissions.

Nonfiction and Photos: General subject matter: "school issues, personal concerns like dating, use of money, drugs, church, volunteer services, youth empowerment, meaning and importance of life, religious themes. Our concept of the magazine is to encourage youth to search for the meaning of life and begin committing themselves to the solving of social problems. We do not want to see boy/girl romance stories, sport stories, historical articles, moralistic articles. We would like to see articles on youth/adult tension and successful ways for overcoming; youth in government; youth and religion; ecology; youth culture, new trends, new school issues." Buys informational, how-to, interview, profile, humor, think, personal opinion, photo, spot news. Length: 1,000 to 1,500 words. Pays 2¢ a word. Photos purchased with mss. Pays $1.50 to $10 for 8x10, 4x5 glossies.

Fiction: Buys experimental, mainstream, fantasy, humorous, and nonmoralistic religious stories. Length: 1,800 to 2,000 words. Pays 2¢ a word.

Poetry: Buys all forms of poetry. Pays $5 per poem.

Fillers: Buys puzzles and short humor. Pays 2¢ a word.

How to Break In: "Best 'how to break in' for us is a simple query letter with a sample of his/her work. Or a couple of column items sent our way."

BOYS' LIFE, Boy Scouts of America, National Headquarters, Route 1, North Brunswick NJ 08902. Editor: Robert E. Hood. For boys 8 to 17 years of age with "the widely diversified interests of that age group." Monthly. Circulation: 2,250,000. Buys all rights. Buys 25 to 35 mss a year. Reports in 2 weeks. Will send free sample copy on request. Pays on acceptance. Enclose S.A.S.E. for return of submissions.

Nonfiction: Adventure, general interest, physical fitness, sports, science, personalities, historical, and how-to articles to interest boys. New phases of any subject, how-to's of sports (preferably by a name athlete or "as told" by a name athlete); vocations presented in interesting and informative fashion, but without a recruiting pitch. Should be written in modern idiom, crisp, fast-moving. Should be written for boys, not down to them. "We welcome variety of types and styles. Contributors should study the magazine." Thorough knowledge of the subject and flair for words required. Length: 2,000 to 2,500 words. Query advisable. Pays $350 and up. Material dealing with a specific season must be submitted six months to one year in advance.

Photos: Occasionally buys photos submitted with mss, seldom with captions only. Most photo features assigned, but editors are always happy to see the work of first-class talent. Neatly prepared folio of pictures desirable. Prefers 8x10 b&w; uses color all sizes. Larger transparencies preferred for cover, but magazine accepts any size if good quality. Pays $100 per page for b&w, $200 per four-color page. Department Editor: Brian Payne.

Fiction: Adventure, mystery, sports, scouting, science fiction, humor, foreign background, animal, special holidays, cars, historical, western, and slanted toward boys 14 to 17. Main characters usually boys of 14 and up or young men. Should present basic principles of good character and citizenship without moralizing. Professional excellence in style and characterizations, imagination and originality in treatment, well-sustained movement of story sequences and strong plot required. Stories: 2,000 to 2,500 words. Serials: two or three installments of 3,000 to 4,000 words. Pays $350 and up. Occasional serials to 9,000 words. Stanley Pashko, Fiction Editor.

How To Break In: "Write a short feature and submit with letter asking for comments."

CAMPUS AMBASSADOR MAGAZINE (CAM), 1445 Boonville Ave., Springfield MO 65802. Six times during college year to students on secular campuses only, by the Christ's Ambassadors Department, Assemblies of God. Circulation: 14,500. Buys all rights. Will send free sample copy on request. Reports in a few weeks or sooner. Enclose S.A.S.E.

Nonfiction: College-age slanted, religious nonfiction on personal evangelism, mis-

sions, Bible doctrines, Christianity and the sciences, devotional material. 800 to 1,200 words. Pays ½¢ to 1½¢ per word.
Photos: Purchased with mss. Prefers 5x7 b&w glossy. Payment varies according to quality and use.
Poetry: To 50 lines. Pays 20¢ per line.
Fillers: Brief quotes. Pays 1½¢ per word.

CAMPUS LIFE MAGAZINE, 4360 N. Main Place, Carol Stream IL 60187. Editor: Harold Myra. For teenagers. Monthly. Buys any rights offered by author. Query first. Enclose S.A.S.E. for reply to queries.
Nonfiction: "Youth activity articles. Material should avoid being preachy." 1,600 words average. Pays 2¢ per word and up.
Photos: Buys 5x7 or larger b&w photos and any size transparency with mss or with captions only, youth-slanted. Pays $5 and up per picture. Also uses four-color. Buys photo stories of unique youth activities.
Fiction: "Main characters should be Christian teenagers in situations that are teen-centered and teen-slanted." 1,700 words average. Pays $50 and more for good material.
How To Break In: "A simple query letter."

CAMPUS NEWS, P.O. Box 21441, Dallas TX 75211. Editor: R. W. Whitney. A bi-weekly newspaper aimed at the university student. Established in 1971. Circulation: 25,000. Rights purchased vary with author and material. May buy all rights but may reassign rights to author after publication. May buy first North American serial rights, first serial rights, second serial (reprint) rights or simultaneous rights. Buys 30 to 40 mss a year. Payment on publication. Will send sample copy to writer for 25¢. Query first for columns, reviews and fiction. Submit complete ms for non-fiction. Will consider photocopied submissions. Submit seasonal material 4 months in advance. Reports on material in 2 to 4 weeks. Enclose S.A.S.E. for return of submissions or reply to query.
Nonfiction and Photos: "Reviews of records and films, how-to articles, columns and articles telling of activities or happenings of interest to the college student. Concerts and events such as film festivals, summer activities; travel. Approach should be casual, open, pointed. We do not want to see the radical diatribe type of article. We prefer exposes to be tempered with fact and logic." Length: 200 to 1,500 words. Pays 25¢ to 60¢ per column inch. Dept. Editor: Paul R. Williams. 8x10 b&w glossy photos purchased with or without mss. Captions required. Pays $2. Dept. Editor: R. W. Whitney.
Fiction: Experimental, mainstream. Length: 500 to 1,500 words. Pays 10¢ to 60¢ per column inch. Dept. Editor: R. W. Whitney.
Poetry and Fillers: Traditional forms, blank verse, light verse, free verse, avant-garde forms. Length: 24 lines maximum. Newsbreaks, puzzles, jokes, short humor. Length: 200 words maximum. Pays 10¢ to 60¢ per column inch. Poetry Dept. Editor: Paul R. Williams. Fillers Dept. Editor: R. W. Whitney.

CATALYST, P.O. Box 179, St. Louis MO 63166. Editor: Jerry O'Malley. Monthly for senior highs. Will send a sample copy to a writer for 25¢. Write for copy of guidelines for writers. Enclose S.A.S.E. for return of submissions.
Nonfiction: Articles dealing with some aspect of religion or of social issues or what high school youth are doing in these areas. Humor, especially meaningful satire. Length: 1,000 to 1,200 words. Pays 1½¢ a word and up.
Photos: 8x10 preferred, but will accept any size of b&w if good photo. Photographers should state "asking price". Less payment for photos in photo features. Mainly wants photos of teenagers of all colors, shapes and sizes engaged in teenage activities. Would also like some abstract and scenery photos.
Fiction: "Using very little fiction now."
Poetry: Same topics as above. Some seasonal poetry also. 16 lines preferred, but longer lengths considered. Payment of 25¢ per line for most poems. Writer queried concerning payment for exceptionally long poems.
How To Break In: "By reading the magazine to see features we carry occasionally written by teenagers, and to write asking to participate in those features."

CHRIST-STYLE (formerly *Spirit Talk*), Concordia Publishing House, 3558 South Jefferson Ave., St. Louis MO 63118. Editor. John E. Schroeder. For "13 to 18 age group, mostly middle-class establishment, all church attenders, but issue oriented and concerned about community action." Educational discussion packet on a specific theme, with multimedia box resources for leader. Quarterly. Circulation: 50,000 pupils, 6,000 teachers. Buys "all rights on originals, second rights on reprints, songs previously copyrighted, photo essays, etc." Buys 50 mss a year. Pays "at point of final layout." Will send a sample pupil packet for $1.50, or a sample teacher kit for $5. Query before submitting. Submit seasonal material 8 months in advance. Enclose S.A.S.E. for reply to queries.

Nonfiction, Photos, Fiction, Poetry, and Fillers: "Short essays, poems, short stories, graphics, posters, filmstrips, plays, songs, etc., on specific themes which are scheduled in the prospectus. We strive for contemporary look, feel, sound, and we want a variety of approaches, not just linear literary material. The emphasis is on tightly written literary material for variety. Mostly affirming morality and positive religious values, but may hit society's standards to point up needs for improvement." Articles and fiction should be 250 to 1,000 words. Payment is $10 minimum. Looking for "issue oriented, church or community action articles involving youth or opinions of interest to them." Photos should be 8x10 b&w glossies or color transparencies. Payment is "$10 up for first use, ½ for re-use." Uses contemporary and avant-garde poetry, and some traditional and light verse, maximum length 2 pages. "Verse drama can go to 5 typewritten pages." Payment is $8 up. Payment is $1 to $10 for puzzles, clippings, jokes, posters, slogans, graffiti. Wants freelance material for "creative, craft, or group activity materials including game designs." Also uses "opticals, liturgies, lightshows, etc."

CIRCLE K MAGAZINE, 101 E. Erie St., Chicago IL 60611. Executive Editor: Andrew Leckey. Published five times yearly by Circle K International, male collegiate organization of Kiwanis International. Circulation: 15,000 members on U.S. and Canadian campuses. Not copyrighted. Pays on acceptance. No query required. Deadlines are 60 days prior to date of publication. Mss should be typed, not stapled, and should show number of words, title, and name of writer. Reports as soon as possible. Enclose S.A.S.E. for return of submissions.

Nonfiction: Authoritative, well-researched articles meaningful to today's collegian. Length: 800 to 1,500 words. Students' attitudes and opinions on what is happening on the college campus; dynamics of leadership or group dynamics; social and political issues, ecology; drug abuse. Offbeat campus humor. Description of service activities rendered by collegians in the vein of the Peace Corps or VISTA. General interest articles for college men such as dating, sports, fashion, and recreation. Pays up 10¢ a word.

Photos: Purchased with mss or with captions only. Also photo stories or essays. B&w glossies preferred. Payment varies.

CO-ED, Scholastic Magazines, Inc., 50 W. 44th St., New York NY 10036. Editor of Manuscript Department: Mrs. Norma Ainsworth. For girls ages 14 to 18. Monthly. Buys all rights. Pays on acceptance. Will send free sample copy on request. Enclose S.A.S.E. Send only one ms at a time for consideration. Do not resubmit a rejected manuscript unless revision is specifically requested.

Fiction: Stories up to 5,000 words for girls in homemaking classes, dealing with problems of contemporary teenagers, home, family, love, personal relationships, boy-girl situations. Humor is welcome. Prefers fall, winter, spring settings rather than summer. Pay starts at $150.

How To Break In: "First, a writer should study our fact sheet for various Scholastic publications. Second, he should read our magazines. Too many authors, even professionals, send us poetry which we don't buy, nonfiction which is usually staff prepared except in special categories, anthropomorphic short stories which we don't like, and adult fiction which we can't use."

CONQUEST, 6401 The Paseo, Kansas City MO 64131. Editor: Paul Miller. Young people's magazine with a point of view that attempts to mold as well as reflect the junior and senior high school Christian teen, sponsored by the youth organization of the Church of the Nazarene. Monthly. Pays on acceptance. Accepts simultaneous submissions. Buys second rights. Will send free sample copy and Editorial Specifications sheet on request. Reports on submissions in 6 weeks. Enclose S.A.S.E.

Nonfiction: Helpful articles in the area of developing the Christian life; first person, "this is how I did it" stories about Christian witness. Length: up to 2,500 words. Articles must be theologically acceptable and make the reader want to turn over the page to continue reading. Should not be morbid or contain excessive moralizing. Looking for fresh approach to basic themes. The writer should identify himself with the situation but not use the pronoun "I" to do it. Also go easy on "you" (unless the second approach is desired). The moral or application should not be too obvious. Also needs articles dealing with doctrinal subjects, written for the young reader. Pays a minimum of 1½¢ per word..Works six months ahead of publication.

Photos: 8x10 b&w glossies of teens in action. Payment is $7.50 and up.

Fiction: "Adventure, school, and church-oriented. No sermonizing." Length: 2,500 words maximum. Payment is a minimum of 2¢ a word.

EDITOR, Catholic School Press Association, 1135 W. Kilbourn Ave., Milwaukee WI 53233. Editor: Warren G. Bovée. Aimed at high school students engaged in school publication work and hopefully planning for career in journalism. Also school publication advisers. Quarterly. Buys all rights. Pays on publication. Will send a sample copy for 75¢. Query preferred. Reports on submissions as soon as possible. Enclose S.A.S.E.

Nonfiction and Photos: Articles for high school or college journalists. Prefers approach of teacher of scholastic journalism and not that of freelancers advocating "how to sell writing." Particularly interested in specific reports of successful innovations in college and high school communications, especially those involving other than the standard school newspaper, magazine or yearbook. These articles should provide school journalists with insights into alternative ways of serving their publics. When possible, pictures or other illustrative material should accompany ms. 2,500 to 3,000 words. Pays $35 per article accepted.

18 ALMANAC, c/o Approach 13-30, 1005 Maryville Pike, S.W., Knoxville TN 37920. Editor: Phillip W. Moffitt. Established in 1972. For high school seniors. Annually. Circulation: 150,000. Buys all rights. Buys about 5 freelance mss per year. Payment on acceptance. Query first. "Since we're an annual, we generally assign topics. Best way to query is to send us a resume of some previous work. We look for writers, not mss. Best time to write us is in July." Will send sample copy to writer for $2. Enclose S.A.S.E. for reply to queries.

Nonfiction and Photos: Informational, how-to, interviews. "Anything that will help high school seniors make the transition from high school to whatever follows, be it work, school, marriage or travel. Our style is tight, factual, structured. Articles are short, easy to read and brimming with facts." Payment "varies, depending on topic; roughly 10¢ a word. Writer is given an assigned length." B&w and color photos are purchased on assignment.

ENCOUNTER, Wesleyan Publishing House, Box 2000, Marion IN 46952. Address submissions to Editor of Sunday School Magazines. For senior teens, ages 15 to 18. Weekly. Special issues for all religious and national holidays. Not copyrighted. Pays on acceptance. Will send a free sample copy to a writer on request. No query required. Submit special material 9 months in advance. Reports in 6 weeks. Enclose S.A.S.E. for return of submissions.

Nonfiction: "Features of youth involvement in religious and social activity, travel, youth of other countries, history, biographies including people of all races, informational articles of educational, religious, or cultural value. Avoid implied approval of liquor, tobacco, theatres, and dancing." Length: 200 to 1,000 words. Payment is "2¢ a word for quality material."

Fiction: Stories with definite Christian emphasis and character-building values, without being preachy. Setting, plot, and action should be realistic. Length: 1,000 to 2,000 words. Serials should be no longer than 8 chapters, about 1,800 words per chapter. Payment is "2¢ a word for quality material."

Photos: 5x7 and 8x11 b&w glossies purchased with mss. Portraying action or the teenage world, or with seasonal emphasis. Payment is $1 to $10 depending on utility and quality.

Poetry: Religious and/or seasonal, expressing action, imagery. Length: 4 to 16 lines. Payment is 25¢ a line.

EQUAL OPPORTUNITY MAGAZINE: THE MINORITY STUDENT MAGA-ZINE, Equal Opportunity Publications Inc., 9130 S. Drexel Ave., Chicago IL 60619. Editor: Alfred Duckett. Audience is "primarily 'Third World'—Black, Latin, Indian, other nonwhite college students interested in employment, careers, 'own your business' opportunities." Three times a year. Buys all rights. Buys minimum of 20 mss a year. Pays on publication. Will send a sample copy for $3.75. Wants "letter of inquiry unless subject material is already written." Submit seasonal material 6 months in advance. Reports in 6 weeks. Enclose S.A.S.E. for reply to queries.

Nonfiction, Photos, and Fiction: Wants "stories, articles, features relating to jobs, racism, humor, etc., which are of special interest to college students." Buys how-to's in the job field, personal experience and inspirational stories, profiles, interviews, successful business operation reports, historical articles, think pieces, exposes, and photo essays. Buys articles on humorous, contemporary problems, and religious fiction. Length: 600 to 3,000 words. Payment is $10 to $50.

Poetry: Buys all kinds of poetry, if "related to 'Third World' interests." No length limitations. Payment "depends on material."

ETC., 6401 The Paseo, Kansas City MO 54131. Editor: Paul Miller. Published by the Church of the Nazarene. For the "18- to 24-year-old student, young professional, and serviceman." Monthly. Circulation: 18,000. Buys first rights or second rights. Buys approximately 50 mss a year. Pays on acceptance. Will send a sample copy to a writer on request. No query required. Submit seasonal material 6 months in advance. Enclose S.A.S.E. for return of submissions.

Nonfiction: "Helpful articles in the area of developing the Christian life, how the Christian meets his world." Writer's style should be "evangelical in emphasis; material should have a real 'bite' in it." Wesleyan doctrine. Buys interviews, profiles, inspirational and think pieces, humor, photo essays. Length: 2,500 words maximum. Pays minimum 1½¢ a word.

Photos: B&w glossies. Pays $5 to $15.

EVENT, 127 9th Ave., N., Nashville TN 37203. Issued monthly for Southern Baptist youth, ages 12 to 17. Circulation: 225,000. Buys all rights, first rights, and simultaneous submissions provided other publications are listed. Pays on acceptance. Will send free sample copy to a writer on request. "Profanity and moral problems such as smoking, petting, and drinking as natural or acceptable behavior are taboo." Mss should be double-spaced and include approximate number of words, rights for sale, and Social Security number of the author. Reports within three to four weeks. Enclose S.A.S.E. for return of submissions.

Nonfiction and Photos: Stories of achievement by high school youth, photo stories of places and persons interesting to youth, sports and sports figures, do-it-yourself and self-development features, vocational information, dating skills, science, human relations, preparation for college, citizenship, travel (limited amount), hobbies (especially for boys). Wants up-to-date subjects, given fresh treatment. Length: 750 to 1,500 words. Query helpful but not required. Pays 2½¢ per word (all rights); 1¼¢ per word (one right). Photos purchased with mss only. No specific size, although 8x10 preferred. Main requirement is that photos be sharp and clear and fit article. No color. Pays $5 to $10.

Fiction: Boy-girl or sports stories with a come-to-realize theme or a situation where a young person faces a problem reflecting the needs of high school youth. Length: 1,500 to 3,000 words. Pays 2½¢ per word (all rights); 1¼¢ per word (one right). Deadline for seasonal material one year in advance of publication.

Poetry: Short poems; humorous, devotional, nature, self-understanding. Length: 4 to 20 lines. Only poems of unusual merit above this length. Pays 35¢ to 50¢ per line.

Fillers: 300 to 500 words on devotional, personality, or humorous subjects. Pays 2½¢ per word. Also general information, puzzles and quizzes. Pays $5 to $10.

EXPLORING, Boy Scouts of America, Rte. #1, North Brunswick NJ 08902. Editor: Robert Hood. Executive Editor: Jack Haring. For "ages 15 to 20. Grade school, high school, some college. Interests are general and wide—indoor, outdoor, career, education, sports, cars, planes, psychology, etc." Published 6 times a year. Buys all rights. Buys about 40 mss a year. Pays on acceptance. Will send a free sample copy to a writer on request. Query first. Submit seasonal material 6 months in advance. Reports in 4 weeks. Enclose S.A.S.E.

Nonfiction: "Subjects: Careers, colleges, exploring, travel, music, contemporary youth activities, sports." Interested in how-to, personal experience, interviews, profiles, humor, think pieces, and photo articles. Consider the ages and education of our readers, yet realize we're not a 'far out' youth magazine. No sex; no particularly controversial themes; nothing below the age-level interest." Length: 2,000 to 2,500 words. Payment is $250 to $500. "Looking for talented young writers, preferably college students." Dept. Editor: Annette Stec.

Photos: Payment is $250 to $350 for cover, $150 a page for inside color, $100 a page for b&w. Purchases one-time use rights for general interest; all rights for assigned articles. Dept. Editor: Brian Payne.

FACE-TO-FACE, 201 Eighth Avenue, South, Nashville TN 37202. Editor: Sharilyn S. Adair. For "15 to 18 year olds in the United Methodist Church." Established in 1971. Special issues at Christmas, Easter, and summertime. Monthly. Circulation: 45,000. Rights purchased vary with author and material. May buy first North American serial rights, first serial rights, or simultaneous rights. Buys about 20 mss a year. Payment on acceptance. Will send free sample copy to a writer on request. Will send editorial guideline sheet on request. Will consider photocopied submissions. Submit seasonal material 8 to 9 months in advance. Reports in 1 to 2 months. Enclose S.A.S.E. for return of submissions.

Nonfiction and Photos: Subject matter consists of think pieces in meditative prose and blank verse relating to teens' personal identity, purpose in life, faith, personal relationships, goals and feelings; paraphrasing of Biblical material in contemporary terms; brief articles encouraging creativity; short stories with teenage protagonists. We seek any style that reflects good writing. We do not want academic sounding rhetoric. Writing should be 9th or 10th grade level, using the Flesch formula. Writing should be both theologically sound and aesthetically pleasing. We are striving to resemble an art piece more than a feature magazine. We are not presently interested in nonfiction feature articles. Buys informational and how-to articles. Pays 2¢ to 3¢ a word. Dept. Editor: Richard H. Rice. Photos purchased with or without mss, on assignment, and captions are optional. "Good b&w low-key, high-impact photos dealing with a broad range of human experience and with the natural world." Pays $15 for one-time use of 8x10 b&w glossy or matte. Pays $35 for one-time use of color transparencies.

Fiction: Buys experimental, mainstream, fantasy, humorous, and religious fiction. Length: 1,200 to 2,400 words. Pays 2¢ to 3¢ a word. Should relate to subject matter.

Poetry: Buys traditional and avant-garde forms, and free and blank verse. Length: 10 to 150 lines. Pays 25¢ per line.

FLIP MAGAZINE, 405 Park Ave., New York NY 10022. Editor: Barbara Benson. Issued monthly to teenage girls, ages 11 to 17. Pays on publication. Buys all rights. Reports in three weeks. Enclose S.A.S.E. for return of submissions.

Nonfiction: Wants medium length exclusive, accurate articles on the pop scene as viewed by teenage girls. Usually based on interviews with top pop personalities. Breezy, intimate, but honest and candid style. Teen pop recording stars and TV personalities emphasized. Query first and state credentials and interest in the field. Pays $50 and up. Address Rickie Kenton, Associate Editor. Enclose S.A.S.E.

Photos: With mss or with captions only. Any size; popular music and TV personalities of teen interest. Payment subject to negotiation. Direct photo queries to Carl Opalek, Creative Director.

FOR TEENS ONLY, 235 Park Avenue, South, New York NY 10003. Editor: B.J. Lange. For "young teenage girls, aged 10 to 16, from all parts of the country." Quarterly. Buys all rights. Buys 28 to 30 mss a year. Pays on acceptance. No queries. Submit seasonal material 3 to 4 months in advance. Reports in 1 month. Enclose S.A.S.E. for return of submissions.

Fiction: "Themes are predominately boy-girl, but we can use friendship, family, growing up, etc.,—anything that relates to a teenage girl's life. Can use mystery and contemporary problem stories. Stories should not be written down to the reader—situations and especially dialog must be realistic. Fiction should be generally geared to the season in which it will be appearing (no school settings in the summer, for example), but we do not zero in on specific holidays." Length: 1,500 to 4,000 words. Payment is $50.

HICALL, 1445 Boonville Ave., Springfield MO 65802. Editor: James R. Erdmann. Issued monthly in weekly parts for high school students belonging to Evangelical churches (Assemblies of God). Will send free sample copy and writer's suggestion sheet on request. Pays on acceptance. Publication not copyrighted. Material should be typed, double-spaced, preferably 10 words per line, 25 lines per page. Include approximate number of words in upper right-hand corner of first page. Enclose S.A.S.E. for return of submissions.

Nonfiction: Human interest, geographical, missionary, nature and scientific articles, or any other topics interesting to teenagers, with emphasis on 15 to 17-year-olds. Articles should have evangelical emphasis, but should not be preachy or have tacked-on moral. Length of 500 to 700 words with 1,000 words maximum. Pays ½¢ to 1¢ per word. Seasonal deadlines are 10 to 12 months prior to publication.

Photos: Purchased with captions only. Teens in everyday activity scenes. Size is not as important as subject matter and clarity of picture. Must be suitable for offset printing. 4x5 or 8x10 b&w. Pays up to $5.

Fiction: Stories, 1,200 to 1,800 words, on any subject interesting to teenagers. Strong evangelical emphasis, but not preachiness, should be inherent part of story. Good plots wanted in which main character solves his problems through putting Biblical principles and Christian values into action. Stories of two, three, and four parts considered. Each should be accompanied by synopsis. Pays ½¢ to 1¢ per word.

Fillers: Must have definite relationship to teenager's spiritual life. Up to 500 words.

HIGH, 1233 Central, Evanston IL 60201. Editor: David Olson. For teenage churchgoers (evangelical churches) of various denominations. Established in 1959. Quarterly issues of 13 weekly parts. Buys all rights. Buys 100 mss a year. Payment on acceptance. Will send sample copy (plus information packet) to writer for 50¢. Query first. Submit seasonal material 9 to 12 months in advance. Must be issue-related. Reports on material in 1 to 2 months. Enclose S.A.S.E. for reply to queries.

Nonfiction and Photos: "Articles that help readers live the Christian life in their own world and understand what commitment to Christ means. All aspects of daily life on which Christiantity has a basic bearing. Contemporary and teen-related." Informational, how-to, personal experience, interview, inspirational, humor. Pays minimum of 3¢ per word. Length: 100 to 1,500 words. 8x10 b&w glossies. Pays $3 to $15. Captions optional.

Fiction: Religious or humorous. Length: 1,000 to 1,600 words. Minimum of 3¢ per word.

HIS, 5206 Main St., Downers Grove IL 60515. Editor: Stephen Board. Issued monthly from October to June for college students, faculty administrators, and graduate students belonging to the evangelical Christian faith. Buys all rights. Enclose S.A.S.E.

Nonfiction: Articles dealing with practical aspects of Christian living on campus, relating contemporary issues to Biblical principles. Should show relationships between Christianity and various fields of study, Christian doctrine, and missions. Query not necessary. Mss up to 1,500 words. Pays 1¢ a word. Reports in 3 months.

Photos, Fiction, and Poetry: Uses b&w singles. Pays $10 per photo. Also uses photo series in which $6 per photo is paid. No color. Rarely accepts illustrated articles. Reports within 10 days or as work permits. Buys first rights, single publication. Payment is made on acceptance. Photos should be original and creative. Poetry occasionally bought. Pays $5 to $10.

JUNIOR BOWLER, 5301 S. 76th St., Greendale WI 53129. Editor: Ed Baur. Monthly. November through April to boys and girls 21 and under. Query first. Enclose S.A.S.E. for reply to queries.

Nonfiction and Photos: Subject matter of articles must be based on tenpin bowling and activities connected with American Junior Bowling Congress only. Audience includes youngsters down to 6 years of age, but material should feature the teenage group. Lengths: 500 to 800 words. Accompanying art preferred. Pays $30 to $50 per article. $5 for each photo used, 8x10 glossies, and more for an exceptional spread.

JUNIOR SCHOLASTIC, Scholastic Magazines, Inc., 50 W. 44th St., New York NY 10036. Address Mrs. Norma Ainsworth, Editor of Manuscript Department. Published weekly during the school year for seventh and eighth grades, ages 12 to

14. Buys all rights. Pays on acceptance. Will send free sample copy on request. Enclose S.A.S.E. for return of submissions. Send only one ms at a time for consideration. Do not resubmit same ms unless revision specifically requested.
Nonfiction: Pays up to $50 for bright features, 500 to 2,000 words, about young teenagers. Hobbies, community activities, various achievements.
Fiction and Drama: Would like 1,000- to 2,000-word original plays or stories, social studies oriented. Government, history, communities, social change. Preferably young characters. Pays from $100. Also pays $50 for 600 words or less.
How To Break In: "A simple query letter for nonfiction; complete ms for fiction."

THE KEYNOTER, 101 East Erie St., Chicago IL 60611. Executive Editor: Andrew Leckey. Published monthly, September through May for high school males, 15 to 18 years. This is the organization publication of Key Club International. Circulation: 95,000. Not copyrighted. Pays on acceptance. Reports as soon as possible. Include S.A.S.E. for return of submissions.
Nonfiction and Photos: Uses material of interest to the high school leaders of U.S. and Canada. Topical material directed to a mature level of young men. Dangers of abusive use of drugs, moral standards of young people, ecology efforts, leadership, humor, fashions, various aspects of college life to be encountered. Also school problems, political and social issues. Length: 2,000 words maximum. Payment "rates vary." Buys some photos; b&w glossies only.

LIGHT AND LIFE EVANGEL, Winona Lake, IN 46590. Editor: Vera Bethel. Free Methodist weekly publication for young people of college age and young adults. Pays on acceptance. Will send free sample copy on request. Write for copy of guidelines for writers. Reports within a month. Enclose S.A.S.E. for return of submissions.
Nonfiction: Pays 2¢ a word for articles, 300 to 2,000 words. Any religious, moral or ethical problems which confront today's young Christians; racial issues, responsibility toward minority groups such as migrants or the Appalachian poor whites, almost any of these social problems which pose some sort of moral decision or responsibility. Also uses human interest articles, 1,000 to 2,500 words.
Fiction: 1,800 to 2,000 words, dealing with the Christian answer to contemporary problems, including the racial problem. Pays 2¢ a word. Stories should have a specific moral or religious message, but not an obvious one. Preferably written from the young person's viewpoint, but not necessarily from the viewpoint of a Christian. Also uses short-shorts.
Photos: Pays $1 to $10 for photos submitted with mss. Can be 3x5, 6x8, or 8x10.
Poetry: From four lines to 25. Religion, nature, personal attitudes. Pays 25¢ per line.
Fillers: Short devotional articles, 100 to 500 words; anecdotal or straight exposition. Fresh, pointed, without trite expressions.

LITERARY CAVALCADE, Scholastic Magazines, Inc., 50 West 44th Street, New York NY 10036. Address mss to Mrs. Norma Ainsworth, Editor of Manuscript Dept. Buys second rights. Enclose S.A.S.E. for return of submissions.
Fiction: "Fiction (reprint only) should have as much of a universal theme as possible and should be written on an upper adult level in style. This doesn't mean that the story can't be about young people; it simply means that the point of view has to have a strong intellectual pull. *Cavalcade* is not looking for deeply introspective or mood pieces: there has to be some story; not necessarily heavily plotted, but somewhere in the first page or two, we have to know what is happening and where the thing is going. *Cavalcade* never prints high school romance stories." Length: 1,500 to 3,500 words. Payment varies.

LIVE, 1445 Boonville Avenue, Springfield MO 65802. Editor: Gary L. Leggett. For "young people and adults in Assemblies of God Sunday Schools." Established in 1928. "Special issues during Easter, Thanksgiving, and Christmas in which we want articles of a devotional nature." Weekly. Circulation: 225,000. Not copyrighted. Acquires first serial rights, second serial rights, and simultaneous rights. Buys about 100 mss a year. Payment on acceptance. Will send a free sample copy to a writer on request. Will send editorial guidelines to a writer on request. Reports on rejected material within 10 days. Reports on accepted material "hopefully within a month to

6 weeks." Submit seasonal material 10 months in advance. Enclose S.A.S.E.

Nonfiction and Photos: General subject matter consists of "short stories and articles that show the reader how to put Bible principles into action in his everyday life." Evangelical approach. "We do not want articles like the self-pitying housewife and mother." Buys personal experience, interview, profile, inspirational, historical, think, and photo articles. Length: 500 to 1,000 words. Pays ½¢ to 1¢ a word "according to the amount of editorial work necessary and the value of the original piece to our readers." Photos purchased with or without mss, on assignment, and captions are optional. "We need color photos showing people in everyday activities suitable for illustrating short stories as well as nonfiction." Pays $35 for 35mm slides or prints (color).

Fiction: Buys mainstream, religious, and historical fiction. Should relate to subject matter. Length: 1,500 to 2,000 words. Pays ½¢ to 1¢ a word.

Poetry: Buys traditional, free, and blank verse. Length: 12 to 20 lines. Pays 10¢ per line.

Fillers: Buys short fillers related to purpose of magazine. Length: 150 to 500 words. Pays ½¢ to 1¢ a word.

THE MODERN WOODMEN MAGAZINE, 1701 1st Ave., Rock Island IL 61201. Editor: Robert E. Frank. Free bimonthly to members of Modern Woodmen of America, for children 6 to 16. Will send free sample copy to a writer on request. Reports in one to three weeks. Not copyrighted. Pays on acceptance. Indicate word count to nearest hundredth on all mss. Mss should be typewritten, double-spaced, on one side of paper only. Enclose S.A.S.E. for prompt ms return.

Nonfiction: Clear, educational, inspirational articles of 1,500 words for children and young people. Prefers secular, educational, inspirational material with appeal for children up to 16. Queries, article summaries or outlines not necessary. Length: 1,500 to 2,000 words. Pays $25 and up. Holiday material must be received several months ahead of publication date.

Photos: Buys photos and artwork that accompany stories. Publication prints b&w and one-color. No transparencies. Photos submitted without mss should be b&w verticals suitable for cover. Pays $25 for vertical front cover photos.

Fiction: Clear, educational, inspirational articles for children and young people. No "first-person" stories. No serials. Length: 1,500 to 2,000 words. Pays $25 and up. Needs "read aloud" and other preschool material. Overstocked with teen adventure.

MY DELIGHT, Box 6059, Cleveland OH 44101. Circulation: 39,000. Nondenominational Christian magazine for teenagers. Will send a free sample copy to a writer on request. Reports approximately within one month. Buys all rights. Pays on acceptance. Send for booklet, "Manual for Writers." Enclose S.A.S.E. for return of submissions.

Nonfiction and Fiction: True-life stories with moral or spiritual emphasis; no slang. 925 to 1,225 words. No query required. Pays 2¢ per word. Fiction requirements same as for nonfiction. Also uses short-shorts of approximately 300 words. Pays 2¢ per word.

Poetry: "We will now accept both blank and free verse, as well as traditional forms of poetry. We would like to see the work of young writers with young ideas. Topics may vary, but they should be primarily inspirational or devotional. Poems should have a 'now' message for teens. Poetry should not exceed 25 lines. Payment is 2¢ a word."

THE NEW INGENUE, 635 Madison Ave., New York NY 10022. Editor-in-Chief: Joanna Brown. Monthly for girls between 15 and 19. Query first. Enclose S.A.S.E.

Nonfiction: Articles involving current trends in activities, attitudes, interests and achievements of teenagers, their life styles and relationships. Topic examples: problems and solutions dealing with personal identity, health, drugs, sex, school, relationships with family and peer groups; travel experiences; participation in sports; involvement in political and social trends. Teen topics with a humorous twist. Young people of interest to a national audience; articles on teenagers of other countries, their fads, life styles, attitudes. Women outstanding in their field with special

appeal for young people. Personality quizzes—fun and analytical. Short articles suggesting and explaining how to do interesting, unique and "now" things. Teenagers' accounts of their own experiences. Articles should be well researched, factually supported in detail, should contain an interesting and/or provocative approach, should be of the moment and slanted to a teenage audience. Pays $15 to $50 for short "how to" articles, $175 to $500 for articles of 700 to 4,500 words.
Fiction: Teenage figure in a dominant role. Can be either girl or boy. Contemporary teen life—problems young people face in growing up and in their relationships with their family and friends (romantic or otherwise), their school, teachers, and community. Stories can be light, but the humor should not be silly, frivolous or incredibly exaggerated. Also interested in high quality science fiction if it involves teenagers. Lengths: 1,500 to 6,500 words. Pays $175 to $500.

NUTSHELL, c/o Approach 13-30 Corp., 1005 Maryville Pike S.W., Knoxville TN 37920. Editor: Phillip W. Moffitt. For college freshmen. Established in 1969. Annually. Circulation: 850,000. Buys all rights. Buys 5 mss a year. Payment on acceptance. Will send sample copy to writer for $2. Query first. "Best month to query is February." Address query to Managing Editor. Enclose S.A.S.E. for reply to query.
Nonfiction and Photos: "We generally assign topics to writers. So best way to query is to send us a resume and some previous work. We look for writers, not manuscripts." Anything that will help a freshman orient himself to college those first few weeks. Style is tightly focused; all articles are short, well-structured, brimming with facts. Length varies. "Writer is given an assigned length, however." Pays 10¢ a word usually, but payment is negotiable. Photos purchased on assignment.

OPUS ONE, Church Music Dept., Baptist Sunday School Board, Nashville TN 37234. Editor: Daniel B. Johnson, Jr. For "12- to 14-year-old members of church youth choirs in Baptist churches." Established in 1970. Quarterly. Circulation: about 55,000. Rights purchased vary with author and material; may buy all rights, but may reassign rights to author after publication. Buys 10 to 15 mss a year. Pays on acceptance. Will send a sample copy to a writer on request. Query first or submit complete ms. Will consider photocopied submissions. Submit seasonal material 12 to 14 months in advance of issue date. Reports in 30 to 60 days. Enclose S.A.S.E. for return of submission or reply to queries.
Nonfiction: "Personal experience—all church music related if at all possible. Remember, these are early adolescents. Lots of these choirs nowadays are making trips to ghetto-type areas to do social ministry-type work with music. Most of the readers would be from the Southeast, or at least from the South. We get more stories of the lives of great composers than we need." Interested in articles on "music used in public places." Buys informational articles, how-to's, personal experience articles, interviews, profiles, inspirational articles, humor, historical and think articles, photo essays. Length: maximum 1,000 words. Pays 2½¢ a word, $15 a page for photo features of 2 pages.
Photos: Purchased with mss, without mss, or on assignment; captions optional. Prefers 5x7 b&w glossies; "strong contrast."
Fiction: Adventure, humorous, religious. "Stories should illustrate what a choir experience has done to help the hero." Must relate to subject matter. Length: up to 1,000 words. Pays 2½¢ a word.
Poetry: Traditional forms, blank verse, free verse, avant-garde forms, light verse. "Needs to relate to church or music."
Fillers: "Word-type puzzles," jokes. Length: "¼ to 1 page." Pays "up to $15 per page; rarely less than $5."

OPUS TWO, Church Music Dept., Baptist Sunday School Board, Nashville TN 37234. Editor: Daniel B. Johnson, Jr. For "15- to 17-year-old members of Southern Baptist youth choirs." Established in 1970. Quarterly. Circulation: about 60,000. Rights purchased vary with author and material; may buy all rights, but may reassign rights to author after publication. Buys 12 to 18 mss a year. Pays on acceptance. Will send a sample copy to a writer on request. Query first or submit complete ms. Will consider photocopied submissions. Submit seasonal material 12 to 14 months in advance of issue date. Enclose S.A.S.E. for return of submissions or reply to queries.

Nonfiction: "Personal experiences—all church-related. We don't need any stories about great composers. More and more church youth choirs go outside the church to sing in shopping areas, etc. Coverage of that trend might be helpful." Buys informational articles, how-to, personal experience articles, interviews, profiles, inspirational articles, humor, historical and think pieces, and photo features. Length: maximum 1,000 words. Pays 2½¢ a word; $15 a page for photo features of 2 pages.
Photos: Purchased with mss, without mss, or on assignment. Prefers 5x7 b&w glossies; "strong contrast."
Fiction: "Fiction must have musical background and/or church connection. Dialog, drama, first person experiences—any format is possible." Buys adventure, humorous, and religious stories. Length: maximum 1,000 words. Pays 2½¢ a word.
Poetry: Traditional forms, blank verse, free verse, avant-garde forms, light verse. "Needs to relate to Church or music."
Fillers: "Word-type" puzzles, jokes. Length: ¼ to 1 page. Pays maximum $15 per page; "never less than $5."

PROBE, 1548 Poplar Ave., Memphis TN 38104. Editor: Mike Davis. Baptist publication. Monthly for boys ages 12 to 17. Usually buys first rights. Will accept simultaneous submissions if there is no conflict in market. Payment on acceptance. Will send a free sample copy to a writer on request. Submit seasonal material at least 5 months in advance. Reports in three weeks. Enclose S.A.S.E. for return of submissions.
Nonfiction: Any subject of special interest to boys in this age group. Buys how-to's, humor, interviews with prominent people, profiles, inspirational and historical articles, sports, outdoors, think pieces, missions, travel. Length: 1,200 words maximum, and shorter lengths preferred. Query not necessary. Pays 2½¢ a word.
Photos: Buys b&w photos, 5x7 or larger, with mss and with captions only. Pays $10 each.
Fiction: Stories, especially mission, adventure, and seasonal, with "boy appeal." 1,200 words maximum. Pays 2½¢ per word. Prefers stories that aren't preachy; that are interesting and exciting, but aren't corny, and that have some conflict in the plot but aren't artificial or strained. Limited need. "Uses very little fiction."
Fillers: Games, handicrafts, campcrafts, puzzles.

REACHOUT, Light and Lift Press, Winona Lake IN 46590. Editor: Vera Bethel. For "young teens, 12, 13, and 14-year-olds." Weekly. Circulation: 35,000. Will buy first, second, or simultaneous rights. Not copyrighted. Buys 250 mss a year. Pays on acceptance. Will send a free sample copy to a writer on request. No query required. Submit seasonal or holiday material 3 months in advance. Reports in 1 month. Enclose S.A.S.E. for return of submissions.
Nonfiction and Photos: Wants articles with photos on youth projects and hobbies. Can be how-to, personal experience, inspirational, or think pieces. Length: 500 to 1,000 words. Payment is 2¢ a word. B&w glossy photos purchased with mss, 8x10 preferred. Payment is $3.50 to $10.
Fiction: "We want stories with a Christian orientation; not secular in tone but definitely not pious; fast-paced and contemporary in style. Stories should involve junior-high interests which center largely around school activities and hobbies." Length: 1,500 to 2,000 words. Payment is 2¢ a word.
Poetry: Payment is 25¢ a line for nature and devotional poetry.

REFLECTION, Pioneer Girls, Box 788, Wheaton IL 60187. Editor: Carole M. Sherman. Published ten times yearly for girls in junior high and senior high school. Buys first and (at times) all rights. Pays on acceptance. Sample copies and writer's packet for 50¢. Query first. Reports in six weeks. Include S.A.S.E. for reply to queries.
Nonfiction: Inspirational articles should indicate practical relevance of Christianity to problems facing age group. Other nonfiction articles range from humorous to informative (careers, hobbies, how-to, recipes, etc.). Address query to Article Editor. "Payment based on material content and length."
Photos: Glossies. For photos not included in ms price, query.
Fiction: Timely and honest stories of 1,000 to 2,500 words. Need not have strong

spiritual emphasis but should be in keeping with Christian point of view. At least one story used every month. "Payment based on material content and length; usually $35 to $50." Address to Fiction Editor.

Fillers: Uses puzzles and games. Query.

SCHOLASTIC SCOPE, Scholastic Magazines, Inc., 50 W. 44th St., New York NY 10036. Editor of Manuscript Department: Mrs. Norma R. Ainsworth. Issued weekly. 4th to 6th grade reading level; 15 to 18 age level. Enclose S.A.S.E.

Nonfiction and Photos: Interested in two kinds of nonfiction articles (400 to 800 words). 1) Personal interviews with fairly young people who have jobs that do not require a college education and are not closed to members of minority groups; include job requirements, advantages and disadvantages, pay, opportunities for advancement, where to write for further information in this field, etc. 2) Articles about teenagers who have accomplished something against great odds, overcome obstacles, performed heroically, or simply done something out of the ordinary. Prefers articles about people outside New York area. Payment is $50 per magazine page. Photos purchased with articles. Pays $10 for every photo used.

Fiction and Drama: 4th through 6th grade reading level; 15 to 18 age level. Subject matter: Problems of contemporary teenagers (dating, drugs, failure in school, prejudice, runaways, family problems, etc.); interests of urban students; relationships between people (interracial, adult-teenage, employer-employee, etc.) in family, job, and school situations. Urban settings. "Strive for directness, realism, and action, perhaps carried through dialogue rather than exposition. Try for depth of characterization in at least one character. Realistic stories, written from viewpoint of a minority group character, not necessarily focusing on race relations, would be helpful. Avoid too many coincidences and random happenings. Even though *Scope* wants action stories, this is not a market for crime fiction. Occasionally we use mysteries and science fiction. We are looking for American Indian, Chicano (Mexican-American), Puerto Rican, and black authors, among others." Stories of 400 to 1,200 words; plays to 3,000 words. Pays minimum of $150.

SCHOLASTIC VOICE, Scholastic Magazines, Inc., 50 W. 44th St., New York NY 10036. Editor of Manuscript Department: Mrs. Norma Ainsworth. For high school students ages 14 to 17. Send only one ms at a time for consideration. Do not resubmit a rejected ms unless revision is specifically requested. Full requirements information available on request. Enclose S.A.S.E.

Fiction and Drama: Stories and plays of 1,500 to 3,000 words about teenagers; strong on plot and characterization, dealing with problems common to teenagers. Steer clear of teenage stereotypes. Boy-girl situations, school situations, adventure, mystery, science fiction, family situations, sports. Problems that confront teenagers, like finding one's own identity, setting standards of conduct, reconciling ideals and reality, bridging the generation gap, etc., are all good. Plays should be suitable for reading in class as well as for stage performance. Pay starts at $150.

SCIENCE WORLD, Scholastic Magazines, Inc., 50 W. 44th St., New York NY 10036. Editor of Manuscript Department: Mrs. Norma Ainsworth. For science students grades 7 through 12. Buys all rights. Pays on acceptance. Will send free sample copy on request. Query first. Enclose S.A.S.E. for reply to queries.

Nonfiction and Photos: Pays up to $125 for articles of about 1,000 words. Articles heavily emphasize concepts and the work of scientists presently engaged in specific research. Articles wanted for "Today's Scientists," a work-in-progress report of prominent contemporary scientists, with emphasis on scientific principles and methods, some brief biography and human interest. Also for "Science World Takes You There," which covers laboratories, observatories, weather stations, expeditions of scientific interest, etc. Author supplies photos.

SEARCH, Scholastic Magazines Inc., 50 West 44th Street, New York NY 10036. Editor of Manuscript Department: Mrs. Norma R. Ainsworth. For "4th to 6th grade reading level; 14 to 17 age level." Enclose S.A.S.E. for return of submissions.

Nonfiction, Drama, Fiction, and Photos: Fiction and nonfiction of 400 to 1,200 words and plays up to 3,000 words; subject matter: relationships between people (inter-racial, intercultural, adult-teenage, employer-employee, etc.) in family, job, and school situations. *Search* is also interested in two kinds of nonfiction articles (400 to 800 words) with photos. (1) Personal interviews with fairly young people who have jobs that do not require a college education and are not closed to members of minority groups; include job requirements, advantages and disadvantages, pay, opportunities for advancement, where to write for further information in this field, etc. (2) Articles with photos about some unusual sociological or psychological aspect of teen life. Note: prefer articles about people outside New York area. Special Note: Since *Search's* needs are subject to change, a careful study of the magazine will help authors. Payment for original short stories is from $150, except for short-shorts (500 to 600 words) amount is $100.

SENIOR SCHOLASTIC, 50 W. 44th St., New York NY 10036. "Completely staff-written."

SEVENTEEN, 320 Park Ave., New York NY 10022. Editorial Director: Merrill Panitt. Managing Editor: Ray Robinson. Monthly. Buys first rights on fiction. Reports in about 2 weeks. Enclose S.A.S.E. for return of submissions.
Nonfiction and Photos: Articles and features of general interest; strong emphasis on topicality and helpfulness. Send brief outline and query, summing up basic idea of article. Length: 2,000 to 3,000 words. Pays $100 to $500. Photos usually by assignment only. Pamela Hoffman, Art Director.
Fiction: Babette Rosmond, Fiction Editor. Top quality stories featuring teenagers—the problems, concerns, and preoccupations of adolescence, which will have recognition and identification value for readers. Does not want "typical teenage" stories, but high literary quality. Avoid oversophisticated material; unhappy endings acceptable if emotional impact is sufficient. Humorous stories that do not condescend to or caricature young people are welcome. Best lengths are 2,500 to 8,000 words. Occasionally accepts 2- or 3-part stories such as mysteries and science fiction with adolescent protagonist and theme. Pays $50 to $300.
Poetry: By teenagers only. Pays $5 to $25.
How To Break In: "The best way for beginning teenage writers to crack the *Seventeen* lineup is for them to contribute suggestions and short pieces to the Free-For-All column, a literary format which lends itself to just about every kind of writing: profiles, puzzles, essays, exposes, reportage, and book reviews."

STAR, 8490 Sunset Blvd., Los Angeles CA 90069. Publisher: Don Berrigan. Edited for girls between the ages of 12 and 18. Estimated circulation: 600,000. Payment on acceptance. Query first with outline. "Samples of writer's previous work will be helpful." Write for copy of guidelines for writers. Enclose S.A.S.E. with all correspondence.
Nonfiction: "*Star* is not a fashion magazine, not beauty/charm, not a fan magazine. It is an entertainment magazine, whose format really compares with no other youth publication available today. Though this is not an exact comparison, one may begin to think of *Star* as being a teenage, female cousin to *Playboy*, or a younger sister of *Cosmopolitan*, who thinks that *Ms.* has a lot right about it. Entertainment, fun and important topics like guys are what *Star* is all about. Articles will average in length from 2,800 to 4,000 words. We purchase three or four per issue. See magazine for sample topics. We also need verbatim (taped) interviews with selected celebrities. Fee on inquiry."
Fiction: "We need at least two fiction stories per issue. They range in length from 2,800 to 4,000 words, or double that if it is published in 2 parts. Stories usually involve very moving teenage romantic entanglements. (However, any piece of fiction that seems appropriate to the audience's interest will be considered.) The lead character should be a teenage female who is involved in two simultaneous processes: finding love and, through that situation, is becoming aware of a new sense of her own individuality and liberated life style. There should be at least two teenage males, one a budding male chauvinist in one of his many guises; the other a genuine, liberated beautiful man-to-be. The purpose of each story, in addition to its paramount one: to entertain, must be to excite a visceral reaction through its sexy (but not carnal) love-suspense situations. Also, it should give the reader a sense of the intense, 'happening' life style, and a glimpse of new personal horizons that can be hers. Stories must always be firmly rooted in everyday language and colloquial, familiar values." Fee on inquiry.

STRAIGHT, 8121 Hamilton Ave., Cincinnati OH 45231. Editor: Mrs. Bee Nelson. Weekly for teenagers; primarily distributed through Christian Sunday schools. Publication not copyrighted. Pays on acceptance. Will send free sample copy to a writer on request. Reports on submissions in 2 to 4 weeks. Query not necessary. Deadline for seasonal material nine months before publication date. Include Social Security number on ms. Enclose S.A.S.E. for return of submissions.

Nonfiction: Christian approach to current events and teen problems. Articles on teen activities, Bible study, Christian sportsmen, missions, group projects, etc. Length: 1,000 to 1,200 words.

Fiction: Must appeal to teenagers and have interesting, well-constructed plots. Stories should have character-building elements without being preachy. Main characters should be teenagers. Need stories to correlate with International Sunday School Lesson Outline. Payment to $35.

Photos: Candid photos of teens in school, church, sports activities; seasonal teen photos. Prefers 8x10 glossies. Pays to $10. Send photos to Mr. Ralph Small, Executive Editor, Standard Publishing, 8121 Hamilton Ave., Cincinnati OH 45231.

Poetry: Teen-written only. Should be submitted to Straight Pens Club. Author must include date of birth, Social Security number and S.A.S.E. Rate of payment determined by quality.

THE STUDENT, 127 Ninth Ave., N., Nashville TN 37234. Editor: Norman L. Bowman. Publication of the Southern Baptist Convention. For college students. Published 9 times during the school year. Circulation: 34,000. Buys all rights; will buy first rights on request. Pays on acceptance. Will send a sample copy to a writer on request "within limits of reasonable demand." Mss should be double-spaced on white paper with 70-space line, 25 lines per page. Reports in 6 weeks. Enclose S.A.S.E. for return of submissions.

Nonfiction: Contemporary questions, problems, and issues facing college students viewed from a Christian perspective. Articles on intellectual questioning that deal with faith in conflict issues. Spiritual and moral values on campus. Material dealing with the struggle for self-concept and with interpersonal relationships. Current events and student involvement. Articles on the Christian life and devotional helps. Length: 1,200 to 1,500 words. Satire and parody on college life, humorous episodes, etc. Length: 500 to 1,000 words. From students only, expressions of opinion on vital issues. Length: 800 to 1,200 words. Payment is 2½¢ per word after editing, with reserved right to edit accepted material.

Fiction: Short stories touching on student interests, activities, life styles, and personal concerns. Length: 500 to 2,000 words. Payment is 2½¢ per word after editing, with reserved right to edit accepted material.

Poetry: Related to student interests and needs. Length: 30 lines. Payment varies.

'TEEN MAGAZINE, 8831 Sunset Blvd., Hollywood CA 90069. Editor and Publisher: Robert MacLeod. Monthly for girls 12 to 18. No verse or fillers. Buys all rights. Pays on acceptance. Reports in 6 weeks. Enclose S.A.S.E. for return of submissions.

Nonfiction: Articles on self-improvement in personality and social areas, with light, anecdotal, nonpreachy approach, 2,500 words and up. Greatest editorial need: full-length features for sex and dating series. Payment up to $200, depending on quality. Feature Editor: Kathy McCoy.

Photos: Purchased with mss only. 5x7 and 8x10 glossy prints of high quality. 'Teen considers photos part of the package when submitted with special features-personality profiles. Rate on needed buyouts $12.50 each. Color for the most part is shot locally under the direction of Barbara Gilbert, Art Director.

Fiction: Stories of up to 3,500 words dealing specifically with teenagers—variety in setting, believable plots, romance and humor wanted. Pays $150. Senior Editor: Roxie Camron.

How To Break In: "Most of our features are staff-written, so a good young fiction writer who sends us a lively, topical story has the best chance of selling. Best prospects for aspiring teen feature writers would be true personal or work experiences that would be of interest and help to other teens. For aspiring teen journalists who would like to be an editorial part of 'Teen, but who don't feel ready to tackle a full article, our Teen Research Gang can be a valuable experience. We send questionnaires and opinion polls to our TRG members when teen opinions are needed for features or roundups. Recent areas covered: parent-teen relations, views on death and grieving, love at first sight, and capital punishment. There is no payment for TRG members, but they often do get their names and opinions in print and are an important part of the 'Teen editorial effort. Interested teens may join TRG by sending S.A.S.E. to T.R.G., c/o 'Teen Magazine, 8490 Sunset Blvd., Los Angeles CA 90069. I would advise anyone, teen or adult, who hopes to sell to 'Teen to please read the magazine before submitting their work! This sounds elementary. However, as an editor and former freelancer, I am continually appalled at how many hopefuls have no idea of our editorial needs or policies, in spite of the fact that 'Teen is readily available on newsstands across the nation and in a number of foreign countries. Roughly 95% of all submissions are rejected instantly because they are completely inappropriate. Many are not even about teenagers. Some are fillers and poems, which we never buy. Others center around long obsolete fads and trends. Still others miss because they talk down to the kids and try to use (and usually misuse) their slang. Any writer who hopes to sell to us must know our editorial tone—in-depth, straight but nonpreachy and with a touch of humor when appropriate. To teenage writers, I say, 'Write about what you know, what you have experienced!' To adult writers, I say, 'If you are out of touch with the teen scene as it is today, if you haven't spoken to a teenager in years, if you don't *like* teenagers . . . please save your time and ours. Write about something else!' "

TEENS TODAY, 6401 The Paseo, Kansas City MO 64132. Editor: Wesley Tracy. Published weekly. For 10th, 11th and 12th graders. Buys "one-time" rights only. Buys 150 to 200 mss a year. Pays on acceptance. Will send a free sample copy to a writer on request. Reports within 6 to 8 weeks. Seasonal deadlines are 10 months prior to publication date. Enclose S.A.S.E. with all submissions.
Nonfiction, Photos, and Fiction: Articles on contemporary teen problems from a Christian perspective. School, home, social and interpersonal relationships and conflicts, devotional tips, witnessing. "We are looking for contemporary, hard-hitting stories and articles. Please send your sticky-sweet moralizing pieces elsewhere. We also need articles of quality on the central truths of the Christian faith. We also use biographical pieces. We use fiction to 2,200 words, articles to 1,200 words." Pays 2¢ per word. Photos purchased with mss. Pays $4 to $15.
Poetry: Poems of 8 to 20 lines on general subjects of interest to teens.

VENTURE/DASH, Box 150, Wheaton IL 60187. Managing Editor: Paul Heidebrecht. For boys 8 to 18 in the Christian Service Brigade program. "Above average students with a wide range of hobbies and interests, outdoor and sports minded, many are college bound." Monthly. Circulation: 60,000. Buys all rights. Buys 12 mss a year. Pays on acceptance. Will send a free sample copy to a writer on request. Reports in 2 months. Enclose S.A.S.E. for return of submissions.
Nonfiction and Fiction: "We publish factual articles, interviews, short stories dealing with a young man's relationship to his world. We desire relevant concepts, character-building motivation. We use articles telling how boys are helping others, learning about themselves and growing in character and purpose. Interviews with Christian athletes, etc. Our world view is a Biblical one and this outlook is frequently expressed in materials used. We don't wish stories that solely entertain, or that offer simple solutions through simple 'believe-ism.' We strive to be relevant to the needs of today's boy, and pull no punches." Length: 500 to 2,000 words for articles, 1,000 to 2,000 words for fiction. Payment is 2¢ to 5¢ a word.
Photos: B&w glossies preferred. Also uses 35mm color and color transparencies. Payment is $7.50 to $15 for 1-time rights.
How To Break In: "Write a true story or fiction about something that has happened to you or something you are very interested in."

WORKING FOR BOYS, 601 Winchester St., Newton Highlands, Boston MA 02161. Editor: Brother Jerome, C.F.X. Send all mss to Mss. Editor: Brother Jason, C.F.X., Xaverian Brothers High School, Westwood, MA 02090. For Catholic junior high students and parents. Quarterly. Circulation: 30,000. Buys all rights. Pays on acceptance. Will send a free sample copy to a writer on request. No query required. Reports in 1 week. Enclose S.A.S.E. for return of submissions.
Nonfiction and Photos: "Human interest, nature, biography, travel, religion, how-to, sports. Readable for early teenagers. No pious legends. Little pure research mat-

ter." Length: 1,000 words. Payment is 3¢ a word. 6x6 b&w photos purchased with mss, "rarely." Payment is $10.

Fiction: "Boy life, sports, adventure, etc." Length: 500 to 1,000 words. Payment is 3¢ a word.

Poetry: "Seasonal, religious (not saccharine). Free or rhymed (but rarely rhymed couplet); dimeter or trimeter preferred." Length: 24 lines maximum. Payment is 25¢ a line.

YOUNG AMBASSADOR, Lincoln NE 68501. Associate Editor: Ruth Johnson Jay. Issued monthly for early teens. Circulation: 90,000. Buys first rights. Pays on acceptance. Will send free sample copy to a writer on request. Reports within one week. Query not necessary. Enclose S.A.S.E. for return of submissions.

Fiction: Stories of interest to early teenagers with strong plots and spiritual tone, although not preachy. Seasonal stories needed. Check magazine for style of writing. Length: 1,800 to 2,000 words. Pays up to 3¢ per word.

YOUNG MISS, 52 Vanderbilt Ave., New York NY 10017. Editor: Rubie Saunders. Monthly, except June and August, for girls 10 to 14. Buys all rights. Pays on acceptance. Will send editorial requirement sheet to a writer, if S.A.S.E. is enclosed with request. Reports on submissions in 3 to 4 weeks. All mss must be typed, double spaced. Enclose S.A.S.E. for return of submissions.

Nonfiction: "No food, fashion or beauty articles are wanted, but practically everything else goes. Hobbies, unusual projects, self-improvement (getting along with parents, brothers, etc.), 'how-to' articles on all possible subjects." Length: about 1,500 words. Do not submit illustrations. Rough sketches may accompany a "how-to" article.

Fiction: "All fiction should be aimed at girls 10 to 14, with the emphasis on the late 12 to 14-year-olds. Stories may be set in any locale or time—urban, western, foreign, past, contemporary, or future. Boys may be involved, even in a romantic way, as long as it is tastefully done. Mystery and adventure stories are also welcomed. Stories of today are particularly desirable. Especially interested in fiction with an urban setting dealing with the *real* problems today's young teens face. Overstocked on stories about middle income, small town girls who seem to have no problems greater than getting a date for a school dance or adjusting to a new neighborhood." Length: 2,000 to 2,300 words. Strongly plotted novelettes up to 6,500 words.

Fillers: Short (100 to 150 words) how-to fillers. Pays $5. Crossword puzzles and short quizzes on general information and personality subjects. Pays $10. Overstocked at present.

YOUTH ALIVE, 1445 Boonville Ave., Springfield MO 65802. Editor: Gayle D. Erwin. "Official youth organ of the Assemblies of God, slanted primarily to late teens." Monthly. Circulation: 27,000. Buys all rights unless specified, but "we are interested in multiple submissions, second rights, and other reprints." Pays on acceptance. Will send a free sample copy to a writer on request. No query required. Reports in 6 weeks. Enclose S.A.S.E. for return of submissions.

Nonfiction, Photos, and Poetry: "Purpose is to provide news of the Pentecostal youth scene, to inspire to Christlike living, and to be used as a witnessing tool. We can use photo features, photos, interviews, forums, biographical features, reports on outstanding Christian youth, how-to-do-it features, satire, humor, allegory, anecdotes, poems, news, motivational articles, testimonies, seasonal material, personal experiences. Avoid clichés, unexplained theological terms, sermonizing, and 'talking down' to youth. Read *Youth Alive* to get our style, but don't be afraid to submit something different if you think we might like it." Length of articles: 300 to 1,200 words. Payment is 1½¢ a word, slightly higher for assigned articles. Teen-slanted human interest photos purchased with mss or with captions. 8x10 b&w glossies or color transparencies. Payment is $5 to $25. Payment for poetry is 20¢ a line. "Annual ms contest open to youth through age 21."

YOUTH IN ACTION, Winona Lake IN 46590. Monthly for church and nonchurch youth, age 14 to 19; servicemen, pastors, youth leaders, and other interested adults. Buys all rights. Pays on publication. Will send free sample copy to a writer on request. Deadlines at least three months prior to publication dates. Reports on submissions in 5 to 6 weeks. Enclose S.A.S.E. for return of submissions.

Nonfiction: Articles designed to help in Christian growth, conduct, witness. Informative articles or religious (Wesleyan Arminian theology); Christian attitude toward: sex, integration, war, self, serving others, sensual literature, ambition, failure, credit buying, politics, etc. Length: about 500 to 1,200 words. Pays 1½¢ per word.

Photos: Purchased mostly as illustrations, sometimes for cover, sometimes with mss. Pays $5 to $15.

Fiction: Should be significant while entertaining the reader. See above (nonfiction) for attitudes favored. Length: 750 to 1,500 words. Pays 1½¢ per word.

Theater, Movie, TV, and Entertainment

Magazines emphasizing music and musician entertainers are classified in Music and Sound Reproduction Equipment.

AFTER DARK, 10 Columbus Circle, New York NY 10019. Editor: William Como For an audience "20 to 55 years old." Monthly. Circulation: 121,000. Buys first rights. Buys about 30 mss a year. Pays on publication. Will send a sample copy to a writer for $1. Query first, including copies of previously published work. Submit seasonal material 4 months in advance. Reports in 3 to 4 weeks. Enclose S.A.S.E.
Nonfiction and Photos: Articles on "every area of entertainment—films, TV, theater, nightclubs, books, records." Length: 2,500 to 3,000 words. Pays $75 to $150. Photos with captions only. B&w glossies, color transparencies. Pays $20 to $50.

AFTERNOON TV, 185 Madison Ave., New York NY 10016. Monthly. For soap opera viewers. Reports at once. Enclose S.A.S.E. for return of submissions.
Nonfiction and Photos: At least four typewritten pages. Star interviews. Pays $50 for a four-page story, $100 for eight-page story. Photos purchased with mss. Afternoon TV stars. Pays up to $15 per photo.

BLACK STARS, 820 South Michigan Ave., Chicago IL 60605. Editor: Ariel Perry Strong. For young housewives, teenagers and persons who are interested in the private lives of entertainers. Established in 1971. Monthly. Circulation: 300,000. Buys all rights. Buys 72 mss a year. Payment on publication. Will send free sample copy to writer on request. Query first. Enclose S.A.S.E.
Nonfiction and Photos: "Only articles pertaining to entertainers. Biographies, movie reviews, television reviews and record reviews. We deal only with black entertainers. B&w photos should accompany articles." Length: 2,000 to 4,000 words. Pays $100 to $200.

CASTLE OF FRANKENSTEIN, c/o Gothic Castle, 509 Fifth Ave., New York NY 10017. Editor: Calvin Thomas Beck. For "those interested in films pertaining to fantasy, horror and science fiction. Also in comic books and science fantasy books." Established in 1961. Bimonthly. Circulation: 110,000. Buys second serial (reprint) rights. Buys 90 to 115 mss a year. Payment on acceptance. Will send free sample copy to a writer on request, "if they enclose S.A.S.E." Submit complete ms. Will consider photocopied submissions "only if original is lost." Reports on materials accepted for publication in 2 to 4 weeks. Returns rejected material in 1 to 3 weeks. Enclose S.A.S.E. for return of submissions.
Nonfiction and Photos: "About 75% of each issue is devoted to essays on fantasy-horror films, their directors, stars, writers, etc. Also, histories of the genre (especially interviews) and reviews are accepted. It's preferable if writer knows and likes fantasy and horror films, whether in theater or TV program form. We're tied of stuff only on Karloff, Lugosi and other oldtimers, unless someone has something new to say or an entirely fresh slant." Pays 1¢ to 6¢ per word, "depending on quality and importance of ms." Pays $3 to $6 for film reviews. "We prefer photos (pertaining to an article-review) accompanying mss, though lack of them will not ruin chances of acceptance, especially when the material is good." Pays $1 to $3 per photo.

Fillers: Newsbreaks ("no free studio releases, please!") and clippings. Pays $1 to $6; "depends on uniqueness."

DANCE MAGAZINE, 10 Columbus Circle, New York NY 10019. Editor: William Como. Monthly. To the dance profession and members of the public interested in the art of dance. Pays on publication. Will send free sample copy to writer on request. Query suggested. Include S.A.S.E.
Nonfiction: Personalities, knowledgeable comment, news. Length: 2,500 to 3,000 words. Pays $25 to $50.
Photos: Purchased with articles or with captions only. Pays $5 to $10.

DRAMATICS, Box E, College Hill Station, Cincinnati OH 45224. Editor: R. Glenn Webb. For "high school students, teachers, directors, plus all those interested in theatre arts. 40,000 Thespian members constitute largest audience." Special issues devoted to "one theme (i.e., mime, puppetry, playwriting, children's theatre, foreign educational theatre)." Established in 1929. Monthly. Circulation: 50,000. Buys first serial rights. Payment on acceptance. Will send free sample copy to writer on request. Reports in 3 months. Enclose S.A.S.E.
Nonfiction: "Subject matter consists of "articles on theatre production (not drama analysis), on educational theatre in general, new trends, interesting approaches of production. Monthly section on practical approach to technical theatre problems. Emphasis is on educational theatre—how to approach a problem, or how to solve one. We welcome freshness of style, no pedagogy. No talking down to students. Always searching for exciting theatre reports, interviews, news of foreign schools' activities, etc. *Dramatics* is the only magazine devoted to theatre on the secondary school level. General content can be similar to any theatrical periodical in other respects. We do not want any material on literary analysis of plays." Also seeks articles on practical approaches to technical theatre problems. Pays $15 for 1,000 words, $25 for 1,500 to 2,000 words.
Photos: Captions required. Does not pay for photos. No color.
Plays: Accepts one-act plays. Length should be running time of 30 minutes.

FILM COMMENT, Box 686, Village Station, Brookline MA 02147. Editor: Richard Corliss. For film students, teachers and scholars. Has select group of writers which usually fills its needs. A few freelance articles.

FILM HERITAGE, College of Liberal Arts, Wright State University, Dayton OH 45431. Editor: F.A. Macklin. Quarterly for those interested in film analysis. Reports on submissions promptly. Buys all rights. Enclose S.A.S.E. for ms return.
Nonfiction and Photos: Articles on film as an art form and on film explication; revaluation of underrated films. No reviews. Length varies. Payment in contributor's copies; occasional minimal stipend when article proposed by *Film Heritage*. Photos are purchased with mss, but not required.

FILM QUARTERLY, University of California Press, Berkeley CA 94720. Editor: Ernest Callenbach. Issued quarterly. Buys all rights. Pays on publication. Enclose S.A.S.E. for reply to queries.
Nonfiction: Articles on style and structure in films, articles analyzing the work of important directors, historical articles on development of the film as art, reviews of current films and detailed analyses of classics, book reviews of film books. No restrictions on length. Must be familiar with the past and present of the art; must be competently, although not necessarily breezily, written; must deal with important problems of the art. Writers should query first, as many topics are assigned far in advance. Payment is about 1¢ per word.
How To Break In: "We are a very specialized journal, so the answer for aspiring writers is that they must specialize; for example, by taking film courses, reading film books and various journals, including ours, and above all seeing movies—not only the current output but the masterpieces of the past which provide the perscpetive in which to analyze what is going on now."

HOMELIFE, 7 East 43 St., New York NY 10017. "Not soliciting freelance material."

JOURNAL OF THE MARYLAND CENTER FOR PUBLIC BROADCASTING, Maryland Center for Public Broadcasting, Owings Mills MD 21117. Editor: William F. Hallstead. Published monthly; purchased by subscription only. Circulation. 10,000. Buys North American serial rights only. Pays on publication. Will send a free sample copy to a writer on request. Deadlines on the 10th; two months prior to month of publication. Query required. Reports within one week. Enclose S.A.S.E.

Nonfiction: Uses articles concerning noncommercial TV on local or national scene for audience of educational television in Maryland. Wants careful, tight writing, no big knocks against commercial TV; will use subtle humor, unusual material on educational TV as it interests the home viewer. Also interviews with "stars" of locally aired national programs, such as Julia Child, Fred Rogers, etc. 700-word maximum. Pays 10¢ per word. Uses one freelance article per issue.

Photos: May illustrate article, but not essential. Purchased with mss for $5 each. Good resolution; no particular size or finish.

MODERN SCREEN MAGAZINE, 1 Dag Hammarskjold Plaza, New York NY 10017. Editor: Joan Thursh. Monthly. No fiction or verse. Buys first serial rights. Will consider photocopied submissions. Query first. Reports in two weeks. Editor will send sample copy on request. Enclose S.A.S.E. with all correspondence.

Nonfiction: Uses true articles on movie stars, TV stars, show business personalities and figures who attract world attention. Length: up to 2,000 words. Query first. Pays a minimum of $200. Immediate payment.

Photos: Buys singles and photo series in b&w and color. Buys pix submitted with mss. Uses contacts up to 8x10. Pays $20 and up on acceptance.

MOTION PICTURE, Macfadden-Bartell Corp., 205 E. 42nd St., New York NY 10017. Editor: Alice Schoninger. Audience is "female high school graduates, 20 to 70 years old." Monthly. Buys all rights. Buys approximately 140 mss a year. Pays on acceptance. Will send a sample copy to a writer on request. Query first. Submit seasonal material 3 months in advance. Reports in 1 week. Enclose S.A.S.E.

Nonfiction: Uses short, interesting stories about top Hollywood stars; sharply angled. These can vary from personality profiles to timely, newsworthy stories, or stories involving the basic emotions and slanted for self-help. "We specialize in 'camera-closeups'." Buys interviews, profiles, exposes. Length: 2,500 to 4,000 words. Payment variable; bonus for exceptional material.

Photos: Wants top-rate black and white; color photography (any size).

MOVIE CLASSICS, 7950 Deering Ave., Canoga Park CA 91304. Editor: Roy T. Pockett. For filmgoers; movie enthusiasts who appreciate the cinema arts of the past, present and future. Established in 1973. Bimonthly. Circulation: 100,000. Buys all rights but will reassign rights to author after publication. Will send sample copy to writer for $1. Query first. Will consider photocopied submissions. Submit material for special issues 3 months in advance. "If a reader knows of a special anniversary coming up and wishes to submit material, it would be appreciated." Reports on material in 1 month. Enclose S.A.S.E. for return of submissions.

Nonfiction and Photos: "All material on films. Articles about movie stars; anecdotes, true stories. Write detailed facts. Make sure the details are correct, remembering the readers are usually very knowledgeable on the subject. We prefer real nostalgia and not erotic gossip." Personal experience, interview, profile, historical, expose. Length: 100 to 500 words. Pays $10 to $50. 8x10 b&w photos. Pays $5 to $15. Color transparencies. Pays $10 to $25. Captions required.

MOVIE MIRROR, 315 Park Avenue South, New York NY 10010. Editor: Seli Groves. Issued monthly for movie and television fans. Also, *Movie Mirror Yearbook* containing top news stories of the year concerning Hollywood screen, television or recording artists. Query first. Pays on acceptance. Reports immediately. Enclose S.A.S.E.

Nonfiction: Interested in stories on the stars with emotional appeal. Refer to recent issues for type and style of material used. Length approximately 3,000 words. Pays $150 to $200.

Photos: Photos are bought only when subject and type is needed; most photos purchased from freelance photographers or assigned photographers, rarely from those submitting mss. Payment varies.

MOVIE STARS, 295 Madison Avenue, New York NY 10017. Editor: Roseann Hirsch. For housewives "ages 22 to 44 with a high school education." Established in

1935. Buys all rights. Buys 100 mss a year. Submit queries, not mss. Payment on publication. Query required. Enclose S.A.S.E.
Nonfiction and Photos: General subject matter consists of "articles on movies and television personalities." Pays $150 for a "7 to 8 page" article. Pays $25 per b&w photo.

MOVIE WORLD, 575 Madison Avenue, New York NY 10022. Editorial Director: Diane Robbens. Fan magazine covering TV and movie fields. Monthly. Buys all rights. Pays on acceptance. Query first on angle and title on unassigned material. Enclose S.A.S.E.
Nonfiction and Photos: "News stories concerning top TV and movie personalities may be submitted in interview or third-person format, although the interview preferred. Articles with melodramatic, emotional impact are acceptable, but writing must be clear, witty, and fresh in its approach. Mss should be gossipy and fact-filled and aimed toward working class adults." Length: 1,500 to 2,500 words. Pays up to $200 for exclusive interviews. Pays up to $35 for b&w and up to $1,000 for color used for cover material.

MOVIELAND AND TV TIME, 21 W. 26th St., New York NY 10010. Editor: Lillian Smith. Not soliciting freelance material.

PERFORMANCE, 425 Lafayette St., New York NY 10003. Editor: Erika Munk. For "practitioners, critics, scholars, students, and everyone interested in the performing arts." Established in 1971. Bimonthly. Circulation: 9,000. Rights purchased vary with author and material. Buys all rights, but will reassign them to author after publication; buys first North American serial rights. Pays on publication. Will send a sample copy to a writer for $2. Will consider photocopied submissions. Query first or submit complete ms. Reports in 2 weeks to 2 months. Enclose S.A.S.E. for return of submissions or reply to queries.
Nonfiction and Photos: "Essays and interviews on the performing arts; analytic articles on developments in avant-garde theater, some photo-portfolios of interesting new work. Reviews of productions and new books in the field. Some of the special issues we have planned include Popular Culture and Mass Media, Sexuality and Performance, New American Dance, the Olympics, and National Theater." Pays 3¢ a word. B&w captioned photos purchased with mss. Pays $15 to $25.
Plays, Filmscripts, TV and Radio Scripts: "New work, including previously unpublished translations. Publish one full-length and 2 to 3 short plays in every issue; one issue a year (July/August) entirely devoted to scripts. Pays 2¢ a word."

PERFORMING ARTS IN CANADA, 49 Wellington St. E., Toronto, Ont., Canada. Editor: Stephen Mezei. For "well-educated persons between 25 and 45 with special interest in theater, music, dance." Quarterly. Circulation: 30,000. Buys first rights. Buys 30 to 40 mss a year. Pays 2 weeks following publication. Will send a sample copy to a writer for 50¢. Query first. Reports in 3 to 6 weeks. Enclose S.A.E. and International Reply Coupons for return of submissions or reply to queries.
Nonfiction: "Articles covering Canadian performing arts." Material for department "What's Going On." Length: 200 to 1,200 words. Pays $20 to $75.

PHOTO SCREEN, 315 Park Avenue South, New York NY 10010. Editor: Barbara Petty. For "all ages; people interested in the private lives of their favorite film and TV personalities." Seasonal material centered around holidays . . . "stories of a star spending Christmas, Mother's Day, etc., in an unusual way." Monthly. Buys all rights. Buys 100 mss a year on the average. Payment on acceptance. Will send editorial guidelines sheet to a writer on request—"only after query is accepted on a tentative basis; that is . . . the idea may be accepted, but the treatment may need to be 'worked on.' " Query first required. Submit seasonal material 3 months in advance. Reporting time varies. Enclose S.A.S.E. for reply to queries.
Nonfiction and Photos: General subject matter consists of "true stories about the entertainment world and its people; most with a theme concerning the more emotional aspects of their lives. We would suggest that a query be made after the writer has looked through a copy of *Photo Screen* as an editorial guide. Our publication does not stress the sensational; rather, the truth. A so-called over-worked theme can be fresh depending on the personality involved. We would like to see interviews with TV and film people asking questions concerning morality changes . . . political

views, etc." Buys informational, interviews, profiles, and nostalgia articles. Length, average 3,000 words. Pays $200 and up. Photo Editor: David Esbin.

PHOTOPLAY, 205 East 42nd St., New York NY 10017. Editor: Bernadette Carrozza. For women, ages 18 to 50. Monthly. Buys all rights. Pays on acceptance. Will send a sample copy to a writer on request. Query first. Reports in 2 weeks. Enclose S.A.S.E. for reply to queries.
Nonfiction: Uses strongly angled stories on "stars"—in all entertainment media, all walks of life—that would appeal to women of all ages. Query essential. Payment varies.
Photos: Buys pix of "stars" with or without ms. Payment varies with pix subject and exclusivity.

PLAYBILL MAGAZINE, 485 Lexington Ave., New York NY 10017. Editor: Joan Alleman Rubin. Issued monthly; free to theatregoers. Buys first and second U.S. magazine rights. Enclose S.A.S.E. for return of submissions.
Nonfiction: The major emphasis is on current theatre and theatre people. On occasion, buys humor or travel pieces if offbeat. Wants sophisticated informative prose that makes judgments and shows style. Uses unusual interviews, although most of these are staff-written. Style should be worldly and literate without being pretentious or arch; runs closer to *Harper's* or *New Yorker* than to *Partisan Review*. Wants interesting information, adult analysis, written in a genuine personal style. Humor is also welcome. Between 1,000 and 2,500 words for articles. Pays $100 to $300 each.

SCREEN ACTOR, 7750 Sunset Blvd., Hollywood CA 90046. Editor: Buck Harris. Quarterly. For the 26,000 members of Screen Actors Guild. Query first. Enclose S.A.S.E. for reply to query.
Nonfiction and Photos: Uses any subject of interest to actors, the motion picture industry, and the entertainment world generally. Approximately 1,200 to 1,600 words in length, but can be 2,000 words if warranted. Photos should be included. Pays up to a maximum of $150 an article.

SCREEN STARS, 575 Madison Avenue, New York NY 10022. Editorial Director: Diane Robbens. Monthly. Buys all rights. Payment on acceptance. Query first on angle and title on unassigned material. Enclose S.A.S.E. for reply to queries or return of submissions.
Nonfiction and Photos: "Fan magazine covering TV and movie fields. News stories concerning top TV and movie personalities may be submitted in third-person format, although the interview is preferred. Articles must contain new material. Stories with melodramatic, emotional impact are acceptable, but writing must be clear, witty, and fresh in its approach. Mss should be gossipy and fact-filled and aimed toward working class young adults." Length: 1,500 to 2,500 words. Pays $100; up to $200 for exclusive interviews. Pays up to $35 for b&w and up to $500 for color used for cover.

SHOW, 866 United Nations Plaza, New York NY 10017. Managing Editor: Art Ford. Associate Editors: Parker Hodges, William Deerfield, and Robert Levine. For a "broad age range with special emphasis on 20 to 35 bracket interested in films, TV and the arts. Writers should check current issues." Rights purchased vary with author and material. Buys 25 to 100 mss a year. Payment on publication. Enclose S.A.S.E. for reply to queries.
Nonfiction: "We only accept letters of inquiry, not mss. Approach should be (1) controversial, (2) exclusive, personal interviews with TV—film, top names, (3) articles that will sell copies on newsstands. We have a distinguished magazine and currently feature it monthly." Pays $150 per article; "pay for reviews negotiated."

SQUARE DANCE, P.O. Box 788, Sandusky OH 44870. Editors: Stan and Cathie Burdick. For square dancers and callers. Special issues include vacations (April) and fashions (July). Monthly. Circulation: 10,000. Buys all rights. Pays on publication. Will send a sample copy to a writer on request. Submit seasonal material 2 to 3 months in advance. Reports in 1 week. Enclose S.A.S.E. for return of submissions.
Nonfiction: Articles about "dancing, leadership and teaching techniques, organizing and conducting clubs, positive attitudes." Buys how-to's, personal experience

and inspirational pieces, interviews, profiles, humor, spot news, think pieces, historical and travel articles, photo essays. Length: 600 to 800 words. Pays 50¢ a column inch (usually averages out to about 1¢ a word).
Photos: Purchased with mss or with caption only. B&w glossy, any size. Pay rate based on $5 per page.
Fiction: Would like a good story related to square dancing. Buys humorous, historical, and contemporary problem stories. Length: 800 to 1,000 words. Pays 50¢ a column inch (usually averages out to about 1¢ a word).
Poetry: Light verse. Pays 50¢ a column inch (usually averages out to about 1¢ a word).
Fillers: Puzzles.

TAKE ONE, Box 1778, Station B., Montreal 110, Que., Canada. Editor: Peter Lebensold. Managing Editor: Michael Goodwin. For anyone interested in films and/or TV in modern society. Not a fan magazine. Bimonthly. Circulation: 20,000. Buys North American serial rights. Pays on publication. Will send free sample copy on request. Query preferred. Reports in 3 weeks. Enclose S.A.E. and International Reply coupons for reply to queries.
Nonfiction: Interviews, articles, photo stories, reviews. Anything having to do with film or TV. Articles on directors, actors, etc. On new or classic films, on aspects of the industry, current or historical, on aesthetic developments. Anything of interest in this broad area of the communication arts. No taboos at all. Style should be lively, informed and opinionated rather than "newspaperese." Length: 700 to 5,000 words; 1,000 words maximum, reviews. Pays about 1¢ per word.
Photos: Purchased with mss. Events, people in film and/or TV. 8x10 b&w glossy. Payment varies.
Fiction: Very rarely buys fiction. Query first. Maximum 5,000 words. Also uses short-shorts under 2,000 words. Must deal with some aspect of film and/or TV. No taboos. Pays about 1¢ per word.
Poetry: Must deal with some aspect of film and/or TV. No taboos.
Fillers: Puzzles. Must deal with some aspect of film or TV. Payment varies.

TV AND MOVIE SCREEN, 315 Park Ave., S., New York NY 10010. Editor: Beryl S. Basher. Monthly. Buys all rights. Pays on acceptance. Query first. Reports in 2 weeks. Enclose S.A.S.E.
Nonfiction: Articles "heavy on dramatic and emotional appeal, featuring articles on TV and movie personalities. Must be factual and all quotes must be accurate." Writers "should have fan magazine experience as well as real contacts with Hollywood personalities, such as the opportunities to do in-depth interviews. We will not accept pieces culled from other published sources. We are not interested in nostalgia; we feature current personalities." Length: 2,000 words. Pays $200 per story.

TV DAWN TO DUSK, 295 Madison Ave., New York NY 10017. Editor: Ronni Warren Ashcroft. For daytime television viewers. Established in 1970. Monthly. Circulation: over 200,000. Buys all rights. Pays on publication. Query first. Study magazine before submitting. Enclose S.A.S.E. for reply to queries.
Nonfiction: Personality pieces with daytime TV stars of serials and quiz shows; main emphasis is on serial stars. Also interested in some women's interest material. Buys interviews, personality pieces, round-up articles, how-to's, profiles, and personal experience articles. Length and payment are to be negotiated.

TV GUIDE, Radnor PA 19087. Executive Editor: Alexander Joseph. Published weekly. Study publication before submitting. Include S.A.S.E. for return of articles, queries and photos.
Nonfiction: Wants offbeat articles about TV people and shows. This magazine is not interested in fan material. Also wants stories on the newest trends of television, but they must be written in layman's language. Writers are advised to query with an outline first. Length: 200 to 2,000 words. Send to Roger Youman, Managing Editor.
Photos: Uses professional high-quality photos, normally shot on assignment, by photographers chosen by *TV Guide.* Prefers color. Pays $150 day rate against page rates—$250 for 2 pages or less.

TV RADIO MIRROR, 205 East 42nd St., New York NY 10017. Editor: Lawrence B. Thomas. For women of all ages. Pays on acceptance. Query first. Reports imme-

diately. Enclose S.A.S.E. for reply to queries.
Nonfiction: "As the largest 'fan' magazine in the TV field (and radio to a lesser extent), we publish each month 12 or so personal articles about the private lives of television's most popular performers, i.e., stars of such shows as 'Marcus Welby,' 'Maude,' 'All in the Family,' 'Mannix,' 'Ironside,' 'Mod Squad,' etc., as well as many of the daytime television dramas. Love, marriage, family life, religion, these are the broad human-interest areas which produce the stories preferred by *TVRM*. Except for standard staff-written features, all stories are from freelancers, usually based in Hollywood or New York. But we are a wide-open market to any writer who can meet our requirements. It is possible that a writer who lives, for example, in the home town of a major TV star could click at *TV Radio Mirror* by doing an in-depth 'home-town report' on this celebrity, derived from interviews with his former teachers, friends, employers, family members, etc. We have in the recent past bought several such stories from local writers, who saw this suggestion in an earlier issue of *Writer's Digest* or *Writer's Yearbook*." Length: prefers 2,000 to 3,000 words. Pays 10¢ a word and up. Photos are bought from top quality freelance photographers.

TV RADIO SHOW, 315 Park Ave., S., New York NY 10010. Editor: Janice Coughlan. For fans of television stars. Monthly. Circulation: 200,000. Buys about 120 mss a year. Pays on acceptance. Query first. Submit seasonal material 3 months in advance. Reports "immediately." Enclose S.A.S.E. for return of submissions or reply to queries.
Nonfiction: This publication is a "fan magazine about television stars." Articles "should avoid real scandal. Prefer dramatic stories." Buys interviews and inspirational pieces. Length: 1,500 to 3,000 words. Pays $200.

TV STAR PARADE, 295 Madison Avenue, New York NY 10017. Editor: Peggy Adam. For "females. 13 to 60 years old. Some high school. Interests in private lives of TV and soap opera stars." Monthly. Circulation: 400,000. Buys all rights. Payment on publication. Will send a free sample copy to a writer on request. Query first required with basic outline of proposed feature. Submit seasonal material 2 months in advance. Reports in 2 to 3 weeks. Enclose S.A.S.E. for reply to queries.
Nonfiction and Photos: General subject matter consists of interviews, "backstage stories," romance, etc. Approach should be a "chatty style with special attention to dialog, quotes from the stars. We like to use as many real interviews as possible. We never publish made up quotes or interviews. We do not want angles that have been dredged up time and again just to fill space. Interested in timely material." Buys informational, personal experience, interviews, profile, expose, nostalgia, photo articles. "I would appreciate new ideas for columns." Length: "5 to 7 typewritten pages." Pays $150 to $200. Photos are purchased without mss and on assignment. Captions are optional. Wants candid b&w. Pays $25 per photo on publication. Also buys color. Pays according to use.

TVBE, P.O. Box 3354, Madison WI 53704. Editor: Patrick Prentice. For television viewers of all ages, politically left of center. Established in 1973. Monthly. Circulation: 10,000. Buys all rights. Payment on publication. Will send free sample copy to writer on request. Write for copy of guidelines for writers. Query first. Will consider photocopied submissions. Reporting time is "variable." Returns rejected material in 2 weeks. Enclose S.A.S.E. for response to query or return of submission.
Nonfiction and Photos: "Articles, interviews, concerning any facet of television; network, public, cable. Sports, children's TV, new TV season, soap operas (daytime TV), news/documentary, guerilla TV, cable TV issues. We'd prefer articles which clearly reveal the writer's personal bias and reasons behind that bias. The ideal *TVBE* article would be a cross between a long letter to a good friend and a muckraking piece for *Ramparts*. Don't be afraid of using first person singular. A heavily researched, fact-crammed article is fine as long as it doesn't come across as academic twaddle. We need reviews of TV shows, regular series, soaps, game shows, talk shows. TV programming, even junk programming, can stimulate and catalyze an enormous variety of perceptions and we want to publish as many differing views as possible. Pays $25 for 200-word minimum reviews, no maximum. We can also use transcribed interviews with common folk about their TV viewing habits, favorite shows, etc., for 'Clarabelle's Revenge.' A photo and brief background notes on the interivewee should be included. Pays $25 for 200 to 1,000-word interviews."

Photos are purchased with accompanying mss or without, or on assignment. Captions optional.

Fiction: Science fiction and fantasy, any length. Should relate to TV. Pays $25 to $150, depending on length.

WHERE MAGAZINE, 770 Lexington Ave., New York NY 10021. Local where to go guide distributed in major hotels in editions for Atlanta, Baltimore, Boston, Chicago, Cleveland, Dallas, Denver, Detroit, Los Angeles, Minneapolis-St. Paul, New Orleans, New York, Philadelphia, St. Louis, San Diego, San Francisco, Washington, Houston, Phoenix, Fort Lauderdale, and Miami. Weekly. "We do not use material from freelance writers; only staff-written."

Travel, Camping, and Trailer Publications

The magazines that follow tell campers and tourists where to go, where to stay, how to get there, how to camp, or how to select a good vehicle for travel or shelter. Publications that buy how-to camping and travel material with a conservation angle are listed in the Nature, Conservation, and Ecology classification. Newspapers and Sunday supplements and Regional magazines are frequently interested in travel and camping material with a local angle. Hunting and fishing and outdoor magazines that buy camping how-to's will be found in the Sport and Outdoor category. Publications dealing with automobiles or other vehicles maintained for sport or as a hobby will be found with the Automotive and Motorcycle magazines.

Many magazines in the Sponsored Publications section (especially those in the Association, Club, and Fraternal; Customers'; Employees'; General Interest; and Miscellaneous Sponsored publications categories) are also in the market for travel and camping articles and photos.

BETTER CAMPING, 500 Hyacinth Place, Highland Park IL 60035. Editorial Director: Paul Foght. For "those concerned with the basic camping and outdoor experience—from the backpacker to the family with a fold-down tent trailer." Established in 1960. Monthly. Buys all rights to mss; one-time use of photos and transparencies. Pays on acceptance; pays on publication for photo stories and fillers. Will send a sample copy to a writer on request. Write for copy of guidelines for writers. Query first. Reports in 6 to 8 weeks. Enclose S.A.S.E. for reply to queries.
Nonfiction: "Good, informative articles on camping and camping-related activities directed at the beginner and the advanced camper: scenic trips, wilderness travel, do-it-yourself ideas, camping equipment, camp cooking, nature subjects, backpacking, canoeing, mountaineering, bicycling, ski touring. Must be authentically written and of practical value." Length: 1,200 to 2,400 words. Pays "a minimum 5¢ a word for illustrated articles."
Photos: "Sharp b&w prints, preferably 8x10 glossies; color transparencies, preferably 2¼ square." Pays $150 for color cover.
Fillers: "Short subjects wanted for 'Overflow' (humorous anecdotes about family camping experiences), 'Voice of Experience' (camping tips), and 'Over an Open Fire' (recipes)." Pays $5 minimum.

BOATING & FISHING ALMANAC, Box 344, Venice CA 90291. Editor: William Berssen. For "boat owners in the Pacific Southwest." Established in 1965. Annual. Circulation: 35,000. Buys all rights. Buys 3 mss a year. Payment on publication. Will send a sample copy to a writer for $2.95. Query first required. Submit seasonal material 3 to 6 months in advance. Reports in 4 weeks. Enclose S.A.S.E. for reply to queries.
Nonfiction and Photos: "This is a cruising guide, published annually in 3 editions, covering all of the navigable waters in the Pacific Southwest. Though we are almost entirely staff-produced, we would be interested in well-written articles on cruising and trailer-boating along the Pacific coast and in the navigable lakes and rivers of the western states from Baja California to Canada inclusive." Payment for nonfiction varies with quality and length. Pays $5 for 8x10 b&w glossies.

BON VOYAGE MAGAZINE, 4700 Belleview, Kansas City MO 64112. Managing Editor; Jane Rosenthal. "Circulated by travel agents to known travelers and to subscribers. Our readers have an extremely high education and income level. Well-traveled and travel consistently. Sophisticated with good taste, they are mature (over 40) and are interested in history, art, regional culinary specialties, customs, etc." Established in 1969. Bimonthly. Circulation: 72,000. Buys all rights. Buys 5 to 10 mss a year. Payment on publication. Will send sample copy to writer for 50¢. Enclose S.A.S.E. when writing for copy of guidelines for writers. Submit only complete ms. "For winter holiday issue (November-December), must have material by April 1." Reports on material accepted for publication in "90 days hopefully." Returns rejected material as soon as it's read. Enclose S.A.S.E. for return of submissions. "Otherwise, material destroyed in 90 days."
Nonfiction, Photos and Fillers: "We are always interested in good travel pieces that come well-illustrated with color transparencies. What, where and when. First or third person, but no family or friends bit. We want interesting, well-written approach to all aspects of travel in all articles. But, no camping, hiking, freighter trips, etc." Length: 1,000 to 1,500 words, or 500- to 800-word fillers. Pays $25 to $100. Pays $3 for 5x7 or 8x10 b&w; $10 for 35mm (or larger) color transparencies.

CAMPER COACHMAN, P.O. Box 500, Calabasas CA 91302. Editor: Bill Estes. For camper owners or prospective camper buyers. Monthly. Circulation: 70,000. Buys first serial rights. Pays on publication. Will send a copy to a writer on request. Write for copy of guidelines for writers. Query first. Reports with acknowledgement card immediately; reports on status of submissions in 1 month. Enclose S.A.S.E. for reply to queries.
Nonfiction: Travel, novelty, human interest features, technical material, personality pieces, how-to-do-it, automotive articles (related to light trucks), all aimed at the camper owner or prospective buyer. Subject matter can range from articles on entertainment personalities, actors who own camping coaches, to technical material on light truck equipment. Travel material must be slanted toward the camper owner, and at least one photo in layout should include a camping coach. Big emphasis on unusual places to go, people enjoying the great outdoors in camping coaches. Length: varies between 500 words for small layouts to 2,500 or 3,000 words for major topics. "Current emphasis is on camper or truck-related do-it-yourself articles." Payment varies between $75 to $150 per article, including photos.
Photos: Purchased with articles and payment included in ms price. B&w of any size accepted; must be good quality; 8x10 preferred. Quality color transparencies of any size accepted.

CAMPING & TRAILERING GUIDE, 316 Hillside Ave., Mill Valley CA 94941. Editor: Bill Shepard. "Our audience is made up of family campers ranging from young marrieds to retirees. Median age is mid-30's. All types of family camping." Established in 1959. Circulation: 90,000. Buys all rights, but will reassign rights to author after publication. Buys 30 to 45 mss a year. Payment on publication. Will send free sample copy to a writer on request. Write for copy of guidelines for writers. Query first. Will consider photocopied submissions. Submit seasonal material "4 months prior to cover date." Reports on material accepted for publication in 1 month. Returns rejected material in 1 month. Enclose S.A.S.E. for reply to queries.
Nonfiction and Photos: "We attempt to provide complete, accurate information about camping destinations as well as about types of camping and travel equipment; places to go, how to do it and attractions to be seen in an area. The entire camping spectrum from backpacking to motor home travel. We are always looking for out-of-the-way camping destination pieces. We try to give enough information that a reader can duplicate trip described in article." Length 1,000 to 2,500 words. Pays $25 for short-shorts. "$50 is average rate for regular articles; $75 to $100 on assignment." Payment for photos (5x7 and larger; sharp prints) is part of article payment. Color: 35mm and larger. $50 to $75 for covers; no payment if used inside as part of article.
Fillers: Camping tips. Length: 25 to 250 words. Pays $2.50 to $10.

CAMPING GUIDE, Rajo Publications Inc., 316 Hillside Ave., Mill Valley CA 94941. Editor: Bill Shepard. Monthly. Circulation: 100,000. Pays on publication. Enclose S.A.S.E.

Nonfiction: Articles dealing with any phase of family camping and the whole range of equipment from back-packing gear through tents, tent-trailers, travel trailers, pick-up campers, van campers and motor homes. "Family camp-travel stories get the most space and this is also the category in which we are most likely to be overstocked. However, an out-of-the-way camping spot or an original treatment always gets close attention. Other welcome subjects include articles about how to build camping equipment, wilderness camping, foreign camping and peripheral activities such as canoeing, small boat camping, cycling, nature photography. First-person style and first-hand experiences are preferred." Length: 1,000 to 2,000 words. Pays from 1¢ to 4¢ a word. Pays $40 to $50 for illustrated full-length article. For technical articles by professional writers, pays up to $100.
Photos: Mss should be accompanied by b&w glossy photos, snapshot size acceptable when sharp and clear. Color prints and 35mm slides acceptable when no other illustration available, but prefers b&w. Buys photos in a package with mss. Also buys 35mm or larger transparencies for cover at $50. When a transparency is used as an insert or in other secondary position, the pay is less. If a writer submits a transparency which can be used on the cover, the cover price is in addition to his payment for the article.
Fillers: Short articles and one or two photos about favorite or unusual campgrounds, or about travel objectives which are especially interesting and are close to public or private campgrounds. Also short how-to articles on almost any subject applicable to family campers. Length: 300 to 500 words. Pays 1¢ to 4¢ a word.

CAMPING JOURNAL, Davis Pub., 229 Park Ave. S., New York, NY 10003. Editor: Carlton Colquitt. For suburbanite couples, in their thirties, with 2 children; they own one type of recreational vehicle or another, or at least a tent; go camping during their vacations and on several weekends through the year. Established in 1962. Monthly. Circulation: 280,000. Buys all rights but may reassign rights after publication. Buys 150 mss a year. Payment on acceptance. Will send free sample copy to writer on request. Write for copy of guidelines for writers. Query first "one year in advance." Reports in 10 days. Enclose S.A.S.E. for reply to queries.
Nonfiction and Photos: "Travel articles, with information included in each article to show where the nearest camping facilities to that attraction may be; how they are equipped; how-to articles, involving basic camping skills, including recreational vehicle-type camping skills as well as backpacking skills; product round-up articles, which are not test reports, but rather general reports on the capabilities of the equipment and its cost. Write concisely, and never repeat yourself. Avoid the vernacular of the 'old-time' camper, because most campers today have never heard of many of those terms. Especially avoid colloquialisms. Intelligent, rather than folksy. Especially interested in new developments in campgrounds, new products, new ways to solve old problems, new insights into some of the more popular places that everyone seems to enjoy going back to every year. Any skills or adventure articles must be set in the context of a family camping situation. This means there must be something in the article that a child can relate to as well as his parents. Regular columns are presently assigned, but if a freelancer wants to offer his services in competition with an existing contributor, he is welcome to try." Length: 750 to 2,000 words. Pays $100 to $250. B&w photos are purchased with mss. 35mm or larger transparencies. Captions required. "First-rate quality only." Nonfiction and Photo Dept. Editor: Ken Grant.
Fillers: Short humor. Length: 750 words. Pays $50 to $150. Dept. Editor: Ken Grant.

CANADIAN MOTORIST, 2 Carlton Street, Toronto 2, Ontario, Canada. Editor: Jerry Tutunjian. For "Canadian car owners who travel extensively in North America and abroad." Established in 1914. Bimonthly. Circulation: 115,000. Buys first Canadian rights. Buys 25 to 30 mss a year. Pays on acceptance. Will send a free sample copy to a writer on request. Will send editorial guidelines sheet to a writer on request. Query first required. Will consider photocopied submissions. Reports in 1 month. Enclose S.A.E. and International Reply Coupons for reply to queries.
Nonfiction and Photos: General subject matter consists of "travel and motoring anywhere in the world." Buys personal experience, photo, and travel articles. Length: 800 to 2,000 words. Pays $40 to $100. Photos are purchased with or without mss and captions are required. Pays $7 for 8x10 b&w and pays $25 for 2¼x2¼, 35mm color transparencies.

CARIBBEAN WORLD COMMUNICATIONS, INC, Suite 312, 1519 Ponce de Leon Ave., Santurce PR 00909. Editor: Al Dinhofer. Produces Sunday Travel section for El Mundo newspaper. Weekly. Circulation: 165,000. Buys 10 to 12 mss a year. Pays on publication. Reports in 2 to 4 weeks. Enclose S.A.S.E. for return of submissions.
Nonfiction and Photos: "Travel features of interest to the local market, with special interest in other areas convenient to this one—United States, Latin America, Mexico, Caribbean, Europe—especially Spanish-speaking areas." Photos purchased with mss. Length: 1,000 to 1,500 words. Payment approximately $15.

FAMILY HOUSEBOATING, 23945 Craftsman Rd., Calabasas CA 91302. Editor: Art Rouse. For owners and prospective buyers of houseboats. Bimonthly. Circulation: 50,000. Buys all rights. Pays on publication. Will send free sample copy on request. Query desirable. Reports in three weeks. Enclose S.A.S.E. for reply to queries.
Nonfiction and Photos: Interested in articles of interest to houseboat owners and prospective buyers, including how-to pieces, personalities, houseboating waterways, technical and maintenance articles. Length: to 2,000 words. Pays $50 to $150, including photos.

FOUR SEASONS TRAILS, 534 N. Broadway, Milwaukee WI 53202. Editor: Glenn Helgeland. For "middle income, active users of recreational vehicles; family people who enjoy all aspects of the outdoors as long as the activity is based around an RV." 9 times a year. Circulation: 275,000. Buys first North American serial rights. Buys 50 to 60 mss a year. Payment made before publication. Will send free sample copy to a writer on request. Write for copy of guidelines for writers. Query first. Will not consider photocopied submissions. Submit seasonal material 6 months in advance. Reports on material in 3 weeks. Enclose S.A.S.E. for reply to queries.
Nonfiction and Photos: "Basically 'where to go' and 'what to do' in the outdoors with recreational vehicles with private campgrounds as the base for the activity. Study a back copy and query us. Stories should have people doing and saying things, having active fun." Informational, how-to, photo and travel. Length: 250 to 2,000 words. Pays $25 to $400. Photos purchased with and without mss. Pays $20 to $35 for 8x10 b&w glossies; $35 to $100 for any size transparency. Captions required.

HANDBOOK AND DIRECTORY FOR CAMPERS, 1999 Shepard Rd., St. Paul MN 55116. Editor: Richard L. Smith. For families whose members range in age from infancy to past retirement, and whose leisure interests are aimed primarily at outdoor recreation and travel with recreational vehicles providing the means to enjoyment of this new life style. Established in 1971. Annual. Circulation: 1,500,000. Buys all rights, but will reassign rights to author after publication. Buys 6 to 12 mss a year. Payment on acceptance. Will send free sample copy writer on request. Write for copy of guidelines for writers. Query first. Will consider photocopied submissions. Reports in 30 days. Enclose S.A.S.E. for reply to query or return of submission.
Nonfiction: "General articles on outdoor living and travel including how to prepare for trip and ways to gain more enjoyment from the going, staying, and coming home portions of it. In all cases, emphasis should be on the positive, fun aspects of travel and camping, not on the problems sometimes encountered. Writing should be readable rather than academic, clever rather than endlessly descriptive, tight rather than verbose. A good lead is considered essential. First-person articles and stories about personal experiences are not acceptable. We try to emphasize that camping is not only fun in itself, but is the means to all kinds of peripheral activities not normally available to the average family. Editorial slant is consistently on the enjoyment aspects of the experience." Informational, how-to, profile, humor, historical, nostalgia, photo, and travel articles. Length: 700 to 1,500 words. Pays $75 to $275.
Photos: Purchased with accompanying mss or on assignment. Captions optional. Uses color; 35mm and larger. Pays $200 for cover; $50 each for inside use.

MOBILE LIVING, P.O. Box 1418, Sarasota FL 33578. Editor: Frances Neel. Monthly. Copyrighted. Pays on publication. Will send a free sample copy to a writer on request. Reports on submissions within 1 month. Enclose S.A.S.E. with all submissions.

Nonfiction: Articles on recreational vehicle experiences and travel via recreational vehicles. In travel articles, include names of parks to stay at while seeing the sights, etc. Hobbies involving recreational vehicles and how-to-do-it articles that apply to a general audience also wanted. Length: 1,500 words maximum. Pays 1¢ per word.

Photos: With captions and illustrating articles. B&w glossies only. Returned after use. Pays $3 each.

MOBILE MODULAR HOUSING TODAY, 400 Hyacinth, Highland Park IL 60035. Editor: Ron Piette. Owners and prospective buyers of mobile homes. "Mainly retirees and young marrieds of average education. Generally, how great mobile home living is; great landscaping ideas, interior decorating ideas, do-it-yourself projects, unusual mobile home parks, unusual interiors, moneysaving ideas, etc." Established in 1971. 3 times a year. Buys all rights. Buys 25 mss a year. Payment on acceptance. Will send sample copy to a writer for $1. Query first. Reports on material accepted in 2 weeks. Returns rejected material within 1 month. Enclose S.A.S.E. for reply to queries.

Nonfiction and Photos: Informational, how-to, personal experience, humor, new product. "The stories should have some personality. Leads should be exciting." Length: 1,500 to 2,500 words. "Payment based on quality of total package, ms and photos. As a rough guide, we pay approximately 4¢ to 5¢ a word plus photos."

MOTOR NEWS, 150 Bagley Ave., Detroit MI 48226. Travel Editor: Len Barnes. For travelers to all parts of the world. Special issues include Florida and the Caribbean (December); Outdoors and Camping (February); the Western United States (April); Michigan (May). Monthly. Buys first serial rights. "We like, but do not insist, on exclusive pictures." Pays on acceptance. Query suggested. Deadlines are 3 months before publication. "Therefore an article on a timely event or area that can be visited only at a certain time must be received well in advance of its intended publication. In some cases we will hold an article in our files until it becomes timely." Reports in 2 weeks. Enclose S.A.S.E. for return of submissions or reply to queries.

Nonfiction and Photos: Articles about "offbeat or well-known tourist objectives in the U.S." Likes material that describes these areas colorfully, yet which avoids travel writing cliches. "In addition to descriptions of things to see and do, articles should contain accurate, current information on costs the traveler would encounter on his trip. Items such as lodging, meal and entertainment expenses should be included, not in the form of a balance sheet but as an integral part of the article. Tips on what to pack and wear and other trip-planning features should be included." Besides straight travel articles, also interested in "things to do"—subjects concerning camping, hunting, fishing, boating and special events. "Always in the market for pieces about Michigan and like an article to have a Michigan slant if possible." Length: 800 to 1,200 words. Pays between $75 and $100. Requires four or five 8x10, b&w glossies with each article of the above-mentioned length. Pays, with 4 or 5 b&w photos, from $100 and $175, and sometimes higher for special subjects.

MOTORHOME LIFE, 23945 Craftsman Rd., P.O. Box 500, Calabasa CA 91302. Editor: Denis Rouse. Monthly. Pays on publication. Query first. Enclose S.A.S.E. for reply to queries or return of submissions.

Nonfiction and Photos: "Articles on motorhomes, self-propelled recreational vehicles; how-to and travel articles involving motorhomes. Subjects pertaining to motorhomes, their use, maintenance and pleasure; where to go and what to do. We need travel stories which should include maps and must include good photos, both b&w and color. Also needed are technical features, how-to-do improvements, self-service projects with photos or good line drawings. Human interest articles about unusual people." Length: 1,500 to 2,000 words. Pays $125 to $175.

POPULAR RECREATION, 26233 Veva Way, Calabasas CA 91302. Editor: Michael G. Laurentis. For "motorhome and outdoor enthusiasts." Established in 1972. Quarterly. Rights purchased vary with author and material. Buys all rights, but will reassign rights to author after publication. Buys about 40 mss a year. Payment on publication. Write for copy of guidelines for writers. "No query required, but suggest submitting outline first." Submit seasonal material 3 to 4 months in advance. Reports in 2 weeks. Enclose S.A.S.E.

Nonfiction: "We're a broad-based outdoor and recreational vehicles magazine. Motorhomes, travel trailers and truck campers. We publish ideas of special interest to the RV user, for example, current issues or situations; how-to word and picture stories; travel articles, etc., as well as entertainment pieces. Good style and ingenuity. Pieces should be well-written and researched; interesting and honest." Personal experience, interview, think articles, photo, travel, new product, technical articles. Length: 1,500 to 2,500 words. Pays up to $125. Address mss to Articles Editor.

Photos: Purchased with accompanying mss. Captions required. 8x10 b&w single weight glossies preferred, but will accept smaller sizes of sharp and clear quality. B&w purchased with ms. Color transparencies of 35mm used for cover. Pays $25 to $50 for color.

Fiction and Fillers: Experimental, adventure, science fiction, and humorous fiction. Open on story theme. Length: 1,500 to 2,000 words with drawing, illustration, or photos. Address mss to Fiction Editor. Pays to $125. Newsbreaks, clippings, jokes, short humor, and novelty fillers. Length: 500 words maximum. Pays 10¢ a word.

RV WORLD, 16200 Ventura Blvd., Encino CA 91316. Editor: Jim Matthews. For recreational vehicle owners, campers, travelers. Established in 1973. Monthly. Circulation: 80,000. Buys all rights. Buys 30 to 40 mss a year. Payment on publication. Will send free sample copy to writer on request. Write for copy of guidelines for writers. Query first. Submit seasonal material at least 4 months in advance (Winter camping and winter RV material needed in midsummer.) Reports on material in 1 week. Enclose S.A.S.E.

Nonfiction and Photos: Travel articles (exclusive of Southwest). How-to articles related to RV repair or maintenance. Semitechnical articles related to RVs. "Fairly breezy style while keeping in mind our audience. Any technical material must be accurate." Personal experience, humor, informational. Length: 1,800 to 3,000 words. Pays $50 per printed page in magazine (with 50 percent photos). "Prefer negatives and contact sheet; crisp focus, uncluttered background." No extra payment for b&w. Color transparencies; 35mm or larger. Pays "$25 extra for color lead."

TRAIL CAMPING, P.O. Box 310, Canoga Park CA 91305. Editorial Director: Don J. Maxwell. Editor: Bill Shepard. "Our audience is between 16 and 60, both male and female and middle or upper class, with a taste for quality and the outdoors. These are busy people seeking the solitude and serenity of the wilderness as an escape from the pressures of modern society." Directed exclusively to the activities related to the wilderness. Monthly. Established in 1972. Buys all rights, but will reassign rights to author after publication. Payment on publication. Will send free sample copy to a writer on request. Write for copy of guidelines for writers. Query first. Will consider photocopied submissions. Submit seasonal material 4 to 6 months in advance. Reports on material accepted for publication in 4 weeks. Returns rejected material in 4 weeks. Enclose S.A.S.E.

Nonfiction: Articles related to hiking, backpacking, snowshoeing, ski-touring, packing with stock, mountaineering and canoeing. Other subject interests, when related to the trail camping situation, are: geology, botany, weather, fishing, orienteering, photography and conservation. Personal experiences should be first-person narratives and may be dramatic, humorous or adventurous, but they must be true. Topical articles must be accurate and authoritative. All articles should be well supported with sketches or photographs and accurate maps where required. Not interested in stories about trail bikes, RV's, snowmobiles. Also uses profiles, humor, historical, nostalgia, book reviews, spot news, new product and technical articles. Length: 500 to 4,000 words. Pays minimum of 3¢ per word.

Photos: 5x7 or 8x10 b&w glossies. Pays maximum of $10. Purchased with or without mss. Captions required. Color: 35mm, 2¼x2¼ transparencies, or larger. Pays up to $35; $50 for covers.

Fillers: Pertinent newsbreaks and clippings; camping tips. Length: 1,000 words maximum. Pays up to $30.

TRAILER LIFE, 23945 Craftsman Road, Calabasas CA 91302. Editor: Art Rouse. Monthly. For owners and potential buyers of trailers, campers and motor homes. Reports within 3 weeks. No manuscripts or photos will be returned unless accompanied by a stamped, self-addressed envelope. Buys all rights. Will send sample copy on request. Enclose S.A.S.E. for return of submissions.

Nonfiction: Uses articles about the art of using a trailer, camper or motor home, and the problems involved. Length: up to 1,500 words. Also uses how-to-do-it articles with step-by-step photos a necessity. Length: no more than 800 words. Combine as many operations in each photo or drawing as possible. Personal experience stories must be truly interesting. Merely living in or traveling by trailer is not enough. Uses travel articles with 3 to 6 good 8x10 glossy prints on trips that are inexpensive or unusual into areas which are accessible by a travel trailer or pickup camper. Length: 1,000 to 1,500 words. Also uses short travel pieces, with a couple of photos, of interesting places off the established routes. Length: 100 to 250 words. Allied interest articles are one of main interests—things that trailerites (people living in mobile homes) or trailerists (people traveling in trailers) do or would like to do—boating, hiking, fishing, spelunking hobbies. When writing about allied sports or activities, a definite tie-in with travel trailers, motor homes or pickup campers is essential; the articles must be linked to the extent that you tell readers how their trailers fit into the sport, and where they can park while there. All travel articles should include basic information on trailer parking facilities in the areas, costs, locations, and time of year, etc. Payment varies, "based on the quality of the material submitted and how it's used, but $100 to $150 per article is present rate."

Photos: "We occasionally buy separate photos or cover shots, but most of these are shot on assignment. A good selection of photos must accompany all articles, but we will occasionally run a photo story by itself. Photos should be 8x10 glossy. Prints should be numbered and the photographer identified on the back, with numbers corresponding to a caption sheet. Photos should show action, not static poses, and should be as close up as the subject matter will allow."

TRAVEL, Travel Bldg., Floral Park NY 11001. Managing Editor: Robert H. Rufa. For "active travelers." Monthly. Circulation: approximately 560,000. Buys first North American serial rights. Pays on acceptance. Will send a sample copy to a writer on request. Query first. "Study magazine. Remember that we work 4 months in advance." Enclose S.A.S.E. with all queries and submissions.

Nonfiction: Wants what-to-do-and-see material in a particular locale or city, but not single sites, with costs and prices worked in wherever appropriate. Information on dining and accommodations is most helpful. Travel may take place either in U.S. or foreign country. Articles should deal with areas or cities rather than museums, landmarks, etc. Length: 1,000 to 2,500 words. Buys photos with articles, preferably with people in the scenes. B&w glossy, 5x7 or larger, 35mm original transparencies or larger. "We are forced to return otherwise acceptable editorial material if photos are of poor quality or if they are improperly captioned, etc. Though we rarely buy photos without a ms, we don't mind hearing from a photographer with an extensive slide or b&w print file, on the possibility of a photo essay or as a source for material." Pays $50 to $150 for a b&w piece, depending on length. Prefer color stories. Pays $150 to $300.

How To Break In: "If you travel and would like to write and do photography, take notes and lots of color slides. You should be quite capable with a camera. Then study our basic requirements. Query us with your idea, and if we think we can use it, we'll let you know. Then put your experiences and observations down on paper, in the format suggested by *Writer's Market,* and send us the manuscript together with a good selection of photos. You'll get the same consideration that experienced writers do. We're always looking for new talent to help develop. There is no single bit of advice I can give a beginning writer. Rather, he or she must take each of the basic steps necessary to get a travel article into print."

TRAVEL AND LEISURE, 132 W. 31st St., New York NY 10001. Editor-in-chief: Caskie Stinnett. Bimonthly. Circulation: 4,000,000. Buys first North American serial rights. Pays on acceptance. Query first. Reports in 1 week. Enclose S.A.S.E.

Nonfiction and Photos: Uses articles on travel and vacation places, food, wine, shopping, sports. Most articles are assigned. Length: 1,000 to 3,000 words. Pays $500 to $3,000.

Photos: Makes assignments to photographers. Pays expenses.

TRAVEL RATES & PLACES, Box 246, Woodside NY 11377. Feature Editor: Dey Wall. General audience interested in travel. Articles on travel. Established in 1972.

Monthly. Buys all rights. Buys 60 mss a year. Payment on publication. Will send free sample copy to a writer on request. Will consider photocopied submissions. Submit seasonal material 2 months in advance. Enclose S.A.S.E.
Nonfiction, Photos and Fillers: "Be factual. Writer must have been to place described." Informational, how-to, personal experience, humor, nostalgia, new product. Length: 1,200 words maximum. Pays $35 maximum. B&w photos purchased with mss. Captions required. Pays $5. Travel crossword puzzles and travel humor.

TRAVELORE REPORT, 225 South 15th Street, Philadelphia PA 19102. For "travel oriented individuals interested in obtaining objective reports on international travel events." Established in 1970. Monthly. Rights purchased vary with author and material. Buys 50 to 100 mss a year. Payment on publication. Will send free sample copy to a writer on request. Enclose S.A.S.E. for return of submissions.
Nonfiction: Publishes "only travel subjects: timely events, places worth visiting, what to do once there; what to avoid, etc. Provide facts—costs, new discoveries, accommodations, etc. Crisp, concise reporting. Most topics held to average 10 lines. Travelore Report adheres to a newsletter format." Payment varies.

WESTINDIES SOCIETY NEWSLETTER, 1519 Ponce de Leon Avenue, Suite 312, Santurce PR 00909. Editor: Al Dinhofer. For "travelers who are interested in the Caribbean area and seek current, unvarnished information—that will facilitate travel, save them money, and take them to where it's happening." Monthly. Buys one-time rights. Payment on publication. Will send free sample copy to writer on request. Query first. Submit seasonal material 2 months in advance. Enclose S.A.S.E.
Nonfiction: "Our monthly newsletter covers all activities, good buys, festivals, complaints, opinions, comments, tips, suggestions, etc. All must be current, accurate and in telegraphic style." Buys 3 to 6 "special reports of 500 words, also news notes of some dozen sentences in newsletter." Pays 50¢ per typewritten line.

WHEELS AFIELD, 8490 Sunset Blvd., Los Angeles CA 90069. Editor: Don I. Mathews. For recreational vehicle enthusiasts; campers, fishermen, hunters, travelers, outdoor people using camping vehicles; ages 25 to over 50; retired; high school and college grads; middle and upper income; male and female. Established in 1967. Monthly. Circulation: 125,000. Rights purchased vary with author and material. Buys all rights; buys first North American serial rights. Buys 150 mss a year. Payment on acceptance; payment on publication for "some department items." Will send sample copy to writer for $1. Write for copy of guidelines for writers. Submit seasonal material 4 months in advance. Reports in 1 month. Enclose S.A.S.E.
Nonfiction: "How-to-do, what-to-do, where-to-go, what-to-buy, how to fix and maintain RV's. Some off-road traveling, boating, etc., as related to towing or other RV approach. Short, concise reporting on the above RV themes. We publish less on travel, more on mechanical how-to aspect. Unusual new products." Length: 75 to 150 words. Pays $5 to $12.50.
Photos: Purchased with or without mss, or on assignment. Captions required. 8x10 b&w glossies; 2¼ or larger 4-color transparencies, or extra sharp 35mm. Pays $5 to $10 each for b&w photos. Pays $25 maximum for inside color; $75 to $150 for cover.

WOODALL'S TRAILER TRAVEL MAGAZINE, 500 Hyacinth Place, Highland Park IL 60035. Editorial Director: Paul Foght. For family campers. Monthly. Buys all rights. Pays on acceptance. Reports on submission within 3 to 4 weeks. Query first. Enclose S.A.S.E.
Nonfiction and Photos: Uses "articles and photo stories concerned with family camping with travel trailers, pickup coaches, camping trailers, motor homes and all recreational vehicles. New recreation areas, step-by-step tours of scenic highways, influence of camping experience on personal and family life, equipment maintenance and improvement, as well as cooking, clothing, and recreational vehicle housekeeping tips are solicited. Recreational vehicles only, not mobile homes. Articles resulting from long tours should avoid log book approach and concentrate on most significant aspect of experience. Preferred writing style is to utilize anecdotal lead and dialog." Length to 2,500 words. Pays 5¢ a word minimum.

Women's Publications

AAUW JOURNAL, 2401 Virginia Ave., N.W., Washington DC 20037. Editor: Jean A. Fox. Publication of the American Association of University Women. For college-educated women. 7 times a year. "Substantive articles used semiannually." Circulation: 175,000. Buys first serial rights. Buys approximately 10 mss a year. Pays on publication. Will send a sample copy to a writer for 75¢. Query first. Submit seasonal material 4 months in advance. Reports in 1 month. Enclose S.A.S.E. for reply to queries.

Nonfiction: "We're looking for new ideas on subjects about which much has been written: women, education (particularly innovative approaches to learning for people of all ages); ecology, government, court reform, international affairs, communication, community problems and the role of the volunteer, cultural interests. Writing style should not be pedantic. We solicit most of our articles from authorities." Buys how-to's and interviews. Length: 1,800 to 2,400 words. Pays $100.

Photos: B&w glossies.

AMERICAN BABY, 10 E. 52nd St., New York NY 10021. Editor: Judith Nolte. For "expectant mothers (from sixth month of pregnancy) and new mothers (until 4 months after baby's birth)." Special issues include early learning and preschool education (August); travel (May). Monthly. Circulation: 1,500,000. Buys first serial rights. Buys about 50 mss a year. Pays on publication; sometimes pays on acceptance. Will send a sample copy to a writer on request. Submit seasonal material 3 months in advance. Reports in 2 weeks. Enclose S.A.S.E. for return of submissions.

Nonfiction: Articles on "pre- and post-natal care and health and humorous features on parenthood." Uses features on "early learning, physical, psychological, and mental development of new baby." Writing style should be "clear, not condescending." Would prefer not to see articles on "breastfeeding and natural childbirth." Buys how-to's, personal experience and inspirational articles, interviews, profiles, historical and think pieces, new product and travel articles. Length: 500 to 2,000 words. Pays $25 to $200.

How To Break In: "For a writer to get started, he or she should submit a manuscript on a topic which interests *them*, and, of course, our readership. Creating a new column idea would be fine, or interviewing some authority in a field. I suggest the interview as a good way for the beginner because he can do research, learn to ask questions, and get some writing and editing experience all at the same time, and the work won't be too complicated. I do believe, however, that a good beginner needs knowledge of English and a lot of drive."

BABY CARE, 52 Vanderbilt Avenue, New York NY 10017. Editor: Maja Bernath. Managing Editor: Evelyn Podsiadlo. For "mothers of babies from birth through the first year." Quarterly. Circulation: 2,300,000. Rights purchased vary with author and material. May buy all rights, first North American serial rights, and second serial rights. Payment on acceptance. Will send a free sample copy to a writer on request. Will send editorial guidelines sheet to a writer on request. Submit seasonal material 5 to 6 months in advance. Reports in 1 to 4 weeks. Enclose S.A.S.E. for return of submissions.

Nonfiction: Feature articles "include basic infant care (bathing, feeding, common illness, safety); emotional and physical development; how-to's; effect of new baby on family relations; seasonal topics (travel, summer or winter care). Shorter features with a humorous, narrative or reflective approach. Articles can be first-person accounts by mothers and fathers, but prefer medical subjects to be written by M.D.'s and R.N.'s or writer who can work well with doctors." Buys informational, how-to, personal experience, inspirational, humor, nostalgia and travel. Length: 1,000 to 1,800 words. Pays $50 to $125; and slightly higher to professionals such as M.D.'s. Regular columns that seek freelance material are: "Family Corner"—short anecdotes about life with the new baby. Pays $10. "Focus on You"—500-word mss focusing on a mother's feelings, personal interests or family relationships in regard to the baby. Pays $25.

Poetry: Uses poetry occasionally; all forms. Length: 4 to 24 lines. Pays $5 to $10. Should relate to subject matter.

BABY TALK, 149 Madison Avenue, New York NY 10016. Editor: Eve Ham moroohmidt. Will send free sample copy to a writer on request. Buys first serial rights. Pays on acceptance. Enclose S.A.S.E. for return of submissions.
Nonfiction: Articles appealing to new and expectant parents. True experiences of pregnancy and life with new babies or children under 3 years of age. Also, short hints on baby care and housekeeping, and valid opinions on child care, and all aspects of motherhood. Payments of $20, $25, $30 and up for manuscripts.
Photos: May be submitted with manuscripts or separately.

THE BRIDE'S MAGAZINE, 420 Lexington Ave., New York NY 10017. Editor-in-chief: Barbara Donovan. For "engaged girls in their early 20's who are preparing for their first marriage. Also read by the bride's family and friends, the groom, and the groom's family." 6 times a year. Circulation: 300,000. Buys all rights. Buys approximately 60 mss a year. Pays on acceptance. Query first to Ann Cynthia Diamond, Copy and Features Editor. Returns rejected material in 1 month. Acknowledges acceptance of material in 6 weeks. Enclose S.A.S.E. for reply to queries.
Nonfiction: "Serious articles with psychological slant on marriage; communication between the bride and groom and between the young couple and their environment, both sociological and physical. Should include statements by authorities and/or interviews with couples. Material should be concise, personal, relevant, young, optimistic, humane, friendly. Keep in mind contemporary reappraisal of role definitions within marriage. All wedding planning, wedding customs, fashion, beauty, decorating, cooking and honeymoon articles are staff-written. No first-person narratives about marital disaster. No bride's biscuit anecdotes. No household hints." Length: 2,000 to 3,000 words. Pays $50 to $350; "occasionally as high as $500."

CHATELAINE, 481 University Ave., Toronto 2, Canada. Editor: Doris McCubbin Anderson. Managing Editor: Jean Y. Wright. For "women, from age 20 up, mainly homemakers, with or without outside jobs." Monthly. Buys first world serial rights in English and French (the latter to cover possible use in *Chatelaine's* sister French-language edition, edited in Montreal for French Canada). Pays on acceptance. Query first. Reports in 2 to 4 weeks. Enclose S.A.E. and International Reply Coupons for reply to queries.
Nonfiction: Articles examining all and any facets of Canadian life especially as they concern or interest Canadian women. Uses material on medical subjects; education. Also full-length personal experience stories with deep emotional impact. Subjects outside Canada need some Canadian tie-in. For all serious articles, deep, accurate, thorough research and rich detail are required. A shallow once-over-lightly treatment will not do for *Chatelaine.* Length: 2,000 to 3,600 words for full-length major pieces; 1,000 words minimum for minor or humorous pieces. Pays minimum $300 for a major article.
Fiction: Settings should be Canadian if at all possible. In demand are slick, light romance; mystery or suspense; down-to-earth, human stories with real character impact. Also new emphasis is being placed on superior adult fiction. Preferably, the central character should be a woman. Very little demand for stories where the central character is a child (though children can be important secondary characters), or animal stories. Length: 3,000 to 4,500 words preferred, though this can vary depending on the story. No short-shorts. Payment starts at $400. Send fiction manuscripts to Miss Almeda Glassey, Fiction Editor.
How To Break In: "A beginner has to query us with a page or two of outline on a specific article idea and with a specific angle. Probably a personal experience story, if the experience is dramatic and different enough, would be a good entre. We usually find that readers can provide one such story from their lifetime although they do not then move on to become writers."

CONGRATULATIONS MAGAZINE, 175 Rock Rd., Glen Rock NJ 07452. Editor: Peg Rivers. For "new mothers within the first weeks or early months of their return home from the hospital with their infants." Established in 1936. Quarterly. Circulation: 385,000. Rights purchased vary with author and material. Buys "very few" mss a year. Pays on publication. Will send a sample copy to a writer on request. Query first. Will not consider photocopied submissions. Reports in 30 days. Enclose S.A.S.E. for reply to queries.

Nonfiction: "General articles on new mother health care and baby care. A reassuring tone about motherhood, an optimistic approach to baby care. No first-person, baby-written articles. The approach is a direct, down-to-earth scientific approach to baby care; no cutesy-pie articles used. Most of our articles are written by doctors, to whom subjects are assigned." Length: 1,000 to 1,500 words. Payment "varies."

CORONET, 7950 Deering, Canoga Park CA 91304. Publisher: Mrs. Leonora Burton. For "women, 20 to 40, family oriented; median income: $12,000 to $15,000." Established in 1936. Monthly. Circulation: 500,000. Buys all rights. Buys 120 mss a year. Payment on acceptance. "Occasionally operate on a 'kill fee' system." Query first required. Submit 100-word to 1-page outline of proposed article. Submit seasonal material 3 months in advance. Reports as soon as possible. Enclose S.A.S.E. for reply to queries.

Nonfiction, Photos, Fiction, and Fillers: General subject matter consists of women; consumer fraud, human interest, sociological trends, public conscience. "We are news oriented. No 'one woman's experience' please. We would like to see more articles on consumer fraud." Buys informational, how-to, inspirational, expose, photo, and new product articles. Length: 1,750 to 2,500 words. Pays $200. Address photos to Art Director. Buys mystery and romance fiction. Poetry should be addressed to Articles Editor. Buys puzzles for women.

COSMOPOLITAN, 224 West 57th St., New York NY 10019. Editor: Helen Gurley Brown; Managing Editor: George Walsh. For career women, ages 18 to 34. Monthly. Circulation: 1,500,000. Buys all rights. Pays on acceptance. Not interested in receiving unsolicited manuscripts or queries, as editorial staff hasn't time to read them. All material is assigned to established, known professional writers who sell regularly to top national markets, or is commissioned through literary agents.

Nonfiction: Not interested in unsolicited manuscripts or queries; for agents and top professional writers, requirements are as follows: "We want pieces that tell a hip, attractive, 18- to 34-year-old, intelligent, good-citizen girl how to have a more rewarding life—'how-to' pieces, self-improvement pieces as well as articles which deal with more serious matters. We'd be interested in articles on careers, part-time jobs, diets, food, fashion, men, the entertainment world, emotions, money, medicine and psychology, and fabulous characters. We don't want very many cosmic pieces—about space, war on poverty, civil rights, etc., but will leave those to more serious general magazines." Uses some first-person stories. Logical, interesting, authoritative writing is a must, as is a feminist consciousness. Length: 1,200 to 1,500 words; 3,000 to 4,000 words. Pays $200 to $500 for short pieces, $750 to $1,500 for longer articles.

Photos: On assignment only.

Fiction: Not interested in unsolicited manuscripts; for agents and top professional writers, requirements are as follows: "Significant themes are not important. Good plotting and excellent writing are. We want short stories dealing with adult subject matter which would interest a sophisticated audience, primarily female, 18 to 34. We prefer serious quality fiction or light tongue-in-cheek stories on any subject, done in good taste. We love stories dealing with contemporary man-woman relationships. Short-shorts are okay but we prefer them to have snap or 'trick' endings. The formula story, the soap opera, skimpy mood pieces or character sketches are not for us." Length: short-shorts, 1,500 to 3,000 words; short stories, 4,000 to 6,000 words; condensed novels and novel excerpts. "We also use murder or suspense stories of about 25,000 to 30,000 words dealing with the upper class stratum of American living. A foreign background is acceptable, but the chief characters should be American." Has published the work of Agatha Christie, Joyce Carol Oates, Evan Hunter, and other established writers. Pays about $1,000 and up for short stories and novel excerpts, $4,500 and up for condensed novels. Fiction Editor: Junius Adams.

EXPECTING, 52 Vanderbilt Ave., New York NY 10017. Editor: Mrs. Maja Bernath. Managing Editor: Evelyn Podsiadlo. Issued quarterly for expectant mothers. Pays on acceptance. Enclose S.A.S.E. for return of submissions.

Nonfiction: Prenatal development, layette and nursery planning, budgeting, diet, health, fashions, husband-wife relationships, naming the baby, minor discomforts,

childbirth, expectant fathers, working while pregnant. etc. Length: 800 to 1,600 words. Pays $50 to $125 for feature articles, somewhat more for specialists.
Fillers: Short humor and interesting or unusual happenings during pregnancy or at the hospital; maximum 200 words, $10 on publication; submissions to "Happenings" are not returned. Other fillers pay up to $50.

FAMILY CIRCLE MAGAZINE, 488 Madison Ave., New York NY 10022. Editor: Arthur M. Hettich. For women/homemakers. Monthly. Buys North American serial rights. Pays on acceptance. Will send a sample copy to a writer for 35¢. Query first. Submit material to Babette Ashby, Articles Editor, or to the editor of the respective department: Food, Child Care, Home Furnishings, Health, Beauty, Fashion, Creative Crafts, Equipment. Reports in 6 weeks. Enclose S.A.S.E. for reply to queries.
Nonfiction and Photos: Women's interest subjects such as family and social relationships, children, humor, physical and mental health, leisure-time activities, self-improvement, popular culture, travel. "We look for human stories, told in terms of people. We like them to be down-to-earth and unacademic." Length: 1,000 to 2,500 words. Pays $300 minimum. Photos purchased with mss; on assignment.
Fiction: "Fiction stories relating to women. Buys short stories, short-shorts, vignettes. Length: 2,000 to 2,500 words. Payment negotiable.
Fillers: Short women's service type or family oriented. Short humor, how-to, or inspirational. 500 words. Pays $100 and up.

FEMININE FITNESS, Suite 213, 16200 Ventura Blvd., Encino CA 91316. Editor: Bonnie Rogers. Established in 1973. For "women from 18 to 80 who are interested in living healthy, active and more beautiful lives." Monthly. Circulation: 200,000. Buys all rights but will reassign rights to author after publication. Buys about 50 mss a year. Payment on publication. Submit complete ms. Submit seasonal material 4 months in advance. Reports on material within 4 weeks. Will send free sample copy to writer on request. Will not consider photocopied submissions. Enclose S.A.S.E. for return of submissions.
Nonfiction and Photos: "Material with an emphasis on nutrition, diet, health, medicine, sports (women's), beauty, exercise, emotional health. (Not puff stuff, but no women's lib, either.) Stories should be bright, with high interest value. Remember that this is a magazine for women. the last thing we want to do is 'dull' them to death." Informational, how-to, personal experience, interview, profile, humor, think pieces, expose and new products. Length: "Depends on how the piece holds up. Most fall between 4 and 12 pages." Pays $50 to $250. "Payment is not based on length, but on quality and exclusivity." B&w and color photos. Pays $5 to $20 for b&w; $10 to $200 for color.
Poetry: Pays $10 to $25 for humorous verse.
Fillers: Scientific quizzes or humorous puzzles and jokes "related to our field." Pays $5 to $25 for humorous puzzles and jokes, "regular story rates" for scientific quizzes.

GIRL TALK, 380 Madison Ave., New York NY 10017. Editor: Berenice Connor Kennedy. For beauty salon patrons. Monthly. Circulation: approximately 4,000,000. Buys all rights "but will release rights for reprint in a book." Buys approximately 150 mss a year. Pays on publication. Submit seasonal material 3 months in advance. Reports "as soon as possible." Enclose S.A.S.E. for return of submissions.
Nonfiction: Social commentary, Hollywood gossip and interviews. 1,500 to 2,000 words. "Light, fast reading for the lady under the hairdryer." Buys interviews, humor. Length: 1,000 to 1,500 words. Pays 8¢ to 10¢ a word.
Fiction: Of general interest to lady in beauty salon. Confessions, mystery, humor. Length: 1,000 to 1,500 words. Pays 8¢ to 10¢ a word.
Poetry: Of interest to beauty salon patrons. Uses very little. Light verse only. Length: 4 to 8 lines. Pays $10.
Fillers: Short humor jokes. Pays 8¢ per word.

GLAMOUR, 350 Madison Ave., New York NY 10017. Editor-in-Chief: Ruth Whitney; Managing Editor: Phyllis Starr Wilson. Monthly. Query first. Enclose S.A.S.E.
Nonfiction and Fiction: Fashion, beauty, decorating and entertaining, travel are

staff-written, but there is a need for current interest articles; helpful, informative material, humorous or serious, on all aspects of a young woman's life (18 to 35 years old); medicine, mental health, travel; social, economic and emotional problems. Freelancers might study the magazine for style, approach. Length: 2,000 to 3,000 words. Short pieces bring $300 to $500. Pays $750 minimum for regular article.

GOOD HOUSEKEEPING, 959 Eighth Ave., New York NY 10019. Editor: Wade H. Nichols. Issued monthly. Query with an informal letter first. Outlines must pinpoint the idea specifically. Enclose S.A.S.E. with queries and submissions.
Nonfiction: Elizabeth Pope Frank, Articles Editor; Robert Liles, Features Editor; Timothy Mulligan, Editor for "The Better Way." Three categories for nonfiction: 1. General articles on subjects of topicality and consequence that concern readers in a meaningful way. This might be anything from a report on a current controversial problem or a vexing social issue to a dramatic personal narrative dealing with unusual experiences of average families. Most writers miss the boat because of lack of impact, warmth and dramatic appeal with which the average housewife can identify. Material must be accurate, honest, bright, comprehensive and imaginatively presented. Depth reporting is a must. Most articles run between 3,000 and 5,000 words. Rates range from $500 for short features to $5,000 for important articles. 2. Short features include small pieces on big celebrities. These miniatures never attempt to tell everything about anyone, but try to explore some single and interesting angle of the subject's life or point of view. Prefer subjects whose names are well-established. Also interested in short humorous essay. 3. Material for "The Better Way": This is the special information section of the magazine. Since it must fit a stylized format, they don't buy a finished article—just ideas and, on occasion, depth research on a subject of practical interest to housewives. Pays $25 to $50 for ideas and up to $350 for research assignments.
Fiction: Naome Lewis, Fiction Editor. Must portray problems which offer a strong element of reader identification. Characterization and thought content count more than plot, but also look for stories which contain practical and believable solutions offered in dramatic contexts. Average length is 4,000 words. Novelettes, book excerpts, condensations and serials also used. Payment starts at $1,000.
Poetry: Usually overstocked in light verse category. Address serious poetry (preferably short) to Leonhard Dowty. Pays $25 and up for verse on basis of $5 a line.
Fillers: Submit to Robert Liles. Humorous short-short prose for "Light Housekeeping" feature needed. Payment $25 to $100. Buys epigrams, short humor.

HADASSAH MAGAZINE, 65 E. 52nd St., New York NY 10022. Editorial Director: Mrs. Roslyn K. Brecher. Executive Editor: Jesse Zel Lurie. For members of Hadassah. Monthly, except July and August. Circulation: 325,000. Buys U.S. publication rights. Pays on publication. Reports in 6 weeks. Enclose S.A.S.E. for return of submissions.
Nonfiction: Primarily concerned with Israeli, the American Jewish community and American civic affairs. Length: 1,500 to 3,000 words. Pays 10¢ a word.
Photos: "We buy photos only to illustrate articles, with the exception of outstanding color from Israel which we use on our covers. We pay $100 and up for suitable color photo."
Fiction: Short stories with strong plots and positive Jewish values. Length: 3,000 words maximum. Pays 10¢ a word.

HARPER'S BAZAAR, 717 Fifth Ave., New York NY 10022. Editor-in-Chief: Anthony Mazzola. Senior News Editor: Barbara Goldsmith. For "women, late 20's and above, middle income and above, sophisticated and aware, with at least 2 years of college. Most combine families, professions, travel, often more than one home. They are active and concerned over what's happening in the arts, their communities, the world." Monthly. Rights purchased vary with author and material. May buy first North American serial rights. Buys 150 mss a year. Payment on publication. Will send free sample copy to a writer on request. Query first. Will consider photocopied submissions. Submit seasonal material two months in advance. Enclose S.A.S.E. for reply to queries.
Nonfiction and Photos: "We publish whatever is important to an intelligent modern woman. Fashion questions plus articles of general news interest—how the changing

world affects her family and herself; how she can affect it; how others are trying to do so; changing mores and life patterns. Query us first." Approach can be "light or serious, short-to-medium length pieces, newsy and controversial. Changes in our milieu, manners and cultural environment. More interested in hard news, journalistic reporting, insights into current events. Factual and light approaches to problems women face. We do not want any long articles, fiction, or poetry. We would like to see features on immediate news events, social problems, interviews and studies of vital personalities." Buys informational, how-to, interviews, profile, humor, think, expose, nostalgia, photo, travel, reviews of film, books, the arts, spot news, successful business operations, and new product articles. Length: 700 to 2,000 words. Pays $250 to $450. Send photo queries to Ruth Ansel, Art Director. Specifications and payment "to be discussed."

LADIES' HOME JOURNAL, 641 Lexington Ave., New York NY 10022. Editor: John Mack Carter. Issued monthly.
Nonfiction: "Articles that talk to readers as women, that deal with the accomplishments and feelings of real people, that aren't self-conscious about being emotional, that tell in 2,000 words a story so compelling that the reader would finish it even at 10,000 words. Send outlines to Richard Kaplan, Managing Editor or Mary Fiore, Articles Editor."
Fiction: Phyllis Levy, Fiction Editor. Short stories from 1,000 to 4,000 words—on life and love.
How To Break In: "The most practical thing I suggest to writers for breaking into the *Journal* is: Read the magazine. And that means page by page, piece by piece, cover to cover. And then—when you know it exactly—go it one better. Start to research and write your own article. I really can't think of anything more downright practical than that. So practical, nobody seems to do it."

LADY'S CIRCLE MAGAZINE, 21 West 26th St., New York NY 10010. Editor: Betty Etter. For housewives. Monthly. Buys all rights. Pays on publication. Will send a sample copy to a writer for 35¢. Query first with brief outline. Will consider photocopied submissions. Reporting time varies from 1 week to 3 months. Enclose S.A.S.E. for reply to queries.
Nonfiction: Articles, 2,500 to 3,000 words. Particularly likes first-person or as-told-to pieces about health and doing good. Also how housewives and mothers make money at home. Hobbies and crafts. Also articles on baby care, home management, gardening, as well as problems of the homemaker. Articles must be written on specific subjects and must be thoroughly researched and based on sound authority. Pays $125.
Photos: Pays $15 for good b&w photos accompanying articles.

MADEMOISELLE, 420 Lexington Ave., New York NY 10017. Editor-in-Chief: Edith Raymond Locke. Circulation: 698,000. Reports on submissions in 3 to 4 weeks. Buys first North American serial rights. Pays on acceptance. Directed to college-educated women between the ages of 18 to 25. Prefers written query plus samples of work, published or unpublished. Include S.A.S.E.
Nonfiction: Particular concentration on articles of interest to the intelligent young woman that concern the arts, education, careers, European travel, current sociological and political problems. Articles should be well-researched and of good quality. Prefers not to receive profile articles of individuals or personal reminiscences. Length: "Opinion" essay column, 1,300 words; articles, 1,500 to 6,000 words. Pays $300 for "Opinion" essay column; articles $350 to $850. Managing Editor: Mary Cantwell.
Photos: Commissioned work assigned according to needs. Photos of fashion, beauty, travel; career and college shots of interest to accompany articles. Payment ranges from no-charge to an agreed rate of payment per shot, job series, or page rate. Art Director: Roger W. Schoening. Buys all rights. Pays on publication for photos.
Fiction: High-quality fiction by both name writers and unknowns. Length: 2,500 to 6,500 words. Pays $300 and up. Uses short-shorts on occasion. "We are particularly interested in encouraging young talent, and with this aim in mind, we conduct a college fiction contest each year, open to men and women undergraduates. A $500 prize is awarded for each of the two winning stories which are published in our Au-

gust issue. However, our encouragement of unknown talent is not limited to college students or youth. We are not interested in formula stories, and subject matter need not be confined to a specific age or theme." Fiction Editor: Mrs. Ellen A. Stoianoff.
Poetry: Must be of very high literary quality, under 65 lines. Pays $25 minimum. Address ms to Mrs. Ellen A. Stoianoff.

McCALL'S, 230 Park Ave., New York NY 10017. Editor: Robert Stein. "Study recent issues." Monthly. Circulation: 7,500,000. Buys North American serial rights. Pays on acceptance. Query first. "All mss must be submitted on speculation and *McCall's* accepts no responsibilty for unsolicited mss." Reports in 4 to 6 weeks. Enclose S.A.S.E. for reply to queries.
Nonfiction: Miss Helen Markel, Editor. No subject of wide public or personal interest is out of bounds for *McCall's* so long as it is appropriately treated. The editors are seeking meaningful stories of personal experience. They are on the lookout for new research that will provide the basis for penetrating articles on the ethical, physical, material and social problems concerning readers. They are most receptive to humor and belles lettres. *McCall's* buys between 200 and 300 articles a year, many in the 1,000- to 1,500-word length. Miss Lisel Eisenheimer is Editor of Nonfiction Books from which *McCall's* frequently publishes excerpts. These are on subjects of interest to women: biography, memoirs, reportage, etc. Address queries for "Right Now" column to Natalie Gittelson. Subjects can be education, medicine, ecology, women doing interesting things, women's liberation, any timely subject. Length: 300 to 500 words. Payment is up to $300. The magazine is not in the market for new columns. Almost all features on food, household equipment and management, fashion, beauty, building and decorating are staff-written.
Fiction: Mrs. Helen DelMonte, Editor. "Again the editors would remind writers of the contemporary woman's taste and intelligence. Most of all, fiction can awaken a reader's sense of identity, deepen her understanding of herself and others, refresh her with a laugh at herself, etc. *McCall's* looks for stories which will have meaning for an adult reader of some literary sensitivity. *McCall's* principal interest is in short stories; but fiction of all lengths is considered." Length: about 4,000 words. Length for short-shorts: about 2,000 words. Payment begins at $1,250.

MD'S WIFE, 535 North Dearborn St., Chicago IL 60610. Editor: Mrs. J. Paul Sauvageot. "The official publication of the Woman's Auxiliary to the American Medical Association, Inc." 6 times a year. Buys first rights. Enclose S.A.S.E. for return of submissions.
Nonfiction and Photos: "Stories of doctors' wives in community action; 'better living' features for doctors' families; think pieces of medico-social subjects. Photos desired, both b&w and 4-color." Pays $100 to $150.

MODERN BRIDE, 1 Park Ave., New York NY 10016. Executive Editor: Cele G. Lalli. Bimonthly. Buys all rights. Pays on acceptance. Reports in 2 weeks. Enclose S.A.S.E. for return of submissions.
Nonfiction: Uses articles of about 2,000 words of interest to brides-to-be. "We prefer articles on etiquette, marriage, planning a home, and travel from honeymoon point of view. *Modern Bride* is divided into three sections: the first deals with wedding dresses; the second with home furnishings; the third with travel. We buy articles for all three; we edit everything, but don't rewrite without permission." Payment is about $150 and up.
Poetry: Buys some poetry pertaining to love and marriage. Pays $15 to $25 for average short poem.

MOTHER'S MANUAL, 176 Cleveland Drive, Croton-on-Hudson NY 10520. Editor: Beth Waterfall. Bimonthly. Buys all rights unless otherwise specified. Will send sample copy to a writer for 50¢. Payment on publication. Christmas issue deadline: June 1; Summer deadline: Jan. 1; Fall deadline: March 1. Reports on submissions in 6 weeks. Include S.A.S.E. with all mss and queries.
Nonfiction: Articles of broad interest to pregnant women, new mothers and mothers of children through age 6. Always interested in new research going on medically or in the fields of education, child psychology and child behavior in articles written by authorities; well-written articles by mothers who have something to say about family life, child rearing, working mothers, the role of the father. Authoritative material

in this field or work where research has been done. Not interested in first-person experiences on childbirth or stories that should be written by authorities in special fields and are not. Read the magazine first. Buys informational articles, how-to's, personal experience articles, interviews and think pieces. Length: 250 to 2,000 words. Pays $200 maximum.

MS. MAGAZINE, 370 Lexington Ave., New York NY 10024. Editor: Gloria Steinem. For "women predominantly; varying ages, backgrounds, but committed to exploring new life styles and changes in their roles and society." Established in 1972. Monthly. Circulation: over 350,000. Rights purchased vary with author and material; may buy first North American serial rights or second serial (reprint) rights. Pays on acceptance. Query first "with ideas and outlines and include samples of previous work." Will consider photocopied submissions. Submit seasonal material at least 3 months in advance. Reports in 2 to 3 weeks. Enclose S.A.S.E. for reply to queries.
Nonfiction: "Articles, features on the arts, women's minds, women's bodies that relate to exploring new life styles for women and changes in their roles and society. We are a how-to magazine—how a woman may gain control of her life. We are hoping to change the status quo—to treat women as human beings, and not to insult their personhood with down-putting editorializing or insensitive advertising. We give women permission to live their lives as unique people, not role players. We would like more input on what women are doing politically in their communities." Buys informational articles, how-to's, personal experience articles, interviews, profiles, inspirational articles, humor, historical articles, think articles, exposes, personal opinion pieces, photo articles, new product articles, coverage of successful business operations, and art, book, and film reviews. Length: 1,000 words minimum. Pays $100 to $500. Dept. Editor: Donna Handly.
Photos: Purchased with mss, without mss, or on assignment. Payment "depends on usage." Dept. Editor: Bea Feitler.
Fiction, Poetry and Fillers: "All material must relate to our editorial philosophy." Experimental fiction, erotica, fantasy, humorous, historical; condensed novels, serialized novels. Dept. Editor: Donna Handly. Traditional forms of poetry, blank verse, free verse, light verse, avant-garde forms. Dept. Editor: Ruth Sullivan. Acrostics, clippings, short humor used as filler material.

NATIONAL BUSINESS WOMAN, 2012 Massachusetts Ave. N.W., Washington DC 20036. Editor: Lola S. Tilden. For "all mature, educated, employed women." Established in 1919. 11 times a year. Buys all rights and second serial rights. Buys 10 or 12 mss a year. Payment on acceptance. Will send a sample copy to a writer for 35¢. Will consider photocopied submissions. Reports on rejected material immediately. Enclose S.A.S.E. for return of submissions.
Nonfiction: "Originality preferred. Written specifically for members of the National Federation of Business and Professional Women's Clubs, Inc. No fiction or poems." Buys informational, think, and successful business operations articles. Length: 1,000 to 1,200 words. Pays $10 to $35.

NEW WOMAN, P.O. Box 24202, Fort Lauderdale FL 33307. Associate Editor: Wendy Danforth. Query first essential; do not submit mss. For "thinking women of all ages, puberty through bifocals; beauty and brains concern them." Monthly. Buys all rights. Pays on publication. Enclose S.A.S.E. for reply to queries.
Nonfiction: "Everything of interest to the self-starting, self-actualizing, career-minded Renaissance woman. The style should be assured, with flair, humor, warmth, sparkle, wit; the outlook should be feminist but refined, and antitraditional sex roles. The status and image of women are particularly important to us. Our readers meet men on a parity basis; she's the new woman, he's the new man. No more interviews in question-and-answer format—we'd like more charm." Buys how-to's, interviews, profiles, personal experience articles, inspirational and think pieces, humor, coverage of successful business operations, exposes, new product articles, photo pieces, travel features, articles on "psychology, sexology, and politics." Seeks material for departments on "child-rearing; finance; the problems of separated, divorced, or widowed new women; new marriage styles." Length: 500 to 3,000 words. "Payment depends on article."

Photos: B&w contacts, color transparencies, 35mm color. Pays $150 for b&w, $250 to $300 for four-color.

NEWS LADY, *Chicago Daily News*, 401 N. Wabash, Chicago IL 60611. A column for women. Buys first North American rights. Pays on publication. Reports in 3 weeks, "sometimes longer." Enclose S.A.S.E. for return of submissions.
Nonfiction: Essays on topics of interest to women. "We prefer essays from women in the Daily News trading zone (Illinois, southern Wisconsin, northern Indiana), but we will accept particularly good essays from all over the U.S. Food, farm, garden, and pet essays are not especially liked, but we have made exceptions. We are trying to get essays with a greater degree of sophistication about women's lib, consumerism, and social problems. We're interested in humor, especially family humor. Please, no reporting or didactic essays." Length: 500 to 600 words. Pays $25 savings bond.

PARENTS' MAGAZINE, 52 Vanderbilt Ave., New York NY 10017. Editor: Genevieve Millet Landau. Monthly. Circulation: 2,150,000. Usually buys all rights; sometimes buys North American serial rights only. Pays on acceptance. Will send free sample copy to a writer on request. Query first. Reports on submissions in 3 weeks. Enclose S.A.S.E. for reply to queries.
Nonfiction: "We are interested in well-documented articles on the problems and success of preschool, school-age, and adolescent children—and their parents; good, practical guides to the routines of baby care; articles which offer professional insights into family and marriage relationships; reports of new trends and significant research findings in education and in mental and physical health; articles encouraging informed citizen action on matters of social concern. We prefer a warm, colloquial style of writing, one which avoids the extremes of either slanginess or technical jargon. Anecdotes and examples should be used to illustrate points which can then be summed up by straight exposition." Length: up to 2,500 words. Query about an article idea (enclosing an outline and sample openings) before submitting a completed ms. Query editor for special issues (September—Education, November—Health).
Fillers: Anecdotes for "Family Clinic," illustrative of parental problem solving with children and teenagers. Pays $10.
How To Break In: "For beginning writers we recommend that they study the magazine, think about articles they would like to see appear in it, and hopefully, article ideas will emerge, not only of interest to our readers, but to the writer as well."

REDBOOK MAGAZINE, 230 Park Ave., New York NY 10017. Issued monthly. Buys first North American rights. Reports in 2 to 3 weeks. Pays top rates, on acceptance. Enclose S.A.S.E.
Nonfiction: Robert J. Levin, Articles Editor. Narratives and exploratory factual pieces are always wanted; conditions which affect the magazine's readers, who are young married women in the 18- to 34-year-old group, and about which they can do something. Inspirational pieces are welcome if they are written from the point of view of an individual or family. Also interested in submissions for "Young Mother's Story" and "Young Woman's Story" features. "If you have had some experience in your family, social or marital life that you feel may be particularly interesting and helpful to other young mothers or young women, we would be interested in seeing your story. Please don't hesitate to send it because you think your spelling or punctuation may be a bit rusty; we don't judge these stories on the basis of technicalities and we do make minor editing changes. For each 1,000 to 2,000 words accepted for publication, we pay $500. Mss accompanied by a stamped, self-addressed envelope, must be signed (although name will be withheld on request), and mailed to: Young Mother's Story or Young Woman's Story, c/o Redbook Magazine. Stories do not have to be typed, but we appreciate it when they are legibly written." Length: articles, 3,500 to 4,500 words; short articles, 2,000 to 2,500 words.
Fiction: Mrs. Neal G. Thorpe, Fiction Editor. Uses a great variety of types of fiction, with contemporary stories appealing especially to women in demand. Short stories of 3,500 to 5,000 words are always needed. Also short-shorts of 1,400 to 1,600 words. Payment for short-shorts begins at $750, and at $1,000 for short stories.

SPHERE/THE BETTY CROCKER MAGAZINE, 625 N. Michigan Ave., Chicago IL 60611. Editor: Joan Leonard. Query first. Unsolicited mss not accepted.

TODAYS FAMILY, P.O. Box 31467, Dallas TX 75231. Editor: Sherry Gish. For "the middle class housewife and mother." Buys first North American serial rights. "No multiple submissions. Payment is on the 28th of the month of issue." Will send a sample copy to a writer for 25¢. Query first for nonfiction. "Include word count with submissions." Will not consider photocopied submissions. Reports "promptly." Enclose S.A.S.E. for response to queries and return of submissions.
Nonfiction and Photos: "All material in good taste for family reading: self-help, creative crafts, decorating, health, child rearing, family relations, and family fun. Fashion, beauty, needlecraft, travel, cooking, and home maintenance are staff-written." Length: maximum 2,000 words. Pays up to $50. Buys "I Faced a Problem and Solved It" articles. Length: maximum 3,000 words. Pays $25. Buys b&w glossies with ms.
Fiction: General family appeal. Length: "up to 3,000 words; shorter lengths preferred." Pays $50 maximum.

VOGUE, 420 Lexington Ave., New York NY 10017. Editor: Grace Mirabella. Issued monthly. For highly intelligent women. Enclose S.A.S.E. for return of submissions.
Nonfiction and Poetry: Uses articles and ideas for features, 2,000 to 2,500 words. Fashion articles are staff-written. Material must be of high literary quality, contain good information. Pays $300 and up, on acceptance. Kate Lloyd, Associate Editor. Very rarely publishes verse.

W, *Women's Wear Daily,* 7 East 12th St., New York NY 10003. Completely staff-written.

THE WOMAN, 235 Park Ave. S., New York NY 10003. Editor: Diana Lurvey. For "married or once-married women whose main interest is their families." Bimonthly. Buys all rights, "but we will sign away for book publication." Buys about 100 mss a year. Pays within 1 week of acceptance. Will send a sample copy to a writer for 50¢. No query required. Submit seasonal material 4 months in advance. Reports in 2 weeks. Enclose S.A.S.E. for return of submissions.
Nonfiction: Articles about family living, problems, medical information, household information and women's interests outside the home. Can be written informally or personally. "Be honest, be frank, be personal, be original. Yes, I know Johnny can't read. And no more anti-women's lib!" Buys how-to's, personal experience and inspirational pieces, interviews, profiles, exposes. Length: open. Pays $50 and up.

WOMAN'S DAY, 1515 Broadway, New York NY 10036. Editor: Geraldine Rhoads. Monthly. Circulation: over 7,800,000. Buys first and second North American serial rights. Pays on acceptance. Submit detailed queries first to Rebecca Greer, Articles Editor. Reports "as soon as possible." Enclose S.A.S.E. for reply to queries.
Nonfiction: Uses articles on all subjects of interest to women—marriage, family life, childrearing, education, homemaking, money management, travel, family health, and leisure activities. Also interested in fresh, dramatic narratives of women's lives and concerns. Length: from 500 to 3,500 words. Pays $350 up.
Fiction: Needs contemporary fiction of quality, genuine human interest romance and humor, in lengths between 1,500 and 3,000 words. Pays good rates. Dept. Editor: Eileen Herbert Jordan.
Fillers: Brief (500 to 1,000 words), factual articles on contemporary life, community projects, unusual activities are used—condensed, sprightly, and unbylined—in "What Goes On Here?" section. No set rate of payment. "Neighbors" column also pays $25 for each letter and $5 for each brief practical suggestion on homemaking or childrearing. Address to the editor of the appropriate section.
How To Break In: "The best way to start selling to our magazine is to write a short feature and submit it for our consideration."

WOMAN'S WORLD, 261 Fifth Ave., New York NY 10016. Editor-in-Chief: Diana Willis. For women: "Middle-American, over 25, to a great extent 'small town.' " Monthly. Circulation: 500,000. Buys first rights. Buys about 55 mss a year. Pays on publication. Will send a sample copy to a writer for 35¢. Submit seasonal material at least 6 months in advance. Reports in 12 weeks. Enclose S.A.S.E. for return of submissions.

Nonfiction and Photos: "Articles of interest to women—interesting personalities; developments of relevance to women, their families, their homes. Don't treat women only as consumers; don't talk down the them. Very interested in craft features, how-to-make items for home use. Must have step-by-step pictures accompanying story." Buys how-to's, interviews, profiles, humor, coverage of women's successful business operations, new product and travel articles. Length: 500 to 2,000 words. Pays $15 to $40. Photos purchased with mss. B&w glossies. Pays $2.50 each if used.

WOMEN IN BUSINESS, 9100 Ward Parkway, Kansas City MO 64114. Editor: Joanne H. Mordus. For "business women in various professional, technical, and service fields." Established in 1949. 9 times a year; combined issues in March/April, July/August, November/December. Special issues include citizenship issue (February) and travel issue (June). Buys about 30 mss a year. Pays on acceptance. Will send a sample copy to a writer on request. Write for copy of guidelines for writers. Query first or submit complete ms. Will consider photocopied submissions. Reports in 4 weeks. Enclose S.A.S.E. for return of submissions or reply to queries.

Nonfiction: "Subjects relating to all aspects of business; educational topics (retirement planning, how to handle your money), guides for working women; emphasis on new office techniques, products, careers, etc. All material is carefully developed to interest the working woman—all levels of business." Interested in material on "fashions for business women (fall and spring), how a woman can best advance in business, employment areas that offer financial benefits to women." Buys informational articles, how-to's, profiles, think pieces, travel articles, new product articles, and articles on merchandising techniques. Length: 1,500 words maximum. Pays 3¢ to 5¢ a word.

Photos: Purchased with mss, without mss; captions required. Uses 8x10 b&w glossies. Pays $20 for photos accompanying articles. Pays $35 for cover photo.

YOUR BABY (service section of *Modern Romances*), 1 Dag Hammarskjold Plaza, New York NY 10017. Buys all rights. Reports in 1 month. Enclose S.A.S.E.
Nonfiction: Uses warmly written, genuinely helpful articles of interest to mothers of children from birth to six years of age, dealing authoritatively with pregnancy problems, child health, child care and training. Editors recommend you study this market before trying to write for it. Lengths used vary from 1,200 to 1,500 words with payment on acceptance at flat rates of $100 and $125 for exceptional material. Submission should be addressed to Service Director, *Modern Romances*.

SPONSORED PUBLICATIONS

Association, Club, and Fraternal

The magazines that follow exist to publicize—to members, friends, and institutions—the ideals, objectives, projects, and activities of the sponsoring club or organization. Club-financed magazines that carry material not directly related to the group's activities (for example, Manage *magazine in the Management and Supervision Trade Journals) are classified by their subject matter in the Consumer, Farm, and Trade Journals sections of this book.*

AAA TEXAS DIVISION TEXAS MOTORIST, P.O. Box 1986, Houston TX 77001. Editor: Rick Timmons. Bimonthly. Circulation: 124,000. Pays on publication. Not copyrighted. Will send free sample copy to a writer on request. Enclose S.A.S.E. for return of submissions.
Nonfiction: Articles on travel, automotive, traffic safety. Deadlines are 25th of month preceding month of publication.

THE AMERICAN LEGION MAGAZINE, 1345 Ave. of Americas, New York NY 10019. Monthly. Circulation: 2.6 million. Reports on most submissions promptly; borderline decisions take time. Buys first North American serial rights. Pays on acceptance. Include phone number with ms. Enclose S.A.S.E. for ms return.
Nonfiction: Most articles written on order. Some over transom. Writers may query for subject interest, but no assignments to writers unknown to editors. Subjects include national and international affairs, American history, reader self-interest, great military campaigns and battles, major aspects of American life, etc. Length: Average of 15 to 20 double-spaced typewritten pages. Pay varies widely with length and worth of work. Research assignments for some skilled reporters. Proven pros only.
Photos: Chiefly on assignment. Very rarely an over-transom photo story or photo clicks.
Poetry and Humor: Limited market for short, light verse, and short, humorous anecdotes, epigrams, jokes, etc. No serious verse. Taboos: old material; bad taste; amateurish work. Short humorous verse: $2.50 per line, minimum $10. Epigrams: $10. Anecdotes: $20.

AWAY, 1047 Commonwealth Ave., Boston MA 02215. Editor: Gerard J. Gagnon. For "members of the ALA Auto & Travel Club, interested in their autos and in travel. Ages range from approximately 20 to 65. They live primarily in New England." Slanted to seasons. Quarterly. Circulation: 230,000. Buys first serial rights. Pays on acceptance. Will send a sample copy to a writer on request. "Although a query is not mandatory, it may be advisable for some articles." Submit seasonal material 6 months in advance. Reports "as soon as possible." Enclose S.A.S.E. for return of submissions or reply to queries.
Nonfiction and Photos: Articles on "travel, tourist attractions, safety, history, etc., preferably with a New England angle. Also, car care tips and related subjects." Would like a "positive feel to all pieces, but not the Chamber of Commerce approach." Buys both general seasonal travel and specific travel articles, for example, "Cape Cod's Winter Season" and "Basketball's National Shrine"; travel related articles (photo hints, etc.); outdoor activities; for example, gravestone rubbing, snow sculpturing; historical articles linked to places to visit; humor with a point, photo essays. "Would like to see more nonseasonally oriented material. Most material now submitted seems suitable only for our summer issue. Avoid pieces on hunting

and about New England's most publicized attractions, such as Old Sturbridge Village and Mystic Seaport." Length: 800 to 2,500 words, "preferably 1,200 to 1,500." Pays approximately 10¢ per word. Photos purchased with mss; with captions only. B&w glossies. Pays $5 to $10 per b&w photo, payment on publication based upon which photos are used. Seasonally oriented cover photos pay higher; payment negotiable.

Fiction: Humor. "Should have a point and, perhaps, a New England flavor, angle or slant." Length: 500 to 800 words. Pays $50 to $80.

CHEVRON USA, P.O. Box 6227, San Jose CA 95150. Editor: Gary A. Williams. For members of the Chevron Travel Club. Quarterly. Buys North American serial rights. Pays within 60 days of acceptance. Will send a sample copy to a writer on request. Query first. Reports in 2 weeks. Enclose S.A.S.E. for reply to queries.

Nonfiction: Travel, particularly auto-oriented in the western U.S. Heavy on facts, dates, seasons, specific instructions on things to do. Each piece should have specific slant—tied to season, event, unusual aspect. In general, we like smaller subjects well-covered rather than the sketchy overall story. Length: 500 to 1,500 words. Pays 15¢ a word and up. "But we'd rather settle on a package price."

Photos: Purchased with mss. Subject matter same as nonfiction. No empty scenics. Virtually all photos must have people in them, doing things or driving or touring or hiking. Top quality 35mm. Prefers 2¼ square or 4x5. Pays $125 full page for color, minimum $50. For b&w pays $50 full page, $35 minimum.

Fillers: Anecdotal material. Must be about travel, personal experiences. Length: about 200 to 250 words. Pays $25 each.

DISCOVERY MAGAZINE, Allstate Plaza, Northbrook IL 60062. Editor: David L. Watt. For motor club members; mobile families with above average income. "All issues pegged to season." Established in 1961. Quarterly. Circulation: 740,000. Buys first North American serial rights. Buys 40 mss a year. Payment on acceptance. Will send free sample copy to writer on request. Write for copy of guidelines for writers. Query first. Submit seasonal material 8 to 12 months in advance. Reports in 3 weeks. Enclose S.A.S.E. for reply to queries or return of submissions.

Nonfiction and Photos: "Primarily travel subjects. Also automotive and safety. First-person narrative approach for travel articles. Short pieces on restaurants must include recipes from the establishment." Length: 1,000 to 2,500 words. Payment varies. Photos purchased with accompanying mss; captions required. Photos also purchased on assignment.

Fillers: True, humorous travel anecdotes. Length: 50 to 150 words. Pays $10.

THE ELKS MAGAZINE, 425 W. Diversey Parkway, Chicago IL 60614. Editor: D.J. Herda. For Elks and their families: "middle-aged, rural Americans." Monthly. Circulation: about 1,500,000. Buys first serial rights. Buys approximately 50 mss a year from freelancers. Pays on acceptance. Returns rejected material within 1 week. Acknowledges acceptance of material in 1 month. Always query first. Will not consider photocopied submissions. Submit seasonal material about 4 months in advance. Will send free sample copy to a writer on request. Enclose S.A.S.E. with queries and for return of submissions.

Nonfiction and Photos: "Anything of general interest to the family man or small businessman. Lead articles must be timely, topical, and of greatest possible interest to average American, well-researched, accurately written, and gripping." Length: about 3,000 words. "We also need top-quality supportive articles, lighter in vein on all sports and general-interest topics." Length: about 2,000 words. Pays 10¢ a word and up. Buys b&w photographs as package with mss. Holds one-time reproduction rights. Photos returned only when requested.

Fiction: "We'll consider suitable fiction only when submitted by proven pros or agents." Pays 10¢ a word and up on spec, more on assignment.

FUTURE MAGAZINE, Box 7, Boulder Park, Tulsa OK 74102. Editor: John Hartman. "Our features are now written primarily by assignment only."

THE KEY, 144 W. 12 Ave., Denver CO 80204. Editor: Lou Thomas. For "the general public, over 18 years old, interested in community activities." 9 times a year. Circulation: 12,000. Buys all rights. Buys about 50 mss a year. Pays on publication.

Will send a sample copy to a writer for 50¢. No query required. "Manuscripts should be double-spaced, with 55-character line." Reports in 3 weeks. Enclose S A S E. for return of submissions.

Nonfiction and Photos: Wants "news summary materials of events and activities happening (or that happened) around the nation. Reports on government, culture, crime, law, fashion, economy, etc. All materials must provide multiple points of view." Seeks freelance book, movie, and concert reviews. Buys interviews, profiles, spot news, historical and think pieces, exposes, new product articles, and photo features. Length: 2,000 to 4,000 words. Pays 1¢ to 3¢ per word. B&w glossies and color transparencies purchased with mss. Pays $5 to $20.

Fillers: Newsbreaks, clippings, letters to the editor. Length: 500 to 1,500 words. Pays $5 to $15.

THE KIWANIS MAGAZINE, 101 E. Erie St., Chicago IL 60611. Executive Editor: Dennis Moore. For business and professional men. Published 10 times a year. Buys first North American serial rights. Pays on acceptance. Will send free sample copy on request. Query first. Reports on submission in 2 weeks. Enclose S.A.S.E. with submissions and queries.

Nonfiction and Photos: Articles about social and civic betterment, business, education, religion, domestic affairs, etc. Emphasis on objectivity, intelligent analysis and thorough research of contemporary problems. Concise writing, absence of cliches, and impartial presentation of controversy required. Length: 2,000 words to 4,000. Pays to $400. Also articles dealing with American and Canadian history. Length: 2,000 to 3,000 words. "No fiction, personal essays, fillers, or verse of any kind. A light or humorous approach welcomed where subject is appropriate and all other requirements are observed. Detailed queries can save work and submission time. We sometimes accept photos submitted with mss, but we do not pay extra for them; they are considered part of the price of the ms. Our rate for a ms with good photos is higher than for one without."

THE LION, York and Cermak Roads, Oak Brook IL 60521. Senior Editor: Dennis Brennan. For North American members of Lions clubs, who by their membership "demonstrate a deep interest in community improvement and service to the less fortunate through volunteer effort." Issued 11 times a year. Circulation: 640,000. Buys all rights. "Do not submit unsolicited articles. All articles are purchased after a query has been submitted and the writer has been instructed on the type of article wanted. A sloppy query will be rejected, no matter how good the story idea may be. We insist on quality." Will send free sample copy to a writer on request. Reports on submissions in 10 days. Pays on acceptance. Submit detailed query. Enclose S.A.S.E.

Nonfiction: Articles in the fields of community betterment and self-improvement. Especially in the market for feature-length stories on unusual and impressive Lions club community service projects. "Except for such taboos as those against partisan politics and liquor in a favorable light, there's really no limitation on acceptable topics—as long as they have appeal and value for an international readership of service-minded men. Prefer solid, anecdotal writing which shows the evidence of thorough research. Lions are positivists, and stories for *The Lion* should reflect this, with emphasis on solutions to dilemmas rather than on the dilemmas themselves." Material must appeal to men of many creeds and political beliefs; must be of general, universal interest; most rejects are on subjects too local or provincial. Length: 1,500 to 2,000 words for articles. Always looking for humor articles. Length: up to 100 words. Pays 10¢ per word and up.

Photos: Purchased with mss. Pays $10 each. Pays up to $300 for photo features suitable for spread layouts on impressive and unusual Lions Club community service projects (such as photo story on Lion-supported school for retarded children; Lion truck-caravan of furniture, etc., for needy American Indians). B&w used almost always; color on very rare occasions.

THE LOOKOUT, Seaman's Church Institute, 15 State St., New York NY 10004. Editor: Carlyle Windley. "Basic purpose is to engender and sustain interest in the work of the Institute and to encourage monetary gifts in support of its philanthropic work among seamen." Monthly, except combined February-March and July-August issues. Buys first North American rights and pays on publication. Reports in one month. Will send free sample copy on request. Query first. Study publication before submitting. Include S.A.S.E. with submissions and queries.

Nonfiction: "We seek a variety of fact pieces relating to both the old and modern merchant marine. We seldom use a first-person adventure piece and never fiction. We are not interested in commercial or pleasure fishing, yachting or pleasure boating." Factual yet exciting adventures, sea and ship oddities used. Length: about 1,000 words with one or two photos. Pays to $40 for well-written piece. If extensive rewriting needed, will pay less. Does not use technical pieces; most readers are lay persons, not seafarers.

Photos: Photos must accompany mss and are purchased with mss. 8x10 b&w glossies. Pays to $30 for cover photo. Vertical format. None depicting fishing vessels, power boats or yachts. Pays lesser amounts for miscellaneous photos used elsewhere in the book.

Poetry and Verse: "A small amount is used; it must have a connection with seafaring, but we do not wish verse about the sea per se or the flora and fauna." Pays $5.

MAIN SHEET, Detroit Yacht Club, Belle Isle, Detroit MI 48207. Editor: Jack Genard. Published by Detroit Publishing Consultants for "members of the world's largest (membership) yacht club. Median age about 45, but members range from 18 to 81. Mostly college graduates and affluent, solid citizens." Established in 1914. Monthly. Circulation: 3,000. Not copyrighted. Buys 2 or 3 mss a year. Pays on publication. Will send a sample copy to a writer for $1. Submit complete ms. Will not consider photocopied submissions. Submit seasonal material 3 months in advance of issue date. Reports in 2 to 4 weeks. Enclose S.A.S.E. for return of submissions.

Nonfiction and Photos: "A few humorous shorts, a few yachting related articles, but most of the material is generated from within the membership. We discourage freelance submissions because we buy very few, but we will give attention to writers." Buys humor and photo features. Length: 500 to 1,500 words. Pays $15 to $50. Photos purchased with mss; captions required. For 4x5 to 8x10 b&w glossies, pays $5 to $15. For 8x10 color prints of 2¼x2¼ or larger transparencies, pays $25 up. "Photos should be yachting scenes."

MINNESOTA AAA MOTORIST, Minnesota State Automobile Association, 7 Travelers Trail, Burnsville MN 55378. Managing Editor: Ron D. Johnson. For "AAA members in Minnesota. Most are middle-aged, have college education, above-average salaries and most of them are professional people, educated farmers, and businessmen and women and are interested in travel." Special Minnesota vacation issue in February. Established in 1957. Monthly. Circulation: 230,000. Buys first North American serial rights. Buys 12 mss a year. Pays on acceptance. Will send a sample copy to a writer on request. Write for copy of guidelines for writers. Submit complete mss. Reports in 3 weeks. Enclose S.A.S.E. for return of submissions.

Nonfiction: Articles on domestic and foreign travel, motoring, car care; material of interest to car owners. "We have our own auto consultant for articles on automobile safety." Wants "well-written, interesting articles on places throughout the world, where our readers would like to go. We receive too many freelance articles on Florida." Submissions should "be readable and entertain and educate our readers." Buys how-to's, personal experience articles, interviews, humor, historical and travel articles, photo essays. Length: 800 to 1,500 words. Pays $150 minimum.

Photos: Good b&w, 8x10, glossy photos purchased with mss. Pays $10 to $15 per photo.

MOTORLAND, 150 Van Ness Ave., San Francisco CA 94101. Editor: William C. Ellis. Publication of California State Automobile Association. Bimonthly. Circulation: 900,000. Buys all rights. Pays on acceptance. Will send a free sample copy to a writer on request. Will send a copy of writer's guidelines on request. Always query first. Reports in 30 days. Enclose S.A.S.E. with all submissions and queries.

Nonfiction and Photos: Buys only professional quality, well-researched, tightly written articles on foreign and domestic travel, special attractions and events, (particularly in the West), recreational activities and the automobile. "Editorial emphasis is on the Western states." Length: 500 to 3,500 words. Pays 15¢ to 30¢ a word. B&w photos or color transparencies, 35mm or larger, considered after query. "Photographers invited to submit subject lists." Pays $20 to $150 per photo.

NATIONAL 4-H NEWS, 59 East Van Buren St., Chicago IL 60605. Editor: Gordon F. Bieberle. For "Young to middle-aged adults and older teens who lead 4-H clubs, most with high school, many with college education, whose primary reason for reading us is their interest in working with kids in informal youth education projects, ranging from aerospace to swimming, and almost anything in between." Monthly. Circulation: 100,000. Buys first serial rights. Buys about 48 mss a year. Pays on acceptance. Will send a sample copy to a writer on request. Write for copy of guidelines for writers. Query first. "We are very specialized, and unless a writer has been published in our magazine before, he more than likely doesn't have a clue to what we can use. When query comes about a specific topic, we often can suggest angles that make it usable." Submit seasonal material 6 months to 1 year in advance. Reports in 3 weeks.
Nonfiction: "Education and child psychology from authorities, written in light, easy-to-read fashion; how-to-do-it pieces about genuinely new and interesting crafts of any kind; almost anything that tells about kids having fun and learning outside the classroom, including how they became interested, most effective programs, etc. Speak directly to our reader (you) without preaching. Tell him in a conversational text how he might work better with kids to help them have fun and learn at the same time. Use lots of genuine examples (although names and dates not important) to illustrate points. Use lots of contractions when applicable. Write in a concise, interesting way—our readers have other jobs and not a lot of time to spend with us. Will not print stories on 'How this 4-H club made good' or about state or county fairs or winners in them, etc." Length: 1,700 to 3,400 words. Payment "up to $100, depending on quality and accompanying photos or illustrations."
Photos: Purchased with mss; with captions only. "Photos must be genuinely candid, of excellent technical quality and preferably shot 'available light' or in that style; must show young people or adults and young people having fun learning something. Closeups generally best."

NATIONAL MOTORIST, 65 Battery Street, San Francisco CA 94111. Editor: Jim Donaldson. For California motorists who are members of the National Automobile Club. Every other month starting from January 1. Usually buys first serial rights. Query first or submit complete mss. Enclose S.A.S.E. for reply to queries or return of submissions.
Nonfiction: Stories about anything that would be of interest to the average motorist who lives in California and does most of his motoring along the Pacific Slope and some of it in the other western states. Stories about car care, techniques for motor travel, interesting places to visit, people and events in western history that help illuminate the current scene; interesting outdoor activities and hobbies in which the reader can directly or vicariously participate; wildlife, hunting, fishing; all are possible stories. Prefers writing in the second or third person. Length: around 500 words or around 1,100 words. Pays 10¢ per word minimum.
Photos: Buys pictures submitted with mss; doesn't buy pictures submitted with captions only. Likes 8x10 b&w glossies, sharp, crisp, and dramatic. Uses some color. Pays $15 and up per b&w picture; $25 and up per color transparency.

OHIO MOTORIST, 6000 S. Marginal Rd., Cleveland OH 44103. Editor: A.K. Murway, Jr. For AAA members in 5 northeast Ohio counties. Established in 1909. Monthly. Circulation: 152,000. Buys one-time publication rights. Buys 20 mss a year. Payment on acceptance. Will send free sample copy to writer on request. Submit only complete ms. Submit seasonal material 2 months prior to season. Reports in 2 weeks. Enclose S.A.S.E. for return of submissions.
Nonfiction and Photos: "Travel, including foreign; automotive, highways, etc.; motoring laws and safety. No particular approach beyond brevity and newspaper journalistic treatment. Articles for travel seasons." Length: 2,000 words maximum. Pays $25 to $75 per article including b&w photos. 8x10 b&w photos preferred. Purchased with accompanying mss. Captions required. Pays $8 to $20 for singles, although "rarely" purchases singles.
Poetry: Light verse. Length: 4 to 6 lines. Pays $6 to $8.

THE OPTIMIST MAGAZINE, Optimist International, 4494 Lindell Blvd., St. Louis MO 63108. Editor: Gary Adamson. For "business and professional men engaged in voluntary service." Monthly. Buys all rights. Pays on acceptance. Will send

free sample copy to writer on request. Study publication. Query first. Reports on submissions in 10 days. Enclose S.A.S.E. for reply to queries.
Nonfiction and Photos: "Articles and photo stories about significant community-serving activity of Optimist Clubs, articles (fully documented) to stimulate thinking toward positive solutions to problems confronting the United States and Canada in the decade of the 70's. Articles oriented to Canadian readers particularly desired. Intelligent objective style necessary, suitable for general consumption. Likes strong lead, sustained interest, accuracy." Length: 800 words. Pays up to $100. Good action photographs should accompany ms. Buys photos with ms or with captions. Pays $5 to $10.

PORTS O' CALL, P.O. Box 530, Santa Rosa CA 95402. Editor: William A. Breniman. Newsbook of the Society of Wireless Pioneers. Society members are mostly early-day wireless "brass-pounders" who sent code signals from ships or manned shore stations handling wireless or radio traffic. Twice yearly. Not copyrighted. Payment on acceptance. Query suggested. Editorial deadlines are May 15 and October 15. Reports on submissions at once. Enclose S.A.S.E. for reply to queries or return of mss.
Nonfiction: Articles about early-day wireless as used in ship-shore and high power operation. Early-day ships, records, etc. "Writers should remember that our members have gone to sea for years and would be critical of material that is not authentic. We are not interested in any aspect of ham radio. We are interested in authentic articles dealing with ships (since about 1910)." Oddities about the sea and weather as it affects shipping. Length: 500 to 2,000 words. Pays 1¢ per word.
Photos: Purchased with mss. Unusual shots of sea or ships. Wireless pioneers. Prefers b&w, "4x5 would be the most preferable size but it really doesn't make too much difference as long as the photos are sharp and the subject interests us." Fine if veloxed, but not necessary. Payment ranges from $2.50 to $10 "according to our appraisal of our interest." Ship photos of various nations, including postcard size, if clear, 25¢ to $1 each. Photo Editor: Dexter S. Bartlett.
Poetry: Ships, marine slant (not military), shipping, weather, wireless. No restrictions. Pays $1 or $2.50 each.

THE PUNCH MAGAZINE, 222 N. Rampart St., New Orleans LA 70112. Editor: J.C. Williams. Publication of New Orleans Athletic Club. For businessmen. Monthly. Circulation: 10,000. Not copyrighted. Buys 6 to 12 mss a year. Pays on publication. Will send a sample copy to a writer for $1. No query required. Will not consider photocopied submissions. Submit seasonal material at least 1 month in advance. Reports in 2 months. Enclose S.A.S.E. for return of submissions.
Nonfiction and Photos: "Articles should be copy that would be interesting to athletic club members, such as articles on the Olympics; national sports events, especially handball; travel, Mardi Gras, how-to's, think pieces, and physical fitness programs." Length: 2 typewritten pages maximum. Pays $5 to $25. B&w glossies purchased with mss.
Fillers: Puzzles, jokes, short humor.

THE ROTARIAN, 1600 Ridge Ave., Evanston IL 60201. Editor: Karl K. Krueger. For Rotarian business and professional men and their families; for schools, libraries, hospitals, etc. Monthly. Circulation: 451,000. Usually buys all rights. Payment on acceptance. Will send free sample copy to writer on request. Query preferred. Reports in 2 to 4 weeks. Enclose S.A.S.E. with queries and submissions.
Nonfiction: "The field for freelance articles is in the general interest category. These run the gamut from inspirational guidelines for daily living to such weighty concerns as world hunger, peace, and control of environment. Articles which in some way help Rotarians help other people. An article may increase a reader's understanding of world affairs, thereby making him a better world citizen. It may educate him in civic matters, thus helping him improve his town. It may help him to become a better employer, or a better human being. We carry debates and symposiums, but we are careful to show more than one point of view. We present arguments for higher levels of politics and solutions to moral and spiritual problems. In short, the rationale of the organization is one of hope and encouragement and belief in the power of individuals talking together." Length: 2,000 words maximum. Payment varies.

Photos: Purchased with mss or with captions only. Prefers 2¼ square or larger color transparencies, but will consider 35mm also. B&w singles and small assortments. Vertical shots preferred to horizontal. Scenes of international interest. Color cover.
Poetry and Fillers: "Presently overstocked." Pays $1 a line. Pays $10 for brief poems. "We occasionally buy short humor pieces."

SCOUTING MAGAZINE, North Brunswick NJ 08902. Editor: Walter Babson. For "men and women who are leaders and committeemen supporting Cub Scout Packs, Scout Troops, and Explorer Posts." Bimonthly. Circulation: 1,500,000. Buys about 25 mss a year from freelancers. Pays on acceptance. Will send a free sample copy to a writer on request. Write for a copy of guidelines for writers. Query first with outline of proposed article. Submit seasonal material 6 months in advance. Reports in 2 weeks. Enclose S.A.S.E. for reply to queries.
Nonfiction: "Scouting Magazine is for adults. We need scouting success stories, American heritage articles, and information on children, including their educational interests, games, etc." Length: 500 to 1,000 words (some up to 2,000 on assignment). Pays $25 to $75 a magazine page (more for longer assigned stories) for how-to, profiles, inspirational, humor, historical, and photo articles. For the "Worth Retelling" column, we also need "information, humor, and human interest about Scouts and their leaders." Pay is $5 an item.
Photos: Purchased with ms or with captions only. Buys first rights. Payment is $5 to $100 for b&w glossies, color transparencies, or 35mm color. Photo Editor: Brian Payne.
Poetry: "We seldom buy poetry, except on assignment." Executive Editor: Dick Pryce.

STEERING WHEEL, 406 E. 11th St., P.O. Box 1169, Austin TX 78767. Editor: Mrs. Kellyn Murray. Published by the Texas Motor Transportation Association for "transportation management, high school libraries, state agencies, doctors, legislators, mayors, county judges, newspapers." Established in 1936. Monthly. Circulation: 5,800. Not copyrighted. Buys about 11 mss a year. Pays on publication. Will send a sample copy to a writer on request. Write for copy of guidelines for writers. Query first. Will consider photocopied submissions. Submit seasonal material 2 months in advance of issue date. Enclose S.A.S.E. for reply to queries.
Nonfiction and Photos: "General interest, travel, transportation, government agencies in Texas, economic articles relating to industry. Articles should be clear-cut, to-the-point, and keyed to transportation." Buys interviews, profiles, historical articles, travel articles, spot news, and coverage of successful business operations. Length: 1,200 to 1,800 words. Pays $20 to $50. Photos purchased with mss; captions required.

V.F.W. MAGAZINE, Broadway at 34th, Kansas City MO 64111. Publisher: John L. Smith. Pays on acceptance. Enclose S.A.S.E. for ms return.
Nonfiction: "Timely and factual articles on any subject of national interest or concern—including features which will aid persons in coping with recurrent problems of daily living. How-to features, preferably illustrated with photographs; stories on personalities and popular activities, such as sports, all desired. Historical pieces liberally sprinkled with action will always be considered. Combat stories in well-defined plot structures based upon personal experience and interest are welcomed, as are factual accounts of military actions of consequence. Length: 1,200-1,500 words. Well-stocked with feature material at this time but always on the lookout for material of interest to V.F.W. members." Pays 5¢ to 10¢ per word.
Photos: For pictures with articles, pays $5 each.

WATERSPORT, 534 N. Broadway, Milwaukee WI 53202. Editor: A. W. Limburg. For "family boatmen who like to cruise, waterski and fish." Sponsored by the Boat Owners Council of America, 401 N. Michigan, Chicago IL 60611. Established in 1966. Quarterly. Circulation: 10,000. Buys first North American serial rights. Buys 12 to 15 mss a year. Payment on acceptance "or as close to acceptance as possible." Will send free sample copy to writer on request. Write for copy of guidelines for writers. Query first. Will not consider photocopied submissions. Submit seasonal material 3 months in advance. Reports on material in 3 weeks. Enclose S.A.S.E. for reply to queries.

Nonfiction and Photos: "Articles on boating; preferably with outboards, but also canoeing, sailing and bigger power. Also features about interesting people (may be oddballs) and events in boating. Not much lone wolf adventure boating. Have people in the story doing and experiencing and enjoying. Don't want itinerary reports, or stories about the great boating opportunities of one specific lake, unless there's a great story peg." Length: 250 to 2,200 words. Pays $50 to $400. 8x10 b&w glossy photos purchased with or without mss or on assignment. Pays $10 to $25; "package price negotiated." Any size color. Pays $35 to $100.

WISCONSIN AAA MOTOR NEWS, 433 West Washington Ave., Madison WI 53703. Editor: Hugh P. (Mickey) McLinden. Aimed at audience of domestic and foreign motorist-travelers. Monthly. Circulation: 204,000. Buys all rights. Pays on publication. Reports immediately. Include S.A.S.E. for return of submissions.
Nonfiction and Photos: Domestic and foreign travel; motoring, safety, highways, new motoring products. Length: 500 words maximum. Photos purchased with mss or captions only. B&w glossy.

WOODMEN OF THE WORLD MAGAZINE, 1700 Farnam St., Omaha NE 68102. Editor: Leland A. Larson. Published by Woodmen of the World Life Insurance Society for "people of all ages in all walks of life. We have both adult and children readers from all types of American families." Established in 1891. Monthly. Circulation: 390,000. Not copyrighted. Buys "about 20" mss a year. Pays on acceptance. Will send a sample copy to a writer on request. Query first or submit complete ms. Submit seasonal material 3 months in advance of issue date. Reports in 5 weeks. Enclose S.A.S.E. for reply to queries or return of submissions.
Nonfiction: "General interest articles which appeal to the American family—travel, history, art, new products, how-to-do-it, sports, hobbies, food, home decorating, family expenses, etc. Because we are a fraternal benefit society operating under a lodge system, we often carry stories on how a number of people can enjoy social or recreational activities as a group. No special approach required. We want more 'consumer type' articles. We do use seasonal material." Buys how-to's, personal experience articles, inspirational articles, humor, historical articles, think pieces, nostalgia, photo articles. Length: 600 to 2,000 words. Pays $10 minimum, 2¢ a word depending on word count.
Photos: Purchased with or without mss; captions optional "but suggested." Uses 8x10 glossies, 4x5 color transparencies ("and possibly down to 35mm"). Payment "depends on use." For b&w photos, pays $20 for cover, $10 for first photo used inside and $5 "if more than 1 bought with story. Color prices vary according to use and quality."
Fiction: Humorous and historical short stories. Length: 600 to 2,000 words. Pays "$10 or 2¢ a word, depending on count."

College, University, and Alumni

The following institutionally sponsored magazines are intended for students, graduates, and friends of the institution. Publications for college students in general are found in the Teen and Young Adult category.

ALCALDE, University of Texas Alumni Magazine, P.O. Box 7278. University Station, Austin TX 78712. Managing Editor: Mrs. Pat Maguire. For persons who have attended the University of Texas: "educated, intelligent men and women ranging in age from 21 to 90, living in every state in the U.S. and 100 countries of the world." Bimonthly. Circulation: 24,000. Buys all rights. Buys 5 to 10 mss a year from freelancers. Pays on acceptance. Will send a sample copy to a writer for 50¢. Query first. "We do not even look at an article unless we have seen a query first." Submit seasonal material at least 3 months in advance. Enclose S.A.S.E. for reply to queries.
Nonfiction and Photos: Everything in this publication "is slanted toward the interests of the University of Texas graduates." Wants articles only. "The writer must know the University of Texas and its alumni intimately. We will consider any query

about any subject that might interest our specialized audience." Length: to 2,000 words. Pays according to the content and research involved in writing article, usually about 4¢ per published word. Photos purchased with mss. Pays $5 and up for b&w glossies.

LOMA LINDA UNIVERSITY SCHOOL OF MEDICINE, ALUMNI JOURNAL OF, 1832 Michigan Ave., Los Angeles CA 90255. Editor: Audrey du Chemin. For alumni of the School of Medicine 1900-1972, and their families. Special issues include Convention issue, January and February; Commencement issue, June; Mission issue, July-August; Directory issue, November. Established in 1931. Published 8 times yearly. Circulation: 5,000. Not copyrighted. Buys "a few" mss a year from freelancers. Pays on publication. Will send a sample copy to a writer on request. Query first. Submit special material 3 months in advance of issue date. Returns rejected material in 1 month. Enclose S.A.S.E. for reply to queries.
Nonfiction and Photos: Uses "mainly articles on graduates of the school, but uses some material on medical history. Information on what's new in medicine." Length: 1,000 to 5,000 words. Pays $10 to $50. Buys photos with accepted ms. B&w glossies with captions only. Pays $3 to $10.

NCSU ALUMNI NEWS, North Carolina State University, Box 5876, Raleigh NC 27607. Editor: Doug Unwin. For North Carolina State University alumni, "graduates from a school that offers liberal arts, but is primarily an engineering and technical school." Bimonthly. Circulation: 9,000. Not copyrighted. Pays on acceptance. Will send a sample copy to a writer on request. Query first. Returns rejected material in 2 weeks. Acknowledges acceptance immediately. Enclose S.A.S.E. for reply to queries.
Nonfiction: Articles "must be about an NCSU alumnus—can be a feature or a technical article on alumnus' work as it relates to people. We are looking for good writing." Buys interviews, profiles, stories on successful business operations as they pertain to alumni. Length: 300 to 2,000 words. Pays $25 to $125.
Photos: Purchased with mss. "Must illustrate story on an alumnus." Also purchased with captions only. Pays $7.50 to $25 for b&w glossies.

UNIVERSITY OF MANITOBA, THE ALUMNI JOURNAL OF, Room 139, University Center, Winnipeg, Manitoba, R3T 2N2, Canada. Editor: Mrs. Susan Currie. For graduates of the University of Manitoba, "age varies from 21 to 86 years." Quarterly. Circulation: 40,000. Buys first rights. Buys 10 to 12 mss a year from freelancers. Pays on publication. Will send a sample copy to a writer on request. Query first. Reports "immediately." Enclose S.A.S.E. for reply to queries.
Nonfiction and Photos: Wants articles on "Canadian education, in-depth student-community relations, human interest." Mss should be "objective, researched, interesting, informative, and educational." No articles on drugs. Buys interviews, profiles, historical articles, think pieces, and exposes. Length: 1,500 to 2,500 words. Pays $35 to $55. Purchases photos with ms. Pays $1 to $5.

WISCONSIN ALUMNUS, 650 N. Lake St., Madison WI 53706. Editor: Thomas H. Murphy. For graduates of the University of Wisconsin who are dues-paying members of the Alumni Association. "Heaviest concentration on ages 30 to 60." 10 times a year. Circulation: 30,000. Not copyrighted. Buys 12 to 15 mss a year from freelancers. Pays on publication. Will send a sample copy to a writer on request. Query first. Submit seasonal material 2 to 3 months in advance. Reports in 2 months. Enclose S.A.S.E. for reply to queries.
Nonfiction: Buys "features on the authoritative views" of UW faculty or alumni "on virtually any subject of public interest (social problems, law, medicine, etc.), features of personal benefit (childbearing, education trends, drugs, etc.) based on interviews with UW authorities or alumni, or biographies of interesting alumni. Currently we use student-authored views on campus issues or national issues affecting them as UW students on a regular basis." Articles must "peg around UW in some way." No "nostalgia." Length: 500 words minimum. Pays $10 to $50.
Photos: Purchased with ms. Buys b&w glossies with captions only. Pays $5 to $10 each; $35 to $50 for photo essay.

Customers'

The company-sponsored publications below are often called "external" house magazines because they circulate to customers. (As against the "internal" ones that go to employees and salesmen.) They exist to promote the company image, products, or services to potential buyers. (For example, Friends publishes material to encourage the use of Chevrolet automobiles; the Duncan Register educates readers about the uses of electricity.) A few magazines in the Employees' and Dealers' classifications also use company-product material.

Company magazines that exist to cultivate good employee relations are classified in the Employees' category. Those that focus on helping dealers, franchisers, and agents run their businesses are listed in the Dealers' category. Company publications that carry general interest material that doesn't tie in with the company or its interests (for example, The American Way) will be found in the General Interest classification.

ACF HORIZONS, ACF Industries, 750 Third Ave., New York NY 10017. Editor: Orlan J. Fox. For "employees and the public." Quarterly. Circulation: 15,000. Pays on publication. Will send a sample copy to a writer on request. Query first. Reports in 1 month. Enclose S.A.S.E. for reply to queries.
Nonfiction, Photos, and Fillers: "Articles related to the products and operations of the divisions of ACF Industries: railroad equipment, automotive fuel systems, valves and fittings. Material must have ACF tie-in." Length: "the shorter the better." Pays $5 minimum. Buys 8x10 single-weight b&w glossies.

AMERICAN YOUTH, 17390 W. Eight Mile Road, Southfield MI 48075. Editor: Robert M. Girling. For "a national audience of 16- to 18-year-old readers. *AY* is sent to new drivers by General Motors Corporation." Hopefuls should write for sample copy and spec sheets. Query first required. Allow 4 to 6 weeks for a report. Enclose S.A.S.E. for reply to queries.
Nonfiction and Photos: "We will accept queries from writers and writer-photographers who can produce, but chances for new writers are slim; most assignments are carried out by writers known to us." Length: about 1,000 words. Payment is $150 to $600. "We must have top quality professional pictures. We can make separate arrangements with professional photographers for exclusive rights. We must have releases (signed by father if subject is a minor) for every person pictured, named, or quoted."

BAUSCH & LOMB FOCUS, 619 St. Paul St., Rochester NY 14602. Editor: R.I. Fiester. For "high school and college science teachers and professors, laboratory and engineering personnel in industry and government, hospitals, school libraries, and Bausch and Lomb dealers and salesmen." Established in 1929. Semiannual. Circulation: 70,000. Buys all rights. Pays "within 2 weeks following acceptance." Will send a sample copy to a writer on request. Write for copy of guidelines for writers. Reports in 2 weeks. Enclose S.A.S.E. for return of submissions.
Nonfiction and Photos: "We are primarily interested in articles dealing with new or unusual uses of scientific optical equipment, new approaches to teaching, or interesting adaptations and accessories devised for use with such equipment. Obviously, we prefer that the story be concerned with Bausch and Lomb equipment, but we will not reject an article simply because it makes a reference to the use of competitive optical equipment. Serious consideration will be given to any article that advances the cause of science in any area—in schools, industry, hospitals, research labs, etc.—whether or not scientific optical equipment is used (although, obviously, that is preferred). How-to stories describing the construction of scientific optical equipment by students are very much to our liking. Such articles should be accompanied by drawings and photographs so that another student can easily duplicate the equipment from information contained in the article. We do not buy highly technical articles that would be understandable to only a small audience or articles delineating unsupported scientific theories. No articles that 'run down' competitive optical equipment, even if unnamed." Length: 1,500 to 3,000 words. Pays "3¢ per word as published. We do pay more for articles, depending on the type of material,

ease of bringing it to finished form, etc." Photos purchased with mss. "A picture story is particularly appealing to us." Uses b&w for inside use, color for cover "if it illustrates a point about an inside article." Pays $4 minimum per photo. "When we give the author permission to have photos taken, we pay the photographer's fee, including the cost of prints, without further reimbursement to the author."

THE BEAVER, 77 Main St., Winnipeg, MB, Canada. Editor: Helen Burgess. Publication of Hudson's Bay Company for "mature students and adults." Established in 1920. Quarterly. Circulation: 37,000. Buys all rights. Buys about 30 mss a year. Pays on acceptance. Will send a sample copy to a writer on request. "Content is quite specialized; suggest query first." Submit seasonal material at least 6 months in advance. Reports in 2 weeks. Enclose S.A.E and International Reply Coupons for reply to queries.
Nonfiction and Photos: "Well-illustrated, authentic articles on life in the Arctic and areas of early Hudson's Bay Company activities; historical and present-day fur trade, nature subjects, Indians, and Eskimos. Accurate information must be presented in a readable way. No more articles on Arctic canoe trips." Buys informational articles, personal experience pieces, profiles, and historical articles. Length: 1,000 to 4,000 words. Pays minimum 5¢ a word. Photos purchased with mss; captions required. Pays minimum $5 for 8x10 b&w glossies. Pays minimum $10 for 35mm or 4¼x4¼ color slides.

BESCO NEWS, 6303 Kenjoy Dr., Louisville KY 40214. Editor: O.J. Schnieders. For retail bakery owners, managers; wholesale bakery production and management; dairy and food processing plant managers and buyers; some management personnel in food service, institutional and grocery industries. Publication of Bessire & Company, Inc. Established in 1939. Bimonthly. Circulation: 6,600. Not copyrighted. Payment on publication. Will send free sample copy to writer on request. Query first. Reports on material within 2 months. Enclose S.A.S.E. for reply to queries.
Nonfiction and Photos: "Articles on outstanding installations of equipment lines (particularly those distributed by Bessire & Co., Inc.) in food/dairy/baking plants; advantages of new equipment, savings in space and production costs, etc. Objective tone; how establishment solved a problem with new equipment, or achieved a much more efficient and economical operation." Length: open. Pays $12 for 500 words or half page, $25 per page. B&w photos purchased with accompanying ms. Captions required.
Fillers: Brief merchandising idea employed by bakery, ice cream store or convenience food mart; new, different. Pays $5.

BIG, P.O. Box 13208, Phoenix AZ 85002. Editor: Frederick H. Kling. Published by Goodyear Tire and Rubber Company for "owners, operators, and distributors of big earth-moving equipment—the type used in construction of roads, highways, dams, and in mining. Stories on assignment only." Not copyrighted.
Nonfiction and Photos: "Freelance writers and photographers are invited to send in their qualifications for assignment of articles on construction projects, contractors, equipment distributors in their territory. Payment from $250 to $300, plus expenses, for complete editorial-photographic coverage. Additional payment for color, if used."
How To Break In: "Send query letter for assignments, stating qualifications."

BUSINESS ON WHEELS, P.O. Box 13208, Phoenix AZ 85002. Editor: Frederick H. Kling. "External house organ of Goodyear Tire and Rubber Company for distribution to owners and operators of truck fleets, both common carrier trucking systems and trucks used in connection with businesses of various types." Quarterly. Not copyrighted. Pays on acceptance. "Stories on assignment only."
Nonfiction and Photos: "Freelance writers and photographers (especially writer-photographer teams or individuals) are invited to send in their qualifications for assignment of articles on truck-fleet operators in their territory. Payment from $250 to $300, plus expenses, for complete editorial-photographic coverage, additional for color, if used."
How To Break In: "Send query letter for assignment, stating qualifications."

CAL MAGAZINE, 3737 West 127th St., Chicago IL 60658. Editor: T.G. Baldaccini. Coe Laboratories, manufacturers of dental supplies. For dentists, dental assistants and dental technicians. Established in 1935. Monthly. Circulation: 50,000. Buys all rights, but will reassign to author after publication. Pays on acceptance. Will send free sample copy on request. Submit complete ms only. Reports in 6 weeks. Enclose S.A.S.E. for return of submissions.
Nonfiction and Photos: Articles pertaining to or about dentists and dentistry; accomplishments of dentists in other fields. History, art, humor, adventure, unusual achievements, successful business operations, new products, merchandising techniques and technical. Length: 1,500 to 2,000 words. Pays $25 to $100. B&w photos only, 8x10 or 5x7 glossy photos purchased with mss or captions only. Pays $25 to $50.
Fiction: "Related in some way to dentistry," Length: 1,500 to 2,000 words. Pays $25 to $100.
Poetry: Light verse.
Fillers: "Related to dentistry." Puzzles, short humor. Pays $3 minimum.

THE CARAVANNER, 600 S. Commonwealth Ave., Los Angeles CA 90005. Address Frank Quattrocchi, public relations. For "owners and others interested in the Airstream travel trailer." Established in 1954. Bimonthly. Circulation: over 400,000. Not copyrighted. Buys about 10 mss a year. Pays on acceptance. Will send a sample copy to a writer on request. Write for copy of guidelines for writers. Query first for nonfiction. Will consider photocopied submissions. Submit seasonal material 3 months in advance. Reports in 6 weeks. Enclose S.A.S.E. for reply to queries or return of submissions.
Nonfiction and Photos: "Pleasureable, beneficial, or interesting uses of the Airstream make of travel trailer. Cannot use downbeat stories. Mention of Airstream should be casual, unobtrusive. Consider us for a second, slightly rewritten version of story submitted elsewhere when the Airstream travel trailer is involved. Be sure you have cleared rights to submit. We can sometimes help authors place stories concerning Airstreams in other publications. Fancy writing isn't important or even helpful but careful attention to writing basics—spelling, grammar—is. We try to encourage new writers by giving helpful advice—no printed rejection slips. Articles must be illustrated with at least 3 photos, 1 of Airstream. We're especially interested in seasonal stories—particularly about the winter months." Buys informational articles, personal experience articles, interviews, nostalgia, travel pieces, and spot news. Length: 500 to 1,500 words. Pays $50 to $100. Photos purchased with mss, "sometimes" without mss; captions required. 5x7 b&w glossies and larger. Pays $5 to $10, "or by arrangement in advance."

CHANNELS OF BUSINESS COMMUNICATION, Northwestern Bell Telephone Co., 100 S. 19th St., Omaha NE 68102. Editor: G.T. Metcalf. For "top level executives." Quarterly. Circulation: 26,000. Buys first North American serial rights. Query first. Reports in 1 month. Enclose S.A.S.E. for reply to queries.
Nonfiction: "Articles on new developments and techniques in business communications, such as WATS, data transmission, time-shared computers, industrial television, etc. Also occasional general interest features on sports, hobbies, personalities, events, and points of interest in Iowa, Minnesota, Nebraska, North Dakota, and South Dakota. Material is drawn almost exclusively from this five-state area. Writers who do not either live or travel frequently in that part of the country have small chance of coming up with the type of material we seek. Writing must be good and tight." Length: 500 to 1,000 words. Pays $100 minimum.
Fillers: "Short material appropriate to format." Pays $10 minimum.

THE COMPASS, Mobil Sales and Supply Corp., 150 E. 42nd St., New York NY 10017. Editor: K.V.W. Lawrence. For "international marine interest." Established in 1920. Quarterly. Not copyrighted. Pays on acceptance. Query first. Will consider photocopied submissions. Reports in 1 week. Enclose S.A.S.E. for reply to queries.
Nonfiction and Photos: "Sea-type yarns on various marine or maritime subjects, with particular emphasis on history and origin." Length: 200 to 4,000 words. Pays $150 to $300. Photos purchased with mss; "must be on marine subjects." B&w glossies, any size; color, 2¼ x 2¼ or larger. Pays $10 for b&w, $50 for color.

Fiction: "Sea stories, particularly about windship days." Length: "short." Pays $150.

CONTINENTAL MAGAZINE, Ford Motor Company, The American Rd., Dearborn MI 48127. Editorial Director: Robert M. Hodesh. For "owners of luxury cars in the U.S." Quarterly. Circulation: 700,000. Buys first North American serial rights. Pays on acceptance. Will send a sample copy to a writer on request. Query first. Reports in 2 weeks. Enclose S.A.S.E.
Nonfiction: "The editorial idea is 'how the reader can spend money,' and every article is based on this. Our readers are not extremely wealthy, but in the $20,000 to $50,000 class. We presume sophistication and cultivated tastes on the part of our readers. The articles should be of service to the well-to-do—suggestions on buying art, trends in home furnishings, travel, cuisine, shopping, sports. Articles must be of top quality and have genuine news value." Length: 1,500 words. Pays 25¢ a word minimum "after final editing."

CORVETTE NEWS, 465 W. Milwaukee, Detroit MI 48202. For Corvette owners in the U.S. and 48 foreign countries. Publication of Chevrolet Division, General Motors Corporation. Established in 1958. Bimonthly. Circulation: 140,000. Buys all rights. All materials published become the property of Chevrolet Division, General Motors Corporation. Buys 36 to 40 mss a year. Payment on acceptance. Will send free sample copy to writer on request. Write for copy of editorial guidelines for writers. Query first. Will not consider photocopied submissions. Deadline for October/November issue: April 1; December/January: June 1; February/March: August 1; April/May: October 1; June/July: December 1; August/September: February 1. Reports on material in 2 to 3 weeks. Enclose S.A.S.E. for reply to queries.
Nonfiction and Photos: "Articles must be of interest to Corvette owners and enthusiasts. Subjects may be Corvette Club activities, unusual uses for Corvettes, 'Vettes in unusual situations or places; customizing. Also profiles of interesting owners, travels in a Corvette, hobbies involving the use of a 'Vette. Technical articles pertaining to any phase of Corvette maintenance, alteration or repair are desired. These must show expert know-how and be readily understood by less technical readers. Quality of writing and depth of research are vital. A light touch or humorous approach welcome where appropriate." Length: 800 to 2,400 words. Pays $50 to $500. Payment for either color or b&w photos included in story payment; "can't use prints; must have transparencies or negatives." Pays additional fee for cover shot (usually 2¼x2¼).

DUNCAN REGISTER, Duncan Electric Co., Box 180, Lafayette IN 47902. For "public utility industry," customers of Duncan Electric Co. Quarterly. Not copyrighted. Pays on acceptance. "Address queries to the Editor." Enclose S.A.S.E. for reply to queries and return of submissions.
Photos: "Scenic photos only, suitable for a magazine cover." 4x5 vertical or 2¼x2¼ color transparencies. Pays $35 to $45.

DU PONT MAGAZINE, Du Pont Company, Advertising Dept., Wilmington DE 19898. Editor: Jack D. Hunter. For "business and industrial executives." Bimonthly. Buys all rights. Pays on acceptance. Query first. "We urge authors and photographers to study the publication before submitting material." Enclose S.A.S.E. for reply to queries or return of submissions.
Nonfiction and Photos: "Articles are almost always staff-written, but freelance pieces of exceptional merit might be purchased. Stories must be researched and developed in depth, describing interesting and significant uses of Du Pont products. They must be entirely objective, free of puffery and ad-type gushing. Our primary purpose is to offer broad-base support for the general sales of Du Pont products. In doing so, Du Pont Company is portrayed as a creative, innovative, forward-looking organization. All articles must be product-oriented, written in an objective, nonpromotional style, and fully approved by both Du Pont product sales departments and outside firms." Length: 2,000 words maximum. Payment negotiable. Photos purchased with mss; b&w and color, 2¼x2¼ and up. "Must be top quality and illustrative of points made in ms." Must be accompanied by model release where pertinent.

THE ENTHUSIAST, 3700 W. Juneau, Milwaukee WI 53208. Editor: T. C. Bolfert. Published by Harley-Davidson Motor Co., Inc. for "motorcycle riders of all ages, education, and professions." Established in 1920. Monthly. Circulation: 115,000. Not copyrighted. Pays on publication. Will send a sample copy to a writer on request. Write for copy of guidelines for writers. Query first or submit complete ms. Will consider photocopied submissions. Submit seasonal material 2 months in advance. Reports in 2 to 4 weeks. Enclose S.A.S.E. for reply to queries or return of submissions.

Nonfiction and Photos: "Stories on motorcycling or snowmobiling—humor, technical, racing, touring, adventures, competitive events. All articles should feature Harley-Davidson products and not mention competitive products. We do not want stories concerning sex, violence, or anything harmful to the image of motorcycling. We use travel stories featuring Harley-Davidson motorcycles, which must be illustrated with good quality photos of the motorcycle and travelers with scenic background taken on the trip. Also needed are stories of off-road usage, e.g., scrambles, racing, motocross, trail riding, or any other unusual usage. We use snowmobile stories in fall and winter." Buys informational articles, how-to's, personal experience articles, interviews, profiles, inspirational pieces, humor, historical articles, photo features, travel articles, and technical articles. Length: 3,000 words. Pays 5¢ "per published word, or as previously agreed upon." Photos purchased with mss and without mss; captions optional. Uses "quality b&w or color 4x5 prints or larger." Pays $7.50 to $15.

Fiction: "Good short stories with the image of clean motorcycling fun. No black leather jacket emphasis." Buys adventure and humorous stories. Length: 3,000 words maximum. Pays 5¢ "per published word, or as previously agreed upon."

Fillers: Jokes, short humor. Length: open. Pays $15.

ESSO AIR WORLD, Esso International Co., Div. of Exxon Corp., 1251 Avenue of the Americas, New York NY 10020. Editor: E.A.C. Wren. For world-wide audience of technical and semitechnical aviation readers. Bimonthly. Buys reprint rights. Payment on publication. Query first. Reports "quickly". Enclose S.A.S.E.

Nonfiction and Photos: Uses articles on aviation in action, world-wide; especially the offbeat aviation operation; technical articles. Style should be "unsensational, Good 'international' English, informative, accurate." Length 300 to 3,000 words. Must be accompanied with good photos. Pays about 5¢ a word. Photos must be of good quality, interesting subject, striking composition, and adequately captioned.

FORD TIMES, Ford Motor Company, The American Road, Dearborn MI 48121. Managing Editor: Hal Butler. "Family magazine designed to attract all ages." Monthly. Circulation: 1,600,000. Buys first serial rights. Buys about 125 mss a year. Pays on acceptance. Will send a sample copy to a writer on request. Write for copy of guidelines for writers. Query first. Submit seasonal material 6 months in advance. Reports in 2 to 4 weeks. Enclose S.A.S.E. for reply to queries and return of submissions.

Nonfiction, Fiction, and Photos: "Almost anything relating to American life, both past and present, that is in good taste and leans toward the cheerful and optimistic. Topics include motor travel, sports, fashion, where and what to eat along the road, vacation ideas, reminiscence, big cities and small towns, the arts, Americana, nostalgia, the outdoors. We strive to be colorful, lively and engaging. We are particularly attracted to material that presents humor, anecdote, first-person discourse, intelligent observation and, in all cases, superior writing. We are committed to originality and try as much as possible to avoid subjects that have appeared in other publications and in our own. However, a fresh point of view and/or exceptionally literary ability with respect to an old subject will be welcomed." Length: 1,500 words maximum. Pays $250 and up for full-length stories. "We prefer to have a suitable ms in hand before considering photos or illustration. Speculative submission of good quality color transparencies and b&w photos is welcomed. We want bright, lively photos showing people in happy circumstances. Writers may send snapshots, postcards, brochures, etc., if they wish."

FORD TRUCK TIMES, 420 Lexington Ave., New York NY 10017. Editor: Warren Weith. For "truck owners." Quarterly. Circulation: over 3 million. Not copyrighted.

Pays on publication. Will send a sample copy to a writer on request. Query preferable. Will consider photocopied submissions. Enclose S.A.S.F. for reply to queries or return of submissions,

Nonfiction and Photos: "General interest articles (sports, adventure, recreation, hobby) with a Ford truck tie-in; success stories about people who employ Ford trucks in connection with truck operation and ownership; new products information of particular value to this audience; unusual uses of Ford trucks; truck body modifications (customizer innovations) relating to Ford trucks; truck-connected business promotion ideas; general information of a lively nature which would concern truck operators (such as safety, taxes, depreciation)." Length: 500 to 1,500 words, or "what it takes to tell the story. Do not pad." Pays $300 to $500, "depending on quality of photos." Prefers 35mm, 2¼x2¼ or larger color transparencies. "The cover photo is usually selected from photos illustrating one of the features of a given issue." For cover photo, pays $100 maximum.

FRIENDS MAGAZINE, Ceco Publishing Co., 5-107 General Motors Building, Detroit MI 48202. Editor: Alexander Suczek. Publication of Chevrolet Motor Division. For customers, general public. Monthly. Circulation: 2,000,000. Rights negotiable. Pays on acceptance; additional payment for extra pages on publication. Will send a sample copy to a writer on request. Write for copy of guidelines for writers. Query first. Submit seasonal material 6 months in advance. Reports in 1 week. Enclose S.A.S.E. for reply to queries and return of submissions

Nonfiction and Photos: "Subjects of interest to our readers include travel, unusual activities, interesting and famous personalities, special newsworthy events, food, sports, and unusual or creative forms of recreation. Contributors are advised not to submit material that follows a well-worn trail or that has been published in similar vein in other national magazines. A story should have an element of sequence or continuity in its development. A travel story for example, would picture not only the colorful scenery of an area but would suggest recreational activities and accommodations that a motoring visitor could expect to find. We use primarily the picture-caption-text treatment for presenting features, with either b&w or color photos. The quality and the style of the photography is always of the utmost importance. Get the whole story on film. The pictures should be able to communicate with a minimum of explanation. At all times, strive to supplement the basic coverage with artistic and visual variations. No photographic assignment for *Friends* can be considered complete unless some daringly different visual approaches, technical or artistic, are used in the process of securing the story. We require a signed release form for everybody who can be identified in a photo and/or whose name is mentioned, and we prefer our release forms to be used. Rate of payment for stories is $75 per page for b&w and $125 per page for color for the first-time rights, $125 per page (plus expenses and material) for b&w and $150 per page (plus expenses and material) for color for exclusive rights. We pay $400 for a cover on assignment, $300 for a stock picture used on the cover, and $200 for a cover pulled from a story. We always look for possible covers in a color story."

GOODYEAR ORBIT MAGAZINE, 1144 E. Market St., Akron OH 44316. Editor: Thomas S. Palmer, Jr. Published by Goodyear International Corp. for "government officials, industry leaders, universities, school libraries, and news media throughout the world." Monthly. Circulation: 35,000. Not copyrighted. Buys 30 to 40 mss a year. Pays on acceptance. Write for copy of guidelines for writers. "Type mss 60 characters wide." No query required. Will consider sharp and clear photocopied submissions. Reports in 6 to 8 weeks. Enclose S.A.S.E. for return of submissions.

Nonfiction and Photos: "Non-Americanized stories about interesting people, events, and things. Story locale: outside the North American continent. No travelogues. We use simply, concisely written human interest stories about specific subjects, or personality sketches about interesting people. Each ms must contain a Goodyear mention as a logical part of the story, either in the central theme or in reference to a Goodyear person or facility. Third-person articles, referring to living persons, are an effective device. First-person articles are acceptable if subtly done." Length: 1,100 to 2,200 words. Pays $125 to $350. "Mss should be accompanied by sharp, clear color transparencies (4x5 or 35mm) preferably, and/or 8x10 b&w glossies containing elements that identify with the locale of the story."

GOULDS PUMPS INDUSTRIAL NEWS, 240 Fall St., Seneca Falls NY 13148. Editor: D.P. Beehler. Published by Goulds Pumps, Inc. for "industrial engineers, maintenance people, designers, purchasing agents for chemical process, paper, marine, mining, utility, municipal industries." Established in 1937. Bimonthly. Circulation: 15,000. Not copyrighted. Write for copy of guidelines for writers. Query first. Enclose S.A.S.E. for reply to queries and return of submissions.
Nonfiction and Photos: "Case histories, industrial pump related human interest: old replaces new, solves the problem, out-of-the-ordinary application, assisting in scientific breakthrough, used in state-of-the art service, etc." Buys humor, historical articles, coverage of successful business operations, and technical articles. Length: maximum 700 words. Payment open. Photos purchased with or without mss.

HOBART WELDWORLD, Hobart Brothers Co., Troy OH 45273. Editor: Daniel Lea. For "men and women with engineering degrees or technical education who are practicing a technical profession related to welding fabrication or who have moved into manufacturing management posts." Established in 1941. Quarterly. Circulation: 100,000. Not copyrighted. Buys "a few" mss a year. Pays on publication. Will send a sample copy to a writer on request. Query first or submit complete ms for nonfiction. Will consider photocopied submissions. Reports in 1 month. Enclose S.A.S.E. for reply to queries or return of submissions.
Nonfiction and Photos: "Technical articles on arc welding applications. The writer should submit items only about exotic or unusual applications, give full technical information, and describe the benefits of equipment or process for the application as compared with other welding methods. Give figures, if possible. Unless a specific product benefit is involved, we worry about the application and let the product references come as they may. We are one of the two largest manufacturers of welding equipment in the world. We're interested in coverage of big construction projects." Length: 300 to 1,000 words. Pays $10 minimum. Photos purchased with mss; captions required. Buys color negatives or transparencies, "which remain the property of the photographer." Pays $7.50 each.

ILLINOIS BELL MAGAZINE, 30-B, 225 W. Randolph, Chicago IL 60606. Editor: Warren E. Logelin. 6 times a year. Not copyrighted. Pays on acceptance. Query first. Enclose S.A.S.E.
Nonfiction: "Freelance material bought only on assignment." Pays $150 minimum.

IMPERIAL OIL REVIEW, 111 St. Clair Ave. W., Toronto Ont. M5W IK3, Canada. Editor: James Knight. Bimonthly. Buys all rights. Pays on publication. Will send a sample copy to a writer on request. Query first. Reports in 1 week. Enclose S.A.E. and International Reply Coupons for reply to queries.
Nonfiction: "Subject matter is general, but we like material that can be tied in to the oil industry. Articles specifically about the oil industry are generally staff-written. Material must be Canadian." Length: 2,500 words maximum. Pays $300 minimum.

INSPECTION NEWS, P.O. Box 4081, Atlanta GA 30302. Editor: H.A. McQuade. For "management employees of most American corporations, especially insurance companies. This includes Canada and Mexico. Pass-along readership involves sub-management and non-management people in these firms. Distributed by Retail Credit Co." Quarterly. Circulation: 135,000. Not copyrighted; "we allow customer publications free reprint privileges. Author free to negotiate fee independently, however." Buys 3 to 5 mss a year. Pays on acceptance. Will send a sample copy to a writer on request. Query first: "present idea in paragraph outline form. Accepted queries should result in authors' submitting doublespaced copy, typed 33 to 35 characters to the line, 25 lines to the page." Reports in 2 to 3 weeks. Enclose S.A.S.E.
Nonfiction and Photos: "Insurance related articles—new trends, challenges, and problems facing underwriters, actuaries, claim men, executives, and agents; articles of general interest in a wide range of subjects—the quality of life, ecology, drug and alcohol related subjects, safe driving, law enforcement, and insurance-related Americana; inspirational articles to help managers and executives do their jobs better. Write with our audience in mind. Only articles of the highest quality will be considered. Especially interested in material written by insurance underwriters, executives, college instructors, and college professors on previously unpublished or updated facets of our area of interest. More than 90% of our readers are customers

of Retail Credit or its various affiliates, and they expect to see articles that help them know and understand the business information business." Buys inspirational articles, think pieces about insurance industry needs for business information services, etc. Length: 1,000 to 2,000 words. Pays 1¢ to 2¢ a word, "depending on quality and importance of material, but not less than $25." B&w glossies relating to theme of article purchased with mss; 5x7 or 8x10. Pays $5 to $15.

KENDALL SPORTS TRAIL, Sports Division of Kendall Company, 20 Walnut St., Wellesley Hills MA 02181. Editor: J.S. O'Neill. For "high school and college athletic directors, coaches, trainers, team physicians and student trainers, amateur and youth league coaches, pro team trainers, sporting goods buyers and dealers." Bimonthly. Circulation: 40,000. Not copyrighted. Pays on acceptance. Will send a sample copy to a writer on request. Query first. Submit with 1 carbon copy. Will consider photocopied submissions. Deadlines are November 1 (January-February issue), January 1 (March-April issue), March 1 (May-June issue), July 1 (September-October issue), September 1 (November-December issue). Reports in 1 month. Enclose S.A.S.E. for reply to queries and return of submissions.
Nonfiction: "Subject matter includes all phases of athletic department and sports management, including game and personnel management, equipment purchasing and maintenance, athletic department finance and budget administration, athletic injury management and sports medicine, legal aspects of athletic administration, coaching psychology, sociology of sports, sports sciences, and current problems in coaching and athletic department administration." Length: 2,500 words maximum. Pays 5¢ a word.
Photos: "Photos to illustrate features on all aspects of school athletics administration. School sports action scenes. Photos of exemplary athletic training room plants and of training room techniques. Prefer dramatic verticals, but we can fit equally dramatic horizontals into our layouts. No girlie stuff. No controversial personalities. No long-haired athletes." B&w glossies, 8x10 or 5x7; color transparencies, 4x5, 35mm or 70mm. Pays $5 to $25 a photo for b&w; $50 to $70 a photo for color.

KUHLMAN KURRENTS, Kuhlman Corporation, P.O. Box 288, Birmingham MI 48012. For "utility engineers and users of utility-type residential and industrial transformers." Quarterly. Circulation: 3,500. Buys all rights. Buys 4 to 8 mss a year. Pays on publication. Query first with outline of article. Submit seasonal material 3 months in advance. Enclose S.A.S.E. for reply to queries and return of submissions.
Nonfiction and Photos: "Engineering articles of interest to utility personnel. Writers should advise editor of utility or electrical engineering background." Length: roughly 6 to 7 pages including photos. Payment: $150 "flat rate." Photos purchased with mss.

THE LUFKIN LINE, Lufkin Industries, Inc., P.O. Box 849, Lufkin TX 75901. Editor: Miss Virginia R. Allen. For men in oil and commercial and marine gear industries; readers mostly degreed engineers. Each issue devoted to different areas where division offices located; that is, West Coast, Canada, Mid-Continent, Rocky Mountain, Texas, Gulf Coast, International. Established in 1924. Quarterly. Circulation: 12,000. Not copyrighted. Buys 4 to 8 mss a year. Payment on acceptance. Will send free sample copy to writer on request. Write for copy of guidelines for writers. Query first for travel articles. Will consider photocopied submissions. Submit seasonal material 3 to 4 months in advance. Reports in 1 month. Enclose S.A.S.E. with queries and submissions.
Nonfiction and Photos: "Travel articles. Subjects dealing with western U.S., Canada, and Gulf Coast areas." Length: 1,000 to 1,200 words. Pays $50 per ms with illustrating photos. Photos purchased with or without mss. Captions required. "Seasonal only, for inside front cover; payment of $7.50." B&w and colorphotos to illustrate travel articles. 8x10 vertical b&w; color transparencies and prints.

THE MILKPAIL, H.P. Hood Inc., 500 Rutherford Ave., Boston MA 02129. For "dairy farmers, agricultural leaders, university extension services, and others interested in New England dairy farming." Quarterly. Not copyrighted. Pays on publication. Will send a sample copy to a writer on request. Reports in 1 month. Enclose S.A.S.E. for return of submissions.

Nonfiction and Photos: "Dairy farms and operations." Length: 800 to 900 words. Pays $10 to $20. Photos purchased with mss or with captions only; 4x5 or larger b&w glossies. Pays $5 to $10.

NEW HOLLAND NEWS, Sperry New Holland Division of Sperry Rand, New Holland PA 17557. Editor: Michael A. Balas. For "an agricultural audience, particularly farmers." 10 times a year. Buys all rights. Pays on acceptance. Will send a sample copy to a writer on request. Query first. Will not consider photocopied submissions. Reports in 2 weeks. Enclose S.A.S.E. for reply to queries and return of submissions.
Nonfiction and Photos: "Articles telling how farmers have been successful in their occupations. The use of New Holland equipment is mentioned secondarily in the article." Length: 700 words maximum. Pays $175 to $200 per article. Photos purchased with mss; with captions only. "Should show New Holland equipment in action on the farm." Uses 8x10 b&w glossies and 2¼x2¼ or 4x5 color transparencies.

NORDEN NEWS, Norden Laboratories, 601 W. Cornhusker Highway, Lincoln NE 68521. Editor: Patricia Pike. For "doctors of veterinary medicine (clinicians, instructors in schools of veterinary medicine) and juniors and seniors in colleges of veterinary medicine." Established in 1929. Quarterly. Circulation: 15,000. Rights purchased vary with author and material. Will buy all rights, first North American serial rights, or second serial (reprint) rights. Buys 4 to 6 mss per year. Pays on publication. Will send a free sample copy to a writer on request. Will send editorial guidelines sheet to a writer on request. Query first or submit complete ms. Submit seasonal material 3 to 4 months in advance. Reports in 1 month. Enclose S.A.S.E. for reply to queries or return of submissions.
Nonfiction and Photos: "Technical articles, particularly in the area of diagnosis and treatment of diseases of animals; business oriented articles relevant to practice management; feature articles about a veterinarian with an unusual approach to the practice of veterinary medicine, unique hobby or role in community activities. Avoid generalities. Articles should include specific details; many rejected because they are either not technical enough, or subject is unique to the laymen, but ordinary to other vets. Attempt to maintain a smoother, easier reading style. We prefer mss 3 to 4 pages long. We are currently paying $100 for ms, plus $7.50 each for photos. $50 for 1-page articles. 8x10 or 5x7 b&w glossies are acceptable." Purchased with or without mss, or on assignment. Captions optional. Color transparencies or prints. Payment depends on use; $7.50 for article illustrations. "We are interested in unusual photos of animals which could be used as title page illustrations, or used with an ad. Of special interest: cats, dogs, feeder cattle, and horses."

OUR SUN, Sun Oil Co., 240 Radnor-Chester Rd., St. Davids PA 19087. For "local, state, and national government officials; community leaders; news and financial communicators; educators; shareholders, customers, and employees of Sun Oil Company." Established in 1923. Quarterly. Circulation: 80,000. Not copyrighted. Buys 3 to 6 articles a year. Pays on acceptance. Will send a sample copy to a writer on request. Write for copy of guidelines for writers. Query first or submit complete ms. Address to "the Editor." Reports in 3 to 6 weeks. Enclose S.A.S.E. for reply to queries or return of submissions.
Nonfiction: "Articles only. Subject matter should be related to Sun Oil Company, oil industry, or national energy situation. Articles should be directed toward a general audience. Style: magazine feature. Approach: nontechnical. Travel themes are currently being overworked." Buys informational articles, personal experience articles, interviews, profiles, historical articles, think pieces, coverage of successful business operations, and new product articles. Length: 1,000 to 3,000 words. Pays $300 to $800.
Photos: Purchased on assignment; captions optional. "We do not buy photos on spec." Pays $100 to $400 a day for photographic assignments.

OUTDOORS, Outdoors Building, Columbia MO 65201. Editor: Lee Cullimore. Published by Mercury for "boaters and water sport enthusiasts." Monthly. Buys first serial rights. Pays "about 1 month prior to publication." Will send a sample copy to a writer on request. Write for copy of guidelines for writers. Query first. Reports in 2 weeks. Enclose S.A.S.E.

Nonfiction and Photos: "*Outdoors* seeks to encourage readers to spend more leisure time enjoying family recreation in outdoor living; to describe new things to do, new places to visit, and new wonders to see. It strives to stimulate the imagination and provide helpful information that will enable more people to realize and share in the benefit of our natural resources. Subject matter accepted for publication in *Outdoors* principally emphasizes boating, snowmobiling, and closely allied themes, such as cruising, water skiing, boating tips, workshop features, camping by boat, camping by snowmobile, snowmobile tips, trailering, fishing, personalities, nature, outdoor health, outdoor cooking, waterway restaurants, area profiles, historical subjects, and outdoor fashions. Writing must be extremely tight and thoroughly researched. Preference is given to informative mss presented in an objective manner. The first-person approach is not recommended. Boat and snowmobile racing material is not accepted. Editorial mention of the Mercury name in articles is not permitted; stories concerned with products are staff-written. While a company tie-in is essential in boating and snowmobiling stories, other subjects may not have this requirement. Please avoid being overly patronizing in this respect." Length: 1,200 words maximum. "Articles are purchased as a package. As a rule of thumb, rates are about $20 per published page for photo spreads. We do not count words in determining amount. The average article runs $80 to $100. All articles must be accompanied by 8x10 b&w professional quality prints; these are purchased with the ms. Color transparencies (2¼x2¼ minimum size preferred) may be submitted for consideration with the article. Rates for color range from $15 to $25 each, depending on content and quality."

POINTS, 465 W. Milwaukee, Detroit MI 48202. Editor: Robert A. Sumpter. Bimonthly. Query before making submission, as articles are generally set for the year ahead. When OK'd for submission (with good color transparencies, any size) submit as soon before deadline as possible. Deadline for copy and photos is 5 months before date of issue. Deadline for September issue is April 1; for November issue, June 1; for January issue, August 1; for March issue, October 1; for May issue, December 1, for July issue, February 1. Enclose S.A.S.E.
Nonfiction: Articles should involve the how and why of hobbies, sports, and other subjects relating to travel. Family action, all types of camping and family outdoor activities in season or year 'round. Stress the how and why and unusual, little known aspects. Travel-related hobbies such as collecting rocks, desert treasures, beachcombing. How the woman of the family can help in various activities. Man-action, such as specific techniques of fishing, mountain climbing, scuba diving. How-to and equipment suggestions for beginner to the practicing enthusiast. Arts and crafts, such as stained glass from travel finds, leathercraft from hunting hides, on-site art such as landscape painting. Also father-children feature such as teaching how to find way with and without compass, canoeing, archery, identifying wildlife by tracks. Action subjects should be able to be done anywhere, or in a broad area, mountains, plains, oceans and gulf, fresh waters, desert, etc. A particular place may be used as a focal point only to show "how it was done" and "why" and equipment and preparation suggestions. Other areas and sources of information should be telescoped into a paragraph or two. Prefers individual styling flair, active prose, good presentation of how-to aspects from beginning stage to advanced. Photos should include how-to illustrations, results, and human interest on-site shot. Length: from 600 to 800 words. For single-page feature with color photos, pays to $150. $100 if color transparencies submitted with ms cannot be used. For two-page story with color photos pays to $300, $200 without photos. For three-page feature with photos pays $400; without photos $300. This size seldom used.
Photos: Purchased with mss. See nonfiction above. Also pays to $150 for transparency for cover. Wherever natural to article, a GMC truck or recreational vehicle should be shown. "All competitive makes will render photo useless."

PROGRESS, Box 383, Milwaukee, WI 53201. Editor: F.M. Hoppert. Published by Nordberg Machinery Group, Rexnord Inc., for "customers and prospects in mining, manufacturing, and power generation fields." Established in 1918. Quarterly. Circulation: 14,000. Buys all rights. Buys 10 to 12 mss a year. Pays on acceptance. Will send a sample copy to a writer on request. Query first. Reports in 3 to 6 weeks. Enclose S.A.S.E. for reply to queries and return of submissions.
Nonfiction and Photos: "Product case histories." Buys informational articles, how-

to's, coverage of successful business operations, new product articles, and technical articles. Length: 500 to 1,500 words. Pays $50 to $500. 8x10 b&w glossies purchased with mss; captions required. Buys 35mm to 4x5 color transparencies and 8x10 color prints. Pays $5 to $10 "if accompanying ms; if separate photo assignment, $15 to $30." Photo subjects should be the same as nonfiction.

RURALITE, P.O. Box 1731, Portland OR 97207. Editor: Aaron C. Jones. For "rural people served by our member utilities in Oregon, Washington, Idaho and Alaska." Established in 1953. Monthly. Circulation: 90,000. Buys first North American serial rights. Buys 300 mss a year. Payment on acceptance. Will send free sample copy to writer on request. Query. Will consider photocopied submissions. Submit seasonal material 3 months in advance. Reports on material in 15 days. Enclose S.A.S.E. for reply to queries and return of submissions.
Nonfiction and Photos: "Human interest stories about member-owners of the public utilities that send *Ruralite* to their members. Articles that offer good advice to rural people; how to repair or how to live more safely, etc. Must have some connection with utility or members of utility." How-to, inspirational, new product. Length: 250 to 2,500 words. Pays $25 to $100. B&w photos purchased with accompanying mss or without ms. Captions required. Pays $7.50.

SEASONS, 1999 Shepard Rd., St. Paul MN 55116. Editor: Richard L. Smith. For customers and prospects of Amoco heating oil, LP-gas and commercial firms using industrial lubricants. Articles on "home improvement, with particular emphasis on heating and cooling comfort." Established in 1970. Circulation: 140,000. Copyrighted. Rights purchased vary with author and material. Usually buys all rights but will reassign rights to author after publication. Will send a free sample copy on request. Query suggested. Will consider photocopied submissions. Reports within a month, but returns rejected material in 1 week. Enclose S.A.S.E. for reply to queries.
Nonfiction: "Any home improvement or decorating articles will be considered. First-person material not acceptable. Receptive to stories about family activities, hobbies, informational, humor, historical, nostalgia, travel and new products, Emphasis is on the 'why' of home improvement rather than the how-to approach used in many pop magazines which address themselves to the homeowner market." Rejects how-to articles about making items from household throw-aways (milk cartons, egg crates, etc.). "Lead story in each issue is usually related to a specific season." No word length limitation. Pays $50 to $250.
Photos: Purchased with accompanying mss and on assignment, with captions optional. B&w not acceptable, but 35mm and larger color photos are purchased for $50 (inside use) and $100 (cover use).

SMALL WORLD, Volkswagen of America, 818 Sylvan Ave., Englewood Cliffs NJ 07632. Editor: Jonathan Fisher. For "Volkswagen owners in the United States." 5 times a year. Buys all rights. Pays on acceptance. Write for copy of guidelines for writers. "If you have a long feature possibility in mind, please query first. Though queries should be no longer than 2 pages, they ought to include a working title, a short, general summary of the article, and an outline of the specific points to be covered. Where possible, please include a sample of the photography available. We strongly advise writers to read at least 2 past issues before working on a story." Reports in 1 month. Enclose S.A.S.E. for reply to queries.
Nonfiction and Photos: "Interesting stories on people using Volkswagens; useful owner modifications of the vehicle; travel pieces with the emphasis on people, not places; Volkswagenmania stories, personality pieces, inspirational and true adventure articles, VW arts and crafts, etc. The style should be light. All stories must have a VW tie-in. Our approach is subtle, however, and we try to avoid obvious product puffery, since *Small World* is not an advertising medium. We prefer a first-person, people-oriented handling." Length: 1,200 words maximum; "shorter pieces, some as short as 450 words, often receive closer attention." Pays "$100 per printed page for photographs and text; otherwise, a portion of that amount, depending on the space allotted. Most stories go 2 pages; some run 3 or 4." Photos purchased with ms; captions required. "We prefer color transparencies, particularly 35mm slides. All photos should carry the photographer's name and address. If the photographer is not the author, both names should appear on the first page of the text. Where possible, we would like a selection of at least 40 transparencies. It is recommended that

at least one show the principal character or author; another, all or a recognizable portion of a VW in the locale of the story. Quality photography can often sell a story that might be otherwise rejected. Every picture should be identified or explained." Model releases required. Pays $250 for cover photo.

Fillers: "Short, humorous anecdotes about Volkswagens." Pays $15.

How To Break In: "There is no easy way for a beginning writer to break into *Small World*. Competition is tough—just as tough for the pro as the amateur. But we are actively looking for new writers. Our advice: get to know our publication intimately. If you have a feel for our market, you've won half the battle. Most stories are rejected because the idea is wrong."

TARHEEL WHEELS, P.O. Box 2977, Raleigh NC 27602. Editor: Jeff B. Wilson. Established in 1954. Monthly. Circulation: 14,000. Rights purchased vary with author and material. Pays after publication. Will send a sample copy to a writer on request. Query first. Reports "on the first to tenth of the month preceding publication." Enclose S.A.S.E. for reply to queries and return of submissions.

Nonfiction and Photos: "General information, preferably about North Carolina." Buys photo articles and travel articles. Length: "not over 1,000 words." Pays $10 maximum for article. $5 maximum per photo; "not over $30 for photos and story." 8x10 or 5x7 b&w glossies purchased with mss; captions required.

Fiction, Poetry, and Fillers: "With a local theme relative to North Carolina." Pays $10 maximum.

TEXACO TEMPO, P.O. Box 1500, Station H, Montreal 107, PQ, Canada. Published by Texaco Canada Ltd. for "employees, shareholders, plant-community leaders, the press." Established in 1959. Quarterly. Circulation: 6,500. Not copyrighted. Buys about 10 mss a year. Pays on acceptance. Will send a sample copy to a writer on request. Write for copy of guidelines for writers. Query first. Address to "Public Relations Dept." Will consider photocopied submissions. Reports in 2 weeks. Enclose S.A.E. and International Reply Coupons.

Nonfiction: "Related to Canadian oil industry and particularly to activities of this company, a fully integrated oil company which explores for crude oil, drills for it, transports it, refines it, transports the products, and sells them at wholesale and retail. The publication tries to meet external and internal readership needs. No articles on cute little local tourist interest sights or happenings which people might drive 25 miles to see, but not 250 or 2,500 miles." Buys informational articles, how-to's, personal experience articles, profiles, humor, historical articles, nostalgia, travel pieces, and coverage of successful business operations. Length: 800 to 2,000 words. Pays $100 to $200. B&w (5x7 upwards) glossy photos purchased with mss; captions required.

TRAINED MEN, ICS, Industrial Training Division of Intext, Scranton PA 18515. To "first echelon, middle, and upper management." Quarterly. Buys all rights. Pays on acceptance. Will send a sample copy to a writer on request. Reports within 1 month. Enclose S.A.S.E. for return of submissions.

Nonfiction and Photos: "Articles and photos should depict employee development through training, personnel problems and solutions, new aspects of training, current topics of an industrial nature, and new industrial improvements." Length: 1,000 to 2,500 words. Pays 2¢ to 3¢ a word. Photos purchased with mss.

Dealers', Agents', and Franchisers'

The company-sponsored publications below exist to help company dealers, franchisers, and agents run their businesses effectively. They carry material on displaying company products, suggestions for increasing sales, etc. A few magazines in the Employees' and Customers' classifications also use material on dealers and franchisers.

Company magazines that exist to cultivate good employee relations with in-house personnel are classified in the Employees' category. Those that focus on promoting the company image, products, or services to potential customers are listed in the Customers' category. Company publications that carry general interest material that doesn't tie in with the company or its interests (for example, The American Way*) will be found in the General Interest classification.*

AMOCO FARM AND HOME MARKETER, Amoco Oil Company, P.O. Box 5910 A, Chicago, IL 60680. Editor: Gerald J. Bayles. For "petroleum agents supplying diesel fuel, heating oil, L-P gas, lube oils, greases, and pesticides to homeowners, small businesses, and farm markets, and for fertilizer plant managers selling fertilizers and pesticides to the farm market." Quarterly. Circulation: 13,000. Buys all rights, but will reassign rights to author after publication. Buys 3 to 4 mss a year. Pays on publication. Query first. Submit seasonal material 3 months in advance. Enclose S.A.S.E. for reply to queries.
Nonfiction and Photos: "Success stories; merchandising, motivational, and educational features on topics of importance and interest to rural marketers. Call first to discuss specific projects; articles submitted on speculation are rarely on target for our readers." Buys interviews, profiles, spot news, coverage of successful business operations and merchandising techniques. Length: 1,000 words maximum. Pays $400 maximum for stories and accompanying captioned photo. B&w glossies, color transparencies, 35mm color, color prints.

CONOCO TODAY, High Ridge Park, Stamford CT 06904. Editor: John H. Walker. Continental Oil Company. Monthly and bimonthly. Copyrighted. Buys all rights. Pays on acceptance. Best to query first. Reports at once. Will send free sample copy on request. Enclose S.A.S.E.
Nonfiction: Conoco service station operation and wholesale distributor operations, news and ideas. Length: 1,000 words. Pays 7¢ a word.
Photos: Purchased with mss. B&w 8x10, pays $10. Also buys color.

INNER CIRCLE, 17390 W. Eight Mile Rd., Southfield MI 48075. Editor: C. James Rash, Jr. For "service station and independent garage operators; distributed by United Delco Division, General Motors Corp." Bimonthly. Buys first serial rights. Pays on acceptance. Will send a sample copy to a writer on request. Enclose S.A.S.E. for return of submissions.
Nonfiction: Articles on "all sports, human interest, wildlife conservation, personalities, hobbies. Also, fresh, timely articles concerning automotive and related industries. Avoid controversial subjects." Releases required from persons named in articles. Length: 300 to 2,000 words. Pays $100 to $500.
Photos: "Releases required for persons identifiable in photos." Pays $25 to $125.

MERCHANDISER, Amoco Oil Company, P.O. Box 5910A, Chicago, IL 60680. Editor: Gerald J. Bayles. For "American Oil service station dealers, jobbers." Quarterly. Circulation: 35,000. Buys all rights, but will reassign after publication. Buys 3 or 4 mss a year. Pays on publication. Query or "call first to discuss specific projects; articles submitted on speculation are rarely on target for our readers." Submit seasonal material 3 months in advance. Enclose S.A.S.E. for reply to queries or return of submissions.
Nonfiction and Photos: "Success stories; merchandising, motivational, educational features on topics of importance or interest to dealers and jobbers." Buys interviews, profiles, spot news, coverage of successful business operations and merchandising techniques. Length: 1,000 words maximum. Pays up to $400 for stories and accompanying photo. B&w glossies, color transparencies, 35mm color, color prints.

THE RECORD, Fireman's Fund American Insurance Co., 3333 California St., San Francisco CA 94119. Editor: William F. Lawler. For "insurance agents and brokers." Annual. Circulation: 20,000. Buys North American serial rights. Pays on acceptance. Will send a sample copy to a writer on request. Submit from May 1 to September 1 only. Reports in 1 month. Enclose S.A.S.E. for return of submissions.
Fiction, Poetry and Fillers: "In the market for anecdotes, short-shorts, poetry, for annual Christmas issue. All must have strong Christmas theme. Will consider only tight, well-presented material with original twist. Payment according to merit of submission." Pays $25 minimum for anecdotes. Pays $75 for short-shorts. Length: 1,000 words or less. Pays $10 for poetry.

ROSEBURG WOODSMAN, 601 Terminal Sales Building, Portland OR 97205, c/o Hugh Dwight Advertising, Inc. for the Roseburg Lumber Company. For "building dealers and distributors. Monthly. Not copyrighted. Pays on publication. Query first. Reports "at once." Enclose S.A.S.E.
Nonfiction and Photos: "Use of wood building material, exterior and interior, in residential and commercial construction and in industry. Prefer a light but lucid approach. No bylines are used." Length: about 300 words. Pays 10¢ a word. Photos purchased with mss; captions required. Pays $10 for b&w glossies; pays $50 for color transparencies.

SAFECO AGENT, Safeco Insurance, Safeco Plaza, Seattle WA 98185. Editor: Bob Sincock; Managing Editor: Jack C. High. For independent insurance agents, multi-line, highly professional; must compete for their favor with other insurance companies they represent, so content is nearly all Safeco-oriented. Established in 1923. Bimonthly. Circulation: 12,000. Copyrighted. Buys 4 to 8 mss a year, maybe more. "Depends on availability of qualified writer to handle assignment in specific geographical area." Payment on acceptance. Will send free sample copy to writer on request. Write for editorial guidelines for writers. Query first. Reports in 2 weeks. Enclose S.A.S.E. with queries and submissions.
Nonfiction: "Interested in articles by assignment only. Agent success articles. Case histories, profiles, interviews. How to prospect, sell insurance, develop accounts. Agency management. All articles related to Safeco products, policies and procedures. Emphasize agent's success as a Safeco representative. Give testimonials." Informational, how-to, personal experience, interview, profile, inspirational, successful business operations, merchandising techniques and technical. Length: 600 to 1,600 words. Pays to "$200 or thereabouts."
Photos: "All photos are either by assignment only, or ordered from stock photo sources." Pays $10 for b&w glossies; $25 for color transparencies.

SOLUTION, 1 Jake Brown Road, Old Bridge NJ 08857. Editor: George S. Bahue. Published by Blonder-Tongue Laboratories for television service technicians. Buys all rights. Pays on publication. Will send a sample copy to a writer on request. Will consider photocopied submissions. Reports in 2 weeks. Enclose S.A.S.E. for return of submissions.
Nonfiction and Photos: "General information on TV distribution system servicing; other related information of interest to service technicians, particularly the merchandising aspects of the business." Length: 1,000 words. Pays $200 to $300. Photos purchased with mss.
Fillers: Puzzles.

SOONER LPG TIMES, 2910 N. Walnut, Suite 114-A, Oklahoma City OK 73105. Editor: John E. Orr. For "dealers and suppliers of LP-gas and their employees." Monthly. Not copyrighted. Pays on publication. Reports in 3 weeks. Enclose S.A.S.E. for return of submissions.
Nonfiction: "Articles relating to the LP-gas industry, safety, small business practices, and economics; anything of interest to small businessmen." Length: 1,000 to 2,000 words. Pays $10 to $15.

SPIRIT OF SEVENTY SIX, Union Oil Company of California, Room 413, Union Oil Center, Los Angeles CA 90017. Editor: Austin Woodward. For "Union service station dealers." Monthly. Buys all rights. Buys 3 to 4 mss a year. Pays on acceptance. Query first; "almost all freelance material accepted is on assignment." Enclose S.A.S.E. for reply to queries.
Nonfiction and Photos: "We occasionally accept articles on civic or business accomplishments of Union 76 dealers." Length: 200 to 1,000 words. Pays $25 to $200, "plus expenses on assignments." Pays $10 minimum per photo.

TILE AND TILL, Eli Lilly Company, Box 618, Indianapolis IN 46206. Editor: B.A. Smith. For "druggists all over the country." Bimonthly. Circulation: 84,000. Buys one-time rights. Pays on acceptance. Enclose S.A.S.E. for return of submissions.
Nonfiction and Photos: "This publication covers the professional side of pharmacy. We can use exceptional human interest stories that have a wide appeal and a pharmacy slant. If you cover personality or salesmanship in 300 to 700 words (occasion-

ally to 1,200 words) and toss in a clear picture or two, your story will rate a careful reading." Pays 4¢ to 5¢ a word.

VICKERS VOICE, Vickers Refining Co., Inc., P.O. Box 2240, Wichita KS 67201. Editor: Quillin Porter. For "dealers and employees." Bimonthly. Circulation: 3,000. Not copyrighted. Pays on publication. Query first. Enclose S.A.S.E.
Nonfiction: "Articles showing, by example, how a service station owner or manager can make more money from an existing outlet; travel articles." Length: 500 words. Pays $15 to $20.
Photos: "Occasionally use 8x10 b&w glossies." Pays $10.

YAMAHA HORIZONS, 3435 Wilshire Blvd., Los Angeles CA 90010. Publication of Yamaha International Corp., Motorcycle Division. Submit all material to: The Editors. For Yamaha dealers and their customers nationwide. Bimonthly. Circulation; 15,000. Not copyrighted. Payment on acceptance. Submit material 6 to 8 weeks in advance.
Nonfiction and Photos: "Human interest, industry and government developments affecting the manufacturer; personalities in the sport. Must be Yamaha oriented, timely; no news of competitors or outlaw groups. Features, with quality color or b&w photos." Length: 500 to 2,500 words. Pays 5¢ a word.

Employees'

The company-sponsored publications below are often called "internal" house magazines because they circulate to employees. (As against the "external" ones that go to customers.) They aim at cultivating good company/employee relations, fostering good work habits, and instilling pride in company products and activities. Most want material closely tied to the company (for example, Harvest *buys material on Campbell Soup products), but many will also accept general interest pieces on topics like safety, travel, family living, etc., that will inform or entertain their readers. A few magazines in the Customers' and Dealers' classifications also use employee-directed material.*

Company magazines that exist to promote the company image, products, or services to potential customers are classified in the Customers' category. Those that focus on helping dealers, franchisers, and agents run their businesses are listed in the Dealers' category. Company publications that carry general interest material that doesn't tie in with the company or its interests (for example, The American Way*) will be found in the General Interest classification.*

AIRFAIR INTERLINE MAGAZINE, 3540 Wilshire Blvd. Suite 747, Los Angeles CA 90010. Editor: James C. Clark. For airline employees. Monthly. Circulation: 50,000. Buys first rights. Buys 10 mss a year from freelancers. Buys no material that is not assigned; query first. Pays on publication. Will send a sample copy for $1. Submit seasonal material 4 months in advance. Reports in 1 month. Enclose S.A.S.E.
Nonfiction and Photos: Interested in travel. Can be how-to or personal experience. Length: 1,500 words. Pays $50 to $100. B&w glossies, color transparencies, and 35mm color purchased with mss and with captions only.

ARCO SPARK MAGAZINE, Atlantic Richfield Co., 515 S. Flower St., Los Angeles CA 90071. Editor: Dave Orman. For employees and retirees. Quarterly. Circulation: 40,000. Not copyrighted. Pays on publication. Will send a sample copy to a writer on request. Query first. "Study publication for style and slant." Reports in 3 weeks. Enclose S.A.S.E. for reply to queries.
Nonfiction and Photos: "Material related to the energy industry, preferably with an Atlantic Richfield tie-in." Length: 2,500 words maximum. Pays about 10¢ a word. Photos purchased with mss; b&w, color. "Should deal with the energy industry, Atlantic Richfield in particular. No special size requirements." Pay "varies according

to the value of material, and whether assigned or unsolicited; minimum of $10 for b&w; $25 for color."

BRICKBATS AND BOUQUETS, P.O. Box 2759, Dallas TX 75221. Editor: Lynn Halbardier. For employees of Employers Insurance of Texas. Monthly. Very limited amount of freelance material purchased. Query first.

THE BUDGETEER, 6420 Wilshire Blvd., Los Angeles CA 90048. Editor: Barbara Johnson. For employees of Budget Finance Plan. Established in 1950. Monthly. Circulation: 1,000. Not copyrighted. Buys 1 ms a year. Payment on publication. Will send free sample copy to writer on request. Query first or submit complete ms. Will consider photocopied submissions. Submit seasonal material 2 months in advance. Reports on material in 2 months. Enclose S.A.S.E.
Nonfiction and Photos: "Everything in *The Budgeteer* has to have some relation to the company—either directly about developments in the business or reporting about an employee and his family. Social concerns and community involvement is welcomed if there is a connection with Budget. Because of space limitation, article must be concise; a good accompanying photograph is a must and a light feature style is fine with emphasis on 1) what makes this a good subject and 2) what connection it has with Budget." Informational, successful business operations, merchandising techniques. "Have just started Lampoon humor page and can use humorous articles about the consumer finance business." Length: 150 to 300 words. Pays 2¢ a word. Photos purchased with or without ms and on assignment. Clear, good contrast b&w. Captions optional. Pays $50 for cover; $5 for other.
Poetry and Fillers: Humorous verse relating to finance business. 4 to 8 lines. Pays $5. Pays $1 to $5 for jokes and short humor. Length: 25 to 50 words.

THE BULLETIN, 227 Church St., New Haven CT 06506. Editor: William R. Weir. For employees of Southern New England Telephone Co. Established in 1907. Monthly. Circulation: 20,000. Not copyrighted. Payment on publication; in some cases, on acceptance. Will send free sample copy to a writer on request. Query first. Will consider photocopied submissions. Submit seasonal material (Christmas) 3 months in advance. Reports on material in 30 days. Enclose S.A.S.E for reply to queries.
Nonfiction and Photos: Articles on "telephone employees and the telephone business in Connecticut. Best areas for freelancers: activities of employees company involvement in community; factors affecting the company or its employees (anything from phone freaks to government regulations). Should try to keep localized to the company and the state of Connecticut. Competition and ecology are a couple that might be worthwile for freelancers to explore." Informational, how-to, personal experience, interview, profile, humor, historical, think pieces, expose, nostalgia, travel. Length: 1,000 to 2,000 words. Pays average of $150 "for simple story." 8x10 glossy b&w photos purchased with mss or on assignment. Captions required. Pays $25 "unless otherwise arranged." Pays $25 to $150 for 35mm transparencies.

C-B MANIFOLD, Cooper-Bessemer Co., N. Sandusky St., Mt. Vernon OH 43050. Editor: J.R. Elliott. For company employees. Quarterly. Not copyrighted. Pays on acceptance. Query first. Reports in 2 weeks. Enclose S.A.S.E.
Nonfiction: "Thoroughly researched articles on Cooper-Bessemer equipment." Length: 500 words. Pays $35 to $50.
Photos: B&w photos with captions. Pays $10 to $15.

CIBA-GEIGY JOURNAL, 4002 Basel, Switzerland. Editor: Stanley Hubbard. For "employees, mainly staff and scientific-technical, of Ciba-Geigy, together with 'opinion leaders,' customers, educational institutions, etc., in most English-speaking countries." Established in 1971. Circulation: 27,000. Rights purchased vary with author and material; may buy all rights, but will reassign rights to author after publication. Buys 4 to 6 mss a year. Pays on publication. Will send a sample copy to a writer on request. Query first. Will consider photocopied submissions. Submit seasonal material 5 months in advance. Reports in 2 weeks.
Nonfiction and Photos: "Popularized scientific and technical presentations, international cooperation subjects, regional and historical contributions related to group activities, human interest—if possible, with product or operational tie-in. The ap-

proach should be literate; no writing down. The mentality must not be provincial; it can be 'American,' but not xenophobic or condescending. Oh-gee breathlessness is not desired. The writer should realize he's addressing a cosmopolitan audience that likes a good read. The internationalism of our company is the basic determining factor here—we are interpreting from continent to continent rather than talking to a homogenous, neatly defined readership." Buys informational articles, humor, historical articles, think pieces, nostalgia, photo features, travel articles, and technical articles. Length: 500 to 3,000 words. Pays minimum of $50. Photos purchased with mss; captions required. For b&w, pays $10. For color ("if prints, only first quality"), pays $10 to $20.

CONSUMERS POWER WORLD, Public Relations Dept., Consumers Power Co., 212 W. Michigan, Jackson MI 49201. Editor: Al Henderson. For "employees and opinion leaders in our service area." Publication of Consumers Power Company. Established in 1973. Quarterly. Circulation: 20,000. Buys all rights. Buys about 20 mss a year. Payment on acceptance. Will send sample copy to writer on request. Query first. Will not consider photocopied submissions. Submit seasonal material at least 6 months in advance. Reports on material in a week or 10 days. Enclose S.A.S.E. for reply to queries.
Nonfiction: Uses material on the energy crisis, human interest, new company/industry developments; service area businesses and personnel; company sponsored civic/education projects. "No general power shortage articles, but one that specifically relates to Consumers Power Company or the Michigan Power Pool. No junk mss; no spinoff articles. Don't bother sending canned articles on new traffic signs or other such pieces that have no specific bearing on our service area." Informational, interview, profile, humor, historical, think pieces, nostalgia, travel, technical. Length: 500 to 4,500 words. Pays $50 to $750. "Our basis of payment varies with length, difficulty of assignment, importance to us, 'name' author."

DIMENSIONS, 414 Nicollet Mall, Minneapolis MN 55401. Editor: Lyle Frost. Published by Northern States Power Company for "current and retired employees of the company, plus community leaders in the company's service area (the central two-thirds of Minnesota, western Wisconsin, portions of North and South Dakota)." Established in 1971. Quarterly. Circulation: 12,500. Rights purchased vary with author and material; may buy all rights (but may reassign rights to author after publication), first serial rights, or second serial rights. Pays on publication. Will send a sample copy to a writer on request. Query first or submit complete ms. Will not consider photocopied submissions. Reports in 1 to 4 weeks. Enclose S.A.S.E. for return of submissions or reply to queries.
Nonfiction and Photos: "In addition to insights about employees—their accomplishments, problems, philosophies—the magazine offers outside as well as inside insights and opinion about major issues affecting Northern States Power, the electric and gas industries, business in general, and the public at large (e.g., ecology, the media). Also, general interest features. Any article should be people-oriented or issue-oriented, or offer intriguing perspectives on a general interest topic. General interest topics should be from within our service area. Avoid technical reports. Our publication avoids the usual company emphasis on miscellaneous employees and company material and hard news stories (such as details of a new power plant)." Buys informational articles, personal experience articles, profiles, interviews, humor, historical articles, think articles, nostalgia, personal opinion pieces, photo features. Length: "general maximum is 2,500 words; will exceed only for exceptional material." Pays 5¢ to 10¢ per published word. Photos purchased with mss "but need not accompany ms; art is also used frequently to illustrate." For 8x10 b&w prints, pays $3 to $7.50. For 8x10 color prints with negatives, 2x2 transparencies, or 35mm slides, pays $5 to $15.
Fiction: "Stories should relate to the energy industry." Buys experimental fiction, adventure stories, science fiction, fantasy, and historical. Length: "2,500 words maximum unless exceptional material." Pays 5¢ to 10¢ per published word.

ENKA VOICE, American Enka Company, Enka NC 28728. Editor: Tom Bennett. For "employees of American Enka Company of all ages, of limited education, and with interests pertaining to hunting, family, nature, and household information." Established in 1928. Monthly. Circulation: 13,500. Not copyrighted. Buys 1 to 5 mss

a year. Pays on acceptance. Will send a sample copy to a writer on request. Submit complete ms. Will consider photocopied submissions. Submit seasonal material at least 2 months in advance. Reports in 1 week. Enclose S.A.S.E. for return of submissions.
Nonfiction and Photos: "Generally, we publish articles dealing in some way with textiles (end-uses), although occasionally we run unrelated stories as well. We like to see textile or fiber end-use articles so our people can see what their products do. The writer should slant the article toward the conservative, patriotic American. We buy some seasonal stories, but only if they pertain to the use of a textile or man-made fiber end-use (such as nylon Christmas trees)." Buys how-to's, interviews, profiles, new product articles, and coverage of successful business operations and merchandising techniques. Length: 300 to 600 words ("2 typewritten pages maximum"). Pays $25. Photos purchased with mss "ideally, but not necessarily"; captions required. Photos should show "any end-use possibility." For b&w glossies, pays $10 minimum.

GOING PLACES, 65 Broadway, New York NY 10006. Editor: Diane Plummer. For American Express Company employees and employees of American Express Company subsidiaries. Bimonthly. Not copyrighted. Pays on acceptance. Will send a sample copy to a writer on request. Query first. Enclose S.A.S.E. for reply to queries.
Nonfiction and Photos: Seldom purchases freelance mss, but sometimes makes assignments for travel or company-oriented articles, especially offbeat locations. Also occasionally makes assignments for company-oriented b&w photos.

HARVEST, Campbell Soup Company, Campbell Place, Camden NJ 08101. Editor: Dan H. Dolack. For Campbell Soup Company employees. Quarterly. Circulation: 30,000. Buys all rights "only to copy and photos; will return photos to the writer after publication on request, but some time may elapse between acceptance and publication." Pays on acceptance. Will send a sample copy to a writer on request. Write for copy of guidelines for writers. Query first. Reports in 2 to 8 weeks. Enclose S.A.S.E. for reply to queries.
Nonfiction and Photos: "Vocabulary is simple, sentence structure uncomplicated, but done well enough that the literate person would consider it readable. We want an easy-to-read flow. Read a sample copy to get the feel of the style. Articles can often be helped by some fiction techniques, good dialog, setting the scene to give atmosphere, a bit of action. We do not want our stories overwritten; the 'literary' story doesn't have a chance. If an article has a strong company tie-in (such as showing a Campbell, Swanson, Pepperidge Farm, Bounty, or other Campbell Soup Company product in use in a natural—not contrived—way), it stands a better chance of acceptance. We seldom buy articles that do not relate to Campbell Soup Company or to food or nutrition. We do not buy recipes." Length: 500 to 1,500 words. Pays 10¢ per word. Color photos purchased with mss. "Photo standards are high; good transparencies (35mm or 2¼x2¼) stand the best chance of acceptance. Photos with mss must tell the story, not just accompany it. We prefer candid, available-light photography, and are not interested in run-of-the-mill flash photography. Photos accepted for publication become the property of Campbell Soup Company; extras returned on request." Pays $50 per transparency.

HUGHES RIGWAY, Hughes Tool Company, P.O. Box 2539, Houston TX 77001. Editor: Wayne Bryant. For "oil and gas drilling personnel." Quarterly. Buys first North American serial rights. Pays on acceptance. Will consider photocopied submissions. Reports in 3 weeks. Enclose S.A.S.E. for return of submissions.
Nonfiction and Photos: "Character-revealing historical narratives about little-known incidents, heroes, or facts, particularly those which contradict conventional concepts. Also, topical reportorial features about people in oil or drilling. Must be thoroughly documented." Length: 2,000 to 2,500 words. Pays 10¢ a word. Photos purchased with mss. "Pays a flat rate of $50 per printed page for features and articles with good photographs or for picture stories."
Fiction: "Top quality fiction in oilfield settings." Length: 2,000 to 2,500 words. Pays 10¢ a word.

IMPERIAL OIL FLEET NEWS, 111 St. Clair Ave. W., Toronto M5W IK3 Ont., Canada. Editor: G.R. McKean. For "seamen of Imperial Oil tankers." Quarterly. Not copyrighted. Pays on publication. Enclose S.A.E. and International Reply Coupons for return of submissions.
Nonfiction and Photos: "Sea-flavored stories written to interest the seamen of the Imperial tanker fleet." Length: 1,500 words maximum. Pays $25 per story, $40 "when illustrations are included."

INLAND, 18 South Home Ave., Park Ridge IL 60068. Editor: Sheldon A. Mix. Published by Inland Steel Company. Quarterly. Circulation: 12,000. Buys first rights. Buys 12 to 15 mss a year. Pays on acceptance. Will send a sample copy to a writer on request. No query required. Submit seasonal material 3 to 4 months in advance. Enclose S.A.E. and International Reply Coupons for return of submissions.
Nonfiction: "Articles on general subjects in the following areas: history, nostalgia, sports, humor, essays on the current scene—customarily with a tie-in to the Midwest (Illinois, Wisconsin, Minnesota, Michigan, Ohio, Missouri, Iowa, and Indiana). Articles on steel subjects are staff-written. We encourage individuality and quality writing, and we're open to different approaches and ideas. No rehashed historical pieces or reminiscences that do not have a broad enough appeal." Buys profiles, humor, historical articles, and think pieces. Length: 1,000 to 4,000 words. Pays about $300.

ITEMS, Federal Reserve Bank of Dallas, 400 S. Akard, Dallas TX 75222. Editor: Mrs. Mildred Hopkins. For "employees, retirees, and others in the banking field." Monthly. Not copyrighted. Pays on publication for nonfiction; pays on acceptance for photos. Will send a sample copy to a writer on request. Enclose S.A.S.E. for return of submissions.
Nonfiction: "We occasionally use an article in *Items*. The subject matter usually pertains to the fields of banking and finance, although other general interest articles would be considered." Length: 800 to 1,000 words. Pays 2¢ a word.
Photos: "We occasionally use cover photos." Should be 5x7 or 8x10 b&w glossies. Pays $10 to $15.

JEFFERSON ISLAND NEWS, P.O. Box 194, New Iberia LA 70560. Editor: Van J. Kojis. For plant and company employees of Diamond Crystal Salt Co. Established in 1950. Monthly. Circulation: 450. Not copyrighted. Will send free sample copy to writer on request. Submit material for special Easter, Thanksgiving and Christmas issues 2 months in advance. Enclose S.A.S.E. for return of submissions.
Nonfiction: "Safety articles, quality of product, general information fillers, articles on new personnel and equipment, think articles." Length: 250 to 500 words. Pays $25 to $50.
Fiction: Mystery, suspense, adventure, erotica, fantasy, humor. Length: 250 to 500 words. Pays $25 to $50.
Fillers: Safety puzzles, clippings, jokes, short humor. Pays $25 to $50.

THE KRAFTSMAN, 500 Peshtigo Court, Chicago IL 60690. Editor: Lee B. Mulder. Company publication of Kraft Foods Co. For employees and retirees of multi-product, multi-national food company, average age 30, interests in travel, outdoors, and family activity. Established in 1923. Every two months. Circulation: 20,000. Buys simultaneous rights. Buys 6 mss per year. Pays on acceptance. Will send free sample copy to writer on request. Query first. Submit seasonal material 3 months in advance. Reports in 2 to 4 weeks. Enclose S.A.S.E. for response to query or return of submission.
Nonfiction and Photos: "Anything with company, employee or product tie-in. Writing must be first class. We work for the human element; foibles, personal anecdotes, always worked into story and company tie-in somehow. Length: 1,000 to 4,000 words. Can use good Christmas stories approximately 2,000 words." "Payment rates vary from $20 to $100 depending upon writing quality." B&w photos purchased with accompanying mss or on assignment. Captions required. Pays $50 per page maximum.

MUTUAL MAGAZINE, Room 359, P.C. Station, Philadelphia PA 19104. Editor: William D. Gorman. For "Penn Central Railroad employees, officials, and their families." Monthly. Circulation: 15,000. Buys first rights. Pays on acceptance. Will send a sample copy to a writer on request. Query first. Submit seasonal material 2 months in advance. Reports "immediately." Enclose S.A.S.E. for reply to queries.
Nonfiction and Photos: "Articles about employees, their business, or the Penn Central Railroad plant. We buy very little freelance material." Pays 2¢ a word. Photos purchased with mss and without mss; captions required. "Must deal with railroading." B&w only. Pays $5 minimum.

NEWS OF THE ENGINEERING DEPARTMENT, Louviers Building, E.I. Du Pont de Nemours & Co., Inc., Wilmington DE 19898. Editor: Michael R. Tyler. For employees. Monthly. Buys one-time rights. Pays on publication. Will send a sample copy to a writer on request. Query first. Will consider photocopied submissions. Reports in 2 weeks. Enclose S.A.S.E. for reply to queries.
Nonfiction and Photos: "General items with Du Pont engineering department tie-in; engineering accomplishments of the company." Length: 2,000 words maximum. Pays $50 to $250. 8x10 b&w glossies purchased with mss and with captions only.

ONAN NEWS, ONAN DISTRIBUTOR NEWS, 1400 73rd Ave. N.E., Minneapolis MN 55432. Editor: Dennis Lynard. For "Onan employees, distributors, dealers, and customers." Monthly (*Onan News*); bimonthly (*Onan Distributor News*). Circulation: 8,000. Not copyrighted. Buys about 12 mss a year. Pays on acceptance. Will send a sample copy to a writer on request. Query first. Will not consider photocopied submissions. Reports on material accepted for publication in 30 days. Returns rejected material in 15 days. Enclose S.A.S.E. for return of submissions.
Nonfiction and Photos: "Application stories on Onan products and feature stories on Onan employees, distributors, and dealers. The story should be readable, informative, and interesting. It should be able to stand alone, and the mention of Onan products should not necessarily be important to the story line." Length: "about 1,000 words, but we will look at anything on the subject, no matter how short. And if it takes 5,000 well-chosen words to put a message across, we'll consider that, too. Remuneration depends on so many things other than the number of words: difficulty in obtaining the material, accompanying photographs (we prefer contact sheets and require negatives—b&w with captions only), quality of article, timeliness, and degree of importance of theme to our audience. Our normal pay for a four-page typed article accompanied by 8 to 12 b&w negatives is $150. This includes expenses, unless an additional allowance is authorized in advance by the editor."

PEN (Public Employee News), 444 Sherman St., Denver CO 80203. Editor: Jean Blair Ryan. For "members of the Federal Postal Employees Association and federal, state, county, city, and public school employees." Monthly. Circulation: 70,000. Buys first North American serial rights. Buys about 100 mss a year. Pays on acceptance. Will send a sample copy to a writer on request. Query first or submit complete ms. "Submit only 1 ms at a time for articles or fiction. When submitting light verse or fillers, no more than 10 per submission and only 1 to a page." Enclose S.A.S.E. for return of submissions or reply to queries.
Nonfiction and Photos: "*Pen* is of general reader and family interest. We publish material on travel, animals, nature, public service agencies (for example, the U.S. Patent Office and the Government Printing Office have been covered in the past), human interest, historical articles, etc. The approach should be straightforward, simple, and informative in order to achieve our magazine goal, which is to inform and entertain. We do not use local personality stories, and we do not wish editorializing or articles on controversial issues that might be offensive to any group. Emphasis is placed on articles relevant to the season or holiday: July, December, Easter, Thanksgiving, and historical dates." Length: 2,500 words maximum; "a length of 1,500 to 2,000 words is preferable." Pays 3¢ a word. Photos purchased with mss; captions required. Prefers "sharp" 8x10 b&w glossies ("4x5 is the absolute minimum size"). Pays $5 "if used for ms illustration; $5 to $10 if used for cover."
Fiction: Mystery, humorous, adventure, stories concerned with contemporary problems, light romantic stories. Length: 1,500 to 2,500 words. Pays 3¢ a word.

Poetry: "Light verse and some serious commemorative poetry." Length: 16 lines maximum. Pays 50¢ a line.
Fillers: Short humor, quips, jests, newsbreaks. Length: 10 to 350 words, fillers; open, jokes. Pays $1 to $2 for jokes, 3¢ a word maximum for fillers.

PGW NEWS, Philadelphia Gas Works, 1800 N. 9th St., Philadelphia PA 19122. Editor: William B. Hall. For "company employees, retirees, suppliers, other gas companies in U.S. and abroad, government officials in Pennsylvania." Monthly. Circulation: 5,000. Not copyrighted. Pays on acceptance. Will send a sample copy to a writer on request. Submit seasonal material 3 to 4 months in advance. Reports in 1 to 2 months. Enclose S.A.S.E. for return of submissions.
Nonfiction: "Material that is related to employees or that could be employee-directed. We put considerable stress on personality features. Nothing from extremist sources will be considered. We are straight and middle-of-the-road in our presentation." Buys how-to's, patriotic pieces, inspirational and some travel articles and think pieces. Length: 1,000 words. Pays $25 minimum.
Photos: B&w glossies. Pays $10 minimum.

SEVENTY SIX MAGAZINE, Union Oil Co., Box 7600, Los Angeles CA 90054. Editor: Peter Craigmoe. For employees of Union Oil Co. Buys all rights. Pays on acceptance. Query first. Enclose S.A.S.E. for reply to queries.
Nonfiction: "Articles with tie-in to company, its products, its customers or economics of petroleum/energy/fertilizer business. We try to achieve a *Reader's Digest* style: use of anecdotes to tell a story. No technical articles. We like conflict, a dark moment, and our hero (either a person or the product), which is well planted, comes to the rescue at the last moment. In short, we like a nonfiction article organized around fiction plotting principles. No dealer stories. No travel articles." Length: 500 to 1,800 words. Pays 10¢ to 30¢ a word.
Photos: "Must have story-telling values." Pays regular professional rates.

SINGER LIGHT, 30 Rockefeller Plaza, New York NY 10020. Editor: Jim Kleckner. For Singer employees. Circulation: 80,000. Usually buys all rights. Pays on acceptance. Will send a sample copy to a writer on request. "It's best to query on major articles." Enclose S.A.S.E. for reply to queries.
Nonfiction and Photos: "News items and feature articles with a Singer product or Singer employee tie-in. Stories should be illustrated with photos." Length: 1,500 words maximum. Pays 10¢ a word for news items of 200 words maximum. Pays $50 to $250 for features, "depending on length, scope, and quality." Photos purchased with mss. Buys picture stories with a Singer product or Singer employee tie-in. "We prefer the available light approach wherever practical." Send b&w contact sheets or 8x10 glossies; "no color." Model releases required. Pays $50 to $250 for picture stories, "depending on number of pictures, scope, and quality." Pays $10 to $25 for single photos with captions, "depending on importance or originality."

UNIROYAL MANAGEMENT, Oxford Management and Research Center, Middlebury CT 06749. Editor: Robert M. Berzok. Published by Uniroyal, Inc. for "management employees, including sales, engineers, scientists, and general management." Established in 1967. 8 times a year. Circulation: 11,000. Buys all rights. Pays on acceptance. Will send a sample copy to a writer on request. Will consider photocopied submissions. Reports in 3 weeks. Enclose S.A.S.E. for return of submissions.
Nonfiction and Photos: "How-to-manage articles, industry and management trend articles. This publication primarily deals with Uniroyal—its people, places, and products—and must relate to Uniroyal employees." Buys informational articles, how-to's, personal experience articles, interviews, profiles, inspirational articles, humor, think pieces, coverage of successful business operations and merchandising techniques. Length: 600 to 1,200 words. Pays $50 to $200. 8x10 b&w glossies purchased with mss; captions required. Pays $20 per photo.

UNIROYAL WORLD, Oxford Management and Research Center, Middlebury CT 06749. Editor: Robert M. Berzok. Published by Uniroyal, Inc. for "wage and salary employees, all ages and educations; they are plant, office, and management employees." Established in 1964. 8 times a year. Circulation: 65,000. Not copyrighted. Pays on acceptance. Will send a sample copy to a writer on request. Will consider photocopied submissions. Reports in 3 weeks. Enclose S.A.S.E. for return of submissions.

Nonfiction and Photos: "This publication deals primarily with Uniroyal—its people, places, and products. We publish general information dealing with specific aspects of Uniroyal and the rubber industry. Articles must relate to Uniroyal employees." Buys informational articles, how-to's, personal experience articles, interviews, profiles, humor, think articles, coverage of successful business operations and merchandising techniques. Length: 600 to 1,200 words. Pays $50 to $200. 8x10 b&w glossies purchased with mss; captions required. Pays $20 per photo.

VULCAN VARIETIES, 6 E. Fourth St., Cincinnati OH 45202. Editor: Carol J. Morris. Publication of Vulcan Corp. for "factory workers who are middle-aged, lower income, and hard working and who have a high school education (or less). They're interested in home life, family projects, and upgrading their standard of living." Established in 1955. Monthly. Circulation: 2,500. Not copyrighted. Pays on acceptance. Will send a sample copy to a writer on request. Submit complete ms for nonfiction. Prefers photocopied submissions. Submit seasonal material 6 months in advance. Reports on material accepted for publication in 1 month. Returns rejected material in 2 weeks. Enclose S.A.S.E. for return of submissions.

Nonfiction and Photos: Articles on "money management, household and do-it-yourself hints; health and nutrition; sewing and fashion hints; low-key inspirational pieces; lawn and garden care; auto maintenance; explanation of federal taxes, benefits; good vacations; hobbies. Articles should incorporate the practical, inspirational, traditional, nostalgic, and helpful. We need short, simple articles with little detail, and might buy a series of articles." Buys how-to's, inspirational and historical articles, humor, nostalgia, photo features, travel articles, and new product articles. Length: 75 to 450 words. Pays $5 to $15. 4x5 glossy b&w photos purchased with mss; captions optional.

WEATHERBALL NEWS, Northwestern National Bank of Minneapolis, Seventh and Marquette, Minneapolis MN 55480. Editor: Teri Willett Hjermstad. For "Northwestern National Bank of Minneapolis employees." Quarterly. Not copyrighted. Pays on publication. Query first or submit complete ms. Will send a sample copy to a writer on request. Enclose S.A.S.E. for return of submissions or reply to queries.

Nonfiction and Photos: "Banking, general office features which apply to our employees. Features with a human interest slant are definitely preferred." Length: 750 words minimum. Pays $100 maximum. Photos purchased with mss. "Must tie in appropriately with the written article. No posed shots—they must look candid; good contrast necessary." 5x7 or larger, or 35mm transparencies. "Payment depends on quality and artistic merit of photo."

General Interest

The magazines in this category publish broad general interest material designed to inform and entertain a wide spectrum of readers. Some are sponsored by individual companies (for example, The American Way) to promote good will among customers and sell company products (flight bags, etc.) through advertising pages. The rest are produced by specialty publishers as a service to businesses that don't publish their own customer magazine, yet want to distribute one. (Either the publisher or the company imprints the name and address of the company on the front cover before the magazines are given away.) Both kinds resemble Consumer General Interest publications or Sunday Supplements, in their editorial content. A few magazines in the Customers' and Employees' classifications also use general interest material.

Some specialty house-magazine publishers also produce magazines geared to certain trades (for example, Perfect Home, for lumber dealers and homebuilders to distribute). These are classified in the Miscellaneous Sponsored category. Customer-directed publications that use material closely tied to an individual company's products or services will be found in the Customers' category.

In-Flight

AIR CALIFORNIA MAGAZINE, Box 707, South Laguna CA 92677. Editor: Sheldon Kilbane. For business executives, salesmen, upper middle-class Californians. Established in 1966. Monthly. Circulation: 100,000. Rights purchased vary with author and material. May buy first North American serial rights, first serial rights or second serial (reprint) rights. Buys 50 mss a year. Payment on publication. Will send sample copy to writer for $1. Query first. Enclose S.A.S.E. for reply to queries.
Nonfiction and Photos: Travel and profile articles; "anything of interest to our audience." Approach should be "breezy and entertaining; never dull or boring. Avoid trite landmarks and cliche travel pieces." Humorous or historical articles; nostalgia, photo, successful business operations. Length: 3,500 words maximum. Pays $25 to $50. 8x10 glossy b&w photos and 35mm color transparencies purchased with or without ms. Captions required. Payment negotiated. Photo Dept. Editor: Thomas Grim.

ALOFT, 4025 Ponce de Leon Blvd., Coral Gables FL 33146. Editor: Karl Wickstrom. For National Airlines passengers. Travel-oriented. Offbeat places, things to see and do along NAL route or connecting areas. Designed for light upbeat entertainment. Quarterly. Rights to be negotiated. Pays on publication. Will send a sample copy to a writer on request. Query first. Will consider photocopied submissions. Reports in 4 to 6 weeks. Enclose S.A.S.E. with queries and submissions.
Nonfiction and Photos: Articles on unusual or little-known places rather than national monuments, historical sites, and the usual commercial attractions and travel brochure type of thing. Each issue contains at least one piece by or about a known personality. Also gourmet dining (with recipes), a children's activity page, book reviews, fashion, etc. No controversial or expose articles. Length: 800 to 1,500 words. Pays $150 and up for articles. Query Ms. Pat Pinkerton, Executive Editor. Color transparencies are purchased with mss or captions on travel, sports, adventure. Must be top quality with imaginative approach. No snapshots or Polaroids. Payment negotiated. Photo Editor: Theodore R. Baker.

THE AMERICAN WAY, 633 Third Ave., New York NY 10017. Editor: Glen Walker. For businessmen and miscellaneous travelers. Monthly. Circulation: 3,600,000 annually. Rights purchased vary with author and material. May buy all rights. Payment on acceptance. Will send free sample copy to writer on request. Query first. Will consider photocopied submissions, "only if we don't have to return them." Submit seasonal material 7 months in advance. Reports 4 months prior to an issue." Enclose S.A.S.E. with queries.
Nonfiction: "*The American Way,* in addition to articles on travel, sports, food and the arts, tries to provide its readers stimulating and thought-provoking material that deals with current issues. First off, we like queries rather than actual mss. Also we like writing samples which more or less show a writer's abilities and scope. These will not be returned. We seek out the unusual aspects of both the relatively unknown and the familiar. We are essentially a news magazine, not a travel magazine. We want articles on ecology and the environment; art, culture; important historical events that may be relatively unknown to the broad spectrum of our readers." Informational, how-to, interview, profile, humor, historical, think articles, nostalgia, travel, successful business operations and new product articles. Regular columns include: Living the Long Weekend, Pointers, The American Way, Yesterday. Length: 2,500 words. Pays $200 minimum, $400 maximum.
Fillers: "We can possibly use short humor pieces." Length: 2,500 words. Pays average of $200 for humor.

EAST/WEST NETWORK, 3540 Wilshire Blvd., Suite 707, Los Angeles CA 90010. Editorial Director: James C. Clark. In-flight magazines for Allegheny Airlines, Aloha Airlines, Continental Airlines, Delta Air Lines, Hughes Airwest, Pacific Southwest Airlines, Pan American World Airways and United Air Lines. Established in 1968. Monthly. Combined circulation of over 8,000,000. Buys all rights. Buys 200 mss a year. Pays on publication. Will send free sample copy to writer for $1. Reports in 1 month. Enclose S.A.S.E. for return of submissions.
Nonfiction: "On business, topical subjects, sports, personalities, future trends, desti-

nations, geared to an international audience. Nothing on airlines or planes or the history of aviation." Length: 1,500 words maximum. Pays $100.

FLIGHTIME MAGAZINES, East/West Network, Inc., 3540 Wilshire Blvd., Suite 707, Los Angeles CA 90010. Editor: James C. Clark. Separate magazines for in-flight travelers on Pacific Southwest Airlines, Hughes Airwest, and Continental Airlines; predominantly affluent businessmen, ages 35 to 55. Monthly. Circulation: over 1,350,000. Buys all rights. Pays within 15 days after publication. Will send a sample copy to a writer for $1. Limited market. Query first. Enclose S.A.S.E. for reply to queries and return of submissions.
Nonfiction and Photos: Variety, sports, travel, business, wines, dining, personalities. Prefers sports and business features. Taboos are partisan politics or religion. Length: approximately 1,500 words. Payment negotiable; $100 maximum. Photos purchased with mss.

NORTHLINER, 1999 Shepard Rd., St. Paul MN 55116. Editor: Don Picard. For male businessmen who are traveling aboard North Central's planes. Established in 1970. Quarterly. Circulation: 80,000. Buys all rights. Buys 10 or 12 mss a year. Payment on acceptance. Will send free sample copy to writer on request. Write for copy of editorial guidelines for writers. Query first or submit complete ms. Will consider photocopied submissions, "as long as piece has not been previously published." Submit seasonal material 3 to 4 months in advance. Reports within 2 to 3 weeks. Enclose S.A.S.E. with queries and submissions.
Nonfiction: "Short, lively pieces either somehow related to the cities along North Central's route system, or appealing to the traveling businessmen. Writing should be readable rather than academic, clever rather than endlessly descriptive, and tight rather than verbose. No travel stories per se, and very few how-to stories." Informational, interview, profile, humor, think articles, nostalgia, and successful business operations articles. Length: 900 to 1,500 words. Pays $75 to $250 per story.
Photos: Purchased with accompanying mss and on assignment. Captions required. 35mm or larger color photos. Pays $200 for cover; $50 each for inside originals.
Fillers: Puzzles, jokes, and short humor. Pays $5 to $35.

ON ARRIVAL, 488 Madison Ave., New York NY 10022. Editorial Director: Lynne Whiteley. Published for Overseas National Airways. Quarterly. Query first. Enclose S.A.S.E.
Nonfiction: "We use both travel and general interest articles. Travel pieces should give details on food, prices, where to stay, etc." For example, articles such as an interview with Gay Talese, a travel article on the Balearic Islands, and a graphology feature. Length: maximum 1,500 words. Pays maximum $250. B&w photos purchased with mss.

PASSAGES, 747 Third Ave., New York NY 10017. Editor: Richard Stewart. For fairly affluent businessmen, 30 to 55, with college education and many outside interests. Established in 1970. Monthly. Circulation: 150,000. Rights purchased vary with author and material. Buys all rights, but will reassign rights to author after publication; second serial (reprint) rights; simultaneous rights. Buys 50 mss a year. Payment on publication. Will send free sample copy to writer on request. Write for copy of guidelines for writers. Will consider photocopied submissions. Submit seasonal material 6 months in advance. Reports in 2 to 3 months. Enclose S.A.S.E. for return of submissions.
Nonfiction and Photos: "Travel articles with added dimension of social significance, such as ecology, lifestyles, profiles, business related, sports, science, aviation-related; historical especially, with reference to Northwest destination points. Special need for humor. Writer's own style preferred, with an easy style generally better for informational pieces such as humor. Writers should look to contribute meaning, understanding to reader. Generally seek constructive pieces. Creative, business-related articles along with constructive ones on environment and city improvement. Ski and other sports. Leisure time activities." Length: 1,000 to 3,000 words. Pays $50 to $300, with more payment ($25) made for transparencies bought with mss. Also, pays more for assigned work. Color transparencies purchased with mss. Captions optional. Art Director: Ken Hine.
Fiction and Fillers: "Humorous fiction." Theme is open. Length: 1,000 to 2,000

words. Pays $50 to $200. Fiction Editor: Ken Zeserson. Also buys varied puzzles. Pays $50. Filler Dept. Editor: Deborah McRoy.

PASTIMES, 4 W. 58th St., Tenth Floor, New York NY 10019. Publisher: Carroll B. Stoianoff. Distributed by Eastern Airlines for "the *New Yorker* reader—top 20% of population in income and education. All travelers, very deep in frequent air travelers. 67% male—average age 39 years. 29% have family income over $25,000 a year." Bimonthly. Circulation: 600,000. Rights purchased vary with author and material; may buy all rights (but may reassign rights to author after publication), first North American serial rights, first serial rights, second serial (reprint) rights, or simultaneous rights. Pays on publication. Write for copy of guidelines for writers. Query first always. Will consider photocopied submissions. Reports in 2 weeks. Enclose S.A.S.E. for reply to queries.

Nonfiction: "Short, intelligent humor or novelty material which will intrigue, hold attention of, and entertain college-educated business and professional people. Must not be overtly or implicitly controversial in any way or rely on shock or satire for its effect. *Pastimes* does not treat general subject matter in the same way as other magazines. It is a bright, relaxed, adult entertainment publication whose primary mission is to interest and amuse intelligent air travelers as a group comprised of intelligent Americans of all persuasions and convictions. We are interested in all topical subjects, but with an original, offbeat, and generally appealing approach rather than the conventional journalistic or didactic approach." Buys interviews, sports articles, profiles, humor, historical articles, think pieces, nostalgia, photo features, travel articles. Length: 1,000 words maximum. Pays $25 to $100.

Photos: Purchased with or without mss or on assignment. Payment "negotiable."

PSA Magazine, 3540 Wilshire Blvd., Suite 707, Los Angeles, CA 90010. Editor: Thomas Shess, Jr. Published by Pacific Southwest Airlines for "California businessmen with incomes averaging $20,000 per annum." Established in 1968. Monthly. Circulation: 500,000. Rights purchased vary with author and material. Buys about 40 mss a year. Pays on publication. Will send a sample copy to a writer for $1. Query first. Reports in 30 days. Enclose S.A.S.E. for reply to queries and return of submissions.

Nonfiction: "California business, restaurants, saloons, cars, travel, sports, construction, fashions. Articles must be by Californians and about California living. Ours is the only statewide publication for high income California businessmen. No articles on air travel, politics, and religion. We'd like to see more articles on California business and businessmen." Buys how-to's, interviews, profiles, humor, historical articles, think pieces, coverage of successful business operations, new product articles, and coverage of merchandising techniques. Length: 1,500 words. Pays $50 to $150. Photos purchased with ms; captions required. For 8x10 b&w glossies, pays $15. For 35mm color, payment "varies, up to $100 for cover."

SOUTHERN SCENE, 2161 Monroe Dr., N.E., Atlanta GA 30324. Editor: Jane R. Leonard. Published by Southern Airways, Inc. "Average reader is a middle-aged family man, well-educated, highly paid, and he lives in the South. He entertains at home frequently and takes long vacations. His bar and wine cellar are well-stocked; he's a sportsman and camera bug." Established in 1968. Quarterly. Circulation: 80,000. Rights purchased vary with author and material; buys all rights, first serial rights, or second serial (reprint) rights. Buys about 30 mss a year. Pays on acceptance. Will send a sample copy to a writer on request. "All articles are specifically assigned. Interested freelancers should submit brief resume on writing background and rates to editor. If possible, tearsheets of published work should be enclosed." Enclose S.A.S.E.

Nonfiction: "Travel articles focusing on cities on the Southern Airways route system (the South, St. Louis, Chicago, and New York). Since the magazine is a public relations piece for Southern Airways, articles should strive to promote good will. The articles should be specifically geared to the Southern businessman and traveler. We're interested in articles on travel, business, special interests with a Southern slant." Buys informational articles, humor, historical articles, photo articles, travel pieces, and coverage of successful business operations. Length: 1,500 to 3,000 words. Pays $150 to $400, "depending on subject and accompanying photos."

Photos: Purchased with mss, "preferably," without mss, or on assignment; captions required. Uses 35mm or 2¼x2¼ Kodachrome. Payment "negotiable with multiple use; $25 to $200 for one-time use."

TWA AMBASSADOR, 1999 Shepard Rd., St. Paul MN 55116. Editor: Bill Farmer. For TWA passengers; top management executives, professional men and women and world travelers. 57.4% men; 42.6% women; technical managers, officials, proprietors, college graduates. Established in 1968. Monthly. Circulation: 321,000. Buys all rights. Payment on acceptance. Will send free sample copy to writer on request. Write for copy of guidelines for writers. Query first. Will consider photocopied submissions. Submit seasonal material at least 4 months in advance. Reports on material accepted for publication in 2 months. Returns rejected material in 6 weeks. Enclose S.A.S.E. for reply to queries.
Nonfiction and Photos: "Most TWA passengers are business oriented, but the airlines serve people of all areas of the world, all strata of society. Therefore, all stories must be in good taste. Keep in mind the international scope of this magazine avoid subjects of provincial interest. Our travel stories must have a specific story angle from a TWA-route city; unique articles from TWA cities in the United States that would be of interest to the international businessman. We do not use general descriptive pieces about a city or area or where-to-shop, where-to-eat, what-to-see, broadbush travel articles. We avoid flying type articles. First-person approach is unacceptable, and because of our lead time, news-type stories are unacceptable. Our goal is to entertain and inform the international reader via an editorial mix consisting of articles on sports, business, personalities, general human interest topics and foreign and domestic travel." Length: 1,000 to 1,500 words. Pays up to $500 per story. Color photos purchased with accompanying ms. 35mm or larger. $50 inside; $250 cover.

WESTERN'S WORLD, 141 El Camino, Beverly Hills CA 90212. Editor: Frank M. Hiteshew. Published by Western Airlines for the airline traveler. Established in 1970. 5 times a year. Circulation: 250,000. Buys all rights. Buys 20 to 25 mss a year. Pays on publication. Query first. Will consider photocopied submissions. Submit seasonal material 12 months in advance of issue date. Reports in 1 to 3 months. Enclose S.A.S.E. for reply to queries and return of submissions.
Nonfiction: "Articles should relate to travel, dining, or entertainment in the area served by Western Airlines: Hawaii, Minneapolis/St. Paul, Alaska to Mexico, and between. Compared to other airline magazines, *Western's World* strives for a more editorial approach. It's not as promotional-looking; all articles are bylined articles. Some top names in the field." Buys photo features and travel articles. Length: 1,000 to 2,000 words. Pays 10¢ a word.
Photos: Purchased with or without mss or on assignment; captions required. Uses 8x10 b&w glossies, but "rarely." Pays $25. Uses 35mm, 4x5, and larger color transparencies. Pays $25 to $125; "more for cover, subject to negotiation." Tom Medsger, Assistant Editor.
Fiction: Western short stories, fantasy, humor. "Rarely printed because we've seen so few good ones. Should relate to *Western's World*." Length: 1,000 to 2,000 words. Pays 10¢ a word.
Fillers: "Travel-oriented or brain-teasers." Pays 10¢ per word. Dept. Editor: Tom Medsger.

Other

ACCENT, 1720 Washington Blvd., P.O. Box 1373, Ogden UT 84402. Editor: Helen S. Crane. For "a wide segment, from the young couple to the retired one." Established in 1968. Monthly. Circulation: 350,000. Buys 10 to 12 mss a year. Pays on acceptance. Will send a sample copy to a writer on request. Query first. Will consider photocopied submissions. Submit seasonal material at least 6 months in advance. Enclose S.A.S.E. for reply to queries and return of submissions.
Nonfiction and Photos: "The large majority of our articles are written on assignment by professional writers knowledgeable in their fields. We do, however, consider interest-capturing, short features from freelancers. Since our emphasis is on pictures, and our copy space very limited, we require concise, informative, yet lively writing that covers a lot in a few words. We want pieces of lasting general interest

suitable for the family. We do not need rambling experience pieces, preachy pieces, or ecology features; nor do we want holiday material. We use a few travel vignettes about exciting yet well-known spots and pieces showing glimpses of life and unusual activities. Writing should be in a fresh, sparkling style." Pays about 5¢ per word. Photos purchased with mss; captions required. "For the most part, we prefer views without people, particularly if they tend to date the views. If people are present, they should be actively engaged in interesting ways. Subjects must be eye-catching and colors sharp." For "at least 5x7" b&w glossies, pays $10 to $15. For color transparencies ("some 35mm, prefer larger"), pays $25 minimum ("more for larger views or covers").

BAROID NEWS BULLETIN, P.O. Box 1675, Houston TX 77001. Editor: Kit van Cleave. Publication of Baroid Division, N L Industries. "The market we serve are primarily employees of the petroleum industry." Established in 1948. Quarterly. Circulation: 18,000. Buys all rights, but will reassign rights to author after publication. Buys 15 to 20 mss a year "but we could buy more." Pays on acceptance. Will send sample copy to writer on request. Submit complete ms. Reports on material in 1 week. Enclose S.A.S.E. for return of submissions.

Nonfiction and Photos: "We prefer articles of the prose feature story type. Travel, sports, the Old West or Civil War, historical material, and humor are some good topics. But we will print anything that is quality, especially if it is oilfield oriented. This is a quarterly of quality writing and art plus technical articles written by our employees. We will not publish any material that is revolutionary politically, or knocks America or the free enterprise system." Informational, humor, historical, nostalgia, travel, and pro-free enterprise articles. Length: 1,000 to 3,000 words. Payment ranges from 3¢ to 10¢ per word. Sharp, clear, creative photos purchased with mss. Pays $5 to $10 for 5x7 or 8x10 b&w. Captions required. Pays $10 to $15 for 5x7 or 8x10 color photos.

Fiction: Should be related to oil field. Also buys suspense, adventure, western, humorous, historical, pro-America. Length: 1,000 to 3,000 words. Pays 3¢ to 10¢ per word.

Poetry: Should relate to the oil field. Traditional, blank verse, free verse and light verse. Length: Not over 2 typewritten pages. Pays minimum of 3¢ per word; maximum depends on quality.

Fillers: "Our 'Celebrations' column uses 3 or 4 math or logical problems per issue. These are petroleum-related puzzles." Length: open. Pays minimum of 3¢ per word.

HOLIDAY INN MAGAZINE, PO Box 18253, Memphis TN 38118. Editor: Lois Crowe. "We are not in the market for freelance material."

IDEAS FOR BETTER LIVING, GOOD LIVING MAGAZINE, 1755 Northwest Blvd., Columbus OH 43212. Editor: Patrick H. Welsh. For "established customers of financial institutions interested in products and ideas for the average home." Consumer oriented material. Established in 1947. Monthly. Circulation: 100,000 (Good Living); 400,000 (Better Living). Not copyrighted. Buys "very few mss a year, mostly because we aren't offered many good ones." Payment on acceptance. Will send a free sample copy to writer on request. Query first. Will consider photocopied submissions. Reports on material accepted for publication in 3 weeks. Returns rejected material within a week. Enclose S.A.S.E. for reply to queries.

Nonfiction and Photos: "How-to stories, primarily, with some general interest educational material every now and then. We don't carry many 'thoughty' stories or essays. Subject matter is not too deep. Standard style is used. Stories should be addressed to homeowners who want to save time/money. Take a casual, informal outlook and try to develop stories quickly. We try not to get too lofty with our ideas. Projects, designs and concepts are usually within the realm of the average American family, not the super-talented, super-sophisticated and super-rich." Length: 200 to 800 words. Pays minimum of $25. Pays $25 on acceptance for 5x7 or larger b&w glossy b&w prints, 8x10 color transparencies, submitted with or without mss. "We buy many 'arty' subjects for our editorial pages."

Fillers: Puzzles, word games, jokes, "interesting facts." Maximum of 50 words. Pays $2.50 each.

INSURANCE MAGAZINE, Allied Publications Inc., P.O. Box 23505, Fort Lauderdale FL 33307. Associate Editor: Louise Hinton. For "the general public, all ages." Bimonthly. Buys North American serial rights only. Pays on acceptance. No query necessary. Reports in 2 to 4 weeks. Enclose S.A.S.E. with all mss.
Nonfiction and Photos: Wants how-to, inspirational, humor, and travel articles. Length: 500 to 1,000 words. Payment is 5¢ a word, and $5 for photos purchased with mss.

THE IRON WORKER, Lynchburg Foundry (A Mead Company), P.O. Drawer 411, Lynchburg VA 24505. Editor: B.J. Hillman. For Lynchburg Foundry's customers and public in general; generally slanted to upper intellectual group. Quarterly. Circulation: 10,000. Buys first rights. Buys approximately 5 mss a year. Pays on acceptance. Will send a sample to a writer on request. Query first. Submit seasonal material 1 year in advance. Returns rejected material in 6 months. Enclose S.A.S.E. for reply to queries.
Nonfiction: Wants significant Virginia-related articles about American history with national appeal. "Articles submitted must show depth of research on a new or unexplored historical topic. Must be well-written." Prefers action-oriented articles. Also buys historical articles with human interest, biographies on significant Virginians if previously unexplored, or other historical incidents, topics or personalities which show original research. "Prefer not to see articles without strong Virginia tie, articles of strictly local interest or subjects which have already received exhaustive treatment." Length: 3,500 to 5,000 words. Pays $200 to $600.

MODERN LIVING, Allied Publications, Inc., P.O. Box 23505, Fort Lauderdale FL 33307. Associate Editor: Louise Hinton. For "the average homeowner." Bimonthly. Buys North American serial rights only. Pays on acceptance. No query necessary. Reports in 2 to 4 weeks. Enclose S.A.S.E. with all submissions.
Nonfiction and Photos: Articles on "home, family, children, teenagers, travel, hobbies, pets, decorating, sports." Buys how-to's, inspirational articles, profiles, humor, spot news, historical and think pieces, travel articles. Length: 500 to 1,000 words. Pays 5¢ per accepted word. Pays $5 for photos purchased with mss.

READER'S NUTSHELL, Allied Publications, Inc., P.O. Box 23505, Fort Lauderdale FL 33307. Associate Editor: Marie Stilkind. Bimonthly. Buys North American serial rights only. Pays on acceptance. Query not necessary. Reports in 2 to 4 weeks. Enclose S.A.S.E. for return of submissions.
Nonfiction and Photos: "Family magazine for all ages." Wants "humorous articles of general interest." Length: 500 to 1,000 words. Pays 5¢ per accepted word. Pays $5 for photos purchased with mss; b&w glossies.

THE SAMPLE CASE, 632 N. Park St., Columbus OH 43215. Editor: James R. Eggert. For members of the United Commercial Travelers of America, located throughout the U.S. and Canada; 18 years of age and older, with a wide range of interests, educations, and occupations. Established in 1891. Monthly. Rights purchased vary with author and material. Buys all rights, but will reassign rights to author after publication; buys first North American serial rights; first serial rights; second serial (reprint) rights; simultaneous rights. Buys 25 to 50 mss a year. Payment on publication. Will send free sample copy to writer on request. Write for copy of guidelines for writers. Will consider photocopied submissions. Submit seasonal material 2 months in advance. Reports in 4 months. Enclose S.A.S.E. for return of submissions.
Nonfiction and Photos: "Especially interested in general interest nonfiction. We pay special attention to articles about mental retardation, youth, safety, and cancer." Informational, personal experience, interview, some humor. Length: 500 to 2,000 words. Pays 1½¢ per word. Additional payment for good quality b&w glossies purchased with mss. Captions required.

VALLEY LIGHTS, Blackstone Valley Electric Co., P.O. Box 1111, Lincoln RI 02865. Editor: Paul Pinkham. Bimonthly. Circulation: 900. Not copyrighted. Buys about 6 mss a year. Pays on publication. Submit seasonal material 2 months in advance. Reports in 4 to 6 weeks. Enclose S.A.S.E. for return of submissions.

Nonfiction and Photos: How-to's, humor, think pieces, new product coverage, photo and travel articles, safety articles. Length: open. Pays $10 to $40. B&w glossies purchased with mss.

Miscellaneous

BUYWAYS, 534 N. Broadway, Milwaukee WI 53202. Editor: Glenn Helgeland. For "families, low-middle to middle income, average education, mid-thirties in age; like to travel, but must economize when doing so. This is the official publication of the National Association of Consumers and Travelers, which is a group formed by Bankers Life Insurance Company." Established in 1972. Quarterly. Circulation: 125,000. Buys first North American serial rights. Buys 10 to 15 mss a year. Pays on acceptance. Will send a sample copy to a writer on request. Write for copy of guidelines for writers. Query first. Will not consider photocopied submissions. Submit seasonal material at least 3 months in advance of issue date. Reports in 3 weeks. Enclose S.A.S.E. for reply to queries.
Nonfiction: "How and where to travel and stay within a reasonable budget. Interesting places to see and trips to take. Non-travel stories must be based on getting the most for the dollar from everyday living and consuming. Travel stories must be spirited; let the reader enjoy and see with the author. Don't want recountings of 'we went here and did this.' Must be cost-conscious; would like stories to have a short sidebar delineating expected or actual costs. Remember our duality of editorial content—travel and wise family finance. We are more cost-conscious in travel stories and less exotic." Buys informational articles, how-to's, personal experience articles, humor, historical articles, and travel pieces. Length: 500 to 1,800 words. Pays $50 to $250.
Photos: Purchased with or without mss; captions optional. Photo subjects should be the same as nonfiction. For 8x10 b&w glossies, pays $10 to $25. For "any size" color transparency, pays $25 to $75.

EXECUTIVE REVIEW, 224 S. Michigan Ave., Chicago IL 60604. Editor: Harold Sabes. For "management of small and middle-sized companies, middle management in larger companies and corporations." Established in 1955. Monthly. Circulation: 25,000. Not copyrighted. Buys about 10 mss a year. Pays on publication. Will send a sample copy to a writer on request. Submit complete ms. Will consider photocopied submissions. Reports in 1 week. Enclose S.A.S.E. for return of submissions.
Nonfiction: "Articles are mainly how-to, dealing with business activities from the reception desk through the office, manufacturing and delivery. We're interested in articles dealing with business activities and with the personal activities of businessmen. *Executive Review* is sold as an external house organ. It is distributed to the customers and prospects of the sponsor-advertiser." Buys informational articles, how-to's, personal experience articles, humor, think articles, coverage of successful business operations, and articles on merchandising techniques. Length: 1,200 to 1,500 words. Pays up to $50 an article.

EXHIBIT, P.O. Box 23505, Fort Lauderdale FL 33307. Associate Editor: Marie Stilkind. For "customers of art and hobby shops." Bimonthly. Buys North American serial rights only. Pays on acceptance. No queries necessary. Reports on submissions in 2 to 4 weeks. Enclose S.A.S.E. for return of submissions.
Nonfiction and Photos: Articles on art techniques and methods, both commercial and fine art; step-by-step demonstrations showing how a work of art is created; how-to articles, techniques in brush work, how to sell your paintings, etc. Also "how to sell art, art history and theory, profiles of really famous artists known to the general public." Prefers b&w glossy photos with articles if possible. Length: 500 to 1,000 words. Pays 5¢ an accepted word, $5 a photo.

FARMLAND NEWS, 3315 N. Oak Trafficway, P.O. Box 7305, Kansas City MO 64116. Editor: Frank C. Whitsitt. For "farm families who belong to cooperatives served by Farmland Industries." Established in 1932. Biweekly. Circulation: 410,000. Not copyrighted. Buys 100 to 150 mss a year. Pays on acceptance. Will send a sample copy to a writer on request. Will not consider photocopied submissions. Submit seasonal material 3 months in advance. Reports in 2 weeks. Enclose S.A.S.E. for return of submissions.

Nonfiction and Photos: "Articles promoting rural and farm life; some nostalgia. Strong emphasis on human interest, how-to-do-it subjects. The appeal should be general, down-to-earth. We strive to be credible, informative, even inspirational. Easter, Thanksgiving, and Christmas themes are useful." Interested in "concrete self-help efforts to booster rural America and stem urban migration." Buys how-to's, inspirational articles, humor, historical articles, and nostalgia. Length: 1,000 words. Pay "varies, but the average is $25 to $100 per article, plus additional amounts for photos, depending on quality."

Poetry: Themes must be "acceptable to a rural audience." Pays $5. Dept. Editor: Rosetta Hudson.

HAIRSTYLIST, Allied Publications Inc., P.O. Box 23505, Fort Lauderdale FL 33307. Associate Editor: Marie Stilkind. Buys North American serial rights only. Pays on acceptance. Query not necessary. Reports in 2 to 4 weeks. Enclose S.A.S.E. with all mss for return.

Nonfiction and Photos: Wants "articles of general interest to the professional beautician." Interested in how-to's, interviews, and profiles. Length: 500 to 1,000 words. Payment is 3¢ a word. Pays $5 for b&w glossy photos of hairstyles.

INDUSTRIAL PROGRESS, P.O. Box 13208, Phoenix AZ 85002. Editor: Frederick H. Kling. For "executives, management, and professional men (designers, engineers, etc.) in all types of industry." Bimonthly. Pays on acceptance. Enclose S.A.S.E. for return of submissions.

Nonfiction and Photos: "Male interest features; hobbies, sports, novelty, mechanical, do-it-yourself, etc. Must be strongly photographic. Some color photos used." Pays "from $25 to $35 for a single photo-caption item to $150 for short feature with 3 or 4 b&w photos; more for color."

How To Break In: "Ask for a copy of the magazine, study it for material and style, then submit something."

INTERLINE REPORTER, 2 W. 46th St., New York NY 10036. Editor: Eric Friedheim. Buys first serial rights. Query first. Enclose S.A.S.E. for reply to queries.

Nonfiction and Photos: Wants nontechnical articles on airline activities; stories should be slanted to the sales, reservations and counter personnel. Personality stories showing how a job has been well done are particularly welcome. Length: up to 1,200 words. Payment is $50 for articles with photographic illustrations.

LOUISIANA CONSERVATIONIST, 400 Royal St., Room 126-D, New Orleans LA 70130. Editor: McFadden Duffy. Publication of Louisiana Wildlife and Fisheries Commission. For the outdoorsman and his family. Established in 1931. Bimonthly. Circulation: 140,000. Not copyrighted. Payment in contributor's copies. Will send free sample copy to writer on request. Write for copy of guidelines for writers. Query first. "We will look at outlines with query letters." Will not consider photocopied submissions. Submit seasonal material (for Christmas issue only) 6 months in advance. Returns rejected material in 2 weeks. Reports on mss accepted for publication in 6 to 8 weeks. Enclose S.A.S.E. for reply to queries.

Nonfiction and Photos: "We use feature-length articles, including how-to's if they are informative and concisely written, of the outdoor variety. We also consider 'offbeat' pieces if they are written to interest a general audience. Studying the style of the staff writers and published authors in the magazine is the best advice interested writers could get. To be avoided are wordiness, cute tricks, writing with adjectives, and the outmoded 'me and Joe' articles. It is important that a writer be active in the outdoor writing field in order to submit to our magazine."Length: 800 to 2,000 words. Mss should be illustrated with color slides (originals only); 35mm or 2¼x2¼. Payment in contributor's copies.

MAGAZINE OF FLOWERS, Allied Publications, Inc., P.O. Box 23505, Fort Lauderdale FL 33307. Associate Editor: Marie Stilkind. Bimonthly. Buys North American serial rights only. Pays on acceptance. Reports in 2 to 4 weeks. Enclose S.A.S.E. for return of submissions.

Nonfiction and Photos: Articles about professional florists, decorating with flowers and plants in the home or office, flowers for special occasions, history of any type of flower, humor with flowers. Must be written from florist's viewpoint. Length: 500 to 1,000 words. Pays 5¢ per accepted word. Pays $5 for b&w glossies purchased with mss.

MANAGEMENT DIGEST, Allied Publications, Inc., P.O. Box 23505, Fort Lauderdale FL 33307. Associate Editor: Louise Hinton. Buys first North American serial rights. Pays on acceptance. Reports in 2 to 4 weeks. Enclose S.A.S.E. for return of submissions.

Nonfiction and Photos: "Articles of interest to executive management personnel." Buys interviews, profiles, inspirational articles, humor, spot news, coverage of successful business operations, think pieces, photo features, and articles on merchandising techniques. Length: 500 to 1,000 words. Pays 5¢ a word. B&w glossies purchased with mss. Pays $5.

MODERN SECRETARY, Allied Publications, P.O. Box 23505, Fort Lauderdale FL 33307. Associate Editor: Marie Stilkind. Monthly. Buys North American serial rights only. Pays on acceptance. Query not necessary. Reports in 2 to 4 weeks. Enclose S.A.S.E.

Nonfiction and Photos: "Office tips, articles and photos about secretaries. Also articles about secretaries to famous personalities, or other material of interest to secretaries." Length: 500 to 1,000 words. Payment is 5¢ a word, and $5 for b&w glossy photos purchased with mss.

PERFECT HOME MAGAZINE, 427 6th Ave., S.E., Cedar Rapids IA 52401. Editor: Donna Nicholas Hahn. For "homeowners or others interested in building or improving their homes." Established in 1929. Monthly. Buys all rights. Pays on acceptance. Query first. Study magazine carefully before submitting. Submit seasonal material at least 6 months in advance. Reports "at once." Will send free sample copy to a writer on request. Enclose S.A.S.E. for reply to queries.

Nonfiction: "Ours is a nationally syndicated monthly magazine sponsored in local communities by qualified home builders, real estate companies, home financing institutions, and lumber and building supply dealers. We are primarily a photo magazine that creates a desire for an attractive, comfortable home. We need home-building, decorating, and remodeling features, decorating idea photographs, complete home coverage, and plans on homes." No do-it-yourself features. Length: 1 to 3 meaty paragraphs. No set price. "Each month we feature one nationally known guest editor on the theme 'What Home Means to Me.' Check with us before contacting a celebrity, since we have had so many of them." Length: 500 to 1,000 words. Pays $50, including copy, photo, signature, and signed release from individual.

Photos: Purchases photos with articles on home building, decorating and remodeling; also purchases photos of interest to homeowners with captions only. Buys either b&w or color; color 3¼x4¼ up. "We return color; keep b&w unless return is requested as soon as issue has been printed. May hold photos 1 year." Photos must be well-styled and of highest professional quality. No models in pictures. Interested in series (for example, several pictures of gates, bay windows, window treatment, fireplaces, etc.). Pays $7.50 and up.

REVUE DES BEAUX ARTS, Allied Publications, Inc. P.O. Box 23505, Fort Lauderdale FL 33307. Associate Editor: Marie Stilkind. For art collectors. Bimonthly. Buys North American serial rights. Pays on acceptance. Reports in 2 to 4 weeks. Enclose S.A.S.E. for return of submissions.

Nonfiction and Photos: "Articles on art history, current trends, media, famous artists; news in the art world." Buys interviews, profiles, historical articles. Length: 500 to 1,000 words. Pays 5¢ per accepted word. Pays $5 for photos purchased with mss.

TRIP AND TOUR, Allied Publications, Inc., P.O. Box 23505, Fort Lauderdale FL 33307. Associate Editor: Marie Stilkind. For customers of travel agents. Bimonthly. Buys North American serial rights. Pays on acceptance. Query not necessary. Re-

ports in 2 to 4 weeks. Enclose S.A.S.E. for return of submissions.
Nonfiction and Photos. Travel articles and photos on places outside the continental U.S.A." Buys humor and travel pieces. Length: 500 to 1,000 words. Pays 5¢ per accepted word. Pays $5 for photos purchased with mss.

WOMAN BEAUTIFUL, Allied Publications, Inc., P.O. Box 23505, Fort Lauderdale FL 33307. Associate Editor: Marie Stilkind. For "students at beauty schools and people who go to beauty salons." Buys North American serial rights only. Pays on acceptance. Reports in 2 to 4 weeks. Enclose S.A.S.E. with all submissions.
Nonfiction and Photos: "Articles on hairstyling, beauty, and fashion." Length: 500 to 1,000 words. Pays 5¢ per accepted word. Pays $5 for photos of hairstyles.

Union

BOOT & SHOE WORKERS JOURNAL, 1265 Boylston St., Boston MA 02215. Editor: William N. Scanlan. Published by the Boot and Shoe Workers Union, AFL-CIO for "members of the union in the shoe industry. Aged from 18 to 70; men and women; skilled and unskilled." Established in 1896. Bimonthly. Circulation: 40,000. Not copyrighted. Pays on publication. Will send a sample copy to a writer on request. Will consider photocopied submissions. Reports in 2 weeks. Enclose S.A.S.E. for return of submissions.
Nonfiction: "Our members are interested in the advantages of union membership in matters of wages, fringes, human dignity and in achievements through membership. We publish articles on personal success in putting kids through school, overcoming employment handicaps, community achievements of a union, etc. We like true case histories of dignity gained through union membership, community betterment created by labor-management cooperation, community contributions by unions in place of antagonism arising from misunderstanding. We go to readers who actually strive for these results and who want to know that such results are not beyond reach. We have been getting material slanted to retail and manufacturing interests; we want shop-oriented viewpoints by workers or writers who have been through the factory work scene. We are interested in stories of one-industry town whose shoe factory has been forced to close because of foreign shoe imports and the workers' stories of the effects of the closing." Also seeks material for the "Who Needs a Union?" department, which "uses stories of successful grievance processing, winning back wages for aggrieved workers, getting job reinstatement for unfairly fired worker, etc." Length: 250 to 1,500 words. Pays $10 to $35, "more in special cases."
Photos: Purchased with or without mss; captions optional. "Photo subjects should generally be the same as nonfiction, but ironic or unusual shots around which we can write a pro union story are okay." For 2¼x3¼ b&w glossy, pays $5.

UNITED TRANSPORTATION UNION NEWS, 15401 Detroit Ave., Cleveland OH 44107. Editor: Jim Turner. For "members of the United Transportation Union." Weekly. Not copyrighted. Pays on publication. Reports "at once." Enclose S.A.S.E. for return of submissions.
Photos: "Current news shots of railroad accidents, especially when employees are killed or injured." Prefers 8x10 b&w glossies. Pays $10 and up.

FARM PUBLICATIONS

Crops and Soil Management

The publications in this category limit themselves to advising farmers on techniques for raising food from the soil and on cultivating the soil effectively. Other magazines that buy material on the raising of crops and soil management will be found in the General Interest Farming and Rural Life classification.

AMERICAN FRUIT GROWER, 37841 Euclid Ave., Willoughby OH 44094. Editor: R.T. Meister. Monthly. Pays on acceptance. Query first. Enclose S.A.S.E.
Nonfiction and Fillers: Buys short articles about commercial fruit, nut, or berry growers and their practical methods of growing fruit; fertilization; laborsaving devices; spraying; planting; thinning; harvesting; pollination; rodent control; irrigation; weed control. Length: 200 to 1,000 words. Payment is about 1¢ a word. Study publication before submitting these. Does not want poetry or household hints.
Photos: Purchased with mss as well as with captions. Payment is $5 a print.

AMERICAN VEGETABLE GROWER, 37841 Euclid Ave., Willoughby Ohio 44094. Editor: R.T. Meister. Pays on acceptance. Enclose S.A.S.E.
Nonfiction and Photos: Short articles about one particular problem a commercial vegetable grower is having and how he overcomes it. May include plant growing, transplanting, fertilizing, spraying, harvesting, laborsaving ideas, packaging. Send photos with ms. Length: 200 to 1,000 words. Pays about 1¢ per word.
Fillers: "Handy Andy" items welcomed. Uses items pertaining to commercial vegetable industry; especially grower-experience items dealing with the specific problem of the commercial grower and how he solved it. Approximately 200 to 300 words. Pays about 1¢ per word.

COTTON FARMING MAGAZINE, 3637 Park Ave., Memphis TN 38111. Editor: Tom Griffin. Buys all rights. Pays on acceptance. Will send a free sample copy to a writer on request. Reports in 1 week. Enclose S.A.S.E. for return of submissions.
Nonfiction and Photos: Continually looking for material on large-acreage cotton farmers (200 acres or more). Likes stories on one phase of a grower's production such as his weed control program, insect control, land forming work, or how he achieves higher than average yields. Length: 800 to 1,000 words, with 2 or 3 in-the-field photos. Payment is about 8¢ a word.

CRANBERRIES MAGAZINE, R-55 Summer St., Kingston MA 02364. Editor: I.S. Cobb. For "cranberry growers—older audience—interested in growing good crops—most are high school educated—some college." Monthly. Circulation: 2,000. Buys first rights. Buys 2 to 3 mss a year. Pays on publication. Will send a free sample copy to a writer on request. Query first. Reports in 2 to 3 weeks. Enclose S.A.S.E.
Nonfiction and Photos: Wants "personal profiles of cranberry growers—new techniques of growing." Uses how-to's, profiles, spot news, successful business operations, new product, and merchandising techniques stories, and photo essays. Payment is "none to $20." 5x7 b&w glossy photos purchased with mss. Payment is $5.

CROPS AND SOILS MAGAZINE, 677 South Segoe Rd., Madison WI 53711. Editor: William R. Luellen. For above-average farmers, county agents, fertilizer and seed dealers. 9 times a year. Pays on publication. Query first. Reports in 1 month. Enclose S.A.S.E.

Nonfiction and Photos: Articles about current research and articles reviewed for accuracy by USDA or state college workers have best chance for acceptance. Interested in material dealing with new or unusual field crops, seed production methods, new cultivation practices, new harvesting methods, irrigation and drainage practices, tillage, weed and insect control. These can be short items of a few paragraphs up to illustrated features of 1,000 to 1,500 words. Pays 2¢ to 4¢ a word.

RICE FARMING MAGAZINE, 3637 Park Ave., Memphis TN 38111. Editor: Tom Griffin. Buys all rights. Pays on acceptance. Will send a free sample copy to a writer on request. Reports in 1 week. Enclose S.A.S.E. for return of submissions.
Nonfiction and Photos: Continually looking for material on large acreage rice farmers (200 acres or more). Like stories on one phase of grower's production such as his weed control program, insect control, landforming work, or how he achieves higher than average yields. Include 2 or 3 in-the-field photos. Length: 800 to 1,000 words. Payment is about 7¢ a word.

SOYBEAN DIGEST, Hudson IA 50643. Editor: Kent Pellett. For American Soybean Association members. 13 issues a year. Not copyrighted. Will send a free sample copy to a writer on request. Query first. Enclose S.A.S.E.
Nonfiction and Photos: Bulk of editorial material is staff-written, but uses good articles on phases of soybean production and usage and personalities when they have a real message for the industry. Length should be up to 2,000 words. Rates are by arrangement. Occasionally uses 8x10 b&w glossies or color.

THE SUGARBEET, Box 1520, Ogden UT 84402. Editor: A. L. Hanline. Publication of The Amalgamated Sugar Company. For readership "strongly involved in beet sugar industry." Established in 1937. Quarterly. Circulation: 6,500. Not copyrighted. Payment on publication. Will send free sample copy to writer on request. Query first. Enclose S.A.S.E. for reply to queries.
Nonfiction and Photos: "Articles dealing with the growing and harvesting of sugar beets; namely, seed bed preparation, fumigating, fertilizing, planting, weed and insect control, fungus control, irrigating, cultivating, mechanical thinning, harvesting; college research in these areas also desired. Should be tight, direct exposition written to the growers, not research personnel. Each issue is devoted to a specific phase of growing sugar beets during that time of the year." How-to, interview, technical, successful business operations with ample photos. Length: 750 to 2,000 words. Pays $25 to $50. 8x10 b&w glossies purchased with mss. Captions required.

THE SUGARBEET GROWER, 112 N. University Drive, Fargo ND 58102. Editor: Al Bloomquist. Buys all rights. Pays on acceptance. Will send a free sample copy to a writer on request. Reports in 2 to 3 weeks. Enclose S.A.S.E. with all mail.
Nonfiction and Photos: Uses features on cultural practices of farmers who grow sugarbeets, personality profiles of growers, and material on the uses of sugar and byproducts of sugarbeets. Length: 1,200 words. Pays $50. Pays $10 for photos.

VEGETABLE CROP MANAGEMENT, P.O. Box 1877, Salinas CA 93901. Publisher: Jack Leonard. For the commercial vegetable production industry in the United States and Canada. Buys North American serial rights only. Will send a free sample copy to a writer on request. Reports immediately. Enclose S.A.S.E. for return of submissions.
Nonfiction and Photos: Grower-oriented articles describing cultural practices involved in production of vegetables and potatoes for both fresh and processing markets; round-up type articles expected to cover all "why" and "how-to" aspects. Wide selection of 8x10 or 4x5 b&w photos essential. Length: 500 to 1,000 words. Pays $40 to $70.
Fillers: News items, up to 6 to 8 paragraphs, regarding new equipment, marketing trends in specific instances, research in progress, etc. Quality photos or explanatory charts desirable. Rate of payment determined by importance of item.

VEGETABLE GROWERS MESSENGER, Preston MD 21655. Editor: Max Chambers. For commercial vegetable growers and marketers. Bimonthly. Buys all

rights. Pays on publication. Query preferred. Reports promptly. Enclose S.A.S.E.
Nonfiction: Uses articles about vegetable production, harvesting, marketing, and packaging aimed at commercial growers only. Pays 3½¢ a word.
Photos: Pays $5 for 4x5, 5x7, and 8x10 b&w glossies.
Poetry: Will use poetry about vegetables.

WESTERN FRUIT GROWER, P.O. Box 1452, Lake Oswego OR 97034. Editor: M. A. Johnson. Monthly. Buys first publication rights; sometimes buys second rights for affiliated publications. Pays on publication. Reports in 1 week. Enclose S.A.S.E. for return of submissions.
Nonfiction and Photos: Original how-to-do-it and experience type stories on commercial fruit operation in 7 western states. Also, articles on new developments in mechanization, chemical applications, and pest control. No backyard or home-gardener appeal. Ms should be accompanied by 4 or 5 photos; 8x10 preferred, but can use 4x5 if photos are sharp. Length: 2,000 words maximum. Pays $40 to $70, including photos.

Dairy Farming

Publications for dairymen are classified here. Publications for farmers who raise animals for meat, wool, or hides are included in the Livestock category. Other magazines that buy material on dairy herds will be found in the General Interest Farming and Rural Life classification. Journals for dairy products retailers will be found under Dairy Products in the Trade Journals section.

DAIRY GOAT JOURNAL, P.O. Box 1908, Scottsdale AR 85252. Editor: Kent Leach. Monthly for breeders and raisers of dairy goats. Generally buys exclusive rights. Pays on acceptance. Sample copy will be sent on request. Query preferred. Reports in ten days. Enclose S.A.S.E.
Nonfiction and Photos: Uses articles, items, and photos that deal with dairy goats, and the people who raise them. Goat dairies and shows. How-to-do-it articles up to 1,000 words. Pays 1½¢ to 2¢ a word on acceptance. Also buys 8x10 pix for $1 to $15.

DAIRY HERD MANAGEMENT, P.O. Box 67, Minneapolis MN 55440. Editor: Fred Tunks. For "major dairymen of the US." Special issues: February, milking; April, waste management; June, summer health; November, nutrition. Established in 1965. Monthly. Circulation: 60,000. Not copyrighted. Buys 30 mss a year. Payment on acceptance. Will send free sample copy to a writer on request. Query first required. Will consider photocopied submissions. Submit seasonal material 2 months in advance. Reports in 2 weeks. Enclose S.A.S.E.
Nonfiction, Photos, and Fillers: General subject matter consists of "management articles in the areas of animal health, milking, feeding, sanitation, housing, waste management. We stress details on how something is done to improve efficiency. All copy is management oriented and designed to appeal only to top, large dairymen. Overworked themes are producer articles which describe everything he does instead of focusing on one specific area of management. We would like articles on waste management, nutrition, artificial insemination, the future for minor breeds, specific designs for barn and lot layouts." Buys informational, how-to, personal experience, interview, profile, think, spot news, successful business operations, new product, and technical articles. Length: 50 to 2,000 words. Pays $10 to $150. Purchases photos with or without mss, on assignment, and captions are required. Pays $5 to $25 for 8x10 b&w glossies. Pays $20 to $50 for 2¼x2¼ color transparencies. Dept. Editor: Neil Tietz. Buys newsbreaks, clippings. Minimum pay of 50¢ per inch. Address to Neil Tietz.

THE DAIRYMAN, P.O. Box 819, Corona CA 91720. Editor: Dolores Davis Miller. For large herd dairy farmers. Monthly. Buys reprint rights. Pays on publication. Will send a sample copy to a writer on request. Reports in 3 weeks. Enclose S.A.S.E. for return of submissions.

Nonfiction and Photos: Uses articles on anything related to dairy farming, preferably anything new and different or substantially unique in operation, for U.S. subjects. Acceptance of foreign dairy farming stories based on potential interest of readers. Pays $1 per printed inch. Buys photos with or without mss. Pays $5 each.

THE SUNBELT DAIRYMAN, P.O. Box 11617, Nashville TN 37211. Editor: Wayne Harr. For dairymen with more than 10 cows. Monthly. Buys North American serial rights only. Pays on publication. Will send a free sample copy to a writer on request. Query first. Reports in 2 months. Enclose S.A.S.E.
Nonfiction and Photos: Wants articles providing dairymen with news of technical, economic, and legislative developments. Also technical dairy material related to the South, and dairy related subjects such as forage production. Length: 1,500 to 2,000 words, with photos. Pays $30 to $50 a feature.

WESTERN DAIRY JOURNAL, 1730 South Clementine St., Anaheim CA 92802. Editorial Director: Aaron Dudley. Issued monthly. Pays on acceptance. Buys first publication rights, but exclusive photos not necessary. Reports in 30 days or sooner. Enclose S.A.S.E. for return of submissions.
Photos: Particularly needs b&w photos of cover quality showing dairy scenes in the 17 western states. These can be scenic shots of pastures, barns, etc., or they may be interiors of modern milking parlors or milk processing. Pays a minimum of $10 for these. Uses single and series, in b&w only. Pays $3.50 to $10, space rates up to $100.

General Interest Farming and Rural Life

The publications listed here aim at farm families or farmers in general and contain material ranging from light farm-related fiction to articles on sophisticated agricultural and business techniques. Magazines that specialize in the raising of crops will be found in the Crops and Soil Management classification; publications exclusively for dairymen are included under Dairy Farming; publications that deal exclusively with livestock raising are classified in the Livestock category; magazines for poultry farmers are grouped under the Poultry classification. Magazines that aim at farm suppliers are grouped under Agriculture in the Trade Journals section.

National

AGRI FINANCE, 1920 Waukegan Rd., Glenview IL 60025. Editor: Gerald L. Wilkins. For "agricultural specialists and loan offices of banks and other lending institutions that deal with farmers and allied businesses." Established in 1959. Bimonthly. Circulation: 15,000. Buys all rights. Buys 18 to 20 mss a year. Payment on publication. Will send free sample copy to a writer on request. Will send editorial guidelines sheet to a writer on request. Query first required. Enclose S.A.S.E.
Nonfiction: Articles that "interpret developments in agriculture as they affect the flow of loanable funds into agricultural businesses and enterprises." Payment open.

AGWAY COOPERATOR, Box 1333, Syracuse NY 13201. Editor: James E. Hurley. For farmers. Monthly. Pays on acceptance. Usually reports in 1 week. Enclose S.A.S.E. for return of submissions.
Nonfiction: Should deal with topics of farm or rural interest. Length: 1,200 words maximum. Payment is $50 to $100, usually including photos.
Photos: Payment is $5 to $15 for photos purchased singly.

THE AMERICAN FARMER, 225 Touhy Ave., Park Ridge IL 60068. Editor: Steve Van Slyke. For "all ages of farmers and ranchers in all states except Alaska. All are members of Farm Bureau." Established in 1925. 9 times a year. Circulation: 2,000,000. Query first. Enclose S.A.S.E. with queries and submissions.
Nonfiction and Photos: Subject matter consists of short articles of general agricultural interest. "We do not use how-to production articles but concentrate on economic issues that affect farmers' day-to-day management decisions. Query with a

definite plan and idea in mind. Our publication covers the business aspect of agriculture stressing new agricultural developments as they affect farmers; developments in nonagricultural subjects that affect agriculture; exports and imports that affect farmers and their management decisions; farm product utilization and utilization research and marketing of products from the farmer's viewpoint." Length: 700 to 1,000 words. Payment varies. Must have illustrative material. Only highest quality 8x10 b&w photos or 2¼ color transparencies or larger considered. Pay for photos varies according to use.

BIG FARMER, 131 Lincoln Hwy., Frankfort IL 60423. Editor: Len Richardson. Published 8 times a year. Pays on acceptance. Query first. Enclose S.A.S.E.
Nonfiction: Articles to help readers improve management skills of large scale farms. No fiction, verse, or poetry. Length from 1,000 to 1,500 words. Pays $50 to $100.
Photos: Livestock color, dramatic large scale farming situations to illustrate general features. Photographic quality requirements very high. Pays $15 for b&w; $50 for color, one-time use inside.

CAPPER'S WEEKLY, 616 Jefferson St., Topeka KS 66607. Editor: Louise F. Roote. For Midwestern residents, especially for farmers and persons living in small towns. Established in 1875. Weekly tabloid newspaper. Circulation: over 460,000. Not copyrighted. Query first. Enclose S.A.S.E.
Nonfiction: Emphasis on human interest material that appeals to readership. Uses material for "In the Heart of the Home," "Open Session"; articles on food, and general news briefs. Length: open. Payment to be negotiated.
Fiction: Publishes a serialized short story in each issue. Length: open. Payment to be negotiated.

THE COUNTRY GUIDE, 1760 Ellice Ave., Winnipeg 21, Manitoba, Canada. Editor: Don Baron. For farm families. Monthly. Most of material is staff-written or contributed by agricultural specialists. Query first required. Buys first North American serial rights; second North American rights considered. Enclose S.A.E. and International Reply Coupons for reply to queries.
Nonfiction, Photos, and Fillers: Purchased articles include how-to-do farm and homemaking features, mostly from 300 to 1,000 words. Pays $25 to $100, sometimes more for illustrated material. Photos purchased with mss and with captions. Prefers 8x10, b&w glossies. Pays $5 and up. Color transparencies for cover; should be 2¼x2¼ or larger. Pays $50 and up for first rights. Transparencies returned after use. No straight scenics, please. Photos must relate to Canada farm conditions.

ELECTRICITY ON THE FARM, 666 Fifth Ave., New York NY 10019. Editor and Publisher: Hugh J. Hansen. For high income farmers. Each issue emphasizes one aspect of farming. Monthly. Buys all rights. Pays on acceptance. Will send a free sample copy to a writer on request. Query first. Articles should arrive at least 10 weeks before publication date. Brief statement should accompany article, giving author's connection, occupation, etc. Reports in 2 weeks. Enclose S.A.S.E. for reply to queries.
Nonfiction: Information on farmers' use of electricity on the farm and how such use has benefited them. "We prefer stories that are simple to read and understand about farm people and their successful experience with electricity-powered machines." Articles on how farmers can do jobs more economically, save labor, and put new electrical equipment or experimental results to use on their farms. Prefers actual farm or home experience stories, backed by records and statements by the farmer, telling how the equipment has helped him. Mention names and towns; quote farm people. Photos and easy-to-understand drawings and charts used with mss. Length: 1,000 words maximum. Pays 2½¢ a word.
Photos: 5x7 or 8x10 b&w glossies purchased with mss and with captions only. Preferably including farmer or livestock, unposed. Pays $7.50 and up. Pays $100 for color transparencies for cover.

FARM JOURNAL, Washington Square, Philadelphia PA 19105. Editor: Lane Palmer. Many separate editions for different parts of the U.S. Material bought for one or more editions depending upon where it fits. Payment made on acceptance and is the same regardless of editions in which the piece is used. Query before submitting material. Will consider photocopied submissions. Enclose S.A.S.E. for reply to querien

Nonfiction: Timeliness and seasonableness are very important. Material must be highly practical and should be helpful to as many farmers as possible. Farmers' experiences may apply to any phase of farming and animal raising, as well as to the farmhouse and the community. Technical material must be accurate. "Pays excellent rate."

Photos: Much in demand either separately or with short how-to material in picture stories and as illustrations for articles. Warm human interest pix for covers—activities on modern farms. For inside use, shots of home-made and handy ideas to get work done easier and faster, farm news photos, and pictures of children on the farm. In b&w, 8x10 glossies are preferred; color submissions should be 2¼x2¼ for the cover, and 35mm for inside use. Pays $50 and up for b&w shot; $75 and up for color.

FREE PRESS WEEKLY REPORT ON FARMING, 300 Carlton St., Winnipeg, Manitoba, R3C 3C1, Canada. Editor: Bruce P. McDonald. For farmers and other agriculturists (research, transportation, marketing, agribusiness). Established in 1880. Weekly. Circulation: 300,000. Buys first serial rights. Buys 25 mss a year. Payment on publication. Will send free sample copy to writer on request. Submit only complete ms. Submit seasonal material for special farming operation sections. 1 to 2 months in advance. Enclose S.A.E. and International Reply Coupons.

Nonfiction and Photos: "Agricultural articles, with emphasis on good, profitable business. Approach farming as a business and an interesting way of life." How-to, personal experience, successful business operations, merchandising techniques, and technical articles. Length: 200 to 2,000 words. Payment varies. Color slides (positives) purchased with accompanying mss; captions required.

THE FURROW, Deere & Co., John Deere Rd., Moline IL 61265. North American Editor: George R. Sollenberger. For upper income farm families. Seven times yearly. Buys international rights. Pays on acceptance. Will send a sample copy to a writer on request. No query required. Reports in 2 weeks. Enclose S.A.S.E. for return of submissions.

Nonfiction and Photos: Uses short articles aimed specifically at upper-income farm audience. Style should be friendly and conversational but dignified. Human and socio-economic features must be genuinely rural—not struggling for a farm slant. Length: 1,500 words maximum. Color negatives or transparencies, including 35mm, purchased with mss. Payment per illustrated feature is $100 to $200.

GOOD FARMING, 1450 Don Mills Rd., Don Mills, Ontario, Canada. Editor: Robert Mercer. For "top Canadian farmers." 10 times a year. Circulation: 120,000. Rights purchased vary with author and material. May buy all rights, or first North American serial rights. Buys 10 mss a year. Payment on publication. Query first required. Submit seasonal material 3 months in advance. Reports in 1 month. Enclose S.A.E. and International Reply Coupons for reply to queries.

Nonfiction and Photos: Subject matter emphasizes methods and farm management. "Farmer to farmer approach, on assignment only. No fiction." Buys informational and farm oriented how-to articles. Length: 500 to 1,500 words. Pays $75 to $125. B&w glossies bought with mss and on assignment only. Captions required.

THE NATIONAL FUTURE FARMER, Box 15130, Alexandria VA 22309. Editor: Wilson Carnes. For youth, 14 to 21 years old, studying vocational agriculture (agribusiness) in high school, members of Future Farmers of America (FFA). Bimonthly. Buys all rights unless otherwise arranged. Pays on acceptance. Will send a sample copy to a writer on request. No query required. Reports in 2 weeks. Enclose S.A.S.E. for return of submissions.

Nonfiction: "Most articles are staff-written, but purchase a few" in three major categories: 1. The FFA: Articles about present and former members who have made unusual or outstanding accomplishments, provided they would be of interest nationally or have inspirational value. These could be success stories on their farming programs, leadership activities, and other worthwhile endeavors. Local chapter or group activities are appropriate if they are unusual or different and contain ideas or suggestions other chapters might use. 2. Agriculture: "Articles must appeal to a variety of interests and involve young people who are getting established in farming, ranching, or other careers in agribusiness. Articles on management, financing, and other ways of developing an adequate resource base for a career in agriculture are particularly appealing. Articles on technology are considered when they are not too specialized and are translated into an easy-to-read form. Some how-to material for this age group is also considered." 3. General interest: Well-written articles which help the reader broaden his education, tips and suggestions for choosing and preparing for a vocation, hobbies, sports and recreation, social and personality improvement. Shorter articles preferred, concisely written and well illustrated. Maximum length: 1,000 words. Pays up to 4¢ a word for well-written articles.

Photos: 8x10 b&w photos and 4x5 color transparencies of FFA scenes wanted. Pays up to $7.50 for b&w, up to $100 for color transparencies for cover; $50 for calendar photo; uses 12 per year.

THE PROGRESSIVE FARMER, 820 Shades Creek Pkwy., Birmingham AL 35209. Buys first publication rights. Will send sample copy for 40¢. Query essential. Will consider photocopied submissions if not simultaneously submitted elsewhere. Reports in 1 month. Enclose S.A.S.E.

Nonfiction and Photos: Buys articles dealing with personal experiences in farming; how-to-do-it articles from the South. Style should be easy-to-read, farm-oriented writing. Also wants freelance material for regular columns Handy Devices (farm), and Jokes. Pays $15 a column and up. Send to Joe A. Elliott, Editorial Director. 8x10 b&w glossy photos purchased with mss. Pays $10 a photo and up.

Fiction: Farm-slanted stories. Payment varies. Send to Eugene Butler, *Progressive Farmer*, 3612 Noble Ave., Dallas TX 75204.

SUCCESSFUL FARMING, 1716 Locust St., Des Moines IA 50336. Editor: Dick Hanson. For top farmers. 12 times a year. Buys all rights. Pays on acceptance. Query first. Will consider photocopied submissions. Enclose S.A.S.E.

Nonfiction: "Most of our material is too limited and unfamiliar for freelance writers—except for the few who specialize in agriculture, have a farm background and a modern agricultural education." Length: about 1,500 words maximum. Pays, on basis of space used, $10 to $300.

Photos: Austin Russell, Art Director, prefers 8x10 b&w glossies to contacts; color should be 2¼x2¼, 4x5 or 8x10. Buys exclusive rights and pays $20 for b&w, more for color. Pays extra rates for accompanying text. Query is advisable. Assignments are given, and sometimes a guarantee, provided the editors can be sure the photography will be acceptable. Pays for meals, phone, lodging.

TOP OPERATOR, 230 West Washington Square, Philadelphia PA 19105. Editor: Roe Black. For owners and operators of farms and ranches throughout the U.S. Established in 1969. Monthly, except December and June, in 4 editions: eastern, southern, and western. Circulation: over 415,000. Buys all rights. Pays on publication. Query first. Enclose S.A.S.E.

Nonfiction: Material about farm and ranch management, new techniques in agriculture, and the profitability of agribusiness. Regional editions appeal to the particular interests of operators in the areas served. Keep in mind that readers are decision-makers for top farms in the nation. Study the magazine before contributing. Length: open. Pays $25 to $400, depending on length, research required, necessary rewriting, difficulty of the subject.

Local

AMERICAN AGRICULTURALIST AND THE RURAL NEW YORKER, P.O. Box 370, Ithaca NY 14850. Editor: Gordon Conklin. Monthly. Not copyrighted. Acquires all rights. Pays on acceptance. Will send a free sample copy to a writer on request. Reports immediately. Enclose S.A.S.E. for return of submissions.

Nonfiction and Photos: Short articles on farm subjects of general interest to farm and suburban dwellers. Pays 2¢ to 3¢ a word. Photos purchased with mss and with captions only. Pays $5.

Poetry: Pays $3 to $5.

BUCKEYE FARM NEWS, 245 N. High St., Columbus OH 43216. Editor: S.C. Cashman. For a rural audience, "mostly farmers with a high school education or better, 21 to 75 years of age." Established in 1922. Monthly. Circulation: 70,000. Buys all rights, but will reassign rights to author after publication; buys first serial rights in the state of Ohio. Buys 12 to 20 mss a year. Pays on publication. Will send a sample copy to a writer on request. Query first or submit complete ms for nonfiction. Submit seasonal material at least 36 days in advance of issue date. Will consider photocopied submissions. Reports in 1 to 3 months. Enclose S.A.S.E.
Nonfiction and Photos: "Articles on agri-marketing, human interest, public affairs material of interest to rural people, farm organization news, etc. Articles must show the value of something to the farm reader or the members of his family. We do not use a lot of material dealing with agri-production, and do not use short stories dealing with farm people. We'd like to see material on farm politics, farm programs, exports and imports, and environmental matters. Material related to the interests and concerns of Ohio people has priority." Buys how-to's, informational articles, personal experience articles, interviews, inspirational articles, and coverage of successful business operations. Length: 400 to 3,000 words. Pays $25 to $100. Photos with captions purchased with mss.

CAROLINA COOPERATOR, 125 E. Davie, Raleigh NC 27601. Editor: M.G. Mann, Jr. For Carolina farmers. Monthly. Buys all rights. Not many freelance articles bought. Pays on acceptance. Will send a free sample copy to a writer on request. Reports as soon as possible. Enclose S.A.S.E. for return of submissions.
Nonfiction: Interested only in material related to Carolina agriculture, rural living, and farmer co-ops. Length: 1,200 words maximum. Payment is $15 to $35.

COUNTRY LIVING MAGAZINE, 4302 Indianola Ave., Columbus OH 43214. Managing Editor: Marcus T. Orr. For consumers of co-op electricity throughout rural Ohio. Monthly. Circulation: 134,600. Not copyrighted. Pays on publication. Will send a free sample copy to a writer on request. No query required. Enclose S.A.S.E. for return of submissions.
Nonfiction: New ideas, applications, and shortcuts for the home and farm, preferably related to the use of electricity. Length: 500 words or less. Pays 3¢ a word minimum.
Photos: Wants shots of electric power use, human interest, and "home-made and handy" electric power use applications. B&w glossies, any size, purchased with mss and with captions only. Pays $5 and up. Occasionally buys color transparency or print for cover. Pays $25.
Fiction: Only vignettes, rural related, of 750 words or less. See "That Demon Tractor," by Lois Smith (Oct. 72). Pays 3¢ a word minimum.
Poetry: Seldom used. Occasionally buys 13 lines or less. Pays 50¢ a line.

THE DAKOTA FARMER, P.O. Box 910, Aberdeen SD 57401. Editor: Charles Henry. For farmers and families in North and South Dakota. "All have agriculturally related occupations and interests." Special issues include Beef issue (August). Monthly. Circulation: 84,000. Rights bought "depend on story and author. We are flexible." Buys 25 to 30 mss a year. Pays on publication. Will send a sample copy to a writer on request. Query first. Submit seasonal material 2 to 3 months in advance. Returns rejected material in approximately 10 days. Enclose S.A.S.E.
Nonfiction: "Human interest features of Dakota farm people, history, or events. Keep in mind we write for Dakotans. Stories should be geared to that audience." Buys how-to's, personal experience stories, interviews, new product articles, photo essays, historical and travel pieces, and successful business operation coverage. Length: 500 to 2,000 words. Pays 4¢ per published word; 2¢ per published word in home section.
Photos: Purchased with mss. With captions only. B&w glossies, color transparencies. Pays $50 maximum for cover photos.
Poetry: Buys traditional and contemporary poetry and light verse. Length: 5 to 15 lines. Pays $5 to $8 per poem. Department Editor: Mary Bennett.

ENCHANTMENT, Box 416, Santa Fe NM 87501. Editor: Holt Priddy. For "members of rural electric cooperatives in New Mexico. They are farmers, ranchers, miners, oil producers, chile pickers, rug weavers—we represent the entire cross-section of New Mexico life." 12 times a year. Circulation: 44,600. Buys all rights. Buys approximately 24 mss a year. Pays on acceptance. Will send a sample copy to a writer for 25¢. Query first. Submit seasonal material 3 months in advance. Reports in 2 weeks. Enclose S.A.S.E.

Nonfiction and Photos: "Articles having to do with New Mexico and life in the pueblos, towns, villages, and small communities and on the farms, ranches, and industrial areas where electric cooperative power is used. We probably are more in favor of underdevelopment than in progress. From a freelancer we want nothing having to do with electricity; we want articles on and about New Mexico and the ones who live here. A New Mexican writer has a better chance to publish in *Enchantment* than anyone else." The writer "must have first-hand experience of living in New Mexico. We don't want articles from someone who passed this way and then went back home and wished he'd stayed here. We don't want to see articles on household tips, how to farm better, politics, or electricity." Length: 300 to 2,000 words. Pays 1¢ a word. Photos purchased with mss. B&w glossies. "We buy all rights and keep the photo." Pays $1.

GEORGIA FARMER, 476 Plasamour Dr., P.O. Box 13755, Atlanta GA 30324. Editor: Elmo Hester. For commercial farmers of Georgia. Monthly. Not copyrighted. Pays on publication. Query helps, but must have meat in it. Reports immediately. Enclose S.A.S.E.

Nonfiction and Photos: Concise how-to and success farm stories localized to Georgia. Subject can vary anywhere within the areas of interest to farm readers or agribusiness readers. Length: 1,200 words maximum. Payment is $5 to $50. Photos are occasionally bought with mss; payment included in price of article. Any size, color used.

IOWA FARM AND HOME REGISTER, 715 Locust St., Des Moines IA 50304. Editor: Charles J. Nettles. For Iowa farmers and agri-businessmen. Weekly. Buys first serial rights. Pays on publication. Reports in 2 weeks. Enclose S.A.S.E. for return of submissions.

Nonfiction and Photos: Articles of interest to Iowa farmers, including experience stories about Iowans, agri-businessmen and how-to stories. Also short, true, humor articles with a farm connection. Length: 1,000 words maximum. Pays $15 to $50. Good farm photos with or without mss, but with Iowa angle.

MICHIGAN FARMER, 4415 N. Grand River Ave., Lansing MI 48906. Editor: Dayton Matlick. Semimonthly. Buys first North American rights. Pays on acceptance. Query first. Reports in 1 month. Enclose S.A.S.E.

Nonfiction: Uses articles of interest and value to Michigan farmers, which discuss Michigan agriculture and the people involved in it. "These are fairly technical. Also articles for home section about Michigan farm housewives and what they are doing. Although articles are technical, lucid easy-to-understand writing is desired. Length depends on topic." Rates are 2¢ a word minimum; special stories bring higher rates.

Photos: Buys some b&w singles; also a few color transparencies, for cover use. Pays $2 to $5 each, depending on quality.

MONTANA FARMER-STOCKMAN, 510 First Avenue North, Great Falls MT 59401. Editor: Leland P. Cade. For "operators of farms and ranches in Montana and northern Wyoming. This is about 25,000 in Montana and 5,000 in Wyoming. They produce two main crops—wheat and barley; and cattle. Average farmer is about 55 years old, but we aim at a younger age." Established about 1900. Biweekly. Circulation: 36,000. Not copyrighted. Buys 50 to 100 mss a year. Payment on acceptance. Enclose S.A.S.E. for return of submissions.

Nonfiction: General subject matter includes "stories from research workers, farmers and ranchers themselves, a few from rural housewives. Stories should relate to practical situations. Writers should just send what they have. We aren't particular about style. We are particular about practical utility; technical correctness. We try to do our stories from the standpoint of a producer; not from the standpoint of someone on the outside looking in. We get too many 'human interest' stories for our use—far more than any other kind, and we use very few of them. Most of our stories are human interest with practical application. We seek mainly local writers, and a rare one from out of state." Pays $15 to $50 per article.

NEW MEXICO FARM & RANCH, 421 North Water St., Las Cruces NM 88001 Editor: Kim Allen. For "farmers and ranchers actively engaged in the field in New Mexico." Monthly. Circulation: 9,500. Not copyrighted. Buys 12 to 24 mss a year. Pays on publication. Will send a free sample copy to a writer on request. Query first. Reports in 2 months. Enclose S.A.S.E.
Nonfiction and Photos: Wants "news stories and features related to farming and ranching in New Mexico. Would like to see material showing innovations in farming—the new and different aspects which have been developed on an individual farm." Uses interviews and successful business operations stories. Length: 250 to 750 words. Payment is 50¢ an inch, and $2.50 to $5 for b&w glossy photos purchased with mss.

OHIO FARMER, 1350 W. Fifth Ave., Columbus OH 43212. Editor: Earl W. McMunn. Semimonthly. Pays on publication. Query first. Reports in a few days. Enclose S.A.S.E.
Nonfiction, Photos, and Fillers: Practical and of interest to general farmers or farmers specializing in some type of Ohio agriculture. Pays average of 5¢ a line. Photos of Ohio scenes and people purchased with mss.

OKLAHOMA RANCH AND FARM WORLD, Box 1770, Tulsa OK 74102. Editor: Herb Karner. For a rural, urban, and suburban readership. Monthly. Buys first serial rights. Pays on publication. Query first. Enclose S.A.S.E.
Nonfiction and Photos: Wants farm and ranch success stories; also suburban living, homemaking, youth, 4-H, and F.F.A. Effective photo illustrations necessary. Preferred length: 700 to 800 words. Pays $7.50 a column, sometimes more for exceptional copy. Photos purchased with mss and occasionally with captions only. Prefers b&w glossies, at least 5x7. Pays $3.50 each.

RURAL ELECTRIC MISSOURIAN, 2722 E. McCarty St., Jefferson City MO 65101. Editor: Don Yoest. For rural readers (farm and nonfarm). Monthly. Not copyrighted. Buys exclusive Missouri first rights. Pays on acceptance. Prefers query. Reports in 30 days. Enclose S.A.S.E.
Nonfiction: Buys articles on electrical equipment—new applications in home, farm, shop, business, or cooperative business. Also uses human interest material, preferably with a humorous rural flavor. Length: 500 to 1,000 words. Payment varies and is negotiated; minimum $10.
Photos: 8x10 b&w glossies occasionally purchased either with mss or with captions only. Payment varies; minimum $5 a photo.
Poetry: "Short, human interest, rural items needed." Pays $5.

SOUTH CAROLINA FARMER-GROWER, 476 Plasamour Dr., P.O. Box 13755, Atlanta GA 30324. Editor: Elmo Hester. For commercial farmers of South Carolina. Monthly. Not copyrighted. Pays on publication. Query helps, but must have meat in it. Reports immediately. Enclose S.A.S.E.
Nonfiction and Photos: Wants concise how-to and success farm stories localized to South Carolina. Subject can vary anywhere within the areas of interest to farm readers or agribusiness readers. Length: 1,200 words maximum. B&w or color photos, any size, occasionally bought with mss. Payment (including photos) is $5 to $50.

WALLACE'S FARMER, 1912 Grand Ave., Des Moines IA 50305. Editor: Alvin F. Bull. For Iowa farmers and their families. Semimonthly. Buys Midwest States rights (Nebraska, Minnesota, Wisconsin, Illinois, Missouri, South Dakota, and Iowa). Pays on acceptance. Reports in 2 weeks. Enclose S.A.S.E. for return of submissions.
Nonfiction and Photos: Occasional short feature articles about Iowa farming accompanied by photos. Payment varies. Length: 500 to 750 words. Pays about $50. Photos purchased with or without mss. Should be taken on Iowa farms. Pays $7 to $15 for 8x10 b&w; $50 to $100 for 4x5, 2¼x2¼ color transparencies. See recent issue covers for examples.

WISCONSIN AGRICULTURIST, 1125 6th St., Racine WI 53401. Editor: Ralph S. Yohe. For Wisconsin farmers. Bimonthly. Buys first rights. Reports in 2 weeks. Enclose S.A.S.E. for return of submissions.

Nonfiction: Articles containing how-to-do-it information useful to Wisconsin farmers. Also uses feature-type material about Wisconsin farmers. Short sentences, simple words, short paragraphs. Stories should run at least three typed, double-spaced pages. Pays $40 and up.
Photos: Wants photos of farm operations, preferably Wisconsin scene with identifiable farmer. Buys some how-to-do-it photo series of farm interest. Pays $5 to $10 a photo for 8x10 b&w glossies; pays $50 to $100 for all rights to 2¼x2¼ or larger color transparencies. "We're buying quite a few color photos now."

WYOMING STOCKMAN-FARMER, 110 E. 17th St., Cheyenne WY 82001. Editor: Herman Dweuke. Buys all rights. Reports in 1 to 10 months. Enclose S.A.S.E. for return of submissions.
Nonfiction: "Feature stories about Wyoming, W. Nebraska, or West." Payment is $25 to $50.

Livestock

In this listing are magazines for farmers who raise cattle, sheep, or hogs for meat, wool, or hides. Publications for farmers who raise other animals are listed in the Miscellaneous category; also many magazines in the General Interest Farming and Rural Interest classification buy material on raising livestock. Magazines for dairymen are included under Dairy Farming. Publications dealing with raising horses, pets, or other pleasure animals will be found under animals in the Consumer Magazines section.

AMERICAN HEREFORD JOURNAL, 715 Hereford Dr., Kansas City MO 64105. Editor: Bob Day. Monthly. Pays on publication. Always query first. Reports in 30 days. Enclose S.A.S.E.
Nonfiction and Photos: Breeding, feeding, and marketing of purebred and commercial Herefords, with accent on well-substantiated facts; success-type story of a Hereford cattleman and how he did it. Length: 1,000 to 1,500 words. Pays average of 2½¢ to 3¢ a word. Buys 5x7 b&w glossy photos for use with articles. Pays $3 each.

ARKANSAS CATTLE BUSINESS, 208 Wallace Bldg., Little Rock AR 72201. Editor: Mary Hinkle. For beef cattlemen. Not copyrighted. Buys 2 to 3 mss a year. Pays on acceptance. Will send a free sample copy to a writer on request. Query first. Reports in 2 weeks. Enclose S.A.S.E.
Nonfiction and Photos: Articles related to beef cattle production and allied interests, with an Arkansas slant. Could also use historical articles on Arkansas. Length: 1,000 to 2,000 words. Pays 2¢ a word maximum. Photos purchased with mss. Payment varies.

BEEF, 1999 Shepard Road, St. Paul MN 55116. Editor: Paul D. Andre. For farmer-feeders and commercial cattle feeders. Monthly. Circulation: 65,000. Buys first North American serial rights. Pays on publication. Query advisable. Reports in 1 week. Enclose S.A.S.E.
Nonfiction: Strictly material dealing with cattle feeding, research in the field, actual on-the-scene features describing how feeding operations are conducted. Material requires depth and scope that assumes considerable knowledge of cattle business on the part of the writer. Word length: up to 2,000 words. Pays up to $100.
Photos: Purchased with mss. Also limited number of color transparencies for cover use. Must be 2¼ square or larger, strict technical standards. Must have cattle industry tie-in. Also helps if picture can be tied to inside story. Pays up to $100 per published transparency.

BIG FARMER CATTLE GUIDE, 131 Lincoln Highway, Frankfort IL 60423. Editor: Guy M. Price. For "cattle feeders and cow-calf operators. To qualify for this controlled circulation publication, the reader must gross $20,000-plus annually." Established in 1970. Monthly, except June, July and December. Circulation: 100,000. Rights purchased vary with author and material; may buy all rights, but will reassign rights to author after publication. Pays on acceptance. Will send a sample copy to a writer on request. Query first or submit complete ms. Will not consider photocopied submissions. "We prefer articles typed at 37 characters wide and no longer than 6 typewritten pages." Submit seasonal material 3 months in advance. Reports in 1 month. Enclose S.A.S.E. for return of submissions or reply to queries.

Nonfiction and Photos: "Management articles for cattle feeders and cow-calf operators on specific areas; not general features about an operator's operation. Articles must be to the point and acceptable for cattlemen across the country. The only failure of most articles is that the writer commonly forgets to ask himself who 'gives a damn.' If a major share of the audience does 'give a damn,' then he's got himself a story. We'd like to see articles on marketing strategies for cattlemen. Ours is the only nationally circulated vertical publication in the ag field going to cow-calf operators and cattle feeders." Buys informational and how-to articles, interviews, and coverage of successful business operations. Length: 2,000 words maximum. Pay "depends on quality and need." Captioned photos purchased with and without mss. Pays $15 for 8x10 or 5x7 glossy prints "if not submitted with ms." Pay "depends on need and quality" for color transparencies "from 35mm and up."

Poetry: "Poems with a 'western taste' regarding cattlemen in general that fit the modern cowman and are humorous."

CATTLEMEN, Room 251, 1632 14th Ave., N.W., Calgary, Alta., Canada. Editor: Frank M. Jacobs. Special issue on animal health in September; deadline: August 10. Monthly. Buys North American serial rights only. Pays on acceptance. Will send a sample copy for 25¢. Always query first. Reports in 2 weeks. Enclose S.A.E. and International Reply Coupons for reply to queries.

Nonfiction: Industry articles, particularly those on raising and feeding beef in Canada. Also how-to-do-it and success stories with good management slant. Writer must be informed. Uses an occasional historical item. Pays $20 to $70; 2¢ a word for historical items, 3¢ a word and up for industry articles, more for special assignments.

Photos: Canadian shots only, purchased with mss and for cover. B&w and color for cover; no 35mm. Pays $2 to $10 for b&w, up to $35 for color.

FEEDLOT MANAGEMENT, P.O. Box 67, Minneapolis MN 55440. Editor: Fred E. Tunks. For agri-businessmen who feed cattle and/or sheep for slaughter. Special issues include waste management (May); feeder cattle (August); nutrition (October). Monthly. Circulation: 20,000. Not copyrighted. Pays on acceptance. Will send a free sample copy to a writer on request. "Many writers will find a query with a good idea worthwhile." Reports in 1 to 5 weeks. Enclose S.A.S.E.

Nonfiction: Wants detailed, thorough material relating to cattle or lamb feeding and related subject areas—waste management, nutrition, marketing and processing, feeding, animal health. "Write for a copy of the magazine. Writers should know something about the industry in order to get the information that's important. We can accept highly technical articles, but there's no room for simple cursory articles. Feature articles on feedlots should include photos." No length restriction. Pays $30 to $150.

Photos and Fillers: 8x10 and 5x7 b&w glossies purchased with mss and with captions only. Pays 50¢ an inch for newsbreaks and clippings.

HOG FARM MANAGEMENT, Box 67, Minneapolis MN 55440. Editor: Fred Tunks. For "large-scale hog producers who make raising hogs their primary business. Average age: 43.5. Average education: 12.5 years. Average investment: $174,000. Average acres farmed: 558.2." Special issue in July seeks farrowing-related material for a farrowing issue. Established in 1964. Monthly. Circulation: 46,000. Buys 12 to 15 mss a year. Payment on acceptance. Will send a sample copy to a writer for $1. Will send editorial guidelines sheet to a writer on request. Will consider photocopied submissions. Submit seasonal material 3 to 4 months in advance. Reports in 2 to 4 weeks. Enclose S.A.S.E. for return of submissions.

Nonfiction and Photos: General subject matter consists of "management-oriented articles on problems and situations encountered by readers. Subjects include marketing, management, nutrition, disease, waste management, buildings and equipment, accounting and recordkeeping." Articles on a hog producer's operation should focus on one unique aspect or angle, and not give a general description of the producer's entire operation. Controversial articles OK, as are industry articles (trends) and round-ups on new developments. Edited for the largest most business-like producers. More semitechnical and in-depth management information. Prefer not to see articles describing a producer's entire operation, written very general and shallow. Look for articles that focus on only one subject. Buys informational, how-to, personal experience, interview, profile, think, personal opinion, photo, spot news, successful business operations, new product, merchandising techniques, and technical articles. Regular columns that seek freelance material are "Swine Research Review," "Industrial Bulletins," and "Crop Management." Length: up to 2,000 words. Pays $75 to $150 "for maximum feature article." Buys 5x7 or 8x10 b&w glossies. Also buys color transparencies that are at least 2¼x2¼. Must relate to subject matter. Pays $10 to $20 per each b&w photo. Pays $25 to $50 for color photos.

THE KANSAS STOCKMAN, 2044 Fillmore, Topeka KS 66604. Editor: Rich Wilcke. For cattle producers and feeders. Established in 1916. Monthly. Circulation: 5,000. Not copyrighted. Payment on publication. Will send sample copy to writer for 50¢. Submit complete ms. Will consider photocopied submissions. Submit seasonal material 2 months in advance. Premier Producer Issue (May). Marketing Issue (September). Reports on material in 2 months. Enclose S.A.S.E. for return of submissions.
Nonfiction: Material on "how-to issues of importance to cattlemen; production management articles. Human interest, humor, Kansas cattle industry history. Writer ought to understand the cattle business." Length: 500 to 1,200 words. Pays 2¢ per word.

NATIONAL WOOL GROWER, 600 Crandall Bldg., Salt Lake City Utah 84101. Associate Editor: Gary Spendlove. Best to query first here. Enclose S.A.S.E.
Nonfiction: Material of interest to sheepmen. Length: 2,000 words. Pays 1¢ per word for material used.

POLLED HEREFORD WORLD, #1 Place, 4700 E. 63rd St., Kansas City MO 64130. Editor: Marilyn Sponsler. For "breeders of polled Hereford cattle—about 80% registered breeders, about 5% commercial cattle breeders; remainder are agribusinessmen in related fields." Established in 1947. Monthly. Circulation: 20,000. Not copyrighted. Buys "very few mss at present." Pays on publication. Will send a sample copy to a writer on request. Query first "for reports of events and activities. Query first or submit complete ms for features." Will consider photocopied submissions. Submit seasonal material "as early as possible; 2 months preferred." Reports in 1 month. Enclose S.A.S.E. for return of submissions or reply to queries.
Nonfiction: "Features on registered or commercial polled Hereford breeders. Some on related agricultural subjects (pastures, fences, feeds, buildings, etc). Mostly technical in nature; some human interest. Our readers make their living with cattle, so write for an informed, mature audience." Buys informational articles, how-to's, personal experience articles, interviews, profiles, inspirational articles, humor, historical and think pieces, nostalgia, photo features, coverage of successful business operations, articles on merchandising techniques, and technical articles. Length: "varies with subject and content of feature." Pays about 5¢ a word ("usually about 50¢ a column inch, but can vary with the value of material").
Photos: Purchased with mss, sometimes purchased without mss, or on assignment; captions required. "Only good quality b&w glossy prints accepted; any size. Good color prints or transparencies." Pays $2 for b&w photos, $2 to $25 for color. Pays $25 for color covers.

WESTERN LIVESTOCK REPORTER, Box 2559, Billings MT 59103. Editor: Clark E. Schenkenberger. For producers and buyers of livestock. Weekly. Buys all rights. Pays on acceptance. Will send a free sample copy to a writer on request. Query first. Reports in 1 week. Enclose S.A.S.E.
Nonfiction and Photos: Factual, timely, practical, illustrated articles concerning purebred beef cattle-feedlot industry, and horses. Stories on how-to-do-it or ranch histories, rangeland, pastures, feeding, short-cuts in ranching, marketing, etc. Prefers that material concern the eight northwest states or Canada. Length: 800 words max-

imum. Payment is $20 to $50 per article, depending on subject. Photos should be b&w glossies, any size. Pays $2.50 to $15.

Miscellaneous

FISH FARMING INDUSTRIES, Sandstone Building, Mount Morris IL 61054. Editor: Bernard E. Heffernan. For "producers, processors and marketers of farm raised fish of all kinds." Established in 1970. Bimonthly. Circulation: 6,700. Not copyrighted. Buys 6 to 10 mss a year. Payment on acceptance. Will send free sample copy to a writer on request. Will send editorial guidelines sheet to a writer on request. Query first required. Enclose S.A.S.E.
Nonfiction and Photos: Material of "an agribusiness nature which stresses the business side of the industry." Approach "should exhibit in-depth investigation of the subject matter in the story. Do not wish to receive articles directed to popular audiences. Our audience is specific—the fish farming industry." Length: 1,000 to 1,200 words. Pays $75 to $100. Purchases photos with mss.

GLEANINGS IN BEE CULTURE, 623 West Liberty St., Medina OH 44256. Editor: John Root. For beekeepers. Monthly. Buys first North American serial rights. Pays on publication. Reports in 15 to 90 days. Enclose S.A.S.E.
Nonfiction and Photos: Interested in articles giving new ideas on managing bees. Also uses success stories about commercial beekeepers. Length: 3,000 words maximum. Pays $23 a published page. Sharp b&w photos pertaining to honeybees purchased with mss. Can be any size, prints or enlargements, but 4x5 or larger preferred. Pays $3 a picture.
Fillers: Items of interest to beekeepers. Pays according to length. No puzzles.

Poultry

The magazines listed here specialize in material on poultry farming. Other publications that buy material on poultry will be found in the General Interest Farming and Rural Life classification.

CANADA POULTRYMAN, 605 Royal Ave., New Westminster, B.C., Canada. Editor: Fred W. Beeson. For "broiler chicken, egg, and turkey producers; government, feed, equipment, drug company representatives; processors, wholesalers." Monthly. Circulation: about 12,000. Not copyrighted. Pays on publication. Will send a sample copy to a writer for 25¢. Submit seasonal material 3 months in advance. Reports in 1 month. Enclose S.A.E. and International Reply Coupons for return of submissions.
Nonfiction and Photos: Factual articles on how to better produce poultry properly on the farm; in-depth interviews with industry leaders. Strong advocate of quota production at farm level through producer marketing boards. Length: 1,000 to 2,000 words. Pays 3¢ per word. Address Kenneth D. Larson, Managing Editor. Photos purchased with mss. B&w glossies, color transparencies, 35mm color, color prints. Pays $3 for b&w, $5 for color. Submit to Kenneth D. Larson, Managing Editor.

GOBBLES, 1563 University Ave., St. Paul MN 55104. Editor: Roy Munsen. Issued monthly for turkey growers, processors, hatcherymen, feed dealers, equipment dealers, and other industry people. Not copyrighted. Query first. Reports in one month. Enclose S.A.S.E.
Nonfiction: "Features must be such that they would capture the interest of turkey growers and persons in allied industries. Most editorial material must be directed

toward growers. Articles, except those of scientific nature, deal with Minnesota and surrounding states." Length: 300 to 500 words. No set rate of payment.

INDUSTRIA AVICOLA, Watt Publishing Co., Mt. Morris IL 61054. Editor: Gary Buikema. For "producers (minimum 1,000 hens and/or 20,000 broilers annually and/or 1,000 turkeys annually) who have direct affiliation with the poultry industry in Latin America, Spain and Portugal." Circulation: 12,100. Buys all rights. Pays on acceptance. Will send a free sample copy to a writer on request. "Prefer mss written in English." Query first. Reports in 10 days. Enclose S.A.S.E.
Nonfiction and Photos: Specialized publication "for poultry businessmen of Latin America, Spain, Portugal. Printed only in Spanish. Emphasis is to aid in production, processing, and marketing of poultry meat and eggs. Keep readers abreast of developments in research, breeding, disease control, housing, equipment, marketing production and business management. Analytical and trend articles concerning the poultry industry in Latin countries are given preference." Length: up to 1,000 to 1,500 words. Pays $40 to $130 depending on content and quality. Photos are purchased with mss. No size requirements.

POULTRY MEAT, P.O. Box 947, Cullman AL 35055. Editor: Charles Perry. For "large broiler producers, processors, and marketers and for those in management or key positions in the broiler or broiler-related supply business." Special issues include marketing, housing, and convention issues. Monthly. Circulation: 7,800. Not copyrighted. Buys 20 to 30 mss a year. Pays on acceptance. Will send a sample copy to a writer on request. Query first. Submit seasonal material 2 months in advance, "but only after a query on the special issues." Reports in 2 weeks. Enclose S.A.S.E.
Nonfiction: "Articles are designed to aid the broiler industry to do a better job in producing, processing, and marketing the product at a profit. Should be detailed and should be about new ideas and practices. Stories about progressive operations could be done in almost any style as long as the articles are concise and detailed. Business management articles come in floods, and are so general that poultry plant manager could be changed to hardware store manager. These do not get published." Buys interviews, coverage of successful business operations and merchandising techniques. Length: 1,200 to 2,000 words. Pays $60 to $100.

TURKEY WORLD, Mount Morris IL 61054. Editor: Bernard Heffernan. Monthly. Reports on submissions in two weeks. Buys all rights. Pays on acceptance. Query first. Enclose S.A.S.E.
Nonfiction and Photos: Clear, concise, simply written, factual articles beamed at producers, processors and marketers of turkeys and poultry meat products. Length: 1,200 to 2,000 words. Pays $50 to $100.

TRADE, TECHNICAL, AND PROFESSIONAL JOURNALS

Because trade journals buy articles that are readily researched in urban localities and require less of a literary style, many freelance writers get their start in this area. Although there are many trade journals in the same field, they vary in what they buy. When you write a trade journal piece, it's important to read copies of each magazine before you even send off a query letter.

What do you look for when you study a trade publication? The same things as in a consumer magazine—audience, article subjects, handling and approach to subjects, and style.

Most trade journals fall into three audience groups: those for retailers, who are interested in unusual store displays that they can apply to their own store, successful sales campaigns, etc.; those for manufacturers, who want stories on how a plant solved an industry problem related to them, how certain equipment performed in production, etc.; and those for educated, skilled professionals or industry experts. The latter group of trade journals buys technical or scientific articles on systems design; new discoveries in biology, chemistry, or physics that affect the reader's job or product; etc.

Basically, all material a trade journal buys will involve the problems that arise in the trade it covers. *Homesewing Trade News*, for example, is not going to be interested in a hardware display. Also, requirements are further limited by whether a journal goes to everyone interested in the trade (like *Communications News*), only to persons who perform one job (like *EDN*), or to some special mix of persons with different but related jobs (like *Broadcast Engineering*).

Trade journal articles are frequently handled in straight reporting fashion, describing in plain language what some business or plant did, and illustrated with photos. The information is practical to the extent that it gives the reader an idea or method that worked for someone else and that he may be able to use. Some journals prefer profiles of entire plants, others like discussions limited to one machine. You'll want to do your own exploring of the editors' preferences. Similarly, some journals use more scientific terminology than others.

Because each magazine has its own singular requirements that, once learned, are relatively easy to fill, many trade writers write for only a few editors who they know well. They regularly suggest articles which will be assigned to them if acceptable and also receive assignments for stories in their territory. Usually the professional will not write an article without a prior go-ahead on a query.

If you're just starting out, you'll want to do a lot of trade journal reading to select your best market and research your story in depth. In fact, you'll start off by giving it more time than it's worth. However, as you talk with individuals in your trades, you'll gain experience that will eventually qualify you to supply the technical journals in your field.

Advertising and Marketing

In this category are journals for professional advertising agyncy executives, ad copywriters, and marketing men. Publications that deal with the advertising and marketing of specific products, such as hardware or clothing, are classified under the name of the product. Journals for salesmen will be found in the Selling and Merchandising category.

ADVERTISING AGE, 708 Third Ave., Chicago IL 60611. Editor: J.J. Graham. Currently staff-produced.

ADVERTISING AND SALES PROMOTION, 740 N. Rush St., Chicago IL 60611. Editor: Louis J. Haugh. Biweekly. Circulation: 30,000. Buys all rights. Pays on acceptance. Will consider photocopied submissions. Query first. Enclose S.A.S.E.
Nonfiction and Photos: "Interesting and unusual case histories of advertising production, promotion, and merchandising that are written from the standpoint of the advertiser. Emphasis on how things are being or will be done. Categories of interest include art and photography; audio and visual aids; direct advertising; labeling and packaging; graphic arts and paper; premiums, prizes, and specialties; shows and exhibits; signs and identification materials; window and store displays. Articles should be on how these various tools are used by sales promotion executives in the planning, design, and promotion of sales promotion programs. Material must be exclusive within the field." Length: 1,000 words maximum. Pays $2 per inch. Photos purchased with mss. Pays $3 each.

THE COUNSELOR, NBS Building, Second and Clearview Aves., Trevose PA 19047. Managing Editor: Carole Wagemaker. For "the specialty advertising industry." Monthly. Buys first North American serial rights and reprint rights; may buy simultaneous rights. Pays on publication. Reports in 10 days. Enclose S.A.S.E. for return of submissions.
Nonfiction and Photos: "Articles on sales management, case histories of specialty programs, interviews with industry suppliers and distributors, other articles of interest to the industry." Length: 2,000 words minimum. Pays $35 to $75. "Illustrative material bought to accompany articles only."

DIRECT MARKETING, 224 Seventh St., Garden City NY 11530. Associate Editor: J. McIlquham. Monthly. Buys all rights. Pays on acceptance. Query first. Enclose S.A.S.E.
Nonfiction and Photos: "Feature articles and case histories of advertising campaigns whose purpose is to obtain a direct response from the reader via a coupon in print media broadcast and/or via a reply card in direct mail media. Best sources of articles for freelance writers are local retail establishments (department stores, food stores), manufacturers, wholesalers, etc. who conduct direct mail campaigns." Pays 5¢ a word. Pays $2.50 per sample of mailing pieces and/or ads "to recognized freelance writers." Photos purchased with mss. Pays $5.
How To Break In: "It's important that writers must know marketing as we are a trade publication. It would be like someone who had never written anything trying to write for *Writer's Digest*. Also note that we buy cassette interviews for $25 and sell the interviews."

INCENTIVE MARKETING, 633 Third Ave., New York NY 10017. Editor: Murray Elman. For "marketing executives in a wide variety of industries who buy and use premiums or incentives as a definite part of their sales programs." Established in 1905. Monthly. Circulation: 30,000. Rights purchased vary with author and material. Buys 125 to 200 mss a year. Pays on acceptance. Will send a sample copy to a writer on request. Write for copy of guidelines for writers. Query first. Will consider photocopied submissions. Submit seasonal material 3 months in advance. Reports in 1 month. Enclose S.A.S.E.
Nonfiction and Photos: "Marketing profiles and case histories of how companies make use of premiums/incentives to promote their products or services. Articles should include information on strategies, tactics, research, planning, promotion, distribution, and servicing of incentive merchandising techniques. Always write

from the point of view of the company using premiums and emphasize the specific results of completed promotions. Articles should never be based on interviews with suppliers. Stress the incentive philosophy in the context of overall marketing strategy. We receive too many case histories on bank promotions." Buys interviews, profiles, travel promotion information, and coverage of successful business operations and merchandising techniques. Length: 1,500 words minimum, "but the longer, the better." Pays $85 to $125. Photos purchased with mss or on assignment.

MAC/WESTERN ADVERTISING, 6565 Sunset Blvd., Los Angeles CA 90028. Editor: Lee Kerry. For "people involved in advertising: media, agencies, and client organizations as well as affiliated businesses." Weekly. Buys all rights. Pays on acceptance. Query first; "articles on assignment." Reports in 1 month. Enclose S.A.S..E.
Nonfiction and Photos: "Advertising in the West. Not particularly interested in success stories. We want articles by experts in advertising, marketing, communications." Length: 1,000 to 1,750 words. Pays $100. Photos purchased with mss.

MAIL ORDER DIGEST, Newsletter of the National Mail Order Association, 429 S. Western Ave., Los Angeles CA 90020. Chairman, Editorial Board: S.M. Hahn. For "individuals and firms engaged in mail order selling of products and/or services." Established in 1972. Bimonthly. Buys all rights. Pays on publication. Will send a sample copy to a writer for $1. Query first or submit complete ms. Enclose S.A.S.E. for return of submissions.
Nonfiction: "Articles on mail order selling, advertising, success stories, case histories of interest to those engaged in mail order sales and promotion. We want factual, practical, how-to-do-it material presented in a straightforward, interesting manner."

MARKETING TIMES, 630 Third Ave., New York NY 10017. Managing Editor: Randy Sheets. "A member-service publication of Sales and Marketing Executive International, a global society throughout 48 nations." Enclose S.A.S.E.
Nonfiction: "A broad-based journal covering all aspects of the marketing profession: research, product development, packaging, distribution, advertising, sales promotion, management. As a rule, successful articles take the form of case histories, marketing strategy outlines, market profiles, do's and don'ts, etc. Articles should be of a how-to nature written in handbook style, brief and to the point." Length: 1,000 to 2,500 words. Payment to be negotiated.

SALES MANAGEMENT: THE MARKETING MAGAZINE, 630 Third Ave., New York, NY 10017. Editor: Robert H. Albert. For "sales/marketing executives in manufacturing or service concerns." Semimonthly. Buys all rights. Pays on publication. Will send a sample copy to a writer on request. Query first. Reports in 1 week. Enclose S.A.S.E. for return of submissions.
Nonfiction: "Feature material concerning sales/marketing executive situations. The best possibility for freelance features lies in exclusive sales/marketing stories about important companies or industries." Pays $200 to $300.

SALES PROMOTION MARK II, 109 Railside Rd., Don Mills, Ont., Canada. Editor/Publisher: Harry Weston. For "Canadian marketing, sales management, advertising, and agency executives." Buys first rights. Pays on publication. Will send a sample copy to a writer on request. Reports "in a few days." Enclose S.A.E. and International Reply Coupons for return of submissions.
Nonfiction and Photos: "Case histories, conceptual articles. Innovative; lively style. Should have a Canadian slant. Not a market for beginners." Length: 1,500 to 2,000 words. Pays 5¢ a word. 8x10 b&w glossies purchased with mss. Pays $5.

VISUAL MERCHANDISING, (formerly *DISPLAY WORLD*) 407 Gilbert Ave., Cincinnati OH 45202. Editor: David E Phillips. For "department and specialty store display directors, exhibitor producers, point-of-purchase producers, store planners. and shopping center promotion directors. Market Week issues twice annually." Monthly. Not copyrighted. Pays on publication. Will send a sample copy to a writer for 80¢. Query first with photo sample; "we do use specific freelancers on an assignment basis and would like to have additional capable writers in southern Cal-

ifornia, Atlanta, Dallas, and Seattle." Reports in 1 week. Enclose S.A.S.E.
Nonfiction and Photos: "Articles showing how to better display merchandise in every retail category. Besides merchandise presentation, features are desired on the subjects of national advertiser's showrooms, store-wide and shopping center promotions and sophisticated point-of-purchase display. Articles showing how national advertisers participate in exhibits, trade shows, expositions, with emphasis on design and construction; articles showing how basic construction materials are employed in professional displays, exhibits, store fixtures, point-of-purchase displays." Length: "should be adequate to comprehensively cover the subject. We also buy articles of 700 words or less, with 2 or 3 photos, on professional displays and exhibits which include a testimonial on the value of the store." Pays $50 to $80. B&w photos purchased with mss or with captions and brief introductory paragraph. Pays $5.
Fillers: Newsbreaks, clippings. Pays $5 to $15.

Agricultural Equipment and Supplies

AG CHEM MAGAZINE, 200 Commerce Rd., Cedar Grove NJ 07009. Editor: Richard T. Nagle. For "small businessmen who sell fertilizers and pesticides to local growers." Monthly. Circulation: 10,000. Rights purchased vary with author and material; may buy all rights, but will reassign rights to author after publication. Buys 6 to 8 mss a year. Pays on publication. Will send a sample copy to a writer on request. Write for copy of guidelines for writers. Query first. Will consider photocopied submissions. Submit seasonal material no later than 3 months in advance. Reports in 2 weeks. Enclose S.A.S.E.
Nonfiction and Photos: "Subjects include entomology, plant pathology, soil analysis, crop planning, manufacturing, warehousing and application technology, environmental protection, personnel safety, management and marketing. Because the chemicals being used today in agriculture are highly customized to local needs, many are manufactured locally by our readers. Keep material concise and explain significance. *Ag Chem* is more technically oriented than other magazines serving the industry. The magazine also reports more international developments than the others. We're not interested in general management material, but we are interested in articles on how local operators are doing a better job of running their businesses." Buys coverage of successful business operations, technical articles, and articles on merchandising techniques. Length: 1,000 to 3,000 words. Pays $50 to $200. Photos purchased with mss; captions required. Uses 8x10 b&w glossies with "higher than average contrast."

CUSTOM APPLICATOR, 3637 Park Ave., Memphis TN 38111. Editor: Tom Griffin. For "firms that sell and custom apply agricultural chemicals." Circulation: 13,500. buys all rights. Pays on acceptance. "Query is best. The editor can help you develop the story line regarding our specific needs." Enclose S.A.S.E.
Nonfiction and Photos: "We are looking for articles on custom application firms that tell others how to better perform jobs of chemical application, develop new customers, handle credit, etc." Length: 1,000 to 1,200 words "with 3 or 4 b&w glossies." Pays $80.

FARM AND POWER EQUIPMENT, 2340 Hampton Ave., St. Louis MO 63139. Editor: Glenn S. Hensley. For "retailers, manufacturers, and wholesalers of farm, light industrial, and lawn and garden power equipment." Monthly. Circulation: 21,000. Buys all rights. Pays on acceptance. Will send a sample copy to a writer on request. "Query mandatory." Reports "usually within 1 week." Enclose S.A.S.E.
Nonfiction and Photos: "Dealership merchandising and management of farm, lawn and garden equipment features. Should be slanted to the retailer, not to the consumer. All features about dealers must be accompanied by a signed notice indicating that the story subject approves the text for publication. Short, to-the-point text should be accompanied by 'full-of-action' photos." Length: 2,000 words maximum.

Pays 2¢ a word. Photos purchased with ms "to tell additional segments of the story. We prefer full blown photo features of 10 to 14 good shots. We prefer the submission of 35mm negatives with contact sheets; will accept 2¼x2¼ negatives and contacts." Pays $5 for b&w; $50 for color.

FARM SUPPLIER, Mt. Morris IL 61054. Editor: Ray Bates. Monthly. Buys all rights. Pays on acceptance. Query first. Reports in 1 month. Enclose S.A.S.E.
Nonfiction and Photos: "Articles on retail management and merchandising achievements by retail farm supply outlets and sales and service men. Product news developments now emphasized in departments, shorts, and features." Length: 1,000 to 1,400 words, "plus 3 or 4 original 8x10 glossies." Pays $5 to $25 "for short articles," $50 to $100 for feature articles. Photos purchased with and without mss; captions required. Pays $5 to $15.

SOUTHERN FARM EQUIPMENT AND SUPPLY, P. O. Box 11017, Nashville TN 37211. Editor: Galen Freeman. Monthly. Buys all rights. Pays on acceptance. "Query editor on an idea or outline." Reports in 2 to 4 weeks. Enclose S.A.S.E.
Nonfiction: "Features or shorts directly related to the retail farm equipment business and dealers in the 18 Southern and Southwestern states. Material should deal with sales or service innovations that are specific to the above—not just the standard 'dealer success' story, unless with a twist or innovation beyond the ordinary. Interested in general farm equipment; also irrigation equipment, lawn and garden equipment, farmstead mechanization." Length: 800 to 1,500 words. Pays 2½¢ to 3¢ a word. Photos purchased with and without mss; captions required. Pays $3 to $5.

Architecture

Publications in this category aim at architects and city planners who concern themselves with the design of buildings and urban environments. Journals for architects that emphasize choice of materials, structural details, and methods of constructing buildings will be found in the Construction and Contracting classification.

ARCHITECTURAL RECORD, McGraw-Hill Building, 1220 Ave. of Americas, New York NY 10020. Editor: Walter F. Wagner, Jr. For "architects and engineers." Monthly. Buys first rights. Pays on publication. "Always query first, identifying the building by architect, location, and owner." Enclose S.A.S.E.
Nonfiction and Photos: "We buy very little material, except by experts in the field. Material must be slanted directly to our reading audience. We're not a good market unless the author is thoroughly oriented to architectural and/or engineering interests." Length: open. Payment: open. Photos purchased with mss "and sometimes without mss, but only if architecturally or technically informative and of the highest quality."

THE CANADIAN ARCHITECT, 1450 Don Mills Rd., Don Mills, Ontario, Canada. Managing Editor: Robert Gretton. For "architects and town planners ranging from final year university students to practicing architects." Monthly. Circulation: 5,000. Buys all rights or first rights. Buys 24 to 30 mss a year. Pays on publication. Will send a sample copy to a writer on request. Query first. Submit seasonal material 2 months in advance. Returns rejected material in 2 weeks. Reports on material accepted for publication in 1 month. Enclose S.A.E. and International Reply Coupons.
Nonfiction and Photos: "Articles with photos on prominent architectural firms or individuals. Predominantly Canadian in approach. Remember the generally high level of sophistication of our readers. No pollution articles." B&w glossies purchased with mss. Pays $5 to $10.

PROGRESSIVE ARCHITECTURE, 600 Summer St., Stamford CT 06904. Editor: John M. Dixon. Monthly. Buys first-time rights for use in architectural press. Pays on publication. Enclose S.A.S.E. for return of submissions.

Nonfiction and Photos: "Articles of technical professional interest devoted to architecture and community design and illustrated by photographs and architectural drawings. Also uses technical articles, which are prepared by technical authorities and would be beyond the scope of the lay writer. Practically all the material is professional, and most of it is prepared by writers in the field who are approached by the magazine for material." Pays $50 to $100. B&w and color photos purchased; uses 4x5 or 8x10 transparencies. Photo Editor: Barbara McCarthy.

Auto and Truck

The journals below aim at automobile and truck dealers, repairmen, or fleet operators. Publications for highway planners and traffic control experts are classified in the Government and Public Service category. Journals for traffic managers and transportation experts (who route goods across the continent) will be found in the Transportation listing.

AUTO AND FLAT GLASS JOURNAL, 6654 Chestnut St., Cincinnati OH 45227. Editor: James B. Colborne. For "professional auto glass replacement dealers." Monthly. Buys all rights, reprint rights, and simultaneous rights. Pays on acceptance. Will send a sample copy to a writer on request. "Query first on longer material." Reports in 3 weeks. Enclose S.A.S.E.
Nonfiction: "Articles should be written to highlight the tools of business that successful auto glass men have used to their advantage. These can be direct mail, personal solicitations, gimmicks, etc. Readers want to know how other glass men operate. Care should be taken not to offend competitors. Material also wanted for 'News of the Trade' section." Length: 1,000 words maximum. Pays 5¢ a word.
Photos: 8x10 glossies; snapshots. Pays $5.

AUTOMOTIVE NEWS, 965 E. Jefferson, Detroit MI 48207. Editor: Robert M. Finlay. For "auto makers and dealers." Weekly. Buys all rights. Pays on publication. "Query essential." Enclose S.A.S.E.
Nonfiction and Photos: "Concerned with the auto market and the problems of new and used car dealers. Current and complete familiarity with the field is essential, so we don't use much freelance material. We use accurate articles with the emphasis on the how rather than the what; ideas that might be helpful to dealers." Pays "$1 an inch of type." [About 50 words.] "Additional compensation when interviews or extra work involved." Photos purchased with mss.

BRAKE AND FRONT END SERVICE, 11 S. Forge St., Akron OH 44304. Editor: Gale Urda. For "brake, front end, alignment shops (not service stations)." Monthly. Buys all rights. Pays on publication. Query first. Reports "at once." Enclose S.A.S.E.
Nonfiction and Photos: "Specialty shops taking on new ideas such as tune-ups; independent auto diagnosis; new merchandising techniques; growth of business, volume; reasons for growth and success. Expansions, any unusual brake shops." Length: "about 1,000 words." Pays 4¢ to 5¢ a word. B&w glossies purchased with mss. Pays $5.

CANADIAN AUTOMOTIVE TRADE, 481 University Ave., Toronto 2, Ont., Canada. Editor: Edward Belitsky. For "automotive wholesale and retail industry." Monthly. Buys first Canadian serial rights. Pays on acceptance. Will send a sample copy to a writer on request. "Query with outline essential." Reports "within reasonable interval." Enclose S.A.E. and International Reply Coupons.
Nonfiction and Photos: "Technical, mechanical, and maintenance articles from knowledgeable sources; how-to articles on automotive service and repair, written for professionals. Must be of interest and value to a purely Canadian audience of technicians. No-nonsense style—facts, crisply told; Canadian angle preferred. Also,

features related to business management, training, and customer relations."
Length: 1,200 to 1,500 words. Pays 5¢ to 7¢ a word, $65 to $100 for two-page spread.
"2 to 4 well captioned photos" purchased with mss; 8x10 b&w glossies preferred.
No color. Pays $5 to $10.

COMMERCIAL CAR JOURNAL, Chilton Way, Radnor PA 19089. Editor: James
D. Winsor. Monthly. Pays on acceptance. "Query first with article outline." Enclose
S.A.S.E.
Nonfiction: "Articles and photo features dealing with management, maintenance,
and operating phases of truck and bus fleet operations. Material must be somewhat
specialized and deal with a specific phase of the operation." Length: open. Pays $50
to $150.
Photos: "Occasionally use separate photos with captions." Pays $5 to $20.

HEAVY DUTY TRUCKING, P. O. Box W, Newport Beach CA 92663. Editor:
Doug Condra. For "heavy (over 26,000 pounds) truck operators." Monthly. Buys
first North American serial rights. Pays on acceptance. "Query preferred." Reports
in 1 week. Enclose S.A.S.E.
Nonfiction and Photos: "Articles on equipment and components dealing with truck
performance." Length: 1,000 to 2,000 words. Pays $75 to $150. Photos purchased
with mss.

HOT ROD INDUSTRY NEWS, 8490 Sunset Blvd., Los Angeles CA 90069. Editor:
Steve Kelly. For "relatively young businessmen with background in cars who now
produce, market, and/or sell performance and custom equipment for cars, trucks,
motorcycles, campers, etc." Established: 1967. Monthly. Circulation: 19,000. Buys
all rights. Buys 20 to 30 mss a year. Payment on acceptance. Will send free sample
copy to writer on request. Query first. Reports on all material within 30 days. Enclose S.A.S.E.
Nonfiction and Photos: "Up to the minute news of pending anti-car laws in various
states. Also how-to articles for dealers. How-to on taxes, accounting, hiring, etc.
Methods for business practices; how to sell more, do it easier, spend less. Features
on successful business. Not too wordy, easy on inside phrases and terms. Skip
making heroes out of everyone. Stick to basics, and don't use seldom heard words."
Length: 1,000 to 5,000 words. Pays $50 to $300. 8x10 b&w glossy photos purchased
with ms. Captions required.

JOBBER NEWS, 287 MacPherson Ave., Toronto 7, Ont., Canada. Editor: Sam
Dixon. For "parts wholesalers and rebuilders in Canada." Monthly. Pays on publication. Query first. Enclose S.A.E. and International Reply Coupons.
Nonfiction: "Management features slanted to auto parts wholesaling are main interest. This is a specialized field and much research is required. Must have authentic
Canadian application; rewrites of American applications not wanted." Length:
1,000 words maximum. "The rate of pay, which is a flat fee per feature, is negotiated
with the author."

JOBBER TOPICS, 7300 N. Cicero Ave., Lincolnwood IL 60646. Articles Editor:
Jack Creighton. For "automotive parts and supplies wholesalers." Monthly. Buys
all rights. Pays on publication. Enclose S.A.S.E. for return of submissions.
Nonfiction and Photos: "Articles with unusual or outstanding automotive jobber
procedures, with special emphasis on sales and merchandising; any phase of distribution. Especially interested in merchandising practices and machine shop operation." Length: 2,000 words maximum. Pays 4¢ a word. 5x7 or 8x10 b&w glossies
purchased with mss. Pays $5.

MILK HAULER AND FOOD TRANSPORTER, 221 N. La Salle St., Chicago IL
60601. Editor: Douglas D. Sorenson. For "tank truck haulers who pick up milk
from dairy farms and transporters who deliver milk to outlying markets." Buys first
rights. Pays on acceptance. Query first. Reports in 2 to 3 weeks. Enclose S.A.S.E.
Nonfiction and Photos: "Particularly interested in success stories on transporters
whose operation includes the hauling of cheese and other dairy products, liquid

sugar, molasses, citrus juice, and other edible foods. Good photos essential. Pays up to $50 an article, $5 each for sharp b&w photos."

MODERN BULK TRANSPORTER, 4801 Montgomery Lane, Washington DC 20014. Editor: Don Sutherland. For "management of companies operating tank motor vehicles which transport liquid or dry bulk commodities." Monthly. Pays on acceptance. Will consider photocopied submissions, but "we're prejudiced against them." Enclose S.A.S.E. for return of submissions.
Nonfiction and Photos: "Articles covering the tank truck industry; stories concerning a successful for-hire tank truck company, or stories about the use of tank trucks for unusual commodities. We especially seek articles on the successful operation of tank trucks by oil jobbers or other so-called 'private carriers' who transport their own products. Approach should be about specific tank truck problems solved, unusual methods of operations, spectacular growth of a company, tank truck management techniques, or other subjects of special interest. Simple description of routine operations not acceptable." Length: 1,000 to 3,000 words, "preferably accompanied by pictures." Pays minimum 5¢ a word. Pays minimum $30 per published page "for general articles exclusive in the trucking field only (such as maintenance and mechanical subjects)." Pays minimum $25 for "reporter assignments—producing fact sheet for rewrite." 8x10 and 5x7 glossies purchased with exclusive features. Pays $7.

MODERN TIRE DEALER, Box 5417, 77 N. Miller Rd., Akron OH 44313. Editor: C.S. Slaybaugh. For "independent tire dealers." Monthly. Buys all rights. Pays on publication. Will consider photocopied submissions. Query first. Reports in 1 month. Enclose S.A.S.E.
Nonfiction, Photos, and Fillers: "How TBA dealers sell tires, batteries, and allied services, such as brakes, wheel alignment, shocks, mufflers. The emphasis is on merchandising. We prefer the writer to zero in on some specific area of interest; avoid the shotgun approach." Length: 1,500 words. Pays $35 to $75. 8x10, 4x5, 5x7 b&w glossies purchased with mss. Pays $5. Buys 300-word fillers. Pays $5 to $10.

MOTOR, 250 W. 55th St., New York NY 10019. Editor: J. Robert Connor. For automobile service and repairshop operators, dealer service managers. Monthly. Buys all rights. Pays on acceptance. Query first. Reports in 1 week. Enclose S.A.S.E.
Nonfiction: Merchandising sales, promotion and management artiales containing ideas that can be adapted by garages and service stations. Emphasis on how-to material, wants stories on wholesalers, jobbers, and interviews with executives. Length: 1,200 to 1,500 words. Pays $75 to $300; sometimes higher for exceptional pieces.
Photos: Purchased with mss or with captions, of interest to readership. 8x10 glossies. Pays $10 each. Will also pay $12 per photo for unusual pictures of happenings in automotive repair field, general interest pictures with automotive angle, and pretty girls with automotive slant.

MOTOR IN CANADA, 1077 St. James St., P.O. Box 6900, Winnipeg, Man., Canada. Editor: Ralf Neuendorff. Monthly. Not copyrighted. Pays on publication. Reports in 2 weeks. Enclose S.A.E. and International Reply Coupons.
Nonfiction and Photos: "Articles on all phases of automobile maintenance and repair operations of the automotive service industry in western Canada; personnel announcements. Material about new processes, products, and supplies for automotive purposes." Pays "$1 per column inch." Photos purchased with mss. Pays $4.

O AND A MARKETING NEWS, P. O. Box 765, LaCanada CA 91011. Editor: Don McAnally. For "service station dealers, garagemen, TBA (tires, batteries, accessories) people, oil company marketing management." Bimonthly. Circulation: 13,000. Not copyrighted. Pays on publication. Query first. Reports in 1 week. Enclose S.A.S.E.
Nonfiction and Photos: "Straight news material; management, service, and merchandising applications; emphasis on news about or affecting markets and marketers within the publication's geographic area of the 7 western states. No restrictions on style or slant." Length: maximum 1,000 words. Pays about 2¢ a word. Photos purchased with or without mss; captions required. Pays $5.

OHIO TRUCKING NEWS, Mezzanine Floor, Neil House Hotel, Columbus OH 43215. Editor: Mary Francis Hewitt. Publication of the Ohio Trucking Association. Quarterly. Buys material for exclusive publication only. Pays on publication. Free sample copy on request. Query not required. Reports in 30 days. Enclose S.A.S.E.

Nonfiction: Modern developments in truck transportation, particularly as they apply to Ohio industry and truck operators. Length: maximum 1,500 words. Pays $25 to $50.
Photos: Purchased with mss or with captions only. Transportation subjects. Pays $10.

OPEN ROAD, 1015 Florence St., Fort Worth TX 76102. Editor: Chris Lackey. For "professional over-the-road truck drivers of America." Monthly. Buys North American serial rights. Pays on publication. Will send a sample copy to a writer on request. Query first. Reports in 2 to 4 weeks. Enclose S.A.S.E.
Nonfiction and Photos: "Pieces on truck drivers—articles about new model heavy trucks and equipment, acts of heroism, humor, unusual events, special driving articles, advice to other drivers, drivers who do good jobs in community life or civic work, etc." Length: "prefer less than 1,000 words, usually." Pays "about 3¢ a word." 5x7 or 8x10 b&w glossies purchased with mss. Pays $5; "more for covers."
Fillers: "Short humor on interesting driver or driver-related matters." Pays about 3¢ a word.

REFRIGERATED TRANSPORTER, 1602 Harold St., Houston TX 77006. Monthly. Not copyrighted. Pays on publication. Reports in 1 month. Enclose S.A.S.E. for return of submissions.
Nonfiction and Photos: "Articles on fleet management and maintenance of vehicles, especially the refrigerated van and the refrigerating unit; shop tips; loading or handling systems, especially for frozen or refrigerated cargo; new equipment specifications; conversions of equipment for better handling or more efficient operations. Prefer articles with illustrations obtained from fleets operating refrigerated trucks or trailers." Pays minimum $45 per page or $2 per inch.
Fillers: Buys newspaper clippings, "Do not rewrite."

SERVICE STATION AND GARAGE MANAGEMENT, 109 Vanderhoof Ave., Suite 101, Toronto, Ont. M4G 2J2, Canada. Editor: Joe Holliday. For "service station operators and garagemen in Canada only." Established in 1956. Monthly. Circulation: 24,000. Buys first Canadian serial rights. Buys 1 or 2 articles a year. Pays on acceptance. Will send a sample copy to a writer for 50¢. Query first. Reports in 2 days. Enclose S.A.E. and International Reply Coupons.

Nonfiction and Photos: "Articles on service station operators in Canada only; those who are doing top merchandising job. Also on specific phases of service station doings: brakes, tune-up, lubrication, etc. Solid business facts and figures; information must have human interest angles. Interested in controversial legislation, trade problems, sales and service promotions, technical data, personnel activities and changes. No general, long-winded material. The approach must be Canadian. The writer must know the trade and must provide facts and figures useful and helpful to readers. The style should be easy, simple, and friendly—not stilted." Length: 1,000 words. Pays 4¢ to 5¢ a word average, "depending on the topic and the author's status." Photos purchased with mss and without mss "if different or novel"; captions required. Pays $5 for 5x7 or 8x10 b&w glossies.

SOUTHERN AUTOMOTIVE JOURNAL, 1760 Peachtree Rd., N.W., Atlanta GA 30309. Editor: William F. Vann. For service stations, auto dealers, garages, body shops, fleets, and parts jobbers. Monthly. Not copyrighted. Will send a sample copy to a writer for $1. Query first. Enclose S.A.S.E.
Nonfiction and Photos: "Articles of interest to the automotive aftermarket." Length: open. Payment varies. Photos purchased with ms.

SOUTHERN MOTOR CARGO, P. O. Box 4169, Memphis TN 38104. Editor: William H. Raiford. For "trucking management and maintenance personnel of private, contract, and for-hire carriers in 16 southern states (Ala., Ark., Del., Fla., Ga., Ky., La., Md., Miss., N.C., Okla., S.C., Tenn., Tex., Va., and West Va.) and the District of Columbia." Special issues include "ATA Convention," October; "Transportation Graduate Directory," December; "Mid-America Truck Show," March. Monthly. Circulation: 35,000. Buys first rights within circulation area. Pays on publication. Will send a sample copy to a writer on request. "No query necessary." Reports "usually in 2 weeks." Enclose S.A.S.E. for return of submissions.

Nonfiction: "How a southern trucker builds a better mousetrap. Factual newspaper style with punch in lead. Don't get flowery. No success stories. Pick one item, i.e. tire maintenance, billing procedure, etc., and show how such-and-such carrier has developed or modified it to better fit his organization. Bring in problems solved by the way he adapted this or that and what way he plans to better his present layout. Try and find a segment of the business that has been altered or modified due to economics or new information, such as 'due to information gathered by a new IBM process, it has been discovered that an XYZ transmission needs overhauling every 60,000 miles instead of every 35,000 miles, thereby resulting in savings of $$$ over the normal life of this transmission.' Or, 'by incorporating a new method of record keeping, claims on damaged freight have been expedited with a resultant savings in time and money.' Compare the old method with the new, itemize savings, and get quotes from personnel involved. Articles must be built around an outstanding phase of the operation and must be documented and approved by the firm's management prior to publication." Length: 2,500 to 3,500 words. Pays minimum 4¢ a word for "feature material."

Photos: "Purchased with cutline; glossy prints." Pays $5.

SPEED AND CUSTOM DEALER, 11 South Forge St., Akron OH 44304. Editor: Gary L. Gardner. For speed shop owners, high performance machine shops. Monthly. Buys all rights and simultaneous rights. Buys 8 to 10 mss a year. Pays on publication. Query required. Study recent issues. Reports in 1 week. Enclose S.A.S.E.

Nonfiction: Wants articles slanted toward the speed shop owner, showing him how to improve his business and overcome problems. Writer must know cars and racing of all kinds. Accepts articles on major race events where the material is slanted toward the dealer, giving him some indication of what the market is going to be. Interested in new products tested at the track or exclusive product test coverage. All stories should be accompanied by 3 to 6 8x10 photos to help explain the story. Pays 4¢ per word.

Photos: Purchased with and without mss. Pays $6 for photos purchased with mss. Also interested in good, sharp photos that tell stories in themselves. Also purchases unusual photos of speed equipment, speed equipment manufacturers, or speed dealers. Wants interesting track photos pertaining to speed dealer. Pays $8.50.

SUPER SERVICE STATION, 7300 N. Cicero Ave., Lincolnwood, Chicago IL 60646. Editor: Charles Boyd, Jr. For service station operators. Monthly. Pays on publication. Query first. Reports in 2 weeks. Enclose S.A.S.E.

Nonfiction and Photos: "Articles on good station management, merchandise displays, servicing at gas stations. Must be practical." Length: maximum 1,500 words; "preferably less." Pays 5¢ a word. Photos purchased with mss. Pays $5.

Fillers: "On display and selling features. One photo with each." Length: 50 to 150 words. Pays 5¢ a word.

TIRE REVIEW, 11 S. Forge St., Akron OH 44304. Editor: William Whitney. For "independent tire dealers and retreaders, company stores, tire company executives, some oil company executives." Monthly. Circulation: 34,000. Buys first rights. Buys 6 or 7 mss a year. Pays on publication. Will send a free sample copy to a writer on request. Query first. Reports in 1 week. Enclose S.A.S.E.

Nonfiction and Photos: "Tire industry news, including new product news, research and marketing trends, legislative news, features on independent tire dealers and retreaders, news of trade shows and conventions, tire and related accessory merchandising tips. All articles should be straightforward, concise, information-packed, and not slanted toward any particular manufacturer or brand name. Must have something to do with tires or the tire industry." Length: "no limitations." Pays 3¢ a word. B&w glossies purchased with and without mss. Pays "$5 a photo with story $8.50 for photos used alone."

TODAY'S TRANSPORT INTERNATIONAL (TRANSPORTE MODERNO), P.O. Box 1256, Stamford CT 06904. Editor: Philip R. Moran. For "vehicle and fleet operators and materials-handling executives in 110 countries of Asia, Africa, Australia, New Zealand, Latin America, the Caribbean, and the Middle East." Bimonthly. Circulation: 41,000. Buys international rights. Buys 15 to 20 mss a year. Pays on acceptance. Will send a sample copy to a writer on request. Query first. Reports in 1 week. Enclose S.A.S.E.
Nonfiction and Photos: "Write for our audience, that is, avoid a U. S.-oriented approach. Our readers mainly are in developing countries." Wants "articles showing new techniques, how-to-do-it approaches, etc., on an administrative plane." Length: 2,000 to 2,500 words. Pays $100 to $150, "for article and accompanying illustrations where applicable (charts, photos, etc.). We translate into Spanish."

TRUCK TRANSPORTATION, 230 Adelaide St. W., Toronto M5H 1W7, Ont., Canada. Editor: Barry M. Holmes. For "enterprises with special interest in heavy-weight trucking." Copyrighted. Pays on publication. Query first. Enclose S.A.E. and International Reply Coupons for reply to query.
Nonfiction and Photos: "Articles dealing with the manufacture of new trucking products and anything dealing with fleet operations of a Canadian flavor." Length: 1,500 words maximum. Pays $50 or 3¢ a word. Photos purchased with mss. Pays $5 each.

WAREHOUSE DISTRIBUTION, 7300 N. Cicero Ave., Lincolnwood, Chicago IL 60646. Editor: Syd Cowan. For "businessmen in the auto parts distribution field who are doing above one million dollars business per year." 8 times a year. Circulation: 25,000. Buys all rights. Pays on publication. Query first. Reports "within a reasonable amount of time." Enclose S.A.S.E.
Nonfiction and Photos: "Business management subjects, limited to the automotive parts distribution field." Length: 1,500 to 2,000 words. Pays 4¢ to 10¢ a word, "based on value to industry and the quality of the article." Photos purchased with and without mss; captions required. Wants "sharp 5x7 prints." Pays maximum $6.
Fillers: Short humor, jokes, cheesecake. Pay: open.

Aviation and Space

In this category are journals for aviation businessmen and airport operators and technical aviation and space journals. Publications for professional and private pilots are classified with the Aviation magazines in the Consumer Publications section.

AIRPORT WORLD, 7315 Wisconsin Ave., Air Rights Building, Washington DC 20014. Editor: Lew Townsend. For "airport operators and managers, fixed base operators, ground service management, government (city, state, federal), air carriers and other transport users, consultants (planners, architects, engineers), manufacturer representatives, etc." Established in 1968. Monthly. Circulation: 27,000. Buys all rights. Buys about 75 mss a year. Pays on acceptance. Will send a sample copy to a writer on request. Query first. Submit seasonal material 2 months in advance. Reports in 2 weeks, "mostly sooner." Enclose S.A.S.E.
Nonfiction and Photos: "Features on individual airports: modernization, expansion, etc. Features on equipment, facilities, maintenance, management, environmental subjects, operations, safety, financing, training, operations, etc. *Airport World* covers both large and small airports and related operations and has the biggest distribution of any airport-related publication. The writer should first get a copy of our magazine. Since our readers are professional, he must be knowl-

edgeable on the subject or have access to knowledgeable sources." Buys informational articles, how-to's, photo features, coverage of successful business operations, new product articles, semi-technical articles, and articles on merchandising techniques. Length: maximum 2,000 words, "but concise enough to tell the story." Pays maximum $300. B&w photos and transparencies purchased with and without mss; captions required.

BUSINESS AND COMMERCIAL AVIATION, One Park Ave., New York NY 10016. Editor: Archie Trammel. For "pilots and business aircraft operators." Monthly. Circulation: 70,000. Buys all rights. Buys "very little" freelance material. Pays on acceptance. Will send a sample copy to a writer for $1. Query first. Reports "as soon as an evaluation is made." Enclose S.A.S.E.
Nonfiction and Photos: "Our readers are pilots and we have found general articles to be inadequate. Writers with a technical knowledge of aviation would be most suitable." Wants "reports on business aviation operations, pilot reports, etc." Length: "no limits." Pays $100 to $300. B&w photos of aircraft purchased with mss. Pays $15 to $20. Pays $300 for cover color photos.

JET CARGO NEWS, 5314 Bingle Rd., Houston TX 77018. Editor: Britt Martin. For "traffic and distribution managers, marketing executives, sales executives, and corporate management who use or may sometime use air transportation to ship their company's products." Established in 1968. Monthly. Circulation: over 21,000. Buys all rights. Buys 6 to 10 mss a year. Pays on publication. Will send a sample copy to a writer on request. Write for copy of guidelines for writers. Submit complete ms. Will not consider photocopied submissions. Submit seasonal material 2 weeks in advance of issue date. Reports "within a month, if postage is included." Enclose S.A.S.E. for return of submissions.
Nonfiction and Photos: "Air marketing success stories, cargo rate changes, new ideas on packaging and/or sales. The writer's message should be to the shipper, not to or about airlines. We feel the shipper wants to know how an airline can help him, and that he's not particularly interested in the airline's economics. Use a tight, magazine style. The writer must know marketing. We want depth, how-to material." Buys informational articles, how-to's, interviews, and coverage of successful business operations. Length: maximum 2,500 words. Pays 5¢ a word. 7x10 b&w glossies purchased with and without mss; captions required. Pays $7.50.

ROTOR AND WING, News Plaza, Peoria IL 61601. Editor: Robert G. Sutton. For "pilots and aircraft owners." Bimonthly. Circulation: 40,000. Buys all rights. Pays on acceptance. Will send a sample copy to a writer on request. Query first. "Study our publication." Reports in 4 weeks. Enclose S.A.S.E.
Nonfiction and Photos: "Dollars-and-cents feature stories on the use of helicopters, STOL aircraft, avionics, and accessories, directed to pilots and V/STOL aircraft owners and prospective buyers of aircraft working in a broad spectrum of business and government. Must be of a commercial nature, not military. Must be technical and must indirectly encourage the purchase and/or use of helicopters." Length: 2,000 words. Pays $125 to $200. Photos purchased with mss; "good selection."

Baking

THE BAKER, P.O. Box 3960, Dallas TX 75208. News Editor: Jack Thiess. For the baking industry. Established in 1931. Monthly. Circulation: 5,000. Not copyrighted. Pays on publication. Submit complete ms. Enclose S.A.S.E.
Nonfiction: "Technical stories about the baking industry only. We don't want general 'how to be a good businessman' articles. How-to's are currently overworked by freelancers submitting to us. Interested in articles on nutrition." Pays about $1 per column inch.

PACIFIC BAKERS NEWS, Route 2, Belfair WA 98528. Publisher: Leo Livingston. Business newsletter for commercial bakeries in the western states. Monthly. Buys first rights. Pays on publication. Will send a sample copy to a writer on request. Reports "at once." Enclose S.A.S.E.

Fillers: Buys only brief "boiled-down news items about bakers and bakeries operating only in Alaska, Hawaii, Pacific Coast and Rocky Mountain states. Welcomes clippings. Needs monthly news reports and clippings about the baking industry from most western cities (except Seattle and Los Angeles areas)." Length: 10 to 200 words. Pays 4¢ a word.

SPECIALTY BAKERS VOICE, 299 Broadway, New York NY 10007. Editor: Irving Walters. For "bakery management." Semimonthly. Not copyrighted. Pays on publication. Will send a sample copy to a writer on request. Query first. Enclose S.A.S.E. for return of submissions.

Nonfiction: "Articles geared to the single unit and multi-unit retail bake shop on topics such as merchandising, management techniques, store layout, production, employee-employer relations, bakery sanitation, customer service. Articles must be concise, business-oriented, and must include examples." Length: 1,000 to 1,500 words. Pays 2¢ a word.

Beverages and Bottling

The following journals are for manufacturers, distributors, and retailers of soft drinks and alcoholic beverages. Publications for bar and tavern operators and managers of restaurants are classified in the Hotels, Motels, Clubs, Resorts, and Restaurants category.

BEVERAGE INDUSTRY, 777 Third Ave., New York NY 10017. Editor: Sam Martin. For "beverage plant management." Special issues on soft drinks, beer, bottled water, trucks, vending packaging, materials-handling. Biweekly. Buys all rights. Pays on publication. Will send a sample copy to a writer on request. Query first, "outlining proposed treatment." Reports in 10 days. Enclose S.A.S.E.

Nonfiction and Photos: "Beverage plant case histories, detailing manner of operation and specific reasons for success of particular marketing or technological venture; promotional campaigns, special sales efforts, methods of introducing new products, sales training, fleet management, product control, etc. Interesting lead paragraph, then straight facts on operations. Also, quotes from management executives." Length: 1,500 to 2,000 words. Pays minimum of 2¢ "per published word." Photos purchased with mss. "Should be sharp b&w glossies, preferably illustrating some pertinent aspect of the article." Pays $5.

Fillers: "Newsbreaks pertinent to the beverage industry." Will buy newspaper clippings, if information useful.

MICHIGAN BEVERAGE NEWS, 7425 E. Jefferson, Detroit MI 48214. Editor: John R. Dagenais. For "owners of bars, taverns, package liquor stores, hotels, and clubs in Michigan." Semimonthly. Buys exclusive rights to publication in Michigan. Pays on publication. Will send a sample copy to a writer on request. Query first. Reports "immediately." Enclose S.A.S.E.

Nonfiction and Photos: "Feature stories with pictures. Unusual attractions and business-building ideas in use by Michigan liquor licensees. Profit tips, success stories, etc., slanted to the trade, not to the general public. Especially interested in working with freelancers in Grand Rapids, Flint, Kalamazoo, and Bay City areas." Length: 500 to 750 words. Pays "50¢ per column inch." Buys photos of Michigan licensees engaged in business activities. Pays "50¢ per column inch."

MID-CONTINENT BOTTLER, 912 Baltimore Ave., Kansas City MO 64105. Publisher: Floyd E. Sageser. For "soft drink bottlers in the 18-state midwestern area." Monthly. Not copyrighted. Pays on acceptance. Will send a sample copy to a writer on request. Reports "immediately." Enclose S.A.S.E. for return of submissions.

Nonfiction and Photos: "Items of specific soft drink bottler interest with special emphasis on sales and merchandising techniques. Feature style desired." Length: 2,000 words. Pays $15 to $30. Photos purchased with mss.

MODERN BREWERY AGE, 80 Lincoln Ave., Stamford CT 06902. Editor: Stanley N. Vlantes. For "brewery executives on the technical, administrative, and marketing levels." Bimonthly. Buys North American serial rights. Pays on publication. Query first. Reports "at once." Enclose S.A.S.E.
Nonfiction and Photos: "Technical and business articles of interest to brewers." Length: "no more than 6 or 7 double-spaced typewritten pages." Pays "$35 per printed page (about 3 to 3½ pages double-spaced typewritten ms)." Photos purchased with mss; captions required. Pays $7.50.
How To Break In: "Learn a lot about something and something about everything!"

SOFT DRINKS, 10 Cutter Mill Rd., Great Neck NY 11021. Editor: Paul Mullins. Monthly. Buys all rights. Pays on publication. Will send a sample copy to a writer on request. Query first. Reports in 1 month. Enclose S.A.S.E.
Nonfiction and Photos: "Articles on any subject pertaining to manufacturers of carbonated and non-carbonated soft drinks, wine or beer. Emphasis should be on sales, distribution, merchandising, advertising, and promotion. Historical articles and 'how-to dissertations' are not desired; no shorts, fillers, or rewritten newspaper clippings." Pays "$35 per printed page (about 1,200 words). Illustrations should be supplied where possible." Pays $5 each for photos.

SOUTHERN BEVERAGE JOURNAL, P. O. Box 1107, 8453 S.W. 132nd St., Miami (Kendall) FL 33156. Editor: John Hiser. For "operators of package stores, bars, restaurants, hotel lounges, and dining rooms in Florida, Georgia, South Carolina, Texas, Tennessee, Arkansas, Kentucky, Louisiana, Mississippi." Established in 1944. Monthly. Circulation: about 23,000. Buys "exclusive rights for the 9 southern states." Buys about 12 mss a year. Pays on acceptance or publication. Will send a sample copy to a writer on request. Write for copy of guidelines for writers. Query first. Will "hardly ever" consider photocopied submissions. Reports in "about a week." Enclose S.A.S.E.
Nonfiction and Photos: "How operators of package stores, bars, restaurants, hotels, and dining rooms merchandise—what they do to attract customers, keep them coming back, and how they promote their operations and the products they sell. We are different from other beverage journals because of our regional circulation and because of our emphasis on merchandising and promotion." Length: open. Pays 3¢ to 4¢ a word, "but it really depends on the article itself; sometimes we don't count words, but we pay for value." Photos purchased with mss only. We prefer 8x10 b&w glossies, but will consider 5x7. Pays $5.

Book and Book Store Trade

CHRISTIAN BOOKSELLER, Gundersen Dr. and Schmale Rd., Wheaton IL 60187. Editor: Robert Hill. For "Christian booksellers." Monthly. Buys all rights. Pays on publication. Will send a sample copy to a writer on request. Query first. "Writers are urged to study the magazine before submitting." Reports in 2 weeks. Enclose S.A.S.E.
Nonfiction and Photos: "Success stories, illustrated with glossy photos, about established Christian booksellers. Stories should highlight specific techniques and managerial policy contributing to the success of the store. We use how-they-did-it articles on phases of bookstore administration and management with an anecdotal approach, and articles presenting proven techniques for seasonal or year-round items. These must be based on actual bookstore experience or sound sales techniques. Features focusing on trends in the Christian book and supply trade; short news articles, with photos if possible, reporting significant developments in the bookstore or publishing field; comprehensive reports on successful store layouts, traffic flow, with glossy illustrations or diagrams. Approach articles from a 'how-

they-did-it' rather than 'how-to-do-it' point of view." Length: 1,500 to 2,000 words "with 2 or 3 photos." Pays $35 per article. Pays $3 to $5 for photos.

COLLEGE STORE EXECUTIVE, 211 Broadway, Lynbrook NY 11563. Editor: Louise Altavilla. For "managers, buyers, and business operators of campus stores." Monthly. Circulation: 9,500. Buys North American serial rights. Pays on publication. Will send a sample copy to a writer on request. Query first. Reports "immediately." Enclose S.A.S.E.
Nonfiction and Photos: "Descriptions of unusual displays, merchandising techniques, etc. used in a specific 'bookstore' on campus. (We refer to these stores as college stores.) Best source of information is the manager of the store." Length: 1,000 words. Pays 5¢ a word. Photos purchased with mss. Should be "of college stores, expansion, unusual displays, unusual lines being carried in the store, etc. Should be sharp and clear." Pay negotiable, generally $5.
Poetry and Fillers: "Can pertain to any phase of bookselling or retailing to college students." Length: open. Pays 5¢ a word.

PUBLISHERS WEEKLY, 1180 Ave. of the Americas, New York NY 10036. Editor-in-Chief: Arnold W. Ehrlich. Weekly. Pays on publication. Reports "in several weeks." Enclose S.A.S.E. for return of submissions.
Nonfiction and Photos: "We rarely use unsolicited mss because of the highly specialized audience and their technical interests, but we can sometimes use news items of bookstores or store promotions for books, or stories of book promotion and design." Pays 4¢ a word. Photos purchased with and without mss "occasionally."

Brick, Glass, and Ceramics

AMERICAN GLASS REVIEW, 1115 Clifton Ave., Clifton NJ 07013. Editor: Donald Doctorow. For manufacturers, fabricators, and distributors of glass and glass products. Monthly. Pays on publication. Reports in 3 to 4 weeks. Enclose S.A.S.E.
Nonfiction and Photos: "Illustrated articles on uses of glass, application in new buildings, new container uses, products using fiber glass, glass factory operations, etc." Pays $25 per printed page.

BRICK AND CLAY RECORD, 5 S. Wabash Ave., Chicago IL 60603. Managing Editor: Phil Jeffers. For "the heavy clay products industry." Monthly. Pays on publication. Query first. Reports in 15 days. Enclose S.A.S.E.
Nonfiction and Photos: "News concerning personnel changes within companies; news concerning new plants for manufacture of brick, clay pipe, refractories, drain tile, face brick, glazed tile, lightweight clay aggregate products and abrasives; news of new products, expansion, new building." Pays minimum 8¢ "a published line. Photos paid for only when initially requested by editor."
Fillers: "Items should concern only news of brick, clay pipe, refractory, or clay lightweight aggregate plant operations. If news of personnel, should be only of top-level plant personnel. Not interested in items such as patio, motel, or home construction using brick; of weddings or engagements of clay products people, unless major executives; obituaries, unless of major personnel; items concerning floor or wall tile (only structural tile); of plastics, metal, concrete, bakelite, or similar products; items concerning people not directly involved in clay plant operation." Pays $3 "per published 2- or 3-line brief item." Pays minimum $3 for "full-length published news item, depending on value of item and editor's discretion. Payment is only for items published in the magazine. No items sent in can be returned."

CERAMIC SCOPE, 6363 Wilshire Blvd., Los Angeles CA 90048. Editor: Mel Fiske. For "ceramic hobby teachers, dealers, and distributors." 10 times a year. Pays on acceptance. Query first. Reports "immediately." Enclose S.A.S.E.
Nonfiction and Photos: "Articles on all phases of studio management (such as merchandising, promotion, pricing, credit and collection, recordkeeping, taxes, display, equipment and layout); case histories of actual studio operation; discussion of ce-

ramic business practices and policies; news about traveling teachers, studios, shows, books, ceramic associations; reports on manufacturers' aids, products, services, displays, and literature." Length: open. Pays 2¢ a word. Photos purchased with mss. "Show interior of ceramic studios, workshops, and classes." Pays $5.

GLASS DIGEST, 15 E. 40th St., New York NY 10016. Editor: Oscar S. Glasberg. Monthly. Buys all rights. Pays on publication "or before, if ms held too long." Will send a sample copy to a writer on request. Reports "as soon as possible." Enclose S.A.S.E. for return of submissions.
Nonfiction and Photos: "Items about firms in glass distribution, personnel, plants, etc. Stories about outstanding jobs accomplished—volume of flat glass, storefronts, curtain walls, auto glass, mirrors, windows (metal), glass doors; special uses and values; who installed it. Stories about successful glass jobbers, dealers, and glazing contractors—their methods, promotion work done, advertising, results." Length: 1,000 to 1,500 words. Pays 4 to 5¢ a word, "occasionally more. No interest in bottles, glassware, containers, etc., but leaded and stained glass OK." B&w photos purchased with mss; "8x10 preferred." Pays $5, "occasionally more."

Building Interiors

DECORATING RETAILER, 9334 Dielman Industrial Dr., St. Louis MO 63132. Editor: Lee C. Russell. For "paint and wallpaper retailers who own or operate independent stores. They are interested in factual, concrete information on how they can improve their businesses." Established in 1964. Monthly. Circulation: 30,000. Buys all rights. Buys about 20 mss a year. Pays on acceptance. Will send a sample copy to a writer on request. Query first or submit complete ms. Will not consider photocopied submissions. Submit seasonal material 2 months in advance. Reports in 2 weeks. Enclose S.A.S.E. for return of submissions.
Nonfiction and Photos: "Articles on the merchandising, display, and sale of paint, wallcoverings, art and craft products, and other allied decorating products. Interested in direct, to-the-point pieces on how retailers can improve their operations. We prefer the interview-type article, telling how one or 2 retailers faced a problem and solved it. Articles should be specific and full of factual, concrete recommendations, preferably coming from other retailers who have had the experience. Quotes, descriptions of stores, displays, promotions, etc. are desirable. No 'abstract' articles on concepts. We want our readers to know how the suggestion has worked for other retailers, how and why it might or might not work for them. No clippings." Buys informational articles, how-to's, personal experience articles, interviews, profiles, coverage of successful business operations, and articles on merchandising techniques. Length: 1,000 to 1,500 words. Pays 5¢ a word. 5x7 b&w photos purchased with mss; captions optional. Pays $7.50.

KITCHEN BUSINESS, 1501 Broadway, New York NY 10036. Editor and Publisher: Patrick Galvin. For "kitchen cabinet and countertop plants, kitchen and bath planning specialists, and kitchen/bath departments of lumber, plumbing, and appliance businesses." Monthly. Buys all rights. Pays on acceptance. Will consider photocopied submissions. Reports in 1 month. Enclose S.A.S.E. for return of submissions.
Nonfiction and Photos: "Factual case histories with illustrative photos on effective selling or management methods; picture tours of outstanding kitchen showrooms of about 1,000 words; articles on management methods for kitchen distributorships which handle a full range of kitchen products; 'how-to' shop stories on kitchen cabinet shops or countertop fabricators, or stories on how they adapt to growth problems." Length: "600 words and 2 photos to 2,000 words and 10 photos." Pays $50 "first published page, minimum $30 each succeeding page, as estimated at the time of acceptance." Photos purchased with mss.
How To Break In: "Just go ahead and do it. Select the best looking kitchen firm in your area, go in and tell the boss you're a writer and want to do a story for *Kitchen*

Business, ask him to let you sit down and read an issue or two, interview him on a single how-to-do-it topic, shoot some pictures to illustrate the points in the interview, and take a chance. Include his phone number so I can check with him. If it's good, you'll get paid promptly. If it shows promise, I'll work with you. If it's lousy, you'll get it back. If it's in between, you might not hear for a while because I hate to send them back if they have any value at all. This worked for me through a dozen years of highly successful freelancing. It will work for anyone who has any reporting talent at all."

WALLCOVERINGS, 209 Dunn Ave., Stamford CT 06905. Editor: Martin Johnson. For wallpaper dealers. Monthly. Buys all rights. Pays on publication. Will send a sample copy to a writer on request. Enclose S.A.S.E. for return of submissions.
Nonfiction: "Articles, preferably based on interviews with wallpaper dealers, describing good merchandising and promotion ideas, effective display methods, business-building policies, etc." Length: maximum 1,200 words. Pays $50 to $75.
Photos: "Photos of store interiors, window displays, persons interviewed. No paint." Pays $5.

WALLS AND CEILINGS, 215 W. Harrison, Seattle WA 98119. Editor: Charles F. Clay. For "contractors involved in lathing and plastering, drywall, acoustics, fireproofing, curtain walls, movable partitions and their mechanics, together with manufacturers, dealers, and architects." Monthly. Circulation: 15,000. Not copyrighted. Buys 25 mss a year. Pays on publication. Will send a sample copy to a writer on request. Query first. Reports in 30 days. Enclose S.A.S.E.
Nonfiction and Photos: "As technical as possible. Should be helpful to professional operator—diagrams, sketches, and detail pictures should illustrate material." Interested in interviews, spot news, successful business operations, new product, merchandising techniques. Length: maximum 1,000 words. Pay "depends upon value to our readers—maximum usually $50 to $75." B&w glossies purchased with and without mss; captions required. Pays $3 to $5.

Business Management

The publications listed here are aimed at owners of businesses and top level business executives. They cover business trends and general theory and practice of management. Magazines that use similar material but have a less technical or professional slant are listed in Business and Finance in the Consumer Magazines section. Journals dealing with banking, investment, and financial management are classified in the Finance category in this section.
Publications dealing with lower level management (including supervisors and office managers) will be found in Management and Supervision. Journals for industrial plant managers are listed under Industrial Management, and also under the names of specific industries such as Machinery and Metal Trade or Plastics. Publications for office supply store operators will be found with the Office Equipment and Supplies Journals.

HARVARD BUSINESS REVIEW, Soldiers Field, Boston MA 02163. Editor: Ralph F. Lewis. 6 times a year. Buys all rights. Pays on publication. Will send a sample copy to a writer on request. Reports in 2 to 6 weeks. Enclose S.A.S.E.
Nonfiction: "Articles on business trends, techniques, and problems." Length: 3,000 to 6,000 words. Pays $100.

MAY TRENDS, 111 S. Washington St., Park Ridge IL 60068. Editor: J.J. Coffey, Jr. For "business executives, trade associations, government bureaus, Better Business Bureaus, educational institutions, newspapers." 3 times a year. Circulation: 10,000. Buys all rights. Buys 15 to 20 mss a year. Pays on publication. Will send a sample copy to a writer on request. Query first. Reports in 1 week. Enclose S.A.S.E.

Nonfiction: "General business and industry trend articles which include projections for at least 4 months. We prefer articles dealing with problems of specific industries—manufacturers, wholesalers, service companies—where contact has been made with executives, whose comments describing their problems can be quoted, particularly if they have used management consultants in the solving of their problems." Length: 1,500 to 3,000 words. Pays $100 to $300.

How To Break In: "As *May Trends* is interested particularly in the problems of specific businesses, a letter from a writer advising he has knowledge of a situation affecting the operations of an industry will bring a prompt reply from us."

Church Administration and Ministry

ADULT BIBLE TEACHER, 6401 The Paseo, Kansas City MO 64131. Editor: John B. Nielson. For teachers of adults. Quarterly. Buys first and second rights; will accept simultaneous submissions. Pays on acceptance. No query required. Will consider photocopied submissions. Reports in 6 weeks. Enclose S.A.S.E.
Nonfiction: "Articles of interest to teachers of adults and articles relevant to the International Sunday School Lessons." Length: 1,300 words maximum. Pays minimum $20 per 1,000 words. Department Editor: A.F. Harper.
Photos: Purchased with captions only. Pays minimum $5.
Poetry: Inspirational, seasonal, or lesson-related (Uniform Series) poetry. Length: 24 lines maximum. Pays minimum 10¢ per line.

C.S.P. WORLD NEWS, P.O. Box 224, Station J, Toronto M4J MYI, Ontario, Canada. Editor: Guy F. Claude Hamel. For clergy and laity. Established: 1965. Monthly. Circulation: 100,000. Not copyrighted. Buys 20 mss a year. Payment on acceptance. Will send free sample copy to writer on request. Query first. Will consider photocopied submissions. Submit seasonal material 2 months in advance. Reports on material on the 15th of each month. Enclose S.A.S.E.
Nonfiction and Photos: Articles on religions, psychology, theology, missionary activities. Informational, personal experience, interview, profile, inspirational, humor, historical, think articles. Length: 1,000 to 5,000 words. Pays $1 per 8x11 double-spaced page. "Printed photos from newspapers only." Pays $1.

CHRISTIAN ADVOCATE, 1661 N. Northwest Highway, Park Ridge IL 60068. Editor: William C. Henzlik. For clergy of United Methodist Church. Established 1826. Every 2 weeks. Circulation: 12,000. Buys all rights for all United Methodist publications, "depending on situation." Buys 6 to 10 freelance mss a year. Payment on acceptance. Will send free sample copy to writer on request. Write for copy of guidelines for writers. Submit complete ms. Will consider photocopied submissions. Submit seasonal material 8 months in advance. Reports on submissions in 1 month. Enclose S.A.S.E. for return of submissions.
Nonfiction: "Professional materials, book reviews of religious publications. Aimed only at our denomination, and only at pastoral subjects. Freelancer should have intimate knowledge of a pastor's life and problems, plus his/her educational challenges and needs. General religious interests are not enough. Specific knowledge is needed." Length: 250 to 1,800 words. Pays $20 to $50.
Poetry: "Occasional poems of religious content and imagery." Traditional forms, blank verse, free verse, avant-garde, light verse. Must relate to magazine's subject matter. Pays $10 to $15.

CHURCH ADMINISTRATION, 127 Ninth Ave., N., Nashville TN 37234. Editor: George Clark. For Southern Baptist pastors, staff, and volunteer church leaders. Monthly. Buys all rights. Will also consider second rights. Uses limited amount of freelance material. Pays on acceptance. Will send a free sample copy to a writer on request. Write for copy of guidelines for writers. Reports in 1 month. Enclose S.A.S.E. for return of submissions.
Nonfiction and Photos: "How-to-do-it articles dealing with church administration,

including church programming, organizing, and staffing, administrative skills, church financing, church food services, church facilities, communication, pastoral ministries, and community needs." Length: 750 to 1,200 words. Pays 2½¢ a word. Pays $7.50 to $10 for 8x10 b&w glossies purchased with mss.

How To Break In: "A beginning writer should first be acquainted with organization and policy of Baptist churches and with the administrative needs of Southern Baptist churches. He should perhaps interview one or several SBC pastors or staff members, find out how they are handling a certain administrative problem such as 'enlisting volunteer workers' or 'sharing the administrative load with church staff or volunteer workers.' I suggest writers compile an article showing how *several* different administrators (or churches) handled the problem, perhaps giving meaningful quotes. Submit the completed manuscript, typed 53 characters to the line, for consideration."

CHURCH MANAGEMENT, Commercial Bldg., 115 N. Main St., 201-12, Mt. Holly NC 28120. Editor: Norman L. Hersey. For ministers. Monthly. Buys first rights usually. Pays on publication. Reports in 2 to 4 weeks. Enclose S.A.S.E.

Nonfiction and Photos: "Articles and features dealing with such topics as church building, church administration, homiletics. Must have professional emphasis." Likes "how-to articles on church management and minister's professional problems." Length: 1,200 words maximum. Pays $7.50 to $25. Pays $1 to $5 for b&w glossies, any size, purchased with mss.

THE EDGE, formerly *Church School Builder*, 6401 The Paseo, Kansas City MO 64131. Editor: Norman J. Brown. For Church of the Nazarene Sunday School teachers, pastors, Sunday school superintendents, supervisors and officers. Special issues cover national holidays and special events in the Church of the Nazarene. Established 1973. Quarterly. Circulation: 45,000. Buys all rights. Buys about 50 mss a year. Pays on acceptance. Will send free sample copy to writer on request. Write for copy of guidelines for writers. Query first. Submit seasonal material 10 months in advance. Reports in 10 to 12 weeks. Enclose S.A.S.E.

Nonfiction: "The function of the magazine is to provide inspiration, information, promotional ideas, methods, and how-to articles. Basic ideas include a true story which motivates, a special project successfully completed by a school, class, or department; an outstanding promotional idea; a human interest story of an outstanding worker; a new way to use an old method; specific accomplishment through the use of Nazarene Graded Bible Lessons; how-to articles related specifically to age group methods and materials; articles which help teachers understand pupils." Length: 1,000 words maximum. Pays 2¢ a word.

Photos: Used when they tell a story. Very few groups of photos are purchased. 5x7 or larger required.

Fiction: Considered if it is short and deals with a problem in the field. Length: 1,000 words maximum. Pays 2¢ a word.

HISWAY MAGAZINE, 1445 Boonvile Ave., Springfield MO 65802. Editor: Glen Ellard. For "ministers of youth (Christian)." Basic Christianity and Christian activism. Special issues at Christmas and Easter. Established 1944. Monthly. Circulation: 7,500. Buys all rights, but will reassign rights to author after publication. Buys first North American serial rights, second serial (reprint) rights and simultaneous rights. Buys 20 to 30 mss a year. Payment on acceptance. Will send free sample copy to a writer on request. Submit only complete ms. Will consider photocopied submissions. Submit seasonal material 6 months in advance. Reports on material in 6 weeks. Enclose S.A.S.E.

Nonfiction: "How to" articles (e.g., "How to Evangelize Youth Through Music," "How to Study the Bible for Personal Application," "How to Use the Media for the Christian Message"); skits and role-plays; Bible raps, original choruses, Bible verses set to music, posters, ideas for youth services, socials, and fund raising; interviews with successful youth leaders. Avoid cliches (especially religious ones); educational philosophy: youth (or student) centered instead of adult (or teacher) centered; relational approach instead of talking down. Length: 500-1500 words. Pays 3¢ a word.

JOURNAL OF THE ACADEMY OF PARISH CLERGY, 3113 Kenwood Blvd., Toledo OH 43606. Editor: Robert Wm. Croskery, D.D., APC. For Catholic priests,

Jewish rabbis and Protestant pastors who work in parish settings. Established: 1972. Quarterly. Circulation: 2,000. Buys all rights but will reassign rights to author after publication. Buys 24 mss a year. Payment on publication. Will send free sample copy to writer on request. Query first. Reports on material accepted for publication within 60 days. Enclose S.A.S.E.

Nonfiction: "Material that relates to the practice of leadership of congregations (any aspect of congregation life); material relating to training of clergy or continuing education. Marriage counseling; changing world of youth, religion and ministry thereto; any unusual ministry." Approach must be "scholarly and readable. Emphasis is put on case studies or other material built on 'hard' data, rather than opinion or philosophizing. Book reviews relevant to the purposes of the Academy of Parish Clergy." Length: 7,500 words maximum; no minimum. Usually pays $25.

KEY TO CHRISTIAN EDUCATION, 8121 Hamilton Ave., Cincinnati OH 45231. Editor: Charles Matthews. For Sunday school leaders. Quarterly. Not copyrighted. Pays on acceptance. Will send free sample copy on request. "Study sample for style and editorial requirements before submitting ms." Reports in 30 days. Enclose S.A.S.E. for return of submissions.

Nonfiction and Photos: How-to articles helpful to teachers, departmental superintendents, youth leaders, Sunday school superintendents, ministers of Christian education. Writing should not be highly technical. "It Worked for Us" is a feature which deals with the various phases of Christian education. Length: 800 to 1,600 words. Pays $20 to $50. Buys 8x10 b&w photos with mss. Pays $5 to $10.

Fillers: "Tested Ideas" type articles on Sunday school plans that have worked. Length: 50 to 75 words. Pays $5 each.

LEARNING WITH (formerly *Resource*), 2900 Queen Lane, Philadelphia PA 19129. Editor: Rev. Carl Linder. For Sunday and weekday Lutheran church school teachers. Monthly. Buys all rights. Pays on publication. Will send a sample copy to a writer on request. Christmas deadline, August 1; Easter deadline, December 1. Enclose S.A.S.E. for return of submissions.

Nonfiction and Photos: Articles in depth on educational methodology as applicable in a church school, and articles on age-level characteristics and problems. Informal style using first person anecdotes to illustrate points of thought development is preferred. Length: up to 1,500 words. Pays 3¢ per word. Buys glossy prints with mss. Pays $5-$15.

Fillers: Short humor and true anecdotes appropriate to format. Length: 50 to 250 words. Pays $5 to $10.

PASTORAL LIFE, St. Paul Monastery, Canfield OH 44406. Editor: Victor L. Viberti, S.S.P. For "priests and those interested in pastoral ministry." Monthly. Circulation: 8,000. Buys first rights. Pays on acceptance. Will send a sample copy to a writer on request. Query first, "as most of the articles are commissioned from priests and ministers." Reports in 7 to 10 days. Enclose S.A.S.E.

Nonfiction: Length: 2,000 to 3,000 words. Pays minimum 2¢ a word.

PREACHING TODAY, 3015 Fourth St., N.E., Washington DC 20017. Acting Editor: Rev. John J. Geaney, C.S.P. Pays on publication. Enclose S.A.S.E. for return of submissions.

Nonfiction: "Intelligent, readable articles that would attract anyone who has a serious interest in preaching. Articles on theory, history, practice, or new experimentation will be considered, so long as the material will truly profit and interest our readership." Length: 500 to 3,000 words. Pays "up to $5 per page."

SUCCESS, Baptist Publications, P.O. Box 15337, Denver CO 80215. Editor: Mrs. Edith Quinlan. For workers in Christian education. Quarterly. Buys first rights "usually." Pays on publication. Will send a sample copy to a writer on request. Write for copy of guidelines for writers. Query first or submit complete ms. "Enclose short biographical sketch with submission, especially if engaged in Christian education work." Reports "as soon as possible." Enclose S.A.S.E.

Nonfiction and Photos: "Our magazine gives ideas, helps, and information to equip Sunday school superintendents, teachers, and youth workers to do a more effective job. Articles may be either of a general nature, slanted to all Sunday school and training time workers, or may be slanted to specific age groups, such as preschool, elementary, youth, and adult. A Baptist publications commercial slant is not desired for *Success* articles, but writing must be in keeping with philosophies of Christian education advocated by the publishing house, such as adherence to the fundamentals of the faith and Baptistic doctrines, consistent use of Baptist teaching literature at all age groups, emphasis on training for service in training union. Articles should be unstilted and easy to read and understand. We are more desirous of receiving articles from people who know Christian education, or workers who have accomplished something worthwhile in Sunday School or training union, than from trained or experienced writers who do not have such experience. A combination of both would be ideal." Length: 500 to 2,000 words. Pays 2¢ to 3¢ a word, "depending on amount of editing required and the value of the article to the total content of the magazine." Photos purchased with mss. "They should be of people in action, not camera conscious, usually posed but looking natural. Sharp jumbo snapshots or Polaroid pictures are acceptable." Pays $1 to $10.

SUNDAY SCHOOL COUNSELOR, 1445 Boonville Ave., Springfield MO 65802. Editor: Harris Jansen. Monthly. "We will accept simultaneous submissions providing the author advises us of the other publications to which he has sent the ms." Limited amount of freelance material bought. Enclose S.A.S.E. for return of submissions.
Nonfiction and Photos: Interested in news with a Sunday school slant, particularly reports of "this is the way we do it" variety which provide ideas that may be adapted by other Sunday schools. "Be specific; avoid generalities; give enough details for clarity." Length: 1,200 words average. Pays 1¢ to 2¢ a word. Articles may be illustrated with photographs; informal action shots of good quality, rather than posed group pictures. Sketches or photographs may also be included with brief items for teachers and department leaders.
Fillers: "Ideas are especially welcome for a monthly feature containing practical how-to-do-it ideas for all departments of Sunday school, from cradle roll through extension. These brief items for teachers and department leaders may be written up in full, in which event the length is 250 words. Or the writer may give only the seed thought with enough information, so that it may be written up in the *Counselor* office." Pays $5 maximum.

TEACH MAGAZINE, Box 1591, Glendale CA 91209. Editor: Cyrus N. Nelson. Address all material to Ron Widman, Managing Editor. For lay Sunday school workers, superintendents and other workers, as well as pastors and Christian education directors. Quarterly. Buys all rights. Pays on acceptance. Will send a sample copy to a writer on request. A detailed outline of the type of article to be submitted is preferred. State church affiliation. "Do not submit contributions without previous assignment." Reports in 1 month. Enclose S.A.S.E.
Nonfiction and Photos: "We prefer articles containing practical methods of teaching in the Sunday school. We also like inspirational articles of a devotional and Biblical nature. The style of writing in *Teach* is simple and as crisp as possible. All materials should be slanted to the lay Sunday school person—or to professionals who have to work with lay Sunday school people. Writer should keep in mind that the average Sunday school workers are volunteers who lack formal training in teaching and who labor under severe handicaps as far as equipment and time are concerned. Devotional outlines for each quarter include 13 weekly devotional suggestions for use in the Sunday school opening worship period. Specification sheet available upon request for these outlines. Workers Conference Plans section provides suggestions for monthly training meetings of all Sunday school workers. By assignment only. Critical book reviews by experienced adults engaged in an effective ministry to preschoolers, primaries, juniors, junior highs, high schoolers, or who are knowledgeable in the general Christian education field by assignment only. Payments are arranged at time of assignments for the above materials." Length: to 2,000 words. Pays 2¢ to 4¢ a word. Photos can be submitted with mss. Prefers at least 5x7 and the negative, which will be returned. Pays $5 to $10.
Poetry: Some very brief, light verse, slanted to Sunday school teachers. Length: 4 to 8 lines. Pays 25¢ a line.
Fillers: "Short teaching tips from actual experience. These cover all age levels. The tips may be from 100 to 500 words on ways to teach, ways to work with students,

instructions for making simple teaching tools, etc. Party ideas and recipes welcomed. For particular age level; include complete plans." Also uses brief, humorous "Kid Stuff" anecdotes of "quotes and misquotes" by small children in Sunday school. "Tips" pays $5 each; "Kid Stuff" pays $2 each. Uses brief quotes of an inspirational nature that would appeal to a Sunday school worker in the conservative evangelical church.

YOUR CHURCH, 192 Allendale Rd. King of Prussia PA 19406. For clergymen and architects concerned with church planning, architecture, building, equipment, and administration. Bimonthly. Circulation: about 200,000. Buys all rights. Pays on publication. Will send a free sample copy to a writer on request. Reports in 2 to 3 weeks. Enclose S.A.S.E. for return of submissions.
Nonfiction and Photos: "Articles on the practical considerations of church planning, building, equipment, administration, and use of audio-visual materials. Also theological and philosophical backgrounds of church architecture. Articles regarding church programming, local ministry, and community involvement are also welcomed. Photos if submitted should be integral part of submitted articles. Rates arrived at by mutual agreement; $25 minimum."

Clothing and Knit Goods

BODY FASHIONS, 757 Third Ave., New York NY 10017. Editor: Mercy Dobell. Monthly. Pays the 15th of the month following publication. Enclose S.A.S.E. for return of submissions.
Nonfiction and Photos: "Feature articles on merchandising and promotions for foundations, brassiere and swimwear divisions of department stores and specialty shops. All material must be factual and written in a quick, easy-to-read fashion. We want merchandising facts—not froth." Pays "9¢ per published word." Photos must accompany mss. Pays $7.50.

EARNSHAW'S INFANTS, GIRLS, BOYSWEAR REVIEW, 393 Seventh Ave., New York NY 10001. Managing Editor: Diane Specht. For "children's wear buyers, merchandise managers, specialty shop owners, children's wear manufacturers and designers." Established in 1917. Monthly. Circulation: 8,500. Buys all rights. Buys 2 or 3 mss a year. Pays on publication. Will send a sample copy to a writer on request. Query first; "we do not want to receive any unsolicited articles." Will consider photocopied submissions. Reports in 2 weeks. Enclose S.A.S.E.
Nonfiction and Photos: "Articles dealing with selling, personnel, store layout, location, advertising and promotion, and display of children's wear. Stories must deal with outstanding retailers." Buys coverage of successful business operations and merchandising techniques. Length: 1,500 to 2,500 words. Pays $60 tm $75. Photos purchased with mss or on assignment; captions required. Wants "clear, sharp 5x7 b&w photos." Pays $5.

HOSIERY AND UNDERWEAR, 757 Third Ave., New York NY 10017. Editor: Trudye Connolly. For "merchandising executives and hosiery buyers in department and specialty stores, variety chains, discount, supermarket and drug stores, resident buying offices; top management in companies manufacturing men's and women's hosiery; production and department heads in knitting mills, fiber plants, machinery companies, etc." Monthly. Buys all rights. Payment on acceptance. Query first. Reports in 10 days. Enclose S.A.S.E.
Nonfiction and Photos: "Articles needed for split readership; one half of magazine deals with marketing, that is the distribution and sale of hosiery items in every kind of outlet; the other half deals with manufacturing, that is, technological developments, production methods and managerial problems of the mill. Marketing features explore display, selling technique, advertising, general merchandising philosophy in all outlets ranging from department and specialty stores to supermarkets, drug stores, discount and variety chains. May include interviews with buyer or merchandise manager. Stories should focus on a specific merchandising angle; general 'store tour' not acceptable. Manufacturing features explore teahnology and produc-

tion of men's and women's hosiery. In-depth mill studies, technical manufacturing articles, new machinery, surveys of manufacturing trends, automation, packaging, new fibers, pollution." Length: 1,000 to 1,300 words. Pays minimum of 5¢ a word. 3x7 b&w glossy photos. Pays $5 to $7.

INTIMATE APPAREL, 757 Third Ave., New York NY 10017. Editor: Mercy Dobell. Pays the 15th of the month following publication. Enclose S.A.S.E. for return of submissions.
Nonfiction and Photos: "Feature articles on merchandising, promotions, and displays for loungewear, lingerie, sleepwear, and at-home fashions. All material must be factual and written in a quick, easy-to-read fashion. We want merchandising facts, not froth." Length: 750 to 1,000 words. Pays about 9¢ a published word. Photos must accompany mss. Pays $7.50.

NONWOVENS & DISPOSABLE SOFT GOODS, 4 Second Ave., Denville NJ 07834. Editorial Director: Hamilton C. Carson. For manufacturers and converters of nonwoven products (hospital supplies, industrial clothing, waddings, diapers, etc.). Established: 1970. Monthly. Circulation: 10,000. Buys all rights but will reassign rights to author after publication. Buys 2 or 3 mss a year. Payment on publication. Will send free sample copy to writer on request. Query first. Will consider photocopied submissions. Reports on material in 1 week. Enclose S.A.S.E.
Nonfiction and Photos: "Stories on manufacturers, equipment, techniques, marketing. Also stories on use of these products in hospitals, nursing homes, hotels/motels, etc. Query first with one or two paragraph description of suggested article." Informational, interview, spot news, successful business operations, new products, merchandising techniques, technical. Length: 250 to 2,000 words. Pays $5 to $125. B&w photos, 5x7 or 8x10. Pays $3 to $5.

STYLE, 481 University Ave., Toronto 2, Ont., Canada. Editor: Pat Porth. For "retailers, suppliers, manufacturers, advertisers, and salesmen in Canadian women's and children's ready-to-wear industry." Biweekly. Buys first Canadian rights. Pays on publication. Will send a sample copy to a writer on request. Query first. Reports "as soon as possible." Enclose S.A.E.
Nonfiction and Photos: "Subject matter should be Canadian or have some Canadian application. Interested in store promotions, urban developments, installation of new inventory control systems, etc., which might set examples for Canadian stores. Not interested in fashion trends or fashion shows in U.S. cities, or in 'how to sell,' 'how to display' stories initiating with the writer." Length: 50 to 600 words. Pays 60¢ "per column inch." Photos "occasionally" purchased with mss or with captions only. 8x10 or 5x7 glossies.

TACK 'N TOGS MERCHANDISING, P. O. Box 67, Minneapolis MN 55440. Editor: Jim Hager. For "retailers of products for horse and rider and Western fashion apparel." Established in 1971. Monthly. Circulation: 14,000. Rights purchased vary with author and material; may buy all rights. Buys 25 to 30 mss a year. Pays on acceptance. Will send a sample copy to a writer on request. Write for copy of guidelines for writers. Query first. Enclose S.A.S.E.
Nonfiction and Photos: "Case histories, trends of industry." Buys informational articles, how-to's, personal experience articles, interviews, profiles, personal opinion articles, coverage of successful business operations, new product pieces, and articles on merchandising techniques. Length: open. Pays "up to $100." B&w glossies and color transparencies purchased with mss.

TEENS AND BOYS, 71 W. 35th St., New York NY 10001. Editor: Mrs. Kathie M. Andersen. For "retailers and manufacturers of boys' and young men's apparel (ages 5 to 20)." Monthly. Not copyrighted. Pays on publication. Will send a sample copy to a writer on request. Query first; "on assignment only. Unsolicited mss will not be returned or read."
Nonfiction and Photos: " 'Store stories'... terse reports with 2 or 3 pictures, ad clips, direct mail samples, indicating the success principles of a flourishing boys' wear or varsity shop department or store." Length: 1,000 to 1,500 words. Pays 5¢ a word.

Pays $5 to $10 per photo "if reproducible." Pays $2.50 per ad clip or direct mail sample.

How To Break In: "If someone were trying to write for *Teens and Boys*, I would advise him to first write for a copy of the magazine, as well as a list of questions I have prepared to help anyone who writes for us. Then he should suggest a story idea (an interview with a particularly good retailer). If we approve the idea, then the interview can take place."

WESTERN APPAREL INDUSTRY, 112 W. 9th St., Los Angeles, CA 90015. Editor: Denyse Selesnick. For "apparel manufacturers west of the Mississippi." Monthly. Pays on acceptance. Reports "immediately." Enclose S.A.S.E.

Nonfiction and Photos: "Articles telling how a western manufacturer of apparel cut costs or boosted efficiency in his plant." Length: about 1,000 words. Pays 3½¢ a word. Photos purchased with mss. Pays $5.

WESTERN OUTFITTER, 5314 Bingle Rd., Houston TX 77018. Publication Manager: Ted Mizwa. For "owners or managers of retail stores or store departments which sell western riding supplies, tack, or clothing." Monthly. Buys all rights. Pays on publication. Query first. Enclose S.A.S.E.

Nonfiction and Photos: "Articles covering all phases of merchandising—product information, selling to horsemen, promotional gimmicks used successfully by Western stores. Writer must know merchandising and selling." Length: 1,008 to 3,000 words. Pays 3¢ a word. Photos purchased with mss. Pays $5.

Coin-Operated Machines

AMERICAN COIN-OP, 500 North Dearborn, Chicago IL 60610. Editor: Eugene Pitts. Owners and operators of coin-operated and drycleaning establishments. Feature articles describing individual stores; promotional activities, special services to customers, unusual store design, efficient or unusual use of laundry and drycleaning equipment. Established 1959. Monthly. Circulation: 23,000. Buys all rights. Buys between 25 and 35 mss a year. Payment on publication. Will send editorial guidelines sheet to a writer on request. Query first. Will not consider photocopied submissions. Submit seasonal material 2 months in advance. Reports on material within a month. Enclose S.A.S.E.

Nonfiction and Photos: "Articles should stress how to conduct all facets of business. Ecology and water pollution are subjects of interest to coin-op owners due to recent legislation. Writer should make his point with a gripping lead and support it with the facts given in the body of the article. A warm, friendly style is acceptable as long as the reader gets the facts. Interview owners. Give a full description of the store and all equipment with price schedules. We are particularly interested in helping our readers operate an efficient and profitable business. Point of view is from owner's and operator's experience. Stories should have facts about how the business operates. Avoid generalizations about a 'nice new store'. What is different about it? How is it being promoted effectively?" Length: 1,000 to 3,000 words. Pays 3¢ to 5¢ a word. Captions required for 8x10 b&w glossies purchased with accompanying ms. Pays $5.

Fillers: Pays $3 for clippings.

BETTER VENDING AND CATERING, Bewdley, Ont., Canada. Editor: Charlotte Clay. For "vending machine operators, vending and hand caterers, and vending machine 'locations.' " Bimonthly. Buys first or second rights. Buys "very few" mss per year. Pays on publication. Will send a sample copy to a writer for $1. Query first. Submit seasonal material at least 1 month in advance of issue date. Enclose S.A.E. and International Reply Coupons.

Nonfiction and Photos: Buys "technical and marketing material related to vending and catering." Length: 200 to 800 words. Pays 2¢ a word. B&w glossies purchased with mss. Pays $3 to $5.

COINAMATIC AGE, 60 E. 42nd St., New York NY 10017. Editor: Jack J. Gubala. For operators and owners of coin-operated laundries and dry cleaners. Monthly. Buys all rights. Pays on publication. "Queries get same-day attention." Enclose S.A.S.E.

Nonfiction and Photos: "We are currently considering articles on coin-operated laundries, or in combination with drycleaners. Slant should focus on the unusual, but at the same time should stress possible adaptation by other coinamat operators. We are interested in promotional and advertising techniques; reasons for expansion or additional locations; attached sidelines such as gas stations, restaurants, and other businesses; Main Street vs. shopping center operations; successes in dealing with permanent press garment laundering and cleaning; ironing services; and, primarily, financial success, personal satisfaction, or any other motivation that the owner derives from his business. Give the story punch, details, and applicability to the reader. Include a list of specifications, detailing the number of units (washers, dryers, etc.), the different pound-loads of each machine and the make and model numbers of all of these, as well as any vending machines, change-makers, etc. 3 action photos (preferably a minimum of 6) must accompany each article. At this time, we are especially interested in combined laundry/drycleaning articles. Submitted photos must include an exterior shot of the installation and interior shots showing customers. Where possible, a photo of the owner at work is also desired. If you have a far-out slant, query first." Pays 3¢ to 4¢ a word, depending on need to rewrite. Photos purchased with mss. Pays $12 for 3 photos and $6 for each additional photo.

COIN LAUNDERER & CLEANER, 525 Somerset Dr., Indianapolis IN 46260. For owners, operators, and managers of coin-operated and self-service laundry and drycleaning establishments. Monthly. Buys all rights. Enclose S.A.S.E. for return of submissions.

Nonfiction: "Our requirements are for self-service coin laundry and drycleaning store management articles which specify the promotion, service, or technique used by the store owners; the cost of this technique; and the profit produced by it. Freelance writers must be familiar with the coin laundry and drycleaning industry to prepare an article of sufficient management significance." Length: open. Pay: 5¢ per printed word.

COIN-OP, 200 Madison Ave., New York NY 10016. Editor: Edward Barnes. For "owners of coin-op laundry and drycleaning stores of any kind." Monthly. Buys all rights. Pays on publication. Reports in 2 weeks. Enclose S.A.S.E.

Nonfiction and Photos: "We prefer articles that develop one facet of operation. Also interested in washer and dryer coin route operation." Pays 3¢ a word "or agreed price." Pays $5 for photos.

VEND, 150 Wacker Dr., Chicago IL 60606. Managing Editor: Ron Bytner. Monthly. Circulation: 11,000. Buys all rights. Pays on acceptance. Will send a sample copy to a writer on request. "Must query first." Reports "immediately." Enclose S.A.S.E.

Nonfiction and Photos: "Feature articles covering some phase of the automatic merchandising business; that is, the selling of products automatically through coin-operated machines and via manual food services. Amusements and recording devices not included. We also want features describing, from a plant management or institutional management point of view, the use of vending machines and non-vending food service (if performed by a vending firm) in industrial, office, college and hospital facilities. We need 2 types of feature stories: the how-to-do-it feature, and the news feature of some significant development in the field of automatic selling." Length: 600 to 1,000 words. Pays 5¢ a word average. 5x7 or 8x10 b&w glossies purchased with mss. Pays $5.

Fillers: "Newsbreaks and clippings of any phase of vending operation with a how-to angle, with or without a photo." Length: maximum 200 words. Pay varies for written news articles. Clipping payment is $1, if used.

VENDING TIMES, 211 E. 43rd St., New York NY 10017. Editor: Arthur E. Yohalem. For operators of vending machines. Monthly. Circulation: 13,500. Pays on publication. Query first; "we will discuss the story requirements with the writer in detail." Enclose S.A.S.E.

Nonfiction and Photos: "We are always willing to pay for good material. Primary interest is photo fillers." Pays $5 per photo.

Confectionery and Snack Foods

CANDY AND SNACK INDUSTRY, 777 Third Ave., New York, NY 10017.Editor: Myron Lench. For confectionery and snack manufacturers. Monthly. Query first. Reports in 2 weeks. Enclose S.A.S.E. for response to queries.
Nonfiction: "Feature articles of interest to large scale candy, cookie, cracker, and other snack manufacturers that deal with activities in the fields of production, packaging (including package design), merchandising; financial news (sales figures, profits, earnings), advertising campaigns in all media, and promotional methods used to increase the sale or distribution of candy and snacks." Length: 1,000 to 1,250 words. Pays 5¢ a word; "special rates on assignments."
Photos: "Good quality glossies with complete and accurate captions, in sizes not smaller than 5x7." Pays $5. Color covers.
Fillers: "Short news stories about the trade and anything related to candy and snacks." Pays 5¢ per word; $1 for clippings.

Construction and Contracting

AMERICAN BUILDING SUPPLIES, 1760 Peachtree Rd., N.W., Atlanta GA 30309. Editor: Sid Wrightsman, Jr. For "lumber and building material dealers who sell lumber and building materials to do-it-yourselfers and building contractors ordinarily in remodeling." Established: 1967. Monthly. Circulation: 34,000. Buys all rights. Buys 25 to 50 mss a year. Payment on acceptance. Will send free sample copy to writer on request. Query first. Enclose S.A.S.E.
Nonfiction and Photos: "Everything newsy about building material producers, distributors and successful dealers in the field. Like to show how 'smart' operators can succeed in the field today, if they put useful ideas to work. We're stressing the profit potential involved in remodeling and modernization for the small dealer. As a tabloid, we prefer a fast paced editorial approach to all our stories." Informational, how-to, personal experience, interview, profile, expose, spot news, successful business operations, new product, merchandising techniques. Length: 1,250 to 2,000 words. Pays 3¢ to 5¢ per word. 8x10 glossies. Pays $6 to $8. Color transparencies. Pays $10 to $25. Captions required.

AMERICAN ROOFER & BUILDING IMPROVEMENT CONTRACTOR, 221 Lake St., Oak Park IL 60302. Editor: Johanna C. Gudas. For "business executives heading roofing contractor firms, architects, engineers, specification writers, and others in the construction industry." Established in 1911. Monthly. Circulation: 17,500. Buys all rights, but will reassign rights to author after publication. Buys 10 to 15 mss a year. Pays on publication. Will send a sample copy to a writer on request. Query first. Will not consider photocopied submissions. Reports "immediately, as a general rule." Enclose S.A.S.E.
Nonfiction and Photos: "Industry news, stories on roofing contractors, business management, estimating, unusual roofing jobs, technical material on any aspect of this industry. Articles should always be written from the viewpoint of the roofing contractor or architect, or in relation to his point of view, rather than construction in general. Management articles on accounting, sales, saving time, etc. are the subjects most submitted and overworked. We prefer application data—we're interested in industry solutions to problems in these areas, with job details, contractor facts, and how the job was handled." Buys how-to's ("only if very unusual"), interviews, profiles, humor ("industry only"), photo features, coverage of successful business oper-

ations ("must relate to problem solving"), articles on merchandising techniques, and technical articles. Length: 800 to 2,000 words. Pays 2¢ a word. B&w photos purchased with mss; captions required. Pay depends on subject matter."

BATIMENT, 625 President Kennedy Ave., Montreal 111, Que., Canada. Editor: Paul Saint-Pierre. Published in French for "contractors, architects." Established in 1927. Monthly. Circulation: 6,000. Rights purchased vary with author and material. Buys about 25 mss a year. Pays on acceptance. Will send a sample copy to a writer on request. Write for copy of guidelines for writers. Enclose S.A.E. and International Reply Coupons for return of submissions.
Nonfiction: "Articles on new techniques in construction and subjects of interest to builders. Interested in residential, apartment, office, commercial, and industrial buildings—not in public works." Length: 500 to 1,000 words. Pays $50 to $75.

BUILDING DESIGN AND CONSTRUCTION, 5 S. Wabash, Chicago IL 60603, Editor-in-Chief: Keith Ray. For "architects, contractors, consulting engineers." Monthly. Buys prior publication rights. Query first. Reports "immediately." Enclose S.A.S.E.
Nonfiction: "Articles and features stressing inter-relationship of architects, contractors, and consulting engineers. Potential contributors must have familiarity with building construction industry." Pays $50 to $75 "per printed page."
How To Break In: "Recognize that we're news-oriented. *Study* the magazine."

CALIFORNIA BUILDER & ENGINEER, 363 El Camino Real, South San Francisco CA 94080. News Editor: Mahlon R. Fisher. For "contractors, engineers, machinery distributors of all ages and education." Seeks material for water development and market issues. Established in 1894. Biweekly. Circulation: 12,500. Not copyrighted. Buys 30 to 40 mss a year. Pays on publication. Will send a sample copy to a writer on request. Query first. Will consider photocopied submissions. Submit seasonal material 2 months in advance. Reports in 2 weeks. Enclose S.A.S.E.
Nonfiction: "How-to articles: how can a contractor save time or money. Compared to similar publications, we give greater California coverage well within the regional framework." Interested in material on "the highway trust fund." Buys "normally only feature-type articles": how-to articles, interviews, profiles, humor, personal experience articles, photo features, coverage of successful business operations. Length: 1,000 to 5,000 words. Pays "$50 a printed page."
Photos: "We prefer 8x10 b&w glossies. By arrangement only."

CONSTRUCTION EQUIPMENT, 205 E. 42nd St., New York NY 10017. Editor: John Rehfield. For "heavy construction contractors, materials suppliers, miners." Monthly. Circulation: 60,000. Buys first rights. Pays on acceptance. Will send a sample copy to a writer on request. Query first. Reports "on receipt." Enclose S.A.S.E.
Nonfiction and Photos: "Factual reports on time-saving, labor-saving, or money-saving use of heavy equipment on major construction jobs; reports of planning and implementation of maintenance and repair work on equipment. News items about innovative design or use of construction equipment. Feature material on planning and field implementation of safety requirements for construction machines. No newspaper clippings; no cartoons or personality profiles." Pays maximum $75 "per printed page." 8x10 single weight glossies purchased with mss "to illustrate use of equipment."

CONSTRUCTION EQUIPMENT OPERATION AND MAINTENANCE, 220 Higley Bldg., Cedar Rapids IA 52401. Editor: C.K. Parks. For users of heavy construction equipment. Bimonthly. Buys all rights. Pays on acceptance. Reports in 1 month. Enclose S.A.S.E. for return of submissions.
Nonfiction: "Articles on selection, use, operation, or maintenance of construction equipment; articles and features on the construction industry in general; job safety articles." Length: "3 to 4 printed pages." Pays $200.

CONSTRUCTION SPECIFIER, 1150 17th St., N.W., Washington DC 20036. Editor: Roger A. Rensberger. Professional society journal for architects, engineers, specification writers, contractors. Monthly. Circulation: 12,000. Buys all rights.

Pays on publication. Will send a sample copy to a writer on request. Query required. Deadlines are 45 days preceding publication on the 10th of each month. Reports in 4 to 7 days. Enclose S.A.S.E.
Nonfiction and Photos: "Articles on building techniques, building products and material." Length: minimum 3,500 words. Pays $100 to $150. Photos "purchased rarely; if purchased, payment included in ms rate." 8x10 glossies.

CONSTRUCTIONEER, 1 Bond St., Chatham NJ 07928. Editor: Ken Hanan. For contractors, distributors, material producers, public works officials, consulting engineers, etc. Established: 1945. Biweekly. Circulation: 18,000. Rights purchased vary with author and material. Buys all rights but will reassign rights to author after publication. Buys 10 to 15 mss a year. Payment on acceptance. Will send sample copy to writer for $1. Write for copy of guidelines for writers. Query first. Will consider photocopied submissions. Submit seasonal material 2 months in advance. Reports on material accepted for publication in 30 to 60 days. Returns rejected material in 30 days. Enclose S.A.S.E.
Nonfiction and Photos: Construction job stories; new methods studies. Detailed job studies of methods and equipment used; oriented around geographical area of New York, New Jersey, Pennsylvania and Delaware. Winter snow and ice removal and control; winter construction methods. Current themes: public works, profiles, conservation. Length: 1,500 to 1,800 words. Pays $100 to $200. B&w photos purchased with or without accompanying ms or on assignment. Pays $5 to $8.

CONSTRUCTOR MAGAZINE, 1957 E St., N.W., Washington DC 20006. Editor: Taylor Gregg. Publication of the Association of General Contractors of America for "men in the age range of approximately 25 to 70 (predominantly 40's and 50's), 50% with a college education. Most own or are officers in their own corporations." Established in 1902. Monthly. Circulation: 23,000. Buys all rights, but will reassign rights to author after publication. Buys about 30 mss a year. Pays on publication. Will send a sample copy to a writer for 50¢. Query first or submit complete ms. Reports in 30 days. Enclose S.A.S.E.
Nonfiction: "Feature material dealing with labor, legal, technical, and professional material pertinent to the construction industry and corporate business. We deal only with the management aspect of the construction industry. No articles on computers and computer technology." Buys informational articles, interviews, think pieces, exposés, photo features, coverage of successful business operations, and technical articles. Length: "no minimum or maximum; subject much more important than length." Pays $50 to $300.
Photos: Purchased with and without mss; captions required. For 8x10 b&w single weight glossies, pays $35 to $50. For color transparencies, pays $200 for the cover.

ENGINEERING AND CONTRACT RECORD, 1450 Don Mills Road, Don Mills, Ont., Canada. Editor: W. J. Crichton. For "superintendents, executives of contracting companies doing in excess of $100,000 business a year." Established: 1889. Monthly. Circulation: over 18,000. Rights purchased vary with author and material. Buys 36 to 50 mss a year. Pays on publication. Will send sample copy to writer for $1. Query first. Send queries to Clifford J. Allum, Managing Editor. Reports in 2 weeks. Enclose S.A.E. and International Reply Coupons.
Nonfiction and Photos: "Job stories. How to build a project quicker, cheaper, better through innovations and unusual methods. Management articles. Stories are limited to Canadian projects only." Length: 1,000 to 1,500 words. Pays average of $50 per printed page, including photos. B&w glossies purchased with mss. 5x7 preferred.

FARM BUILDING NEWS, 733 N. Van Buren, Milwaukee WI 53202. Editor: John R. Harvey. For farm structure builders and suppliers. 6 times a year. Buys all rights. Pays on acceptance. Will send a free sample copy on request. Query suggested. Deadlines are at least 4 weeks in advance of publication date; prefers 6 to 8 weeks. Reports immediately. Enclose S.A.S.E. for response to queries and return of submissions.
Nonfiction and Photos: Features on farm builders and spot news. Length: 600 to 1,000 words. Pays $150 to $200. Buys color and b&w photos with ms.

FENCE INDUSTRY, 307 N. Michigan Ave., Chicago IL 60601. Editor: Ben Newman. For "manufacturers, wholesalers, dealers and erectors of fencing installation equipment, accessories, garden accessories." Established. 1938. Monthly. Circulation: 10,000. Rights purchased vary with author and material. Buys all rights, but will reassign rights to author after publication. Buys 75 to 100 mss a year. Payment on acceptance. Will send free sample copy to writer on request. Query first. Will consider photocopied submissions. Submit seasonal material 3 months in advance. Reports on material accepted for publication in 3 weeks. Returns rejected material in 2 weeks. Enclose S.A.S.E.
Nonfiction and Photos: "Publish trade-slanted editorial about manufacturers, dealers, installers. Related articles on good business practices; i.e., bookkeeping, advertising, hiring, unique merchandising practices. General story on company may be acceptable if not covered previously. Story should emphasize particularly unusual method of doing business; manufacturing methods, display methods, delivery systems, etc. Promotion and sales success stories of fence companies. How fencing plays a vital role in swimming pools and playgrounds. Will send complete editorial schedule on request." Length: 2,000 words maximum. Pays maximum of 4¢ a word. 2¼x2¼ b&w photos purchased with or without accompanying ms or on assignment. Pays $5. 35mm color transparencies. Pays $50.

HIGHWAY BUILDER, 800 N. Third St., Harrisburg PA 17102. Editor: Robert A. Haynos. For "highway and heavy construction industry." Monthly. Pays on acceptance. Enclose S.A.S.E. for return of submissions.
Nonfiction and Photos: "We are interested mainly in highway, airport, and heavy construction work in Pennsylvania, Maryland, New York, New Jersey, Delaware, West Virginia, and Ohio. The majority of our readership is confined to this area. No news clippings." Length: maximum 800 words. Pays "standard rates." Pays $1 to $3 for photos when used with story. Pays $5 for cover photos.

HOMEBUILDING BUSINESS, Gralla Publications, 1501 Broadway, New York NY 10036. Editor: Ronald Derven. For builders and developers of single family homes and "for-sale" townhouses. Business articles dealing with every phase of single-family development. Established 1972. Monthly. Circulation: 56,000. Buys all rights. Payment on acceptance. Will send free sample copy and editorial guidelines to a writer on request. Query first. Will not consider photocopied submissions. Reports within 2 to 3 weeks on accepted or rejected material.
Nonfiction: Marketing, zoning, design and business management. Length: open. Pays $50 to $250.

JOURNAL OF COMMERCE, 2000 W. 12th Ave., Vancouver, B.C., Canada. Editor: A.H.A. Brown. For Canadian construction men. Established in 1910. Semiweekly. Buys all rights. Pays on publication. Query first. Will not consider photocopied submissions. Enclose S.A.S.E. and International Reply Coupons.
Nonfiction and Photos: "Articles on construction." Length: 100 to 2,000 words. Pays 2¢ to 5¢ a word. B&w glossies purchased on assignment; captions required. Pays $5.

MID-WEST CONTRACTOR, Box 766, 2537 Madison Ave., Kansas City, MO 64141. Editor: Gilbert Mullzy. Biweekly. Buys all rights. Pays on acceptance. Query first. Enclose S.A.S.E.
Nonfiction and Photos: "Limited market for articles relating to large construction contracts in the Midwest only—Iowa, Nebraska, Kansas, and Missouri. Such articles would relate to better methods of handling various phases of large contracts, ranging anywhere from material distribution to labor relations. Also interested in articles of outstanding construction personalities in territory." Length: "no limitations." Pay: open. Photos purchased with and without mss; captions required.

MODERN STEEL CONSTRUCTION, American Institute of Steel Construction, 101 Park Ave., New York NY 10017. Editor: Mary Anne Donohue. For architects and engineers. Quarterly. Not copyrighted. Pays on acceptance. Query first. Enclose S.A.S.E.
Nonfiction and Photos: "Articles, with pictures and diagrams, of new steel-framed buildings and bridges. Must show new and imaginative uses of structural steel for

buildings and bridges; new designs, new developments." Length: "1 and 2 pages."
Pays $100. Photos purchased with mss.

NAHB JOURNAL—SCOPE, 1625 L St., N.W., Washington DC 20036. Editor: Albert B. Manola. For the housing industry. Weekly. Buys all rights. Pays on publication. Query first. Reports in 10 days. Enclose S.A.S.E.
Nonfiction and Photos: "Qualified writers in construction and real estate may submit inquiries regarding interest in new outstanding townhouse, apartment, single family, cluster, quad, mobile, PUD, or commercial buildings and/or projects developed, designed, or built by NAHB members. We pay $100 to $300 and up, with photos. Slides and transparencies related to inside features are ordered from writers."

ROADS AND STREETS, 222 South Riverside Plaza, Chicago IL 60606. Associate Editor: Elwood Meschter. For "contractors, engineers, and officials who are involved with nation's highway, earthmoving, and heavy construction projects (but not any type of residential, office, or other building)." Special Management issue (March) "features case histories of good management practice for contractors." Monthly. Circulation: over 65,000. Buys all rights. Buys 40 to 60 mss a year. Pays on publication. Will send a sample copy to a writer on request. Query first. "Query often leads to specific assignment to cover construction project at a critical stage later rather than at its current stage." Submit seasonal material no later than 3 months in advance. Reports as soon as possible. Enclose S.A.S.E.
Nonfiction: "Limited to detailed descriptions of specific projects of roads, streets, bridges, airfields, and other jobs. The innovations of a project are of prime interest, as is the organization of equipment, men, and the planning of actual construction. Do not cover legal, financial, or political problems. The point, highlight, or conclusion of the article must be stated in the first paragraph. Extensive quotations from project manager, engineer, or other site supervisor desirable to authenticate difficult or controversial points. For special issue, usually need more coverage of small contractors who run tight ships or focus on highly specialized work. Avoid ribbon-cutting and dedication ceremonies. Usually swamped with run-of-the-mill articles on asphalt or concrete paving." Pays minimum of $50 per page published.
Photos: Purchased with mss; captions required. B&w glossies, color transparencies. Does not use 35mm color or color prints. Payment "with mss package as negotiated in advance."

RSI (ROOFING, SIDING, INSULATION), 757 Third Ave., New York NY 10017. Editor: John Sutton. For subcontractors and dealers in the roofing, siding, and insulation trades. Monthly. Circulation: 12,500. Not copyrighted. Pays on acceptance. Will send free sample copy on request. Enclose S.A.S.E.
Nonfiction: Industry developments, new materials, application and construction problems and procedures, merchandising techniques, convention reports and contractor case histories. Written in third person. Use generic terms. Average length: 2,000 words. Pays 3¢-5¢ a word.
Photos: With mss. B&w 5x7 or 8x10. Pays $5.
Fillers: Occasionally buys timely industry news of four or five paragraphs.

WESTERN CONSTRUCTION, 609 Mission St., San Francisco CA 94105. Editor: R. L. Byrne. For "heavy constructors and their job supervisors." Monthly. Buys all rights and simultaneous rights. Pays on acceptance. Will send a sample copy to writers on request. Query first. Enclose S.A.S.E.
Nonfiction and Photos: "Methods articles on street, highway, bridge, tunnel, dam construction in 13 western states. Engineer's byline helps." Length: 1,500 to 2,500 words and 6 photos. Pays minimum $35 "per printed magazine page."

WORLD CONSTRUCTION, 666 Fifth Ave., New York NY 10019. Editor: Donald R. Cannon. For "English-speaking engineers, contractors, and government officials in the Eastern hemisphere." Monthly. Buys all rights. Pays on publication. Will send a sample copy to a writer on request. Query first. Reports in 1 month. Enclose S.A.S.E.

Nonfiction and Photos: "How-to articles which stress how contractors can do their jobs faster, better, or more economically." Length: about 1,000 to 6,000 words. Pays $50 per magazine page, or 4 typed ms pages. Photos purchased with mss; b&w glossies not smaller than 4x5.

Dairy Products

DAIRY RECORD, 141 East Fourth St., St. Paul MN 55101. Editor: Don Merlin. Monthly. Any reports which do not deal with events 10 days prior to publication dates are unacceptable. Pays on publication. Enclose S.A.S.E. for return of submissions.
Nonfiction: Contributions must be confined to spot news articles and current events dealing with the dairy industry, especially news and news commentary of fluid milk distribution and the manufacturing and processing of dairy products. Pays minimum of 40¢ per column inch.

WESTERN MILK AND ICE CREAM NEWS, 55 Mitchell Blvd., San Rafael CA 94903. Editor: Sally Taylor. For dairy executives in the western part of the U.S. Buys all rights. Pays on publication. Will send a sample copy to a writer on request. Write for copy of guidelines for writers. Enclose S.A.S.E. for return of submissions.
Nonfiction and Photos: Wants "news stories and photos pertaining to distribution of milk and cream and manufacture and distribution of manufactured dairy products in eleven western states, plus Alaska and Hawaii. Also news stories pertaining to meetings, legal actions and other activities connected with dairy industry in this area, including news of people in industry—promotion, retirements, deaths, etc." Length: open. Pays 1¢ a word for articles (50¢ a column inch). Photos purchased with mss; with captions only. B&w glossies, color transparencies. Pays $5 for b&w photos.

Data Processing

COMPUTER DESIGN, 221 Baker Ave., Concord MA 01742. Editor: John A. Camuso. For digital electronic engineers. Monthly. Buys all rights and simultaneous rights. Pays on publication. Will send sample copy on request. Query first. Reports in 4 to 8 weeks. Enclose S.A.S.E.
Nonfiction: Publishes engineering articles on the design and application of digital and analog/digital circuits, equipment, and systems used in computing, data processing, control and communications. Pays $25 to $35 per page.

COMPUTERWORLD, 797 Washington St., Newton MA 02160. Managing Editor: Y. J. Farmer. For the computer community; the people who analyze how computers are to be used, those who program, those who manage. Weekly. Circulation: 55,000. Buys all rights. Pays on publication. Will send sample copy on request. Prefers query, but will consider unsolicited submissions if writer knows his subject. Monday a.m. is deadline for weekly issue. All copy submitted should be triple-spaced. Reports within two weeks. Enclose S.A.S.E. for return of submissions.
Nonfiction: Buys limited number of news and feature articles on key developments in computer application techniques, software, equipment design, industry developments and job trends. Human interest articles welcomed but must pertain to computer industry. Length: 750 words maximum for articles. 500 words tops for news stories. Pays 5¢ a word for unsolicited material, more if assigned or writer is known to them.
Photos: Purchased with mss and with captions. Computer theme. Prefers glossies. No color. Pays $5.

EPIC, 338 Mountain Rd., Union City NJ 07087. Manuscript Editor: Harry Kickey. For "executives of companies with annual sales between $500,000 and $5,000,000." Monthly. Buys all rights. Pays on publication. Will send sample copy to a writer on request. Query first. Reports in 2 weeks. Enclose S.A.S.E. with all queries and submissions.

Nonfiction: "Articles on the use of computers by small companies. Should be written in English rather than computerese. Articles are addressed to nontechnical general executives. No company puffs, but can discuss equipment of manufacturers by name. Articles on comparison of capabilities of competing peripheral equipment, particularly input devices. Heavy use of visuals and illustrating diagrams." Charts purchased with mss. Length: 1,000 to 2,000 words. Pays 5¢ per printed word. Pays $10 for charts "if usable as is," $5 "if they need to be re-rendered."

Photos: Purchased with mss; with captions only. 8x10 glossies. Pays $5.

INFOSYSTEMS, Hitchcock Building, Wheaton IL 60187. Editorial Director: Thomas J. Trafals. Edited for people who manage and use information and information systems . . . design and operate information systems . . . develop and sell products and services to those who use, design and operate information systems.

JOURNAL OF ASSOCIATION FOR SYSTEMS MANAGEMENT, 24587 Bagley Road, Cleveland OH 44138. Managing Editor: William Ripley. For systems and procedures and administrative people. Monthly. Buys all serial rights. Pays on publication. Will send a free sample copy on request. Query first. Reports as soon as possible. Enclose S.A.S.E.

Nonfiction: Uses articles on case histories, projects on systems, forms control, administrative practices, computer operations. Length: 3,000 to 5,000 words. Maximum payment is $25.

MODERN DATA, 3 Lockland Ave., Framingham MA 01701. Editor: Alan R. Kaplan. For data processing managers, computer systems analysts, etc. Established 1968. Monthly. Circulation: 92,000. Buys all rights but usually shares republication rights with author. Buys very few mss. Payment 30 to 60 days after publication. Will send sample copy to a writer for $1. Query first. Will consider photocopied submissions. Reports in 30 days. Enclose S.A.S.E.

Nonfiction and Photos: "Equipment surveys, application stories, expository articles on general methods and techniques. Will consider short (500 words) items on social consequences of computer technologies; humorous, actual accounts of computer experiences, etc." Informational, historical, think pieces, reviews of computer equipment, successful business operations, new products, technical. Length: 1,500 words maximum. Pays $25 to $35 per magazine page. "What Hath Babbage Wrought?" department pays $10 for short, humorous, original items. 4x5 or 8x10 b&w photos are purchased with accompanying mss. Captions optional.

Fillers: Pays $2 for clippings.

Dental

AMERICAN DENTAL ASSOCIATION NEWS, 211 E. Chicago, Chicago IL 60611. Editor: Glenn E. Medcalf. For the dental profession. Biweekly. Circulation: 115,000. Buys all rights. Pays on acceptance. Query first. Enclose S.A.S.E. with submissions and queries.

Nonfiction: Articles cover news, interviews, features of interest to all dentists, including material on public health field, health insurance, etc. Length: maximum 750 words. Pays up to $100 per article.

Photos: Purchased with mss and with captions only. Dental subjects of interest to entire profession. Pays $5 to $25.

DENTAL ECONOMICS, 1603 Orrington Ave., Evanston IL 60201. Editor: E. James Best, D.D.S. For practicing dentists in the U.S., senior dental students and

dental suppliers. Established: 1911. Monthly. Circulation: 104,000. Buys first North American serial rights. Buys 40 mss a year. Payment on acceptance when material has been assigned. Payment on publication for unsolicited material. Will send free sample copy to writer on request. Query first or submit complete ms. Reports on material in 1 to 2 weeks. Enclose S.A.S.E. for return of submissions.
Nonfiction and Photos: "Practice administration material; patient and personnel relations, taxes, investments, professional image; original 'case history' articles on means of conducting a dental practice more efficiently or more successfully (preferably with a D.D.S. byline). Lively writing style; in-depth coverage. Must be oriented to the dental profession." Length: 1,000 to 2,500 words. Pays 5¢ to 15¢ a word "depending on material." B&w glossy photos; contact prints. Captions required. Pays $5.

DENTAL MANAGEMENT, Ridgeway Center Bldg., Stamford CT 06905. Editor: M.J. Goldberg. For practicing dentists. Monthly. Buys all rights. Buys two or three articles per issue. Pays on acceptance. Query first. Enclose S.A.S.E.
Nonfiction and Photos: "No clinical or scientific material. Magazine is directed toward the business side of dentistry—management, collections, patient relations, fees, personal investments and life insurance. Writing should be clear, simple, direct. Likes lots of anecdotes, facts and direct conclusions." Pays 5¢ to 15¢ per word, depending on quality and research. Photos purchased with ms. Pays $10.
How To Break In: "First step is to read the magazine, as many issues as you can get hold of. Second step is to speak to dentists, and learn something about their business problems. Third step is develop some article ideas, and query us."

PROOFS, The Magazine of Dental Sales, Box 1260, Tulsa OK 74101. Editor: Richard Henn. Monthly. Pays on acceptance. Will send free sample copy on request. Query first. Reports in a week. Enclose S.A.S.E.
Nonfiction: Uses short articles, chiefly on selling to dentists. Pays about $20.

TIC MAGAZINE, Box 407, North Chatham NY 12132. Editor: Joseph Strack. For dentists, dental assistants, and oral hygienists. Monthly. Pays on acceptance. Reports in 2 weeks. Enclose S.A.S.E.
Nonfiction: Prefers a simple, almost popular style. Uses articles (with illustrations, if possible) as follows: 1. Lead feature: Dealing with major developments in dentistry of direct, vital interest to all dentists; 2. How-to-do-it pieces: Ways and means of building dental practices, improving professional techniques, managing patients, increasing office efficiency, etc.; 3. Special articles: Ways and means of improving dentist-laboratory relations for mutual advantage, of developing auxiliary dental personnel into an efficient office team, of helping the individual dentist to play a more effective role in alleviating the burden of dental needs in the nation and in his community, etc.; 4. General articles: Concerning any phase of dentistry or dentistry-related subjects of high interest to the average dentist. Length: 800 to 3,200 words. Payment negotiable.
Photos: Photo stories: four to ten pictures of interesting developments and novel ideas in dentistry. B&w only. Payment negotiable.

Drugs, Health Care, and Medical Products

DRUG TOPICS, 550 Kinderkamack Rd., Oradell NJ 07649. Editor: David W. Sifton. For retail drug stores and wholesalers, manufacturers, and hospital pharmacists. Monthly. Circulation: over 50,000. Buys all rights. Query first. Pays on acceptance. Enclose S.A.S.E.
Nonfiction: News of local, regional, state pharmaceutical associations, legislation affecting operation of drug stores, news of pharmacists in civic and professional activities, etc. Query first on drug store success stories which deal with displays, advertising, promotions, selling techniques. Length: 1,500 words maximum. Pays $5 and

up for leads, $25 and up for short articles, $50 to $200 for feature articles, "depending on length and depth."
Photos: May buy photos submitted with mss. May buy news photos with captions only. Pays $20.

HEARING DEALER, 1 E. First St., Duluth MN 55802. Editor and Publisher: Marjorie Skafte. Monthly. Buys all rights. Pays on acceptance. Query first. Enclose S.A.S.E.
Nonfiction and Photos: Uses articles about successful hearing aid dealers with a selection of photos illustrating the article. Most articles on current industry problems are of technical nature and must be staff-written or contributed by experts. Occasionally buys personal interviews with leading dealers from coast to coast, outlining specific ways in which they sell or service aids. No humor or consumer-interest material wanted. Articles should be brief, to-the-point, and completely objective. Pays 5¢ per word, $5 to $7 per glossy photo used depending on its relevance to the article.

N.A.R.D. JOURNAL, 1 E. Wacker Dr., Chicago IL 60601. Editor: Louis E. Kazin. Semimonthly. Query first. Buys all rights. Enclose S.A.S.E.
Nonfiction and Photos: Uses success stories about independent retail druggists; novel methods used in promotion of business; community contributions of individual druggists. Length: about 500 words. Pays $50. Occasionally buys 8x10 photos with mss. Pays $25 for photos from professional photographers.

PATIENT AID DIGEST, 2009 Morris Ave., Union NJ 07083. Editorial Director: Albert L. Cassak. For "pharmacists who have home health care departments and manufacturers of patient aid products." Bimonthly. Circulation: 11,000. Pays on publication. Will send a sample copy to a writer on request. Query first. Submit seasonal material 3 months in advance. Enclose S.A.S.E.
Nonfiction and Photos: "Can range from articles on existing home health care centers to opportunities for proprietors, to human interest stories pertaining to home health care." Approach should be "nontechnical." Buys interviews, profiles, humor, coverage of successful business operations and merchandising techniques. Length: 1,500 words maximum. Pays $10 to $60. Photos purchased with mss.

SURGICAL BUSINESS, 2009 Morris Ave., Union NJ 07083. Editorial Director: Albert L. Cassak. For "businessmen, dealers in medical products, distributors, and manufacturers of medical-surgical products." Monthly. Circulation: 5,000. Buys about 12 mss a year. Pays on publication. Will send a sample copy to a writer for $1. Query first. Submit seasonal material 3 months in advance. Enclose S.A.S.E.
Nonfiction and Photos: "Articles on business, financial, personal, or medical topics of interest" to dealers, retailers, and manufacturers of surgical items. Buys interviews, humor, coverage of successful business operations and merchandising and selling techniques. Length: 3,000 words maximum. Pays $10 to $75. Photos purchased with mss.

WHOLESALE DRUGS, 1100 Waterway Blvd., Indianapolis IN 46207. Editor: William F. Funkhouser. Bimonthly. Buys first rights only. Query first. Enclose S.A.S.E.
Nonfiction and Photos: Wants features on presidents and salesmen of Full Line Wholesale Drug Houses throughout the country. No set style, but subject matter should tell about both the man and his company—history, type of operation, etc. Pays $50 for text and pictures.

Dry Goods, Variety, and Department Stores

HOMESEWING TRADE NEWS, 129 Broadway, Lynbrook NY 11563. Editor: Nat Danas. For "retailers of fabrics, sewing notions, etc." Monthly. Pays on publication. Query first. Enclose S.A.S.E.

Nonfiction and Photos: Reports on stores doing on outstanding job in the homesewing trade. Length: 750 to 1,000 words. With 2 to 4 b&w photos. Pays $35 to $50. Photos purchased with mss. Buys photos with captions of display windows.

JUVENILE MERCHANDISING, Columbia Communications, Inc., 370 Lexington Ave., New York NY 10017. Editor: Lee Clark Neumeyer. For juvenile hard goods retailers, whether they are independent stores, juvenile sections of department stores, or discount houses. Monthly. Circulation: 10,000. Buys about 75 mss a year. Will send a sample copy to a writer on request. Query first. Reports in 1 week. Enclose S.A.S.E.
Nonfiction: "Solid features about a phase of juvenile operation in any of the above-mentioned retail establishments. Not interested in store histories. Mss on successful displays, methods for more efficient management; also technical articles on stock control or credit or mail promotion—how a specific juvenile store uses these, why they were undertaken, what results they brought. Illustrated interviews with successful dealers." Length: 1,000 to 1,500 words. Pays $50 to $75.

MILITARY MARKET, 475 School St., S.W., Washington DC 20024. Editor: Kenneth E. Rankin. For military and key civilian buyers and managers of military exchanges (retail stores) and commissaries (food stores). Copyrighted. Pays on acceptance. Will send a sample copy to a writer on request. "Query for approval first." Reports "in 24 hours." Enclose S.A.S.E.
Nonfiction and Photos: "Articles on how to do a better job of buying, displaying, merchandising, and selling in military exchanges (retail stores) and commissaries (food markets). How-to-do-it is more important than fine writing. Slant strictly to retail store and trade merchandising." Length: 500 to 3,000 words. Pays 5¢ a word and up. Photos purchased with and without mss; captions required. 8x10 or 5x7 b&w glossies, "with or without people, featuring merchandise on shelves, displays." Pays $5 minimum.

MODERN RETAILER, 50 Hunt St., Watertown MA 02172. Editor: Sidney L. Davis. For discount department stores and suppliers. Monthly. Rights purchased vary with author and material. Usually buys all rights. Pays on publication. "Query first. If idea is accepted, a sample copy will be sent." Enclose S.A.S.E.
Nonfiction and Photos: "Interviews with discount executives about their specific fields of emphasis." Pays minimum $1 "per inch. Average of $75 to $125 for story and photos." Photos purchased with or without mss; captions required.

PET AGE, 2561 North Clark St., Chicago IL 60614. Editor: Richard L. Shotke. For "professionals in the pet industry: wholesalers, manufacturers, suppliers, retailers, etc." Monthly. Circulation: 21,000. Buys all rights. Buys 25 to 35 mss a year. Pays on acceptance. Will send a sample copy to a writer on request; "postage must accompany request." Query first "with an outline of the specific slant or peg suggested." Submit seasonal material at least 3 to 4 months in advance. Reports in 1 month. Enclose S.A.S.E.
Nonfiction and Photos: "Features which describe innovative approaches, success stories, how-to's, etc., for pet industry personnel on subjects such as pet shop advertising, creating pet promotion projects, pet salesmanship, shop design, use of products, etc. Concentrate on features which provide specific practical methods of improving merchandising. No visits to local pet shops unless particularly innovative, with unusual success story in some phase. No interest in cute stories or poetry or other consumer-oriented material." Buys how-to's, coverage of successful business operations, new product coverage, articles on pet merchandising techniques. Length: 250 to 2,500 words. Pays $5 to $40. Photos purchased with mss; captions required. Pays $2 to $10.

PSM—PETS/SUPPLIES/MARKETING, 1 East First St., Duluth MN 55802. Editor: Paul A. Setzer. For "retailers, wholesalers, and manufacturers of pet supplies." Monthly. Circulation: 14,700. Buys all rights. Buys about 120 mss a year. Pays on acceptance. Will send a sample copy to a writer on request. Write for copy of guidelines for writers. Query first. Submit seasonal material 3 months in advance. Reports in 1 month. Enclose S.A.S.E.

Nonfiction and Photos: "Success and how-to's of merchandising pets and pet supplies; care articles on pets." Buys interviews, profiles, humor, spot news, historical and new product articles, coverage of successful business operations and merchandising techniques. Length: 1,000 to 2,000 words. Pays $10 to $150 (5¢ per word). Photos purchased with mss; captions required. B&w glossies, color transparencies, 35mm color. "No pix of pets. Must combine shots of pets and pet supplies in merchandising context." Pays $6 to $40.

SEW BUSINESS, 1271 Avenue of the Americas, New York N.Y 10020. Editor: Mary Colucci. For retailers of home-sewing merchandise. Monthly. Circulation: 14,000. Not copyrighted. Buys about 100 mss a year. Pays on publication. Will send a sample copy to a writer on request. Query first. Reports in 1 month. Enclose S.A.S.E.
Nonfiction and Photos: Articles on department store or fabric shop operations, including coverage of art needlework, piece goods, patterns, sewing accessories and all other notions. Interviews with buyers/retailers on their department or shop. "Unless they are doing something different or offbeat, something that another retailer could put to good use in his own operation, there is no sense wasting their or your time in doing an interview and story. Best to query editor first to find out if a particular article might be of interest to us." Length: 500 to 1,500 words. Pays $50 minimum. Photos purchased with mss. "Should illustrate important details of the story." Sharp 8x10 b&w glossies. Pays $5.
Fillers: $2.50 for news items less than 100 words. For news item plus photo and caption pays $7.50.

Education

Publications in this listing are for professional educators, teachers, coaches, and school personnel. Magazines for parents or the general public interested in education topics are classified under Education in the Consumer Publications section.

AMERICAN SCHOOL & UNIVERSITY, 134 N. 13th St., Philadelphia PA 19107. Editor: Jeremy L. Fergusson. For administrators in education (chief officers to directors of buildings and grounds) from elementary through college level. Established: 1928. Monthly. Circulation: 45,000. Buys all rights but will reassign rights to author after publication. Buys 50 mss a year. Payment on publication. Will send free sample copy to writer on request. Query first. Submit seasonal material 6 months in advance. Reports on material in 3 weeks. Enclose S.A.S.E.
Nonfiction and Photos: Material on "planning, designing, constructing, equipping, maintaining, operating and renovating school and college facilities." Informational, how-to, interview, successful business operations, technical. Length: 500 to 2,000 words. Pays $25 to $200. B&w glossies and color transparencies purchased wtih mss. Captions optional.

AMERICAN SCHOOL BOARD JOURNAL, National School Boards Association, State National Bank Plaza, Evanston IL 60201. Editor: James Betchkal. Monthly. Rights purchased vary with author and material. Pays an honorarium. Enclose S.A.S.E. for return of submissions.
Nonfiction: "Articles on problems arising out of organization and administration of city, town, and county school systems, with special emphasis upon administrative work of boards of education and superintendents of schools, and school business managers and problems of financing and school planning." Length: 400 to 800 words.

AMERICAN TEACHER, 1012 14th St., Washington DC 20005. Editor: Dave Elsila. For "members of the American Federation of Teachers, AFL-CIO, and other classroom teachers." Monthly except July and August. Buys first North American serial rights; will buy simultaneous rights. Pays on publication. Will send a sample copy to a writer on request. Prefers query first. Reports in 1 month. Enclose S.A.S.E.

Nonfiction and Photos: "We want material directly concerned with our primary interests: educational innovation, academic freedom, the teacher union movement, better schools and educational methods, legislation concerning teachers, etc. Pays $25 to $70. Photos purchased with and without mss; captions required. "Stock photos of classroom scenes." Subjects must be in range of subject interest. No specific size. Pays $15.

ARTS AND ACTIVITIES, 8150 N. Central Park Ave., Skokie IL 60076. Managing Editor: Morton Handler. For "art teachers in elementary, junior high, and senior high schools." Monthly, except July and August. Buys all rights. Pays on publication. Will send a sample copy to a writer on request. Reports in 1 month. Enclose S.A.S.E. for return of submissions.

Nonfiction and Photos: "Articles on creative art activities for children in elementary, junior high, and senior high schools, with illustrations such as artwork or photos of activity in progress. Payment is determined by length and educational value." Pays minimum $30.

ATHLETIC JOURNAL, 1719 Howard St., Evanston IL 60202. Editor: M.M. Arns. For "high school and college coaches, athletic directors, and athletic trainers." Established in 1921. Monthly, except July and August. Circulation: 32,000. Buys all rights. Buys "very few" mss a year. Pays on publication. Will send a sample copy to a writer on request. Query first: "state subject of article and material covered." Will not consider photocopied submissions. Reports in 1 month. Enclose S.A.S.E.

Nonfiction and Photos: "Highly technical material on sports. No general interest articles. Note that the author must be active in coaching or administration of high school or college athletics for men. Most articles submitted by freelancers are too general for our purposes." Length: "about 1,500 words." Pays minimum $25; "varies greatly, depending on professional qualifications (coaching ability) of writer." Photos purchased with mss; captions optional.

BUSINESS EDUCATION WORLD, 1221 Avenue of the Americas, New York NY 10020. Editor: Susan Schrumpf. For "business and office education instructors, classroom teachers, teacher educators and state and local supervisory personnel." 5 times a year. Circulation: 80,000. Buys all rights, but will reassign rights to author after publication. Buys 30 to 40 mss a year. Pays on publication. Will send a sample copy to a writer on request. Write for copy of guidelines for writers. Submit complete ms. Will not consider photocopied submissions. Reports in 3 weeks. Enclose S.A.S.E. for return of submissions.

Nonfiction: "Business, office education, innovative classroom techniques and curricula, professional news, methodology." Interested in freelance material for " 'Post-12,' a column devoted to educators at collegiate and business school levels, and for 'Continuing Education,' a column on adult and continuing education programs." Length: 900 to 1,200 words. Pays $5 to $25.

CHANGING EDUCATION, 1012 14th St., N.W., Washington DC 20005. Editor: Dave Elsila. For classroom teachers at all levels and in all subject areas. Quarterly. Circulation: 325,000. Not copyrighted. Buys 20 mss a year. Payment on publication. Will send free sample copy to writer on request. Query first. Will consider photocopied submissions. Reports on material in 4 months. Enclose S.A.S.E.

Nonfiction and Photos: "Articles on subjects of interest to classroom teachers, especially on topics related to academic freedom, more effective schools, the labor movement, and so on. Our examination of issues is generally from the teacher-union viewpoint." Informational, how-to, personal experience, interview, profile, historical, think articles, expose, personal opinion, reviews of educational books. Length: 1,000 to 2,000 words. Pays $50 to $150. 8x10 b&w glossies. Pays $15 to $30.

CHRISTIAN TEACHER, Box 550, Wheaton IL 60187. Editor: Phil Landrum. For "members of the National Association of Christian Schools. They are mostly grade school teachers; also, high school teachers, principals, board members, parents." Established in 1964. Bimonthly, except during summer. Circulation: 7,000. Not copyrighted. Pays on acceptance "or shortly after." Will send a sample copy to a writer on request. Query first. Reports "quickly." Enclose S.A.S.E.

Nonfiction and Photos: "Educational trends, reports, how-to—mostly informative or inspirational. Our publication deals with education from a Christian point of view." Length for articles: 500 to 2,000 words. Payment: "no set rate; work on assignment only." Photos purchased with and without mss.

COLLEGE MANAGEMENT, 22 West Putnam Ave., Greenwich CT 06830. Editor: Paul K. Cuneo. For "top administrators (presidents, deans, provosts, faculty members, business and financial officers, and plant managers) in the nation's junior colleges, colleges, and universities with enrollment over 2,500." Monthly. Pays on acceptance. Will send a sample copy to a writer on request. Query first. Enclose S.A.S.E.

Nonfiction and Photos: "Magazine's purpose is to inform and guide; its stock-in-trade is the case history that shows how an institution is handling a particular problem. No straight news reporting, but subjects for features should be timely and solutions should have current application." Length: 1,500 to 3,000 words. Pays minimum 3¢ a word.

FORECAST MAGAZINE FOR HOME ECONOMICS, 50 W. 44th St., New York NY 10036. Address mss to Edith McConnell, Editor. For teachers of home economics in junior and senior high schools. Monthly, September through May-June. Buys all rights. Pays on publication. "Query or outline strongly recommended." Reports in 2 months. Enclose S.A.S.E.

Nonfiction: "Articles of interest to home economics teachers in education, family relations, child development, clothing, textiles, grooming, foods, nutrition, and home management." For example, a recent article is, "When Students Choose the Course . . . ." Pays average $50, "depending on the author and length."

INDUSTRIAL EDUCATION, 22 W. Putnam Ave., Greenwich CT 06830. For administrators and instructors in elementary, secondary, and higher education for industrial arts, vocational, and technical education. Monthly, except July and August and combined May/June issue. Buys all rights. Pays on publication. Will send a sample copy to a writer for $1.25. Write for copy of guidelines for writers. Deadline for Shop Planning Annual is Dec. 29; for Back to School and Projects is July 1. Reports in 5 weeks. Enclose S.A.S.E. for return of submissions.

Nonfiction and Photos: "Articles dealing with the broad aspects of industrial arts, vocational, and technical education as it is taught in our junior and senior high schools, voacational and technical high schools, and junior college. We're interested in analytical articles in relation to such areas as curriculum planning, teacher training, teaching methods, supervision, professional standards, industrial arts or vocational education philosophy or practice, relationship of industrial education to industry at the various educational levels, current problems, trends, etc. How-to-do, how-to-teach, how-to-make articles of a very practical nature which will assist the instructor in the laboratory at every level of industrial education. Typical are the 'activities' articles in every instructional area. Also typical is the article which demonstrates to the teacher a new or improved way of doing something or of teaching something or how to utilize special teaching aids or equipment to full advantage—activities which help the teacher do a better job of introducing the industrial world of work to the student." Length: maximum 2,500 words. Pays $15 "per printed page." 8x10 b&w photos purchased with ms.

Fillers: Short hints on some aspect of shop management or teaching techniques. Length: 25 to 250 words.

INSTRUCTOR MAGAZINE, 7 Bank St., Dansville NY 14437. Editor: Dr. Ernest Hilton. For elementary classroom teachers and supervisors. Established: 1891. Monthly except July and August. Circulation: 304,000. Rights purchased vary with author and material. Buys all rights. Buys first serial rights. Payment on acceptance. Will send free sample copy to writer on request. Write for copy of guidelines for writers. Submit complete ms. Submit seasonal material 6 months in advance. Reports on material accepted for publication in 3 months. Returns rejected material in 1 month. Enclose S.A.S.E. for return of submissions.

Nonfiction and Photos: Professional articles on various aspects of education; ideas and suggestions about effective teaching activities. Descriptive work about a program, emphasizing the specific techniques necessary for teachers to follow. Need seasonal articles on teaching suggestions and art activities. Informational and technical. Interviews." Length: 600 to 1,000 words. Pays $20 to $50 depending on length and quality. 8x10 glossies and 4x5 color transparencies purchased with ms.

Fiction: Fantasy. Mystery. Real life situations. "All for children." Length: 600 to 1,000 words. Pays $20 to $50. Department Editor: Kathryn Eldridge.

INTELLECT/The Magazine of Educational and Social Affairs, 1860 Broadway, New York NY 10023. Editors: William W. Brickman and Stanley Lehrer. For professors and administrators of nation's major schools and colleges. Monthly, October through May. Buys world rights. Although 90% of material is freelance, editors occasionally commission articles. Reports in 1 month. Enclose S.A.S.E.

Nonfiction: Wants "articles concerning all phases of college and university activities, such as administration, teaching, curriculum, financing, controversies, trends and developments, profiles of leaders in educational field, etc." Length: 1,500 to 2,500 words. No payment.

Photos: Photos or illustrative artwork concerning some aspect or topic covered by the article are used, if commissioned by the editors. Pays $5 and up for 8x10 glossy prints, horizontal and vertical view, but check first with editors for appropriate size.

THE JOURNAL OF AESTHETIC EDUCATION, University of Illinois Press, Urbana IL 61801. Editor: Ralph A. Smith. For teachers at all levels. Quarterly. Circulation: 1,300. Buys all rights. Reports promptly. Enclose S.A.S.E.

Nonfiction: Articles on the arts, mass media, and environment. Length: 5,000 words.

LEARNING, 530 University Ave., Palo Alto CA 94305. Managing Editor: Morton Malkofsky. For elementary school teachers. Established 1972. Monthly. Circulation: 225,000. Buys all rights, but will reassign rights to author after publication. Buys 50 to 100 mss a year. Payment on acceptance. Query first. Will consider photocopied submissions. Reporting time "depends on story." Rejected material is returned in 1 day to 3 weeks. Enclose S.A.S.E.

Nonfiction and Photos: "We publish material about learning, what it is and isn't. Longer articles, public affairs, more research reports, wide range of editorial content. Suggest writer read the magazine." Especially interested in seeing articles on "accountability and race relations in the classroom." Length: 300 to 7,500 words. Pays $50 to $500. Photos purchased with accompanying mss or on asignment. Captions required. "Contact sheets and negs."

THE LIVING LIGHT, 1312 Massachusetts Ave., N.W., Washington DC 20005. An interdisciplinary review for "professionals in the field of religious education, primarily Roman Catholics." Established in 1964. Quarterly. Buys all rights but will reassign rights to author after publication. Buys 4 mss a year. Payment on publication. Will send sample copy to writer for $2.50. Submit complete ms. Reports on material in 30 to 60 days. Enclose S.A.S.E. for return of submissions.

Nonfiction: Articles that "present development and trends, report on research and encourage critical thinking in the field of religious education and pastoral action. Academic approach." Length: 2,000 to 5,000 words. Pays $40 to $100.

THE MASSACHUSETTS TEACHER, 20 Ashburton Place, Boston MA 02108. Editor: Russell P. Burbank. For Massachusetts educators. Monthly, October through May. Buys all rights. Pays on publication. Will send a sample copy to a writer on request. Query first. Reports in 1 month. Enclose S.A.S.E.

Nonfiction and Photos: "We want provocative education articles, features on classroom innovations that are two steps above the ordinary; well-researched authoritative articles (we check your facts) on items of interest to teachers in general or Massachusetts classroom public school teachers in particular." Pays $25 and up. Occasionally buys photos with mss. Prefers at least 5x7.

MOMENTUM, National Catholic Education Association, One Dupont Circle, Suite 350, Washington DC 20036. Editor: Carl Balcerak. For "Catholic educators—superintendents, principals, teachers." Quarterly. Circulation: 16,000. Buys all rights. Buys 28 to 36 articles a year. Pays on publication. Will send a sample copy to a writer on request. No query required. Submit seasonal material at least 2 months in advance. Reports in 2 weeks. Enclose S.A.S.E. for return of submissions.
Nonfiction and Photos: "In-depth articles on innovative programs in Catholic schools, primarily elementary and secondary schools. The articles should be objective, with pros and cons of the program and with lots of quotes from people involved in the program—reactions to the program from parents, teachers, etc. Also, articles on current topics of interest to Catholic educators. Freelancers tend to overwork general articles, such as how to improve Catholic education, what's wrong with Catholic education." Length: 2,000 to 2,500 words. Pays 2¢ a word. B&w glossies purchased with mss. Pays $5.

NEWS FOR YOU, Box 131, 1320 Jamesville Ave., Syracuse NY 13210. Editor: Nancy Gridley. For "adults and teenagers with poor reading skill." Established: 1959. Weekly paper for adult education classes. Circulation: 40,000. Buys all rights, but will reassign rights to author after publication. Buys about 75 mss a year. Payment on acceptance. Will send free sample copy to writer on request. Query first. Enclose S.A.S.E. for return of submissions.
Nonfiction and Photos: "We publish feature articles in two series. One is an 'Occupations' series featuring a person on a particular job. The second is a 'Life Is an Opportunity' series that features people, particularly young people, in activities that make life more worthwhile for them. Short words and sentences, but not as though writing for children." Length: 200 to 500 words. Pays $10 to $20. 8½x10 b&w photos. Pays $10.

NJEA REVIEW, 180 W. State St., Trenton NJ 08608. Editor: George M. Adams. Aimed at entire educational community in New Jersey, from nursery through higher education. Monthly. Circulation: 95,000. Buys all rights. Pays on publication. Does not pay for articles by New Jersey teachers. Will send a sample copy to a writer on request. Write for copy of guidelines for writers. Query required. Reports in 5 days. Enclose S.A.S.E. for response to queries and return of submissions.
Nonfiction: Prefers articles describing successful educational practices to theorizing on "what should be." Articles should be timely, broad enough in scope to appeal to entire profession, well researched, but not too technical and not footnoted. Writing should be imaginative, crisp and unaffected, with use of human interest appeal and humor. Needed are pieces on new trends in education, such as teaching and curriculum experimentation, as well as subject area articles. Articles especially valuable if based on experience in a New Jersey school or college. Length: 500 to 1,000 words.
Photos: B&w photos purchased with captions. Pays $5.

SCHOLASTIC COACH, 50 W. 44th St., New York NY 10036. Editor: Herman L. Masin. Monthly, except July and August. Buys first rights. Pays on publication. Reports in 10 days. Enclose S.A.S.E. for return of submissions.
Nonfiction: This magazine is directed to the coaches and physical education directors in colleges and high schools. Uses authoritative, technical articles on football, basketball, track and field, tennis, baseball, soccer, swimming, and all physical education activities. Length: 1,000 to 2,000 words. Pays $30 per article.
Photos: Single photos used must have dramatic action. Pays $5 to $15 per photo.

SCHOLASTIC TEACHER, 50 W. 44 St., New York NY 10036. Editor: Loretta Hunt Marion. For "teachers of grades 1 to 12 (all subject areas at the elementary level); teachers of language arts, social studies, science, and humanities at the junior/senior high levels." Established: 1946. Monthly during school year. Circulation: 440,000 (in 2 editions). Rights purchased vary with author and material. Buys all rights but will reassign rights to author after publication. Buys first North American serial rights. Buys second serial (reprint) rights. Buys 25 to 30 mss a year. Payment on acceptance. Will send free sample copy to writer on request. Write for copy of guidelines for writers. Query first. Will consider photocopied submissions. Submit seasonal material 3 to 4 months in advance. Reports on material in 6 weeks. Enclose S.A.S.E.

Nonfiction and Photos: "Major articles interpret and report on major trends and issues in American education; curriculum developments like population education; controversies like IQ testing, compulsory education. *Scholastic Teacher*'s editors identify these subjects, then make assignments to freelance writers specializing in education." Good education writers are requested to send "a letter of introduction to the editor, giving background about themselves, where they have been published, and send sample feature articles. It's also helpful to know what areas of education they're interested in." Length: 1,000 to 2,500 words. Pays $50 to $300. There is an annual travel issue in March with summer travel ideas for teachers. "Potpourri" is a monthly column of short items on innovative educational programs, educational news items, etc. Length: 250 to 500 words. Pays $15 to $25. 8x10 b&w glossy photos purchased with or without mss or on assignment. Captions optional. Pays minimum of $10. "Looking mostly for photos of school situations, and special travel photos for the March issue." Payment for color transparencies varies with use. Art Director: Richard Leach.

SCHOOL ARTS MAGAZINE, 72 Printers Bldg., Worcester MA 01608. Editor: George F. Horn. For art and craft teachers and supervisors from grade through high school. Monthly, except July and August. Will send a sample copy to a writer on request. Pays on publication. Reports in 90 days. Enclose S.A.S.E. for return of submissions.
Nonfiction and Photos: Articles, with photos, on art and craft activities in schools. Length: 1,000 words. Payment is negotiable.

SCHOOL MANAGEMENT MAGAZINE, 22 W. Putnam Ave., Greenwich CT 06830. Editor: Paul K. Cuneo. For public school superintendents, board members, principals. Buys North American serial rights. Pays on acceptance. Will send a sample copy to a writer on request. "Study issues." Reports in 2 to 4 weeks. Enclose S.A.S.E. for return of submissions.
Nonfiction: Articles which provide readers with practical, proven solutions to school management problems. Length: 1,500 to 3,000 words. Pays 3¢ per word and up.

SCHOOL PROGRESS, 481 University Ave., Toronto, Ont., M5W 1A7 Canada. Editor: Margaret Gayfer. For educational administrators and curriculum planners (administrators, business officials, directors of education, school principals, superintendents). Established in 1931. Monthly. Circulation: 16,500. Buys all rights. Buys about 30 mss a year. Pays on publication. Will send a sample copy to a writer on request. Query first. Reports in 1 month. Enclose S.A.E. and International Reply Coupons.
Nonfiction and Photos: Articles about what schools and school boards are doing in curriculum and organization; why they are doing it and how. Length: 500 to 2,000 words. Pays 5¢ a word. For b&w glossies, pays $5.

SCHOOL SHOP, 416 Longshore Dr., Ann Arbor MI 48107. Editor: Lawrence W. Prakken. For "industrial and technical education personnel." Special issue in April deals with varying topics for which mss are solicited. Monthly. Circulation: 44,000. Buys all rights. Pays on publication. Will send a sample copy to a writer on request. Query first; "direct or indirect connection with the field of industrial and/or technical education preferred." Submit mss to Howard Kahn. Managing Editor. Submit seasonal material 3 months in advance. Reports in 2 months. Enclose S.A.S.E.
Nonfiction and Photos: Uses articles pertinent to the various teaching areas in industrial education (woodwork, electronics, drafting, machine shop, graphic arts, computer training, etc.). "Outlook should be on innovation in educational programs, processes, or projects which directly apply to the industrial-technical education area." Buys how-to's, personal experience and think pieces, interviews, humor, coverage of new products. Length: 500 to 2,000 words. Pays $15 to $40. 8x10 photos purchased with ms.

SCIENCE ACTIVITIES, 8150 Central Park Ave., Skokie IL 60076. Editor: Charles A. Martin. Monthly, September through June. Circulation: 29,000. Buys North American serial rights. Pays on publication. Will send a free sample copy on

request. No query required. Reports in 2 weeks. Enclose S.A.S.E.
Nonfiction and Photos: "Articles on practical science activities and projects for junior high and high school teachers." No length specifications. Pays $50 and up. 8x10 photos purchased with ms. Pays $10.

TEACHER, (formerly *Grade Teacher*), 22 W. Putnam Ave., Greenwich CT 06830. Editor: Harold Littledale. For teachers of kindergarten through junior high grades. Monthly, except July and August. (May/June, combined issue.) Pays on acceptance. Query first "with brief outline of material and picture of illustration availability." Enclose S.A.S.E.
Nonfiction and Photos: "Articles of current educational interest, accounts of actual uses of new teaching techniques, classroom-tested units of work. Also needed are original children's songs. Articles should be long on fact, short on preachy material. Historical subjects must be authenticated with sources given." Length: maximum 2,500 words. Pays 1¢ a word. "Photos may be included as illustrations or sent separately wtih captions. Pays minimum $5, depending on size and usage." Also buys art projects, creative arts and crafts, children's art, accompanied by clear b&w glossies when possible. Pays 1¢ a word.

THE TEACHER PAPER, 2221 N.E. 23rd St., Portland OR 97212. Editors: Robin and Fred Staab. For parents, teachers, and administrators of public schools. Quarterly. Circulation: 5,000. Pays on publication. Will send a sample copy for 75¢. No query required. "Submissions by classroom teachers of preschool through twelfth grade only." Enclose a brief biographical note of where presently teaching or have taught. Editorial deadlines are on the first of Aug., Oct., Jan. and March. Reports in 2 months. Enclose S.A.S.E. for return of submissions.
Nonfiction: Wants articles and features containing candid anecdotes from the classroom, playground, faculty lounge on present teacher problems, successes and failures. Articles should be written in English language, not "Ed-speak" jargon. The magazine is "an unconventional, unrestrained publication which begins where most education periodicals stop. The only magazine to print only teachers is exposing—and suggesting solutions to—the persistent human, educational, and political problems facing students and their teachers." No taboos. Interested in "rocking the boat" of public schools. For example, recent articles include "Sexism in Schools" and "Madman in the Classroom." Also uses book reviews on education subjects. Length: 500 to 2,000 words. Pays 1¢ per word.
Fiction: Short-shorts or vignettes. Length: 500 to 2,000 words. Pays 1¢ a word.
Poetry: Length: 20 lines. Pays $5.
How To Break In: "The best thing for a beginning writer to do is: Teach in a classroom full of real children, and then write honestly about it."

TODAY'S CATHOLIC TEACHER, 38 W. 5th St., Dayton OH 45402. Editor: Ruth A. Matheny. For teachers and administrators in Catholic and other nonpublic schools, as well as CCD schools of religious. Monthly, September through May, except December. Buys all rights. Pays on acceptance. Will send sample copy for 50 cents. Send for "Information for contributors." Query first and study publication before submitting mss. Reports in 6 to 8 weeks. Enclose S.A.S.E.
Nonfiction and Photos: Subject matter may cover any topic of practical help or interest to the nonpublic classroom teacher or administrator, and to school boards and parish councils. Typical examples of subject matter treated include: helpful observations on the teaching of curriculum subjects (language arts, math, religion, art, etc.), retarded readers, guidance, the qualities of a good teacher, new developments in reading, television as it affects the school, testing, faculty relationships, parent-teacher relationships, school problems, school and community needs, civil rights, school boards, administration as it affects the classroom, creative teaching, etc. Magazine style desired, direct, concise, informative, accurate; enjoyable to read, informal, and free of educational jargon. Subjects should be handled concretely with specific examples when needed. Problems raised in articles should be accompanied by solutions. Length: 600-800 words or 1,000-1,500 words. Pays $20 to $75, with premium payment for superior content and writing presentation. Photos purchased with mss.
Fillers: Teaching tips and classroom experiences. Length: 100-500 words. Pays $5 to $20.

TODAY'S EDUCATION: NEA JOURNAL, National Education Association, 1201 16th St., N.W., Washington DC 20036. Editor: Dr. Mildred S. Fenner. Does not pay for submissions, except photos. No query necessary. Enclose S.A.S.E. for return of submissions.
Nonfiction: Articles on teaching methods and practices; human interest, popular style. Length: 800 to 2,000 words. No payment.
Photos: Buys singles and photo series of school situations and scenes. Requires model releases. 8x10 b&w or 35mm color. Pays $25 for b&w, $150 for color. Photo Editor: Walter Graves.

WHAT'S NEW IN HOME ECONOMICS, 666 Fifth Ave., New York NY 10019. Editor: Donna Newberry Creasy. For "home ec college grads; most are teachers; all ages and levels of experience; broad interest range—virtually anything regarding the practical aspects of family life and education." Established in 1936. 8 times during the school year. Circulation: about 62,000. Buys all rights. Buys "very few" mss a year. Pays on publication "in special cases; otherwise, pays in contributors' copies." Query first. Will consider photocopied submissions. Submit seasonal material 6 months in advance. Enclose S.A.S.E.
Nonfiction and Fiction: "As a rule, we only accept material from home economists. Exceptions are recognized authorities in special areas (for example, an M.D. on a health topic). We're quite interested in short-short stories appropiriate for classroom use for junior and senior high and on topics of general interest to teachers. The approach must be straightforward, with an informative orientation. Nonfiction must all be related to home economics, consumer education, etc." Length: 3000 to 1,500 words. Pays $25, "but we rely heavily on the free contributions of our readers."

Electricity

Publications classified here aim at electrical engineers, electrical contractors, and others who build, design, and maintain systems connecting and supplying homes, businesses, and industries with power. Journals dealing with generating and supplying power to users will be found in the Power and Power Plants category. Publications for appliance servicemen and dealers will be found in the Home Furnishings classification.

ELECTRICAL APPARATUS, 400 N. Michigan Ave., Chicago IL 60611. Address Editorial Department. Monthly for electrical apparatus service specialists. Circulation: 18,000. Buys all rights. Pays on acceptance. Will send a sample copy to a writer for $1. Query first; uses assigned articles only. Reports in 2 weeks. Enclose S.A.S.E.
Nonfiction: Uses technical and semitechnical illustrated features on specific phases of operation of industrial, electrical apparatus, service firms and in-plant departments; any material directly applicable to maintenance operations. Length: 500 to 2,000 words. Pay "varies, depending on article, but generally runs between $75 and $100."
Photos: Purchased with ms or with captions only. 8x10 or 5x7 glossies that show equipment details or single photos with captions describing an event of interest, people in the industry, meetings of associations. Pays $5 minimum.

ELECTRICAL CONSULTANT, 1760 Peachtree Rd., N.W., Atlanta GA 30309. Editor: Paula Scherer Stephens. For "consulting electrical engineers; both those in private practice and employed by others." Monthly. Buys first rights. Pays on acceptance. "Queries relating to proposed subjects answered promptly." Reports promptly. Enclose S.A.S.E.
Nonfiction: Wants "well-written articles relating to the design and specification of electrical systems for commercial and industrial buildings, institutions, and special projects such as airports, expositions, stadiums, etc. Articles must be based on interviews with consulting electrical engineers." Pays $35 to $75.

ELECTRICAL CONTRACTOR, 7315 Wisconsin Ave., Washington DC 20014. Editor: Larry C. Osius. For electrical contractors. Monthly. Buys first rights, reprint rights, and simultaneous rights. Will send free sample copy on request. Freelance material bought on assignment following query. Usually reports in 1 month. Enclose S.A.S.E.

Nonfiction and Photos: Installation articles showing informative application of new techniques and products. Slant is product and method contributing to better, faster, more economical construction process. Length: "1 column to 4 pages." Pays $60 per printed page, including photos and illustrative material. Photos should be sharp, reproducible glossies, 5x7 and up.

ELECTRICAL CONTRACTOR & MAINTENANCE SUPERVISOR, 481 University Ave., Toronto, Ont., Canada. Editor: George McNevin. For "middleaged men who either run their own businesses or are in fairly responsible management positions. They range from university graduates to those with public school education only." Established in 1952. Monthly. Circulation: 13,000. Rights purchased vary with author and material. "Depending on author's wish, payment is either on acceptance or on publication." Will send a sample copy to a writer on request. Query first. Enclose S.A.E. and International Reply Coupons.

Nonfiction and Photos: "Articles that have some relation to electrical construction or maintenance and business management. The writer should include as much information as possible pertaining to the electrical field. We're not interested in articles that are too general and philosophical. Don't belabor the obvious, particularly on better business management. We're interested in coverage of labor difficulties." Buys informational articles, how-to's, profiles, coverage of successful business operations, new product pieces, and technical articles. Length: "no minimum or maximum." Pays "7¢ a published word or 5¢ a word on submitted mss, unless other arrangements are made." Photos purchased with mss or on assignment; captions optional. Pays "$7 for the first print and $2 for each subsequent print, plus photographer's expenses."

ELECTRICITY IN BUILDING MAGAZINE, 2132 Fordem Ave., Madison WI 53701. Editor: Sheila W. Bingham. Monthly. Pays on acceptance. Query first. Reports in 2 weeks. Enclose S.A.S.E.

Nonfiction and Photos: Wants informative-type story directed toward builder that will tell him how to increase profits, trim losses, and/or utilize new techniques and ideas. Length: 200 to 1,000 words. Pays $60 to $100, "depending on quality." Include 8x10 glossy photos with the article.

Electronics and Communications

Listed here are publications for electronics engineers, radio and TV broadcasting managers, electronic equipment operators, and builders of electronic communication systems and equipment, including stereos, television sets, and radio-TV broadcasting systems. Journals for professional announcers or communicators will be found under Journalism; those for electronic appliance retailers will be found in Home Furnishings; publications on computer design and data processing systems will be found in Data Processing.

Publications for electronics enthusiasts or stereo hobbyists will be found in Popular Science, Hobby and Craft Magazines or in Music and Sound Reproduction Equipment in the Consumer Publications section.

BROADCAST ENGINEERING 1014 Wyandotte, Kansas City MO 64105. Editor: Ron Merrell. For "owners, managers, and top technical people at AM, FM, TV stations, cable TV operators, educational and industrial TV, as well as recording studios." Established in 1959. Monthly. Circulation: 30,000. Buys all rights, but will reassign rights to author after publication. Buys about 50 mss a year. Pays on acceptance; "for a series, we pay for each part on publication." Will send a sample copy to a writer on request. Write for copy of guidelines for writers. Query first. Will not consider photocopied submissions. Submit seasonal material at least 3 months in advance. Reports in 2 weeks. Enclose S.A.S.E.

Nonfiction and Photos: Wants technical features dealing with design, installation, modification, and maintenance of radio and television broadcast station equipment; interested in features on educational and cable TV systems, other material of interest to communications engineers and technicians, and on self-designed and constructed equipment for use in broadcast and communications fields. "Currently looking for cable TV and instructional TV how-to's with pictures; articles on overcoming problems. Articles start with the evolution of the problem and resolve with the solution. We use a technical, but not textbook, style. Our publication is mostly how-to and it operates as a forum, talking with readers, not down to them. We're overstocked with build-it-yourself articles, except for our 'Engineer's Exchange' column, where we take short-shorts and pay up to $25. We're especially interested now in cable TV articles on public access and on recording studios improving facilities and techniques. Length: 1,500 to 2,000 words for features, with drawing and photos, if possible; 200 to 400 words for "Engineer's Exchange." Pays $75 to $150 for features and $15 to $25 for "Engineer's Exchange." Photos purchased with and without mss; captions required. Pays $5 to $10 for b&w, pays $10 to $35 for color (2¼x2¼ color transparencies or larger).

BROADCASTER, 77 River St., Toronto, Ont., M5A 3P2 Canada. Editor: Doug Loney. For the Canadian "communications industry—radio, television, cable, ETV, advertisers, and their agencies." Buys all rights. Pays on acceptance. Will send a sample copy to a writer on request. "Queries and all material will be acknowledged within a month, and I will endeavor to offer constructive criticism where necessary." Enclose International Reply Coupons.

Nonfiction: "We are looking for articles illustrating how the various communicators conduct their business; controversies, inventions, and innovations of broadcast engineers; profiles or interviews on successful men and women; development of program ideas; industry news and technical news in layman's language. Writers should be familiar with the Canadian scene. No consumer-oriented material." Length: 500 to 3,000 words. Payment is $25 up.

CANADIAN ELECTRONICS ENGINEERING, 481 University Ave., Toronto M5W 1AF, Ont., Canada. Editor: Cliff Hand. For technically trained users of professional electronics products. Monthly. Buys Canadian serial rights. Pays on acceptance. Will send free sample copy to a writer on request. Query first with brief outline of article. Reports in 2 to 4 weeks. Enclose S.A.E. and International Reply Coupons.

Nonfiction: Science and technology involving professional electronic products and techniques. Must have direct relevance to work being done in Canada. Length: maximum about 1,500 words. Pays 5¢ to 8¢ per word depending on importance of subject, amount of research, and ability of writer.

Photos: Purchased with mss. 4x5 to 8x10 b&w glossy prints; must provide useful information on story subject. Pays average professional rates for time required on any particular assignment.

COMMUNICATIONS MAGAZINE, 1900 W. Yale, Englewood CO 80110. Editor: Paul Sylvan Maxwell. For "anyone interested in private business communications; management types." Monthly. Circulation: 20,000. Buys all rights. Buys 12 to 20 mss a year. Pays on publication. Will send a sample copy to a writer on request. Query first. Reports in 1 week. Enclose S.A.S.E.

Nonfiction: Market-oriented articles on "radio and communications in public safety, petroleum, health, utilities, marine, military, microwave, RCC, telephone, telegraph, manufacturing, engineering, etc." Wants "in-depth feature material." Buys how-to's, interviews, humor, spot news, historical and think pieces. Exposes, travel and merchandising techniques articles, photo essays. Length: open. Pays $15 to $25 per printed page.

Photos: Purchased with mss; with captions only. B&w glossies, color transparencies, 35mm color, color prints. Payment negotiable.

COMMUNICATIONS NEWS, 402 West Liberty Drive, Wheaton IL 60187. Editor: Bruce Howat. For "managers of communications systems ... business, police, transportation, utility, broadcast, hospital, school, bank, and so on." Established in 1964. Monthly. Circulation: 30,000. Buys all rights. Buys about 6 mss a year. Pays on publication. Will send a sample copy to a writer on request. Query first or submit complete ms. Will consider photocopied submissions. Submit seasonal material 2 months in advance of issue date. Reports in 3 weeks. Enclose S.A.S.E.
Nonfiction and Photos: "New developments in communications—case histories, technical how-to articles. The technique or system described must be new, and improved service or cost savings must be detailed. Our publication covers all types of voice, signal, and data communications." Buys how-to's, new product articles, and technical articles. Length: 100 to 1,000 words. Pays $5 to $25. Photos purchased with and without mss; captions required. Pays $5 to $10 for 8x10 glossies.

EDN, 221 Columbus Ave., Boston MA 02116. Editor: Frank T. Egan. For electronic design engineers. Semimonthly. Buys all rights. Payment when material is published. Will send free sample copy to a writer on request. Reports "immediately." Enclose S.A.S.E. for return of submissions.
Nonfiction and Photos: News from the field, concepts, developments, events; articles on microelectronics, design, materials, instrumentation and measurement, packaging, etc. Articles must be original, practical, accurate, pertinent and free of sales promotion. Length: up to 5,000 words, average 1,000-1,200 words. Pays flat rate based on quality of article ($20 per printed page); no payment for news, new product or new literature releases. Photos purchased with mss; b&w glossy. Color transparencies or prints.

ELECTRONIC SERVICING, 1014 Wyandotte St., Kansas City MO 64105. Editor: C.H. Babcoke. Monthly. Circulation: 55,000. Buys all rights. Pays on acceptance. Will send a free sample copy on request. Write for author's guide before submitting. Query required. Reports in 1 to 3 weeks. Enclose S.A.S.E. with all submissions and queries.
Nonfiction and Photos: Articles and illustrating photos with step-by-step procedures for diagnosing, repairing or installing consumer electronic products. Length: 1,000 to 1,500 words. Pays $125 to $200.

ELECTRONICS, 1221 Avenue of the Americas, New York NY 10019. Editor: Kemp Anderson. Biweekly. Buys all rights. Query first. Reports in 2 weeks. Enclose S.A.S.E.
Nonfiction: Uses copy about research, development, design and production of electronic devices and management of electronic manufacturing firms; articles on "descriptions of new circuit systems, components, design techniques, how specific electronic engineering problems were solved; interesting applications of electronics; step-by-step, how-to design articles; nomographs, charts, tables for solution of repetitive design problems." Length: 1,000 to 3,500 words. Pays $30 per printed page.

ELECTRONIC/TECHNICIAN DEALER, 1 East First St., Duluth MN 55802. Editor: Phillip Dahlen. For professional TV-radio, hi-fi, communications and industrial electronics service dealers and technicians. Buys all rights. Query first. Prompt reports. Enclose S.A.S.E.
Nonfiction: Technical articles concerning the maintenance of consumer electronic products (plus some commercial electronics), plus related sales and business principles. Pays $25 per estimated magazine page.

TELEPHONY MAGAZINE, 53 W. Jackson Blvd., Chicago IL 60604. Managing Editor: Joseph J. Aiken. For people employed in the telephone and communications industry. Weekly. Buys all rights. Pays on publication. Query preferred but not necessary. Enclose S.A.S.E.
Nonfiction: Technical articles, features or briefs about the industry; what is new, or a better way of doing something. Length: 1,500 words.
Photos: Buys photos relating to communications, but this is infrequent. Always needs cover quality photography.

Engineering and Technology

Publications for electrical engineers are classified under Electricity; journals for electronics engineers are classified with the Electronics and Communications publications.

CANADIAN CONSULTING ENGINEER, 1450 Don Mills Rd., Don Mills, Ontario, M3B 2X7 Canada. Managing Editor: Tom Davey. Buys exclusive rights preferably; occasionally exclusive to field or country. Pays on publication. Reports in 15 days. Enclose S.A.E. and International Reply Coupons for return of submissions.
Nonfiction: "Business, professional, and ethical problems faced by professional engineers when they hang up a shingle as businessmen. Relationships with others (architects, mechanical trade, etc.), fees, legal performance standards, etc. Capsule reports of Canadian projects of special significance (either their magnitude, or because of a special engineering feature). Payment dependent on length and extent of research required." Pays usually $50 to $175.

DETROIT ENGINEER, 643 Notre Dame, Grosse Pointe MI 48230. Editor: Jack Grenard. For "members of the Engineering Society of Detroit. They are engineers, architects, and persons in other related fields. The median age is about 42; mostly affluent, with wide-ranging interests." Established in 1945. Monthly. Circulation: 7,000. Rights purchased vary with author and material; may buy all rights, but will reassign rights to author after publication. Buys less than 4 mss a year. Pays on publication. Will send a sample copy to a writer for $1. Submit complete ms. Will not consider photocopied submissions. Submit seasonal material 3 to 4 months in advance. Returns rejected material in "usually 2 weeks." Acknowledges acceptance of material in 4 to 6 weeks. Enclose S.A.S.E. for return of submissions.
Nonfiction: "*Detroit Engineer* publishes articles on subjects of regional, southeastern Michigan interest not covered in other publications. We are only interested in the unusual and highly specific technical or man-oriented pieces, such as an expose on the Wankel engine or a new way to harness solar energy—subjects of wide interest within the scientific community." Buys exposes and technical articles. Length: 500 to 2,000 words. Pays $50 to $100.
Photos: Buys 4x5 to 8x10 b&w glossies; "any surface." Pays $5 to $15. Buys 8x10 color prints or 2½x2¼ or larger transparencies for cover use. Pays minimum $25.

ELECTRO-OPTICAL SYSTEMS DESIGN MAGAZINE, Room 900, 222 W. Adams St., Chicago IL 60606. Editor: Robert D. Compton. Monthly. Circulation: 26,000. Buys all rights. Pays on publication. Will send a sample copy to a writer on request. Write for copy of guidelines for writers. Query required. Editorial deadlines are on the 5th of the month preceding publication. Enclose S.A.S.E.
Nonfiction and Photos: Articles and photos on lasers, laser systems, and optical systems aimed at electro-optical scientists and engineers. "Each article should serve a reader's need by either stimulating ideas, increasing technical competence, improving design capabilities, helping solve practical design problems, or improving testing capabilities in the following areas: natural light and radiation sources, artificial light and radiation sources, light modulators, optical components, image detectors, energy detectors, information displays, image processing, information storage and processing, system and subsystem testing, materials, support equipment, and other related areas." Pays $30 per page. Submit 8x10 b&w glossies with ms.

ENGINEERING GRAPHICS, 25 West 45th St., New York NY 10036. Editor: A.V. Lesmez. For supervisory personnel in the "engineering, reproduction, architectural drafting, and all other types of drafting fields." Monthly. Circulation: 68,000. Buys first rights. Pays on acceptance. Will send sample copy to a writer for $1. Query not required. Type copy with generous margins either side. Reports in 2 weeks. Enclose S.A.S.E. for return of submissions.
Nonfiction and Photos: Drafting and engineering drawings. Shortcuts and time-savers in the drafting field. New techniques. How the drafting department is set up and run. Length: 1,000 to 2,000 words. Pays $50 honorarium for complete article with photos and/or artwork, samples.

ENGINEERING NEWS-RECORD, 1221 Sixth Ave., New York NY 10020. Editor: Arthur J. Fox. For those "interested in construction, architecture, civil engineering, pollution control, city planning, transportation and financing." Established: 1874. Weekly. Circulation: 115,000. Buys all rights. Buys 10 mss a year. Payment on publication. Query first. Reports on material within 2 weeks. Enclose S.A.S.E.
Nonfiction and Photos: News stories and articles dealing with construction. Interview, profile, spot news, successful business operations, merchandising techniques, technical. Length: 2,500 words maximum. Pays 7¢ per word. B&w photos purchased with ms. Department Editor: J. F. Wilkinson.

LIGHTING DESIGN & APPLICATION, 345 E. 47th St., New York NY 10017. Editor: Chuck Beardsley. For "lighting designers, architects, consulting engineers, and lighting engineers." Established in 1971. Monthly. Circulation: 17,500. Rights purchased vary wtih author and material. Buys about 5 mss a year. Pays on acceptance. Query first. Will not consider photocopied submissions. Enclose S.A.S.E.
Nonfiction: "Lighting application, techniques, and trends in all areas, indoors and out. Our publication is the chief source of practical illumination information." Buys informational and think articles. Length: 500 to 2,000 words. Pays $100.

NEW ENGINEER, 555 Madison Ave., New York NY 10022. For "engineering school students at the graduate and undergraduate levels and young professional engineers, recent graduates, engineers in management." 10 times a year combined June/July, August/September issues. Circulation: 63,000. Buys first rights. Buys 20 to 30 mss a year. Pays on publication. Will send a sample copy to a writer on request. Query first with outline or abstract. Submit seasonal material 4 months in advance. Enclose S.A.S.E.
Nonfiction and Photos: Articles on "engineering trends, employment patterns, outlook, profiles of successful engineers, social responsiblity, engineering education. Articles should interest young engineers in general. Our publication approaches the engineer as a professional person—as a member of an elite group." Seeks material for "Closed Loop" department—"short items on engineering schools or developments"—and "Off Hours"—"section on travel and leisure." Publishes issues on "minority groups and engineering and environment and the engineer." Buys how-to's, personal experience articles, interviews, profiles, humor, coverage of successful business operations, and new product articles. Length: 1,500 to 4,000 words. Pays 6¢ to 10¢ a word. B&w glossies, 35mm color, and color transparencies purchased with mss. Payment "usually $20 to $25."
Fiction: Humorous; "engineering related." Length: 1,000 to 2,000 words. Pays 6¢ to 10¢ a word.

TECHNOLOGY REVIEW, Massachusetts Institute of Technology, Cambrdige MA 02139. Editor: John J. Mattill. For M.I.T. alumni and other scientists, engineers, and managers. 8 times a year. Buys first magazine rights. Pays on publication. Query first. Reports promptly. Enclose S.A.S.E.
Nonfiction: Articles on subjects in science, engineering, social science, and relation of these to current affairs. Length: open. Pays 10¢ per word.
Photos: Buys photos; pays $15 to $25.

Equipment Rental and Leasing

RENTAL EQUIPMENT REGISTER, 2048 Cotner Ave., Los Angeles CA 90025. Editor: Leslie Murray. For owners of rental stores and yards of do-it-yourself equipment, sickroom and party goods, and light contractor equipment. Monthly. Not copyrighted. Query first. Enclose S.A.S.E.
Nonfiction: Wants "articles that treat some specific aspect of such a rental firm, in depth: advertising and promotion, branch operations, employee training, equip-

ment maintenance, etc. Information must be accurate." Length: maximum 1,500 words. Pays minimum 5¢ a word.
Photos: Pays $5. Also buys photos with captions only for "Idea Grab Bag" Section. Pays $10. Prefers 8x10 glossies; no color.

Finance

The magazines listed below deal with banking, investment, and financial management. Magazines that use similar material but have a less technical or professional slant are listed in the Consumer Publications under Business and Finance.

BANK SYSTEMS & EQUIPMENT, 1501 Broadway, New York NY 10036. Editor: Alan Richman. For bank and savings and loan association operations executives. Monthly. Circulation: 20,000. Buys all rights. Pays on publication. Query first for style sheet and specific article assignment. Mss should be triple spaced on one side of paper only with wide margin at left hand side of the page. All illustrations should be captioned. Enclose S.A.S.E.
Nonfiction: Third-person case history articles and interviews as well as material relating to systems, operations and automation. Charts, systems diagrams, artist's renderings of new buildings, etc. may accompany ms and must be suitable for reproduction. Prefers one color only. Length: open. Pays $75 for first published page, $45 for second page, and $40 for succeeding pages.
Photos: 5x7 or 8x10 single-weight glossies. Candids of persons interviewed, views of bank, bank's data center, etc.

BURROUGHS CLEARING HOUSE, Box 418, Detroit MI 48232. Managing Editor: Norman E. Douglas. For bank and financial officers. Monthly. Buys all publication rights. Pays on acceptance. Will send a sample copy on request. Query first on articles longer than 1,800 words. Enclose S.A.S.E. for return of submissions.
Nonfiction: Uses reports on what banks and other financial institutions are doing; emphasize usable ideas. Length: 1,000 to 2,000 words; also uses shorter news items. Pays 10¢ a word. Additional payment of $5 for usable illustrations.
Photos: Should be 8x10 glossy b&w. Also buys pix with captions only. Pays $5.
How To Break In: "A beginning writer would be given the same degree of consideration a recognized writer would be given when submitting material to our magazine. We look for factual accounts of ideas that can be of help to our readers, so it's the subject matter that counts."

THE CANADIAN BANKER, Box 282, Royal Trust Tower, Toronto Dominion Centre, Toronto, Ont., Canada. Editor: William Ivens. For bankers and businessmen. Bimonthly. Pays on publication. Will send sample copy on request. Query not necessary but desirable. Reports in 6 weeks. Enclose S.A.E. and International Reply Coupons.
Nonfiction and Photos: History of banking in Canada, international agencies, banking biographies, industries, government developments related to finance and business, legislation. "We generally reject articles that relate only to the U.S. banking system and not to the Canadian banking system." Pays about $175. Prefers photos with articles.

CREDIT AND FINANCIAL MANAGEMENT, 475 Park Ave., S., New York NY 10016. Editor: Thomas C. Cowlan. Special issues: Insurance (Oct.), Financing (Nov.), Convention (April). Monthly. Buys all rights. Pays on acceptance. Will send free sample copy to a writer on request. Query first. Enclose S.A.S.E.
Nonfiction: Articles on credit office practices for manufacturers and wholesalers; should be specific, to the point. Wants articles dealing with credit and finance; not consumer or personal credit. Length: 2,000 to 3,000 words. Pays $100 to $200.
Photos: Purchased with captions only. Pays $15 to $25.

FINANCIAL QUARTERLY, P. O. Box 14451, North Palm Beach FL 33408. Editor: Thomas A. Swirles. For "bank and savings and loan presidents, vice-presidents, etc." Established in 1969. Quarterly. Circulation: 64,000. Rights purchased vary with author and material. Pays on publication. Will send a sample copy to a writer on request. Submit complete ms. Will consider photocopied submissions. Reports on material accepted for publication "at closing." Returns rejected material in 1 month. Enclose S.A.S.E. for return of submissions.
Nonfiction and Photos: "Bank product information, trends in banking, etc." Buys informational articles, how-to's, interviews, and coverage of merchandising techniques. Length: 500 to 750 words. Pays $200 to $500. Photos purchased with mss.

THE INDEPENDENT BANKER, Box 267, Sauk Centre MN 56378. Editor: Bill McDonald. For bankers. Monthly. Buys all rights, but will consider simultaneous rights. Pays on acceptance. Will send free sample copy to writer on request. Query first. Reports in 1 month. Enclose S.A.S.E.
Nonfiction and Photos: Human interest or how-to-do-it articles that will appeal to officers of independent banks in small communities. Avoid articles slanted toward large branch or holding company banks and savings and loans. Length: open. "Our top rate (for articles professionally written that do not require extensive rewriting) is 5¢ a word. Less professional articles or 'top of the head' pieces, of course, would not receive the top rate. Maximum payment for any article, regardless of word count, is $100, unless we negotiate for a story with a recognized authority in the field." Photos purchased with mss. 8x10 or 5x7 b&w glossies. Pays $5.

INSTITUTIONAL INVESTOR, 140 Cedar St., New York NY 10006. Editor: Peter Landau. For "professional investors, financial officers, security analysts, etc." Monthly. Circulation: 20,000. Rights purchased vary with author and material. Buys about 20 mss a year. Pays on acceptance. Query first. Reports on query in 2 to 6 weeks. Enclose S.A.S.E.
Nonfiction: "Articles of interest to money managers. Bought only under specific assignment from us." Length: 1,000 to 3,000 words. Pays $300 to $400.

INVESTMENT DEALERS' DIGEST, 150 Broadway, New York NY 10038. Editor: Alfred J. Naylor. Weekly. Buys all rights. Pays on acceptance. Will send free sample copy to a writer on request. Reports in 1 month. Enclose S.A.S.E. for return of submissions.
Nonfiction and Photos: Articles of interest to professional investment men—banks, bankers, investment trusts, insurance companies; new developments in the investment field. Length: 1,500 words. Pays 3¢ a word. Photos purchased with ms. Must have action.

THE MAGAZINE OF BANK ADMINISTRATION, P.O. Box 500, Park Ridge, IL 60068. Editor: F.G. McCabe. For bank operating officers, controllers, auditors. Monthly. Buys all rights or reprint rights. Pays on publication. Will send sample copy on request. Query first. Enclose S.A.S.E.
Nonfiction and Photos: Case studies of new or improved banking procedures, equipment, or methods. Payment depends on amount of research, and value of article. Payment for photos usually included with manuscript.

MERGERS & ACQUISITIONS, 1621 Brookside Rd., McLean VA 22101. Editor: Stanley Foster Reed. For presidents and other high corporate personnel, financiers, buyers, stockbrokers, accountants, and related professionals. Quarterly. Buys all rights. Pays 21 days after publication. Will send a free sample copy to a writer on request. Highly recommends query with outline of intended article first. Include 50-word autobiography with ms. Enclose S.A.S.E. for response to queries and return of submissions.
Nonfiction: "Articles on merger and acquisition techniques (taxes, SEC regulations, anti-trust, etc.) or surveys and roundups emphasizing analysis and description of trends and implications thereof. Articles should contain 20-60 facts per 1,000 words (names, dates, places, companies, etc.). Accurate research is a must and footnote references should be incorporated into text. Avoid 'Company A, Company B' ter-

minology." Length: maximum 10,000 to 15,000 words. Pays $50 to $100 per 1,000 printed words for freelance articles; $200 honorarium or 200 reprints for articles by professional business persons, such as lawyers, investment analysts, etc.

MICHIGAN INVESTOR, 1629 W. Lafayette Blvd., Detroit MI 48216. Editor: George A. Harding. For bankers, brokers, executives. Query first. Enclose S.A.S.E.
Nonfiction: Articles dealing with new bank procedure, machines, supplies, etc. Also building or equipment innovations; special bank openings or service promotions; personality sketches. Length: 500 to 1,500 words. Pay varies.
Photos: Buys 8x10 photographs with mss and with captions only. Pays $5.

PACIFIC BANKER AND BUSINESS, 1 Yesler Way, Seattle WA 98104. Editor: David C. Rankin. For banking and finance people. Monthly. Buys all rights. Pays on acceptance. Will send sample copy on request. Query first. Reports in 2 weeks. Enclose S.A.S.E.
Nonfiction: Uses features pertaining to finance and business. Length: 1,000 words. Pays $35 to $100.

Fishing

CANADIAN FISHERMAN AND OCEAN SCIENCE, Gardenvale, Que., Canada. Editor: Allan Muir. Not copyrighted. Pays on publication. Will send a sample copy to a writer on request. Reports in 1 month. Enclose S.A.E. and International Reply Coupons for return of submissions.
Nonfiction: Articles describing new developments in commercial fisheries and oceanography. Will also consider sketches and controversial articles about Canadian fisheries and oceanological developments. Style should be strictly factual and easy to read. Length: up to 1,000 words. Pays 3¢ to 5¢ per word.
Photos: Buys photos with mss and with captions only. Pays $3 and up.

FISHING GAZETTE, 461 Eighth Ave., New York NY 10001. Editor: Robert J. Burns. For "commercial fishermen, processors, wholesalers, distributors. They are in their 40's and 50's and have an average education." Established in 1879. Monthly. Circulation: 19,000. Buys all rights. Buys 8 to 12 mss a year. Pays on publication. Will send a sample copy to a writer on request. Query first. Will not consider photocopied submissions. Reports on material accepted for publication in 2 to 3 weeks. Returns rejected material in 1 week. Enclose S.A.S.E.
Nonfiction and Photos: "Articles related to commercial fishing operations of the world. The emphasis should be on how-to or 'this is the secret of our success." Buys informational articles, how-to's, coverage of successful business operations and merchandising techniques. Length: "2 to 3 printed pages (about 750 words to a page), including photos." Pays $75 average. Captioned b&w glossies purchased with mss; 5x7 minimum. No fillers or cartoons.

NATIONAL FISHERMAN, Camden ME 04843. Editor: David R. Getchell. For commercial fishing and boat building readership. Monthly. Buys one time rights. Pays on acceptance. Will send free sample copy to a writer on request. Data sheets available. Article proposals should be accompanied by sample of work. Reports in 2 to 3 weeks. Enclose S.A.S.E.
Nonfiction: "Features and articles pertaining to commercial fishing, boat building and general marine subjects. Prefers informal style, human interest, unpretentious approach. Some technical detail necessary in certain stories." Length: maximum 3,000 words. Pays 50¢ per column inch; more for text and photo package.
Photos: Purchased with mss or with captions. Good quality, size varies. Prefers 5x7 or 8x10 b&w; can use b&w snapshots. Pays $5.
Fillers: Long or short news items pertaining to commercial fishing, boat building and general marine subjects. Pays 50¢ per column inch.

Florists, Nurserymen, and Landscaping

FLORAFACTS, Box 9, Leachville AR 72438. Director of Publications: Ron Looney. Free to Florafax International members: wholesalers, retailers, and associations in the floral industry. Monthly. Circulation: 8,500. Buys second serial rights. Pays on publication. Will send a free sample copy to a writer on request. No query required. Returns rejected material "immediately; others held for consideration." Enclose S.A.S.E. for return of submissions.
Nonfiction: Wants articles that will help improve the retail flower business. Would like interesting pieces on successful advertising promotions, merchandising, interior decorating and worthwhile business innovations for the small retail shop. Not necessary, but prefers articles about members of Florafax International when specific case histories are handled. Pays 3¢ a word.
Photos: Pays $5 each for 8x10 b&w glossies with mss.

FLORIST, 900 West Lafayette, Detroit MI 48226. Editor: Frank J. Baccala. For retail and wholesale florists. Monthly. Circulation: 21,000. Buys all rights. Pays on acceptance. Will send a sample copy to a writer on request. No query required. Submit seasonal material 3 months in advance. Reports in 3 weeks. Enclose S.A.S.E.
Nonfiction and Photos: Shop management, sales promotion, developments in flower culture. "No articles that glorify the individual florist." Length: 500 to 1,200 words. Pays 4¢ a word. Photos purchased with mss. B&w glossies, color transparencies. Pays $5 to $30.

FLOWER NEWS, 549 W. Randolph St., Chicago IL 60606. Editor: Barbara Gilbert. Weekly. Enclose S.A.S.E. for return of submissions.
Nonfiction: Uses retail advertising, merchandising, how-to articles of interest to retail florists. "We accept articles already researched and complete on subjects having to do with promotional ideas, holiday business, how to set up a flower shop. No articles on specific flower shops. Also accept articles of a technical nature." Pays $10.

SEED TRADE NEWS, 5100 Edina Ind. Blvd., Edina MN 55435. Publisher: S.M. Dean. For "grower, wholesaler, and retail seedsmen." 40 times a year. Not copyrighted. Will send a sample copy to a writer on request. Enclose S.A.S.E.
Nonfiction: Articles which pertain to the seed industry. Length: about 500 words. Pay negotiable.

SOUTHERN FLORIST AND NURSERYMAN, P.O. Box 1868, Fort Worth TX 76101. Executive Editor: Jim Martin. Weekly. Not copyrighted. Pays on publication. Enclose S.A.S.E. for return of submissions.
Nonfiction: Good promotion, sales methods, management, etc., being used successfully by full-time florists, landscapemen, nurserymen and garden center operators. Articles should be written on trade journal level, aimed at specific group. Art where applicable.

TELEFLORA SPIRIT, 35 E. Wacker Dr., Chicago IL 60601. Editor: Robert Harker. Official publication of Teleflora, Inc. for retail florist subscribers to Teleflora's flowers-by-wire service. Monthly. Circulation: about 12,000. Buys one-time rights in floral trade magazine field. Pays on acceptance. Query first. Reports in 2 weeks. Enclose S.A.S.E.
Nonfiction: Articles dealing with selling, designing, managing, bookkeeping, remodeling, etc., slanted to the retail florist. Avoid growing, wholesaling aspects. Any florist mentioned must be a Teleflorist. Length: 800 to 1,000 words. Pays 5¢ a word.
Photos: Purchased with mss or captions only; 8x10 glossies preferred. Pays $5. Captions required.

WEEDS, TREES AND TURF MAGAZINE, 9800 Detroit Ave., Cleveland OH 44102. Editor: James A. Sample. For "the field of vegetation maintenance including turf management, weed and brush control, and tree care." Established: 1961. Monthly. Circulation: 35,000. Rights purchased vary with author and material. Buys all rights but will reassign rights to author after publication. Buys 20 mss a year. Payment on acceptance. Will send free sample copy to writer on request. Write for copy of guidelines for writers. Query first. Submit seasonal material 3 months in advance. Reports on material accepted for publication in 30 days. Returns rejected material immediately. Enclose S.A.S.E.

Nonfiction: Articles on "cultural practice pertaining to commercial turfgrass maintenance and production; maintenance and production of trees, plus weed control practices." Informational, how-to, personal experience, interview, successful business operations, merchandising techniques and technical. Length: 500 to 1,500 words. Pays $50 to $200.

Food Products, Processing, and Service

In this list are journals for food wholesalers, processors, warehousers, caterers, institutional managers, and suppliers of grocery store equipment. Publications for grocery store operators are classified under Groceries. Journals for food vending machine operators will be found under Coin-Operated Machines.

CANNER/PACKER, P.O. Box 664, Barrington IL 60010. Editor: R.L. McKee. Buys all United States rights. Pays on publication. Enclose S.A.S.E.
Nonfiction and Photos: "Short, punchy articles on canned, dehydrated, or frozen food processing." Pays "$25 to $50, including photos."

CATERING EXECUTIVE NEWSLETTER, P.O. Box 788, Lynbrook NY 11563. Editor: Janet J. Kimmerly. For "social caterers, 40 to 60 years old, most educated with one or two years of college." Established in 1965. Bimonthly. Not copyrighted. Buys about 6 mss a year. Pays on publication. Will send a sample copy to a writer on request. Write for copy of guidelines for writers. Query first. Will consider photocopied submissions. Returns rejected material in 2 weeks. Reports on a ms accepted for publication in 1 month. Enclose S.A.S.E.
Nonfiction and Photos: "News and news features on catering of affairs and catering operations nationwide. The writer should emphasize the specifics of how an individual caterer operates." Buys informational articles, interviews, profiles, and technical articles. Length: 300 to 400 words. Pays 4¢ a word. B&w glossies purchased with mss; captions optional. Pays $5.

FOOD MANAGEMENT, 757 Third Ave., New York NY 10017. Editor: William B. Patterson. For the institutional foodservice field (schools, colleges, nursing homes, hospitals, contract feeders). Monthly. Circulation: 45,000. Buys all rights. Payment on acceptance. Write for copy of guidelines for writers. Query first. Enclose S.A.S.E.
Nonfiction and Photos: Articles on food purchasing and storage, menu planning, food preparation and cooking, methods of serving, sanitation, employee motivation, security, legislation. Length: 2,000 to 3,000 words. Pays 7¢ per word. Strong, action type b&w photos and 35mm color. Pays $5 for b&w; $7.50 for color.

FREEZER PROVISIONING, 10225 Bach Blvd., St. Louis MO 63132. Editor: Albert Todoroff. For meat processors, locker plant operators, freezer provisioners, portion control packers, meat dealers, and food service (food plan) operators. Monthly. Pays on acceptance. Reports in 2 weeks. Enclose S.A.S.E. for return of submissions.
Nonfiction, Photos, and Fillers: Buys feature-length articles and shorter subjects pertinent to the field. Length: 1,000 words for features. Pays 1½¢ a word. Pays $3.50 for photos.

GROUPS & CHAINS MAGAZINE, 1100 Jorie Blvd., Oak Brook IL 60521. Editor: Richard W. Mulville. For "executives with food wholesalers and corporate food chains." Established: 1931. Monthly. Circulation: 15,000. Buys all rights, but will reassign rights to author after publication. Buys 40 to 60 mss a year. Payment on publication. Will send free sample copy to writer on request. Write for copy of

guidelines for writers. Query first. Reports on material in 1 week. Enclose S.A.S.E.
Nonfiction and Photos: Only assigned articles are accepted. Length: 1,500 to 2,500 words. Pays $100 per article. B&w photos purchased with ms. Captions required.

KITCHEN PLANNING, 757 Third Ave., New York NY 10017. Editor: Freda Barry. Buys all rights. Pays on acceptance. Query first. Enclose S.A.S.E.
Nonfiction and Photos: How-to, in-depth articles on designing institutional food service—installations based on actual experience of specific operation—with quotes, facts, figures. Length: 1,000 to 1,500 words. Kitchen floor plans must accompany ms. B&w glossies purchased with ms.

PRODUCE NEWS, 6 Harrison St., New York NY 10013. Editor: Walter H. Preston. For "commercial growers and shippers, receivers, and distributors of fresh fruits and vegetables, including chain store produce buyers and merchandisers." Established in 1897. Weekly. Circulation: 5,000. Not copyrighted. Pays on publication. Will send a sample copy to a writer on request. Query first. "Our deadline is Wednesday afternoon before Friday press day each week." Enclose S.A.S.E.
Nonfiction and Photos: "News is our principal stock in trade, particularly trends in crop growing, distributing, and marketing. Tell the story clearly, simply, and briefly." Buys informational articles, how-to's, profiles, spot news, coverage of successful business operations, new product pieces, articles on merchandising techniques. Length: "no special length." Pays 40¢ a column inch. 8½x11 b&w glossies purchased with ms.

QUICK FROZEN FOODS, 757 Third Ave., New York NY 10017. Editor/General Manager: Joseph V. Angione. Monthly. Buys all rights but will release any rights on request. Pays on publication. Query first. Will give guaranteed assignments by special arrangement. Will accept names for standing file of correspondents who would be given assignments when and if story broke in their locality. Reports in 30 days. Enclose S.A.S.E.
Nonfiction and Photos: Uses feature articles and short articles on frozen food operations in processing plants, wholesalers' warehouses, chain stores and supermarkets. Good articles on retailing of frozen foods. Can also use articles (all lengths) and photos on frozen foods in any foreign country, whether packer, retailer, distributor, or warehouse level. Pays 2¢ to 3¢ a word. Pays $5 a photo.
Fillers: $1 minimum for clippings.

Fur

FUR TRADE JOURNAL, Bewdley, Ont., Canada. Editor: Charles Clay. For fur ranchers in mink, chinchilla, rabbit, nutria; and for all aspects of fur pelt sales, garment manufacture, garment retailing. Monthly. Buys First Canadian rights. Pays on publication. Will send free sample copy on request. Query required. Limited amount of freelance material used. Reports "immediately." Enclose S.A.E. and International Reply Coupons.
Nonfiction: Articles on anything of practical value and interest to fur ranchers. Length: up to 1,500 words. Pays 2¢ per word.
Photos: Purchased with mss; dealing with fur ranching. Pays $3-$5.

U.S. FUR RANCHER, 3055 N. Brookfield Rd., Brookfield WI 53005. Publisher: Bruce W. Smith. For mink farmers. Monthly. Pays on publication. Will send free sample copy on request "by letter, not postcard. Market extremely limited for 1974; queries imperative, including names and addresses of proposed interview subjects." Reports "immediately." Enclose S.A.S.E. for return of submissions.
Nonfiction and Photos: "Articles and photos on mink-ranch operations, based on interviews with manager or owner. Not interested in any fur-bearing animals except

mink. Opportunities for freelancers traveling to foreign nations in which mink are raised." Length: 1,000 to 2,000 words. Pays $30 to $75 per article, including four contact prints at least 2¼ square.

Gas

BUTANE-PROPANE NEWS, P.O. Box 3027, Arcadia CA 91006. Editor-Publisher: William W. Clark. For LP-gas distributor dealers with bulk storage plants, LP bottled gas dealers and manufacturers of appliances and equipment. Monthly. Buys all rights. Pays on publication. Will send free sample copy on request. Query preferred. Reports in 1 week. Enclose S.A.S.E.
Nonfiction: Articles on advertising and promotional programs; plant design, marketing operating techniques and policies; management problems; new, unusual or large usages of LP-gas. Completeness of coverage, reporting in depth, emphasis on the why and the how are musts. "Brevity essential but particular angles should be covered pretty thoroughly." Pays 3¢ per word or $30 per page.
Photos: Purchased with mss. 8x10 desired but not required; can work from negatives. Pays $5.
Fillers: Clippings and newsbreaks pertinent to LPG industry. Clippings regarding competitive fuels (electricity, oil) with relationship that would have impact on LPG industry. Pays $4 minimum for clippings.

GAS APPLIANCE MERCHANDISING, 1 East First St., Duluth MN 55802. Editor: James Couillard. For gas appliance dealers, builders, plumbers, contractors, and gas utility personnel. Bimonthly. Buys all rights. Pays on acceptance. Will send free sample copy on request. Write for copy of guidelines for writers. Reports in 1 week. Enclose S.A.S.E. for return of submissions.
Nonfiction: "Gas appliance dealer case histories. Articles on gas utility promotions. Marketing trends, displays." Length: 800 to 1,500 words. Pays 5¢ to 6¢ per word.
Photos: Purchased with mss or with captions only. 5x7 glossies. Pays $5 to $7.

GAS FUTURE, 3910 Lindell Blvd., St. Louis MO 63108. Editor: Robert Tibbs. Gas utility employees and executives. Expository articles. Established 1967. Monthly. Circulation: 15,000. Buys all rights, but will reassign rights to author after publication. Buys 10 mss a year. Payment on publication. Query first. Will consider photocopied submissions. Submit special or seasonal material 2 months in advance of issue date. Reports on material accepted for publication in 2 weeks. Returns rejected material immediately.
Nonfiction and Photos: "Must cover natural gas industry subject matter." Informational, how-to, personal experience, interview, profile, inspirational, humor, historical, think, expose, nostalgia, spot news, new product. Length: open. Pays $5 to $100. B&w photos purchased with accompanying ms or without ms. Captions required. Pays $10 to $50 for the latter.

LP-GAS, 1 East First St., Duluth MN 55802. Editor: James Couillard. For liquefied petroleum gas marketers. Monthly. Buys all rights. Pays on acceptance. Query first. Enclose S.A.S.E.
Nonfiction: Uses dealer and LP-gas utilization articles, "how-to" features on selling, delivery, service, etc. Tersely written, illustrated by photo or line for documentation. Length: maximum 1,500 words. Pays 5¢ a word.
Photos: Pix with mss or captions only not less than 4x5. Pays $5 to $7.

NLPGA TIMES, 79 W. Monroe St., Chicago IL 60603. Editor: Charles J. Huck, Jr. For LP-gas dealers. Quarterly, supplemented by periodic newsletters. Buys first publication rights, reprint rights and possibly simultaneous rights. Pays on publication. Will send a sample copy to a writer on request. Query first. Reports in 10 days. Enclose S.A.S.E.
Nonfiction: Wants articles on reports of new sales promotions, and new operating practices by LP-gas dealers. Length: 500 to 750 words. Pays $25 per published page.

Photos: Uses 8x10 glossies with mss or captioned photos, which must be sharp and have good contrast for reproduction. Pays $7.50 each.

Government and Public Service

Below are journals for individuals who provide governmental services, either in the employ of local, state, or national governments or of franchised utilities. Included are journals for city managers, politicians, civil servants, firemen, policemen, public administrators, urban transit managers, utilities managers, etc.

Publications that emphasize the architectural and building side of city planning and development are classified in Architecture. Publications for lawyers are found in the Law category. Journals for teachers and administrators in the schools are found in Education. Publications for private citizens interested in politics, government, and public affairs are classified with the Politics and World Affairs magazines in the Consumer Publications section.

THE CALIFORNIA HIGHWAY PATROLMAN, 1225 8th St., Suite 150, or P.O. Box 2631, Sacramento CA 95812. Editor: Joseph L. Richardson. "Half of our audience are California highway patrolmen, the other half are citizens interested in traffic safety: parents, driver education teachers, doctors (for their waiting rooms), lawyers, truckers, businessmen, and more. We are the nation's only traffic safety magazine published for the entire family." Monthly. Circulation: 11,500. Buys all rights, but will reassign rights to author after publication. Buys 72 mss a year. Pays on publication. Will send a free sample copy to a writer on request. Write for copy of guidelines for writers. Submit seasonal material 3 months in advance. No query required. Reports in 1 month. Enclose S.A.S.E. for return of submissions.
Nonfiction and Photos: "We are not a technical journal." Articles should be written in "magazine free style." Wants "general interest articles on traffic safety and drivers education. Also Old West and travel pieces—usually one per issue." No poetry, fiction, or fillers. "Not interested in law enforcement subjects unless they deal with traffic safety." Length: 800 to 3,500 words. Pays 2¢ a word. Payment is $2.50 a photo for b&w glossies purchased with mss.

CAMPAIGN INSIGHT, Petroleum Bldg., Wichita KS 67202. Editor: Hank Parkinson. For "persons who are politically oriented who are interested in staying abreast of the latest political techniques." Established: 1969. Every 2 weeks. Circulation: 4,000. Buys first North American serial rights. Buys 35 to 40 mss a year. Payment on acceptance. Will send free sample copy to writer on request. Query first. Will consider photocopied submissions. Reports on material in 30 days. Enclose S.A.S.E.
Nonfiction and Photos: "Strictly how-to material. We like profiles on campaigns at all levels—city to the White House—as long as they're liberally laced with specific techniques that lead to the win or loss. No partisan material or philosophy wanted—just the nuts and bolts of good campaigning. We only assign from queries. Any facet of any political technique will get a good hearing from us." Length: 800 to 1,200 words. Pays 3¢ per word. B&w photos; 5x7 minimum. Pays $5 per half-tone.

FIRE CHIEF MAGAZINE, 625 N. Michigan Ave., Chicago IL 60611. Editor: William Randleman. For chiefs of volunteer and paid fire departments. Buys all rights. Will not consider simultaneous submissions or material offered for second rights. Pays on publication. Reports in 10 days. Enclose S.A.S.E. for return of submissions.
Nonfiction: Wants articles on fire department administration, training, or firefighting operations. Will accept case histories of major fires, extinguished by either volunteer or paid departments, detailing exactly how the fire department fought the fire and the lessons learned from the experience. "Prefer feature articles to be bylined by a fire chief or other fire service authority." Writing must be simple, clear, and detailed, preferably conversational in style. Pays $1 to $1.50 per column inch.
Photos: Used with mss or with captions only. 4x5 or larger; Polaroid or other small

prints of individuals or small subjects accepted. Pays up to $35 for acceptable color photos. Pays nothing for public domain photos, up to $5 for exclusives, $1 for mug shots.

FIRE ENGINEERING, 666 Fifth Ave., New York NY 10019. Editor: James F. Casey. For commissioners, chiefs, senior officers of the paid, volunteer, industrial, and military fire departments and brigades. Buys all rights. Pays on publication. Reports in 3 weeks. Enclose S.A.S.E. for return of submissions.
Nonfiction and Photos: Wants articles on fire suppression, fire prevention, and any other subject that relates to fire service. Length: 750 to 1,500 words. Pays minimum 2¢ a word. Good photos with captions always in demand. Particular need for color photos for cover; small print or slide satisfactory for submission, but must always be a vertical or capable of being cropped to vertical. Transparency required if accepted. Pays $15 and up, depending on quality and strength of shot.

FOREIGN SERVICE JOURNAL, 2101 E St., N.W., Washington DC 20037. Editor: Shirley R. Newhall. For Foreign Service officers and others interested in foreign affairs and related subjects. Monthly. Pays on publication. Query first. Enclose S.A.S.E
Nonfiction: Uses articles on "international relations, internal problems of the State Department and Foreign Service, informative material on other nations. Much of our material is contributed by those working in the fields we reach. Informed outside contributions are welcomed, however." Length: 2,500 to 4,000 words. Pays 2¢ to 3¢ a word.

GOOD GOVERNMENT, 1825 K St., N.W., Room 508, Washington DC 20506. Editor: Ada R. Kimsey. For "public personnel and manpower specialists; concerned citizens." Established in 1881. Quarterly. Circulation: 5,000. Acquires all rights, but will reassign rights to author after publication. No payment is made. Will send free sample copy to writer on request. Query first. Will consider photocopied submissions. Returns rejected material in 1 month. Reporting time on material accepted for publication varies. Enclose S.A.S.E. for reply to queries.
Nonfiction and Photos: Articles on "public manpower issues of our times; collective bargaining; fair employment, federal manpower subsidies. *Good Government* serves as a forum for the informed opinions of public manpower leaders and decisionmakers." Informational articles, interviews, think pieces and book reviews. Length: 4,000 to 6,000 words. Captions are required for b&w glossies.

MANPOWER, Dept. of Labor, ML 2212, Washington DC 20210. Editor: Ellis Rottman. For job training, poverty and education specialists. Monthly. Circulation: 30,000. Not copyrighted. Pays on publication. Will send a free sample copy on request. Query preferred. Enclose S.A.S.E.
Nonfiction: Articles on government and private efforts to solve manpower, training, and education problems, particularly among the disadvantaged. Length: 600 to 4,000 words. Payment negotiable.

MODERN GOVERNMENT (SERVICIOS PUBLICOS), P.O. Box 1256, Stamford CT 06904. Editor: Philip R. Moran. For government officials, private contractors and executives of public utilities and corporations in Latin America and Spain (Spanish) and Asia, Australasia, Africa, the Middle East and the Caribbean (English). 9 times a year. Circulation: 42,000. Buys international rights. Pays on acceptance. Will send free sample copy on request. Query advised. Reports in 1 week. Enclose S.A.S.E.
Nonfiction and Photos: All material should be of interest to government officials in developing nations. Strong "how to do it" (but not highly technical) angle on infrastructure development, public works, public transportation, public health and environmental sanitation, administrative skills, etc. Avoid strictly U.S. orientation. Publications go only overseas. Articles are bought in English and translated into Spanish. Length: 1,500 to 2,000 words. Pays $100 to $150 for article with up to 6 photos.

NATION'S CITIES, 1620 Eye St., Washington DC 20006. Managing Editor: Raymond L. Bancroft. For municipal officials, mayors, city managers, councilmen, and department heads. Monthly. Buys first North American serial rights. Pays on acceptance. Will send a sample copy to a writer on request. Query first. Reports in 1 month. Enclose S.A.S.E.

Nonfiction and Photos: Limited budget for freelance material. Wants "articles covering role of city government in improving community development through better administration, new techniques, and cooperation with public and other governments." Prefers mss illustrated with photos or charts and graphs so as to be "quickly meaningful to the harried city executive." Welcomes "pro and con treatment of important subjects and new ideas. We try to run articles which would be of interest to not only city officials in the large metropolitan areas, but also those in smaller and scattered regions. Articles should be fresh, vigorous, active, and accurate, as well as friendly, lucid, easy-to-read, interesting, and valuable to urban affairs decision-makers." Length: 750 to 1,250 words. Pays $50 to $100.

PASSENGER TRANSPORT, 465 L'Enfant Plaza, Room 2900, Washington DC 20024. Editor: Albert Engelken. Published by the American Transit Assn. for those in urban mass transportation. Pays on publication. Very little material bought. Enclose S.A.S.E. for return of submissions.

Nonfiction: Uses short, concise articles which can be documented on urban mass transportation. Latest news only. No airline, steamship, intercity bus or railroad news. Pays 40¢ per column inch.

Photos: Sometimes buys photographs with mss and with captions only, but standards are high. 8x10's preferred. No color.

POLICE TIMES MAGAZINE, 1100 N. E. 125th St., N. Miami FL 33161. Editor: Gerald S. Arenberg. For "law enforcement officers; federal, state, county, local, and private security." Bimonthly. Circulation: 50,000. Buys all rights. Buys 10 to 20 mss a year. Pays on publication. Will send a free sample copy to a writer on request. No query required. Reports "at once." Enclose S.A.S.E. for return of submissions.

Nonfiction and Photos: Interested in articles about local police departments all over the nation including Mexico and Canada. In particular, short articles about what the police department is doing, any unusual arrests made, acts of valor of officers in the performance of duties, etc. Also articles on any police subject from prisons to reserve police. "We prefer newspaper style. Short and to the point. Photos and drawings are a big help." Length: 300 to 1,200 words. Payment is "$5 to $15— up to $25 in some cases based on 1¢ a word." Payment for photos is from $1 for b&w Polaroid to $15 for 8x10 b&w glossies, "if of particular value."

Fillers: Puzzles.

RESERVE LAW, 210 West Olmos, San Antonio TX 78212. Editor: Otto Vehle. Publication of Reserve Law Officers Association of America. For sheriffs, chiefs of police, other law enforcement officials and their reserve components. Established in 1969. Bimonthly. Circulation: "over 10,000." Not copyrighted. Payment on publication. Will send free sample copy to writer on request. Submit complete ms. Will consider photocopied submissions. Enclose S.A.S.E. for return of submissions.

Nonfiction and Photos: "Articles describing police reserve and sheriff reserve organizations and their activities should be informative and interesting. Style should be simple, straightforward, and with a touch of humor when appropriate. We need current features on outstanding contemporary lawmen, both regular officers and reserves." Length: 500 to 2,000 words. "In most cases, ms should be accompanied by high contrast 8x10 b&w action photos, properly identified and captioned." Pays minimum of $10; plus $5 for first photo and $2.50 for additional photos used in same article. Also seeks material for the following columns: "Ichthus," a chaplain's column dealing with Christian law officers (100 to 500 words); "Law-Haw," humorous anecdotes about police work (40 to 60 words); "Fundamentals," basic "how-to's" of law enforcement (100 to 500 words). Payment in contributor's copies or a maximum of $50.

Fiction: "Fictionalized accounts of true police cases involving reserve officers will be accepted if they meet our needs." Length: 200 to 800 words. Pays maximum of $50.

Fillers: Jokes and short humor "of the law enforcement type." Length: 20 to 80 words. Pays maximum of $10.

ROLL CALL, 636 Pennsylvania Ave., S.E., Washington DC 20003. Editor: Sidney L. Yudain, "Nonpartisan Congressional paper for political pros and office holders." Special editions: Welcome Congress, (Jan.); Anniversary, (June); Christmas, (Dec.). Weekly. Circulation: 8,000. Buys first rights. No query required. Reports in 1 week. Enclose S.A.S.E. for return of submissions.

Nonfiction: Political satire, political lore, anecdotes, bright biography, statistics, history. Political vignettes, little-known political events, background on current news (censure, seniority, etc.). Style is breezy, authoritative, but not pedantic. Nothing anti-Congress unless done with a light touch. Length: 250 to 1,500 words. Pays $2.50 to $20.

Photos, Poetry, and Fillers: Subject matter must be political, Congressional. Pays $1 to $5. 8x12 b&w glossies purchased with mss. Wants good satirical poetry on current events. Short humor and puzzles used as fillers.

STATE GOVERNMENT ADMINISTRATION, 20371 Bluffwater, Huntington Beach CA 92646. Editor: David A. Reed. For "top officials, managers, and administrators at the state level in the government of all 50 states." Seeks material for the following special issues: data processing (March/April), personnel management (May/June), highway construction (July/August). Established in 1966. Bimonthly. Circulation: 8,500. Buys all rights. Buys 4 or 5 mss a year. Pays on publication.. Will send a sample copy to a writer on request. Query first or submit complete ms. Submit seasonal material at least 2 months in advance of issue date. Reports in 4 to 6 weeks. Enclose S.A.S.E. for return of submissions.

Nonfiction and Photos: "Innovative methods that states are employing to increase the efficiency of administration, personnel management and training, revenue programs, issues facing states, new methods, procedures, and systems to reduce costs. We are management and administration oriented, as opposed to public works oriented. We are interested in environmental/pollution coverage." Length: 1,000 to 2,000 words. Pays 3¢ a word. 8x10 b&w glossies purchased with mss; captions required. Pays $2.50.

VIRGINIA MUNICIPAL REVIEW, Travelers Bldg., Richmond VA 23201. Editor: Ralph L. Dombrower. For governmental officials. Monthly. Circulation: 10,000. Buys all rights. Pays on publication. Will send a free sample copy on request. Query first. Reports in 10 days. Enclose S.A.S.E.

Nonfiction: Articles on subjects affecting public administration. Length: 500 words. Pays 10¢ a word.

Photos: Purchased with mss. Federal, state, city, town or county governmental subjects. Pays $5.

Groceries

The journals that follow are for owners and operators of retail food stores. Journals for food wholesalers, packers, warehousers, and caterers are classified with the Food Products, Processing, and Service journals. Publications for food vending machine operators are found in the Coin-Operated Machines category.

CANADIAN GROCER, 481 University Ave., Toronto M5W 1A7, Ont., Canada. Publisher: F.M. Shore. Monthly. Buys first rights. Pays on acceptance. Sample copy will be sent on request. Query first. Reports in 2 weeks. Enclose S.A.E. and International Reply Coupons.

Nonfiction and Photos: Articles on solving merchandising problems. Needs correspondents from some regions of Canada, so a Canadian writer should query first to learn if his region is covered. Length: 500 to 1,000 words. Pays 5¢ a word minimum for features, $1.50 an inch for news. Photos purchased with mss: 1 to 4 "clear, well-captioned photos." Pays $5.

THE CAROLINA FOOD DEALER, 1 Charlettetown Center, P.O Box 6066, Charlotte NC 28207. Editor: G. Everett Suddreth, Jr. For retail grocery, general mer-

chandise, wholesale, and manufacturing grocery trade. Monthly. Enclose S.A.S.E.
Nonfiction: Only news of interest to the grocery trade in North Carolina accepted.

CONVENIENCE STORE JOURNAL, 1100 Jorie Blvd., Oak Brook IL 60521. Editor: Richard W. Mulville. For executives of convenience store chains; owners of convenience stores; franchised operators of convenience stores. Established: 1965. Monthly. Circulation: 15,000. Buys all rights. Buys 30 to 40 mss a year. Payment on publication "unless we intend to hold article for undue length of time." Will send free sample copy to writer on request. Write for copy of guidelines for writers. Query first. Reports on material immediately. Enclose S.A.S.E.
Nonfiction and Photos: "In-depth corporate profiles; case history merchandising and operations stories; trend stories. Writer must submit qualifications. We accept only assigned articles." Length: 2,000 words. Pays $100. 4 to 5 b&w photos purchased with ms. Captions required.

DELI NEWS, P.O. Box 706, Hollywood CA 90028. Editor: Michael Scott. For supermarket delicatessen buyers, retail store owners, chain store executives in southern California. Special issues: May, Dairy; June, Hot Dog; July, Sandwich; Sept., Fall Cheese Festival; Dec., Christmas holidays. Monthly. Circulation: 4,000. Not copyrighted. Pays on acceptance. Will send sample copy to writer for $1. Query not required. Enclose S.A.S.E. for return of submissions.
Nonfiction: Delicatessen foods and store operations in southern California. Success stories. How products are made. Personal profile or company stories. Length: 1,500 words minimum. Pays $15 to $40.
Photos: Purchased with mss or captions only. B&w, clear, sharp, glossy. Pays $5 to $25.
Fiction: Humorous, with some connection or relation to supermarkets or food, preferably refrigerated products. Length: minimum 500 words. Pays $15 to $40.
Poetry: About supermarket deli departments or operators. Pays $5 to $10.
How To Break In: "I occasionally do an industry-wide research article on a deli food item. I tried but was unable to get material for an article on herring, which comes out of the Atlantic. Consumer or industry-executive interviews on various industry subjects are always good. I may do one on what is the best location for a deli within the supermarket. Retailers are always interested in merchandising and promotional ideas—including the pros and cons of various advertising methods, in-store displays, couponing, pricing, etc. Product packaging is another important subject. Humorous fiction that is funny, and in some way connected to the food business is always welcome. Every year we need a Christmas feature that deals with foods."

FOODSMAN, 1001 E. Main St., Richmond VA 23219. Attn: Managing Editor. Buys all rights. Query first. Queries handled immediately. Enclose S.A.S.E.
Nonfiction: Uses articles reporting on developments, news, new sales techniques or other features on, or about, middle-Atlantic region food stores and warehouse distribution facilities. Payment varies.
Photos: Buys good, glossy b&w photographs with mss and with captions only.

GROCERY COMMUNICATIONS, 436 W. Colorado St., Glendale CA 91204. Editor: D. David Dreis. For "food retailers in the 11 western states. Their interest: how to make a profit." Special issues: Store equipment/security equipment (February); candy and tobacco (March); health food sales in supermarkets (June); pet products (December). Established in 1970. Monthly. Circulation: 36,000. Buys all rights. Buys about 20 mss a year. Pays on acceptance. Query first. Submit seasonal material 2 months in advance of issue date. Reports in 2 weeks. Enclose S.A.S.E.
Nonfiction and Photos: "We need short news stories on local operators, food brokers, enterprising retailers, new products given a push in local markets, new departments. Local meetings are covered. The writer should take an informative, objective marketing approach. We are very marketing oriented; we do need stringers in the 11 western states." Length: maximum 5,000 words. Pays $25 to $200. Pays $1 for local news clippings. 5x7 b&w photos purchased with mss; captions required.

NON-FOODS MERCHANDISING, 1372 Peachtree St., N.E., Suite 211, Atlanta GA 30309. Editor: Reuben Guberman. For middle to high level executives in the non-food merchandising field and field personnel. Established: 1955. Monthly. Circulation: 15,000. Not copyrighted. Buys 15 to 20 mss a year. Payment 10 days to 3 weeks after acceptance. Will send free sample copy to writer on receipt of 9x12 S.A.S.E. "We suggest reading our booklet 'Entering the Non-Foods Market' (16 pages). It is available to writers for 50¢. Some understanding of our business is essential." Query first. "A calendar of our seasonal themes is available on receipt of 9x12 S.A.S.E. with 16¢ postage." Reports on material within 2 weeks. Enclose S.A.S.E.

Nonfiction and Photos: "Stories of successful approaches to the merchandising of non-foods, that can be emulated. Our orientation is to in-store merchandising; practical, pragmatic ways to increase volume and profits. No 'think' pieces; no 'expert' advice. We have solid sources for these field-reported articles. Read the magazine and follow basic pattern." Length: 500 to 2,000 words. Pays minimum of 3¢ a word. 3 to 6 b&w 5x7 glossy photos purchased with ms. Pays minimum of $5. Color is on assignment only. Pays $10 to $15.

PACIFIC COAST REVIEW, 33 Reed Blvd., Mill Valley CA 94930. Editor: Nina Hamilton. For "those responsible for decisionmaking in the operation of retail food stores, from corner markets and convenience stores to great supers." Established: 1928. Monthly. Circulation: 5,500. Buys first North American serial rights. Payment on publication. Free sample copy on request. Query first. Will consider photocopied submissions. Reports on material in 1 month. Enclose S.A.S.E.

Nonfiction and Photos: "We want tightly written articles with valid facts and figures on individual market operation, or well done articles to give retailers helpful insight into consumer's viewpoint. All material to help operator assess his market position, his competition and the trends that will affect his business. We're strictly regional, concentrated in northern California and the Pacific Northwest, Alaska and Hawaii. Want only personalities and businesses in this area." Length: 300 to 1,500 words. Pays $10 to $100. 4x5 or 8x10 b&w glossy photos purchased with ms or on assignment. Captions required. Pays $5.

Poetry: Light verse related to this field. Length: 4 to 16 lines. Pays $5 to $10.

PROGRESSIVE GROCER, 708 Third Ave., New York NY 10017. Editor: Robert W. Mueller. For supermarket management. Established: 1922. Monthly. Circulation: 90,000. Rights purchased vary with author and material. Buys all rights, but will reassign rights to author after publication. Buys first North American serial rights. Buys first serial rights. Buys 20 to 30 mss a year. Payment on acceptance. Will send free sample copy to writer on request. Write for copy of guidelines for writers. Query first. Will consider photocopied submissions. Reports on material accepted for publication in 2 to 4 weeks. Returns rejected material immediately. Enclose S.A.S.E.

Nonfiction and Photos: Articles on merchandising and industry trends; store operations, unusual successes. Informational, how-to. Should be "simple, factual, unfanciful." Length: 100 to 500 words for short articles; maximum of 1500 words for full-length features. Pays minimum of 5¢ a word. B&w photos purchased with ms. Department Editor: Joseph S. Coyle.

SUPERMARKET MANAGEMENT, 209 Dunn Ave., Stamford CT 06905. For supermarket managers. Quarterly. Buys all rights. Pays on publication. Will send free sample copy on request. Articles on assignment only. Pays $100 to $150. Reports "promptly." Enclose S.A.S.E. for return of submissions.

Grooming Products and Services

AMERICAN HAIRDRESSER/SALON OWNER, 100 Park Ave., New York NY 10017. Editor: Marguerite Buck. For beauty shop owners and operators. Monthly. Buys all rights. Pays on publication. Reports "6 weeks prior to publication." Enclose S.A.S.E. for return of submissions.

Nonfiction: "Technical material; is mainly staff-written." Pays $25 per magazine page.

PROFESSIONAL MEN'S HAIRSTYLIST, 100 Park Ave., New York NY 10017. Editor: John Gangi. For "men and women serving the men's hairstyling and barbering profession." Monthly. Circulation: 70,000. Rights purchased vary with author and material. Buys 10 to 12 mss a year. Pays on publication. Will send a sample copy to a writer on request. Write for copy of guidelines for writers. Query first. Submit seasonal material 2 months in advance of issue date. Enclose S.A.S.E.

Nonfiction and Photos: "Matter only relating to the hairstyling profession. Material should be technical—written from the viewpoint of professionals. Currently overworked are articles on female barbers or hairstylists and unisex salons. We're interested in articles on new trends in men's hairstyling." Buys informational articles, how-to's, interviews, coverage of successful business operations, articles on merchandising techniques, and technical articles. Length: 750 to 2,500 words. Pays $25 to $75. 8x10 b&w glossies purchased with mss and on assignment. Pays $25.

Hardware

In this classification are journals for general hardware wholesalers and retailers, locksmiths, and retailers of miscellaneous special hardware items. Journals specializing in the retailing of hardware for a certain trade, such as plumbing or automotive supplies, are classified with the other publications for that trade.

CHAIN SAW AGE, 3435 N.E. Broadway, Portland OR 97232. Editor: Norman W. Raies. For "mostly chain saw dealers (retailers); small businesses—typically small town, typical ages, interests, education." Monthly. Circulation: 10,000. Not copyrighted. Buys "very few" mss a year. Payment on acceptance or publication—"varies." Will send a sample copy to a writer on request. Query first. Will consider photocopied submissions. Enclose S.A.S.E.

Nonfiction and Photos: "Must relate to chain saw use, merchandising, adaptation, manufacture, or display." Buys informational articles, how-to's, personal experience articles, interviews, profiles, inspirational articles, personal opinion articles, photo features, coverage of successful business operations, and articles on merchandising techniques. Length: 500 to 1,000 words. Pays $20 to $50 ("2½¢ a word plus photo fees"). Photos purchased with mss, without mss, or on assignment; captions required. For b&w glossies, pay "varies."

CHAIN SAW INDUSTRY AND POWER EQUIPMENT DEALER, Louisiana Bank Bldg., P.O. Box 1703, Shreveport LA 71166. Editor: O.M. Word. For chain saw and outdoor power equipment dealers. Bimonthly. Buys first rights. Pays on publication. Will send free sample copy on request. Reports in 1 week. Enclose S.A.S.E. for return of submissions.

Nonfiction: Articles on successful or unusual chain saw and other small outdoor power equipment dealers, explaining factors which make them so. Human interest material necessary. Articles on unusual uses or unusual users of these tools. Articles on dealers whose profits have increased through diversification of stock. Information on new markets and accessory items. Slant to help dealers do a better job of merchandising. Reader audience varies from large hardware dealers in major cities to crossroad filling station shops in rural areas. Length: 1,000 to 1,500 words. Pays 3½¢ a word.

Photos: Purchased with mss or with captions. B&w, sharp, action if possible; caption must include identification. Pays $5.

HARDWARE AGE, Chilton Way, Radnor PA 19089. Editor: John J. Sullivan. For "manufacturers, wholesalers, and retailers in the hardware/housewares/ lawn and garden industry. About half of our circulation is independent hardware retailers, and another significant portion is mass merchandisers." Established in 1857. Monthly. Circulation: 50,000. Buys all rights. Buys about 10 mss a year. Pays on acceptance. Will send a sample copy to a writer for $1. Write for copy of guidelines for writers. Query first or submit complete ms. Will not consider photocopied submissions. Submit seasonal material 3 months in advance. Reports in 3 weeks. Enclose S.A.S.E. for return of submissions.

Nonfiction: "Articles relating how hardlines retailers increase sales and profits through better management, merchandising, etc. Generally these articles are built around a specific product category. Field research by our own editorial staff is quite thorough." Does not want to see "the round-up story on a single store which tells how that one store does a good job—usually, a good job on everything! Tell us how one store does one thing well. Better yet, tell us how several stores in different parts of the country do one thing well. We have a strong emphasis on the large volume hardlines outlet. Also, we aim for features that are more in-depth—both in the information and the geographic coverage. We have on occasion covered such non-merchandising subjects as product liability, consumerism, and black employment in the hardware industry." Length: open. Pays $100 to $125 "for a good piece with text and photos filling three pages." Captioned photos purchased with mss, without mss, or on assignment. "Photo subjects should be the same as nonfiction, and no people in the photos, please." For b&w, submit enlargements or proof sheets and negatives. Pays $10 to $15 per b&w photo, "more for series of related photos." Pays $15 minimum for color enlargements or transparencies. Dept. Editor: Jon Kinslow, Managing Editor.

Fillers: "Short fillers on management/merchandising." Pays $10 to $15. Dept. Editor: Jon Kinslow, Managing Editor.

HARDWARE MERCHANDISING, 481 University Ave., Toronto 1, Ont., Canada. Associate Editor: Starr Smith. For "hardware retailers and hardware and houseware buyers across Canada." Monthly. Circulation: 8,900. Rights purchased vary with author and material. Buys about 12 mss a year. Pays on acceptance. Query first. Enclose S.A.E. and International Reply Coupons.

Nonfiction: "Any articles demonstrating ways to increase profit for the above audience. The approach must be geared to management improving profit/image picture in retailing. This is a Canadian book for Canadians." Buys informational articles, how-to's, coverage of successful business operations and merchandising techniques, new product articles, and technical articles. Length: open. Pay: open. 8x10 b&w glossies purchased with mss; captions optional.

NORTHERN HARDWARE MARKETING, 6121 Excelsior Blvd., Suite 202, Minneapolis MN 55416. Editor: Edward Gonzales. For "owners, managers of hardware and discount stores and lumber yards; hardware, sporting good, wholesalers." Special issues include lawn and garden (Jan., Feb.), fishing tackle (March, April), and hunting equipment (June, July). Established in 1971. Monthly. Circulation: 13,300. Not copyrighted. Buys about 12 mss a year. Pays on publication. Will send a sample copy to a writer on request. Query first or submit complete ms. Submit seasonal material 3 months in advance of issue date. Enclose S.A.S.E. for return of submissions.

Nonfiction and Photos: "Case histories on successful retail stores." Buys how-to's and articles on successful business operations. Pays 4¢ a word. B&w photos purchased with mss. Pays $5.

OUTDOOR POWER EQUIPMENT, 3339 W. Freeway, P. O. Box 1570, Fort Worth TX 76101. Publisher: Bill Quinn. Enclose S.A.S.E. for return of submissions.

Nonfiction and Photos: Photo-story of a single outstanding feature on power equipment stores (lawnmower, snowblower, garden tractors, chain saws, tiller, snowmobiles, etc.). Feature can be a good display, interior or exterior; sales tip; service tip; unusual sign; advertising or promotion tip store layout; demonstrations, etc. Photos must be vertical. One 8x10 photo sufficient. Length: 200 to 300 words. Pays $32.50.

OUTDOOR POWER PRODUCTS, 481 University Ave., Toronto 2, Ont., Canada. Associate Editor: Starr Smith. 8 times a year. Pays on acceptance or on publication "as per agreement." Query first. Enclose S.A.E. and International Reply Coupons.

Nonfiction: "We're interested in any new approach to increase the profitability of an outdoor power products dealer." Length: open. Pay: open.

SOUTHERN HARDWARE, 1760 Peachtree Rd., N.W., Atlanta GA 30309. Editor: Ralph E. Kirby. For retailers of hardware and allied lines. Established: 1900. Monthly. Circulation: 16,000. Buys all rights. Buys 50 mss a year. Payment on acceptance. Will send free sample copy to writer on request. Write for copy of guidelines for writers. Query first. Submit seasonal material 3 to 4 months in advance. Reports on material accepted for publication in 30 days. Returns rejected material immediately. Enclose S.A.S.E.

Nonfiction and Photos: "Articles dealing with the sales and merchandising activities of specific southern hardware retailers; new home centers and stores serving do-it-yourself customers." Successful business operations; merchandising techniques. Bulletin on special seasonal issues should be requested. Length: 4 double-spaced pages, maximum. Pays $30 to $100. 5x7 or 8x10 b&w photos purchased with ms, or without ms. Captions required. Pays $5 to $20, depending on quality.

Home Furnishings and Appliances

APPLIANCE MANUFACTURER, 5 South Wabash Ave., Chicago IL 60603. Editor: William Wingstedt. Buys first North American serial rights. Pays on acceptance. Will send sample copy to qualified writer on request. Query first. Reports promptly. Enclose S.A.S.E.

Nonfiction and Photos: Stories on product design, research and development, use of plastics, new materials, fasteners, adhesives, new packaging of appliances, new ways of materials handling, solutions to appliance problems; any story that will show how something was accomplished and will be of interest to the men and women who design, engineer, manufacture, market major appliances, electric housewares and radio, TV-electronic products. Best to review current issues. Pays $35 per page. "Photos must accompany articles."

AUDIO TIMES, INC., 155 E. 78th St., New York NY 10021. Editor: Robert Angus. For retailers of high fidelity components, tape recorders and related products. Bi-weekly. Pays on publication. Query first. Reports in 1 week. Enclose S.A.S.E.

Nonfiction: Business surveys of specific high fidelity markets, dealer interviews on business conditions, local issues, etc. Dealer stories; how a specific retailer solves a particular high fidelity component sales problem, advertising approach, etc. News regarding audio-industry dealer personnel shifts, new store openings, etc. "We are very much interested in finding stringers in cities in the South, Midwest and Southwest. We will make definite assignments at regular intervals to stringers for which we guarantee payment." Length: 500 to 1,000 words. Pays $10 to $50.

Photos: Purchased with captions only. Pays $5.

BEDDING, 1150 17th St., N. W., Washington DC 20036. Editor: Charles McKee. For manufacturers and suppliers of mattresses, springs, and dual-purpose sleeping equipment. Monthly. Buys North American serial rights. Buys about 12 mss a year. Pays on acceptance. Will send a sample copy to a writer on request. Write for copy of guidelines for writers. Query first. Reports in 2 weeks. Enclose S.A.S.E.

Nonfiction: "Articles on management, manufacturing, and merchandising techniques applicable to the bedding industry; articles on peripheral subjects slanted specifically to bedding industry (for example, packaging as related to mattresses, etc.); articles general enough to be as applicable to mattress makers as to any other industry. Although the industry is specialized and unfamiliar terrain for many writers, queries are encouraged. We would rather redirect a writer's effort than not hear from him at all." Length: 500 to 4,000 words. Pays about 3¢ a published word; "rates for assigned article negotiable."

Photos: B&w glossies purchased with mss and with captions only. Query editor regarding color transparencies. Pays $5 minimum.

CASUAL LIVING MAGAZINE, Time & Life Bldg., 1271 Avenue of the Americas, New York NY 10020. Editor: Marvin L. Wilder. For retailers and manufacturers of

summer and casual furniture and accessories. Monthly. Circulation: 10,500. Buys
all rights. Pays on publication. Query first. Reports in 2 weeks. Enclose S.A.S.E.
Nonfiction: "Articles on how various department stores, discount houses and specialty stores used advertising, promotion, display to improve business. Should be well-written, well-slanted, non-blurb material with good b&w photos." Length: 500 to 1,000 words. Pays $50 to $75.
Photos: Anything pertaining to outdoor and casual furniture industry; purchased with mss. Pays $5 each for 8x10's.

CHINA GLASS AND TABLEWARES, 1115 Clifton Ave., Clifton NJ 07013. Editor: Donald Doctorow. Monthly. Pays on publication. Query first. Reports within 4 weeks. Enclose S.A.S.E.
Nonfiction and Photos: Interested in articles on department store and specialty shop china, glass, silverware and tableware merchandising ideas; special promotion, display techniques, advertising programs, and retail activities in this field. Length: 1,000 to 2,000 words. Pays $30 a published page. Photos with suitable captions should accompany articles.

CONSUMER ELECTRONICS, 155 East 78th St., New York NY 10021. Managing Editor: Cathy Ciccolella. Buys first rights. Pays on publication. Query first. Enclose S.A.S.E.
Nonfiction: Publishes "news stories dealing with successful promotions of home electronics products. New store openings and other news of interest to retailers of radio, TV, high fidelity, tape and other consumer electronics." Pays 5¢ a word as a basic rate, more with photos.

FLOORING MAGAZINE, 757 Third Ave., New York NY 10017. Editor: Michael Korsonsky. For floor covering retailers, wholesalers, floor covering specifiers, architects, etc. Monthly. Circulation: 20,000. Buys all rights. Buys 10 to 20 mss a year. Payment on acceptance. Will send free sample copy to writer on request. Query first. Reports on material in 2 months. Enclose S.A.S.E.
Nonfiction and Photos: "Merchandising articles, new industry developments, etc. Conversational approach; snappy, interesting leads; plenty of quotes." Informational, how-to, interview, successful business operations, merchandising techniques, technical. Length: 1,500 to 2,500 words. Pays 5¢ to 10¢ a word. 5x7 or 8x10 b&w photos. Pays $5. Color transparencies (when specified). Pays $7.50. Captions required.

FURNITURE & FURNISHINGS, 1450 Don Mills Rd., Don Mills, Ont., M3B 2X7 Canada. Editor: Ron Shuker. For "retailers of furniture, furnishings, floor and wall coverings, draperies, and accessories in Canada only." Established in 1910. 10 times a year. Circulation: 11,000. Buys first serial rights. Buys 10 to 15 mss a year. Pays on publication. Will send a sample copy to a writer on request. Write for copy of guidelines for writers. Query first or submit complete ms. Submit seasonal or special material at least 2 months in advance. Enclose S.A.S.E. for return of submissions.
Nonfiction: "Furniture styles and trends; also, floor and wall coverings, contract furnishing; retail success stories: successful promotions, merchandising, displays, etc. Concentrate on details, examples, promotions, etc., that will help a retailer build a strong business. No articles on general management topics without any retailing or personal examples." Buys how-to's, personal experience articles, interviews, profiles, coverage of successful business operations, and articles on merchandising techniques. Length: "depends on factual content." Pays $2.50 per published column inch. Photos purchased with mss; captions required.

FURNITURE DESIGN AND MANUFACTURING, 7373 N. Lincoln Ave., Chicago IL 60646. Editor: Raymond A. Helmers. For furniture manufacturers and designers. Monthly. Usually buys first publication rights. Pays on publication. Query first. Reports in 2 weeks. Enclose S.A.S.E.
Nonfiction and Photos: "Most material is staff-produced. Very, very limited market for freelance writers; then only those with proven technical knowledge." Wants technical and management articles dealing only with the volume mass production

of furniture of all kinds—the methods, materials and tools used by modern, progressive plants. Length: 3,000 words. Pay: open. Photos purchased with ms.

FURNITURE METHODS AND MATERIALS, P.O. Box 16528, Memphis TN 38116. Editor: James D. Powell. For furniture manufacturers and suppliers. Monthly. Not copyrighted. Pays on publication. Query required. Send queries to I. Leon Powell, Managing Editor. Deadline is 10th of month preceding publication. Reports in 1 month. Enclose S.A.S.E.
Nonfiction: Technical articles on furniture manufacturing, processes and materials used. Clear, lucid prose. Length: 2,000 words maximum. Pays 3¢ to 4¢ a word.
Photos: Purchased with mss. Must be appropriate to article. Pays $5.

GIFTS & DECORATIVE ACCESSORIES, 51 Madison Ave., New York NY 10010. Editor: Phyllis Sweed. For the "quality gift and decorative accessories retailer, independent store and department store." Established: 1917. Monthly. Circulation: over 25,000. Buys all rights. Buys 10 to 12 mss a year. Payment on publication. Will send sample copy to writer for $1. Write for copy of guidelines for writers. Query first. Submit seasonal material 2 to 3 months *in advance* of the following deadlines: Bridal, February 15 or July 15; Christmas, July 1; resort merchandising, January 15. Reports on material in 3 months. Enclose S.A.S.E.
Nonfiction and Photos: "We talk about store management, merchandising, interesting promotions and display, dynamic store design and new merchandising. We use stories about stores that do any of the above in a unique, profitmaking way. We are particularly interested in ways that gift retailers promote sales with the bridal market; interesting Christmas shops and promotions; good social stationery and greeting card departments that deviate from the standard company-planned departments. The emphasis should be on merchandising; how big is the store, what kind of customer does it sell? What is the volume, the turnover, the particular selling pitch? What helps the store do its business best? What makes it a successful gift store? We approach the quality market from a merchandising point of view. We do not want stories on discounters or mass merchants. We do not cover antique shops per se. We do not want general store merchandising stories without examples. We do want to see stories on the emerging creative and decorative craft revival as it is being utilized in the gift shop ... the merchandising of ecology ... the year-round resort shop that is not just a souvenir shop." Length: 1,000 to 5,000 words. Pays $25 to $100. 5x7 or 8x10 clear and sharp b&w photos purchased with ms. Pays $7.50. 4x5 transparencies (sharp color prints) or 35mm can be used. Pays $7.50 for 35mm; $15 for 4x5 color photos.

GIFT & TABLEWARE REPORTER, 165 W. 46th St., New York NY 10036. Editor: Jack McDermott. For "merchants (department store buyers, specialty shop owners) engaged in the resale of giftwares, china and glass, decorative accessories." Biweekly. Circulation: 20,000. Buys all rights. Buys 150 to 200 mss a year. Pays on acceptance. Will send a sample copy to a writer on request. Query first or submit complete ms. Will consider photocopied submissions. Reports "immediately." Enclose S.A.S.E. for return of submissions.
Nonfiction: "New store announcements, retail store success stories. Be brief, be factual, describe a single merchandising gimmick. Our distinguishing factor is conciseness, fast-moving factuality. We are a tabloid format—glossy stock. Descriptions of store interiors are less important than a sales performance. We're interested in articles on aggressive selling tactics." Buys coverage of successful business operations and merchandising techniques. Length: 300 words. Pays "minimum $2.50 for first inch on galley, $1 for each additional inch."
Photos: Purchased with and without mss and on assignment; captions optional. "Individuals are to be identified." For b&w glossies, pays $6.
Fillers: "Newsbreaks on new store openings." Length: 50 to 100 words. Pays "$2.50 for first inch, $1 for each additional inch."

LINENS, DOMESTICS AND BATH PRODUCTS, 370 Lexington Ave., New York NY 10017. Editor: Ruth Lyons. For department store, mass merchandiser, specialty store and bath boutique. 6 times a year. Buys all rights. Pays on publication. Query first. Will not consider photocopied submissions. Reports in 4 to 6 weeks. Enclose S.A.S.E.

Nonfiction and Photos: Merchandising articles which educate the buyer on sales trends, legislation, industry news, styles; in-depth articles with photos on retail sales outlets for bath products, linens and sheets, towels, bedspreads. Length: 700 to 900 words. Pays $30 a published page ("the average article is 1 to 3 pages long"). Photos purchased with mss. For b&w glossies, pays $5. For Ektachrome color, pays $30.

MART MAGAZINE, Berkshire Common, Pittsfield MA 01201. Editor: Jack Adams. For retailers, distributors, and manufacturers of home appliances and home electronic items. Semimonthly. Circulation: 54,000. Buys exclusive rights in retailing field. Buys 25 mss a year. Pays on acceptance. Will send free sample copy on request. Query first. Special Christmas Merchandising Issue, deadline Sept. 10; Gift Giving Issue, deadline March; Air Conditioning Issue, deadline Jan. 20. Reports in 3 weeks. Enclose S.A.S.E.

Nonfiction: Articles and case histories showing how retailers successfully merchandise home appliances or home electronic items. Length: 500 to 750 words. Pays $50 to $100.

Photos: Uses photos of good displays, especially Christmas displays. 8x10 glossy preferred; 2¼x2¼ or 4x5 color shots also used. For b&w, pays $10.

NHFA REPORTS, National Home Furnishings Assn., 1150 Merchandise Mart, Chicago IL 60654. Editor: Peggy Heaton. Monthly. Buys North American serial rights. Pays on publication. Reports in 2 to 3 weeks. Enclose S.A.S.E. with query.

Nonfiction: Service articles directed to all phases of furniture store operation—merchandising, selling, display, customer services, promotion, expense control, warehousing, etc. Information must be based on experiences of others in this field. Aim for practicality, "how-to," how others have done it; for "hard-headed merchant" readership. Special articles must be preceded by a query which also describes photo possibilities. Style: tight, crisp, clear. Length: 800 to 2,000 words. Pays 4¢ a word.

Photos: Purchased with mss and occasionally with captions only. 8x10 glossies. Pays $5.

RETAILER AND MARKETING NEWS, P.O. Box 57149, Dallas TX 75207. Editor: Michael J. Anderson. For "retail dealers and wholesalers in appliances, television, and furniture." Monthly. Circulation: 10,000. Buys all rights. Buys 3 mss a year. Pays on publication. Will send a free sample copy to a writer on request. No query required. Will consider photocopied submissions. Mss will not be returned unless S.A.S.E. is enclosed.

Nonfiction: "How a retail dealer can make more profit" is the approach. Wants "sales promotion ideas, advertising, sales tips, business builders, and the like, localized to the southwest and particularly to North Texas." Length: 100 to 500 words. Payment is $5 to $20.

Fillers: Newsbreaks, jokes, short humor.

UPHOLSTERING INDUSTRY MAGAZINE, 600 S. Michigan Ave., Chicago IL 60605. Editor: Kathleen Schmitz. For "upholstery manufacturers, custom upholsterers, furniture designers, fabric distributors." Established in 1888. Monthly. Circulation: 16,000. Buys first North American serial rights. Buys about 6 mss a year. Pays on publication. Will send a sample copy to a writer on request. Query first or submit complete ms. Will not consider photocopied submissions. Submit seasonal material 2 months in advance. Reports "at once." Enclose S.A.S.E. for return of submissions.

Nonfiction and Photos: "Straightforward articles dealing with technical and mechanical aspects of furniture manufacturing, fabric manufacturing and distribution ... businesslike." Buys informational articles, how-to's, interviews, profiles, exposes, coverage of successful business operations, and operations of upholstering and reupholstering. Length: "sufficient for story." Pays $85. Photos purchased with mss; captions required. For b&w glossies, pays $5.

Hospitals, Nursing, and Nursing Homes

In this listing are journals for nurses; medical and nonmedical nursing home, clinical, and hospital staffs; and laboratory technicians and managers. Journals for physicians in private practice or that publish technical material on new discoveries in medicine will be found in the Medical category.

DOCTORS' NURSE BULLETIN, 9600 Colesville Rd., Silver Spring MD 20901. Editor: Evelyn W. Bickford. Quarterly. Occasionally copyrighted. Pays on publication. Reports in a few days. Enclose S.A.S.E. for return of submissions.
Nonfiction: Uses articles of interest to the doctor's nurse. Pays from $5 to $50, depending on length and value.
Photos: Buys photographs with mss and with captions only. No color.

HOSPITAL PHYSICIAN, 550 Kinderkamack Road, Oradell NJ 07649. Editor: Bruce Millar. For physicians in academic medicine or full-time hospital practice, residents and interns. Monthly. Buys all rights. Send for Guide for Contributors. "Study of the magazine is indispensable to the would-be contributor. We welcome informal summaries of proposed articles (with sufficient detail to make clear the intended theme and how it will be developed) as well as completed mss. Every *Hospital Physician* article is founded on a solid base of research or personal experience built around a well-defined clinical, diagnostic treatment. If a ms has these qualities, we'll buy it even in an unfinished state and have our own staff rewrite or supplement the story. We use articles written by physicians only." Address submissions to Assignments Editor. Enclose S.A.S.E. for return of submissions.
Nonfiction: Occasionally buys "penetrating articles that reflect the vitality and ferment in medicine today. Also fast-moving, helpful articles giving practical advice on socio-economic aspects of a young doctor's life and education. Possible subjects could be training, pay, workload, diagnosis, clinical developments, medico-legal problems, career guidance; personal relationships with patients, the public, students; savings, investments, family life, establishing private practice. Our articles contain lots of anecdotes, for-instances, case histories, illustrations. We write about people rather than about things. We like to quote a doctor's actual words, rather than use generalized statements about what he thinks." Length: to 2,000 words. "Factors in evaluating acceptable copy and determining payment (which usually ranges from 5¢ to 20¢ a word) include the nature and importance of the subject matter, and the amount of staff supplementation required."

HOSPITAL PROGRESS, 1438 S. Grand Blvd., St. Louis MO 63104. Editor: Robert J. Stephens. For hospital administrators, paramedical personnel in Catholic hospitals. Monthly. Buys all rights. Query first. Submit ms in duplicate with summary of article enclosed. Reports in 6 months. Enclose S.A.S.E.
Nonfiction and Photos: Uses limited amount of freelance material. "Articles concerning management, with specific application to hospital problems. Also articles dealing with X-ray, public relations, law of hospitals, pharmacy, purchasing, laundry, dietary, lab, housekeeping, etc. Simple, direct writing necessary. Should be well-researched analysis of current problems affecting hospital personnel, written in third person." Length: 1,500 to 3,000 words. Uses 1 to 4 illustrations. Pays $1 per column inch or by previous arrangement.

HOSPITAL SUPERVISOR'S BULLETIN, 681 Fifth Ave., New York NY 10022. Editor: Leslie Brennan. For hospital supervisors of non-medical areas: clerical, laundry, kitchen, maintenance, etc. Semimonthly. Pays on acceptance. Query recommended. Enclose S.A.S.E.
Nonfiction: Interview-based articles, quoting by name topnotch hospital supervisors in public and voluntary hospitals who tell what today's problems are in hospital supervision, how they solve these problems, what results they're getting, illustrated by examples from daily hospital life. Emphasis on good methods of "getting things done through others." Problem areas: motivation, communication, self-development, planning, absenteeism and tardiness, job enrichment, goal-setting, supervising the undereducated, training, disciplining, personnel shortages, getting

employees to accept change. Wants factual, accurate reporting; no "atmosphere" needed. Length: prefers 2- to 3-page articles; a page has about 450 words. Pays $25 a printed page.

LABORATORY MANAGEMENT, 750 Third Ave., New York NY 10017. Editor: Jon W. Mohr. For supervisory scientists in biomedical research and clinical practice. Circulation includes hospital, foundation, government, academic and pharmaceutical laboratory personnel. Monthly. Buys all rights. Pays on publication. Reports in 1 week. Enclose S.A.S.E. for return of submissions.
Nonfiction and Photos: Articles on biomedical research; laboratory techniques; management of laboratory equipment; new or improved instrumentation; laboratory design and facilities; case histories; interviews with research personalities. Length: 1,500 words maximum. Pays $50 per printed page, including photos.
Fillers: News items on life sciences. Length: 2 paragraphs.

MEDICAL LAB, 750 Third Ave., New York NY 10017. Editor: Margaret Howell. Monthly. Pays on publication. Query first. Reports in 1 week. Enclose S.A.S.E.
Nonfiction and Photos: New medical advances as applied to the clinical laboratory. Straight technical material, operational features, economics in the lab, and how-to features are also invited. Length: maximum 1,500 words. Photos should accompany ms. Pays $25 to $100, plus $5 a photo.

MEDICAL RECORD NEWS, 875 N. Michigan Ave., Suite 1850, John Hancock Building, Chicago IL 60611. Editor: Mary J. Waterstraat. For "persons (of all ages) in hospitals and other health care facilities who are responsible for the medical record department; also edited for hospital administrators, information scientists, medical educators; biostatisticians, insurance representatives, systems analysts, medico-legal authorities, federal and state health officials, medical record students, etc." Established in 1928. Bimonthly. Circulation: 12,000. Buys all rights. Buys 3 or 4 mss a year. Pays on acceptance. Will send a sample copy to a writer for $2. Query first. Will consider photocopied submissions. Reports in 2 to 3 weeks. Enclose S.A.S.E.
Nonfiction: "Articles deal with recording and transcribing systems and equipment, record retention, record retrieval, photocopying, microfilming and microfiche, analyzing, summarizing, computerizing, and making available patient case histories for medical research. Do not just play up a specific product or manufacturer—if a system is being utilized which is unique or somewhat unusual, tell why and how, etc., then end the article. Use a fresh, intelligent, instructive, informative approach. We are interested in new systems being put to use or recently initiated; articles that are bylined by registered record administrators or accredited record technicians concerning new products or systems." Buys informational articles, how-to's, coverage of successful business operations, and technical articles. Length: 1,200 to 3,500 words. Pays $45 to $125. Department Editors: Kay Conlon and Marshall Dick.
Photos: Purchased with or without mss or on assignment; captions optional. For 5x7 or 8x10 "sharp, interesting" b&w photos, pays $5 to $10.

MODERN NURSING HOME, 230 W. Monroe St., Chicago IL 60606. Editor: Jane Barton. Monthly. Buys all rights unless special arrangements made. Query first. Send queries to Linda Harper, Managing Editor, or Jane Barton. Enclose S.A.S.E.
Nonfiction: Articles on administration and management, business operation, nursing care, architecture, rehabilitation techniques relating to nursing homes, giving some degree of nursing care. Not interested in material dealing with homes for the aged or retirement developments that offer no care of chronically ill. Pays $35 to $100.
Photos: Pays $10 for 8x10 b&w glossies.

NURSING CARE (formerly *Bedside Nurse*), 250 West 57th St., New York NY 10019. Editor: John J. Johnston. For licensed practical nurses. 12 times a year. Circulation: 65,000. Buys North American serial rights. Pays on publication. Will send free sample copy on request. Query first. Enclose S.A.S.E.

Nonfiction and Photos: Nursing articles geared specifically to licensed practical nurses and their profession. Length: maximum 2,500 words. Pay: open.

PROFESSIONAL MEDICAL ASSISTANT, One East Wacker Dr., Chicago IL 60601. Editor: Esther A. Strom. "About 95% of our subscribers belong to the American Association of Medical Assistants. They are professional people employed by a doctor of medicine." Established in 1957. Bimonthly. Circulation: 18,000. Rights purchased vary with author and material. Buys about 3 mss a year. Pays on acceptance. Will send a sample copy to a writer on request. Submit complete ms. Will consider photocopied submissions. Reports in 2 weeks. Enclose S.A.S.E. for return of submissions.
Nonfiction and Photos: "Articles dealing with clinical, clerical, and administrative procedures in a physician's office. Request our publication to study for the style we require." Buys informational articles, how-to's, and humor. Length: 500 to 2,500 words. Pays $15 to $50. 8x10 b&w glossies purchased with mss; captions required. Pays $20 to $50.
Fillers: Jokes, "crosswords for allied health personnel." No payment.

Hotels, Motels, Clubs, Resorts, Restaurants

Journals which emphasize retailing for bar and beverage operators are classified in the Beverages and Bottling category. For publications slanted to food wholesalers, processors, and caterers, see Food Products, Processing, and Service.

AMERICAN MOTEL-HOTEL-RESORT-HOSPITALITY MAGAZINE, 614 Superior Ave., Cleveland OH 44113. Editor: Martin Judge. For motel and hotel operators. Monthly. Pays on publication. Query first. Enclose S.A.S.E.
Nonfiction: "This is not a travel magazine. We buy articles that contain ideas other lodging operators have found practical and helpful in lowering costs, saving time, serving the public better." Pays 4¢ a word.
Photos: Purchases captioned photos, 5x7 or larger, of superior ways of doing things in hotel, motel, or resort. Pays $10.

THE BAR SERVER HANDBOOK, 820 Second Ave., New York NY 10017. Editor: Allen Schwartz. For bar owners and managers of bar-restaurants, hotels and clubs. Annual. Buys first North American serial rights. Pays on acceptance. Query first. Reports in 1 month. Enclose S.A.S.E.
Nonfiction: "Emphasis here is on merchandising and promotion of the bar operation in quality restaurants, clubs, and hotels. If possible, articles should highlight one or two outstanding merchandising ideas. Good private club operation articles needed." Length: 2,000 words. Pays $100 to $125.

CLUB EXECUTIVE, 1028 Connecticut Ave. N.W., Washington DC 20036. Editor: Paul E. Reece. For military club managers. Monthly. Pays on publication. Reports in 2 weeks. Enclose S.A.S.E. for return of submissions.
Nonfiction: Articles about food and beverages, design, equipment, promotional ideas, etc. Length: 1,500 to 2,000 words. Pays 4¢ a word.

FOOD EXECUTIVE, 508 IBM Building, Fort Wayne IN 46805. Associate Editor: Christian L. Brasher. For restaurant, hotel, cafeteria owners and managers. Bimonthly. Pays on acceptance. Enclose S.A.S.E. for return of submissions.
Nonfiction: Material dealing with restaurant, institutional, industrial, and catering food service (includes government and military) operation and techniques such as cost control, personnel, portion control, layout and design, decor, merchandising. Also new trends in the food service industry, general economic problems, labor situations, training programs for personnel. Must be written for professionals in the

field. Length: 500 to 2,000 words. Pays 15¢ per word.
Photos: "Pertinent photos." Pays $3 to $5.

HOTEL & MOTEL MANAGEMENT, 845 Chicago Ave., Evanston IL 60202. Editor: Robert C. Freeman. Monthly. Buys all rights. Pays on acceptance. Will send free sample copy on request. Query required. Reports in 1 to 2 weeks. Enclose S.A.S.E.
Nonfiction and Photos: Articles on hotel and motel management. Length: 1,000 to 2,000 words. Pays 6¢ a word. Photos purchased with mss. B&w, 8x10 glossies. Pays $5.

KANSAS RESTAURANT MAGAZINE, 359 South Hydraulic St., Wichita KS 67211. Editor: Neal D. Whitaker. For food service operators. Special issues: Christmas, October Convention, Who's Who in Kansas Food Service, Beef Month, Dairy Month, Wheat Month. Monthly. Circulation: 1,400. Not copyrighted. Pays on publication. Will send sample copy for 50¢. Reports "immediately." Enclose S.A.S.E. for return of submissions.
Nonfiction and Photos: Articles on food and food service. Length: 1,000 words maximum. Pays $10. Photos purchased with ms.

MEETING MAKERS, P. O. Box 828, Burbank CA 91503. Editor: Patrick A. Terrail. For "hotel sales managers, passenger traffic coordinators, association executives, convention organizers, meeting planners." Established in 1971. Biweekly. Circulation: over 500. Rights purchased vary with author and material. Pays on publication. Enclose S.A.S.E. for return of submissions.
Fillers: "Short news items."

NATION'S RESTAURANT NEWS, 2 Park Ave., New York NY 10016. Associate Editor: Fred Germain. National business newspaper for "executives of major restaurant chains and owners of the country's better, more prosperous restaurants." Biweekly. Circulation: 48,000. Buys all rights. Buys "several hundred" mss a year. Pays on acceptance. Will send a free sample copy to a writer on request. Reports in 10 days. Enclose S.A.S.E. for return of submissions.
Nonfiction: "News and newsfeatures, in-depth analyses of specific new types of restaurants, mergers and acquisitions, new appointments, commodity reports, personalities. Problem: Most business press stories are mere rehashes of consumer pieces. We must have business insideness. Sometimes a freelancer can provide us with enough peripheral material that we'll buy the piece then assign it to staff writers for further digging." Length: 2,000 words maximum. Pays $5 to $75.
Photos: B&w glossies purchased with mss and with captions only. Pays $10 and up.

RESORT MANAGEMENT, P.O. Box 4169, Memphis TN 38104. Editor: Allen J. Fagans. For "the owners and/or managing executives of America's largest luxury vacation resorts." Monthly. Buys first rights only. Pays on publication. Will send free sample copy on request. Query first. "Editorial deadline is the 1st of the month; i.e., January material must be received by December 1." Reports in 10 days. Enclose S.A.S.E.
Nonfiction and Photos: Articles on how to improve resort operation with examples of successful application; advertising and promotion, entertainment and recreation, operation and maintenance, personnel, furnishings, guest activities, etc. "Length is relatively unimportant—quality is important. Style of writing is unimportant—the idea and facts are all important." Length: average 800 to 1,000 words. Pays up to $50 for article, 60¢ per 20 em, 40¢ per 13 em column inch for news. B&w glossy photos purchased with mss. "Photos of the resort, of its manager, and of the subjects being discussed in the article are a must." Pays $5 per photo.
Fillers: Uses material for the following departments: " 'Resort Report' (a roundup of general news concerning resorts, resort areas, tourism in states, etc. We pay $1 to $5 depending on the length used); 'Resort Personalities' (announcements regarding individuals in the business. Usually job changes, awards, obits, etc. We pay $1 per item, regardless of length); and 'Coming Events' (a calendar of upcoming events of resort interest. We pay $1 per item)." Buys "clippings on business promotions or changes, new developments. Not interested in restaurants or motels and city hotels which are outside resort areas. Clippings must be pasted onto individual sheets of

paper. Paper must include the typewritten or printed name of the individual, address, source, and date. Any clipping not received in this manner will not be paid for. No entire pages from newspapers. Clippings will not be returned." Pays $1.

TAP AND TAVERN, 117 S. 13th St., Philadelphia PA 19107. Editor: Morris Nissman. Biweekly. Circulation: 14,000. Buys rights to exclusive use in Pennsylvania. Pays on publication. Will send a free sample copy on request. Query first to see if promotion conforms to Pennsylvania liquor laws. Reports in 2 weeks. Enclose S.A.S.E.
Nonfiction: Wants merchandising articles featuring promotions designed to build business at bars. Articles should tell of promotion, how it improves business, proprietors' and patrons' reactions, approximate percentage of increased volume, identity and address of bar. Length: 400 to 600 words. Pays 70¢ per inch of published material.
Photos: Pictures illustrating promotions. Pays $5.

Industrial Management

The journals that follow are for industrial plant managers, executives, distributors, and buyers; some industrial management journals are also listed under the names of specific industries, such as Machinery and Metal Trade. Publications for industrial supervisors are listed in Management and Supervision.

AUTOMATION, Penton Plaza, 1111 Chester Ave., Cleveland OH 44114. Editor: Lee D. Miller. For "men who engineer production; interested in concepts, procedures and hardware involving production processes and machines, handling equipment, controls, and manufacturing and information handling plus personal and professional development." Established in 1954. Circulation: 48,473. Buys all rights. Buys less than 20 mss a year. Payment on publication. Will send sample copy to writer for $1. Write for copy of guidelines for writers. Query first or submit complete ms. Will consider photocopied submissions. Submit seasonal material 4 months in advance. Reports on material in "about a month." Enclose S.A.S.E.
Nonfiction and Photos: "Feature articles and short items describing new equipment, new components and free new literature related to our readers' interests. Keep the interests and characteristics of our readers in mind. Try to supply illustrations or ideas for good graphics." Length: 3,000 to 5,000 words. Pays average of $25 per printed page. 8x10 b&w glossies; 3x5 or larger transparencies (8x10 prints) purchased with mss. Captions required.
Fiction: Humorous fiction related to subject matter. Length and payment are the same as for nonfiction.

BUSINESS ILLUSTRATED, 10169 Sherman Rd., Chardon OH 44024. Editor: Donald H. Cornish. 6 times a year. Not copyrighted. Pays on acceptance. Enclose S.A.S.E. for return of submissions.
Photos: Captioned photos of new products and product applications; also pretty girls with products for cover. 8x10 b&w glossies preferred. Payment is $5 to $20.
How To Break In: "What are men interested in as businessmen and in their private life? Unusual 'featurettes' with good photos, captions and information-packed 200-word article might click!"

COMPRESSED AIR, 942 Memorial Pkwy., Phillipsburg NJ 08865. Editor: S. M. Parkhill. For "management and upper management men concerned with the production, distribution and utilization of compressed air and other gases in all industries." Established: 1896. Monthly. Circulation: 100,000. Buys all rights, but will reassign rights to author after publication. Buys 18 mss a year. Payment on publication. Will send free sample copy to writer on request. Write for copy of guidelines for writers. Query first. Will consider photocopied submissions. Reports on material in 2 weeks. Enclose S.A.S.E.
Nonfiction and Photos: "Case histories of pneumatic applications; in-depth articles about companies using pneumatics in construction and mining projects. Unusual

and unique applications of air power. Must be factually and technically accurate, but in a quasi-technical style. This is not a 'how-to' magazine." Informational, historical, think articles, successful business operations, technical. Length: open. Pays $10 to $25 per published page. Photos purchased with ms. Captions required.

ELECTRONIC DISTRIBUTING (formerly *Electronic Distributing & Marketing*), 33140 Aurora Rd., Cleveland OH 44139. Editor: James C. Kincaid. For "the nation's electronic distribution outlets, plus their management and sales personnel." Established in 1937. Monthly. Circulation: 17,500. Buys first North American serial rights. Buys about 6 mss a year. Pays on acceptance. Will send a sample copy to a writer on request. Write for copy of guidelines for writers. Query first. "The writer should provide a basic outline covering the subject to be covered and the people directly involved with the subject." Will consider photocopied submissions. Submit seasonal material 75 days in advance of issue date. Reports in 15 days. Enclose S.A.S.E.
Nonfiction: "Articles that show new management techniques, or which show how product features can be turned into sales benefits. We are marketing and sales oriented; we do not feature technical subject matter. We turn technical matter into language that a layman consumer could understand." Buys informational articles, how-to's, personal experience articles, interviews, exposes, photo features, spot news, coverage of successful business operations, and articles on merchandising techniques. Length: 1,200 words. Pays minimum 2¢ a word or $25 per published page for features.
Photos: Purchased with or without mss or on assignment; captions required. Pays $5 minimum; color rarely used.
Fillers: Clippings. Pays $4.

HANDLING AND SHIPPING, 614 Superior Ave. W., Cleveland OH 44113. Executive Editor: John F. Spencer. For operating executives with physical distribution responsibilities in transportation, material handling, warehousing, packaging and shipping. Monthly. Buys all rights. Pays on publication. "Query first with 50-word description of proposed article."
Nonfiction: "Features case histories and articles on theory. Writer must know field and publications in it; not for amateurs and generalists." Length: 2,000 words. Payment depends on material.

INDUSTRIAL DISTRIBUTION, 16 W. 61st St., New York NY 10023. Editor: George J. Beerkwitt. Monthly. Buys all rights. Enclose S.A.S.E.
Nonfiction: "Articles aimed at making industrial distributors better sales-creating and profit-producing business organizations; wide range of ideas, information, and know-how for the improvement of distributor's overall effectiveness; designed to put distributor management and sales personnel in stronger position to render economic services, on continuing basis, to ultimate users of products they sell and to manufacturers who sell their products through distribution channels." Length: 900 words minimum. Pays "minimum $50 a book page."

INDUSTRIAL DISTRIBUTOR NEWS, 1 West Olney Ave., Philadelphia PA 19120. Features Editor: Brent W. Rosenberger. For industrial distributors, wholesalers of industrial equipment and supplies; business managers and industrial salesmen. Established: 1959. Monthly. Circulation: 31,000. Buys all rights. Buys 15 to 20 mss a year. Payment on publication. Will send free sample copy to writer on request. Write for copy of guidelines for writers. Query first. Reports on material within 6 weeks. Enclose S.A.S.E.
Nonfiction and Photos: "Factual feature material with a slant toward industrial marketing. Case studies of distributors with unusual or unusually successful marketing techniques. Avoid triteness in subject matter. Be sure to relate specifically to industrial distributors." Informational, how-to, interview. Length: 500 to 3,000 words. Pays $50 to $200. 8x10 b&w glossies purchased with ms. Pays $10. 2¼x2¼ color transparencies, but query must precede submission. Pays $20.

INDUSTRIAL WORLD, 386 Park Ave., S., New York NY 10016. Editor and Publisher: S.W. Kann. For plant managers abroad. Monthly. Buys first world rights. Pays on publication. Will send a sample copy to a writer on request. Write for copy of guidelines for writers. Query first. Formal outlines not required; paragraph of copy sufficient. Reports in 30 days. Enclose S.A.S.E.

Nonfiction and Photos: "Interested primarily in articles dealing with application of U.S. industrial machinery and know-how abroad. Clear, factual data necessary. Articles of more than passing interest to plant managers on production tools, techniques, unusual installation, new or novel solutions to production problems, etc. Should be slanted for the overseas plant manager." Length: 1,000 to 3,000 words. Pays "$50 for first printed page of article, $35 for each subsequent page." Photos purchased with mss. 5x7 or 8x10 glossies only; must be clean, professional, quality. ("If necessary, we will make prints from author's negatives which will be returned. Photos supplied, however, are usually not returned.")

MATERIALS MANAGEMENT AND DISTRIBUTION, MacLean-Hunter Ltd., 481 University Ave., Toronto 2, Ont., Canada. Editor: John M. O'Keefe. For materials handling and physical distribution management. Monthly. Buys first North American serial rights. Pays on publication. Will send sample copy on request. Query first. Reports in 1 month. Enclose S.A.E. and International Reply Coupons.

Nonfiction: Uses "articles dealing with the technical aspects and basic fundamentals of the materials handling and physical distribution field. Occasionally job articles are used but these must be specifically oriented to the field. Payment subject to negotiation."

Photos: Photos are bought with mss or with captions only. 8x10 glossies; pays $5 per print.

Fillers: Industrial News, department runs short features on topics related to the field. Length: 200 words. Pays 10¢ a word.

MODERN PLANT OPERATION AND MAINTENANCE, 209 Dunn Ave., Stamford, CT 06905. Editor: Kenneth V. Jones. For plant engineers and managers. Quarterly. Circulation: 55,000. Buys all rights. Pays on acceptance. Will send sample copy on request. "We do not accept any unsolicited work. All assignments come from us and we can use only the people who truly know the field. Send letter stating qualifications and availability." Enclose S.A.S.E. for response to queries.

Nonfiction and Photos: Length: 600 to 1,000 words. Pays $100 to $150.

PURCHASING, 205 E. 42nd St., New York NY 10017. Editor: Walter E. Willets. Biweekly. Buys all rights. "Most material is prepared on specific assignment. Best to query editor regarding acceptability of idea first." Reports in 10 days. Enclose S.A.S.E.

Nonfiction and Photos: Uses "articles on industrial purchasing methods and policies, industrial materials and commodity markets. All material is factual, based on actual practices in representative purchasing departments, preferably derived through interviews with purchasing executives." Length: maximum 1,500 words. Pays $25 per printed page and up. Uses photographs as illustrations for articles.

WORLDWIDE PROJECTS AND INDUSTRY PLANNING, P. O. Box 1256, Stamford CT 06904. Editor: Richard Lurie. For persons in management positions involved in constructing and managing projects abroad. Established in 1966. Bimonthly. Circulation: 20,500. Buys all rights, but will reassign rights to author after publication. Buys about 20 mss a year. Pays on acceptance. Will send a sample copy to a writer on request. Write for copy of guidelines for writers. Query first. Will consider photocopied submissions. Reports in "1 week to 2 months." Enclose S.A.S.E.

Nonfiction: "Sophisticated non-technical articles which will appeal to sophisticated engineers, manufacturers, and contractors working abroad. We're interested in case histories." Length: 3,000 to 4,500 words. Pays $200 to $300.

Insurance

BUSINESS INSURANCE, 740 N. Rush Street, Chicago IL 60611. Editor: Stephen D. Gilkenson. For "corporate risk managers, insurance brokers and agents, insurance company executives. Generally middle-aged (40 to 65). Most have college degrees. Interested in insurance, safety, security, consumerism, employee benefits, investments. Special issues on safety, pensions, health and life benefits, international insurance. Biweekly. Circulation: 38,000. Buys all rights. Buys 75 to 100 mss a year. Pays on publication. Query required. Submit seasonal or special material 2 months in advance. Reports in 2 weeks. Enclose S.A.S.E.

Nonfiction: We publish material on corporate insurance and employee benefit programs and related subjects. We take everything from the buyers' point of view, rather than that of the insurance company, broker, or consultant who is selling something. Items on insurance company workings do not interest us. Our special emphasis on corporate risk management and employee benefits administration requires that freelancers discuss with us their proposed articles before going ahead. Length is "subject to discussion with contributor." Payment is $1.50 a column inch.

INSURANCE JOURNAL, 3200 Wilshire Blvd., Suite 805, Los Angeles CA 90010. Editor: Mark Wells. For "independent insurance agents and brokers, corporate risk managers, insurance adjusters, attorneys, insurance company executives." Established in 1923. Biweekly. Circulation: 4,300. Buys all rights, but will reassign rights to author after publication. Buys "very few" mss a year. Pays on publication. Will send a sample copy to a writer on request. Query first. Submit seasonal material at least 1 month in advance of issue date. Enclose S.A.S.E.

Nonfiction: "News, interviews, feature articles about property/casualty insurance." Buys informational articles, how-to's, interviews, profiles, humor, historical articles, think pieces, spot news, coverage of successful business operations, articles on merchandising techniques, and technical articles. Length: open. Pays $50.

THE SPECTATOR, Chilton Way, Radnor PA 19089. Managing Editor: Leland Witting. For "executives and key brokers in insurance-related fields." Monthly. Query first. Enclose S.A.S.E.

Nonfiction: "In-depth observations relevant to the insurance and financial community, including broad-based statistical studies." Pays $25 to $50.

UNITED STATES REVIEW, 617 West Ave., P. O. Box 505, Jenkintown PA 19046. Publisher: Robert R. Dearden IV. Editor: John C. Duncan and Diane L. Miles. For "insurance agents and brokers who are independent agents and all insurance-related industry in the Middle Atlantic region." Established in 1868. Weekly. Circulation: 5,000. Not copyrighted. Buys about 20 mss a year. Pays on publication. Will send a sample copy to a writer for 25¢. Submit seasonal material 3 months in advance. Enclose S.A.S.E. for return of submissions.

Nonfiction: Buys coverage of successful business operations and articles on merchandising techniques. Length: open. Pay: open.

Jewelry

AMERICAN JEWELRY MANUFACTURER, Biltmore Hotel, Suite S-75, Providence RI 02902. Editor: Steffan Aletti. For manufacturers of supplies and tools for the jewelry industry; their representatives, wholesalers and agencies. Established: 1956. Monthly. Circulation: 5,000. Buys all rights (with exceptions). Buys 2 to 5 mss a year. Will send free sample copy to writer on request. Write for copy of guidelines for writers. Query first. Will consider photocopied submissions. Submit seasonal material 3 months in advance. Reports on material within a month. Enclose S.A.S.E.

Nonfiction and Photos: "Topical articles on manufacturing; company stories; economics (i.e., rising gold prices). Story must inform or educate the manufacturer. Occasional special issues on timely topics, i.e., gold; occasional issues on specific processes in casting and plating." Informational, how-to, interview, profile, historical, expose, successful business operations, new product, merchandising techniques, technical. Length: open. Payment "usually around $25." B&w photos purchased with ms. 5x7 minimum.

INDEPENDENT JEWELER, P. O. Box 3960, Dallas TX 75208. Publisher and Editor: Pat Eskew. For independent jewelry store owners and watchmakers in Arkansas, Louisiana, Mississippi, New Mexico, Oklahoma, and Texas. Established in 1968. Monthly. Circulation: 8,000. Buys first rights. Pays on publication. Submit complete ms. Reports in 1 week. Enclose S.A.S.E. for return of submissions.
Nonfiction and Photos: "Success stories of independent jewelers. News articles about jewelry store owners or employees in its circulation area. Store openings, remodelings, disasters, success stories, retirements, awards. Journalistic style. Taboos are items about chain jewelry stores and crime (unless death or bodily injury occurs, then mention briefly, but do not describe the crime). We want tips from writers in circulation area about independent jewelers in their home towns." Length: 100 to 200 words, news stories; 700 words, features. Pays 3¢ a word. B&w glossy photos purchased with mss. Pays 50¢ a square inch published space.

JEWELER'S CIRCULAR-KEYSTONE, Chilton Company, Radnor PA 19089. Editor: Donald S. McNeil. For "retail jewelers doing over $30,000 annual volume." Monthly. Circulation: 22,000. Buys all rights. Buys 10 or 12 mss a year. Pays on publication. Will send a free sample copy to a writer on request. Query first. Reports "immediately." Enclose S.A.S.E.
Nonfiction and Photos: Wants "how-to-articles, case history approach, which specify how a given jeweler solved a specific problem. No general stories, no stories without a jeweler's name in it, no stories not about a specific jeweler and his business." Length: 1,000 to 2,000 words. Payment is $75 to $100. Also wants "items about promotion or management ideas implemented by a jeweler" for department "Ideas that Pay." Length: 150 to 300 words. Payment is $15. Photos purchased with mss.

MODERN JEWELER, 15 W. 10th St., Kansas City MO 64105. Managing Editor: Dorothy Boicourt. For retail jewelers and watchmakers. Monthly. Pays on acceptance. Will send sample copy only if query interests the editor. Reports in 30 days. Enclose S.A.S.E.
Nonfiction and Photos: "Articles with 3 or 4 photos about retail jewelers—specific jewelers, with names and addresses, and how they have overcome certain business problems, moved merchandise, increased store traffic, etc. Must contain idea adaptable to other jewelry operations; 'how-to' slant. Informal, story-telling slant with human interest. We are not interested in articles about how manufacturing jewelers design and make one-of-a-kind jewelry pieces. Our readers are interested in retail selling techniques, not manufacturing processes. Photos must include people (not just store shots) and should help tell the story." Pays average $70 to $90 for article and photos.

NATIONAL JEWELER, 1501 Broadway, New York NY 10036. Editor-in-Chief: Irving Sherman. For "retail jewelers." Monthly. Buys all rights. Buys about 24 mss a year. Pays on publication. Will send a sample copy to a writer on request. Query first. Enclose S.A.S.E.
Nonfiction: "How-to promotions, new ideas in merchandising, store design, advertising. Our publication presents news in tabloid form." Length: open. Pays 7½¢ a word.

THE NORTHWESTERN JEWELER, Washington and Main Sts., Albert Lea MN 56007. Associate Editor: John R. Hayek. Monthly. Not copyrighted. Pays on publication. Enclose S.A.S.E. for return of submissions.
Nonfiction and Photos: Uses news stories about jewelers in the Northwest and Upper Midwest and feature news stories about the same group. Also buys retail jeweler "success" stories with the "how-to-do" angle played up, and occasionally a technical story on jewelry or watchmaking. Pictures increase publication chances. Pays 1¢ a published word. Pays $2.50 per photo.

SOUTHERN JEWELER, 75 Third St., N.W., Atlanta GA 30308. Editor: Charles Fram. For southern retail jewelers and watchmakers. Monthly. Not copyrighted. Submit seasonal material by the 15th of the month preceding issue date. Enclose S.A.S.E. for return of submissions.
Nonfiction: Articles relating to southern jewelers regarding advertising, manage-

ment, and merchandising. Buys spot news about southern jewelers and coverage of successful business operations. Prefers *not* to see material concerning jewelers outside the 14 southern states. Length: open. Pays 1¢ per word.
Photos: Buys b&w glossies. Pays $4.
Fillers: Clippings "on southern retail jewelers and stores." Pays 50¢ "if used."

Journalism

Because many writers are familiar with the journals of the writing profession and might want to submit to them, those that do not pay for contributions are identified in this list. Writers wishing to contribute material to these publications should write the editors for their requirements or query before submitting work.

AMERICAN PRESS, 651 Council Hill Rd., Dundee IL 60118. Editor: Clarence O. Schlaver. "We do not accept freelance material."

ARMED FORCES WRITER, George Washington Station, Alexandria VA 22305. For military and civilian writers and journalists, public relations personnel with membership in Armed Forces Writers League, Inc. Bimonthly. Not copyrighted. Buys about 20 mss a year. Pays on acceptance. Will send free sample copy on request; send self-addressed 9x12 envelope. Query first or submit complete ms. Will consider photocopied submissions. Reports in 30 days. Enclose S.A.S.E.
Nonfiction: "Articles on writing or other forms of communications (art, photography, public relations, etc.). Material must have positive educational and professional content (how to write and sell); must be authoritative by reason of author's recognized professional achievement. No room for humorous, flippant or trite material." Buys informational and how-to articles. Length: 500-word "shorticles"; 800-1,500-word features. Pays $5 to $10; "better rate depends on quality, significance or timeliness."
Fillers: "Newsbreaks of interest to writers and artists." Length: 300 words. Pays $2.

BLACK WRITERS' NEWS, 4019 S. Vincennes Ave., Chicago IL 60653. Editor: Alice C. Browning. "At present we are not paying."

THE CALIFORNIA PUBLISHER, 9841 Airport Blvd., Los Angeles CA 90045. Editor: Mrs. Peggy Plendl. Does not pay.

CANADIAN AUTHOR AND BOOKMAN, 8726 116th St., Edmonton 61, Alberta, Canada. Editor: Mary E. Dawe. Does not pay.

THE CATHOLIC JOURNALIST, 432 Park Ave. S., New York NY 10016. "We are no longer buying freelance material."

CHICAGO JOURNALISM REVIEW, 11 E. Hubbard, Chicago IL 60611. Editor: Ron Dorfman. No payment.

THE COLLEGIATE JOURNALIST, Box 2707, East Carolina University, Greenville NC 27834. Editor: Ira L. Baker. "We do not pay."

COLUMBIA JOURNALISM REVIEW, 700 Journalism Building, Columbia University, New York NY 10027. Editor: Alfred Balk. All articles are assigned.

CONTENT, 1411 Crescent St., Montreal 107, Que. Canada. Editor: Dick MacDonald. For "working journalists in all media in all parts of Canada, public relations and advertising personnel, journalism students and faculty, and government officials." Established in 1970. Monthly. Circulation: 5,000. Rights purchased vary with author and material; may buy all rights, but will reassign rights to author after publication. Buys about 60 mss a year. Pays on publication. Will send a sample copy to a writer on request. Write "by letter" for copy of guidelines for writers. Query first "with brief 50- to 100-word outline, of suggested article." Will consider photocopied submissions. Enclose S.A.E. and International Reply Coupons.

Nonfiction: "All material deals in one way or another with the profession of journalism and related media activities. By and large, material should deal with Canadian events. There is no other journalism review of national stature in Canada." Seeks freelance material for "Speak-out," which carries "guest editorials and opinionated material regarding the profession," and for "Watering Hole," which carries "light-hearted accounts of refreshment spots." Length: 500 to 3,000 words. Pays $15 to $250.

Photos: Captioned photos purchased without mss. "Subjects should ideally be the same as nonfiction." Prefers 8½x11 b&w glossies. "Also open to photo spreads." Pays $10 to $25 per photo, but fee is negotiable.

Fillers: Newsbreaks and short humor "regarding the profession." Length: open.

EDITOR AND PUBLISHER, 850 Third Ave., New York NY 10022. Managing Editor: Jerome H. Walker, Jr. Weekly. Query first. Enclose S.A.S.E.
Nonfiction: Uses newspaper business articles and news items; also newspaper personality features.
Fillers: "Amusing typographical errors found in newspapers." Pays $2.

FOLIO, 125 Elm St., P.O. Box 696, New Canaan CT 06840. Editor: Charles I. Tannen. For publishing company executives. Query first. Enclose S.A.S.E.
Nonfiction: "Covers 6 specific areas of interest to executives of magazine publishing companies: management, sales, circulation, production, editing, and graphics. All material should be written with our audience in mind. Above all, we are a how-to magazine, and every story should have information that can be applied by magazine publishers." Length: about 3,500 words; "articles for each of the departments (1 department for each of the areas mentioned above) run to about 1,800 words." Payment to be negotiated.

THE JOURNALISM EDUCATOR, Department of Journalism, University of Nevada, Reno NV 89507. Editor: LaRue W. Gilleland. For journalism professors and a growing number of news executives in the U.S. and Canada. Published by the Association for Education in Journalism. Quarterly. Enclose S.A.S.E. for return of submissions.
Nonfiction: Uses articles dealing with problems of administration and improvement of teaching in journalism education at the university level. Maximum length: 2,500 words. Does not pay.

JOURNALISM QUARTERLY, School of Journalism, University of Minnesota, Minneapolis MN 55455. Editor: Edwin Emery. No payment.

JOURNALISM QUARTERLY, School of Journalism, Ohio University, Athens OH 45701. Acting Editor: Guida H. Stempel, III. For members of Association for Education in Journalism; also, other academicians and journalism practitioners. Established: 1923. Quarterly. Usually acquires all rights. Circulation: 4,000. Write for copy of guidelines for writers. Submit only complete ms. Will consider photocopied submissions. Reports in 4 to 6 months. Enclose S.A.S.E. for return of submissions.
Nonfiction: Research in mass communication. Length: 4,000 words maximum. No payment.

THE MILITARY JOURNALIST, Public Affairs Office, Defense Information School, Ft. Harrison IN 46216. Editor: John S. Alfeld. Does not pay.

MORE, A Journalism Review, P.O. Box 2971, Grand Central Station, New York NY 10017. Editor: Richard Pollak. For "both men and women active in media and readers and viewers interested in how media operates." Monthly. Circulation:

9,000. Rights purchased vary with author and material. Buys all rights, but will reassign them to author after publication. Buys 70 mss a year. Pays on publication. Will send a copy to writer for $1. Query first. Reports promptly. Enclose S.A.S.E.
Nonfiction: Publishes "critical evaluations of the media—print and electronic, overground and underground. Heavy emphasis on solid reporting and good writing. Essayists need not apply. With the exception of the generally scholarly *Columbia Journalism Review*, there is no publication doing what we do." Length: "ordinarily 4,000 words." Pays 10¢ a word.

THE PEN WOMAN, 1300 17th St., N.W., Washington DC 20036. Editor: Mrs. Lee M. Waldrop. Principally for members of the National League of American Pen Women, Inc., professional women writers, artists and composers; libraries and schools. Monthly, except July, August and September. Editorial content supplied mostly by members. Does not pay for submissions.

PHILATELIC JOURNALIST, P.O. Box 150, Clinton Corners NY 12514. Editor: Gustav Detjen, Jr. For "journalists, writers, columnists in the field of stamp collecting." Established in 1971. Bimonthly. Circulation: 1,000. Not copyrighted. Pays on publication. Will send a sample copy to a writer on request. Query first. Will consider photocopied submissions. Submit seasonal material 2 months in advance. Reports in 2 weeks. Enclose S.A.S.E.
Nonfiction and Photos: "Articles concerned with the problems of the philatelic journalists, how to publicize and promote stamp collecting, how to improve relations between philatelic writers and publishers and postal administrations. Philatelic journalists, many of them amateurs, are very much interested in receiving greater recognition as journalists. Any criticism should be coupled with suggestions for improvement." Buys profiles and personal opinion articles. Length: 250 to 500 words. Pays $15 to $30. Photos purchased with ms; captions required.
Fillers: Jokes, short humor. Length: 2 to 5 lines. Payment negotiated.

PHOTOLITH, Box 17344, Memphis TN 38117. Editor: N.S. Patterson. For student journalists and their adviser-teachers. Established: 1950, 8 issues through school year. Circulation: 3,000 plus schools and colleges. All rights reserved. Will send sample copy to writer on receipt of 25¢ for postage. Submit complete ms. Submit seasonal material 2 months in advance. Reports "promptly." Enclose S.A.S.E. for return of submissions.
Nonfiction: "Articles on how to prepare and edit materials for the school/college publication; how to plan and get photos, how to lay out pages and sections and books and how to make up newspapers; how to finance publications, with illustrations drawn from prize-winning publications, (glossy prints, layouts, copy from the publications, spreads of actual books and newspapers). About half of each issue is staff-prepared; the rest contributed." Length: 600 to 1,000 or 1,200 words. No payment, but "we 'reward' with biographies of writers and, where pictures are available, the photos of writers. We also run an annual contest and award about $250 in prizes, mostly cash, for first-experience articles."

PNPA PRESS, 2717 N. Front St., Harrisburg PA 17110. Editor: Ruth E. Kuhn. No payment.

THE QUILL, National Magazine for Journalists, 35 E. Wacker Dr., Chicago IL 60601. Editor: Charles Long. For newspaper personnel, broadcasters, magazine writers and editors, freelance writers, journalism educators and students, public relations and advertising executives and others interested in journalism. Established: 1912. Monthly. Circulation: 25,000. Rights purchased vary. Will send free sample copy to writer on request. Query first. Enclose S.A.S.E.
Nonfiction: "Articles relating to all aspects of journalism; nuts and bolts type features, freedom of the press articles, profiles of people and places in the media; news items. Regardless of the subject matter, write in a readable style and a structure understandable to a lay audience; nothing that appears like a term paper or thesis." No payment.

ST. LOUIS JOURNALISM REVIEW, P. O. Box 3086, St. Louis MO 63130. A critique of St. Louis media, print and broadcasting, by working journalists. No payment.

SCHOLASTIC EDITOR GRAPHICS/COMMUNICATIONS, 18 Journalism Bldg., University of Minnesota, Minneapolis MN 55455. Editor: Kristi Hedstrom. For high school and college student publications editors, staffs and advisers; mass media people. Established: 1921. 8 issues a year. Circulation: 3,000. Buys all rights but will reassign rights to author after publication. Buys 25 to 30 mss a year. Payment in contributor's copies. Will send sample copy to writer on request. Will consider photocopied submissions. Submit seasonal material 3 months in advance. Reports on material in 2 to 4 weeks. Enclose S.A.S.E. for return of submissions.
Nonfiction and Photos: "How-to articles on all phases of publication work, photography, classroom TV, and the general field of communications; e.g., 'how to save money setting up a darkroom'; 'make your yearbook layouts exciting with press-on lettering,' etc. Especially interested in articles that suggest interesting illustration possibilities, such as 'Caging the Censorship Dragon.' Emphasis is on a lively, exciting approach. Avoid using first person. Articles on summer journalism workshops would be appropriate for the summer workshop issue published in April." Informational, personal experience. Length: 10 to 20 typed double-spaced pages. Payment 5 contributor's copies. Departmental needs include: Book reviews for "Reading Between the Lines"; news releases for "Publicity" and new product news for "Conglomerate." 8x10, b&w glossy photos purchased with and without ms. Captions required. Occasionally use mood photos in "Ed-Lib" (editor's column).

THE WRITER, 8 Arlington St., Boston MA 02116. Editor: A.S. Burack. Monthly. Pays on acceptance. Uses very little freelance material. Enclose S.A.S.E.
Nonfiction: Articles of instruction for writers. Length: about 2,000 words. Pays minimum $25.

WRITER'S DIGEST, 9933 Alliance Rd., Cincinnati OH 45242. Editor: Skip Weiner. For writers. Established in 1919. Monthly. Circulation: 120,000. Buys first magazine rights and book rights. Buys about 50 mss a year. Pays on acceptance. Will send a sample copy to a writer on request. "Query first for in-depth features." Will consider photocopied submissions. Submit seasonal material at least 3 months in advance of issue date. Reports in 3 weeks. Enclose S.A.S.E.
Nonfiction: "Practical instructional features on specific types of writing for the freelance market. In-depth market features on major magazine and book publishing houses; interviews with outstanding writers. Discussions of specialized fields of writing, such as greeting cards, wire service reporting, comedy writing, script writing, new potential freelance markets, etc. Regular columns cover poetry, cartooning, photojournalism, TV, law and the writer, and New York markets. We also publish articles on subjects related to the business aspects of writing for publication." Length: 500 to 3,000 words. Pays 3¢ a word; "more for outstanding pieces."
Photos: "Well-known writers, the New York scene, the writing life; for inside and cover use." B&w only. Pays $15 to $35.
Poetry: Uses some light verse related to writing. Pays 50¢ per line.
Fillers: Clippings, etc., about well-known writers. Will not be returned unless accompanied by S.A.S.E. Pays $2 to $5.

WRITER'S YEARBOOK, 9933 Alliance Rd., Cincinnati OH 45242. Editor: Skip Weiner. For writers. Established in 1930. Annual. Buys first magazine and book rights. Buys 20 mss a year. Pays on acceptance. Will send a sample copy to a writer for $1.75. "Most articles are on assignment, but will look at queries from July to September each year." Will consider photocopied submissions. Enclose S.A.S.E.
Nonfiction: "In-depth reports on magazine and book publisher requirements; articles of instruction on type of writing; exclusive interviews with top writers." Length: 1,000 to 4,000 words. Pays 5¢ a word; "more for outstanding pieces."
Photos: Purchased with and without mss; captions required. "B&w glossies of extremely well-known U.S. writers; New York street scenes. Depending on use, we pay $15 to $35."

Laundry and Dry Cleaning

Some journals in the Coin-Operated Machines category are also in the market for material on laundries and dry cleaning establishments.

AMERICAN DRYCLEANER, 500 N. Dearborn St., Chicago IL 60610. Editor: Paul T. Glaman. For professional drycleaners. Monthly. Circulation: 30,000. Buys all rights. Pays on publication. Will send free sample copy on request. Reports "promptly." Enclose S.A.S.E. for return of submissions.
Nonfiction and Photos: Articles on merchandising, diversification, sales programs, personnel management, consumer relations, cost cutting, workflow effectiveness, drycleaning methods. "Articles should help the drycleaner build his business with the most efficient utilization of time, money and effort, inform the drycleaner about current developments within and outside the industry which may affect him and his business, introduce the drycleaner to new concepts and applications which may be of use to him, teach the drycleaner the proper methods of his trade. Tight, crisp writing on significant topics imperative. Eliminate everything that has no direct relationship to the article's theme. Select details which add depth and color to the story. Direct quotes are indispensable." Pays 3¢ to 5¢ per word. Photos purchased with mss; quality 8x10 b&w glossies. Photos should help tell story. No model releases required. Pays $5.

AMERICAN LAUNDRY DIGEST, 500 N. Dearborn St., Chicago IL 60610. Editor: Ben Russell. For management of all types of laundries: family service, industrial, linen supply, diaper service, coinop and institutional. Monthly. Buys first rights. Pays on publication. Will send free sample copy on request. Write for copy of guidelines for writers. Queries preferred. Reports "promptly." Enclose S.A.S.E.
Nonfiction: "Plant stories or interviews with heads of plants relating to either a single subject or a wide range of subjects, including production, cost cutting, workflow, marketing, sales, advertising, labor, etc. In short, articles that will help our readers run their own plants more profitably. We like for writers to explore the whys and why nots as well as the whats and hows." Pays minimum 3¢ a word.
Photos: Purchased with mss or with captions only. Candid action shots. Prefers 8x10 b&w glossy; 5x7 acceptable. Pays $5.
Fillers: Newsbreaks, clippings. Length: 10 to 300 words. Pays minimum $3.
How To Break In: "A beginning freelancer should: (1) familiarize himself with the magazine; (2) research the field by contacting editors, associations and perhaps his local library, for background information; (3) decide honestly if he can write and wants to write about some of the activities engaged in by industry firms; (4) try to find a story possibility in his locale that would fit in with the editorial approach of our magazine. Then query, suggesting a slant and including a list of questions that he thinks should be asked. Also include a list of suggested photos. Any editor worth his salt will be delighted to work with a beginning writer who goes to this trouble, and he will undoubtedly suggest other questions and, in general, give all the help he can."

Law

JURIS DOCTOR MAGAZINE FOR THE NEW LAWYER, 555 Madison Ave., New York NY 10016. Editor: Wendy Moonan. For "young lawyers, ages 24 to 35." 10 times per year. Circulation: 95,000. Buys first rights. Buys 20 mss a year. Pays on publication. Will send a free sample copy to a writer on request. Query first "with 2 short writing samples and an outline." Reports in 3 weeks. Enclose S.A.S.E.
Nonfiction: Wants articles relating to law, as well as travel items and leisure items. Writer should show a knowledge of law, but should not be overly technical. Willing to research. "Most articles are muckraking pieces about the profession—the organized bar, law schools, foundations giving legal grants. We also run book reviews

and interesting leisure time activities: travel, male-oriented hobbies, how to live."
Interested in how-to, interviews, and profiles, Length: 1,500 words. Book reviews,
900 words. Payment is $100; $30 for reviews.
Photos: B&w glossies and color transparencies purchased with mss and with captions only. Payment is $25.

LAWYER'S NEWSLETTER, 1180 S. Beverly Dr., Los Angeles CA 90035. Editor:
Stephan Z. Katzan. For "attorneys." Monthly. Buys all rights. Pays on publication.
Will send a sample copy to a writer on request. Reports in 2 weeks. Enclose S.A.S.E.
Nonfiction: "Our publication's main purpose is to increase the efficiency of attorneys and of law office operations. We are interested in suggestions and ideas for
improvement of office operations as well as articles on legal economics. We also accept practice suggestions which meet a specific legal problem." Length: 2,000 words
maximum. Pays 10¢ a word.

Leather Goods

BOOT & SHOE RECORDER, Chilton Way, Radnor PA 19089. Editor: Bob Haf-
tel. For "footwear retailers and manufacturers." Monthly. Circulation: 30,000.
Buys all rights. Buys about 18 mss a year. Pays "60 days after acceptance." Will send
a sample copy to a writer for $1. Write for copy of guidelines for writers. Query first
or submit complete ms. Will consider photocopied submissions. Submit seasonal
material at least 3 months in advance of issue date. Returns rejected material in 2
weeks. Reports on material accepted for publication in 30 days. Enclose S.A.S.E. for
return of submissions.
Nonfiction and Photos: "We are primarily a merchandising book, but usually carry
one feature each issue on a manufacturing operation. These are usually, although
not exclusively, staff-written. We do not want features about fashion. Although we
cover a wide variety of topics, more than 90% of the freelance material we buy deals
with individual operations—one store, one chain, one man, etc. A knowledge of
footwear is not absolutely essential, but it helps. The writer must be familiar with
merchandising, however. Our stories stress the 'how to' and the 'why.' Our mission:
to help our reader (the footwear retailer) to perform more efficiently, more profitably and with more direction. So, we are interested in success stories—but only when
the 'hows' and 'whys' are fully detailed. We like stories to mention all pertinent
points of the retailer's policy and procedure—store hours, employee policy, decor
and displays, advertising, marketing, sale policy, etc.—but each story must have a
distinctive hook or angle. Ask yourself what singular thing there is about this operation that makes it stand out from the rest. Don't write down to our readers. We
have established a high degree of literacy in our product and we demand skillful
writing, alive with imagery. No hack stuff. We consider ourselves in competition
with all the consumer books our readers get and we have to be at least that good."
Length: 600 to 800 words, profiles; 800 to 1,500 words, coverage of successful business operations and merchandising techniques. Pays $50 to $100. Photos purchased
with and without mss; captions required. "Stories without pictures are rarely
bought. Pictures must be clear and sharp. We prefer pictures showing people in a
store to those showing only displays or merchandise. (By the way, brand names are
not important to us unless they are some way related to the hook of the story.) We
can use color transparencies." For 5x7 or 8x10 b&w glossies ("excellent quality
only"), pays $10. Color transparencies purchased with ms. Department Editor:
Edith E. Stull, Managing Editor.
Fillers: For "Pulse," wants "bright, interesting short takes. Whimsy. Opinion. Facts
of interest to shoemen. Gags. Interesting promotions. Unusual operations or ways
of doing business. Bits of news, the flotsam and jetsam that doesn't warrant publication in our 'News' section, but that can be written brightly to stimulate reader interest. No filler material will be returned unless S.A.S.E. is enclosed." Pays $5.

HANDBAGS AND ACCESSORIES, 80 Lincoln Ave., Stamford CT 06904. Editor:
Renee Prowitt. For "buyers, retailers, store owners, and merchandising managers."

Monthly. Circulation: 5,000. Buys 10 to 12 mss a year. Pays on acceptance or on publication. Will send a sample copy to a writer on request. Query first. Enclose S A S E

Nonfiction and Photos: "Articles about accessories which are retail- and fashion-oriented." Length: "3 to 15 double-spaced typed pages." Pays "$50 per half page of published text; about $100 per major feature or article."

LUGGAGE AND LEATHER GOODS, 80 Lincoln Ave., Stamford CT 06904. Editorial Director: Howard Kelly. Monthly. Pays on acceptance. Query first on feature articles. Enclose S.A.S.E.

Nonfiction: "Personal feature articles and case histories of successful luggage departments, personal leather goods departments and luggage shops. In-depth articles on major business topics of interest to retailers and buyers. Buyer-oriented merchandising publication. Stress on subjects and approaches of vital interest to the luggage and leather goods buyer, such as displays, ideas, ads, merchandising and promotional innovations." Pays $30 per published page.

Photos: Uses one-photo shorts showing and describing an unusual merchandising or display idea in luggage or leather goods. Pays $5 for photo and $5 for caption.

Fillers: News items. Pays $2.50 for the first inch and $1 per inch thereafter.

Library Science

AMERICAN LIBRARIES, 50 E. Huron St., Chicago IL 60611. Editor: Gerald R. Shields. For librarians. "A highly literate audience. They are for the most part practicing professionals with high public contact and involvement interests." 11 times a year. Circulation: 35,000. Buys first North American serial rights. Buys 11 mss a year. Will send free sample copy to writer on request. Query first. Will consider photocopied submissions if not being considered elsewhere at time of submission. Submit seasonal material 2 months in advance "if author has been accepted to provide ms." Reports on material accepted for publication within 8 weeks. Returns rejected material in 2 weeks. Enclose S.A.S.E.

Nonfiction and Photos: "Any material that reflects the special interest of the library profession, which will raise the professional abilities of the reader." Current interest is in "the entire question of who is going to pay for needed information services, the impact of revenue sharing on libraries, the effect of the copyright revision, the impact of cassette TV, the use of cable TV franchises for libraries; the loss of services to the poor and rural areas, the needs of minority service in libraries. We are interested in forecast material on library materials on a spring and fall basis. We prefer that a writer send us a sample of style and explain the idea in mind for an article. We might not buy the idea, but the style may give us an idea for the writer to consider." Length: 3,000 to 5,000 words. Pays $50 to $250. 5x7 (minimum) glossy b&w photos. Pays $5 for unsolicited; $10 for assignment. No "artsie-craftsie," full flood or flash.

THE HORN BOOK MAGAZINE, 585 Boylston St., Boston MA 02116. Editor: Paul Heins. For librarians, teachers, parents, authors, illustrators, publishers. Bimonthly. Circulation: 27,500. Buys all rights, "subject to author's wishes." Buys 24 mss a year. Pays on publication. Will send a free sample copy to a writer on request. No query required. Reports in 3 months. Enclose S.A.S.E. for return of submissions.

Nonfiction: Uses four or five articles per issue about children's books or children's pleasure reading, both in this country and others. Material must have originality and the ability to give inspiration to those working with children and books. Does not want articles on techniques of reading or articles aimed at the education market. Read the magazine before submitting. "It is a literary magazine. Good writing required as well as suitable subject." Length: 3,000 words maximum. Pays "$5 a page."

Poetry: Traditional, contemporary, and light verse. Payment is $10 a page.

MEDIA: LIBRARY SERVICES JOURNAL, 127 Ninth Avenue, North, Nashville TN 37234. Editor: Wayne E. Todd. For "adult leaders in church organizations and people interested in library work, especially church library work." Quarterly. Circulation: 20,000. Buys all rights. Pays on acceptance. Will send a free sample copy to a writer on request. Query first. Enclose S.A.S.E.
Nonfiction: "Articles related to media, especially that related to church libraries, audiovisuals available. The materials should definitely be practical for church library staffs or stories related to the use of media with persons." Interested in how-to, personal experience, inspirational. No length limitations. Payment is 2½¢ a word.

MICROFORM REVIEW, P. O. Box 1297, Weston CT 06880. Editor: Allen B. Veaner. For "librarians and educators at the college and university level." Established in 1972. Quarterly. Circulation: over 1,000. Rights purchased vary with author and material; may buy all rights. Buys "a few" mss a year. Pays on acceptance. Will send free sample copy to a writer on request. Write for copy of guidelines for writers. Query first. Will consider photocopied submissions. Reports in 3 weeks. Enclose S.A.S.E.
Nonfiction and Photos: "Articles dealing with micropublications, libraries and research using micropublications. We're interested in problems libraries have using microforms and the solutions to those problems." Buys informational articles, how-to's, personal experience articles, interviews, profiles, historical articles, reviews of micropublications, coverage of successful business operations, new product articles, articles on merchandising techniques, and technical articles. Length: 2,000 to 8,000 words. Pays $20 to $50. Photos purchased with and without mss; captions required.

WILSON LIBRARY BULLETIN, 950 University Ave., Bronx NY 10452. Editor: William R. Eshelman; Associate Editor: Arthur Plotnik. For professional librarians and those interested in the book and library worlds. Monthly, September through June. Circulation: 37,000. Buys North American serial rights only. Pays on publication. Sample copies may be seen on request in most libraries. "Ms must be original copy, double spaced; additional Xerox copy or carbon is appreciated. Deadlines are a minimum 2 months before publication." Reports in 2 to 8 weeks. Enclose S.A.S.E. for return of submissions.
Nonfiction: Uses articles "of interest to librarians throughout the nation and around the world. Style must be lively, readable and sophisticated, with appeal to modern, professionals; facts must be thoroughly researched. Subjects range from the political to the comic in the world of media and libraries, with an emphasis on the human as well as the technical aspects of any story. No condescension: no library stereotypes." Length: 3,000 to 6,000 words. Pays about $50 to $150, "depending on the substance of article and its importance to readers."

Lumber and Woodworking

THE BRITISH COLUMBIA LUMBERMAN, 2000 West 12th Ave., Vancouver 9, B.C., Canada. Editor: Martin A. Keeley. For forest industries (logging, sawmilling, plywood, marine and forest management). Monthly. Buys first rights. Pays on acceptance. Reports in 2 weeks. Enclose S.A.E. and International Reply Coupons for return of submissions.
Nonfiction: In-depth research articles on new developments, theories, practical applications, new methods, equipment usage and performance, etc., in the industry. Must be specific and accurate; especially applicable to forestry in British Columbia. Length: maximum 1,500 words. Pays 3¢ to 5¢ a word.
Photos: Purchased with mss (see above) or with captions only. B&w glossy; minimum 4x5 (8x10 preferred). Pays $3 to $5.

CANADIAN FOREST INDUSTRIES, 1450 Don Mills Rd., Don Mills, Ont., Canada. Editor: Steve Trower. Monthly. Query first. Enclose S.A.E. and International Reply Coupons.
Nonfiction: Uses "articles concerning industry topics, especially how-to articles that

help businessmen in the forest industries. All articles should take the form of detailed reports of new methods, techniques and cost-cutting practices that are being successfully used anywhere in Canada, together with descriptions of new machinery and equipment that is improving efficiency and utilization of wood. It is very important that accurate descriptions of machinery (make, model, etc.) be always included and any details of costs, etc., in actual dollars and cents can make the difference between a below-average article and an exceptional one." Pays 5¢ a word.
Photos: Buys photos with mss, sometimes captions only. Should be 8x10, b&w glossies or negatives.

NATIONAL HARDWOOD MAGAZINE, P. O. Box 18436, Memphis TN 38118. Editor: Floyd Keith. For "hardwood lumber mills and furniture manufacturers; their education varies, as do their interests." Established in 1927. Monthly. Circulation: 5,000. Buys all rights. Buys 12 to 24 mss per year. Pays on acceptance. Will send a sample copy to a writer on request. Write for copy of guidelines for writers. Query first. Will not consider photocopied submissions. Returns rejected material "usually right away." Reports on ms accepted for publication "usually within 3 to 4 months." Enclose S.A.S.E.
Nonfiction and Photos: "Furniture plant stories on those using large amounts of hardwood lumber; also, other plants that use hardwoods: casket firms, etc. We're the only publication dealing exclusively with hardwood lumber producers and users." Buys informational articles, how-to's, photo features, technical articles. 5x7 or smaller b&w glossies purchased with mss; captions required. Pays $100 "for complete story and photographs, usually."

PLYWOOD AND PANEL MAGAZINE, 1100 Waterway Blvd., Indianapolis IN 46202. Editor: James F. Burrell. For manufacturers and industrial fabricators of plywood and veneer. Monthly. Buys all rights. Pays on publication. Enclose S.A.S.E. for return of submissions.
Nonfiction: "Factual and accurate articles concerning unusual techniques or aspects in the manufacturing or processing of veneer, plywood, particle board, hardboard; detailing successful and/or unusual marketing techniques for wood panel products; or concerning important or unusual industrial end-uses of these materials in the production of consumer goods." Length: maximum 1,500 words. Pays maximum 5¢ a word.
Photos: Of good quality and directly pertinent to editorial needs. Action photos; no catalog shots. No in-plant photos of machinery not operating or not manned in natural fashion. Must be completely captioned; 5x7 b&w or larger preferred. Pays up to $5 per photo.

SOUTHERN LUMBERMAN, 2916 Sidco Drive, Nashville TN 37204. Editor: S.F. Horn. Semimonthly. Pays on publication. Reports in 1 week. Enclose S.A.S.E. for return of submissions.
Nonfiction: Uses articles dealing with logging production or manufacturing and marketing of lumber, new developments in use of wood, news of industry, etc. Any length. Pays $1 an inch.
Photos: Buys photographs.

WESTERN LUMBER AND BUILDING MATERIALS MERCHANT, 573 S. Lake Ave., Pasadena CA 91101. Editor: David Cutler. For retail lumber and building material dealers. Monthly. Not copyrighted. Enclose S.A.S.E.
Nonfiction: "Interested in articles and features on how to merchandise and sell to specified audience; light, easy style." Length: 1,000 words. Pays $20 to $25.

WOOD & WOOD PRODUCTS, 300 W. Adams St., Chicago IL 60606. Editor: James D. Saul. "For management and operating executives of all types wood product manufacturers normally employing minimum of 20 persons." Monthly. Circulation: 30,000. Buys first rights. Pays on acceptance. Will send fact sheet on request. "Detailed query imperative." Reports in 2 to 4 weeks. Enclose S.A.S.E.
Nonfiction: "Semitechnical to technical articles, manufacturing process descriptions, safety, management. No handicraft, forestry or logging articles. Must be en-

tirely factual and accurate. Photos essential." Length: 1,500 words maximum. Payment is $50 for first printed page, and 6¢ to 8¢ a word for each word after the first 500. "Expenses only on prior approval."

Photos: Purchased with mss. "Must have complete descriptive captions, flow diagram of operation desirable. Photos of employees and machinery in natural operating poses. No mug shots, no catalog shots wanted. Any size negative from 35mm up; prints 5x7 or 8x10." Payment is $4 to $10 for first 6 used, and $3 to $5 for each additional; more if used on cover. "Color only on assignment."

WOODWORKING & FURNITURE DIGEST, Hitchcock Bldg., Wheaton IL 60187. Editor: E.R. Gillis. For industrial manufacturers whose products employ wood as a basic raw material. Monthly. Buys all rights. Pays on publication. Will send free sample copy to serious freelancer on request. Query first. Reports in 10 days. Will sometimes hold ms for further evaluation up to 2 months, if it, at first, appears to have possibilities. Enclose S.A.S.E.

Nonfiction and Photos: "Articles on woodworking and furniture manufacturing with emphasis on management concepts, applications for primary raw materials (including plastics, if involved with wood), technology of remanufacturing methods and machines, and news of broad industry interest. Articles should focus on cost reduction, labor efficiency, product improvement, and profit. No handcraft, do-it-yourself or small custom shopwork. Present theme, or why reader can benefit, in first paragraph. Cover 'feeds and speeds' thoroughly to include operating data and engineering reasons why. Leave reader with something to do or think. Avoid mechanically handled case histories and plant tours which do not include management/engineering reasons." Photos, charts and diagrams which tell what cannot be told in words should be included. "We like a balance between technical information and action photos." Length: "no length limit, but stop before you run out of gas!" Pays $35-$50 per published page. Photos purchased with mss. Good technical quality and perception of subject shown. No posed views. Prefers candid action or tight closeups. Full color cover photo must be story related.

WORLD WOOD, 500 Howard St., San Francisco CA 94105. Editor: William E Davis. For production people: loggers, foresters, sawmills, plywood plants, particle board plants outside U.S. 13 times per year. Buys exclusive rights for one year in the field. Pays on acceptance. Query first. Reports "within 5 working days of receipt of material." Enclose S.A.S.E. for response to query and return of submissions.

Nonfiction and Photos: Needs "operating articles about logging operations, mills, etc., outside U.S. No U.S. material used. Should be on-the-spot, technical material including full details of production and equipment. Production articles to show how to do a job more efficiently, faster, safer, cheaper, etc. Also descriptions of specific operations which might not be particularly new but will show industry man in another country how things are done in other countries than his own. Needs all trade names and equipment specifications. Should be efficient operations, possibly showing new production ideas. Author need not be an expert but must have expert sources of material. Uses very few of the general forest resource type articles. Our readers are very equipment-minded." Wants details of specific operations. Pays minimum of $30 per published page (including photos), with occasional higher rates for outstanding material. Photos should be 8x10 glossies; color covers.

Fillers: Short items of general industry news outside U.S.A. Pays $2.50 to $5.

Machinery and Metal Trade

ASSEMBLY ENGINEERING, Hitchcock Publishing Co., Wheaton IL 60187. Editor: Robert T. Kelly. For design and manufacturing engineers and production personnel concerned with assembly problems in manufacturing plants. Monthly. Buys first publication rights. Pays on publication. Sample copy will be sent on request. "Query first on leads or ideas. We report on ms decision as soon as review is completed and provide edited proofs for checking by author, prior to publication." Enclose S.A.S.E.

Nonfiction and Photos: Wants features on design, engineering and production practices for the assembly of manufactured products. Material should be submitted on "exclusive rights" basis and, preferably, should be written in the third person. Subject areas include selection, specification, and application of fasteners, mounting hardware, electrical connectors, wiring, hydraulic and pneumatic fittings, seals and gaskets, adhesives, joining methods (soldering, welding, brazing, etc.), and assembly equipment; specification of fits and tolerances; joint design; design and shop assembly standards; time and motion study (assembly line); quality control in assembly; layout and balancing of assembly lines; assembly tool and jig design; programming assembly line operations; working conditions, incentives, labor costs, and union relations as they relate to assembly line operators; hiring and training of assembly line personnel; supervisory practices for the assembly line. Also looking for news items on assembly-related subjects, and for unique or unusual "ideas" on assembly components, equipment, processes, practices and methods. Requires good quality photos or sketches, usually close-ups of specific details. Pays $30 per published page.

AUTOMATIC MACHINING, 65 Broad St., Rochester NY 14614. Editor: Donald E. Wood. For metalworking technical management. Buys all rights. Query first. Enclose S.A.S.E.
Nonfiction: "This is not a market for the average freelancer. Articles deal in depth with specific job operations on automatic screw machines, chucking machines, high production metal turning lathes and cold heading machines. Part prints, tooling layouts always required, plus written agreement of source to publish the material. Without personal background in operation of this type of equipment, freelancers are wasting time." Length: "no limit." Pays $20 per printed page.

CANADIAN MACHINERY AND METALWORKING, 481 University Ave., Toronto M5W 1A7, Ont., Canada. Editor: A. Whitney. Monthly. Buys first Canadian rights. Pays on publication. Query first. Enclose S.A.E. and International Reply Coupons.
Nonfiction: Technical and semitechnical articles dealing with metalworking operations in Canada and in the U.S., if of particular interest. Accuracy and service appeal to readers is a must. Pays minimum 5¢ a word.
Photos: Purchased with mss and with captions only. "Color for covers only."

CUTTING TOOL ENGINEERING, P.O. Box 937, Wheaton IL 60187. Editor: N.D. O'Daniell. For metalworking industry executives and engineers concerned with design, function, and application of metal cutting tools. Monthly. Circulation: 25,000. Buys all rights. Pays on publication. Will send free sample copy on request. Query required. Enclose S.A.S.E.
Nonfiction: "Intelligently written articles on specific applications of all types of metal cutting tools—mills, drills, reamers, etc. Articles must contain all information related to the operation, such as feeds and speeds, materials machined, etc. Should be tersely written, in-depth treatment. In the Annual Diamond Directory, published in July, we cover the use of diamond cutting tools and diamond grinding wheels." Length: 1,000 to 2,500 words. Pays "$35 per published page, or about 5¢ a published word."
Photos: Purchased with mss. 8x10 b&w glossies. No Polaroids.

THE FABRICATOR, 3813 Broadway, Rockford IL 61108. Editor: Milo J. Pituin. For "managers of metal fabricating plants; superintendents, plant owners, etc." Established in 1970. Bimonthly. Circulation: 50,000. Rights purchased vary with author and material; may buy all rights but reassign rights to author after publication, or first North American serial rights. Buys 12 to 16 mss a year. Pays on publication. Query first or submit complete ms. Will consider photocopied submissions. Submit seasonal or special material at least 6 weeks in advance of issue date. Reports in 2 weeks. Enclose S.A.S.E. for return of submissions.
Nonfiction and Photos: "Technical articles on metal fabricating, punching, shearing, forming, bending, welding, material handling, estimating. The writer may use any style which is short, punchy, to-the-point. Make good use of photos and line drawings. We're interested in articles on labor problems." Buys informational articles, how-to's, interviews, profiles, think articles, coverage of successful business op-

erations, new product articles, and technical articles. Length: 750 to 1,000 words. Pays $200 to $300 for a "good, technical article." Photos purchased with mss or on assignment; captions required. For b&w glossies, pay is "negotiated."
Fillers: Newsbreaks, clippings. Pays $10.

FINISHERS MANAGEMENT, 248 Lorraine Ave., Upper Montclair NJ 07043. Editor: P. Peter Kovatis. Monthly. Buys all rights. Pays on publication. Enclose S.A.S.E. for return of submissions.
Nonfiction and Photos: Wants management how-to articles as related to operating a metal finishing company. Length: 2,000 to 3,000 words. Pays about $25 minimum; "negotiated." 8x10 glossy photos purchased with mss.

FOUNDRY MAGAZINE, Penton Plaza, Cleveland OH 44114. Editor: J.C. Miske. Monthly. Reports in 2 weeks. Enclose S.A.S.E. for return of submissions.
Nonfiction and Photos: Uses articles describing operating practice in foundries written to interest companies producing metal castings. Length: maximum 3,000 words. Pays $35 a printed page. Uses illustrative 8x10 photographs with article.

INDUSTRIAL FINISHING, Hitchcock Building, Wheaton IL 60187. Editor: Matt Heuertz. Monthly. Circulation: 35,000. Buys first rights. Buys 3 or 4 mss a year. Pays on acceptance. Will send a free sample copy to a writer on request. Query first. Enclose S.A.S.E.
Nonfiction and Photos: Wants "technical articles on finishing operations for oem products." Style should be "direct and to the point." Photos purchased with mss, "as part of the complete package which we purchase at $100 to $150."

INDUSTRIAL MACHINERY NEWS, P.O. Box 727, Dearborn MI 48121. Editor: Lucky D. Slate. For "metalworking manufacturing managers and engineers who plan and select methods of manufacturing design equipment for manufacturers, or create or refine manufacturing techniques and work in metalworking plants." Established in 1952. Monthly. Circulation: 65,000. Buys all rights. Pays on publication. Will send a sample copy to a writer for $1. Write for copy of guidelines for writers. Query first or submit complete ms. Will consider photocopied submissions. Reports in 1 to 3 months. Enclose S.A.S.E. for return of submissions.
Nonfiction and Photos: Articles on "metal removal, metal forming, assembly, finishing, inspection, application of machine tools, technology, measuring, gauging equipment, small cutting tools, tooling accessories, materials handling in metalworking plants, safety programs. We give our publication a newspaper feel—fast reading with lots of action or human interest photos." Buys how-to's. Length: open. Pay: open. Photos purchased with mss; captions required.
Fillers: Newsbreaks, puzzles, jokes, short humor.

MODERN MACHINE SHOP, 600 Main St., Cincinnati OH 45202. Editor: Fred W. Vogel. Monthly. Pays 30 days following acceptance. Query first. Reports in 5 days. Enclose S.A.S.E.
Nonfiction: Uses articles dealing with all phases of metal manufacturing and machine shop work, with photographs. Length: 1,500 to 2,000 words. Pays current market rate.

NC SCENE, 183 Loudon Road, Concord NH 03301. Editor: Mary A. DeVries. For "numerical control users, producers, educators, students, and other interested persons, from programmer to company president. Age 18 to retirement. Usually college graduates with engineering, math, or business background. Interested in NC uses—applications of NC machine tools and processes—and anything affected by NC, such as design, marketing, management." Monthly. Circulation: 2,500. Buys first rights. Buys 24 mss a year. Pays on publication. Will send a free sample copy to a writer on request. Query preferred. Reports in 2 to 3 weeks. Enclose S.A.S.E.
Nonfiction and Photos: "Case histories of successful use of NC machine tools or processes. New developments in NC technology. Role of government in NC industry. NC education and training. Techniques and trends in NC design, programming, production, justification, and management. Economic and social influences." Interested in how-to, personal experience, interviews, profiles, successful business

operations, think pieces, new product, and photo articles. "Style should be straight-forward, factual, and to the point. Avoid generalities. Emphasize NC rather than organization that builds or uses it. Professional and technical aspects receive more emphasis than companies or product specifications. Product promotion is taboo." Length: 500 to 2,000 words. Payment is up to $25 a page. B&w glossy photos purchased with mss.

POWER TRANSMISSION DESIGN, 614 Superior Ave. West, Cleveland OH 44113. Editor: Jay Myers. For design engineers and persons who buy, operate, and maintain motors, drives, and bearings. Monthly. Circulation: 42,000. Buys all rights, but may reassign rights to author after publication. Pays on acceptance. Reports in 2 weeks. Enclose S.A.S.E. for return of submissions.
Nonfiction and Photos: "The article should answer these questions: What does the machine do? What loads and load changes, speed and speed changes, does the operation impose upon the drive system? What drive system do you use and why? What were the alternatives, and why did you reject them? How did the operating environment affect the selection of motors, drives, bearings, and controls? How is the machine designed for easy maintenance? What are the sizes and capacities of the motors, drives, bearings, and controls? How does the drive system design make the machine superior to competitive machines? To previous models of your manufacture? What specific advances in motors, drives, bearings, and controls have led to improvements in machines like this one? What further advances would you like to see? Accompany your write-up with a photo of the machine and close-ups of the drive system and schematic drawings and blueprints, if necessary." Length: 600 to 6,000 words; "anything longer we'll break up and serialize." Pays $25 "per published magazine page (about 600 words to a page)."

PRODUCTION, Box 101, Bloomfield Hills MI 48013. Editor: Robert F. Huber. For "managers of manufacturing." Monthly. Circulation: 80,000. Rights purchased vary with author and material. Buys "a few" mss a year. Pays on acceptance. Query first. Enclose S.A.S.E.
Nonfiction and Photos: "Trends, developments, and applications in manufacturing." Length: open. Pays $50 to $350. Photos purchased with mss; captions required.

PRODUCTS FINISHING, 600 Main St., Cincinnati OH 45202. Editor: Gerard H. Poll, Jr. Monthly. Buys all rights. Pays within 30 days after acceptance. Reports in 1 week. Enclose S.A.S.E. for return of submissions.
Nonfiction: Uses "material devoted to the finishing of metal and plastic products. This includes the cleaning, plating, polishing and painting of metal and plastic products of all kinds. Articles can be technical and must be practical. Technical articles should be on processes and methods. Particular attention given to articles describing novel approaches used by product finishers to control air and water pollution, and finishing techniques that reduce costs."
Photos: Wants photographs dealing with finishing methods or processes.

SOUTHAM'S METALWORKING, 1450 Don Mills Rd., Don Mills, Ont., Canada. Editor: Don R. Endicott. Buys first publication rights. Query first. Enclose S.A.E. and International Reply Coupons.
Nonfiction and Photos: "Articles with illustrations on machine production and management techniques in Canada. Magazine readership covers management, production, engineering, and purchasing functions of all industry wherever any metal is worked. Submission should detail a manufacturing process involving metal; report on metallurgical discoveries having a manufacturing management relative to production." Length: 600 to 1,500 words. Pays 2¢ to 5¢ a word, "depending on quality."

STAMPING/DIEMAKING, 45 Crosby St., New York NY 10012. Editor: Arthur Salsberg. For engineers, technical managers. Bimonthly. Circulation: 45,000. Buys all rights. Pays on publication. Will send free sample copy on request. Enclose S.A.S.E. for return of submissions.

Nonfiction: Technology of stamping, diemaking, tooling, forming. Innovations in same. Highly technical articles. Length: 4,000 words maximum. Pay "negotiated."

STEEL FACTS, 1000 16th St., N.W., Washington DC 20036. Editor: Thomas D. Patrick. For "opinion leaders; all ages and professions." Established: 1933. Quarterly. Circulation: 180,000. Not copyrighted. Buys 10 to 20 mss a year. Payment on publication. Will send free sample copy to writer on request. Query first. Submit special material 6 months in advance. Reporting time varies on material accepted for publication. Returns rejected material in 2 weeks. Enclose S.A.S.E.
Nonfiction and Photos: Articles on the environmental, foreign trade, economics, international trade, new technology aspects of the steel industry. "No product articles." Interviews, think pieces, technical. Length: 50 to 2,000 words. Pays $25 to $400. Photos purchased with or without accompanying ms or on assignment. Proofsheets and negatives. Color transparencies. Pays $15 to $100. Captions required.

33 MAGAZINE, 22 Bank St., Summit NJ 07901. Editor: Joseph L. Mazel. For "operating managers (from turn foreman on up), engineers, metallurgical and chemical specialists, and corporate officials in the steelmaking industry. Work areas for these readers range from blast furnace and coke ovens into and through the steel works and rolling mills. 33's readers also work in nonferrous industries." Monthly. Buys all rights. Pays on publication. Will send free sample copy on request. Query required. Reports in 3 weeks. Enclose S.A.S.E.
Nonfiction and Photos: Case histories of primary metals producing equipment in use, such as smelting, blast furnace, steelmaking, rolling. "Broadly speaking, *33 Magazine* concentrates its editorial efforts in the areas of technique (what's being done and how it's being done), technology (new developments), and equipment (what's being used). Your article should include a detailed explanation (who, what, why, where, and how) and the significance (what it means to operating manager, engineer, or industry) of the techniques, technology or equipment being written about. In addition, your readers will want to know of the problems you experienced during the planning, developing, implementing, and operating phases. And, it would be especially beneficial to tell of the steps you took to solve the problems or roadblocks encountered. You should also include all cost data relating to implementation, operation, maintenance, etc., wherever possible. Benefits (cost savings; improved manpower utilization; reduced cycle time; increased quality; etc.) should be cited to gauge the effectiveness of the subject being discussed. The highlight of any article is its illustrative material. This can take the form of photographs, drawings, tables, charts, graphs, etc. Your type of illustration should support and reinforce the text material. It should not just be an added, unrelated item. Each element of illustrative material should be identified and contain a short description of exactly what is being presented." Pays $25 per published page. Minimum 5x7 b&w glossies purchased with mss.

THE WELDING DISTRIBUTOR, Box 128, Morton Grove IL 60053. Editor: Donald Jefferson. For wholesale and retail distributors of welding equipment and safety supplies and their sales staffs. Bimonthly. Buys all rights. Pays on publication. Enclose S.A.S.E. for return of submissions.
Nonfiction: Categories of editorial coverage are: management, process/product knowledge, profiles, selling and safety. Recent articles included features on the following: preventing employee pilferage; cylinders for liquified gas; mistakes in selling and cylinder retesting. Pays 2¢ a word.

WELDING ENGINEER, P.O. Box 128, Morton Grove IL 60053. Editor: R.A. Mate. Monthly. Buys first American serial and reprint rights. Pays on publication. Editorial interest guide available on request. Query first. Enclose S.A.S.E.
Nonfiction: Technical articles dealing with the use of welding and related processes in various industries. Magazine is edited to inform readers of new developments in equipment and materials, new techniques and "state of the art" in metalwork where fabrication is completed by welding, brazing or soldering. Length: 500 to 3,000 words. Pays 2¢ to 3¢ a word, "depending on type and content of copy." Articles should be illustrated with photos and/or drawings.

Photos: "Photos of interesting welding and cutting applications, with captions." Pays minimum $5.

Maintenance and Safety

BUILDING SERVICES CONTRACTOR, 101 West 31 St., New York NY 10001. Editorial Director: John Vollmuth. For contract cleaners, owners, officers, managers in the field. Established: 1964. Bimonthly. Circulation: 5,800. Not copyrighted. Payment on publication. Will send free sample copy to writer on request. Query first. Will consider photocopied submissions. Reports on material "immediately." Enclose S.A.S.E. for return of submissions.
Nonfiction and Photos: "Articles on new products, building services contractors, new developments and ideas in the field. Straightforward accounts, concise news stories, telling of new developments, methods, expansion and diversification of building services contractors. Time and motion studies." Informational, how-to, personal experience, interview, profile, historical, think pieces, personal opinion, successful business operations, merchandising techniques, technical. Length: 1,500 words maximum. Pays $1 to $110. B&w glossy photos purchased with or without ms. Pays $5 unless on assignment, in which case payment is negotiated. Captions required.
Fillers: Newsbreaks, clippings, short humor. Pays 3¢ to 5¢ a word.

MAINTENANCE SUPPLIES, 101 W. 31 St., New York NY 10001. Editorial Director: John Vollmuth. For manufacturers and distributors of sanitary supplies. Monthly. Circulation: 10,000. Not copyrighted. Payment on publication. Will send free sample copy to writer on request. Submit complete ms. Reports "as soon as possible." Enclose S.A.S.E. for return of submissions.
Nonfiction and Photos: "Articles pointing out trends in the sanitary supply fields; stories about manufacturers and distributors, possible markets and merchandising. We expect a writer to turn out an article about some aspect of the sanitary supply field for readers who sell the products of this industry. General sales articles are sometimes accepted, but stories geared to the specific industry are much preferred." Length: 1,500 words. Pays $90. 8x10 b&w photos purchased with accompanying ms. Captions required.

OCCUPATIONAL HAZARDS, 614 Superior Ave. W., Cleveland OH 44113. Editor: Peter J. Sheridan. Monthly. Buys first rights in field. Pays on publication. Reports in 30 days. Enclose S.A.S.E. for return of submissions.
Nonfiction: "Articles on industrial health, safety, security and fire protection. Specific facts and figures must be cited. No material on farm, home, or traffic safety. All material accepted subject to sharp editing to conform to publisher's distilled writing style. Illustrations preferred but not essential." Length: 300 to 2,000 words. Pays minimum 3¢ a word.
Photos: Accepts 4x5, 5x7 and 8x10 photos with mss or with captions only. Pays $5.

PEST CONTROL, 9800 Detroit Ave., Cleveland OH 44102. Editor: Donald D. Miller. For the pest control industry. Established: 1935. Monthly. Circulation: 13,000. Rights purchased vary with author and material. Buys all rights but will reassign rights to author after publication. Buys 20 mss a year. Payment on acceptance. Will send free sample copy to writer on request. Query first. Submit seasonal material 3 months in advance. Enclose S.A.S.E.
Nonfiction: Technical and semitechnical articles. Operator experience articles. Informational, how-to, personal experience, interview, successful business operations, merchandising techniques. Special emphasis issues include the following: Termite, Chemicals, Flying Insect Control, Equipment Directory, Cockroach, Rodent, Convention Promotion, NPCA Convention/Trade Show and Annual Business and Index. Length: 500 to 1,500 words. Pays $50 to $200.

SDM: SECURITY DISTRIBUTING & MARKETING, 2639 South La Cienega Blvd., Los Angeles CA 90034. Editor: Robert J. Bargert. For alarm dealers, installers, manufacturers and distributors. Established 1971. Monthly. Circulation: 15,000. Buys all rights. Buys 10 to 12 mss a year. Payment on publication. Will send free sample copy to writer on request. Query first. Reports in 4 weeks. Enclose S.A.S.E.

Nonfiction and Photos: "Stories on marketing, sales, training, case histories, etc. Clean, crisp copy. Management overview articles." Informational, how-to, think pieces, successful business operations, new product, merchandising techniques, technical. Length: 500 to 3,000 words. Pays $1.50 per published inch. 8x10 b&w glossy photos purchased with accompanying ms. Captions required. Pays $10.

Management and Supervision

This category includes trade journals for lower level business and industrial managers, including supervisors and office managers. Journals for business executives and owners are classified under Business Management. Those for industrial plant managers are listed in Industrial Management.

LE BUREAU, 625 President Kennedy, Montreal 111, Que., Canada. Editor: Paul Saint-Pierre. For "office executives." Established in 1965. Monthly. Circulation: 7,500. Buys all rights, but will reassign rights to author after publication. Buys about 20 mss a year. Pays on acceptance. Will send a sample copy to a writer on request. Query first or submit complete ms. Submit seasonal material "between 1 and 2 months" of issue date. Enclose S.A.E. and International Reply Coupons for return of submissions.

Nonfiction and Photos: "Our publication is published in the French language. We use case histories on new office systems, applications of new equipment, articles on personnel problems. Material should be exclusive and above-average quality." Buys personal experience articles, interviews, think pieces, coverage of successful business operations, and new product articles. Length: 500 to 1,000 words. Pays $50. B&w glossies purchased with mss. Pays $5.

CONSTRUCTION FOREMAN'S & SUPERVISOR'S LETTER, 24 Rope Ferry Rd., Waterford CT 06385. Editor: Frank Berkowitz. For "field supervisors and craft foremen for construction companies of all kinds." Established in 1965. Semi-monthly. Circulation: 9,000. Buys all rights. Buys 100 mss a year. Pays on acceptance. Will send a free sample copy to a writer on request. Write for copy of guidelines for writers. Query first or submit complete ms. Reports in 2 weeks. Enclose S.A.S.E. for return of submissions.

Nonfiction and Photos: Wants "interviews with working supervisors, dealing with techniques used in directing employees," written up as "tightly written, unrepetitious, newspaper or feature-style articles, free of editorializing or irrelevancies." No think pieces. "We prefer regular stringer coverage of areas and give preference to their submissions. We rely exclusively on the direct interview." Length: 800 words maximum. Payment is 6¢ a word minimum, "as edited." B&w glossy "head-and-shoulders" photos purchased with mss. "Minimum 1 inch from ear to ear." Pays $4.

THE FOREMAN'S LETTER, National Foremen's Institute, 24 Rope Ferry Rd., Waterford CT 06385. Editor: Frank Berkowitz. For industrial supervisors. Semi-monthly. Buys all rights. Pays on acceptance. "Query preferred only if out-of-pocket expenses may be involved." Interested in regular stringers (freelance) on area exclusive basis. Enclose S.A.S.E. for return of submissions.

Nonfiction: Interested primarily in direct interviews with industrial (including construction and public utilities companies) foremen in the U.S. and Canada, written in newspaper feature or magazine article style, with concise, uncluttered, non-re-

petitive prose as an essential. Subject matter would be the interviewee's techniques for managing people, bolstered by illustrations out of the interviewee's own job experiences. Slant would be toward informing readers how their most effective contemporaries function, free of editorial comment. "Our aim is to offer information which, hopefully, readers may apply to their own professional self-improvement." Length: maximum 1,000 words. Pays 6¢ to 7½¢ a word "after editing."
Photos: Buys photos submitted with mss. "Captions needed for identification only." Head and shoulders, any size glossy from 2x3 up. Pays $4.

MANAGE, 9933 Alliance Rd., Cincinnati OH 45242. "Official publication of the National Management Association. Most readers are members of company or city chapters of this organization. They are primarily middle management, first line supervisors, or scientific-technical managers." Established in 1925. Bimonthly. Circulation: 70,000. Buys first North American serial rights "with reprint privileges," or "sometimes" second serial or simultaneous rights. Buys about 24 mss a year. Pays on acceptance. Will send a sample copy to a writer on request. Write for copy of guidelines for writers. Query first or submit complete ms for nonfiction, quizzes, puzzles. Submit complete ms for short humor. Address mss to Managing Editor. Will consider photocopied submissions. Returns rejected material in 2 weeks. Reports on mss accepted for publication in 1 month. Enclose S.A.S.E. for return of submissions.
Nonfiction and Photos: "Content shows how to advance the management abilities and status of our readers. Most articles concern 1 or more of the following categories: communications, economics and cost reduction, executive abilities, health and safety, labor-human relations, leadership and motivation, professionalism. Articles must be practical and tell the manager how to apply the information to his job. Be specific and back up statements with facts and, where possible, charts and illustrations. Include pertinent anecdotes and examples. In general, we want lively, interesting articles of immediate value to our readers. *Manage* also contains articles dealing with NMA's clubs, activities, and members, but these are staff-written. We do not want academic reports, essays, personal opinion pieces, overt promotions, or 'how my company did this.'" Buys informational articles, how-to's, interviews, humor "relating to management," think articles, coverage of successful business practices. Length: 600 to 2,500 words for articles; under 500 words for humor. Pays 3¢ to 5¢ a word. 8x10 or 5x7 b&w glossies purchased with mss; captions required. "No mug shots." Pays $5 for inside use, $15 if used for cover.
Poetry: "Not published previously, but light verse relating to management might be considered." Length: 2 to 4 lines. Pays $5.
Fillers: Puzzles, quizzes "in same areas as nonfiction." Pays $2 to $5, "depending on length and quality."

OFFICE SUPERVISOR'S BULLETIN, Bureau of Business Practice, 681 Fifth Ave., New York NY 10022. For first and second line office supervisors. Semi-monthly. Buys all rights. Pays on acceptance. Will send a free sample copy to a writer on request. Query first. Address mss to the Editor. Reports in 1 week. Enclose S.A.S.E.
Nonfiction: Wants "interview-based articles, quoting, by name, topnotch office supervisors in business and industry, who tell what today's problems are in office supervision, how they solve those problems, what results they're getting, illustrated by examples from daily office life. Uses freelance work to give publication geographic balance. Interested in interviews from Canada, the Midwest, South, West. Offices with data processing, word processing, accounting, reproduction departments, and banks are all good subjects, as well as traditional personnel, purchasing, typing and filing. Writers will find it useful to do a little reading in the library on basic management theory and supervisory techniques to gain background understanding and to get ideas for interview topics and questions. Articles should deal with 'people problems' and how they can be solved, not about equipment or techniques unless related to people problems. Public relations departments of large corporations headquartered near you can be helpful in finding an experienced, verbal supervisor to interview if you have a topic in mind. Sample subjects: the 'whole job' concept; experiences with affirmative action programs for women, minorities, religious and ethnic groups; corporate security; adapting older workers to new equipment; safety problems solved; transactional analysis; positive reinforcement; motivation, controls,

discipline; planning, delegating, absenteeism and tardiness; training. Use plenty of quotes. No bylines. Factual, accurate reporting; no 'atmosphere' needed. Since the office supervisor's boss is paying for the publication, magazine prints nothing against him, nor does it encourage the supervisor to change jobs." Length: "2 or 3 pages." Pays "$25 per printed page or approximately 450 words."

SUPERVISION, 424 N. 3rd Street, Burlington IA 52601. Editor: G.B. McKee. For foremen, personnel managers, supervisors, and department heads. Monthly. Buys all rights. Pays on publication. Sample copy sent on request. Query first. Reports in 10 days. Enclose S.A.S.E. for response to queries and return of submissions.
Nonfiction and Photos: Wants "how-to articles dealing with manufacturing plant situations relating to improving production, cutting costs, handling grievances, eliminating waste, building morale. Case study situations preferred, showing how a specific problem was overcome and what benefits resulted. Clear style wanted; article must contain practical information." Length: 1,500 to 2,000 words. Payment is 2¢ a word. Occasionally buys b&w photos with mss. Payment is $5.

TRAINING IN BUSINESS AND INDUSTRY, 33 W. 60th St., New York NY 10023. Editor: Wallace Hanson. For executives and instructors in American business and industry. Monthly. Enclose S.A.S.E. for return of submissions.
Nonfiction and Photos: "We seek information on the management and techniques of employee training. Material should discuss a specific training problem; why the problem existed; how it was solved, the alternative solutions, etc. Should furnish enough data for readers to make an independent judgment about the appropriateness of the solution to the problem. Articles are written from the viewpoint of a practitioner for other practitioners. No 'gee whiz' approach which might be suitable for general-audience magazines. We want names and specific details of all techniques and processes used." Pays $30 per printed page. No extra payment for photos.

UTILITY SUPERVISION, National Foremen's Institute, 24 Rope Ferry Rd., Waterford CT 06385. Editor: Frank Berkowitz. For "first-line supervisors for public utilities companies (electric & gas companies, water companies, sewerage departments, municipal mass transportation, etc.)." Semimonthly. Buys all rights; buys first rights for photos. Buys 100 mss a year. Pays on acceptance. Will send a free sample copy to a writer on request. Query first. Reports in 2 weeks. Enclose S.A.S.E.
Nonfiction and Photos: Wants "interviews with working supervisors, dealing with techniques they utilize in directing employees." Approach should be "tightly written, unrepetitious, newspaper or magazine feature-style, free of any editorializing, free of irrelevancies." Does not want think pieces. "We rely almost exclusively on the direct interview." Length: 800 words maximum. Payment is 6¢ a word minimum, "as edited." B&w glossy "head and shoulders" photos purchased with mss. Payment is $4.

Marine Industries and Water Navigation

In this list are journals for seamen, boatbuilders, navigators, boat dealers, and others interested in water as a means of travel or shipping. Journals for commercial fishermen are classified with Fishing journals. Publications for scientists studying the ocean will be found under Oceanography.

THE BOATING INDUSTRY, 205 E. 42nd St., New York NY 10017. Editor: Charles A. Jones. For "boating retailers and distributors." Established in 1929. Monthly. Circulation: 26,000. Buys all rights, but will reassign rights to author after publication. Buys 10 to 15 mss a year. Pays on publication. Will send a free sample copy to a writer on request. "Best practice is to check with editor first on story ideas for go-ahead." Submit seasonal material 3 to 4 months in advance of issue date.

Returns rejected material in 2 months. Acknowledges acceptance of material in 1 month. Enclose S.A.S.E.

Nonfiction and Photos: Uses "boat dealer success stories." Pays 7¢ to 10¢ a word. B&w glossy photos purchased with mss. Payment for photos is $5 to $35 for covers.

CNE MAGAZINE, 250 Park Ave., New York NY 10017. Editor: Leo G. Sands. For "dealers, distributors, manufacturers, technicians, engineers, and maintainers of land mobile and marine radio equipment, avionics, and marine navigation equipment." Monthly. Circulation: 10,000. Buys all rights. Buys about 12 mss a year. Pays on publication. Will send a sample copy to a writer for $1,50. Query first. Will consider photocopied submissions. Submit seasonal material at least 3 months in advance. Reports in 1 month. Enclose S.A.S.E.

Nonfiction and Photos: "*CNE* is the technical journal of the communication and navigation electronic industry. Its function is to provide comprehensive and authentic information not available in any other single publication. Types of feature articles published include those on system design, equipment design, technology, FCC reports, servicing, installation, applications, and case histories. Technical information should be written in plain language." Buys how-to's, coverage of successful business operations, historical articles, and new product articles. Length: 500 to 3,000 words. Pays $15 to $150. B&w glossies purchased with mss.

THE DOMESTIC MARITIME JOURNAL, 3750 Nixon Rd., Ann Arbor MI 48105. Editor: Jacques LesStrang. For "firms and individuals involved in some aspect of water transportation which is not international. Business executives, mostly; perhaps some ship buffs. Government officials." Established: 1973. Quarterly. Circulation: 5,000. Rights purchased vary with author and material. Buys first serial rights; buys second serial (reprint) rights. Payment on publication. Will send sample copy to writer for $1. Query first. Will consider photocopied submissions. Reports on all material within 2 weeks. Enclose S.A.S.E.

Nonfiction and Photos: "Nonfiction relating to water transportation; rivers, all U.S. ports, labor situation on water, ships of all kinds, shipbuilding, river facilities (locks, channels). Container traffic (includes Puerto Rico, Hawaii and Alaska)." Length: 500 to 3,500 words. Pays $50 to $250. 8x10 b&w glossy photos purchased with or without ms or on assignment. Pays $5 to $25. Color: 2½x2½ smallest acceptable. Pays $25 to $100. "We are interested in photos of ships on the rivers or in the river ports of the U.S.; container ships in open waters. Virtually any U.S. flagship may be of potential interest to us. We are probably the best market for maritime photos in the industry."

FLORIDA JOURNAL OF COMMERCE/SEAFARER, P.O. Box 4728, Jacksonville FL 32201. Editor: David A. Howard. For those engaged in shipping, transportation and foreign trade in southeastern U.S. Established: 1958. Monthly. Circulation: 4,265. Not copyrighted. Will send free sample copy to writer on request. Query first. Seasonal and special material done only on assignment. Reports on material accepted for publication in 1 month. Returns rejected material immediately. Enclose S.A.S.E.

Nonfiction and Photos: "In-depth features. Analytical pieces (based on original data or research). Port finances. Other transportation and export items (in-depth) with solid figures. News approach, basically. No 'old salt' human interest." Length: "depends solely on subject." Pays $1 per column inch. 8x10 b&w glossy photos purchased with ms. Pays $1 per column inch "as used." Pays $25 for color.

MARINE ENGINEERING LOG, 350 Broadway, New York NY 10013. Editor: Robert Ware. For shipbuilding and ship repair companies; ship operating companies, owners, agents and brokers; naval architects and marine engineers; other readers associated with the marine field. Monthly except June, when publication is semimonthly. Buys exclusive rights "unless specific arrangements are made to the contrary." Pays on publication. Reports "immediately." Enclose S.A.S.E. for return of submissions.

Nonfiction and Photos: Wants "articles of a technical or semitechnical nature on all aspects of shipbuilding and ship operation." Length: 500 to 4,000 words, "depending on the subject." Pays 5¢ per published word. Pays $5 per 8x10 glossy photo purchased with ms.

NAVAL ENGINEERS JOURNAL, Suite 807, Continental Bldg., 1012 14th St. N.W., Washington DC 20005. Editor: Captain Frank G. Law, USN (Ret). For "individuals, firms, or organizations concerned in any way with the design, construction, operation, maintenance, or repair of naval vessels and their installed equipment." Subject matter is "all engineering disciplines involving vessels: design, construction, maintenance, installed equipment, propulsion, control, electronics, navigation, oceanography, aircraft, habitability, etc." Special issue in June "covers society's annual ASNE Day symposium/meeting." Bimonthly. Circulation: 6,000. Copyrighted. Will send a sample copy for $4 ($6 outside U.S.). No query required. Submit seasonal or special material 4 to 6 months in advance. Reports in 3 months. Enclose S.A.S.E.

Nonfiction and Photos: Wants "up-to-date technical papers on naval engineering and naval architecture. Also, from time to time, general articles of interest to those people of the engineering community: management, technical histories, shipyards, etc. No special limitations; desire technically sound treatment of subject in a readable and logical presentation. Provide 100-word biographical sketch and, if applicable, an abstract to a technically oriented paper." Length: 3,000 words preferred. "Shorter or longer may be acceptable." B&w glossy photos with mss.

SEAWAY REVIEW, 3750 Nixon Rd., Ann Arbor MI 48105. Editor: Jacques LesStrang. Professional journal dealing with the St. Lawrence Seaway, Great Lakes, Lake ports and shipping. Quarterly. Buys North American serial rights. Pays on acceptance. Sample copy available for $1. "Query first on features as these are usually assigned to experts in their respective fields. From time to time will have assignments for writers in the states covered by the journal and will keep on file the names of qualified writers in these areas. Writers should support their listings with either credits or samples of their work. Deadlines fall on the 10th of the months preceding April, July, Oct. and Jan." Reports in two weeks. Enclose S.A.S.E.

Nonfiction: Articles of a professional nature relating to Great Lakes shipping, the economics of the eight states which comprise the Seaway region (Minnesota, Ohio, Wisconsin, Michigan, New York, Pennsylvania, Indiana and Illinois), port operation, the Seaway's role in state economic development, etc. Length: 1,000 to 1,500 words, short features; minimum 3,000 words, articles. "Payment varies with the knowledgeability of the author and the value of the subject matter; up to $250."

Photos: Purchased both with mss and with captions only. 8x10 glossy b&w or 4x5 Ektachrome on Lake shipping or port activity, if newsworthy. Pays $25 per accepted b&w photo, and "$100 for color—scenic as well as news photos."

Fillers: Uses spot news items relating to Lake ports. Length: 50 to 500 words. Pays $5 to $50.

SHIPPING NEWS AND MARITIME REVIEW, P.O. Box 22, Cary IL 60013. Editor: Captain Walter N. Larkin. For maritime industry. Monthly. Buys all rights. Pays on publication. Reports "immediately." Enclose S.A.S.E. for return of submissions.

Nonfiction: Articles on research pertaining to marine and maritime industry. On order only.

Photos: Uses 5x7 pix with captions only.

THE WORK BOAT, P.O. Box 52288, New Orleans LA 70150. Managing Editor: Philip C. Sperier. Monthly. Buys first rights. Pays on acceptance. Query first. Reports in 1 week. Enclose S.A.S.E.

Nonfiction and Photos: "Articles on waterways, river terminals, barge line operations, work boat construction and design, barges, dredges, tugs. Best bet for freelancers: One-angle article showing in detail how a barge line, tug operator or dredging firm solves a problem of either mechanical or operational nature. This market is semitechnical and rather exacting. Such articles must be specific, containing firm name, location, officials of company, major equipment involved, by name, model, power, capacity and manufacturer; with b&w photos." Length: 1,000 to 5,000 words. Payment "varies according to value of article."

Medical

Publications that are aimed at private physicians or which publish technical material on new discoveries in medicine are classified here. Journals for nurses, laboratory technicians, hospital resident physicians, and other medical workers will be found with the Hospitals, Nursing, and Nursing Homes journals. Publications for druggists and drug wholesalers and retailers are grouped with the Drugs, Health Care, and Medical Products journals.

AMERICAN FAMILY PHYSICIAN, 1740 W. 92nd St., Kansas City MO 64114. Publisher: Walter H. Kemp. Monthly. Circulation: 126,000. Buys all rights. Pays on publication. Query first. Reports in 2 weeks. Enclose S.A.S.E.
Nonfiction: Interested only in clinical articles. Length: 2,500 words. Pays $50 to $200.

AUDECIBEL, Journal of the National Hearing Aid Society, 24261 Grand River, Detroit MI 48219. Editor: Anthony DiRocco. For "otologists, hearing aid dealers, educators of the deaf and hard of hearing, audiologists, and others interested in hearing and audiology." Established in 1951. Quarterly. Circulation: 11,900. Buys all rights. Buys about 4 mss a year. Pays on publication. Will send a sample copy to a writer on request. Write for copy of guidelines for writers. Query first or submit complete ms. Enclose S.A.S.E. for return of submissions.
Nonfiction and Photos: "Purpose of the magazine is to bring to the otologist, the clinical audiologist, the hearing aid audiologist and others interested in the field authoritative articles and data concerned with research, techniques, education and new developments in the field of hearing and hearing aids. In general, *Audecibel's* editorial policy emphasizes a professional and technical approach rather than a sales and merchandising approach. Seven types of articles are used: technical articles dealing with hearing aids themselves; technical articles dealing with fitting hearing aids; case histories of unusual fittings; technical articles dealing with sound, acoustics, etc.; psychology of hearing loss; medical and physiological aspects; professional standards and ethics. We are not interested in human interest stories, but only in carefully researched and documented material." Length: 200 to 2,000 words; "will consider longer articles if content is good." Pays 1¢ to 2½¢ a word, "minimum of $5." Photos purchased with mss; captions optional. Pays $3 to $5.

CANADIAN DOCTOR, Gardenvale 800, Que., Canada. Editor: David Elkins. Associate Editor: Irwin Stephen. For registered doctors of medicine in private, group, industrial, hospital and institutional practice in Canada. Monthly. Pays on publication. "Freelance articles are written mainly on assignment basis. Query first. Study back issues before submitting material." Enclose S.A.E. and International Reply Coupons.
Nonfiction: "Articles concerning doctors' business procedures, facilities for practicing (office planning and design, financing, equipment, etc.), medical economics, ethics, legal matters, and similar strictly nonclinical material. Canadian viewpoint only." Length: about 2,000 words. Pays 3¢ to 5¢ a word.
Photos: Buys photographs with mss and, very seldom, with captions only. 8x10 preferred. Pays $3 to $5 per photo when price not included in rate for article.

MEDICAL OPINION, 575 Madison Ave., New York NY 10022. Executive Editor: Patrick Flanagan. For physicians primarily in private practice. Monthly. Circulation: 170,000. Buys all rights. Buys 30 to 55 mss a year. Payment on acceptance. Query first. Reports in 4 to 6 weeks. Enclose S.A.S.E.
Nonfiction: "Interested primarily in humor with sympathetic view toward physicians and their problems. Keep in mind the chronic interests and problems of the average practitioner. Example: Anything showing sympathy to his worries over paperwork, taxes, unruly patients, etc. *Medical Opinion* takes a consumer magazine approach, avoiding any hint of style used in technical journals. Also interested in serious, controversial articles concerning medicine or physicians, written by doc-

tors. Hard-hitting, opinionated articles, think pieces, or exposes with plenty of facts and points well made in organized, magazine article format (written by physicians) receive special attention." Length: 1,200 to 2,500 words. Pays up to $350.

THE MEDICAL POST, 481 University Ave., Toronto 1, Ont., Canada. Editor: Earl Damude. For the medical profession. Semimonthly. Will send sample copy to medical writers only. Send query first to John Shaughnessy, Managing Editor. Buys first North American serial rights. Pays on publication. Enclose S.A.E. and International Reply Coupons.
Nonfiction: Uses "newsy, factual reports of medical developments, technical advances, professional appointments. Must be aimed at professional audience, and not written in 'popular medical' style." Length: 300 to 800 words. Pays 8¢ a word.
Photos: Uses photos with mss or captions only, of medical interest; pays $5 and up.

PHYSICIAN'S MANAGEMENT, 26 Sixth St., Ridgeway Center, Stamford CT 06905. Editor: M.J. Goldberg. For "practicing physicians and senior medical students." Monthly. Circulation: 250,000. Buys all rights, but will reassign rights to author after publication. Buys 12 to 24 mss a year. Pays on acceptance. Write for copy of guidelines for writers. Query first recommended. Will not consider photocopied submissions. Submit seasonal material 4 months in advance of issue date. Reports in 2 weeks. Enclose S.A.S.E.
Nonfiction and Photos: "No clinical material. Interested only in the business side of conducting a medical practice: office management, patient relations, handling assistants, collections, personal investments, taxes and insurance. Use a simple, direct, anecdotal approach, emphasizing the human and practical side of medical practice and the political, social, and economic aspects of medicine." Buys informational articles, how-to's, personal experience articles, interviews, humor, exposes, personal opinion articles. Length: 1,500 to 2,500 words. Pays 5¢ to 15¢ a word, "depending on research, quality, etc." Photos purchased with mss; captions required. For 8x10 b&w glossies, pays $10.
Fillers: Short humor. Length: 50 to 200 words. Pays $5 to $25.

PRIVATE PRACTICE, 1029 United Founders Tower, Oklahoma City OK 73112. Editor: Marvin Henry Edwards. For "medical doctors in private practice." Monthly. Buys first North American serial rights. Pays on publication. Will send a free sample copy on request. No query required. Enclose S.A.S.E. for return of submissions.
Nonfiction and Photos: "Articles which indicate importance of maintaining freedom of medical practice or which detail outside interferences in the practice of medicine, including research, hospital operation, drug manufacture, etc. Straight reporting style. No clichés, no scare words such as 'socialists,' etc. No flowery phrases to cover up poor reporting. Stories must be actual, factual, precise, correct. Copy should be lively and easy-to-read." Length: up to 2,000 words. Pays "usual minimum $100." Photos purchased with mss only. B&w glossies, 8x10. Payment "depends on quality, relevancy of material, etc."

Milling, Feed, and Grain

FEED INDUSTRY REVIEW, 3055 Brookfield Rd., Brookfield WI 53005. Publisher: Bruce W. Smith. For manufacturers of livestock and poultry feed. Quarterly. Circulation: 8,000. Buys all rights. Pays on publication. Will send a free sample copy on receipt of letter only, no postcards. Query preferred. Reports in one week. Enclose S.A.S.E.
Nonfiction: "Profile articles on progressive feed manufacturing operations, including data on plant layout and equipment, research, and distribution. This is a market for factual reporters, not creative writers. Market extremely limited in 1974; queries imperative prior to submitting completed articles." Length: 1,500 to 2,200 words. Pays $20 to $75.

Photos: Buys usually only with mss, occasional exceptions. Subject matter should be agribusiness, plants, or other physical facilities. Wants b&w glossies, horizontal prints. Pays $7 to $10.

THE WHEAT SCOOP, 510 First Ave. N., Great Falls MT 59401. Editor: Joe Renders. Bimonthly. Not copyrighted. Query first. "Very little freelance material purchased." Enclose S.A.S.E.
Nonfiction: Uses "articles on grain research, freight rates, fertilizers, domestic markets and foreign markets as they pertain to Montana. Clarity and precision necessary. Authenticity, definite Montana tie-in are musts." Length: 100 to 1,000 words. Payment negotiated.
Photos: Buys photos with mss and with captions only.

Mining and Minerals

COAL AGE, 1221 Avenue of the Americas, New York NY 10021. Editor: Harold Davis. For supervisors, engineers and executives in coal mining. Monthly. Circulation: 15,100. Buys all rights. Pays on publication. Reports in two to three weeks. Enclose S.A.S.E. for return of submissions.
Nonfiction: Uses some technical (operating type) articles; some how-to pieces on equipment maintenance.

MINING EQUIPMENT NEWS, P.O. Box 225, Clarendon Hills IL 60514. Editor: Marsha M. Bailey. For "operating management of coal, metallic and nonmetallic minerals mines, pits, quarries." Established: 1923. Monthly. Circulation: 8,500. Buys all rights. Buys 6 to 12 mss a year. Payment on publication. Will send free sample copy to writers on request. Query first. Will consider photocopied submissions. Enclose S.A.S.E.
Nonfiction: Articles "strictly pertaining to mining machinery and processes. Simple, straightforward style with no literary gimmicks. State problem and solution first. *No* theory, geology, rock mechanics, labor-management politics, legal problems. *No* think pieces on ecology, mine politics, etc." Informational and how-to. Length: 500 to 1,000 words. Pays minimum of 3¢ a word.

Miscellaneous

THE ANTIQUES DEALER, 1115 Clifton Ave., Clifton NJ 07013. Editor: Gayle D. Aanensen. For dealers, show managers, others doing business with dealers in antiques. Monthly. Buys all rights unless otherwise arranged. Pays on publication. Free sample copy on request. Reports in 3 weeks. Enclose S.A.S.E. for return of submissions.
Nonfiction: Merchandising articles and articles about antiques and the antiques trade. Strictly a business magazine. Material must be geared to the trade; news of the trade, including upcoming antique shows, changes in shop operation, deaths of important members of the trade, dealer's associations news, changes in import excise taxes, etc. Length: 1,000 to 2,000 words. Pays 4¢ per word.
Photos: Purchased with mss; pays $5 per photo used. Also purchased with brief caption. Pays $5.50.
Fillers: Newsbreaks to interest antique dealers. Pays $1.50 and up.

BRUSHWARE, 330 Main St., Madison NJ 07940. Editor: C.D. Baldwin. For manufacturers and suppliers in the brush, broom, mop, and roller industries. Monthly. Circulation: 1,800. Pays on publication. Reports in 30 days. Enclose S.A.S.E. for return of submissions.

Nonfiction and Photos: Length: 800 to 1,000 words. Pays 2¢ per word. Photos purchased with mss. Payment varies.

CANADIAN TECHNICAL & SCIENTIFIC INFORMATION NEWS JOURNAL, Suite 2A, 1509 Sherbrooke St., W., Montreal, Quebec 109, Canada. Editor: Ronald A. Javitch. Established in 1972. For "universities and colleges, industrial libraries, government agencies (all levels), research centers, scientific and engineering institutions, consultants, design and research technologists, science editors." Biweekly. Circulation: "approximately 5,000." Not copyrighted. Time of payment "depends on agreement with writer." Query first. Reports in 60 to 90 days. Will send sample copy to writer for $3.50. Will consider photocopied submissions. Enclose S.A.E. for reply to queries.
Nonfiction: "News about breakthroughs and developments in science and technology in Canada primarily. Also news about unique scientific and engineering discoveries throughout the world. Notes on the decisions made on a science policy in Canada by the government and its agencies. Oceanography and oceanology; breakthroughs in cancer research and cold research. Advances in medical electronics applied to aiding the blind and the mute. Very clear and concise scientific style, understood by all readers whether technical, academic or lay. Parallel to style of *Scientific American.*" Length: 2,500 words maximum. Pays $20.

COM-ART, P.O. Box 128, Philadelphia PA 19150. Editor: Donald Sobwick. For art college graduates, professional and student commercial artists. "Art is their business and they approach it in a business-like manner." Established in 1972. Monthly. Circulation: 10,000. Rights purchased vary with artist and material. Buys all rights or first North American serial rights. Payment on publication. Write for copy of guidelines for authors. Query first for interviews. Submit complete ms for balance of material. Submit seasonal material 3 to 4 months in advance. Reports on material in 3 weeks. Enclose S.A.S.E. for return of material or reply to queries.
Nonfiction and Photos: "Interviews with top illustrators and commercial artists, up and coming artists, and those in a position to buy a commercial artist's product; articles about new or unusual aspects of the commercial art field; humorous sketches; helpful hints. Style should be easily read material with a minimum of technical jargon. Articles should emphasize the artist's contribution, but should also include a good account of how the material or process is used." Length: 6,000 words maximum. Pays 3¢ to 5¢ a word. 8x10 b&w glossy photos purchased with mss or on assignment. Pays $10.
Fillers: Jokes, short humor. Length: 250 words maximum. Pays $5 to $10.

HOUSEHOLD AND PERSONAL PRODUCTS INDUSTRY, 4 Second Ave., Danville NJ 07834. Editor: Hamilton C. Carson. For "manufacturers of soaps, detergents, cosmetics and toiletries, waxes and polishes, insecticides, and aerosols." Established in 1964. Monthly. Circulation: 12,000. Not copyrighted. Buys 3 to 4 mss a year, "but would buy more if slanted to our needs." Pays on publication. Will send a sample copy to a writer on request. Query first. Will consider photocopied submissions. Submit seasonal material 2 months in advance. Enclose S.A.S.E.
Nonfiction and Photos: "Technical and semitechnical articles on manufacturing, distribution, marketing, new products, plant stories, etc., of the industries served. Some knowledge of the field is essential in writing for us." Buys informational articles, interviews, photo features, spot news, coverage of successful business operations, new product articles, coverage of merchandising techniques, and technical articles. Length: 500 to 2,000 words. Pays $5 to $125. 5x7 or 8x10 b&w glossies purchased with mss. Pays $3 to $5.

JOURNAL OF THE AMERICAN CANDLEMAKER, 2010 Sunset Dr., Pacific Grove CA 93950. Editor: Michael E. Whitton. For "anyone concerned with candlemaking." Monthly. Circulation: 2,200. Not copyrighted. Buys 100 mss a year. Payment on acceptance. Will send free sample copy to writer on request. Submit complete ms. Submit seasonal material 2 months in advance. Reports on material in 2 weeks. Enclose S.A.S.E. for return of submissions.
Nonfiction and Photos: "Descriptive manuscripts about unique candles and the process of their manufacture written to where the average person can understand."

How-to, personal experience, historical, travel, successful business operations, new product, merchandising techniques, technical. Length: 500 to 2,500 words. Pays 2¢ a word. 8x10 b&w glossy photos purchased with accompanying mss. Captions required. Pays $3 to $5.
Poetry: Traditional forms, blank verse, free verse, avant-garde forms and light verse. 10 lines. Pays $2 per poem.

MODEL NEWS OF HOUSTON, Box 13447, Houston TX 77019. Editor: K. White. For "models, agents, clients." Established in 1971. Monthly. Circulation: 2,500. Rights purchased vary with author and material. Pays on acceptance. Will send a sample copy to a writer for $1. Query first for all material. Will not consider photocopied submissions. Submit seasonal material 2 months in advance of issue date. Reports in 5 days. Enclose S.A.S.E.
Nonfiction: "Relates to modeling techniques, training, shows." Buys informational articles, how-to's, photo features, new product articles, and coverage of merchandising techniques. Length: 300 to 1,000 words. Pays 1¢ to 2¢ a word.
Photos: Purchased with and without mss or on assignment; captions optional. For 5x7 b&w glossies, pays $10 to $25.

NATIONAL MALL MONITOR, 5615 Westfield Ave., Pennsauken NJ 08110. Editor: Robert J. Goldberg. Publisher: Robert A. Norins. For realtors, builders, developers, contractors, bankers, investors, managers, promotion directors, public relations consultants, leasing agents, department store executives. Established in 1971. Monthly. Circulation: 18,651 (monthly average). Not copyrighted. Payment on publication. Will send free sample copy to writer on request. Write for copy of guidelines for writers. Query first. Enclose S.A.S.E. for reply to queries.
Nonfiction: "This is a newspaper serving all facets of the shopping center industry. A typical assignment would involve contacting a specific person or company in this field for an interview. All inquiries pertaining to freelance work should be directed to the attention of the publisher." Recommended article length: 500 to 1,500 words. Pays 5¢ a word.

THE NATIONAL PUBLIC ACCOUNTANT, 1717 Pennsylvania Ave., N.W., Suite 1200, Washington DC 20006. Managing Editor: Linda A. Taxis. For "professional accountants in public practice; also lawyers, educators, banking officials, data processing supervisors, and finance executives." Monthly. Circulation: 16,000. Buys no rights, but "may request reprint with credit line." Usually does not pay, "but we are willing to venture into this, depending on relative value." Will send a free sample copy to a writer on request. Write for copy of guidelines for writers. Submit 2 typed copies of mss. Reports in 2 to 4 weeks. Enclose S.A.S.E.
Nonfiction and Photos: "Practical articles with valuable insight into our business area are preferred to mss that deal only with theory and academic rhetoric." Interested in personal experience, interviews, profiles, humor, and successful business operations. Sometimes uses b&w glossy photos as illustrations with articles. Length: 750 to 1,000 words. "We pay only under extremely special circumstances."

OCCULT TRADE JOURNAL, 240 Main St., Danbury CT 06810. Editor: R.C.H. Parker. For "the directors, owners, publishers, and interested business leaders involved in some field relating to the occult/metaphysical industry and personal development and spiritual awareness, which encompasses groups, associations, research, and societies." Monthly. Circulation: 3,200. Buys all rights. Buys 60 to 100 articles a year. Pays on publication; pays in copies "for first articles." Will send a sample copy to a writer on request. Reports in 60 days. Enclose S.A.S.E. for return of submissions.
Nonfiction and Photos: "Business articles of interest to bookstores, occult stores, and metaphysical centers. Organizational plans, advertising, public relations. News and book reviews. Short, to-the-point business articles with photos which cover basic skills in running small operations—less than $200,000 a year. This is the only trade publication in an unorganized industry having sales estimated at $500 to $800 million and including such areas as publishing, games, gifts, and the teaching of occult sciences. Most individuals in this field are very independent. No articles that take a childish approach or 'if you knew what you were doing' approach." For Directory of Suppliers, uses "5 business articles, 1,500 words each, on accounting, dis-

play, merchandising, advertising, and customer service." Buys how-to's, interviews, profiles, inspirational articles, humor, spot news, coverage of successful business operations and merchandising techniques, exposes, new product articles, and photo and travel features. Length: 250 to 1,200 words. Up-to-date, personal business items on insurance, family expense, etc. Length: 800 words maximum. Pays $5 to $75. B&w glossies and negatives purchased with ms. Photo Editor: Gilles Rousseau.
Poetry: "Mystic. Very little used." Pays $10. Dept. Editor: Aelbert Clark.
Fillers: Clippings, short humor. Length: 100 words. Pays $5.

PHONOGRAPH RECORD MAGAZINE, 8824 Betty Way, West Hollywood CA 90069. Editor: Martin Robert Cerf. For "music buyers." Established in 1970. Monthly. Circulation: 78,000. Buys all rights, but will reassign rights to author after publication. Buys about 450 mss a year. Pays on publication. Will send a sample copy to a writer for 25¢. Write for copy of guidelines for writers. Submit complete ms. Will consider photocopied submissions. Submit seasonal material 6 weeks in advance. Reports in 3 weeks. Enclose S.A.S.E. for return of submissions.
Nonfiction: "Music reviews, features." Length: 300 to 3,500 words. Pays $15 to $65. 8x10 b&w photos purchased with or without mss. Pays $8.

SCALE JOURNAL, 1327 Seventh St., Rockford IL 61108. Editor: David M. Mathieu. Buys first North American rights. Reports in 2 weeks. Enclose S.A.S.E.
Nonfiction: "Stories on product design, research and development of scales amd meters; new ways to use scales and meters, unique applications; anything that will show how something was accomplished and will be of interest to men who design, service, and sell weighing and measuring equipment. Also use articles on weighing and measuring officials—their job, how they do it; general interest articles on selling, management, etc." Pays 3¢ to 5¢ a word.

TOBACCO REPORTER, 424 Commercial Square, Cincinnati OH 45202. Editor: F. Lee Stegemeyer. For tobacco growers, processors, warehousemen, exporters, importers, manufacturers of cigars, cigarettes, and tobacco products. Monthly. Buys all rights. Pays on publication.Enclose S.A.S.E. for return of submissions.
Nonfiction and Photos: Uses original material on request only. Pays 2½¢ a word. Pays $3 for photos purchased with mss.
Fillers: Wants clippings on new tobacco product brands, local tobacco distributors, smoking and health, and the following relating to tobacco and tobacco products: job promotions, obituaries, honors, equipment, etc. Pays minimum 25¢ a clipping.

Music

THE CHURCH MUSICIAN, 127 Ninth Ave. N., Nashville TN 37234. Editor: William Anderson. Southern Baptist publication. For Southern Baptist church music leaders. Monthly. Circulation: 20,000. Buys all rights. Pays on acceptance. Will send a sample copy to a writer on request. No query required. Reports in 1 month. Enclose S.A.S.E. for return of submissions.
Nonfiction: Leadership and how-to features, success stories, articles on Protestant church music. Length: maximum 1,300 words. Pays up to 2½¢ a word.
Photos: Purchased with mss; related to mss content only.
Fiction: Inspiration, guidance, motivation, morality with Protestant church music slant. Length: to 1,300 words. Pays up to 2½¢ a word.
Poetry: Church music slant, inspirational. Length: 8 to 24 lines. Pays $5 to $10.
Fillers: Puzzles, short humor. Church music slant. Pays $3 to $5.
How To Break In: "I'd advise a beginning writer to write about his or her experience with some aspect of church music; the social, musical, and spiritual benefits from singing in a choir; a success story about their instrumental group; a testimonial about how they were enlisted in a choir—especially if they were not inclined to be enlisted at first. A writer might speak to hymn singers—what turns them on and what doesn't. Some might include how music has helped them to talk about Jesus as well as sing about him. We would prefer most of these experiences be related to the church, of course, although we include many articles by freelance writers whose af-

filiation is other than Baptist. We are delighted to receive their manuscripts, to be sure. A writer might relate his experience with a choir of blind or deaf members. Some people receive benefits from working with unusual children—retarded, or culturally deprived, emotionally unstable, and so forth. Photographs are valuable here."

CLAVIER, 1418 Lake Street, Evanston IL 60204. Editor: Mrs. Dorothy Packard. 9 times a year. Buys all rights. Pays on publication. Sample copy will be sent on request. "Suggest query to avoid duplication." Reports in 2 weeks on very good or very bad mss, "quite slow on the in-betweens." Enclose S.A.S.E.
Nonfiction and Photos: Wants "articles aimed at teachers of piano and organ. Must be written from thoroughly professional point of view. Avoid, however, the thesis-style subject matter and pedantic style generally found in scholarly journals. We like fresh writing, practical approach. We can use interviews with concert pianists and organists. An interview should not be solely a personality story, but should focus on a subject of interest to musicians. Any word length. Photos may accompany ms." Pays $15 to $18 per printed page.

HIGH FIDELITY TRADE NEWS, 25 W. 45th St., New York NY 10036. Editor: J. Bryan Stanton. For "retailers, salesmen, manufacturers, and representatives involved in the high fidelity/home entertainment market." Established in 1956. Monthly. Circulation: 15,000. Buys all rights. Buys about 36 mss a year. Pays on acceptance. Will send a sample copy to a writer on request. Query first; "all work by assignment only." Enclose S.A.S.E.
Nonfiction: "Dealer profiles, specific articles on merchandising of high fidelity products, market surveys, sales trends, etc." Length: "open." Pay varies.

THE INSTRUMENTALIST, 1418 Lake St., Evanston IL 60204. Editor: Kenneth L. Neidig. For instrumental music educators. Extablished: 1946. Monthly except in July. Circulation: 16,500. Buys all rights. Liberal permission to reprint. Buys 200 mss a year. Payment on publication. Will send sample copy to writer for $1 postpaid. Query first. Will consider photocopied submissions. Submit seasonal material 3 months in advance. Summer Camps, Clinics, Workshops (March); Nostalgia/History (June); Back to School (September); Music Ind. (August). Reports on material accepted for publication within 4 months. Returns rejected material within 3 months. Enclose S.A.S.E.
Nonfiction and Photos: "Practical information of immediate use to instrumentalists. Not articles 'about music and musicians,' but articles by musicians who are sharing knowledge, techniques, experience. 'In-service education.' Professional help for instrumentalists in the form of instrumental clinics, how-to articles, new trends, practical philosophy. Most contributions are from professionals in the field." Interpretive photojournalism. Length: open. Pays $10 to $100, plus 3 contributor's copies. Quality b&w prints. Pays $5. Color: 35mm and up. Pays $25.

JOURNAL OF CHURCH MUSIC, 2900 Queen Lane, Philadelphia PA 19129. Editor: Robert A. Camburn. For "church musicians with limited background; organists and directors of adult, youth, and children's choirs." Also for ministers and members of music committees. Circulation: about 4,000. Buys all rights. Buys 40 to 50 mss a year. Pays on acceptance. Will send a sample copy to a writer on request. Query first. Submit seasonal material 6 months to a year in advance. Reports in 2 to 3 months. Enclose S.A.S.E.
Nonfiction: "Practical suggestions and how-to articles on church service playing and choir training, modern trends in all phases of church music, some music history and literature, newsy items, church music administration, personal experience story if somehow unique." Taboos include "articles engaged more in philosophizing about a problem rather than suggesting a plan to attack it; also scholarly and analysis-of-the-score articles. To be avoided are the heartwarming, sentimental type pieces." Length: 1,000 to 3,000 words. Pays 2¢ a word.
Photos: B&w glossies. Pays $15.
Fiction: Humorous, contemporary problems and religious as applicable to music. Length: 1,000 to 1,500 words. Pays 2¢ a word.
Fillers: Puzzles, jokes, short humor. Length: 300 to 500 words. Pays 2¢ a word.

KORD, 735 Mayfield Ave., Stanford CA 94305. Editor: Eric Kriss. For "professional and aspiring musicians with strong interests in American musical forms, especially blues, jazz, rhythm and blues, folk and electronic music." Established: 1969. Quarterly. Circulation: 1,000. Rights purchased vary with author and material. Buys all rights. Buys first North American serial rights. Payment on publication. Will send sample copy to writer for $1.25. Query first. Will consider photocopied submissions, but not for musical compositions. Reports on material accepted for publication in 3 weeks. Returns rejected material in 1 week. Enclose S.A.S.E.
Nonfiction and Photos: "Interviews with musicians; technical articles on instruments, music theory; instructional articles; record and book reviews; music history pieces; a few general articles on music and society. Also publish original songs and compositions (in musical notation). No special style or approach; just clear, sensitive, creative, knowledgeable writing." Length: 200 to 6,000 words. Pays minimum of 1¢ a word. B&w glossy photos, 8½x11 or 5x7. Pays minimum of $1.

MUSIC MINISTRY, 201 Eighth Ave. S., Nashville TN 37202. Editor: H. Myron Braun. Affiliated with United Methodist Church. For church musicians, pastors, educators. Monthly. Circulation: 13,000. Buys all rights; occasionally buys first rights only. Buys 20 to 25 mss a year. Pays on acceptance. Will send a sample copy to a writer on request. No query required. Submit seasonal material 7 to 8 months in advance. Reports in 2 to 3 months. Enclose S.A.S.E. for return of submissions.
Nonfiction: Articles that deal with philosophy, history, and practice of music in the life of the organized church. Pays 2¢-2½¢ per word minimum.
Photos: Purchased with mss, 8x10. Pays $7.50.
Fiction: Very limited use of short-shorts that illustrate "right attitudes or practices" with regard to music and its relationship to life. Pays 2¢-2½¢ per word minimum.

MUSIC TRADES, 80 West St., P. O. Box 432, Englewood NJ 07631. Editor: John F. Majeski, Jr. For "music store owners and salesmen; manufacturers of pianos, organs, band instruments, guitars, etc." Monthly. Circulation: 7,000. Pays on publication. Enclose S.A.S.E. for return of submissions.
Nonfiction and Photos: Uses news and features on the musical instrument business. Also uses case history articles with photos, dealing specifically with musical instrument merchandising, not including record or hi-fi shops. No limit on length. Payment negotiable.
Fillers: Clippings of obituaries of music store people. Music store openings.

THE MUSICAL NEWSLETTER, Box 250, Lenox Hill Station, New York NY 10021. Editor: Patrick J. Smith. For "amateur and professional music lovers who wish to know more about music and be given more specific information." Established in 1971. Quarterly. Circulation: 400. Rights purchased vary with author and material; may buy first serial rights in English or second serial rights. Pays on acceptance. Will send a sample copy to a writer for $1. Query first for nonfiction, "giving list of subjects of possible interest and outlines, if possible." Will consider photocopied submissions. Enclose S.A.S.E. for return of submissions.
Nonfiction: "Articles on music and the musical scene today. The bulk of articles are on 'classical' music, but we also publish articles on jazz and pop. Articles need not pertain to music directly, such as socio-economic articles on performing entities. As the level of our publication is between the musicological quarterly and the record review magazine, what we want is readable material which contains hard-core information. We stress quality. We are always happy to examine freelance material on any aspect of music, from articles on composers' works to philosophical articles on music or reportorial articles on performing organizations. We discourage reviews of performances and interviews, which we feel are adequately covered elsewhere." Length: 3,000 words maximum. Pays 10¢ a word.

PTM MAGAZINE, 434 S. Wabash Ave., Chicago IL 60605. Editor: Robert E. Allan. For "music retailers, musical instrument manufacturers, music educators." Monthly. Circulation: about 13,000. Buys all rights. Buys 24 to 36 mss a year. Pays on publication. Will send a sample copy to a writer on request. Query first. Submit seasonal material 3 months in advance. Reports in 3 to 4 weeks. Enclose S.A.S.E.
Nonfiction and Photos: Articles must be specifically geared to musical instrument

retailing in a "relaxed" unstilted news-feature magazine style. "We like signed articles to have opinion and personality. And we don't mind pointing out to the industry its inadequacies in sales, advertising, merchandising, or other critical areas of marketing." Length: 2,000 words. Pays $10 to $55 depending on length and quality. "We use cover features of successful retailers with emphasis on a unique selling, advertising, promotion, etc., idea." Photos purchased with mss; with captions only. 8x10 or 5x7 b&w glossies.

SOUTHWESTERN MUSICIAN, P.O. Box 9908, Houston TX 77015. Editor: J.F. Lenzo. For music teachers. Monthly (August through May). Buys all rights. Pays on acceptance. Reports in 30 days. Enclose S.A.S.E. for return of submissions. **Nonfiction:** Wants "professional-slanted articles of interest to public school music teachers." Pays $25 to $50.

Oceanography

The journals below are intended primarily for scientists who are studying the ocean. Publications for ocean fishermen will be found under Fishing. Those for persons interested in water and the ocean as a means of travel or shipping are listed with the Marine Industries and Water Navigation journals.

OCEAN INDUSTRY, Box 2608, Houston TX 77001. Editor: Donald M. Taylor. For ocean-oriented technical personnel. Monthly. Circulation: 30,000. Buys all rights. Pays on acceptance. Will send free sample copy on request. Query required. Reports in 1 month. Enclose S.A.S.E.
Nonfiction: New developments relating to industry in ocean. No historical material; nothing that begins, "Over 70% of the earth is covered with water. . ." Length: 500 to 3,000 words. Pays "$30 to $50 per published page, or $1 per inch for short world report items."
Photos: Purchased with mss. "New ideas; new developments relating to industry in the ocean."

SEA FRONTIERS, 10 Rickenbacker Causeway, Virginia Key, Miami FL 33149. Editor: F. G. W. Smith. For "members of the International Oceanographic Foundation. People with an interest in the sea; professional people for the most part; people in executive positions and students." Established: 1954. Bimonthly. Circulation: 70,000. Buys all rights. Buys 20 to 25 mss a year. Payment on publication. Will send free sample copy to writer on request. Write for copy of guidelines for writers. Query first. Will consider photocopied submissions "if very clear." Reports on material within 6 weeks. Enclose S.A.S.E.
Nonfiction and Photos: "Articles (with illustrations) covering explorations, discoveries or advances in our knowledge of the marine sciences, or describing the activities of oceanographic laboratories or expeditions to any part of the world. Emphasis should be on research and discoveries rather than personalities involved." Length: 500 to 3,000 words. Pays 5¢ to 8¢ a word. 8x10 b&w glossy prints and 35mm (or larger) color transparencies purchased with ms. Pays $25 for color used on front and back cover. Pays $15 for color used on inside covers.
How To Break In: "The best way for a beginning writer to break into *Sea Frontiers* would be to study our style, query us concerning a subject and then submit a short article, with photographs. Before being submitted, the manuscript should be checked by a scientist doing work in the area with which the manuscript is concerned. The writer should also be sure that his sources are authoritative and up to date."

Office Equipment and Supplies

GEYER'S DEALER TOPICS, 51 Madison Avenue, New York NY 10010. Editor: Neil Loynachan. For individual office equipment and stationery dealers, and special purchasers for store departments handling stationery and office equipment. Monthly. Buys all rights. Pays on acceptance. Query first. Reports "immediately." Enclose S.A.S.E.

Nonfiction and Photos: Articles on merchandising and sales promotion; case histories of stationery and office equipment dealers. Length: 300 to 1,000 words. Rate on articles and photos negotiated.

MARKING INDUSTRY, 18 E. Huron St., Chicago IL 60611. Editor: A.W. Hachmeister. For dealers and manufacturers of marking devices—rubber stamps, stencils, badges, numbering machines, etc. Monthly. Buys all rights. Pays on publication. Reports in 1 week. Enclose S.A.S.E.

Nonfiction: Articles on the applications of marking products. News of related products, applications, people in marking industry; sales advice and techniques.

Photos: Buys glossy photos of marking products in use. Payment varies.

OFFICE PRODUCTS, Hitchcock Building, Wheaton IL 60187. Editorial Director: Thomas J. Trafals. For "independent dealers who sell all types of office products— office machines, office furniture, and office supplies." Established in 1904. Monthly. Circulation: 24,000. Buys all rights, but will reassign rights to author after publication. Pays on acceptance. Write for copy of guidelines for writers. Query first. Article deadlines are the 1st of the third month preceding date of issue. News deadlines are the 1st of each month. Will consider photocopied submissions. Reports in 3 to 4 weeks. Enclose S.A.S.E.

Nonfiction: "We're interested in anything that will improve an office product dealer's methods of doing business. Some emphasis on selling and promotion, but interested in all phases of dealer operations. Also news of the field—new stores, expansions, remodelings of OP dealerships." Length: "that which tells the story, and no more or less." Pays $25 to $125, "based on quality of article."

Photos: Purchased with and without mss. "Some news photos. Also, photos of new stores, promotions, etc., but we're not actively looking for these now." Pays $10.

OFFICE PRODUCTS INDUSTRY REPORT, 1500 Wilson Blvd., Suite 1200, Arlington VA 22209. Editor: Robert Kruhm. For "office product dealers." Established in 1970. Biweekly. Circulation: 6,000. Rights purchased vary with author and material. Pays on acceptance. Write for copy of guidelines for writers. Query first. Will consider photocopied submissions. Submit seasonal material 2 months in advance. Reports in 3 to 4 weeks. Enclose S.A.S.E.

Nonfiction and Photos: "Articles on new concepts of merchandising management and marketing in office products stores; not only retail, but also wholesale and manufacturers." Pays $25 to $75. Photos purchased with mss; captions required. For 5x7 or 8x10 b&w glossies, pays $10.

OFFICE WORLD NEWS, 645 Stewart Ave., Garden City NY 11530. Editor: Stan Warren. For manufacturers, distributors, retailers of office furniture, equipment and supplies. Established: 1973. Biweekly. Circulation: 25,000. Buys all rights. Buys 50 to 100 mss a year. Will send free sample copy to writer on request. Write for editorial guidelines. Query first. Will consider photocopied submissions. Reports on material in 2 weeks. Enclose S.A.S.E.

Nonfiction and Photos: "Generally feature articles concerning a dealer, distributor, or manufacturer, with a news slant to the lead." Informational, interview, profile, successful business operations, impact and application of new products; merchandising techniques, technical. Length: 250 to 750 words. Pays 5¢ to 7½¢ per word. B&w photos purchased with accompanying mss, without mss, or on assignment. "Tri-X. Send negs. We make proofs and prints." Captions required. Pays up to $20. Color transparencies. "Prefer Ektachrome or its equivalent in reproductive quality." Pays up to $20.

SOUTHERN STATIONER AND OFFICE OUTFITTER, 75 Third St. N.W., Atlanta GA 30308. Editor: Earl Lines, Jr. For retailers of office products in the Southeast and Southwest. Monthly. Not copyrighted. Pays on publication. Will send free sample copy on request. Query required. Reports promptly. Enclose S.A.S.E.

Nonfiction: Can use articles about retailers in the Southeast and Southwest regard-

ing problems solved concerning store layout, inventory, personnel, etc. "We want articles giving in-depth treatment of a single aspect of a dealer's operation rather than superficial treatment of a number of aspects." Must be approved by subject. Length: 1,000 to 1,400 words. Pays 2¢ to 4¢ a word.
Photos: Purchased with mss. Pays $5.

Optical

THE DISPENSING OPTICIAN, 1980 Mountain Blvd., Oakland CA 94611. Editor: Robert L. Pickering. Buys first rights. "Queries on special articles suggested by opticians welcomed." Enclose S.A.S.E.
Nonfiction: Interested in "articles on successful operation of optical dispensing business. (These are not to be confused with optometrists, oculists or ophthalmologists. Dispensing opticians are the people who make and fit the glasses on ophthalmologists' prescriptions.) Articles may deal with factors making for success of outstanding optical dispensing companies, technical aspects of adjusting glasses, economic factors in the business, relations with prescribing doctors (how does the optician get to the busy ophthalmologist; how does he ask for referrals); design of new dispensing establishments; merchandising sun glasses. Also will consider articles on advertising directed to doctors and to the public." Length: maximum 2,000 words. Pays 4¢ a word.

OPTICAL JOURNAL AND REVIEW OF OPTOMETRY, Chilton Way, Radnor PA 19089. Editor: John F. McCarthy. Semimonthly. Buys exclusive rights in the field. Pays on publication. Enclose S.A.S.E. for return of submissions.
Nonfiction: Uses technical articles, authoritatively written, on optometry and ophthalmic optics. News and activities of optometrists, opticians, and optical manufacturers, importers, and wholesalers. Pays 60¢ per printed inch minimum.
Photos: Photos may be singles or to illustrate articles; b&w only. Pays $5.

Packing, Canning, and Packaging

Journals in this category are for packaging engineers and others concerned with new methods of packing, canning, and packaging foods in general. Other publications that buy similar material will be found under the Food Processing, Products, and Services heading.

FOOD AND DRUG PACKAGING, 777 Third Ave., New York NY 10017. Editor: Ben Miyares. For packaging decisionmakers in food, drug, cosmetic firms. Established in 1959. Biweekly. Circulation: 40,000. Rights purchased vary with author and material. Pays on acceptance. Will send free sample copy on request. "Queries only." Enclose S.A.S.E.
Nonfiction and Photos: "Looking for news stories about packaging legislation, and its impact on the marketplace, new packages, easy opening devices, spectacular successes, etc. Newspaper style." Length: under 1,000 words; usually 500 to 750 words. Pays 5¢ a word. Photos purchased with mss. 5x7 glossies preferred. Shots should illustrate unusual aspect of container. Pays $5.
How To Break In: "1) Get details on local packaging legislation's impact on marketplace/sales/consumer/retailer reaction, etc. 2) Keep an eye open for *new* packages. Query when you think you've got one. New packages move into test markets every day, so if you don't see anything new this week, try again next week. Buy it; describe it briefly in a query."

MODERN PACKAGING, 1221 Avenue of the Americas, New York NY 10021. Editor: Thomas M. Jones. For product manufacturers who package or have contract-packaged their product lines; suppliers of packaging materials and equipment. Established: 1927. Monthly plus annual encyclopedia. Circulation: 46,000 domestic; 7,000 foreign. Buys all rights. "Very little freelance material bought; mostly on assignment." Payment on publication. Will send free sample copy to writer on request. Write for copy of editorial guidelines (technical/engineering only). Query first, with brief description of subject and available illustration. Reports "immediately." Enclose S.A.S.E.
Nonfiction: "Trend reports, how-to, news, engineering and technical reports." Length: open. Pays $30 per printed page.

PACKING AND SHIPPING, 437 E. Fifth St., Plainfield NJ 07060. Editor: C.M. Bonnell, Jr. For "packaging engineers, traffic managers, shipping managers, and others interested in physical distribution, industrial packaging and shipping." 9 times a year. Buys all rights. Pays on publication. A sample copy will be sent on request. Query first. Reports "promptly." Enclose S.A.S.E.
Nonfiction: Packing, handling and physical distribution procedure by land, sea and air as related to large company operations. Length: 1,000 words. Pays ½¢ to 1¢ a word.
Photos: Uses photographs of new products. Pays $1 each for size 5x7.

Paint

Additional journals that buy material on paint, wallpaper, floor covering, and decorating products stores are listed under Building Interiors.

AMERICAN PAINT AND WALLCOVERINGS DEALER, 2911 Washington Ave., St. Louis MO 63103. Editor: John Rogers. Monthly. Buys first North American serial rights. Pays on publication. Sample copy will be sent on request. Write for copy of guidelines for writers. Reports in 3 weeks. Enclose S.A.S.E. for return of submissions.
Nonfiction and Photos: Interested in articles that tell how paint and wallpaper, hardware, lumber and building supply dealers have built their decorating products businesses or have sold specific classes of merchandise such as: Paints, alkyd finishes, latex paints, masonry and specialty paints, enamels, wood finishes; wallpaper and fabrics, scenics, photomurals, metallic papers; rental equipment such as floor sanders and edgers, steamers; window shades and venetian blinds; spray guns and equipment; artist's materials, crafts, toys, ladders, floor tile, linoleum, carpeting, unfinished furniture and window glass. Also wants articles about remodeled or new stores, advertising and promotional programs, window displays, etc. Don't include "names of manufacturers and their brands. Identify products by generic names." Do include "the full name and address of the store and the name of the owner or manager who was interviewed." Pictures are a necessity. Pays 2¢ to 3¢ a word for text, $5 to $6 for photos.

AMERICAN PAINT JOURNAL, 2911 Washington Ave., St. Louis MO 63103. Editor: Fred Schulenberg. Weekly. Pays on publication. Reports "promptly." Enclose S.A.S.E. for return of submissions.
Nonfiction: Uses news, features, etc. covering the paint, varnish and lacquer industry—new plants, facilities, management, sales, etc. Pays 75¢ per printed inch.
Photos: Buys pix with mss and captions only. 5x7 or 8x10. Pays $3 to $5 each.
How to Break In: "Either query letter or short features, provided author sticks to publication requirements."

AMERICAN PAINTING CONTRACTOR, 2911 Washington Ave., St. Louis MO 63103. Editor: Erwin L. Below. For professional painting contractors, architects, specification writers, and industrial maintenance engineers. Monthly. Circulation: 45,000. Buys 40 to 50 mss a year. Pays on publication. Will send a sample copy to a writer on request. Query first. Mss must be double-spaced on good grade soft paper; "mss submitted on 'butcher-grade' paper will be returned." Reports in 1 to 2 months. Enclose S.A.S.E.

Nonfiction and Photos: Technical descriptions of large-scale painting projects, such as buildings, apartment projects, hotels, etc.; unusual decorating applications in commercial and residential jobs; industrial maintenance coatings applications; running a painting contracting business. Professional painting only; do-it-yourself taboo. Buys how-to's, interviews, profiles, spot news, coverage of merchandising techniques and successful business operations. Length: 2,000 to 2,400 words. Pays "average 4¢ a word and up, with extra compensation for good spadework, original research, and complexity of assignment." Photos purchased with mss. B&w glossies and color transparencies. Pays $5 each.

How to Break In: "Absolutely mandatory to study publication to determine the type of readership to which it is aimed and the business interests and needs of that readership. This simple 'homework' requirement would increase chances of consideration at least 50 percent."

CANADIAN PAINT AND FINISHING MAGAZINE, 481 University Ave., Toronto 2, Ont., Canada. M5W 1A7 Editor: B. Rogers. Monthly. Pays on acceptance for mss, on publication for photos. Query first. Reports "at once." Enclose S.A.E. and International Reply Coupons.

Nonfiction: "Semitechnical and news articles on paint manufacturing, industrial finishing techniques, new developments. Also interested in electroplating. Mostly Canadian material required." Accompanied by photos. Length: 800 to 1,500 words. Pays minimum 5¢ a word.

Photos: 8x10 glossy. Pays $5.

WESTERN PAINT REVIEW, 1833 W. 8th St., Suite 206, Los Angeles CA 90057. Editor: Ernest C. Ansley. For painting and decorating contractors, retail paint dealers and paint manufacturers. Established 1920. Monthly. Circulation: 18,000. Buys 25 to 30 mss a year. Payment on publication. Query first. Will consider photocopied submissions. Submit seasonal material 2 months in advance. Reports on material within 3 weeks. Enclose S.A.S.E.

Nonfiction and Photos: Articles on successful busines operations, merchandising techniques. Technical articles. Length: 500 to 3,000 words. Pays 3¢ a word minimum. 4x5 minimum glossy b&w photos purchased with ms. Captions required. Pays $3.

Paper

PAPERBOARD PACKAGING, 777 Third Ave., New York NY 10017. Editor: Joel J. Shulman. For "managers, supervisors, and technical personnel who operate corrugated box manufacturing and folding cartons converting companies and plants." Established in 1916. Monthly. Circulation: 8,200. Buys all rights. Pays on publication. Will send a sample copy to a writer on request. Query first. Will consider photocopied submissions. Submit seasonal material 3 months in advance. Enclose S.A.S.E.

Nonfiction and Photos: "Application articles, installation stories, etc. Contact the editor first to establish the approach desired for the article. Especially interested in packaging systems using composite materials, including paper and other materials." Buys technical articles. Length: open. Pays "$50 per printed page (about 1,000 words to a page), including photos. Will not pay photography costs, but will pay cost of photo reproductions for article."

SOUTHERN PULP AND PAPER MANUFACTURER, 75 Third St., N.W., Atlanta GA 30308. Editor: Vincent F. Waters; Associate Editor: Gary W. Johnston. For "those actively associated with a pulp and/or paper manufacturing or converting operation." Monthly. Pays after publication. Reports in 2 weeks. Enclose S.A.S.E. for return of submissions.
Nonfiction and Photos: Production, new methods, processing, and new mill or mill expansion stories written to interest pulp and paper companies' personnel. Length: up to 2,000 words. Pays 35¢ per column inch or more, depending upon importance of subject matter and quality of material. Pays $2 per photo.

Petroleum

CANADIAN PETROLEUM, 6 Crescent Rd., Toronto 5, Ont., Canada. Editor: James D. Hilborn. For oil and gas industry. Monthly. Buys all rights. Pays on acceptance. Will send sample copy on request. Query first. Reports in two weeks to one month. Enclose S.A.E. and International Reply Coupons.
Nonfiction: Oil refining operations, petrochemical production operations, natural gas exploration, drilling, pipelining, producing, processing, petroluem products marketing. Uses how-to pieces slanted to Canadian operators. No U.S. statistics. Writer must have engineering know-how. Length: 800 to 2,500 words. Pays $25 to $50 per published page.
Photos: Purchased with mss or with captions.

EM REPORT, P.O. Box 1589, Dallas TX 75221. Editor: Ernestine Adams. For executives and technical managers in the oil and gas industries. Monthly. Pays on publication. Reports in 1 month. Enclose S.A.S.E. for return of submissions.
Nonfiction: Articles about management and economics in petroleum and natural gas industries. Payment varies.

FUEL OIL NEWS, 1217 Kennedy Blvd., Bayonne NJ 07002. Editor: T. R. Byrley. Monthly. Circulation: 15,000. Buys all rights. Pays on publication. Will send a free sample copy on request. Prefers outline first, then assignment. Reports in 10 days. Enclose S.A.S.E.
Nonfiction and Photos: Articles with photos about dealer operations and technical pieces on heating. Pays $35 to $50 per printed page, depending on material.

FUELOIL AND OIL HEAT, 200 Commerce Rd., Cedar Grove NJ 07009. Feature Editor: M.F. Hundley. For distributors of fueloil, heating equipment dealers. Monthly. Buys first rights. Pays on publication. Reports in 2 weeks. Enclose S.A.S.E. for return of submissions.
Nonfiction: Management articles dealing with fueloil distribution and equipment selling. Length: up to 2,500 words. Pays $25 to $35 a printed page.

HYDROCARBON PROCESSING, P.O. Box 2608, Houston TX 77001. Editor: Frank L. Evans. For personnel in the oil, gas, petrochemical processing or hydrocarbon processing industries, including engineering, operation, management phases. Special issues: January, Maintenance; April, Natural Gas Processing; September, Refining Processes; November, Petrochemical Processes. Monthly. Buys all rights. Write for copy of guidelines for writers. Enclose S.A.S.E.
Nonfiction: Wants technical manuscripts on engineering and operations in the industry which will be of help to personnel. Also nontechnical articles on management, safety and industrial relations that will help technical men become managers. Length: open, "but do not waste words." Pays about $25 per printed page.
Photos: Buys photos as part of nonfiction package; and infrequently, with captions only. Prefers 8x10 but can use 5x7 or even smaller if extremely sharp.

NATIONAL PETROLEUM NEWS, 1221 Avenue of the Americas, New York NY 10020. Editor: Frank Breese. For "independent businessmen and oil company marketing personnel who require information about developments, trends, problems and issues in oil marketing." Established: 1909. Monthly. Circulation: 22,000. Buys all rights. Buys 6 mss a year. Payment on publication. Will send free sample copy to writer on request. Query first. Enclose S.A.S.E.

Nonfiction and Photos: Articles on "current developments in storage, warehousing, transportation, merchandising of oil products (motor fuels, fuel oils, lubricants, TBA); also management, training, pricing and marketing research and legislative activity. How-to; merchandising techniques. Send a brief query with suggestion and do nothing until a reply is received." Length: 2,000 words maximum. No minimum. Pays $40 a printed page. Purchases b&w photos with or without accompanying ms or on assignment. Captions required.

OFFSHORE, P.O. Box 1941, Houston TX 77001. Editor: Robert G. Burke. For companies involved in drilling, producing, exploration, pipelining, in the oil and gas industry; engineering-construction, shipbuilding, oceanography, underwater mining, marine services, oilwell services, equipment manufacturers and supply companies. June 20 is Annual Drilling and Production Issue. Major offshore oil areas of the world are reviewed. Established in 1954. Monthly. Circulation: 16,000. Buys first North American serial rights. Buys 15 to 20 mss a year. Pays on publication. Query required. Reports in 2 to 4 weeks. Enclose S.A.S.E.

Nonfiction and Photos: Informative, explanatory material on how a project was accomplished. Aim at the working engineer, middle management, workmen, and persons interested in commercial offshore projects and commercial oceanography. Buys informational articles, personal experience articles, interviews, profiles, and spot news. Length: 500 to 3,500 words. Pays $1 per column inch. Photos purchased with mss.

THE OIL AND GAS JOURNAL, 211 S. Cheyenne, Tulsa OK 74101. Editor: George Weber. Weekly. Buys all rights. Enclose S.A.S.E. for return of submissions.

Nonfiction: Uses only spot oil and gas industry news and technical engineering-operating articles covering specific oil exploration, drilling, production, refining, pipelines, petrochemical operations. Pays $1 to $2 per column inch.

PETROLEUM ENGINEER INTERNATIONAL, PIPELINE & GAS JOURNAL, P.O. Box 1589, Dallas TX 75221. Monthly. Buys all rights. Query first. Enclose S.A.S.E.

Nonfiction and Photos: "Technical and semitechnical articles about the petroleum industry, but not about the marketing of oil. Must concern methods in drilling, production, pipeline construction and operation, and gas distribution. Knowledge of the oil industry is essential. Pictures and illustrations help." Length: 2 to 10 typed pages. Pays $35 to $250.

PETROLEUM INDEPENDENT, 1101 Sixteenth St., N.W., Washington DC 20036. Editor: Tony Simmons. For "independent petroleum drillers, operators, producers, bankers, and oil company personnel." Bimonthly. Circulation: about 11,000. Buys first rights. Buys about 10 mss a year. Guaranteed payment on acceptance. Will send a sample copy to a writer on request. Query first. Reports promptly. Enclose S.A.S.E.

Nonfiction: "Anything of political or economic interest to our audience. Most material solicited from experts in their fields. Will consider any unusual, interesting oil drilling/ producing events. We frequently print articles about towns with a strong petroleum background or round-up stories describing a particularly active exploration area. Not wanted are articles on foreign production, refining, marketing, and other segments of the industry, each of which has its own magazine." Buys how-to's, interviews, and profiles; occasionally, historical and photo articles. Ironic and/or unusual situations regarding energy shortages (oil, gas) in particular areas. Length: maximum 2,500 words. Pays $50 to $75 per magazine page.

Photos: Purchased with mss; with captions only. B&w glossies, color transparencies, color prints. Pays $5 to $25 for photos not accompanying mss.

Fiction: "Rarely bought, but will consider it if well-done and slanted toward petroleum politics or economics." Length: maximum 2,500 words. Pays $50 to $75 per magazine page.

PETROLEUM MARKETER, 636 First Ave., West Haven CT 06516. Editor: Richard J. Myers. For "independent oil jobbers, major oil company operations and management personnel, and petroleum equipment distributors." Bimonthly. Circulation: 20,000. Buys North American serial rights. Pays on publication. Will send a sample copy to a writer on request. Query first. Reports "within 3 days of receipt." Enclose S.A.S.E.
Nonfiction and Photos: "Success stories on how an oil jobber did something; interpretive marketing stories on local or regional basis. We want straightforward, honest reporting. Treat the subject matter with dignity." Length: 1,200 to 1,500 words. Pays "$35 per printed page." Photos purchased with and without mss; captions required. "Glossies for reproduction by engraving; subject matter decided after consultation." Pays $5.

PETROLEUM TODAY, 1801 K St., N.W., Washington DC 20006. Editor: Cynthia Riggs Stoertz. For "mostly men, in their early fifties; what we call opinion leaders; may be clergymen, legislators, newspapermen, club leaders, professors; but few oil industry people." Established: 1959. Quarterly. Circulation: 110,000. Not copyrighted. Buys 8 to 10 mss a year. Payment on publication. Will send free sample copy to writer on request. Query first. Reports on material in 2 to 6 weeks. Enclose S.A.S.E.
Nonfiction and Photos: "Articles on issues that currently face the petroleum industry on the energy crisis, marine drilling, the environment, taxation, the Alaska pipeline, offshore drilling, consumerism, coastal zone management. Also like to use a few short, light articles; oil-related." Informational, personal experience, interview, profile, think pieces. Length: open. Pays $200 to $750. 8x10 b&w glossy photos purchased with or without accompanying mss, or on assignment. Captions required. Pays $25. 35mm (or larger) color transparencies. Pays $50 a quarter page; $200 for cover. Must be petroleum-related.
How to Break In: "We want absolute honesty in dealing with a subject, and we want it carefully researched. Before anyone submits an article, please ask us for a copy of *Petroleum Today*. Then read it! 90 percent of our rejections are for material completely unsuited to our magazine. Some are extremely well-written. Don't waste postage, your time or ours, plus wear and tear on your manuscript, unless you're pretty sure your article is aimed at us."

PIPE LINE INDUSTRY, P.O. Box 2608, Houston TX 77001. Editor: Don E. Lambert. For gas and oil pipeline and distribution industry. Monthly. Circulation: about 20,000. Buys all rights. Pays on publication. Will send free sample copy to a writer on request. Query preferred; include outline indicating approach, depth, and probable photos or other illustrations to be submitted. Reports in 10 days. Enclose S.A.S.E.
Nonfiction: Short technical features; ideas for doing a job easier, cheaper, and safer; operating hints, etc. Length: "varies." Pays $25 per page; higher rates upon advance agreement. Gas and Engineering Editor: Robert E. Stiles; Associate Editor-Construction: Dave Deason.
Photos: Purchased with mss; construction and operations of facilities in the gas and pipeline industry. 8x10 glossies preferred. Payment depends on space and manner in which photo is used.

WORLD OIL, P.O. Box 2608, Houston TX 77001. Editorial Director: Donald E. Kliewer. For "petroleum exploration, drilling, and production people and their managements; average age, 41; education, 1 degree." Established in 1916. Monthly, except semimonthly in February and August. Circulation: 26,500. Rights purchased vary with author and material; may buy all rights, but may reassign rights to author after publication. Buys about 50 or 60 mss a year. Pays on acceptance. Will send a sample copy to a writer on request "if query is about an article in our editorial area." Write for copy of guidelines for writers. Query first. Reports in 2 weeks. Enclose S.A.S.E.
Nonfiction: "Engineering/operating articles, primarily. We're more oriented to en-

gineering and field operations articles than other publications in our field." Buys technical articles. Length: 750 to 2,000 words. Pays $17.30 per magazine page.

Photography

AMERICAN CINEMATOGRAPHER, 1782 N. Orange Dr., Hollywood CA 90028. Editor: Herb A. Lightman. For motion picture directors of photography and film production personnel. Monthly. Buys all rights. Query first. Enclose S.A.S.E.
Nonfiction and Photos: Uses articles dealing with the photography and allied technology of motion pictures in all fields of film production. Treatment must be technical or semitechnical, describing unusual problems encountered and how solved, with substantial emphasis on the equipment and mechanical techniques used. Length: 1,500-2,500 words. Pays up to $75. Photos purchased with ms.

BUSINESS SCREEN, 757 Third Ave., New York NY 10017. Editor: Bob Seymour. For sponsors, producers and users of business, commercial advertising and industrial motion pictures, slidefilms and related audio-visual media. Bimonthly. Buys all rights. Pays on publication. Query first. Reports in 2 weeks. Enclose S.A.S.E.
Nonfiction: "Short articles on successful application of these 'tools' in industry and commerce, but only when approved by submission of advance query to publisher's office. Technical articles on film production techniques, with or without illustrations, science film data and interesting featurettes about application or utilization of films in community, industry, etc., also welcomed." Pays up to 5¢ a word.

GOVERNMENT PHOTOGRAPHY, 2000 P St., N.W., Washington DC 20036. Editor: John Ncubauer. For government photographers and government employees in photography-related jobs. Monthly. Buys one-time rights. Pays on acceptance. Query essential. Enclose S.A.S.E.
Nonfiction: Articles must deal with how-to's for government photographers, with specific government slant. Pays $25 minimum.
Photos: Only those taken by government photographers in conjunction with government assignment.
How To Break In: "Too many freelancers write around the bush for us, forgetting that we direct our efforts toward government photographers and a-v specialists. Often, they don't know a thing about photography or the a-v field. We've found staff-written pieces are best for us, and on the few occasions when we use a freelance piece that it be handled by someone in government who is a photographer or a-v specialist. But if we ever get a good idea from a freelancer we always consider it, and sometimes assign it. With us, queries are always essential."

INDUSTRIAL PHOTOGRAPHY, 750 Third Ave., New York NY 10017. Editor: Natalie Canavor. For industrial photographers, scientists, educators and other professionals interested in industrial photograpy (various ages; college-trained specialists). Established: 1952. Monthly. Circulation: 41,000. Rights purchased vary with author and material. Buys first North American serial rights, first serial rights and second serial (reprint) rights. Pays on publication. Will send sample copy to writer for $1. Query first. Will consider photocopied submissions. Submit material for special issues 3 months in advance. Reports on material in 2 weeks to 1 month. Enclose S.A.S.E.
Nonfiction and Photos: Articles on "any area in industrial photography. Techniques and approaches in still photography; motion pictures, audiovisuals, video. New ideas for using photography department administration. All writing must be for professional level audience of photographers, relevant to their work as staff members of communications departments of business, industry, government installations, hospitals, research facilities, etc." Special issues include: Bio-Medical Photography, Underwater Photography, Photojournalism, Law Enforcement Photography, Lighting, Industrial Audiovisuals. Length: open. Pays $50 to $200, depending on material. 8x10 b&w glossy photos purchased with ms.

PHOTOJOURNALIST, P.O. Box 1466, Columbus MS 39701. Editor: Dr. Richard Logan. For freelance photojournalists. 10 times a year. Pays on acceptance. Will send two sample copies to a writer for 25¢. Enclose S.A.S.E.
Nonfiction: "Short items on successful and unusual ways to make money in photography. Letters or short articles about successful photographers and how they make money, short cuts in photographic methods, etc. Must be tried and proven successful." Length: "1 to 2 pages, doublespaced." Pays "$15 to $25 worth of photo books we have in stock for longer and unusual items, $5 worth of photo books we have in stock for short items."

PMI/PHOTO METHODS FOR INDUSTRY, 33 W. 60th St., New York NY 10023. Editor: Merwin Dembling. For photographers in industry, engineers who use photography in their work, executives dealing with photography. Established: 1958. Monthly. Circulation: 50,000. Buys first North American serial rights. Buys about 25 mss a year. Payment on publication. Will send free sample copy to writer on request. Query first. Will consider photocopied submissions. Enclose S.A.S.E.
Nonfiction and Photos: "Need how-to stories that show solutions to problems faced by photographers in the field and in the darkroom. Must be from the point of view of the working professional photographer." Length: 100 to 5,000 words. Pays $35 per printed feature page. B&w photos purchased with ms. Captions required.

THE PROFESSIONAL PHOTOGRAPHER, 1090 Executive Way, Oak Leaf Commons, Des Plaines IL 60018. Publisher: Frederic Quellmalz. Managing Editor: Fred Schmidt. Monthly. Circulation: 20,000. Buys all rights. Pays on acceptance. Will send free sample copy to a writer on request. Query required. Reports in 2 weeks. Enclose S.A.S.E.
Nonfiction and Photos: Business articles; business methods for small businesses; photographic styles and trends; operations of successful studios; profiles on photographic personalities and studios. Do not send clippings, or items on homemade equipment. Length: 500-2,000 words. Payment usually about 2¢ per word. Photos purchased with mss. 8x10 glossy preferred. pays $2 to $100.

THE RANGEFINDER MAGAZINE, 3511 Centinela Ave., Los Angeles CA 90066. Editor: Janet Marshall Victor. For career photographers and photofinishers. Established in 1952. Monthly. Circulation: 35,000. Not copyrighted. Buys about 20 mss a year. Pays on publication. Will send a sample copy to a writer for $1. Write for copy of guidelines for writers. Query first "for major features; no query required on secondary material." Will consider photocopied submissions "if legible." Reports in 2 weeks. Enclose S.A.S.E. for return of submissions.
Nonfiction and Photos: "Features encompass all phases of professional photography—solutions to technical problems, business practices, handling assignments, equipment testing, processing techniques, future trends—anything to help improve the status quo, both business-wise and quality-wise. We like a variety of brief articles. We're interested in unique methods of marketing photography. We don't want to see biographies in which there is no real knowledge to help our readers increase their quality and profit. We need to know specific techniques which the subject successfully applied to a problem." Length: 1,000 to 2,000 words. Pays 2¢ a word; "3¢ a word if illustrations accompany articles." Photos purchased with mss; captions optional. Uses 8x10 matte or glossy b&w photos. Uses color.

Plastics

CANADIAN PLASTICS, 1450 Don Mills Rd., Don Mills, Ont., Canada. Editor: Lyn Hamilton. For management people in the plastics industry. Monthly. Pays on publication. Query first. Reports on acceptance. Enclose S.A.E. and International Reply Coupons.
Nonfiction: Wants accurate technical writing. Accuracy is more important than style. "Our readers are businessmen looking for guidance and information." Pays 7¢ a word.

Photos: Buys photos submitted with ms. Pays $5.
Fillers: Buys newsbreaks.

PLASTICS TECHNOLOGY, 630 Third Avenue, New York NY 10017. Editor: Malcolm W. Riley. For plastic processors. Circulation: 40,000. Buys all rights. Pays on publication. Will send free sample copy on request. Query preferred. Reports in 2 weeks. Enclose S.A.S.E.
Nonfiction and Photos: Articles on plastics processing. Length: "no limits." Pays $30-$35 per published page. Photos purchased with ms.

Plumbing, Heating, Air Conditioning, and Refrigeration

Publications for fuel oil dealers who also install heating equipment are classified with the Petroleum journals.

BUILDING SYSTEMS DESIGN, 235 Duffield St., Brooklyn NY 11201. Managing Editor: W. Edmond Gutman. For "consulting design engineers in the air conditioning, heating, and ventilating fields (non-residential market); architects, mechanical contractors, and original equipment manufacturers' engineering staff. It is a mature, highly sophisticated engineering audience." Established in 1904. Monthly. Circulation: 26,000. Buys all rights. Buys about 36 mss a year. Pays on publication. Will send a sample copy to a writer on request. Query first or submit complete ms. Submit seasonal material 2 to 3 months in advance. Reports in 1 week. Enclose S.A.S.E.
Nonfiction and Photos: "Technical applications in the air conditioning, heating, and ventilating fields, with a special eye toward environmental control and energy conservation. Articles on process piping, exotic refrigeration systems, etc. The writer should have a sound knowledge of the particular theme treated. Especially interested in unusual applications in our field. No press release story treatment—ugh!" Buys how-to's, new product articles, and technical articles. Length: 1,500 to 6,000 words. Pays $25 "per printed page, including photos." Captioned b&w glossies purchased with ms.

DE/JOURNAL, 450 E. Ohio St., Room 800, Chicago IL 60611. Editor: Stephen J. Shafer. For plumbing, heating, piping, air conditioning contractors. Monthly. Circulation: 30,000. Buys all rights. Pays on publication. Will send a sample copy to a writer on request. Query first. Reports in 1 month. Enclose S.A.S.E.
Nonfiction: Management, marketing or technical articles keyed to the interest of mechanical contractors. Freelancers who sell consistently to this magazine are usually able professionals with a knowledge of the field, although editors are willing to work with any serious freelancer who shows ability. Major features must deal with significant aspects of current industry problems and trends. Articles showing how a mechanical contractor has solved a specific management problem. Short features on unusual contractor merchandising promotions and programs. Pays $25 per published page.

ELECTRIC COMFORT CONDITIONING JOURNAL, 2132 Fordem Ave., Madison WI 53701. Editor: Donald J. Jonovic. For architects, consulting engineers, electrical and heating contractors, builders, and their allies. Monthly. Circulation: 40,000. Buys all rights. Pays on acceptance. Will send a free sample copy to a writer on request. Query suggested. "Mostly staff-written because of a shortage of acceptable freelance submissions." Reports in 10 days. Enclose S.A.S.E.
Nonfiction and Photos: "Articles and photos on unusual electric heating system designs, electric heating experimental projects, electrical contractors or heating contractors with strong, intelligent sales programs, and new developments in electric

heating. Articles should be tightly written, pointed, and intelligent. We try to give our readers clear, readable stories on all aspects of electric comfort conditioning. Stories on advanced equipment, new ideas in the field, how-to's on power saving, interviews, and anything else that's efficient would be smiled upon. Good photos are always manna from heaven, but only when accompanying articles." Length: maximum 1,500 words. Pays $75 to $150.

ELECTRIC HEAT, 400 N. Michigan Ave., Chicago IL 60611. For "heating contractors, electric utility heating specialists, builders, architects, consulting engineers." Established in 1955. Bimonthly. Circulation: 11,000. Buys all rights. Pays on acceptance. Will send a sample copy to a writer for $1. Query first. Reports in 2 to 3 weeks. Enclose S.A.S.E.
Nonfiction and Photos: "Specific case histories of ways and means of selling or installing electric heating equipment, components and accessories for electric heating. Illustrated articles of new and converted electrically heated industrial, commercial, and residential buildings." Length: 750 to 1,500 words. Pays $75 to $200. 8x10 or 5x7 b&w glossies purchased with mss. Pays minimum $5.

HEATING AND PLUMBING MERCHANDISER, P.O. Box 343, E. Paterson NJ 07407. Editor: George V. Larabee. For heating and plumbing contractors and wholesalers. Bimonthly. Pays on acceptance. Reports immediately. Enclose S.A.S.E. for return of submissions.
Nonfiction and Photos: Wants articles dealing with new products; merchandising; selling. No standard rate of payment.

HEATING/PIPING/AIR CONDITIONING, 10 S. LaSalle St., Chicago IL 60603. Editor: Robert T. Korte. Monthly. Buys all rights. Pays on publication. Query first. Reports in 2 weeks. Enclose S.A.S.E.
Nonfiction: Uses engineering and technical articles covering design, installation, operation, maintenance, etc., of heating, piping and air conditioning systems in industrial plants and large buildings. Length: 3,000-4,000 words maximum. Pays $30 per printed page.
Photos: Sometimes buys photographs.

HEATING, PLUMBING, AIR CONDITIONING, 1450 Don Mills Rd., Don Mills, Ont., Canada. Managing Editor: Nick Hancock. For mechanical contractors; plumbers; warm air heating, refrigeration and air conditioning contractors; wholesalers; architects; consulting and mechanical engineers who are in key management or specifying positions in the plumbing, heating, air conditioning and refrigeration industries in Canada. Biweekly. Circulation: 14,500. Buys North American serial rights only. Pays on publication. Will send free sample copy to a writer on request. Reports in 1-2 months. Enclose S.A.S.E. and International Reply Coupons.
Nonfiction and Photos: News, technical, business management and "how-to" articles which will inform, educate and motivate readers who design, manufacture, install, service, maintain or supply fuel to all mechanical components and systems in residential, commercial, institutional and industrial installations across Canada. Length: 1,000-2,000 words. Pays 5¢ per word. Photos purchased with mss. Prefers 5x7 or 8x10 glossies.

ILLINOIS MASTER PLUMBER, 140 S. Dearborn St., Chicago IL 60603. Editor: J.E. Fitzgerald, Jr. For members of plumbing and heating, cooling trade, architects, engineers, union officials, manufacturers and wholesalers in industry. Monthly. Buys all rights. Pays on publication. Will send free sample copy to a writer on request. Reports in 30 days. Enclose S.A.S.E. for return of submissions.
Nonfiction: Articles on tax problems, accounting, service; humorous articles. Subjects of interest to readers in the plumbing, heating and cooling trade. Length: 1,200 words. Pays $1.50 per 100 words.

IOWA PLUMBING, HEATING, COOLING CONTRACTOR, Box 56, Boone IA 50036. Editor: R.G. Canier. For those in the plumbing-heating-cooling contracting industry plus state procurement authorities. Monthly. Circulation: 1,100. Not copyrighted. Pays on publication. Will send sample copy to a writer on request. "Study

publication." Enclose S.A.S.E. for return of submissions.
Nonfiction, Photos, and Fiction: Articles on development, engineering problems and improvements in general covering new equipment, new materials, legal review, state news, national news, and other topics. Also buys photos and fiction appropriate to format.

REEVES JOURNAL OF PLUMBING, HEATING, & COOLING, 2048 Cotner Ave., Los Angeles CA 90025. Managing Editor: Leslie Murray. Buys first rights. Pays on acceptance. Enclose S.A.S.E. for return of submissions.
Nonfiction: "Articles on wholesaler or contractor operations in the western U.S. Prefers that articles take a specific slant rather than taking the general, 'success story' approach." Length: 1,200 to 1,500 words. Pays 5¢ a word.
Photos: 5x7 or 8x10 b&w glossies. Pays $5.

SNIPS MAGAZINE, 407 Mannheim Rd., Bellwood Il. 60104. Editor: Nick Carter. For sheet metal, warm air heating, ventilating, air conditioning, and roofing contractors. Monthly. Buys all rights. "Write for detailed list of requirements before submitting any work." Enclose S.A.S.E. for return of submissions.
Nonfiction: Material should deal with information about contractors who do sheet metal, warm air heating, air conditioning, ventilation and roofing work; also about successful advertising campaigns conducted by these contractors and the results. Length: "prefers stories to run less than 1,000 words unless on special assignment." Pays 2¢ each for first 500 words, 1¢ each for additional words.
Photos: Pays $2 each for small snapshot pictures, $4 each for usable 8x10 pictures.

SOUTHERN PLUMBING, HEATING AND COOLING, P.O. Box 9377, Greensboro NC 27409. Publisher and Editor: Emmet Atkins, Jr. Monthly. "Please query." Enclose S.A.S.E.
Nonfiction: Features about individual plumbing and heating contractors in the 14 southern states, who are doing a good job along such lines as merchandising, advertising, modernization, etc. Length: about 1,000 words. Pays 2¢ a word.
Photos: Pays $2.50 for photos.

Power and Power Plants

Publications in this listing aim at company managers, engineers, and others involved in generating and supplying power for businesses, homes, and Industries. Journals for electrical engineers who design, maintain, and install systems connecting users with sources of power are classified under the heading Electricity.

DIESEL AND GAS TURBINE PROGRESS, P.O. Box 7406, 11225 West Blue Mound Rd., Milwaukee WI 53213. Editor: Bruce W. Wadman. For engineers, purchasers, and users of diesel and natural gas engines and gas turbines. Monthly. Pays on acceptance. Will send free sample copy to a writer on request. "Query with brief details about engine system and location. Send queries to Tony Alberte, Managing Editor." Reports in 4 weeks. Enclose S.A.S.E.
Nonfiction and Photos: Illustrated on-the-job articles detailing trend-setting application of diesel, gas (not gasoline) engines, gas turbine engines in industrial and commercial service: Material must thoroughly describe installation of the prime mover and auxilary equipment, special system requirements, and controls. Articles must be slanted to the viewpoint of the user. Length: 2,500 words. Pays $55 and up per page.

ELECTRIC LIGHT AND POWER, Cahners Building, 221 Columbus Ave., Boston MA 02116. Editorial Director: Robert A. Lincicome. 2 editions (Energy/Generation and Transmission/Distribution) for electric utility engineers, engineering management and electric utility general top management. Monthly. Buys all rights. Pays on publication. Will send free sample copies to a writer on request. "Query not

required, but recommended." Reports in 1 week. Enclose S.A.S.E.
Nonfiction and Photos: Engineering application articles, management subjects, electric utility system design, construction and operation, sales, etc. Articles may be case histories, problem-solutions, general roundups, state-of-the-art, etc. Must be technically oriented to industry. Length: 500-3,000 words. Pays $35 first published page, $25 second published page, $15 third published page, $10 fourth and succeeding pages. Photos purchased with mss as package; no separate photos accepted. Prefers 8x10 glossy prints, b&w; color transparencies, 2¼x2¼ or larger.

POWER, 1221 Ave. of the Americas, New York NY 10020. Editor: J.J. O'Connor. Monthly. Enclose S.A.S.E. for return of submissions.
Nonfiction: Uses editorial material from men of engineering training and experience only, and writers without such experience should not submit. Needs practical engineering articles dealing with boilers, turbines, large diesels, refrigeration machinery, electrical equipment, and similar energy systems equipment. Rates vary, but run about $25 per magazine page.

POWER ENGINEERING, 1301 S. Grove Ave., Barrington IL 60010. Editor: Ray Schuster. Monthly. Buys first rights. "Must query first." Enclose S.A.S.E.
Nonfiction and Photos: Articles on electric power field design, construction, and operation. Length: 500 to 1,500 words. Pays $80 to $200, "depending on published length." Uses 8x10 glossies with mss.

PUBLIC POWER, 2600 Virginia Ave., N.W., Washington DC 20037. Editor: Ron Ross. Bimonthly. Pays on publication. Enclose S.A.S.E. for return of submissions.
Nonfiction: News and features on municipal and other local publicly owned electric systems. Pays $10 to $60.
Photos: Pays $3 each for 8x10 glossy prints.

RURAL ELECTRIFICATION, 2000 Florida Ave., N.W., Washington DC 20009. Editor: Robert S. Trotter. For managers and boards of directors of rural electric systems. Monthly. Buys all rights or reprint rights. Pays on acceptance. Will send sample copy on request. Query first. Reports in one month. Enclose S.A.S.E.
Nonfiction: Uses articles on the activities of rural electric systems which are unusual in themselves or of unusually great importance to other rural electric systems across the country. Length: "open." Pay "negotiable, but usually in $50 to $250 range."
Photos: Uses photos with or without mss, on the same subject matter as the articles; 8x10 glossies. Pays $5 for b&w; $10 for color.

Printing

AMERICAN INK MAKER, 101 W. 31st St., New York NY 10001. Editor: John Vollmuth. For those in managerial and technical positions in the printing ink and pigment industries. Monthly. Circulation: 3,300. Buys all rights. Pays on acceptance. Will send free sample copy to a writer on request. Query first. Reports "immediately." Enclose S.A.S.E.
Nonfiction: Articles on new products for printing inks and pigment producers; articles on companies in these fields. Length: 1,200 words. Pays 3¢ per word; extra for photos.
Photos: Pays $5 per b&w photo (unless on assignment, in which case payment is negotiated).
Fillers: Newsbreaks, clippings, short humor on ink and pigment industries.

BUSINESS GRAPHICS, 7373 North Lincoln Ave., Chicago, IL 60646. Editor: Roy D. Conradi. Buys first rights. Reports "on the first of the month preceding publication date." Enclose S.A.S.E. for return of submissions.

Nonfiction and Photos: "Feature stories on internal reproduction departments, mailrooms, or visual communications systems." Pays $50. Photos purchased with ms

GRAPHIC ARTS MONTHLY, 7373 N. Lincoln Ave., Chicago IL 60646. Editor: Dr. Paul J. Hartsuch. Monthly. Query first. Pays on acceptance. Reports in 30 days. Enclose S.A.S.E.
Nonfiction: Uses articles of interest to management, production executives, and craftsmen in printing and allied plants. Length: maximum 2,500. Pays average of $85.
Photos: Purchased with mss.

GRAPHIC ARTS SUPPLIER NEWS, 134 North 13th St., Philadelphia PA 19107. Editor: William L. Edgell. For dealers, salesmen, and manufacturers of printing equipment and supplies. 6 times a year. Buys first publication rights. Query preferred. Reports in 2 months. Enclose S.A.S.E.
Nonfiction: Feature articles with heavy emphasis on sales, marketing, profiles and promotion techniques, and some news related to graphic arts supply. Pays 4¢ per word; assignments, flat fee $75.
Photos: On assignment only; payment varies with assignment.

INDUSTRIAL ART METHODS, 25 West 45th St., New York NY 10036. Editor: A.V. Lesmez. For supervisory personnel in in-house art departments. Monthly. Circulation: 23,000. Buys first rights. Pays on acceptance. Will send sample copy to a writer for $1. Query not required. Enclose S.A.S.E. for return of submissions.
Nonfiction and Photos: Application standards. On the spot reports on how Art Department is run. How to apply new techniques in industrial art. In-house reports. Visual aids. New approaches to old problems. Graphic arts in industry. Length: 1,000 to 2,000 words. Pays $50 honorarium fee for complete article with illustrations (photographs and/or art work, samples, etc.).

THE INLAND PRINTER/AMERICAN LITHOGRAPHER, 300 W. Adams St., Chicago IL 60606. Editor: Jack Homer. For qualified personnel active in any phase of the graphic arts industry. Established in 1882. Monthly. Circulation: 54,000. Buys all rights, unless otherwise specified in writing at time of purchase. Pays on publication. Will send free sample copy to a writer on request. Query first. Submit seasonal material 2 months in advance. "Study publication before writing." Enclose S.A.S.E.
Nonfiction: Articles on management; technical subjects with illustrations. Must have direct bearing on graphic arts industry. Length: 1,500 to 3,000 words. Pays $50 to $200.
Photos: Purchased with mss; also news shots of graphic arts occurrences. 5x7 or 8x10 glossy. Pays $5 to $10.
Fillers: Newsbreaks, clippings, short humor; must relate to printing industry. Length: 100 to 250 words. Payment varies.

MID-ATLANTIC GRAPHIC ARTS REVIEW, 134 N. 13th St., Philadelphia PA 19107. Editor: Robert W. Hardy. For "printers, print shops, in-plant printing manufacturers, etc." Special issues include In-Plant Printing (April), Book Printing (May), Key Personalities (July or August), Lithography (September), Directory (December). Monthly. Circulation: over 3,500. Buys all rights. Buys 4 or 5 mss a year. Pays on publication. Will send a sample copy to a writer on request. Query first. Submit seasonal material 2 to 3 months in advance. Reports in 10 days. Enclose S.A.S.E.
Nonfiction: Articles should be on local printing, the needs of printing buyers, profiles on management of local printers (Eastern Pennsylvania, New Jersey, Delaware, Maryland, Northern Virginia, Washington, DC) and marketing. "Style should be in-depth and detailed, but give the human interest approach. The informal approach is favored." Buys how-to's, personal experience and new product pieces, photo essays, coverage of successful business operations and merchandising techniques. Length: 50 to 5,000 words. Pays 4¢ a word.
Photos: Purchased with mss. B&w glossies. Pays $5.
Fillers: Newsbreaks. Length: 200 words maximum. Pays 4¢ a word.

MODERN LITHOGRAPHY, 8150 Central Park Ave., Skokie IL 60076. Editor: Jerome Rakusan. For "management, supervisors, employees of lithographic plants." Established in 1935. Monthly. Circulation: 16,000. Buys first North American rights. Buys 15 to 20 mss a year. Pays on publication. Will send a sample copy to a writer on request. Submit complete ms. Will not consider photocopied submissions. Submit seasonal material at least 3 months in advance. Reports in 2 to 3 weeks. Enclose S.A.S.E. for return of submissions.
Nonfiction and Photos: "Technical articles on new developments in lithography; success stories of litho plants and manufacturers. Concentrate on material of interest to our readers within the story structure. We specialize in only the lithographic segment of the printing industry, so we cover details in greater depth." Buys informational articles, interviews, historical articles, coverage of successful business operations, and technical articles. Length: 500 to 1,000 words. Pays 3¢ to 4¢ a word. 8x10 b&w glossies purchased with mss; captions required.

PLAN AND PRINT, 10116 Franklin Ave., Franklin Park IL 60131. Editor: James C. Vebeck. For blue print, photocopy, offset, microfilm, diazo and allied reproduction firms; dealers in architects', engineers', and draftsmen's supplies and equipment; in-plant reproduction department supervisors, and design and drafting specialists. Monthly. Circulation: 19,000. Buys all rights. Pays on acceptance. Will send a sample copy to a writer on request. Query preferred. Reports in 2 weeks. Enclose S.A.S.E.
Nonfiction: Wants features on commercial reproduction companies and in-plant reproduction departments, on a specific theme such as offset, microfilm, diazo; the promotion of these services, solving of problems with regard to these services; technical articles on techniques involved in reproduction work, and how commercial reproduction companies work with the captive in-plant reproduction departments; articles relating to areas of design and drafting. Do not send articles on "how a company grew from 2 employees to 500, etc." Pays $20 to $100. Photos purchased with mss; b&w glossies. Pays $5 to $10.
Poetry: Uses humorous verse related to reproduction industry, design, and drafting. Length: 4 to 12 lines. Pays $5 to $7.50, depending upon length and quality.
Fillers: Epigrams, anecdotes, and short humor on the above topics. Pays $5.

PRINTING MAGAZINE, 475 Kinderkamack Rd., Oradell NJ 07649. Editor: Jeremiah E. Flynn. For commercial printers and lithographers. Monthly. Pays after publication. Query first. "Best procedure for writers is to contact a local printer and find out whether or not he would have the time to tell him about his operations. Then check with us, telling us what sort of plant it is and what the owner would be willing and able to talk about. We can then suggest questions, angles, points of view, photo possibilities, etc." Enclose S.A.S.E.
Nonfiction and Photos: "Interested in specific, detailed information on actual printing plants of 10 or more employees and their management, production and marketing problems. Knowledge of printing is necessary, but more important is the ability to interview plant owners intelligently, so they would discuss specific issues, programs, operations, etc. Story must give facts, not generalizations." Length: about 1,500 words. "We pay roughly $35 per printed page, after publication. Many printers will take pictures themselves and send to us. This would facilitate sale of article."
Fillers: Interested in clippings and fillers on printing plants and personnel changes, as well as relocations. Pays $1 minimum.

PRINTING MANAGEMENT MAGAZINE, P.O. Box 417, Berea OH 44017. Editor: Edward H. Owen. For management executives in the printing business who function as company owners, general managers, vice-presidents, plant managers, production managers, superintendents and mechanical department foremen in commercial, magazine, and private plants, including engraving and electrotype plants. Monthly. "A query is appreciated before submission." Reports in 2 weeks. Enclose S.A.S.E.
Nonfiction: Articles must be of value to management. Length: around 1,500 words, although it varies depending on value of subject. Payment "depends on subject."

PRINTING SALESMAN'S HERALD, Champion Papers, a division of Champion International, 245 Park Avenue, New York NY 10017. Editor: Michael Corey. For

printing, graphic arts industries. Bimonthly. Buys all rights. Pays on acceptance. Reports in 1 to 4 weeks. Enclose S.A.S.E. for return of submissions
Nonfiction: Articles on salesmanship as applicable to the selling of printing; technical pieces relating to printing production; sales incentive material as seen from both sides of the desk. Material must be valid to the publication's audience and well-written. Pays $50 if material is worth developing but needs rewriting: $75 to $100 if copy is meaty and well-written.

REPRODUCTIONS REVIEW & METHODS, 134 N. 13th St., Philadelphia PA 19107. Editor: Wayne Riley. For managers and supervisors of in-house reproduction and communications departments. Established: 1955. Monthly. Circulation: 43,000. Not copyrighted. Buys 60 mss a year. Payment on publication. Will send free sample copy to writer on request. Will consider photocopied submissions. Reporting time varies. Enclose S.A.S.E. for return of submissions.
Nonfiction and Photos: "Good, down-to-earth management articles; good, down-to-earth technical articles pertaining to the graphic arts. Articles on specific installations if there's really a story there. Articles on technology transfer and possibility of effect on individual members of graphic arts. No special style, but field is hard to grasp without studying the magazine or learning it first-hand. Prefer concise statements and articles to flowery puff." Length: 1,000 to 1,500 words. Pays $50 to $100. B&w photos (good, sharp prints any size to 8x10) purchased with ms. Color transparencies, 35mm up. Pays $50 for cover use of color.
Fillers: Newsbreaks. 100-500 words. Pays $15. Short humor. Length: open. Payment varies.

SCREEN PRINTING MAGAZINE, 407 Gilbert Ave., Cincinnati OH 45202. Editor: R.O. Fossett. For screen printers, suppliers, ad agencies, industries allied with screen printing in any way. Established in 1953. Monthly. Circulation: 8,000. Not copyrighted. Pays on publication. Will send a sample copy to a writer on request. Write for copy of guidelines for writers. Query first "always. Ordinarily, work is done on assignment." No S.A.S.E. needed, but does return material.
Nonfiction and Photos: "Subject matter desired may vary with trend of industry. Feature must illustrate specifically some phase of the screen printing industry. Generally, technical articles are required; but prior discussion is necessary, with prospective writers. Concise, factual reporting is essential—leave out padding. Technical and operational articles on phases of screen printing." Buys informational articles, how-to's, interviews ("assigned only"), successful business operations ("assigned only"), coverage of merchandising techniques, and technical articles. Length: 1,500 to 2,000 words for features, "with illustrations." Pays $50 to $75. 4x5 b&w glossies purchased with mss; "no Polaroids. Photos should pertain to technology in text."

SOUTHERN PRINTER & LITHOGRAPHER, 75 Third St., N.W., Atlanta GA 30308. Editor: Charles Fram. For commercial printing plant management in the 14 southern states. Established: 1924. Monthly. Circulation: 3,000. Not copyrighted. Payment on publication. Will send free sample copy to writer on request. Write for copy of guidelines for writers. Query first. Will consider photocopied submissions. Reporting time on submissions varies. Enclose S.A.S.E.
Nonfiction and Photos: Feature articles on commercial printing plants in the 14 southern states and their personnel. Length: 1,000 to 1,500 words. Pays 1¢ a word. B&w photos. Pays $4.

Railroad

RAILWAY SYSTEM CONTROLS, 29 E. Madison St., Chicago IL 60602. Editor: Robert W. McKnight. Monthly. Query first. Enclose S.A.S.E. for return of submissions. Buys all rights.
Nonfiction: Uses small amount of freelance material. Wants articles about installations of signaling, communications, computer usage and system control on railroads—factual descriptions with technical details; engineering approach. Also tech-

nical material of general interest to engineers working in the field. Length: 500 words minimum. Pays 50¢ per column inch.
Photos: Sometimes buys 5x7 or larger b&w glossies as article illustrations.

THE SIGNALMAN'S JOURNAL, 2247 W. Lawrence Ave., Chicago IL 60625. Editor: J.W. Walsh. Monthly. Buys first rights. Query first. Reports in 3 weeks. Enclose S.A.S.E.
Nonfiction: Can use articles on new installations of railroad signal systems, but they must be technically correct and include drawings and photos. Length: 3,000 to 4,000 words. Pays $10 per printed page, and up.
Photos: Photographs dealing with railroad signaling. Pays $5.

Real Estate

AREA DEVELOPMENT, 114 East 32nd St., New York NY 10016. Editor: Albert H. Jaeggin. For chief executives of nation's leading firms faced with problems of finding new sites, building new plants or relocating existing facilities. Monthly. Buys all rights, reprint rights, and possibly simultaneous rights. Enclose S.A.S.E. for return of submissions.
Nonfiction: Wants articles on all subjects related to facility planning, including: finding new sites, building new plants and/or expanding and relocating existing facilities; community and employee relations; political climate; transportation, recreational and educational facilities; financing; insurance; plant design and layout; safety factors; water and air pollution controls; case histories of companies which have moved or built new plants. Must be accurate, objective (no puffery) and useful to executives. Must avoid discussions of merits or disadvantages of any particular community, state or area. Also carries news items on activities, people, areas, books on facility planning, based on releases. Pays $35 per printed page.
Photos: Buys glossy photos. Pays $35 per page.

HOUSING AFFAIRS LETTER, Community Development Services, Inc., 1319 F St., N.W., Washington DC 20004.
Fillers: Pays $1.10 for each used in steady arrangement for contributions of newspaper clippings on low-income housing, urban renewal, Model Cities, community development substantive actions, and litigation, that would be of interest to housing and community development professionals beyond immediate area. Particularly want regular contributors for multistate region, or at least a full state. Query first. Write Editor Ash Gerecht for fact sheet, typical usage.

PROPERTIES MAGAZINE, 4900 Euclid Ave., Cleveland OH 44103. Editor: Gene Bluhm. Monthly. Pays on publication. Query first. "Limited amount of freelance material bought." Enclose S.A.S.E. for return of submissions. Buys all rights.
Nonfiction and Photos: Wants articles of real estate and construction news value. Length: 400 to 500 words. Pays $25. Buys photographs with mss, 8x10 preferred.

SHOPPING CENTER WORLD, 461 Eighth Ave., New York NY 10001. For "developers, real estate agents for chains, major lenders, financiers, investors, architects, etc. They are extremely knowledgeable and educated." Established in 1972. Monthly. Circulation: 15,000. Buys all rights, but will reassign rights to author after publication. Pays on publication. Will send a sample copy to a writer on request. Query first. "Stories generally on assignment." Will consider photocopied submissions. Submit seasonal material 4 to 5 months in advance of issue date. Reports in 2 weeks. Enclose S.A.S.E.
Nonfiction and Photos: "How-to articles on specific centers or subjects—cutting costs of construction, promoting a center, increasing its cash flow, selecting a site, etc." Buys informational and how-to articles. Length: 1,000 to 3,000 words. Pays $75 to $150. B&w photos purchased with mss; captions required.
How To Break In: "Most of our material comes from seasoned reporters and journalists who are doing a little moonlighting on the side. I would advise someone trying to write for us to go overboard on detail: gather as much information on dollars

and cents and specifics as possible and include it within the article. Too much of the material we get is superficial. The beginner must get so involved in the basics of whatever he is writing about that when he is finished he knows almost as much about it as his sources of information."

Recreation Park and Campground Management

CAMPGROUND AND RV PARK MANAGEMENT, 1 Willow St., Mill Valley, CA 94941. Editor: Mary Matheson. 8 times a year. Circulation: 14,000. Buys all rights. Pays on publication. Will send a free sample copy on request. "Best to query first." Reports in 1 month. Enclose S.A.S.E.
Nonfiction and Photos: Success stories and management information articles for owners of campgrounds and recreation vehicle parks. News stories about campgrounds, campground associations, campground chains and any other subjects helpful or of interest to a campground operator. Also uses features about such subjects as a specialized bookkeeping system for campground operations, an interesting traffic circulation system, an advertising and promotion program that has worked well for a campground, an efficient trash collection system. Successful operation of coin operated dispensing machines, successful efforts by a campground owner in bringing in extra income through such means as stores, charge showers, swimming fees, etc. Use newspaper style reporting for news items and newspaper feature style for articles. Length: 500 to 700 words, news stories; 300 to 1,200 words, features. Pays 4¢ to 10¢ a word. "B&w photos should accompany articles whenever practicable."
Fillers: Pays $2 to $5 for ideas which eventually appear as stories written by staff or another writer; $5 to $10 for newsbreaks of one paragraph to a page.

PARK MAINTENANCE, P.O. Box 409, Appleton WI 54911. Editor: Erik L. Madisen, Jr. For administrators of areas with large grounds maintenance and outdoor recreation facilities. Special issues include March, Swimming Pool and Beach; July, Turf Research and Irrigation Annual; October, Buyer's Guide issue. Established in 1948. Monthly. Circulation: 17,000. Buys all rights. Buys 4 or 5 mss a year. Pays on acceptance. Will send a sample copy to a writer on request. Write for copy of guidelines for writers. Query first. "Outline material and source in letter, and include S.A.S.E." Will consider photocopied submissions "if exclusive to us." Deadlines are the first of the month preceding publication. Reports in 2 weeks. Enclose S.A.S.E.
Nonfiction: How-to, case history, technical or scientific articles dealing with maintenance of turf and facilities in parks, forestry, golf courses, campuses. These may be new or unique ideas adopted by park systems for greater use or more efficient and economical operation. Also, methods of dealing with administrative, financial, personnel and other problems; new phases of landscape architecture and building design. Buys how-to's and interviews. Length: up to 1,000 words. Pays 2¢ a word.
Photos: Purchased with mss if applicable; 8x10 or 5x7 b&w glossies. "Captions required." Pays minimum of $2 each; $5 for front cover.

Secretarial

M.S. FOR MEDICAL SECRETARIES, 681 Fifth Avenue—10th Floor, New York NY 10022. Editor: Mrs. Irene R. Stone. "*M.S.* goes to the secretary—not the medical aide or nurse—in the doctor's office. Usually the office is small (1 doctor, 1 girl) although we do have some readers in clinics and hospitals." General subject matter is "educational, how-to articles containing information that can be put to use by the reader in her office." Biweekly. Circulation: 7,500. Buys all rights. Buys 25 mss a year. Will send a free sample copy to a writer on request. Query first. Reports "usually in 2 to 4 weeks." Enclose S.A.S.E.
Nonfiction: Needs material for grammar columns, lead stories, and clinics. "Aim is to motivate, as well as educate. We offer skill-oriented articles and articles on coping

with explicit job problems, and particular human relations problems. Possible subjects: Billing procedures, collection procedures, handling emergencies, etc. Fast, easy-to-read, crisp style is necessary. Subject of article should be narrowly pinpointed—not 'Patient Relations' but rather 'How to Cope with Terminal Patients.' In an interview story, we're not interested in discussing the secretary's personal background, and we talk about her job only insofar as it relates directly to—and illustrates—the point of the article. Since *M.S.* is going to the doctor's secretary rather than his nurse or aide, the articles should be confined to secretarial subjects rather than technical, laboratory material. For example, we're not interested in articles on taking blood counts, injection techniques, microscopic urinalysis, etc." Length: "Grammar column, 450 words; lead, 900 words; clinic, 1,500 words—all approximate." Payment: "Grammar columns, $35; lead stories, $50; 4-page clinics, $75."

P.S. FOR PRIVATE SECRETARIES, 681 Fifth Ave—10th Floor, New York NY 10022. Editor: Mrs. Irene R. Stone. For "executive secretaries and administrative assistants who are career-oriented and anxious to expand the scope of their jobs. They enjoy being secretaries and want to learn how to do the best job possible for their bosses." Biweekly. Circulation: 35,000. Buys all rights. Buys 50 mss a year. Pays on acceptance. Will send a free sample copy to a writer on request. Query first. Reports in 2 to 4 weeks. Enclose S.A.S.E.
Nonfiction: Needs material for grammar columns, lead stories, clinics, and supplements. All should be "educational 'how-to' articles containing information that can be put to use by the reader on her job. We offer skill-oriented articles, articles on coping with explicit job problems, articles on particular human relations problems. Possible subjects: How to set up conferences; how to deal with visitors; how to organize your workload; how to build good will. Fast, easy-to-read crisp style is necessary. Subject of article should be narrowly pinpointed—writer must keep in mind that he is teaching the secretary how to do a particular part of her job better. We're not interested in discussing the secretary's personal background in an interview story, and we talk about her job only insofar as it illustrates points made in the article." Length: "grammar column, 450 words; lead, 900 words; clinic, 1,500 words; supplement, 3,000 words—all approximate." Payment: "Grammar column, $35; lead stories, $50; 4-page clinics, $75; 8-page supplements, $100."

THE SECRETARY, 616 E. 63rd St., Kansas City MO 64110. Editor: Shirley Englund. For women in the secretarial profession. Established: 1942. 10 times a year. Circulation: 50,000. Buys all rights. Buys about 20 mss a year. Payment on publication. Will send free sample copy to writer on request. Submit complete ms. Reports on material in 2 to 3 months. Enclose S.A.S.E. for return of submissions.
Nonfiction and Photos: "Articles on the secretarial profession; secretarial procedures and human interest stories on secretaries; secretaries in management positions." Informational, how-to, personal experience, interview, profile, expose, personal opinion, travel, new product. Length: 750 to 2,500 words. Pays 3¢ per word. B&w photos purchased with ms. Captions required.

TODAY'S SECRETARY, 1221 Avenue of the Americas, New York NY 10020. Editor: Ann Roberts. For secretarial students, 15 to 19 years of age; high school or business school students; interests in business, human relations, fashion, beauty, and communications. Established 1899. Monthly. October through May. Circulation: 65,000. Buys all rights. Buys 24 mss a year. Payment on acceptance. Will send free sample copy to writer on request. Write for copy of guidelines for writers. Query first for nonfiction. Submit complete ms for fiction. Will consider photocopied submissions. Submit seasonal material 6 months in advance. Reports in 2 months. Enclose S.A.S.E. for reply to query or return of submission.
Nonfiction and Photos: "We carry features about professional secretaries, office procedure, secretarial skills, self-awareness, human relations, personal communications, business communications, technological developments, business trends, economics, consumerism, health, beauty, and fashion. Style should be simple and relaxed; easy going talk; motivational but not preachy. Young outlook, feminist approach." Regular columns include The Human Side and Think It Out. Length: 800 to 1,000 words. Pays $35 to $100. Photos purchased on assignment.
Fiction: Mainstream, mystery, suspense, adventure, and humorous fiction considered. Theme: open. Length: 600 to 800 words. Pays $25.

Selling and Merchandising

In this category are journals for salesmen and merchandisers that publish general material on how to sell products successfully. Journals in nearly every other category of this Trade Journal section will also buy this kind of material if it is slanted to the specialized product or industry they deal with, such as clothing or petroleum. Publications for professional advertising and marketing men will be found under Advertising and Marketing journals.

SALESMAN'S OPPORTUNITY MAGAZINE, 1460 John Hancock Center, Chicago IL 60611. Editor: Jack Weissman. For "people who are eager to increase their incomes by selling or through an independent business of their own." Established: 1923. Monthly. Buys all rights. Buys about 50 mss a year. Payment on publication. Will send free sample copy to writer on request. Write for copy of guidelines for writers. Submit complete ms. Will consider photocopied submissions, but must have exclusive rights to any article. Enclose S.A.S.E. for return of submissions.
Nonfiction: "Our editorial content consists of articles dealing with sales techniques, sales psychology and general self-improvement topics that are inspirational in character." Should be tightly written, very specific. "We prefer case history type articles which show our readers how to do the same things that have helped others succeed in the direct selling industry. We are particularly interested in articles about successful women in the direct selling door-to-door field, particularly for our annual women's issue which is published each August." Length: 250 words for column features; maximum of 1,000 words for full-length articles. Pays $20 to $35.
How To Break In: "A well-written, to-the-point article dealing with an appropriate subject will be given every consideration. There is no 'secret' formula for writing for our magazine."

SMOKESHOP MERCHANDISER, P.O. Box T, 265 Sunrise Highway, Rockville Centre NY 11571. Managing Editor: Ted Glasser. For "high-grade smokeshop owners; some store managers." Established: 1969. Quarterly plus a special convention issue in September. Circulation: 4,000. Not copyrighted. Buys 6 to 10 mss a year. Payment on acceptance. Will send free sample copy to writer on request. Write for copy of guidelines for writers. Query first. Submit seasonal material 2 to 3 months in advance. Reports on material in 1 month. Enclose S.A.S.E.
Nonfiction and Photos: " 'How it's done' articles that tell what a successful dealer does to attract people to his store. Articles should be helpful; that is, applicable to other smokeshops. Father's Day and Christmas make for special articles, although the issues do not gear themselves entirely to these holidays." Profile. Informational, how-to, successful business operations and merchandising techniques. Length: 500 to 1,500 words. Pays 4¢ per word. 5x7 or 8x10 b&w photos. Pays $5 to $10. Captions required.

SPECIALTY FOOD MERCHANDISING, 29 Park Ave., Manhasset NY 11030. Editor: Saul Tarter. For "professional buyers of specialty foods representing such outlets as department stores, gourmet food stores, cheese shops, supermarket chains, variety chains, discount stores." Established: 1971. Monthly. Circulation: 7,700. Buys all rights. Buys 18 to 24 mss a year. Payment on publication. Will send free sample copy to writer on request. Editorial guidelines sent to writer with first assignment. Query first. Reports in 10 days. Enclose S.A.S.E.
Nonfiction and Photos: Merchandising stories on unusual or outstanding successful distributor/retail firms within the quality food field. "Advise if writer is particularly knowledgeable in the field or in any related field (i.e., supermarket merchandising) and if he has professional ability with a camera. Will provide specific assignment, arranging beforehand for necessary interview with subject firm." Length: Up to 2,000 words, with 5 to 8 photos. Pays 5¢ per word. 5x7 or 8x10 b&w photos. Pays $5. 2x2 color mount or 2x2 transparencies, unmounted. Pays $20.

SPECIALTY SALESMAN AND FRANCHISE OPPORTUNITIES MAGAZINE, 307 N. Michigan Ave., Chicago IL 60601. Editorial Director: Ben Newman. For salesmen selling "direct." Monthly. Buys all rights. Pays on acceptance. Will send free sample copy to a writer on request. Reports in 2 weeks. Enclose S.A.S.E. for return of submissions.

Nonfiction and Photos: Articles about people involved in direct selling. Subject matter may fall into these three categories: stories of successful direct salesmen; advice by men and women who have sold successfully Fuller Brush, Avon, Stanley, etc.; and inspirational or motivational articles. Likes good photos to illustrate stories. Length: 500 to 1,500 words. Pays 3¢ per word; extra for photos. Photos purchased with mss. Pays $5.

How To Break In: "Best approach is to read the magazine; send a query letter or a short feature. And write, and write and write!"

STATIONERY & SCHOOL SUPPLIES MERCHANDISING, 1372 Peachtree St., N.E., Suite 211, Atlanta GA 30309. Editor: Nancy Horne. For stationery and school supplies buyers and merchandisers. Established: 1974. Monthly. Circulation: 15,000. Not copyrighted. Acquires all rights. Will buy minimum of 12 mss a year. Payment on acceptance. Will send free sample copy to writer on request if 9x12 S.A.S.E. plus 21¢ postage are enclosed. Write for copy of editorial guidelines for writers, enclosing S.A.S.E. Query first. Reports immediately on material. Enclose S.A.S.E. for return of submissions.

Nonfiction and Photos: "Photo-illustrated articles about successful merchandising ideas readers can use." Length: 500 to 2,000 words. Pays 3¢ per word. 5x7 glossy photos purchased with ms. Pays $5. Color: 2¼x2¼ transparencies; 5x7 prints. Pays $15. Department Editor: Reuben Guberman.

Show People and Amusements

THE BILLBOARD, 9000 Sunset Blvd., Los Angeles CA 90069. Editor-In-Chief: Lee Zhito. Music Editor: Ian Dove (New York). Coin Machine Editor: Earl Paige (Chicago). Weekly. Buys all rights. Pays on publication. Enclose S.A.S.E.

Nonfiction: "Correspondents are appointed to send in spot amusement news covering phonograph record programming by broadcasters and music machine operators; record merchandising by retail dealer, and the music-games coin-operated machine industry. We are extremely interested in blank tape, and tape playback, and record hardware stories." Length: "short." Pays 25¢ to $1 per published inch.

VARIETY, 154 W. 46th St., New York NY 10036. Editor: Abel Green. Does not buy freelance material.

Sport Trade

AMERICAN BICYCLIST AND MOTORCYCLIST, 461 Eighth Ave., New York NY 10001. Editor: Stan Gottlieb. For bicycle sales and service shops. Monthly. Enclose S.A.S.E. for return of submissions.

Nonfiction and Photos: Typical story describes (very specifically) unique traffic-builder or merchandising idea used with success by an actual dealer. Emphasis is on showing other dealers how they can follow a similar pattern and increase their business. Articles may also be based entirely on repair shop operation, depicting efficient and profitable service systems and methods. Length: 1,800 to 2,500 words. Pays 3¢ a word. Relevant b&w photos illustrating principal points in article purchased with ms. 5x7 minimum. No transparencies. Pays $5 to $20.

Fillers: Short items on repair shop hints for workbench page. Length: 50 words maximum.

BICYCLE JOURNAL, 3339 W. Freeway, Fort Worth TX 76101. Publisher: Bill Quinn. Enclose S.A.S.E. for return of submissions.

Photos and Fillers: Stories of a single outstanding feature of bike store, such as a good display, interior or exterior; sales tip; service tip; unusual sign; advertising or promotion tip; store layout, etc. Photo must be vertical. One 8x10 photo is sufficient. Length: 200 to 300 words. Pays $32.50.

THE BOWLING PROPRIETOR, 375 W. Higgins Rd., Hoffman Estates IL 60172. Editor: Marjorie A. Paul. For owners and managers of bowling establishments. Established: 1954. Monthly except July. Circulation: 5,000. Buys all rights and second serial (reprint) rights. Buys 3 or 4 mss a year. Payment on acceptance. Will send sample copy to writer for 35¢. Write for copy of guidelines for writers. Query first. Will consider photocopied submissions if of good quality. Submit seasonal material 3 months in advance. Reports on material in 6 to 8 weeks. Enclose S.A.S.E.
Nonfiction and Photos: "Articles on management helps; products; individual proprietor or proprietor group promotions or programs. Remodeling, furnishings; game machines including billiards; restaurants. Straight reporting style; simple language, simple sentences." Length: 1,200 words. Pays $35 to $50. 3x7 b&w photos purchased with or without accompanying ms. Captions required. Pays $5 to $10.

GOLF SHOP OPERATIONS, 88 Scribner Ave., Norwalk CT 06856. Managing Editor: Jim Achenbach. For golf professionals at public, private, and resort courses and driving ranges. 6 times a year. Buys all rights. Pays on publication. Will send free sample copy to a writer on request. Reports in 2 weeks. Enclose S.A.S.E. for return of submissions.
Nonfiction: Articles that describe how golf pros are buying, promoting, displaying, and merchandising their wares; articles of practical value to other professionals; teaching, tournament management, golf industry developments, etc. Length: 500-1,500 words. Pays 5¢ per word.
Photos: Purchased with mss and with captions only. Pays $7.50.
Fillers: Newsbreaks appropriate to format. Pays $25.

GOLFDOM, 235 E. 45th St., New York NY 10017. Editor: Vincent J. Pasterna. For the golf trade—country club management, maintenance, merchandising. 10 times a year. Mostly freelance. Buys all rights. Pays on acceptance. Query first. Reports in 1 month. Enclose S.A.S.E.
Nonfiction: Uses technical articles on club maintenance, management, pro shop merchandising, course equipment, driving ranges. Pays $75 minimum.
Photos: Purchased with mss; with captions only. Pays minimum $12.50.

MOTORCYCLE DEALER NEWS, P.O. Box 288, South Laguna CA 92677. Editor: David Seaver. For "motorcycle dealers and key personnel of the industry." Monthly. Buys first serial rights. Pays on publication. Will send a free sample copy to a writer on request. Write for copy of guidelines to writers. Query first. Reports within 4 weeks. Enclose S.A.S.E.
Nonfiction: "In-depth articles regarding liability insurance, warranty, land usage, noise pollution, and advertising have been handled recently. Usually, in-depth articles about current problems are staff-written; however, do not hesitate to query. The editors are also looking for articles that examine problems of dealers and offer a solution. These dealer articles are not a history of the business, but one unique aspect of the store and its attempt to hurdle an obstacle that may aid other dealers in a similar situation. This is not to be success story, but rather a fresh look at tackling problems within the industry. Tips for dealers on selling merchandise, creating new displays, and upgrading the basic level of the dealer are also needed. We do not use articles of general or unspecific nature. Concrete thoughts and examples are a must. Photos help sell the article." Length: 1,000 to 1,500 words. Pays minimum $75 for articles about specific problems facing the industry; $45 to $75 for dealer articles; "however, rates are negotiable."
Photos: Purchased with mss or with captions only. Modern stores, dealer awards, etc. Prefers 8x10 glossy. Pays $4 and up.
Fillers: "Clippings regarding dealer promotions, business news, etc." Pays "$1 per column inch used."

NATIONAL BOWLERS JOURNAL AND BILLIARD REVUE, 1825 N. Lincoln Plaza, Suite 214, Chicago IL 60614. Editor: Mort Luby, Jr. For proprietors of bowling centers, dealers and distributors of bowling and billiard equipment. Also for professional bowlers and billiard players. Monthly. Circulation: 17,000. Buys first rights. Buys 20 to 30 mss a year. Pays on publication. Will send a free sample copy to a writer on request. Query editor first. Reports in 2 to 3 weeks. Enclose S.A.S.E.

Nonfiction and Photos: Uses illustrated articles about successful bowling and billiard room proprietors who have used unusual promotions to build business, profiles of interesting industry personalities (including bowlers and billiard players), and coverage of major competitive events, both bowling and billiards. "We publish some controversial matter, seek out outspoken personalities." Length: 1,500 to 2,500 words. Pays $50 to $75. Photos purchased with mss. B&w glossies. Pays $10.

POWERBOAT INDUSTRY, 16216 Raymer, Van Nuys CA 91406. Editor: Bill Ames. For members of the industry. Established: 1972. Bimonthly. Circulation: 27,000. Buys all rights. Buys 12 mss a year. Payment on publication. Will send free sample copy to writer on request. Query first. Reports on material in 2 to 3 weeks. Enclose S.A.S.E.

Nonfiction and Photos: "Interviews with industry leaders, roundtable discussions, marketing techniques, promotional ideas. Our premise is that the power boat industry is an industry within the industry. We devote our efforts to those concerned with power only." Length: 1,500 to 2,500 words. Pays $100 to $150. "Will consider column idea suggestions." 8x10 b&w glossies (no Polaroid) purchased with accompanying ms.

RECREATIONAL VEHICLE RETAILER, 23945 Craftsman Rd., Calabasas CA 91302. Editor: Art Rouse. For recreational vehicle retailers, and related accessory and appliance dealers. Established: 1972. Monthly. Circulation: 26,000. Rights purchased vary with author and material. Buys all rights. Buys first North American serial rights. Buys 150 mss a year. Payment on publication. Will send free sample copy to writer on request. Write for copy of guidelines for writers. Query first. Reports on material in 3 weeks. Enclose S.A.S.E.

Nonfiction and Photos: Articles on "how to sell and service recreational vehicle market today; improve profits, train salesmen." Length: 1,500 to 2,000 words. Pays $75 to $150. B&w and color photos purchased with ms. "Good prints; any size." Captions required.

SELLING SPORTING GOODS, 717 N. Michigan Ave., Chicago IL 60111. Editor: Thomas B. Doyle. For owners and managers of retail sporting goods stores. Established: 1945. Monthly. Circulation: 15,000. Buys all rights. Buys 12 mss a year. Pays on acceptance. Will send free sample copy to writer on request. Query first. Submit seasonal material 3 months in advance. Enclose S.A.S.E.

Nonfiction and Photos: Articles on "full-line and specialty sporting goods stores. Buys informational articles, how-to's; articles on retail sporting goods advertising, promotions, in-store clinics/workshops; employee hiring and training; photo articles, coverage of successful business operations and merchandising techniques. Articles related to the retailing of particular sports products are the most desired." Length: 750 to 1,000 words. Pays 4¢ to 7¢ a word. B&w glossy photos purchased with or without accompanying ms. 5x7 minimum. Captions required. Color transparencies, 2¼x2¼. Pays $15 to $25.

How To Break In: "Practice photography! Most stories, no matter how good, are useless without quality photos. They can be submitted as contact sheets with negatives to hold down writers' work."

THE SHOOTING INDUSTRY, 8150 N. Central Park Blvd., Skokie IL 60076. Editor: J. Rakusan. For manufacturers, dealers, sales representatives of archery and shooting equipment. 12 times a year. Buys all rights. Buys about 135 mss a year. Pays on publication. Will send free sample copy to a writer on request. Reports in 2 to 3 weeks. Enclose S.A.S.E. for return of submissions.

Nonfiction and Photos: Articles that tell "secrets of my success" based on experience of individual gun dealers; articles of advice to help dealers sell more guns and shooting equipment. Also, articles about and of interest to manufacturers and top manufacturers' executives. Length: up to 3,000 words. Pays $50 to $150. Photos essential; b&w glossies. Purchased with ms.

SKI AREA MANAGEMENT, Box 242, North Salem NY 10560. Editor: David Rowan. For ski area managers. Quarterly. Circulation: 6,000. Buys all rights. Buys about 10 mss a year. Pays on publication. Will send a sample copy to a writer on request. Query first. Reports immediately. Enclose S.A.S.E.
Nonfiction: "Articles on restaurant management, slope grooming, lift maintenance, lift construction, ski schools, snowmaking, marketing, insurance." Length: 1,000 to 5,000 words. Pays $50 to $200.
Photos: Purchased with mss. B&w glossies.

SKI BUSINESS, 235 E. 45th St., New York NY 10017. Editor: Richard L. Needham. For ski retailers. 7 times a year. Circulation: 12,000. Buys all rights. Pays on publication. Will send two free sample copies to a writer on request. Reports in 1 month. Enclose S.A.S.E. for return of submissions.
Nonfiction: Anything that has to do with retail business, especially sporting goods and ski retailing business.

SPORTING GOODS BUSINESS, 1501 Broadway, New York NY 10036. Editor: Howard S. Rauch. For "sporting goods retailers: full-line stores, hardware chains, department store chains, discounters, etc." Established in 1968. Monthly. Circulation: 20,000. Not copyrighted. Buys 12 to 14 mss a year. Pays "shortly after publication." Will send a sample copy to a writer on request. Query first "for everything. We send detailed written instructions for each specific assignment. Please do not send unsolicited mss. We do not return them." Will not consider photocopied submissions. Reports "immediately." Enclose S.A.S.E.
Nonfiction and Photos: "We are newsy in format. We prefer features emphasizing growth of sporting goods (if a discount or department store chain) or organizational expansion (if a full-line sporting goods chain). We want hard news. We are not interested in the buyer's personal history or other extraneous material." Pays "$60 for first published page, $40 for each successive page." Photos purchased with mss.

THE SPORTING GOODS DEALER, 1212 N. Lindbergh Blvd., St. Louis MO 63166. Editor: Roland Burke. For sporting goods dealers, wholesalers, manufacturers, and sales representatives. Monthly. Buys all rights in its field. Buys about 20 mss a year. Pays on publication. Will send a sample copy to a writer for $1. No query required. Submit seasonal material at least 2 months in advance; "seasonal emphasis on merchandise in advance of dealer's buying season—such as July for next year's fishing tackle." Reports as soon as possible. Enclose S.A.S.E.
Nonfiction: Articles featuring news about sporting goods stores and their merchandising policies and techniques; also personality sketches and authoritative articles that are of special help to sporting goods dealers. Length: 300 to 400 words. Pays 2¢ per word and up.
Photos: 4x5 b&w glossy or larger. Photos of selling techniques, displays, signs, etc. of sporting goods stores. Buys photos with mss or as single; b&w. No model releases required. Pays $3.50 to $7.
Fillers: Pertinent newspaper clippings. Pays 1¢ per published word.

SWIMMING POOL WEEKLY/SWIMMING POOL AGE, P.O. Box 11299, Fort Lauderdale FL 33306. Managing Editor: Dave Kaiser. For "swimming pool dealers, distributors, manufacturers, and those in fields related to above-ground pools." Established in 1971. Monthly. Circulation: 15,000. Rights purchased vary with author and material; may buy all rights, but will reassign rights to author after publication. Buys about 100 mss a year. Pays on publication. Will send a sample copy to a writer on request; enclose S.A.S.E. Query first "always." Will not consider photocopied submissions. Submit seasonal material 2 months in advance. Reports in 1 week. Enclose S.A.S.E.
Nonfiction: "Articles on any aspect of the pool industry—from marketing to learn-to-swim programs. Always interested in unique merchandising techniques, dealer success stories, or new uses for pools." For annual edition, buys features "describing new techniques, facilities, and advances in pool technology." Length: maximum 500 words. Pays 3¢ to 6¢ a word, $20 per article.
Photos: Purchased with mss or as photo stories. "Pictures of unique store displays or merchandising layouts welcome." 5x7 or 8x10 glossies. Pays $5.
Fillers: Newsbreaks, clippings. Length: 50 to 100 words. Pays $5.

TENNIS INDUSTRY, 14965 N.E. 6th Ave., No. Miami FL 33161. Editor: Michael Keighley. For "those responsible for the management of tennis clubs and related tennis operations." Established: 1972. Monthly, January through October. Circulation: 12,000. Buys all rights. Buys 10 to 15 mss a year. Payment on publication. Will send free sample copy to writer on request. Query first. Will consider photocopied submissions. Reports on material within 2 months. Enclose S.A.S.E.
Nonfiction and Photos: "Articles on the business aspects of tennis with emphasis on the financial. Latest information about tennis products, new court surfaces, recreational center planning, the effect of tennis facilities on hotel occupancy; the costs of creating and operating tennis complexes at schools, in cities and at resorts and country clubs." Length: 900 to 1,500 words. Pays 5¢ a word. 8x10 b&w, 35mm color purchased with ms.

TENNIS TRADE, 3000 France Ave. S., Minneapolis MN 55416. Managing Editor: Robert Gillen. For "owners and managers of indoor and outdoor tennis clubs; teaching professionals; retailers, jobbers, and distributors of tennis equipment; pro shops; public relations department heads; selected coaches and other educational institutions with tennis program responsibilities." Established in 1972. Monthly. Circulation: 25,000. Rights purchased vary with author and material. Buys over 50 mss a year. Pays on publication. Will send a sample copy and guidelines for writers to those who meet qualifications described below. Submit seasonal material 45 to 60 days prior to issue date "or earlier if possible." Reports in 30 days. Enclose S.A.S.E.
Nonfiction: "Articles outlining tennis club management procedures, tennis marketing techniques, instruction methods, tennis business 'success' stories; also news on new products, market trends and statistics, and people in the industry. Freelancers should have business writing background and a good working knowledge of the business and sport of tennis. All our features should have a news peg taken from the experience of a club manager, teaching professional, or store owner/manager, and using actual 'successes' to illustrate management/instruction suggestions." Interested in freelance material for "Learning the Trade" department; "writer must be a working tennis professional." Length: 250 to 2,500 words. Pays $20 to $75.
Photos: Purchased with or without mss or on assignment; captions required. Subjects should be the same as nonfiction. Uses 8x10 b&w glossy prints ("or negatives and contact sheet on special assignment"). Uses 35mm color transparencies. Pays $5 to $10 per b&w photo and $10 to $20 for color photo; "for color cover, $50 to $100."
How To Break In: "The most important consideration in getting a piece of writing into *Tennis Trade* magazine is knowledge of the business of tennis—retailing, teaching techniques or club management. If a person desires to write for our publication, and has good writing and reporting skills, he should thoroughly research what is being done in tennis in his area—visiting tennis clubs, retailers, pros, school and recreation program heads, and tournament directors. If something strikes him as newsworthy (in a national sense), it may so strike us and he would have a sale. We are not interested in tournament results, celebrities playing the game, features on national and international stars (unless they have just opened a tennis business and if they have we probably already know it) or instruction tips from non-professionals. Story queries are always welcomed, always considered and often acted on."

Stone and Quarry Products

ASBESTOS, 131 North York Road (P.O. Box 471), Willow Grove PA 19090. Editor: Mrs. Doris M. Fagan. For the vertical asbestos industry. Monthly. Pays on publication. Will send free sample copy to a writer on request. Query first. Enclose S.A.S.E.
Nonfiction: "Interested only in items concerning some phase of the international asbestos industry, i.e., new asbestos mines and mills, progress reports on asbestos mines and mills, new or improved techniques in processing asbestos fiber and the manufacture of asbestos-based products, personnel changes and expansions within asbestos firms, asbestos vs. industrial and public health (including techniques to control the emanation of asbestos dust), findings from research into new uses for asbestos (including utilization of the fiber as a reinforcement to improve the effectiveness of plastics, synthetics, and composite materials), improvements in already

existing asbestos-based products, etc. We are not interested in news of the asbestos workers union or in advertisements. We make little use of photographs or other graphics." Length: 500 to 2,000 words. Pays 1¢ to 1½¢ per word "as the article appears in the journal."

Fillers: Newsbreaks and clippings related to asbestos industry. Length: maximum 500 words. Pays 1¢ a word.

CONCRETE CONSTRUCTION MAGAZINE, P.O. Box 555, Elmhurst IL 60126. Publisher: William M. Avery. For building and concrete contractors, engineers, and architects. Monthly. Buys all rights. Pays on acceptance. Will send free sample copy to a writer on request. Reports in 2 weeks. Enclose S.A.S.E.

Nonfiction and Photos: Relatively short, well-illustrated items on improved methods and equipment for handling, forming, reinforcing, curing and finishing concrete on the job. Any item that tells the user of job-placed concrete how to do his job better, or easier, or at less cost. Length: 1,500 to 3,000 words. Pays 5¢ per printed word. Photos purchased with mss. 8x10 glossy. Pays $5.

MODERN CONCRETE, 105 W. Adams St., Chicago IL 60603. Editor: Donald T. Papineau. For producers of concrete—ready mix, concrete block, prestressed, pipe concrete, precast, etc. Monthly. Buys exclusive rights in the field. Pays on publication. Enclose S.A.S.E. for return of submissions.

Nonfiction and Photos: Prefers material providing an authoritative description of a concrete producer's plant, citing trade names of equipment, methods, and capacities. Should be technical in style. Length: 2,000 to 4,000 words. Payment varies, but averages about $25 a page.

Fillers: Also uses short features and fillers covering the news of the associations in the field, including briefs of meetings, officers, elections, and highlights in the industry. Length: 25 to 500 words. Pays $15 per printed page, including illustrations.

ROCK PRODUCTS, 300 W. Adams St., Chicago IL 60606. Editor: Sidney Levine. For nonmetallic minerals mining producers. Monthly. Pays on publication. Query first. Enclose S.A.S.E.

Nonfiction and Photos: "Covers the construction minerals segment of the non-metallic (industrial) minerals industry. Uses articles on quarrying, mining, and processing of portland cement, lime, gypsum, sand and gravel, crushed stone, slag, and expanded clay and shale. Other non-metallic metals covered include dimension stone, asbestos, diatomite, expanded flyash, vermiculite, perlite. Equipment and its applications are emphasized in the operating and technical coverage. Feature articles describe complete plant operations, design and planning, company profiles, marketing, and management techniques." Length: open. Pays 3¢ per published word; $5 each for photos.

How To Break In: "Articles for *Rock Products* are prepared by specialists or authorities in their particular field. For the beginning writer, an engineering or technical background is a major prerequisite. For 'professional' freelancers, I suggest what the pro already knows: 'Study the book.'"

Textile

AMERICA'S TEXTILE REPORTER/BULLETIN, P.O. Box 88, Greenville SC 29601. Editor: Laurens Irby. For "officials and operating executives of manufacturing corporations and plants in the basic textile yarn and fabric industry." Established in 1878. Monthly. Circulation: 22,000. Not copyrighted. Buys "very few" mss a year. Pays on publication. Will send a sample copy to a writer for $1. Write for copy of guidelines for writers "only if background is suitable." Query first. "It is extremely difficult for non-textile industry freelancers to write for us." Enclose S.A.S.E.

Nonfiction: "Technical and business articles about the textile industry." Length: open. Pays $25 to $50 per printed page.

FIBRE AND FABRIC, P.O. Box 401, Acton MA 01720. Editor: Vincent A. Paradis. For textile executives. Monthly. Buys all rights. Pays on acceptance. "Query saves time." Reports in 10 days. Enclose S.A.S.E.

Nonfiction: Articles on textile manufacturing slanted to the production or management executive. Also first-person accounts of practical solutions to production problems in the card, spin, weave, dye, and finish rooms of textile manufacturers. Length: 1,500 to 3,000 words. Pays 2¢ to 5¢ per word.

SOUTHERN TEXTILE NEWS, Box 1569, Charlotte NC 28201. Editor: Ernest E. Elkins. For textile and apparel industries. Weekly. Pays on publication. Will send free sample copy on request. Enclose S.A.S.E. for return of submissions.
Nonfiction: Articles and features on industry and textile industry-oriented personalities. Must have textile tie-ins. Length: up to 2,000 words. Pays minimum 35¢ per column inch.
Photos: Uses 8x10 photos related to textile industry; good contrast and quality. Pays up to $5 for good photos.
Fillers: Spot news of industry; textile fillers; topical, current clippings related to textile industry. Length: up to 200 words. Pays minimum 35¢ per column inch.

TEXTILE WORLD, 1175 Peachtree St., N. E., Atlanta GA 30309. Editor-in-Chief: Laurence A. Christiansen. Monthly. Buys all rights. Pays on acceptance. Enclose S.A.S.E. for return of submissions.
Nonfiction, Photos, and Fillers: Uses articles covering textile management methods, manufacturing and marketing techniques, new equipment, details about new and modernized mills, etc., but avoids elementary, historical, or generally well-known material.

Toy, Novelty, and Hobby

MODEL DEALER MAGAZINE, 733 Fifteenth St., N.W., Washington DC 20005. Editor: David Boynton. For retail model stores stocking and selling models and model supplies (small retail establishments). Established: 1970. Monthly. Circulation: 4,400. Rights purchased vary with author and material; usually buys "industry only" rights. Buys 60 mss a year. Payment on publication. Will send sample copy to writer for 50¢. Query first. Will consider photocopied submissions. Reports on material in 2 weeks. Enclose S.A.S.E.
Nonfiction and Photos: "We print a great number of general business articles which are relevant to small businessmen and retailers. In addition, we carry some technical articles intended to broaden the knowledge of hobby retailers about various areas of modeling. We also are interested in pictorial type stories about specific hobby stores. Articles on how to file and collect shipping damage claims; taxes for the small businessman; retail bookkeeping." Length: 500 to 5,000 words. Pays 4¢ per word. B&w photos (any size) purchased with ms. Captions required. Pays $5.

PROFITABLE CRAFT MERCHANDISING, Pleasantville NY 10570. Editor: Jack Wax. For retailers and wholesalers of craft merchandise. Monthly. Not copyrighted. Pays on publication. Prefers query. Reports "at once." Enclose S.A.S.E.
Nonfiction: Wants articles describing how a craft dealer (name and address must be included with article) used a unique, different, interesting, sales-making idea to boost profits or sales of some specific craft item or process. Tear pages containing specific examples showing style and slant will be sent on request. Pays 3¢ per word.
Photos: All mss should have good, clear glossy photos, 5x7 or larger. Stories about craft stores should have good shot of window display or in-store display. Pays $5 per usable photo.

SOUVENIRS AND NOVELTIES, Bldg. 30, 20-21 Wagaraw Rd., Fair Lawn NJ 07410. Editor: Martin Dowd. For "owners and managers of tourist attractions and souvenir shops who buy and sell souvenirs and novelties at resorts, parks, museums, airports, etc." Special issues include parks, museums, attractions (April), tourist travel terminals shops (June), free attractions (December). Established in 1962. Bimonthly. Circulation: 6,500. Buys first North American serial rights. Buys about 15 mss a year. Pays on acceptance. Will send a sample copy to a writer on request.

Write for copy of guidelines for writers. Query first or submit complete ms. Will consider photocopied submissions. Submit seasonal material 2 months in advance of issue date "if possible." Reports in 1 week. Enclose S.A.S.E.

Nonfiction and Photos: "Articles about how to buy and sell souvenirs and novelties. How to manage a souvenir or novelty shop. How to handle inventory, pilferage, prices, etc. The writer should interview managers and owners and report on what they say about how to sell and buy souvenirs and novelties. How to display merchandise, how to train employees, etc. We specialize in a narrow field of merchandising for tourists, generally. I am not really interested in travel articles." Buys informational articles, how-to's, interviews, and coverage of successful business operations. Length: 500 to 1,500 words. Pays 4¢ to 5¢ a word. Photos purchased with ms; captions required. For 8x10 or 5x7 b&w glossies, pays $5 "for amateur photos" and $10 "for professional photos. Will pay for photos even if they are supplied by the park or attraction or museum, as long as we use them and the writer obtains them."

Fillers: Clippings. "Must be about souvenir or novelty business, or don't bother to send them, please. We pay 80¢ a published inch if we use the clipping."

THE STAMP WHOLESALER, P.O. Box 529, 217 Church St., Burlington VT 05401. Editor: Lucius Jackson. For dealers in postage stamps for collectors. Established: 1936. 21 issues a year. Circulation: 9,483. Buys all rights but releases book rights on request by author. Buys 40 to 50 mss a year. Payment on acceptance. Will send free sample copy to writer on request. Query first. Submit seasonal material 3 months in advance. Reports on material within 6 months. Enclose S.A.S.E.

Nonfiction and Photos: How-to articles. "Down to earth; no charts; no footnotes." Informational, personal experience, interview, profile, inspirational, humor, historical, think pieces, expose, nostalgia, personal opinion, travel, spot news, successful business operations, merchandising techniques. Length: "We like 1,500 words or more; often buy less." Pays minumum of 3¢ per word. 6x9 b&w photos purchased with accompanying ms, without ms or on assignment. Captions required. Pays $5 minimum.

TOY AND HOBBY WORLD, 1312 Peachtree St. N.E., Suite 211 Atlanta, GA 30309. Editor: David Kreissman. Established in 1962. Biweekly. Circulation: 17,000. Not copyrighted. Buys about 12 mss a year. Pays on publication. Will send a sample copy to a writer on request. Write for copy of guidelines for writers. Query first or submit compete ms. Will not consider photocopied submissions. Submit seasonal material at least 2 months in advance of issue date. Returns rejected material "on request." Enclose S.A.S.E. for return of submissions.

Nonfiction: Wants "features and news items directed specifically to those concerned with the manufacture, buying and selling of toys, hobbies and related items. Includes technical articles for manufacturers, features about wholesalers, retailers, chains, department stores, discount houses, etc., concerned with their toy operations. Prefers stories on toy wholesalers or retailers who have unusual success with unusual methods. Also interested in especially successful toy departments in drug stores, supermarkets, hardware stores, gas stations, etc. No interest in mere histories of run-of-the-mill operators. Mss of general interest to retailers on advertising, finances, etc., must be slanted to the industry in particular, and must be worthwhile and interesting. Particularly in the market for technical articles for manufacturers and feature articles on the mass merchandisers." Use a news style. Length: 1,000 to 3,000 words, features; "shorter for news items." Pays 4¢ a word.

Photos: Buys photographs with mss and with captions only. 8x10 preferred; must be glossy, on single-weight paper. No color. Pays $6 plus word rate. Prefers captions.

TOYS, 757 Third Ave., New York NY 10017. Editor: William W. Troeber. For "retail buyers and wholesalers serving outlets with toy/hobby/craft departments." Publishes "2 special selling Christmas decorations issues; the deadlines are Jan. 1 and April 1." Established in 1909. Monthly. Circulation: 15,000. Buys all rights. Buys 12 to 15 mss a year. Pays on publication. Will send a sample copy to a writer on request. Query first. Will not consider photocopied submissions. Submit seasonal material at least 2 months in advance. Reports in 15 days. Enclose S.A.S.E.

Nonfiction and Photos: "How-to-do-it for retailers, interviews with buyers and wholesalers, successful toy or hobby retail articles. Articles with specific facts of interest to others in this industry and 'quotable quotes.' We carry more in-depth reporting. No puff articles. Manufacturer stories are currently overworked by freelancers submitting to us. We're interested in articles about successful hobby retailers and Christmas decoration retailers." Buys how-to's, interviews, and coverage of successful business operations. Length: 500 to 2,000 words. Pays 9¢ a word. 5x7 or 8x10 b&w glossies purchased with mss; captions required. Pays $5 to $15.

Trailers

MOBILE AND RECREATIONAL HOUSING MERCHANDISER, 300 W. Adams St., Chicago IL 60606. Editor: Lynn P. Landberg. For dealers, manufacturers, and suppliers in the mobilehome-recreational vehicle industries. Monthly. Buys all rights. Pays on publication. "Query a must." Enclose S.A.S.E.
Nonfiction: Interested in factual accounts, with accompanying photos, about how specifically named mobilehome dealer or recreational vehicle dealer successfully performs some operation of business or sales management. Length: 1,500 words or less. Pays $35 per published page, including text and photos; about $140 per article.
Photos: Purchased with mss and with captions only. Should be 4x5 or larger, glossy, well-composed and exposed, properly printed.

MOBILE-MODULAR HOUSING DEALER, 6229 Northwest Highway, Chicago IL 60631. Editor: James J. Kennedy. For "mobile-modular housing dealers, manufacturers, and suppliers." Established in 1949. Semimonthly. Circulation: 17,500. Rights purchased vary with author and material; may buy all rights. Buys about 75 mss a year. Pays 10 days after publication. Will send a sample copy to a writer on request. Query first. Will not consider photocopied submissions. Submit seasonal material at least 2 months in advance of issue date. Reports in 10 days. Enclose S.A.S.E.
Nonfiction and Photos: "Success stories on dealers, highlighting their promotion, service, accessory, sales programs. Not interested in general sales articles. We're interested in articles on modular housing as seen by the dealer." Buys interviews, coverage of successful business operations, and technical articles. Length: 700 to 1,500 words. Pays $1 to $2 a column inch. Photos purchased with mss; captions required. For 4x5 or 7x10 b&w glossies, pays $7.
Fillers: Clippings, jokes, short humor.

TRAILER/BODY BUILDERS, 1602 Harold St., Houston TX 77006. Editor: Paul Schenck. For the manufacturers and builders of truck trailers, truck bodies, truck tanks, vans, cargo containers, plus the truck equipment distributors. Monthly. Not copyrighted. Pays on publication. Will send free sample copy to a writer on request. Reports in 30 days. Enclose S.A.S.E. for return of submissions.
Nonfiction: "Material on manufacturers of truck trailers, and truck bodies, school bus bodies, also their sales distributors. These also go under the names of semitrailer manufacturing, custom body builders, trailer sales branch, or truck equipment distributor. No travel trailers, house trailers, mobile homes, or tire companies, transmission people or other suppliers, unless it directly affects truck body or truck trailer. Needs shop hints and how-to features. Many stories describe how a certain special truck body or truck trailer is built." Pays $2 per inch or $40 per page.
Photos: Buys photos appropriate to format. Study publication.
Fillers: "New products and newspaper clippings appropriate to format. Do not rewrite clippings: send as is." Pays $1.50 per inch or better on news items.

Transportation

The journals below aim at traffic managers and transportation experts (who route goods across the continent). Publications for automobile and truck dealers, repairmen, or fleet operators are classified in the Auto and Truck category. Journals for highway planners and traffic control experts will be found in the Government and Public Service listing.

CANADIAN TRANSPORTATION AND DISTRIBUTION MANAGEMENT, 1450 Don Mills Rd., Don Mills, Ont., Canada. Editor: Douglas W. Seip. For "industrial traffic managers and rail, road, air, marine, and transit carriers." Monthly. Buys all rights. Pays on publication. Will send a sample copy to a writer on request. Reports in 6 weeks. Enclose S.A.E. and International Reply Coupons.
Nonfiction and Photos: "This publication covers the complete spectrum of innovations in transport service and equipment related to the Canadian scene. Of particular interest are stories describing how shippers and carriers work together to mutual advantage. Field is changing rapidly due to technological change, world competition, etc., and cooperation between shippers and carrier is being forced by these conditions. All of this is reflected in our editorial content." Length: 1,000 to 3,000 words. Pays 5¢ a word minimum. 8x10 b&w photos purchased with mss. Pays $6.

DEFENSE TRANSPORTATION JOURNAL, 1612 K St., N.W., Washington DC 20006. Editor: Jo Anne M. Thompson. For "transportation executives and managers of all ages and military transportation officers. Generally educated with college degree." Established in 1945. Bimonthly. Circulation: 13,000. Rights purchased vary with author and material; may buy all rights, but may reassign rights to author after publication. Buys 5 to 10 mss a year. Pays on publication. Will send a sample copy to a writer on request. Write for copy of guidelines for writers. Submit seasonal material 2 to 3 months in advance. Reports in 2 to 3 weeks. Enclose S.A.S.E.
Nonfiction: "Articles on transportation, distribution, and traffic management in the U.S. and abroad. This publication emphasizes transportation as it relates to defense and emergency requirements." Buys informational and personal experience articles. Length: 1,000 to 2,500 words. Pays $100 to $125.
How To Break In: "Study the magazine very carefully, perhaps even discuss the editorial goals with the editor, and then come up with creative ideas or a new approach to an old idea, that would be valuable to the magazine. Whether it be a new column, a research article or new ideas along other lines, I believe a fresh, imaginative view is the most helpful to an editor."

HIGHWAY USER, 1776 Massachusetts Ave., N.W., Washington DC 20036. Editor: Cullison Cady. For "an adult readership interested in all aspects of highway transportation." Established in 1963. Bimonthly. Circulation: 20,800. Buys all rights. Buys about 3 mss a year. Pays on acceptance. Will send a sample copy to a writer on request. Submit complete ms. Enclose S.A.S.E. for return of submissions.
Nonfiction and Photos: "Interested in all subjects related to highway transportation." Buys informational articles, historical articles, think articles, photo features, new product pieces, and technical articles. Length: 1,000 to 5,000 words. Pays $100 to $250. Photos purchased with or without mss; captions required. Pays "about $10."

TRANSPORTATION AND DISTRIBUTION MANAGEMENT, 815 Washington Building, Washington DC 20005. Editor: Kenneth Marshall. For "management men involved with distribution." Monthly. Buys all rights. Pays on publication. Will send a sample copy to a writer on request. Reports in 2 weeks. Enclose S.A.S.E.
Nonfiction: "Articles dealing with new equipment, management innovations, computer applications, etc., in the field of transportation and physical distribution management. Rate of payment variable."

Travel

ASTA TRAVEL NEWS, 488 Madison Ave., New York NY 10022. Editor: Lynne Whiteley. For "an international readership of travel industry management—particularly travel agents." Monthly. Circulation: 13,500. Buys all rights. Pays on acceptance. Will send a sample copy to a writer for 50¢. "It is imperative to query first. Travel articles are assigned in advance." Reports in 6 weeks. Enclose S.A.S.E.

Nonfiction and Photos: "How-to articles for better travel agency management, specialized travel articles and highly specialized travelguides, interviews with government and industry leaders, special reports on new travel developments. Most travel agency owners have a college education. Their major interest is in running their business more profitably. We are totally a feature magazine. We carry industry news only in staff-written departments. Our features should have a consumer flavor, as opposed to dry, dull, statistic-filled articles. Since the travel industry is highly specialized, the only way to write for our publication is to study it, then query. We do not want anything that smacks of 'what I did on my vacation,' or 'it's just the most beautiful place in the world.'" Buys how-to's, interviews, profiles, and coverage of successful business operations. Length: 1,000 to 2,000 words; more for travelguides. Pays $50 to $200, "depending on quality of writing, depth of research, and whether or not the writer has photos to illustrate." B&w glossies, color transparencies, and 35mm color photos are purchased with mss.

GROUP TRAVEL MAGAZINE, 380 Madison Ave., New York NY 10017. Editorial Director: Harry Graff. For "decisionmakers in group travel: the travel agent, travel organizers in clubs, companies." Monthly. Payment covers right to reprint in any form. Pays on publication. Query first. Issues close the 10th of the month preceding month of release. Suggests that mss be typed with 40 characters to a line. Reports in 1 month. Enclose S.A.S.E.

Nonfiction: Articles on "group travel in all its aspects, from airlines and other carriers to hotels." Interested in "organization of such groups, ideal destinations, problems encountered. Slant toward organizations interested in the group market." Length: 500 to 5,000 words. Pays 2½¢ a word; average per article, $50 to $100. "Would pay established travel writers up to $150."

Photos: Purchased with mss. "Action, nonposed, close-cropped." B&w glossies.

PACIFIC TRAVEL NEWS, 274 Brannan St., San Francisco CA 94107. Editor: Shirley Fockler. For travel trade—travel agencies, transportation companies. Monthly. Buys one-time rights for travel trade publications. Pays on publication unless material is for future use; then on acceptance. Will send sample copy on request. Most material purchased on assignment following specific outline. Query about assignment. "Do not send unsolicited mss or transparencies." Reports in 1 to 3 weeks. Enclose S.A.S.E.

Nonfiction: Writer must be based in a country in coverage area of the Pacific from Hawaii west to India, south to Australia and New Zealand. "We are not interested in how-to articles, such as how to sell, decorate your windows, keep your staff happy, cut costs." Pays $200 maximum.

Photos: Purchased with mss or captions only. Related to travel attractions, activities within Pacific area. Sometimes general travel-type photos, other times specific photos related to hotels, tours, tour equipment, etc. Buys mainly b&w glossy, 5x7 or larger. Also buys about 24 color transparencies a year, 35mm top quality. Pays up to $10 for b&w; up to $50 for inside color; $75 for color used on cover.

THE STAR SERVICE INC., Sloane Agency Travel Reports, P. O. Box 17 205, West Hartford CT 06117. Editor: Robert D. Sloane. Editorial manual sold to travel agencies on subscription basis. Buys all rights. Buys about 2,000 reports a year. Pays on publication. Write for instruction sheet and sample report form. Query first. Initial reports sent by a new correspondent will be examined for competence and criticized as necessary upon receipt, but once established, a correspondent's submissions will not usually be acknowledged until payment is forwarded, which can often be several months, depending on immediate editorial needs. Enclose S.A.S.E.

Nonfiction: "Objective, critical evaluations of worldwide hotels suitable for North Americans, based on inspections. Forms can be provided to correspondents so no special writing style is required, only perceptiveness, experience, and judgment in travel. No commercial gimmick—no advertising or payment for listings in publication is accepted." With query writer should "outline experience in travel and forthcoming travel plans, time available for inspections. Leading travel agents throughout the world subscribe to Star Service. No credit or byline is given correspondents due to delicate subject matter often involving negative criticism of hotels. We would like to emphasize the importance of reports being based on current experience and the importance of reporting on a substantial volume of hotels, not just isolated stops (since staying in hotel is not a requisite) in order that work be profitable for both publisher and writer. Experience in travel writing is desirable." Length: "up to 200 words, if submitted in paragraph form; varies if submitted on printed inspection form." Pays $5 per report used. "Guarantees of acceptance of set numbers of reports may be made on establishment of correspondent's ability and reliability up to about $250, usually, but always on prior arrangement."

THE TRAVEL AGENT, 2 W. 46th St., New York NY 10036. Editor: Eric Friedheim. For "travel agencies and travel industry executives." Established in 1929. Semiweekly. Circulation: 15,000. Not copyrighted. Pays on acceptance. Query first or submit complete ms. Reports "immediately." Enclose S.A.S.E.
Nonfiction and Photos: Uses trade features slanted to travel agents, sales and marketing people, and executives of transportation companies such as airlines, ship lines etc. No travelogues such as those appearing in newspapers and consumer publications. Articles should show how agent and carriers can sell more travel to the public. Length: up to 2,000 words. Pays $50 to $100. Photos purchased with ms.

Veterinary

VETERINARY ECONOMICS MAGAZINE, 2828 Euclid Ave., Cleveland OH 44115. Editorial Director: John D. Velardo. For all practicing veterinarians in the U.S. Monthly. Buys exclusive rights in the field. Pays on publication. Enclose S.A.S.E. for return of submissions.
Nonfiction and Photos: Uses case histories telling about good business practices on the part of veterinarians. Also, articles about financial problems, investments, insurance and similar subjects of particular interest to professional men. Pays $15 to $25 per printed page depending on worth. Pays maximum $100. Photos purchased with ms. Pays $7.50.

VETERINARY MEDICINE/SMALL ANIMAL CLINICIAN, 144 North Nettleton Ave., Bonner Springs KS 66012. Editor: Dr. C.M. Cooper. For graduate veterinarians, research, libraries, schools, government agencies and other organizations employing veterinarians. Monthly. Circulation: 13,500. Buys North American serial rights. Pays on publication. Reports in 2 weeks. Enclose S.A.S.E.
Nonfiction and Photos: Accepts only articles dealing with practice management, business, taxes, insurance, investments, etc. Length: 1,500 to 2,500 words. Pays $15 per printed page. Dept. Editor: Ray E. Ottinger, Jr.
How To Break In: "Write up clinical reports for local veterinarians."

Water Supply and Sewage Disposal

GROUND WATER AGE, 110 N. York Rd., Elmhurst IL 60126. Editor: Gene Adams. For water well drilling contractors and water well drilling business owners. Established: 1965. Monthly. Circulation: 15,000. Rights purchased vary with author and material. Buys all rights but will reassign rights to author after publication. Buys first North American serial rights, first serial rights (reprint) and simultaneous rights. Buys 12 to 18 mss a year. Payment on acceptance. Will send free sample copy to writer on request. Query first. Will consider photocopied submissions. Submit seasonal material 3 to 6 months in advance. Reports on material within 2 weeks. Enclose S.A.S.E.

Nonfiction and Photos: Technical articles on business operation. Informational, how-to, interview, historical, merchandising techniques. Length: open. Pays 4¢ to 8¢ a word. B&w photos. Minimum 4x5. Prefers 8x10. Pays $5 to $15. Purchased with accompanying ms. Captions required. Pays $20 to $40 for color.

IRRIGATION JOURNAL, P.O. Box 29168, Columbus OH 43229. Editor: Alfred Bessesen. For "service dealers, distributors, and engineers of both turf and agricultural irrigation equipment." Established in 1951. Bimonthly. Circulation: 8,000. Buys all rights, but will reassign rights to author after publication. Buys about 12 mss a year. Pays on publication. Will send a sample copy to a writer on request. Query first. Will consider photocopied submissions. Submit seasonal material 2 to 3 months in advance. Reports in 1 month. Enclose S.A.S.E.
Nonfiction and Photos: Articles "of special interest to irrigation contractors, including business and legal aspects, humorous human interest pertaining to irrigation, some historical and technical articles, news items of national interest. The only trade journal in the field dealing only with irrigation—no other agricultural news or engineering articles. Use a simple, readable style." Buys informational articles, how-to's, personal experience pieces, interviews, profiles, humor, historical articles, nostalgia, coverage of successful business operations and merchandising techniques, and technical articles. Length: 500 to 2,000 words. Pays 2¢ a word minimum; "maximum $25 per page of printed matter, with 600 to 1,000 words to a page." B&w glossies purchased with mss; captions required. Uses "almost any size photo from 2 inches square on up. Do not want contact sheets." Pays "$4 per single photo, $3 for each additional photo."

WATER AND SEWAGE WORKS, 4601 W. Saginaw St., Lansing MI 48917. Editor: V.W. Langworthy. For technicians in water and waste-water field. Monthly. Buys all rights. Pays on publication. Write for copy of guidelines for writers. Query preferred. Reports in 2 weeks. Enclose S.A.S.E.
Nonfiction and Photos: Wants articles such as "Self-Contained Sanitation at Kincheloe AFB," "Automatic Network Analysis by Microcomputer," and "Riley Helps Save the Wabash and Erie Canal" which appeared in recent issues. Length: 2,500 words. Pays 2½¢ per word. Photos purchased with mss.

WATER WELL JOURNAL, P.O. Box 29168, Columbus OH 43229. Managing Editor: Sylvia H. Ross. For "water well drillers, manufacturers, and suppliers of water well equipment, geologists, engineers, and other technical people in the ground water field." Established in 1949. Monthly. Circulation: about 15,000. Buys all rights, but will reassign rights to author after publication. Buys about 12 mss a year. Pays on publication. Will send a sample copy to a writer on request. Query first. Will consider photocopied submissions. Submit seasonal material 2 to 3 months in advance of issue date. Reports in 1 month. Enclose S.A.S.E. for return of submissions.
Nonfiction and Photos: "Articles of special interest to water well contractors, including business and legal angles, humorous instances; some historical interest, some technical articles. News items of national interest. Simple, readable style." Buys informational articles, how-to's, personal experience articles, interviews, profiles, humor, historical articles, nostalgia, coverage of successful business operations, and technical articles. Length: 500 to 2,000 words. Pays "up to $25 per page of printed matter. There are 600 to 1,000 words per page. Minimum 2¢ a word." B&w photos purchased with mss; captions required. Pays $4 for single photo, $3 for each additional photo in set.

BOOK PUBLISHERS

Before you send off your finished book manuscript to a publisher, here are some of the special angles you should keep in mind about this field.

Keep a carbon. If your manuscript is lost, regardless of whether you sent it registered mail, the publisher will not bear the cost of retyping. Therefore, always retain a carbon. Do not bind or staple a manuscript. Enclose return postage.

What you have to say belongs in the book. Any matter enclosed in a covering letter that is not specifically important cannot help you. A covering letter should list your previously published works *only* if of some importance and issued by a respected publisher.

How long does a publisher take to report on a manuscript? The best you can expect is three weeks from the time you mail the manuscript. If you get a decision within a month after mailing, you are lucky. Seven weeks is average. Three months is not unusual. After that length of time, send a brief query, enclosing a stamped, self-addressed envelope.

What rights? Since you are selling a book, the logical thing is to offer "book rights only." If you are a beginner, you are in a tough bargaining position regarding movie, syndicate, paperback and book club rights. But try to hold on to as many of these rights as possible. You cannot copyright a book manuscript until it is actually printed; and then the publisher does it in your name. No specific rights are typed in on the title page of your manuscript. The rights you are asked to sell will be contained in the book contract.

CONTRACTS AND ROYALTIES

Many publishers offer a writer an advance against royalties to be paid on sales. The size of the advance varies with the subject matter of the book, the publisher's evaluation of its sales potential, your reputation as a writer and your or your agent's success in negotiating with the publisher. An advance on a juvenile might be only $500, while very successful authors may receive several hundred thousand dollars as an advance against royalties on a multiple-book contract. However, some rental library book publishers pay as little as $250 total outright fee for a book, as do some racy fiction paperback publishers.

Generally speaking, trade books—the kind that are sold in book stores: novels, nonfiction books, etc.—have a standard minimum royalty payment of 10% on the first 5,000 or 10,000 copies, 12½% on the next several thousand copies, and 15% thereafter. This percentage is based on the retail price of the book. For subsidiary rights, first book authors are usually offered 50% of what the publisher receives for paperback and book club rights; 90% on movie and TV sales. For paper-back originals, the standard minimum royalty is 4% on the first 150,000 copies and 6% thereafter.

In the textbook field, college textbooks have a royalty based any-where between 8% and 12% of the net price the publisher receives. Al-though a book is listed at $6, for example, no one pays $6 for the book since the school is given a bulk order price. The author receives his roy-alty then, based on the net amount of money that the publisher has re-ceived for his book. In the case of elementary and secondary school textbooks, the author's royalty will be much less—3% to 5%, based on the amount of illustration cost and staff work the publisher has had to prepare this textbook for purchase by schools.

In the case of juveniles, two situations obtain. On some picture books, the royalties range between 10% and 15%, with author and illustrator getting 5%-7½% each. In other cases, the author gets the full royalty and the illustrator is paid a flat fee by the publisher.

Who makes money on a first novel? Nobody. Once in a while light-ning will strike and a first novel will sell 50,000 copies or more.

Is it worth it? A novel teaches you a great deal. It builds up a profit-able audience for your later books. It gives you prestige if you get good reviews. Book publishers are willing to gamble because the "names" of today were the unknown first novelists of ten and fifteen years ago.

MARKETING A FIRST NOVEL

The easiest way to dispense with all thought and trouble of market-ing is to ship the novel off to an agent. But asking an agent to handle a first novel without the payment of any fee is rather presumptuous. A first novel generally sells from 500 to 2,000 copies and if the author re-ceives a royalty of 10% of the retail price of $4.50, he will receive a gross of up to $900. This means the agent gets a gross of $90 (10% of author's gross). That's not bad for the agent. All he has to do is call up the pub-lisher, send over the novel, collect $900, and send the author $810. Would that it were so!

First, the agent must, in fact, read the novel to determine the publish-ers to whom he should send it. Second, if it is a first novel the agent may find passages that can be cut, chapters that can be improved and dialog that can be shortened. This often necessitates returning the novel to the author and dictating several pages of comment.

After the agent sends the novel to the publisher, he makes a note on his calendar to follow up the publisher in thirty days. He must also keep his eyes open for some sort of sales channels which will particularly jus-tify the publisher's purchase of the book. If the first, second and third publishers do not buy the book, the agent then must proceed to send it to the fourth, fifth and sixth publishers.

That's why an agent is not too anxious to handle a first novel on a 10% commission basis without an advance fee. Further, even with the fee for handling, a first novel is not a profitable proposition. The only excuse for an agent's being willing to handle it is that he feels, along with the publisher who buys it, that the author will be able to produce subsequent novels which will find an increasingly larger market.

The author may want to market his first novel himself. How?

The traditional way is to bundle the novel off to some publisher who includes in his current catalog a book or books somewhat similar in their sales appeal to your own. Certainly, you would not send a first novel in the detective field to a publisher who issues only juveniles; and you would not send a juvenile novel to a publisher who issues only Bibles. This is fundamental, but unhappily, not all authors examine the publisher's current catalog before sending the novel off. You can examine the publisher's current catalog at any large book store, at your local library, or by simply writing the publisher and asking for his current catalog. (Information about the availability of a catalog appears in each of the following listings.)

THE OUTLINE AND SAMPLE CHAPTER METHOD

A somewhat different procedure from the foregoing is followed by a good many professionals to save postage and speed up results. This method is preferred by most of the publishers in the following listings.

Type a synopsis of your novel (or nonfiction book) in one or two pages. Attach with this synopsis the first two or three chapters of your book, and, in addition, one other chapter which you believe to be well-written, dramatic, and with some sort of a sales hook that a copy writer can use when he writes the ads on your book to go to the consumer and trade press. This package containing, at the most, four chapters and a brief synopsis of the novel, should go to the editor of the publishing house which you believe is now in the field in which your book is located—that is, juvenile, western, detective, light love, etc. Enclose a letter stating as briefly as possible that you are working on a book and here is a sample of what you have, and would the publisher like to see more? If he expresses interest, send him the works; if he does not, your material will be returned in the self-addressed, stamped envelope (S.A.S.E.) you enclosed with the manuscript. You are able to circulate ten publishers in ten months, whereas if you send your entire book, you would be lucky to reach four publishers in ten months. In addition, your book will not get shopworn.

Asterisk preceding a listing indicates that subsidy publishing (in addition to the firm's regular lines) is also available. Those firms that specialize in subsidy publishing are listed at the end of the book publishers' section.

ABBEY PRESS, St. Meinrad IN 47577. Editor: John J. McHale. Publishes hardcover and paperback originals, reprints, and anthologies. "Royalty schedule variable; usually 7% of retail price with reasonable advance." Usual advance is $300, but average varies, depending on author's reputation and nature of book. Pub-

lished 10 books last year. Will send a catalog to a writer on request. Send query with outline and sample chapter. Reports in 3 weeks. Enclose return postage with ms.
Nonfiction: "Dealing with marriage and family life, as well as books of general religious interest." Current titles include *The Sexual Christian.*

ABC-CLIO, INC. (American Bibliographical Center—Clio Press), Riviera Campus, 2040 Alameda Padre Serra, Santa Barbara CA 93103. Publisher and Editor: Dr. Eric H. Boehm; Managing Editor: Lloyd W. Garrison. Publishes hardcover and paperback originals. Published 10 titles last year. Pays 10% on sales price for first 5,000 copies sold, 12½% for next 5,000 copies, 15% for following 5,000 copies, per contract. Will send a catalog to a writer on request. Query first with prospectus. Enclose return postage. Reports within 2 months.
Biography, History, and Politics: Interested in historical bibliography, history, business, economics, library, biography, political science, current affairs. No length limitations. Is seeking material for a series in comparative politics and one in war/peace bibliographies.

ABELARD-SCHUMAN, LTD., 257 Park Ave. S., New York NY 10010. Publishes hardcover and paperback originals and translations. Offers standard royalty contract. Published 28 titles last year. Send outline and complete ms. Address department editor. Reports in 4 to 6 weeks. Enclose return postage.
General: Publishes fiction, nonfiction, science, biography, garden, cookbooks, children's books. Current titles include *The Entertaining Woman's Cookbook* (Athearn); *The Grande Lapu-Lapu* (Drachman); *Harry Truman* (Faber). Address all juvenile mss to Frances Schwartz.

ABINGDON PRESS, 201 Eighth Ave. S., Nashville TN 37203. Senior Editor: Emory S. Bucke; College Editor: Pierce S. Ellis, Jr.; Editor of Religious Books: Paul M. Pettit; Editor of General Books: Robert J. Hill, Jr.; Juvenile Editor, Nashville: Ernestine Calhoun; Editor of Fine Arts: Richard Loller; Editor of Research Projects: Jon Setzer. Payment in royalties. No advance. Published 90 titles last year. Write for guide to preparation of mss. Query first. Reports in 1 month. Enclose return postage.
Nonfiction, Juveniles, and Textbooks: Publishes religious (United Methodist), children's and general books (biography, philosophy, art, music, religion), and college texts. Wants books on marriage, the family, Americana, recreation, and social concerns. Length: 200 pages.

ACADEMIC PRESS, INC., 111 Fifth Ave., New York NY 10003. Editorial Vice-President: James Barsky. Royalty varies. Published 360 titles last year. Will send copy of current catalog to a writer on request. Submit outline, preface and sample chapter. Reports in 1 month. Enclose return postage.
Science: Specializes in scientific works. Textbooks and reference works in natural sciences at college and research levels.

ACADEMY PRESS, 515 Westchester, Campbell CA 95008. Editor-in-Chief: E.A. Foster. Publishes hardcover and paperback originals. Offers standard 10-12½-15% royalty contract. Query first. Reports in 3 months. Enclose return postage and self-addressed envelope.
Americana, Scientific, Self-Help, Sports, and Technical: "Subject open. Prefer nonfiction technical material of greater interest to smaller market; unusual subject. Discussions must be complete, verified, documented." For Survival Series, wants "books pertaining to various aspects of preserving life, liberty, and independence." For Aquarian Library, wants "books of psychic development, ESP, parapsychology." Looking for a book on "economics: the minimum wage concept." Length: "not over 300 pages." May publish dissertations after thorough study of subject and ms.

ACE BOOKS, 1120 Avenue of the Americas, New York NY 10036. Publishes paperback originals and reprints. "All royalty terms depend on material. Standard advances against standard royalty contracts, varying with the quality and nature of the material." Published 244 titles last year. Will send a catalog to a writer on request. Will consider photocopied submissions "if clearly readable." Query first.

Address all queries to Evelyn B. Grippo, Vice-President, Editorial. "Include a 1-page or less synopsis of the plot. The editor can then tell quickly if story line is suitable for publication." Reports in 6 weeks. Enclose return postage.
Fiction: "Gothic suspense, mysteries, science fiction, westerns, war novels, nurse novels, modern novels, historicals, double westerns, double science fiction." Length: 55,000 words minimum, "except for doubles." Wants "no short story collections or anthologies." For Silhouette Series, wants "realistic romances that project real life situations. These are novels about women of any age who face mature problems, as opposed to romance as we currently know it on the young adult level: nurse-intern-rich patient; coed-student-young instructor, etc. There is not necessarily a romantic triangle: one story is about the classic mother who won't let go of her three grown children. What Ace is actually doing is providing a long-needed category for women readers who are too mature for the usual type of romance and not quite oriented toward the heavier, blockbuster type of fiction. All the stories will be in modern settings, whether here or abroad. The mss should be between 60,000 to 65,000 words. We have no objection to sex, if it's an integral part of the plot; sex for sex's sake is out. Any mature problem within the realm of validity and good taste is acceptable; the issues involved should be as identifiable to a woman in mid-America as to one in New York or San Francisco."
Nonfiction: "Occult, cookbooks, puzzle books, contemporary problems (ecology, etc.), nostalgia. No books of limited local interest." Length: 55,000 words minimum.

ADDISONIAN PRESS AND YOUNG SCOTT BOOKS, Juvenile Division of Addison-Wesley Publishing Co., Inc., Reading MA 01867. Editor-in-Chief: Ray Broekel. Publishes hardcover originals. Contracts "vary." Advance is negotiable. Published 25 titles last year. Will send a catalog to a writer on request. Send complete ms for fiction; send outline and sample chapter for nonfiction. Reports in 2 to 3 weeks. Enclose return postage.
Juveniles: Publishes picture books and nonfiction for 4- to 16-year-olds. "Especially interested in school-oriented enrichment books in social studies and language arts curriculum areas."

ADVANCE HOUSE PUBLISHERS, P.O. Box 334, Ardmore PA 19003. Manager: S.N. Davis. Publishes paperback originals. Offers 7½% royalty contract. Published 2 books last year. "We promote sales through direct mail bulletins. We never advertise. Book dealers sell about ⅓ of our work." Query first for law, science, and business; send outline and 1 sample chapter with outline of chapter headings. Will consider photocopied submissions. Enclose return postage.
Business, Law, Scientific, and Technical: "We publish books in 3 fields: science, law and patents, and business. Our books are specific and are directed to selected audiences. The writer should take a serious approach, based on research or experience. Recent titles include *How to Profit in the Far East; The Literature of Licensing; Taxation of Industrial Property Transfers.*

AERO PUBLISHERS, INC., 329 Aviation Road, Fallbrook CA 92028. Editor-in-Chief: L.W. Reithmaier. Offers 10% royalty contract. No advance. Published 6 titles last year. Submit chapter outline and sample chapters. Reports in 3 months. Enclose return postage.
Aviation and Science: General science nonfiction: books dealing with aviation and space. Length: 50,000 to 100,000 words.

ALBA HOUSE, 2187 Victory Blvd., Staten Island NY 10314. Editor-in-Chief: Anthony L. Chenevey, S.S.P. Royalties negotiable. Advance (in some cases) is $500, but this varies, depending on author's reputation and nature of book. Published 19 titles last year. Will send catalog on request. Reports in 4 weeks. Enclose return postage.
Nonfiction: Books in the Biblical, spiritual, philosophical, sociological and religious fields. Length: 30,000 to 100,000 words. Current leading titles: *History of the Old Testament; Minority Religions in America.*

ALDINE-ATHERTON, INC., 529 S. Wabash Ave., Chicago IL 60605. Managing Editor: Curt Johnson. Publishes hardcover originals. Royalty schedule varies. Pub-

lished 90 titles last year. Query first. Enclose return postage.
Textbooks: Publishes high school and college textbooks.

*ALLEGHENY PRESS, Box 1652, Pittsburgh PA 15230. Publishes hardcover and paperback originals. Offers 10-12½%-15% royalty contract "except on rare occasions"; no advance. "Planning to publish a poetry series by subsidy only." Published 4 titles last year. Query first. Will consider photocopied submissions. Reports in 1 month. Enclose return postage.
Scientific: "Lab manuals and books on geography, geology, and earth science—other fields may be considered."

ALLIANCE PRESS (LONDON) LTD., P.O. Box 593, Times Square Station, New York NY 10036. Affiliate of Diplomatic Press, Inc. Pays 10% of net price. Prefers query letters with outlines and sample chapters be sent to the Editor. Reports in 2 months. Enclose return postage.
Fiction and Nonfiction: Publishes books in every field of human interest—adult fiction, juvenile, history, biography, science, philosophy, the arts, religion and general nonfiction. Length requirements: 65,000 to 125,000 words.

ALLYN & BACON, 470 Atlantic Ave., Boston MA 02110. Editor-in-Chief: Philip Parsons. Publishes hardcover originals. Royalties vary. Query first. Enclose return postage.
Textbooks: Texts for elementary and high schools and colleges.

AMERICAN CLASSICAL COLLEGE PRESS, P.O. Box 4526, Albuquerque NM 87106. Pays a flat sum plus royalties of 10%-15%. Prefers queries. Enclose return postage.
Nonfiction: Publishes history, biography, scientific phenomena, and philosophy books pertaining to Wall Street and the stock market. Length: 25,000 to 50,000 words. Publishes The Science of Man Research Books series.

AMERICAN ELSEVIER PUBLISHING CO., INC., 52 Vanderbilt Ave., New York NY 10017. President and Publisher: Paul B. Hoeber. Published 186 titles last year. Enclose return postage.
Reference, Scientific, and Technical: Publishes scientific, medical and technical reference books; scientific textbooks; multilingual technical dictionaries and glossaries.

AMERICAN HERITAGE PRESS (division of McGraw-Hill Inc.), 330 W. 42nd St., New York NY 10036. Editor-in-Chief: Gladys J. Carr. Publishes hardcover and paperback originals, translations, and anthologies. Payment in royalties. "Usual advance is $3,500 to $7,500, but average varies, depending on author's reputation and nature of book. We prefer submission through leading literary agents, but will reply to direct queries. Query first with prospectus and sample text and/or illustrations. No unsolicited mss." Reports in 4 to 6 weeks.
General Nonfiction and Juveniles: "Books of enduring literary and cultural distinction. All subject areas, particularly those reflecting American life style, past and present. Especially interested now in contemporary themes. Prefer established writers."

THE AMERICAN HUNGARIAN REVIEW, 5410 Kerth Road, St. Louis MO 63128. Editor: Leslie Konnyu. Wants originals only. Offers royalty contract. Usual advance is $250, but average varies, depending on author's reputation and nature of book. Prefers queries, outlines, sample chapters. Reports in 1 month. Enclose return postage.
Nonfiction: Publishes history, biography, science, and the arts dealing with American-Hungarian relations. No set rule on length.

*AMERICAN LIBRARY ASSOCIATION, Publishing Services, 50 E. Huron St., Chicago IL 60611. Editor: Pauline A. Cianciolo. Publishes hardcover and paperback originals, reprints, translations, anthologies. Royalty contract terms negotiable; usually 10%. Advance varies. Does some subsidy publishing; less than 1%. Published 29 titles last year. Will send a catalog to a writer on request. Send outline with sample chapter or complete ms. "Request author follow Chicago *Manual of Style*." Reports in 2 months. Enclose return postage.

Reference, Technical, Business and Professional, and Textbooks: "On subjects related to library and information science: bibliographies, reference tools and textbooks; monographs and research studies on issues and concepts of library service, intellectual freedom, history of books and printing, publishing and communications, and relationship of other disciplines to librarianship." For technical titles, wants "conceptual works and theory, as well as state of the art and syntheses." For business and professional titles, needs "monographs and studies—germinal and provocative works as well as state of the art." Textbooks "for graduate and undergraduate studies in library and information science." Current leading titles include *Sources of Information in the Social Sciences*; *Serial Publications, Library Materials in Service to the Adult New Reader*.

THE AMERICAN WEST PUBLISHING COMPANY, 599 College Ave., Palo Alto CA 94306. Editor: Donald E. Bower. Publishes originals and reprints. Payment on royalty basis. Advances are negotiated. Published 6 books last year. Submit query with outline and sample chapter before submitting complete ms. Reports in 2 months. Enclose return postage.

History and Biography: Natural history, ecology. Emphasis on the trans-Mississippi West. Standards of writing style and historical scholarship are extremely high; exceptional in terms of literary merit and scholarship. Some interest in the literary and artistic West, the general subject of the "Western." painting; also in pictorial history, large picture-and-text books. Length: 100,000 words maximum for standard works of history; 80,000 words for pictorial history. Current titles include *This Living Earth* (Cavagnaro); *The Great Southwest* (Bakker and Lillard); *Hippocrates in a Red Vest* (Beshoar); *The Magnificent Rockies*.

AMPHOTO, (American Photographic Book Publishing Co., Inc.), East Gate and Zeckendorf Blvds., Garden City NY 11530. Editor-in-Chief: John C. Wolf. Publishes hardcover and paperback originals. Offers standard technical royalties contract. Usual advance is $250, but average varies, depending on author's reputation and nature of book. Published 50 titles last year. Send outline and sample chapter. For technical works, a reading by another qualified expert is mandatory for acceptance. Reports within 10 weeks. Enclose return postage.

Photography: Mss by professional persons: illustrated texts on photography; detailed texts on photographic processes, fields, techniques. Data is what is wanted here. Minimum length: 25,000 words, excluding captions, introduction. Current leading titles are *Minolta Systems Handbook*; *Principles of Composition in Photography*; *Amphoto Pocket Data Guides*.

THE W.H. ANDERSON CO., 646 Main St., Cincinnati OH 45201. Editor-in-Chief: John L. Mason. Offers royalty contract. Send outlines and sample chapters. Reports in 6 weeks. Enclose return postage.

Nonfiction: Mss dealing with law and police science.

ANTI-DEFAMATION LEAGUE OF B'NAI B'RITH, 315 Lexington Ave., New York NY 10016. Contact: Stan Wexler, Publications Dept. Publishes hardcover and paperback originals and paperback reprints. "We usually pay flat fee of $50 to $250." Published 8 titles last year. Current catalog available. Does not use fiction or poetry. For nonfiction send query and outline or entire work. Will consider photocopied submissions. Reports in 2 months. Enclose return postage.

History, Religion, Sociology: Books "in the field of intergroup relations. Social science nonfiction on race and prejudice, dealing with human relations and understanding, programs in the field of human relations.

Juvenile: Interested in nonfiction material for young people dealing with human relations and understanding, showing the importance of dealing with all people as human beings. Elementary school level.

APOLLO EDITIONS, INC., 666 Fifth Ave., New York NY 10019. Publishes paperback originals and reprints. Royalty schedule: 5%. Prefer query with outline and sample chapter. Enclose return postage.

Nonfiction: Current titles include *The Apollo Library of Computer Science*; *The Politics of Broadcasting* (Barrett).

APPLETON-CENTURY-CROFTS, 440 Park Ave. S., New York NY 10016. Publishes hardcover originals. Royalty schedule varies. Published 160 titles last year. Query first. Enclose return postage.
Textbooks: Elementary school textbooks and college textbooks. Dept. Editors: Antenor Willems, General Manager, College Dept.; Thomas Aloisi, Editorial Director, New Century School.
Medical: Publishes medical and nursing books. Dept. Editor: David W. Stires.
Professional and Reference: Dept. Editor: Thomas L. Begner.

ARBOR HOUSE PUBLISHING CO., INC., 757 Third Ave., New York NY 10017. President and Publisher: Donald I. Fine. Senior Editor: Evelyn Gendel. Director of Publicity and Promotion: Wendy Webber Nicholson. Published 23 titles last year. Enclose return postage with ms.
Fiction and Nonfiction: "General works of adult fiction and nonfiction."

ARCHITECTURAL BOOK PUBLISHING CO., INC., 10 E. 40th St., New York NY 10016. Editor: Walter Frese. Royalty is percentage of retail price. Prefers queries, outlines and sample chapters. Reports in 2 weeks. Enclose return postage.
Architecture and Industrial Arts: Publishes architecture, decoration, and reference books on city planning and industrial arts. Also interested in history, biography, and science of architecture and decoration.

ARCO PUBLISHING CO., INC., 219 Park Ave. S., New York NY 10003. Editor-in-Chief: David Goodnough; Education Editor: Edward Turner. Publishes hardcover and paperback originals and reprints. Offers standard 10-12½-15% royalty contract; average advance is $1,000. Published about 100 titles last year. Query first. Will consider photocopied submissions. Reports in 4 to 6 weeks. Enclose return postage.
General Nonfiction: Books on all subjects—history, biography, science, the arts (with emphasis on the do-it-yourself approach, instructions, etc.) Interested in educational books, programmed learning, etc. Also study guides, laws for the layman, sports, self-improvement, hobbies, English language, reference, health, antiques. Especially interested in mss on "health and nutrition, sports, and horses." No humor. Length: 60,000 words and up. Recent titles include: *Introduction to African Arts* (Parrott); *America's Historic Inns and Taverns* (Haas).

ARLINGTON HOUSE, 81 Centre Ave., New Rochelle NY 10801. Associate Editor: Malcolm Wright. Publishes hardcover originals, reprints, translations, and anthologies. Offers standard royalty contract. Average advance: $1,500. Published 35 titles last year. Will send a catalog to a writer on request. Query first. Reports in 1 to 3 months. Enclose return postage.
General Nonfiction, Religion and Philosophy, Business and Professional, and History and Biography: "Conservative political books, financial books, nostalgia books dealing primarily with the period from 1920 to 1955. No personal reminiscences. Length: 50,000 words, minimum." Current titles include *J. Edgar Hoover* (de Toledano); *The Golden Age of Movie Musicals: The MGM Years* (Thomas). Department Editors: Malcolm Wright and Llewellyn Rockwell, General Nonfiction, Religion and Philosophy; Martin Gross, Business and Professional; David Franke, History and Biography.

THE ASHLAND POETRY PRESS, Ashland College, Ashland OH 44805. Editors: Robert McGovern, Richard Snyder. Publishes paperback originals. Offers 10% royalties. "In anthologies, we buy poems at a small price (normally $5)." Publishes 4 to 7 titles per year. Query first. Will consider photocopied submissions of poetry "for anthologies, with proper credit." For anthologies, include information on prior magazine publication. In making our calls for the anthologies, we try to maintain a list of all practicing poets in the country. If a writer has not received material from us, he should let us know who he is in order to get on the list. For the anthologies, we pay when the book earns the money necessary. This has fortunately been very quickly. We do not read unrequested material." Enclose return postage.

Poetry: "We publish both anthologies and full-length mss by individual writers. The individual writers that we publish are on an invitational basis only. Each year we publish an anthology of members of the Ohio Poets' Association. About every other year, we do an anthology of public poems, and for these books we solicit the best poetry we can find. The only criteria are the ones we lay down for the theme of the book. Our first such anthology was *60 on the 60's: A Decade's History in Verse*."

ASHLEY BOOKS, INC., Box 768, Port Washington NY 11050. Editor-ic-Chief: Sy Paget. Publishes hardcovers. Standard royalties. Published 5 titles last year. Query first for fiction; submit complete ms for nonfiction. Will consider photocopied submissions "if readable." Reports in 8 weeks. Enclose return postage.
General Fiction and General Nonfiction: "We are seeking fiction and nonfiction mss that relate to the world today. Mainly, if a book turns us on, we believe the public will be turned on too. We are interested in mass market appeal. We're interested in controversy and headliners. No college campus subjects. We have enthusiasm and contacts." Current titles include *The Mystery of the Phantom Billionaire* and *The Cookout Conspiracy*. Dept. Editors: Gwen Costa, adult trade fiction and medicine and psychiatry; Robert Young, book trade and self-help and how-to; Billie Young, cookbooks, cooking, and foods; Paul Korea, erotica. No juveniles.

ASSOCIATED BOOKSELLERS, 147 McKinley Ave., Bridgeport CT 06606. Sometimes purchases mss on outright basis. Royalty schedule 10% for up to 5,000 books; 12% for up to 10,000; 15% for over 10,000. Nominal advance. Address queries to Alex M. Yudkin. Reports promptly. Enclose return postage.
Occult and Psychiatry: Psychiatry books: 20,000 to 25,000 words; occult, hypnotism, handwriting: 20,000 words.
Americana and Hobbies: "Antiques, flea market material, nostalgia books (with photos or illustrations), price guide books (coins, antiques, etc.), and books for collectors." Length: 5,000 words minimum.

ASSOCIATED PUBLISHERS' GUIDANCE PUBLICATIONS CENTER, 355 State St., Los Altos CA 94022. Editor-in-Chief: George Pfeil. Publishes paperback originals. "We are more or less typical on royalty contracts, but would consider special arrangements. The writer would have to have an exceptional offering to expect an advance." Published 2 titles last year. Will send a catalog to a writer on request. Query first with outline and sample chapters for nonfiction. Will consider photocopied submissions. Reports in 30 days. Enclose return postage.
Education: "Guidance materials for schools, especially materials suitable for high schools. Could use a series of publications in pamphlet form, such as occupational briefs, social drama (role playing). These might be quite short; the brief might be 4 8½x11 pages only; the drama, 10 to 20 pages in smaller format, perhaps 5x9 inches or less. The briefs might be illustrated with drawings or photographs. We are open to all materials of this kind, in addition to larger materials, but are not able to market college textbooks or heavy professional materials. We prefer materials suitable for grade 7 and up, for student use individually or in groups. We bring together materials from over 1,000 sources, including the federal government, scholarly societies, and private or commercial publishers. We will not publish something that competes with good materials on the market, unless we think it significant, although it has been rejected by major publishers. We often suggest appropriate publishers for materials we prefer not to take. Some of our guidance publications could be classified as economics, sociology, self-help, psychiatry, but on secondary level."

ASSOCIATION PRESS, 291 Broadway, New York NY 10007. Managing Editor: Robert Roy Wright. Publishes hardcover and paperback originals. Pays 5% royalty for paperbacks; 10% for hardcover. Advance varies, depending on author's reputation and nature of book. Published 30 titles last year. Prefers query with outline and sample chapter. Will consider photocopied submissions. Reports in 5 weeks. Enclose return postage.
General Nonfiction, Education, Religion, Sociology, and Sports: Publishes general nonfiction, religious education, youth leadership, youth problems, recreation, sports, national and international affairs, physical fitness, marriage and sex, crafts and hobbies, social work and human relations. "Word length is a function of the

subject matter and market of each book"; ranges from 20,000 words up. Current titles include *Clock Repairing As a Hobby*; *Jewelry Making As a Hobby*; *The Sensuous Christian.*

ATHENEUM PUBLISHERS, 122 E. 42nd St., New York NY 10017. Editor-in-Chief: Herman Gollob. Published 120 titles last year. For unsolicited mss prefer query, outline, or sample chapter. Submit complete ms for juveniles. All freelance submissions, with the exception of juveniles, should be addressed to "The Editors." Reports in 4 weeks. Enclose return postage.
General Fiction and Nonfiction: Publishes adult fiction, history, biography, science (for the layman), philosophy, the arts and general nonfiction. Length: over 40,000 words.
Juveniles: Juvenile nonfiction books for ages 3 to 18. Length: open. Picture books for ages 3 to 8. "No special needs; we publish whatever comes in that interests us. No bad animal fantasy." Dept. Editor: Miss Jean Karl.

ATHLETIC PRESS, P.O. Box 2314-D, Pasadena CA 91105. Editor-in-Chief: Donald Duke. Publishes paperback originals. Royalty contract "varies, from 5% to 10%, depending on editing required for publication. No advances." Published 4 books last year. Will send a catalog to a writer on request. Query first. Reports in 2 weeks. Enclose return postage.
Sports: "Athletic training manuals with exercises, diet, etc. for participant improvment in the sports of track and field, wrestling, football, etc. Our books are published for the participant—not the coach." Length: open. Dept. Editor: Nancy Danielson.

ATLANTIC MONTHLY PRESS, 8 Arlington St., Boston MA 02116. Director: Peter Davison; Associate Director: Upton Birnie Brady; Editor of Children's Books: Emilie McLeod. "Advance and royalties depend on the nature of the book, the stature of the author, and the subject matter." Query letters welcomed. Mss preferred, but outlines and chapters are acceptable. Send outline and sample chapters for juvenile nonfiction; send complete ms for juvenile picture books.
General Fiction and Nonfiction: Publishes, in association with Little, Brown and Company, fiction, general nonfiction, juveniles, biography, autobiography, science, philosophy, the arts, belles lettres, history, world affairs and poetry. Length: 50,000 to 200,000 words. For juvenile picture books for children 4 to 8, looks for "literary quality and originality."

AUERBACH PUBLISHERS, 121 N. Broad St., Philadelphia PA 19107. Publishes hardcover and paperback originals. Published 40 titles last year. Will send a catalog to a writer on request. Send outline with query; include sample chapter for nonfiction. Will consider photocopied submissions "only if as sharp and clear as ribbon copies." Reports in 2 months. Enclose return postage.
Technical, Medical, and Scientific: "Supplementary texts for high school use; how-to texts for adult readers." Current leading titles include *Computer Techniques in Biomedicine and Medicine* (Haga); *Artificial Intelligence* (Jackson). Department Editor: Orlando Petrocelli.

AUGSBURG PUBLISHING HOUSE, 426 S. Fifth St., Minneapolis MN 55415. Director, Book Dept.: Roland Seboldt. Payment in royalties on larger books; purchases short books outright. Published 40 titles last year. Prefers queries, outlines and sample chapters. Reports in 1 month. Enclose return postage.
Fiction, Nonfiction, Juveniles, Poetry, and Religion: Publishes primarily religious books. Also nonfiction and fiction, juveniles, and some poetry. Specializes in Christmas literature; publishes "Christmas," an American Annual of Christmas Literature and Art. Length: "varied." Juveniles are usually short.

*AURORA PUBLISHERS, INC., 118 16th Ave. S., Nashville TN 37203. Publisher: Dominic de Lorenzo. Publishes hardcover and paperback originals and reprints. Offers standard royalty contract. Usual advance is $500 to $1,000 but this varies, depending on author's reputation and nature of book. Does about 10% subsidy publishing. Published 3 titles last year. Query first or submit outline and sample chapters. Will consider photocopied submissions. Reports on material within 10 days. Enclose return postage.

General Fiction and Nonfiction: Science fiction, sociology, law, art, how to, religious philosophy, history, cookbooks. Current titles include *Sex, Schools and Society* (Fraser); *Suffer the Little Ones* (Ryan). Dept. Editor: Bonnie McCloy.

Academic: Casebooks on literary works and authors.

Juvenile: Ethnic values; especially American Indian. Current title: *Moon of the Red Strawberry* (Irwin/Reida). Dept. Editor: Linda Duke.

*AVI PUBLISHING CO., P.O. Box 831, Westport CT 06880. Editor-in-Chief: John J. O'Neil. Publishes hardcover originals. Offers 12% royalty contract. No advance. 15% of books are subsidy published. Published 18 titles last year. Will send a catalog to a writer on request. Submit outline and sample chapters. Will consider photocopied submissions. Reports in 3 weeks. Enclose return postage.

Food: "Our principal field is technical books concerned with foods (analysis, composition, production, preservation, science, and technology). We also publish a few books in the food service field for hotels and restaurants. A few of our books are concerned with agriculture and agricultural engineering. We also publish a few concerned with biochemistry, horticulture and nutrition. We are interested in mss from recognized specialists in the field of food science technology service, agriculture, and horticulture. All mss must be authoritative and technical to receive any consideration. We are greatly interested in receiving mss of technical books on human and animal nutrition. If we can get technical mss on nutrition, food, microbiology, toxicology, and chemistry, we will give them careful consideration for publication in the latter part of 1974. We are also bringing out a series of *Food Product Formularies* which present formulas and methods of preparing several thousand food products." Length: 75,000 to 500,000 words.

AVIATION BOOK COMPANY, 565½ West Glenoaks Blvd., P.O. Box 4187, Glendale CA 91202. Editor: Walter P. Winner. Specialty publisher. Publishes hardcover and paperback originals and reprints. No advance. Published 8 titles last year. Will send a catalog to a writer on request. Query with outline. Reports in 2 months. Enclose return postage.

Nonfiction: Aviation books, primarily of a technical nature and pertaining to pilot training. Young adult level and up. Also aeronautical history. Current titles include *Airman's Information Manual* and *Pilot's Guide to an Airline Career.*

AVON BOOKS, 959 Eighth Ave., New York NY 10019. Editor-in-Chief: Peter M. Mayer. Executive Editor: Robert Wyatt. Publishes originals and reprints. Minimum royalties: 4% of retail price for first 150,000 copies, 6% thereafter; "frequently higher. Minimum payment is $1250, but have paid as high as $25,000 for original mss. Usual advance is $3,000." Published 266 titles last year. Send query for nonfiction and fiction. "For science fiction, contact Charles Platt. For juveniles, contact Nancy Coffey, Senior Editor." Current catalog available on request. Reports in 4 to 6 weeks. Enclose return postage.

General Fiction and Nonfiction: Adult fiction, general nonfiction including biography and juveniles. Interested in original contemporary novels set in America or with American characters. Particularly interested in published authors, especially science fiction. Length: 50,000 to 150,000 words. General nonfiction with the popular touch. Recent titles include *Jonathan Livingston Seagull; The Flame and The Flower.*

Juvenile: Books of interest to ages 7 to 14 and biographies about present-day public figures, personality books, etc. Length: 30,000 to 50,000 words.

AWARD BOOKS (formerly Universal Publishing & Distributing Corp.), 235 E. 45 St., New York NY 10017. Editorial Director: Mrs. Agnes Birnbaum. Publishes paperback originals and reprints. "Our payment rates vary from title to title and are not necessarily set." Pays 4% and 6% on paperbacks. Usual advance is $1,500, but this varies, depending on author's reputation and nature of book. Submit outline and sample chapters. Will consider photocopied submissions. Enclose return postage.

Fiction: "Science fiction, gothics, westerns, sweet romance and sorcery."

Nonfiction: "Special interest paperbacks. Books of special interest in the following areas: diet, nutrition, health foods, consumer guides, offbeat cookbooks, health and

physical fitness, reference and how-to, sports and games, books for women."
Length: 60,000 words.

BAKER BOOK HOUSE, 1019 Wealthy St., Grand Rapids MI 49506. Publishes originals and reprints. Royalty schedule: 10% on case bound and 5% on paperbacks with escalation clause, except for 150 copies for promotional purposes. Published 120 titles last year. Query first with outline and sample chapter to Cornelius Zylstra. Will send catalog on request. Reports in 4 to 6 weeks. Enclose return postage.
Religion: Religious juveniles, devotions, Bible study aids, reference, and gift books.

BALE BOOKS, Box 50, Sioux Falls SD 57101. Editor-in-Chief: Don Bale, Jr. Publishes hardcover and paperback originals and reprints. Offers standard 10-12½-15% royalty contract; "no advances." Sometimes purchases mss outright for $500. Published 10 titles last year. "Most books are sold through publicity and ads in the coin newspapers." Will send a catalog to a writer on request. Will consider photocopied submissions. "Send ms by registered or certified mail. Be sure copy of ms is retained." Reports in 1 to 2 months. Enclose return postage with ms.
Nonfiction and Fiction: "Our specialty is coin books, especially coin investment books and coin price guides. We now are especially interested in any self-help or how-to books and are open to any new ideas in any area. We are considering humor, politics, other financial and investment books. The writer should write for a teenage through adult level. Lead the reader by the hand like a teacher, building chapter by chapter. Our books sometimes have a light, humorous treatment, but not necessarily. May publish adult trade fiction, primarily light fiction, biography, business, economics, humor, politics, reference, sociology, hobbies, textbooks, and travel." A recent title is *Paper Money of the United States* (Friedberg).

BALLANTINE BOOKS, INC., 201 E. 50th St., New York NY 10022. Editor-in-Chief: George A. Young. Publishes hardcover and paperback originals and reprints. Royalty contract varies. Published 300 titles last year; about 1/3 were originals. Query first. Enclose return postage.
General: General fiction and nonfiction, with a special interest in the environment and ecology. Also publishes gift books. Recent titles include: *Only a Little Planet; Fantastic Art.*

BANTAM BOOKS, INC. 666 Fifth Ave., New York NY 10019. Senior Vice President and Editorial Director: Marc H. Jaffe; Assoc, Editorial Director: Allan Barnard. Executive Editor: Grace Bechtold. Principally reprint. "Query first always. No longer accept unsolicited mss. Mss will be returned unread unless they are sent at our request." Published 381 titles last year. "Will consider, in special cases, mss, both fiction and nonfiction, which are aimed specifically at our market, but query first." Current catalog available on request. Reports in 1 month.
General Fiction and Nonfiction: Publishes adult fiction and general nonfiction education titles. Length: 75,000-100,000 words. A recent title is *The Day of the Jackal.*

BARCLAY HOUSE, 21322 Lassen Ave., Chatsworth CA 91311. Editor: George Karnaookh. Publishes paperback originals. Offers contract for outright sale. "The average advance is $850." Published 72 books last year. Will send a catalog to a writer on request. Send outline and sample chapter. "Basically we try to conform to the University of Chicago Press *Manual of Style* (12th Ed.) and, of course, *Webster's Unabridged.*" Reports within 4 weeks. Enclose return postage.
Nonfiction: Wants material "dealing with human sexual deviate behavior. The presentation is made in case history form and first-person narrative," and should include "authoritative commentary by the author that draws upon established psychiatric and psychological sources. Our readership is adult and predominantly male. The slant, style, and emphasis of our books may be best gathered from copies of current titles; the only change, hopefully, will be in the improved quality of the writing."
Fiction: High-quality, well-plotted adult novels with contemporary characters, settings and problems. Length: 45,000 to 50,000 words.

BARLENMIR HOUSE, 2180 Bolton St., New York NY 10062. Publishes hardcover and paperback originals. Offers standard royalties. Advance varies. Query

first "with samples of work, brief biography, and S.A.S.E." Query first with sample chapters for fiction. "No unsolicited mss are invited."
Fiction, Nonfiction, Juveniles, and Poetry: "No adheren·· ·· ·· special schools of writing, age, or ethnic group. Acceptance based solely on original and quality work." For Gallery Series, wants "fine, quality books and discovery literature, an exciting fusion of contemporary prose, poetry, children's literature. Themes range from narrative writing on the American Indian, cosmic and visionary philosophy, San Quentin, drug addiction, found poems, comic strips, TV, wrestlers, love, war, peace . . . in diverse free forms, ranging from surreal to real via explosive, original work." Length: approximately 50,000 words for fiction and nonfiction; 15 to 60 ms pages (with illustrations) for juveniles; 80 to 160 ms pages for poetry.

A.S. BARNES AND CO., INC., Cranbury NJ 08512. Editor: Mrs. Doreen Ferazzgra. Publishes hardcover and paperback originals and reprints; occasionally publishes translations and anthologies. Contract negotiable: "each contract considered on its own merits." Advance varies, depending on author's reputation and nature of book. Published 200 titles last year. Will send a catalog to a writer on request. Query first. Reports as soon as possible. Enclose return postage.
General Nonfiction: "General nonfiction with special emphasis on history, art, cinema, antiques, sports."

BASIC BOOKS, INC., 10 E. 53rd St., New York NY 10022. President and Publisher: Erwin A. Glikes. Publishes hardcover originals. Offers standard 10-12½-15% royalty contract. Published 80 titles last year. Will send a catalog to a writer on request. Query first. Enclose return postage.
General Nonfiction: "Books on behavioral and social sciences, belles-lettres, history and general nonfiction."

WILLIAM L. BAUHAN PUBLISHER, Dublin NH 03444. Editor: W.L. Bauhan. Publishes hardcover and paperback originals and reprints. Royalty schedule: 10% as a rule. Less on poetry and small editions. No advances. Published 8 titles last year. Query first, describing subject, with brief outline and sample chapter if possible. Current catalog available on request. Reports in 4 to 8 weeks. Enclose return postage.
Nonfiction: "New England regional books (including history, art, biography, crafts, etc., with regional basis or appeal)." Recent titles include *New Hampshire Town Names* (Hunt); *Old Vermont Houses* (Congdon); *The Arnold Arboretum* (Sutton).

BEACON PRESS, 25 Beacon St., Boston MA 02108. Director: Gobin Stair. Publishes hardcover and paperback originals. Average royalties are 7½% for paperback, 10% for hardcover. Published 63 titles last year. Query first. Prefers complete ms rather than outlines. Reports in 4 to 6 weeks. Enclose return postage.
Nonfiction: Beacon is the publishing wing of the Unitarian-Universalist Association. Publishes world affairs, ethics, liberal religion, history, social science, biography, philosophy, the arts.

BEAU LAC PUBLISHERS, Chuluota FL 32766. Editor: Mary Preston Gross. Query first.
Nonfiction: "Military subjects."

BELISLE EDITEUR, INC., 35-39 rue Sault-au-Matelot, Quebec 2, Canada. Royalties are paid according to translation rates, mainly 5%—or mss are purchased outright for translation and/or adaptation in French, for Canada. Usual advance is $100, but this varies, depending on author's reputation and nature of book. Market is forcibly limited. Published 6 books last year. Enclose S.A.E. and International Reply Coupons with ms.
Nonfiction: All books published in French. Presently looking for a good marketing manual, a fundamental text on transistors, and a good one on real estate purchasing and management. Length: 250 to 500 pages (5x7).

BELLHAVEN HOUSE LIMITED, 1145 Bellamy Rd., Scarborough, Ont., Canada. Editor-in-Chief: Miss Carol J. Fordyce. Royalty schedule varies. Usual advance is $100, but average varies, depending on author's reputation and nature of book.

Published 9 titles last year. Send queries, outlines, sample chapters. Reports in 4 to 6 weeks. Enclose S.A.E. and International Reply Coupons.
Textbooks: Publishes educational textbooks for Canadian elementary and high schools only.

CHAS. A. BENNETT CO., INC., 809 West Detweiller Dr., Peoria IL 61614. Editor: Paul Van Winkle. Payment is on royalty basis. Published 15 titles last year. Reports in 2 months. Enclose return postage with ms.
Textbooks: Particularly interested in high school textbook mss on industrial education and home economics.

BERKLEY PUBLISHING CORPORATION, 200 Madison Ave., New York NY 10016. Editor-in-Chief: George Ernsberger; Managing and Juveniles Editor: Karen Levine. Publishes paperbacks. "Usual paperback royalties." Published 144 titles last year. Query first. Current catalog available on request. Reports in 1 month. Enclose return postage.
Fiction and Nonfiction: "All categories except westerns."

BETTER HOMES AND GARDENS BOOKS, 1716 Locust St., Des Moines IA 50336. Editor-in-Chief: Donald J. Dooley. Publishes hardcover originals and reprints. "We have our own basic contract and forms with details keyed to the individual situation. There is an advance, and this too is keyed to the circumstances and requirements. Ordinarily we pay an outright fee for work (amount depending on the scope of the assignment). Then if it's a complete author work, we offer royalties." Published 10 titles last year. Will send a catalog to a writer on request. Prefers outlines and sample chapters. Will accept complete ms. Will consider photocopied submissions. Reports in 4 weeks. Enclose return postage.
Home Service: "We publish nonfiction in many family and home service categories, including gardening, decorating and remodeling, sewing and crafts, family legal matters, money management, entertaining, handyman's topics, cooking and nutrition, and other subjects of home service value. Emphasis is on how-to and on stimulating people to action. We require concise, factual writing. There are no specific length requirements. Audience considerations: primarily husbands and wives with home and family as their main center of interest. Style: informative, somewhat lively copy with a straightforward approach. Outlook: stress positive aspects of things. Emphasis is entirely on reader service. We approach the general audience with a confident air, instilling in them a desire and the motivation to accomplish things. We use a great deal of the imperative in our books, and we try to get the reader to assume, right in the beginning, that he or she can do this or that. Food book areas that we have already dealt with in detail are currently overworked by writers submitting to us. We are interested in several larger works, sometimes of a multi-volume nature, serving the same categories that can serve mail order and book club requirements (to sell at least for $6.95 and up). Rarely is our first printing of a book less than 100,000 copies. Then, new titles must compete with our other BH&G titles. Our books fall into basic lines: 96-page books, 128-, 160-, 208- and 400- are ordinarily the way our various lines run. Each is heavily interspersed with illustrations ranging from 2-page spreads to 1 column, 5-inch pix."

BINFORDS & MORT, PUBLISHERS, 2505 S.E. 11th Ave., Portland OR 97242. Editor-in-Chief: L.K. Phillips. Publishes hardcover and paperback originals and reprints. Offers standard 10-12½-15% royalty contract. Usual advance is $500, but average varies, depending on author's reputation and nature of the book. Published 14 titles last year. Writer should "query us first regarding his ms. We prefer complete mss, but will consider partially finished ones." Will consider photocopied submissions. Reports in 6 to 12 weeks. Enclose return postage.
Nonfiction and Fiction: "Books about the Pacific Northwest—historical, scientific, travel, biography, Northwest Americana, geological, archaeological, botanical, marine, etc. Our emphasis is on nonfiction or on strongly historical fiction. Length should be around 60,000 words, but type of ms will determine length in many cases. We are always interested in new material on this region." Recent titles include *Swan Among the Indians* (McDonald) and *Indian Wars of the Pacific Northwest* (Glassley).

BLACK LETTER PRESS, 1201 Butler S.E., Grand Rapids MI 49507. Editor: Donald D. Teets. Publishes hardcover originals and hardcover and paperback reprints. "We buy any material outright, if possible, or will pay per book printed." Published 4 titles last year. Will send a catalog to a writer on request. Query first with outline and sample chapters. Reports in 3 months. Enclose return postage.
Fiction and Nonfiction: "Historical material. No shorts. Heavy on Michigan and Great Lakes material. Adult material suitable for school or collectors of Americana. Our books are more in the line of private press books. Our runs are from 500 to 1,000 copies. Our best seller and only work of fiction has been a historical fur trade novel of the Great Lakes region." Interested in mss on "Americana in general. We are also looking for someone to write new introductions to our reprints. Person would have to read book and should be interested in American history. Will pay 6¢ to 10¢ per word for material used."

BLACK ORPHEUS PRESS, INC., 322 New Mark Esplanade, Rockville MD 20850. Editor-in-Chief: Alfred L. Black. Publishes hardcover and paperback originals. Offers standard 10-12½-15% book contract. "We do not give advances, except in special cases." Published 12 titles last year. Will send a catalog to a writer on request. "Please send a letter outlining project before sending ms." Enclose return postage with all correspondence.
Fiction and Nonfiction: "Generally, we are interested in nonfiction books on the African and Afro-American experience, and on the third world in general. Also interested in fiction with social themes. We are especially interested in mss by young black writers. Our goal is to present relevant books which throw new light both on the history and on the present situation of African, Afro-American, Afro-Caribbean, and Afro-Brazilian thought. Our emphasis is on the world of the black intellectual—the poet, professor, philosopher, novelist, and artist; our primary interest is in the history, context, and implications of the ideas, art, and culture of Africans, both on the continent and in the diaspora." Also interested in books on "China and the third world." Recent titles include *Batouala: A True Black Novel; The Social Psychology of the Black African Child.*

JOHN F. BLAIR, PUBLISHER, 1406 Plaza Dr., Winston-Salem NC 27103. Editor-in-Chief: John F. Blair. Publishes hardcover originals; occasionally paperbacks and reprints. Royalty to be negotiated. Published 5 titles last year. Will send a catalog on request. Submit complete ms. Reports in 6 weeks; "authors urged to inquire if they have not received an answer within that time." Enclose return postage.
General Fiction, Nonfiction, Juveniles, and Poetry: Adult fiction, juvenile, history, biography, philosophy, the arts, religion, general nonfiction and occasionally poetry. In juveniles, preference given to books for ages 10 through 14 and up; in history and biography, preference given to books having some bearing on the southeastern United States. Does not want anything very technical in philosophy nor very expensive art books. First volumes of poetry should be about 64 pages, complete. No length limits for juveniles. Other mss may be 140 pages or more.

BLAKISTON COLLEGE BOOKS, McGraw-Hill Book Co., 1221 Avenue of the Americas, New York NY 10020. Publisher: Joseph J. Brehm. Pays on royalty basis. Published 10 titles last year. Enclose return postage with ms.
Textbooks: Publishes textbooks, major reference books and audio-visual materials in the fields of medicine, dentistry, nursing, and allied health.

THE BOBBS-MERRILL CO., INC., 4 W. 58th St., New York NY 10019. Editor-in-Chief: Eugene Rachlis. Publishes hardcover originals. Offers standard 10-12½-15% royalty contract. Advances vary, depending on author's reputation and nature of book. Published about 81 titles last year. Query first. Send outlines with sample chapters or complete ms for juvenile nonfiction; send complete ms for juvenile picture books. "Follow Chicago *Manual of Style.*" Reports in 4 to 5 weeks. Enclose return postage.
General Fiction, General Nonfiction, and Juveniles: Publishes American and foreign novels, suspense, popular science, art criticism, theatre, film; politics, history, and current events, biography/autobiography. Material determines length. Is interested in receiving material for Black Bat Mysteries series. Dept. Editors: Walter

Myers, adult trade fiction; Miriam Chaikin, juveniles; Barbara Norville, Black Bat series.

THE BOND WHEELWRIGHT COMPANY, Freeport ME 04032. Editor: Thea Wheelwright. Offers 10% royalty contract. No advance. Query first. Enclose return postage.
Nonfiction: "We are interested in nonfiction only—books that have a regional interest or specialized subject matter (if the writer is an authority), or how-to-do-it books." Publishes books on Americana, art, biography, book trade, cookbooks, foods, cooking, history, sports, hobbies, recreation, and pets. "Length can vary from 50,000 words up, or start at less if there are a lot of illustrations (b&w only)."

THE BOOK SOCIETY OF CANADA, LTD., 4386 Sheppard Ave., E. Agincourt, Ontario M1S 3B6, Canada. Editor: Sybil Hutchinson. Royalty schedule varies. Query first. Enclose S.A.E. and International Reply Coupons.
Fiction, Nonfiction, and Drama: Seeking good quality short stories, one-act plays, and essays suitable for reading and study in secondary schools. Could be previously unpublished, or would buy anthology rights, if material suitable. Also in the market for novels suitable for study in senior public and secondary schools. Must be well-written.

BOOKCRAFT, INC., 1848 W. 2300 South, Salt Lake City UT 84119. Editor: H. George Bickerstaff. Publishes hardcover originals and reprints. Offers standard 10-12½-15% royalty contract. "We rarely make an advance to a new author." Published 20 titles last year. Will send a catalog to a writer on request. Query first. Will consider photocopied submissions. "Include contents page with ms." Reports in 2 to 3 months. Enclose return postage.
Nonfiction: "We publish for members of the Church of Jesus Christ of Latter-Day Saints (Mormons). Most of our books are directly related to the faith and practices of that church. We will be glad to review such mss and those having an indirect relationship, but mss having merely a general religious appeal are not acceptable. Ideal book lengths range from about 64 pages to 300 or so, depending on subject, presentation, and age level. We look for a fresh approach—rehashes of well-known concepts or doctrines not acceptable. Mss should be anecdotal unless truly scholarly or on a specialized subject. Outlook must be positive. We do not publish anti-Mormon works. We are glad to consider mss in any form, except plays or music."
Teen and Young Adult: "We are particularly desirous of publishing short books for Mormon youth, about ages 14 to 19. Must reflect LDS principles without being 'preachy'; must be motivational. 18,000 to 20,000 words is about the length, though we would accept good longer mss. This is a tough area to write in, and the mortality rate for such mss is high."

BOOKS FOR BETTER LIVING, 21322 Lassen St., Chatsworth CA 91311. Editor-in-Chief: Richard G. Laugharn. Publishes paperback originals. Offers "standard paperback royalties, average advance is $1,500. Thrust of marketing is toward supermarket and drugstore bookstand sales." Submit outline and sample chapters for nonfiction, complete ms for fiction. Will not consider photocopied submissions. "Helpful if writer conforms to University of Chicago Press *Manual of Style*. Style should be toward clear, easily read and understood material that is well researched and documented where necessary. Positive outlook essential." Reports in 1 month. Enclose S.A.S.E.
Biography: "We are particularly interested in receiving books by Negro authors. Biography or autobiography of general interest to both the Negro and white reader." Length: 60,000 words minimum.
Cookbooks, Nonfiction, Reference: "How to improve (income, health, credit buying, nutrition, protecting self and property, etc.), plus works on astrology, numerology that improve or assist in improving the human condition, i.e., Books for Better Living." Length: 60,000 words minimum.

THOMAS BOUREGY AND CO., INC., 22 E. 60th St., New York NY 10022. Editor: Miss Reva Kindser. Offers $300 advance on publication date; 10% of retail price on all copies after the original printing of 3,000, to which the $300 applies.

Published 60 titles last year. Query first. Reports in 1 month. Enclose return postage.
Fiction: For teenagers and young adults. Publishes romances, nurse and career stories, westerns and gothic novels. Sensationalist elements should be avoided. Length: 50,000 to 55,000 words. Also publishes Airmont Classics Series.

R.R. BOWKER CO., 1180 Avenue of the Americas, New York NY 10036. Editor-in-Chief, Reference Books: David Biesel; Managing Editor, General and Trade Books: R. Cary Bynum. Royalty basis by contract arrangement. Published 38 titles last year. Query first. Reports in 2 to 4 weeks. Enclose return postage.
Book Trade and Reference: Publishes books for the book trade and library field, reference books, and bibliographies.

BOWLING GREEN UNIVERSITY POPULAR PRESS, 101 University Hall, Bowling Green State University, Bowling Green OH 43403. Editor: Ray B. Browne. Publishes hardcover and paperback originals. Offers 10% royalties; no advance. Published 10 titles last year. Will send a catalog to a writer on request. Send complete ms. "Follow MLA style manual." Enclose return postage.
Nonfiction: "Popular culture books generally. We print for the academic community interested in popular culture and popular media." Interested in nonfiction mss on "science fiction, folklore, black culture." Length: 10 to 12 pages, double-spaced.

BOWMAR, 622 Rodier Dr., Glendale CA 91201. Editor in Chief: Karle Lindstrom. Publishes hardcover and paperback originals. Offers standard minimum book contract of 10-12½-15%. Books marketed by direct national sales force. Query first. Catalog available on request. Will consider photocopied submissions. Reports in 1 month. Enclose return postage.
Textbooks: "Special emphasis on early childhood materials. Must be geared to classroom use, textbooks, supplementary reading; writer must be acquainted with latest educational philosophy." Recently published Monster Books, a series of 12 softcover books; text is taken from children's sentence patterns, written by children, compiled by authors; appropriate for discussion, language development, creative writing and reading. Material must be typed.

*THE BOXWOOD PRESS, 183 Ocean View Blvd., Pacific Grove CA 93950. Editor-in-Chief: Dr. Ralph Buchsbaum. Publishes hardcover and paperback originals. Offers "mostly 10% royalty, more if material looks especially good." Does some (5%) subsidy publishing "if ms is excellent in scholarship but low in market potential." Usual advance is $100, but this varies, depending on author's reputation and nature of book. Published 2 titles last year. "Our best market is the college, junior college market," reached by direct mail. Will send a catalog to a writer on request. Submit outline and sample chapters before submitting complete ms. Wants "neat, clean, proofread, original copy. No biography, poetry, novels, or autobiography." Reports in 1 to 4 weeks. Enclose return postage.
Science: Original scholarly works or new teaching materials, especially for use in high schools and colleges. "We prefer books on special subjects where the readership can be reached by a specialized mailing list. For example, ecologists, psychologists, historians, judges, sociologists, etc. Writer should show good scholarship (be accurate) that is relevant to the problems of today or to certain groups." Needs material for series on " 'basic' subjects: botany, pathology, vertebrate biology, ecology, and life sciences in general." Length: 50,000 words or less. Recently published title is *Man, Money and Markets* (Bangs).

BRANDEN PRESS, INC., 221 Columbus Ave., Boston MA 02116. Editor: Edmund R. Brown. Publishes hardcover and paperback originals and reprints. Standard royalty schedule. Usual advance is 10%, but this varies, depending on author's reputation and nature of book. Published 64 titles last year. Will send a catalog on request. Complete mss wanted. Reports in 2 weeks. Enclose return postage.
Nonfiction and Fiction: All categories of nonfiction; some novels. Length: open. Recent titles include *The Myth of America's Military Power* (Chodes); *When Mercy Seasons Justice: The Spock Trial* (Michalek); *Cherokee Woman* (Daves).

BRANDON BOOKS, 21322 Lassen St., Chatsworth CA 91311. Senior Editor: Larry T. Shaw. Publishes paperback originals. "Payment varies according to quality. Standard paperback royalties; $1,000 minimum. In the past, we bought more books for an outright fee, but are now writing more royalty contracts." Usual advance is $1,000, but this varies, depending on author's reputation, and nature of book. Published 60 titles last year. Prefers a query with outline and three sample chapters. "Before submitting, check our latest releases at newsstands or bookstores in order to understand our market requirements." Enclose return postage.
Fiction: Fiction of mass-market appeal, strong male interest and frankly adult in treatment. Novels should be strong on plot, characterization and motivation. Length: 60,000 words and up. Recent titles include *The Sin Preacher; The Savage Body.*

CHARLES T. BRANFORD CO., 28 Union St., Newton Centre MA 02159. Editor: Mrs. Leo L. Jacobs. Pays on royalty basis (10% on retail price when sold at regular discount). Published 29 titles last year. Query before submitting. Reports in 45 days. Enclose return postage.
General Nonfiction: Publishes general nonfiction and books on arts, crafts, natural history, needlework, dolls, antiques, sports, gardening.

GEORGE BRAZILLER, INC., 1 Park Ave., New York NY 10016. Editor-in-Chief: Edwin Seaver. Offers standard 10-12½-15% royalty contract. Advance varies, depending on author's reputation and nature of book. Published 28 titles last year. Prefers completed mss. Reports in 6 weeks. Enclose return postage.
General Fiction and Nonfiction: Publishes fiction and nonfiction; literature, art, philosophy, history, science. Length: 70,000 to 90,000 words.

BRIGHAM YOUNG UNIVERSITY PRESS, 209 University Press Bldg., Provo UT 84601. Director: Ernest L. Olson. Managing Editor: Gail W. Bell. Publishes hardcover and paperback originals. "Royalties based on net cost of book." No advance. Published 13 titles last year. "We have a complete sales department and our own advertising agency." Will send a catalog to a writer on request. Submit complete ms "with an accompanying abstract." Reports in 1 to 2 months. Enclose return postage.
Nonfiction: "Serious nonfiction in all fields; emphasis on works adding to the scholarly community. No length preferences." Publishes books on Americana, biography, book trade, business, history, juveniles, nature, politics, reference, religion, science, sociology, textbooks, and travel. Length: 30,000 words minimum. Maximum varies. Recent titles include *Outdoor Survival Skills* (Olsen) and *The Golden Legacy: A Folk History of J. Golden Kimball* (Cheney).

BROADMAN PRESS, 127 Ninth Ave. N., Nashville TN 37234. Manager: Ras Robinson. Publishes hardcover originals. Offers standard 10% royalty contract. Submit query or synopsis with sample chapters. Submit fiction and inspirational and popular mss to William Stephens. Submit general religious and church leadership mss to W.J. Fallis. Enclose return postage.
Religious Nonfiction and Fiction: Publishes religious nonfiction which is inspirational, sermonic, expository; primary appeal to Protestant readers. Some fiction.

WILLIAM C. BROWN CO., PUBLISHERS, 2460 Kerper Blvd., Dubuque IA 52001. Executive Editor: Richard C. Crews. Progressive royalty scale. Published 100 books last year. Enclose return postage.
Textbooks: Publishes textbooks, laboratory manuals, workbooks, and other supplementary books for college text use.

BRUCE BOOKS, Division of Benziger Bruce and Glencoe, Inc., 8701 Wilshire Blvd., Beverly Hills CA 90211. Publishes hardcover originals. Usually offers royalty contract of 10%. Query first with outline and sample chapters. Reports in 1 month. Enclose return postage.
Textbooks: Publishes instructional materials for vocational, career and industrial education at school, college and adult levels.

BUDLONG PRESS, 5915 Northwest Hwy., Chicago IL 60631. Editor: H.T. Milgrom. Pays flat fee. Query first. Reports in 30 days. Enclose return postage.
Medical: Publishes medically related paperback books that are distributed by physicians to their patients. The main purpose of these books is to simplify the doctor's problems by having enlightened patients. Each book covers a specific field (examples: *A Doctor Discusses Learning How to Live With Heart Trouble; A Doctor Discusses Allergy: Facts and Fallacies.*) Authors with medical degrees preferred, but will consider mss co-authored with a physician. Length: around 30,000 words.

BUTTERWORTHS, 14 Curity Ave., Toronto 16, Ont., Canada. Chief Executive: Dennis D. Beech. Sliding scale royalty. Flexible advance. Published 15 titles last year. Current catalog available on request. Prefers query with outline and sample chapters. Reports in 2 to 4 weeks. Enclose S.A.E. and International Reply Coupons.
Nonfiction: Publishes professional and educational books of any length.

*C.S.S. PUBLISHING COMPANY, 628 South Main St., Lima OH 45804. Editor: Wesley T. Runk. Publishes paperback originals. "We either buy a ms outright or offer a 10% royalty, depending on the book. We pay on publication when we buy outright. Royalty is paid twice a year. No advance." 1% subsidy. Published 50 books last year. Will send catalog to writer on request. Write for copy of guidelines for writers. Submit complete ms or outline and sample chapters for nonfiction. Query first for fiction. Will consider photocopied submissions. Reports in 2 to 3 months. Enclose S.A.S.E.
General: "Religious books, largely of a practical nature to help the parish clergyman and lay leaders in worship, education, youth work, evangelism, stewardship, preaching, and all other phases of congregational life. We look for practical aids that have been field-tested by authors themselves in their own contexts. Greatest demand is for contemporary worship materials and dramas suitable for performance in the church. We publish for all denominations, so do not look for a special emphasis. We do not have length requirements. Some of our books are as small as 24 pages, some as large as 200 pages. Our consideration of length concerns the specific subject or purpose of the particular book. Emphasis on practical aspects of religious life, materials that have been field-tested and do work." Multimedia material, plays, religion, self-help and how-to books. Recent titles include: *Bulletin Board ers* (Eisenberg), 2,000 quips and quotes for use on bulletin boards, as fillers, etc.; *Matters of Life and Death* (Valbracht), sermons on life and death that captivate the reader and carry the reader along, giving a helpful message.

CAHNERS BOOKS, 89 Franklin St., Boston MA 02110. Editor: Sanford M. Herman. Publishes hardcover originals. Royalty contract "negotiable. Advance can range from $50 to $5,000, depending on nature of the work, author's reputation, etc." Published 75 titles last year. Will send a catalog to a writer on request. Query first. Will consider photocopied submissions. Reports in 2 to 4 months.
Business and Technical: "Aimed primarily at the practicing professional. Subjects of interest include building and construction, electronics, engineering, manufacturing, management, food service and lodging, ceramics, materials handling, packaging, plastics, purchasing, distribution and transportation. Should be written by experts in these fields or by coauthors, one of whom should be expert. Special attention given to careful editing, attractive production and packaging. No poetry, fiction, or general interest books."

JOHN W. CALER, SCHOLARLY PUBLICATIONS/AERONAUTICA CORP., 7506 Clyborn Ave., Sun Valley CA 91352. Royalty schedule open. Prefers queries, outlines and sample chapters. Address to John W. Caler. Reports in 3 to 5 weeks. Enclose return postage.
Aviation: Publishes books on aviation history and on aeronautics/low speed aerophysics. Aviation fiction considered.

*CAPSTONE BOOK PRESS, 6126 West 64th Ave., Arvada CO 80002. Hardcover and paperback originals. "Royalty schedule open to negotiation; will buy books of outstanding value. Will also publish cooperatively, with some investment by the author. Will also publish books with guaranteed sales and complete subsidy of limited editions." Send complete mss. Reports within 3 weeks. Enclose return postage with ms.

Business, General Nonfiction and Fiction, and History: Publishes adult fiction, general nonfiction including history. Interested in books for business and industry; Western Americana. No taboos, but no cheap sex books. Adult fiction: under 100,000 words; history: under 50,000 words; general nonfiction: anything from manuals to hardcover books. Representative title: *Standard Manual of Paperwork Flowcharting.*

CAROLRHODA BOOKS INC., 241 First Ave. N., Minneapolis MN 55401. Publishes hardcover and paperback originals. Royalty schedule or direct payment dependent on quality. Will send catalog to writer on request. Send complete ms, with or without art, to Miss Rebecca Poole, General Manager. Reports in 10 to 12 weeks. Number of titles published last year: 11. Enclose return postage with ms.

Juveniles: Specializes in fiction picture storybooks for children. No seasonal or religious material. Length: open. Recent titles: *Lancelot the Ocelot; The Bridge to Blue Hill; The Little Painter.*

JAMES F. CARR BOOKS, 227 E. 81st St., New York NY 10028. Editor-in-Chief: James F. Carr. Publishes hardcover originals and reprints. Royalty schedule varies. Published 2 titles last year. Query first. Enclose return postage.

Art: Books in the areas of historical Americana and American art history. Currently compiling a multi-volume biographical dictionary of artists in North America. Always interested in biographical work on American artists. Length is flexible.

CATHOLIC UNIVERSITY OF AMERICA PRESS, 620 Michigan Ave. N.E., Washington DC 20017. Manager: Miss Marian E. Goode. 10% royalty schedule. Query first with sample chapter plus outline of entire work. Reports in 60 days. Enclose return postage.

Nonfiction: Publishes history, biography, languages and literature, philosophy, religion, church-state relations. Length: 100,000 to 500,000 words.

THE CAXTON PRINTERS, LTD., P.O. Box 700, Caldwell ID 83605. Publisher: Gordon Gipson. Pays royalties of 10%. Usual advance is $500 on paperbacks; minimum of $1,000 on hardcovers. Published 10 titles last year. Catalog available on request. Query before submitting ms. Publisher does not pass on excerpts or synopses, only complete mss. Reports in 4 to 6 weeks. Enclose return postage.

Americana and Politics: Publishes adult books of nonfiction western Americana or of conservative political nature. No fiction, scientific mss. Length: 40,000 words and up. Recent titles include *Selected American Game Birds* and *Colorado Ghost Towns—Past and Present.*

CBS PUBLICATIONS—SPECIAL INTEREST PUBLICATIONS, (formerly Holt, Rinehart, Winston, Inc. Special Interest Publications), 383 Madison Ave., New York NY 10017. Editor: Bill Kirkpatrick. "Payment varies, depending on quality of work submitted." Has paid $3,000 for mss of about 30,000 words with illustrations. "Query in detail first. Don't waste your time or ours unless you really know what you're talking about." Enclose return postage.

Nonfiction: "We publish annual special interest magazines in the areas of hunting, fishing, camping, outdoor recreation, and home building, improvement and furnishings. Each magazine is usually prepared by one author, ideally a recognized authority in his or her field. Ms should be nontechnical, faultlessly accurate, and of interest to both expert and beginner. Average length is 30,000 words. Package must include illustrations, photos, and captions."

*CELESTIAL ARTS, 231 Adrian Rd., Millbrae CA 94030. Editor-in-Chief: Harold Kramer. Publishes hardcover and paperback originals. "We offer standard royalty contract with no general provision for advances. Subsidy publishing would be considered under some circumstances. None of our current titles are in this classification. We market through gift and card shops as well as through conventional accounts." Will send catalog to writer on request. Query first and submit outline and sample chapters on mss over 150 pages. Submit complete ms on those under 150 pages. Include descriptions or examples of artwork and photographs. Will consider

photocopied submissions. Reports on material within 4 weeks. Enclose S.A.S.E.
General nonfiction: "Subjects generally fall into 2 classifications: 1) awareness/sensitivity poetry and philosophy utilizing illustrative photography and/or original artwork, and 2) instructional, Introductory level texts on various subjects of unique interest or uniquely approached subjects of general interest. Manuscripts falling into the first category reflect the new humanism and are primarily addressed to the young. The second category represents the 'turn-on' series, addressing the inaugural or cursory student. Our standard book format is 5½x8½ in size; 80 to 128 pages in length." Interested in philosophy, self-help, how-to and sociology. Prefers not to see fiction or "self-serving poetry expressing loneliness and fatigue." Recent titles include *You and I* (Nimoy) and *Chairman Mao's Four-Minute Physical Fitness Plan* (Howell).

*CENTURY HOUSE, INC., Affiliated with the Yorker Yankee Village Museum and Preservation Projects, Watkins Glen NY 14891. Editor: John C. Freeman. Standard royalty contract. Preservation Press, related to Century House, does some subsidy publishing. "Preservation Press will report on such publication costs and related distribution problems if such requests accompany mss." Books published last year: 10. Enclose return postage with ms.
Americana and Hobbies: Publishes Americana and books on American decorative arts; history, historical biography, American arts, books on antiques and other collector subjects; hobby handbooks. Pictorial preferred. No fiction. Interested in old children's picture books as well as biography on the subject. Books should be relevant "primarily in our regional area."

CHAIN STORE PUBLISHING CORP., 2 Park Ave., New York NY 10016. Editor-in-Chief: Marilyn Greenbaum. Publishes hardcover and paperback originals. Standard minimum book contract considered individually. No advance. Books marketed through house ads and direct mail. Will send catalog to writer on request. Write for copy of guidelines for writers. Query first or submit outline and sample chapters. Will consider photocopied submissions. Reports on accepted material in 2 months. Immediate reports on rejected material. Enclose return postage.
Business: "Reference, guideline or how-to books dealing with all aspects of management, administration and planning in mass retailing, including supermarket, drug store, variety and general merchandise and discount and restaurant fields. Books aimed at store management, regional management and/or top management. Length 256 to 400 pages. Also paperbacks on topical problems and issues in the same retail fields. Length: 128 to 150 pages. Training manuals for all levels of employees in the same fields. Length: 90 to 160 pages. Also interested in material on sanitation. Mss should be practical and factual, giving concrete suggestions. Follow Chicago *Manual of Style.*" Recent title is *How to Make Ecology Work for You* (Pinto).

CHARTERHOUSE BOOKS INCORPORATED, 145 East 49th St., New York NY 10017. Publisher: Richard Kluger. Publishes hardcover and paperback originals. Offers standard royalty contract. Distributes books through David McKay Co., Inc. Will send catalog to a writer on request. Query first or submit outline and sample chapters for nonfiction, submit outline and sample chapters for other material. Will consider clean photocopied submissions. Reports in 3 to 4 weeks. Enclose return postage.
General Nonfiction and Fiction: "We publish general trade books, with emphasis on quality fiction and works of social interest, especially in the political, historical, and economic fields; also a strong interest in biography. We're not aiming at any special audience. We want anything really good of its kind. We don't want custom-tailored books, but works that grow out of a strong impulse on the writer's end. We're looking especially for nonfiction that has an on-going life, both in backlist sales of hardcover editions and a quality paperback edition." Length varies between 40,000 and 120,000 words.

*THE CHATHAM PRESS, INC., 15 Wilmot Lane, Riverside CT 06878. Editor: Christopher Harris. Publishes hardcover and paperback originals, reprints, and anthologies. "Standard book contract does not always apply if book is heavily illustrated. Average advance is low." Does some subsidy publishing. Published 14 titles last year. Will send a catalog to a writer on request. Send query with outline and sample chapter. Reports in 2 weeks. Enclose return postage.

General Nonfiction, The Arts, and History and Biography: Publishes mostly "regional history and natural history, involving almost all regions of the U.S., all illustrated, with emphasis on conservation and outdoor recreation, photographic works, the arts." Current titles include *Haunted New England; A Guide to Atlantic Canada.* Department Editor, General Nonfiction and the Arts: Christopher Harris. Department Editor, History and Biography: John V. Hinshaw.

CHILDRENS PRESS, 1224 W. Van Buren Ave., Chicago IL 60607. Managing Editor: Joan Downing. "Outright purchase, or $500 advance against 10¢ to 20¢ per book, for juvenile picture books. Outright purchase only for juvenile nonfiction books." Published 40 titles last year. Send outline with sample chapters or complete ms for juvenile nonfiction; send complete ms for picture books. Do not send finished artwork with ms. Reports in 3 to 6 weeks. Enclose return postage.

Juveniles: Publishes only children's books. Nonfiction, curriculum-oriented material for supplementary use in elementary classrooms, and easy picture books for beginners. For juvenile nonfiction, wants "easy-to-read curriculum-oriented books. Unusual social studies for grades 2 to 5." Length: 50 to 2,000 words. For picture books, needs are "very broad, but no fantasy or rhyme. Simple folk tales in a second grade vocabulary. Picture books should be geared to kindergarten to grade 3." Length: 50 to 1,000 words. Current titles include *I Live in So Many Places* (Hengesbaugh); *Explorers in a New World* (McCall).

CHILTON BOOK COMPANY, Chilton Way, Radnor PA 19089. Editorial Director: Michael J. Hamilton. Publishes hardcover originals; "sometimes" paperback originals. Offers standard royalty contract; advance is negotiable. Published 69 titles last year. Will send catalog to a writer on request. Query first with outline and 2 sample chapters for nonfiction. Will consider photocopied submissions. Reports in 6 to 8 weeks. Enclose return postage.

General Nonfiction: "Arts and crafts, automotive, technical, science, history, current affairs. No fiction and no juveniles. The author's tone and approach should be appropriate to subject matter and audience." Current titles include *Sculptured Sandcast Candles; Children in the Learning Factory; The Art of Body Surfing.*

CHRONICLE BOOKS, 54 Mint St., San Francisco CA 94103. A division of the *San Francisco Chronicle.* Editor: Phelps Dewey. Publishes hardcover and paperback originals, reprints, and anthologies. Offers standard royalty contract. No advance. Published 6 titles last year. Send query with outline and sample chapter or complete ms. "We prefer outline and sample chapter to complete ms." Reports in 1 month. Enclose return postage.

General Nonfiction: Current titles are in the fields of animals, architecture, conservation, food, history, the outdoors, sports, travel. Length: 60,000 to 100,000 words.

CITADEL PRESS, 120 Enterprise Ave., Secaucus NJ 07094. Publishes hardcover and paperback originals and reprints. Royalty schedule: 10% of list price on first 7,500 copies sold; 12½% of list on copies sold between 7,501 and 12,000, and 15% on copies sold above 12,000. Published 52 books last year. Query with outline, sample chapter, and S.A.S.E. Address all queries to Allan J. Wilson. Reports in 6 to 10 weeks.

Fiction: In adult fiction, looks for characters of depth and color in finely plotted, well-paced works that engross and that expose the accepted and unrecognized in daily life. Length: 60,000 words minimum. Recent title: *Black Triumvirate.*

Biography: Subject must be a figure of universal significance, and whether living or deceased, perspective must be the keynote in the recording of the life. Length: 60,000 words minimum. A recent title is *Lana: The Public and Private Lives of Miss Turner.*

The Arts and Philosophy: Only those thoughts and words which have the depth of meaning that makes them applicable to almost any peoples at any time. Word length varies according to subject and theme. Arts, techniques and developments within either the visual or the performing arts. Word length varies. Recent title: *The Making of No, No Nanette.*

THE ARTHUR H. CLARK CO., 1264 S. Central Ave., Glendale CA 91204. "Standard contract on limited edition publications; 10% royalty. No advance." Published 6 titles last year. Current catalog available on request. Send query, outline and sample chapter. Editorial Dept. Reports in 8 weeks. Enclose return postage.
Nonfiction: Research work, history and biography relating to Western North America. Length: 50,000 to 140,000 words.

CLARKE, IRWIN & CO., LTD., 791 St. Clair Ave. W., Toronto, Ont., M6C 1B8 Canada. Publishes originals and reprints in hardcover and paperback. Royalty schedule varies. Published 35 titles last year. Will send catalog to writer on request. Send outline plus sample chapter, or completed mss. Reports in 8 weeks. Enclose S.A.E. and International Reply Coupons.
Fiction, Nonfiction, and Poetry: General nonfiction, fiction, 60,000 words and up; short story, poetry collections. Current titles include *Four Decades: The Canadian Group of Painters and Their Contemporaries, 1930-1970* (Duval); *The Case Against the Drugged Mind* (Malcolm); *Canadian Defense Priorities* (Gray).

CLIFF'S NOTES, INC., Box 80728, Lincoln NE 68501. Editor: Harry Kaste. Publishes paperback originals. Outright purchase, with full payment upon acceptance of ms. Published 9 titles last year. Current catalog available on request. Query. Contributors must be experienced teachers with appropriate special interests; usually have Ph.D. degree. Reports in 4 weeks. Enclose return postage.
Nonfiction: Publishes paperback study aids on literary classics and works of ideas for high school and college students. Length: 35,000 to 50,000 words. Currently emphasizing new series of subject matter course outlines with compensation to be on royalty basis. Also occasional trade or textbooks of special merit.

COLGATE UNIVERSITY PRESS, Hamilton NY 13346. Editor-in-Chief: R.L. Blackmore. Publishes hardcover originals and reprints. Offers standard royalty contract; "rarely an advance." Published 3 titles last year. Will send a catalog to a writer on request. Query first. Will consider photocopied submissions. Reports in 1 month. Enclose return postage.
Biography: "Books by or about the Powyses: John Cowper Powys, T F Powys, Llewelyn Powys. Our audience is general and scholarly." Length: open.

COLLIER-MACMILLAN CANADA, LTD., 1125 B Leslie St., Don Mills, Ont., Canada. Publishes both originals and reprints in hardcover and paperback. Advance varies, depending on author's reputation and nature of book. Always send query with outline and sample chapter to David Liebman, Managing Editor. Include table of contents where applicable. Reports in 4 weeks. Enclose S.A.E. and International Reply Coupons.
General Nonfiction: "Topical subjects of special interest to Canadians; how-to books."
Textbooks: The editorial department has recently inaugurated a strong emphasis on school and college text publication. History, geography, science, economics, and social studies: mainly texts conforming to Canadian curricular requirements. Also resource books, either paperback or pamphlet for senior elementary and high schools. Length: open. Current titles include *The Collier Macmillan Canadian History Program.*

COLORADO ASSOCIATED UNIVERSITY PRESS, University of Colorado, 1424 Fifteenth St., Boulder CO 80302. Editor: Margaret C. Shipley. Publishes hardcover and paperback originals. Offer standard 10-12½-15% royalty contract; "no advances." Published 10 titles last year. Will send a catalog to a writer on request. Query first. Will consider photocopied submissions "if not sent simultaneously to another publisher." Reports in 3 months. Enclose return postage.
Nonfiction: "Scholarly and regional. No poetry or fiction." Length: 250 to 500 ms pages. Recent titles include *Air and Water Pollution; Cosmology, Fusion and Other Matters.*

COLUMBIA UNIVERSITY PRESS, 562 W. 113th St., New York NY 10025. Editor: Robert J. Tilley. Publishes hardcover and paperback originals. Royalty con-

tract to be negotiated. Published 102 titles last year. Query first. Enclose return postage.
Nonfiction: "General interest nonfiction of scholarly value."
Scholarly: Books in the fields of literature, philosophy, fine arts, Oriental studies, history, social sciences, science, law.

COMSTOCK PUBLISHING ASSOCIATES, 124 Roberts Pl., Ithaca NY 14850. Pays standard royalty rates. Enclose return postage with ms.
Biology: A division of Cornell University Press, publishing books on biological science subjects. Wants scientific, accurate treatment, not popularization. Length should be governed by material and sales possibilities.

CONCORDIA PUBLISHING HOUSE, 3558 S. Jefferson Ave., St. Louis Mo. 63118. Pays 10% royalty on retail price; outright purchase in some cases. Current catalog available on request. Published 50 titles last year. Send outline and sample chapter for nonfiction; complete mss for fiction. Reports in 3 months. Enclose return postage.
Religion, Juveniles, and Fiction: Publishes Protestant, general religious, theological books and periodicals; music works, juvenile picture and beginner books and adult fiction.

CONSTRUCTION PUBLISHING CO., INC., 2 Park Avenue, New York NY 10016. Editor-in-Chief: William H. Edgerton. Publishes originals and reprints in both hardcover and paperback. Offers "negotiable" royalty. Published 6 titles last year. Markets by direct mail only. Will send catalog to a writer on request. Query first, or submit outline and sample chapters or complete ms. Will consider photocopied submissions. Reports in 1 to 2 weeks. Enclose return postage.
Technical: "Anticipated titles will cover the subject areas of construction management, value engineering, computer applications in design and construction, management of the professional design firm, minority group contractors, and trade-by-trade estimating handbooks. In addition the firm will publish pricing books in other subject areas overlapping construction such as coverage of machinery and equipment prices. Subject should be construction related." Recent title is *1973 Building Cost File.*

DAVID C. COOK PUBLISHING CO., 850 N. Grove Ave., Elgin IL 60120. Standard royalty contract. Usual advance is $1,000, but this varies, depending on author's reputation and nature of book. Published 12 titles last year. Will send catalog to a writer on request. Submit outline and sample chapters to attention of Book Department. Reports in 6 weeks to 6 months. Enclose S.A.S.E.
Religion: "We publish a limited number of books on contemporary religious-oriented issues of interest to ministers, Christian educators, and laymen—youth and adult." Recent titles include *Strange Things Are Happening.* "We will also look at manuscripts for children's paperbacks, (ages 9 to 12 years); good stories, but not preachy." Length: 42,000 to 60,000 words.

CORNELL MARITIME PRESS, INC., Box 109, Cambridge MD 21613. Publisher: Robert F. Cornell. Hardcover and quality paperbacks, both originals and reprints. Payment is on regular trade publishers' royalty basis: 10% for first 5,000 copies, 12½% for second 5,000 copies, 15% on all additional. Revised editions revert to original royalty schedule. Published 7 titles last year. Will send catalog on request. Send queries first, accompanied by writing samples and outlines of book ideas. Reports in 2 to 4 weeks. Enclose return postage.
Marine: Nonfiction relating to marine subjects, highly technical; manuals; how-to books on any maritime subject. Current leading titles: *Advanced First Aid Afloat* (Eastman); *Whips and Whip Making* (Morgan).

R.D. CORTINA CO., INC., 136 W. 52nd St., New York NY 10019. General Editor: MacDonald Brown. Pays on a fee and a royalty basis. Published 37 titles last year. Do not send unsolicited mss; send outline and sample chapter. Reports in 2 months or less. Enclose return postage.
Textbooks: Publishes language teaching textbooks for self-study and school; also

publishes language teaching phonograph records and tapes. Other books in self-instruction also of interest. Word length varies.

COWARD, McCANN & GEOGHEGAN, 200 Madison Ave., New York NY 10016. President and Editor-in-Chief: John J. Geoghegan. Pays on a royalty basis. For juveniles, offers 5% to 10% royalties; for juvenile nonfiction, advance is $500 to $3,000. Unsolicited mss will be returned unread. Query the editor, who will advise whether to submit ms. Enclose return postage.
General Fiction and Nonfiction: Publishes novels, including mysteries (no westerns or light or salacious love stories); outstanding nonfiction of all kinds; religious, history, biography (particularly on American figures). Also interested in humor. All should have general appeal. Length: 60,000 words and up.
Juveniles: "We will look at anything. Our needs vary considerably." Want picture books for ages 4 to 12. Want nonfiction for ages 4 and up.

CRANE, RUSSAK & COMPANY, INC., 52 Vanderbilt Ave., New York NY 10017. Editor-in-Chief: Ben Russak. Publishes hardcover originals. On monographs, offers no royalty for first 1,000 copies sold, 7% on the second 1,000 copies, and 10% on all copies sold after the first 2,000. No advances. "We promote our books by direct mail to the exact market for which each book is intended." Submit outline and sample chapters. Reports in 1 month. Enclose return postage.
Technical and Reference: "We publish scientific and scholarly works at the graduate and reference level: post graduate textbooks and reference books for scholars and research workers. Our publications also appeal to members of professional societies. We'd like to see manuscripts on large scale systems analysis in relation to solution of large scale social problems. But do not send any popular material or matter which is intended for sale to the general public." Length: 60,000 to 120,000 words. Recent titles include *Current Practice in Program Budgeting; Power, Law and Society; Ocean Development.*

CREATION HOUSE, INC., 499 Gunderson Ave., Carol Stream IL 60187. Editor: Robert Weber. Publishes hardcover and paperback originals. Offers standard royalty contract. Published 7 titles last year. Will send a catalog to a writer on request. Send query with outline and sample chapter. Follow Chicago *Manual of Style.* Reports in 1 to 2 months. Enclose return postage.
Religion and Philosophy: "We publish exclusively evangelical Christian literature, primarily mss dealing with contemporary issues or subjects of interest to a wide spectrum of readers of religious books. This would include social problems, personal ethics, biography, autobiography, devotional, some religious fiction, and studies of the Bible in general. We publish mostly popular type books although we do have a few of a more scholarly nature." Current titles include *Joy: A Homosexual's Search for Fulfillment* (Boone); *The Backside of Satan* (Cerullo); *For This Cross, I'll Kill You* (Olson).

CRESCENDO PUBLISHING CO., 48-50 Melrose St., Boston MA 02116. Publishes both originals and reprints in hardcover and paperback. Offers standard 10-12½-15% royalty contract. "Advances are rare; sometimes made when we seek out an author." Will send catalog on request. Will look at queries or completed mss. Address submissions to Robert L. Bell. Reports in 2 to 3 weeks. Enclose return postage with ms.
The Arts: Trade and textbooks in music and the arts. Length: open.

*CRESTLINE PUBLISHING CO., Box 48, Glen Ellyn IL 60137. Editor-in-Chief: George H. Dammann. Publishes hardcover originals. Offers 10% royalty on each book sold. "Would consider some subsidy publishing." Usual advance is $1,000 upon completion of ms, but this varies, depending on author's reputation and nature of book. Published 2 titles last year. Will send a catalog to a writer on request. Query first required. Do not submit through agent. Reports within a month. Enclose return postage.
History: "We publish highly specialized photographic histories of automobiles and trucks. Our audience is very special, consisting of antique auto enthusiasts primarily, car buffs in general secondarily. Use special format that we will not stray from, so potential authors would have to virtually work under our direction. We use a

minimum of 1,500 photos per book to trace *complete* lineage of car being described. We're planning a wide range of historical-type books on American cars and trucks. We do not want hodge-podge collections of old ads or photos, reprints of old road tests—the book must tell a definite history from start to finish." Length: 1,000 to 2,000 words with captioned photos. Recent titles include *60 Years of Chevrolet; 70 Years of Buick.*

CRITERION BOOKS, 257 Park Ave. S., New York NY 10010. Publishes hardcover originals. Offers standard royalty agreements and advances. Published 5 titles last year. Catalog available from Publicity Dept. Query first with outline. Reports in 8 weeks. Enclose return postage.
Fiction: Quality fiction, both historical and contemporary, including science fiction, mysteries, adventure stories.
Nonfiction: Select authoritative nonfiction, including crafts books and how-to's. A current title is *Baseball: Diamond in the Rough* (Leitner).
Juveniles: Juveniles for ages 9 through 14 and up. Prefers 20,000 words for younger groups, 25,000 to 35,000 for junior and senior high level mss. A current title is *Kodi's Mare* (Highsmith).

CROFT EDUCATIONAL SERVICES, 100 Garfield Ave., New London CT 06320. Editor-in-Chief: Carl J. Buehler. Royalty schedule by arrangement. Also buys copy at 6¢ a printed word for newsletters. Send query with S.A.S.E. for reply to query. Reports in 4 weeks.
Education: Publishes newsletters, in-service programs, and books for teachers, school administrators, and school boards. Quality of the mss and specific audience determines length. Mss must not be over 800 to 1,000 words in length and must deal with successful and tested teaching practices, administrative practices in public schools and school board actions.

THOMAS Y. CROWELL CO., 666 Fifth Ave., New York NY 10019. Editor-in-Chief, Trade and Reference Dept.: Paul Fargis; Trade Editor for submissions: Hugh Rawson; Reference Editor for submissions: Pat Barrett. Offers standard 10-12½ to 15% royalty contract. Publishes over 100 books a year. Always query first with outline and sample chapter. Reports in 1 to 2 months. Enclose return postage.
Fiction, Nonfiction, Juveniles, and Textbooks: "Trade and reference books, children's books, college and secondary school reference books. Interested in general books of an informational nature as well as fiction."

CROWN PUBLISHERS, 419 Park Ave., S., New York NY 10016. Editor-in-Chief: Herbert Michelman. Contracts offered on basis of stature of writer, outline, subject and sample material. For juveniles, offers "10% against catalog retail price on books for older children; for picture books, 5% of the catalog retail price to the author and 5% to the artist. However, royalty scales may vary. Advance varies, depending on author's reputation and nature of book." Books published last year: 130. Will send catalog on request. Prefers queries. Send complete ms for juvenile picture books. Address mss to department editor. Reports in 2 to 6 weeks. Enclose return postage.
General Fiction and Nonfiction: General fiction and nonfiction; pictorial histories, popular biography, science, books on decorative arts and antiques, some on music, drama and painting. Recent title: *Joy of Sex* (Comfort). Senior Editors: Millen Brand, David McDowell; Special Projects: Brandt Aymar; Collector's Books: Kay Pinney. Service: Paul Nadau.
Juveniles: For juvenile nonfiction for all ages, wants "contemporary issues of a social and political nature. Length depends on the book." Picture books for pre-schoolers to children 7 years old "should be approached in terms of telling a good story. Length depends on the book." Children's Books Editor: Norma Jean Sawicki.

CUSTOMBOOK, INCORPORATED, The Custom Bldg., South Hackensack NJ 07606. A new opportunity for writer-reporters has been developed by Custombook, Inc., nationwide publishers of color editions for churches. "These limited editions are published in conjunction with special occasions such as anniversaries, construction, renovations or for general education. As a result of major technical breakthroughs, such limited color editions are now practical for the first time. The books feature full-color photographs and the story of each church, its history, stained glass, symbolism, services, and organizations. Writers are being sought in most regions of the country to work. Recommendations are being sought from talented writers as to which churches would be the best subject for their initial Custombook. Older churches with major anniversaries (10th, 25th, 50th, 100th), new construction, or renovations (church, religious school, or convent), would be good subjects. The company will then contact the churches recommended by writers. $50 will be paid to any individual whose recommendation of a church eventually results in a Custombook. The organization will at the same time evaluate previous written efforts of this individual. If their editorial staff engages the writer to prepare the ms for the book, and the writer completes the ms himself, he will be paid $200 for his initial effort. Additional assignments may then follow from our own sources or from additional recommendations by the writer." Further details on the program are available from Mrs. Joan Curtis, Editor, at the above address.

DARTNELL CORPORATION, 4660 North Ravenswood Ave., Chicago IL 60640. Editorial Director: John Steinbrink. Publishes hardcover originals. Royalties: 10% of net monies received. Books published last year: 12. Send outline and sample chapter. Reports in 4 weeks. Enclose return postage with ms.
Business: Interested in new material on business skills and techniques in management, supervision, administration, advertising sales, etc.

DASEIN-JUPITER HAMMON PUBLISHERS, G.P.O. Box 2121, New York NY 10001. Editor-in-Chief: A. Rini. Offers standard 10-12½-15% royalty contract. Books published last year: 20. Query first. Reports in 60 days. Enclose return postage for response to query or return of ms.
Nonfiction and Fiction: Trade books. Recent titles include *Dictionary of Shakespearean English.*

DAVIS PUBLICATIONS, INC. 50 Portland St., Worcester, MA 01608. Books published last year: 4. Enclose return postage with ms.
Art and Reference: Publishes art and craft books.

DAW BOOKS, INC., 1301 Avenue of the Americas, New York NY 10019. Editor: Donald A. Wollheim. Publishes paperback originals and reprints. Standard paperback book contract with advances starting at $1,500. Published 36 books last year. Books are distributed nationally and internationally by The New American Library. Submit complete ms. Will not consider photocopied submissions. Reports in 2 to 6 weeks. Enclose return postage with ms.
Fiction: "Science fiction only, about 4 titles a month. About 70% are original works. Mainly novels with occasional collections of the short stories of one author (name authors only). Space flight, future adventure, scientific discovery, unusual concepts, and all the vast range of s-f conceptions will be found in our works. We prefer good narrative presentation without stress on innovations, avant-garde stunts, etc." Length: 55,000 to 75,000 words.

THE JOHN DAY COMPANY, INC., 257 Park Ave. South, New York NY 10010. Publishes hardcover originals. Royalty schedule varies. Will send a catalog to writer on request. Send outline and sample chapters to the editor. Enclose return postage.
General: Publishes adult fiction, juveniles, history, biography, science, and books on the arts. "Adult fiction is not a large field for us; we have never published anything approaching 'pulp' fiction, so we have a rather high general standard of excellence in this field's requirements. Our juvenile books are primarily of an educational-supplementary materials nature, or story books which are unique; 'classic' enough to merit special attention."

JOHN DE GRAFF, INC., 34 Oak Ave., Tuckahoe NY 10707. Royalty schedule: 10% of retail. Reports in 3 to 4 weeks. Enclose return postage with ms.
Sports: Nonfiction mss on nautical and pleasure boating themes.

DELL PUBLISHING CO., INC., (including Delacorte Press), 245 E. 47th St., New York NY 10017. Editorial Director: Ross Claiborne. Publishes hardcover and paperback originals and reprints. Standard royalty schedule. Published 431 books last year. Query first always. "Mss that arrive without a preceding query answered in the affirmative by a member of our staff will have to be returned unread. On fiction queries, we would like to know what sort of book the author has written or proposes to write—whether straight novel, romance-suspense, mystery, historical, or Gothic. A paragraph further describing the story would also be helpful." Send complete ms for juveniles. Reports in 8 to 10 weeks. Enclose return postage.
General Fiction and Nonfiction: Publishes adult fiction; general nonfiction including philosophy, biography, history, religion, science, the arts; juvenile.
Juveniles: Delacorte Press children's books: poetry, history, sports and science for ages 12 and over; history, social science and fiction for intermediate level; picture books for the very young. Length: 30,000 to 50,000 words for ages 12 to 16. Juvenile Editor: Ronald Buehl.

DELMAR PUBLISHERS, Division of Litton Educational Publishing, Inc., Mountainview Ave., Albany NY 12205. Director of Publications: Alan N. Knofla. Publishes softcover originals. Royalty schedule up to 10%. No advance. Published 38 titles last year. Query first. Length: About 500 pages, written to Delmar manuscript specifications.
Textbooks: Publishes trade, industrial, and technical books for middle and secondary schools and two-year colleges. Publishes softcover lab textbooks.

T.S. DENISON AND COMPANY, INC., 5100 W. 82nd St., Minneapolis MN 55431. Editor: Lawrence M. Brings. Publishes hardcover and paperback originals. "Flat rate royalty per thousand copies sold. Some mss purchased outright. No advance." Will send a catalog to a writer on request. Submit complete ms. Will not consider photocopied submissions. Enclose return postage with ms.
Education and Juveniles: Juveniles: 300 to 1,500 words, Early Childhood Series, controlled vocabulary; Primary and Upper Grades, coordinated with units of classroom study. Biography: Men of Achievement Series, on assignment only. From 200 to 400 standard page length. Subject must give consent and agree to approve the finished ms. Also science books for elementary and high school classroom use. Length varies. Publishes all types of aids for teachers, particularly in elementary grades. Representative titles are *The Speaker's and Toastmaster's Handbook; The New Teacher's Complete Reference Guide; Alton S. Newell, Recycling Expert.*

DENLINGER'S PUBLISHERS, P.O. Box 76, Fairfax VA 22030. Editor-in-Chief: Mrs. R. Annabel Rathman. Royalty varies, depending upon type of ms; averages 10%. Specific information given upon receipt of query indicating type of projected ms. No advance. Reports in 3 months. Enclose return postage.
Fiction and Nonfiction: Publishes fiction, nonfiction, general publications, books on dog breeds (not dog stories). Length varies, depending upon type of publication.

THE DIAL PRESS, INC., 1 Dag Hammerskjold Plaza, New York NY 10017. Editor-in-Chief: Richard Marek. Pays on a royalty basis. Usual advance is $1,500 minimum, depending on author's reputation and nature of book. Books published last year: 72. Query first. Reports in 6 weeks or sooner. Enclose return postage.
General Fiction and Nonfiction: "No definite rule governing types of material published." Length: 65,000 words minimum. Recent titles: *The Matlock Papers; Vacation Houses.*
Juvenile: Editor of Children's Books: Phyllis Fogelman.

THE DIETZ PRESS, INC., 109 E. Cary St., Richmond VA 23219. Editor: August Dietz, III. Requires preliminary letter stating the subject and briefly outlining the material. Enclose return postage.
Nonfiction: Publishes biography, books of an historical nature, Americana, unusual cook and hostess books. Length: 40,000 to 50,000 words. No poetry.

DIGEST BOOKS, INC., 540 Frontage Road, Northfield IL 60093. President: Milton Klein. Editor: John T. Amber. Publishes paperback originals and reprints. Query first with outline, sample chapter, photos and/or illustrations. Generous ad-

vance, royalties or outright purchase. Enclose return postage.
Sports: Wants to see submissions on sports—mainly hunting, shooting, fishing, camping, outdoor vocations, recreation vehicles and boats. No personal experience stories. Length: 2,500 to 5,000 words.

DILLON PRESS, 106 Washington Ave. N., Minneapolis MN 55401. Editor-in-Chief: Mrs. Gerald R. Dillon. Publishes hardcover originals. Offers royalty or straight fee, depending on title; no advance. Published 6 titles last year. Will send a catalog to writer on request. Submit complete ms or outline and sample chapters. Will consider photocopied submissions. Follow the Chicago *Manual of Style.* Reports in 6 weeks. Enclose return postage.
Juveniles: "We need mss for our upper elementary/junior high reader series: (1) Looking Forward to a Career. Emphasizes opportunities within a field; is an introduction to the variety of jobs available in each field—no specifics or dated information (current salaries, etc.). Average length: 25,000 words. Recent title is *Advertising* (Larranaga). (2) The Story of an American Indian. Biographies of contemporary and historical Indians to acquaint children with the varied contributions of American Indians. Average length: 15,000 words. Recent title is *Osceola* (Johnson). (3) Contributions of Women. Each volume includes the stories of 6 to 8 women who have made significant contributions in a particular field (medicine, art, business, etc.). Average length: 45,000 words. (4) Environment. Each title describes the development of a certain feature of the environment (eg, a lake, a mountain, a forest), then tells how this feature maintains itself under ideal conditions, what happens when the natural balance is affected by man, and, finally, what must be done to restore the subject to an acceptable condition. Average length: 20,000 words."
General Nonfiction: "For the adult market, we need ms for the 'Ethnic' series. Each Ethnic book describes 'old country' customs and beliefs to acquaint and re-acquaint readers with the ethnic roots of Americans." Average length: 65,000 words.

DIMENSION BOOKS, INC., P.O. Box 811, Denville NJ 07834. Regular royalty schedule. Advance is negotiable. Books published last year: 39. Current catalog available if S.A.S.E. is enclosed. Send query first to editorial office. Address mss to Thomas P. Coffey. Reports in 1 week on requested mss. Enclose return postage with ms.
General Nonfiction: Publishes general nonfiction including religion, principally Roman Catholic. Also psychology and music. Length: 40,000 words and over. A recent title is *Prayer Is a Hunger* (Farrell).

*DIPLOMATIC PRESS, INC., 1102 Betton Rd., Tallahassee FL 32303. Editor: George Alexander Lensen. Publishes hardcover originals. "No royalties on first printing." No advance. 10% of books are subsidy published. Published 4 titles last year. Will send a catalog to a writer on request. Query first. Reports in 1 month. Enclose return postage.
History: "Memoirs, diaries, letters, and dispatches of diplomats in the Far East and Russia, or scholarly studies of Russo-Asian relations. Maximum ms length is normally 300 pages. The ms should be scholarly in content and documentation, lucid and graceful in style. We place a greater emphasis on primary source material than some publishers do." Interested in mss on "history of Russian relations with Japan, China, and other Asian countries." Recent titles include *Witnesses of Tsushima* (Westwood); *Japanese Foreign Policy on the Eve of the Pacific War, A Soviet View* (Kutokov); *Faces of Japan: A Photographic View* (Alexander).

DIPLOMATIC PRESS, INC., Address all communications to: P.O. Box 604, Times Square Station, New York NY 10036. Royalty schedule: 10% off published price. Reports in 6 months. All subsidiary companies of Diplomatic Press consider mss at the New York headquarters only. Wants mss only from professional or skilled, if not established, writers. "Unsolicited mss must be accompanied by self-addressed and stamped envelopes or label."
General Nonfiction and Fiction, Textbooks: General adult nonfiction and fiction. Textbook publisher to different universities and colleges. Considers publications in French, German, Italian and Spanish languages if they are of scholastic or universal appeal. Length: 50,000 to 75,000 words.

DODD, MEAD AND CO., 79 Madison Ave., New York, NY 10016. Executive Editor: Allen T. Klots, Jr. Royalty basis: 10% to 15%. Advances vary, depending on the sales potential of the book. Books published last year: 150. A contract for nonfiction books is offered on the basis of a query, a suggested outline and a sample chapter. Write for permission before sending mss. Adult fiction, history, philosophy, the arts, and religion should be addressed to Editorial Department. Reports in 1 month. Enclose return postage.

General Fiction and Nonfiction: Publishes book-length mss, 70,000 to 100,000: fiction and nonfiction of high quality, mysteries and romantic novels of suspense, biography, popular science, travel, yachting and music. Very rarely buys photographs or poetry.

Juvenile: Length: 1,500 to 75,000 words. Children's Books Editor: Mrs. Joe Ann Daly.

THE DORSEY PRESS, 1818 Ridge Rd., Homewood IL 60430. Publishes hardcover and paperback originals. Royalty schedule varies. Address all material to: W. E. O. Barnes, Assistant Vice-President. Prefers queries, outlines and sample chapters. Reports in 6 to 8 weeks. Enclose return postage.

Textbooks: Publishes college textbooks in the social sciences (anthropology, sociology, history, political science, psychology).

DOUBLEDAY & CO., INC., 277 Park Ave., New York NY 10017. Editor-in-Chief: Stewart Richardson. Publishes hardcover and paperback originals; publishes paperback reprints as Anchor Books only. Offers standard 10-12½-15% royalty contract. Advance varies. Published about 750 books last year. Query first with outline and sample chapters for nonfiction. Submit complete ms for fiction. Reports in 1 month. Enclose return postage.

General Fiction and Nonfiction: "Adult fiction, history, biography, science, philosophy, religion, general nonfiction, cookbooks, westerns, science fiction, and mysteries." Length: "usually 75,000 words and up." Department Editors: Maureen Mahon, Science; John Delaney, Catholic Religious; Alexander Liepa, Protestant and Jewish; Loretta Barrett, Anchor Books; John Kinney, Dolphin Books. Submit cookbooks to Cookbook Dept.

Juvenile: "Lengths vary. Submit to Books for Young Readers."

DOUBLEDAY CANADA LTD., 105 Bond St., Toronto 2, Ont., Canada. Managing Editor: Douglas M. Gibson. Publishes hardcover originals. Offers standard royalty contract. Advance varies. Published 10 titles last year. Will send a catalog to a writer on request. Send query, outline and sample chapters. Reports in 1 to 2 months. Enclose return postage.

General Nonfiction and Fiction, and Juveniles: "We publish trade books of all sorts that are either about Canada or written by Canadian residents." Recent titles include: *The Great Canadian Novel; Hockey Showdown; The Twelfth Mile* and *Where the Wagons Led.* Lengths: 60,000 to 100,000 words for nonfiction; 55,000 to 90,000 words for fiction; open for juveniles.

DOW JONES-IRWIN, INC., 1818 Ridge Rd., Homewood IL 60430. Publishes originals only. Royalty schedule 10% of net. Advance negotiable. Published 14 titles last year. Send completed mss to the attention of Editorial Director. Enclose return postage with ms.

Nonfiction: Business and industrial subjects.

DRAKE PUBLISHERS, INC., 381 Park Ave. S., New York NY 10016. Senior Editor: Kenn Harris. Offers standard 10-12½-15% royalty contract; "all advances are arranged individually." Ms must be typewritten on 8½x11 bond paper and must be presented with a carbon or a Xerox. Reports in 30 days. Enclose return postage with ms.

Cookbooks, Self-Help and How-To, and Hobbies: "Publishes general nonfiction books, including auto repair manuals, woodworking, craft and how-to books, cookbooks, travel guides, etc. The books are geared in general to home craftsmen or home repairmen, although our books are often bought, used, and praised by professionals. We are flexible about length, but prefer our books to be at least 132 pages long. Craft books of any sort should be characterized by conciseness and clarity of presentation—step-by-step instructions, diagrams when necessary, and photos are most desirable. Drake books are noted for their thoroughness and for the excellence of the directions found in them. New lines include film biographies, exercise, and biographies of World leaders."

DRAMA BOOK SPECIALISTS/PUBLISHERS, 150 West 52nd St., New York NY 10019. Publishes hardcover and paperback originals. Royalties usually 10%. Advance varies. Published 26 titles last year. Send query to Ralph Pine, Managing Editor. Reports in 4 to 8 weeks. Enclose return postage.
Drama: "Theatrical history, texts, film, and books dealing with the performing arts." Representative titles include *People's Theatre in America; Plays, Politics and Polemics; Comden and Green on Broadway.*

DREENAN PRESS LTD., P.O. Box 165, Croton-on-Hudson NY 10520. Editor-in-Chief: Michael J. Dillon. Publishes hardcover and paperback originals. "On hardcover titles, we offer a straight 10% on copies sold at discounts up to 49% off list and 10% of net on sales at 50% or more. Paperbacks receive a straight 5% of list. In addition to the usual trade channels like bookstores and libraries, our output will also be marketed in tack shops and feed stores." Will send catalog to writer on request. Submit outline and sample chapters. Will consider photocopied submissions. Enclose return postage.
General Nonfiction: "Horse and horsemanship books only. Books on individual breeds as well as technical, reference and how-to-do-it titles on all subjects of horsemanship. Also posters, prints and graphic aids in the same area. No specific length required. Since the largest part of the horse enthusiast market is composed of young adults and children, the writing should lean toward that audience while not excluding the adult market. Generally, a good deal of photos or drawings should accompany the text." In process are works on the Appaloosa, Painted horse, Welsh pony, Trakener and other breeds; anatomy and conformation of the horse; grooming for the show ring; tack and other equipment.

DROKE HOUSE/HALLUX, INC., 1372 Peachtree St., Atlanta GA 30309. Editor: Alan Whitten. Publishes hardcover originals. Offers standard royalty contract with small advances. Published 18 titles last year. Will send a catalog to a writer on request. Send outline and sample chapter. Reports in 6 to 8 weeks. Enclose return postage.
General: "National book publishers—fiction and nonfiction books of all types, from novels to the occult to inspiration, self-help, etc." Length: 30,000 to 120,000 words. Current leading titles include *The Psychic World of Doc Anderson; Brighten Your Corner; The Purpose of Love.*

DUNELLEN PUBLISHING CO. INC., 386 Park Ave., S. New York NY 10016. Acquisitions Editor: Diana Bryant. Publishes hardcover and paperback originals. "Our royalty rate is 7½-10-12½%. We do not issue any advance to authors." Publishes 15 to 20 books a year. "Our distribution is mainly in the academic fields and the libraries, not so much to the general public bookstores." Submit outline and sample chapters. "We send out an authors' guide to anyone preparing a manuscript." Will consider photocopied submissions. Reports in 2 to 3 weeks. Enclose return postage.
General Nonfiction: "We deal mainly in the social sciences. Subjects include the legal field, economics, international politics, urban affairs, etc.; occasionally books in the experimental and theoretical psychology field; black studies. We prefer original studies, which have been well researched, with a scholarly approach. We plan to start an empirical studies line as opposed to the more theoretical University Press of Cambridge Series. We would prefer not to see any more books on either World War II or the Vietnam War." Other publishing interests include business, law, multimedia material, sociology, urban and environmental, labor and diplomacy. No limit on length. Recent titles include: *Health Services for Tomorrow: Trends and Issues* (Burns).

DUQUESNE UNIVERSITY PRESS, Pittsburgh PA 15219. Royalty schedule is 10%. No advance. Query first. Reports in 6 months or less. Enclose return postage.

Nonfiction: Scholarly books on philosophy and philology and psychology. Length: open.

E.P. DUTTON AND CO., INC., 201 Park Ave. S., New York NY 10003. Editor-in-Chief, adult publications: Hal Scharlatt; Juvenile Department: Ann Durell. Dutton Paperback: Cyril Nelson; other categories handled by John Macrae III. Pays by advances and royalties. Queries welcomed for nonfiction of high quality on almost any subject for the general reader. Before sending mss query with outline and sample chapters. Enclose return postage.
General Fiction and Nonfiction: Publishes novels of permanent literary value; mystery, nonfiction, religious, travel, fine arts, biography, memoirs, belles lettres, history, science, psychology, translations, and quality paperbacks.

DUXBURY PRESS (Division of Wadsworth Publishing Co.), 6 Bound Brook Court, North Scituate MA 02060. Publishes hardcover and paperback originals. Contract varies "depending on number of authors involved and degree of involvement. Usually offers 10 to 15% with advance arrangements on a limited basis." Published 17 titles last year. Will send catalog to writer on request. Submit outline, publishing rationale, and sample chapter. Uses Chicago *Manual of Style.* Enclose return postage.
General Nonfiction: "Social science and quantitative methods college texts. Also geography, environmental studies, and interdisciplinary studies; economics, history, politics, sociology, criminal justice, and sex education. Some books in these areas of a semi-trade nature as well. Emphasis on pedagogy and quality of thought. Authors mostly PH.D's but some work in collaboration with professional writers, researchers, etc., whom we hire. Emphasis on new and exciting approaches to knowledge in these areas: novel formats and varying lengths. We accept a wide latitude of styles, outlooks and structures, as long as each is accompanied by a detailed and thorough rationale and is the embodiment of a responsible trend in the academic field." Length: 50,000 to 200,000 words. Recent titles include: *A Georgraphy of Economic Behavior* (Eliot-Hurst) and *Much Is Taken, Much Remains* (Bryan).

EASTERN ORTHODOX BOOKS, P.O. Box 302, Willits CA 95490. Editor-in-Chief: Vladimir Anderson. Publishes originals and reprints in both hardcover and paperback. Published 17 titles last year. "Our publications are purchased by Eastern Orthodox, Anglicans, traditional Roman Catholics, and institutional libraries." Will send catalog to a writer on request. Query first preferred. Will consider photocopied submissions. Reports in 2 to 3 weeks. Enclose return postage.
Religion: "We publish manuscripts on religion—Eastern Orthodox orientation: including Church history, ritual and dogma; lives of saints, spiritual works, Fathers of the Church, and family religious life. Emphasis is on traditional Eastern Orthodoxy, however, pre-Schism Western material is quite acceptable. Any length acceptable. All works must be conservative—ecumenism, Death of God, rationalism, questioning traditional Church teaching, are all taboo. We are especially looking for translations of works from Russian, Greek, Latin, and Syraic: patristica, theological works, etc.; either material of our selection, or of the translator's choice. Do not send Orthodoxy treated as being 'quaint,' 'how I was saved,' Protestant orientation, fiction."

LES EDITIONS DE L'ETOILE, 325-327 Mont-Royal Est., Montreal 151 PQ, Canada. (formerly John Desgranges). Offers 10% royalty contract. No advance. Enclose S.A.E. and International Reply Coupons for return of submissions.
General Fiction and Nonfiction: General publisher of all types of books in French language only.

*LES EDITIONS PAULINES, 250 Nord, Boul. St.-Francois, Sherbrooke, Quebec, Canada. Editor-in-Chief: Laurent Foletto. Publishes paperback originals in French and translations into French. Offers standard royalty contract. "We also do subsidy publishing (25%)." Usual advance is 8% to 10%, but this varies, depending on author's reputation and nature of book. Will send a catalog to a writer on request. Send complete ms or query and outline. Reports in 5 to 8 weeks. Enclose International Reply Coupons for return postage.
Social Sciences, Philosophy, and Religion: "Mass oriented books in psychology, hu-

man relations, youth problems, social work, marriage and sex, etc. Philosophy and religious problems. Length may vary according to subject; usually 20,000 words and up."
Juveniles: "Sciences, hobbies, travels or fiction."

JOHN EDWARDS PUBLISHING CO., 61 Winton Place, "Appledore," Stratford CT 06497. Editor: William B. Jacobs, Jr. Publishes hardcover originals and reprints. Offers average advance of $600 to $1,000. "Standard minimum book contracts are offered on the basis of the stature of the writer and material." Published 32 books last year. Will send a catalog to a writer on request. Query first required. Reports in 2 to 4 weeks. Enclose postage.
Art, General Fiction and Nonfiction, and Hobbies: "We publish general fiction and nonfiction, pictorial histories, books on decorative arts, hobbies, and antiques." Recent titles include *Collector's Guide to English Furniture; The Complete Clock Book; Collector's Guide to Mechanical Banks.*

WILLIAM B. EERDMANS PUBLISHING CO., 255 Jefferson, S.E., Grand Rapids MI 49502. Editor: Marlin J. Van Elderen. Pays 10% of retail, sometimes graduated to 15% after the first 5,000 copies; 5% on paperback; sometimes graduated to 7½%. No advance. Books published last year: 65. Send sample chapters and outlines. Reports in 3 months. Enclose return postage with ms.
History and Religion: Publishes Michigan and Great Lakes regional histories and Church history of 60,000 words and up; biographies of Christian figures in past and current church history of 60,000 words and up; works on Christianity and science of 60,000 words and up; Christian philosophy of 60,000 words and up; Christian perspectives on the arts and history of Christian art, of 60,000 words and up; and other works such as Bible studies, commentaries, history, philosophy, and psychology of a generally Christian nature.

ELK GROVE PRESS, INC., P.O. Box 1637, Whittier CA 90603. (Subsidiary of Children's Press, 1224 W. Van Buren St., Chicago, IL 60607.) Editor: Mrs. Ruth Shaw Radlauer. Publishes juveniles; hardcover originals. Overstocked at present. "Please query first to see if your project fits our long-range plans."

ENGLEWOOD CLIFFS COLLEGE PRESS, Hudson Terrace, Englewood Cliffs NJ 07632. Executive Director: Vincent Dolan. Publishes hardcover and paperback originals and reprints. Offers standard book contract, advance is negotiated. Established in 1972, published 2 titles last year. Will send a catalog to a writer on request. Submit complete ms for fiction and nonfiction. Reports in 2 to 3 weeks. Enclose S.A.S.E. for return of ms.
Nonfiction and Fiction: "We'll publish Americana, biography, business, economics, history, nature, philosophy, politics, religion, scientific, self-help and how-to, sociology, and travel books; textbooks, and mainstream fiction. Inspirational and philosophical books should have a Catholic point of view. Positive outlook a must. No mss that are nihilistic, salacious, or anti-American." Recent title is *Chasing Rainbows* (Sister Madeleine, C.S.J.)

PAUL S. ERIKSSON, INC., 119 W. 57th St., New York NY 10019. Editor: Paul Eriksson. Publishes hardcover and paperback originals. Pays standard royalty. Published 7 titles last year. Query first with outline and sample chapters. Reports within 1 month. Enclose return postage.
Fiction and Nonfiction: Trade nonfiction and fiction. Also nature and bird lore. Current leading titles include *At a Bend in a Mexican River* (Sutton); *Before the Age of Miracles* (Johnston); *Find a Falling Star* (Niningon).

ETC PUBLICATIONS, 18512 Pierce Terrace, Homewood IL 60430. Editor-in-Chief: Richard W. Hostrop. Publishes originals and reprints in both hardcover and paperback. Standard minimum book contract. "Rarely are advances given, but exceptions of up to $1,200 are occasionally made, depending on author's reputation and nature of book." Published 12 books last year. Will send a catalog to a writer on request. Submit outline and sample chapters for nonfiction. Will consider photocopied submissions of good quality. Reports in 1 month. Enclose S.A.S.E.

Education: "We publish material on all subjects at all levels in the fields of education, educational technology, and educational communications. Mss must be geared to reach a wide number of professional educators, on timely topics. Would like to see both fiction and nonfiction works on education." Length: 50,000 to 150,000 words. Recent titles include *The ABC's of the Open Classroom* (Gingell); *The Year-Round School at Work* (Hermansen and Gove).

M. EVANS AND COMPANY, INC., 216 E. 49 St., New York NY 10017. Editor-in-Chief: Herbert M. Katz. Publishes hardcover originals. Royalty schedule to be negotiated. Publishes 20 books a year. Query first. Will consider photocopied submissions. No mss should be sent uncolicited. A letter of inquiry is essential. Reports on rejected material in 6 to 8 weeks. Reporting time on accepted material varies. Enclose return postage.
General Fiction and Nonfiction: "We publish a general trade list of adult fiction and nonfiction, cookbooks and semireference works. The emphasis is on selectivity since we publish only 20 books a year. Our fiction list represents an attempt to combine quality with commercial potential. Our most successful nonfiction titles have been related to the behaviorial sciences. No limitation on subject. A writer should clearly indicate what his book is all about: frequently the task the writer performs least well. His credentials, although important, mean less than his ability to convince this company that he understands his subject and that he has the ability to communicate a message worth hearing." Recent titles include: *The Whore Mother* (Herron) and *Bloodletters and Badmen* (Hash). Length: open.
Juveniles: "We are always in the market for a new juvenile series, particularly in the sciences at the younger age levels." Length: open.

FAIRCHILD PUBLICATIONS, INC., Book Division, 7 East 12th St., New York NY 10003. Manager: Ed Gold. Pays 10% of net sales distributed twice annually. No advance. Books published last year: 8. Query first, giving subject matter and brief outline. Enclose return postage.
Business and Textbooks: Publishes business books and textbooks relating to fashion, electronics, marketing, retailing and management. Length: open.

FAIRLEIGH DICKINSON UNIVERSITY PRESS, Rutherford NJ 07070. Editor: Charles Angoff. Royalty by arrangement. Usually offers no advance. Books published last year: 25. Reports within 6 months. Enclose return postage with ms.
Nonfiction: "Only works of the highest scholarship; real contributions to their fields." Length: open.

FAMILY LAW PUBLICATIONS, P.O. Box 2192, Madison WI 53701. Editor: N.C. Kohut. Publishes hardcover and paperback originals. Offers standard 10-12½-15% royalty contract. May do some subsidy publishing "later." Published no books last year. Will send a catalog to a writer on request. Query first with outline and sample chapters for nonfiction. Enclose return postage.
Law: "Socio-legal books on marriage and divorce. Interested in books on divorce reform." Length: 2,500 to 7,500 words. A recent title is *Therapeutic Family Law (Kohut)*.
Sociology: "Serious books on upgrading family life, including research studies."

FAR EASTERN RESEARCH AND PUBLICATIONS CENTER, 7404 Rose Court, Camp Springs MD 20022. Publishes hardcover and paperback originals and reprints. "Royalty is based on the standard rate or outright purchase. Pays up to $2,000 advance against standard royalties." Submit a synopsis or table of contents with sample chapter, along with biographical sketches, to editor-in-chief. Reports in 2 months. Enclose return postage with ms—"enough postage to cover a registered mail return."
Nonfiction: Subject emphasis: reference materials on the Far East, especially on the Chinese, Japanese, and Korean people. All lengths.

FARNSWORTH PUBLISHING CO., INC., 78 Randall Ave., Rockville Centre NY 11570. President: Lee Rosler. Publishes hardcover originals. "Standard royalty applies, but 5% is payable on mail order sales." Published 11 titles last year. Will send a catalog to a writer on request. Send query. Reports in 1 to 5 weeks. Enclose S.A.S.E.

General Nonfiction and Business and Professional: "Our books generally fall into 2 categories: 1. Books which appeal to executives, lawyers, accountants, and life underwriters. Subject matter may vary from selling techniques, estate planning, taxation, money management, etc. 2. Books which appeal to the general populace which are marketable by direct mail and mail order, in addition to book store sales." Current leading titles include *America Is for Sale; Anatomy of a Successful Salesman.*

FARRAR, STRAUS AND GIROUX, INC. (including Hill and Wang), 19 Union Square W., New York NY 10003. Editor-in-Chief: Henry Robbins. Variable advance and royalty arrangements. Books published last year: 150. Prefers queries. Enclose return postage.

General Fiction, Nonfiction, and Juveniles: Publishes general fiction, nonfiction, juveniles. New emphasis on nonfiction, primarily biography. Publishes Ariel Books (Claire Costello, Editor), Noonday Books (Andree Conrad, Editor), Octagon Books (Henry Schlanger, Editor).

FAWCETT PUBLICATIONS, INC./GOLD MEDAL BOOKS, 1515 Broadway, New York NY 10036. Editor-in-Chief: Joseph Elder. Gold Medal Books publishes paperback originals. Pays 4% royalty on every copy printed up to 200,000; 6% for every copy printed above 200,000. Usual advance is $2,500. Query is essential. Will consider photocopied submissions. Reports in 3 to 8 weeks. Enclose return postage.

General Fiction: "Strongly plotted, contemporary mainstream novels. Literate, freshly conceived Gothics; science fiction; westerns; medical novels; novels of the occult and supernatural; novels of high adventure in the Alistair MacLean tradition. Apart from literary quality, we look for books with potential in the mass paperback market; books that do not appeal to highly specialized or regional interests." Length: 50,000 words and up.

General Nonfiction: "Topical nonfiction with mass market appeal." Humor, self-help and inspirational; biography, cookbooks; medicine and psychiatry; reference, how-to, sports and hobbies.

FEDERAL LEGAL PUBLICATIONS INC., (including Aberdeen Press), 95 Morton Street, New York NY 10014. Editor: Martin Greenberg. Publishes hardcover and paperback originals, reprints, and translations. "Royalty schedule arranged with author." No advance. Published 5 titles last year. Will send a catalog to a writer on request. Send query with outline and sample chapter. "Direct all material to Martin Greenberg. If material is unsolicited, enclose S.A.S.E."

General Nonfiction and Textbooks: Aberdeen Press publishes "texts and professional books in the areas of drug abuse, urban problems, and psychiatry/psychoanalysis. Also, trade nonfiction lending itself to mail exploitation." Length: open.

Law: Publishes "law texts, treatises, source material, material about the law for laymen and law-allied professionals, scholarly journals on various aspects of law, pamphlets on law for mail order sales, information services, material of practical use to practicing attorneys such as 'black letter' law, treatises, hand books, loose leaf services, etc." Also history and biography, "suitable for the Law Market." Length: open. Current leading title is *The Electrical Conspiracies* (Banc); *Antitrust and the U.S. Supreme Court* (Duggan); *God Bless Our Second Mortgage* (Cabbell).

FREDERICK FELL, INC., 386 Park Ave. S., New York NY 10016. Royalty basis. Books published last year: 27. Offers "standard minimum book contract with variations in isolated cases. Advance depends on author's reputation and nature of book." Reports in 4 to 6 weeks. Enclose return postage with ms.

General Nonfiction: "Interested in high-quality books for the general public. We prefer that medical and/or technical subjects be written by authorities in those fields. We are constantly extending our Fell's Guide Series. We now have books on stamps, coins, judo, diving, antiques, etc. Query Roger Blair, Editor of Fell's Guide Series, to avoid duplication."

Fiction: "Although we publish very little adult fiction, we are on the lookout for unusual, controversial, high-quality mss. Queries or outlines and sample chapters should be sent to Margaret Brilant, Editor."

Business: "In Fell's Business Book Shelf, we publish books on all aspects of busi-

ness: Success in leadership, management, financial growth, investments, and experiences in the business world. Material in those categories should be sent to Frederick Fell, Editor-in-Chief."
Health: "Books for Fell's Better Health Series should deal with both physical and mental health and well-being. Query Roger Blair, Health Editor."

FIDES PUBLISHERS, INC., Box F, Notre Dame IN 46556. Editor: James F. Burns. Originals and reprints. Pays 10%, 11%, 12% royalties; reprint in Dome or Spire, 5%, 6%, 7%. No advance. Books published last year: 20. Current catalog available on request. Send outline and sample chapter. Reports in 6 weeks. Enclose return postage.
Religion: Publishes religious books (Christian and ecumenical) and general nonfiction with theological, spiritual, pastoral implications. The new look in religion and religious education, and the attitude of freedom and personal reponsibility. Length: religious, 20,000 words and up; general nonfiction, 20,000 words and up. Representative titles: *The Hidden Hinge; Self-Development in Early Childhood; Pray to Live.*

FIELDING PUBLICATIONS, INC., 105 Madison Ave., New York NY 10016. Editor: Eunice Riedel. Books published last year: 8. Send outline and sample chapter. Reports in 3 weeks. Enclose return postage.
Travel: Interested in general nonfiction books in the field of travel. Minimum length: 60,000 words.

FILTER PRESS, Box 5, Palmer Lake CO 80133. Editor: G.L. Campbell. Publishes paperback originals or reprints. Pays 10% net sales. No advance. Books published last year: 8. Will send a catalog to a writer on request. Query with outline. Will consider photocopied submissions "if legible." Reports on query in 1 week; on solicited mss in about 3 weeks. Enclose return postage.
Americana: Western Americana. Books on Western motif. Also publishes Western history books about Indians, early explorations, ghost towns, national parks. Length: 5,000 to 20,000 words (48 to 68 illustrated pages). "We have built our Wild and Woolly West series around reprints of 19th century travel materials, using the antique wood engravings as well as other illustrations to preserve the Victorian atmosphere which is so much a part of the Old West. Indians, miners, bad guys, explorers, and other residents of the Old West are suitable material. While a casual, humorous, or light style is acceptable, the subject should be treated with whatever respect it merits. Writing should be competent. Research should be accurate. We prefer to avoid footnotes except where the ideas cannot be placed in the narrative. A bibliography may be desirable in many cases, but it is not essential. We will do more on American Indians. Too many people are finding notes or diaries written by Uncle Charlie; these are coming to us with little or no added work on them, and nothing to relate them to the past or present. Too many are working on Jesse James-buried treasure sorts of things, with nothing really new. Because we are small, we are not the publisher for a book that should be aimed at the mass market." Length: 5,000 to 20,000 words (48 to 68 pages). Recent titles include: *Buffalo Bill's Wild west; Game Cookery Recipes; Indian Weapons.*
Nonfiction: "We departed from the Wild and Woolly West series to some extent in publishing *In Case I'm Found Unconscious,* a non-technical medical book for the diabetic and his family. We will do other non-Western books whenever they appeal to us." Interested in cookbooks, history, medicine, western pioneer, poetry, scientific, self-help and how-to, sport, hobbies, recreation, pets, technical, textbooks, and travel.

FINNEY COMPANY, 3350 Gorham Avenue, Minneapolis MN 55426. President: Horace J. Finney. Publishes originals. "Contract terms negotiable. No advance." Query first, "include writing experience."
Textbooks: Informative textbook-workbooks for students of special classes (slow learners). Subject matter should relate to jobs or the working world. Current leading titles include *Your Money—Going or Growing?* Editors: Mrs. Jo Ann Osmer, Mrs. Charlotte Nolan, and Mrs. Marjorie Loper.

FITZHENRY & WHITESIDE, LIMITED, 150 Lesmill Rd., Don Mills, Ontario, Canada. Editor-in-Chief: Robert Read. Publishes hardcover and paperback originals and reprints. Royalty contract "varied." No advance. Published 20 titles last year. Submit outline and sample chapters. Will consider photocopied submissions. Reports on material accepted for publication in 1 month. Returns rejected material within 2 months. Enclose return postage.
General Nonfiction: "Especially interested in topics of interest to Canadians." Biography; business; cookbooks, cooking and foods; history; medicine and psychiatry; nature; politics. Canadian plays and poetry are also of interest. Recent titles include *Before the Age of Miracles* (biography of a country doctor); *Canadian Voter's Guidebook.* Length: open..
Textbooks: Elementary and secondary school textbooks in social studies and reading.

FLEET PRESS CORPORATION, 156 Fifth Ave., New York NY 10010. Editor: Susan Nueckel. Publishes hardcover and paperback originals and reprints. Royalty schedule "varies." Advance "varies." Published 32 titles last year. Will send a catalog to a writer on request. Send query and outline. Reports in 6 weeks. Enclose return postage with ms. Will not evaluate unsolicited mss.
General Nonfiction: "History, biography, arts, religion, general nonfiction, sports." Length: 45,000 words.
Juveniles: Nonfiction only. Stress on minority subjects; for ages 8 to 12. Length: 25,000 words.

*FLORHAM PARK PRESS, INC., P. O. Box 303, Florham Park NJ 07932. Editor: Vincent Mott. Publishes hardcover and paperback originals. Offers standard 10-12½-15% royalty contract "with this reservation. Royalties are not due or payable until 500 of our paperback originals and 1,000 copies of clothbound books have been sold and paid for. No advance. About 50% of our books are subsidy published." Published 3 titles last year. Will send a catalog to a writer on request. Query first. Will consider photocopied submissions. Reports in 1 month. Enclose return postage.
Textbooks and Scholarly: "College textbooks in the fields of sociology, economics, and marketing. Scholarly books and booklets in the fields of sociology, economics, and marketing. Writers must be experts in the fields in which they write." New series—"Marketing Monographs short (50 to 150 pages) scholarly works, emphasizing marketing research projects." Mss on "consumer sociology and consumer psychology. No mss on mathematical economic analysis." Recent titles are *Philosophy in Economic Thought* (Chirovsky & Mott); *The American Consumer: A Sociological Analysis* (Mott).

FOLLETT PUBLISHING CO., 1010 W. Washington Blvd., Chicago IL 60607. Editorial Director, Children's Book Department: Ms. Marci Ridlon Carafoli. Royalties: "percentage of net receipts." Send outline with sample chapters or send complete ms. Enclose return postage.
Juveniles: "We seriously consider all mss of top professional quality. No heavily moralistic stories. No juvenile fluff or teen romances. No religious material. No biographies that have been done over and over." Wants juvenile nonfiction books for ages 8 to 10, 10 to 12, 12, 14, 16. "Length varies according to subject matter and age group."

FORTRESS PRESS, 2900 Queen Lane, Philadelphia PA 19129. Senior Editor: Norman A. Hjelm. Publishes hardcover and paperback originals. Offers 7% to 8½% paperback royalties; offers 10% hardcover royalty. Advances are negotiable, depending on author's reputation and nature of book. Published about 50 titles last year. Will send a catalog to a writer on request. Query first. "Use Chicago *Manual of Style.*" Reports in 2 months. Enclose return postage.
Religion and Philosophy: "Fortress Press is a major publisher of general religious and theological books. Our academic listing—books in the field of Biblical studies, systematic theology, ethics, church history, etc.—is extensive and well known. The major portion of published titles, however, is for a more general reading audience—laity and clergy of all denominations. Book length varies, from 27,500 to 125,000 words. Books should be readable in style (for 'general religious' books, the reading

level should be from ninth to twelfth grades, according to the Fogg Standard); academic books must be in proper scholarly form (apparatus, etc.) and must reflect awareness of current theological trends and methods. We have high standards of editing, a willingness to use visual materials other than print, and a serious religious commitment without denominational or confessional limitations. New series in the area of pastoral counseling. Mss must be devoted to specific areas—e.g., counseling the drug addict, alcoholic, divorced person, etc. They should be concrete and designed to help clergy in the development of counseling ministries. In books for the lay person, we would like to see coverage of the crisis of authority in American society; new forms of viable parish life for American churches, the question of law and freedom, books for creative worship, books of value for senior citizens. No standard 'daily devotions' or unsolicited sermons." Recent titles include *The Fragile Presence* (Killinger); *The Johannine Epistles* (Bultmann, Hermeneia series).

FOUNTAINHEAD PUBLISHERS, INC., 475 Fifth Ave., New York NY 10017. Director: Rose P. Portugal. Offers standard 10-12½-15% royalty contract; advance "depends on author's reputation and subject." Published 5 titles last year. "Author must request permission to submit ms with full personal biography as to education and profession; must enclose list of chapters, short outline indicating scope of book and have ms in clean, double-spaced typed pages, fully paginated." Send query to Frances Diane Robotti, Editor-in-Chief. Royalty payments semiannually—statements submitted during February and August of each year as of December 31 and June 30, and payable April 30 and October 31. Usually reports in 1 month. Enclose return postage.
General Nonfiction: Publishes history, biography, law, religion, political science, social science, general education, etc.
Fiction: "Some factual, adult, clean fiction."

FRANCISCAN HERALD PRESS, 1434 West 51st St., Chicago IL 60609. Editor: Rev. Mark Hegener, O.F.M. "Royalty schedule—10% and up with volume. Advance: depending on nature and length of ms." Published 24 titles last year. Send query and outline. Use University of Chicago *Manual of Style.* Reports in 30 days. Enclose return postage.
Religion: "A Catholic publishing house with a wide range of interests in theology, sociology, culture, art and literature, reflecting, interpreting, directing the socio-religious and cultural aspects of our times." Synthesis Series of booklets (10,000 word maximum) in the field of religion and psychology. Church history, biography and specialized publications on history, purpose and personages of the Franciscan Order. Lengths run from 5,000 to 60,000 words. Current leading titles include *Two Say Why* (von Balthasar and Ratzinger); *The Problems of Religious Faith* (Mackey). Religion and Philosophy Editor: Albert J. Nimeth. Arts Editor: Marion A. Habrig.

FRANCONIA PUBLISHING CO., 475 Fifth Ave., New York NY 10017. Editor: J. Russell Tippett. Publishes hardcover originals. Offers standard 10-12½-15% royalty contract. "$1,000 advance upon delivery of finished mss." Published 2 titles last year. "Suggest descriptive letter first with outline of ms, etc. Do not submit ms unless requested." Reports in 30 days. Enclose return postage.
Nonfiction, Americana, and Juveniles: "Full-length (about 250-plus pages) books on nonfiction subjects of novel or unusual interest. Currently interested in subjects of broad interest in human relationships, such as strange traditions or practices, unusual historical or nostalgic facts; humorous customs, beliefs, or events; disclosures of fallacious history; folk heroes, adventures, etc. Facts must be authenticated. Interested in debunking the Western hero. History, use, and problems of the metric system. Nostalgia related to today's living (with pictures). No astrological books that emphasize character interpretation but avoid the astronomy and facts of astrology."

FRANKLIN PUBLISHING CO. INC., P.O. Box 765, Palisade NJ 07024. Editor: Irene E. Berck. Publishes hardcover originals. Pays 10% on list. No advance. Prefers queries with table of contents and a sample chapter. Reports within a month. Enclose return postage.
Science: Publishes science books. Length: 45,000 words minimum.

THE FREE PRESS, a Division of the Macmillan Publishing Company, 866 Third Ave., New York NY 10022. President: Edward W. Barry. Royalty schedule varies, Books published last year: 66. Send sample chapter, outline, and query letter before submitting mss. Reports in 3 weeks. Enclose return postage.
Nonfiction and Textbooks: Publishes college texts and adult educational nonfiction in the social sciences and humanities.

*FREEMAN PUBLISHING COMPANY, LTD., Saskatoon, Canada. Editor: Dr. Walter B. Hoover. Publishes hardcover and paperback originals. Offers "standard royalty contracts 10-12½%" except on poetry. Published 6 titles last year. "Query editor before mailing mss." Reports in 30 days. Enclose Canadian postage or International Reply Coupons for return postage.
Religion, Philosophy, History, and Biography: "Looking for well-documented history books, inspirational biographies, philosophy, religious and theological works in the classical orthodox Christian tradition." Length: 40,000 to 80,000 words.
Poetry: "We can publish poetry only upon the basis of some degree of subsidation, and it has to be top-flight poetry at that."

FRIENDSHIP PRESS, 475 Riverside Dr., New York NY 10027. Editor-in-Chief: William C. Walzer. Payment by negotiated flat fee plus royalty. Seldom takes unsolicited mss; query first with brief outline. Reports in 30 days. Enclose return postage with query.
Religion: Wants mss only in the field of religion. Especially wants mss in the field of Christian mission and social issues with Christian emphasis. Also interested in biographies and drama related to Christian mission. Adult and Youth Editor (including biographies): Ward Kaiser. Juveniles and Drama Editor: Dorothy Weeks.

GARRARD PUBLISHING CO., 1607 N. Market St., Champaign IL 61820. Editorial Offices: 2 Overhill Rd., Scarsdale NY 10583. "We solicit established authors to write a book to meet our editorial specifications." Query first.
Textbooks: "We publish books planned for the elementary classroom and school library to coordinate with the reading, social studies, and science curriculum."

GINN AND COMPANY, 191 Spring St., Lexington MA 02173. Editor-in-Chief: James R. Squire. Royalty schedule: from 10% of net on a secondary book to 6% on elementary materials. Sample chapters, complete or partially complete mss will be considered. Reports in 2 to 6 weeks. Enclose return postage.
Textbooks: Publishers of textbooks for elementary and secondary schools.

GOLDEN GATE JUNIOR BOOKS, 8344 Melrose Ave., Los Angeles CA 90069. Address sample chapters or complete ms to the attention of Miss Marjorie Thayer. Enclose return postage.
Juveniles: Publishers of juvenile books.

GOLDEN PRESS (Whitman/Western Publishing Co.), 850 Third Ave., New York NY 10022. Editor: Jack B. Long. Submit all material to: Bruce Butterfield, Assistant to Editorial Director. Publishes hardcover and paperback originals and reprints. "Our royalty rates vary with each title. Advance varies." Write for copy of guidelines to authors. Submit complete ms. Will consider photocopied submissions. Reports in 3 months. Enclose S.A.S.E.
Juveniles and General: "The juvenile books that originate in our New York office cost over $1 and are written for ages of 2 to 12. We do not publish fiction for teens and we do not publish fiction novels. We publish large picture books and nonfiction books for upper elementary junior high school readers. We strongly recommend that writers study our publications thoroughly before submitting material." Recent titles include: *The City Book* (Corcos), breathtaking views of the city scape from high above rooftops, mysterious glimpses of subways, cross-sections of office buildings, stores, apartments, factories, etc, all combined with informative text to reveal the excitement, joys, and problems of city life, for readers ages 4 to 10; *Miss Jaster's Garden* (Bodecker), a story about the experiences of a shy little hedgehog and a garden loving old lady who become tender friends and experience quite a calamity when flowers start to grow on the hedgehog's back, for readers ages 4 to 8.

THE GOLDEN QUILL PRESS, Francestown NH 03043. Pays 10% royalty in most cases on a guarantee by author of minimum sales. Send complete ms. Reports in 30 to 60 days. Enclose return postage with ms.
Poetry: Publishes poetry books only.

GOLDEN WEST BOOKS, P.O. Box 8136, San Marino CA 91108. Publisher: Donald Duke. Royalty schedule: 5%-10%, depending on work. No advance. Send outline or sample chapter. Reports in 2 weeks. Enclose return postage.
Nonfiction: "We are concerned only with transportation history: railroads, steamships, transportation Americana." Length: open.

GORDON & BREACH, SCIENCE PUBLISHERS, INC., One Park Ave. S., New York NY 10016. Editor-in-Chief: Edmund H. Immergut. Publishes hardcover and paperback originals. Royalty contract to be negotiated. Published 156 titles last year. Query first.
Scientific and Technical: Publishes scientific and technical books; business, behavioral science, social sciences.
Textbooks: Publishes college textbooks and graduate texts.

***GORDON PRESS,** P.O. Box 459, Bowling Green Station, New York NY 10004. Editor: R. Gordon. Publishes hardcover originals and reprints. Offers standard 10% royalty contract; "author should submit camera-ready copy." 40% of books are subsidy published. Published 12 titles last year. Submit outline and sample chapters or complete ms. Will consider photocopied submissions. Reports in 4 to 6 weeks. Enclose return postage.
Fiction: "Exceptional fiction."
Nonfiction: "Scholarly books, including literary criticism, history, sociology, social history, biography, philosophy, music, cinema, cooking, general literature, problems of minority groups, theater, drama, religion, travel, occult, education, sex, humor, photography, sexual problems, feminism, women's rights, anarchism and libertarian literature. Our approach is generally more adult, scholarly-oriented." Series for which material is needed include "women's liberation series, oriental literature series, occult series, cinema-movie-history series, libertarian literature series, Americana series."

GRAY'S PUBLISHING LTD., Box 2160, Sidney, BC, Canada. Editor: Gray Campbell. Publishes hardcover originals. Offers standard royalty contract. No advance. Published 6 titles last year. Will send a catalog to a writer on request. Query first with outline. Reports in 6 to 10 weeks. Enclose return postage.
Nonfiction: Wants "nonfiction, Canadiana" geared to high-school age audience, adults. Length: 60,000 to 120,000 words.

GREAT OUTDOORS PUBLISHING CO., 4747 28 St. N., St. Petersburg FL 33714. Editor: Charles F. Allyn. Publishes paperback originals. Offers 5% royalty contract. "Seldom advances." Published 10 titles last year. Will send a catalog to a writer "if in stock." Send outline. Reports in 2 weeks. Enclose return postage.
General Nonfiction and Natural History: "Books on fish, aquariums, seashells, reptiles, crafts, regional cookbooks, and how-to-do-it books on leisure time activities." Material should have Florida background.

***WARREN H. GREEN, INC.,** 10 S. Brentwood Blvd., St. Louis MO 63105. Editor: Warren H. Green. Publishes hardcover originals. Offers "12½% to 20% sliding scale of royalties based on quantity distributed. All books are short run, highly specialized, with no advance." About 1% of books are subsidy published. Published 43 titles last year. "45% of total marketing is overseas." Will send a catalog to a writer on request. Submit outline and sample chapters. "Publisher requires 300- to 500-word statement of scope, plan, and purpose of book, together with curriculum vitae of author." Will consider photocopied submissions. Reports in 60 to 90 days. Enclose return postage.
Medical and Scientific: "Specialty monographs for practicing physicians and medical researchers. Books of 160 pages upward. Illustrated as required by subject. Medical books are non-textbook type, usually specialties within specialties, and no gen-

eral books for a given specialty. For example, separate books on each facet of radiology, and not one complete book on radiology. Authors must be authorities in their chosen fields and accepted as such by their peers. Books should be designed for all doctors in English-speaking world engaged in full- or part-time activity discussed in book. We would like to increase publications in the fields of radiology, anesthesiology, pathology, psychiatry, surgery, and orthopedic surgery, obstetrics and gynecology, psychology, and speech and hearing. Recent titles include *Surgery of the Liver and Intrahepatic Bile Ducts* (Fagarasance); *Non-Operative Aspects of Pediatric Surgery* (Owings).

Education: "Reference books for elementary and secondary school teachers. Authors must be authorities in their fields. No textbooks."

STEPHEN GREENE PRESS, P.O. Box 1000, Brattleboro VT 05356. Standard royalty basis. Books published last year: 20. Will send a catalog on request. Address all queries to Orion M. Barber, Managing Editor; outlines with sample chapters in all cases. Reports in 45 days. Enclose return postage.

General Nonfiction: Publishes general adult nonfiction: Americana, regional (New England) literature, biography, sports (especially horse and individual sports like cross-country skiing, snowshoeing), humor, railroads, cooking, aviation, nature and environment, how-to, self-reliance. Must meet high literary standards. Recent titles include *The Morgan Horse Handbook; A Peep Into the Past; The Most of John Held, Jr.*

GREENLEAF CLASSICS, INC., 3511 Camino Del Rio South, San Diego CA 92128. Originals only. Outright purchase on acceptance. Royalty contracts open to discussion. Publishes over 400 titles each year. Interested only in the work of established writers. Sample and outline preferred. Reports in 2 weeks. Enclose return postage.

Erotica: Publishes erotic fiction. Length: minimum 47,000 words, maximum 62,000 words.

GREENWICH PRESS, 335 Bleecker St., New York NY 10014. Editor: Anton Hardt. Publishes hardcover originals and reprints. Query first. Enclose return postage.

Nonfiction: "Books only on the subject of antiques and possibly allied fields."

GREENWOOD PRESS, INC., 51 Riverside Ave., Westport CT 06880. Managing Editor: Jeannette Lindsay. Publishes hardcover and paperback originals; hardcover reprints. Contracts are "usually standard; sometimes vary. Each contract written according to its own merit. Advance varies." Published 25 original books last year; 500 reprints. Books marketed by direct mail and advertising in scholarly journals. Will send catalog to writer on request. Query first. Will consider photocopied submissions. Reports in 2 to 8 weeks. Enclose return postage.

General Nonfiction: Monographs, reference and professional books basically of an academic nature; biography. Business, economics, history, library, politics, sociology. Recent titles include: *The Age of Great Corporations; A Microcosmic History of American Business* (1914-1970) (Sobel).

GREGG DIVISION, McGraw-Hill Book Co., 1221 Ave. of the Americas, New York NY 10020. Vice-President and General Manager: Donald L. Fruehling. Publishes hardcover originals. "Contracts negotiable; no advances." Query first. "We accept very few unsolicited mss." Reports in 1 to 2 months. Enclose return postage with query.

Textbooks: "Textbooks and related instructional materials for the career education market." Publishes books on typewriting, office education, shorthand, accounting and data processing, distributing and marketing, trade and industrial education, health and consumer education.

GRIFFIN HOUSE PUBLISHERS, 455 King Street West, Toronto, Ontario, Canada. Publishes hardcover and paperback originals. Offers standard royalty contract. No advance. Published 9 titles last year. Will send a catalog to a writer on request. Send complete ms. Enclose return postage with ms.

General Fiction, General Nonfiction, Religion and Philosophy, History and Biogra-

phy, and Textbooks: Interested in school texts and general interest, religious, and Canadiana books. Current leading titles include *My Brother, My Sister* (Mosteller); *Only Farmers Need Apply* (Troper).
Juveniles: "Very interested in juvenile books of a Canadian interest; basically something with stories for children between the ages of 9 and 15."

GROSSET AND DUNLAP, INC., (including Tempo Teenage Paperbacks and Universal Library), 51 Madison Ave., New York NY 10010. Editor-in-Chief: Robert Markel. Publishes hardcover and paperback originals and reprints, as well as a "very few" translations, and anthologies "on occasion." Royalty and advance terms generally vary. Published "close to 400" titles last year. Will send a catalog to a writer on request. Send query letter, outline, or sample chapter only; do not send complete ms. Reports in 3 to 5 weeks. Enclose return postage with query.
General Fiction: "Very seldom—usually only via literary agent."
General Nonfiction and Reference: "No limits—anything and everything that would interest the 'average' American reader: sports, health, ecology, etc." Interested in history, science, religion, biography, the arts, and literature. Favors writers with strong experience and good credits.
Juveniles and Teen: Editor-in-Chief, Children's Picture Books: Doris Duenewald.

GROVE PRESS, INC., 53 E. 11th St., New York NY 10003. Senior Editor: Fred Jordan. Publishes hardcover and paperback originals. Royalty contract to be negotiated. Published 93 titles last year. Query first. Enclose return postage.
General: Publishes general adult fiction and nonfiction; books on art.

GULF PUBLISHING COMPANY, P.O. Box 2608, 3301 Allen Parkway, Houston TX 77001. Editor: Clayton A. Umbach, Jr. Publishes hardcover originals. Royalty schedule: 8%-15%. "Generally we do not have any advance." Published 20 titles last year. Will send a catalog to a writer on request. Write for copy of *Author's Handbook* ($2) for details on proper ms submission. Send query with outline. Reports in 6 to 8 weeks. Enclose return postage.
General Nonfiction, Technical and Scientific, Business, and Textbooks: "Scientific, technical, college texts, management, training, self-help. We attempt to reach untapped technical, training, and managerial markets."

H.P. BOOKS, P.O. Box 50640, Tucson AZ 85703. Editorial Coordinator: Bill Fisher. Publishes paperback originals and reprints. Royalty schedule "varies with title and distribution requirements. We rarely offer an advance unless we have a 'handle' on it. We do not believe in 'front money' per se. We don't use the standard contract. This is worked out with author when written." Published 4 titles last year. Will send a catalog to a writer on request. Send query and outline. "No mss without prior correspondence to determine whether there is a fit."
Hobbies: "General how-to titles related to hobbies, especially automotive, art and craft, photography, gardening, landscaping, cooking, etc. Our books are heavily illustrated and copy-only books are not being solicited." Current leading titles include *How to Hotrod Small Block Chevrolets; Holley Carburetors; Central America: On and Off the Beaten Path.*

WALTER R. HAESSNER AND ASSOCIATES, INC., P.O. Box 89, Newfoundland NJ 07435. Editor: Walter R. Haessner. Publishes hardcover originals. Offers standard 10-12½-15% royalty contract. Advance varies. Published 12 titles last year. Will send a catalog to a writer on request. Query first with outline and sample chapters for nonfiction. Will consider photocopied submissions "sometimes. Follow Ayer Style Book. Pica type preferred; 60 character count per line, 25 lines deep." Reports on ms accepted for publication in 6 weeks. Returns rejected material in 4 weeks. Enclose return postage.
Nonfiction: Transportation (antiques, motorsports, boating, how-to-do-it). Travel, sports, art, reference. Recent titles include *Fast Rolling Ships; Africa on Wheels.*

HARCOURT BRACE JOVANOVICH, INC., 757 Third Ave., New York NY 10021. Editor-in-Chief: Julian P. Muller. Publishes hardcover and paperback originals and paperback reprints. Offers standard 10-12½-15% royalty contract. Published about 150 trade books for adults, 50 trade books for children, and 26 paperbacks last year. Query first with sample chapters for juvenile nonfiction. Enclose return postage.

General: "Fiction, nonfiction, poetry, plays for adults and children; textbooks for elementary and high schools and colleges and universities; medical and scientific books." Editor of Paperbacks: John Ferrone.

Juveniles: "We are going to try to do more nonfiction. Our lists will probably contain fewer picture books, translations, and imports." Fiction must be of exceptional quality.

HARIAN PUBLICATIONS, 1000 Prince St., Greenlawn NY 11740. Editor: Frederic Tyarks. Advances paid on royalties. Books published last year: 20. Will send copy of current catalog on request. Query first. Include S.A.S.E. with query. Reports in 1 week.

Nonfiction: Books on travel, retirement, investments, and health. Length: 50,000 words minimum for completed mss.

HARPER AND ROW, PUBLISHERS, INC., (including Torchbooks, Colophon, and Perennial Library), 10 E. 53rd St., New York NY 10022. Publishes hardcover and paperback originals and reprints. Royalty schedule subject to negotiation, but generally 10% to 5,000; 12½% to 10,000; 15% thereafter. Query letters, sample chapters and outlines preferred. For fiction, prefers completed ms. Address General Trade Dept. for fiction and nonfiction. Address Children's Book Dept. for juveniles. Reports in 4 to 6 weeks. Enclose return postage.

General Fiction and Nonfiction: Publishes books between 40,000 and 200,000 words in the following departments: college, elementary and high school, mail order, medical, nature and outdoor, religious, social and economic, and trade. Trade books can cover any subject of general interest, fiction or nonfiction, rather than specialized or scholarly works.

Juveniles: Ursula Nordstrom, Juvenile Editor.

Textbooks: Publishes elementary and high school textbooks. Address Ray Sluss, Publisher, El-Hi Division, 2500 Crawford Ave., Evanston IL 60201.

HARVARD UNIVERSITY PRESS, 79 Garden St., Cambridge MA 02138. Director: Arthur J. Rosenthal. Books published last year: 189. Prefers queries with outlines. Enclose return postage.

General Nonfiction: Publishes general nonfiction including history, science, religion, philosophy and the arts. Publishes books of scholarly research directed toward a scholarly audience.

HARVEST HOUSE, LTD., PUBLISHERS, 1364 Greene Ave. (Westmount), Montreal 215, PQ, Canada. Editor: Maynard Gertler. Publishes hardcover and paperback originals, reprints, and translations. Royalty schedule varies between 6% and 12%. Prefer completed ms. Reports in 6 weeks. Enclose return postage with ms.

Nonfiction: History, biography, philosophy, science, education, public affairs, and general nonfiction. "We prefer nonfiction to fiction and deal with mss concerning Canadian and general world interest." Minimum length is 35,000 words. Recent titles include *The History of City Planning: A Survey* (Hugo-Brunt); *The Last Refuge* (Nelson).

HARVEY HOUSE, INC., Irvington-on-Hudson, NY 10533. Editor: Mrs. Jeanne Gardner. Publishes hardcover originals. Offers 10% royalty, usually $500 advance; "5% split with artist on younger age bracket where pictures are abundant." Published 12 titles last year. Will send a catalog to a writer on request. Query first or submit complete ms. Reports in 3 to 12 weeks. Enclose return postage.

Juveniles: "Children's books primarily—fiction and nonfiction. Strong interest in subject matter that supplements science and social studies curriculums in elementary and junior high schools." Story of Science series geared to grades 5 to 8; Science Parade series, grades 2 to 6. Length for juvenile nonfiction books: 35,000 to 40,000 words maximum. Wants easy-to-read books for K-3 and 2-5. Recent titles include *Skeezer, Dog With a Mission; The Boy Drummer of Vincennes; Cochise, Chief of the Chiricahuas.*

HASTINGS HOUSE PUBLISHERS, INC., 10 E. 40th St., New York NY 10016. Editor: Walter Frese. Offers 10% minimum royalty contract. Published 85 titles last year. Query first, "describing ms." Reports in 4 weeks. Enclose return postage. **Nonfiction:** Publishes general nonfiction, biography, history, the graphic arts, architecture and decoration.

HAWTHORN BOOKS, INC., 260 Madison Ave., New York NY 10011. Editor-in-Chief: Charles N. Heckelmann. Editor, Children's Book Dept.: Carolyn Trager. Publishes hardcover and paperback originals, translations, and anthologies. Normal advance and royalty schedule, "but we do negotiate contracts for lower than normal royalties depending on the size of the market and the risk involved. Nonfiction on a wide variety of types: health, psychology, sports, cookbooks, biography and autobiography, business, history, politics, self-help, religion and inspiration. Length: 45,000 to 75,000 words. Query first before submitting." Will send a catalog to a writer on request. Strongly suggests consulting catalog before making any submission. Prefers submission through agents, but will consider query with outline and sample chapter.

HAYDEN BOOK COMPANY, INC., 50 Essex St., Rochelle Park NJ 07662. Editorial Director: Irving Lopatin. Advance and royalty arrangements vary; generally 10 to 15% of net. Published 24 titles last year. Will send a catalog to a writer on request. All book proposals should include complete outline, preface and two representative chapters. Reports in 4 weeks. Enclose return postage.
Technical: Publishes technician-level and engineering texts and references in many subject areas (emphasis on electronics); texts and references for hotel, restaurant and institution management and other personnel (emphasis on management, food preparation, handling). Recent titles: *Statistical Pattern Recognition* (Chen). *Ocean Wealth: Policy and Potential* (Doumani). Editor, Technical Program: W.W. Yates.
Textbooks: Texts, references, and visual aids for junior and senior high schools, technical institutes and community colleges in English, mathematics, social studies and other subject areas. Recent titles include *Introduction to Tragedy* (Gordon); *The Feminine Image in Literature* (Warren). Editor, Academic Programs: S.W. Cook.
Education: "Books on education and other subjects of interest to teachers, college faculty and students, and the general public." Recent title is *The Celluloid Curriculum: How to Use Movies in the Classroom* (Maynard).

D.C. HEATH & CO., 125 Spring St., Lexington MA 02173. Editor, College Division: John T. Harney. Publishes hardcover and paperback originals. Offers standard royalty rates for textbooks. Advance is negotiated. Published about 80 titles last year. Will send a catalog to a writer on request. Query first. Returns rejected material in 2 weeks. "Finished mss accepted are published within 1 year." Enclose return postage.
Textbooks: "Texts at the college level in sociology, psychology, history, political science, chemistry, math, physical science, economics, education, modern language, and English." Length varies. Editor, Economics: Beverly Singleton; Editor, Foreign Language: Valdemar Hempel; Editor, History: Barbara Hamelburg; Editor, Sociology: Michael Zamcyzk; Editor, Technical: Michael McCarroll.

HELIOS BOOK PUBLISHING CO., INC., 150 W. 28th St., New York NY 10001. Editor: Fred Weissman. Publishes originals. "The rate of royalties varies and depends largely on the market potential of the individual book. Generally, we start with a very low royalty percentage (5% to 10%) in an effort to first recover our production cost. After that, the percentage will increase, with the sales volume, up to 25%." Prefers complete ms. Reports in 4 weeks. Enclose return postage with ms.
General: "Publish books on every subject, primarily nonfiction. The preferred length is 75,000 to 100,000 words." Recent titles include *Before Olympus* (Suhr); *Friends, Not Outcasts* (Gill); *Voice From the Cement Desert* (Mendola). Length: 4,000 to 25,000 words.

HELLER & SON, 90 Daisy Farms Dr., New Rochelle NY 10804. Editor: Richard H. Heller. Publishes hardcover and paperback originals. Offers standard 10-12½-

15% royalty contract with advance for hardcovers, and 4% and 6% for paperbacks. Query first with outline and sample chapters. Will consider photocopied submissions. Reports in 5 to 6 weeks. Enclose return postage for response to queries and return of ms.

General: "Use mostly nonfiction, with some fiction; books on contemporary subjects, women's liberation, exposes, biography, show business, sex, cookbooks, education, how-to, suspense, romance, books that appeal to the 'now' generation, natural foods, inspirational, ecology, etc. Books receive my personal attention and experience as a writer, editor, and publisher for 20 years. We publish only a limited number of books and therefore can give more time, care and attention to each book we do. We co-published *The New Earth Catalog* with G. P. Putnam's Sons and Berkeley and (in all) will do from 15 to 20 books this year, including books on how to 'trip' without drugs; women's sex fantasies and private lives of Hollywood's greatest stars."

HELLRIC CHAPBOOK SERIES, 32 Waverly Street, Belmont MA 02178. Editor: Ottone M. Riccio. "Mostly works by 1 author, but at times anthologies, memorial volumes, etc." Buys first North American rights only on material used in anthologies. Pays in "copies plus royalties on copies sold on chapbooks by one author; copies on anthologies." Printing run is 500 copies. Publishes 3 to 6 titles a year. Query first for nonfiction except humor; send complete ms for humor, poetry, fiction, plays. Reports in 2 to 4 weeks. Enclose S.A.S.E.

General: "No restrictions on subjects, form, etc. Prefer avant-garde and experimental. Looking for collections of poems, short stories, plays, novellas, etc. We're interested in material that makes something happen in the reader's mind and emotional apparatus. We try to search out the promising but unestablished writers. We'll look at anything because we're more interested in how the writer writes than what he writes about—though he should write about something." Length: fiction, 20 to 80 pages (250 words a page); nonfiction, 20 to 40 pages; poetry, at least 20 pages. For Pyramid Pamphlet series, uses poetry of 12 to 20 pages.

HENDRICKS HOUSE, INC., 103 Park Ave., New York NY 10017. Editorial Office: Putney VT 05346. Editor: Walter Hendricks. Publishes hardcover originals and hardcover and paperback reprints. Published 5 titles last year. Will send a catalog to a writer on request. Submit complete ms. Will consider photocopied submissions. Reports in 1 month. Enclose return postage with ms.

Nonfiction: "Mainly educational." Publishes Americana, biography, history, philosophy, reference, and textbooks.

HERALD HOUSE, P.O. Box 1019, Independence MO 64051. Editor: Paul A. Wellington. Publishes original hardbacks. Standard royalty contract. Usual advance is $500, but this varies, depending on author's reputation and nature of book. Books published last year: 12. Query first. Reports in 2 months. Enclose return postage.

Religion: Publishes religious books for adults and children. Fiction, poetry, doctrinal texts, history, etc. All books must be relevant to the Reorganized Church of Jesus Christ of Latter Day Saints. Length: 30,000 to 60,000 words.

HERALD PRESS, 616 Walnut Ave., Scottdale PA 15683. (A division of Mennonite Publishing House.) Book Editor: Paul M. Schrock. Publishes hardcover and mass market paperback originals. Pays 10% of retail price on first 10,000 copies, 12% for next 10,000, and 15% thereafter for hardcover books. Mass market paperbacks bring 6% of retail price on first 75,000 copies, 7% for next 75,000, and 8% thereafter. Usually does not provide an advance, but depending on the author's reputation and the nature of the book, is willing to consider payment of an advance against royalties. "An average advance in such cases would probably be $500." Publishes 25 titles per year. Catalog on request. Query first with brief summary. Reports on queries in 3 weeks; allow 5 months for report on complete ms. Enclose return postage with queries and ms.

General Fiction and Nonfiction: "We are interested in fiction which deals with such themes as strengthening family life; coping with such issues as abortion, racial tension and mistreatment of minority groups; stories growing out of the Amish and Mennonite traditions; narratives that emphasize the role of the Christian as a peacemaker in a troubled world; and historical fiction on important persons and events in the Christian past. Length: "We would like the writer to develop his material with integrity in whatever length seems appropriate." Recent titles include *Happy As the Grass Was Green* (Good); *Drama of the Amish* (Yoder). **Juveniles:** For ages 9 and up. Length: 25,000 to 30,000 words.

HERDER AND HERDER, 1221 Ave. of the Americas, New York NY 10020. Editori-in-Chief: Justus G. Lawler. Publishes hardcover and paperback originals. Royalty contract to be negotiated. Published 105 titles last year. Query first. Enclose return postage.
General: Publishes general adult fiction and nonfiction; art books, gift books. Publishes crime and detective novels, mainstream novels; biography, autobiography, sociology, how-to, psychology.

HERMAN PUBLISHING SERVICE DIVISION, Cahners Publishing Co., 89 Franklin St., Boston MA 02110. Editor: M.J. Philips. Publishes hardcover and paperback originals and reprints. "Standard 10% royalty up to break-even point; higher beyond." Books published last year: 16. Advance varies, depending on author's reputation and nature of book. Will send copy of current catalog on request. Send query, outline and sample chapter to C.A. Herman. Reports in 3 months. Enclose return postage.
General Nonfiction, Business, and Technical: Business, technical and general nonfiction; reference, science, hi-fi, music, antiques, gardening, cooking, the arts, religion, history, biography, ships, audio, acoustics, electronics, radio, TV. "It might be worth noting that we also perform a unique service. We will market to the book trade (and elsewhere possibly), books which may have been privately published by the author or by a small publisher. Naturally, we must first see a sample copy and be satisfied that we can market it." Writing must be factual and authoritative. No length limits. Representative titles: *Building and Flying Scale Model Aircraft; Pocket Book of American Pewter.*

HOBBY HOUSE PRESS 4701 Queensbury Rd., Riverdale MD 20840. Royalty schedule: 10%. Will send catalog on request. Prefers query. Reports in 6 weeks. Enclose return postage.
Nonfiction: Books on antiques collecting, doll collecting, and doll making.

*HOGARTH PRESS-HAWAII, Box 6012, Honolulu HI 96818. Editor: J. Patrick O'Connell. Publishes hardcover and paperback originals and reprints. "We share the profits after costs are recovered 50-50. No advance." About 25% of books are subsidy published. Published 8 titles last year. Query first. Will consider photocopied submissions. Reports in 3 weeks. Enclose return postage.
Fiction, Biography, and History: "Hawaiiana and Pacific Island—anything on the subject. Novels, history, autobiography, etc. No special requirements except good writing. Books should be innovative."

HOLIDAY HOUSE, INC., 18 E. 56th St., New York NY 10022. Editor: Eunice Holsaert. Books published last year: 18. Reports in 4 to 6 weeks. Enclose postage with ms.
Juveniles: Publishes children's books only—fiction and nonfiction, for pre-school through teenage boys and girls.

HOLLOWAY HOUSE PUBLISHING CO., 8060 Melrose Ave., Los Angeles CA 90046. Editor: Donald Shepherd. Publishes originals, reprints and translations. "Our payment is comparable to that of all paperback book publishers. We promote heavily, giving each book individual attention. You must query first on all nonfiction. Also prefer query on fiction, but will accept unsolicited fiction, complete, or outline-synopsis with 2 sample chapters. We try to report in 2 weeks if rejected and in 2 months if interested, but this is subject to the volume of mss received. We do not publish poetry, short stories or plays." Enclose S.A.S.E. with queries or submissions.
Nonfiction: "We're looking for extraordinary works on all subjects which have something to say and which say it well. Prefer 50,000 to 100,000 words. You must

query first and all queries or mss must be accompanied by a brief synopsis of the work. For our Black Experience line, we're particularly interested in seeing the work of black authors on the black experience."

Fiction: "We're looking for general novels; science fiction (no science fantasy or formula stuff); and European erotic classics, either new translations or translations never published in the U.S. We are not in the market for sex books. Also interested in novels about life in the black ghetto for our Black Experience line."

*A.J. HOLMAN COMPANY East Washington Square, Philadelphia PA 19105. Editor: Dr. Russell T. Hitt. Publishes hardcover originals. "Generally, we stick to the standard 10-12½-15% royalty contract. Advance depends on the ms." Does some subsidy publishing. Published 10 titles last year. Will send a catalog to a writer on request. Submit outline and sample chapters or complete ms. Will consider photocopied submissions "for outlines only." Reports on ms accepted for publication in 30 to 60 days. Returns rejected material in about 6 weeks. Enclose return postage.

Religion: "We are the religious division of the J.B. Lippincott Company. The type of book we are most interested in is written for the man on the street and not necessarily for the theologian. Interested in books on current subjects as they relate to the religious aspects of life, biographies, how-to-do-it books, etc. Most books we publish are in the 128- to 156-page length. Our primary market is the conservative religious layman rather than the minister/educator. This should be given the greatest consideration. Many writers write over the heads of this audience when approaching a religious subject." Interested in material on "how a person's life has been changed by faith in God." Current titles include *How Come, God?* (Howard); *How to Face Your Fears* (Hubbard); *The Family Album* (DeMoss).

HOLT, RINEHART AND WINSTON, INC., 383 Madison Ave., New York NY 10017. Royalty plus advance paid. Published 562 titles last year. Enclose return postage with query or ms.

General: Publishes outstanding fiction and distinctive nonfiction—adult fiction, juvenile, history, biography, philosophy, religion and poetry.

HOLT, RINEHART AND WINSTON OF CANADA, LTD., 55 Horner Ave., Toronto 18, Ontario, Canada. Director, Research and Product Development: J.C. Mainprize. Publishes hardcover and paperback originals and anthologies. Offers standard royalty contract. "Advance depends on material. Flat fee only in anthologies." Published 120 titles last year. Will send a catalog to a writer on request. Send complete ms "for fiction, etc."; send query with outline and sample chapter for nonfiction and textbooks. Reports in 1 to 3 months. Enclose Canadian postage or International Reply Coupons.

General Fiction and Poetry: "Short stories and poems for anthologies only."

General Nonfiction: "Canadian authors preferred." Buys some religion and philosophy, business and professional, arts, history and biography.

Juveniles: "We are interested in materials by Canadian authors, or those dealing with Canada or Canadians. We are looking for a great deal of material (probably in the vicinity of 45 juvenile novels and collections of short stories). Short novels, short stories, collections of related short stories. Should abound with bright, vivid description and lively conversation exhibiting a realistic approach to life situations that is comprehensible to 8- to 14-year-olds." Sports, adventure, animal life, exploration and discovery, fantasy, science fiction, mythology and legends, mystery, growing up, biography, the world around us, historical romance. Length: short novels, 13,000 to 16,000 words; short stories, 1,500 to 3,000 words. Specifics for this new juvenile publishing program are: "The ms must be typed double spaced on 1 side of 8½x11 paper with a 2-inch margin. It should be a copy, not the original. No illustrations are necessary, but documentation is, if the material is historical. Immediate acknowledgement will be made of the manuscript's receipt, but further word may take up to a year. Upon acceptance for publication, single short stories will be bought outright for $3,000. An 8% royalty contract will follow acceptance of manuscripts of novels or short story collections."

Textbooks: "All fields—elementary, secondary, and college levels. Must be by Canadians or dealing specifically with Canadian materials."

HOOVER INSTITUTION PRESS, Stanford University, Stanford CA 94305. Royalty schedule is negotiated with author and is dependent upon factors surrounding publication of the ms, though generally about 10% on first edition. Usual advance is 8%, but this varies, depending on author's reputation and nature of book. Prefers to see an outline first. Should be addressed to Secretary, Publications Committee. Reports in 6 to 10 weeks. Enclose return postage.
Economics, History, and Political Science: History and political science, primarily 20th century, concerning any part of the world; biographies relating to persons connected with 20th century political, social or economic change; documentaries, studies, or bibliographies relating to 20th century political, social or economic change. Length: 40,000 words minumum.

*HOPKINSON & BLAKE, 329 Fifth Ave., New York NY 10016. Editor-in-Chief: Len Karlin. Publishes clothbound and paperback originals. Offers standard 10-12½-15% royalty contract; average advance, $1,500. Does subsidy publishing "occasionally." Published 6 titles last year. Query first. Will consider photocopied submissions. Reports in 2 weeks. Enclose return postage.
Nonfiction: "Mainly for college market. We plan to continue to publish books on motion pictures. Also going into travel." A recent title is *The Traveler's Africa.*

HORIZON PRESS, 156 Fifth Ave., New York NY 10010. Prefers complete ms. Royalty schedule standard scale from 10% to 15%. Books published last year: 26. Will send catalog. Reports in 4 weeks. Enclose return postage with ms.
Nonfiction: History, science, biography, the arts, general. Length: 40,000 words and up. Recent titles include *Chaplin: Last of the Clowns.*

HOUGHTON MIFFLIN CO., 2 Park St., Boston MA 02107. Editor-in-Chief: Austin J. Olney. Publishes hardcover and paperback originals and reprints. Pays by royalty contract. Books published last year: 318. Queries welcomed on basis of at least 50 mss pages plus an outline. Enclose return postage with query and outline. Reports within 1 month.
General: Publishes general literature, fiction, biography, autobiography, history. Length: 25,000 words minimum; 70,000 to 140,000 words for biographies. Poetry; children's books. Also publishes Sentry Editions, which are reprints of titles of permanent interest in a soft-backed edition. Recent titles include *Green Darkness* (Seton); *A China Passage* (Galbraith); *The Defection of A.J. Lewinter* (Littell).
Textbooks: Elementary, secondary, and college textbooks.

HOWELL BOOK HOUSE, INC., 845 Third Ave., New York NY 10022. President and Editor-in-Chief: Elsworth S. Howell. Royalty schedule: 10% of list sales made up to 49% discount; 5% of list on sales made at over 49% discount. Published 14 books last year. Catalog on request. Query first with outline. Do not send unsolicited mss. Reports in 2 weeks. Enclose return postage with query.
Technical: Technical books (nonfiction only) about purebred dogs; individual breed books and books on care, training, breeding, etc. Length: 50,000 words minimum.

HOWELL-NORTH BOOKS, 1050 Parker St., Berkeley CA 94710. President: Mrs. Morgan North. Publishes hardcover and paperback originals. Pays 10% of retail price; no advance. Books published last year: 7. Current catalog available. Send query, outline and sample chapter. Reports in 10 weeks. Enclose return postage with query.
Nonfiction: Publishes railroadiana, works on transportation, steamboating, mining, California, marine nonfiction pictorials, histories, Americana, and especially influence of the west. Length: 30,000 words minimum. Recent titles include *Remain to Be Seen—Historic California Houses Open to the Public* (Richey); *The Search for Steam* (Collias).

HUBBARD PRESS, Publishers of Donohue/Hampton Books, P.O. Box 442, 2855 Shermer Road, Northbrook IL 60062. Editor: Richard J. Whittingham. Query before sending mss. Enclose return postage.
Juveniles and Science: Publishes juvenile books and science publications.

HUDSON-COHAN PUBLISHING COMPANY, 1780 Fremont, Suite A (P.O. Box 816), Seaside CA 93955. Editor: Rowena K. Cohan. Publishes paperback originals and reprints. Offers standard 10-12½-13% royalty contract; "no advance." Published 2 titles last year. Query first for nonfiction. Submit outline and sample chapter for trade books. "We will not accept a complete ms." Will consider photocopied submissions. Enclose return postage.
Nonfiction: "Trade books: parapsychology, self-help, philosophy. Length: maximum 300 pages."

HUMANITIES PRESS, INC. 450 Park Ave. S., New York NY 10016. Editor: Simon Silverman. Publishes 10 to 15 books per year. "Do not send ms without authorization from publisher."
Philosophy: "Books on philosophy and related subjects. We are primarily importers of scholarly and academic books."

HURRICANE HOUSE PUBLISHERS, INC., 14301 S.W. 87th Ave., Miami FL 33158. Editor: Marjory Stoneman Douglas. Publishes hardcover and paperback originals and reprints. Offers standard 10-12½-15% royalty contract; "advance varies." Published 5 titles last year. Query first. Will consider photocopied submissions. Reports in 6 weeks. Enclose return postage.
Nonfiction: "Historical, nature, wildlife, horticultural, medical, legal, financial, humor, real estate, and hobbies. Special interests: feminist and black history."

HURTIG PUBLISHERS, 225 Birks Bldg., Edmonton, Alta. T5J 1Z1, Canada. Editor: Jan Walter. Publishes hardcover and paperback originals and reprints. Usual advance is $500, but this varies, depending on author's reputation and nature of book. "Royalties start at 10%." Published 9 titles last year. Will send a catalog to a writer on request. Query first. Reports in 6 weeks. Enclose S.A.E. and International Reply Coupons.
Nonfiction: "Interested in topical Canadian nonfiction of a political or social comment nature, also Canadian history and biography." Length: 50,000 to 200,000 words. Recent titles include *Nunaga, My Land, My Country* (Pryde); *The Canadian Rockies: Early Trade and Explorations* (Fraser); *Bleeding Hearts . . . Bleeding Country* (Smith).

INDIANA UNIVERSITY PRESS, 10th and Morton Sts., Bloomington IN 47401. Managing Editor: Miss Miriam S. Farley. Publishes hardcover originals and paperback reprints. Normally pays 10% royalty. Books published last year: 59. Queries should include as much descriptive material as is necessary to convey scope and market appeal of ms. Reports on rejections in 6 weeks or less; on acceptances, in 3 months. Enclose return postage.
Nonfiction: Scholarly books on humanities, social science; regional materials, serious nonfiction for the general reader.

INTERNATIONAL INSURANCE MONITOR, 150 W. 28th St., New York NY 10001. Royalty schedule depends on terms of the contract. Prefers complete mss. Reports in 4 weeks. Enclose return postage with ms.
Nonfiction: Publishes insurance books of every kind.

INTERNATIONAL MARINE PUBLISHING COMPANY, 21 Elm St., Camden ME 04843. Editor: Peter Spectre. Publishes hardcover and paperback originals and reprints. "Standard royalties, with advances." Published 8 titles last year. Will send a catalog to a writer on request. "Material in all stages welcome. Query invited, but not necessary." Reports in 4 weeks. Enclose return postage with ms.
Marine Nonfiction: "Marine nonfiction only—but a wide range of subjects within that category: fishing, boatbuilding, yachting, sea ecology and conservation, maritime history, cruising, true sea adventure, etc.—anything to do with boats, lakes, rivers, seas, and the people who do things on them, commercially or for pleasure. No word length requirements. Pictorial books with short texts are as welcome as 60,000-word mss." Current leading titles include *Celestial Navigation Step by Step* (Norville); *Sea Sense* (Henderson); *Boatbuilding and Repairing With Fiberglass* (Willis).

INTERNATIONAL WEALTH SUCCESS, Box 186, Merrick NY 11566. Editor: M.B. O'Brien. Offers royalty schedule of 10% of list price. Usual advance is $1,000, but this varies, depending on author's reputation and nature of book. Query first. Will consider photocopied submissions. Reports in 4 weeks. Enclose return postage. **Self-Help and How-to:** "Techniques, methods, sources for building wealth. Highly personal, how-to-do-it with plenty of case histories. Books are aimed at the wealth builder and are highly sympathetic to his problems." Length: 60,000 to 70,000 words.

THE INTERSTATE PRINTERS AND PUBLISHERS, INC., 19-26 N. Jackson St., Danville IL 61832. Editorial and Marketing Manager: Paul A. Sims. Royalty schedule varies; however, it is usually 10% of wholesale price. Books published last year: 61. Will send a current catalog to a writer on request. Prefers queries, outlines, or sample chapters. Reports in 30 to 60 days. Enclose return postage.
Textbooks: Publishes textbooks primarily, in agriculture, industrial arts, home economics, athletics, and special education. Preferred word length varies according to content covered. Recent titles include *Land Speculation; Readings in Evaluation; Construction: Principles, Materials and Methods.*

INTER-VARSITY PRESS, Box F, Downers Grove IL 60515. Editor: Dr. James W. Sire. Publishes hardcover and paperback originals, reprints, translations, and anthologies. Royalty schedule "varies with the ms and the author." Published 25 titles last year. Will send a catalog to a writer on request. Send outline and sample chapter. Reports in 16 weeks. Enclose return postage.
Religion and Philosophy and Textbooks: "Publishes books geared to the presentation of Biblical Christianity in its various relations to personal life, art, literature, sociology, philosophy, history, etc.; college, university, and seminary-level textbooks on any subject within the general religious field. The audience for which the books are published is composed primarily of university students and graduates. The stylistic treatment varies from topic to topic and from fairly simplified popularization for college freshmen to extremely scholarly works primarily designed to be read by scholars." Current leading titles include *The Dust of Death* (Guinness); *Genesis in Space and Time* (Schaeffer).

INTEXT PRESS, 257 Park Ave. S., New York NY 10010. Editor-in-Chief: Samuel D. Stewart. Publishes hardcover and paperback originals and paperback reprints. Offers standard 10-12½-15% royalty contract; "advances are spread over a wide range." Will send a catalog to a writer on request. Query first for fiction and poetry. Submit outline and sample chapters for nonfiction. Will consider photocopied submissions "but prefer typed. Address mss to Fiction Editor or Nonfiction Editor." Reports in 2 to 4 weeks. Enclose return postage.
General: "Quality fiction and nonfiction of book length for general trade audience on any and all subjects. We want anything that is well-written." Categories include adult trade mainstream fiction, biography, business, cookbooks, cooking, foods, economics, history, nature, photography, poetry, politics, scientific, self-help and how-to, sports, hobbies, recreation, pets, travel." A recent title is *In the Beginning, Love* (Van Doren and Samuel).
Juveniles: "Quality fiction and nonfiction."

IOWA STATE UNIVERSITY PRESS, Ames IA 50010. Director: Merritt Bailey. Payment on royalty basis; 10%, 12½%, 15%. No advance. Books published last year: 26. Prefers outline or full table of contents with query letter. Reports in 30 to 60 days. Enclose return postage.
Nonfiction: Publishes books of science, agriculture, humanities, engineering, home economics, veterinary medicine—authoritative, professional. Length: 40,000 words, minimum. Recent titles include *Grant Wood and Marvin Cone; Mr. Piper and His Cubs.*
History and Biography: Some regional history and Iowa biographies. Length: 200 or more ms pages.
Textbooks: Textbooks of modern appeal, mostly college level.

RICHARD D. IRWIN, INC. (including Dorsey Press), 1818 Ridge Road, Homewood IL 60430. Executive Editor: John R. Young. Minimum payment is 10% of net; maximum is 15% of list. Books published last year: 84. Prefers queries, outlines, and sample chapters, before the finished ms is submitted. Usually reports in 6 to 8 weeks. Enclose return postage.

Textbooks: Publishes college textbooks in the fields of accounting, business management, economics, insurance, marketing, finance and information processing, of 100,000 words and over.

Social Sciences: Under Dorsey Press imprint, also publishes in social sciences.

ISLAND PRESS, 175 Bahia Via, Ft. Myers Beach FL 33931. Editor-in-Chief: Rolfe F. Schell. Offers standard 10-12½-15% royalty contract; "on unknown authors and children's books, some start at 7%." No advance. Query first with outline. Will consider photocopied submissions. Enclose return postage.

Fiction and Nonfiction: "Are interested only in fiction and nonfiction about Florida at the moment." Recent titles include *Southwest Florida's Vanished People; Guide to Southeastern Mexico.*

ITHACA HOUSE, 314 Forest Home Dr., Ithaca NY 14850. Senior Editor: Baxter Hathaway. "Since our first printings are planned and priced to yield at best no more than production costs, royalties are involved only if there are later printings. No advances." Enclose return postage with ms.

Poetry: "To date we have published 12 books of poetry in the development of a poetry series which we hope represents the very best work being done in America today. We are a cooperative of writers with much editorial experience collectively, and we are willing to trust our critical judgments with relatively unknown poets provided that we are confident that what they are writing is the real thing. Our orientation is not strongly commercial, and poets whom we publish are not likely to make much if any money out of the venture. Some of our books we print ourselves, hand-set; some we do offset. We do not wish to be limited to any one school or fashion. We are, however, more interested in new forms and new voices than in the last gasps of the old and the security of the staid and all-too-well understood." Length: 50 to 100 pages.

Fiction: "Books of significant fiction. We are interested only in high literary quality." Length: 20,000 to 40,000 words.

JARROW PRESS, INC., 29 Commonwealth Ave., Boston MA 02116. Editor: Philip Deemer. Publishes hardcover and paperback originals. Offers standard 10-12½-15% royalty contract; "advance varies." Published 6 titles last year. "Query first; no unsolicited mss considered." Will consider photocopied submissions "only after a query." Reports in 3 to 4 weeks. Enclose return postage.

Religion: "We have changed our emphasis in the last year and are no longer doing trade books; we are now publishing reference and research books in the religious field only. We are basically Episcopal Church oriented, but we are interested in considering mss involving ecumenicity and liturgical reform. We are interested in publishing books about the increasing evangelism movement growing among individual people of faith when the institutional churches are losing members. No inspirational material."

THE JEWISH PUBLICATION SOCIETY OF AMERICA, 222 N. 15th St., Philadelphia PA 19102. Editor: Chaim Potok. Payment is on royalty basis. 25¢ per book unit on membership sales. Usual advance is $1,000, but this varies, depending on author's reputation and nature of book. Books published last year: 10. Reports in 4 to 8 weeks. Enclose return postage with ms.

Nonfiction: Publishes scholarly history, scholarly biography, fiction, Jewish philosophy, material of Jewish interest on the arts, religion, general essays and translations of foreign work; reprints and originals. Approximately 80,000-100,000 words.

Juvenile: Also publishes biographies of juvenile interest, about important Jewish historical figures. Should run 50,000 words. Subjects to be chosen in consultation.

THE JOHNS HOPKINS UNIVERSITY PRESS, Baltimore MD 21218. Editorial Director: J.G. Goellner. Publishes scholarly books and nonfiction for the intelligent reader—history, science, philosophy, the arts, and general nonfiction, especially literary criticism, international affairs and economics. Paperback originals and reprints. Payment varies; contract negotiated with author. Mss must be over 40,000 words. Prompt report, usually 8 weeks. Prefers query letter first. Books published last year: 92.

JONATHAN DAVID PUBLISHERS, 68-22 Eliot Ave., Middle Village NY 11379. General Editor: Alfred J. Kolatch. Publishes hardcover and paperback originals. Offers standard 10-12½-15% royalty contract; "advances according to credentials." Published 20 titles last year. Will send a catalog to a writer on request. Send query with outline and sample chapter. Reports in 2 to 4 weeks. Enclose return postage.
General Nonfiction: "General nonfiction for adults. Because we are new in the general book field, we feel that we can give the author a more personal relationship than he ordinarily would receive. Our titles must have a mass audience potential. We're always open to solid ideas. We generally recruit our top authors, but we are interested in hearing from able writers with nonfiction book ideas. Recent titles include *The Football Playbook; I Couldn't Stand My Wife's Cooking, So I Opened a Restaurant.*
Juvenile: "We restrict ourselves to nonfiction for the 8-to-12 age group. We are currently interested in writers interested in writing for our 'Let's Talk about . . .' series. Recent titles include *Let's Talk About the New World of Medicine.*"
Reference: Current leading title is *Names for Boys & Girls.*

MARSHALL JONES COMPANY, Francestown NH 03043. Editor: Clarence E. Farrar. Enclose return postage with ms.
Nonfiction: Publishes nonfiction, worthy of publication, written to interest a specific market.
Textbooks: Progressive school, junior college, and college textbooks.

JUDSON PRESS, Valley Forge PA 19481. Managing Editor: Harold L. Twiss. Publishes hardcover and paperback originals. Generally 10% royalty on first 7,500 copies; 12½% on next 7,500; 15% above 15,000. "Payment of an advance depends on author's reputation and nature of book." Books published last year: 27. Catalog available on request. Prefers a query letter accompanied by outline and sample chapter. Reports in 3 months. Enclose return postage.
Religion: Adult religious nonfiction of 30,000 to 200,000 words.

KEATS PUBLISHING, INC., 212 Elm St., New Canaan CT 06840. Editor: A. Keats. Publishes hardcover and paperback originals and reprints. Offers standard 10-12½-15% royalty contract. Advance varies. Will send a catalog to a writer on request. Query first with outline and sample chapter. Reports in 2 months. Enclose return postage.
Nonfiction: "Natural health, special interest; industry-subsidy. Also, mss with promotion and premium potential. In natural health, anything having to do with the current interest in ecology, natural health cookbooks, diet books, organic gardening, etc." Length: open. Recent titles include *Food Additives and Your Health* (Hunter).
Religion: "Largely in the conservative Protestant field."

KENT STATE UNIVERSITY PRESS, Kent State University, Kent OH 44242. Editor: Mrs. Josephine Zuppan. Publishes hardcover and paperback originals and reprints. Standard minimum book contract; rarely gives an advance. Published 9 titles last year. Will send a catalog to a writer on request. "Please always write a letter of inquiry before submitting mss. We can publish only a limited number of titles each year and can frequently tell in advance whether or not we would be interested in a particular ms. This practice saves both our time and that of the author, not to mention postage costs." Reports in 10 weeks. Enclose return postage.
Nonfiction: Especially interested in "scholarly works in history of high quality, particularly any titles of regional interest for Ohio. Also will consider scholarly biographies of the highest quality and original scientific research. Publications also in philosophy, the arts, and general nonfiction."

DALE STUART KING, PUBLISHER, 2002 N. Tucson Blvd., Tucson AZ 85716. Publishes hardcover and paperback originals. Royalty schedule: usually 12% of gross sales. Books published last year: 1. Current catalog available on request. Send query first, then outline and sample chapter. Reports in less than 30 days. Enclose return postage.

Nonfiction: Publishes specialized history, biography, science, and general nonfiction on the Southwest only. Length: around 60,000 words.

KIRKLEY PRESS, INC., P.O. Box 200, Timonium MD 21093. Editor: Alan Dugdale. Publishes paperback 16-page booklets. "We buy mss outright and pay upon acceptance. Payment (total) varies between $200 and $300, depending on subject and strength with which written." Will send a sample copy to a writer on request. Send complete ms. "Try to answer in 2 weeks." Enclose S.A.S.E. for return of submissions.

Business: "We publish small booklets which are sold to businesses for distribution to the employee. They attempt to stimulate or motivate the employee to improve work habits. Basically they are pep talks for the employee. We need writers who are so close to the problems of present-day employee attitudes that they can take one of those problems and write about it in a warm, human, understanding, personal style and language that will appeal to the employee and which the employer will find it to his advantage to distribute to the employees." Length: 2,400 to 2,600 words. Current leading titles include *Stop Kidding Yourself About Mistakes; Let's Keep America Great.*

B. KLEIN PUBLICATIONS INC., 11 Third Street, Rye NY 10580. Editor: Bernard Klein. Publishes hardcover and paperback originals. "Standard royalty usually 10%. No advances—until ms is in our hands. This must be negotiated with author, and could vary a great deal." Published 6 titles last year. Send query and outline. Reports in 30 days. Enclose return postage.

General Nonfiction and Reference: Specializes in "business and educational directories and reference books. Only nonfiction." Length: open.

ROBERT R. KNAPP, PUBLISHER, P.O. Box 7234, San Diego CA 92107. Editor: Robert R. Knapp. Publishes hardcover and paperback originals. "Pays on a royalty basis." Published 3 titles last year. Will send a catalog to a writer on request. "Always query first." Reports in 30 days. Enclose return postage.

Nonfiction and Textbooks: "Scholarly nonfiction, especially the social sciences, psychology, education, and statistics."

ALFRED A. KNOPF, INC., 201 East 50th St., New York NY 10022. Managing Editor: Ashbel Green. Payment is on royalty basis. Books published last year: 113. Send query letter for nonfiction; query letter or complete mss for fiction. Will consider photocopied submissions. Reports in 2 to 4 weeks. Enclose return postage.

Fiction: Publishes book-length fiction of literary merit by known or unknown writers. Length: 30,000 to 150,000 words.

Nonfiction: Book-length nonfiction, including books of scholarly merit on special subjects. Preferred length: 40,000 to 150,000 words. A good nonfiction writer should be able to follow the latest scholarship in any field of human knowledge, and fill in the abstractions of scholarship for the benefit of the general reader by means of good concrete, sensory reporting.

Juveniles: No minimum length requirement for juvenile books. Juvenile Editor: Pat Ross.

JOHN KNOX PRESS, P.O. Box 1176, Richmond VA 23209. Editor: Dr. Richard A. Ray. Publishes hardcover and paperback originals, reprints, and translations. Royalties: paperbacks, 8% of retail price; hardbacks, 10% of retail price." Published 122 titles last year. Will send a catalog to a writer on request. Send query with personal vita, outline and sample chapter. "It would be helfpul if the author's covering letter includes a brief description of the book's potential market and its uniqueness in the field." Ms should be double-spaced, 60 characters to a line, 25 lines per page. Conform to *A Manual of Style* (12th edition), The University of Chicago Press." Reports in 3 months. Enclose S.A.S.E.

Religion and Philosophy: "We are looking for books dealing with personal faith; family and interpersonal relationships; inspiration; Biblical and theological scholarship; and the relation of religion to social, cultural, ethical, or aesthetic concerns. The audience varies with the book. Primarily, we are interested in reaching church professionals (ministers, directors of Christian education, etc.), the college and seminary markets, and the elusive 'general' audience. Length: 15,000 to 60,000 words (15,000 to 36,000 preferred)." Current leading titles include *Barefoot in the Church* (Allen); *Mark of the Taw* (Finegan).

LADYSMITH PRESS, Ladysmith, Quebec, Canada. Editors: Sean Haldane and Marnie Pomeroy. Publishes hardcover and paperback originals and anthologies. "10% standard royalty." No advance. Published 5 titles last year. Send a dozen pages of ms. Reports in 2 months. Enclose return envelope and Canadian postage or International Reply Coupons.
Poetry: "Books of poetry. Collections of poems. Length: 32 pages minimum; 34 lines per page. Occasionally prose books in the field of poetry (biographies of poets, essays, etc.). But no other prose." Current leading title is *The Speck* (Pomeroy).

LANCER BOOKS, INC., 1560 Broadway, New York NY 10036. Editorial Director: Rochelle Larkin. Editors: John Holt, Charlotte Hastings, Kathy Dobkin. Publishes paperback originals and reprints. Also anthologies, but these are "usually not open to freelancers." Offers "standard paperback contract, advances from $1,000 up, less for reprint Westerns." Published approximately 320 titles last year. Will send a catalog to a writer on request. "Prefer full ms with synopsis from new or unknown writers; established professionals, will consider portion and outline (2 to 3 chapters). Always prefer query before submission." Reports "usually within 30 days, occasionally longer if taking several readings." Enclose S.A.S.E. with mss and with query letter.
General: "General paperback list, including nonfiction and standard categories of fiction (science fiction, fantasy, mystery-suspense, gothic romance, erotica, westerns). Also non-category fiction, but this is mostly reprint." Length: 55,000 to 60,000 words. Recent titles include *Murder Mission, Soldato #4* (Conroy); *The Evil Children* (Roberts).

LANTERN PRESS, INC., 354 Hussey Rd., Mount Vernon NY 10552. Payment is on royalty basis, or outright purchase, if preferred. Usual advance is $250 on signing, $250 on publication, but this varies, depending on author's reputation and nature of book. Books published last year: 5. No mss should be sent unless authorized. Reports in 3 to 4 weeks. Enclose return postage.
Nonfiction: Publishes adult nonfiction, self-help, mail-order books. Length: 2,000 to 30,000 words.
Juveniles: Especially interested in juveniles for all ages. Juvenile Editor: J.A.L. Furman.

LARK PUBLISHING CO., INC., 636 E. 80th St., Brooklyn NY 11236. President: Gerald Rubinsky. Publishes hardcover and paperback originals. Offers standard 10-12½-15% royalty contract; "average advance, $1,000 to $2,000." Published 2 titles last year. Query first. Will consider photocopied submissions. Reports on ms accepted for publication in 1 month. Returns rejected material in 2 weeks. Enclose return postage.
Nonfiction: "Primarily nonfiction, specializing in psychology and inspirational titles. In addition, we create and publish Gemini-Lark Make-It-Yourself kits, such as *How to Make Your Own Books.* We prefer mss that appeal to an audience looking for inspiration and assistance and self-help." Length: 60,000 to 75,000 words.

LAW-ARTS PUBLISHERS, INC., 453 Greenwich St., New York NY 10013. Editor: Joseph Taubman. Publishes hardcover and paperback originals. Offers standard 10-12½-15% royalty contract. Usual advance is $500, but this is totally dependent on author's reputation and nature of book. Published 6 titles last year. Will send a catalog to a writer on request. Submit outline and sample chapters. Will consider photocopied submissions. Reports in 1 to 2 months. Enclose return postage.
The Arts: Books on "management of the arts (performing and graphic arts). Should appeal to the performing artist and the arts managerial staff. Books are specifically chosen for their unique qualities—should fill existing lacunae." Length: open. A recent title is *Performing Arts Management and Law.*

Law: "Books on law which appeal to the businessman lawyer. No books on legal oddities."

SEYMOUR LAWRENCE, INC., 90 Beacon St., Boston MA 02108. Publisher: Seymour Lawrence. Editor: Merleyd Lawrence. Publishes hardcover originals. Seymour Lawrence books are published in association with the Delacorte Press. Royalty schedule: 10% to 5,000 copies; 12½% to 10,000; 15% thereafter on adult hardcover books; 10% on children's books. Send outline and sample chapters. Enclose return postage.
Fiction: Adult fiction.
Nonfiction: Child care and child development books for the general reader (no textbooks).
Juveniles: Juvenile fiction and picture books.

LE ROI PUBLISHERS, P.O. Box 1165, Jefferson City MO 65101. Editor: A.H. Stainback. Publishes hardcover and paperback originals. "Our present contracts are a straight 10%." Published 2 titles last year. Will send a catalog to a writer on request. Query first with outline and sample chapters. Will consider photocopied submissions. Enclose return postage with ms.
Religion: "We publish conservative religious books only. These may be studies, sermons, novels, illustrations, etc. The writer should present his material as he would present it to a conservative group of Bible teachers or preachers." Length: open. Recent titles include *A New Heaven and a New Earth* (Lawrence); *The Gosepl According to . . .* (LaFavre).

*LEARNING TRENDS, 115 Fifth Ave., New York NY 10003. Editor-in-Chief: William Shanahan. Publishes hardcover and paperback originals. Contract and advance "subject to negotiation; usual advance is $1,000." Does some subsidy publishing. Published 16 titles last year. Will send a catalog to a writer on request. Submit outline and sample chapters. Will consider photocopied submissions. Reports in 3 weeks. Enclose return postage.
Textbooks: "Textbooks, grades K to 12; emphasis on slow learner material. Especially interested in special education, career education, and other areas lending themselves to a high interest, low reading level approach. Other media besides print welcome. Short chapters and study aids recommended. Interested in relevant, original materials in social studies, language arts, science, mathematics, and other fields represented in school curricula. The high conceptual level and slow learner approach is recommended."

LENOX HILL PRESS, 419 Park Ave. S., New York NY 10016. Editor: Alice Sachs. Pays $150 for westerns, $250 for romances. Books published last year: 72. Address query letters to Phyllis Fleiss, Editorial Department; entire mss when possible. Reports in 6 weeks. Enclose return postage with ms.
Fiction: Publishes sweet romances, gothics, old-time western yarns. Prefers 55,000 to 60,000 word lengths.

LERNER PUBLICATIONS CO., 241 First Ave. N., Minneapolis MN 55401. Books published last year: 23. Current catalog available on request. Query unnecessary; prefers complete ms. Send ms to Jennifer Martin. Will consider photocopied submissions. Reports in 10 to 12 weeks. Enclose return postage with ms.
Juveniles: Publishes fiction and educational books for children from preschool through high school, including books in the following subject areas: K-3 reading and language arts, remedial reading, art appreciation, music, mathematics, science, social science, family living and medical topics, career education, sports, picture storybooks. Representative series include: *In America Books* (immigrant groups), *Mr. Bumba, Mrs. Moon and Mr. & Mrs. Bumba Easy-Readers, Fine Art Books for Young People* (topical approach to art history), *The Real World of Economics, The Real World of Pollution, The Being Together Books* (sex education), *Medical Books for Children, The Math Concept Books, The Racing Books, The Early Career Books, The Pull Ahead Books* (remedial biographies), *Musical Books for Young People, The Science-Hobby Books, Felipe Adventure Stories* (multi-ethnic readers), *General Juvenile Books* (selected fiction and picture storybooks), *Real Life Books* (biographies), *The Real World Books* (contemporary social and political topics).

LIBRA PUBLISHERS, INC., 391 Willets Rd., P.O. Box 165, Roslyn Hts., L.I. NY 11577. Pays royalties of 10% and up. No advance. Books published last year: 10. Wants queries with outlines and sample chapters. Send inquiries to Editor-in-Chief. Reports in 2 weeks. Enclose return postage.
Nonfiction: Books on history, biography, science, philosophy, religion, psychology, psychiatry. No word length requirements.
Fiction and Poetry: Some books of fiction and poetry.

LIBRARIES UNLIMITED, INC., P.O. Box 263, Littleton CO 80120. President: Bohdan S. Wynar. Publishes hardcover and paperback originals. Offers standard 10-12½-15% royalty contract. No advance. Published 25 titles last year. Will send a catalog to a writer on request. Send complete ms. Follow Chicago *Manual of Style*. Reports in 4 weeks. Enclose return postage with ms.
Library and Reference: "Library science, reference books, information science." Reference Books Dept. Editor: Christine L. Wynar.
Textbooks: Publishes textbooks in library science on graduate and technician levels. Monographs and research studies in the area of library science and reference books in all areas. Dept. Editor: Dr. Bohdan S. Wynar.

LIBRARY PRESS, INCORPORATED, Box 599, LaSalle IL 61301. Editor: Melvin J. Lasky. Published 20 titles last year. Query before submitting.
General: "Library Press, Incorporated is an American publishing house dedicated to original works of quality and special public interest in biography, history, literary criticism, current affairs, and imaginative writing, and, above all, to maintaining the authentic relationship between the author and his reader. Distinctly international in spirit, we are based both in Chicago and London. Library Press publishes books of scholarship and general interest, including art books, cookbooks, history, humor and how-to books, sport books, poetry, and plays. Adult books for adults. And children's books for children. It is a publishing house run as a cultural enterprise, even as a literary handicraft, and not as an anonymous, assembly-line industry." Current titles include *Nine Lies Against America* (Beichman); *Psychology Is About People* (Eyeenck); *On Proust* (Revel).

*LINACRE PRESS, INC., Box 38, Greens Farms CT 06436. Editor-in-Chief: Ethel Paul. Publishes hardcover and paperback originals and reprints. Outright purchase; average fee, $500. 90% of books are subsidy published. Usual advance is $500 to $1,000, but this varies, depending on author's reputation and nature of book. Published 5 titles last year. Query first. Enclose return postage with ms.
Social Sciences: "Books on psychiatry, psychology; sexual manuals." Length: open.

LINKS BOOKS, 33 W. 60th St., New York NY 10023. Editors: Daniel Moses and Carol Fein. Publishes paperback originals. Query first with sample chapters. Enclose return postage.
Nonfiction: "This is a book operation by serious freaks. We're going to be publishing things we care about, books that will be sold in college bookstores and stores catering to other youth groups, including the counter-culture." Current titles include *Einstein and Beckett: A Record of an Imaginary Discussion with Albert Einstein and Samuel Beckett* (Schlossberg); *Time Out's Book of London: An Alternate Guide*.

J.B. LIPPINCOTT CO., E. Washington Square, Philadelphia PA 19105. General Adult Book Editor: Edward L. Burlingame. Publishes hardcover and paperback originals and reprints. Standard royalty schedule. "Juvenile royalty schedule is 10% (shared equally with author and artist for picture books). Books published last year: 228. Will send catalog on request. Reports in 3 to 4 weeks. Enclose return postage with ms.
General: Publishes general nonfiction; also history, biography, nature, sports, the arts, adult fiction.
Juveniles: For juvenile nonfiction, "the subjects should be closely tied to the school curriculum for the age group. The book should supplement and expand textbook exposure to a subject. Writing style must be interesting and non-condescending." Considers nonfiction book mss for grades 3 to 5 and for junior high school. "No

books on 'in' subjects, such as drugs, ecology, etc. We are well-supplied in such areas." Length: 25,000 words, grades 3 to 5; 35,000 to 40,000 words, junior high. For picture books, wants "high quality writing on any good subject. We have a special interest in easy- or beginning-readers at this time. Gear picture books to preschool and K to 3." Length: "under 1,500 words." Recent titles include *A Twister of Twists, A Tangler of Tongues* (Schwartz). Editor-in-Chief, Juvenile Trade Books: Dorothy S. Briley.

LITTLE, BROWN AND COMPANY, 34 Beacon St., Boston MA 02106. Editorial Director: J. Randall Williams. Publishes hardcover and paperback originals and reprints. Offers royalty contract. Published 150 titles last year. "Contracts for nonfiction offered on basis of an outline and 3 or 4 sample chapters." Reports in 1 month. Enclose return postage.
General: "Fiction and general nonfiction book-length mss."
Juveniles: "All ages." Editor of Children's Books: John G. Keller.

LIVERIGHT PUBLISHING CORP., 386 Park Ave. S., New York NY 10016. Editorial Director: Margot Schutt. Publishes hardcover and paperback originals, reprints, and anthologies. "Payment is on a royalty basis." Published 36 titles last year. Will send a catalog to a writer on request. Send a synopsis and brief biographical sketch. Do not send complete ms. Contracts offered for good nonfiction material on the basis of an outline and several sample chapters. Reports in 60 days. Enclose return postage.
General: "Publishes good nonfiction and fiction over 60,000 words." Subjects for nonfiction include art (should be "big, biographical, illustrated"), architecture, criticism, history, biography. Especially interested in politics. Wants "good fiction for 'New Writers Series'."

LIVING BOOKS, LTD., P.O. Box 593, Times Square Station, New York NY 10036. An affiliate of Diplomatic Press, Inc. Pays "the usual 10% of the published price in accordance with Author's Guild requirements." Advance varies, depending on author's reputation and nature of book. Prefers query letters with outlines and sample chapters be sent to the Editor. "Unsolicited mss must be accompanied by S.A.S.E. or label." Reports in 2 to 3 months. Enclose return postage.
General: Publishes books in every field of human interest—adult fiction, history, biography, science, philosophy, the arts, religion, and general nonfiction. "List for fiction closed for the time being." Length: 65,000 to 125,000 words.

LLEWELLYN PUBLICATIONS, Box 3383, St. Paul MN 55165. Editor: Ronald Wright. Publishes hardcover and paperback originals, reprints, and translations. 10% royalty contract. No advance. Published 20 titles last year. Will send a catalog to a writer on request. Send complete ms. Reports in 2 to 4 months. Enclose return postage with ms.
Occult Fiction and Nonfiction: "We focus on occult subject matter—astrology, witchcraft, mysticism, magic, divination (Tarot, I Ching), etc. Our audience consists of segments of every economic, social, age, and religious group." Interested in "occult-oriented fiction, parapsychological studies, Eastern religions, mysticism, etc." Length: open. Current leading titles include *Astrology Reveals Life and Love* (Burroughs); *Magic Without Tears* (Crowley).

LONGMAN CANADA LTD., 55 Barber Greene Rd., Don Mills, Ont., Canada. Managing Editor: Alistair Hunter. Query on general nonfiction and science; completed mss preferred in all other categories. Do not need to include return postage. Does return mss and respond to queries.
Fiction: Publishes adult fiction. Fiction mss should run 80,000 words or more.
Nonfiction: History (Canadian preferred), biography (lives of Canadians preferred), popular science, general nonfiction.
Juveniles: Juveniles at the teenage level. Length: 50,000 words or more.
Textbooks: Textbooks on all levels.

LOTHROP, LEE AND SHEPARD CO., 105 Madison Ave., New York NY 10016. Editor-in-Chief: Mrs. Edna Barth. Publishes hardcover originals, translations, and anthologies. Royalty schedule varies. Published 56 titles last year. Send outline and sample chapters for nonfiction; complete ms for fiction. Reports in 6 to 8 weeks. Enclose return postage.

Juveniles: "Fiction and nonfiction for children and young people, mainly for ages 3 to 14. Particularly interested in fiction at present. Seeking fiction of originality by members of minority groups or others. Distinctive picture book scripts for younger children; any good nonfiction for the youngest." Length: 3 to 4 pages to about 40,000 words. Also "interested in good poetry for children"; interested in history and biography "if written with new approach and not on wornout subjects." Current leading titles include *The Carp in the Bathtub* (Cohen); *Mouse Cafe* (Coombs).

ROBERT B. LUCE INC., 2000 N Street, N.W., Washington DC 20036. Offers standard 10%-12½%-15% royalty contract. Published 10 titles last year. Will send a catalog to a writer on request. Reports in 4 weeks. Enclose return postage.

General Fiction: "Publishes limited fictional works."

General Nonfiction: "Books dealing with current affairs: books of personal experience that are meaningful to general readers; how-to-do-it, self-help books that are authoritative and written for the popular audience. Books on controversial subjects. Mss should be 60,000 words and up; outline and sample chapters preferred initially." Current leading titles include *Our Soviet Sister* (St. George). Dept. Editor: Ms. Virginia Wheaton.

History and Biography: "Mss should be 60,000 words and up; outline and sample chapters preferred initially." Current leading title is *Hussein* (Snow). Dept. Editor: Joseph Binns.

Public Affairs and Social Problems: "Query first with outline and sample chapters." Dept. Editor: Robert van Roijen.

LYONS AND CARNAHAN, Educational Publishers, 407 E. 25th St., Chicago IL 60616. Vice President and Editorial Director: Sylvan Wiley. Pays either a royalty fee after sales or a flat fee on acceptance. Books published last year: approximately 50. Query first, enclosing description of materials and brief professional resume. Reports in 1 month. Enclose return postage.

Textbooks: Elementary-high school, part of the educational division of Meredith Corporation. Most activities centered on basic learning materials usually written by teachers or other persons connected with education.

THE MACMILLAN CO., 866 Third Ave., New York NY 10022. Publishes hardcover and paperback originals and reprints. Books published last year: 304. Send query letter before sending ms. Address all mss except juveniles to Trade Editorial Department; children's books to Children's Book Department. Will consider photocopied submissions.

Fiction and Nonfiction: Publishes adult fiction and nonfiction. Length: at least 75,000 words.

Juveniles: Children's books.

MACMILLAN COMPANY OF CANADA, LTD., 70 Bond St., Toronto, Ont., Canada. M5B 1X3 Trade Editor: K.A. McVey. Payment by arrangement. Desirable but not necessary to query first. Reports in 6 weeks. Enclose return postage.

General: Publishes Canadian books of all kinds.

Textbooks: Educational Editor: Gladys Neale.

Scientific and Technical: College, Medical, Nursing Editor: Mrs. Diane Mew.

MACRAE SMITH COMPANY, 225 S. 15th St., Philadelphia PA 19102. Pays 10% of list price. Published 14 titles last year. Will send a catalog on request. Send outline and sample chapters or complete ms and letter reviewing relevant background and experience of author. Address mss to Ruth Allan Miner. Reports in 4 to 6 weeks. Enclose return postage.

General: "Adult trade books, fiction and nonfiction. Current issues and topical concerns, adventure, mysteries and gothics, history and science, biography."

Juveniles: For nonfiction books, interested in "biographies, history of world cultures, impact of the sciences on human affairs, cultural anthropology, scientific and medical discoveries, ecology, current social concerns and theory, peace research, international cooperation and world order, controversial issues, sports. Future-oriented subjects. For all ages, but prefer 8 to 12 and junior and senior high school."

Also buys adventure stories, mysteries, history and science, biography, and girls' fiction. Length: 40,000 to 60,000 words. Recent titles include *The U.S. Congress: Men Who Steered Its Course, 1787-1876* (Fribourg); *When Reason Fails: Psychotherapy in America* (Liston); *Ralph Nader's Crusade* (Curtis).

MANOR BOOKS (including Macfadden-Bartell Books), 329 Fifth Ave., New York NY 10016. Editor-in-Chief: Donald A. Schrader. Publishes paperback originals and reprints. Royalty contract to be negotiated. "Each is discussed on its own merits." Published 75 titles last year. Query first. Enclose return postage.
General: Adult fiction and nonfiction trade books; category fiction. Current titles include *Shelter* (Ljorka); *Cock A Doodle Dew* (Davis); *How to Make Liquers at Home.*

*MANYLAND BOOKS, INC., 84-39 90th St., Woodhaven NY 11421. Editor-in-Chief: Stepas Zobarskas. Publishes hardcover and paperback originals. Offers standard 10-12½ 15% royalty contract; average advance, $250 to $2,500. About 33% of books are subsidy published. Published 6 titles last year. Will send a catalog to a writer on request. Submit complete ms. Will consider photocopied submissions. Reports in 6 weeks. Enclose return postage with ms.
Fiction, Nonfiction, Poetry, and Juveniles: "Manyland is concerned primarily with the literature of the lesser known countries. It has already published a score of novels, collections of short stories, folk tales, juvenile books, works of poetry, essays, and historical studies. Most of the publications have more than local interest. Their content and value transcend natural boundaries. They have universal appeal. We are interested in both new and established writers. We will consider any subject as long as it is well-written. No length requirements. We are especially interested in memoirs, biographies, anthologies." Current titles include *Modern Stories From Many Lands* (Decker & Angoff); *Sin at Easter* (Vaizgantas); *Two Seas* (Field).

MASTERCO PRESS, INC., P. O. Box 382, Ann Arbor MI 48107. Editor: Thomas S. Roberts. Publishes hardcover and paperback originals. Offers standard 10-12½-15% royalty contract; no advance. Marketing by direct mail. Will send a catalog to a writer on request. Query first, then send outline and sample chapters. Will consider photocopied submissions "as long as we can read it." Reports in 3 months. Enclose return postage.
Business: Books on "business, economics, finance and management. Emphasis on the practical, how-to-do-it approach. The writer must have authority in fields covered since ours is primarily a management audience. Interested in books on marketing by objectives and hospital management."

McCLELLAND AND STEWART, LTD., 25 Hollinger Rd., Toronto 16, Ont., Canada. Royalties are standard, but often individually negotiated. "15% straight royalty for very prestigious authors; 5% or 8% royalty on less expensive paperback editions." Usual advance is $500, but this varies, depending on author's reputation and nature of book. Books published last year: 125. Will send catalog on request. Include with ms an outline plus brief history of writing credits. Send all mss to Editor-in-Chief. Reports in 5 to 8 weeks. Enclose return postage with ms.
Fiction: Interested in Canadian writing of outstanding quality. Adult fiction: 60,000 to 75,000 words.
Nonfiction: General nonfiction: 40,000 to 75,000 words. Religion: 60,000 to 70,000 words. History: 60,000 to 85,000 words. Biography: 60,000 to 85,000 words. Science: 40,000 to 75,000 words. Philosophy: 40,000 to 60,000 words. The arts (illustrated): 3,000 to 60,000 words. Recent titles include *The National Dream; The Last Spike; The Barn.*
Juveniles: Length: 40,000 to 60,000 words.

McCORMICK-MATHERS PUBLISHING COMPANY, 450 W. 33rd St., New York NY 10001. A subsidiary of Litton Educational Publishing, Inc. Enclose return postage with ms.
Textbooks: Publishes elementary and secondary textbooks.

McGILL-QUEEN'S UNIVERSITY PRESS, 3458 Redpath Street, Montreal 109, Quebec, Canada. Editor: Miss Beverly Johnston. Publishes hardcover and paperback originals. "Standard royalty is 10% of list. Advances are given only in exceptional cases." Send outline. "If invited to submit work, send in ms typed double-spaced throughout, with double-spaced notes at the back of the ms." Reporting time "depends on whether ms is to be read by specialists." Enclose International Reply Coupons for return postage.

General Nonfiction: "Books based on original scholarly reasearch and serious non-fiction of general interest."

McGRAW-HILL BOOK COMPANY, 1221 Ave. of the Americas, New York NY 10020. Publishes hardcover and paperback originals, reprints, translations, and anthologies. Offers standard royalty contract: 10% to 5,000, 12.5% to 10,000, 15% thereafter. On textbooks, "royalties vary from 3% net to 15% list." Published 609 titles last year. Will send a catalog to a writer on request. Send outline and sample chapter. "Unsolicited mss rarely accepted. No poetry, mysteries or science fiction." Reports in 3 weeks. Enclose return postage.

General: Trade nonfiction and fiction. Current titles include *Group Portrait With Lady* (Boll); *Transparent Things* (Nabokov). Dept. Editors: Fred Hills, General Fiction, General Nonfiction, Reference; Tyler Hicks, Technical and Scientific; Paul Schneider, Medical; Samuel Bossard, Religion and Philosophy; William Mogan, Business and Professional.

Juveniles: Editor-in-Chief, Junior Books: Eleanor Nichols.

College and University Textbooks: The College and University Division publishes college textbooks. "We aim for superior editorial content geared to course level and type of student. The writer must know the college curriculum and course structure. No 'relevance' readers and anthologies." Also publishes "scientific texts and reference books in medicine, nursing, the physical sciences, and mathematics. Material should be scientifically and factually accurate. Most, but not all, books should be designed for existing courses offered in various disciplines of study. Books should have superior presentations and be more up-to-date than existing textbooks." Dept. Editors: Joseph J. Brehm, Editor-in-Chief, Medicine and Psychiatry and Nursing; Bradford Bayne, Scientific, Mathematics, and Statistics textbooks.

Community College Textbooks: For Community College Division, wants material in the areas of "remedial/basic skills education, occupational education, technologies education, general/academic education in all media. The treatment must relate or conform to two-year college curriculums and course outlines specifically. The author must either be a teacher in a two-year college or an instructor in a business-industry training program. Clearly stated objectives, both macro and micro, must be an integral part of the ms." Dept. Editors: E.E. Byers, Editor-in-Chief, Business and Management; A.W. Lowe, Senior Editor, Electricity, Electronics, and Computer Science; R. Buchanan, Senior Editor, Engineering Technologies, Applied Math and Science; A. Cleverdon, Editor, Human Service Occupations; E.B. Fuchs, Editor, Basic Skills programs; G.O. Stone, Manager, General/Academic programs; P. Walker, Publisher, Professional Reference.

McGRAW-HILL RYERSON, LTD. 330 Progress Ave., Scarborough 707, Ont., Canada. Editor: Mr. Toivo Kiil. Publishes hardcover and paperback originals and reprints. Royalty schedule varies: 10% and more on list for trade titles; average advance is $1,000 for biographies. Published 30 titles last year. Will send a catalog to a writer on request. Query first with outline and sample chapter for nonfiction; send outline for fiction. Reports in 90 days. Enclose return postage.

General Fiction and Nonfiction: "Adult fiction; general fiction, history, science, philosophy, sports. Length for history: 50,000 to 90,000 words. A recent title is *Lives of Girls and Women.*

Biography: "Good market for book-length Canadian biographies." Length: 60,000 to 120,000 words. A recent title is *Alexander Mackenzie.*

Juveniles: Buys some illustrated juveniles.

DAVID McKAY CO., INC., 750 Third Ave., New York NY 10017. Chairman of the Board: Maxwell Geffen; President and Editor-in-Chief: Kennett L. Rawson; Editorial Director: James O'Shea Wade; Executive Editor: Ms. Eleanor S. Rawson. Publishes hardcover originals and translations; also anthologies, but "rarely—only if stunning idea." Publishes paperbacks "only if previously established as strong in hardcover, such as the Euell Gibbons books." Offers standard royalty contract.

"Rarely vary royalty scale, but all contracts negotiated individually and vary so today that there is no blanket answer." Published 119 titles last year. Prefers that writer send complete ms, but will consider outline with sample chapters, or query. Ms should be cleanly typed, and accompanied by S.A.S.E. and postage, and "informative covering letter giving any details about genesis of book and author's background which will help in evaluating material." Reports in approximately 3 weeks.

General Fiction: "Adult fiction tied to contemporary life and concerns; occasional innovative fiction if strong enough to command review attention. Particularly interested in fiction with a strong central idea which lends itself to promotion and advertising; novels with exciting and appealing central characters; strong story lines, pace and tension."

General Nonfiction: "Adult nonfiction in all areas. Strong emphasis on contemporary affairs and concerns in fields of human behavior, popular psychology, psychiatry, medicine, science; explorations of new life styles, new fields of knowledge; popular history and biography if of contemporary interest and relevance; social commentary; exposes of all kinds; books celebrating nature; current affairs both domestic and international; military and diplomatic memoirs; philosophy; arts; the rare inspirational work of a general nature. Also how-to's—cookbooks, diet books, etiquette, craft, sewing—if they have strong organizing editorial ideas behind them and good promotional pegs. Particularly appreciate nonfiction books from experts who have writing talent. As an example, Dr. Robert Atkins, an expert on obesity, whose first book was *Dr. Atkins' Diet Revolution—The High Calorie Way to Stay Slim Forever.*

Juveniles: "Fiction and nonfiction of a general nature for young adults; mature tone and innovative ideas."

Reference and Textbooks: "Reference books, foreign language manuals and dictionaries, educational books at college level." Director and Editor, College Dept.: Gordon G. Hill.

MEDICAL EXAMINATION PUBLISHING COMPANY, INC., 65-36 Fresh Meadow Lane, Flushing NY 11365. Royalty schedule is negotiable. Will send catalog on request. Send outlines to Editor. Reports in 1 month. Enclose return postage.
Medical: Medical texts and medical review books; monographs and training material for the medical and paramedical professions.

MELMONT PUBLISHERS, 1224 W. Van Buren St., Chicago IL 60607. Managing Editor: Joan Downing. Enclose return postage with ms.
Juveniles: Publishes easy-to-read nonfiction for early grades.

CHARLES E. MERRILL PUBLISHING CO., a Bell & Howell Co., 1300 Alum Creek Dr., Columbus OH 43216. Publishes hardcover and paperback originals. Payment is on acceptance or on a royalty basis. "Our textbooks generally offer 6% at elementary school level; 8% at secondary school level; 10% to 15% at college level. Books published last year: 192. Send brief outline and sample chapter. Reports in 4 to 6 weeks. Enclose return postage.
Textbooks: Education Division publishes texts, workbooks, instructional tapes, overhead projection transparencies and programmed materials for elementary and high schools in all subject areas (no juvenile stories or novels). The College Division publishes texts and instructional tapes in all college areas, specializing in education, sociology, business and economics, engineering and technology, science, political science, speech and drama, health and physical education, career education. Editor-in-Chief, Educational Division: Ralph Hoyashida; Editor, College Division: John Buterbaugh.

MERRY THOUGHTS, INC., P.O. Box 2, Bedford Hills NY 10507. Editor-in-Chief: Mrs. A. Kahn. Publishes hardcover originals. Offers standard royalty contract. No advance. Send complete ms for fiction. Reports in 6 weeks minimum. Enclose return postage with ms.
Juveniles: "Gift type of editions." Interested in books on "Christmas or the American Revolution." Length: 1,000 to 4,000 words.

JULIAN MESSNER, Division of Simon & Schuster, Inc., 1 W. 39th St., New York NY 10018. Books published last year: 32. Will send catalog on request. Query first

with outline. Reports in 1 month. Enclose return postage with ms.
Juveniles: Publishes nonfiction books for young people. Miss Jo Ann White, Editor of Books for Young People, considers mss of 53,000 to 55,000 words for biographies, nonfiction, and books on careers for junior and senior high. Miss Lee Hoffman, Editor, Books for Boys and Girls, looking for nonfiction for elementary grades, or ages 7 to 12.

MIDWOOD BOOKS, 185 Madison Ave., New York NY 10016. Editor-in-Chief: Karen Williamson. Publishes paperback originals. Payments range from $600 to $1,000. Published 132 titles last year. Submit complete mss with outline. Write for copy of guidelines for writers. Will not consider photocopied submissions. Reports in 3 to 5 weeks. Enclose return postage with ms.
Erotic Fiction: "We are particularly interested in strong, well-thought-out plots and realistic characters. The sex scenes should be well motivated, lengthy, graphic and explicit. No male homosexuality. No fantasy, occult or science fiction sex books. No satire." Length: 55,000 to 60,000 words. Current titles include *Lena Learns Fast* (Hoffer); *Sinful Sisters* (Santagata).

MILITARY MARKETING SERVICES, INC., 2300 S. 9th St., Suite 504, Arlington VA 22204. President: Mrs. Ann Crawford. Publishes originals. "Usually purchase books outright. Royalties are negotiable if outright purchase is not made. Advance is also negotiable." Enclose return postage with ms.
Nonfiction: "Information-type books for military families. Books which show the military family, active or retired, how to save money are needed. Also, books explaining reservist and retiree benefits will be given special consideration. We're looking for more titles which will help make the military family's life easier and more enjoyable." Length: open. A recent title is *Europe on Less Per Day.*

*MIMIR PUBLISHERS, INC., Hilldale State Bank Building, Box 5011, Madison WI 53705. Each book is arranged on a special contract with the author. "Some are subsidy published. Division of costs and returns on the basis of prime and secondary costs. Authors given preference. Minimal advance." Send query letters, outline of book, sample chapters. Reports in 10 days to 3 weeks depending on time of year and nature of subject. Enclose return postage.
Nonfiction: Publishes history, biography, social science, and philosophy books. Specializes in the fields of economics, sociology, journalism, and related studies as political science and social institutions. Also has an interest in any worthy work relating to markets and problems of distribution (e.g., speculation, stock markets, commodity exchanges, cooperation, etc.).

MITCHELL PRESS LIMITED, 1706 W. 1st Ave., Vancouver, B.C., Canada. Editor-in-Chief: Howard T. Mitchell. Publishes hardcover and paperback originals. Standard royalty contract. No advance. Published 6 titles last year. Will send catalog to writer on request. Query first. Enclose return postage.
General Nonfiction: "We specialize in British Columbia history and travel." Recent titles include: *We've Killed Johnny Ussher!* (Rothenburger), the story of the "wild McLeans" and Alex Hare who ran a murderous course in the Nicola Valley and were captured by a settlers' posse.

MODERN WRITERS PRESS, 16 Maple Lane, Denville NJ 07834. Editor: Lee Rousseau. Publishes hardcover and paperback originals. Offers standard 10-12½-15% royalty contract; "usual advance is $2,000, but advance varies, depending on author's reputation and nature of book." Published no books last year. Query first with outline and sample chapters. Will consider photocopied submissions. Reports in 2 weeks. Enclose return postage.
Fiction: "Novels. No pornographic material."

MONTHLY REVIEW PRESS, 116 West 14th St., New York NY 10011. Director: Harry Braverman. Royalty schedule. Books published last year: 46. Current catalog available on request. Send query letter, table of contents and two sample chapters; enclose return postage. Reports in 1 to 3 months.
Economics, History, and Politics: Publishes books on history, economics, political

science, world events. Books should reflect or be compatible with the socialist point of view on world problems.

MOODY PRESS, 820 North LaSalle St., Chicago IL 60610. Editor: Leslie H. Stobbe. Publishes hardcover and paperback originals. Royalty schedule is usually 10% of the retail. No advance. Books published last year: 130. Send query with outline and sample chapters. Reports within 3 months. Enclose return postage.
Religion: Publishes books that are definitely Christian in content. Christian education, Christian living, inspirational, theology, missions and missionaries, pastors' helps. Conservative theological position. Clothbound between 45,000 and 60,000 words.
Fiction: Adult; mostly paperback. Length: 25,000 to 40,000 words.
Juveniles: Fiction; mostly paperback. Length: 25,000 to 40,000 words.

MOREHOUSE-BARLOW COMPANY, 14 East 41st St., New York NY 10017. Editor: E. Allen Kelley. Hardbound and paperback originals and reprints. On royalty basis. "Advance depends entirely on author's reputation and nature of book." Books published last year: 15. Send sample chapter and outline with query. Gives preliminary report in 4 to 6 weeks. Enclose return postage.
Nonfiction: Publishes nonfiction trade and textbooks, in religion and allied fields, for adults and children. Length: 20,000 to 25,000 words and up.

WILLIAM MORROW AND CO, 105 Madison Ave., New York NY 10016. Editor: John C. Willey. Payment is on standard royalty basis. Published 171 titles last year. Query on all books. For nonfiction include outline and three sample chapters. For fiction send 50 pages or completed mss. Address to specific department. Reports in 4 weeks. Enclose return postage.
General: Publishes fiction, nonfiction, history, biography, arts, religion, poetry, how-to books, and cookbooks, all high-quality. Length: 50,000 to 100,000 words. Recent titles include *Harry S. Truman.*
Juveniles: Juvenile Editor: Connie C. Epstein.

MULTIMEDIA/BIOGRAF (including Rudolf Steiner Publications), 100 South Western Highway, Blauvelt NY 10913. Editor: Paul M. Allen. Publishes paperback originals and reprints. "We offer only 5% to 7% royalty; average advance, $300." Published 18 titles last year. Will send a catalog to a writer on request. Query first with outline and sample chapters for nonfiction. Will consider photocopied submissions. Reports on ms accepted for publication in 60 days. Returns rejected material in 3 weeks. Enclose return postage.
Nonfiction: "Spiritual sciences, occult, philosophical, metaphysical, E.S.P. These are for our Steiner books division only. Scholarly and serious nonfiction. How-to-do or make books using our patented format of Biograf Books. Examples: origami, breadbaking, calendar. We prefer not to see any more Tarot or religious books." Dept. Editor, Multimedia Materials and Self-Help: Beatrice Garber; Dept. Editor, Philosophy and Spiritual Sciences: Paul M. Allen.

NASH PUBLISHING CORPORATION, 9255 Sunset Blvd., Los Angeles CA 90069. Editor-in-Chief: Sylvia Cross. Hardcover and paperback originals and reprints. "Contract varies. We have given lower rates to authors of books that were very risky, or authors who were being published for the first time." Books published last year: 75. Send query first to Sylvia Cross for juveniles; to Cynthia Swan for fiction. If query brings positive reply, may send outline and sample chapter. Reports within six to eight weeks. Enclose S.A.S.E. with sample.
General: Publishes mainly nonfiction: how-to, self-help, self-improvement, current issues, controversial subjects. Aim toward broad lay-readership; 60,000 to 80,000 words. Publishes very little fiction. Life assertive themes and controversial subject areas, but no pornography. Recent titles include *The Lovomaniacs* (Barrett); *Contact* (Zunin).

NATIONAL COUNSELOR REPORTS, INC., Task Building, Kerrville TX 78028. Editor: J.N. Ledbetter. Publishes hardcover originals. "$500 advance; royalties negotiable." Query first. Reports in 4 weeks. Enclose S.A.S.E.
Nonfiction: "We are interested in finished self-help, money opportunity, and busi-

ness opportunity with meaty how-to-do-it style and content. Must contain self-help benefits to reader. Must be salable to year-after-year market. Will consider training courses."

NATIONAL TEXTBOOK COMPANY, 8259 Niles Center Rd., Skokie IL 60076. Editorial Director: Leonard I. Fiddle. Pays 6% to 10% royalties. Books published last year: 18. Current catalog available on request. Send sample chapter. Reports in 2 to 3 weeks. Enclose return postage.
Textbooks: Primarily publishers of supplementary texts and readers in the fields of speech, French and Spanish, and music. "As an outgrowth of our speech activities, we are fast getting into what might be termed 'communications,' from an educational point of view. For example, we now have in the works a book on creative or effective writing for high school students. We will undoubtedly be coming out with titles on playwriting, theatrical production, etc. Inasmuch as television and motion picture departments are becoming more and more numerous in our colleges, we would be interested in titles along these lines. The subject of music, as it applies to the classroom, is also one we want to become involved in to a greater degree. As far as our foreign language program is concerned, we are especially interested in children's books written in French or Spanish, which are appropriate for youngsters on the elementary school level." Also wants original stories in Spanish and French for elementary and junior high school students. No length requirements. Recent titles include *Dynamics of Acting; Journalism for Today; Philosophers on Rhetoric.*

NATUREGRAPH PUBLISHERS, 8339 West Dry Creek Rd., Healdsburg CA 95448. Editor-in-Chief: Vinson Brown. Publishes hardcover and paperback originals. Offers 10% royalty contract; 15% after 10,000 copies; no advance. Published 5 titles last year. Will send a catalog to a writer on request. Query first. Reports in "several months." Enclose return postage.
Nature and History: "Our published list consists of books on natural history and observations which serve as guides to identification of seashore and inland plants. For example, wildflowers and moss; creatures such as insects, common wild animals, and birds; inanimate objects such as rocks, minerals, fossils, gems and shells. Additional publications are on the American Indian and his legends, religion, history and customs. Books on hobbies in connection with natural history or Indian culture. Length, 64 minimum, 312 pages maximum. 128 to 160 pages best. Must be factual, generally verified by authoritative person in that field of natural science. Can be narrative or textbook style descriptive for a guide. Can be general to cover a whole field (all the birds of one state, or whole southwest area) or just one species, but emphasis on natural state instead of a captured pet. Indian books with emphasis on rediscovering art, crafts and ways of life of all tribes (for example, clothes worn, type of homes, trails and hunting area). Well-illustrated work with choice of original art, color Kodachromes, good clear photographs or descriptive drawings are vital. Have used historical photos. Books should have appeal to persons who want to learn about natural sciences, Indians or hobbies. Easy-to-understand language; reasonably priced for students of natural sciences. Some of our books are used as a general guide to be used along with more specialized books, or as a supplement to other books, showing a general overall picture. Could use material for American Wildlife Region series, Indian Map Book series, and Ocean Guidebook series. Also, books on pollution and conservation."

NAUTILUS BOOKS, Division of Galloway Corp., 5 Mountain Ave., North Plainfield NJ 07060. Editor: Howard P. Galloway. Publishes hardcover and paperback originals and reprints. Offers "standard advance and royalty arrangement." Published 2 titles last year. Send query. Reports in 6 weeks. Enclose S.A.S.E.
General Fiction and Nonfiction: "Primarily interested in books related to youth work and youth work organizations."

*THE NAYLOR COMPANY, 1015 Culebra, P.O. Box 1838, San Antonio TX 78201. Publisher: Mrs. Joe O. Naylor. Royalty and subsidy contracts. Books published last year: 64. Current catalog available on request. Send completed ms. Reports in 3 to 8 weeks. Enclose return postage with ms.
Americana: Specializes in Western Americana items—history, legend, cookbooks, and poetry.

*NAZARENE PUBLISHING HOUSE, Box 527, Kansas City MO 64141. Trade name: Beacon Hill Press of Kansas City. Editor: J. Fred Parker. Publishes hardcover and paperback originals and reprints, Offers "standard contract (sometimes flat rate purchase). Advance on royalty is paid only on assignments or when book is held over for a year. Some (10%) subsidy publishing." Pays 10% on first 5,000 copies and 12% on subsequent copies "Advance on first 2,000 on assignment only; otherwise paid at the end of each calendar year." Published 50 titles last year. Send complete ms or query "on larger books." Follow Chicago *Manual of Style.* Address all mss to Book Editor. Reports in 2 to 5 months. " Book Committee meets quarterly to select, from the mss which they have been reading in the interim, those which will be published." Enclose S.A.S.E. for return of mss or reply to query.

General Fiction and Juvenile Fiction: "Must have religious content germane to plot not artificially tacked on. At the same time not preachy or moralistic." Publishes 1 adult fiction and 1 juvenile a year. "Currently have backlog of approved mss on hand."

General Nonfiction, Juvenile Biography, Religion and Philosophy, and Textbooks: "Basically religious, but of wide scope from college textbook level to puzzles and juvenile. Doctrinally must conform to the evangelical, Wesleyan tradition. Conservative view of Bible. Personal religious experience. We want the accent on victorious life, definitely upbeat. Social action themes must have spiritual base and motivation. Use both textbook and popular style books, the latter 128 pages and under except in unusual circumstances." Interested in business and professional books on church administration, Sunday school, etc., and church related history and biography. Textbooks are "almost exclusively done on assignment. Send query first." Length: 10,000 to 30,000 words. Current leading titles include *Every Day With the Psalms; A Return to Christian Culture; Contemporary Portraits From the Old Testament; Behold, I Come!*

THOMAS NELSON, INC., 30 E. 42nd St., New York NY 10017. Editor: Gloria Mosesson. Publishes hardcover and paperback originals, reprints, translations, and anthologies. Offers standard royalty contract. Advance varies. Published 40 titles last year. Will send a catalog to a writer on request. Send query with outline and sample chapter. Query letters for juveniles should include description of ms, length, subject matter, age group, and sample of writing. Reports in 2 months. Enclose return postage.

General Nonfiction: "Publishes general nonfiction, history, biography, science, philosophy, the arts. Specialties—religious, antique collectors' books."

Juveniles: "Junior books department publishes fiction and nonfiction for boys and girls 7 through 12 and for teenagers on just about every subject imaginable—treatment, writing, etc., matter most." Length: 15,000 to 50,000 words. "We do not publish juvenile picture books."

NELSON-HALL COMPANY, 325 West Jackson Blvd., Chicago IL 60606. Editor: V. Peter Ferrara. Standard royalty schedule. Rarely offers an advance. Books published last year: 80. Send query accompanied by outline. "Soundness of subject matter and its treatment more important than just 'good writing.'" Reports in about 3 weeks.

Social Sciences, Psychology, and Applied Psychology: Publishes serious works in the behavioral sciences. Also more popular books on practical, applied psychology written by qualified writers; business subjects, employment and personnel, general self-improvement, techniques relating to memory efficiency, retirement, investment, hobbies, etc. Length: 50,000 to 100,000 words.

NEW AMERICAN LIBRARY, (including Mentor Books and Signet Books), 1301 Avenue of the Americas, New York NY 10019. Editor-in-Chief: Elaine Geiger. Publishes paperback originals and reprints. "Pays substantial advances with standard paperback royalties. Requires queries prior to sending mss. Send queries to Edward T. Chase, Editorial Vice President. Reports in about 2 weeks."

General: "Publishes reprint adult fiction, chiefly modern contemporary novels, and lively, topical nonfiction under the Signet Books imprint. Also paperback originals along the same lines." Length: 75,000 to 400,000 words. Current leading titles include *Eleanor and Franklin; The Boys of Summer.*

*NEW IDEA PUBLISHING CO., P.O. Box 1237-EG, Melbourne FL 32935. Editor: Harold Pallatz. Publishes hardcover and paperback originals and reprints. Offers "10% on hardcover, 5% on softcover; specific contracts can go higher or lower, depending upon material. No advance is ever given." About 25% of books are subsidy published. Published 4 titles last year. Query first. Will consider photocopied submissions. Reports in 2 to 4 weeks. "No material will be returned unless S.A.S.E. is attached."

Health: "Natural approaches to good health through nutrition, herbs, vegetarianism, vitamins, unusual medical approaches for specific ailments, particularly from authorities in the field. Any style is acceptable, but it must hold the reader's attention and make for fairly smooth nonintensive (no brain taxation) requirements. Ideas should be in a simple, easygoing pace."

Self-Help and How-To: "Special approaches are of interest, from viewpoint of new products to manufacture, easy things to manufacture, tax approaches for the small business."

Technical: "Relating to television, electronics, space, chemistry, medicine, dentistry."

NOBLE AND NOBLE, PUBLISHERS, INC., 1 Dag Hammarskjold Plaza, New York NY 10017. Editor-in-Chief: Warren Cox. Royalty and advance varies. Books published last year: 46. Prompt initial reply; subsequent replies may take several months. Enclose return postage with ms.

Textbooks: Elementary and secondary textbooks.

NORTH STAR PRESS, P.O. Box 451, St. Cloud MN 56301. Editor: John N. Dwyer. Publishes hardcover originals. "New or unknown authors are offered a flat 10% for first printing. Advance is dependent on amount of funds author spent for art or photos, etc. Accepted authors will get advance only if their other books have been well-received." Published 4 titles last year. Will send a catalog to a writer on request. Query first "with outline or sample chapter in duplicate copy only—no original material on first inquiry." Reports in 2 weeks. Enclose return postage.

Americana: "Subject is middle western Americana; mainly nonfiction of historical interest to an adult. Style can be author's own, provided he can write complete and connected sentences. For out-of-doors, sports, etc., style is casual or folksy. Professional material must not contain professional jargon. We are open to camping specialty books or books on muzzle-loading guns used in middle western frontier—especially gun books which detail the gunmaker or his art by name and location." Recent titles include *Help—A Teacher's Guide to Teaching Religion; Valuable You—Personality Development Through Games.* Dept. Editor, History and Sports: Jim Kain.

Juveniles: "Will read good, adapted historical material for children, especially if well-illustrated for youth."

NORTHLAND PRESS, P.O. Box N, Flagstaff AZ 86001. Editor: James K. Howard. "Query before sending outline, ms, or illustrative material." Enclose return postage.

Americana: "A small organization concentrating on fine books on western Americana, heavily illustrated, and priced, therefore, for the special rather than the general reader."

NORTHWESTERN UNIVERSITY PRESS, Evanston IL 60201. Director: Robert P. Armstrong. Offers 7½-10-12½% royalty contract. No advance. Books published last year: 34. Enclose return postage with ms.

Nonfiction: Scholarly books, chiefly Africana, philosophy, political science, social sciences, literary criticism.

*W. W. NORTON & COMPANY, INC., 55 Fifth Ave., New York NY 10003. Publishes hardcover originals. "Occasionally we offer a variation of the standard book contract, but almost never below the minimum. 10% are subsidy published." Published about 200 titles last year. "We service the general trade market audience and market through bookstores. Special interest, small market books are not for us." Will send catalog to writer on request. Query with resume or outline for nonfiction;

query, outline and several sample chapters for fiction. Reports in 4 weeks. Enclose return postage.

General Fiction and Nonfiction: Material in most areas: Mainstream, biography, economics, history, humor (novels only), psychiatry, music, nature, philosophy, politics, scientific, sociology, sports, hobbies, recreation, textbooks (for college only); travel. No sex or violence. No cookbooks, medical, juvenile or religious books. Length: "If shorter than book length (under 200 pages), it's not for us." Recent titles include *Dragon by the Tail* (Davies); *A Sort of a Saga* (Mauldin); *Power and Innocence* (May).

NOYES DATA CORPORATION (including Noyes Press), Noyes Bldg., Park Ridge NJ 07656. Publishes hardcover originals. Pays 12% domestic; 6% foreign royalties. Advance varies, depending on author's reputation and nature of book. Books published last year: 65. Current catalog available on request. Address mss to Editorial Dept. Query first. Reports in 1 to 2 weeks. Enclose return postage.

Nonfiction: "Art, architecture, archaeology, history, other nonfiction. Material directed to the intelligent adult and the academic market."

Technical: Publishes practical industrial processing science; technical, economic books pertaining to chemistry, chemical engineering, food and biology, primarily those of interest to the business executive; books relating to international finance. Length: 50,000 to 250,000 words.

OCEANA PUBLICATIONS, INC., Dobbs Ferry NY 10522. President: Philip F. Cohen; Managing Editor: William W. Cowan; Legal Editor: Edwin S. Newman; "Docket Series" Editor: Julius Marke; Editor, Reprint Bulletin: Sam P. Williams. Royalty schedule is 10% of list price, regardless of method of sales. No advance. Pays $500 fee for legal and business almanac titles. Books published last year: approximately 50. Send outline and sample chapter. Reports in 60 days. Enclose return postage.

Nonfiction: Publishes nonfiction books with emphasis on law, world affairs, and other selected political, historical and semilegal matters for the professional and layman. Length: 30,000 to 75,000 words. Publishes legal and business almanac titles. Length: about 30,000 words.

OCTOBER HOUSE, INC., 160 Sixth Avenue, New York NY 10013. Royalty schedule: 10% cloth, 5% paper. Published 10 titles last year. Catalog on request. Query David Way. Enclose return postage.

General: Publishes books on music, general trade books, poetry, bilingual anthologies, regional and nonfiction. Recent titles include *The Selected Poems of Jacob Glatstein* and *The Passion of Lizzie Borden* (Whitman).

ODDO PUBLISHING, INC., P.O. Box 68, Beauregard Blvd., Fayetteville GA 30214. Managing Editor: Genevieve Oddo. Publishes hardcover and paperback originals. "Only successfully proven authors are considered for royalty. Scripts from new authors are purchased outright." Published 11 titles last year. Will send a catalog to a writer on request. Send complete ms, typed clearly. Reports in 90 to 120 days. Enclose return postage with ms.

Juveniles and Textbooks: Publishes "language arts, workbooks in math, writing (English), photo phonics, science (space and oceanography), and social studies" for "schools, libraries, and trade." Interested in "children's supplementary readers in the areas of language arts, math, science, social studies, etc. Text runs from 1,500 to 7,500 words. Presently we are searching for mss carrying the positive mental attitude theme—how to improve oneself, without preaching. Americanism is also a subject we are looking for. Who made America great and how? Such material must be different from what is on the market now or we will not be interested. Ecology, space, oceanography, and pollution are subjects we are interested in. Ms must be easy to read, general, and not set to outdated themes. It must lend itself to illustration. No books on domestic animals or grandmother-long-ago stories. No love angle, permissive language, or immoral words or statements." Recent titles include *The Alphabet Zoo* (Laird); *A Delightful Day With Bella Ballet* (Utz).

ODYSSEY PRESS, A Division of The Bobbs-Merrill Company, Inc., 4300 West 62nd St. Indianapolis IN 46268. "No unsolicited mss at this time but queries are acceptable."

J. PHILIP O'HARA, INC., 20 East Huron, Chicago IL 60611. Publishes hardcover and paperback originals and reprints. Royalty schedule. Will send a catalog to a writer on request. Send complete ms. Reports in 4 weeks. Enclose return postage with ms.
Nonfiction and Fiction: Adult books. Adult Editor: Howard Greenfeld.
Poetry: Poetry Editor: John Ashbery.
Juveniles: Originals only. Interested in juvenile nonfiction and fiction. Dept. Editor: Mrs. Paula J. Orellana.

OHARA PUBLICATIONS, INC., 5650 West Washington Blvd., Los Angeles CA 90016. Editor: M. Uyehara. Publishes hardcover and paperback originals, reprints, and translations. Offers standard 10-12½-15% royalty contract; "advance depends on the quality of the book." Published 6 titles last year. Query first with outline and sample chapters. Reports in 2 weeks. Enclose return postage.
Nonfiction and Fiction: "We publish books primarily on the Oriental way of life, such as the Oriental martial arts, philosophy, literature. The only fiction mss we accept are direct translations from the Japanese and Chinese and historical narratives based on history and legend. Our audience is persons with a college education and, naturally, the Oriental." Interested in books on "the history of Japan—particularly immediately preceding World War II until the present. Not scholarly, but for general reader interest. Interested in books on Oriental religions and philosophy, e.g., Buddhism, Confucianism, Taoism; philosophy of Japan and the Orient in general (Bushido). Our main interests are Japan, China, Korea in that order. Most interested in Japanese samurai and other legendary and historical heroes." Recent titles include *Pineapple White* (Shirota); *Wing Chun Kung-Fu* (Lee). Dept. Editor, Nonfiction: Pat Alston.
Juveniles: "Nonfiction only. Would have to deal specifically with the Orient. Primarily interested in nonfiction with illustrations."

OHIO STATE UNIVERSITY PRESS, 2070 Neil Ave., Columbus OH 43210. Director: Weldon A. Kefauver. Payment on royalty basis. Query letter preferred with outline and sample chapters. Reports within two months. Ms held longer with author's permission. Enclose return postage.
Nonfiction: Publishes history, biography, science, philosophy, the arts and general scholarly nonfiction. No length limitations.

OLD TIME BOTTLE PUBLISHING COMPANY, 611 Lancaster Dr., Salem OR 97301. Editors: B.J. Blumenstein and Lynn Blumenstein. Publishes hardcover and paperback originals. Offers standard royalty contract with average $500 advance. Published 3 titles last year. Send outline. Reports in 30 days. Enclose return postage.
Hobbies: "Generally new hobbies and any new approach to old hobbies such as treasure hunting, bottle collecting, and artifact collecting. Audience: general public, all ages. Approach is how to get started. Writing should be condensed, very informative, with simple, flowing manner. Step by step instructions with inspirational matter and purpose contained in forward. Profusely illustrated with photos of high quality and identification of items. Average page count (book) 100 to 200 pages." Current titles include *Remade in America; The Grand Tour of Europe and Asia Within the U.S.A.*

*OPEN COURT PUBLISHING CO., Box 599, LaSalle IL 61301. Editor-in-Chief: Jameson G. Campaigne, Jr. Publishes hard cover and paperback originals and reprints. Offers standard minimum book contract. Usual advance is $1,000, but this varies, depending on author's reputation and nature of book. "Have done some subsidy publishing but only for a scholarly book of exceptional quality and cost." Books marketed through national sales organization and direct mail selling. Will send catalog to writer on request. Query essential. Will consider photocopied submissions. Reports in 6 weeks. Enclose return postage.
General Nonfiction: "While Open Court has a backlist from the 1880's that specializes in science, philosophy and religion, it has branched out in the 1970's to a more

general kind of nonfiction including books on education, politics, art and literary criticism, biography, economics; books for the serious reader. Would like an economic analysis of whether the New Deal liberal ascendancy has been helpful or harmful to the poor (whether government intervention in the economy has been positive or negative as far as the economic fortunes of the poor are concerned). Would like a good political-economic history of the Corn Law Reforms in England and subsequent economic results; good study of textbook publishers versus the problem of our growing illiteracy. Have they helped or retarded the fight against our national reading problem? Poetry, analytical philosophy, X-rays from outer space sapping the vital juices of the human race. Author should write us with his idea and discuss it; we may then either encourage or discourage the ms depending on the quality of the concepts involved." Americana, art, politics, religion, sociology, biography, economics, history. Dept. Editor: Jameson Campaigne, Jr. Juveniles Dept. Editor: Ms. Marianne Carus. Philosophy Dept. Editor: Eugene Freeman. Textbooks Dept. Editor: M. B. Carus. Length in all departments is open. Recent titles include *Hoffer on America* (Koerner); *The Uses of Liberal Education* (Blanchard).

ORBIS BOOKS Maryknoll NY 10545. Editor: Philip Scharper. Publishes hardcover and paperback originals. Offers standard 10-12½-15% royalty contract; "standard advance, $500." Published about 20 titles last year. Query first with outline, sample chapters, and prospectus. Reports in 4 to 6 weeks. Enclose return postage.
Nonfiction: "Christian orientation in the problems of the developing nations. Transcultural understandings, mission theology and documentation." Current titles include *Church and Power in Brazil; Worship and Secular Man.*
Juveniles: "On all age levels, but only with a third world theme."

OREGON STATE UNIVERSITY PRESS, P.O. Box 689, Corvallis OR 97330. Director: J.K. Munford. Hardcover and paperback originals and reprints. "Royalties vary." Published 6 titles last year. Will send a catalog to a writer on request. "Query before submitting ms." Reports in 2 months. Enclose return postage.
General Nonfiction: Wants "well-written mss of regional interest" on Pacific Northwest history, biography, and geography. Also "books on higher education for professional and lay audience."
Technical and Scientific: "Biological science for professional and advanced reader." Also geology and geography.

OUTERBRIDGE & LAZARD, INC., 200 W. 72nd St., New York NY 10023. Editor: Paul DeAngelis. Publishes hardcover and paperback originals and translations. Offers standard royalty contract with $1,500 average advance. Published 15 titles last year. Will send a catalog to a writer on request. Always send outline, plus sample chapter for fiction. Reports in 4 weeks. Enclose return postage with ms.
General: "Trade books with special emphasis on American life—education, music, politics, law, social science. Lay adult and professional audience." Current leading titles include *The Fred Astaire and Ginger Rogers Book* (Croce); *The Sorrow and the Pity.*

OXMOOR HOUSE, (a division of The Progressive Farmer Co.), P.O. Box 2463, Birmingham AL 35202. Director: Les Adams. Editor: Mrs. Betty Ann Jones. Publishes hardcover originals. "Payment on royalty basis or fee." Published 5 titles last year. "Address all inquiries to Les Adams." Send outline and sample chapter. Reports in 10 days. Enclose return postage.
General Nonfiction: "Publishes books of general interest to Southern readers—cookbooks, garden books, interior decorating, architecture, history, travel, etc. Also publishes technical and nontechnical agricultural books." Current leading titles include *Southern Country Cookbook; Party Cookbook; Needlepoint Patterns; Vegetable Gardening.*

PACE & PACE, LTD., Room 1438, 150 Nassau St., New York NY 10038. Editor: Robert Scott Pace II. Publishes hardcover and paperback originals and reprints. "We offer a sliding scale with royalties up to 25%, depending on the number of copies sold. Advances depend on type of material, background of author, and any guaranteed sales." Published 6 titles last year. Will send a catalog to a writer on request. Query first for fiction, poetry, or books on economics. Submit outline and sample chapters for nonfiction, anthologies, reprints. "If available, we would prefer to see the complete book for nonfiction." Will consider photocopied submissions, "but would like to know if other publishers are considering." Reports in 1 month. Enclose return postage.

Textbooks: "On all subjects especially on the college or advanced high school level. Interested in all areas of economics. Pace & Pace Ltd. is owned by Pace College, but is operated as a profit oriented subsidy at the present time, rather than a university press, and would consider wide based type textbooks as well as scholarly works with smaller markets. Most of our titles to date are in the area of business, but we are interested in expanding into all academic areas. We look for books with a fresh approach to learning and which meet the demands of quickly changing curriculums and changing information in every discipline. We are interested in books that are new and fresh in approach by authors who have some market for their product. We will look at books by people who are academically qualified, but who are not now teaching in the subject area they wish to write about. We are trying to use the facilities of Pace College to classroom test all materials before they are put into final published form. We also publish several looseleaf books to meet the rapidly changing demands of accounting and tax courses that change from year to year. Interested in material for a series on well-known modern authors (a kind of critical biography approach to writers of the late nineteenth and twentieth centuries). Also remedial material in all areas of English, science, math, social science, history to meet the requirement of students in programs such as "Seek" and open enrollment in the New York City University and elsewhere." Length: open. Recent titles include *Quantitive Methods in Business Decisionmaking*.

*PACESETTER PRESS (a division of Gulf Publishing Co.), 3301 Allen Pkwy., P.O. Box 2608, Houston TX 77001. Editor-in-Chief: Robert Hudspeth. Publishes hardcover and paperback originals. "Each author's contract considered on an individual basis." 50% subsidy. Submit outline and sample chapters. Enclose return postage.

General Fiction and Nonfiction: "Trade titles of a general or regional interest. This includes corporate histories, personal testimonies, photography and how-to books. Will also consider general interest fiction and nonfiction titles." Recent titles include *Dutch Oven Cookbook* (Ragsdale), for use on camping excursions—particularly for youth groups. *An Oilman's Oilman: The Story of Walter William Lechner*.

PACIFIC BOOKS, PUBLISHERS, P.O. Box 558, Palo Alto CA 94302. Editor: Henry Ponleithner. Royalty schedule varies with book. No advance. Books published last year: 10. Will send catalog on request. Send complete ms. Reports promptly. Enclose return postage with ms.

Nonfiction: General interest, professional, technical and scholarly nonfiction trade books. Specialties include western Americana and Hawaiiana. Recent titles include *The Invisible Core: A Potter's Life and Thoughts* (Wildenhain); *Frontiers of Advertising Theory and Research* (Sargent).

Textbooks and Reference: Publishes text and reference books; high school and college.

PACIFICA HOUSE, INC., P.O. Box 2131, Toluca Lake CA 91602. Submit mss to Paul Wegmann, President. Publishes originals in hardcover and softcover. 10% royalty contract. Advance "negotiable". Published 5 titles last year. Prefers mss with illustrations. Reports in 4 to 6 weeks. Enclose return postage with ms.

Cookbooks: Publishes cookbooks with a minimum 150 recipes. Current titles include *Mother Had a Way With Food*.

MAX PADELL, INC., 830 Broadway, New York NY 10003. Editor: Avram C. Freedberg. Publishes hardcover and paperback originals. "We have always purchased our mss outright (minimum fee, $800). For mss, even when purchased outright, author receives a minimum of 10% of all subsidiary rights sales." Will send a catalog to a writer on request. Submit outline and sample chapters. Will consider photocopied submissions. Reports in 8 weeks. Enclose return postage.

Self-Help and How-To: "Basically a how-to list—how to play the horses and win, how to make lampshades, how to make foreign dolls. We would also consider works for specialty markets. The minimum length is 40,000 words. Preferential treatment is given to mss which are written by experts, or in the case of professional writers, with an expert whose name we can use in promotion. Copy should be aimed at the layman. When ms is approved for publication, camera-ready illustrations and/or permission-free photographs are expected to be furnished and/or paid for by the author. Publisher may pay for illustration; however, author's fee or advance may be affected. We are looking for new titles in the self-defense field, sports, gambling, bicycle and motorcycle repair; leathercraft, patchwork, quiltmaking. Recent titles include *Key to Basic Crocheting; How to Win at Pinochle; ABC Shorthand.*

PAGURIAN PRESS, LTD., 10 Whitney Ave., Toronto 5, Ont., Canada. Editor: Christopher Ondaatje. Publishes hardcover and paperback originals and reprints. "All contracts vary. Usual advance is $500 to $1,500." Published 22 titles last year. Will send a catalog to a writer on request. Send outline and sample chapters for nonfiction or complete ms. Will consider photocopied submissions. Reports in 1 month. Enclose International Reply Coupons for return postage.
General Nonfiction: "General interest subjects, i.e., history, biography, sports, crafts, business and finance, home economics." Current leading titles include *Wilderness Survival; The Pocket Hobby Encyclopedia; Nancy Greene, an Autobiography; Sewing Without Tears; 1001 Ways to Have Fun With Children.*

PALADIN PRESS, Box 1307, Boulder CO 80302. Editor: Robert K. Brown. Publishes originals and reprints. 10% to 15% royalty. No advance. "Length of ms is immaterial and should be submitted to editor. At least 2 sample chapters and outline are required. We submit mss to members of our Advisory Board who are located throughout the world and therefore cannot give definite reply before 2 months." Enclose return postage.
Military: Primarily concerned with publishing works on unconventional warfare and counterinsurgency. "We are interested in mss dealing with guerrilla and unconventional warfare, weapons and espionage. It is desirable that the author have first-hand experience with the subject about which he writes. We are also looking for mss by former Air America or Continental Air Service employees, ex-CIA or intelligence agents, soldiers-of-fortune, etc." Recent titles include *Silencers, Snipers and Assassins; The Quiet Killers* (Truby).

PANETH PRESS LTD., P.O. Box 593, Times Square Station, New York NY 10036. Pays the usual 10% of the published price in accordance with Author's Guild requirements. Advance varies. Insists that query letters with outlines and sample chapters be sent to the Editor. Reports in 2 to 3 months. Enclose return postage and label.
General: Publishes books in every field of human interest—adult fiction, history, biography, science, philosophy, the arts, religion and general nonfiction. Length requirements: 65,000 to 125,000 words.

PANTHEON BOOKS, Random House, Inc., 201 E. 50th St., New York NY 10022. Managing Editor: Andre Schiffrin. Published over 40 books last year. Query first. Send outline and sample chapters for fiction. Enclose return postage with ms.
Fiction: Publishes a few novels each year.
Nonfiction: Books mostly by academic authors. Emphasis on international politics and radical social theory.
Juveniles: Publishes some juveniles.

PANTHER HOUSE, LTD., Box 3552, New York NY 10017. Creative Director: S.O. Battle. Publishes hardcover and paperback originals and reprints. Offers standard 10-12½-15% royalty contract; "no advance." Query first. "Prefer Xerox or carbon copies to avoid loss or damage in mails. We prefer that ms conform to MLA style book." Reports in 1 week to 10 days. Enclose return postage.
General: "Fiction and nonfiction of all kinds including, but not limited to, the area of African and Afro-American literature and problems. We are especially interested in book-length (40,000 words plus) mss of a humorous content. Mss must be of high creative standards, but not necessarily in the tradition of 'literature.' We prefer highly unusual and original treatments which most publishers consider

unpublishable or unsellable. We are not interested in purely erotic material or material which deals solely with violence. Our printings are generally small—a maximum of 5,000 copies."

PAPERBACK LIBRARY, INC., 315 Park Ave. S., New York NY 10010. Editorial Director: Jerry Gross. Publishes paperback reprints and originals. Pays 4% and 6% royalty; half advance on acceptance. Advances of $1,500 and up. "No subsidy publishing, but will do premium publishing." Published 250 titles last year. Send query accompanied by outline and three sample chapters for both fiction and nonfiction. Reports in 1 to 2 months. Enclose return postage.
General: Publishes adult fiction and general nonfiction. Strong contemporary novels on controversial themes. The occult; humor. Send Gothic romances and cookbooks to Mrs. Kathy Malley. Length: 40,000 to 120,000 words; 65,000 to 80,000 for Gothics. Should have commercial, mass-audience appeal.

PARENTS' MAGAZINE PRESS, 52 Vanderbilt Ave., New York NY 10017. Editor: Alvin Tresselt. Address queries to Mrs. Lillian McClintock. Address mss to Alvin Tresselt. Usual advance is $750 minimum, but this varies, depending on author's reputation and nature of book. Reports in 6 weeks. Enclose return postage with ms.
Juvenile: "Picture books, 500 to 1,500 words, for ages 4 to 8. Although there are no vocabulary restrictions, these stories must combine a high interest level with simplicity of style. It is, of course, essential that the material offer excellent possibilities for illustrations." Recent titles include *While the Horses Galloped to London* (Watts) and *Splish, Splash* (Kessler).
Young Adult: Publishes the Background Books series for high school and college trade. Timely subjects.

PARKER PUBLISHING CO., West Nyack NY 10994. Publishes a few paperback originals and reprints. Royalty: 10%; 5% on mail order and book clubs. No advance. Books published last year: 60. Will send catalog on request. Reports in two to four weeks. Enclose return postage with ms.
Nonfiction: General nonfiction. Length: 65,000 words. Representative titles: *Spare-Time Fortune Guide; The Cosmic Power Within You, Healing Beyond Medicine, Telecult Power.*

PARNASSUS PRESS, 2721 Parker St., Berkeley CA 94704. Editor-in-Chief: Herman Schein. Publishes hardcover and paperback originals. Offers standard 10-12½-15% royalty contract, "including subsidiary rights and advance. Suggest query in advance, especially for nonfiction." Enclose return postage.
Fiction and Nonfiction: "Adult and juvenile fiction and nonfiction."

PAULIST/NEWMAN PRESS, 1865 Broadway, New York NY 10023. Publishes hardcover and paperback originals and reprints. Standard trade contract with basic royalty open to negotiation. Advance depends on length of ms. Books published last year: 50. Send outline and sample chapter first to Editorial Department. Reports in 4 weeks. Enclose return postage.
Religion: Catholic and Protestant religious works, both popular and scholarly. Length: 30,000 words and up. "Photo books and multimedia materials, large amounts of contemporary religious education materials." Material tends to avant-garde; no homespun philosophy or pious rehashes. Current titles: *Hope for the Flowers* (Paulus); *Christ Among Us* (Wilhelm); *Free to Be Faithful* (Padavano).

PEACOCK PRESS, 3550 N. Lombard, Franklin Park IL 60131. Editor: Joseph Cooper. Publishes paperback originals and reprints. "Because most of our titles are reprints, we pay an outright fee. However, we would use a standard royalty contract for new works." Published 12 titles last year. Query first with outline and sample chapters. Will consider photocopied submissions. Reports in 2 to 4 weeks. Enclose return postage.
Nonfiction: "Self-improvement, how-to, games (adult and kids'), diets if different. Ours are in 8x10 magazine size and illustrated more than most paperbacks. Copy should be concise, to-the-point, informative, and entertaining." Recent titles in-

clude *How to Solve Your Marital Problems With Hypnotism; 261 Things to Do When There's Nothing to Do* (for preschool ages); *How to Improve Your Personality.*

PEGASUS, (A Division of The Bobbs-Merrill Co., Inc.), 4300 West 62nd Street, Indianapolis IN 46268. "We are not interested in unsolicited mss at this time but queries are acceptable."

*PELICAN PUBLISHING CO., INC., 630 Burmaster St., Gretna LA 70053. Editor-in-Chief: James Calhoun. Publishes hardcover and paperback originals and reprints. Offers standard 10-12½-15% royalty contract. No advance. "Will consider subsidy publishing only if a book meets our standards but is not economically feasible." Published 12 titles last year. Will send a catalog to a writer on request. Query first. Will consider photocopied submissions ; "must state whether it is being simultaneously submitted elsehere." Reports in 6 months. Enclose return postage.
Nonfiction: "General trade books with emphasis on history, biography, and how-to-do-it books; guide books for tourists on states, cities, or areas; picture books on cities, states, and subjects; scholarly monographs suitable for classroom supplementary reading. The subject should be well-researched, absolutely accurate, but not stuffy. A style that will suit the lay reader but also be of value to the professional." Interested in how-to-do-it books on "the role of the South in the political life of contemporary America." Needs material for Pelican Guide series, such as the *Pelican Guide to Plantation Houses in Louisiana.* Publishes books on Americana, biography, book trade, cookbooks, cooking, foods, foreign language, history, medicine and psychiatry, poetry, politics, self-help and how-to, sports, hobbies, recreation, pets, textbooks, travel, and architecture. Length: open. Recent titles include *Make Believes* (Fleming); *Toledo Bend* (Nims).
Poetry: "For our requirements, see Robert Graves' philosophy of poetry. No poetry that has no thought, rhyme, or beauty."

THE PENNSYLVANIA STATE UNIVERSITY PRESS, University Park PA 16802. "There are many variations offered on the standard royalty contract. Some authors are not given a royalty on the first 500 to 1,000 books. Others are given a 5-10-12½-15% contract. Advances are seldom given. Sometimes permission fees are paid and charged as advance royalties." Books published last year: 31. Send outlines and sample chapters to Chris W. Kentera. Reports within 3 months. Enclose return postage.
Nonfiction: Publishes history, biography, science, philosophy, general nonfiction and art history. Length: 40,000 to 100,000 words.

THE PEQUOT PRESS, INC., Old Chester Road, Chester CT 06412. Publications Director: Robert W. Wilkerson. Publishes both hardbound books and several series of paperback monographs; originals and reprints. 7½-10-12½% royalty contract for casebound books; 5-7½% for paperback. Advances individually arranged. Send query with sample chapter. Books published last year: 16. Current catalog available. Reports in two weeks. Enclose return postage.
Nonfiction: Publishes history, biography, special interest, and "how-to" books. Special field is genealogies, stories of towns from beginnings, interesting personalities in history of New England, New England historical sidelights, railways, maritime, New England arts and crafts, including antiques and architecture. Interested in Connecticut history, biography, the arts. "For book trade and elementary and high school markets." Length: open.

PERGAMON PRESS, INC., Maxwell House, Fairview Park, Elmsford NY 10523. Managing Editor: Gerald Deegan. Publishes hardcover and paperback originals. Royalties vary. Published 220 titles last year. Query first with outline and sample chapter. Reports in 1 to 2 months. Enclose return postage.
Scientific and Technical: Critical studies, biography, autobiography, psychology, sociology. Length for science mss: 100,000 words. Recent titles include *The Early Window: The Effects of TV on Children and Youth* (Liebert); *Survival: Black/White* (Halpern); *The Cybernetic Society* (Parkman); *Encounters in Organizational Behavior* (Joyce).
Textbooks: High school and college textbooks.

PFLAUM/STANDARD 38 W. 5th St., Dayton OH 45402. Publishes paperback originals. Published 17 titles last year. Royalties: "5% up; advance from $250 up." Will send a catalog to a writer on request. Send query with outline and sample chapter to John M. Heher. Reports in 4 weeks. Enclose return postage with ms.
General Education and Religion: "Books in the fields of guidance/mental health, personal and social development, cinema, religion (especially Catholic), religious education. Filmstrip scripts and visuals on any of these topics welcomed." A recent title is *The Media Works,* a secondary level text on mass media (Valdes and Crow).

PHAEDRA INC. PUBLISHERS, 49 Park Avenue, New York NY 10016. Editor: Janet Jamar. Publishes hardcover and paperback originals, reprints, translations and anthologies. Offers standard royalty contract. Published 26 titles last year. Will send a catalog to a writer on request. Send complete ms. Reports in 5 weeks. Enclose S.A.S.E. for return of submissions.
General: "Quality fiction, history, plays, biography, poetry, criticism, belles-lettres, science, art, current events."

S.G. PHILLIPS, INC., 305 West 86th St., New York NY 10024. Editor: Sidney Phillips. Publishes hardcover originals. "Graduated royalty schedule varies where artists or collaborators share in preparation." Published 10 titles last year. Will send a catalog to a writer on request. "Query first; no unsolicited mss." Reports in 30 to 60 days.
General and Juvenile: "Fiction and nonfiction for children and young adults. Particular interests—contemporary fiction, mysteries, adventure, science fiction; nonfiction: biography, politics, urban problems, international affairs, anthropology, archaeology, geography. Length depends on age group." Recent titles include *Simple Printing Methods* (Cross); *Child in the Bamboo Grove* (Harris); *Code Name, Valkyrie: Count von Stauffenberg and the Plot to Kill Hitler* (Forman).

PIERIAN PRESS, P.O. Box 1808, Ann Arbor MI 48106. Editor-in-Chief: C. Edward Wall. Publishes hardcover and paperback originals and reprints. Standard royalty contract. No advance. Published 8 titles last year. Books marketed by "extensive advertising in our own journal (*Reference Services Review*)." Will send catalog to writer on request. Query first. "Writer should contact us first with his idea to set up parameters and reach a publication agreement." Reports in 2 weeks. Enclose return postage.
General Nonfiction: Books for libraries, especially reference and referral types; bibliographies, indexes, guides, directories, handbooks, etc. Indexes and reference manuals in multi-media. Current titles include: *Multi-Media Reviews Index* and *Reference Services Review*.

PILOT BOOKS, 347 Fifth Ave., New York NY 10016. Publishes paperback originals. Offers standard royalty contract. Usual advance is $2,500, but this varies, depending on author's reputation and nature of book. Published 12 titles last year. Send outline. Reports in 4 weeks. Enclose return postage.
General Nonfiction, Reference, and Business: "Publishes financial, business, and personal guides, training manuals. Directories and books on moneymaking opportunities." Wants "clear, concise treatment of subject matter." Length: 12,000 to 20,000 words. Current leading titles include *Preparing for Your Retirement Years* (Corrick); *Blueprinting Your Coaching Career* (Fuoss); *A Checklist to Successful Acquisitions* (Harold). General Nonfiction Editor: Samuel Small. Reference Editor: Robert S. Levy.

PINNACLE BOOKS, 275 Madison Ave., New York NY 10016. Editor: Andrew Ettinger. Publishes paperback originals and reprints. "Contracts and terms are standard and competitive." Publishes an average 12 to 14 titles a month. Will send a catalog, brochure, and requirements memo to a writer if S.A.S.E. is enclosed. "Will no longer accept unsolicited mss. Most books are assigned to known writers or developed through established agents. However, an intelligent, literate, and descriptive letter of query will often be given serious consideration." Enclose return postage with query.
General: "Books range from general nonfiction to commercial trade fiction in most popular categories. Pinnacle's list is aimed for wide popular appeal, with fast-

moving, highly compelling escape reading, espionage, historical intrigue and romance, popular sociological issues, topical nonfiction." Recent titles include *The Karamanov Equations* (Goldberg); *The Erotic Fantasies of Women* (Lee), *Jonathan Segal Chicken* (Weinstein and Albrecht); *Inside Linda Lovelace* (Lovelace).

THE PIPER COMPANY, 120 North Main St., Blue Earth MN 56013. Executive Editor: John M. Sullivan. Publishes hardcover and paperback originals. Standard minimum book contract "but we consider each publishing contract as an individual matter and make equitable variances for each author." Send outline or complete ms. Reports in 6 weeks. Enclose return postage with ms.
Sports, History, Politics, and Biography: Current leading titles are *Hand Me That Corkscrew, Bacchus* (a "fun" book on the wine industry); *Almost to the Presidency* (biography of Hubert H. Humphrey and Eugene J. McCarthy).

PITMAN PUBLISHING CORPORATION, 6 East 43 St., New York NY 10017. Managing Editor: Ms. Carol Schneider. Publishes hardcover and paperback originals. Standard minimum book contract. Published 19 titles last year. Write for copy of editorial guidelines. Query first. Will consider photocopied submissions. Reporting time "varies greatly." Enclose return postage.
General Nonfiction: "Economics and environment, consumerism, academia, chess, sociology and various nonfiction works with an aim at an intellectual, not a mass, audience." Length: open. Recent titles include *Those Vintage Years of Radio; Rhodesia: Little White Island* (Parker).
Textbooks: "Pitman is always interested in new educational approaches and unusual teaching aid methods, and our editors work closely with authors to help develop all texts to work in the intended approach of the author; work with a general outlook for a specific business education audience." Business education, distributive and consumer education, data processing, economics, accounting, secretarial sciences. Length: open. Americana, history, politics, reference, sociology. Dept. Editor: Jerome S. Ozer. Art, biography, book trade, cookbooks, cooking and food; law, library, technical and textbooks. Dept. Editor: Ms. Carol Schneider.

PLATT & MUNK, 1055 Bronx River Ave., Bronx NY 10472. Editor: Ken Roberts. Standard minimum book contract "or flat fee anywhere from $2,000 to $6,000 depending on size of book and its complexity." Usual advance is $2,000 to $3,000, but this varies, depending on author's reputation and nature of book. Books published last year: 20. "We take on very few unsolicited mss and generally commission what we publish. All books aimed at Pre-K to Grade 6 market." Send ms or outline and sample chapter to Associate Editor. No art, except sample to Associate Editor. Reports in approximately four weeks. Enclose reture envelope and postage.
Juveniles: Publishes juveniles, including picture books, fiction, nonfiction, biographies and photographic books; ages 2 to 12. Also publishes Peggy Cloth Books, washable cloth books and novelty books for children.

PLAYBOY PRESS, Division of Playboy Enterprises, Inc., 919 Michigan Ave., Chicago IL 60611. New York office: 747 Third Ave., New York NY 10017. Editorial Director (hardcover): Edward Kuhn, Jr.; Editorial Director (softcover): Mary Ann Stuart. Publishes hardcover and paperback originals and reprints. Royalty contract to be negotiated. Published 64 titles last year. Query first. Enclose return postage.
General: Fiction and nonfiction slanted to the adult male who reads *Playboy* magazine. Recent titles include *The Playboy Gourmet* (Mario); *Mafia U.S.A.* (Gage); *Killer, Autobiography of a Mafia Hitman.*

PLENUM PUBLISHING CORP., 227 W. 17th St., New York NY 10011. Imprints: Da Capo Press, Consultants Bureau, IFI/Plenum Data Corporation, Plenum Press. Published 450 titles last year. Query R.N. Ubell. Enclose return postage.
Nonfiction: Books on history, biography, science, the arts.

POCKET BOOKS, 630 Fifth Ave., New York NY 10020. Paperback originals and reprints. Books published last year: 300. Reports in one month. Enclose return postage with ms.
General: History, biography, philosophy, inspirational general nonfiction and

adult fiction (mysteries, science fiction, gothics, westerns). Some biography, reference books, joke books, puzzles. Recent titles include *The Winds of War* (Wouk), *Nemesis* (Christie) *Report to the Commissioner* (Mills).

POET GALLERY PRESS, 224 W. 29th St., New York NY 10001. Editor: E.J. Pavlos. Publishes paperback originals. Offers standard 10-12½-15% royalty contract. Published 5 titles last year. Submit complete ms "only." Enclose return postage with ms.
General: "We are a small specialty house, and we place our emphasis on publishing the works of young Americans currently living in Europe. We are interested in creative writing rather than commercial writing. We publish for writers who live overseas, who write and live, who produce writings from the self. Our books might turn out to be commercial, but that is a secondary consideration. We expect to emphasize poetry; however, our list will be concerned with all aspects of literature: the novel, plays, and cinema, as well as criticism."

POPULAR LIBRARY, INC., 355 Lexington Ave., New York NY 10017. Editor-in-Chief: James A. Bryans. Publishes originals and reprints. Royalty contract to be negotiated. Published 242 titles last year. Query first. Enclose return postage.
General: Publishes adult general fiction and nonfiction.

POPULAR SCIENCE–OUTDOOR LIFE BOOK CO., Division of Popular Science Publishing Co., Inc., 355 Lexington Ave., New York NY 10017. Editor: William B. Sill. "We offer a royalty of so many cents per copy because of the nature of publishing original books for book club use. Details are discussed with each author. Royalties and advance according to size and type of book." Wants outlines, sample chapters, author information. Enclose return postage.
How-To and Self-Help: Publishes books in Popular Science field: home repair and improvement, workshop, hand and power tools, automobile how-to. In the Outdoor Life field: hunting, especially big game and deer; fishing, camping, firearms. Small books to 30,000 words; large books to 150,000 words.

BERN PORTER BOOKS, P.O. Box 209, Belfast ME 04915. Buys on outright purchase, 10% royalty, or combination, depending on value. Send complete ms. Enclose return postage with ms.
Fiction, Nonfiction, and Poetry: Looking for adult fiction and nonfiction including American vanguard expression—poetry, drama, experimental work. Interested only in mss in complete, final version; 40,000 words and up. Highest possible literary quality demanded.

POTOMAC BOOKS INC., P.O. Box 40604, Palisades Sta., Washington DC 20016. Publishes hardcover and paperback originals and reprints. Royalty schedule arranged. Published 6 titles last year. Will send a catalog to a writer on request. Send query with outline first. Reports in 3 weeks. Enclose return postage.
General Nonfiction: Specializes in books about the Washington area. Some general nonfiction books. No fiction, juveniles, science, or philosophy.

CLARKSON N. POTTER, INC., 419 Park Ave., S., New York NY 10016. Editor-in-Chief: Clarkson N. Potter. Senior Editor: Jane West. Production Editor: Donna Greenberg. Royalty schedule varies with each book. Books published last year: 18. Query first. Reports in two weeks. Enclose return postage.
Nonfiction: General trade books, especially Americana, science, art, contemporary scene. "No fiction."

PRAEGER PUBLISHERS, INC., 111 Fourth Ave., New York NY 10003. Editor-in-Chief: Arnold Dolin. Publishes hardcover and paperback originals and reprints. Royalty contract to be negotiated. Published 347 titles last year. Query first. Enclose return postage.
General Nonfiction: Quality general nonfiction books; especially books on history, art, psychology, contemporary problems, social sciences, music.

PRENTICE-HALL, INC., Englewood Cliffs NJ 07632. Editor-in-Chief, Trade Division: John Grayson Kirk. Publishes hardcover and paperback originals and reprints. Offers standard 10-12½-15% royalty contract; advance usually $2,500 to $7,000. "A flat royalty is occasionally offered in the case of highly specialized hard-cover series. A flat royalty is always offered on house paperbacks. Children's book contracts tend to average around 8% to 10% royalty rate. The advance depends on cost of artwork, but does not usually exceed anticipated first year royalties." Published 80 trade titles and 20 children's book titles last year. Will send a catalog to a writer on request. Submit outlines and sample chapters for nonfiction; submit complete ms for fiction. Will consider photocopied submissions. "Always keep 1 or more copies on hand in case original submission is lost in the mail." Reports in 4 to 6 weeks on trade books; reports in 4 to 8 weeks on juveniles. Enclose return postage with ms.

General: "All types of fiction and trade nonfiction, save poetry, drama, and westerns. Average acceptable length: 80,000 words. The writer should submit his work professionally and be the subject of a first-class book, provided the author were first class. The author should be prepared to participate to the extent required in the books promotion." Publishes adult trade mainstream fiction, Americana, art, biography, business, cookbooks, history, humor, medicine and psychiatry, music, nature, philosophy, politics, reference, religion, science, self-help and how-to, sports, hobbies and recreation. Length: 80,000 to 90,000 words. Recent titles include *The Presidential Character* (Barber); *The Peking Incident* (Acheson).

Juveniles: "Contemporary older fiction for ages 10 and up; magic books up to age 12; joke books up to age 12; puzzle books up to age 12; high interest, low reading level fiction; nonfiction picture books for ages 5 to 8; biography, natural science; science project books, up to age 12. Style, outlook, and structure requirements vary with each ms. They are as much an integral part of the book as the subject matter itself. In general, writers should make their material as interesting, alive, and simple as possible." May need material for "possibly a line of vocational career books: auto mechanic, etc. There is still a great need for contemporary books on minority groups such as Indians and Mexican Americans, fiction and nonfiction. If a book is really good, it can usually survive the fact that the subject has been worked over. However, at this point there seems to be an excessive number of ecology-protest books on the market. There does seem to be room, though, for constructive ecology books that are city- and urban-oriented. Because children's books are so expensive to produce and therefore expensive to buy, the trade market is limited. Libraries are the primary market. At this point, they seem to be showing a decided preference for books in which the child can participate—instructive books, involving books." Length: 500 to 750 words and pictures (for picture books); 25,000 to 30,000 words for teenage novels. Senior Editor, Juvenile Books: Kathryn F. Ernst.

THE PRESS OF CASE WESTERN RESERVE UNIVERSITY, Frank Adgate Quail Building, Cleveland OH 44106. Director: William R. Crawford. Standard minimum book contract. No advance. Books published last year: 25. Query first. Reports in 3 months. Enclose return postage.
Scholarly: Publishes work resulting from scholarly research only; not a general freelance market. Mostly history, biography, some science, philosophy, the arts, religion and general nonfiction (political science, sociology, English criticism, foreign languages and literature, and law). Minimum length: 40,000 words.

PROFIT PRESS, INC., 400 East 89th St., New York NY 10028. President: Julian Handler. Offers standard 10-12½-15% royalty contract. Published 2 titles last year. Send query with outline. Reports in two weeks. Enclose return postage.
Business: Publishes books on marketing, advertising and merchandising. Expanding into nonfiction for specialized reader interests; also interested in business books; will outline special needs to freelance writers interested in creating books filling these requirements. No length requirement.

PRUETT PUBLISHING CO., P.O. Box 1560, Boulder CO 80302. Publishes hardcover and paperback originals. "No advance on royalties. 10-12½-15% based on price received by us, rather than on retail price." Published 12 titles last year. Will send a catalog to a writer on request. Send query. Use Chicago Manual Style. Reports in 30 to 60 days. Enclose S.A.S.E. for return of submissions.
General Nonfiction: "Books on the history and development of the American West; railroad books; books slanted toward such outdoor activities in the Rocky Moun-

tain states, such as climbing, hiking, camping, etc. No fiction." Dept. Editor: Gerald Keenan.
Textbooks: "Specialized textbooks and material aimed at the slow learner, as well as el-hi and college textbooks." Production Editor: Nikki Debrouwer. Promotion Director: Natalie Noll.

PSI PRESS, 8131 Manchester, St. Louis MO 63144. Editor: Edward T. Wright. Publishes hardcover originals "and notebooks." Offers standard 10-12½-15% royalty contract; "no advance." Published 4 titles last year. Will send a catalog to a writer on request. Submit outline and sample chapters. Will consider photocopied submissions. Reports in 2 weeks. Enclose return postage.
Nonfiction: "We publish books for municipal officials and other nonfiction books. Approach is entirely up to author. We are always looking for ways to serve municipal officials and the public. Through our association with Practical Seminar Institute, we reach municipal officials directly." Publishes books on economics, humor, law, politics, self-help and how-to, sociology, textbooks, and general nonfiction. Recent titles include *Citizens Requests and Meeting File.*

G.P. PUTNAM'S SONS, 200 Madison Ave., New York NY 10016. Editor-in-Chief: William Targ. Publishes hardcover and paperback originals. Payment is on standard royalty basis. Books published last year: 181. Well-known authors may submit outline and sample chapter. Lesser known authors should submit at least half the book for inspection. Reports in 2 to 4 weeks. Enclose return postage with ms.
Fiction: Publishes novels, 50,000 words and up, of all types.
Nonfiction: Nonfiction in history, biography, exploration, etc.
Juveniles: Juvenile fiction and nonfiction. Dept. Editor: Thomas MacPherson.

THE PYNE PRESS, 92A Nassau St., Princeton NJ 08540. Editor: Lawrence Grow. Publishes hardcover originals and hardcover and paperback reprints. Offers standard 10-12½-15% royalty contract; "on heavily illustrated books involving particularly heavy costs, we start at 8%." Published 11 titles last year. "We market quite heavily through direct mail promotion." Will send a catalog to a writer on request. Query first. "We would prefer to receive an outline of a book, and no more than 2 or 3 sample chapters. We will then advise the author as to our interest and possible terms of publication. Sample illustrations are also appreciated, as is information on the writer's background, credentials, etc." Will consider photocopied submissions. Reports in 4 to 6 weeks. Enclose return postage.
The Arts and History: "Books in the fields of social history, architecture and antiques. Great emphasis is given to books having an American theme or subject. Approximately one-quarter of the titles published each year originate within the house and are assembled by members of the staff. All Pyne Press books are illustrated editions, and a small number make extensive use of color photos. Although not a university press, our titles, at best, match their scholarly counterparts in terms of research and authoritativeness."

PYRAMID COMMUNICATIONS, INC. (formerly Pyramid Books), 919 Third Ave., New York NY 10022. Vice President/Associate Publisher: Norman Goldfind. Publishes hardcover and paperback originals and reprints. "We offer royalties (based on the paperback cover price) ranging from 4% to 8% (with rare exceptions over this amount). Advances range from $1,000/$1,500 on up." Published 300 titles last year. "Primarily a mass market, paperback house. We do have a hardcover line. However, it is reserved for selected titles." Will send catalog to writer on request. Query first for nonfiction. Send outline and sample chapter for fiction. Reports on accepted material within 8 weeks. Returns rejected material in 4 weeks. Enclose return postage.
General Nonfiction and Fiction: "Publishes books in all the traditional categories, i.e., mystery, suspense, adventure, science fiction, gothics, romance, historical; biographies, autobiographies. We do not publish poetry as a rule. The prime exception to this would be in the religious and inspirational categories. It should be noted with special emphasis that Pyramid is the leading paperback publisher in the health, nutrition, religious and inspirational categories. Books of this sort should be directed to Jean-Louis Brindamour, Director of Special Projects. We have recently launched

The Aren Books, a line of higher priced, quality titles primarily oriented toward the college/education market, but with definite book store appeal. For the present, we are looking for books in the social sciences: psychology, human behavior, etc." Mainstream, cookbooks, history, humor, juveniles, psychiatry, politics, reference, self-help and how-to. Length: 60,000 to 200,000 words. Representative titles include *King in Hell* (Balin); *Pieces of a Hero* (Overgard); *Weep No More My Lady* (Deans/Pinchot); *Acupuncture* (Duke).

QUADRANGLE/THE NEW YORK TIMES BOOK CO., a subsidiary of the New York Times Co., 330 Madison Ave., New York NY 10017. Publishes hardcover and paperback originals and reprints. Royalty contract to be negotiated. Published 80 titles last year. Query first. Enclose return postage.
Nonfiction: "We are interested in generally serious nonfiction for the intelligent lay audience." Special emphasis on current affairs and information books, by recognized authorities.

RAND McNALLY, P.O. Box 7600, Chicago IL 60680. Trade Division and Education Division at this address. Variable royalty and advance schedule. Payment on royalty basis or outright, except for mass market books which are outright. Books published last year: 200. Adult mss should be sent to Steven P. Sutton, Editor, Adult Books, Trade Division, but he should first be queried on the subjects of Americana, natural history, personal adventure, exploration and travel. Contracts on nonfiction are sometimes offered on the basis of an outline and sample chapter. Query Executive Editor, Education Division, for books of an educational nature. Reports in 6 to 8 weeks. Enclose return postage.
General Nonfiction: Publishes general nonfiction including travel, geography, adventure; all for the general reader.
Juveniles: Mass market books (Elf and Start-Right Elf). Picture book scripts, six years and under. Realistic stories, science, fantasy; not to exceed 600 words and must present varied illustration possibilities. Editor: Roselyn Berger. Trade Books: Picture books for ages 3 to 8; fiction and nonfiction, ages 8 to 12; special interest books (no fiction) for young adults. Send picture book manuscripts for review. Query on longer mss. Editor: Dorothy Haas.
Textbooks: Education Division publishes texts, maps and related material for elementary, high schools and colleges in restricted fields.

RANDOM HOUSE, INC., 201 East 50th St., New York NY 10022. Also publishes Vintage Books. Editor-in-Chief: James H. Silberman. Publishes hardcover and paperback originals and reprints. Payment as per standard minimum book contracts. Send complete ms. Enclose return postage with ms.
Fiction and Nonfiction: Publishes fiction and nonfiction of the highest standards. Not interested in circulating library material.
Poetry: Some poetry volumes.
Juveniles: Editor-in-Chief: Walter Retan. Publishes a broad range of fiction and nonfiction for young readers, including Beginner Books, Step-up Books, Gateway Books, Landmark Books. Particularly interested in high-quality fiction for children.

RED DUST, INC., 218 East 81st St., New York NY 10028. Editor: Joanna Gunderson. Publishes hardcover and paperback originals and translations. Also publishes recordings. Books printed either simultaneously in hard and paper covers or in hardcover alone, in editions of 1,500 to 2,500. The author generally receives $300 on the signing of the contract, either outright (with 30% of the profits after the publisher's costs have been met) or as an advance against royalties (using the regular royalty schedule). Books published last year: 4. Current catalog available on request. Query with sample chapter. Reports within a month. Enclose return postage.
Fiction: Novels and short stories.
Nonfiction and Poetry: Scholarly, art, art history, film and poetry (in book or record form). Specializes in quality work by new writers.

REGENTS PUBLISHING COMPANY, INC., Two Park Ave., New York NY 10016. Pays 10% to 15% royalty based on net sales. Usual advance is $500, but this varies, depending on author's reputation and nature of book. Books published last

year: 46. Prefers queries, outlines, sample chapters. Reports in 3 to 4 weeks. Enclose return postage.
Textbooks: Publishes foreign language texts, multi-media packages, English books for the foreign-born. Dept. Editors: Jacqueline Flamm. Editor of English as a Second Language Publications; Argentina Palacios, Editor of Foreign Languages.

HENRY REGNERY CO., 114 W. Illinois Chicago IL 60610. Vice President, Editorial: Dominick Abel. Publishes hardcover and paperback originals, paperback reprints; juveniles. Offers standard 10-12½-15% royalty contract. Advance varies. Books published last year: 90. Query first with outline and sample chapters. Will consider photocopied submissions. Reports in 1 to 3 weeks. Enclose return postage.
General Nonfiction: Publishes general nonfiction; books on crafts, hobbies, sports, biography, entertainment, automotive repair, Americana, business, cookbooks, cooking, foods, history, medicine and psychiatry, nature, multimedia material, politics, self-help and how-to; adult education and text preparation materials. Length: open.

FLEMING H. REVELL COMPANY, Old Tappan NJ 07675. Editor-in-Chief: Dr. Frank S. Mead. Payment usually on royalty basis. Books published last year: 54. Reports in a month to six weeks. Enclose return postage with ms.
Religion: Publishers of inspirational and religious books. Also books related to Sunday school and church work. Occasional biography and more general books that might appeal to the religious market. Length: usually 40,000 to 60,000 words.

THE RIO GRANDE PRESS, INC., La Casa Escuela, Glorieta NM 87535. President: Robert B. McCoy. Standard royalty schedule; advance negotiable. Books published last year: 12. Current catalog available on request. Send query accompanied by outline and sample chapter. Address mss to Editor-in-Chief. Reports in two weeks. Enclose return postage.
History: Interested in American historical subjects only; Americana specializing in the Southwest. Wants authentic source material; sources must be cited. Length: minimum 35,000 words; prefers 50,000 words and up. Current titles: *Unknown Mexico; Incidents of Travel in Yucatan.*

THE WARD RITCHIE PRESS, 3044 Riverside Dr., Los Angeles CA 90039. Editor: Russ Leadabrand. Offers standard 10-12½-15% royalty contract. Advance varies, depending on author's reputation and size of book. Published 30 titles last year. Will send a catalog to a writer on request. Query first and submit outline. "Submit complete ms only after query." Enclose return postage.
Cookbooks: "Original, menu-tested, and carefully thought-out cookbooks. Distinctive cookbooks; only unique mss will be considered. They must have a special angle.
Juveniles: "Very limited interest; must be all ages and most unusual."
Travel: "Strong interest in short Western travel/guidebooks. Likes moody, factual, fresh, imaginative, journalistic approach in expanding line of travel books." Recent title is *Great Bike Tours in Northern California* (Ross).

RONALD PRESS, 79 Madison Ave., New York NY 10016. Publishes hardcover originals. Royalty contract to be negotiated. Published 35 titles last year. Query first. Enclose return postage.
Reference and Textbooks: Publishes college textbooks. Also publishes encyclopedias and reference books.

RICHARDS ROSEN PRESS, 29 E. 21st St., New York NY 10010. Editor: Ruth C. Rosen. Publishes hardcover originals. "Each project has a different royalty setup." Books published last year: 48. Wants queries with outline and sample chapter. Reports within three weeks. Include S.A.S.E.
Nonfiction: "Our books are geared to the young adult audience whom we reach via school and public libraries. Most of the books we publish are related to guidance-career and personal adjustment." Preferred length: 40,000 words. Representative title: *The Theatre Student and Scenery.*

SAYRE ROSS, INC. (formerly Lion Books), 461 Park Ave., South, New York NY 10016. Publishes hardcover and paperback originals. "No royalty. $500 to $750 to $3,000 straight on acceptance." Published 30 books last year. Will send catalog to writer on request. Will consider photocopied submissions. Query first with outline and sample chapters. Reports on material accepted for publication in 8 weeks. Returns rejected material in 1 week. Enclose return postage.
Nonfiction: "Style is less important than interesting facts with good research." Americana, art, cookbooks, nature, religious, self-help and how-to; sports (preferably specific teams), hobbies, recreation and pets. Length: 30,000 to 50,000 words. Recent titles include *Soccer: The Game and How to Play It* (Rosenthal); *Super Hoop—Basketball All-Stars* (Liss); *Ins and Outs of Gardening* (Fenten).
Juveniles: Mysteries and suspense for ages 8 to 12.

ROUTLEDGE & KEGAN PAUL, LTD., 9 Park St., Boston MA 02108. Editorial Director: Brian Southam. Publishes hardcover and paperback originals and reprints. Offers standard 10-12½-15% royalty contract "on clothbound editions, if the books are not part of a series"; usual advance is $250 to $1,000. Published over 200 titles last year. Will send a catalog to a writer on request. Query first with outline and sample chapters. Submit complete ms "only after going through outline and sample chapters step." Returns rejected material in 1 to 2 months. Reports on ms accepted for publication in 1 to 6 months. Enclose return postage.
Nonfiction: "Academic, reference, and scholarly levels: English and European literary criticism, drama and theater, social sciences, philosophy and logic, psychology, parapsychology, oriental religions, mysticism, history, political science, education. Our books generally form a reputable series under the general editorship of distinguished academics in their fields. The approach should be similar to the styles adopted by Cambridge University Press, Harvard University Press, and others." Interested in material for Routledge Author Guides, the International Library of Sociology, Authors and Critics series, Birth of Modern Britain series, International Library of Social Policy, and the International Library of the Philosophy of Education. Dept. Editors: Norman Franklin, Chairman (sociology, philosophy, politics, history, economics); Brian Southam (education, literature). Length: 30,000 to 250,000 words. Recent titles include *The Rosicrucian Enlightenment* (Yates); *The New Criminology* (Taylor/Walton/Young).

THOMAS J. ROWEN BOOKLET SERVICE, 986 Camino Drive, Santa Clara CA 95050. Editor: Tom Rowen. Publishes paperback originals. "We pay 40% for each booklet sold. No advance. Our books sell for $1.50, but 25¢ comes off for mailing and handling. We pay 40¢ per booklet." Published 3 booklets last year. Will send catalog to writer on request. Query first. Will consider photocopied submissions. Reports in 1 month. Enclose return postage.
General Nonfiction: "We publish booklets on how to do different skills involved in sports; travel, history and other nonfiction subjects. The sports book are done in interviews with coaches, athletes involved in the sport. The travel books should tell location, what to do and what to see and go into history of the area. Same with the historical booklets. Writers should make the booklet informative and the style simple. Main market is involved with libraries in high schools, colleges and city libraries. Writers shouldn't write too high for audience but should keep it on average level. We are receptive to any new series that writers will send to us. We would like to get into home repairs, travel and historical places. We don't use pictures but need good description of the processes involved in carrying out the different skill or technique." Recent titles include *Let the Experts Speak on Baseball* (interviews with leading high school and college coaches); *Let the Experts Speak on Football*; *Tips From the Coaches on Basketball.* Length: approximately 10,000 words.

ROY PUBLISHERS, INC., 30 East 74th St., New York NY 10021. Editor: Mrs. Hanna Kister. Books published last year: 12. Query first. Unsolicited mss refused. Enclose return postage.
General: Publishes general fiction and nonfiction. "Standard book length." Representative titles: *Elizabeth, Queen and Woman; A Crash in Time; The Story of Ghengis Khan.*
Juveniles: "Standard book length."

RUTGERS UNIVERSITY PRESS, 30 College Ave., New Brunswick NJ 08901. Pays approximately 10% royalty on most books. Books published last year: 30. Catalog on request. Prefers queries. Final decision depends on time required to secure competent professional reading reports. Enclose return postage.
Nonfiction: Books with a New Jersey or regional aspect. Also scholarly books on history, science, biographies, philosophy, and the arts. Regional nonfiction must deal with mid-Atlantic region with emphasis on New Jersey. Length: 80,000 words and up. Recent titles include *Anne Royall's U.S.A.* (James); *Manner of Speaking* (Ciardi).

RUTLEDGE BOOKS, INC., 17 East 45th St., New York NY 10017. Editor: Doris M. Townsend; Creative Director: John T. Sammis. Hardcover and paperback originals. Royalty schedule varies. "Each book is negotiated individually." Advance varies. Books published last year: 38. Send query accompanied by outline and sample chapter. Reports in 3 to 4 weeks. Enclose return postage.
General Nonfiction: Publishes general nonfiction; science; biography; history; sports. Length: open. Recent titles include *The Gladiators; Golf for Women; American Revolution: Mirror of a People.*
Cookbooks and Self-Help: Cookbooks and general do-it-yourself books of any length. A recent title is *Great Classic Recipes of Europe.*

ST. MARTIN'S PRESS, 175 Fifth Ave., New York NY 10010. Books published last year: 20 to 30 original works; 200 to 300 foreign-originated works. Query Editorial Secretary. Reports promptly. Enclose return postage.
General: Publishes general fiction and nonfiction; major interst in adult nonfiction, history, political science, popular science, biography, music and musicians, archaeology, gardening, boats and boating, scholarly, technical reference, etc. St. Martin's list is primarily American, but encompasses the facilities of Macmillan, Ltd., London, Australia, and India.
Juveniles: Major interest in juveniles.
Textbooks: High school and college textbooks.

ACHILLE J. ST. ONGE PUBLISHER, 7 Arden Rd., Worcester MA 01606. Pays flat fee ($300 to $500) or 10% royalty with no advance. Prefers that queries with outlines or sample chapters be sent to Achille J. St. Onge. Include return postage with queries and outlines. Reports in one week.
History and Biography: History and biography books. Also miniature books. Length: approximately 3,000 words.

ST. WILLIBRORD'S PRESS, Box 528, Zuni NM 87327. Editor: Rev. Karl Pruter. Publishes paperback originals and reprints. Offers 5% royalty contract. Published 20 titles last year. Will send a catalog to a writer on request. Always send complete ms. Reports in 3 weeks. Enclose return postage with ms.
General Nonfiction: "We are in the market for ms on any phase of old Catholicism. We are also interested in material of a more general Catholic interest."
Religion and Philosophy, History and Biography: "Wanted: studies on the various free Catholic churches around the world." Also wants "books and pamphlets on the history of the old Catholic movement and accounts of the lives of old Catholic leaders. Any length."

HOWARD W. SAMS & CO., INC., 4300 W. 62nd St., Indianapolis IN 46268. Manager, Book Division: C.P. Oliphant. Payment depends on quantity, quality, salability. Offers both royalty arrangements or outright purchase. Prefers queries, outlines, and sample chapters. Usually reports within 30 days. Enclose return postage.
Technical, Scientific, and How-To: "Publishes technical and scientific books for the electronics industry; Audel books for the homeowner, craftsman, and handyman; and books for the amateur radio field."
Textbooks: "Textbooks for industrial arts, technical, and vocational education."

SANDLAPPER PRESS, INC., P.O. Box 1668, Columbia SC 29202. Editorial Vice President: Delmar L. Roberts. Publishes hardcover and paperback originals and reprints. Offers standard 10-12½-15% royalty contract; "advances are presently low

($300 to $500) and limited chiefly to published authors." Published 8 titles last year. Will send a catalog to a writer on request. Query first "on all submissions, including a broad outline of the material and the approach. Submit outline and sample chapters as requested, following query. The editor may consider samples on an unfinished ms. Submit complete ms only on the request of the editor." Will consider photocopied submissions "if unavoidable." Reports in 2 to 3 months. Enclose return postage .

Fiction: "Will consider adult fiction only if of exceptional quality and interest to a regional audience."

Nonfiction: "In general, a Southern regional emphasis on all books—presently concentrating on subject matter close to home (the two Carolinas and Georgia), but open to mss with broader scope (either wide regional or general trade interest). The majority of our books are nonfiction, including Americana, history-related books, cookbooks, hobby and collector interests. Although we are regional publishers, we are not interested in books with such limited subject appeal that marketing limitations are severe. No scholarly approaches." A recent title is *The Green Dragoon: The Lives of Banastre Tarleton and Mary Robinson* (Bass).

Juveniles: "In juvenile nonfiction, presently concentrating on biographies of well-known Southerners, but open to other approaches. The age level and approaches may vary for the biography series. Interested in juvenile fiction with a strong regional tie-in of some sort. We're interested in publishing ghost stories, natural history and nature study, ecology, folklore, sports, all within regional limitations." A recent title is *Turning the World Upside Down: The Story of Sarah and Angelina Grimke* (Willimon), a juvenile biography of the daughters of a prominent Charleston family.

PORTER SARGENT PUBLISHER, 11 Beacon St., Boston MA 02108. Publishes hardcover and paperback originals, reprints, translations, and anthologies. "Each contract is dealt with on an individual basis with the author." Published 5 titles last year. Will send a catalog to a writer on request. Send query with outline and sample chapter or complete ms. "It is helpful if label indicates it is a new, unsolicited ms, but it is not necessary." Enclose return postage.

General Nonfiction, Reference, Philosophy, and Textbooks: "Handbook Series and Special Education Series offer standard, definitive reference works in private education and writings and texts in special education. The Extending Horizons Series is an outspoken, unconventional series which presents topics of importance in contemporary affairs, viewpoints rarely offered to the reading public, methods and modes of social change, and the framework of alternative structures for the expansion of human awareness and well-being." Contact F. Porter Sargent. Current leading title: *The Seventies: the Politics of Nonviolent Action.*

SAUCERIAN PRESS, INC., P.O. Box 2228, Clarksburg WV 26301. Pays standard book royalty rates. No advance. Books published last year: 5. Current catalog available on request. Send query to Gray Barker. Reports in 30 days. Enclose return postage.

Nonfiction: Publishes books about unidentified flying objects; actual sightings of flying saucers; theories about flying saucers, etc. Must be true experiences. Books are of a limited circulation and are designed for a specialized audience which enjoys reading about and collecting information on flying saucers. Length: open. Representative titles: *The Subterranean World* (Beckley); *Your Part in the Great Health Plan* (Michael X).

SCHENKMAN PUBLISHING CO., INC., 3 Revere St., Cambridge MA 02138. Editor: Alfred S. Schenkman. Publishes hardcover and paperback originals and reprints. "Sliding scale for royalties; all cases evaluated individually. Generally no advance, or small advance (determined individually)." Published 50 titles last year. Will send a catalog to a writer on request. Reports in 4 weeks. Enclose return postage with ms.

Social Sciences: Books on "sociology, anthropology, political science, history, and philosophy." Length: Open. Recent titles include *Republic or Empire (American Resistance to the Philippine War); Out of Discontent.*

SCHMITT, HALL & McCREARY CO., Book Division, 110 N. 5th St., Minneapolis MN 55403. Editor: Rosemary J. Letofsky. Publishes hardcover originals. Royalty contract varies. Usual advance is $150 to $300, but this varies, depending on author's reputation and nature of book. Published 8 titles last year. Query first with outline and sample chapters for nonfiction. Submit complete ms for fiction. Returns rejected material in 2 months. Reports on material accepted for publication in 4 months. Will consider photocopied submissions. Enclose return postage.

Juveniles: Children's books, preschool through junior high; school library and curriculum oriented. Craft hobby books, special subject fiction, picture books. "We have a hobby/craft series for early elementary grades that stress very simple instructions, heavily illustrated for high interest. Our first list in this series included a cookbook and a book for young, beginning stamp collectors. We're still in the planning stages for specific series and are open for suggestions." Length: open. "We do *not* want short, short moralistic picture book formats, romantic novels, topical subjects that will be passe within the year." Recent titles include *A Merry Christmas to You and a Happy Chanukah* (about a young Jewish boy who feels out of place in his new classroom as Christmas approaches).

SCHOLASTIC BOOK SERVICES, 50 West 44th St., New York NY 10036. Includes Four Winds Press, See-Saw Book Club, Teen Age Book Club, Lucky Book Club, Campus Book Club, Arrow Book Club and Citation Press. Scholastic's standard contract for paperback rights provides for an advance against royalties which ranges, depending on the book's market potential, upward from $500. Paperback royalties start at 4% of the selling price. Scholastic's contracts are often made for both hard and softcover publications. Hardcover royalties begin at 10%. Address mss and inquiries to Mrs. Norma R. Ainsworth, Editor of Manuscript Department. Enclose return postage.

Juveniles: See-Saw Book Club for grades kindergarten and first needs science picture books. Lucky Book Club for grades second and third interested in science, mystery, adventure. Arrow Book Club for fourth, fifth and sixth grade readers wants science, biography and mystery. The elementary clubs also looking for authors interested in writing books on Negro history or Negro contributions in general. Also fiction with an honest minority group point of view or with legitimate minority group characters. Length: A minimum of 32 pages for a picture book with a few words on each page; middle grade books should be about 30,000 words.

Teen and Young Adult: Scope/Action Books needs fiction of 8,000 to 12,000 words written for secondary school students who read at second to fourth grade level. No writing down. Settings and characters with which average teens can identify. Emphasis on action, as the title suggests. Teen Age Book Club for grades 7-9 needs humor (fiction and nonfiction) and nonfiction on pop music, cars, hot-rodding, movie and TV personalities, beauty tips, teen grooming, pro sports. Fiction needed about adolescent concerns of school, friends, family, dating; also mystery and suspense novels. Campus Book Club for grades 10-12 needs humor, superior romances for older girls, nonfiction about the contemporary scene, suspense novels, fiction and nonfiction about adolescent problems, action-filled nonfiction for boys about man's efforts to survive. All these should be written on fairly adult level. Books for young adult readers should be limited to 60,000 words; maximum 100,000 words or more for a full-length adult book.

Science: Editorial requirements for science mss: nonfiction, curriculum oriented, on the juvenile or young adult level, suitable for supplementary reading or use in class as project material. Mss should deal with research and involve the work of scientists today. Style should be lively, colorful, informative; not textbookish.

Education: Citation Press focuses on trends, innovations and new programs at all levels of education for teachers, administrators, and college students in teacher education.

SCOTT, FORESMAN AND COMPANY, 1900 E. Lake Ave., Glenview IL 60025. Senior Vice-President, Editorial: Landon H. Risteen (elementary and high school); Vice President and General Manager, College Division: David Halfen. Books published last year: 300. Enclose return postage with ms.

Textbooks: Publishes textbooks and related instructional material in most of the basic subject fields.

CHARLES SCRIBNER'S SONS, 597 Fifth Ave., New York NY 10017. Editor-in-Chief: Burroughs Mitchell. Publishes hardcover originals and hardcover and paperback reprints. "Our contract terms, royalties and advances vary, depending on the nature of the project." Published 300 titles last year. Will send a catalog to a writer on request. Query first for nonfiction (juvenile and adult), adult fiction, and poetry; complete ms preferred for juvenile fiction, "but will consider partial ms and outline." Will consider photocopied submissions. Reports in 1 to 2 months on ms accepted for publication. Returns rejected adult material in 4 to 6 weeks; returns rejected juveniles in 3 to 4 weeks. Enclose return postage.
General: Publishes adult fiction and nonfiction, poetry, practical books, garden books, subscription sets, cookbooks, history, science. Adult Trade Editors: Elinor Parker, Norman Kotker, Ann Murphy, Harris Dienatfray. Science Editor: Kenneth Heuer.
Juveniles: "We publish books for children of all ages—pre-kindergarten up through high school age. We publish picture books, fiction, and nonfiction in all subjects. We have no special requirements in regard to special treatment or emphasis and length requirements. We're interested in books on any topical subject or theme, assuming we feel the material is exciting enough."

SCROLL PRESS, 22 E. 84th St., New York NY 10028. Juvenile Editor: Margaret B. Glos. Publishes hardcover originals. Royalty schedule open. Will send catalog to writer on request. Submit outline. Reports within 2 to 3 months. Enclose return postage.
Juveniles: Picture books for children ages 2-10 years. Maximum length: 1,000 words.

SEABURY PRESS, 815 Second Ave., New York NY 10017. Editor-in-Chief, Books for Young People: James C. Giblin. Publishes hardcover originals. "Most new authors of our Books for Young People receive a 5% royalty on picture books, 10% on older age books. Average advance is $750 or $1,000, depending on the type of book." Publishes 15 to 20 titles a year. Send outline with sample chapter for nonfiction; complete ms for fiction. Enclose return postage.
Juveniles: Picture books for ages 5-8, 2,000 words or under. Fiction and nonfiction for ages 8-12, 20,000 to 30,000 words. Fiction and nonfiction for ages 12 and up, 30,000 words and up. Special stress is put on contemporary fiction and nonfiction in the social studies area—biography, history, natural sciences. "We have avoided straight how-it-works nonfiction and concentrated more on the humanistic and interpretive. For picture books, especially interested in fresh, amusing, and/or contemporary stories for ages 3 to 7. Currently overworked are animals who want to be something else and verse that doesn't read smoothly or effectively. If writers don't find the verse form comfortable, they'd be better off telling their stories in prose." Current titles include *Fog* (Lee); *Turnabout* (Wiesner).

RICHARD SEAVER BOOKS, Viking Press, 625 Madison Ave., New York NY 10022. Editor: Richard Seaver. Publishes originals. "Royalties and advances for each book are negotiated separately." Queries only; no complete mss. Enclose return postage.
Fiction and Nonfiction: "My main interest right now is in serious nonfiction. I'll be doing some new fiction too, but nonfiction is of primary interest."

SENTINEL BOOKS PUBLISHERS, INC., 17-21 East 22nd St., New York NY 10010. President: Louis Sackman. Outright purchase or 10% royalty. Usual advance is $250, but this varies, depending on author's reputation and nature of book. Books published last year: 4. Query with outline. Reports in ten days. Enclose return postage.
Hobbies, Science, and Sports: Publishes hobby, science and sports books of about 18,000 words for adults and teenagers.

SHEED AND WARD, INC., 64 University Place, New York NY 10003. Editor: A.F. Geoghegan. Standard royalty schedule. Advance negotiable. Books published last year: 12. Query with outline and sample chapter. Reports in 4 to 6 weeks. Enclose return postage.
Nonfiction: Publishes all types of nonfiction from Christian or ecumenical view

point: theology, philosophy, history. No fiction. Minimum length: 40,000 words. Representative titles: *Darkness and Light; Prison of Love; Neither East Nor West.*

SHERBOURNE PRESS, INC., 1640 S. La Cienega Blvd., Los Angeles CA 90035. Editor-in-Chief: Mr. Shelly Lowenkopf. Publishes hardcover and paperback originals. Offers standard 10-12½-15% royalty contract; "advance varies." Published 20 titles last year. Will send a catalog to a writer on request. "Query first on all material, but please be prepared to send complete ms." Will consider photocopied submissions "if highly readable. Our style is according to the Chicago *Manual of Style*, our usage adheres strictly to *American Heritage Dictionary.* Put the title on each page, please. We try to sell a great deal to institutions—libraries, schools, etc. We enjoy mail order success. Books must have a built-in point-of-sales clout. We do good to excellent advertising and promotion, so mss must have a good built-in promotion basis. Authors should understand the difference between California and eastern publishing before they submit tired eastern themes to a California publisher. The west is a cultural focal point; approach us with a sound voice of your own, make us listen, and we will—with great sympathy." Reports on a ms accepted for publication in 1 to 2 months. Returns rejected material in 1 month. Enclose return postage.

Nonfiction: "We want strong emphatic materials on personal dependencies, group dependencies, teaching and learning techniques, annotated handbooks, checklists, readings selected on viable, important themes. We want consumer-oriented nonfiction, books related to diet but not fad diet or recipe or cookbooks; supplementary readings for a broad-based, adult-young adult level; challenging ideas that students of all ages will bring into the classroom as an adjunct to their learning. Our books have author involvement—we do not shun author participation, and we emphasize the need for documentation, annotation, exploration, proper preparation." Interested in publishing books on "psychochemical reactions, diet, eating habits, the new anthropology, humanism, western history (but not the Gold Rush and the railroad sort of thing—histories of banking, say, or histories of important industrial growth); histories of political activism, the new astrology, social reform, social experimentation, survival." Publishes books on Americana, biography, business, history, medicine and psychiatry, multimedia material, nature, politics, reference, self-help and how-to. Recent titles include *The Cholesterol Controversy* (Pinckney); *Modern Astrology* (Williams); *How to Get Your Money's Worth From Psychiatry* (Lazarus).

SHINN MUSIC AIDS, 5090 Dobrot Way, Central Point OR 97501. Editor: Duane Shinn. Publishes hardcover and paperback originals and reprints. Pays flat rate for accepted mss (minimum of $300; maximum, $1,000). Advance of 50% of either sum. Published 4 titles last year. Send query with outline. Reports in 1 week. Enclose return postage.

How-To: "How-to books in the music field. Must show reader in step-by-step style how to play a guitar, tune a piano, write a song, etc. Any length considered, but short mss are preferred. Action photos will definitely help to sell the ms. Try us! We are a young company specializing in how-to books about music, and we want to attract new writers who are knowledgeable in the music field." Current leading titles include *How to Play Chord Piano; Instant Harmony.*

THE SHOE STRING PRESS, INC., (Archon Books, Linnet Books), 995 Sherman Ave., Hamden CT 06514. President: Mrs. Frances T. Rutter. Pays 10% of net. "Advances in royalty are not offered as a rule, but special circumstances may be considered." Books (including reprints) published last year: 84. Query first and include table of contents and sample chapters. Reports in 4 to 6 weeks. Enclose return postage.

Nonfiction: Publishes scholarly books in limited editions, cloth-bound, etc.; history, biography, science, philosophy, religion, bibliographies, information science, library science, general scholarly nonfiction. Preferred length is 50,000 to 100,000 words, though there is no set limit.

GEORGE SHUMWAY, Publisher, R.D. 7, York PA 17402. Editor: George Shumway. Publishes hardcover and paperback originals, reprints, and translations. "We are very flexible in arranging contracts with authors. Advances are minimal because of the specialized nature of our publishing." Published 6 titles last year. Will send a catalog to a writer on request. Query first. Reports in 3 weeks. Enclose return postage.

General Nonfiction. "Particularly in the field of antique art, antiques, and Americana.

SIERRA CLUB BOOKS, 597 Fifth Ave., New York NY 10017. Editor: John G. Mitchell. Publishes hardcover and paperback originals. "On paperbacks, royalty starts at 7%; average advance is $4,000." Published 12 titles last year. Query first. Reports on ms accepted for publication in 3 months. Returns rejected material in 1 month. Enclose return postage.
Nonfiction: "Environmental, ecological, with special emphasis on critical issues and human interest in the out-of-doors. Length: 35,000 words and up. Audience demands quality writing and a philosophy consistent with environmental protection and wilderness preservation. We hit harder on specific conservation issues in our books, and our color photo reproductions are superior." Current titles include *Floor of the Sky; Snake Wilderness.*

SILVER BURDETT CO., a division of General Learning Corp., 250 James St., Morristown NJ 07960. Editor-in-Chief: Harrison B. Bell. Enclose return postage with ms.
Textbooks: Publishes elementary and secondary textbooks and supplementary materials.

*SILVERMINE PUBLISHERS INCORPORATED, Comstock Hill, Silvermine, Norwalk CT 06850. Editor: Joan Adler. Publishes hardcover and paperback originals. Royalty schedule varies but usually starts at 8%-10%; no advances. "No subsidy publishing at this time, but will undertake if requested." Books published last year: 3. Current catalog available. Send outlines and sample chapters. "We'd rather consider photocopied submissions. Send two copies, doublespaced, of everything." Reports in 2 to 3 months. Enclose return postage.
Nonfiction: Publishes general nonfiction, biography, and books dealing with fine arts and architecture. "We are not interested in name authors, but insist on good writing. Our books are designed to last (that is, they are not 1-season phenomena). Thus, a typical book over a period of 3 to 5 years may earn $3,000 to $6,000 royalties. It is our opinion that books that are solid text, unillustrated, are not salable any longer unless they are news or topical (which we are not interested in), fiction by established writers (which we are not interested in), or books on special subjects."

SIMON AND SCHUSTER, Trade Books Division of Simon and Schuster, Inc., 630 Fifth Ave., New York NY 10020. "If we accept a book for publication, business arrangements are worked out with the author or his agent and a contract is drawn up. The specific terms vary according to the type of book and other considerations. Royalty rates are more or less standard among publishers. Special arrangements are made for anthologies, translations and projects involving editorial research services." Published 256 titles last year. Catalog available on request. "All unsolicited mss will be returned unread. Only mss submitted by agents or recommended to us by friends or actively solicited by us will be considered. Our requirements are as follows: All mss submitted for consideration should be marked to the attention of the editorial department. Mystery novels should be so labeled in order that they may be sent to the proper editors without delay. It usually takes at least three weeks for the author to be notified of a decision—often longer. Sufficient postage for return by first-class registered mail, or instructions for return by express collect, in case of rejection, should be included. Mss must be typewritten, double-spaced, on one side of the sheet only. We suggest margins of about one inch all around and the standard 8½-by-11-inch typewriter paper." Prefers complete mss.
General: "Simon and Schuster publishes books of adult fiction, history, biography, science, philosophy, the arts and religion, running 50,000 words or more. We also publish poetry and juveniles. Our program does not, however, include school textbooks, extremely technical or highly specialized works, or, as a general rule, plays. Exceptions have been made, of course, for extraordinary mss of great distinction or significance."

SINCERE PRESS, Box 10422, Phoenix AZ 85016. Editor: William Ewers. Publishes hardcover originals. "We pay on a straight 10% basis; advance contingent on the work." Published 8 books last year. Will send a catalog to a writer on request. Query first with outline and sample chapters. Reports in 30 days. Enclose return postage.
Self-Help and How-To: "Our line is basically directed toward the do-it-yourself and vocational training markets. Our marketing has been directed toward public libraries and schools. Style and slant should be directed toward the working man mentality. Mss should be around 50,000 words, or whatever is required to adequately cover the subject. Include a minimum of technical terms so that the average do-it-yourselfer or person in vocational training can comprehend and retain. All mss must be well-illustrated with either drawings or b&w glossies." Recent titles include *Home Cleaning Guide* (Melle and Charlos); *Mini-B.C. Service* (Ewers and Charlos).

THE SMITH, 5 Beekman St., New York NY 10038. Publishes hardcover and paperback originals. Royalty schedule: 10% up to 2,500 copies; 12½% for 2,500 to 5,000 copies; 15% thereafter. Usual advance is $500, but this varies, depending on author's reputation and nature of work. Books published last year: 18. Will send catalog on request. Send query first for nonfiction; sample chapter preferred for fiction. Reports within six weeks. Enclose return postage.
Fiction: No specific categories or requirements. Editor of Adult Fiction: Harry Smith.
Nonfiction: Nonfiction Editor: Sidney Bernard.

SMITHSONIAN INSTITUTION PRESS, Washington D.C. 20560. Director: Gordon Hubel. Publishes hardcover originals and reprints. Pays 10% of list price on domestic sales, 7% on foreign sales and 50% of subsidiary rights income. Books published last year: 6. Send sample chapters or entire ms. Reports in four weeks. Enclose return postage with ms or sample chapters.
Nonfiction: On the history of science and technology, zoology, tropical biology, cultural anthropology at semiprofessional or professional level (50,000 to 100,000 words); and art history, fully illustrated. Representative titles: *The New Deal Art Projects: An Anthology of Memoirs*; *The Papers of Joseph Henry*; *Continental Drift: The Evolution of a Concept*; *Gems in the Smithsonian*; *The Horse in Blackfoot Indian Culture.*

SMYRNA PRESS, Box 327, Glen Gardner NJ 08826. Publishes paperback originals, reprints. "We offer a per poem price which varies from anthology to anthology but is minimal payment at any rate. No advance. We do give 10 author's copies." Publishes 4 books a year. Query first. Enclose S.A.S.E. with query letter. Reports in 2 weeks.
Poetry: "We remain dedicated to the full-time, seriously committed writer who knows what has gone before and is ready to forge ahead. No dilettantes please. No rhyme and rhythm stuff. We are not for the poet who does not know what is going on now. We get too many submissions from amateurs who have never gotten beyond their high school anthologies. They need not waste time submitting to us." Shorter lengths preferred. Department Editor: Dan Georgakas.
History and Biography: "We publish a limited number of political pamphlets. Most of these are solicited. Needs here are very special and knowledge of Smyrna Press is essential." Pamphlet length. Department Editor: Elias Bokhara.

*SOCCER ASSOCIATES, P.O. Box 634, New Rochelle NY 10802. Editor: Jeff Miller. Books published last year: 185. Send finished book to Milton Miller. Enclose return postage.
Sports, Hobbies, and Recreation: Publishes sports, recreation, leisure time, and hobby books under Sport Shelf and Leisure Time Books imprints. Most of their titles are British and Australian although they do have a special service for authors who publish their own books and desire national and international distribution, promotion, and publicity.

SOUTHERN METHODIST UNIVERSITY PRESS, Dallas TX 75222. Director: Allen Maxwell; Associate Director and Editor: Margaret L. Hartley. Payment is on royalty basis: 10% of list up to 2,500 copies; 12½% for 2,500-5,000 copies; 15% there-

after. No advance. Books published last year: 5. Catalog available on request. Appreciates query letters, outlines and sample chapters. Reports tend to be slow for promising mss requiring outside reading by authorities. Enclose return postage.
Nonfiction: Regional and scholarly nonfiction. Length: open.

SOUTHERN PUBLISHING ASSOCIATION, Box 59, Nashville TN 37202. Pays straight 5% royalty "and nominal advance royalty." Prefers queries with outlines and sample chapters. "Examine some previously published titles for approach and subject interest." Address material to the Book Editor. Usually reports within 3 months. Enclose return postage.
Nonfiction: Biographies and religiously oriented books only. "Our most popular books are on Biblical characters and events, medical advice for laymen, practical religious application to today's problems and biography on important religious figures in history." Length requirements: 20,000 to 60,000 words.
Juveniles: Religiously oriented juveniles only.

SPORTS CAR PRESS, LTD., Sylvester Ct., E. Norwalk CT 06855. Editor: Joe Christy. Publishes paperbacks. Pays 12% of net: ½ on mail order; no ascending scale. $300 advance against royalties. Publishes 5 to 10 titles a year. Query Mrs. J.W. Greenberg. Will send catalog to writer on request. Reports in three weeks. Enclose return postage.
Nonfiction: On sports car and small aircraft subjects, sports and recreation. Recent titles include *Chassis Tuning* (Nordyke); *Parachuting for Sport* (Greenwood).

STACKPOLE BOOKS, Cameron and Kelker Sts., Harrisburg PA 17105. Executive and Editorial Director: Clyde P. Peters. Standard royalties. Usual advance is $1,000, but this varies, depending on author's reputation and nature of book. Send query with sample chapter and outline. Reports in less than one month. Enclose return postage.
Nonfiction: Major publisher of outdoors, guns, camping, fishing, recreation, military, military-political, history fields for adults. Also publishes philosophy, leisuretime, current affairs. Seeking new book-length mss that add new sales and content dimensions to these and related fields. Length: 20,000 words and up. Recent titles include *Beginner's Guide to Archaeology; Sailplanes and Soaring; Guide to Caves and Caving.*

STANDARD PUBLISHING, 8121 Hamilton Ave., Cincinnati OH 45231. Product Planner: Shirley Beegle. Publishes paperback originals. Offers "a cash payment ($100 to $200) only for mss for children's books." No royalty. Published 30 titles for children last year. "The majority of our books are sold through Christian bookstores." Will send a catalog to a writer on request. Query first for nonfiction; submit complete ms for fiction. Will not consider photocopied submissions. Reports in 2 months. Enclose return postage.
Juveniles: "The majority of our books are storybooks for children from 3 to 10. The material should be Bible-based or contain a definite Christian teaching." Length: open.

STATE HISTORICAL SOCIETY OF WISCONSIN PRESS, 816 State St., Madison WI 53706. Editor: Paul H. Hass. Publishes hardcover originals. Pays 10% of gross income. No advance. Books published last year: 6. Send complete ms. (No corrasable bond, please.) Reports in eight weeks. Enclose return postage with ms.
History: Research and interpretation in history of the American Middle West—broadly construed as the Mississippi Valley. Must be thoroughly documented. 150,000 to 200,000 words of text, exclusive of footnotes and other back matter.

STECK-VAUGHN COMPANY, Box 2028, Austin TX 78767. For juveniles, offers "10% of net when we provide illustration, 10% of list for author-illustrator or author and illustrator team. We pay a $500 advance against royalties on juvenile sports books—advances not offered on other types of juveniles." Books published last year: 75. Prefers complete mss and sample illustrations and dummy (if prepared by author-artist team). Enclose return postage with ms.
Textbooks: "Elementary and secondary school textual and supplementary mate-

rials; adult education materials." Dept. Editor: Paul C. Craig, Vice-President, Editorial.

Juveniles: Little League baseball stories: 28,000 to 33,000 words (ages 8-12); football, basketball, baseball stories for early teens: 40,000 to 45,000 words; informational books: length varies. For juvenile nonfiction books for ages 6-10 and 8-13, is interested in mss on "wildlife, particularly endangered species; environmental subjects." Length: "3,000 to 5,000 words or more. We do not publish seasonal books." Recent titles include *The North American Eagles; The Pronghorn; The Food Crisis.* Children's Book Editor: Jane Moseley.

STEIN AND DAY, 7 E. 48th St., New York NY 10017. Offers standard royalty contract. Books published last year: 80. Not interested in unsolicited mss. Nonfiction, send outline or summary and sample chapter; fiction, send first chapter only. Enclose return postage.

General: Publishes general trade books; no juveniles or college. All types of nonfiction except technical. Quality fiction. Length: 75,000 to 100,000 words. Representative titles include: *Knifeman* (Craig); *The History of World Cinema* (Robinson).

STORY HOUSE CORP., Charlotteville NY 12036. Editor: D. Steven Rahmas. Publishes paperback originals. Offers outright fee: "$150 upon completed and corrected final ms, and $150 after sale of 6,000 books. Fee includes research, proofreading, and lengthening or shortening of the text to conform with required length." Publishes about 100 books a year. Write for copy of guidelines for writers. Query first; "do not begin writing until subject is confirmed. Subject is exclusive for 60 days. The right to assign the subject to another author is reserved if the work is not completed within 60 days if other arrangements have not been made. Please submit 3 or more subjects in order of preference." Enclose return postage.

Nonfiction: For "high school and college students," material is wanted for "Outstanding Personalities series (biographies), Great Events of our Times series (study of single great events), Topics of Our Times series (study of topics of special current interest), and Handcraft and Hobby series. In each of these series, the aim is creation of a basic research tool for assigned areas of interest. Work should be a concise description, but still interesting and intriguing. To be written in a free-flowing, interesting style, not a scholarly style. Must contain all basic facts about area of interest assigned, as contained in information guidelines for prospective authors. No chapter or other subdivisions. For biography series, ms should be basic research tool for the assigned personality. Should cover information chronologically from birth to death or present. For the Events of Our Times series, each work should be devoted to only one single event, not to any movement or trend. The term 'event' is meant to include all occurrences leading to the event and all results flowing therefrom. For Handcraft and Hobby series, material should depict a craft or art by means of explanation and diagrams. For Topics of Our Times series, we are interested in any areas of interest that are currently of more than average interest to the common person, such as women's rights, ecology, population problem." Length: 9,500 to 10,500 words. Recent titles include *The Mai Lai Massacre* (Aurland) *The Abortion Controversy* (Keast). Managing Editor: Barbara Burgower.

STRAIGHT ARROW BOOKS, 625 Third St., San Francisco CA 94107. Publishes hardcover and paperback originals and reprints. Offers standard 10-12½-15% royalty contract; "advances vary depending on author and circumstances, from $500 up." Published 18 titles last year. Will send a catalog to a writer on request. Query first with outline and sample chapters or submit complete ms. Reports in 1 month. Enclose return postage.

General Fiction: "Novels on all topics, short story collections."

Nonfiction: "We specialize in youth and so-called 'counter-culture' books. We publish a regular, but limited, number of nonfiction titles each season, including books on history, politics, how-to-do-it books for self-sufficient living, music books, picture books, spiritual and religious works, novels and reference works—a complete line of connections within a community of sensibility we feel ourselves a part of, a market of readers 'no longer concerned with just entertainment or conventional wisdom, but rather, enlightenment and survival.'" Recent titles include *Strike* (Brecher); *Kerouac* (Charters); *Fear and Loathing on the Campaign Trail 1972* (Thompson); *Independent Filmmaking* (Lipton).

STRUCTURES PUBLISHING CO., P.O. Box 423, Farmington MI 48024. Editor: R.J. Lytle. Publishes hardcover originals. Offers standard 10-12½-15% royalty contract. Usual advance is $500, but this varies, depending on author's reputation and nature of book. Published 3 titles last year. Will send a catalog to a writer on request. Submit outline and sample chapters. Will consider photocopied submissions. Reports in 4 to 6 weeks. Enclose return postage.
Technical: "Construction-related books of the handbook type for architects, builders, suppliers, etc. Mss should be practical, ready reference manuals." Length: open. Recent titles include *Kitchen Planning Guide for Builders and Architects* (Galvin).

SUMMY-BIRCHARD COMPANY, 1834 Ridge Ave., Evanston IL 60204. Enclose return postage with ms.
Music: Publishes educational music and musical methods, texts, and collections.

SUNSTONE PRESS, P.O. Box 2321, Santa Fe NM 87501. Editor: Jody Ellis. Publishes paperback originals; "sometimes hardcover originals." Offers 10% royalty contract. Advance varies. Will send a catalog to a writer on request. Query first. Will not consider photocopied submissions. Reports in 1 month. Enclose return postage.
Nonfiction: "Cookbook series, humorous series, how-to series, educational series, southwest series. No special audience considerations. We try to hit new ideas." Length: open. Recent titles include *Sir* (Cram); *Mountain Villages* (Bullock); *Adobe Architecture* (Stedman).
Poetry: "Any poetry which is well constructed and in good taste." Dept. Editor: Marcia Miller.

SWALLOW PRESS, INC., 1139 S. Wabash Ave., Chicago IL 60605. Editor: Durrett Wagner; Literary Editor: Michael Anania. Publishes hardcover and paperback originals and reprints. Royalty varies. Books published last year: 20. Catalog on request. Reports in 6 months. Enclose return postage with ms.
Nonfiction and Poetry: General nonfiction, Western Americana nonfiction; poetry.

SWEDENBORG FOUNDATION, 139 East 23rd St., New York NY 10010. Chairman, Editorial and Publications Committee: C. S. Priestnal. Publishes hardcover and paperback originals and reprints (limited to Swedenborgiana). Royalties negotiable. Published 4 titles last year. Catalog available on request. Query first. Will consider photocopied submissions. Reports in 1 month. Enclose return postage with query.
Nonfiction: The life and works of Emanuel Swedenborg. Studies of Swedenborg's scientific activities as precursors of modern developments. Studies of Swedenborg's contributions to the mainstream of religious thought. Also related history, science, philosophy, religion, parapsychology, sociology. "Objective and scholarly analysis. Our audience is ecumenical; serious students of all religions."

SYRACUSE UNIVERSITY PRESS, Box 8, University Station, Syracuse NY 13210. Associate Director and Editor: Arpena Mesrobian. The royalty schedule varies, but generally a royalty is paid on every title. Books published last year: 14. Catalog available on request. Query first with outline or sample chapters. If the ms is not rejected outright, a decision may be expected in 3 to 4 months. Enclose return postage.
Nonfiction: Publishes nonfiction, scholarly books, including biography, regional (especially on New York State and Iroquois), technical, literary criticism, history, philosophy, politics, religion, and educational books. Approximate minimum length: 50,000 words.

TAB BOOKS, Blue Ridge Summit PA 17214. Pays on fee or royalty basis. Advance varies. Distribution through bookstores, libraries, schools, advertising, direct mail, etc. Wants queries sent to Verne M. Ray; include title, chapter outline, and one-page synopsis describing who book is written for and why. List other books on the subject and how book differs from the others. Reports in 1 to 4 weeks. Enclose return postage.
Technical: Publishes technical books. Distribution reaches electronic engineers and

technicians; radio and TV broadcasters (chief engineers and managers, program directors, etc.); hobbyists and experimenters, cable TV owners, operators, managers, engineers and technicians; also electric motor service shops, both independent and in-plant. "We are looking for up-to-date book mss for technical people in these fields, or for nontechnical managers and executives in these fields." Length: "Depends on illustrative content."

Self-Help and How-To: "We are seeking books for the do-it-yourselfer, including crafts, on virtually all subject areas."

TAFNEWS PRESS, Box 296, Los Altos CA 94022. Editor: Bert Nelson. Publishes hardcover and paperback originals. Pays 10%. No advance. Published 10 books last year. Query first or submit outline and sample chapters. Will send catalog to writer on request. Will consider photocopied submissions. Enclose return postage with queries and submissions.

General Nonfiction: "Track and field titles only. Technique, training, biographies, etc. Sports, hobbies, recreations and pets." Recent titles include: *Runners & Races: 1500m/Mile* (history of mile); *Track & Field Dynamics* (introduction to body mechanics involved in track and field events).

TEACHERS COLLEGE PRESS, 1234 Amsterdam Ave., New York NY 10027. Publishes originals and reprints. Royalty schedule varies. No advance. Books published last year: 44. Current catalog available on request. Send outline and sample chapter addressed to the Director. Enclose return postage.

Nonfiction: Publishes scholarly and professional books in education and allied subjects (psychology, sociology, social studies, etc.) as well as testing materials. Length: open.

TEMPLEGATE, 302 E. Adams St., Springfield IL 62705. Executive Editor: Hugh M. Garvey. Books published last year: 10. "Unsolicited mss not returned unless return postage accompanies ms."

General: General fiction and nonfiction.

TEXAS WESTERN PRESS, The University of Texas at El Paso, El Paso TX 79968. Director: E.H Antone. Publishes hardcover and paperback originals. "We are a university press, not a commercial house; therefore, payment is in books and prestige more than money. Most of our books are sold to libraries, not to the general reading public." Published 10 titles last year. Will send a catalog to a writer on request. Query first. Will consider photocopied submissions. "Follow MLA Style Sheet." Reports in 1 to 3 months. Enclose return postage.

Nonfiction: "Scholarly books. Historic accounts of the Southwest (west Texas, southern New Mexico, and northern Mexico). Some literary works, occasional scientific titles. Our Southwestern Studies use mss of 20,000 words. Our hardback books range from 30,000 words up. The writer should use good exposition in his work. Most of our work requires documentation. We favor a scholarly, but not overly pedantic, style. We specialize in superior book design." Recent titles include *The Lasater Philosophy of Cattle Raising* (Lasater).

CHARLES C. THOMAS, PUBLISHER, 301-27 E. Lawrence Ave., Springfield IL 62717. Editor: Payne E.L. Thomas. Publishes hardcover originals. Royalty contract varies with type of book, whether it is in a series, and the number of books. No advance. Published 308 titles last year. Query first. Reports in 2 weeks. Enclose return postage with query.

Business, Medical, and Professional: Publishes medical, business, police, agricultural, and law books. Length depends on subject.

TIDEWATER PUBLISHERS, Box 109, Cambridge MD 21613. Editor: Mary Jane Cornell. An imprint of Cornell Maritime Press, Inc. Publishes hardcover and paperback originals and reprints. Offers standard 10-12½-15% royalty contract. Published 5 titles last year. Will send a catalog to a writer on request. Query first with outline and sample chapters. Will not consider photocopied submissions. Reports in 2 to 3 weeks. Enclose return postage.

Nonfiction: "General nonfiction on Maryland and the Delmarva Peninsula." A recent title is *Wye Oak: The History of a Great Tree.*

TIME-LIFE BOOKS, Time & Life Building, New York NY 10020. Editor: Jerry Korn. Publishes hardcover originals. "We have no minimum or maximum fee because our needs vary tremendously. Advance, as such, is not offered. Author is paid as he completes part of contracted work." Book distribution is primarily through mail order sale. Query first to Oliver Allen, Director of Editorial Planning. Enclose return postage.
Nonfiction: "General interest books. Most books tend to be heavily illustrated (by staff), with text written by assigned authors." Length: open. Recent titles include *The Cowboys* (first book in The Old West series); *The Neanderthals* (The Emergence of Man series).

TIMES CHANGE PRESS, Penwell Rd., Washington NJ 07882. Editors: Su Negrin and Tom Wodetzki. Publishes hardcovers, paperbacks and pamphlets. A nonprofit press, paying very little for material. "Most of our writers now accept 50 or 100 copies of their book, and no money." Maximum payment of $100 is made in rare cases. Publishes 6 to 10 titles per year. Query first. Enclose return postage.
Nonfiction: "The press is a tool to change ourselves/America/the world, individually and politically. Interested in alternate culture, women's and gay liberation, new models for social organization and personal growth, creative approaches to racism, classism and ageism. Simple, clear writing preferred. Imaginative approaches welcome." Length: 100,000 words maximum. Recent titles include: *Begin at Start: Some Thoughts on Personal Liberation and World Change; Great Gay in the Morning: One Group's Approach to Communal Living and Sexual Politics.*

TOUCHSTONE PRESS, P.O. Box 81, Beaverton OR 97005. Editor: Thomas K. Worcester. Publishes paperback originals. "Our contracts are somewhat negotiable, but in recent years we have tended to use a straight 10% of the retail price." Advances are rare." Published 3 books last year. Will send a catalog to a writer on request. Query first with outline, samples of photography, and sample chapters; "do not submit ms." Reports in 3 to 5 weeks. Enclose return postage.
Nature: "We publish only trail guides and field identification guides at this time and this will probably remain the strong base of our operation. We insist on complete coverage by the author in person. The first book of a new series, *Short Trips and Trails: The Columbia Gorge,* is a combination travel guide/walking guidebook to a relatively small region, with some mention of local history. Very interested in expanding this series; two more in progress on other geographic areas at this time. We suggest potential authors study our published books for overall style, although each individual author will naturally have variations." Also cookbooks and ecology; self-help, how-to and history. Length: 20,000 to 40,000 words with photographs. Recent titles include *Wildflowers 1, The Cascades* (Horn); *100 Southern California Hiking Trails* (Lowe).

TRAIL-R-CLUB OF AMERICA, Box 1376, Beverly Hills CA 90213. Editor: R.H. Nulsen. Publishes paperback originals. Offers standard royalty contract. No advance. Published 10 titles last year. Will send a catalog to a writer on request. Query first. "Let us know topic and how you will treat it. We'll request outline if interested." Will consider photocopied submissions. Reports in 1 month. Enclose return postage.
How-To: "How-to-do-it books for the mobile home and recreation vehicle market. The heavily-illustrated books are 8½x5½ and run 200 to 400 pages." Recent titles include *Motor Home Manual; Alaska by Pickup Camper.*

TRANSACTION BOOKS, Rutgers University, New Brunswick NJ 08903. Editor: Mary E. Curtis. Publishes hardcover and paperback originals, reprints, translations, and anthologies. Offers standard 10-12½-15% royalty contract; "advance varies, depending on author's reputation and nature of book." Published 12 titles last year. Will send a catalog to a writer on request. Send complete ms. Reports in 3 months. Enclose return postage with ms.
Social Sciences: "Books in the social sciences, social research, and urban studies." Length: 150 to 500 ms pages.

TRANS-ANGLO BOOKS, P.O. Box 38, Corona del Mar CA 92625. Editorial Director: Spencer Crump. Royalty of 5%-10%. Books published last year: 5. Catalog on request. Query required; do not send mss until requested. Reports in three weeks to one month. Enclose return postage.

Nonfiction: Publishes Americana, ecology, Western Americana, and railroad books. Most books are 8½x11 hardcover with many photos supplementing a good text of 5,000 to 100,000 words.

TREND HOUSE, P.O. Box 2350, Tampa FL 33601. Publishes hardcover and paperback originals. "We offer standard royalty arrangements and, occasionally, an advance, depending on the nature of the book and our interest in it." Published 15 titles last year. "Many of our books are sold through *Florida Trend* magazine in addition to the usual means. Query, outline, or ms is acceptable." Will consider photocopied submissions. Reports in 2 to 3 weeks. Enclose return postage.

Nonfiction: "We publish books related to Florida in all fields. Books about Florida real estate, business, estate planning on Florida, condominiums, birds, retiring in Florida, and figures about Florida, Florida cooking, history of the south, famous men. Looking for Florida school material for use in Florida public schools. No special length requirements. Also publish titles that are aimed at special markets, e.g., *300 Most Abused Drugs,* for law enforcement officers. Interested in seeing school and textbook materials for any individual state."

TROUBADOR PRESS, 126 Folsom St., San Francisco CA 94105. Editor: Malcolm K. Whyte. Publishes hardcover and paperback originals. "Royalties vary from 5% to 10%. Advances vary from $200 to $1,000." Published 7 titles last year. Will send a catalog to a writer on request. Query first with outline. Address mss to Gregory Frazier. Reports in 3 to 4 weeks. Enclose return postage.

General Nonfiction and Juveniles: "Troubador publishes a line of coloring books, cookbooks, game and activity books, and humor books. The coloring books are of the highest quality 'art' type and are very popular in gift shops and boutiques. Cookbooks are readable and contain quality, original artwork. They might be termed 'coffee table' books. Troubador will consider any material of a light nature. Interested in how-to books and juveniles (not 'Funny Bunny' style or poems). No novels, story books or technical works." Current leading titles: *Maze Craze, Nature Crafts.*

CHARLES E. TUTTLE CO., INC., Publishers & Booksellers, 26-30 S. Main St., Rutland VT 05701. Publishes originals and reprints. Pays $250 against 10% royalty. Advance varies. Books published last year: 83. Current catalog available for 50¢. Send queries accompanied by outlines or sample chapters to Charles E. Tuttle. Reports in 4 to 6 weeks. Enclose return postage.

Nonfiction: Specializes in publishing books about Oriental art and culture as well as history, literature, cookery, sport and children's books which relate to Asia, Hawaiian Islands, Australia and the Pacific areas. Also interested in Americana, especially antique collecting, architecture, genealogy and Canadian. Not interested in travel, sociological or topical works even when in subject field. No interest in poetry and fiction except that of Oriental theme. Normal book length only. Recent titles include *Crisis in Identity and Contemporary Japanese Novels; Alien Rice: A Novel of Mixed Marriage.*

Juveniles: Juvenile books are to be accompanied by illustrations.

TWAYNE PUBLISHERS, INC., 31 Union Sq., New York NY 10003. Editor: Jacob Steinberg. Payment is on royalty basis. Query first. Reports in three weeks. Enclose return postage.

Nonfiction: Publishes scholarly books.

TYNDALE HOUSE PUBLISHERS, 336 Gundersen Dr., Wheaton IL 60187. Publishes hardcover and paperback originals. Royalty contract to be negotiated. Published about 50 titles last year. Query first. Enclose return postage.

Nonfiction: Publishes religious books.

FREDERICK UNGAR PUBLISHING CO., INC., 250 Park Ave. S., New York NY 10003. Publishes about 35 books a year. Query first.

Nonfiction: "Scholarly books mainly in fields of literature and literary criticism. We do not encourage submission of mss by nonscholars."

UNITED CHURCH PRESS (including Pilgrim Press Books), 1505 Race St., Philadelphia PA 19102. Editor-in-Chief: Theodore A. McConnell. Publishes hardcover and paperback originals. Royalty schedule: 10% of retail. No advance. Books published last year: 20. Catalog on request. Query letter, full outline of ms, and not less than 2 sample chapters preferred. Reports in 8 to 15 weeks. Enclose return postage.
Nonfiction: Publishes books on education, theology, history, biography, the arts and religion, social action and Biblical literature. "Books on value issues of society, business, government, and communications." Length: 25,000 words minimum. Representative title: *The New Consciousness in Science and Religion.*

UNITED SYNAGOGUE BOOK SERVICE, 218 E. 70th St., New York NY 10021. Hardcover and paperback originals. Royalty schedule: 10% of list price. No advance. Books published last year: 6. Catalog on request. Send query, outline, sample chapter first. Address juveniles and history to Dr. Morton Siegel; biography, philosophy and adult religion to Rabbi Marvin Wiener. "Address general inquiries to George L. Levine, Director." Reports in one to eight weeks. Enclose return postage.
Religion: Publishes religious books only: textbooks, readers, Hebrew language books, history, picture books. No length requirements. Recent titles are *If I Am Only for Myself—the Story of Hillel* (Blumenthal); *More of the Songs We Sing* (Coopersmith).

*UNIVERSE BOOKS, 381 Park Ave. S. New York NY 10016. Editor: Louis Barron. Publishes hardcover originals. "No significant variation on standard 10-12½-15% royalty contract; our average advance varies from $1,000 to $10,000. Perhaps 5% or less of books are subsidy published." Published 25 titles last year. Will send a catalog to a writer on request. Query first with outline and sample chapters. Will consider photocopied submissions. Reports in 2 weeks. Enclose return postage.
The Arts, History, and Politics: Books on "art, art history, architecture, design, natural history, social history, and contemporary affairs. Most of our books are for a serious market—college and university students—and are for supplementary rather than text use. However, our books on social history and contemporary affairs are for a larger general market, and such books should be well-researched but more popularly written. Some consideration should be given to the illustrations and their sensible amplification of the text. Even in our illustrated books, the emphasis is always on the informative nature of the text rather than pictures." Recent titles include *Vienna: City of Dreams* (Stradal); *Art of the Nineteenth Century* (Vogt); *Women in Greece and Rome* (Zinserling).

UNIVERSITY OF ALABAMA PRESS, Drawer 2877, University AL 35486. Editor: James Travis. Publishes hardcover originals. "Maximum royalty is 12½%; no advances made." Published 21 titles last year. Will send a catalog to a writer on request. Submit outlines and sample chapters. Will consider photocopied submissions, "although these are suspect." Reports in "about 6 months." Enclose return postage.
Nonfiction: "Scholarly nonfiction. Categories include biography, business, economics, history, philosophy, politics, religion, and sociology." Considers upon merit almost any subject of scholarly investigation, but specializes in linguistics and philology, political science and public administration, literary criticism and biography, philosophy, and scholarly history (especially southern). Also interested in biology, medicine, and agriculture.

*UNIVERSITY OF ARIZONA PRESS, Box 3398, Tucson AZ 85722. Director: Marshall Townsend. Publishes hardcover and paperback originals and reprints. "Contracts are individually negotiated, but as a 'scholarly publishing house' operating primarily on informational works, does not pay any advances. Also, royalty starting point may be after sale of first 1,000 copies, by virtue of the nature of the publishing program." Occasionally does subsidy publishing. Published 20 titles last year. Marketing methods "are based on 'what is considered best for the book,' giving individual treatment to the marketing of each book, rather than a generalized formula." Will send catalog to writer on request. Write for copy of editorial guidelines sheet. Query first and submit outline and sample chapters. Will consider photocopied submissions if ms is not undergoing consideration at another publishing house. "Must have this assurance." Reports on material within 90 days. Enclose return postage.

Nonfiction: "Significant works of a regional nature about Arizona and the Southwest; books of merit in subject matter fields strongly identified with the universities in Arizona; i.e., anthropology, arid lands studies, Asian studies, Southwest Indians, Mexico, etc. Each ms should expect to provide its own answer to the question, 'Why should this come out of Arizona?' The answer would be that either the work was something that ought to be made a matter of record as a service to Arizona and the Southwest, or that it was presenting valuable information in a subject matter field with which the Arizona institutions hold strong identification. The Press strongly endorses 'the target reader' concept under which it encourages each author to write for only *one* reader, then leave it up to the publisher to reach the thousands—as contrasted with the author's trying to write for the thousands and not 'hitting home' with anyone. The Press believes this approach helps the author come to a consistent level of subject matter presentation. The Press also insists upon complete departure of 'time-dating' words such as 'now,' 'recently,' and insists that the author consider how the presentation will read three years hence." Americana, art, biography, business, history, nature, scientific, technical. Length: "what the topic warrants and demands." Not interested in "personal diary types of Western Americana, mainly directed only toward family interest, rather than broad general interest." Recent representative titles include *Southwest Indian Painting: A Changing Art* (Tanner); *Cowboys Under the Mogollon Rim* (Ellison).

UNIVERSITY OF CALIFORNIA PRESS, Berkeley CA 94720; Los Angeles CA 90024. Director: August Frugé. Los Angeles address is 60 Powell Library, Los Angeles CA 90024. Editor: Robert Y. Zachary. New York Office, Room 513, 50 E. 42 St., New York NY 10017. London Office IBEG, Ltd., 2-4 Brook St., London W1Y 1AA, England. Publishes hardcover and paperback originals and reprints. On books likely to more than return their costs, a standard royalty contract beginning at 10% is paid; on paperbacks it is less. Titles published last year: 150. Queries are always advisable, accompanied by outlines or sample material. Address to either Berkeley or Los Angeles address. Reports vary, depending on the subject. Enclose return postage.

Nonfiction: "It should be clear that most of our publications are hardcover nonfiction written by scholars." Publishes scholarly books including art, literary studies, social sciences, natural sciences and some high-level popularizations. No length preferences.

Fiction and Poetry: Publishes fiction and poetry only in translation. Usually in bilingual editions.

UNIVERSITY OF CHICAGO PRESS, 5801 Ellis Ave., Chicago IL 60637. Publishes Phoenix Books. Royalties are paid on sliding scale, beginning at 10% on net receipts. Books published last year: 180. Write for guide for writers. Send queries and outlines before submitting any portion of mss. Mss are immediately acknowledged and reported on within three months. Enclose return postage.

Nonfiction and Textbooks: Serious nonfiction in all fields; emphasis on basic research in social science, humanities, and natural science; advanced textbooks; scholarly journals.

UNIVERSITY OF FLORIDA PRESS, 15 N.W. 15th St., Gainesville FL 32601. Director: William B. Harvey. Basically 10% royalty payment on net sales—except on works with limited sales appeal. Books published last year: 30. Catalog available on request. Send query letters, outlines, and sample chapters to William B. Harvey. Reports in 8 to 10 weeks. Enclose return postage.

Nonfiction: Publishes scholarly books and monographs; works of regional, inter-American, and general interest. Mss are selected for publication by Board of Managers composed of faculty members. Length: minimum 25,000 words; average 75,000 words.

UNIVERSITY OF IOWA PRESS, Graphic Services Building, Iowa City IA 52240. Director: John Simmons. Publishes hardcover originals. Offers standard, 10-12½-15% royalty contract; "no advances." Published 6 titles last year. Will send a catalog to a writer on request. Query first with outline and sample chapters. Will consider

photocopied submissions. "Follow the Chicago *Manual of Style*." Reports in 3 months. Enclose return postage.
Scholarly: "Scholarly books, usually on academic subjects. Also, translations of significant works into English. Special series: The Iowa Translation series (the International Writing Program and translators outside its formal program provide significant literary works from other languages in English translations)." Length: minimum 40,000 words; no maximum. General Editor, Iowa Translation Series: Paul Engle.

UNIVERSITY OF MASSACHUSETTS PRESS, Amherst MA 01002. Publishes original works and reprints. Typical royalties: none on first run; 10% of retail thereafter. Advances are rare. Books published last year: 18. Address mss to the Editor. Initial reports in six to twelve weeks. Enclose return postage with ms.
Nonfiction and Poetry: Scholarly and esthetic merit, including American philosophy and history, black studies, biography, science, poetry, art, and studies of regional interest. Current leading titles: *Frost: A Time to Talk, Conversations and In discretions Recorded by Robert Francis; Conjure: Selected Poems, 1963-1970* (Reed); *The Education of Black People: Ten Critiques, 1906-1960* (Du Bois).

UNIVERSITY OF MIAMI PRESS, P.O. Drawer 9088, Coral Gables FL 33124. Publishes hardcover originals and translations. Royalty schedule: generally 10% of retail. Books published last year: 40. Catalog on request. Always send query, outline and sample chapter. No carbon copies or handwritten mss. Mss should be typed, double-spaced, on one side only with approximately 28 lines of 65 characters each per page. Address to E.A. Seemann, Director. Reports on mss within 12 weeks. Enclose return postage with ms.
Nonfiction: In the fields of history, science, philosophy, the arts and general nonfiction. Must be scholarly. No fiction or poetry. No specific length requirements.

UNIVERSITY OF MICHIGAN PRESS, 615 E. University, Ann Arbor MI 48106. Acting Director: John Scott Mabon. Royalty varies with the market potential. Books published last year: 32. Reports quickly. Enclose return postage with ms.
Nonfiction and Textbooks: Publishes general nonfiction and textbooks. Interested in history, biography, science, philosophy, art, music, drama, etc.

UNIVERSITY OF MINNESOTA PRESS, 2037 University Ave., S.E., Minneapolis MN 55455. Royalties vary. Books published last year: hardcover, 27; paperback, 9. Query letters highly important. Mss should be addressed to Editorial Department. Reports in three weeks to four months. Enclose return postage with ms.
Nonfiction: Publishes scholarly nonfiction in any field; interpretations for a more general audience. No word length requirement, except that only book-length mss are acceptable. Representative title: *Lifeway Leap: The Dynamics of Change in America.*

UNIVERSITY OF NEBRASKA PRESS, 901 N. 17th St., Lincoln NE 68508. Publishes hardcover and paperback originals and reprints. Royalty paid annually; 6% on paperback originals and reprints. Usual advance is $300, but this varies, depending on author's reputation and nature of book. Books published last year: 48. Send query accompanied by one-page outline for all mss. "All copy should be double-spaced, including footnotes and extracts. Footnotes should not be on page, but on separate pages grouped after each chapter or at the end of the mss. Be sure to put your address on the first page as well as on the wrapper. Number pages consecutively throughout the ms. Make a list of any illustrative matter included." Address all queries to Editor. Reports within 8 to 12 weeks. Enclose return postage.
Nonfiction: Work in all fields of scholarship: history, biography, literary criticism, science, philosophy, and the arts. Does not publish poetry or current fiction. Length: 60,000 words and up. Recent titles include *Huerta: A Political Portrait* (Meyer); *Rolvaag: His Life and Art* (Reigstad); *Bernard Shaw's Marxian Romance* (Hummert).

UNIVERSITY OF NOTRE DAME PRESS, Notre Dame IN 46556. Editor: Ann Rice. Publishes hardcover and paperback originals and paperback reprints. Offers

standard 10-12½-15% royalty contract; no advance. Published 18 titles last year. Will send a catalog to a writer on request. Query first. Will consider photocopied submissions. Reports in 2 to 3 months. Enclose return postage.
Nonfiction: "Scholarly books, serious nonfiction of general interest; book-length only. Especially in the areas of philosophy, theology, history, sociology, English literature (Middle English period, and modern literature criticism in the area of relation of literature and theology), government, and international relations. Lately, especially Mexican-American studies, American Indian studies. Also interested in books on the heritage of American beliefs and ideas suitable for junior college or high school students."

UNIVERSITY OF OKLAHOMA PRESS, Norman OK 73069. Director: Edward A. Shaw; Editor: Mary Stith. Pays on royalty basis. Paperbacks, 5%; for some highly scholarly books with very limited markets, other arrangements are made other than the standard contract, but these vary with circumstances. No advance. Books published last year: 41. Reports in 2 months. Query before sending ms. Enclose return postage.
Nonfiction: Publishes nonfiction books from 50,000 to 125,000 words in such fields as history, folklore, the American Indian, Western Americana, exploration and travel, farming, ranching, archaeology, anthropology, American literature; in fact, all of the fields of permanent interest which an American university press should cultivate.

UNIVERSITY OF PENNSYLVANIA PRESS, 3933 Walnut St., Philadelphia PA. 19104. Director: Fred Wieck. Publishes hardcover and paperback originals, reprints, and translations. Published 25 titles last year. Query first with outline and sample chapter. Reports in 1 to 3 months. Enclose return postage.
General Nonfiction, Technical, Medical and Scientific, Religion and Philosophy, History and Biography: "Scholarly books aimed at the academic fields."

UNIVERSITY OF SOUTH CAROLINA PRESS, University of South Carolina Campus, Columbia SC 29208. Director: Robert T. King. Royalties start at 5% of net receipts. Books published last year: 38. Submit queries, outlines, and sample chapters to Managing Editor. Reports in 20 weeks. Enclose return postage.
Nonfiction: Publishes scholarly books.

UNIVERSITY OF TEXAS PRESS, P.O. Box 7819, Austin TX 78712. Royalty schedule varies. Books published last year: 40. Query first to the Editor. Reports in 2 months. Enclose return postage.
Nonfiction: History, biography, science, the arts, philosophy, scholarly and/or regional (southwestern scene) nonfiction, and translations into English of notable books from Latin America. No word length requirements.

UNIVERSITY OF UTAH PRESS, University of Utah, Building 513, Salt Lake City UT 84112. Director: Norma B. Mikkelsen. Publishes hardcover and paperback originals, reprints, and translations. Offers no royalty payment on first 500 copies sold; 10% on 501 to 2,000 copies sold; 12½% on 2,001 to 4,000 copies sold; 15% thereafter. No advance royalties. Published 8 titles last year. Will send a catalog to a writer on request. Query first with outline and sample chapter. "If extremely long ms, indicate number of typewritten pages in query." Reports in 2 to 4 months. Enclose return postage.
Nonfiction: Scholarly books on history, biographies, science, philosophy, religion, the arts and general nonfiction. Length: author should specify word length in query.

UNIVERSITY OF WISCONSIN PRESS, P.O. Box 1379, Madison WI 53701. Director: Thompson Webb, Jr. Editor: Joan M. Krager. Publishes hardcover and paperback originals, reprints, and translations. Offers standard royalty contract. No advance. Published 30 titles last year. Send complete ms. Follow Modern Language Association Style Sheet. Reports in 3 months. Enclose return postage with ms.
Nonfiction: Publishes general nonfiction based on scholarly research.

UNIVERSITY PARK PRESS, Chamber of Commerce Bldg., Baltimore MD 21202. Hardcover originals in medicine, science and economics. Royalty schedule: from 7½%-15%. Advances for books in medicine and science are not generally offered, but are negotiated in certain cases depending on circumstances, as when the author needs to hire research or secretarial assistance to complete his ms." Books published last year: 142. Catalog on request. Send query and outline to Editorial Director. Reports in two weeks. Enclose return postage.
Nonfiction: Publishes postgraduate works in the biological and medical sciences, as well as national and international symposia and conferences. Length: 35,000 words minimum; no maximum. Current titles: *Public Budgeting Systems; Cardiomyopathies; Sociological Framework in Pharmacy Practice.*

UNIVERSITY PRESS OF KANSAS, 366 Watson Library, Lawrence KS 66044. Editor-in-Chief: Mrs. Yvonne Willingham. Publishes hardcover originals and paperbacks. Royalties, 5% and 10% of list. No advance. Publishes about 12 titles per year. Catalog available on request. Write for guide for writers. Query first. Address Mr. John H. Langley, Director. Reports in 8 weeks. Enclose return postage.
Nonfiction: History, biography, science, philosophy, the arts, religion, general nonfiction. Emphasis is on scholarly and regional material. No special requirements other than competence, accuracy, and consistency of style. Length: open.

THE UNIVERSITY PRESS OF KENTUCKY, Lexington KY 40506. Editor: Wm. Jerome Crouch. Hardcover and paperback originals and reprints. Pays royalties of 10% after first 1,000 copies. No advance. Books published last year: 16. Current catalog available on request. "Writers should query first, sending outline and describing their mss." Reports in approximately three months. Enclose return postage.
Nonfiction: Publishes general nonfiction including philosophy, biography, history, science and the arts. "This is the scholarly publishing arm of 13 Kentucky colleges and universities and its policy restricts it to the publishing of scholarly works, works which make some form of contribution to knowledge. All mss submitted to us must receive a favorable evaluation from a scholar in field covered by any particular ms before they can be accepted for publication. The Press does not publish works of fiction, poetry, or drama as such." Length: approximately 30,000 words and up.

THE UNIVERSITY PRESS OF VIRGINIA, Box 3608, University Station, Charlottesville VA 22903. Publishes hardcover and paperback originals and reprints. "Royalty schedule varies with title, depending upon cost, potential sale, etc." No advance. Books published last year: 30. Catalog on request. Send query letters to the Director. Reports in 8 weeks. Enclose return postage.
Nonfiction: History, biography, science, philosophy, the arts, religion, general nonfiction and monographs. Requires book-length mss.

THE VIKING PRESS, INC., PUBLISHERS, 625 Madison Ave., New York NY 10022. Royalties paid on all books. Books published last year: over 200. Juvenile mss should be addressed to Viking Junior Books. Adult mss should be addressed to The Viking Press. Studio mss should be addressed to Viking Studio Books. Reports in 4 to 6 weeks. Enclose return postage with ms.
General: Publishes adult and studio books. Also publishes Viking Portable Library and Viking Critical Library.
Juveniles: Publishes juvenile books.

WADSWORTH PUBLISHING COMPANY, INC., 10 Davis Dr., Belmont CA 94002. Managing Editor: James McDaniel. Publishes hardcover and paperback originals. Offers standard 10-12½-15% royalty contract. Published about 100 titles last year. Query first. Enclose return postage.
Textbooks: Publishes only college textbooks for most disciplines in the undergraduate college and university curriculum. "The writer should have taught the subject matter for some time before writing."

HENRY Z. WALCK, INC., 19 Union Square West, New York NY 10003. Editor: Mrs. Patricia C. Lord. Books published last year: 37. Enclose return postage with ms.
Juveniles: Publishes juveniles.

WALKER AND CO., 720 Fifth Ave., New York NY 10019. Publishes hardcover originals. Offers standard 10-12½-15% royalty contract. Published about 80 titles last year. Query first. Send complete ms for juvenile picture books. Will consider photocopied submissions. Reports in 6 weeks. Enclose return postage.
Fiction: Publishes adult fiction; all mystery categories (puzzle, chase, crime, espionage); science fiction. Length: 50,000 words minimum.
Nonfiction: History, biography, science, the arts, international affairs, military history, anthropology, archaeology, current affairs, psychology.
Juveniles: "For nonfiction, we are interested in science books for young readers and, occasionally, in biography and nonfiction that is relevant or controversial. We will consider nonfiction mostly for preschoolers through age 12. Length depends on the age group: anywhere from 2,000 words to 20,000 words. We are always open to many ideas for picture books for ages 3 to 8. Length for picture books: 1,500 to 4,000 words." Science Editor, Children's Books: Millicent E. Selsam; Associate Editor of Children's Books (fiction): Margery Cuyler.

WARBROOKE PUBLISHERS, 4050 Grey, Montreal 260, Que., Canada. Editor: Alfred Warkentin. Publishes hardcover and paperback originals. Royalty schedule varies. Send outline and sample chapter for nonfiction; complete ms for fiction. Reports in 2 months. Enclose return postage with ms.
Fiction: "Adult fiction. We will look at all fiction mss, from science fiction to the blockbuster." Length: 82,000 to 246,000 words.
Nonfiction: "Economics, cookbooks, the occult, astrology." Length: 82,000 to 246,000 words.
History: "History mss might deal with thought-provoking North American, European, and world political themes. We're especially interested in early exploration subjects." Length: 82,000 to 246,000 words.
Biography: "Interested in biographies of North American or European subjects." Length: 82,000 to 246,000 words.
Religion: "Controversial religious subjects on the Church and comparative religion." Length: 82,000 to 205,000 words.
Juveniles: Length: 8,200 to 61,500 words.

IVES WASHBURN, INC., 750 Third Ave., New York NY 10017. Subsidiary of the David McKay Co., Inc. Payment is on royalty basis. Books published last year: 11. Enclose return postage with ms.
General: Publishes novels, nonfiction, personal experience accounts for adults.
Juveniles: Nonfiction for children and young adults.

WASHINGTON SQUARE PRESS, Published by Pocket Books, a Division of Simon & Schuster, Inc., 630 Fifth Ave., New York NY 10020. Editor-in-Chief: Linda Lewin. Publishes paperback originals and reprints. Pays standard royalty rates. Advances against standard paperback royalties paid in part upon signing of contract and in part upon acceptance of ms. Books published last year: 50. Current catalog available on request. Send query, outline, sample chapter or complete ms to Laurie Brown, Assistant Editor. Reports in 1 to 2 months. Enclose return postage with ms.
General Nonfiction: Publishes works on all phases of the humanities, philosophy, biography, history, the arts, social sciences and physical sciences, oriented toward high school and college audiences, as well as to the general public. Does not publish original fiction or poetry. Length: 80,000 to 100,000 words. Problems of American Society Series, Gerald Leinwand, General Editor; Enriched Classics, Henry Shefter, General Editor; Myths for Modern Man, Gene and Barbara Stanford, Editors.

WATSON-GUPTILL PUBLICATIONS, One Astor Plaza, New York NY 10036. Publishes originals. Reprints foreign or out-of-print art instruction books. Pays, for originals, 10% of first 10,000; 12½% on next 5,000; 15% of selling price for all following 1,000's. Usual advance is $1,000, but average varies, depending on author's reputation and nature of book. Books published last year: 40. Address queries (followed by outlines and sample chapters) to Hal Miller, Managing Editor. Reports on queries within 10 days. Enclose return postage.
Art: Publishes art instruction books. Interested only in books of a how-to-do-it nature in any field of painting, crafts, design, etc. Not interested in biographies of painters, art history books, aesthetic appreciation. Length: open.

FRANKLIN WATTS, INC., 845 Third Ave., New York NY 10022. Editor in Chief: Jean Reynolds. Royalty schedule varies according to the type of book. Usual advance is $1,000, but average varies, depending on author's reputation and nature of book. Books published last year: 130. Current catalog available on request. Prefers queries on nonfiction and complete book on fiction. Reports in one month. Enclose return postage.

Juveniles: Publishes a wide variety of quality juveniles—from the young, to and including teenagers. Especially interested in fiction with a contemporary, especially a city, background. Interested in "contemporary biography, middle group and teenage fiction, good sports fiction and nonfiction. No formula novels. Would suggest that writers check our catalog before submitting any nonfiction ideas, since our First Book Series is 300 volumes and has covered a wide variety of subjects. Length depends on the subject and age group for which it is written." Recent titles include *Grandma Didn't Wave Back* (Blue); *The Killing Tree* (Bennett); *Cosmonauts in Orbit* (Gurney); *Experiments in Ecology* (Stone/Collins).

WAYNE STATE UNIVERSITY PRESS, Detroit MI 48202. Director: Herbert M. Schueller. Publishes hardcover originals and reprints. Royalty schedule standard, but separately negotiated for each book. No advance. Books published last year: 26. Current catalog available on request. Send query accompanied by outline and complete ms. Address mss to the Director. Reports in 1 to 6 months. Enclose return postage.

Nonfiction: Publishes scholarly and nonfiction books including biographies, history, religion, science, and the arts. Length: 40,000 words and up. Recent titles include *The Christian Humanism of Flannery O'Connor* (Eggenschwiler); *Freud As We Knew Him* (Rutenbeek); *Walt Whitman: A Study in the Evolution of Personality* (Smiths/McLeod).

WEBSTER DIVISION, McGraw-Hill Book Co., 1221 Ave. of the Americas, New York NY 10020. General Manager: Alexander J. Burke, Jr. Editorial Director: Roger E. Egan. Royalties vary. "Our royalty schedules are those of the industry, and advances are not commonly given." Books published last year: 136. Always query. Will consider photocopied submissions. Reports in 2 to 4 weeks. Enclose return postage.

Textbooks: Publishes school books, films, equipment and systems for elementary and secondary schools. Juveniles, history, science, the arts, mathematics. "Material is generally part of a series, system, or program done in connection with other writers, teachers, testing experts, etc. Material must be matched to the psychological age level, with reading achievement and other educational prerequisites in mind. Interested in a Mathematics Laboratory program and Career Education program for the elementary schools. Recent titles include *Personal Perspectives* (Paolucci et al); *Challenges to Science* (Smallwood et al).

WESTERN ISLANDS, 4 Hill Rd., Belmont MA 02178. Royalty is usually straight 10% on cloth editions; 4% on paper editions. Query first. Reports in two months. Enclose return postage.

Nonfiction: Specializes in books that have a conservative-political orientation: current events, essays, history, criticism, biography, memoirs, etc. No word length requirement.

WESTERN PUBLISHING CO., INC., 1220 Mound Ave., Racine WI 53404. Publishes hardcover and paperback juvenile books only; originals and reprints. Mss purchased outright. Books published last year: 95. Complete ms may be sent for picture books; query with outline and sample chapter on all mss over 1,000 words. Address mss and query letters for picture books to Miss Betty Ren Wright; query letters for novels to William Larson. Mss should be typed, double spaced, with S.A.S.E. enclosed. Reports in two to five weeks.

Juveniles: Picture book lines include Whitman Tell-a-Tale books, Big Golden books, Little Golden books, Golden Play and Learn books, Golden Shape books, and Golden Touch and Feel books. Material should be concerned with familiar childhood experiences, early learning concepts, favorite subjects (animals, cars and trucks, play activities). Urban, suburban and rural settings welcome. Unless specifically indicated, books are planned to be read to children, but vocabulary should be simple enough for easy understanding and for young readers to handle themselves if they wish. "We are interested in a limited number of very simple beginning readers, preferably falling into the late first grade category. We are also looking for stories about animals, humorous stories, and stories that emphasize concepts important to preschool-primary learning. We have board books and cloth books for children two and under; most of our picture books are intended for ages 3 to 6. While we are definitely interested in stories that combine fun and learning, we see too many mss that are forced or uninteresting because the writer has tried too hard to make them 'educational.' Also, we see many stories that are about children without being for children. We would encourage writers to consider always whether the story is genuinely meaningful to children. We are also interested in seeing stories about little girls that enlarge upon the position of women in our society. It is easy to turn out a 'message' story, and we do not want to do that, but we would like to publish stories in which girls play a wide variety of roles." Length for picture books: 200 to 800 words. Also publishes novel-length hardcover books and story anthologies for ages 8-14. These should be 35,000 to 60,000 words. Material should deal with subjects of genuine interest to pre-teens and early teens—mystery, adventure, and stories about high school activities.

WESTERNLORE PRESS, 5117 Eagle Rock Blvd., Los Angeles CA 90041. Editor: Paul D. Bailey. Pays standard royalties except in special cases. Query first. Unsolicited mss returned. Reports in 60 days. Enclose return postage with query.
Americana: Publishes Western Americana of the scholarly and basically researched type. "Volumes fitting our Great West & Indian Series, American Survey Series, Ghost Town Series, or Desert Series." Republication of rare and out-of-print books. Scholarly studies of the great West. Length: 25,000 to 65,000 words.

WESTMINSTER PRESS, 900 Witherspoon Bldg., Philadelphia PA 19107. Editor, chilren's fiction and nonfiction books: Barbara Bates. "Royalty rate depends on type of book, proportion of illustration, expected sales, previous record of author. No longer give escalating royalties in standard contract. Advance varies, depending on author's reputation and nature of book and author's need and preference." Current catalog available on request. Juvenile books published last year: 19. Query first with outline and sample chapter. Enclose return postage.
Juveniles: Fiction and nonfiction for children 9 years of age and up. No picture books, articles, gags, poetry, collections of stories. No mss over 40,000 words."

WESTOVER PUBLISHING CO., INC., 333 E. Grace St., Richmond VA 23219. Director: Edward H. Harrell. Publishes hardcover and paperback originals. Offers standard royalty contract; "advance varies with author." Published 17 titles last year. Will send a catalog to a writer on request. Query first with outline and sample chapter (must be typewritten). Reports in 3 weeks. Enclose return postage.
General Nonfiction and Fiction: "General subject matter; adult." Recent titles include *How to Defend Yourself at Auctions; Entertaining and Cooking With American Wines; America Awakes: A New Appraisal of the Twenties.*

WEYBRIGHT AND TALLEY, 750 Third Ave., New York NY 10017. President: Truman M. Talley. Publishes hardcover originals and text paperbacks. Usually offers standard 10-12½-15% royalty contract; "there is no average advance—usually $2,000 on up, depending on many factors." Published 30 titles last year. Will send a catalog to a writer on request. Query first with outline and sample chapters. Will consider photocopied submissions "if clear." Reports in 1 to 3 weeks. Enclose return postage.
General Fiction: "One-third very selective fiction." Publishes mainstream fiction, historical novels, science fiction, and espionage.
General Nonfiction: "Two-thirds nonfiction." Publishes books on Wall Street, business economics, history, politics, and is expanding its nature publishing. Length: 100,000 to 120,000 words. Recent titles include *The Money Lords* (Josephson); *The Go-Go Years* (Brooks).

DAVID WHITE INC., 60 East 55th St., New York NY 10022. Publishes hardcover and paperback orginals. Offers standard royalty schedule. Books published last year: 10. Current catalog available. Query first; for nonfiction send outline and

sample chapter. Address mss to Mr. David White. Reports in four weeks. Enclose return postage.
General Nonfiction. Diography and history; nature and natural sciences, and cook books.
Juveniles: Fiction and nonfiction.

ALBERT WHITMAN AND COMPANY, 560 West Lake St., Chicago IL 60606. Editor: Caroline Rubin. Publishes hardcover originals. Royalty payment. "There is some variation in what we offer, as when the author is also the artist in the case of picture books, for example. "There is a rather wide range in advances, depending on our relationship with the individual." Published 18 titles last year. Send queries and outlines for fiction and nonfiction. Do not query on picture books. Reports in two to four months. Enclose return postage.
Juveniles: Books retail for $2 or more. List usually includes several 32 to 40-page picture books for pre-school through grade one, and for grades one through three. Has some nonfiction, often related to social studies for the middle and upper grades. At present buying fewer than five mss from unpublished authors. "We are not interested in verse, fantasy, science fiction, religion, textbooks, synthetic folklore. We prefer realistic picture books and easy-to-read mysteries, sports stories, and historical material. An element of humor is a plus, but the fanciful or whimsical is usually not successful. Most of our books are used in school libraries. Therefore we look for a plus value in information, character development, or appeal to the less able reader." Length: picture books, 32 to 48 pages; easy-to-read fiction, 128 pages; folklore, 128 to 160 pages. Recent titles include *Mothers Can Do Anything* (Lasker); *The Mystery of the Missing Suitcase* (Heide).

WHITMORE PUBLISHING COMPANY, 35 Cricket Terrace, Ardmore PA 19003. Standard royalty contract or outright purchase. Send queries and sample chapters or poems to Blair A. Simon, Managing Editor. Reports in two to three weeks. Enclose return postage.
General Nonfiction: Publishing interest focused on books that will provide the reader with insight and techniques to manage his life more effectively. Interests include nutrition, education, community life, philosophy, self-improvement, family study and planning, career planning; explanations of significant science and technology not broadly understood.

WHITSTON PUBLISHING CO., INC., P.O. Box 322, Troy NY 12181. Editor: Stephen Goode. Publishes hardcover originals. Offers 10% royalty contract; "no advance. Our runs are almost never over 2,000." Published 15 titles last year. Will send a catalog to a writer on request. Query first. Reports "immediately." Enclose return postage.
Nonfiction: "We publish principally bibliographies, indexes, checklists, and the like, involving the humanities, social sciences, and in some instances those that are technical-medical. We have accepted bibliographies in card form, but generally prefer completed mss. Our audience is exclusively college and research libraries and larger public libraries reference and serials collections. Style and structure of each index or bibliography is unique to the book. Interested in unique indexes (original) and bibliographies and in cumulations of existing serial bibliographies, as in our *Bibliography of the Thoreau Society Bulletin Bibliographies.* A smaller emphasis is put on scholarly critical material, mostly essay collections by individuals or groups, involving the avant-garde of the 20th century. Creative avant-garde matter is in the form of anthologies, generally—not individual's canons." A recent title is *A Descriptive Catalog of the Bibliographies of 20th Century British Writers* (Mellown).

WILDERNESS PRESS, 2440 Bancroft Way, Berkeley CA 94704. Editor: Thomas Winnett. Publishes paperback originals. "We offer 8% to authors who have not published before. Our average advance is $200." Published 5 titles last year. Query first. Will consider photocopied submissions. Reports in 2 weeks. Enclose return postage.
Nature: "We publish books about the outdoors. So far, almost all our books are trail guides for hikers and backpackers, but we will be publishing how-to books about the outdoors and personal adventures. The ms must be accurate. The author must research an area thoroughly in person. If he is writing a trail guide, he must walk all the trails in the area his book is about. The outlook must be strongly conservationist.

The style must be appropriate for a highly literate audience." Recent titles include *Ski Tours in California; Backpacking for Fun.*

JOHN WILEY AND SONS, 605 Third Ave., New York NY 10016. Publishes hardcover and paperback originals. Royalty contract to be negotiated. Published 484 titles last year. Query first. Enclose return postage.
Technical and Textbooks: Publishes scientific works, business texts, research works, reference books; publishes college textbooks.

THE WILLIAMS AND WILKINS COMPANY, 428 E. Preston St., Baltimore MD 21202. Vice President and Editor-in-Chief: Dick Hoover. Payment is on royalty basis. Books published last year: 170. Send outlines and prefatory statement. Reports in 1 week to 60 days. Enclose return postage.
Medical: Publishes professional books in medicine, dentistry, veterinary medicine, both pre- and post-graduate, nursing books in closely allied fields.
Scientific: Books on the life sciences for general college courses.

WILSHIRE BOOK COMPANY, 12015 Sherman Rd., North Hollywood CA 91605. Editor: Melvin Powers. Publishes paperback originals and reprints. Royalty schedule is 5% of retail price. No advance. Published 50 titles last year. Query first with outline and sample chapters. Will consider photocopied submissions. Reports in 3 weeks. Enclose return postage.
Self-Help and How-to: Inspirational and psychological, self-help books of all types. Also interested in how-to-do-it books of all kinds. Interested in "books about horses, particularly instruction books." Length: 40,000 to 70,000 words. Recent titles include *Practical Horse Psychology; Way to Self-Realization; Psych Yourself to Better Tennis.*

WINTER HOUSE, LTD., 1123 Broadway, New York NY 10010. Publishes both hardcover and paperback originals and reprints. Individual royalty schedules. Send query and outline for nonfiction; outline, and sample chapter for fiction. Enclose S.A.S.E if return expected. Address all queries to Sarah Nichols Smith, Editor. Reports in 4 weeks. Enclose return postage.
General: Fiction and nonfiction "of the eclectic sort. No Gothic novels, westerns, or sex books. Should be of lasting literary merit."

WM. H. WISE AND CO., INC., 336 Mountain Rd., Union City NJ 07087. Editor: Harry Kickey. Publishes hardcover originals. "Buys all rights outright; buys titles outright at a price negotiated with author. Usual advance is $1,000, but this varies, depending on author's reputation and nature of book." Published 20 books last year. Query first with outline. Reports in 1 week. Enclose return postage.
General Nonfiction, Technical, Medical, and Scientific: Publishes home reference how-to-do-it books. Length: 200,000 to 300,000 words. Current titles include *Handy Guide for Car Owners; Consumer's Guide to Insurance.* General Nonfiction Editor: John Crawley Jr. Technical, Medical, and Scientific Department Editor: Harry Kickey.

*WOODBRIDGE PRESS PUBLISHING CO., P.O. Box 2053, Beverly Hills CA 90213. Editor-in-Chief: Howard B. Weeks. Publishes hardcover and paperback originals. Standard royalty contract. Rarely gives an advance. Will consider subsidy publishing. Published 2 titles last year. Books marketed by conventional methods. Query first. Will consider photocopied submissions. Returns rejected material immediately. Reports on material accepted for publication in 2 months. Enclose return postage with query.
General Nonfiction: "How-to books on personal health and well-being. Should offer the reader valuable new information or insights on anything from recreation to diet to mental health that will enable him to achieve greater personal fullfillment, with emphasis on that goal. Should minimize broad philosophy and maximize specific, useful information." Length: Books range from 96 to 240 pages. Also publishes cookbooks. Recent titles include *Hydroponic Gardening* (Bridwell); *Prayer Therapy* (Parker).

WORLD PUBLISHING COMPANY, a subsidiary of The Times Mirror Company, 110 East 59th St., New York NY 10022. (Also 2231 West 110th St., Cleveland OH 44102.) Publishes Meridian Books. President: Christopher J.H.M. Shaw; Executive Vice President and Publisher: Leonard R. Harris; Vice President, Dictionary and Encyclopedia Division: David B. Guralnik; Vice President, General Publishing Division: Peter V. Ritner. Published about 250 titles last year. Will send a catalog to a writer on request. Send complete ms. Reports in 4 weeks. Enclose return postage with ms.
General: Publishes Bibles, dictionaries, encyclopedias, reference books, adult fiction and nonfiction in all categories, religious and inspirational books.
Juveniles: Publishes juvenile fiction and nonfiction. "We want to move into serious books and expand our school and library line. We'll add more information books, too."

THE WRITER, INC., 8 Arlington St., Boston MA 02116. Editor: A.S. Burack. Publishes hardcover originals. Standard royalty schedule. Advance varies. Books published last year: 6. Catalog on request. Query first. Reports within three weeks. Enclose return postage.
Nonfiction: Books on writing for writers. Length: open.

WRITER'S DIGEST, 9933 Alliance Rd., Cincinnati OH 45242. Publishes hardcover and paperback originals. "Usual royalty contract is 10% of net. Books are sold in bookstores, by direct mail, and through regular advertising in *Writer's Digest* magazine." Send completed mss, outline and sample chapters, or query; query followed by outline and sample chapters preferred. Reports in 8 weeks. Enclose S.A.S.E. or return postage with all correspondence.
Nonfiction: "Looking for down-to-earth how-to books offering practical advice to beginning and professional writers on the techniques of writing. Authors should be established, selling writers. Possible topics are writing the confession story, writing the science fiction novel, writing religious articles, careers in writing, playwriting, case histories of books by 'big name' writers. Style should be conversational and anecdotal. Also interested in collections of interviews with writers, biographies of well-known writers, discussions of the current literary climate, and all other material relating to writers and writing." Current leading titles include *Writing and Selling Nonfiction* (Hayes B. Jacobs); *Writing Popular Fiction* (Koontz); *The Greeting Card Writer's Handbook* (H. Joseph Chadwick); *The Creative Writer* (Aron Mathieu).

XEROX EDUCATION PUBLICATIONS (formerly American Education Publications), 245 Long Hill Rd., Middletown CT 06457. Offers flat fee of $40 to $90 (depending on line count), or standard royalty contracts. Enclose synopsis and return postage with ms.
Fiction and Nonfiction: Needs range from children's picture or easy-to-read books to material appropriate for high school light reading. Grades 4, 5 and 6 needs specifically include activity books (games, puzzles and crafts) and ghost/mystery fiction. Length: children's picture or easy-to-read books, 32 pages; activity books, 96 pages; ghost/mystery fiction, 128 pages. Also, teaching aid materials for secondary school English teachers.

YESHIVA UNIVERSITY, 185th St. and Amsterdam Ave., New York NY 10033. Editor: Dr. Leon D. Stitskin. Enclose return postage with ms.
Religion and Philosophy: Publishes books and monographs on philosophy and religion, studies in Torah Judaism, and studies in Judaica.

YOSEMITE NATURAL HISTORY ASSOCIATION, P.O. Box 545, Yosemite National Park CA 95389. Editor: Henry Berrey. Publishes paperback originals and hardcover and paperback reprints. "Royalties range from 5% to 15%, depending on circumstances; we don't ordinarily make advances." Published 1 title last year. Will send a catalog to a writer on request. Query first. Will consider photocopied submissions. Reports in 2 months. Enclose return postage.
History and Nature: "We publish human history, natural history (botany, geology, etc.) of Yosemite and Sierra Nevada. These are illustrated pamphlets, 12 to 50 pages; 1,500 to 10,000 words. Accuracy is paramount."

ZONDERVAN PUBLISHING HOUSE, 1415 Lake Dr., S.E., Grand Rapids MI 49506. Managing Editor: T. Alton Bryant. Publishes hardcover and paperback originals. Royalty schedule: 10%. Books published last year: 120. Will send current catalog on request. Writers should follow the University of Chicago *Manual of Style.* "Always send inquiry and keep in mind the conservative, evangelical audience and readership." Prefers query with outline and sample chapter. Reports in 6-10 weeks. Enclose return postage.

Fiction: Adult fiction. Contemporary life, oriented to the Chistian life. Length: 60,000 words.

Religion: Length: 60,000 words. Books on teenage problems and interest areas. Missionary emphasis. Recent titles include *Satan Is Alive and Well on Planet Earth* and *No Pat Answers.*

Philosophy: Material making the Christian life relevant and meaningful in the arena of the modern world. Length: 60,000 to 90,000 words.

Science: Material that shows the harmony of science and the Scriptures. Length: 60,000 to 90,000 words.

Biography: Prominent religious leaders of the past and the present, emphasizing the spiritual secret of their lives. "Subject (missionary, Christian statesman, etc.) must be known and have a following." Length: 50,000 to 100,000 words. Recent titles include *On Duty in Bangladesh; The Richest Lady in Town.*

SUBSIDY BOOK PUBLISHERS

Subsidy book publishing, sometimes called "vanity publishing," is the process of printing books for a fee which the writer pays. If a writer submits a book manuscript to a standard royalty book publishing company they will either reject it or accept it for publication. If they accept it for publication they will usually pay the author an advance check on receipt of his signed contract and always make royalty payments subsequently based on the sale of the book.

Many writers who have tried unsuccessfully to interest a standard royalty book publisher in their book decide to pay to have the book published themselves. How much does it cost? Here are some examples of estimates from subsidy publishers: but there are variations: 500 copies of a 48-page book of poetry, $900; 2,500 copies of a 96-page book, $2,160; 3,000 copies of a 176-page book, $3,360. The books are professionally printed, bound and usually have an attractive dust jacket. While the subsidy book publishing contract agrees to pay 40% royalty to the author rather than the 10% offered by most standard book publishers, the problem is that the subsidy book publisher does not have book salesmen calling on bookstores to sell the book, is usually not able to get national review media to review the book, and can engage in only a certain amount of promotion and advertising. All of the subsidy publishers who advertise in *Writer's Digest* adhere to the advertising policies the magazine has established which require that they state specifically in their contract what they are offering and spell out to the writer exactly what he is getting for his payment. They will deliver everything that is promised in the contract. The following is a list of book publishers who specialize in subsidy publishing and who have agreed to abide by the *Writer's Digest* advertising policies.

Dorrance and Company, 1617 J. F. Kennedy Blvd., Philadelphia PA 19103.

Exposition Press, 50 Jericho Turnpike, Jericho NY 11753.

Mojave Books, 7040 Darby Ave., Reseda CA 91335.

Pageant-Poseidon Ltd., 644 Pacific St., Brooklyn NY 11217.

Thom Henricks Associates, P.O. Box 1024, Birmingham AL 35201.

Vantage Press, 516 W. 34th St., New York NY 10001.

William-Frederick Press, 55 East 86 Street, New York NY 10028.

MISCELLANEOUS FREELANCE MARKETS AND SERVICES

Audiovisual Markets

Because producers of "software"—the trade term for nonprint materials like records, filmstrips, tape cassettes, etc., as opposed to "hardware," which refers to the machines on which they are viewed or played—frequently have highly individualized editorial requirements, freelance writers are encouraged to seek firm assignments from audiovisual producers before writing or submitting finished scripts. A good query letter should outline the writer's credentials (as an educator, specialist in some subject, or professional scriptwriter), include a sample of his writing, and give details of his proposed script or series of scripts.

Many of the companies currently active in the audiovisual field are working with staff writers and do not actively seek freelance contributions. Those who are interested in staff positions will find a more complete list of audiovisual producers in the excellent Audiovisual Market Place *(published by R.R. Bowker).*

Software producers pay on a flat fee or royalty basis, depending on the company and the quality of the writer's material. The sponsored film production company, operating on a contract basis to produce audiovisuals for the government, business, or private organizations, offers a flat fee payment, which varies according to the nature of the project and the writer's credentials. If a company produces and markets its own audiovisual products (usually to the elementary and secondary school and college markets), payment is most often according to a royalty contract with the writer, but a flat fee is sometimes paid. The flat fees vary widely, but royalty agreements usually approximate the ones offered for school texts. Based on the net money the publisher receives on sales, this is 3% to 5% for elementary and secondary school materials and 8% to 12% for college textbooks. A few producers offer an even higher percentage, some going as high as 18.75% for college materials.

ADDISON-WESLEY PUBLISHING CO., Reading MA 01867. Contact: Leslie J. Wilson. "It's likely that most of our scripts would come from corporate managers or training directors, or from university educators—largely because such people would be able to draw upon their practical experience in developing training material. We would be glad to consider submissions from anyone, on our usual royalty basis (10%), provided it was understood we're not aiming at a general consumer market." Consult current Addison-Wesley "Training Publications Catalog" before submitting. Query first. Enclose S.A.S.E. for response to queries or return of submissions.

Business: "We probably will have some audio cassettes produced for us. These would be aimed at professional or managerial self-development, or designed for course use by in-company training programs of managers, supervisors, etc. We aim at a professional education and rather formalized corporate training market."

ADMIRAL FILM PRODUCTIONS, INC. (formerly Associated Film Consultants), 369 Lexington Ave., New York NY 10017. Contact: B. S. Greenberg. For general TV audience, school audience (primary, secondary and college level), specialized audiences. Copyrighted. Writer should have background in film script writing of the specific subject area required. Query first, enclosing resume of experience. Enclose S.A.S.E. for response to queries.
Education and General: Broad range of subjects including science, research, food, fashion, home furnishings, social issues, etc. Film loops, silent filmstrips, sound filmstrips, motion pictures, phonograph records, prerecorded tapes and cassettes, slides (35mm). All lengths, from one-minute news films to 60-minute documentaries. Average script fee ranges between 5% and 10% of gross billing of project.

AERO PRODUCTS RESEARCH, INC., 11201 Hindry Ave., Los Angeles CA 90045. Contact: J. Parr. For pilot training schools, private and public schools from K through college. Copyrighted. Write for copy of guidelines for writers. "Writer would have to be qualified in specific project." Enclose S.A.S.E. for response to queries or return of submissions.
Education: "Developing and editing both technical and nontechnical material. Charts, silent filmstrips, models, multimedia kits, overhead transparencies, phonograph records, prerecorded tapes and cassettes, slides and study prints. Royalty arrangements are handled on an individual project basis."

AFI-ATELIER FILMS, INC., 293-5 N. Fulton Ave., P.O. Box 8, Mount Vernon NY 10552. Producer-Director: Desi K. Bognár. For "professional and/or general audience. Usually copyrighted. We work with freelance people. If material and subject requires, we assign projects. We prefer to contact writers (we keep their names and specialty fields on file), depending on subject matter. For our overseas work, we like our people to speak a few languages. We must deal individually with subjects." Enclose S.A.S.E. for response to queries.
General: Editorial requirements "depend on type and sponsor. We do documentaries, TV films and video tapes, medical films, promotion shorts, some educational films. Also preparing for feature and featurette. We are open-minded and flexible. Length varies according to kind of material." Produces silent filmstrips; sound filmstrips; 16mm, 35mm, and super 8mm motion pictures; slides. Pays in fees or royalties—"either or both, depending on type, length and purpose of film."

ANIMATION ARTS ASSOCIATES, INC., 1539 Race St., Philadelphia PA 19102. Contact: Harry E. Ziegler, Jr. Copyrighted. For "government, industry, engineers, doctors, scientists, dentists, general public, military." Send "resume of credits for motion picture and filmstrip productions. The writer should have scriptwriting credits for training, sales promotion, public relations." Enclose S.A.S.E. for response to queries.
Business: Produces 3½ minute, 8mm and 16mm film loops; 16mm and 35mm motion pictures (ranging from 5 to 40 minutes), 2x2 or 4x5 slides and teaching machine programs for training, sales, industrial and public relations. Fee arrangements dependent on client's budget.

HAL MARC ARDEN AND COMPANY, Executive Offices: 1 Gardiner's Bay Drive, Shelter Island NY 11964; Production Facility: 245 W. 55th St., New York NY 10019. President: Hal Marc Arden. Copyrighted. "Writer must have experience in writing for motion pictures. Scripts are not solicited, but we welcome resumes." Query first. Enclose S.A.S.E. for response to queries.
General: "Specialize in sponsored publications only: documentary, educational, public service." Produces silent and sound filmstrips, 16mm motion pictures, multimedia kits, phonograph records, prerecorded tapes and cassettes, and slides. "No royalties. Fees negotiated."

AUDIO VISUAL PRODUCTIONS, INC., 1233 N. Ashland Ave., Chicago IL 60622. Contact: Robert M. Rubel. For "lower primary grades." Copyrighted. Query first. Enclose S.A.S.E. for response to queries.
Education: Produces "single concept teaching" materials for lower primary grades. Produces super 8mm film loops, silent filmstrips, sound filmstrips, super 8mm motion pictures, multimedia kits, phonograph records, prerecorded tapes and slides.

BACHNER PRODUCTIONS, INC., 501 Madison Ave., New York NY 10010. Contact: Annette Bachner. Audience is "corporate personnel, sales people, perspective clients for corporations." Writer should "submit list of credits or sample films. Experience in film writing, working with spot sheets, etc., is needed. We do not keep staff writers and use freelance writers only." Query first. Enclose S.A.S.E. for response to queries.
Business: "Sales training and motivational fields. Subject matter varies. Length of films from 5 to 30 minutes."

EZRA BAKER FILMS, INC., Village Square Building, Bronxville NY 10708. Contact: Ezra R. Baker. For "general motion picture theater audiences; also, TV." Copyrighted. Writer must have "the ability to think in a subdued, humorous vein." Enclose S.A.S.E. for return of submissions or reply to query.
General: Looking for ideas for 10-minute motion picture short subjects. "Simple subject matter having rapport with general motion picture theater audiences. All important is the twist ending. Most always humorous in nature. The idea can be as little as 1 paragraph or as much as 10 pages. The idea and the twist ending must be apparent. I always do the screenplay." Pays "$750 for an acceptable idea. Meaning, if I like it and my backers like it and we decide to go ahead on production, the writer gets paid. The writer will get a screen credit. The fee can go up if additional stories by the writer are accepted."

BILLY BARNES PRODUCTIONS, 407 Severin St., Chapel Hill NC 27514. Contact: Billy E. Barnes. For persons "from kindergarten to specialized professions, like physicians." Copyright "depends on material. Have never bought a script from the outside, but would be interested in seeing good, well-researched scripts on a current subject for which there is a provable market. Tell me about the potential market as well as the subject." Query first. Enclose S.A.S.E. for response to queries.
General: "Documentaries in social action fields, training films for nonprofit organizations, fund-raising films, information-sharing films on programs such as new methods in therapy for retarded children, low income housing, etc. We also produce filmstrips for west coast educational distributors; varying subjects. Geography no consideration—recent productions ranged to Wisconsin, Arkansas, Kentucky, Tennessee." Produces silent and sound filmstrips, kinescopes, 8mm and 16mm motion pictures, phonograph records, prerecorded tapes and cassettes, slides, study prints. "Filmstrips and slide-tape shows average 16 minutes generally; motion pictures, 28 minutes. BB Productions markets many of its own properties, and it is interested in new products for which there is a promising, promotable market." Prefers a flat fee payment, "depending on length, subject, and market potential."

BARR FILMS, P.O. Box 7-C, Pasadena CA 91104. President: Donald Barr. For "classroom audience, grades K through secondary." Not copyrighted. Query first. "We are only marginally interested in outside scripts at this time, but will consider scripts that are of special interest to us. Send completed visual/dialog script." Enclose S.A.S.E. for return of submissions.
General: Produces 16mm motion pictures for "all curriculum areas. Supply visual treatment and proposed voice over, dialog, etc." Pay "negotiable; have paid $400 and up, depending on our interest."

BEAR FILMS, INC., 805 Smith St., Baldwin NY 11510. Contact: Frank Bear. For elementary and secondary schools; some general adult." Copyrighted and not copyrighted material. Will assign projects to qualified writers. "Credentials according to project." Query first. Enclose S.A.S.E. for response to queries.
Education and General: Requirements "varied, according to subject matter and audience." Produces silent and sound filmstrips, 16mm motion pictures, multimedia kits, slides. "Fee according to project."

BORG-WARNER EDUCATIONAL SYSTEMS, 7450 North Natchez, Niles IL 60648. Contact: William A. LaPlante. For "kindergarten through adult basic education." Copyrighted. Will send a catalog to a writer on request. Query first. Enclose S.A.S.E. for response to queries.
Language Arts and Mathematics: "Language arts and beginning math programmed instruction designed for System 80 audiovisual unit. Material presented must be educationally sound." Produces sound filmstrips, prerecorded tapes and cassettes. Length: 300 to 500 words. Offers outright fee or royalties.

STEPHEN BOSUSTOW PRODUCTIONS, 1649 Eleventh St., Santa Monica CA 90404. Contact: Penny Bergman. For "public schools, libraries, industries." Buys all rights. Will send a catalog to a writer on request. "Submit one- to two-paragraph concept proposal. A background in entertainment films would be helpful for the writer. Writers should submit concepts for series of films, keeping in mind an entertainment style, lots of action, fast pacing and timing, dealing with contemporary problems, social injustices." Query first. Enclose S.A.S.E. for response to queries.
Language Arts and Social Sciences: "Our general subject matter is language arts and social sciences. The style should be right for visual action in outline form. 'Parables' are useful too." Produces 8mm film loops, sound filmstrips, 16mm motion pictures. Pays 5% of gross sales.

GERT BUNCHEZ AND ASSOCIATES, INC., 7730 Carondelet, St. Louis MO 63105. Contact: Gert Bunchez, President. For radio audiences. Enclose S.A.S.E. for return of submissions.
Radio Programs: "We feel that the time is propitious for the return of stories to radio. It is our feeling that it is not necessary to 'bring back' old programs, and that there certainly should be contemporary talent to write mystery, detective, suspense, soap operas, etc. We cast, produce, tape, and sell these properties to clients and radio stations. We need sustaining material with main characters. There will be a need for 52 30-minute plays, for 15-minute 5-days-weekly 52-weeks soapies, or 30-minute weekly soapies. Rates start at $100 per script."

CAMPBELL FILMS, Academy Ave., Saxtons River VT 05154. Contact: Michael Campbell. For elementary or high school level. "Usually copyrighted." Query first. "Writers should have experience in motion picture production." Enclose S.A.S.E. for response to queries.
Education: For children, art crafts, societal problems. 8mm film loops, sound filmstrips, 16mm motion pictures. Pays 5% to 15%.

CHAMBA PRODUCTIONS, INC., 155 Chamber St., New York NY 10007. President: St. Clair Bourne. For "general audiences, minority audiences. We make films for all levels (high school and adult)." Write for copy of guidelines for writers. Will assign projects to writers with "creativity, sensitivity. We prefer submission of film treatments first." Query first. Enclose S.A.S.E. for response to queries.
Education: "We make educational, motivational, and documentary films. However, I am beginning to branch out into feature-type films (story line, actors, etc.). Our films are usually social action oriented." Produces 16mm motion pictures. Payment "negotiable"; minimum, $1,000.

CINE-GRAFIX, INC., 8404 Indian Hills Drive, Omaha NE 68114. Contact: Dennis Burrow. "Would like to hear from writers who are experienced in the field." Query first. Enclose S.A.S.E. for response to queries.
General: "Most of material is documentary or point-of-purchase sales." Produces sound filmstrips; 16mm, 35mm, super 8mm motion pictures; prerecorded tapes and cassettes, slides, and multimedia kits. Payment "negotiated."

CINEMATOGRAPHY ASSOCIATES, INC., 600 Barrymore Lane, Mamaroneck NY 10543. Contact: Bert Spielvogel. Wants writers with "talent." Query first. Enclose S.A.S.E. for response to queries.
General: "Treatments and scripts suitable for theatrical audience, TV audience, documentaries, and for children. Be creative. I'm looking for film designers." Produces 16mm and 35mm motion pictures. Length for features: 5 to 90 minutes. Length for industrial films: 5 to 20 minutes. Pays "$400 to $1,500 for 8- to 10-minute

industrial film; fee plus percentage for feature or TV series script. Have paid as high as $2,500 for a treatment, script and shooting script combination for industrial, education films."

CLOSE PRODUCTIONS, INC., 2020 San Carlos Blvd., Fort Myers Beach FL 33931. President: E. Burt Close. For "businessmen, training managers, students of high schools, technical schools, and occupational training classes." Rights purchased "for filmstrip and cassette tape purposes. Will consider only experienced writers who can do a thoroughly professional job. Writer should first query as to what assignments are open and submit complete resume of experience with samples of published writing, if possible. Will not accept or examine any ms sent without first querying." Send query to E. Burt Close and enclose S.A.S.E. for reply.
Business and Education: "Subject matter: business and educational training. Style: filmstrip narration with direct explanation or conversational style, double-spaced by frame. The emphasis should be toward training, teaching, or demonstrating. Length: 60 to 100 frames." Produces silent filmstrips, sound filmstrips, prerecorded tapes and cassettes, and slides. Offers "royalty of 5% to 10% of the sales income received by producer, or fee to be negotiated on each assignment."

CONTEMPO PRODUCTIONS INC., 25 West 68th St., New York NY 10023. Contact: Joan Marshall. "Our audiences vary widely, from top management to consumers. We use topnotch freelance writers who are experienced in business communications, as well as related fields of TV, MP and theatre. Submit a detailed resume accompanied by a sample of your best work in each medium." Enclose S.A.S.E. for response to queries.
Business: "Our field is business communications in such areas as sales meetings, management conferences, sales promotion, public relations, new product introduction, sales training. We frequently use music and lyrics and comedy writing." Sound filmstrips, 16mm motion pictures, multimedia kits, phonograph records, prerecorded tapes and cassettes, and 35mm and super slides. "We work on a very high quality level and require strong creative concepts, as well as excellent writing skills. In-person contact imperative. Fees are paid on a per project basis and vary according to overall budget for the project."

CONTEMPORARY DRAMA SERVICE, Box 457, Downers Grove IL 60515. Contact: Editor. For high school age religious education groups. Enclose S.A.S.E. for return of submissions.
Religion: "Will consider filmstrip scripts that deal with subjects of contemporary religious importance for high school religious education groups. Liberal approach preferred. Professional quality only. Author paid on a royalty basis."

CONTINENTAL FILM PRODUCTIONS CORPORATION, 2320 Rossville Blvd., Chattanooga TN 37408. Contact: James E. Webster. "Our audiences are all types as we do custom films, syndications, and various industrial applications." Produces copyrighted and not copyrighted material; "all syndicated films are copyrighted." Will send a catalog to a writer on request. Write for copy of guidelines for writers. "We would be interested in using outside writers. They must have experience in writing filmstrips or industrial and technical motion picture scripts. We would require specimen of previous scripts that the writer has written to determine his capabilities, and a list of his clients." Query first. Enclose S.A.S.E. for response to queries.
General: "Each one of our scripts is written on information supplied by our customers and by us for our syndicated films." Produces 8mm and 16mm film loops, silent filmstrips, sound filmstrips, 16mm and 35mm motion pictures, multimedia kits, phonograph records, prerecorded tapes and cassettes, and slides. "We do not work on a royalty basis. We purchase the script outright. Custom sound filmstrips, $6 per frame; custom motion pictures, 5% of basic production cost."

DAVID C. COOK PUBLISHING CO., 850 N. Grove Ave., Elgin IL 60120. Editor: Mrs. Sylvia Tester. For "teachers of children in preschool and/or the elementary and middle grades. Stories and poetry are slanted toward children in these grades. These materials are used both in public schools and parochial or private schools." Buys all rights. Will send a catalog to a writer on request. Write for copy of guide-

lines for writers. "Since all our work is done on an assignment basis, we ask prospective writers to contact us. We then give them a sample assignment, for which a modest fee is paid. Future assignments are given as they arise on basis of the quality of the samples. Writers should have at least a B.A. degree, preferably more, several years experience in teaching, and the ability to write for both adults and children." Query first. Enclose S.A.S.E. for response to queries.
Education: Produces "teaching pictures with comprehensive manuals for teachers. Subject matter for teachers' manuals must be correlated with visuals. Each ms includes background information on subject (encyclopedia style), classroom learning activities with specific instructions, some stories for children, and some good poetry for children. Stories and poetry are sometimes assigned separately." Length for stories: 500 to 1,500 words. Length for entire ms: 25,000 to 35,000 words. "We pay fees, which vary depending on the assignment." Average fees: children's story, $60; children's poems, $1 per line; $1,000 to $1,200 for an entire teacher's manual.

DEFENSE PRODUCTS COMPANY, 8608 Irvington Ave., Bethesda MD 20034. Contact: Harry A. Carragher. For general audience, TV audience, school audience, national trade audiences, and government. Not copyrighted. Will send catalog to writer on request. Write for copy of guidelines for writers. Query first, with sample scripts and proposals. Enclose S.A.S.E. for response to queries.
General: 10- to 28-minute scripts and motion pictures, 16mm film loops, silent filmstrips, sound filmstrips, models, 16 and 35mm motion pictures, phonograph records, prerecorded tapes and cassettes, slides and radio spots and TV commercials. Pays 10% fee.

T.S. DENISON AND CO., INC., Textbooks Division, Minneapolis MN 55437. Contact: Editor-in-Chief. Educators who feel their school systems might qualify are advised to query. Enclose S.A.S.E. for response to queries.
Education: "We are planning a series of instructional packages or cassettes that will include a variety of materials to make a complete teaching program in the classroom. We are getting tested materials from school systems who have originated programs." Payment by "outright purchase or a flat fee on copies sold."

FRANZ EDSON, INC., P.O. Box 503, Huntington NY 11743. Contact: Franz Edson. For general audience. Copyrighted. Will assign audiovisual projects to "talented" writers. Query first. Enclose S.A.S.E. for response to queries.
General: Subject matter varies. "No special format. Every film has its own style." Industrial, public relations, documentary educational, etc. Produces 16mm film loops, silent filmstrips, sound filmstrips, 16mm motion pictures, multimedia kits, manuals, brochures, catalogs. Pays $200 to $2,000, "depending on stories."

EDUCASTING SYSTEMS, INC., 770 Lexington Ave., New York NY 10021. Contact Norman S. Livingston, President. For "entry level employees to veterans." Copyrighted. Buys all rights. Will send catalog to writer on request. Query first. "We'd like to know past work done and for whom." Enclose S.A.S.E.
Education: "Career education and industrial training materials. Sound filmstrips, prerecorded tapes and cassettes, 35mm slides and teaching machine programs." No length limit. Pays fee only; no royalties. "Fee depends on size of job and number of modules required."

EMC CORPORATION, 180 E. 6th St., St. Paul MN 55101. Contact: Northrop Dawson, Jr., Editor-in-Chief. Kindergarten through college audience. Copyrighted. Will send catalog to writer on request. Write for copy of guidelines for writers. Query first, enclosing S.A.S.E. for reply. Would like to see samples of previously produced educational programs before making assignment.
Education: All curriculum areas. Filmstrips; multimedia kits. Controlled vocabulary in language arts program. Charts, prerecorded tapes and cassettes. Payment "varies from outright purchases to royalties that rise per number of units sold."

ENVISION CORPORATION, 323 Newbury St., Boston MA 02115. Contact: Mrs. Susan McIntosh. For first graders through college. Copyrighted. Will send catalog to writer on request. Query first. Enclose S.A.S.E. for response to queries.
Education: "Everything from first grade to college chemistry." Sound filmstrips,

16mm motion pictures, multimedia kits, phonograph records, prerecorded tapes and cassettes. "Fee is negotiated for each assignment and depends entirely on project."

FAIRCHILD VISUALS, 7 E. 12th St., New York NY 10003. Contact: Ed Gold. For high school and post-secondary training audiences; includes fashion, vocational careers, consumerism. Approximately 20% of audiovisual materials designed for junior college and university courses in business and fashion. Copyrighted. Will send catalog to writer on request. Query first, with a resume and writing samples. "Writer must be able to demonstrate ability to think visually either in past work or in a proposed storyboard. Teaching experience a help, but journalistic researching skills most important strength. Writer must be able to accompany photographer during shooting sessions." Enclose S.A.S.E. for response to queries.

Education: "Currently considering freelance material in the following vocational and career areas: hotel-motel, transportation, advertising, sales promotion and government employment. Multimedia kits, prerecorded tapes and cassettes and 35mm slides. Standard rate is 7½% of net proceeds."

FAMILY FILMS/COUNTERPOINT FILMS, 5823 Santa Monica Blvd., Hollywood CA 90038. Contact: Paul R. Kidd, Director of Product Development. For all age levels from preschool through adult. Copyrighted. Will send a catalog to writer on request. Query first. "We don't encourage submission of mss. Majority projects are assigned and developed to our specifications. Writers are welcome to submit their credentials and experience. Some experience in writing film and filmstrip scripts is desired. A teaching credential or teaching experience valuable for our school materials. Active involvement in a mainstream church desirable for our religious projects."

Education and Religion: "Sound filmstrips, 16mm motion pictures and prerecorded tapes and cassettes for schools, universities, public libraries, and for interdenominational religious market. Motion pictures vary from 10 minutes to 30 to 40 minutes. Filmstrips about 50 to 60 frames with running time of 7 to 10 minutes. Emphasis on the human situation and person-to-person relationships. No royalty arrangements. Outright payment depends on project and available budget. As an example, usual filmstrip project requires 4 scripts, for which we pay $150 to $250 each."

FIREBIRD FILMS, 203 Glen Ave., Sea Cliff NY 11579. For "K to 12." Copyrighted. Writer must have "good background in films, with emphasis on educational experience; educator background, with some communications skills. Age unimportant, but must have a young mind—flexibility plus craftsmanship." Query first. Enclose S.A.S.E. for response to queries.

Language Arts and Social Studies: Editorial requirements "vary with each unit type produced." Produces silent filmstrips, sound filmstrips, 16mm motion pictures, prerecorded tapes and cassettes. Pay "varies; 1% to 5% royalties, depending on nature of script and quality of budget."

GAMCO, Box 1911, Big Spring TX 79720. Contact: Auriel LaFond. For "public schools, elementary to college levels." Copyrighted. Will send a catalog to a writer on request. Write for copy of guidelines for writers. Writer must have "teaching experience, knowledge of subject, preferably experience in preparation of a-v materials." Query first. Enclose S.A.S.E. for response to queries.

Education: "All subject areas. Requirements to be worked out according to project." Produces overhead transparencies, prerecorded tapes, cassettes and filmstrips. Pays "10% royalty on first 20,000 net sales, 8% next 80,000 net sales, 7% over 100,000 net sales."

GENERAL LEARNING CORPORATION, 250 James St., Morristown NJ 07960. For "elementary and high school students, 2-year and 4-year college students, students of all ages in career education, teachers and administrators." Copyrighted. Assigns audiovisual projects to qualified writers "on occasion. Write to editor-in-chief proposing an idea; complete submission form. Writer must have understanding of school market and general school texts and materials." Query first. Enclose S.A.S.E. for response to queries.

Education: Editorial requirements "vary with purpose and audience." Produces silent filmstrips, sound filmstrips, 16mm motion pictures, multimedia kits, overhead transparencies, phonograph records, prerecorded tapes and slides, and manipulative devices for early learners. "Depending on grade level of material, involvement as major or minor author, and other considerations, usual royalty percentage averages perhaps 5% to 6%."

HARPER AND ROW PUBLISHERS, INC., 10 E. 53 St., New York NY 10022. Director of Media: R.L. Berman. For "college and high school students." Copyrighted. Will send a catalog to a writer on request. Writer must have "knowledge of subject, willingness to coauthor with academician, and experience in appropriate format." Proposal "must be relatively well structured with sufficient detail to permit evaluation, and some samples of final script." Query first. Enclose S.A.S.E. for response to queries.
Education: Requirements "vary, but must be curriculum-oriented. Sensitivity to market needs and teaching methods important. Stick to established media. Not interested in 'far out' or television-type material." Produces 8mm film loops, sound filmstrips, 16mm motion pictures, multimedia kits, phonograph records, prerecorded tapes and cassettes, slides. Payment "varies with work done. May be straight fee or royalty."

ROBERT BRUCE HICKS AND ASSOCIATES, Suite LL-6, O'Hare Inn, 6600 N. Mannheim Rd., Des Plaines IL 60018. Contact: B.B. Hicks. For "mostly business corporations and trade associations." Copyrighted "sometimes." Writer must have "good writing ability. Acquaintance with the job-at-hand can come with the research. I like to know a writer's background and see samples of his work. We return samples." Query first. Enclose S.A.S.E. for response to queries.
General: "Each project is different, customized to the requirements of a specific client—corporation or trade association." Produces sound filmstrips, 8mm and 16mm motion pictures, phonograph records, prerecorded tapes and cassettes, slides, and "industrial printed materials—catalogs, sales brochures, etc." Pays $1,000 to $2,000 (depending on research, etc., required) for script for 1-hour industrial show with actors; $1,500 to $3,000 (depending on complexity) for 30-minute motion picture script; $500 to $1,000 for script for 15-minute slide presentation.

HUBBARD SCIENTIFIC CO., Box 105, Northbrook IL 60062. Editor: R. W. Wittingham. "Our major audience is the junior and senior high school student (grades 6 to 12)." Copyrighted. "Writer must be able to furnish samples of professional work, preferably in our subject and media areas. We only work with writers on specific assignments and do not want unsolicited mss." Query first. Enclose S.A.S.E. for response to queries.
Science and Social Sciences: "Subject matter: science, social studies. Style should be logical, clear, concise. We're looking for writers who can follow instructions and write a logical, easy-to-follow, and accurate script, student booklet, or teacher's guide. Teaching experience and knowledge of the subject is desirable, but the ability to organize information into a logical presentation is more important." Produces charts, dioramas, 8mm film loops, sound filmstrips, models, multimedia kits, overhead transparencies, prerecorded tapes and cassettes, slides, and study prints. Payment on fee basis.

IMAGE PUBLISHING CORPORATION, 15 E. 26th St., New York NY 10010. Contact: Kenneth E. Baranski. For schools. Copyrighted. "When approached, we will deal with a potential freelance writer on the basis of what work, if any, we have. It is helpful if the writer has written instructional materials before; it may even be helpful if he has taught. The basic requirement, however, is intelligence, a respect for the English language, and a compulsion to write clear, graceful sentences. We provide direction and guidance for each project." Query first. Enclose S.A.S.E. for response to queries.
Education: "We publish instructional materials, mainly audiovisual, for schools, mainly elementary schools. Such materials obviously should be written in a language understandable to young children. The accompanying teacher's materials should reveal some awareness of educational practices." Produces sound filmstrips, multimedia kits, overhead transparencies, phonograph records, prerecorded tapes

and cassettes, slides, and teacher's guides. "We prefer a fee arrangement, which is negotiable."

IMPERIAL INTERNATIONAL LEARNING CORPORATION, Box 548, Rt. 54 South, Kankakee IL 60901. Contact: Mrs. Kathryn Ring, Director of Product Development. For boys and girls in the intermediate grades (approximately 8 to 12 years old). "Even though we do buy a fair amount of material from freelancers, our needs are quite specialized and we discourage speculative submissions of completed stories or scripts. Instead, we prefer a letter from potential writers stating their background in terms of the types of material they have written and marketed and any special qualifications which would suit them for our type of material (for example, a writer who is also an educator, or a person whose background includes scripting or audio material for tape, radio or dramatic productions)." Query first. Enclose S.A.S.E. for response to queries.

General: "We are producers of audio materials (in both cassette and reel-to-reel forms) and sound filmstrips for the school, library, and consumer markets. Our materials are marketed under the Imperial International trademark in the education field and under the trademark of Grademaker in the consumer field. Filmstrips are short (30 to 50 frames) and are written on assignment only. Experienced writers should query first, enclosing S.A.S.E. for reply. Regarding our needs, we buy considerable freelance material for use both on tape and in print. (Our materials, especially in the reading field, involve printed stories and articles and tape scripts to accompany them. The two media are used together to form an entire lesson.) Thus, we are actually two different kinds of markets—a market for audio scripts and a market for short stories and articles. Some of our particular needs are children's stories of under 1,500 words, both for young children and for children up to the age of 12; stories and articles written to meet the interests of older children (from fourth through tenth grade) but with a simple vocabulary. Humor, adventure; stories which deal empathetically with social issues and relevant problems (pollution, minority groups, disappearing resources and species, space travel). Looking for a lively style. Characters to identify with. No preaching. No fairy tales, folk tales or legends. No talking animals. Regarding lengths and payment arrangements: these are individually negotiated but tend to follow the current practices of the industry. Fees for stories range from $50 to $100. Audio script payment depends on length and amount of research required."

INDIVIDUALIZED INSTRUCTION INCORPORATED, 1901 Walnut, P.O. Box 25308, Oklahoma City OK 73125. Contact: Jerome P. Welch, Vice-President. Query first. Enclose S.A.S.E. for response to queries.

Language Arts: "As a rule, we are interested in complete educational programs in the language arts area of elementary education. The number of lessons will vary, from as few as 20 to as many as 50. Presently, our main venture into the audiovisual world is with prerecorded lessons on cassettes with corresponding folders, books, etc. We are currently very much in the market for new programs. However, prospective producers must be interested in and capable of writing programs for education. Too, our programs must be written to complement the automatic stop feature of our tape player. This feature allows the pupil to respond at his own pace and frees him from the frustrations and distractions of group instructions." Pays 5% royalties on net sales of software.

INSTRUCTIONAL IMAGE CORPORATION, 25 Broadway, Pleasantville NY 10570. Contact: G. Wolf. For "medical and paramedical trainees, students in grades 4 to 12, and users of advertising and promotional specialties." Copyrighted. Write for copy of guidelines for writers. "Credentials needed depend on assignment." Query first. Enclose S.A.S.E. for response to queries.

Education, Medicine, and Promotion: Material on "medical and paramedical and reading improvement subjects; promotional specialties, posters." Produces charts, silent filmstrips, sound filmstrips, prerecorded tapes and cassettes, study prints, and concealed image response systems. "Royalties and/or fees are negotiated. Minimum fee is 20¢ a word."

INSTRUCTOR CURRICULUM MATERIALS, 7 Bank St., Dansville NY 14437. Editor-in-Chief: Mrs. Ruth Ann Hayward. "U.S. and Canadian school supervisors, principals, and teachers purchase items in our line for instructional purposes." Buys all rights. Will send a catalog to a writer on request. Writer should have "experience in preparing materials for elementary students, including suitable teaching guides to accompany them, and demonstrate knowledge of the appropriate subject areas, or demonstrable ability for accurate and efficient research and documentation. Please query." Enclose S.A.S.E. for response to queries.

Education: "Elementary curriculum enrichment, all subject areas. Display material, copy, and illustration should match interest and reading skills of children in grades for which material is intended. Production is limited to printed matter: pictures, charts, duplicating masters, workbooks, teaching guides." Length: 6,000 to 12,000 words. "Standard royalty contract, but fees vary considerably, depending on type of project."

KEN-DEL PRODUCTIONS, INC., 111 Valley Rd., Richardson Park, Wilmington DE 19804. Contact: Ed Kennedy. For "elementary, junior high, high school, and college level, as well as interested organizations and companies." Will assign projects to qualified writers. Query first. Enclose S.A.S.E. for response to queries.

General: Wants material for "topics of the present (technology, cities, traffic, transit, pollution, ecology, health, water, race, genetics, consumerism, fashions, communications, education, population control, waste, future sources of food, undeveloped sources of living, food, health, etc.); topics of the future; how-to series (everything for the housewife, farmer, banker, mechanic on music, art, sports, reading, science, love, repair, sleep—on any subject)." Produces dioramas; sound filmstrips; 8mm, 16mm, and 35mm motion pictures; 16mm film loops; phonograph records; prerecorded tapes and cassettes; slides. Pays a flat fee.

WALTER J. KLEIN CO., LTD., 6301 Carmel Rd., Charlotte NC 28211. Contact: Richard A. Klein. Audience "varies, from general to specific, such as women's clubs, schools, gardeners, veterans, conservationists." Copyrighted. Will send a catalog to a writer on request. Will assign projects to writers "with superb and successful previous scripts to present. Send sample script with simple letter." Enclose S.A.S.E.

General: "Public relations films for organizations, industry, government. Require good research, heavy on facts, national and international scope. Often need to respect multiple and conflicting clients. Documentary style. Do not underestimate intelligence of audiences. They are ready for serious and interesting writing and are beyond simplistic, arty scripts." Length: filmstrips and motion pictures, 13 to 27 minutes; tapes and cassettes, 4 to 12 minutes. Pays $1,000 to $2,500 per project.

LANSFORD PUBLISHING COMPANY, 2516 Lansford Ave., San Jose CA 95125. For "teachers in colleges and universities throughout the United States and Canada." Will send a catalog to a writer on request. "We are willing to assign audiovisual projects to qualified writers. We are always looking for new ideas to improve the effectiveness of the college teacher." Query first. Enclose S.A.S.E. for response to queries.

Education: "The subject matter should deal with educational material that could be used in college and university classrooms." Produces charts, dioramas, film loops, silent filmstrips, sound filmstrips, models, motion pictures, multimedia kits, overhead transparencies, prerecorded tapes and cassettes, slides, and study prints. "Payment varies with the subject." Usually offers royalty of 10% of retail price.

LeCRONE RECORD CO., 819 N.W. 92nd, Oklahoma City OK 73114. Contact: A.B. LeCrone. For preschool through 6th grade elementary. Copyrighted. Will send catalog to writer on request. Query first. "Writer needs no special credentials; just produce excellent material." Enclose S.A.S.E. for response to queries.

Education: Teaching aids, activities, physical fitness, square dance, learning records; colors, shapes, ABC's, counting activities. 15 to 17 minutes on each side of record. "We negotiate payment. We have never paid less than $300 and have paid as much as $1,200, but this is not our base either way."

LE ROY MOTION PICTURE PRODUCTION STUDIOS, 1208 E. Cliveden St., Philadelphia PA 19119. Contact: Charles Roy. For "general audiences: women, children, etc. Projects assigned. Resume required." Query first. Enclose S.A.S.E. for response to queries.

General: "We create and produce TV commercials and television programs and series. We create and produce documentary and theatrical motion pictures. Assignments might be on speculation or by negotiated contract. Payment varies with specific projects."

LEARNING MACHINES, INC., Box 86, Pinos Altos NM 88053. Contact: Paul Morgan. For "K to 18, special audiences." Copyrighted. Will assign projects to writers "qualified in content field, or else they must be a teacher, or both. Audio and picture scripts (if any) must be submitted. Operational testing with students is desirable." Query first. Enclose S.A.S.E. for response to queries.

Education: Produces "audio tape programs, audio tape slide (2x2) programs, and programmed instruction lessons for public schools, from nursery school to graduate school." Pays royalties of "10% of sale price for college and/or high school (7 to 18), 5% of sales price for elementary or combined elementary-secondary materials."

MARSH FILM ENTERPRISES, INC., P.O. Box 8082, Shawnee Mission KS 66208. Contact: Joan K. Marsh, President. For children; primary, intermediate, and high school. Copyrighted. Will send catalog to writer on request. Query first, with sample of previous work. "Writer should be able to take very rough, raw, factual material, and transpose it into simple, clear and interesting format." Enclose S.A.S.E. for response to queries.

Education: Educational material for elementary, and secondary school children. Variety of subjects; approach varies with subject. "We produce sound filmstrips, usually about 4 filmstrips per year, on current topics of news interest." Pays no royalty; straight fee commensurate with ability. Pays $200 for 10- to 15-minute script.

McGRAW-HILL FILMS/CONTEMPORARY FILMS, 1221 Avenue of the Americas, New York NY 10020. Contact Suzanne T. Isaacs or Anne Schutzer. For elementary students, high school students; colleges, public libraries, government, business and industry. Copyrighted. Buys all rights. Will send catalog to writer on request. Query first; "then if we notify you positively, send in material." Enclose S.A.S.E.

Education and Language Arts: "Social studies, science, language arts, career education, economics for elementary and high market. Film loops (8mm), sound filmstrips, 16mm motion pictures, and prerecorded tapes and cassettes." Pays 5% to 25% depending on investment terms.

CAMERON MC KAY PRODUCTIONS, 6850 Lexington Ave., Hollywood CA 90038. Contact: Olga Nichols. For "pre-kindergarten through eighth grade." Copyrighted. Will send a catalog to a writer on request. Write for copy of guidelines for writers. Query first. Enclose S.A.S.E. for response to queries.

Education: "Primary and elementary educational material." Produces silent filmstrips, sound filmstrips, motion pictures, phonograph records, and prerecorded tapes and cassettes. Length: 1,200 to 2,000 words. "We buy outright or pay percentage of gross sales."

MRC FILMS, INC., 71 W. 23rd St., New York NY 10010. Executive Producer: Larry Mollot. "Audience varies with subject matter, which is wide and diverse." Writer "should have an ability to visualize concepts and to express ideas clearly in words. Experience in motion picture or filmstrip script writing is desirable. Write us, giving some idea of background. Submit samples of writing. Wait for reply. We will always reply, one way or another. We are looking for new talent. No unsolicited material accepted. Work upon assignment only." Query first. Enclose S.A.S.E. for response to queries.

General: "Industrial, documentary, educational, and television films. Also, public relations, teaching, and motivational filmstrips. Some subjects are highly technical in the fields of aerospace and electronics. Others are on personal relationships, selling techniques, ecology, etc. A writer with an imaginative visual sense is important." Produces silent and sound filmstrips, 16mm motion pictures, and prerecorded tapes and cassettes. "Fee depends on nature and length of job. Typical fees: $500 to $1,000 for script for 10-minute film; $1,000 to $1,400 for script for 20-minute film;

$1,200 to $2,000 for script for 30-minute film. For narration writing only, the range is $200 to $500 for a 10-minute film; $400 to $800 for a 20-minute film; $500 to $1,000 for a 30-minute film. For script writing services by the day, fee is $60 to $100 per day."

THE WALTER G. O'CONNOR COMPANY, P.O. Box Y, Sipe Avenue, Hershey PA 17033. Contact: John P. Hudak, Executive Producer. For all levels; K through 12 in education; adult and professional. Copyrighted. Query first. "Write for requirements. Unsolicited materials will be returned unopened. Writer must have a high degree of professionality and proven ability." Enclose S.A.S.E. for response to queries.
Education and Business: "We produce materials with a wide range of subject areas for education, public relations, industry, and business." 8mm film loops, silent and sound filmstrips, 16 and 35mm motion pictures, multimedia kits, and slides. Pays 7% to 10% of budget for motion pictures; $500 to $800 for filmstrips.

OUR SUNDAY VISITOR, INC., Audiovisual Department, Noll Plaza, Huntington IN 46750. Contact: John E. Covell. For students (K to 12), adult religious education groups, and teacher training. Copyrighted. Will send catalog to writer on request. Query first. "We are looking for well-developed total packages only. Programs should display up-to-date audiovisual technique and cohesiveness." Enclose S.A.S.E. for response to queries.
Education and Religion: "Broadly speaking, material should deal with religious education, including liturgy and daily Christian living, as well as structured catechesis. Must not conflict with sound Catholic doctrine. Should reflect modern trends in education. Word lengths may vary." Produces charts, sound filmstrips, overhead transparencies, phonograph records, prerecorded tapes and cassettes and 2x2 slides. Royalties vary from 5% to 10% of price received, depending on the product and its market. Fee arrangements also; for example, so many dollars per each 100, 500, or 1,000 sets or projects produced at time of production.

PACE FILMS, INC., 411 E. 53rd St., New York NY 10022. Contact: Mr. R. Vanderbes. For "TV and theatrical audience in the U.S. and worldwide." Buys all rights. "Writing assignments are handled through agencies, but independent queries or submissions are considered. Enclose S.A.S.E. for response.
General: "Documentaries and feature motion pictures for TV and theaters." Pays "Writers Guild of America minimums and up."

OUTDOOR PICTURES, Box 277, Anacortes WA 98221. Contact: Ernest S. Booth, Ph.D. Interested in the junior high school and the senior high school level. Would accept materials for lower grades. "Copyrights are unimportant to us; we can do it if you wish to prepare a filmstrip or slidefilm for use in public schools, that you work closely with one or several public school teachers in whom you have confidence. Do not attempt to work up the material on your own without the help and advice from several teachers in the selected grade level."
Education: "We would like to have qualified persons design the filmstrips and/or slide sets, take the photos or obtain the artwork, write the scripts, and submit to us the entire package ready to produce. We will make the internegative filmstrip master from which the final prints are made. We will record the narration and take care of the narration tapes, but the script should be furnished. We are interested in all subjects, but are especially anxious to obtain filmstrips on social studies, especially geography in foreign countries. We want the material complete, at least rough edited, and all elements ready to go. Examine and listen to a number of existing filmstrips in the area in which you would like to work. See and hear what others have done, so you will be acquainted with the competition." Film loops (8mm and 16mm); silent and sound filmstrips; motion pictures (8mm and 16mm); prerecorded tapes and cassettes and 2x2 slides. "We prefer to pay 10% royalty on gross sales. You furnish all elements of the production, but we will return the original pictures to you, after a reasonable time to make negatives, so you are free to borrow material from experts."

PANORAMIC STUDIOS, 179 W. Berks St., Philadelphia PA 19122. Contact: Leonard N. Abrams. Copyrighted. Will send a catalog to a writer on request. "All of our work is based on actual client requirements; speculative submissions are useless." Query first. Enclose S.A.S.E. for response to queries.
General: Requirements vary according to project. Produces dioramas, models, relief maps, and relief globes. Pays straight fee.

TED PETOK STUDIOS, INC., 20169 James Couzens, Detroit MI 48235. Contact: Ted Petok. For adults. Copyrighted. Assigns projects for writers "with an ability to write for the screen. Contact us first as to the nature of the material." Query first. Enclose S.A.S.E. for response to queries.
Cartoons: "Animated cartoons for theatrical release of an adult nature." Produces 16mm and 35mm motion pictures. Payment "dependent on the project."

PFLAUM/STANDARD, 38 W. Fifth St., Dayton OH 45402. Contact: J.M. Heher. For "first graders through adults." Usually buys all rights. Will send a catalog to a writer on request. Will assign projects to qualified writers "if they have a proven track record." Query first. Enclose S.A.S.E. for response to queries.
Communications, Personal Development, and Social Sciences: "History, techniques, and social effects of media—cinema, television, print. Personal and social development materials. Social concerns." Produces silent filmstrips, sound filmstrips, prerecorded tapes and cassettes, slides, and study prints. "Flat fee payment preferred, but royalty possible."

PLAYETTE CORPORATION, 301 E. Shore Rd., Great Neck NY 11023. Contact: Sidney A. Evans. For "all school levels, teachers, and libraries." Copyrighted. Writer must have "a complete and thorough knowledge of the subject with practical applied usage. Material must have been classroom tested before submission. Use MLA format." Query first. Enclose S.A.S.E. for response to queries.
Education and Foreign Languages: Requirements "depend on subject selected." Produces charts, silent filmstrips, sound filmstrips, multimedia kits, overhead transparencies, phonograph records, prerecorded tapes and cassettes, slides, study prints, and foreign language training aids and games. "Payment for each subject on a separate basis."

PROFESSIONAL EDUCATION PRODUCTS, 4116 Farnam St., Omaha NE 68005. Contact: Stanley L. Teutsch. For dental patients, children and adults. Copyrighted. Will send catalog to writer on request. Query first. Enclose S.A.S.E. for response to queries.
Education: "Patient education filmstrip and sound programs for the dental profession. Cover a variety of dental procedures, such as bridgework, etc. Also have preventive dentistry films on how to brush, floss, etc. Some films are slanted toward children, others on the adult level. Prerecorded tapes and cassettes. Our work is usually contracted out for a set fee, rather than paying royalties. Fees depend upon complexity of work."

Q-ED PRODUCTIONS, 2921 W. Alameda Ave., Burbank CA 91505. Contact: Michael Halperin. For "elementary through senior high school students for in-class use. Growing need for preschool material." Copyrighted. Will send a catalog to a writer on request. "Previous experience required as a filmstrip writer. Samples for screening preferred." Query first. Enclose S.A.S.E. for response to queries.
Education: "Any material which will fit within the school curriculum, elementary through senior high school. Currently producing mostly sound filmstrips, length up to 80 frames per strip. Prefer filmstrip sets of 4 or more. We are interested in inquiry-inductive materials which will stimulate children to make further investigation into the subject area. We believe it is more important to affect children than merely feeding them a multitude of facts." Produces sound filmstrips, 16mm motion pictures, and multimedia kits. "Our normal procedure is to pay a fee only for writing services. If a complete project is brought in by a writer-producer, we will consider a royalty arrangement."

RANDOM HOUSE, INC., School Division, 201 E. 50th St., Fifth Floor, New York NY 10022. Contact: Susan Tucker. For "elementary and junior high school students." Rights to be negotiated. "We are always interested in receiving resumes and project proposals, and will make every effort to respond within a reasonable length of time. Credentials should include experience in writing, experience in academic fields. Send one-page letter briefly describing the subject matter, grade level, point of view, scope of material, type of visuals the writer thinks should go with material, etc." Enclose S.A.S.E. for response.

Language Arts, Vocational Guidance, Science, and Social Studies: Requirements "vary. Subject matter includes English, social studies, guidance and vocational education, and science." Produces charts, sound filmstrips, multimedia kits, phonograph records, and prerecorded tapes and cassettes. Pay "varies."

REGENTS PUBLISHING COMPANY, INC., Two Park Ave., New York NY 10016. Contact: Julio I. Andujar, President. For foreign language students, in school and at home. Copyrighted. Will send catalog to writer on request. Query with description of material, table of contents and sample portions. Enclose S.A.S.E. for reply. No unsolicited mss. "It would be helpful if writer has done previous audiovisual work, has taught or is currently teaching."

Education: English as a second language. Spanish, French, German. Supplementary materials, cultural aspects of wide appeal in foreign language classes. Vocabulary within the range of foreign language students. Sound filmstrips, multimedia kits, phonograph records, prerecorded tapes and cassettes. Pays 6% of list price.

RHYTHMS PRODUCTIONS, Whitney Bldg., Box 34485, Los Angeles CA 90034. Contact: R.S. White. "Our audience is generally educational, with projects ranging from early childhood through adult markets." Copyrighted. Query first. "We need to know a writer's background and credits and to see samples of his work." Enclose S.A.S.E. for response to queries.

Education: Sound filmstrips, 16mm motion pictures, multimedia kits, phonograph records, prerecorded tapes and cassettes, and study prints. "Our firm specializes in creative productions, so though content is basic to the productions, a creative and imaginative approach is necessary." Usually pays $250 for filmstrip script.

RIDDLE VIDEO AND FILM PRODUCTIONS, INC., 507 Fifth Ave., New York NY 10017. President/Executive Producer: William Riddle. For "general public for television shows, young and old alike. Also for theater distribution." Material may be copyrighted or not copyrighted. Write for copy of guidelines for writers. Writer "must be experienced and well-qualified in the subject in order to handle work assignments satisfactorily. We must see a sample of his or her work." Query first. Enclose S.A.S.E. for response to queries.

General: "Story boards and scripts are needed." Produces 8mm and 16mm film loops; silent filmstrips; sound filmstrips; kinescopes; models; 8mm, 16mm, and 35mm motion pictures; multimedia kits; prerecorded tapes and cassettes; slides; study prints; videotape productions. Pays "standard going rates, with bonus on super work performed."

RIVIERA PRODUCTIONS, 6610 Selma Ave., Hollywood CA 90028. For "theatrical" audience. Will assign projects to qualified writers "provided samples of previous work of professional quality can be submitted. We prefer to see a short treatment prior to reading full screenplay. Material is not returned unless accompanied by return postage." Query first. Enclose S.A.S.E. for return of submissions and reply to queries.

General: "Full-length shooting scripts (screenplays). Must be professional in quality. And forget about the 'R' or 'X' rated material. Leave out the sex and profanity; that is too easy to write and does not indicate quality or depth in content. Pays 10% royalty."

ROUNDTABLE PRODUCTIONS, INC., 113 N. San Vicente Blvd., Beverly Hills CA 90211. Contact: Leon Gold. For "supervisors and middle level managers in large organizations; beginning and experienced salesmen." Copyrighted. Writer "must have experience in our field of specialization." Query first. Enclose S.A.S.E. for response to queries.

Business: "Management and sales training films." Produces 16mm motion pictures. Payment arrangements "vary."

HOWARD M. SAMS & CO., INC., Education Division, 4300 W. 62nd St., Indianapolis IN 46268. Contact: John Obst, Managing Editor. Query first. Enclose S.A.S.E. for response to queries.
Education: Seeking scripts for "industrial arts and vocational/technical education subjects at the junior and senior high school and technical school levels." Payment by royalty arrangement.

WARREN SCHLOAT PRODUCTIONS, INC., 115 Tompkins Ave., Pleasantville NY 10570. Contact Mrs. Barbara Martinsons. For k-14 and special education students. Copyrighted. Will send catalog to writer on request, "if warranted." Query first, "with proposal and possibly an outline." Enclose S.A.S.E.
Education and Language Arts: "Social studies, language arts, early childhood, science, math, career education, inservice. 8mm film loops, sound filmstrips, possibly models, and multimedia kits. Style should be stirring. Format exciting. Slant will vary." Length: 12 to 16 minutes for filmstrips. Pays $500 to $700 per script, or advance and royalty.

SCOPE PRODUCTIONS, INC., P.O. Box 5515, Fresno CA 93755. Contact: P. McKim, Traffic Manager. Audience includes "K through university; retired persons; general audience (novice approach); government, educational, industry, business clientele; local and major markets in U.S., Europe, Asia, Africa, South America." Copyright "depends on assignment." Will send a catalog to a writer on request. "We make assignments strictly on previous work and we require samples from pros. In the commercial field, must have broad experience in radio and TV and motion pictures. No educators, please. No novices. Must provide release prints and copyrighted scripts. The writer must be able to synthesize quickly, meet deadlines without hassling. No prima donnas. The writer doesn't have to have a name, just a demonstrated ability to deliver. Length of experience not important. No hack stuff. No old audiovisual or industrial writers. Do not send your only original film. Send copy print only. Do not send original script which has not been copyrighted.
General: "All types of assignments, including light breeze spots (30/60's in TV/radio); product description; process/skill/sequence/order format for self-instruction and group generalizations; Italian, Spanish, French, German, English. We need excellent analogies, objective analysis, fresh up-tempo pacing; not pedantic or esoteric. The work must be highly imaginative, showing a sense of current trends in philosophy of communications and thought." Produces charts, super 8mm film loops, sound filmstrips, VTR/film transfers, models, 16mm motion pictures, multimedia kits, overhead transparencies, phonograph records, prerecorded tapes and cassettes, slides, study prints, documentaries, commercials, corporate image programs, training formats. Payment "completely dependent on individual contracts by client; usually 10% of total production billing."

SILVERMINE PUBLISHERS INCORPORATED, Comstock Hill, Silvermine, Norwalk CT 06850. Contact: Joan Adler, Editor. For "a general audience at various ages and both sexes who are interested in learning more about how to paint or draw, how to improve handicraft techniques, how to play tennis, golf, or play other sports better." Will send a catalog to a writer on request. Query first. Enclose S.A.S.E. for response to queries.
The Arts, Handicrafts, and Sports: Material on "how to draw, paint, sculpt; how to sew, embroider, weave; how to play golf, tennis, etc." Produces prerecorded tapes and slides ("20 to 40 color slides and audio tape of 18 to 45 minutes"). "We have a contract arrangement based on a negotiated advance and commission on sales."

SNAPDRAGON PRODUCTIONS, 7785 S.W. 86th St., Miami FL 33143. Contact: Steven Cohen. Will assign projects to qualified writers. "We will have to see work." Query first. Enclose S.A.S.E. for response to queries.
General: Requirements "vary by job. Motion picture script format. Feature length." Pays "flat rate per script."

SWIMMING WORLD PUBLICATIONS, 5507 Laurel Canyon Blvd., North Hollywood CA 91607. Contact: Albert Schoenfield. For swimmers and divers, age 12 to 20. Copyrighted. Query first. Enclose S.A.S.E. for response to queries.
Sports: "Instructional films on swimming and diving technique. 8mm motion pic-

tures and sport cassettes for action viewers. Length of films usually 15 to 20 minutes. Payment depends on how films are produced."

TALCO PRODUCTIONS, 279 E. 44th St., New York NY 10017. President: Alan Lawrence. "We almost always assign scripts to freelance writers. In addition, we work with authors in developing ideas for television presentation. Generally, we like to review some of the writer's previous work in the medium." Query first, enclosing S.A.S.E. for reply.
General: "We produce documentary, industrial, and public relations presentations as well as educational programs (art, fashion, food, politics, labor, anthropology, archaeology). Our area of concentration is in business and industry." Produces sound filmstrips, 16mm and 35mm motion pictures, prerecorded tapes and cassettes, slides, multimedia kits, kinescopes, and quad and helical videotape. "Monetary arrangements depend on project."

BOB THOMAS PRODUCTIONS, 23 Broad St., Bloomfield NJ 07003. President: Robert G. Thomas. Buys all rights. "Send material with introductory letter explaining ideas. Submit outline or rough draft for motion picture or business matter. If possible, we will contact the writer for further discussion." Enclose S.A.S.E.
Business, Education, and General: "We produce 3 types of material for 3 types of audiences: 8mm film loops in sports and pre-teen areas (educational); 8mm and 16mm motion pictures for business (educational, distributed by agencies); 35mm motion pictures for entertainment for a general audience (theater type). General subject matter may be of any style, any length. For the future, 35mm theatrical shorts for distribution." Payment "depends on agreements between both parties. On 8mm and 16mm matter, one free arrangement. On 35mm shorts, percentage or fee."

ROGER TILTON FILMS, INC., 241 West G St., San Diego CA 92101. Contact: Roger Tilton. For "usually military audiences, or those about to become associated with the military. General audiences of all ages as well." Copyrighted. Will send a catalog to a writer on request. Will assign projects to qualified writers "providing our experience requirements are met." Query first. Enclose S.A.S.E. for response to queries.
Military and General: "Government training films—simple, to-the-point. Nothing elaborate. Lengths usually vary. We also do other than military films, and our editorial requirements would vary accordingly." Produces sound filmstrips, 8mm and 16mm motion pictures, and slides. "Fees negotiable."

TOMORROW ENTERTAINMENT, INC., 777 Third Avenue, New York NY 10017. Contact: Tom Moore. "We are not exclusively working with specific assigned writers and producers and are wide open for original programming ideas from professional freelance writers in the area of TV and motion pictures; in fact, we look forward to receiving them. We receive scripts both through talent agents and directly from individual writers who are anxious for us to consider their material." Query first. Enclose S.A.S.E. for response to queries.

TROLL ASSOCIATES, 320 Route 17, Mahwah NJ 07430. Contact: Marian Francis. For students. Copyrighted. Will send a catalog to a writer on request. Writers "need to be educators or creative writers or both. Write first to explain project." Query first. Enclose S.A.S.E. for response to queries.
Education: "Requirements depend on media. General subject matter should be relevant to the elementary school or high school audience. All subject matters considered within that range." Produces film loops, silent filmstrips, sound filmstrips, multimedia kits, overhead transparencies, and prerecorded tapes and cassettes. "Fee depends on media. Usually outright purchase."

UNITED METHODIST COMMUNICATIONS, 1525 McGavock St., Nashville TN 37203. Contact: Edgar A. Gossard, Director, Dept. Audiovisual Media. For children, from nursery age to 6th graders; youth, junior high to college age; young adults, middle adults, older adults, usually in church settings. Educational level for adults would range from high school graduate through college graduate. Copyrighted. "Normally, all rights purchased." Query first. "Writers should have professional experience in scripting for media. Background in Christian education and/or theology would be necessary for many projects, helpful for most, not required for some. Samples of previous work are most helpful to us in considering writers." Enclose S.A.S.E. for response to queries.

Education and Religion: "Subject areas are very broad, although much of our audiovisual production is done for use in church-school or Christian education settings. Interpersonal relationships, ethics, Bible study, church history, human growth and potential, theology, are some content areas in which we produce materials. Silent filmstrips, sound filmstrips, 16mm motion pictures, phonograph records, and prerecorded tapes and cassettes. All material written to specifications; requirements for scripts are transmitted with assignment. We are seldom, if ever, able to utilize unsolicited manuscripts. Projects vary from scripts for very short (3 to 4 minutes) recordings to scripts for 15- to 20-minute motion pictures. The bulk of the work is in 8- to 20-minute recordings and 70- to 80-frame filmstrips. Fees are paid on a per project basis. Minimum fees $50; maximum $1,500. No royalty arrangements.

VIDEO FILMS INC., 1004 E. Jefferson Ave., Detroit MI 48207. President: Clifford Hanna. For "adult, industrial audience." Send "resume of credentials with sample scripts." Query first. Enclose S.A.S.E. for response to queries.
Industry: Wants "shooting scripts." Produces silent filmstrips, 8mm and 16mm motion pictures, prerecorded tapes and cassettes, and slides. Payment "negotiable, usually $150 for proposal; $5,000 for script."

VIDEORECORD CORPORATION OF AMERICA, Videorecord Bldg., Westport CT 06880. Contact: Mrs. D. Millais. For volunteer, professional and paraprofessional personnel in health care; training of business personnel and those in dealer and customer relations; all levels of education. Copyrighted. Will send catalog to writer on request. Query first, enclosing S.A.S.E. for reply. "Writer's formal credentials preferred, but not vital. Nothing should be submitted except on the basis of prior agreement."
Business, Education and Medicine: Videocassette programs for health care, education, business and civic, social and community organizations. Payment negotiated; advance against royalty.

VISUAL TEACHING, 79 Pine Knob, Milford CT 06460. Contact: James A. Cunningham. For elementary through college level; most junior high level. Copyrighted. Query first. "Writers should be educators with photographic abilities as well." Enclose S.A.S.E. for response to queries.
Science: "Texts to accompany 2x2 slide sets. 20 slides per set. Approximately 1,000 words. Prerecorded tapes and cassettes and slides. So far, all our topics have been nature and science. We would consider other topics if photographic materials were available or could be obtained." Pays 10% to 25%.

VISUALS FOR TEACHING, INC., P.O. Box 8455, Universal City CA 91608. Contact: Douglas F. George. For "primary grades to high school." Copyrighted. Will send a catalog to a writer on request. Write for copy of guidelines for writers. Will assign projects to writer "with a track record. Must have educational experience. Must deliver on time." Query first. Enclose S.A.S.E. for response to queries.
Education: Requirements "vary." Produces sound and silent filmstrips, multimedia kits, phonograph records. Pays $100 per 15-minute script.

VOCATIONAL EDUCATION PRODUCTIONS, c/o California Polytechnic State University, San Luis Obispo CA 93401. Contact: Clyde Hostetter, Director. For students who have an interest in occupational education, career education and the like. Copyrighted. Will send catalog to writer on request. "Because our program's scope is changing so rapidly, we would prefer to have writers, artists and photographers query us first. We are interested primarily in West Coast freelancers, but anything is possible. Credentials needed are simply the proven ability to produce professional work within a specified time-line. The writer must have a good visual sense, so that he thinks in terms of the total words-and-pictures impact of the material. An artist and/or photographer who can write well would probably be the ideal person to prepare our audiovisuals."
Education: "Most of our audiovisuals relate to occupational or vocational areas,

slanted for use in an educational setting from grades 7 through college. There is a wide variety of requirements." Charts, sound filmstrips, multimedia kits, overhead transparencies, prerecorded tape and cassette, and 2x2 slides. "Payment would depend upon the type of material involved, but would usually be on a flat payment basis rather than royalties. We pay $100 to $500 for filmstrip scripts."

Authors' Agents

Because an agent must receive a certain amount in commissions each year to justify his handling a writer's work, many agents will take on only those new clients who have been recommended to them by editors or other professional writers. Such writers, these agents reason, are the most likely to achieve the minimum yearly sales figure that will enable the agent to make a profit (for example, an agent's commission would be $200 on a writer's $2,000 sales). Other agents are willing to read unsolicited mss from new writers, though some charge a reading fee—this pays for their time if a submission turns out to have little or no sales potential. Each agent's policy on new writers is given in the listings below.

It's generally a good idea for a new writer to market his material himself at first. Marketing experience is invaluable to a writer. It gives him direct contact with editors and producers, and he learns firsthand what they want and how close his work comes to their requirements.

Eventually, after he is successfully selling articles or fiction to quality and top-paying magazines; after he has sold a book; or after he has obtained several local productions of plays and/or publication by a play publisher; the writer may want an agent to handle his business. Some writers prefer to write full time, some like their marketing to be handled by a marketing specialist, some dislike seeing rejections, or have other reasons. Once the writer has established a "name," so that his work is in demand, an agent may also secure better contracts for him.

However, many successful professional writers continue to market their own material even after they've established a "name." Why? Because they prefer to keep the 10% of royalties that an agent charges, they like personal contact with editors, they feel their writing stays closer to the market this way, or they have other personal reasons.

Writers are reminded that an agent cannot sell material that isn't right for today's market, or that is of low quality. All an agent can do is submit work he considers salable to those editors and producers whom he judges likely to be interested enough to buy it.

The television market is an exception to the general rule that a writer can act as his own agent. Television producers will not read unsolicited manuscripts for fear of possible charges of plagiarism; and all TV scripts are submitted through agents. Writers interested in finding a television agent should know that most successful television writers live in Los Angeles, where they can work directly with producers once their agents have sold their scripts or ideas.

ADAMS, RAY, AND ROSENBERG, 9220 Sunset Blvd., Suite 210, Los Angeles CA 90069. Agency Representatives: Sam Adams, Rick Ray, Lee Rosenberg, Robert Wunsch. Established in 1963. Handles novels, nonfiction books, motion pictures (screenplays), plays, TV scripts plus services of writers, producers and directors. "Our firm functions primarily in the representation of creative individuals and material in the motion picture and television fields." 10% standard commission. New clients by referral. Not interested in unsolicited mss, but a new writer could "submit a fairly detailed letter of explanation upon which we can judge sales potential and whether to accept his material." Enclose S.A.S.E. for reply.

DOROTHY ALBERT, 162 W. 54th St., New York NY 10019. Established in 1959. Handles novels, motion pictures, stage plays, and TV scripts. Interested in TV pilot series, drama and comedy plays, original drama for motion pictures, and novels which are "well-plotted suspense; quality drama; adult fiction; human relations." 10% standard commission. New writer should send "letter of introduction, description of material, and resume of background. Enclose S.A.S.E. for reply. The writer should have some foreknowledge of structure and endurance, whether it be motion pictures, plays, TV, or novels." Will not read unsolicited mss.

MAXWELL ALEY ASSOCIATES, 145 E. 35th St., New York NY 10016. Agency Representative: Mrs. Ruth Aley. Established in 1938. Handles magazine fiction "if exceptional," nonfiction books, "top teenage fiction," and novels "if exceptional. I prefer books that have strong promotional possibilities that bear on current problems. The work should be totally professional and preferably of current interest." Recent sales for clients include *Two in Galilee* (Holmes); *Judaka* (Norwood). 10% standard commission. New clients "through recommendation from publishers or other authors." Will consider only mss of established writers that come with special professional recommendation. A writer preferably should have achieved $5,000 in sales and interest from major magazine or book publishers. Will read unsolicited queries or outlines accompanied by biographical data "if very professional." Enclose S.A.S.E. for reply.

AMERICAN PLAY CO., INC., 52 Vanderbilt Ave., New York NY 10017. Est. in 1890's. Specializes in motion pictures, TV and Broadway stage. Works with new writers on fiction and nonfiction book mss. Will read unsolicited mss and provide a detailed, written critique for a $45 fee.

JOSEPH ANTHONY AGENCY, 530 Valley Road, Upper Montclair NJ 07043. Established in 1962. Specializes in books, motion pictures, short stories and plays. Charges reading fee of $10. Will work with a writer who wants to work hard. Enclose S.A.S.E. for return of submissions.

AUTHORS' AND PUBLISHERS' SERVICE, 146-47 29th Ave., Flushing NY 11354. Director: Miriam Gilbert. Established in 1940. "We handle all types of scripts for book and magazine publication: fiction, nonfiction, juveniles, articles, short stories, etc. Special department for plays and TV scripts. Our primary business is selling mss, not criticizing them. We welcome new writers." 10% standard commission. "Nominal reading fee on scripts under 5,000 words (minimum $10) is charged if a comprehensive editorial analysis is required. All fees are dropped as soon as one sale is made." Query first. Enclose S.A.S.E. for reply to query and return of submissions.

BILL BERGER ASSOCIATES, INC., 535 East 72nd St., New York NY 10021. Established in 1962. Specializes in books in all areas. Writer must have achieved minimum sales of $5,000 and must have been recommended. No reading fee. Will not read unsolicited mss.

LOIS BERMAN, 530 E. 72nd St., New York NY 10021. Established in 1971. Handles magazine fiction, novels, motion pictures, and plays. "Most of our clients are playwrights, so most of the material I handle is dramatic in form. If, however, my clients choose to turn to narrative writing, I handle it, too. I now represent primarily young playwrights with workshop or off-Broadway credits." 10% standard commission. Will represent a writer whose "work must be interesting to me. And I am interested in quality material. The writer should have full-length theater work for initial consideration." Obtains new writers "from seeing productions and by referral." Will "sometimes" read unsolicited mss "on basis of letter outlining writing background." Enclose S.A.S.E. for reply to query and return of submissions.

BEST SELLER LITERARY & MUSIC AGENCY, P.O. Box 8136, San Jose CA 95125. President: Sharlene Reid. Established in 1969. Handles "textbooks, novels, how-to, handbooks, religious, juvenile, children's picture books, autobiography, poetry, philosophy, controversial novels, sports, occult, ecology, history, westerns, mysteries, science fiction, political, natural science, music books, art books, romances, cookbooks, sex stories, medical, law, scientific research, picture books, poems, jokes, greeting card verse, cartoons, crossword puzzles, articles, short stories, pamphlets, stage plays, screen plays, radio scripts, motion pictures, lyrics, sheet music, demo records, TV scripts, biographies. Send for brochure." Standard commission 10% of U.S. sales, 15% of Canadian sales, 20% of foreign sales. Welcomes new writers who have confidence in their writing. No reading fees for selling writers and inmates. Charges reading fees from $5 to $25 per ms, depending on material. "Reading fee is deducted from commission if material brings in over $2,000 in first royalties." Enclose S.A.S.E. "with all correspondence."

MEL BLOOM & ASSOCIATES, 328 South Beverly Dr., Suite C, Beverly Hills CA 90212. Established in 1966. Handles novels, motion pictures, plays, scripts for TV movies and nonfiction books. Recent sales for clients include *The Sting* (Ward); *The Terminal Order* (Miller). 10% standard commission. New clients "by recommendations from people in the industry." Will read unsolicited mss. "Send us a finished piece of good material in play, novel, or screenplay form. No outlines or treatments." Enclose S.A.S.E. for return of submissions.

GEORGES BORCHARDT, INC., 145 E. 52nd St., New York NY 10022. Established in 1953. Specializes in novels and short stories of high literary quality. "Will represent new clients if recommended by someone whose judgment we trust." Will not read unsolicited mss.

AARON BOWMAN ENTERPRISES, 1517 Joy, Granite City IL 62040. Contact: Aaron Bowman. "Very interested in new talent, especially in poetry, nonfiction and fiction book lengths 40,000 words and up. No reading fee for those with $5,000 earned royalties last 24 months. Others enclose reading and critical analyses fee: articles, $20; short stories, $15; poetry collections, $25; book manuscripts, $50. Reports in two weeks. We either submit the work to editors, consider it for our own publications, or react with detailed, constructive criticism or advise otherwise. Reading-critique fee refunded upon sale or purchase. Upon sale, we contract 10% of royalties for placing manuscript. Enclose S.A.S.E. please."

CELINE BREVANNES, 28 Bauer Place, Westport CT 06880. Established in 1936. Specializes in children's books—mostly science from age 10 and up. Looks for quality of writing and subject matter. Charges reading fee. Will not read unsolicited mss. Enclose S.A.S.E. for reply to query.

ANITA HELEN BROOKS ASSOCIATES, 155 E. 55th St., New York NY 10022. Established in 1956. Specializes in fiction, nonfiction, mystery, books written by newspapermen and radio-TV executives and personalities, biographies, radio, TV scripts. 10% standard commission. Will not read unsolicited mss. Query first. Enclose S.A.S.E. for reply.

BROOME AGENCY, INC., P.O. Box 848, Columbus MT 59019. Established in 1957. Directors: Sherwood and Mary Ann Broome. "We read unsolicited books, stories and articles (teen material, but no children's) of national or wider interest and handle on professional percentage basis under exclusive contract when work is acceptable to us. No reading or handling fees. We charge fees based on time when author wishes us, by prior arrangement, to analyze, edit, revise, rewrite or collaborate. We handle all rights worldwide, but we must place material for publication before trying to sell TV or movie rights. No poems, young children's material, fillers, newspaper or trade magazine material or screen originals. Standard commission 10% on U.S. sales, 15% on Canadian sales, 20% on other foreign rights. "Offers $1,000 annual prize for fiction, nonfiction or unpublished mss of 50,000 words or more." Enclose return postage.

CURTIS BROWN, LTD., 60 E. 56th St., New York NY 10022. Established in 1914. Handles "fiction, nonfiction, plays. No unsolicited mss."

JAMES BROWN ASSOCIATES, INC., 22 E. 60th St., New York NY 10022. Established in 1949. Handles books primarily; handles stage plays for the writers it represents and sells short stories and articles, but does not work with writers devoting all of their time to articles and short stories. No poetry. Writer must be professional, but not necessarily published. 10% standard commission. "Writers should query us first with a statement, not a long description, of the book and the writer." Does not charge reading fee. Enclose S.A.S.E. for reply.

NED BROWN ASSOCIATED, 407 North Maple Dr., Beverly Hills CA 90210. Established in 1936. Handles nonfiction books, novels, motion pictures, and plays; also TV scripts and packages, but these "only by established writers." A recent sale is *Journey to Ixtlan* (Castaneda). 10% standard commission. Works with writers who are earning at least $5,000 yearly from writing. Will work with new writer on occasion if highly recommended or if published by an established publisher. Will not read unsolicited mss.

SHIRLEY BURKE, 370 E. 76th St., Suite B-704, New York NY 10021. Established in 1948. Handles magazine fiction, novels, nonfiction books. Clients obtained through recommendation. Must have some writing experience. 10% standard commission. Will read unsolicited queries or outlines only. "Please inquire. Do not send mss without letter of inquiry." Enclose S.A.S.E. for return of outlines or reply to queries.

CCRLA WRITERS LITERARY AGENTS, Division of Best Seller Literary and Music Agency, P.O. Box 8064, San Jose CA 95125. President: Sharlene Reid; Director: H. Russ. Established in 1970. Welcomes new writers who have confidence in their writing. No reading fees for selling writers or inmates. Handles fiction and nonfiction, textbooks, novels, how-to, handbooks, religious, juvenile, children's picture books, biography, autobiography, poetry, sports, philosophy, controversial novels, occult, ecology, history, westerns, mysteries, science fiction, political, natural science, music books, art books, romances, cookbooks, sex stories, medical, law, scientific research, picture books, magazine articles, juvenile articles, short stories, stage plays, motion pictures, TV and radio scripts, screenplays, poems, jokes, cartoons, greeting card verses, crossword puzzles. Charges reading fees of $5 to $25 per manuscript. Reading fee is deducted from commission if material brings in over $2,000 in first royalties. Standard commission of 10% U.S. sales, 15% Canadian sales, 20% foreign sales. "Material should be submitted as outlined in *Writer's Market.* For the best selling novel of the year, we award a one-year subscription to *Writer's Digest.* Send for brochure. Enclose S.A.S.E. with all correspondence."

THE CAMBRIDGE COMPANY, 9000 Sunset Blvd., Suite 319, Los Angeles CA 90069. Agency Representative: Lee Atkinson. Established 1963. Handles novels, nonfiction books, motion pictures, TV scripts. Enclose S.A.S.E. for return of submissions.

RUTH CANTOR, Room 1005, 156 Fifth Ave., New York NY 10010. Established in 1952. Handles "trade books, juvenile books, good fiction and nonfiction. I'm probably the best agent for children's books in the country. I prefer really good, solid novels and am allergic to potboilers. I am badly in need of really good nonfiction with broad market appeal." Standard commission 10% for domestic sales, 20% for foreign sales. New clients through referrals, recommendations, and direct contact with writers. To be represented by this agent, a new writer "must have proven talent, which means that he has published at least something, or else that some responsible person (such as an editor, another writer, a teacher) recommends him to me. Even then, I will represent only such people as I think I can sell, but will give a promising writer a free reading and appraisal of his ms. A new writer should write me a letter, giving me a concise writing history and description of what he wishes to send me. Enclose return postage in stamps both with query letter and with ms."

JANET COHN, Hotel Royalton, 44 W. 44 St., New York NY 10036. Established in 1968. Handles novels, motion pictures, plays, TV scripts. Recent sales for clients include *Finishing Touches* (Kerr); *No Enemy But Winter* (Allen). 10% standard commission. Advises writers to "give proof of professional experience or ability." New clients accepted "through recommendations by other clients or letters of inquiry." Will not read unsolicited mss "unless author seems promising." Will read unsolicited mss for fee of $10. Enclose S.A.S.E. for return of submissions or reply to queries.

TOBY COLE, 234 W. 44th St., Suite 402, Sardi Building, New York NY 10036. Established in 1957. Handles stage plays only. Standard commission 10% professional, 20% nonprofessional. Obtains new clients "in cooperation with agents abroad." Will read unsolicited mss. Enclose S.A.S.E. for return of submissions.

SHIRLEY COLLIER AGENCY, 1127 Stradella Road, Los Angeles CA 90024. Established in 1943. Handles magazine articles, magazine fiction, novels, nonfiction books, motion pictures, plays, comedy and satire. Recent sales for clients include *The Goliath Head* (Calitri/Brettschneider). Advises writers to "polish your material to the highest degree. Never let a rough or first draft be seen by an agent." Standard commission 10% "of all avenues of revenue on domestic royalties and subsidiaries. 20% of all foreign rights." Writer "should earn a minimum of $5,000 a year from his work. Only occasionally can we find time to develop a promising newcomer." Clients accepted by recommendations from writers or editors. Will read unsolicited queries or outlines. Will not read unsolicited mss "except when the first few pages are really interesting." Query first, "setting down your qualifications for writing." Enclose S.A.S.E. for reply to query.

COLTON, KINGSLEY, & ASSOCIATES, INC., 321 S. Beverly Dr., Beverly Hills CA 90212. Established in 1934. Specializes in TV, theater and motion pictures. Represents only recognized, established writers.

BEN CONWAY AND RUMAR ASSOCIATES, 999 N. Doheny Dr., Los Angeles CA 90069. Established in 1967. Handles magazine fiction, novels, motion pictures, stage plays, and TV scripts. "We handle mostly film properties. New writers must have reached some degree of achievement." 10% standard commission. Obtains new clients by referral. New writers should "write at least a full-length screenplay or ms." Will not read unsolicited mss. Enclose S.A.S.E. for reply to queries.

BILL COOPER ASSOCIATES, INC., 16 E. 52nd St., New York NY 10022. Established in 1964. Interested in original plays for theatre, motion pictures, and series ideas for television, dramatic, comedy, and daytime game and panel show areas. Advises writers to "write original material, not adaptations." 10% standard commission. Clients accepted by "recommendation and solicitation." Will read unsolicited mss "if S.A.S.E. is enclosed."

HAROLD CORNSWEET LITERARY AGENCY, P.O. Box 3093, Beverly Hills CA 90212. Established in 1950. Specializes in screenplay adaptations for motion pictures. 10% standard commission. Only talented writers need apply for literary representation. Ask for information card before submitting. Will read unsolicited mss. Fee required for new writers. Enclose S.A.S.E. for response to queries and return of submissions.

CREATIVE MANAGEMENT ASSOCIATES, 600 Madison Avenue, New York NY 10022. Established in 1933. Specializes in theater, television, motion pictures, and publishing. No unsolicited mss.

CREATIVE WRITERS AGENCY P.O. Drawer 2480, 1128 S. Patrick Dr., Satellite Beach FL 32937. Agency Representatives: John C. Roach, Jr., Verda L. Veatch. Established in 1971. Handles novels, nonfiction books, textbooks, motion pictures, plays, TV scripts. Is interested in "novels and plays with movie potential. A property recently placed is *The Stumblebum Saga* (Richardson/Ross). 10% standard commission. Will criticize unsolicited mss for a fee of $7.50 (to 7,500 words), $15 (to 25,000 words), $25 (25,000 words and up; all plays). Enclose S.A.S.E. for return of submissions.

JEANNE DARLING ASSOCIATES, 4425 Mayfield Rd., South Euclid OH 44121. Established in 1969. Prefers established writers; however, will consider prolific new writers if they demonstrate potential. 10% standard commission. Professional writers are handled on a straight commission basis. Rates for reading and analysis are available upon request. Query first. Enclose S.A.S.E. for response to queries and return of submissions.

JOAN DAVES, 515 Madison Ave., New York NY 10022. Established in 1951. Handles magazine articles, magazine fiction, juvenile fiction, novels, nonfiction books. Negotiates dramatic, TV and film rights on behalf of clients, but does not handle original scripts. 10% standard commission on all domestic income. 20% commission on all foreign income. Advises writers to "query. Give details about background and professional achievement. Do not give plots of fiction in endless detail." Will read unsolicited queries and outlines. Will not read unsolicited mss. Enclose S.A.S.E. for reply to queries.

ANITA DIAMANT, THE WRITERS WORKSHOP, INC., 51 E. 42 St., New York NY 10017. Established in 1917. Handles magazine articles, magazine fiction, juvenile fiction, novels, nonfiction books. "We handle both U.S. and foreign rights." Recent sales for clients include *Sappho Was a Right-On Woman* (Love/Abbott); *Africa A to Z* (Shane), 10% standard commission. Will represent a writer if he has sold a book within past 2 years or $1,500 worth of magazine material within past year. New clients accepted through recommendations from publishers and other clients. Advises writers to "always query, giving experience and history of mss to be submitted." Will read unsolicited queries and outlines. Enclose S.A.S.E. for reply.

ANN ELMO AGENCY, INC., 52 Vanderbilt Ave., New York NY 10017. Handles short stories, articles, books, fiction and nonfiction, teleplays, and plays for stage use. Enclose S.A.S.E. for return of submissions.

FRIEDA FISHBEIN, 353 W. 57th St., New York NY 10019. Established in 1941. Handles novels, nonfiction books, children's books, motion pictures, plays, TV scripts. Works on a 10% commission and an exclusive option for two years. Will read unsolicited mss and work with new writers. Reading fees vary, depending on whether ms is a play or a book. Enclose S.A.S.E. for return of submissions.

BARTHOLD FLES, 507 Fifth Ave., New York NY 10017. Established in 1933. Specializes in fiction, nonfiction, juveniles (no picture books). No magazine material except for clients. Recent sales for clients include *The American Inquisition* (Belfrage); *Buttes Landing* (Rikhoff). 10% standard commission for domestic rights; 15%, British; 20%, translation. New clients accepted through "recommendation by clients and/or editors." Will not read unsolicited mss. Enclose S.A.S.E. for reply to queries.

THE FOLEY AGENCY, 34 E. 38th St., New York NY 10016. Agency Representatives: Joan and Joseph Foley. Established in 1956. Handles novels and nonfiction books; handles some magazine articles and magazine fiction. 10% standard commission. New clients by recommendation. Will not read unsolicited mss. Will read unsolicited queries and outlines; "give all pertinent details." Enclose S.A.S.E. for reply.

HAROLD FREEDMAN BRANDT & BRANDT DRAMATIC DEPT., INC., 101 Park Ave., New York NY 10017. Established in 1927. Specializes in theater. Reads some unsolicited mss, but inquire first. Enclose S.A.S.E. for reply to queries.

PEGGY LOIS FRENCH, 12645 Norwalk Blvd., Norwalk CA 90650. Established in 1952. Handles novels, juvenile books (for an older age group), and TV scripts. Material must be high in quality. 10% standard commission. Will develop a writer with talent. "If a writer shows promise, I work with him until he makes a sale." Will read unsolicited mss. Charges $1.50 reading fee per 1,000 words (flat rate for longer mss) for unsolicited mss and new writers; none for professionals. Enclose S.A.S.E. for return of submissions.

JAY GARON-BROOKE ASSOC., INC., 415 Central Park West, New York NY 10025. Established in 1951. Handles novels, nonfiction books, textbooks, motion pictures, and stage plays. 10% standard commission. "Writer must be referred to us by an editor or one of our clients. We rarely accept a client who does not earn $10,000 a year. The writer should write to us, if established, and give his credits." Will not read unsolicited mss. Enclose S.A.S.E. for reply.

MAX GARTENBERG, 331 Madison Ave., New York NY 10017. Established in 1954. Handles novels and nonfiction books. 10% standard commission. Will not read unsolicited mss. "However, any writer, published or unpublished, who submits a grammatical, coherent letter describing what he has to sell will receive a reply if Mr. Gartenberg is interested." Enclose S.A.S.E. for reply.

PHIL GERSH AGENCY, INC., 222 North Canon Drive, Beverly Hills CA 90210. Established in 1959. 10% standard commission. Specializes in motion pictures, TV packaging, development of book projects for motion pictures. "Established novelists and screen writers only."

LARNEY GOODKIND, 30 E. 60 St., New York NY 10022. Established in 1948. Handles magazine articles, novels, nonfiction books, motion pictures, and stage plays. 10% standard commission. "We accept only previously published (or produced) writers. We require a query letter detailing past credits. Give all the facts of prior experience with other agents, publishing contracts, credits, commitments. No material welcome otherwise." Will not read unsolicited mss. Will read unsolicited queries and outlines. Enclose S.A.S.E. for response to queries.

IVAN GREEN AGENCY, 1900 Ave. of the Stars, Suite 840, Los Angeles CA 90067. Established in 1954. Handles novels, nonfiction books, motion pictures, stage plays, and TV scripts. 10% standard commission. New clients through recommendations. Will not read unsolicited mss.

SANFORD J. GREENBURGER ASSOCIATES, INC., 757 Third Ave., New York NY 10017. Agency Representative: Mr. Francis Greenburger. Established in 1932. Handles novels, nonfiction books, textbooks, motion pictures, juvenile fiction and nonfiction. Recent sales for clients include *The Pit* (Church/Carnes); *The Escalator Effect* (Patori); *Oh, My Aching Back* (Kiernan). 15% standard commission. New clients "through recommendations from publishers and other authors and through unsolicited mss." Will read unsolicited mss or outlines; "send query and short autobiographical information." No reading fee. Enclose S.A.S.E. for return of submissions and reply to queries.

BLANCHE C. GREGORY, INC., 2 Tudor City Place, New York NY 10017. Established in 1950. Specializes in fiction (novels and stories) for the major national magazines and nonfiction books. Prefers an author who has already sold to a first-class market. Query first. Enclose S.A.S.E. for reply.

VANCE HALLOWAY, Box 518, Pearblossom CA 93553. Established in 1956. Handles novels and nonfiction books. Recent sales for clients include *Murder Master* series. Will read unsolicited queries, outlines, and mss to 50,000 words. Enclose S.A.S.E. for return of submissions and reply to queries.

REECE HALSEY AGENCY, 8733 Sunset Blvd., Los Angeles CA 90069. Established in 1957. Handles novels, nonfiction books, and motion pictures. Handles novels, "after the subject matter has been discussed, and full screenplays, preferably contemporary but non-drug oriented." 10% standard commission. New clients through "referrals by other clients." Will not read unsolicited mss. Send "a query letter outlining the background of the writer." Enclose S.A.S.E. for response to query.

SHIRLEY HECTOR AGENCY, 29 West 46th St., New York NY 10036. "We request that a writer send us a brief account of what he has had published and a description of the work he wishes to submit. We do not encourage a writer to send us his ms unless he queries first." Enclose S.A.S.E. for response to query.

KURT HELLMER, 52 Vanderbilt Ave., New York NY 10017. Established in 1952. Handles novels, nonfiction books, textbooks, motion pictures, stage plays, and TV scripts. Recent sales for clients include *The Professional* (Buchanan); *The Yellow Jersey* (Hurne). Standard commission 10% domestic, 20% foreign. New clients by "word of mouth, inquiries, and recommendations. A new writer must show promise." Will read unsolicited mss for a fee of $25 for books and $15 for plays. Query first. Enclose S.A.S.E. for response to queries and return of submissions.

DICK IRVING HYLAND ASSOCIATES, 8961 Sunset Blvd., Los Angeles CA 90069. Agency Representatives: Dick Hyland, Wende Hyland, Paula Stoppa. Established in 1951. Handles published novels for motion picture sale, plays, original screenplays, TV series. Recent film sales for clients include "The Brownsville Raid." 10% standard commission. To be accepted, a writer "must be firmly established as a professional, or must win our respect after his material has been read, such material having been recommended by a respected professional or client of this office." Will not read unsolicited mss "unless recommended by a present client or a respected professional. Enclose S.A.S.E. for reply to queries.

GEORGE INGERSOLL AGENCY, 7167½ Sunset Blvd., Hollywood CA 90046. Established in 1949. Specializes in motion picture and television scripts. Will not read unsolicited mss.

CAROLYN JENKS AGENCY, 55 Seventh Ave., Brooklyn NY 11217. Established in 1966. Handles magazine articles, nonfiction books, poetry, and stage plays. Interested in "material oriented to social change, women's issues, humanist philosophy." Recent sales include *Jane Castle Manuscript* (Greene); *Ants, Wild Animals and Plants* (Batten). 10% standard commission. To be represented by this agency, a new writer "must be interested in achieving artistic and craftsmanlike work goals. My writers are committed to the art of writing for life." Usually obtains new clients "through other writers I represent." Will read unsolicited queries or outlines. Will not read unsolicited mss. Enclose S.A.S.E. for response to queries.

KAHN, LIFFLANDER, & RHODES, 853 Seventh Ave., New York, NY 10019. Agency Representative: Barbara Rhodes. Established in 1968. Handles juvenile fiction, novels, nonfiction books, motion pictures, and stage plays. Recent sales for clients include *Theodore Johnson Wainwright Is Going to Bomb the Pentagon* (Phillips); *Second Wives' Tales* (Cassidy). 10% standard commission. To be represented by this agency, a writer must have "either theatrical/movie performance or previous publication and some professional writing experience." Usually obtains new clients through recommendations. Will read unsolicited queries. Will read unsolicited mss "only after query." Enclose S.A.S.E. for response to queries.

VIRGINIA KIDD, 1 Sheridan Sq., Apt. 3-A, New York NY 10014. Established in 1965. Handles magazine fiction, juvenile fiction, novels, nonfiction books, motion pictures, TV scripts. Specializes in "speculative fiction (science fiction and fantasy), also experimental work; high-quality mainstream." 10% standard commission. Will represent new writers who "have earned at least $1,000 (from writing) during the preceding year, and the quality of the work must be outstanding. Some exceptions are made in the former instance, none in the latter." New clients accepted by referrals. "I have been refusing 'slush pile' applicants for 3 years with few exceptions—no room on my list." Will not read unsolicited mss.

BERTHA KLAUSNER, INTERNATIONAL LITERARY AGENCY, INC., 71 Park Ave., New York NY 10016. Established in 1938. Handles novels, nonfiction books, textbooks, motion pictures, plays, TV scripts. 10% standard commission. New clients accepted through "recommendations from publishers and authors." Will work with a writer who is "established or passes a reader's appraisal." Query first. Enclose S.A.S.E. for reply to queries.

LUCY KROLL AGENCY, 390 West End Ave., New York NY 10024. Established in 1950. Specializes in full-length plays, nonfiction and fiction. No unsolicited mss accepted; inquiries only, with S.A.S.E. for reply.

ROBERT LANTZ–CANDIDA DONADIO LITERARY AGENCY, INC., 111 W. 57th St., New York NY 10019. Established in 1968. Represents a limited number of writers and playwrights in all fields.

LASTER'S LITERARY AGENCY, 204 E. 45th Place, Tulsa OK 74105. Contact: Clara Laster. Established in 1971. Handles magazine articles, fiction, juvenile articles and fiction, novels, nonfiction books, textbooks, and specializes in poetry. Will read unsolicited mss for a fee of $25. Will criticize unsolicited mss for a fee of $25. No fee taken out of sales up to $250, then 10%. Standard commission is 10% with $25 paid in advance. Enclose S.A.S.E. with all correspondence.

LENNIGER LITERARY AGENCY, INC., 437 Fifth Ave., New York NY 10016. Established in 1923. Handles fiction and nonfiction books for adults and young readers. Handles magazine fiction and articles "only if we can expect a minimum commission of $25 on any sale. We refuse to handle writers who will not earn us at least $100 annually in commissions." Standard commission: 10%, American sales; 15%, Canadian sales; 20%, British sales; 30%, first $100 of foreign translation, 20% over $100; 10%, audiovisual. "Writers must have $1,000 sales minimum from any national magazines or book publishers within past year to be considered on commission basis. Preliminary letter from prospective clients should state publication credits, describe works to be offered. Await agency's invitation before sending mss. New writers can only be considered on reading fee basis. Preliminary letter describing writer's experience and prospective offering will bring agency's terms for evaluation fee if material described might be salable." Will not read unsolicited mss. Enclose S.A.S.E. for reply to queries.

HENRY LEWIS AGENCY, 9172 Sunset Blvd., Hollywood CA 90069. Established in 1950. Specializes in television scripts for filmed series and motion picture scripts. 10% standard commission. Will read unsolicited mss. Enclose S.A.S.E. for return of submissions.

LESTER LEWIS ASSOCIATES, INC., 156 E. 52nd Street, New York NY 10022. Agency Representative: Mrs. Carolyn Willyoung Stagg, Literary Department. Established in 1952. Specializes in fiction and nonfiction in book and magazine fields. Occasionally looks at unsolicited mss, but query must be sent first. No reading fee—hopes for "enough knowledge of the rudiments of writing to indicate a potential writer." Enclose S.A.S.E. for reply to queries. "Return postage is a must."

PATRICIA LEWIS, 450 Seventh Ave., Room 602, New York NY 10001. Established in 1951. Handles juvenile fiction and nonfiction books. Specializes in "teen-age fiction and nonfiction and general nonfiction; very few novels." 10% standard commission. "Query first. Do not send material without okay from agent." Will read book length unsolicited mss "only if 1) writer has taken courses of study in writing or has been recommended by an editor or teacher; 2) payment of $25 is made for a complete detailed criticism and suggestions to make the manuscript more salable. If the author is accepted as a client and the material is sold, the reading fee of $25 is refunded and the usual agency fee of 10% is charged." Enclose S.A.S.E. for reply to queries.

LITERA AGENCY, 11901 Laurel Hills Road, Studio City CA 91604. 10% standard commission. Agency Representative: Eve Duggan Alter. Handles motion picture and TV scripts only. "Will read and evaluate new writers' mss, but require minimum reading fee of $5 and up, depending on length involved, which will be returned if product is marketable." Enclose S.A.S.E. for return of submissions.

STERLING LORD AGENCY, INC., 660 Madison Avenue, New York NY 10021. Established in 1951. Handles magazine articles, magazine fiction, novels, nonfiction books, motion pictures, stage plays, TV scripts, and syndicated material. 10% standard commission. "No minimum sales are required, but writer must have previously published." Enclose S.A.S.E. for return of submissions.

WILL LOZIER, 134-35 Cherry Ave., Flushing NY 11355. Established in 1957. Specializes in books and short stories. 10% standard commission. Will read unsolicited mss in conformity with his established and advertised terms. Enclose S.A.S.E. for return of submissions. "Evaluation fees: $5 for short stories under 2,000 words. $10 for novelettes. $25 for plays and $15 for books."

DONALD MacCAMPBELL, INC., 12 East 41 Street, New York NY 10017. Established in 1940. Contact: Maureen Moran. Handles novels and nonfiction books for adult market only. "All sales on an assignment basis." Recent sales for clients include *How to Turn a Woman On and Off* (Cambrai); *Assignment: Ceylon* (Aarons). 10% standard commission for domestic rights, 20% for foreign rights. New writer must have previously published 1 book (send brief biography and record of past sales). Will read unsolicited queries and outlines, but will not read unsolicited mss. "No fees for reading," but enclose S.A.S.E. for return of submissions and always query first.

BETTY MARKS, 51 E. 42 St., Suite 1406, New York NY 10017. Established in 1969. Handles magazine articles, magazine fiction, juvenile articles, juvenile fiction, novels, nonfiction books. Recent sales for clients include *The Art Crowd* (Burnham); *In Their Own Good Time* (Kaufman). 10% standard commission. Will represent new writer whose work is "of good quality in research, writing, and subject matter." Will read unsolicited queries and outlines. Will read unsolicited mss (maximum 100,000 words) for a fee of $50. Enclose S.A.S.E. for return of submissions.

HAROLD MATSON COMPANY, INC., 22 East 40 St., New York NY 10016. Established in 1930. Specializes in any area in which a successful author's output can be exploited. Will represent a new writer if they are convinced of his potential possibilities. Does not read unsolicited mss; query first. No reading fee charged. Requires recommendation of an editor, writer, or professor. Enclose S.A.S.E. for response to queries.

McINTOSH AND OTIS, INC., 18 E. 41st St., New York NY 10017. Established in 1931. Handles magazine articles, magazine fiction, juvenile fiction, novels, nonfiction books. 10% standard commission for domestic rights; 15% for British rights; 20% for continental rights. Advises writers to "write, describing material offered, previous publication, etc. Do not ask for personal interview." Enclose S.A.S.E. for response to queries.

SCOTT MEREDITH LITERARY AGENCY, INC., 580 Fifth Ave., New York NY 10036. Established in 1941. Handles magazine articles, magazine fiction, juvenile fiction, novels, nonfiction books, textbooks, poetry collections, motion pictures, plays, TV scripts, columns and other material for syndication. Recent sales for clients include *Marilyn Monroe* (Mailer), *The Treasure Hunter* (Moore), and *My Country* (Eban). 10% standard commission on American sales, 15% on Canadian sales, 20% on all other foreign sales. Charges a fee in working with writers who are not now selling regularly to major markets, and works on commission basis with regularly selling writers. If a writer has sold to a major book publisher in the past year or has begun to make major national magazine or television sales with some regularity, "we drop fees and proceed on a straight commission basis." Booklet describing agency and terms available free on request. Will read unsolicited mss. Enclose S.A.S.E.

ROBERT P. MILLS LTD., 156 E. 52 St., New York NY 10022. Established in 1960. Specializes in general trade book publishing and general magazines; more emphasis on fiction than nonfiction. 10% standard commission. A writer "must come to me recommended by a respected source or have established himself in some way as a professional writer; no minimum sales required, but I must have faith in the writer." Will not read unsolicited mss.

MOLSON-STANTON ASSOCIATES AGENCY, INC., 10889 Wilshire Blvd., Los Angeles CA 90024. Contact: Gordon Molson. Established in 1943. "The only unsolicited mss we can read are completed novels, plays or motion picture screenplays from writers who have sold in a major market in the last few years. Also required is a 5- to 10-page double-spaced outline, giving the main characters and the full story line, including the ending. These outlines help us in learning the possible story potential in advance. We do not handle single TV series episode scripts for out-of-town writers." 10% commission. No reading fees. Recent sales include *Night World* (Bloch) and *Panic* (Pronzini). "Please list professional writing experience and sales and enclose return mailer."

HOWARD MOOREPARK, 444 East 82nd St., New York NY 10028. Established in 1946. Handles magazine articles, magazine fiction, novels, nonfiction books and motion pictures. 10% standard commission; 19% overseas. New clients accepted through recommendations. Also will read unsolicited queries, outlines, and mss. Enclose S.A.S.E. for return of submissions and response to queries.

WILLIAM MORRIS AGENCY, 1350 Avenue of the Americas, New York NY 10019. Enclose S.A.S.E. for return of submissions.

NATIONAL LAUGH ENTERPRISES, Box 835, Grand Central Station, New York NY 10017. Agency Representative: George Q. Lewis. Established in 1945. Will read unsolicited mss only if they are less than 10 pages in length. Will represent a writer "if he has great talent." Specializes in humor. Interested in the performing arts primarily: radio, TV, stage, off-Broadway, etc. 15% standard commission. Conducts "College of Comedy" for gagwriters and comedians in New York City, and guest teaches "The Art of Laughmaking" at varied schools in the Metropolitan New York area (including New Jersey) and does mini-courses in creative comedy. These courses provide a humor laboratory where skills and techniques are examined and tested, then channeled to members of Humor Exchange Network. Also invites membership in Humor Exchange Network, which sponsors Comedy Workshop activities in communities throughout the country. Also each month invites gagwriters to compete for Gagwriter-of-the-Month title, a showcase of 50 original jokes which is sent to prominent columnists and broadcasting executives to focus attention on new talented gagwriters. Enclose S.A.S.E. for return of submissions.

CHARLES NEIGHBORS, INC., 240 Waverly Place, New York NY 10014. Established in 1967. Handles magazine articles, magazine fiction, juvenile articles, juvenile fiction, novels, nonfiction books, textbooks, poetry, motion pictures. Recent sales for clients include *Acts of Love* (Berge) and *Alternatives to College* (Hecht). 10% standard commission. New writer must have "written and had published high quality material. I will, however, be willing to consider the work of unpublished writers on recommendation of existing clients or editors." Will also read unsolicited queries and outlines, provided that S.A.S.E. is enclosed.

B.K. NELSON LITERARY AGENCY, 210 E. 47 Street, New York NY 10017. Established in 1968. Nonfiction; current events for trade book publication. Also handles key novels with movie sale potential. Will read unsolicited mss. Charges $25 reading fee. Enclose S.A.S.E. for return of submissions.

NICHOLAS LITERARY AGENCY, 161 Madison Avenue, New York NY 10016. Agency Representative: Georgia C. Nicholas. Established in 1934. Handles books and plays. 10% standard commission. "Until first sale together, we charge a nominal handling fee for book lengths, refundable after first sale. We're not seeking new clients but would be intersted in novels adaptable to Disney films. Queries with no S.A.S.E. take months to answer." Enclose S.A.S.E. for response to queries and return of submissions.

HAROLD OBER ASSOCIATES, INC., 40 E. 49 St., New York NY 10017. Handles magazine articles, magazine fiction, novels, nonfiction books. In business over 40 years. 10% standard commission, U.S. sales; 15%, British sales; 20%, translations. "Writer doesn't necessarily have to have been published before, but we must feel strongly about a person's potential before taking anyone new on." Will read unsolicited queries and outlines. Enclose S.A.S.E. for reply to queries.

DOROTHEA OPPENHEIMER, 866 United Nations Plaza, Rm. 471, New York NY 10017. Established in 1959. Handles book-length adult fiction and nonfiction "of exceptional quality." 10% standard commission. Query first "with a brief outline of the work and a couple of sample pages to give an idea of the style." Enclose S.A.S.E. for response to queries.

ETHEL PAIGE AGENCY, 155 E. 34 St., New York NY 10016. Established in 1935. Handles novels, nonfiction books, poetry, motion pictures, stage plays, TV scripts, and radio scripts. Will also represent songwriters and singers for special fee. Recent sales for clients include *Scarlet Children* (Keys) and *Play Your Hunch, Make It a Miracle* (Brown). 10% standard commission; 15% foreign. Usually obtains new clients by recommendations. Will read unsolicited queries, outlines, or mss. Resumes of writing experience helpful. Will read and criticize unsolicited mss for a fee "according to the script." 10% commission, U.S.; 15%, foreign. Enclose S.A.S.E. for return of submissions and response to queries.

PARK AVENUE LITERARY AGENCY, 230 Park Ave., New York NY 10017. Agency Representative: Marie Wilkerson. Established in 1960. Handles nonfiction books primarily. 10% standard commission. "Looking for new writers with good potential. It is not necessary that they have been previously published." Advises writers to "write full query letters, giving background information." Enclose S.A.S.E. for response to queries.

JUNE PARKER LITERARY AGENCY, 16601 N. 29th St., F 18, Phoenix AZ 85032. Established in 1964. Specializes in TV, movies and publishers' material of all kinds. Query first. Will look at professionally written unsolicited mss. Charges "small reading fee. Enclose S.A.S.E. for reply to queries.

MARJORIE PETERS, PIERRE LONG, 5744 S. Harper, Chicago IL 60637. Est. 1953. Specializes in poetry and fiction. 10% standard commission. Works with new writers of calibre; no minimum sales requirement. Does not read unsolicited mss; query first. $30 reading fee charged for book length mss of 200 pages or less; more for longer mss. For short stories, articles and essays of not more than 15 pages double-spaced, poetry of not more than four pages double-spaced, and 15 minute TV plays, charges $15; more for longer plays. Enclose S.A.S.E. for response to queries.

PISCEAN PRODUCTIONS, Suite 105, Executive Bldg., 1135 Pasadena Ave., S., St. Petersburg FL 33707. President: Tom Milner. Established in 1972. Handles novels, television plays, and motion picture scripts. 10% standard commission. Query first. "Unpublished writers are sometimes charged a reading fee. Non-established writers should enclose S.A.S.E. when writing."

SIDNEY PORCELAIN, Box J, Rocky Hill NJ 08553. Established in 1951. Handles magazine articles, magazine fiction, juvenile fiction, novels, nonfiction books, TV scripts. Recent sales for clients include *Belvaux, The Return of Kavin.* 10% standard commission. New clients accepted by referrals. Will read unsolicited queries, outlines, and mss. Enclose S.A.S.E.

Q E D LITERARY AGENCY, 7032 Willis Ave., Van Nuys, Los Angeles CA 91405. President: Vincent J. Ryan. Established in 1966. Handles "scholarly or serious nonfiction; subject areas include philosophy, anthropology, theology, sociology, psychology, phenomenology, linguistics, ethnology, ethnomusicology, natural history, ecology, education, history, literature." Recent sales for clients include *Twentieth Century Literature* (Mueller) and *Pastoral Psychology* (Zavalloni). 10% standard commission. New writer should "send outline and list of contents and possibly 1 or 2 chapters of ms. Make submission on exclusive basis. If in process of writing, submit ms piecemeal." Will read unsolicited mss. "About 15%" of annual income is obtained from ms reading or criticism fees. Enclose S.A.S.E. for return of submissions. Will also undertake computerized typesetting and indexing and camera ready copy preparation

THERON RAINES AGENCY, 244 Madison Ave., New York NY 10016. Established in 1961. Has juvenile department. Will work with new writers. Will not read unsolicited mss. Query first. Enclose S.A.S.E. for response to queries.

PAUL R. REYNOLDS, INC., 599 Fifth Ave., New York NY 10017. Established in 1893. Handles magazine articles, magazine fiction, juvenile fiction, novels, nonfiction books, motion picture rights and novels. 10% standard commission. New clients accepted through recommendations. Advises new writer to "write a ms or part of a ms that we are wildly enthusiastic about." Will read unsolicited queries and outlines. Rarely reads or handles unsolicited mss. Enclose S.A.S.E. for response.

VIRGINIA RICE, 301 East 66th St., New York NY 10021. Established in 1928. Handles magazine articles, magazine fiction, juvenile fiction, novels, nonfiction, textbooks, poetry. Query first. Enclose return postage for response to queries.

BETTY J. RUSSELL, Russylvania-Suman Rd., Route 1, Valparaiso IN 46383. established in 1951. Handles juvenile fiction. 10% standard commission. No minimum sales needed. Will read unsolicited queries, outlines, and ms. Enclose S.A.S.E. for return of submissions or response to queries.

LEAH SALISBURY, INC., 790 Madison Ave., New York NY 10021. Specializes in theatre and films. 10% standard commission. "Interested in writers of superior talent. Evaluation in terms of quality and potential rather than dollars." Reading fee is generally required for unpublished writers but returned if mss is accepted. Query first. Enclose S.A.S.E. for response to queries.

IRVING SALKOW AGENCY, 450 North Roxbury Dr., Beverly Hills CA 90210. Established in 1963. Handles motion pictures, plays, TV scripts. "The opportunities for writers in motion pictures and television are as strong as ever, if not a little more so, with the many pictures now being made for television exhibition. To expedite matters, writers who have original material should present it in the form of completed screenplays." 10% standard commission. New writer must have "a willingness to write and demonstrate that, with written material in the form of scripts, treatments, or outlines intended for dramatic, motion picture, television, or stage production." New clients accepted through referrals. Will read unsolicited queries, outlines, and mss. Enclose S.A.S.E. for return of submissions or response to queries.

AD SCHULBERG LITERARY AGENCY, 300 East 57 St., New York NY 10022. Established in 1931. Handles magazine articles, magazine fiction, novels, nonfiction books, motion pictures, stage plays, and TV scripts. Recent sales for clients include *Sanctuary V* and *A Face in the Crowd*. New clients by recommendation. Will read unsolicited manuscripts only under special circumstances; inquire first. No minimum sales required for talented new writers. Enclose S.A.S.E. for response to queries.

SELIGMANN AND COLLIER, 280 Madison Ave., New York NY 10016. Agency Representative: Oscar Collier. Established in 1960. Handles novels and nonfiction books. Will consider work of new writers; no minimum sales volume required. No unsolicited mss. No reading fee. Query first. Enclose S.A.S.E. for response to queries and return of submissions.

A. FREDERICK SHORR, INC., 1717 No. Highland Ave., Hollywood CA 90028. Agency Representative: A. Frederick Shorr. Established in 1971. Handles motion pictures and TV scripts. 10% standard commission. New clients through "referrals from other clients or friends." Will not read unsolicited mss.

H.E. SHUSTER AND COMPANY, 4930 Wynnefield Ave., Philadelphia PA 19131. Agency Representative: Harold Shuster. Established in 1961. Handles fiction and nonfiction books, magazine stories and articles, stage plays, television scripts and motion pictures. "Specializes in well-written, well-plotted, and well-characterized books." 10% standard commission on American sales, 15% on Canadian sales, 20% on foreign sales. No minimum sales required. "Will read unsolicited ms if writer has attained professional status, is recommended by an editor or author whose judgment we respect." No reading fee charged. Enclose S.A.S.E. for return of submissions.

MAX SIEGEL AND ASSOCIATES, 154 E. Erie St., Chicago IL 60611. Established in 1959. Handles magazine articles, magazine fiction, juvenile articles, juvenile fiction, novels, nonfiction books, textbooks, poetry, motion pictures, plays, TV scripts. "We are particularly interested in increasing our juvenile and textbook representation. These 2 areas have tended to handle their contracts without agents and are, as a result, subject to minimum contracts in royalty, rights, advances, and overseas edition income." Advises writers to "be explicit about publishing background, both in preparation and experience that relates to writing, and about all publishing success. Make the first contact by mail. A serious writer should write." 10% standard commission. "We encourage new talent and work with it as aggressively as we do established writers. We prefer publishing experience, but the real test of a new writer is the quality of the ms offered." Will read unsolicited mss for a fee. Enclose S.A.S.E. for return of submissions or response to queries.

EVELYN SINGER LITERARY AGENCY, P.O. Box 163, Briarcliff Manor NY 10510. Established in 1951. Handles adult and juvenile novels and nonfiction books and magazine fiction and articles. Handles magazine material only in the form of subsidiary rights, or for clients represented in the past. Does not take on short material from new clients. Write, giving pertinent writing background and/or authority in the case of nonfiction. Do not phone. Briefly describe material you would like to send. Type queries; do not write in longhand. Will not read unsolicited mss. Will review contracts for $100 fee. This does not include any negotiation. A written evaluation of the contract will be made. Any resulting consultation will be prorated. 10% standard commission. Will work with writer who has earned $10,000 minimum from past sales. Reads book manuscripts (adult or juvenile, fiction or nonfiction) on recommendation of any professional writer or editor. Writer should contact by letter, giving his background and a description of work before sending ms. "Outline past publication history succinctly, include jackets if available, and describe briefly projects on hand. Do not phone." Will not read unsolicited mss. Enclose S.A.S.E. for response to query.

ELYSE SOMMER, INC., Box E, Woodmere, Long Island NY 11598. Specializes in juveniles, how-to books, paperbacks, and confessions. 10% standard commission. Writer should have made at least three independent sales (not including fillers, poems, or such). Query first. Enclose S.A.S.E. for response to queries.

PHILIP G. SPITZER LITERARY AGENCY, 111-25 76th Ave., Forest Hills NY 11375. Established in 1969. Handles novels, nonfiction books, motion pictures; handles magazine articles and magazine fiction "when the writer is also working on book-length material." Recent sales for clients include *The Decline and Fall of America* (DeMaria) and *The Secton Women* (Heely). 10% standard commission. Obtains new clients "primarily through recommendations of editors and established clients." Will read unsolicited queries or outlines. Enclose S.A.S.E. for response to queries.

DAVID STEIN, 1400 Sawyerwood Rd., Orlando FL 32809. Established in 1970. Handles juvenile fiction, novels, and nonfiction books. "Presently handling mostly fiction in adult line. This covers detective, western, adventure, sex. Nonfiction is scarce, but will handle if well-written and covers a timely subject. Main outlet right now is sex, and can place many of these almost at will, providing they adhere to the rules of writing in all areas and handle sex properly. My clients are all men except for 2. They are published writers, but not necessarily well-known." 10% standard commission. New clients "through newspaper ads, editors, and word of mouth." To be represented by this agent, a writer must "know the mechanics of writing and be able to tell an interesting story in an up-to-date manner. A story must move and not wander. Writer must also be willing to rewrite, cut, or add when necessary." Will read unsolicited queries or outlines. Will read unsolicited mss for a fee of $10 to $25. Enclose S.A.S.E. for return of submissions or response to queries

C.M. STEPHAN, JR., 918 State St., Lancaster PA 17603. Established in 1971. Handles magazine fiction and novels. Recent sales include *Way Station* (Van Cort); *My Secret Life* (Burns). Writing must display potential or be competitive. 10% standard commission. Charges $10 reading fee. Enclose S.A.S.E. for return of submissions.

LARRY STERNIG, 2407 N. 44th St., Milwaukee WI 53210. Established in 1953. Handles magazine articles, magazine fiction, juvenile articles, juvenile fiction, novels, nonfiction books. Recent sales for clients include *The Linnet Estate* (Polk) and *Sidewalk Indian* (Holt). 10% standard commission. Will represent a new writer "only if sent by some editor or valued client." Will not read unsolicited mss.

GUNTHER STUHLMANN, 65 Irving Place, New York NY 10003. Est. 1956. Specializes in book and magazine fiction and nonfiction. Also, quality juveniles for older age group. 10% standard commission in U.S. and Canada, 15% in Great Britain, 20% elsewhere. Previous sale to national market required. Query first. Enclose S.A.S.E. for response to query.

HAROLD SWOVERLAND, PERSONAL MANAGEMENT, 3246 Isabella Dr., Oceanside CA 92054. Contact: Harold Swoverland. Established in 1945. Handles novels, motion pictures, stage plays. 10% standard commission. Material must be "well-written, readable, with good story line; suitable for films; well-motivated. I want a writer who writes every day." Will read unsolicited mss for a fee of $100. Will criticize unsolicited mss for a fee of $200. Will read unsolicited queries or outlines. Enclose S.A.S.E. ¢for reply to queries, or return of submissions.

TWIN PINES LITERARY AGENCY, 72 Truesdale Dr., Croton-On-Hudson NY 10520. Contact: Marty Lewis. Established in 1970. Magazine articles, fiction, juvenile articles and fiction, novels, nonfiction books, textbooks, motion pictures, stage plays, TV scripts, radio scripts, and syndicated material. "We specialize in motion picture, stage plays and TV scripts. New writers will have to pay reading fee depending on the material submitted. Established writers, no fee. Only requirement is that material be submitted in professional manner ready to be submitted to publishers. All material must be geared toward commercial market." Query first. Enclose S.A.S.E.

GEORGE ULLMAN AGENCY, 8450 De Longpre Ave., Los Angeles CA 90069. Established in 1927. Specializes in motion picture features and television. Dollar sales not important. Writer should have published some material and have television or feature credits. Enclose S.A.S.E. for return of submissions.

J.H. VAN DAELE, 225 E. 57th St., New York NY 10022. Agency Representative: Jacqueline H. Van Daele. Established in 1971. Handles nonfiction books. "I handle only psychiatrically oriented books, including all the behavioral sciences, aimed at the popular market." 10% standard commission. Obtains new clients "through recommendations." To be represented by this agency, a new writer "must be either an M.D. (psychiatrist) or a Ph.D. (psychologist). I only represent professional people. I will read outlines of potential mss only. I also create ideas for books for a higher percentage of commission." Enclose S.A.S.E. for return of submissions.

AUSTIN WAHL AGENCY, INC., 21 E. Van Buren St., Chicago IL 60605. Agency Representatives: Thomas Wahl, Paul Carson, Joel Rittley, Robert Restivo. Established in 1935. Handles motion pictures, TV scripts, novels, nonfiction books (including educational, reference, and technical), stage plays, short stories, and articles; adult and juvenile material. 10% standard commission. Sometimes charges reading fee. "New clients by referral and solicitation." Will read queries and brief outlines. Will not read unsolicited mss. Enclose S.A.S.E. for reply to queries and return of submissions.

A. WATKINS INC., 77 Park Ave., New York NY 10016. Established in 1908. Specializes in all areas except juveniles and poetry. Enclose S.A.S.E. for return of submissions.

W. B. AGENCY, INC., 156 E 52 St., New York NY 10022. Agency Representatives: Warren Bayless, Roberta Kent. Established in 1969. Specializes in fiction, nonfiction, plays, films. "Author and materials must be recommended by competent editor, educator, writer, etc." Query first, Attention: Miss Kent. Enclose S.A.S.E. for response to query.

WENDER & ASSOCIATES, INC., 30 E. 60 St., New York NY 10022. Agency Representative: Karen Hitzig. Established in 1968. Handles magazine articles, magazine fiction, novels, nonfiction books, poetry, motion pictures, plays, TV scripts. 10% standard commission for U.S. and Canada; 15% for Britain; 20% for foreign countries. Commission for plays: 10% for off-Broadway and Broadway; 15% for stock; 20% for amateur. Will read unsolicited mss. Enclose S.A.S.E. for return of submissions.

WRITERS: FREE-LANCE, 426 Pennsylvania Ave., Fort Washington PA 19034. Director: Robert M. Cullers. Secures assignments for writers of all types who can produce the material needed by business, industry, science, technology, education, institutions and government. These assignments include advertising for print, broadcasting and direct mail, speeches, public relations, house organs, annual reports, audio/visual presentations, industrial films, business and educational books. Technical assignments include training manuals, instruction handbooks, control cataloging and all types of documentation. Writers are paid promptly on terms contracted in advance. No speculative writing is requested. Registration for assignments requires qualified writers to send detailed resumes, stressing their specializations. The Writers: Free-Lance network currently consists of over 2,500 writers in cities and towns across the United States, Canada and 50 countries overseas and can cover local writing and photographic assignments for commercial news events. Send resumes and samples which can be kept in writer's file. Enclose S.A.S.E.

MARY YOST ASSOCIATES, 141 E. 55th St., New York NY 10022. Established in 1958. Handles magazine articles, magazine fiction, novels, nonfiction books. Recent sales for clients include *Open Marriage* (O'Neill/Evans) and *Power and Innocence* (May/Norton). 10% standard commission. Will read brief, unsolicited queries and outlines. Will not read unsolicited mss. Enclose S.A.S.E. for response to queries.

Contests and Awards

The contests and awards listed below are conducted annually. For information on irregular and "one shot" competitions, see the "Writer's Market" column in Writer's Digest *magazine. Deadlines are given for the year 1974; ordinarily, deadlines will fall around the same time from year to year for a specific competition.*

Some of the listed contests and awards—like the National Book Awards—do not accept entries or nominations direct from writers. They are included because of their national or literary importance. When a competition accepts entries from publishers, and the writer feels his work meets its requirements, he may wish to remind his publisher to enter his work.

Always enclose a business-sized self-addressed, stamped envelope when writing for entry blanks or further information.

A.I.P.-U.S. STEEL FOUNDATION SCIENCE WRITING AWARD. Write Press Relations Section, American Institute of Physics, 335 E. 45th St., New York NY 10017. Awards $1,500, a certificate, and a symbolic device representing the prize. Deadline: January 31, annually.
Nonfiction: The purpose of the award is "to stimulate distinguished reporting and

writing of advances in physics and astronomy. Any article on physics or astronomy may be submitted for the award provided it has been published in a newspaper or a magazine or a book between January 1 and December 31, of the previous year. The entries must have been printed in any recognized international, national, or local medium of communication such as newspapers, magazines, or books. The media should normally be available to and intended for the general public—purely scientific, technical, and trade publications are excluded. No more than three entries may be submitted by any one individual. Persons other than the author may submit entries on behalf of an author in accordance with the rules. Each entry must be accompanied by an official entry blank."

AAAS-WESTINGHOUSE SCIENCE WRITING AWARDS. Write Grayce A. Finger, AAAS-Westinghouse Science Writing Awards, 1515 Massachusetts Ave. N.W., Washington DC 20005. Awards three $1,000 prizes for science writing in newspapers and general circulation magazines. Deadline: October 10.

Nonfiction: The award "recognizes outstanding writing on the natural sciences, and their engineering and technological applications (excluding medicine), in newspapers and general circulation magazines. Entries are judged on the basis of their initiative, originality, scientific accuracy, clarity of interpretation, and value in promoting a better understanding of science by the public. The three prizes are given for writing in daily newspapers with daily circulation of more than 100,000; for writing in newspapers with circulation of less than 100,000; for writing in general circulation magazines. Each entrant in a newspaper award competition and each entrant in the magazine award competition may submit three entries. An entry for a newspaper competition may be any of the following: a single story; a series of articles; or a group of three unrelated stories, articles, editorials, or columns published during the contest year. A magazine entry may be a single story or series published during the contest year. Each entry must have been published in a newspaper or general magazine within the United States during the contest year—October 1 through September 30. A completed entry blank must be submitted together with five copies of each entry in the form of tearsheets, clippings, reprints, or syndicate copy (not over 8½"x11"), showing name and date of the publication."

HERBERT BAXTER ADAMS PRIZE. Contact: Committee Chairman, Herbert Baxter Adams Prize, American Historical Association, 400 A St., S.E., Washington DC 20003. Awards $300 annually "for an author's first book in the field of European history." Write to Committee Chairman for more information. Deadline: June 1.

AMERICAN ACADEMY OF FAMILY PHYSICIANS JOURNALISM AWARDS. American Academy of Family Physicians, P.O. Box 8723, Wornall Station, Kansas City MO 64114. A total of $2,000 will be awarded in this annual medical writing competition. Deadline: May 25.

Nonfiction: Reporters, feature writers, syndicated staff writers, freelance writers, or any members of the press who write medical news and features are eligible. Entries will be judged on their effectiveness in stimulating critical public awareness of the role of the family doctor in helping families benefit from the American health care structure; new thought and approaches to improvements and changes in the health care structure and the role of the family doctor, to better serve the families of the nation in the future. All entries must be accompanied by entry blank. All entries for the calendar year must have been published during the previous year. None of the entries will be returned. Send for submission requirements and entry blank.

AMERICAN DENTAL ASSOCIATION SCIENCE WRITERS AWARD. Write Science Writers Award Committee, American Dental Association, 211 E. Chicago Ave., Chicago IL 60611. Awards two $1,000 prizes plus air fare and per diem expenses for winners' attendance at the annual session of the American Dental Association. Deadline: August 31, 1974.

Nonfiction: "Articles should broaden and deepen public understanding of dental disease, dental treatment, or dental research and be published in the period from July 1, 1973 to June 30, 1974. The award is made for the best article, feature, or editorial in general circulation magazine and newspaper categories . Entries will be judged on the basis of scientific accuracy, public interest, impact, clarity, originality of presentation and significance. All entries must be submitted with a cover page containing the following information: title of entry, name and address of entrant, publication in which article appeared, date of publication, category (magazine or newspaper) in which entry is submitted. Two copies of each entry must be submitted. Neither can be returned."

AMERICAN MEDICAL ASSOCIATION MEDICAL JOURNALISM AWARDS. Write Medical Journalism Awards Committee, American Medical Association, 535 N. Dearborn St., Chicago IL 60610. Awards $1,000 in each of 5 categories. Deadline: February 1.

Nonfiction, Radio, and TV: The award is made "for distinguished contributions to a better understanding of medicine and health through magazines, newspapers, television, radio, and in editorials." The 5 categories of competition include "magazines: (for an article or articles in a U.S. magazine of general circulation published at regular intervals. Sunday magazines with national distribution will be judged in this category), newspapers (for a news story, feature story or series in a U.S. newspaper of general circulation published at least once a week), television (for reporting on medicine or health on a U.S. television station or network), radio (for reporting on medicine or health on a U.S. radio station or network), editorial (for editorial writing in a U.S. newspaper of general circulation published at least once a week or on a U.S. radio or television station or network). Entries must have been published or broadcast during the calendar year preceding the deadline date. Entries will be considered for accuracy, significance, quality, public interest, and impact. Successful communication of an idea will be the basis for judgment rather than the length or elaborateness of presentation. The awards will not be given for work, however excellent, that involves primarily the relaying of medical knowledge to the medical and allied professions. Members of the medical profession, medical associations and their employees are not eligible. Entries for newspaper and magazine articles must be submitted in triplicate: at least one copy must be a tearsheet validating the date of publication and showing the material as it appeared when published. All entries must be accompanied by the following information: Title of entry, writer or producer, publication in which article appeared or station or network over which program was broadcast, date of publication or broadcast, category for which entry is submitted, name, address, and title of person submitting entry."

AMERICAN OPTOMETRIC ASSOCIATION JOURNALISM AWARD. Write Division of Public Information, American Optometric Association, 7000 Chippewa St., St. Louis MO 63119. Awards four $500 prizes and medallions. Deadline: July 1.

Nonfiction, Radio, and TV: The purpose of the awards is "to recognize outstanding articles and broadcasts on the subject of vision as contributing to a better understanding of the importance of vision and its care; to honor writers of articles and radio and television scripts that focus public attention upon the significance and need for proper vision care; and to create increased public and professional interest in programs for the care, improvement, and preservation of vision." Categories for the competition include the following: press (newspapers, feature syndicates, wire services), magazine, radio, and television. "All entries must have been published or broadcast during the period beginning June 1 of the preceding year and ending May 31 of the year in which the award is presented. Each entry must be accompanied by an exhibit and properly completed official entry form. Exhibits of entries submitted in the categories of press and magazine must include one copy of the published news story or magazine article. This copy must validate the date of publication and show the material as it was presented to the public. Exhibits of entries submitted in the categories of radio and television must include a typed summary of the script, a copy of the full script, and a recording of the radio broadcast, or in the case of television, a 16mm film, kinescope or tape of the telecast. A concise statement summarizing any reactions by readership or audience indicating response to the article or broadcast must be included as a part of all entries. No entries will be returned with the exception of films, tapes, recordings, and similar materials accompanying entries in the radio and television categories."

AMERICAN OSTEOPATHIC JOURNALISM AWARDS. Write Journalism Awards Competition, American Osteopathic Association, 212 E. Ohio St., Chicago IL 60611. Awards three $100 prizes. Deadline: March 1.

Nonfiction: "The purpose of the awards is to recognize the growing corps of competent journalists who are reporting and interpreting the contributions of osteopathic medicine to the scientific community and the general public. Competition for the awards is open to writers on newspapers, magazines, or other regularly published periodicals. Members of the osteopathic profession and their employees are not eligible. Entries may deal with any aspect of the osteopathic profession, including scientific advances, college and hospital programs, or activities of individual osteopathic physicians. The accepted standards of good journalism and the contribution which the article makes toward a fuller understanding of the osteopathic profession will be the criteria upon which entries will be judged. All entries become the property of the AOA. Permission to reprint winning entries in AOA publications with full credit is implicit. Clippings should be mounted on white paper with the name of the author and the publication typed in the upper right corner." All entries must have been published during the calendar year preceding the deadline date.

AMERICAN PSYCHOLOGICAL FOUNDATION NATIONAL MEDIA AWARDS. Contact Jim Warren, Public Information Officer, American Psychological Association, 1200 Seventeenth St., N.W., Washington DC 20036. Deadline: May 15.

Films, Radio, Television, Magazine Writing, Newspaper Reporting, Books/Monographs: Six awards are presented to recognize and encourage outstanding, accurate reporting which increases the public's knowledge and understanding of psychology. In addition, a Grand Prix winner will be selected from the winners of the six categories. Entrants in film, radio, television categories must send preview copies of their show to the American Psychological Association before June 1, 1974. Prints of tapes do not have to accompany the nomination. Video tapes accepted but 16mm film preferred. Entrants in magazine writing and books/monographs competition should submit at least two copies of the material to be judged at the time the nomination is made or shortly thereafter. No textbooks will be considered. Newspaper entrants need only supply one set of materials, preferably at the time of nomination. Materials must have been produced sometime between May 1, 1973 and May 1, 1974. Award winners will be honored at the annual convention of the APA. Entries must be accompanied by an entry blank.

ARK RIVER AWARDS, *The Ark River Review*, 440 N. Yale, Wichita KS 67208. Prizes of $50 and $20 for poetry. One $100 prize for fiction. No deadline.
Nonfiction: To be considered for the awards simply submit manuscripts to the *Ark River Review* for publication in the usual fashion. Winners will be selected from the material published in each volume of the *Ark River Review*. Mss should be typed, original and unpublished. S.A.S.E. must be enclosed. Regular rates of payment for poetry published is 20c per line; minimum $5 per poem. Fiction, $3 per printed page, minimum $20 per story.

THE ATHENAEUM OF PHILADELPHIA LITERARY AWARD. Write the Literary Award Committee, Athenaeum of Philadelphia, East Washington Square, Philadelphia PA 19106. Awards a bronze medal. Nomination must be made on or before December 31 of each year.
Nonfiction, Fiction, Poetry, Drama: "Any volume of general literature (fiction, history, biography, drama, belles lettres) written by a Philadelphian; or persons resident in Philadelphia at time of writing; technical, scientific, exclusively educational and juvenile books are not included. An award may be given to both a fiction and a nonfiction title in any year, at the discretion of the judges. Nominations of candidate books for this annual prize shall be made in writing to the Literary Award Committee of the Athenaeum of Philadelphia, by the author, the publisher or a member of the Athenaeum, on or before December 31 of each year and shall be accompanied by a copy of the book or books in question. Consideration of nominations is to be on the basis of their significance and importance to the general public as well as on literary excellence. Decision of the judges shall be final and all books submitted shall become the property of the Athenaeum of Philadelphia."

AVIATION/SPACE WRITERS ASSOCIATION WRITING AWARDS. Write Aviation/Space Writers Association, 101 Greenwood Ave., Jenkintown PA 19046. Awards $100 and engraved scroll in 6 categories. Deadline: January 15.

Nonfiction, Photography, Radio, and TV: Awards for writing on aviation and space. Categories include newspapers over 200,000 circulation, newspapers under 200,000 circulation, magazines, television and radio, photography, and books (nonfiction). There is a separate award for aviation and space in each category. Entries must have been published during the year preceding the contest year. Entry blanks are preferred.

EMILY CLARK BALCH PRIZES. Write the *Virginia Quarterly Review*, One West Range, Charlottesville VA 22903. Awards $500, first prize; $250 each, second prizes. Deadline: March 1.
Fiction and Poetry: "Made possible through the generous bequest of Emily Clark Balch to the University of Virginia for the purpose of stimulating appreciation and creation of American literature." Prizes are offered in even-numbered years for poetry and in odd-numbered years for short stories. Prize-winning entries are published in an issue of *Virginia Quarterly Review*. The prizes will be in addition to payment for publication at the magazine's usual rates. Envelopes should be marked plainly "Emily Clark Balch Prize Contest." Manuscripts will be returned if accompanied by S.A.S.E.

BANCROFT PRIZES. Write Secretary, 311 Low, Columbia University, New York NY 10027. Awards $12,000 for outstanding books on American history.
Nonfiction: Three prizes of $4,000 are awarded for books in the categories of U.S. international relations, American diplomacy, and biography. 4 copies of each book entry must be submitted by January 1 of the year following publication.

GEORGE LOUIS BEER PRIZE. Contact: Committee Chairman, George Louis Beer Prize, American Historical Association, 400 A St., S.E., Washington DC 20003. Awards $300 annually "for the best work by a young scholar (first book) in the field of European international history since 1895." Deadline: June 1.

STEPHEN VINCENT BENET NARRATIVE POETRY AWARDS. Write *Poet Lore*, 52 Cranbury Road, Westport CT 06880. Awards 5 prizes: $500, $100, and 3 $25 prizes for narrative poetry, plus one Honorable Mention and 10 Special Mentions. Deadline: December 31.
Poetry: Narrative poems only are eligible for this competition established to honor the poetic tradition of Stephen Vincent Benet. "Contestants need not be subscribers to *Poet Lore*, though they are urged to become familiar with *Poet Lore*'s criteria of excellence: 'clarity, beauty, profundity'; also, in a narrative poem, 'characters, movement and drama.' " Length: 200 lines maximum. "Every sheet of each ms must bear the name and address of the author. Each ms and each envelope must carry the words 'Benet Award.' Only unpublished mss will be accepted. No mss of poems submitted will be returned."

BEST SPORTS STORIES AWARDS. Write Edward Ehre, 1315 Westport Ln., Sarasota FL 33580. Offers 3 story prizes of $250 each and 2 photo prizes of $100 each. Deadline: December 31.
Nonfiction and Photos: For the annual *Best Sports Stories*, published by E.P. Dutton & Co., sports stories and photos which have appeared in a magazine or newspaper during the preceding calendar year are sought and prizes are awarded for the top entries. "Three story prizes will be awarded for the best news-coverage story, best news-feature story or column, and best magazine story. Two photo prizes will be awarded for the best feature photo and for the best action photo. All newspaper stories should be pasted on a backing of some sort, either cardboard or copy paper, and should have name of publication. Photos preferably should be 8x10 glossies and must be completely captioned. Please enclose a 50-word biography with your entries and also your home address, with zip code, so that the book, if you are included, may reach you more readily and safely. To help in obtaining permission to reprint, please include the name of the person on your publication who can grant such permissions. We cannot return clippings or photos. We will accept Xerox copies of stories if you prefer."

ALBERT J. BEVERIDGE AWARD. Contact: Committee Chairman, Albert J. Beveridge Award, American Historical Association, 400 A St., S.E., Washington

DC 20003. Awards $5,000 annually for "the best book in English on American history (history of the United States, Canada, and Latin America)." Deadline: June 1.

BLACK COLLECTIVE THEATRE PLAYWRIGHTING CONTEST, c/o The Black Collective Theatre and Film Company, 4309 So. Broadway, Los Angeles CA 90037. Contact: Esther Vance. Prizes of $100, $75, and $50. Deadline: April 30.
Drama: Manuscripts on the life or lives of any one of the following black heroic figures: Biddy Mason, Ida B. Wells, Harriet Tubman, Frederick Douglass, W.E.B. DuBois, Marcus Garvey, William Monroe Trotter, Henry Highland Garnet, Martin Luther King, Jr., or Malcolm X. Winning plays will be produced by The Black Collective Theatre Group.

HOWARD W. BLAKESLEE AWARDS. For official entry blank, write Chairman, Managing Committee, Howard W. Blakeslee Awards, American Heart Association, 44 E. 23rd St., New York NY 10010. Awards $500 honorarium and a citation to each winning entry, which may be a single article, broadcast, film, or book; a series; or no more than 5 unrelated pieces. Deadline: Midnight, May 1, following the contest year.
Nonfiction, Fiction, Films, Radio and TV: "Entries will be judged on the basis of their accuracy and significance, and on the skill and originality with which knowledge concerning the heart and circulatory system and advances in research or in the treatment, care and prevention of cardiovascular disease are translated for the public; and on the basis of what the writer hoped to achieve. The judges will consider entries from all media. Judges are free to make awards in one or more categories, as determined by the quality of entries. Entries must have been published or broadcast in the U.S. or its territorieq during the period from March 1 through February 28, which constitutes the contest year. Published entries must be in the form of clippings, tearsheets, photostats, photographs, reprints or books. Television entries must include a film or, if a film is not available, a video tape and, preferably, a copy of the script. Radio entries must include a transcription or tape of the program, and a script if available. Collaborative efforts will be considered as a single entry. Persons other than the author may make nominations, with the author's consent. Contestants may submit any number of entries. Unless return is requested, all entries shall be considered the American Heart Association's property.

HEYWOOD BROUN AWARD. Write Broun Award Committee, Newspaper Guild (AFL-CIO, CLC), 1125 15th St. N.W., Washington DC 20005. Awards $1,000 and a citation. Deadline: January 15.
Nonfiction and Photos: "For outstanding journalistic achievement in the spirit of Heywood Broun, who was distinguished by unceasing devotion to the public interest and an abiding concern for the underdog. All good work in the public interest, including photographs and cartoons, will receive consideration, particularly if it has helped right a wrong. One year, for example, the Award was won by a series of institutional advertisements." The award is given for work done or completed between January 1 and December 31 of the preceding calendar year. "Eligible are employes in the Guild's jurisdiction on newspapers, news services, news magazines, radio and TV stations in the U. S., Canada and Puerto Rico, whether they are members of the Guild or not. Anyone may submit an entry on his own or another's behalf. Entries should be submitted in scrapbook form with an accompanying letter describing the circumstances under which the work was done, particularly the initiative and ingenuity shown by the candidate. Important factors influencing judges' decisions in past years have been disinterestedness of the candidate, significance and quality of the work and technique. All entries become the property of the Award Committee and will not be returned except upon specific request."

RAY BRUNER SCIENCE WRITING AWARD, American Public Health Association, 1015 Eighteenth St., N.W., Washington DC 20036. Annually awards a fellowship. Deadline: August 1 to September 1.
Nonfiction: "The purpose of the fellowship is to give recognition to a writer in the mass media with less than 2 year's full-time science writing experience whose preferred professional ambition is full-time science/medical reporting. Each year's winner is selected by an independent committee of working science reporters. Nominations must include samples of published material from each nominee."

CALIFORNIA LITERATURE MEDAL AWARD. Write Durward S. Riggs, Secretary, Literature Medal Award Jury, Commonwealth Club of California, Monadnock Arcade, 681 Market St., San Francisco CA 94105. Awards medals for fiction, nonfiction, and poetry books written by residents of California. Deadline: January 31.

Nonfiction, Fiction, and Poetry: Entries are not restricted to California themes, although one medal is given for "the best book of fiction or nonfiction of historical import or significance relating to California." Another medal is given for "the best book suitable for reading by children under 18." Entries "may be made by the author or the publishers, who must mail at least two copies of each book entered, together with entry blank."

CAROLINA QUARTERLY. Write to Fiction Contest, *Carolina Quarterly*, P.O. Box 1117, Chapel Hill NC 27514. Sponsored by the North Carolina Arts Council and the *Carolina Quarterly*. Awards annual prizes of $200, $100, $50, and several honorable mentions. Submit from September 15 to February 15.

Fiction: Fiction contest for young writers. Entrants must be under 30 years old and may not have published a book-length ms. Only original, unpublished mss under 6,000 words are eligible. Entries must be in standard ms form and labeled as fiction contest entries. Winning entry will be published in the Spring issue of the *Carolina Quarterly*. Enclose S.A.S.E. for return of submissions.

RUSSELL L. CECIL WRITING AWARDS IN ARTHRITIS. Write Russell L. Cecil Awards, The Arthritis Foundation, 1212 Ave. of the Americas, New York NY 10036. Offers 4 $1,000 prizes in 4 categories. Deadline: January 31.

Nonfiction, Radio, and TV: The purpose of the award is "to recognize and encourage the writing of news stories, articles and radio and television scripts for general circulation newspapers, magazines and broadcast media on the subject of arthritis. Entries are judged on their accuracy, clarity, originality, and potential for stimulating greater public knowledge, understanding, and concern about the nationwide problem of arthritis and other rheumatic diseases. The four media categories are newspaper, magazine, television, and radio writing. "Entries may be a single story, feature or a series; or a broadcast script. A writer may submit more than one entry. All entries eligible for cash prize awards must have been published or broadcast in media available to the general public. Honorable mentions may be awarded in any category at the discretion of the judges. Entries may be made by the writer or, in his behalf, by the editor, publisher, radio or television official or by a chapter of The Arthritis Foundation. Each entry must consist of a properly completed entry blank and six copies mf the story, article or script, showing the name and the date of the publication or, in the case of a radio or TV program, the date, station and place of the broadcast. In special situations, a single tape or kinescope of a broadcast will be acceptable. It is understood that entries may be reproduced or published in part or in full by The Arthritis Foundation." Entries must have been published between January 1 and December 1 of the year preceding the deadline date. Entries must be accompanied by an official entry blank.

CHILDREN'S BOOK AWARD. Child Study Association of America/Wel-Met, 50 Madison Ave., New York NY 10010.

Fiction:"Given annually to a book for children or young people which deals realistically with problems in their contemporary world. The book, published in the past calendar year, must offer an honest and courageous treatment of its theme. To present its ideas and characters effectively the book must be well written, though it need not be great literature. It must be convincing and realistic in its approach and have integrity in the development of its theme. It should be a book which children will find enjoyable reading, and in which they will also recognize the deeper implications. The Children's Book Committee's year-round reviewing of all of the children's books as they come from the publishers culminates in an annual selected list: Books of the Year for Children. The award book is selected from this listing."

CHRISTOPHER AWARDS. Write William J. Wilson, Associate Director, 12 E. 48th St., New York NY 10017.

Books, Motion Pictures, Television: Awards are given for motion pictures (producer, director, writer), television (producer, director, writer), and books (author, editor, illustrator, photographer) executed during the calendar year for which the awards are given. "The awards are aimed at recognizing individuals who have used their talents constructively, in the hope that they and others, will continue to produce high quality works that reflect sound values. The work must affirm the highest human and spiritual values; it must be artistically and technically proficient; it must have received a significant degree of public acceptance." Awards bronze medallions.

COMMUNITY CHILDREN'S THEATRE OF KANSAS CITY PLAYWRITING FOR CHILDREN AWARD. Write Mrs. Fred A. Rice, Jr., 1404 N. 81 St., Kansas City KS 66112. Awards $500. Deadline: February 1.
Drama: "The Playwriting for Children Award has been sponsored in the hope it will yield the best trouping scripts from which to choose the finest dramatic fare for our children. Suggested subjects for plays are legends, folklore, historical incidents, biography, adaptation of children's classics, famous stories, and original scripts. Please do not send seasonal plays as our plays are trouped for about 6 or 7 months during the year. Plays must be written for a youthful audience—grades first through sixth. Plays should have preferably 8 characters or fewer. Plays must be written with the idea that they will be acted by adult women. They should not contain too many parts for virile characters for this reason. The children will be the audience and not the actors. Plays must be of a technical nature that will allow them to be easily rigged in the average elementary school auditorium. Plays must run 55 to 60 minutes playing time. Mss should be double-spaced and securely bound. Author's name and address must appear on the fly-page. A very brief resume of play is requested at the beginning of the ms." Enclose S.A.S.E. for return of entries.

ALBERT B. COREY PRIZE IN CANADIAN-AMERICAN RELATIONS. Contact Office of the Executive Secretary, American Historical Association, 400 A St., S.E., Washington DC 20003. Awarded jointly by the Canadian Historical Association and the American Historical Association. Deadline: June 1. For the best book on the history of Canadian-United States relations, or on the history of both countries. Cash award "not exceeding $1,000."

THE COUNCIL ON INTERRACIAL BOOKS FOR CHILDREN, INC., FIFTH ANNUAL CONTEST, 29 West 15th St., New York NY 10011. Open only to African Americans, American Indians, Asian Americans, Chicanos and Puerto Ricans. $500 in prizes offered for each group. Deadline: October 1.
Nonfiction, Fiction and Poetry: Original manuscripts for children's books, limited to writers who are unpublished in the children's book field. Story book, picture book, poetry, fiction and nonfiction acceptable. Mss will be judged for literary merit, and characterization presented without racist, sexist or religious stereotyping, authenticity of ethnic experience described, relevancy to struggles for minority liberation, and characterizations that provide positive images for reader identification. Write for entry blank and contest rules. Enclose S.A.S.E.

DECORATIVE ARTS BOOK AWARD. Write L.M. Goodman, Coordinator, American Life Foundation and Study Institute, Watkins Glen NY 14891. Deadline: October 15. "Given to the author of a book in English which has most advanced the fields of antique collecting and decorative arts appreciation." Submission by publishers only.

EDUCATOR'S AWARD. Write Miss Catherine Rathman, Executive Secretary, The Delta Kappa Gamma Society, P.O. Box 1589, Austin TX 78767. Awards $1,000. Deadline: March 1.
Nonfiction: "The award aims at recognizing women and their contribution to education which may influence future directions in the profession. The contribution may be in the fields of research, philosophy, or any other area of learning which is stimulating and creative. The work must be written by one woman or by two women in the U.S., Canada, Norway, or Sweden, and copyrighted in its first edition, during the calendar year preceding the deadline date."

ENCORE NATIONAL POETRY CONTEST, *Encore Magazine,* 1121 Major Ave. N.W., Albuquerque NM 87107. For students of junior and senior high schools. Address all correspondence to Alice Briley, Editor. Cash prizes of $10, $5, and $2 will be awarded in junior and senior category. Deadline: May 15.

Poetry: "Type, double spaced, two copies of your poem. Put your name and address on one copy and no identification on the second copy which goes to the judge. Only one entry per student. Limit is 20 lines. On the copy which bears your name and address students please add the following statment: This poem is my own original work; sign your name. Under the statement, add this information: Age as of April 15, name of school and school address, grade you are in this school year and name of your English teacher. Please write at the top of your paper whether you are in junior or senior high school category. Mss will not be returned."

EPILEPSY FOUNDATION OF AMERICA JOURNALISM AWARD. Write Journalism Award, Epilepsy Foundation of America, 1828 L St., N.W., Suite 406; Washington DC 20036. Awards $500. Deadline: November 1.

Nonfiction: For "the journalist whose writing has been outstanding in advancing the cause of epilepsy" during the contest calendar year. "Any writer who has written an article or series of articles in excess of 1,000 words which was published in a newspaper or magazine of general circulation or was aired on TV or radio is eligible. The author should submit a copy of his article (or series) in script or published form, along with a brief letter outlining his reasons for writing the piece. TV and radio scripts should indicate stations, dates, and times of airing."

EXPLICATOR PRIZE COMPETITION. Write *The Explicator*, Virginia Commonwealth University, Richmond VA 23220. Awards $200 and a bronze plaque. Deadline: April 1.

Nonfiction: The award is given "for the best book of *explication de texte* published in the field of English or American literature" during the calendar year preceding the contest deadline. "Authors and publishers are invited to submit books for the competition. One book should be sent directly to each judge." Names and addresses of the judges are available from *The Explicator*.

CHARLES W. FOLLETT AWARD. Write Follett Publishing Co., 1010 W. Washington Blvd., Chicago IL 60607. Annually awards $3,000 and royalties for a fiction or nonfiction ms. Deadline: June 1.

Fiction and Nonfiction: For children ages 9 to 12 or for readers 12 years old and up. The book-length ms must be 25,000 to 35,000 words long if geared to the younger age group, 40,000 to 60,000 words for ages 12 and older.

GEORGE FREEDLEY MEMORIAL AWARD. Submit nominations to Dr. Robert M. Henderson, President, Theater Library Association, 111 Amsterdam Ave., New York NY 10023. Awards a plaque. Deadline: January 15.

Nonfiction: "The Award honors a work in the field of theatre published in the United States. A plaque is presented to the author on the basis of scholarship, readability, and general contribution to the broadening of knowledge. Only books on theatre per se will be considered—biography, history, criticism, and related fields. Excluded from the category of theatre are vaudeville, puppetry, pantomime, motion picture, television, radio, opera, circus, dance and ballet, plays, and similar dramatic forms. Other works considered ineligible are textbooks, bibliographies, dictionaries and encyclopedias, anthologies, collections of articles and essays published previously and in other sources, and reprints of publications."

FRIENDS OF AMERICAN WRITERS AWARDS. Write Mrs. Donald Smyth, 1040 Lake Shore Dr., Chicago IL 60611. Awards $1,000. Deadline: December 31.

Nonfiction and Fiction: "For a book, published during the current year, with a midwestern locale or by a native or resident author of the middle West. Books for consideration submitted by publishers only."

FRIENDS OF LITERATURE AWARD. Write Mrs. Hazel R. Ferguson, President, 1500 Chicago Ave., Evanston IL 60201. Awards prizes totaling $1,100 annually in 4 categories for "writers who must have identity with Chicago, metropolitan area included." Deadline: March 1.

Nonfiction, Fiction, Poetry, and Juvenile: Awards $500 for fiction, $500 for nonfiction, $100 for poetry or essay. Contestants must be presently or formerly residents of the metropolitan Chicago area. "Work must be published by trade publisher. Submit books."

CHRISTIAN GAUSS AWARD. Write Phi Beta Kappa, 1811 Q St., N.W., Washington DC 20009. Awards $2,500 annually for a book of literary criticism or scholarship published in the United States. Books submitted by publisher only. Deadline: June 30.

SIDNEY HILLMAN PRIZE AWARD. Write Sidney Hillman Foundation, Inc., 15 Union Square, New York NY 10003. Awards $500 annually for each outstanding contribution. Deadline: January 31.
Nonfiction, Fiction, Radio, and TV: "Contributions dealing with themes relating to the ideals which Sidney Hillman held throughout his life. Such themes would include the protection of individual civil liberties, improved race relations, a strengthened labor movement, the advancement of social welfare and economic security, greater world understanding, and related problems. Contributions may be in the fields of daily or periodical journalism, fiction, nonfiction, radio and television. All written contributions must have been published. Radio and television contributions must have been produced under professional auspices."

DON HOLLENBECK AWARD. Write Professor M.L. Stein, Chairman, Don Hollenbeck Award Competition, Department of Journalism and Mass Communications, Washington Square College of Arts and Sciences, New York University, 1021 Main Bldg., Washington Square, New York NY 10003. Awards $500. Deadline: September 1.
Nonfiction, Radio, and TV: Given "for the best newspaper article, magazine article, television or radio script, or book evaluating the mass media or any particular publication or news organization. Three copies of the article, script, or book must be submitted. Entries must have been published or broadcast after September 1 of the previous year. Only published or broadcast material will be considered. Broadcasts must be submitted in script form."

HOUGHTON MIFFLIN LITERARY FELLOWSHIP. Write Houghton Mifflin Co., 2 Park St., Boston MA 02107. Awards $2,500 grant and $5,000 as an advance against royalties to help authors complete projects of outstanding literary merit. No deadline.
Fiction and Nonfiction: "Candidates should submit at least 50 pages of the actual project, an informal description of its theme and intention, a brief biography, and examples of past work, published or unpublished. Enclose return postage with submission."

INGAA-MISSOURI BUSINESS JOURNALISM AWARDS. Write Lyle E. Harris, Director, INGAA-University of Missouri Business Journalism Awards Program, Neff Hall, School of Journalism, Columbia MO 65201. Awards $1,000 in each of 4 categories. Deadline: June 10.
Nonfiction: "The awards program honors excellence in reporting and interpreting business, economic, trade and financial news. It was established to encourage a greater public understanding of the American economic system through coverage of U.S. business in newspapers and magazines. Entries are limited to U.S. publications. Subject matter must concern itself with American business and its contribution to modern society. Entries may be in areas of straight news reporting, feature articles, columns, or editorials in each category. Items appearing only in professional journals, company publications, or annual reports will not be considered. Each winner will receive a cash award and trophy, and the publication will receive a plaque. Distinguished runners-up will receive certificates of outstanding merit plus $150." Entries must be published between June 1 of the preceding year and May 30 of the current year. "All entries must be accompanied by an official entry form or a letter from a publication's editor stating the position held by the contestant."

IOWA SCHOOL OF LETTERS AWARD FOR SHORT FICTION. Write Iowa School of Letters Award for Short Fiction, English-Philosophy Building, University of Iowa, Iowa City IA 52242. Awards $1,000. Deadline: September 30.
Fiction: "Book-length collections of short stories by writers who have not published

a book. The winning ms will be published by the University of Iowa Press. The Press reserves the right to consider for publication any ms submitted." Recent winner: *The Itinerary of Beggars* (Francis). "Return postage should be enclosed with ms."

JOSEPH HENRY JACKSON AWARD. Write The San Francisco Foundation Awards Office, 425 California St., Suite 1602, San Francisco CA 94104. Awards $2,000. Deadline: "competition opens November 1 and closes January 15."
Nonfiction, Fiction, Poetry: "An award will be made to the author of an unpublished, partly completed work of fiction, nonfictional prose, or poetry; those types of writing in which Mr. Jackson was most interested during his many years in San Francisco as a book reviewer, critic, author, and editor of numerous volumes. Applicants must be residents of northern California or Nevada for 3 years immediately prior to deadline. Applicants must be from 20 through 35 years of age on deadline date. Their writings need not concern California. Applications must be made on forms provided for that purpose."

JEWISH BOOK COUNCIL OF AMERICA AWARD FOR A BOOK OF JEWISH THOUGHT. National Jewish Welfare Board, 15 E. 26th St., New York NY 10010. Awards $500 and a citation. Deadline: January 15.
Nonfiction: "Presented in the name of Frank and Ethel S. Cohen to the author of a work dealing with some aspect of Jewish thought, past or present, which in the opinion of the judges combines knowledge, clarity of thought, and literary merit. The award will be given to the author of a book published during the preceding calendar year."

JEWISH BOOK COUNCIL OF AMERICA AWARD FOR A BOOK ON THE NAZI HOLOCAUST. National Jewish Welfare Board, 15 E. 26th St., New York NY 10010. Awards $500 and a citation. Deadline: January 31.
Nonfiction: "Presented in the name of Mr. Leon Jolson to the author of a nonfiction book dealing with some aspects of the Nazi holocaust period. The first year the award will be given for a book published in English, the next year for a book published in Yiddish, and the third year for a book published in Hebrew. The award will be given to the author of a book published during the three preceding calendar years."

JEWISH BOOK COUNCIL OF AMERICA AWARD FOR BOOKS OF POETRY. National Jewish Welfare Board, 15 E. 26th St., New York NY 10010. Awards $500 and a citation. Deadline: January 15.
Poetry: "Presented in memory of Harry and Ethel Kovner to the author of a book of poetry of Jewish interest. Starting in 1970, the award will be given for a book published in Yiddish, the next year for a book published in English, and the third year for a book published in Hebrew. The award will be given to the author of a book published during the three preceding calendar years."

JEWISH BOOK COUNCIL OF AMERICA FICTION AWARD. National Jewish Welfare Board, 15 E. 26th St., New York NY 10010. Awards $500 and a citation. Deadline: January 15.
Fiction: The award will be given to the author of a work of fiction of Jewish interest, either a novel or a collection of short stories, which in the opinion of the judges combines high literary merit with an affirmative expression of Jewish values. The award will be given to the author of a book published during the preceding calendar year."

JEWISH BOOK COUNCIL OF AMERICA JUVENILE AWARD. National Jewish Welfare Board, 15 E. 26th St., New York NY 10010. Awards $500 and a citation. Deadline: January 15.
Juvenile: "Presented in the name of Charles and Bertie G. Schwartz to the author of a Jewish juvenile book. Prayer books and textbooks are not eligible. The award will be given to the author of a book published during the previous calendar year."

JOHN HANCOCK AWARDS FOR EXCELLENCE IN BUSINESS AND FINANCIAL JOURNALISM. Write "Awards for Excellence," B-21, John Hancock Mu-

tual Life Insurance Co., 200 Berkeley St., Boston MA 02117. Awards $1,000 in 6 categories. Deadline: January 31.
Nonfiction: The objectives of the contest are "to foster increased public knowledge of and interest in business and finance; to recognize editorial contributions to a better understanding of personal money management; to clarify the significance of political and social developments as they relate to the nation's economy; to stimulate discussion and thought by bringing together, in an academic environment, newsmakers, reporters, faculty, and students. Material for the consideration of the selection panel must have been published in the 12-month period ending December 31. Six unmounted tearsheets of the published article must be submitted, including publication date (or tearsheet and five photocopies). Do not submit mounted clips or tearsheets. Wire service writers may submit teletype copy and photocopies. A series of articles may be entered in the same manner as individual stories (six tearsheets or photocopies). An entrant may submit more than one entry, but it is requested that entrants be reasonably selective. It is not necessary for the article to have appeared in the business section of the publication, and entries can be made by any staff reporter or editor. Entries submitted must be from publications published in the United States. Entries will not be returned. Each entry must be accompanied by a completed entry form."

KANSAS CITY POETRY CONTESTS. Write Poetry Contests Directors, P.O. Box 5313, Kansas City MO 64131. Awards prizes totaling $1,600. Deadline: February 1.
Poetry: "Top prize is the Devins Award, which is a $500 cash prize and publication of a book-length poetry ms by the University of Missouri Press. Hallmark Honor Prizes of $100 each are awarded to 6 college undergraduate poets for individual poems. Kansas City Star Awards of $100 each are given to 4 poets. Sharp Memorial Awards of $25 each are given to 4 high school pupils from Missouri or adjoining states. Send S.A.S.E. for complete contest rules."

FRANK KELLEY MEMORIAL AWARD. Write American Association of Petroleum Landmen, P.O. Box 1984, Fort Worth TX 76101. Awards $250 and a plaque. Deadline: May 15.
Nonfiction: "Presented in appreciation for excellence in reporting oil and gas industry information to the public. Printed newspaper articles entered must have been written and published in the United States or Canada between April 1 of the preceding year and March 31 of the current year. Entries will be judged on the basis of accuracy, style of presentation, selection of subject matter, reader interest, and overall quality. For handling convenience, entries which consist of a large number of articles should be submitted in a standard size (12x14) scrapbook or mounted and bound in some other suitable manner. Single newspaper articles should be sent in as tearsheets or pasted on sheets of plain paper when a scrapbook is not used. All entries must be accompanied by the following data: title of entry, writer, name of publication, and name, address, and title of person submitting the entry."

LAMONT POETRY SELECTION. Write The Academy of American Poets, 1078 Madison Avenue, New York NY 10028. Awards purchase of 1,000 copies of the winning book of poetry, thus insuring publication of the winning ms. Deadline: April 15.
Poetry: "The Academy of American Poets sponsors The Lamont Poetry Selection, 'for the discovery and encouragement of new poetic genius.' Manuscripts of poetry must be submitted by a publisher, and must be by an American poet who has not yet had a book of poems published other than in a limited, private, or subsidized edition. The Academy purchases 1,000 copies of the winning book for distribution to its membership. The award was made possible by a generous bequest of the late Mrs. Thomas W. Lamont, and is offered annually."

JERRY LEWIS MDAA WRITING AWARD, c/o Stan Silverman, Director, Department of Public Health Education, MDAA Inc., 810 Seventh Ave., New York NY 10019. Deadline: December 1.
Nonfiction: An award and prize of $1,000 is given to the writer whose work is considered most effective in stimulating public interest in the fight against muscular dystrophy and related diseases of the neuromuscular system. Only material which has been published or broadcast in the U.S. between January 1 and November 30

will be considered. The Muscular Dystrophy Association of America reserves the right to utilize, with the permission of those involved, winning entries or excerpts therefrom in reprint form or in radio or television broadcasts.

ELIAS LIEBERMAN STUDENT POETRY AWARD. Write the Poetry Society of America, 15 Gramercy Park, New York NY 10003. Awards $100 for the best poem by a high or preparatory school student of the U.S.A. Deadline: June 15.
Poetry: "Only one poem by each writer may be submitted, typed and in triplicate, with his or her name and address as well as that of the school attended in a sealed envelope, on the face of which is written the title of the submitted poem. Poems may be on any subject in any form or length. No poems will be returned nor will notification be made of their arrival."

G.M. LOEB AWARDS. Write Robert O. Harvey, Secretary, G.M. Loeb Advisory Board, The University of Connecticut, Storrs CT 06268. Three awards of $1,000 and a bronze plaque. Deadline: January 20.
Nonfiction: "The purpose of The University of Connecticut G.M. Loeb Awards is to encourage the highest possible standards of responsibility, accuracy, clarity, and insight in the writing and interpretation of news on investment, finance, and business. Prizes awarded include The Loeb Newspaper Award for a single newspaper article, The Loeb Magazine Award for a single magazine article, Each entry must contain four copies of the articles, columns or editorials nominated. At least one copy must be a tearsheet, syndicated proof or wire service duplicate validating date of publication and showing the written material as it appeared before the public. Do not submit entries in bound form. The Loeb Column/Editorial Award for outstanding financial columns or editorials. Each entry must be accompanied by a completed entry blank."

MADEMOISELLE COLLEGE FICTION COMPETITION. Write College Fiction Competition, *Mademoiselle*, 350 Madison Ave., New York NY 10017. Awards two prizes of $500 each and publication of winners' stories in the August issue. Deadline: February 1.
Fiction: "Original short stories under 5,000 words in length. Open to undergraduate students (under 26 years old) enrolled for a degree in an accredited college or junior college."

MADEMOISELLE COLLEGE POETRY COMPETITION. Write College Poetry Competition, *Mademoiselle*, 350 Madison Ave., New York NY 10017. Awards two prizes of $100 each and publication of the winners' poems in the August issue. Deadline: February 1.
Poetry: "Original poems under 30 lines long. The contest is open to undergraduate students (under 26 years old) enrolled for a degree in an accredited college or junior college."

THE MAN IN HIS ENVIRONMENT BOOK AWARD. Write The Man in His Environment Book Award, E.P. Dutton and Co., Inc., 201 Park Avenue South, New York NY 10003. Awards annually a guarantee of a minimum of $10,000 as an advance against earnings. Deadline: December 31.
Nonfiction: "In the hope of stimulating the writing of good books on ecological themes, Dutton offers a book award for the best ms submitted in any given year dealing with the past, present or future of man in his environment, natural or man-made. The award will be given for a single work of adult nonfiction. The contest is open to new authors and to authors whose works have already been published, to authors in the United States and to foreign authors. Mss must be typewritten, in English, double-spaced, on one side of a page only. Mss not originally in English must be submitted in an English translation in order to be eligible. No work containing less than fifty thousand words will be eligible. The words 'man in his environment' are used in the most inclusive possible sense, the basic requirement of entries for the award being that the subject matter explicitly encompass both terms. Mss submitted for the award should be so written as to be readily intelligible to the nonspecialist reader. Authors are not limited to one entry. Novels, or mss primarily for children, will not qualify. All mss submitted are to be considered available for possible publication by E.P. Dutton & Co., subject to contractual terms to be agreed

upon. A work written by two or more authors in collaboration will be eligible; if such a manuscript wins the award, the prize money and royalties will be divided btwn th llbrtr. A hh h b pblhd rl dd form in a magazine or which has been developed from an article in a magazine will be eligible, provided it has never been published in book form in the United States." On the/ms itself this statement should appear: "Submitted for The Man in His Environment Book Award." Enclose S.A.S.E. for return of submissions.

HOWARD R. MARRARO PRIZE IN ITALIAN HISTORY. For submission details, write to Office of the Executive Secretary, American Historical Association, 400 A St. S.E., Washington DC 20003. Deadline: June 1. For the book or article which treats Italian history in any epoch of Italian cultural history, or of Italian-American relations. Competitors must be resident citizens of the United States or Canada. Cash Award: $500.

JOHN MASEFIELD MEMORIAL AWARD. Write The Poetry Society of America, 15 Gramercy Park, New York NY 10003. Awards $500. Deadline: January 15.
Poetry: Award "is for an unpublished narrative poem written in English not to exceed 200 lines, in memory of the late Poet Laureate of England, honorary member of the Society. Only one poem is to be sent in by each contestant and any poet writing in English, member or non-member of the Society, of any country is eligible. Copies should be retained by the poet, for none will be returned." Mss should be typed or copied in triplicate (with identity and address of author in an accompanying sealed envelope on the face of which the title of the poem appears) and mailed first class. The outside mailing envelope should be marked 'John Masefield Memorial Award.'"

JOHN H. McGINNIS MEMORIAL AWARD. Write *Southwest Review*, Southern Methodist University, Dallas TX 75222. Awards $500. For 1975, the award will be given for the best article published in the magazine in 1973 and 1974.
Nonfiction and Fiction: This award, perpetuating the memory of the man who served as editor of the Southwest Review from 1927 to 1942, is made in alternate years for fiction and nonfiction pieces published in the *Southwest Review*.

EDWARD J. MEEMAN CONSERVATION AWARDS. Write Meeman Conservation Awards, Scripps-Howard Foundation, 200 Park Ave., New York NY 10017. Awards $10,000: $2,500 first prize and various other lesser prizes to be determined by judges. Deadline: February 15.
Nonfiction: Awards are given "to newspapermen and women on U.S. newspapers in recognition of outstanding work in the cause of conservation published in newspapers during the preceding calendar year. Conservation, for the purposes of these awards, embraces the environment and the forces that affect it. For example, this could include control of pollution, future technological developments, over-population, recycling. In broader terms, it could also include the conservation of soil, forests, vegetation, wildlife, open space, and scenery. Conservation of mineral resources and oil, important though it is, is not included. Any U.S. newspaperman or woman may be nominated for an award by a newspaper or newspaper reader. Nominations should include clippings or tearsheets of candidate's work published in a newspaper during the contest year and a biographical sketch of author."

FREDERIC G. MELCHER BOOK AWARD. Write Edward Darling, Director, Melcher Book Award, 25 Beacon St., Boston MA 02108. Awards $1,000 and bronze medallion.
Nonfiction: "For a work published in America during the previous calendar year judged to be the most significant contribution to religious liberalism. Submission usually by publishers only."

FRANK LUTHER MOTT-KAPPA TAU ALPHA RESEARCH AWARD IN JOURNALISM. Write Dr. William H. Taft, Chief, Central Office KTA, School of Journalism, University of Missouri, Columbia MO 65201. Awards $200 and a hand-lettered scroll. Deadline: February 1.
Nonfiction: "For the best book published during the previous year."

NATIONAL BOOK AWARDS, National Book Committee, Inc., One Park Avenue, New York NY 10016. Awards of $1,000 are made for literature written or translated by American citizens and published in the United States during the preceding year. **Nonfiction, Fiction, Poetry, Juveniles:** "The Awards were originated in 1950 as the book industry's first joint effort to honor outstanding creative writing by Americans and bring national attention to the literary arts and their contribution to the nation's cultural life." Categories include arts and letters, biography, contemporary affairs, children's books, fiction, history, poetry, philosophy and religion, science, and translation. Does not accept submissions from authors.

NATIONAL COUNCIL FOR THE ADVANCEMENT OF EDUCATION WRITING CONTEST. Write Cynthia Parsons, National Council for the Advancement of Education Writing, Box 233, McLean VA 22101. Awards grand prize of $1,000, six first prizes of $250 each, and a second prize of $100 "when appropriate." Deadline: January 15.
Nonfiction, Radio, and TV: "The awards honor the best education writing and broadcasting in the mass media. There are 6 newspaper prizes: prizes for breaking news, for feature articles, and for investigative reporting for newspapers over 150,000 circulation and under 150,000 circulation. There is a prize for the best articles or series of articles in a mass circulation magazine (no trade journals) and a prize for the best TV or radio program. All material must have appeared during the previous calendar year. Entries must be clearly labeled and mounted for ease in handling; they may not exceed 12x14."

NATIONAL FEDERATION OF STATE POETRY SOCIETIES, INC. CONTEST. Write Lee Mays, Contest Chairman, 310 Cedarcrest Dr., Ripley WV 25271. Awards $10 to $500, depending on the contest. Deadline: April 15.
Poetry: Sponsors 34 poetry contests, 12 of which are open to non-members of the society.

NATIONAL HISTORICAL SOCIETY BOOK PRIZE IN AMERICAN HISTORY. Write Board of Judges, Box 1831, Harrisburg PA 17105. Awards $1,000. Deadline: April 1.
Nonfiction: "Through this award, NHS hopes to encourage promising historians, young and old, in producing the sound but readable history that is so necessary for portraying our past to the general public. Books eligible include biographies, general histories, and works dealing with the nation's past from its beginnings to recent times. Submissions must be books published in the calendar year preceding the deadline date. Each entry must be the first book published by the respective author. No mss, theses, or dissertations are eligible. Entries may be submitted either by the author himself or by his publisher. Three copies must be submitted."

NATIONAL INSTITUTE OF ARTS AND LETTERS AWARDS. Contact Felicia Geffen, Assistant Secretary, National Institute of Arts and Letters, 633 W. 155th St., New York NY 10032.
Nonfiction and Fiction: Annual awards include the Rosenthal Award ($2,000 "for the best novel of the year which, though not a commercial success, is a literary achievement"), the National Institute and American Academy Awards ($3,000 awarded to "10 non-members to further their creative work"), and the Morton Dauwen Zabel Award ($2,000 "to a poet, writer of fiction, or critic, in rotation"). None of the awards may be applied for.

NATIONAL MEDAL FOR LITERATURE. National Book Committee, Inc., One Park Avenue, New York NY 10016. Awards $5,000 and a bronze medal annually to honor a living American writer for the excellence of his total contribution to the world of letters. Does not accept submissions from authors.

NATIONAL SOCIETY OF PROFESSIONAL ENGINEERS ANNUAL JOURNALISM AWARDS. Write Leonard J. Arzt, Director of Public Relations, National Society of Professional Engineers, 2029 K St. N.W., Washington DC 20006. Awards $500, $300, and $200. Deadline: January 15.
Nonfiction: "Awarded to newspaper writers who during the course of the calendar year make the most significant contribution (in one or a series of stories) to public

knowledge and understanding about the role of engineers and creative technology in contemporary American life. Articles should deal with engineering subject matters—as distinguished from science. Articles will be judged primarily on the extent and manner in which the writer relates engineers to the subject matter. Entries must have been published in a daily or weekly newspaper during the calendar year. An entrant may send as many entries as he wishes. No entry blank is needed."

ALLAN NEVINS PRIZE. Write Secretary-Treasurer, The Society of American Historians, 706 Hamilton Hall, Columbia University, New York NY 10027. Awards $1,000 and publication of winning ms. Deadline: December 31.
Nonfiction: For the best written doctoral dissertation in the field of American history. "The Society defines history broadly and welcomes the submission of manuscripts dealing historically with American arts, literature, and science, as well as biographical studies of Americans in any walk of life. Mss should be submitted by the Chairman of the Department concerned and, except in unusual circumstances, no department may nominate more than one ms. While the prize is for the best written ms, only dissertations that meet high standards of scholarship and make a significant contribution to historical knowledge should be offered. Although the prize money is free and clear and not an advance against royalties, the winning manuscript will be published by one of the 8 major publishers which currently support the Nevins Prize (Bobbs-Merrill; Harper and Row; Little, Brown; McGraw-Hill; Prentice-Hall; Random House-Alfred A. Knopf; Harcourt, Brace, Jovanovich; W. W. Norton."

NEW YORK DRAMA CRITICS' CIRCLE AWARD, New York Drama Critics Circle, c/o T. E. Kalem, Time, Inc., Time & Life Bldg., Rockefeller Center, New York NY 10020.
Plays: Awards a scroll annually for the best play of the year. The Circle also customarily gives a non-mandatory award for the best musical. The awards are not open to application.

NEW YORK POETRY FORUM AWARDS. Write for complete rules to Dorothea Neale, Director, New York Poetry Forum Inc. P.O. Box 655, Madison Square Station, 149 E. 23 St., New York NY 10010. Deadline: November 1.
Poetry: Sponsors 12 or more contests open to all poets. Awards $10 to $50, depending on the contest, plus memberships and readings.

NORTH CAROLINA LITERARY AND HISTORICAL ASSOCIATION. Write North Carolina Literary and Historical Association, 109 E. Jones St., Raleigh NC 27611. Awards 4 cups in literary competitions for North Carolina authors. Deadline: July 15.
Nonfiction, Fiction, Poetry, and Juvenile Literature: The following prizes are awarded: The Mayflower Cup for Nonfiction, The Sir Walter Raleigh Award for Fiction, the Roanoke-Chowan Award for Poetry, and The American Association of University Women Award in Juvenile Literature. "For a work to be eligible, it must be an original work published during the twelve months ending June 30 of the year for which the award is given. Its author or authors must have maintained either legal or physical residence, or a combination of both, in North Carolina for the three years preceding the close of the contest period. Three copies of each entry must be submitted to the secretary of the North Carolina Literary and Historical Association. In reaching a decision, members of each Board of Award will consider creative and imaginative quality, excellence of style, universality of appeal, and relevance to North Carolina and her people. For the Mayflower award, the extent to which the author has covered his subject, making use of all available source materials, giving a well-balanced presentation, and accomplishing the purpose he set out to achieve will also be considered. All works will be judged without regard to length. Technical and scientific works are not eligible."

OVERSEAS PRESS CLUB OF AMERICA NEWS AWARDS. Overseas Press Club, 3 W. 51 St., New York NY 10020. Awards scrolls, a gold medal, or cash, depending on the classification of entries. Deadline: February 1.
Nonfiction, Photos, Radio, and TV: Awards are made in the following classes: "best

daily newspaper or wire service reporting from abroad; best daily newspaper or wire service interpretation of foreign affairs; best daily newspaper or wire service photographic reporting from abroad; best photographic reporting or interpretation from abroad in a magazine or book; best radio spot news reporting from abroad; best radio interpretation of foreign affairs; best radio documentary on foreign affairs; best TV spot news reporting from abroad; best TV interpretation of foreign affairs; best TV documentary on foreign affairs; best magazine reporting from abroad; best magazine interpretation of foreign affairs; best book on foreign affairs; best cartoon of foreign affairs, $250; best article or report on Latin America (any medium); Bache & Co. Award ($500) for best business news reporting from abroad (any medium); best article or report on Asia (any medium); Robert Capa gold medal (*Time*) for superlative still photography requiring exceptional courage and enterprise abroad; OPC George Polk Memorial Award ($500 CBS) for best reporting, any medium, requiring exceptional courage and enterprise abroad. Madeline Ross Award for international reporting in the field of health and welfare, $250." Entry blank required.

P.E.N. TRANSLATION PRIZE. Write Chairman, Translation Committee, P.E.N., 156 Fifth Ave., New York NY 10010. Sponsored by the Book-of-the-Month Club. Deadline: December 31.
Translations: Awards $1,000 for the "best translation into English from any language which is published in the United States in the current calendar year. Technical, scientific, or reference works are not eligible."

PARIS REVIEW FICTION CONTEST. Write The *Paris Review*, Fiction Contest, 541 E. 72nd St., New York NY 10021. Awards $500. Deadline: April 30.
Fiction: For the Aga Khan Fiction Contest, will consider mss "of any length. All mss will be considered for the magazine's usual rates."

FRANCIS PARKMAN PRIZE. Write Professor Kenneth T. Jackson, Secretary, The Society of American Historians, 706 Hamilton Hall, Columbia University, New York NY 10027. Awards $500 and a bronze medal. Deadline: December 31.
Nonfiction: "To give recognition and reward to the author who best epitomizes the Society's purpose—the writing of history with literary distinction as well as sound scholarship, this award was established. Books are to be submitted by the publisher and must deal with the colonial or national history of what is now the United States." To enter the competition, publishers must mail copies of each entry directly to each of 3 judges and send a fourth copy to the secretary of the Society.

DREW PEARSON PRIZE. Write the Drew Pearson Foundation, 1156 15th St., N.W., Washington DC 20005. Awards $5,000.
Nonfiction: Awarded "for excellence in investigative reporting by a Washington correspondent. The winner is selected each year by the Board of Directors of the Foundation. The award is given at the National Press Club on December 13 of each year."

PENNEY-MISSOURI MAGAZINE AWARDS. Write Penney-Missouri Magazine Awards, School of Journalism, University of Missouri-Columbia, Columbia MO 65201. Awards six $1,000 prizes. Deadline: May 1.
Nonfiction: Awarded "to honor excellence in women's interest journalism in the nation's magazines." Categories include the following: contemporary living (to a writer of an article concerned with family activities enhancing the quality of life; innovations in design and decor; the arts, crafts and creative home activities); consumerism (to a writer of an article in relevant areas such as current consumer concerns, product safety, fair pricing, warranties, guarantees, and consumer protection); health (to a writer of an article in the field of health. Articles may deal with advances in medicine, nutrition, mental health, pediatrics, geriatrics, rehabilitation, therapy, gynecology, and efforts to combat disease); personal life style (to a writer of an article about today's changing lifestyle that stresses individuality and freedom in dress, appearance, and the search for quality in life); expanding opportunities (to a writer of an article about the new status, involvement, and achievement of women in contemporary society); excellence in smaller magazines (to a writer whose work appears in a magazine with circulation under 400,000). Articles on any of the above

categories may be submitted. Entries must have been published during the preceding calendar year. All entries must be accompanied by official entry forms.

PFIZER AWARD. Write The Pfizer Award, c/o Isis Editorial Office, Smithsonian Institution, Washington DC 20560. Awards $650. Deadline: May 1.
Nonfiction: The award is given to "an American scholar for the best published work related to the history of science published during the previous year."

JAMES D. PHELAN AWARDS. Write The San Francisco Foundation Awards Office, 425 California St., Suite 1602, San Francisco CA 94104. Awards $2,000. Deadline: January 15.
Nonfiction, Fiction, Poetry, and Drama: "Awards in literature and art, to bring about a further development of native talent in California. Competition opens November 1. Open to persons born in California and from 20 to 35 years old."

EDGAR ALLAN POE AWARDS. Write Mystery Writers of America, Inc., 105 E. 19th St., New York NY 10003. Deadline: nominations must be received by January 31.
Fiction and Nonfiction: Awards Edgar Allan Poe statuettes annually in 9 categories: best mystery novel published in America, best first mystery novel by an American author, best fact crime book, best juvenile mystery, best paperback mystery, best mystery short story, best mystery motion picture, best TV mystery, best mystery book jacket.

POETRY SOCIETY OF AMERICA AWARDS. Write The Poetry Society of America, 15 Gramercy Park, New York NY 10003. Awards cash prizes of $100 to $3,500 to Poetry Society of America members in 15 categories; 4 contests open also to nonmembers. Deadline: January 15.
Poetry: Contests open to nonmembers and members include The John Masefield Award ($500 for a narrative poem), the Melville Cane Award ($500 for the best book published by an American on poetry or on a poet), the Elias Lieberman Memorial Award ($100 for a poem by a U.S. high or preparatory school student on any subject), and the Shelley Memorial Award ($1,800 to an American poet of merit and in need). Only one poem may be sent by each competitor. Poems are to be typed in triplicate. Mailing envelopes should be marked with the name of the award for which the submission is to be considered. No poem will be returned.

POETS' CLUB OF CHICAGO SHAKESPEAREAN SONNET CONTEST. Chairman: Mary Torode, 1541 N. Avers Ave., Chicago IL 60651. Awards $20, $10, and $5. Deadline: September 1.
Poetry: Open to all poets. 3 copies of each entry must be submitted. "No name on poem sheet. Enclose name and address on 3x5 card in separate envelope. Type first line of poem on outside of envelope."

GEORGE POLK MEMORIAL AWARDS, Professor Jacob H. Jaffe, Awards Curator, Department of Journalism, Long Island University, Brooklyn NY 11201. Deadline: January 15.
Nonfiction: Bronze plaques and special citations for outstanding reporting, writing, editing, criticism, photography and production manifested through newspapers, magazines, books and radio/television. Submit entries with explanatory letters.

PULITZER PRIZES. Write Secretary, Advisory Board on the Pulitzer Prizes, 702 Journalism, Columbia University, New York NY 10027. Deadline for nominations: November 1, literary prizes; February 1, journalism prizes.
Nonfiction: Awards prizes in 16 categories in journalism and letters for distinguished work by U.S. newspapers, for distinguished work in journalism, and for distinguished achievement in literature.

PUTNAM AWARDS. Write The Putnam Awards, G.P. Putnam's Sons, 200 Madison Ave., New York NY 10016. Awards $7,500 advance against royalties. No deadline.
Fiction and Nonfiction: Award is given for outstanding fiction and nonfiction book mss not less than 65,000 words long.

ERNIE PYLE MEMORIAL AWARD. Write Ernie Pyle Memorial Award, Scripps-Howard Foundation, 200 Park Ave., New York NY 10017. Awards $1,000 and a plaque. Deadline: January 15.
Nonfiction: Given "for newspaper writing which was published in U.S. newspapers during the contest year most exemplifying the style and craftsmanship of Ernie Pyle. The judges' concern will be that entries capture the compassion of Pyle's work. He knew people, he knew words, and was sensitive to his treatment of both."

REGINA MEDAL, Catholic Library Association, 461 W. Lancaster Ave., Haverford PA 19041.
Juveniles: "The Regina Medal award was established in 1959 by the Catholic Library Association to dramatize its standards for the writing of good literature for children. It has been made possible through the generosity of an anonymous donor. The only criterion for the award is that of excellence. The silver medal is presented at the annual convention of CLA at a special luncheon to an individual whose lifetime dedication to children's literature has made him an exemplar of the words of Walter De La Mare, '... Only the rarest kind of best in anything can be good enough for the young. ...' The award is given without regard to the recipient's religion, country, or birth, or nature of contribution (author, publisher, editor, illustrator, etc.)."

SUMMERFIELD G. ROBERTS AWARD. Write the Sons of the Republic of Texas, 2426 Watts Rd., Houston TX 77025. Awards $1,000. Deadline: January 15.
Nonfiction, Fiction, and Poetry: "The purpose of the award is to encourage literature pertaining to the period of the Republic of Texas. The judges will determine which entry best portrays the spirit, character, strength and deeds of men and women during the Republic of Texas days. The book or ms must pertain to the Republic of Texas events and personalities. It must be written or published during the calendar year for which the award is given. There is no word limit on the material submitted for the award. Mss may be either fiction or nonfiction, poems, essays, short stories, novels or biographies. The authors do not have to be Texas residents nor must publishers be in Texas. A copy of each entry must be mailed to the State Office of The Sons of the Republic of Texas and to each judge. No entries will be returned."

THE HENRY SCHUMAN PRIZE IN THE HISTORY OF SCIENCE, c/o *Isis,* Editorial Office, Smithsonian Institution, Washington DC 20560. Deadline: September 1.
Nonfiction: $250 prize for an original essay on the history of science and its cultural influences. Open to graduate and undergraduate students in any American or Canadian college, university, or institute of technology. Papers submitted for the prize should be approximately 5,000 words in length, exclusive of footnotes and thoroughly documented. It is hoped that the prize-winning essay will be suitable for publication in *Isis.* Papers may deal with ideas and accomplishments of scientists in the past; trace the evolution of particular scientific concepts; study historical influences of one branch of science upon another. Essays dealing with medical subjects are not acceptable, although papers dealing with relations between medicine and natural sciences will be welcome.

SEQUOYAH CHILDREN'S BOOK AWARD. Write Sequoyah Children's Book Award Committee, P.O. Box 12311, Oklahoma City OK 73112. Awards plaque.
Nonfiction and Fiction: For juvenile book on a select list judged favorite by Oklahoma school children. "The Sequoyah Children's Book Award Program is a reading program designed to encourage the children of Oklahoma in grades four through eight to read a variety of distinguished books and to think about them critically. The books included on a masterlist, released annually, are selected according to literary standards for evaluation adopted by the Children's Services Division of the American Library Association for the Notable Children's Books. Each child having read at least two of the books on the masterlist is eligible to cast a vote for his favorite book. Deadline for voting is January 31st of each year, with the author of the winning book announced in February. The following qualifications for entries must be met: (a) the author must be a living United States citizen; (b) the book must be written for use by children in grades four through eight; (c) no textbooks or pic-

turebooks will be considered; (d) books must bear copyright of the second and third years previous to the dates of the list."

SEVENTEEN'S ANNUAL PHOTOGRAPHY CONTEST. Write *Seventeen*, 320 Park Ave., New York NY 10022. Awards 6 $100 prizes. Deadline: entries must be postmarked by midnight, July 15.
Photography: Only boys and girls at least 13 and less than 20 years old on the July 1 immediately preceding the deadline date are eligible to compete for the six $100 prizes. Contestants may submit color or b&w photos "illustrating themes of love, communication, reverie, nature, and social issues. You may send as many pictures as you wish; every effort will be made to return all prints except winning photographs. Be sure to indicate your name, address, and birth date on the back of each print. Save the negatives from which the submitted prints are made, but send no negatives until requested. Do not mount pictures or retouch in any way the prints or the negatives from which they are made. Cropping and enlarging are permissible." Photos must be unpublished and original. Winning photos will be published with poems in the January issue. Judging will be based on "photographic quality and appropriateness for publication." Winning entries will become the property of Triangle Communications, Inc.

SEVENTEEN'S ANNUAL SHORT STORY CONTEST. Write *Seventeen*, 320 Park Ave., New York NY 10022. Awards nine prizes totalling over $1,000. Deadline: entries must be postmarked by midnight, July 1.
Fiction: Only young people at least 13 and less than 20 years old on the deadline date are eligible to compete for the prizes: $500 first prize, $300 second prize, $200 third prize, and 6 honorable mentions of $50 each. Stories will be judged on the basis of "literary worth, originality, plot development, naturalness of dialogue, convincing characterization, and suitability for *Seventeen*." The 3 top prize-winning stories will be published in the January issue of *Seventeen*. Stories must be unpublished, approximately 2,000 to 5,000 words in length, and accompanied by a notarized statement on the age of entrant and the originality of the story. There is no limit to the number of stories a contestant may submit, but each must be accompanied by a notarized statement. Mss cannot be acknowledged or returned.

JOHN GILMARY SHEA PRIZE. Write The American Catholic Historical Association, The Catholic University of America, Washington DC 20017. Awards $300. Deadline: October 14.
Nonfiction: "Anyone who is a citizen or resident of the United States or Canada may be entered in the competition, regardless of his religion and of his membership in the Association. The book, however, must deal in some way with the history of the Church broadly considered. 3 copies of each work entered in the contest must be sent to the executive office or directly to the contest judges. The book entry must have been published since October 1 of the previous year."

SHELLEY MEMORIAL AWARD. Sponsored by the Poetry Society of America, 15 Gramercy Park, New York NY 10003. Awards about $1,800. Deadline: January 15.
Poetry: This award, given for a poet's entire work, as well as his or her financial need, is noncompetitive. The money was left by the late Mary P. Sears of Waltham, MA. The jury does its own selection of the poet, in consultation. Applications for the award are not acceptable. Members and nonmembers of the Poetry Society of America are eligible.

SIGMA DELTA CHI AWARDS IN JOURNALISM. Write Sigma Delta Chi Awards in Journalism, 35 E. Wacker Dr., Suite 3108, Chicago IL 60601. Deadline: February 1.
Nonfiction: Awards bronze medallions and plaques in 16 categories "for outstanding achievements in journalism during a calendar year. Each nomination must be accompanied by a nomination form."

SOCIETY OF COLONIAL WARS AWARD. Write Awards Committee, Society of Colonial Wars, 122 East 58th St., New York NY 10022. Awards bronze medallion and citation. Deadline: June 1.

Nonfiction and Fiction: The award is "presented each year in recognition of contributions of outstanding excellence, produced during the previous calendar year, in the field of literature, drama, music or art relative to colonial Americana (1607-1775). Literary or dramatic entries should be in bound volumes or pamphlet form. The purpose of the award is twofold: to promote a wider knowledge of the era in which the Society has a vital and hereditary interest and to encourage the production of important material concerned with the life and times of early America."

SOUTHWESTERN LITERARY AWARD. Write NLC Committee, 30529 Terminal Annex, Los Angeles CA 90030. Awards $2,500 biannually.
Fiction: Awarded "to the author of a book-length fiction work for outstanding achievement in the field of creative writing. Any American author is eligible. The book must be an original novel, set anywhere within the United States, on any subject or theme. All works nominated for the award will be judged solely on literary merit, regardless of commercial success. Although the deadline is June 1, books with fixed publication dates to August 1 will be considered. May not be applied for by solicitation of books, titles, etc."

SPUR AWARDS. Western Writers of America, Inc. Deadline: December 31. For information, write Nellie S. Yost, Secretary, 1505 West D. St., North Platte NE 69101. Do not send entries to this address. Current rules will be provided by the secretary.
Fiction, Nonfiction, Juveniles: Awards the Spur Award Trophy for the best achievement in 6 areas: Western nonfiction book, Western novel, Western juvenile nonfiction book, Western juvenile fiction book, Western TV script, Western short material. "Any number of entries permitted by the same publishers, agents, or authors. Publication during the preceding calendar year qualifies entry for awards of the current year."

STANLEY DRAMA AWARD, Wagner College, Staten Island NY 10301. Contact: Dr. J.J. Boies. Write for applications. Deadline: May 15.
Plays: $500 award for an original full-length play or musical which has not been professionally produced or received tradebook publication. Consideration will also be given to a series of 2 or 3 thematically connected one-act plays. Plays must be recommended by a teacher of drama or creative writing, a critic, an agent, a director, or another playwright or composer. Former Stanley Award winners are not eligible to compete. Book and lyric writers are urged to submit full musicals (including music) for the award.

JESSE STUART CONTEST. Write Jesse Stuart Contest, *Seven*, 21½ North Harvey (Terminal Arcade), Oklahoma City OK 73102. Awards prizes of $25, $15, $10 and $5. Deadline: February 1.
Poetry: "For the best unpublished poems in the Jesse Stuart tradition; any form or free verse; no restrictions as to length. Must communicate Mr. Stuart's poetry and/or prose: embodying basic factors and emotions simply and directly without being obtuse, crude, or depressive. Send triplicate copies on 8x11 paper (carbons acceptable if clear and readable). Entries must be typed. Sign each copy with pen name. Include title of poem, pen name, real name, and address inside a sealed envelope. On outside of sealed envelope put title of poem and pen name. No entries will be returned."

TEXAS INSTITUTE OF LETTERS COMPETITION. Write Martin Shockley, Secretary-Treasurer, The Texas Institute of Letters, N.T. Box 5712, Denton TX 76203. Awards 8 prizes, from $200 to $1,000. Deadline: January 2.
Nonfiction, Fiction, Poetry, and Juveniles: "Books by Texas authors or books about Texas are eligible. A 'Texas author' may be one who was born in Texas, who presently resides in Texas, or who spent formative years in Texas. In general, entries may deal with any subject, but preference will be given to books bearing on Texas or the Southwest." Awards include the following: Carr P. Collins Award ($1,000 for the best nonfiction book), Jesse H. Jones Award ($1,000 for the best book of fiction), Friends of the Dallas Public Library Award ($500 for the most useful and informative book in the field of general knowledge), short story award ($250), Stanley Walker Journalism Award ($500 for the best work of journalism), Voertman's Po-

etry Award ($200 for the best book of poetry), Steck-Vaughn Award ($200 for the best book for children), and Texas Collectors' Institute Award ($250). One copy of each entry must be mailed to each of the three judges.

UNITED STATES AWARD. Write International Poetry Forum's United States Award, University of Pittsburgh Press, Pittsburgh PA 15213. Awards $2,000 and publication of the winning ms by the University of Pittsburgh Press. Deadline: April 1.
Poetry: "A United States citizen who has not published a volume of poetry is eligible. Private printing of a limited edition does not disqualify the writer; however, poems published in the private edition are not eligible for inclusion in the contest ms. Revised mss which have been previously entered in this contest may be resubmitted. University of Pittsburgh Press in cooperation with the International Poetry Forum retains the right of first refusal on all mss submitted for the award. Entries must be original poetry in English and at least forty-eight typewritten pages. Poems that have been previously published in periodicals are eligible for inclusion. No more than one poem may appear on a page, but the poems may extend for more than one page; pages should be numbered consecutively throughout the ms." Entries should be submitted between February 1 and April 1 of the contest year. "S.A.S.E. must accompany the ms."

VETERANS' VOICES AWARDS, *Veterans' Voices,* 4801 Linwood Blvd., Kansas City MO 64128. Local contests close 3 times a year: March 15, June 15, and October 15. If there is no local contest, any staff member can mail selected entries to *Veterans' Voices.*
Nonfiction, Fiction, Poetry: For hospitalized or outpatient veterans only. Mss must be submitted through local hospital staff. Hospitalized Veterans Writing Project and *Veterans' Voices* award prizes and cash for mss about true experience (facts, your opinion); story (fiction, imagination); light verse and humorous rhymes; poetry (mood, interpretation); patriotic essay (way to help a problem). Keep it short: 1 to 4 pages for story or article, 4 to 24 lines for verse or poem. In upper left corner of first page put date, month and year, "original, unpublished," approximate number of words of prose, number of lines of poetry. In upper right corner put your name, hospital address, home address. Type double space. Set machine 60 spaces wide for story or article. Make original and 3 carbon copies, original and 1 copy for *Veterans' Voices,* 1 copy for hospital, keep 1 copy for yourself. No entries are returned. Give entries to your hospital HVWP representative. $10 for story or article, $5 for poetry, special rates for short original fillers, paid on publication.

EDWARD LEWIS WALLANT BOOK AWARD. Submit to Dr. Lothar Kahn, Central Connecticut College, New Britain CT 06150. Awards $125 and citation. Deadline: October 15.
Fiction: "The award is conferred annually for a creative work of fiction by an American writer which has been published during the current year and which has significance for the American Jew. The novel (or collection of short stories) should preferably bear a kinship to the writing of Wallant and, when possible, the award will seek out the writer who has not yet achieved literary prominence."

W.D. WEATHERFORD AWARD. Write Thomas Parrish, Chairman of the Award Committee, Appalachian Center, CPO 2336, Berea KY 40403. Awards $500 and $200. The $200 prize may be divided into two $100 prizes. Deadline: December 31.
Nonfiction, Fiction, and Poetry: "For the work that best illustrates the problems, personalities and unique qualities of the Appalachian South—the published book or short piece of any kind that does this most effectively for the readers. The writing may be of any kind, tone and point of view—somber, analytical, poignant, optimistic—so long as it rings true and says it best in that year for Appalachia. We realize that this is a difficult assignment, one calling for knowledge and understanding of the region and—quite significantly—for impact on readers. This is not a purely literary award, which is the reason that unpublished works are not eligible. Works submitted for the prize may be fact, fiction or poetry, and they may be of any length, from magazine article or story length to book length. They may consist of one individual piece or a series of pieces. They may be published in newspapers, magazines or anthologies, or they may in themselves be complete books. However, the winning

work must have been first published during the year for which the award is made. A work may be nominated by its publisher, by a member of the Award Committee, or by any reader. We ask that, where it is possible, persons making nominations send at least one and preferably several copies of the nominated work. Where this cannot be done, we ask for full information about the source of the work (publisher, date, etc.)"

WESTERN HERITAGE AWARDS. Write Western Heritage Awards, National Cowboy Hall of Fame, 1700 N.E. 63rd St., Oklahoma City OK 73111. Awards Wrangler trophies. Deadline: January 15.
Nonfiction, Fiction, Juveniles, Radio, and TV: "Any individual, organization, or company may enter in the appropriate category its best Western productions, publications, or compositions. Categories include western documentary film; factual television program; fiction television program; motion picture; music; art book; juvenile book; magazine article, short story, or poetry; nonfiction book; novel." Entries must be released or published between January 1 of the preceding year and April 1 of the contest year. Each entry must be accompanied by an entry form. Entry forms are available in November.

WILMETTE CHILDREN'S THEATRE PLAYWRITING CONTEST. Write Wilmette Children's Theatre Playwriting Contest, 825 Green Bay Rd., Wilmette IL 60091. Awards $150 and $100. Deadline: May 1.
Drama: Award is given "to encourage authors to increase the material available for production with child actors or with both child actors and adults. Authors are encouraged to write scripts which would offer the greatest amount of participation for as many children as possible. Authors of the first and second prize-winning scripts must agree to grant the Wilmette Children's Theatre first production rights on a royalty-free basis for the following two seasons. Honorable mention winners must agree to grant Wilmette Children's Theatre first production rights for the following season, for which a token royalty will be paid. Only unpublished mss will be accepted for this contest which is open to professional and amateur writers. The plot may be original or adapted. Plays with original music are acceptable. Plays should interest elementary school age children and should be up to 1½ hours long. The author's name should not appear on the ms, but should be attached to a separate sheet containing author's name, address, and play title. If adapted, source and release from publisher and author or a statement that the story is in the public domain must accompany script. Pages should be numbered and fastened together with brass fasteners. (No paper clips, please.) Scenes and Cast of Characters should be listed at the beginning of the script. Mss will not be returned unless S.A.S.E. is enclosed."

THOMAS J. WILSON MEMORIAL PRIZE. Write Harvard University Press, 79 Garden St., Cambridge MA 02138. Awards a cash prize. No deadline.
Nonfiction: The memorial prize is awarded to the author of a first book by a beginning author accepted by Harvard University Press and judged "outstanding in content, style, and mode of presentation."

WINE & HEALTH WRITING AWARDS. Write Administrator, Wine & Health Writing Awards, 2729 W. Lunt Ave., Chicago IL 60645. Awards 3 $1,000 prizes. Deadline: January 31.
Nonfiction: The purpose of the award is to bring attention to both the modern scientific confirmation of wine's ancient medical uses and to new discoveries of wine's beneficial uses, through the media of mass communication to the general public (Category 1), and through the media of medical communication to the health professions (Category 2), and through the media of radio and television (Category 3). Articles and broadcasts to be submitted must have been published or broadcast during the calendar year preceding the contest deadline. Entries for Category 1 must have been published in a newspaper, newspaper magazine supplement, or magazine intended for the general public and available to the general public through newsstand sales or through subscription, or both. Entries for Category 2 must have been published in a recognized journal or magazine intended for such members of the health professions as physicians, surgeons, nurses, and hospital or nursing-home administrators. Entries for Category 3 must have been broadcast or

telecast to the public by an FCC-licensed station (commercial or educational) and not solely used on closed-circuit transmission, as at a medical convention or medical center. Each published entry must be submitted in triplicate, of which one copy should be the original, showing the name of the publication, or station, and the date of issue or presentation. Each copy of the entry should have affixed to it information as to the category of entry, name of the article, name and date of the publication, name of person submitting the article, his address and title. Do not bind entries. In the cases of radio-television, each entry should include three copies of the script, and, in the case of radio, a disc or tape, and, in the case of television, a sound film or kinescope. Except for films, entries will not be returned.

AUDREY WOOD AWARD IN PLAYWRITING. Write Kenneth Baker, Director of Theater, The American University, Washington DC 20016. Awards $500 and production of play. Deadline: December 15.
Drama: The award will be presented "for the best original (unproduced) script of any length. All scripts must be accompanied by a synopsis. Please send a duplicate copy, not the original. A contestant may submit one entry only. All production and publication rights remain the property of the playwright. Scripts will not be returned unless accompanied by S.A.S.E."

WRITER'S DIGEST CREATIVE WRITING CONTEST. Write *Writer's Digest*, 9933 Alliance Rd., Cincinnati OH 45242. Awards 300 prizes worth over $7,500 (in cash value) for the best article, short story, and poetry entries. Deadline: midnight, May 31.
Nonfiction, Fiction, and Poetry: All entries must be original, unpublished, and not previously submitted to a *Writer's Digest* contest. Length: short story, 2,000 words maximum; article, 2,500 words maximum; poetry, 16 lines maximum. Entries must be typewritten, double-spaced, on 8½x11 paper with the name and address in the upper left corner. An entry form must accompany each entry. Each contestant is entitled to submit one entry in each category. All entries may be submitted elsewhere after they are sent to *Writer's Digest*. No acknowledgement will be made of receipt of mss. Mss will not be returned and enclosure of S.A.S.E. will disqualify the entry. Announcement of this contest is made yearly in the January through April issues of *Writer's Digest*.

WRITERS GUILD OF AMERICA, WEST AWARDS. Write Allen Rivkin, Public Relations, Writers Guild of America, West, 8955 Beverly Blvd., Los Angeles CA 90048. Deadline: "first week in January, TV submissions; mid-January, screenplays."
Radio, TV, Movies: Awards plaques in screen, television, and radio categories for "best written" scripts.

YALE SERIES OF YOUNGER POETS. Write Editor, Yale Series of Younger Poets, Yale University Press, 92A Yale Station, New Haven CT 06520. "The winning manuscript is published by the Yale University Press and the author receives the usual royalties." Deadlines: "Mss should not be sent to the editor before March 1 and will not be accepted after May 1."
Poetry: "The Yale Series of Younger Poets competition is open to any writer under forty years of age who has not previously published a volume of poetry. The winning ms is published by the Yale University Press, and the author receives the usual royalties. No application form is required, but the ms must be of the highest professional quality. The format of the Series calls for a ms of from 48 to 64 pages, with no more than one poem on a page. Illustrations are not accepted. Mss must be typewritten, either single or double spaced, and only a good xerox copy should be submitted. There should be a title page bearing the author's full name and address, and a table of contents. Ms pages should be numbered consecutively throughout, beginning with the title page. All verse must be original. There are no limitations on the kind of poetry or the subject matter, though translations are not acceptable. Acknowledgments should be included for all poems previously published in newspapers or periodicals. A contestant may submit more than one ms in one year's competition. An unsuccessful ms may be revised and resubmitted the next or subsequent years. An addressed return envelope must accompany the ms, as well as

sufficient postage to cover its return if it is not selected. If no postage accompanies the ms, it will not be returned."

YANKEE POETRY AWARDS. Write *Yankee* Magazine, Dublin NH 03444. Awards $175 in prizes for poetry appearing in *Yankee* during the calendar year. Deadline: December 1.
Poetry: Prizes of $100, $50, and $25 for the best poems appearing in *Yankee*. Submissions may be rhymed or unrhymed and need not necessarily be about New England. Length: "we prefer verse of no more than 30 lines."

Gag Markets

The following markets include information about cartoonists who are looking for gags. Submissions to cartoonists should be made on 3x5 slips of paper. Briefly suggest the scene and then add the gagline. For convenience in identifying the gag, include some identifying code number at the upper left of the gag slip. (See sample gag slip below). Your name and address should be typed on the reverse side of the gag slip, in the upper left hand corner.

A Sample Gag Slip

```
409 A

Supermarket.  Man pushing loaded shopping
cart for his wife, says to another man:

"I estimate the cost per mile to operate
one of these things is around $300!"
```

```
Your name goes here _____
Your address goes here _____
```

BOB ARENTS, 4025 N. Federal Hwy., Apt. 122 C, Ft. Lauderdale FL 33308. "I can use general stuff—but it must be good enough for at least the $25 markets before I'll draw it up." Interested in general, family, adventure, sports, and medical gags. Does not want to see "two-line jokes, old cliches." Pays 25% commission. Returns rejected material "as soon as possible, usually in 2 weeks." May hold gags "for as long as 1 year." Enclose S.A.S.E. for return of submissions.

ART ASKUE, 132 S. Cherry St., Poughkeepsie NY 12601. Cartoonist since 1950. Interested in "general, contemporary (environment, family problems, money) gags; switches on history, myths, nursery rhymes, etc. Gags should be visually funny, not verbally. They should be clever—for average to smarter-than-average folks." Has sold to *New York Times*, and trade journals. Pays 25% commission on net. Will send a sample cartoon to a gagwriter on request. Also interested in collaborating with writer on humorous articles or books, including children's market. Will work for 10% and three good repros from published work or articles. Returns rejected material "immediately." Enclose S.A.S.E. for return of submissions.

RAE AVENA, 186 Pearl Harbor St., Bridgeport CT 06610. Cartoonist since 1965. Likes to see all types of gags. Has sold to *True, Official Detective*, and *Weight Watchers*. "Gagwriters should send around 12 gags. Keep descriptions short." Pays 25% commission. Bought about 6 gags from gagwriters last year. Returns rejected material "as soon as possible—no more than 1 week later." Enclose S.A.S.E. for return of submissions.

AARON BACAL, 305 Ocean Parkway, Brooklyn NY 11218. Cartoonist since 1965. Wants "clever generals and/or trade journal gags on specific topics, i.e., insurance, medical, chemical, etc. Also male slant gags and topical humor. Please, no tired and trite situations. Shun verbosity. Double-space gags and make them humorous. A nonhumorous gag is a contradiction in terms." Has sold to *Medical Economics, Sir, New Yorker* and trade journals. Bought about 30 gags from freelancers last year. 30% commission. Reports in 1 week. Enclose S.A.S.E. for return of submissions.

FRANK BAGINSKI, Box 108, Village Station, New York NY 10014. Cartoonist since 1962. Only buys gags (old, unsold, beaten up) for a flat $1 apiece. Major markets include *True, Cavalier*, and *True Detective*. Enclose S.A.S.E. for return of submissions.

HERBERT BENNETT, P.O. Box 41, Michigan City IN 46360. Cartoonist since 1947. Interested in "general and trade journal gags; specifically trade journal. Gags must not criticize professions." Has sold to *American Machinist, Adventure, Medical Economics*, and others. Pays 25% commission; "will pay substantially more for good gags." Bought about 180 gags from gagwriters last year. Will send a sample cartoon to a gagwriter for $2. Returns rejected material "immediately." Returns unsold gags "when requested." Enclose S.A.S.E. for return of submissions.

NICHOLAS F. BOHN, 35380 Mound Rd., Apt. 2, Sterling Heights MI 48077. Cartoonist since 1952. Interested in "girly, adventure-type gags. Also some teenager gags; medical and science fiction gags and gags suitable for a gag-a-day comic strip, but no kid or family types. "I don't care for gags with animals in them, except for dogs now and then." Has sold to *Humorama* and *California Supreme*. Wants batches of 6 to 12 gags. Pays 25% commission. Bought about 50 gags from gagwriters last year. Illustrates gags for writers at the rate of $1 per full (8½x11) page cartoon, and puts the writer's name on the drawing. Is interested in ghosting a strip or single panel feature. Will send a sample cartoon to a gagwriter for $1. Returns rejected material "immediately." Enclose S.A.S.E. for return of submissions.

DOROTHY BOND ENTERPRISES, 2450 N. Washtenaw Ave., Chicago IL 60647. Cartoonist since 1944. "We carefully look at every submission. We want good, funny, family gags with a new, humorous slant and sell to top paying markets. Please, no pornography, no cannibal, monkey or elephant gags. Keep your gags brief. Submit on small, numbered cards, with self-addressed stamped envelope. If we sell your gag, we send you 40% of the sale price the same day we get the payment. If we reject your gag, we send it back to you within 3 days after receipt, without fail.

You're important to us." Bought about 200 gags from freelancers last year. Unsold gags are returned within 3 months.

BILL BOYNANSKY, 230 W. 76 St., New York NY 10023. Cartoonist for over 30 years. "General subjects. No sports, political gags or any gag idea that's been done to death. Prefer the writer first write me, giving me a brief background of his ability and sales as a gag cartoon writer, etc. Am always interested in new ideas for a good comic strip. Am also interested in writers who can write humorous articles to be illustrated." Pays 25% for regular gags; 35% for captionless. Returns unsold gags "as promptly as possible. In fact, I rarely take a gag unless I'm reasonably sure of selling it." Returns rejected material within 3 days. Will send a sample cartoon to a gagwriter for $1. Enclose S.A.S.E. with all correspondence.

CHARLES D. BREMSER, 4343 Chateau de Ville Dr., St. Louis MO 63129. Cartoonist since 1953. Interested in "general, girly, male gags." Has sold to *Boys' Life*, and others. Pays 25% commission. Bought about 137 gags from gagwriters last year. Will send a sample cartoon to a gagwriter on request. Returns rejected material "within a week or two." May hold unsold gags for "6 months to a year." Enclose S.A.S.E. for return of submissions.

FRANCIS H. BRUMMER, Box 100, Missouri Valley IA 51555. Cartoonist since 1954. Interested in gags for "machine shop, welding, construction, teenage, religious teen, church, insurance, banking, stocks and bonds, printing, and other house organs and trade journals." Does not want general gags. Has sold to magazines like *American Machinist, VFW, Christian Century*. Submit in batches of 10 to 20 gags. Pays 25% and 30% commission "to the top trade journal writers." Returns rejected material "normally within 3 days." May hold unsold gags for approximately 2 years. Enclose S.A.S.E. for return of submissions.

JOE BUSCIGLIO, 420 W. North Bay, Tampa FL 33603. Cartoonist since 1943. Interested in "sports gags with topical themes (involving 'name' sport personalities, teams, etc.) and sports in general for 'Sportoons.' No other type of material, please." Query first. Pays 25% commission. Will promptly return rejected material if not suitable for format. Enclose S.A.S.E. with all correspondence or submissions. "None returned, otherwise."

ROBERT E. CANNAVA, 33 Myrtlewood Ln., Willingboro NJ 08046. Cartoonist since 1971. Interested in "general, medical (from doctor's viewpoint), salesman, and business travel gags. They should be sophisticated—*New Yorker* or *Cosmo* type." Has sold to *Medical Opinion, Pageant*, and others. Pays 25% commission. Will send a sample cartoon to a gagwriter on request. Returns rejected material within 10 days. Enclose S.A.S.E. for return of submissions.

BILL CHAMBERS, 1032 Beloit, Forest Park IL 60130. Cartoonist since 1971. "I need funny stuff for top market sales and male markets. Simple, funny, but no captionless." Pays 25% commission. Enclose S.A.S.E. for return of submissions.

DON COLE, P.O. Box 378, Cape Canaveral FL 32920. Cartoonist since 1960. Wants gags "of all types, any amount. Submitted to top markets on down." Pays 25% commission. Enclose S.A.S.E. for return of submissions.

EUGENE CRAIG, The *Columbus Dispatch*, 34 S. Third St., Columbus OH 43215. Interested in batches of family gags, with accent on feminine foibles. "I want original cartoon gags—visual gags where part of the humor is in the drawing, not a one-liner with the humor in the words and the picture superfluous. No one-liners from TV." Submit any number of gags in a batch. Pays $3 each. Bought about 100 gags from gagwriters last year. Returns rejected material at once. Enclose S.A.S.E. for return of submissions.

A. CRAMER, 1909 Quentin Rd., Brooklyn NY 11229. Cartoonist since 1942. Wants family gags. Gags must have funny situations. Sells to the major markets. Prefers batches of 15 to 20. Pays 25% commission. Enclose S.A.S.E. for return of submissions.

CREATIVE CARTOON SERVICE, 3109 West Schubert Ave., Chicago IL 60647. Contact: Peter Vaszilson. Cartoonist since 1965. "Creative Cartoon Service is a cartoon agency that channels the work of over 42 cartoonists to major and minor markets. We are seeking gagwriters to assist our various cartoonists. Write us, stating qualifications." Pays 25% commission, "unless gagwriters can prove themselves otherwise." Enclose S.A.S.E. for return of submissions and response to queries.

JAMES CROAK, Hutton Heights Village #63, Green River WY 82935. Wants generals, sports, construction and girlies. Sells to trade journals and newspapers. Has been selling cartoons for 3 years. Pays 50% commission. Returns rejected material immediately. Will send a sample cartoon to a gagwriter on request. Enclose S.A.S.E. for return of submissions.

THOMAS W. DAVIE, 3715 N. 11th, Tacoma WA 98406. Cartoonist since 1960. Interested in general, male, medical, hunting, and fishing themes. Sells to *American Legion, Sports Afield,* King Features, *Medical Economics,* and others. Prefers batches of 5 to 25. Pays 25% commission. Enclose S.A.S.E. for return of submissions.

LEE DeGROOT, Bethlehem Pike and Tennis Ave., Ambler PA 19002. Cartoonist since 1960. Interested in general gags. Major markets include *Holiday,* and trade magazines. Interested in humorous studio card ideas. "I draw up each studio card idea in full-color before submitting to greeting card publishers." Looks at batches of fifteen. 25% commission. Enclose S.A.S.E. for return of submissions.

ROY DELGADO, P.O. Box 50241, Tucson AZ 85703. Cartoonist since 1953. Interested in "sophisticated, erotic, clever, offbeat, sarcastic, 'way out' material. Sold cartoons in 6 countries last year." Pays 25 to 30% commission. Holds unsold gags for "approximately 2 years." Returns rejected material in 10 days. Query first. Will send sample cartoon to a gagwriter for $1. Enclose S.A.S.E. for response to queries.

GEORGE DOLE, P.O. Box 1396, Portland ME 04104. Cartoonist since 1952. Interested in "general situation gags." Has sold to *Playboy, Parade, Cosmopolitan, Good Housekeeping, Argosy.* Pays 25% commission. Returns rejected material in 1 week. Enclose S.A.S.E. for return of submissions.

JAMES ESTES, 1916 Karen, Amarillo TX 79106. "Primarily interested in seeing good, funny material of a general nature. Most themes are acceptable, but the usual taboos apply. Submit on 3x5 cards or paper, 10 to 20 gags per submission; clear, concise ideas set down without excessive wordiness. Wholesome, family, general material wanted." Has been selling cartoons for 3 years. Returns rejected material as quickly as possible, usually in 2 to 3 days. Pays 25% of what cartoon sells for. Enclose S.A.S.E. for return of submissions.

GATES FEATURES, INC., 35-63 88th St., Jackson Heights NY 11372. Contact: Art Gates. Interested in "funny ideas suitable for family audience. No risque material. Home life, cars, school, church, teens, kids, office, shopping, sports, suburbia, etc., are possible subjects. Cartoons are to amuse. No unpleasant subjects. No bad taste or risque gags for us. We like sight gags—topical, if possible. We do not like Indian smoke signal gags, but we've bought them if they made us laugh. Overworked subjects include Hindus on beds of nails, cars out of gas. No old gags. I've been syndicating my service for over 11 years to more than 200 newspaper subscribers. In addition to our humor service, we now syndicate a daily panel (8 gags a week). We also buy ideas for cartoon advertising campaigns. Car dealers and sporting goods stores are our prime users. Will expand to TV and banks." Will send a sample cartoon to a gagwriter on request. Pays "from $10 to $20; I've paid more." Returns rejected material in 1 week. Enclose S.A.S.E. for return of submissions.

MAL GORDON, 29 Monroe Ave., Worcester MA 01602. Cartoonist since 1955. Interested in dental (avoid anything derogatory to dentistry); medical, pharmaceutical, grocery, law, photography, sports, golf, fishing; educational, parochial, college and grade school level subjects; family, male and female. Has sold to *Today's Education, Progressive Grocer, Dental Survey* and others. Bought about 25 gags from freelancers last year. Pays 25% commission. Returns rejected material in 10 days. Holds unsold gags for 1 to 2 years.

ROBERT M. HAGEMAN, 769 Wesley St., Baldwin, L.I. NY 11512. Cartoonist since 1964. Looking for gags of all types for middle and major markets. Has sold to such markets as *McCall's, American Legion, True, Medical Economics,* King Features and all male markets. Will consider batches of 15. Pays 25% commission. Enclose S.A.S.E. for return of submissions.

CHARLES HENDRICK, JR., Old Fort Ave., Kennebunkport ME 04046. Cartoonist since 1942. Interested in family, sports, adventure, and general gags. No sex gags. Prefers batches of 6 to 10. Pays 25% commission. Will send a sample cartoon to a gagwriter on request. Returns rejected material "immediately." May hold unsold gags for about 3 months. Enclose S.A.S.E. for return of submissions.

WILLARD A. HOPE, 4774 College View Ave., Los Angeles CA 90041. Cartoonist since 1936. Interested in trade journal and house organ gags. Has sold to *Prosecutor,* Singer Features, Inc. and others. Pays 50% commission. Bought about 20 gags from gagwriters last year. Will send a sample cartoon to a gagwriter on request. Returns rejected material in 1 week. Enclose S.A.S.E. for return of submissions.

LARRY "KAZ" KATZMAN, 101 Central Park West, Apt. 4B, New York NY 10023. Cartoonist since 1949. Wants only medical, nurse, hospital, drug store, and drug gags. "Mild sex is okay in a medical category." Uses hundreds of these per year for regular Nellie Nifty, R.N. feature and other medical and drug features. Any number per batch. Pays 25% commission plus bonus when gags are re-used in his Dell paperback collections. Enclose S.A.S.E. for return of submissions.

JEFF KEATE, 8 Maple Grove, Westport CT 06880. Cartoonist since 1936. Interested in general situation and timely gags, sports gags (all sports in season) for "Time Out" sports panel and "Today's Laugh," general situation panel. "Be Funny. No puns, No oldies. No old hat situations." Has sold to *Golf Digest,* Register-Tribune Syndicate and King Features. Pays 25% commission. Bought close to 200 gags from freelancers last year. Holds unsold gags for "approximately 2 years unless gagwriter requests gag back sooner." Returns rejected material immediately. Enclose S.A.S.E. for return of submissions.

REAMER KELLER, P.O. Box 195, Sea Bright NJ 07760. Cartoonist since 1935. Interested in "M.D.-hospital stuff and general gags." Seeks gags for daily doctor panel. Has sold to *McCall's, Playboy, Medical Economics, American Legion* and others. Pays 25% commission. Returns rejected material in 1 month. Holds unsold material for 1 year before returning. Enclose S.A.S.E. for return of submissions.

MILO KINN, 1413 S.W. Cambridge St., Seattle WA 98106. Cartoonist since 1942. Interested in male slant, girly, captionless, adventure, and family gags. Wants anything that is funny. Sells trade journals, farm, medical, office, and general cartoons. Wants batches of 10. Pays 25% commission. Enclose S.A.S.E. for return of submissions.

C.W. LEGGETT, 4790 Lawrence Dr., Sacramento CA 95820. Cartoonist since 1966. "I would like to see a lot of material slanted to particular trades and occupations, but will look at all kinds if top quality. I favor short, captioned sight gags and captionless material. No illustrated joke types." Has sold to *National Enquirer, American Machinist,* and others. Pays 30% commission. Returns rejected material in 1 week. May hold unsold gags for about 6 months. Enclose S.A.S.E. for return of submissions.

LO LINKERT, 1333 Vivian Way, Port Coquitlam, B.C., Canada. Cartoonist since 1957. Interested in clean, general, male, medical, family, office, outdoors gags; captionless ideas. "Make sure your stuff is funny. No spreads." Wants "action gags—not two people saying something funny." Has sold to *Reader's Digest, Good Housekeeping, Family Circle, Boys' Life, Better Homes and Gardens.* Prefers batches of 10 to 15 gags. Pays 25% commission. Bought about 450 gags from gagwriters last year.

Returns rejected material in 1 week. Enclose S.A.E. and International Reply Coupons for return of submissions or 8¢ U.S. postage.

MASTERS AGENCY, P.O. Box 655, Capitola CA 95010. Cartoonists since 1953. Interested in gags on banking, business, farm, medical, religious and industrial safety themes. Pays $5 for these. Gags for "Simpkins" ($7.50) and "Belvedere" ($5) panels. Will look at typers, bur prefer scribbles or sketches, however crude, drawn on 3x5 gag slips. It is our opinion that gagwriters would all greatly increase their sales average by this method. We also purchase cartoonists' inked roughs ($5) and previously published clips ($15). Bought "many hundreds" of gags from freelancers last year. Returns rejected material in 2 weeks. Will send sample cartoon to gagwriter on request. Enclose S.A.S.E for return of submissions.

ART McCOURT, 3819 Dismount, Dallas TX 75211. Cartoonist since 1952. Interested in general and family gags. "Keep them current with the times." Has sold to *Argosy, American Legion, Arizona Republic* and others. Pays 25% commission. Enclose S.A.S.E. for return of submissions.

J. GORDON McLACHLAN (GORDON/JOHNNY MAC), 25 Calhoun St., Trenton NJ 08618. Cartoonist since 1965. Interested in "captionless gags, young, modern woman or late teenage girls, good medicals and some generals. Can use a few top-notch girlies, but they have to be really good as I write 95% of my own male slant stuff." Has sold to *Stag, Man to Man, Army Fun* and others. Pays commission of 25% for sales up to $50; 30% for sales of $50 and over; 35% for sales of $100 or more. Holds unsold gags for about 2 years. Returns rejected material within a week. Enclose S.A.S.E. for return of submissions.

ROLAND MICHAUD, 201 E. Ridgewood Ave., Ridgewood NJ 07451. Cartoonist since 1958. Interested in all kinds of gags. "Avoid submissions that are too wordy and unnecessarily descriptive. A couple of lines usually suffice." Has sold to *Playboy, Look, True, Ladies' Home Journal, McCall's,* and others. Will look at batches of 10. Pays 25% commission. Returns rejected material in 1 to 2 weeks. "As all gags are always potential sales and are circulated and recirculated constantly, I do not return." Enclose S.A.S.E. for return of rejected submissions.

RAY MORIN, 140 Hamilton Ave., Meriden CT 06450. Interested in general gags submitted on 3x5 slips. Has sold to *Saturday Evening Post, Weight Watchers, Family Circle* and others. Will look at batches of 8 or 10 gags. Pays 25% commission. Returns rejected material in 2 weeks. Holds unsold gags "indefinitely." Enclose S.A.S.E. for return of submissions.

IRV PHILLIPS, 2807 East Sylvia St., Phoenix AZ 85032. Cartoonist since 1934. Interested in general, pantomime, and word gags. Also interested in social satire. For a daily feature panel, wants gags on "politics, taxes; youth, ecology, demonstrations; the daily problems, conflicts, and annoyances of the common man." Submit on 3x5 cards. No limit to number of gags submitted. Pays 25% commission; $10 minimum on syndication. "A greater percentage to anyone who can produce a steady supply." Enclose S.A.S.E. for return of submissions.

ROBERT A. PODEWILS, 2225 N. 44th St., Milwaukee, WI 53208. Cartoonist since 1933. Interested in girly gags. "They should be to the point, but not smart. General subjects are good, but I don't care for trade journal or house organ type material. I like the underdog—dumb, clumsy, poor, bum—and the painted lady stuff. I also like sophistication if it has a point or moral, such as the *New York* type. Could use some gags about music and/or musicians. Nothing to downgrade music, but can be dumb or stupid or way out. I'm not much for enigmatic gags, although the subtle type might be okay if it's not too conservative." Seeks gags for "a four-panel strip without captions. Also, hard-hitting explosive type material for sex-o-grams." Pays "25% after expenses; could drop on some to 10%, but seldom, if ever, do. Could increase to 50% before expenses, but don't see too many that good." Returns rejected material in 2 to 4 weeks. May hold unsold gags for 6 months. Enclose S.A.S.E. for return of submissions.

DOM RINALDO, 411 Lafayette Ave., Brooklyn NY 11238. Cartoonist since 1960. Interested in "general, girly; all subjects as long as they are funny." Seeks gags for "a strip called 'Scratch Sheet,' about a bunch of characters who love to gamble and are always trying to think of ways to win. Anyone interested in writing for my strip should get in touch with me for further details. Will consider any type except racial gags." Has sold to *Man, Stag, Modern Medicine,* and others. Pays "25% for the first 2 gags that I've sold, then 40% thereafter. Pay varies for comic strip material." Bought about 45 gags from gagwriters last year. Will send a sample cartoon to a gagwriter on request. Returns rejected material "the same day I receive them. I hold the ones that I like at least 6 months to a year." Enclose S.A.S.E. for return of submissions.

LEE RUBIN, 9 Murray Ave., Port Washington NY 11050. Wants gags for trade journals only. Gags for regular panel: eyeglasses, eye doctors, vision, contact lenses, eye examinations, and vision. Has been selling cartoons for 7 years. Returns rejected material immediately. Pays 25%. Will send a sample cartoon to gagwriter on request. Enclose S.A.S.E. for return of submissions.

PERRY W. SCHAEFFER, Rural Route 2, Box 72A, Britt IA 50423. Cartoonist since 1969. "I can always use farm, medical, office, youth, and electronics gags. No generals or girlies. Each batch of around 12 gags should be heavily slanted to one subject. I'm mainly a minor market man and need gags that indicate inside knowledge of the subject area. I'm mainly a minor market man and need gags that indicate inside knowledge of the subject." Has sold to *Radio Electronics, Modern Secretary, Teens Today* and others. Pays 25% commission. Holds unsold gags "around 6 months; sometimes longer." Returns rejected material in 1 week. Enclose S.A.S.E. for return of submissions.

FRANK "DEAC" SEMATONES, 5226 Mt. Alifan Dr. San Diego CA 92111. Interested in "anything new, fresh, and funny—preferably with a male and girly slant." Has sold to *National Enquirer* and male and girly magazines. Pays 25% commission. Bought 200 to 250 gags from gagwriters last year. Returns rejected material "immediately. Will keep unsold gags going forever unless return is requested." Enclose S.A.S.E. for return of submissions. Also acts as cartoonists' agent, paying 50% commission on cartoon sales under $25; 70% on cartoon sales of $25 and up. Enclose S.A.S.E. with submittals to agency (Deacon's Features at same address).

JOSEPH SERRANO, Box 42, Gloucester MA 01930. Cartoonist since 1950. Interested in sophisticated gags. Seasonal and social comment preferred. Has sold to most major and middle markets. Pays 25% commission. Enclose S.A.S.E. for return of submissions.

PAUL M. SHARPE, 636 Williamsburg Dr., Holly Hill FL 32017. Cartoonist since 1935. Interested in gags on "the church, school, marriage, kids, pets, drunks and drinking, the Armed Forces, hospitals, and the presidency. The gags must be compelling, simple, contemporary, and about foibles. I have my own weekly panel called 'Sharpie' for weekly newspapers." Pays 40% commission first time out, 30% commission second time out, 25% commission third time out. If I rework a gag which I really believe in where mailing is a big cost, I never pay less than 20%." Bought about 85 gags from gagwriters last year. Will send a sample cartoon to a writer on request. May hold unsold gags for about 3 months. Enclose S.A.S.E. for return of submissions.

GODDARD SHERMAN, 6302 Central Ave., Tampa FL 33604. Cartoonist since 1952. Interested in "general, male, teen, medical, some trade journal gags. Funny action as well as funny caption. No gags about desert islands or prisoners hanging in a dungeon." Has sold to *American Legion, Medical Economics, Writer's Digest, Boys' Life,* and others. Pays 33⅓% commission. Bought about 210 gags from gagwriters last year. Returns rejected material "usually in 1 week." Does not return unsold gags; "I keep on trying if I think it's a good gag." Enclose S.A.S.E. for return of submissions.

SHOW-BIZ COMEDY SERVICE, 1735 East 26th St., Brooklyn NY 11229. "We are looking for topical, satirical, one-line gags to sell to comedians, deejays, etc."

Send on 3x5 cards to George Schindler. Pays $2 per single gag line. Enclose S.A.S.E. for return of submissions.

JOHN W. SIDE, 335 Wells St., Darlington WI 53530. Cartoonist since 1940. Interested in "small town, local happening gags with a general slant." Pays 25% commission. Will send a sample cartoon to a gagwriter for $1. Does not return unsold gags. Returns rejected material "immediately." Enclose S.A.S.E. for return of submissions.

CAIRO STURGILL, P.O. Box 107, Milford OH 45150. Cartoonist since 1955. Wants family gags. Needs gags on coal mining, as seen from the union worker viewpoint, and safety in the coal mines. Girly gags are strictly out. Has sold to farm, banking, coal mining, safety, and office magazines. Would like to see batches of 10 gags pertaining to each subject. Also interested in gags that can be used in advertising cartoons (batches of 10). Pays 25% commission. Enclose S.A.S.E. for return of submissions.

PAUL SWAN, 2930 Randy Ln., Dallas TX 75234. Interested in "medical, dental, fishing, flying, science, camping, safety, TV repair, farmers, antique collecting, and office gags. I want medicals and dentals from the doctor's viewpoint. I use gags for 'Sideliners by Swan,' weekly pro football panel, and 'Tommy Trader,' monthly antique strip. No team put-downs. I don't need generals or girlies, and don't use joketoons. That is, the caption by itself should not be funny." Has sold to *Modern Medicine, Collector's News, Air Progress, National Enquirer* and others. Pays 25% commission quarterly. Bought about 600 gags from gagwriters last year. Will send sample cartoon to gagwriter for $1. Returns rejected material "same day received." May hold unsold gags "for a year or so." Enclose S.A.S.E. for return of submissions.

BOB THAVES, P.O. Box 67, Manhattan Beach CA 90266. Cartoonist since 1950. Interested in gags "dealing with anything except raw sex. Also buys gags for syndicated (daily and Sunday) panel, 'Frank & Ernest.' Prefer offbeat gags (no standard, domestic scenes) for that, although almost any general gag will do." Has sold to King Features, trade journals, *Cosmopolitan*, and others. Will look at batches containing any number of gags. Pays 25% commission. Returns rejected material in 1 to 2 weeks. May hold unsold gags indefinitely. Enclose S.A.S.E. for return of submissions.

MARVIN TOWNSEND, 631 West 88th St., Kansas City MO 64114. Cartoonist since 1947. Interested in gags with a trade journal or business slant. "Religious and children gags also welcome. Caption or captionless. Don't waste postage sending worn out gags or nonprofessional material." Sells mostly to business and trade magazines of all types. Prefers batches of 12 gags. Pays 25% commission. Enclose S.A.S.E. for return of submissions.

CHARLES W. TROTTER, 1336 N. Rogers, Springfield MO 65802. Cartoonist since 1962. Interested in "girlies, generals, and men's books. Gags should be *Playboy*-type." Has sold to "most of girly markets." Pays 25% commission. Bought about 50 gags from gagwriters last year. Returns rejected material "promptly. I never return unsold gags, but I always tell gagwriter I'm through." Enclose S.A.S.E. for return of submissions.

BARDULF UELAND, Halstad MN 56548. Cartoonist since 1968. Interested in general, family, education, farm, business, and some medical gags. "Something with a punch—that which employs a universal truth. No sex—I don't work the male markets." Has sold to *National Enquirer, Parade and Pageant.* Pays 25% commission. Currently making extensive use of gagwriters. Returns rejected material in 2 to 3 days. May hold unsold gags "until I have worked all possible markets, which could be 2 to 3 years." Enclose S.A.S.E. for return of submissions.

VIRGIL WILSON, 11014 Pepperidge Circle, Dallas TX 75228. Cartoonist since 1969. Interested in "general material and office and factory gags. Make material fairly close to reality. I don't go for much far-out material. Please don't send me a deluge of gags about the boss chasing the secretary. I am developing a comic strip about an office and plant situation. All types of office gags will be used, with particular emphasis on poking fun at the establishment (office bosses, plant foremen, etc.)." Has sold to *Modern Medicine*, *King Features*, *Inside Detective*, *For Men Only*, and others. Pays 25% commission on magazine cartoons. "If the comic strip is syndicated, I will probably pay about $10 each, payable when the particular gag is published. I will consider paying a higher rate if a writer's gags are outstanding." Bought about 10 gags from gagwriters last year. Will send a sample cartoon to a gagwriter on request. Enclose S.A.S.E. for return of submissions.

ART WINBURG, 21 McKinley Ave., Jamestown NY 14701. Cartoonist since 1936. Will look at all types of gags; general, house organs, trade journals, children's magazines. Gagwriter should "use variety, be original, and avoid old cliches." Would prefer not to see gags about "smoke signals, flying carpets, moon men, harems, or cannibals with some person in cooking pot." Has sold to *American Legion Magazine*, *Girl Talk*, *Boys' Life*, *Snow Goer* and *Archery World*. Pays 25% commission, "sometimes 30%." Returns rejected material "usually within a week, sometimes same day as received." Will return unsold gags "on request. Always a possibility of eventually selling a cartoon." Enclose S.A.S.E. for return of submissions.

ANDY WYATT, 213 Tech Rd., Pittsburgh PA 15205. Cartoonist since 1960. Interested in general, topical, girly, and male slant gags. "I like visual gags, but any good gag is okay. There is always a better gag on the same old topic. Some of the funniest material comes from trying to top old cliches." Has sold to *Wall Street Journal*, *Man to Man*, *Mr.*, and others. Pays 25% commission. Bought "over 100" gags from gagwriters last year. Will send a sample cartoon to a gagwriter on request. Returns rejected material in "1 to 2 weeks if I definitely can't use; sometimes longer if I feel there's a possibility in the material." May hold unsold gags "until I sell, unless a writer specifies he wants gags back at a certain time." Enclose S.A.S.E. for return of submissions.

Government Information Sources

The administrative, judicial, and legislative offices of the United States government offer the writer an excellent source of statistics and information on just about any subject, including commercial fisheries (The National Marine Fisheries Service), management training (The Small Business Administration), or measurement in the physical and engineering sciences (The National Bureau of Standards). Often a writer can locate a fact that eludes his library research by writing a letter to the proper government agency and asking them to supply it or suggest where he might find it. The government offices described in the listings that follow have indicated a special willingness to assist writers with research in their areas of expertise; for a more comprehensive directory of government offices, see A Directory of Information Resources in the United States in the Federal Government (available from the U.S. Government Printing Office).

In addition, many of the agencies described here issue booklets about their operations. Writers can get copies of these, often at no cost, by requesting them from individual agencies.

The research done by these government offices is usually published in booklet or book form by the U.S. Government Printing Office. Details on getting copies of this material are given in the entry for that office.

ACTION, 806 Connecticut Ave., N.W., Washington DC 20525. Contact: Office of Public Affairs, c/o Lee Mullane. "ACTION is the citizens' service corps, formed by President Nixon to coordinate federal volunteer programs in the United States and abroad. ACTION is designed to expand the testing and innovations in voluntary actions. ACTION programs include the Peace Corps, Volunteers in Service to America (VISTA), Foster Grandparent Program, Retired Senior Volunteer Program (RSVP), Service Corps for Retired Executives (SCORE), Active Corps of Executives (ACE), and University Year for Action. ACTION programs deal with meeting human needs in the areas of education, nutrition, health, legal services, city planning, business, recreation, community development, world friendship, and world peace. At present, ACTION is able to provide writers with photos of project areas, volunteers in service, and the people with whom they work. Bibliographies of Peace Corps material are also available. Writers may also obtain biographies of personnel and contacts for additional information. ACTION publishes feature stories, press releases, reports, brochures, flyers and program fact sheets.

AGRICULTURAL MARKETING SERVICE, U.S. Department of Agriculture, Washington DC 20250. Contact: Director, Information Division. This agency is responsible for the grading of agricultural commodities, market regulation, purchase of agricultural products for family and child feeding programs, designation and promotion of foods which are plentiful, inspection of egg products for wholesomeness, and transportation and warehousing activities. The agency is concerned with all food commodities, seed, feed, and fibre. It can provide publications, photos, a catalog of available publications, and other assistance to writers.

AGRICULTURE, DEPARTMENT OF, Independence Ave. between 12th and 14th Sts., S.W., Washington DC 20250. Contact: Director of Communication. The U.S. Department of Agriculture is directed by law to acquire and diffuse useful information on agricultural subjects in the most general and comprehensive sense. The Department performs functions relating to research, education, conservation, marketing, regulatory work, agricultural adjustment, surplus disposal, and rural development. It conducts research in agricultural and industrial chemistry, the industrial uses of farm products, entomology, soils, agricultural engineering, agricultural economics, marketing, crop and livestock production, production and manufacture of dairy products, human nutrition, home economics, forestry, and conservation. It provides crop reports, commodity standards, Federal meat and poultry inspection service, and other inspection, grading, and marketing services. It administers many regulatory laws designed to protect the farmer and the consumer. See listings for individual agencies, bureaus, and services to locate best sources of information.

AIR FORCE, DEPARTMENT OF THE, The Pentagon, Washington DC 20330. Contact: Public Information Office. The Secretary of the Air Force is responsible for and has the authority to conduct all affairs of the Department of the Air Force, including those necessary or appropriate for the training, operations, administration, logistical support and maintenance, welfare, preparedness, and effectiveness of the Air Force, including research and development, and such other activities as may be prescribed by the President or the Secretary of Defense, as authorized by law.

ARMY, DEPARTMENT OF THE, The Pentagon, Washington DC 20310. Contact: Public Information Officer. The Department of the Army is responsible for providing support for national and international policy and the security of the United States by planning, directing, and reviewing the military and civil operations of the Department of the Army. This includes the organization, training, and equipping of land forces of the United States for the conduct of prompt and sustained combat operations on land in accordance with plans for national security.

ATOMIC ENERGY COMMISSION, Washington DC 20545. Contact: Office of Information Services. The Atomic Energy Commission is responsible for providing by national policy that the development, use, and control of atomic energy be directed to make the maximum contribution to the general welfare and to the common defense and security, and to promote world peace, increase the standard of living, and strengthen free competition in private enterprise.

CENSUS, BUREAU OF THE, U.S. Department of Commerce, Washington DC 20233. Contact: Public Information Officer. This agency conducts and reports results of censuses and surveys of U.S. population, housing, agriculture, business, manufacturing, mineral industries, construction, foreign trade and governments.

Statistical information is available for the U.S.; for each state, county, city, metropolitan area, and for portions of cities and metropolitan areas.

CENTRAL INTELLIGENCE AGENCY, Washington DC 20505. Contact: Assistant to the Director. To coordinate the intelligence activities of the Government departments and agencies in the interest of national security, the Agency, under the direction of the National Security Council, advises and makes recommendations to the National Security Council in matters concerning such intelligence activities of the Government departments and agencies as relate to national security; correlates and evaluates intelligence relating to the national security; and provides for the appropriate dissemination of such intelligence within the Government using, where appropriate, existing agencies and facilities; performs, for the benefit of the existing intelligence agencies, such additional services of common concern as the National Security Council determines can be more efficiently accomplished centrally; performs such other functions and duties related to intelligence affecting the national security as the National Security Council may from time to time direct.

CIVIL SERVICE COMMISSION, 1900 E Street, N.W., Washington DC 20415. Contact: Office of Public Affairs for general information. For employment information, contact Job Information Center at same address. As the central personnel agency of the U.S. Government, the Civil Service Commission administers the civil service merit system. It is responsible for competitive examinations for entry into the Federal civil service. This Commission issues examination announcements; administers programs of job classification, pay, training, retirement, health and life insurance, occupational health, veteran preference, promotion, equal employment opportunity, and appeals from certain personnel actions; compiles figures on the Federal work force by occupation, grade and salary, and geographical location; regulates assignment of personnel between Federal, state, and local governments and institutions of higher learning. Library at central office of Commission in Washington DC is outstanding location for research in personnel administration. Research must be accomplished at the library; material does not circulate.

COPYRIGHT OFFICE, Library of Congress, Washington DC 20559. Contact: Public Information Office. The business of the Copyright Office is directed by the Register of Copyrights, who is appointed by the Librarian of Congress. The office registers claims to copyright and provides copyright searches, information on copyright questions, and other related services.

DEFENSE, DEPARTMENT OF, The Pentagon, Washington DC 20301. Contact: Chief, Magazine and Book Branch, Office of the Assistant Secretary of Defense for Public Affairs. The primary function of this branch of the Defense Department is to assist magazine and book editors and writers in the gathering and preparation of material about the Department of Defense and its components. It provides or arranges technical advice, research help, and information about where such material may be obtained. Such information includes location of retired miltary records, illustrative materials, interviews, briefings, and any other assistance which is authorized and warranted.

ECONOMIC ANALYSIS, BUREAU OF, U.S. Department of Commerce, Washington DC 20230. Contact: Public Information Officer. This bureau provides basic economic measures of the national economy (such as the gross national product), current analysis of the economic situation and business outlook, and general economic research on the functioning of the economy.

ECONOMIC OPPORTUNITY, OFFICE OF, 1200 19th St., N.W., Washington DC 20506. Contact: Office of Public Affairs. The Office of Economic Opportunity was established to strengthen, supplement, and coordinate efforts to further the policy of the United States to "eliminate the paradox of poverty in the midst of plenty in this Nation by opening to everyone the opportunity for education and training, the opportunity to work, and the opportunity to live in decency and dignity." Does not purchase ms.

ENVIRONMENTAL PROTECTION AGENCY, Washington DC 20460. Available literature includes popular booklets and leaflets on water and air pollution, solid waste management, radiation and pesticides control as well as noise abatement and control. Literature available by contacting Public Inquiries Branch of Office of Public Affairs at above address. 16mm color films on pollution control and photographs of pollution problems available by contacting Communications Division of Office of Public Affairs at address above.

FARM CREDIT ADMINISTRATION, 485 L'Enfant Plaza, S.W., Washington DC 20578. Contact: Joel Greeneisen, Director of Information. This agency is responsible for "the supervision and coordination of activities of the farm credit system, which consists of the federal land banks and federal land bank associations, federal intermediate credit banks and production credit associations, and the banks for cooperatives. Writers should confine areas of questions to agricultural finance and farm credit."

FEDERAL COMMUNICATIONS COMMISSION, 1919 M St., N.W., Washington DC 20554. Contact: Director of Information. The responsibility of this agency is the regulation of all nongovernmental communications—radio, television, telegraph, telephone, cable, satellite, and two-way radio communications: aviation, marine and public safety, amateur and citizens band radio. The agency's Information Bulletin No. ED 1 is a list of all available publications.

FEDERAL RESERVE SYSTEM, BOARD OF GOVERNORS OF THE, 20th and Constitution Avenue, N.W., Washington DC 20551. Contact: Public Information Office. The Federal Reserve System is the central bank of the United States consisting of a seven-man Board of Governors in Washington, DC, and 12 Federal Reserve Banks, 24 Branches and one facility located throughout the country. It is the responsibility of the Federal Reserve System to contribute to the strength and vitality of the U.S. economy through the monetary policy it conducts and, through its bank supervisory and regulatory functions, to help maintain banking institutions stable and flexible enough to be responsive to the nation's domestic and international financial needs and objectives.

FEDERAL TRADE COMMISSION, Sixth St. and Pennsylvania Ave., N.W., Washington DC 20580. Contact: Office of Public Information. The purposes of the commission are "to protect the public (consumers and businessmen) against abuses caused by unfair competition and unfair and deceptive business practices; to guide and counsel businessmen, consumers, and federal, state, and local officials, promoting understanding among them and encouraging voluntary compliance with trade laws; to develop and administer a nationwide consumer education program. The Commission makes every effort to assist a researcher with reprints, copies of speeches, or other documents pertinent to his subject. We can be most helpful when a writer's questions are specific rather than general. Publications include *News Summary*, a biweekly roundup of news stories emanating from the Commission, and *Consumer Alert*, a monthly publication directed at editors, consumer columnists, and other 'multipliers' with a large consumer constituency."

FISH AND WILDLIFE SERVICE, Room 3242, Interior Building, Washington DC 20240. Contact: Office of Conservation Education. In meeting America's ecological crisis, this agency provides for and engages in hunting and fishing license sales statistics, Federal aid to fish and wildlife restoration, fish and wildlife research, duck stamp data, and migratory bird hunting regulations. Recreational use of National Wildlife Refuges and National Fish Hatcheries, river basin studies, pesticide research related to fish and wildlife, and rare and endangered wildlife are also under the jurisdiction of this agency.

FOOD AND DRUG ADMINISTRATION, Rockville MD 20852. Contact: Press Office. It is the responsibility of the Food and Drug Administration to "protect the health of American consumers by insuring that foods are safe, pure, and wholesome; that drugs are safe and effective; that cosmetics are harmless; that all these products are honestly and informatively labeled and packaged. FDA administers the Federal Food, Drug and Cosmetic Act; sections of the Public Health Service

Act dealing with biologic drugs, milk, shellfish and restaurant sanitation, and sanitary facilities for interstate travel; the Radiation Control for Health and Safety Act, the Tea Importation Act, and the Import Milk Act. FDA also enforces those parts of the Fair Packaging and Labeling Act which apply to foods, drugs, and other products within FDA jurisdiction. Press releases are issued on all major actions of the agency and there are individual publications on its varied programs. Requests should indicate specific subject of interest.

FOREST SERVICE, U.S. Department of Agriculture, 12th and Independence Ave., S.W., Washington DC 20250. Contact: George Castillo, Press Officer, Room 3229, South Agriculture Bldg., Washington DC 20250. The Forest Service is responsible for "management of the 187 million acres of lands in the national forest system; forestry research, and cooperation with state and private foresters. The agency works on multiple-use management programs, including forest recreation, timber management, range, watershed, wilderness, fire control, etc. Writers preparing material on specific subjects within the above areas may write the press officer."

GENERAL ACCOUNTING OFFICE, 441 G St., N.W., Washington DC 20548. Contact: Roland Sawyer, Information Officer. The U.S. General Accounting Office is a nonpolitical, nonpartisan agency of the Congress. Through audits, GAO examines the manner in which nearly all U.S. agencies and departments discharge their responsibilities—managerial, financial, and legal. GAO reports at all times its findings to the Congress and recommends ways in which the 12 executive departments and 60 agencies can carry out programs and operations more effectively, efficiently, and economically. It does so in some 250 public reports each year. These are summarized in a *Monthly List of GAO Reports* issued by the agency. GAO also makes special audits, surveys, and investigations at the request of congressional committees and members of the Congress and provides reports. Sometimes these reports are released to the public.

GENERAL SERVICES ADMINISTRATION, 19th and F Sts., N.W., Washington DC 20405. Contact: Public Information Officer. The Administrator of the General Services Administration directs 39,000 employees and a wide range of responsibilities including the construction and operation of Federal buildings, procurement and distribution of common-use supplies and the issuance of procurement regulations, operation of the national Archives and Federal Records Centers, utilization and disposal of excess and surplus property, management of stockpiles of strategic and critical materials for use in national emergencies, and transportation and communications management.

GEOLOGICAL SURVEY, Department of the Interior, Washington DC 20242. Contact: Information Officer. Principal Federal agency concerned with preparation of accurate maps of the physical feature of the country and providing of scientific information essential to development of the Nation's land, mineral, and water resources. Responsible for preparation of national topographic map series; for assessing the quantity and quality of surface and ground water resources; for supervision of mining and oil and gas development on Federal and Indian lands; and for fundamental research in topography, hydrology, geology, geochemistry, geophysics, and related sciences. Publishes numerous and wide variety of maps, charts, atlases, circulars, bulletins, professional papers, and special reports summarizing results of investigations. "Press releases, photo services, and nontechnical literature available for news media. Writers may obtain press releases, supporting photos, and nontechnical literature relating to our work and the earth sciences in general. We invite inquiries from writers as to how they may receive press releases and other nontechnical information."

GOVERNMENT PRINTING OFFICE, Public Documents Department, Washington DC 20402. This office publishes all the documents issued by the various agencies of the Federal Government. Any person may receive a free, biweekly list of selected Government publications by sending his request, with his name and address, to the above address. The December issue each year of the GPO's monthly catalog contains an annual index by subject of the publications issued that year. This issue varies in price. Free listings of Government publications on various subjects, such as Geology, Insects, Weather, or American History (write for subject list), are available on request. The *Monthly Catalog of U.S. Government Publications* is a comprehensive listing of all publications issued by the various departments and agencies of the U.S. Government each month; a yearly subscription is $12.50.

HEALTH, EDUCATION, AND WELFARE, DEPARTMENT OF, Room 1528 North, 330 Independence Ave., S.W., Washington DC 20201. Contact: Office of Public Affairs. Striving to "promote the general welfare," this Department is divided into 9 agencies. Some of its broad areas of responsibility are education of the disadvantaged and the handicapped; insuring the safety and truthful labeling of foods, drugs, and cosmetics; research into the causes and early prevention of illness; income support through Social Security and public assistance payments; combatting other conditions in life which prevent people from reaching their potential.

HOUSE OF REPRESENTATIVES, The Capitol, Washington DC 20515. Contact: Public Information Office.

HOUSING AND URBAN DEVELOPMENT, DEPARTMENT OF, Washington DC 20410. Contact: Office of Public Affairs. The special concerns of this agency include community planning and development; production and financing of housing; equal opportunity in housing; flood insurance, crime insurance, and riot reinsurance; and interstate land sales registration.

INDIAN AFFAIRS, BUREAU OF, Room 52, 1951 Constitution Ave., Washington DC 20242. Contact: Communications Director. Gives information on Indians and their relationship to the Federal Government, tribes when the tribe is specified, location of specific reservations, and ceremonials and celebrations of interest to visitors of all ages on these reservations.

INFORMATION AGENCY, Department of State, 1750 Pennsylvania Ave., N.W., Washington DC 20547. The role of the U.S. Information Agency is to support the foreign policy of the United States by explaining it to people in other countries, to build overseas understanding of United States institutions and culture, and to advise the U.S. Government on public opinion abroad and its implications for U.S. policy. The Agency also administers the Department of State's cultural and educational exchange program overseas. To achieve these purposes, USIA employs all the aboveboard techniques of modern mass communications: press, radio, film, television, libraries, exhibits, the arts, and personal contact by its officers overseas. Over 1,300 Agency officers in over 100 countries throughout the world serve as spokesmen for America. "The Agency's materials, with but few exceptions, are not available in the United States."

INTERIOR, DEPARTMENT OF THE, Interior Building, Washington DC 20240. Contact: Director of Communications. "As the nation's principal conservation agency, the Department of the Interior has basic responsibilities for water, fish, wildlife, mineral, land, park, and recreational resources, and Indian and territorial affairs." Since this Department is responsible for a variety of natural resource activities, requests for information can be met more rapidly and effectively if they are directed to the office most concerned with the specific subjects of interest. See listings for individual bureaus and agencies to locate the best source for information materials.

INTERNAL REVENUE SERVICE, 1111 Constitution Ave., N.W., Washington DC 20224. The Internal Revenue Service is decentralized. The headquarters organization functions to develop nationwide policies and programs for the administration of the internal revenue laws and to provide overall direction to the field organization.

INTERSTATE COMMERCE COMMISSION, 12th and Constitution Ave., Washington DC 20423. Contact: Public Information Office. This agency has the regulatory responsibility for interstate surface transportation by railroads, trucks, buses, barges, coastal shipping, oil pipe lines, express companies, freight forwarders, and transportation brokers. Jurisdiction includes rates, mergers, operating rights, and issuance of securities. "Free list of publications available."

JUSTICE, DEPARTMENT OF, Constitution Ave. and 10th St., N.W., Washington DC 20530. Contact: Public Information Officer. Under the Attorney General's office are these divisions: Antitrust, Civil, Civil Rights, Criminal, Internal Security, Lands and Natural Resources, Office of Legal Counsel, Office of Legislative Affairs, Tax, and Administrative. Other bureaus and agencies in the department include FBI, Law Enforcement Assistance Administration, Prisons, Narcotics and Dangerous Drugs, Office of Drug Abuse Law Enforcement, Community Relations Service, Immigration and Naturalization Service, Parole Board, Pardon Attorney, Bureau of Immigration Appeals, U.S. Attorneys, and U.S. Marshals.

LABOR, DEPARTMENT OF, 14th and Constitution Ave., N.W., Washington DC 20210. Contact: Office of Information, Publications, and Reports. The U.S. Department of Labor was established by Congress in 1913 "to foster, promote, and develop the welfare of the wage earners of the United States, to improve their working conditions, and to advance their opportunities for profitable employment." Areas of major concern include job training, counseling and placement, occupational safety and health, equal opportunity in employment, labor research and statistics, collective bargaining, unemployment insurance and workmen's compensation, apprenticeship, wages and working hours, and international labor.

LAND MANAGEMENT, BUREAU OF, U.S. Department of the Interior, Washington DC 20240. Office of Public Affairs provides information and photographs on the management of 451 million acres of National Resource Lands (Public Domain) mostly in 10 western states and Alaska; on forest, range, water, wildlife, and recreation resources; on resource uses including camping, hunting, fishing, hiking, rockhounding, off-road vehicle use; and on primitive, historic, natural and scenic areas.

LIBRARY OF CONGRESS, Washington DC 20540. The Library of Congress serves as a research arm of Congress and as the national library of the U.S. In direct services to individuals, the Library maintains reading rooms open to scholars for research on the premises. It provides bibliographic and reference information by mail only in cases where individuals have exhausted the library resources of their own region. Such reference information should be sought from the General Reference and Bibliography Division. A free list of Library of Congress publications can be obtained from the Central Services Division. Photoduplicates of materials in the collections (not subject to copyrights or other restrictions) are available at set fees from the Photoduplication Service.

MANAGEMENT AND BUDGET, OFFICE OF, Old Executive Office Building, Washington DC 20503. Contact: Information Office. The Office of Management and Budget was established to "provide the President with an institutional staff capability in the various areas of executive management—particularly in program evaluation and coordination, Government organization, information and management systems, and development of executive talent. The Office continues to perform the key function of assisting the President in the preparation and execution of the Federal budget."

MARINE CORPS, Headquarters Marine Corps, Washington D.C. 20380. Contact: Director of Information. "The Director of Information is the representative of the Commandant of the Marine Corps in all matters of public information and is responsible to the Commandant for the Public Affairs program of the Marine Corps."

MINES, BUREAU OF, 2611 Interior Building, Washington DC 20240. Contact: Chief, Office of Mineral Information. The Bureau is the U.S. Government's principal mineral technology agency, responsible for enforcing Federal health and safety standards in the nation's mines and for conducting a broad program of research on mineral resource conservation, environmental technology, and mineral industry occupational safety and health. The Bureau maintains a free-loan library of 16mm sound-and-color motion pictures, several of which illustrate mineral and other natural resources—such as parks and scenic attractions—of various states. It also publishes technical literature on mining, mineral, and recycling technology and, in some cases, may provide photos.

THE NATIONAL ACADEMY OF SCIENCES, NATIONAL ACADEMY OF ENGINEERING, NATIONAL RESEARCH COUNCIL, INSTITUTE OF MEDICINE, 2101 Constitution Ave., N.W., Washington DC 20418. Contact: Public Information Officer. "The National Academy of Sciences is a private organization which acts as an official, but independent, adviser to the Federal government in matters of science and technology. In 1964 a National Academy of Engineering was organized under the charter of the NAS to identify those who have made outstanding contributions to engineering theory and practice and bring their leadership to bear in dealing with engineering problems of national importance. The National Research Council, organized in 1916, serves as an operating agency for both Academies. Its work is conducted through boards and committees composed of thousands of U.S. scientists and engineers serving without compensation to foster the sound development of all aspects of science and engineering. In 1970, the NAS established the Institute of Medicine to enlist members of medical and other professions to address the larger problems of medicine and health care. For writers on assignment, the Academies often can be helpful by identifying authorities in various scientific disciplines and, sometimes, by providing state-of-the-art reports on broad scientific and environmental subjects prepared by the organization's committees."

NATIONAL AERONAUTICS AND SPACE ADMINISTRATION, Washington DC 20546. Contact: Public Information Office. In carrying out the policy of Congress that activities in space should be devoted to peaceful purposes for the benefit of all mankind, the principal statutory functions of NASA are these: conduct research for the solution of problems of flight within and outside the earth's atmosphere and develop, construct, test, and operate aeronautical and space vehicles; conduct activities required for the exploration of space with manned and unmanned vehicles; arrange for the most effective utilization of the scientific and engineering resources of the United States with other nations engaged in aeronautical and space activities for peaceful purposes; provide for the widest practicable and appropriate dissemination of information concerning NASA's activities and their results.

NATIONAL AIR AND SPACE MUSEUM, Smithsonian Institution, 900 Jefferson Dr. S.W., Washington DC 20560. Contact: Librarian, NASM. According to Public Law 722, the National Air Museum "shall memorialize the national development of aviation; collect, preserve, and display aeronautical equipment of historical interest and significance; serve as a repository for scientific equipment and data pertaining to the development of aviation; provide educational material for the historical study of aviation." The Museum's Historical Library has books, drawings, photographs, films, scrapbooks, and oral history tape records on all aspects of aviation.

NATIONAL ARCHIVES AND RECORDS SERVICE, Pennsylvania Ave. at 8th St., N.W., Washington DC 20408. Contact: Public Information Officer. The National Archives is the repository for the permanently valuable, official records of the United States Government. All treaties, laws, proclamations, executive orders, and bills are retained. It is also authorized to accept private papers. Administering all presidential libraries from Herbert Hoover to Lyndon Johnson and 15 Federal Records centers across the nation, the National Archives was created to serve the government, scholars, writers, and students. Among its holdings are sound recordings, motion pictures, still pictures, and some artifacts.

NATIONAL CREDIT UNION ADMINISTRATION, Washington DC 20456. Contact: Herman Nickerson, Jr., Administrator. The agency has the regulatory responsibility "to charter, supervise, examine, and insure up to $20,000 per individual shareholders' account some 13,000 Federal credit unions, and to provide such insurance to qualifying state-chartered credit unions requesting it. Reference information, photos, etc., are available on request. Available free on request are *Credit Union Statistics* (monthly), occasional *Research Reports*, and certain other publications dealing with the credit union industry. Also free to individuals is the *NCUA Annual Report*. The quarterly *NCUA Bulletin* is $1 a year from the Government Printing Office. Writers interested in the credit union story are offered assistance in developing their articles."

NATIONAL ENDOWMENT FOR THE ARTS, 806 15th St., N.W., Washington DC 20506. Contact: Office of Program Information. The National Endowment for the Arts is an independent agency of the federal government created to aid and encourage cultural resources in the United States through matching grants to nonprofit organizations and nonmatching grants to individuals of exceptional talent in the following areas: architecture and environmental arts, dance, education (does not include art history research projects which are handled through the National Endowment for the Humanities), expansion arts (community based, professionally directed arts programs), literature, museums, music, public media (film, television, radio), theatre, visual arts, and special projects. A separate program provides matching grants to official State arts agencies. The Endowment is advised by the 26 presidentially appointed members of the National Council on the Arts. Available materials: information brochure, latest annual report.

NATIONAL MARINE FISHERIES SERVICE, National Oceanic and Atmospheric Administration, Department of Commerce, Washington DC 20235. Contact: Public Affairs Office. Biological and technical research, market promotion programs, statistical facts on commercial fisheries, marine game fish, and economic studies are the responsibilities of this Service. It also administers the Fisheries Loan Fund and Commercial Fisheries Research and Development Act and manages the fur-seal resources of the Pribilof Islands, Alaska, and sections of the Marine Mammal Protection Act of 1972.

NATIONAL PARK SERVICE, Room 3043, Interior Building, Washington DC 20240. Contact: Office of Information. This agency of the Department of the Interior provides information on more than 290 areas of the National Park System which the Service administers. Information available includes park acreage and attendance statistics; data on camping, swimming, boating, mountain climbing, hiking, fishing, winter activities, wildlife research and management, history, archeology, nature walks, and scenic features. Photographs of many areas and activities are available.

NATIONAL SCIENCE FOUNDATION, 1800 G St., N.W., Washington DC 20550. Contact: Office of Public Affairs. The National Science Foundation has the broad general mission of fostering the progress of science and science education in the United States. A major activity of the foundation is providing support for scientific research. It also serves to strengthen education in the sciences to assure the continuing availability of well-trained scientists to meet the requirements of industry. It also leads a national program to improve scientific information services. "We can supply some photographic materials, printed information about some programs, and can refer writers to various experts for information related to specific fields of science. Because of staff limitations, we cannot perform detailed research projects for writers. We will be happy to receive and answer specific questions related to projects supported by the National Science Foundation, but cannot respond to encyclopedic questions, the answers to which can be found in a local community or university library."

NATIONAL TRANSPORTATION SAFETY BOARD, 800 Independence Ave., S.W., Washington DC 20591. The responsibility of this agency is "the investigation and cause determination of transportation accidents and the initiation of corrective measures. The Safety Board's work is about 80% in the field of U.S. civil aviation; the balance is in selected cases involving highways, railroad, pipeline, and marine accidents. We provide writers with accident reports, special studies involving transportation safety, and accident photos. The case history details of all cases available for review are in the Public Docket section of the Safety Board in Washington DC."

NATIONAL WEATHER SERVICE, National Oceanic and Atmospheric Administration, Department of Commerce, 8060 13th St., Silver Spring MD 20910. Contact:

Public Affairs Officer. This Service reports the weather of the United States and its possessions, provides weather forecasts to the general public, and issues warnings against tornadoes, hurricanes, floods, and other weather hazards. In addition, the Weather Service develops and furnishes specialized information which supports the needs of agricultural, aeronautical, maritime, space, and military operations. Its services are supported by a national network of surface and upper-air observing stations, satellite systems, communications, and computers. Some 300 Weather Service offices in cities across the land maintain close contact with the general public to ensure prompt and useful dissemination of weather information.

NAVY, DEPARTMENT OF THE, The Pentagon, Washington DC 20350. Contact: Office of Information. Under the direction, authority, and control of the Secretary of Defense, the Secretary of the Navy is responsible for the policies and control of the Department of the Navy, including its organization, administration, operation, and efficiency.

OCCUPATIONAL SAFETY AND HEALTH REVIEW COMMISSION, 1825 K St., N.W., Washington DC 20006. Contact: Linda Dodd, Director of Information. "The commission is an independent agency of the executive branch of the government. It functions as a court system by adjudicating contested cases under the Occupational Safety and Health Act of 1970. The Review Commission operates under the mandates of the Freedom of Information Act. Therefore, its files are open to anyone who wishes to inspect them. The Review Commission publishes press releases and a guide to our Rules of Procedure written in laymen's language. We prefer that requests for information be put in writing."

OUTDOOR RECREATION, BUREAU OF, Room 4024, Department of the Interior, Washington DC 20240. Contact: Office of Information. The Bureau serves as Federal coordinator of public and private outdoor recreation programs and activities; as administrator of the Land and Water Conservation Fund; and as conveyor of Federal surplus properties to state and local governments for public recreation use. It provides information on national and statewide outdoor recreation planning; assistance available from other government and private sources; the L&WCF's Federal recreation land acquisition and state grant programs; Congressionally authorized resource studies for potential Federal recreation areas including national trails, wild and scenic rivers, lakeshores and seashores; off-road vehicle regulations; the Federal recreation area fee system; and sources of technical assistance, literature and research on outdoor recreation.

PATENT OFFICE, U.S. Department of Commerce, Washington DC 20231. Contact: Public Information Officer. This office administers the patent and trademark laws, examines applications, and grants patents when applicants are entitled to them under the law. It also publishes and disseminates patent information, maintains search files of U.S. and foreign patents and a Patent Search Room for public use, and supplies copies of patents and official records to the public. This Office performs similar functions relating to trademarks.

POSTAL SERVICE, Washington DC 20260. Contact: Communications Department. The U.S. Postal Service operates the government's nationwide network of services and facilities to collect, process, dispatch, and deliver mail on a continuous basis.

RECLAMATION, BUREAU OF, Department of the Interior, Room 7642, Interior Building, Washington DC 20240. Contact: Information Officer. Information on Federal development of water and associated land resources in the 17 western states and Hawaii, including widespread recreational use of more than 100 reservoirs— fishing, water sports, boating, swimming; scenic tours and camping areas; sightseeing attractions at dams and related works; recreational development and plans on basin-wide pattern.

SALINE WATER, OFFICE OF, Room 5022, Department of the Interior, 18th and C Sts., N.W., Washington DC 20240. Contact: Information Officer. The Office of Saline Water conducts an information program for keeping the public informed and making technical data readily available to the desalting industry and other individuals or organizations interested in desalting as an alternative source of fresh water. Visitors are welcome at the OSW field installation at Wrightsville Beach NC.

SECRET SERVICE, 1800 G Street, N.W., Washington DC 20226. Contact: Office of Public Affairs. The United States Secret Service is the oldest general law enforcement agency of the Federal Government. Created in 1865 to suppress the counterfeiting of U.S. currency, the primary responsibility of the Secret Service is the protection of the President of the United States. In addition, the Secret Service is authorized to protect the immediate family of the President of the United States, the President-elect, the Vice President, the Vice President-elect, former Presidents and their wives, widows of former Presidents until their death or remarriage, children of former Presidents until they reach 16 years of age, major Presidential and Vice Presidential candidates, visiting heads of a foreign state or foreign government, and, at the direction of the President, other distinguished foreign visitors to the United States and official representatives of the United States performing special missions abroad. The Secret Service is also authorized to detect and arrest individuals violating federal laws relating to the coins, currency, obligations and securities of the United States and foreign governments (e.g., counterfeiting and forgery). Information regarding the history and responsibilities of the Secret Service is available from the Office of Public Affairs.

SENATE, The Capitol, Washington DC 20510.

SMALL BUSINESS ADMINISTRATION, 1441 L Street, N.W., Washington DC 20416. Contact: Director, Office of Public Information. The Small Business Administration has four main functions: to help finance small businesses through guaranteed bank loans, bank-participation, and direct government loans; to help small businesses sell their products or services to the Federal government; to promote improved management among small businesses through various publications and management training courses; to license and help finance privately owned small business investment companies that help finance small businesses.

SMITHSONIAN INSTITUTION, Washington DC 20560. Contact: Director of Public Affairs. The Smithsonian is at once a private and public organization with headquarters centered in Washington DC. It also operates major facilities across the country and overseas. Under its auspices museums, educational programs, scientific research organizations, and art galleries have been established and maintained. Funds are received annually from Congress and private sources.

SOCIAL SECURITY ADMINISTRATION, 6401 Security Blvd., Baltimore MD 21235. Contact: Russell R. Jalbert, Assistant Commissioner for Public Affairs. The Social Security Administration administers the Federal retirement, survivors, and disability insurance programs and health insurance for the aged (Medicare). Under the new amendments to the social security law, a new program of Supplemental Security Income for aged, blind, and disabled people will be administered by the Social Security Administration. It is responsible for studying problems of poverty, insecurity, and the health care needs of the aged as well as the contributions that can be made to their solution by social insurance and related programs. Among its duties is the responsibility to make recommendations as to the most effective methods of improving social and economic security through social insurance. "Publications on all social security programs are available free of charge from any social security office, or from the Office of Public Affairs at the Social Security Administration headquarters in Baltimore. Writers may also obtain statistical and historical information, news releases, photographs, biographies of top SSA officials, and other information materials from the Office of Public Affairs. We cannot provide information about any individual social security account or beneficiary. Under the law, all social security records are confidential."

SOIL CONSERVATION SERVICE, U.S. Department of Agriculture, Washington DC 20250. Contact: Hubert W. Kelley, Jr., Director, Information Division. The purpose of this agency is "to help landowners and operators to use their land and water in the best possible manner. This includes assistance with soil and water conservation measures on cornfields, cattle pastures, and construction sites. This also includes assistance to local groups with flood, drought, excessive sedimentation, or other water problems. Our main concerns are soil, water, plant, and wildlife conservation; flood prevention; better use of water by individuals and communities; improvement of rural communities through better use of natural resources. We are happy to work with writers interested in conservation and environmental issues. We have an extensive b&w photo file. The Soil Conservation Service magazine is not available for widespread distribution, but individual copies may be obtained on a limited basis. At irregular intervals, the agency puts out brochures containing technical information or providing information on aspects of SCS work. Individual copies are available."

SOUTHEASTERN POWER ADMINISTRATION, U.S. Department of the Interior, Samuel Elbert Bldg., Elberton GA 30635. Contact: Miss Mary George Bond, Administrative Officer. This agency is responsible for "transmission and disposition of electrical energy generated at reservoir projects under the control of the Corps of Engineers in the southeastern United States, and for water sources development. Will answer inquiries from writers regarding the bureau."

SOUTHWESTERN POWER ADMINISTRATION, P.O. Drawer 1619, Tulsa OK 74101. Contact: Wanda M. Cantrell, Public Information Specialist. "SWPA, a bureau of the Department of the Interior, is designated marketing agent for power and energy produced at 23 multi-purpose projects constructed and operated by the U.S. Corps of Engineers. Power is wholesaled at rates approved by the Federal Power Commission to cooperatives, municipalities, investor-owned utilities, and other government agencies in a six-state area. Specific requests for information are answered."

STANDARDS, NATIONAL BUREAU OF, U.S. Department of Commerce, Washington DC 20234. Contact: Special Assistant, Public Affairs. The National Bureau of Standards is the nation's central measurement laboratory. It is charged with maintaining and refining the standards and technology on which our measurement system is based. Because measurement is fundamental to all phases of scientific research, to all the operations of manufacturing and production, and to all the exchanges of goods and services in commerce, the research program of the National Bureau of Standards covers the entire spectrum of the physical and engineering sciences. NBS also provides the technical base for federal programs in environmental management, consumer protection, health, and other areas. Bureau publications are available through the Government Printing Office.

STATE, DEPARTMENT OF, Washington DC 20520. Contact: Bureau of Public Affairs, Office of Media Services. As principal foreign affairs agency, the Department of State, under the direction of the Secretary of State, is responsible for the conduct of U.S. foreign policy including U.S. relations and negotiations with other countries and with the United Nations and other international organizations. Publications, available from the Superintendent of Documents, concerning the activities and interests of this department include the annual report of the Secretary of State to the Congress, background notes on 164 foreign countries, historical volumes covering the years 1861-1948, and a weekly periodical. Films may be borrowed from the Office of Media Services, Room 4831, Department of State, Washington DC 20520.

SUPREME COURT, No. 1 First St., N.E., Washington DC 20543. Contact: Public Information Officer. This highest court in the land has the primary duty of deciding cases and controversies of national importance and of overseeing a uniform application of the laws throughout the nation. It also serves as the final arbitrator of the Constitution.

TELECOMMUNICATIONS POLICY, OFFICE OF, Executive Office of the President, Washington DC 20504. Contact: Brian P. Lamb, Assistant to the Director. The responsibilities of the office are three-fold: "the Director of the Office is the President's principal adviser on electronic communications policy; the Office develops the executive branch positions and speaks for the administration on national communications matters as a partner in policy discussion with Congress, the FCC, the industry, and the public; the Office formulates new policies and coordinates operations for the Federal Government's own extensive use of electronic communications. The Office has occasional reports, news releases, speeches, and staff research papers on a variety of communications topics."

TERRITORIAL AFFAIRS, OFFICE OF, C St. between 18th and 19th, N.W., Washington DC 20240. Contact: Deputy Assistant Secretary for Territorial Affairs. Concerned with travel, sightseeing, recreation, fishing, water sports, and boating in the Virgin Islands, Guam, Trust Territory of Pacific Islands, and American Samoa.

TRANSPORTATION, DEPARTMENT OF, 400 Seventh St., S.W., Washington DC 20590. Contact: Public Information Officer. The Department of Transportation purposes are "to develop national transportation policies and programs conducive to the provision of fast, safe, efficient, and convenient transportation at the lowest cost consistent therewith and with other national objectives, including the efficient utilization and conservation of the nation's resources; to provide general leadership in identification and solution of transportation problems; to develop and recommend to the President and the Congress for approval national transportation policies and programs to accomplish these objectives with full and appropriate consideration of the needs of the public, users, carriers, industry, labor, and the national defense."

TREASURY DEPARTMENT, Room 2313, 15th St. and Pennsylvania Ave., N.W., Washington DC 20220. Contact: Public Information Office. The Department was established to superintend and manage the national finances. The Secretary of the Treasury is charged with the preparation of plans for the improvement and management of the revenue and the support of the public credit. He prescribes the forms for keeping and rendering all manner of public accounts and for the making of returns. He may grant, subject to the limitations of the amended act, all warrants for moneys to be issued from the Treasury pursuant to legal appropriations, and to furnish information, upon request, to either or both branches of Congress on any matter referred to him or pertaining to his office. The Treasury Department now embraces a score or more of diversified bureaus, divisions, and offices, and its charge includes the coinage and printing of money.

UNITED NATIONS EDUCATIONAL, SCIENTIFIC AND CULTURAL ORGANIZATION, UNESCO, Office for Liaison with the United Nations, Room 2201, United Nations Building, New York NY 10017. Contact: Information Officer. The purpose of the Organization, as defined in its Constitution, is "to contribute to peace and security by promoting collaboration among the nations through education, science, and culture in order to further universal respect for justice, for the rule of law, and for the human rights and fundamental freedoms which are affirmed for the peoples of the world, without distinction of race, sex, language or religion by the Charter of the United Nations." According to the Organization, "We always welcome enquiries from writers, providing they have a definite assignment. Due, however, to the limitation of staff, we cannot help those working on spec, however much we would like to." A list of Unesco publications is available from UNIPUB, Box 433, New York NY 10016. *Introduction to Unesco* is available free of charge.

VETERANS ADMINISTRATION, 810 Vermont Ave., N.W., Washington DC 20420. Contact: Public Information (063). The Veterans Administration administers laws authorizing benefits principally for former members and certain dependents of former members of the Armed Forces. The VA also administers certain limited benefits authorized by law to individuals currently on active duty and to certain dependent wives and children. Major VA programs include education and training, compensation, pension, loan guaranty, and insurance. The VA medical system currently includes 170 hospitals. Publications include *Summary of Benefits for Veterans and Servicemen with Service since Jan. 31, 1955 and Their Dependents* (VA mailing symbol 232), *Federal Benefits for Veterans and Dependents* (send 20¢ to Superintendent of Documents, Washington DC 20420), and *VA: What It Is, Was, and Does* (VA mailing symbol 232). Specialized pamphlets are also available.

WHITE HOUSE OFFICE, 1600 Pennsylvania Ave., N.W., Washington DC 20500. Contact: Public Information Officer. The staff of the White House Office maintains communications with the Congress, the heads of the executive departments and agencies, the press and other information media, and the general public. The various assistants to the President are personal aids who assist the Chief Executive in such matters as he may direct.

WOMEN'S BUREAU, Employment Standards Administration, U.S. Department of Labor, Washington DC 20210. Contact: Chief, Information and Publications Division. The functions of the Women's Bureau are primarily educational and promotional in nature. The Bureau seeks to improve the economic and legal status of women by eliminating discrimination in employment against them, improving their employability, and increasing job opportunities for them. It also promotes legislation to improve their wages and working conditions. The Bureau prepares and distributes publications, holds conferences, provides advisory services, and serves as a clearinghouse for information on women's participation in the labor force and on their economic and legal status.

Greeting Card Publishers

Greeting card companies have specialized editorial needs, just as magazines and publishing houses do, so the successful greeting card writer must learn what kinds of cards each company buys. Many companies produce only a few kinds of cards; even big companies which produce all the standard kinds of cards may have staff writers to prepare some categories, so that they buy only a few kinds from freelance writers.

The listings below give the publishers' requirements for verse, gags, or other product ideas. Artwork requirements are also given for companies that are interested in buying a complete card from a greeting card specialist who can supply both art and idea.

To submit conventional greeting card material, type or neatly print your verses on either 4x6 or 3x5 slips of paper or file cards. For humorous or studio card ideas, either use file cards or fold sheets of paper into card dummies about the size and shape of an actual card. Neatly print or type your idea on the dummy as it would appear on the finished card. Put your name and address on the back of each dummy or card, along with a code number of some type, such as 1, 2, 3, etc. The code number makes it easier for the editor to refer to your idea when writing to you, and also helps you in keeping records. Always keep a file card of each idea. On the back of each file card, keep a record of where and when the idea was submitted. Submit from 10 to 15 ideas at a time (this makes up a "batch"); be sure to include a stamped, self-addressed return envelope. Keep the file cards for each batch together until the ideas (those rejected) come back. For ideas you write that use attachments, try to get the actual attachment and put it on your dummy; if you cannot, suggest the attachment. For mechanical card ideas, you must make a workable mechanical dummy. Most companies will pay more for attachment and mechanical card ideas.

A.B.M. CORP., 1137 East Janis, Carson CA 90746. Editor: John H. Gilbert. Buys all rights. Submit seasonal material 4 months in advance. Reports in 2 weeks. May hold ideas for 1 month. Enclose S.A.S.E. for return of submissions.
Conventional, Informal, Soft Line, Sensitivity, and Humorous: "All seasons and occasions, and animal (stuffed) cards." Pays $5 to $50.
Promotions: "Interested in promotion ideas for our Panda Bear cards."

AFRICA CARD CO., INC., 303 W. 42nd St., New York NY 10036. Editor: Vince Jordan. Buys all rights. Pays on acceptance. Send for list of current needs. Submit seasonal material in March. Sometimes holds material for 2 weeks. Enclose S.A.S.E. for return of submissions.

Inspirational, Informal, Soft Line and Promotions: Birthday cards for children. Pays $15 for card ideas.

AMBERLEY GREETING CARD CO., 1738 Tennessee Ave., Cincinnati OH 45229. Editor: Herb Crown. Buys all rights. Send for list of current needs. Seasonal material (Christmas and Valentine's Day only) is bought all year long. Submit ideas on regular 3x5 cards. "We always take a closer look if artwork [a rough sketch on a separate sheet of paper that shows how the card would appear] is submitted with the gag. It gives us a better idea of what the writer has in mind." Do not send conventional cards. Reports in 3 to 4 weeks. May hold ideas for approximately 1 week. Enclose S.A.S.E. for return of submissions.
Humorous, Studio and Promotions: Buys all kinds of studio and humorous everyday cards, "including relative and odd captions such as promotion, apology, etc. General studio is still the best selling caption. We never get enough. We look for belly laugh humor, not cute. All types of risque are accepted. No ideas with attachments. We prefer short and snappy ideas." Would prefer not to see "friendship titles, Easter, Mother's Day, and Father's Day ideas." Pays $10 to $25. Occasionally buys promotion ideas. Payment negotiable, "depending entirely upon our need, the quantity, and work involved."
Other Product Lines: Buys "motto ideas with me-to-you thoughts." Pay is $10 a motto. Also buys ideas for bumper stickers.

AMERICAN GREETINGS CORPORATION, 10500 American Rd., Cleveland OH 44144. Managing Editor: Frank Merrill. Buys all greeting card rights. Pays on acceptance. Send seasonal material "any time." Submit on 3x5 cards "or dummies if they are professional." Do not send conventional verse, as "our staff handles all of that," and don't send juvenile book mss. Reports in 4 to 6 weeks. Enclose S.A.S.E. for return of submissions.
Sensitivity, Humorous, and Promotions: Publishes all kinds of everyday cards. "We're billed as the Fresh Idea Company, and we're always interested in new, fresh approaches (yet salable) to anything we make . . . or don't make. Idea people will do best here." Pay is $20 and up for humorous material. Buys greeting card promotion ideas, "especially humorous." Must be "something that looks, sounds, or feels different from the usual card in the racks. From a card manufacturer's viewpoint, it is something that will bring him plus business. We do not want to see reworks of other companies' promotions." Some recent promotions include Teddy Bears, Urchins, Soft Touch books. Payment open.
Studio: Send studio ideas to Jack Clements, Editor. Must be of professional quality. Not a large freelance market, mostly staff-written material, but does purchase a limited number of highly original studio ideas. "We do like to keep the door open for interesting, unusual material." Pay is $25 and up for studio ideas.
Other Product Lines: "Always in the market for new product ideas (figurines, puzzles, calendars, books, games, etc.). Also in the market for strong ideas for $1 and $2 greeting books. Generally have a 'from-me-to-you' message, i.e., missing you, love you, happy birthday, etc. Many of a friendship nature, paying a compliment to a friend or offering inspiration. Special books for holiday greetings. Copy should be simple and charming. Suggests study books available in department stores, etc. Rates vary with the idea, but normally run between $100 to $250." Send ideas to Frank Merrill.

J. & L. BARDINA, 25-34B 14th St., Long Island City NY 11102. Editor: Ligia Bardina. Buys all rights. Submit seasonal and occasional material 1 year in advance. Artists should "send sample to see if style blends with the line of cards we have." Does not want to see humorous studio cards. Reports in 8 weeks. May hold ideas for approximately 2 weeks. Enclose S.A.S.E. for return of submissions.
Soft Line, Sensitivity, Humorous, and Juvenile: Everyday cards published include birthday, anniversary, get well, bon voyage, congratulations, wedding, baby birth, friendship. Needs contemporary animal and children designs with soft look. "Payment varies, depending on idea, etc."

BARKER GREETING CARDS, Box 9010, Cincinnati OH 45209. Editor: George Wilson. Buys all rights. Pays on acceptance. Send for list of current needs. Buys Christmas, Halloween, and Thanksgiving ideas in May and June; Valentine's Day,

St. Patrick's Day, and Easter in September and October; Mother's Day, Father's Day, and Graduation in December and January. Reports in 2 weeks. Enclose S.A.S.E. for return of submissions.

Soft Line and Studio: "Complete line of studio cards for all occasions and seasons. Want fresh ideas with general sendability and a me-to-you message. Some risques if they are funny. For the soft line, we need ideas with general sendability and a me-to-you message. Get wells and birthday ideas should be identifiable on the outside of the card. Always need good sendable get well cards. Will buy a good Mother's Day or Father's Day card any time. Age gags have a chance only if very very funny. Brief verse is best." Pays $20 "beginner's rate. Goes up when you show you are a consistent contributor. Extra for ideas with mechanicals or new attachments."

Other Product Lines: "Always glad to look at promotions and non-greeting card promotions, too." Also buys ideas for lines other than greeting cards—"make me an offer!"

BERLINER & McGINNIS, 109 N. Pine St., Nevada City CA 95959. Editor: Malcolm Nielsen. Buys all rights. Pays on publication. Write for specifications sheet. Submit Christmas material any time. "Initial offering should be in the rough. Will not publish risque or 'cute' art." Reports in 2 weeks. Enclose S.A.S.E.

Conventional, Inspirational, and Studio: Interested in submissions from artists. Publishes everyday cards in a "very specialized series using verse from Shakespeare and a series of cards imprinted with college names. Our major line is Christmas. We avoid the Christmas cliches and attempt to publish offbeat type of art. We can use either finished art which we will separate or can use the artist's separations. Our studio lines are a complete series with a central theme for the series. We do not try to compete in the broad studio line, but only in specialized areas. We do not purchase verse alone, but only complete card ideas, including verse and art." Payment for art on "royalty basis, depending on the form in which it is submitted."

Other Product Lines: Bookplates, note papers, stationery. Payment negotiated.

BRILLIANT ENTERPRISES, P.O. Box 14285, San Francisco CA 94114. Editor: Ashleigh Brilliant. Buys all rights. Will send a catalog and sample set for $1. Submit seasonal material any time. "Submit words and art in black on 5½x3¼ horizontal thin white paper. Regular bond okay, but no card or cardboard." Does not want to see "topical references, subjects limited to American culture, or puns." Reports "usually in 10 days." Enclose S.A.S.E. for return of submissions.

Other Product Lines: Postcards. "All our cards are everyday cards in the sense that they are not intended only for specific seasons, holidays, or occasions." Messages should be "of a highly original nature, emphasizing subtlety, simplicity, insight, wit, profundity, beauty, and felicity of expression. Accompanying art should be in the nature of oblique commentary or decoration rather than direct illustration. Messages should be of universal appeal, capable of being appreciated by all types of people and of being easily translated into other languages." Limit of 17 words per card. Pays $25 for "complete ready-to-print word and picture design."

SIDNEY J. BURGOYNE AND SONS, INC., 2120 W. Allegheny Ave., Philadelphia PA 19132. Enclose S.A.S.E. for return of submissions.

Artwork: Conventional. "Christmas only. No verse. Company uses 4-color process, embossing, gold lead stamping, die-cutting, tipping in reproductive processes. Quote price for outright purchase when submitting designs."

BUZZA, 1500 S. Anaheim Blvd., Anaheim CA 92803. Freelance writing for humor and studio greeting cards, seasonal and everyday. Dick Weger, Art Director.

COLOURPICTURE PUBLISHING CO., 76 Atherton St., Boston MA 02130. Editor: O.D. Freedgood. Buys all rights. Reports in 1 month. Enclose S.A.S.E.

Studio: Publishes studio and photographic cards. "Any kind of good, contemporary idea. Our line is for the traveling and souvenir business. Therefore, cards should be slanted for a traveler or tourist sending cards back home." Pays $25.

COMPAC INDUSTRIES, INC., P.O. Box 29663, Atlanta GA 30329. Editor: B.T. Corbin. Buys all rights. Buys seasonal material any time. "We are not responsible for unsolicited work unless accompanied by S.A.S.E. and release." May hold ideas

for approximately 2 weeks. Enclose S.A.S.E. for return of submissions.
Other Product Lines: Humorous greeting booklets. "Imagine a 24-page booklet, animated by art or photos and humorous. The punchline is on the last page. Customer will be flipping pages to get motion. The message appears on the last page. For example, two mountain climbers are depicted climbing. The rope begins to break. The last page says 'Bon Voyage!' " Does not want to see verse or sensitivity themes. Prefers 1 or 2 lines. Interested in ideas for promotions and in "any unusual new stationery and/or gift-oriented themes." Pays minimum $5.

CREATIVE SOUL DESIGN STUDIO, INC., P.O. Box 29101, Cincinnati OH 45229. Editor: Yvette L. Dalton. Buys all rights. Reads material for Christmas and photograph line in September. Does not want to see anything risque. Reports in 1 month. May hold ideas for 6 weeks. Enclose S.A.S.E. for return of submissions.
Soft Line and Studio: "People humor or sentiments leaning toward black ethnic." For example, a recent card has a picture of a black astronaut and the verse "Happy Birthday" on the outside. Inside is the sentiment: "To the swingingest soul in the solar system." Interested in material for a Christmas and photograph line. Verse should be "short but sweet." Interested in ideas for promotions. Pays $25 to $45.

FEITH, STRAUSS & ASSOCIATES, INC., 530 Fort Washington Ave., New York NY 10033. Editor: Steven R. Strauss. Buys all rights. Pays on acceptance. "No seasonals or occasionals." Reports in 1 to 3 weeks. Sometimes holds material for 2 or 3 weeks. Enclose S.A.S.E. for return of submissions.
Soft Line: "We are seeking material for our new expanded line of friendship cards called Flubbies. We're interested in short, whimsical copy based on birthday, get well, thank you, love, friendship, and 'I miss you' lines." For example, recent sentiments include "Happy birthday! Remember it's not the present that counts—it's the thought . . . I'm thinking . . . I'm thinking!" Wants "no harsh lines, verses, sex lines. No artwork. No ideas for promotions." Pays $10.

D. FORER AND CO., INC., 18 West 18th St., New York NY 10011. Editor: B. Schaeffer. Buys all rights. Pays on acceptance. Sometimes holds material for up to 4 weeks. Enclose S.A.S.E. for return of submissions.
Informal and Humorous: "Whimsical and warm cards; all everyday; some Christmas (short lines, not verse). No poetry. No conventional verse. The shorter the better. Submissions must have release as to originality of idea." Pays $15 and up for card ideas.

FRAN MAR GREETING CARDS, LTD., 630 S. Columbus Ave., Mt. Vernon NY 10550. Editor: Stan Cohen. Buys all rights. Write for list of current needs. Submit seasonal material (Valentine's Day, Mother's Day, Father's Day) any time. Reports in 2 to 10 days. Enclose S.A.S.E. for return of submissions.
Informal, Studio, and Humorous: All copy should be on the cute side. It should be short and whimsical, and not verse. It should appeal to the teen and college market primarily—no juvenile copy. Publishes birthday, get well, anniversary, friendship cards, and special titles (engagement, travel, general, goodbye, etc.). "We have an image (Moppets) and try to maintain that image with appropriate copy. We do not use topical or dramatic copy. We rely on soft and sensitive copy. We prefer copy that does not rhyme—short prose of no more than 4 lines." Pays $10 to $25 for humorous and sensitivity ideas.
Other Product Lines: Plaques and posters. "Ideas for plaques should be short and strictly friendship." Pays $10 to $15 for plaque ideas.

FRAVESSI-LAMONT, INC., Edison Place, Springfield NJ 07081. Enclose S.A.S.E. for return of submissions.
Humorous: A few humorous and sentimental verses bought for everyday. Pays $2.50 to $5.

FREEDOM GREETINGS, Box 6274, Philadelphia PA 19136. Editor: Jerome Wolk. Buys all rights. Pays on acceptance. Send for list of current needs. Submit seasonal ideas 1 year ahead of holiday. Enclose S.A.S.E. for return of submissions.
Conventional, Inspirational, Soft Line, Sensitivity, and Humorous: All categories, all

holidays. Prefer 8 lines (2 and 4 line rhyme and 6 and 8 line rhyme). Interested in inspirational birthday and free poetry. Pays $1 a line.

GALLANT GREETINGS CORP., 2725 W. Fullerton, Chicago IL 60647. Editor: Bob Roth. Buys all rights. Submit on 3x5 cards. "No more than 12 to 15 ideas at a time, please." Uses Christmas and Valentine's Day seasonals. Reports in 1 week. Enclose S.A.S.E. for return of submissions.
Sensitivity and Studio: Wants "sensitivity type for our 'Brief Encounter' line and snappy studios, some risques, for our 'Gi Gi' and 'Can Can' series." Pays $12 to $20.

GEMINI RISING, INC., 7 W. 57th St., New York NY 10019. Editor: Ed Weiss. Buys all rights. Reports immediately. Enclose S.A.S.E. for return of submissions.
Other Product Lines: Buys poster ideas. "Posters in any form." Likes sensitivity, poetry and philosophy type ideas. Pays $150 minimum per poster for original artwork.

GIBSON GREETING CARDS, INC., 2100 Section Road, Cincinnati OH 45237. Buys exclusive rights. Pays on acceptance. Address Editor. Reports within 10 days. Enclose S.A.S.E. for return of submissions.
Humorous, Studio, and General: Interested in outstanding studio, humorous, and general material. Prices increase when accompanied with unusual design and/or mechanical ideas such as trick folds, die cuts, shapes, or attachments and little or no reworking is required. Conventional verse, $3 per line. "Cutes" and "soft" types, $20 per idea. Humorous, $25. Studio, $30. Small books, $100. Currently overstocked on book mss.

GREENBRIAR PAPERS, Box 473, Spring Green WI 53588. Editor: Frank Leach. Buys all rights. Reports in 2 weeks. May hold ideas for 3 weeks. Enclose S.A.S.E. for return of submissions.
Inspirational, Sensitivity, and Other Product Lines: "Inspirational verse, Christmas verse. Artwork for notes and cards for one- to three-color printing." Pays $10 minimum.

HALLMARK CARDS, INC., Contemporary Department, 25th & McGee, Kansas City MO 64141. Managing Editor: Kent DeVore. Buys all rights. "Needs lists are included with ideas returned. Seasonal ideas may be submitted any time during the year." Deadlines are January 15 for St. Valentine's Day; March 15 for St. Patrick's Day, April Fool's, and Easter; April 15 for Mother's Day, Father's Day, and Graduation; August 15 for Halloween; September 15 for Thanksgiving; October 15 for Hanukkah and Christmas; and November 15 for New Year's Day. Does not want to see finished artwork or poetic verse sentiments. Puns and slams are currently being overworked by freelancers submitting to Hallmark. Submit on 4x9 folded dummies or typed note cards. "Hallmark is currently reading all contemporary (studio) card ideas from the freelance market. We are unable to read other freelance submissions, except those received from writers working on assignment. Those freelancers who are regularly publishing their greeting card verse and who wish to receive assignments from us are welcome to acquaint us with their experience by letter." Reports in 1 to 3 weeks. Enclose S.A.S.E. for return of submissions.
Studio: "Good, funny, sendable gags with strong 'me-to-you' sending situations" for seasonal and everyday lines. Wants "less explicitly risque ideas, less insulting humor, and more complimentary cards." Pays $50 for studio ideas.
Other Product Lines: "One-line slogan-mottos for posters, buttons, bumper stickers, calendar gags, etc., on love, graffiti, and ecology themes. Payment is usually between $25 and $50."

HAMBLY STUDIOS, 1093 Memorex Dr., Santa Clara CA 95050. Editor: Harry Hambly. Buys all rights. Submit seasonal and occasional ideas "any time." Enclose S.A.S.E. for return of submissions.
Inspirational, Informal, Soft Line, Sensitivity, Studio, and Artwork: Interested in "words to live by; hope, love, life." For example, a sentiment like "It isn't what you do but how you do it that counts." No "sweet, ordinary" sentiments. Also buys artwork. Pay "depends on the material."

HAPPINESS, INC., P.O. Box 434, 300 Happiness Ln., Kingman KS 67068. Buys all rights. Will send a current needs list to a writer on request. Send ideas to Bob Redmon, President. Submit ideas "on 3x5 index cards only." Reports in 3 weeks. Enclose S.A.S.E. for return of submissions.
Informal, Soft Line, Studio, Sensitivity: "We are presently buying for a full-line of 'soft touch' type of greeting card line. We manufacture a standard studio line and have a Caressable line of cute little boys and girls. In our Caressable line, we use cute, subtle humor—nothing harsh. We are always in need of birthday and get well ideas in our studio and Caressable lines. All occasion and friendship ideas seem to be overworked. Pays $15 per idea.

HB PRODUCTIONS, 5780 Federal St., Detroit MI 48209. Editor: Charles H. Hightower. Department Editors: Roy Stewart, Production; U. Burney, Creative. Buys all rights. Will send current needs list to a writer on request. Buys Christmas, Valentine's Day, and Mother's Day seasonals. Reports "at least 6 months in advance of the season." May hold material for 1 month. Enclose S.A.S.E. for return of submissions.
Conventional: "Our cards are geared to a specific market—black Americans across the country. We are currently seeking sentiments for sympathy, Valentine's Day, Christmas, Mother's Day, and baby congratulations. Verse should be normal length for greeting cards." Not interested in ideas for promotions. Pays $10 to $40.

HEBREW PUBLISHING COMPANY, 79 Delancey St., New York NY 10002. Editor: Mr. Barish. Enclose S.A.S.E. for return of submissions.
Conventional and Humorous: "Humorous Jewish American cards for everyday occasions." Length: 4 to 6 lines. Pays $5 to $10.

HOLIDAY PUBLISHING CO., INC., 9947 Franklin Ave., Franklin Park IL 60131. Editor: Cel Smith. Buys all rights. Reports in 10 days. Enclose S.A.S.E. for return of submissions.
Conventional: Publishes baby gift and shower cards. Pays $12 for 4-line verse, $35 for art.

JOLI GREETING CARD CO., 220 W. Chestnut St., Chicago IL 60610. Editor: Lori Jay. Art Director: Herb Ruud. Buys all rights. Will send current needs list to a writer on request. Submit Christmas and Valentine's Day seasonals at any time. Reports in 2 weeks. Enclose S.A.S.E. for return of submissions.
Humorous, Studio: Wants ideas for "Pudgies" and "Nostalgia" lines. Birthday, friendship, get well, anniversary, travel, risque. Prefers short, snappy punch lines. "Always looking for new ideas, new concepts."Does not want to see sensitivity ideas. Pays $25.

KEEP 'N TOUCH. P.O. Box 912, Framingham MA 01701. Editor: Ruth Fishel. Buys all rights. Will send a current needs list to a writer on request if S.A.S.E. is enclosed. "Ideas most easily read when typed on 3x5 file cards, or roughed out on studio card size." Submit seasonal material 6 to 8 months in advance. Reports in 1 month. Sometimes holds material for 2 months. Enclose S.A.S.E. for return of submissions.
Studio Humorous, Soft Line, Sensitivity: Welcomes punch lines for sophisticated, humorous contemporary greeting cards with or without artwork. Ideas must be original. All cards are clean humor. No off-color. Does not use any slam cards. Aims for the sophisticated, offbeat, and the unusual card that says something nice in a humorous vein. Also has collegiate line. Pays $12 for ideas, $15 for art, and $25 and up for complete card. "We are now interested in sensitive photography in full color."

LAKESHORE ARTISANS, P.O. Box 160, Belgium WI 53004. Editor: Earl Sherwan. "All rights are preferred, but we will purchase second rights if previous use is defined and we see no conflict in our use. Pays on acceptance. Advance query is essential and should contain detailed description of material available. We will not necessarily respond to queries unless they evoke further interest on our part." Will furnish sample notes at 10¢ per sample. Reports in 2 weeks. Enclose S.A.S.E. for return of submissions.

Photos: "Our product line is highly specialized, consisting of correspondence notes featuring dogs, cats, and wildlife in that order of current importance. We need sharp, extremely detailed, professional quality photos of dogs and cats for use in preparing original art. We do not reproduce the photos per se, but reproduce resulting art for both notes and for framing size prints. Expert knowledge of official conformation standards for these animals is a prerequisite. While candid shots are preferred, these must purposefully and obviously illustrate excellent conformation to the individual breed standard. In addition, expressions should be appealing, 'adorable.' 35mm color slides may show the entire animal, but the head is all important because most of our art involves only the head. 8x10 b&w prints must be head-only shots, unretouched. All subjects must be sharply delineated with no detail lost to shadow or background interference. Use of head only does not apply to wildlife shots which are desired only in the form of 35mm color slides. Mammals and birds preferably are in natural environmental situations and settings. Consumers use our notes for correspondence, everyday cards, and for greeting cards as well. Christmas card versions of the notes have been published in the past, but discontinued. We may consider reviving this idea if new and unusual treatments are suggested in query form." Pays $5 to $7.50. "Might pay considerably higher for exceptional material."

LOOART PRESS, INC., Box 2559, Colorado Springs CO 80901. Art Director: Joe Russo. Buys all rights and retains art. Write Art Director for detailed specifications. Submit material in March, June, September. Reports in 2 weeks. Enclose S.A.S.E. for return of submissions.
Conventional, Inspirational, Humorous, and Other Product Lines: Christmas cards only. "Highly professional finished art, both gently humorous and general and/or religious interpretations of the Christmas theme." Pays $250 for art.

LUCAS STUDIO GREETINGS, Stevens Building #1716, 17 N. State St., Chicago IL 60602. Pays fee and royalty. Send for list of current needs. Submit seasonal material 90 days in advance. Submit ideas typed on 3x5 cards. No risque. Reports on publication. May hold ideas for 2 to 3 weeks. Enclose S.A.S.E. for return of submissions.
Soft Line, Sensitivity, Humorous, and Studio: Publishes birthday and get well, everyday cards. "We design and publish black ethnic greeting cards. However, ideas do not have to reflect such. Art design, on the other hand, should include black or white or both" Pays $10 to $15 for verse and humorous ideas. Pays $50 for art.

MEXICARD DESIGNERS, 1201 Hoffman Ave., Suite 6, Long Beach CA 90813. Editors: Raymond Sanchez and Augustine Berthe. Buys all rights. Will send current needs list to a writer on request. Reports in 4 weeks. Enclose S.A.S.E. for return of submissions.
Humorous and Studio: "Humorous. Verses only; we have art department." Buys birthday, general, friendship, anniversary, and get well cards. "Payment negotiable on imagination and good taste of verse"; pays $10 to $25.

MILLEN CARDS, INC., 230-03 Linden Blvd., Jamaica NY 11411. Editor: Stanley B. Millner. Pays 30 days after acceptance. May hold ideas for approximately 2 weeks. Enclose S.A.S.E. for return of submissions.
Seasonal and Studio: Ideas for Jewish everyday studios, birthdays, anniversaries, get wells. Pays $25.

MILLER DESIGNS, 336 Sabin Pl., River Vale NJ 07675. Buys all rights. Submit Christmas ideas "any time." Enclose S.A.S.E. for return of submissions.
Conventional, Inspirational, Informal, Sensitivity, and Other Product Lines: Interested in all everyday or special sentiment cards. Expecially interested in "birthday, anniversary, get well, and friendship cards." Pay "open."

MISTER B. GREETING CARD CO., 3500 N.W. 52nd Street, Miami FL 33142. Editor: Alvin Barker. Buys all rights. Pays on acceptance. Submit seasonal material any time. Does not want to see "belated birthday, 'why don't you write?,' and long verses over 4 lines." Reports in 3 to 4 weeks. Enclose S.A.S.E. for return of submissions.

Conventional, Inspirational, Informal, Humorous, and Studio: "We are always in the market for greeting card verses and ideas, either humorous, novelty, mechanical or anything above the average." Also buys short verses for sentimental cards. Pays highest prices for good usable ideas. Submit rough art. "Suggested copy would be helpful." Pays $10 to $100.

Other Product Lines: "Cute mottos, plaques, and inspirational mottos. Notes and stationery, thank you; invitations and announcements."

MODERNE CARD CO., INC., 3855 Lincoln, Chicago IL 60613. Editor: W.D. Harris. Buys all rights. Reports in 1 week. Enclose S.A.S.E. for return of submissions.
Soft Line, Sensitivity, and Studio: Publishes contemporary cards only. Pays $10 to $12.

NORCROSS INC., 244 Madison Ave., New York NY 10016. Buys all rights. Will send current needs list to a writer on request. Schedule for submission of seasonals: "Submit Halloween, Thanksgiving and Christmas material from February through June; Valentine and St. Patrick's, June through August; Easter and Graduation, September through November; Mother's Day, Father's Day, November through January." Submit on 3x5 cards unless gag depends on illustration or dummy. Reports in 2 weeks. Sometimes holds material for 3 weeks. Enclose S.A.S.E. for return of submissions.
"Inasmuch as Norcross is moving in mid-1974, it is suggested that submissions be sent by certified mail or insured mail until the new address is announced."
Conventional, Inspirational, Informal, Soft Line, Humorous, Studio, Juvenile: Seeks "conversational verse; 2, 4 or 8 lines, for general or relative cards; contemporary prose, light and complimentary, for general and relative cards; studio and regular humor." Does not buy "risque humor or forced gags that aren't really funny. Mild sex is good if the gag line is dependent on a sexy slant." Pays $1.50 to $3 a line for regular verse, $20 to $50 for humor and studio ideas.

THE PARAMOUNT LINE, INC., Box 678, Pawtucket RI 02862. Editors: Mrs. Dorothy M. Nelson and Bernice Gourse. Buys all rights. Interested in everyday material at all times. Seasonal verses read on approximately the following schedule: Christmas: March through August; Valentine's Day and St. Patrick's Day: August through November; Easter: November through January; Mother's Day, Father's Day, and graduation: January through March. Reports in 2 weeks. Enclose S.A.S.E. for return of submissions.
Conventional, Informal, Soft Line, Sensitivity, Humorous, and Promotions: "Conversational for all seasons and everydays." Verses should not exceed 8 lines in length. Each verse should be typed on a 3x5 card. Number each verse and keep a duplicate with corresponding number for your own records. Rate of payment starts at $1 a line. For humorous ideas, ability to present your ideas in the form of a rough sketch substantially increases the rate of payment. For promotions, "we are interested in anything that is new and different in the way of greeting cards." May buy photography from freelancers. Payment to be negotiated. "Range is $50 to $150."

PLASTIC LACE, INC., 65 Walnut St., Peabody MA 01960. Editor: I.T. Kutai. Buys all rights. Enclose S.A.S.E. for return of submissions.
Other Product Lines: "Wall hangings, 7x9 or 11½x17½. Sensitivity, humorous, and juvenile captions to accompany characters. Not more than 10 words to a caption. Placemats: sketch, $10; finished b&w, $50. Wall hanging: sketch, $5; finished b&w, $20. Caption must accompany illustrations. We also accept placemat designs, one color only. Pencil sketch okay."

REED STARLINE CARD CO., 3331 Sunset Blvd., Los Angeles CA 90026. Editor: Reed Stevens. Buys all rights. Pays on acceptance. Send for list of current needs. Submission deadlines for seasonal ideas: March 31 (Valentine's Day and St. Patrick's Day), August 1 (Easter, Mother's Day, Father's Day, Graduation), January 1

(Halloween, Thanksgiving, Hanukkah, Christmas). Submit ideas on 3x5 cards. Reports in "about 2 weeks on everyday copy. Seasonal copy might require 30 days reporting time after deadline dates." Enclose S.A.S.E. for return of submissions. **Studio and Promotions:** Needs original studio card copy that is short, conversational in tone, and written for sophisticated adults—including the 18- to 25-year-olds—smart and humorous. Copy must convey a message. "Copy should definitely convey a 'me to you' message and be conversational in tone." Does not want to see copy with "a play on words, mention of money matters, highly topical material, or insulting humor." Categories include birthday, friendship, get well, anniversary, thank you, travel and congratulations, plus all seasons. Pays $40 per idea on acceptance. Monthly cash prizes for top-selling "everyday" copy. Seasonal prizes for copy: $100, $50 and $25. "We like submissions regarding counter card promotions or any closely related subject matter." Payment to be negotiated.

ROTH GREETING CARDS, 7900 Deering Ave., Canoga Park CA 91304. Editor: Charles Roth. Buys all rights. Each idea should be written or typed on a 3x5 card. Christmas and Valentine ideas accepted all year. Reports in 2 to 3 weeks. Enclose S.A.S.E. for return of submissions.
Humorous, Studio, and Other Product Lines: Publishes humorous, contemporary, studio cards, love cards; also humorous plaques. Pays $35.

RUST CRAFT GREETING CARDS, INC., Rust Craft Road, Dedham MA 02026. Editor: Dolores Riccio. Buys all rights. Pays on acceptance. Send for list of current needs and enclose S.A.S.E. Include name, address, and numerical code on each contribution. Submit humorous and studio ideas to Norman Miller. Reports promptly. Enclose S.A.S.E. for return of submissions.
Conventional, Humorous, Studio, Juvenile, Promotions, and Other Product Lines: "We are interested in contemporary and original material only. Please do not send finished artwork or photos. Quick sketches to put across humorous or juvenile ideas are okay, but what we're buying is the idea, not the artwork. We're buying material for all kinds of cards, but we're especially interested in 'Tenderness' sentiments (prose), informals, and books. The books should be about 24 pages long, 12 to 24 pages with copy, usually slanted toward the kind you buy to give somebody. Writers of informals, humorous, and studios should send us material that lends itself to 'lively' illustration. We still buy conventional verse, but we prefer not to see verses which are very similar to the thousands we have on file." Interested in ideas for promotions. "We recently purchased material for our 'Naughty 'n' Nice' promotion." Pays $1.25 a line and up for conventional verse, $10 and up for informals, $10 and up for "Tenderness" prose, $30 for humorous verse, $30 for juvenile "idea cards," $25 for studio cards, $50 and up for books. "Payment for promotions to be negotiated."

SANGAMON COMPANY, Route 48 West, Taylorville IL 62568. Editor: Stella Bright. Buys all rights. Reports in 2 weeks. Enclose S.A.S.E. for return of submissions.
Everyday and Humorous: Verse for "everyday" and all seasons; also cute and humorous gags. Payment depends on quality, usually $1.50 a line for verse, and up to $20 for gags. Length: 4 and 8 lines.

SAWYER PRESS, P.O. Box 46-578, Los Angeles CA 90046. Editor: Eric Matlen. Buys all rights or will negotiate on rights. Reports immediately. May hold ideas for consideration for approximately 1 month. Enclose S.A.S.E. for return of submissions.
Informal, Sensitivity, and Studio: Needs "mechanicals on ecology, love, togetherness, and political" themes for greeting card line. "Handles politically strong statements" and "wants to see everything." Publishes R. Cobb note cards. Pays $2.50 to $10 for verse and sensitivity ideas.
Other Product Lines: "Note card art, poster art, editorial cartoons." Pays $10 and up for art.

STANITA DESIGNS, INC., 657 Broadway, New York NY 10017. Editor: Norman Drittel. Buys all rights. Reports in 3 to 4 weeks. Enclose S.A.S.E. for return of submissions.

Studio: "We are seeking captions for black-oriented studio cards. We need captions for birthday, get well, all occasion, seasonal captions, Christmas, Valentine's Day, Mother's Day, and Father's Day." Pays $15 for verse, $15 for humorous or studio ideas, $35 to $50 for art.

SUBWAY, 12 Irving St., Framingham MA 01701. Editor: Dick Summer. Buys all rights. Submit ideas for Christmas "early." Enclose S.A.S.E. for return of submissions.
Sensitivity: "Pictures of young couples." Pays $50 to $75.

SUNSHINE ART STUDIOS, INC., 45 Warwick St., Springfield MA 01172. Editor: W.S. Robbins. Enclose S.A.S.E. for return of submissions.
Conventional, Soft Line, Sensitivity, Humorous, Studio, and Juvenile: "Birthday and get well. Christmas designs and verses." Pays $1.50 a line.

UNITED CARD COMPANY, 1101 Carnegie St., Rolling Meadows IL 60008. Editor: Mr. Edward Letwenko. Buys all rights. Submission deadlines for seasonal material: December (St. Patrick's Day, Valentine's Day), July (Easter, Mother's Day, Father's Day, graduation), September (Halloween, Christmas). Does not buy artwork. Submit on 3x5 index card or dummy studio card. Reports in 3 to 4 weeks. Enclose S.A.S.E. for return of submissions.
Studio and Sensitivity: Publishes studio cards, funny and/or risque. Also buys verse for "Love Touch" photo line. "Will at times buy freelance photography." Pays $25 for verse or humorous studio ideas.

VAGABOND CREATIONS, 2560 Lance Drive, Dayton OH 45409. Editor: George F. Stanley, Jr. Buys all rights. Submit seasonal material any time; "we try to plan ahead a great deal in advance." Submit on 3x5 cards. "We don't want artwork—only ideas." Reports within same week usually. May hold ideas 3 or 4 days. Enclose S.A.S.E. for return of submissions.
Soft Line and Studio: Publishes contemporary cards. Studio verse only; no slams, puns, or reference to age or aging. Emphasis should be placed on a strong surprise inside punch line instead of one that is predictable. Also prefers good use of double entendre. "Mildly risque." Purchases copy for Christmas, Valentine's and Graduation. Wants "1 short line on front of card and 1 short punch line on inside of card." Pays $10 "for beginners; up to $15 for regular contributors."
Other Product Lines: Interested in receiving copy for mottos and humorous buttons. "On buttons we like double-entendre expressions—preferably short. We don't want the protest button or a specific person named. We pay $10 for each button idea." Mottos should be written in the "first person" about situations at the job, about the job, confusion, modest bragging, drinking habits, etc. Pays $10 for mottos.

VISUAL CREATIONS, 18434 Oxnard St., Tarzana CA 91356. Editor: David Lieberstein. Buys all rights. Send for current needs list. Sometimes holds material for 3 to 6 weeks. Enclose S.A.S.E. for return of submissions.
Inspirational, Informal, Soft Line and Sensitivity: Short, simple, sincere messages for birthday, anniversary, friendship, get well, travel. 1 line only. Photos must have people in natural situations that all ages can identify with. Buys all year. "We are also interested in ideas or art styles to develop a card line around." Pays $10 a card for verse. Pays $25 for b&w photos with byline on each card. Original artwork for special card lines. Pays $50 per design and 2% royalty of gross sales.

WARNER PRESS PUBLISHERS, Fifth at Chestnut St., Anderson IN 46011. Product Editor: Dorothy E. Smith. Pays on acceptance. Submit to attention of Product Editor. Schedule for reading is as follows: everyday sentiments (friendship, birthday, get-well, sympathy, baby birth, congratulations, etc.), September 1; Christmas sentiments, November 1. Enclose S.A.S.E. for return of submissions.
Conventional and Inspirational: Publishes Sunshine line, Regent line, and Christian Faith Greetings. "Greeting card sentiments must be religious, but not preachy or doctrinal. Please suggest Scripture text for each sentiment. (We make no payment for this.)" Length: 4 to 6 lines. Pays $1 per line.

WHITE CARD CORP., 76 Atherton St., Boston MA 02130. Editor: K. Patricia Mann. Buys all rights. Pays on acceptance. Reports within 1 month. Enclose S A S E for return of submissions
Humorous and Studio: Imprinted travel cards. "Greetings from Anytown, U.S.A." Must be general, so that any locale can be imprinted. Should be positive. Don't knock the vacation spot." Pays $25 for card ideas.

Play Producers

ALABAMA SHAKESPEARE FESTIVAL, Martin L. Platt, Artistic Director, P.O.B. 141, Anniston AL 36201. For classical theater audiences; professional cast, summer theater. "Will consider any full-length plays, historical and contemporary, dealing with major themes and human problems." Large casts. Episodic, epic theater, Brechtian or Robert Bolt-type history. No nudity, sex, overt violence. Produces 1 new play annually. No rights retained. Pays "performance and $50 to $75 per performance." Send complete script only. Reports in 4 weeks. Enclose S.A.S. E. for return of submissions.

ANTIQUE FESTIVAL THEATRE, Box 26, Buhl ID 83316. Producer-Director: Aldrich Bowler. Produces plays of 1½ hours playing time in parks, conventions, and summer recreation areas of small towns in the Rocky Mountain region. Produces "comedies and folk plays that will appeal to families; comedies of irony, paradox, situation, satire. Plays should be short, in daylight outdoor settings. Strong characterizations. We have usually a balanced company of 6 to 8 males and 6 to 8 females." Produces about 3 full-length summer plays and 5 to 10 winter readings. Pays 10% "or we would be interested in a company playwright traveling and contemporizing." Send complete script only. "Rehearsals start June 5 to 10 annually." Enclose S.A.S.E. for return of submissions.

APPLE HILL PLAYHOUSE, Box 60, Delmont PA 15626. Producers: Jack Zaharia, Nancy Chesney, Harry Cauley. Produces full-length plays. Interested in plays that will appeal to "the public of all ages from the Pittsburgh area." Wants "commercial comedies." Does not want to see "political satire, avant-garde plays. Prefer small cast (under 10 characters), one set or very simple sets." Produces about 8 to 10 plays a year. Does not copyright plays. Pays $150 a week. "Apple Hill gets 5% of play if produced after playing Apple Hill." Query first with synopsis only. Enclose S.A.S.E. for reply to queries.

STEPHEN ARCHER, 129 Fine Arts, University of Missouri-Columbia, Columbia MO 65201. Produces plays of any length for university students. "Major production program or workshop production series. Interested in any kind of play on any topic in any style. We are looking for creativity and originality. No imitations of established playwrights. We will not accept any plays not copyrighted by their authors. We wish rights to 1 production." Recent productions include *The King and His Cup* (Lynch) and *Therapy* (Morris). Produces 1 major play and up to 20 short plays in a year. Pay "varies. For major productions, $25 per performance or more. For one-acts, $5 per performance or more." Query first with synopsis. Reports in 1 to 3 months. Enclose S.A.S.E. for reply to queries.

RUTH BAILEY, Cherry County Playhouse, Box 661, Traverse City MI 49684. Winter address: Spring Hill Lane, Cincinnati OH 45226. Produces three-act plays for "middle class TV watchers on vacation in large resort area." Wants plays with "small cast; 1-set comedies. Conventional Neil Simon type of comedies. No serious plays." Recent productions include *A Frog He Would A-Wooing Go.* Produces 9 plays a year. Purchases all Broadway, film, and stock rights. Pays percentage of gross. Send complete ms only. Reports in September and April. Enclose S.A.S.E. for return of submissions.

STEVEN BAKER, Dramatis Personae, 114 W. 14th St., New York NY10011. Prefers dramas with casts of under 6, themes of social significance on present problems or avant-garde and futuristic. "Plays should run 2 acts, 90 minutes. The theme should be serious and universal. Emphasis on daring and frankness; sex and nudity when called for. No all male plays. We like to use a Greek chorus, dancers, musical emphasis, fantasy. No plain, drab, realistic plays for 2 people. Nothing that cannot be handled well arena-style on a stage 14x22 with 1 scenic wall. Use a reasonable amount of props and costumes. We have excellent lighting." Produces about 2 plays a year. Copyrights plays. Purchases rights for "run of the play and option on movie rights." Pays "nothing for first 3-week showcase; percentage of gross for a run, or $5 per performance." Send complete script only. Reports in 4 to 6 weeks. Enclose S.A.S.E. for return of submissions.

THE BARN, 8204 Highway 100, Nashville TN 37221. Produces plays of 2 and 3-acts; 1 hour, 45 minutes. Dinner theatre and professional plays, mostly comedies. For a public audience, 8 to 80. "We like fast pace, sight gags, clean comedy; no filthy language or nudity. Most plays adapted for theatre in round, maximum 2 set changes, 10 cast members." Recently produced titles include: *How the Other Half Loves* (Ayckbourn); *The Gazebo* (Coppel); *Natalie Needs a Nightie* (Shaffner). Pays flat fee, weekly. Produces 12 plays a year. Send complete script only. Enclose S.A.S.E. for return of submissions.

BARTER THEATRE, Main St., Abingdon VA 24210. Producer: Rex Partington. Looks for good plays, particularly comedies. Three acts, preferably, but will consider good quality plays of other lengths. Pays 5% royalties. Submissions through an agent. Reports vary; "very limited staff to read mss." Enclose S.A.S.E. for return of submissions.

BOARSHEAD PLAYERS, LEDGES PLAYHOUSE, Box 96, Grand Ledge MI 48837. For the adult public who dislike "causy" and preachy plays. Winter and summer professional stock company. Two-act and three-act plays. Good plays of any kind. Plays are copyrighted. Buys right to further performance elsewhere and agent fee for other productions. For winter, small proscenium stage, small budget; cast usually no greater than 12. For summer, large thrust stage, moderate budget; cast usually no greater than 20. Produce over 13 plays a year. Recent productions include a rewrite of *The Italian Straw Hat, She'd Rather Kiss,* (original), *Mistress of the Inn* (original). *Waiting for Godot.* Pays minimum "author's transportation out here and room and board." to maximum of $300 per week. Send complete script only. Reports in 2 months. Enclose S.A.S.E. for return of submissions.

OSCAR L. BROWNSTEIN, University Theatre, University of Iowa, Iowa City IA 52240. Produces one-act and three-act plays for a "generally young audience" at the University of Iowa. The plays are performed at the University Theatre and Studio Theatre by amateur and professional training students. We are especially interested in original conceptions of drama and theatre—the fresh, imaginative perception, not novelty for its own sake. We do not want plays previously produced for a paying audience. We do not want plays whose authors will not agree to be here for 1 week of the run. The purpose of our productions of original scripts is to provide the playwright an experience useful to his subsequent revision of the script. This is the out-of-town tryout for non- or not-yet-commercial scripts." Recent productions include *The Fire, The Spider* (Bell), and *Chamber Piece.* (O'Keefe). Produces 2 original plays a year and 8 standard plays. Pays $35 a performance "during the run—7 to 10 performances." Send complete script only. Reports in 6 months. Enclose S.A.S.E. for return of submissions.

LAWRENCE CARRA, Great Lakes Shakespeare Festival, Carnegie-Mellon University, Pittsburgh PA 15213. For a public audience, paid admission, with preference toward classical theatre. Summer theatre with potential for Broadway; professional cast. Three-act or full-length plays. Open as to style, content and genre. Interested only in effective dramatic works. Buys class A rights. Not interested in plays with sex themes per se. Limitations in cast, approximately 20. Recent productions include *Godspell, Marowitz Hamlet,* and *R UR.* Produces 5 plays per summer season. Payment is negotiable. Query first with synopsis only. Reports within 1 month. Enclose S.A.S.E. with query and synopsis.

CASA MANANA MUSICALS, INC., P.O. Box 9054, Fort Worth TX 76107. Producer: Melvin O. Dacus. Produces two-act musicals "basically for over-30 audience; for people who enjoy shows like *Oklahoma*, *Fiddler on the Roof*, *Sound of Music* and who don't like shows like *The Fantasticks* and avant-garde stuff. The musicals should be noncontroversial. We want entertainment for the broadest based of people—we're not educators of public taste. No rock musicals; no racial themes; no revues. The style should be melodic, with the emphasis on singable tunes, easily remembered, with comedy and fun as main ingredients. We use an arena theatre that seats 1,832 and has an oval 24x28 stage." Produces about 8 plays a year. Pay is "negotiable." Send complete script and score only. Enclose S.A.S.E. for return of submissions.

CENTER THEATRE GROUP (Mark Taper Forum and Ahmanson Theatre), 135 North Grand Ave., Los Angeles CA 90012. Script Coordinator: Marian Barnett. Center Theatre Group's season presents a mixture of classics and contemporary works. Additionally, the "New Theatre for Now" program seeks "explorative drama with special interest in work which is unconventional in style and structure." Contracts individually negotiated. Reports in 4 to 8 weeks. Enclose S.A.S.E. for return of submissions.

CHELSEA THEATER CENTER, 30 Lafayette Ave., Brooklyn NY 11217. Artistic Director: Robert Kalfin. Looking for full-length plays "that stretch the bounds of the theater in form and content and are related to contemporary society—where it is and where it is going. No limitations as to size of cast or physical production." Pays usually "$100 for an option to produce a play in workshop; $500 for a 6-month option for an off-Broadway production." Works 10 months in advance. Query first with synopsis. Enclose S.A.S.E. for reply to queries.

ALFRED CHRISTIE, 405 E. 54th St., New York NY 10022. "The theatre is a summer stock theatre and many of the people in the audience are on vacation, most are over age 30." Professional cast. Two-act or three-act plays. "We would like funny situation, contemporary farces or light comedies. Scripts that are sensational in theme, that can compete with today's frank and modern films are also possible. Also, we do children's shows. We like a well-written play with interesting switches or avant-garde scripts that are based on reality and make sense. We would expect the author to copyright the play but if the show moves on to other theatres or Broadway or to a film, etc., we would like a small percentage of the action. We want no family situation shows, no period plays involving many period costumes. We prefer small cast, single-set shows, but if a script is good we would do a larger cast and multiple set production." Recent productions include *The Gingerbread Lady*, Father's Day, and *Last of the Red Hot Lovers*. Produces 6 to 10 full productions and several children's plays yearly. Payment varies. A percentage or a flat fee is possible. "Does the author want to come and work with the people and on the play?" Send synopsis or complete script. "We like scripts by April of each year because we must arrange publicity, hire actors, etc." Enclose S.A.S.E. for return of submissions.

CLARION PREMIERE THEATRE SERIES, Department of Speech Communication and Theatre, Clarion State College, Clarion PA 16214. Business Manager: Charles L. Marlin. Produces one-act, two-act, and three-act plays "in a modern, fully equipped theater, directed by professionals and acted by college theater majors. Audiences are a combination of college and community with a generally sophisticated outlook, and they tend to be predominantly in their 20's and few past middle age. We will consider a wide variety of plays: musical, revue, comedy, serious drama, multimedia, farce, experimental. We are not particularly interested in historical pageant or opera. We have no predetermined bias toward any one format or style. We like both traditional and experimental scripts. We only consider scripts which have not received a fully staged production either in the United States or abroad. There are no limitations in cast, stage, or technical production." Recent productions include *The American War Women* (Greth). Produces 2 to 3 plays a year. "Royalty ranges from $200 to $300, with an additional honorarium of $100 if the playwright visits the campus during the production." Send complete script only. Enclose S.A.S.E. for return of submissions.

CLEVELAND PLAY HOUSE, 2040 East 86th St., Cleveland OH 44106. Director: Richard Oberlin. A professional resident theater. Produces plays of "all types. We are interested primarily in full-length plays. One-acts are rarely used." Looks for special qualities in characterization and theme. "Our season of about 15 productions encompasses a wide range, from classics to current Broadway and Off-Broadway successes, plus new plays, to appeal to a wide interest range in our audience. Recent premiere: *The Rabinowitz Gambit* (Goldemberg). We must keep in mind that the Play House is a family theater, supported by subscriptions and gifts. Blatant vulgarity and tastelessness would not be acceptable." Produces about 1 or 2 plays a year from freelancers. "Royalties are negotiated with individual authors or agents. In the case of new scripts, authors are usually in attendance during the rehearsal period and financial arrangements are made for this period." Send complete script to Robert Snook. Reports in 6 weeks. Enclose S.A.S.E. for return of submissions.

E.P. CONKLE WORKSHOP FOR PLAYWRIGHTS, University of Texas at Austin, College of Fine Arts, Austin TX 78712. Director: Webster Smalley, Chairman of Drama. "A summer project during which we produce 3 new scripts which are two- or three-act and full-length. Performances are for the general public. We also do new scripts on our major and experimental bills. Playwrights should be recommended by a recognized member of the educational theater, the professional theater, or by an agent. Playwrights are offered $1,000 fellowships to make it possible for them to be present for rehearsals and performances, which are held during June and the first 2 weeks of July. Financial arrangements for scripts on our major and experimental bills are worked out." Enclose S.A.S.E. for return of submissions.

COUNTRY CLUB THEATRE, 4700 West Rand Rd., Mt. Prospect IL 60056. Produces two-act and three-act plays in "year-round equity for persons in upper middle class suburbs. Interested in comedy, but also in experimental productions. We have a 3-quarter round stage which is quite small and have very little wing space. No curtain." Produces 4 to 6 plays a year. Does not copyright plays. Pays "flat rate per week plus percentage." Send synopsis or complete script. Enclose S.A.S.E. for return of submissions.

JEAN DALRYMPLE, 130 W. 56th St., New York NY 10019. Produces stage and television shows, sometimes 3 or 4 a year. She is the producer of the musical and drama revivals at New York's City Center. Payment in royalties according to Dramatists Guild contract. Submit original material through agents only.

THE DRAMA GUILD, Dr. H. Adrian Rehner, Kennedy-King College, 6800 South Wentworth Ave., Chicago IL 60621. For a public audience, all ages, all types of people in a city. "The Professional Performing (Equity) Company of the Drama Guild of Kennedy-King College is always interested in new plays, to be produced in one of our theatres." Full-length plays. "We are very much interested in seeing plays by black writers that deal with black living and are hopeful that some involvement with whites is in the script. We use integrated casting sometimes. However, plays using all blacks will be welcome, too. We do not copyright plays. The play remains with the writer unless we negotiate otherwise. If the show is going to be extremely costly to us, then we might need to retain some rights of future production but that is not the usual procedure." Produce 9 to 10 full-length plays yearly. Pays standard royalty payments. Query first with synopsis only. "No set time for reporting. If rejected by first reader it goes back very fast, if all of our readers read the play, it takes some time." Enclose S.A.S.E. for reply to query. "We will not return plays if correct postage and addressed envelope are not enclosed."

DAVID EASTWOOD, Wilton Rd., Greenfield Center NY 12833. For general public. Summer theatre, professional cast. All kinds of plays, "Neil Simon style, the subject is 'life'. I believe future plays, because of costs, will be one set, with contemporary costumes." Does not copyright plays. Limitations are 1 set, cast of 9 maximum. Produces 4 plays a year. "Payment is negotiable, usually $25 per night." Query first with synopsis only. Enclose S.A.S.E.

ELKINS PRODUCTIONS INTERNATIONAL CORP., 19½ E. 62nd St., New York NY10021. Specializes in musicals, comedies, and dramas for films and the theater. A recent film is *A Doll's House.* Will not look at unsolicited scripts. Works through agents only. Enclose S.A.S.E. for return of submissions.

ZELDA FICHANDLER, 6th and M Sts., S.W., Washington DC 20024. Wants original plays preferably (but not necessarily) submitted through agents. "Plays with relevance to the human situation—which cover a multitude of dramatic approaches—are welcome here." Pays 5 percent of gross. Reports in 6 months. Enclose S.A.S.E. for return of submissions.

FRANK PRODUCTIONS, INC., 119 West 57th St., New York NY10019. Specializes in musicals. Enclose S.A.S.E. for return of submissions.

ROY FRANKLYN, 29 W. 65th St., New York NY10023. Produces two-act and three-act plays for "possibly off-Broadway, possibly summer theater, for commercial-type audiences." Interested in "good plays, small casts, simple sets." Recent production is *Diary of a Summer Scandal* (Kemp). Buys subsidiary rights. Produces 2 plays a year "at most." Pays 5% of gross receipts. Query first with synopsis only. Reports in 3 weeks. Enclose S.A.S.E. for reply to queries.

JOSEPH N. FRENCH, Edison Institute, Dearborn MI 48121. Interested in two-act plays for "museum theater and semi-professional company." Audience is "middle-aged rural Americans." Wants "historical or patriotic plays in Restoration style (Delsartean). No depressing or downbeat themes; no anti-hero. Should have cast of 12 or less." Produces about 6 plays a year. Buys no rights. Pays $20 a performance. Send complete script only. Reports in 6 months. Enclose S.A.S.E. for return of submissions.

GALWAY PRODUCTIONS, Suite 1010, 701 Seventh Ave., New York NY10036. Director: Paul Barry. Looks for avante-garde, controversial plays for a modern small cast. Pays standard Dramatists Guild royalty percentage. Synopsis or full-length play. No one-acts. Enclose S.A.S.E. for return of submissions.

J. GORDON GREENE, UNC-G Theatre, Greensboro, NC 27412. Produces one-act ("greatest need"), two-act, and three-act plays. "Talented preprofessional student casts perform our shows. We have 4 theaters, ranging in size from 60 to 1,500 seats. We produce plays for the university community in a middle-sized urban area and for a summer resort mountain area (the Parkway Playhouse). Any well-written play is worth our time. We are especially interested in finding scripts for and about college-age young people. Would like to see well-developed characters inter-relating around a solid dramatic conflict situation. Plays with acting opportunities for females receive priority treatment, but any well-written, well-structured play interests us. Avoid intentionally esoteric treatments. Small cast plays with simple set requirements have a much better chance of being selected for our purposes. Most of our productions are plays by well-established playwrights, such as Neil Simon, Williams, Miller." Produces 15 to 20 one-act plays and 5 to 12 full-length plays a year. Pays $10 to $25 per performance, "depending on length and quality of script." Send complete script only. Reports in 4 to 8 weeks. Enclose S.A.S.E. for return of submissions.

GUBER FORD GROSS PRODUCTIONS, 32 E. 57th St., New York NY10022. Produces three-act plays for professional Broadway and summer theater. Interested in musicals and comedies. "No noncommercial subjects." Produces 1 or 2 plays a year. Buys world rights, motion picture rights, and television rights. Pay "open." Send complete script only. Enclose S.A.S.E. for return of submissions.

HALFPENNY PLAYHOUSE, 155 Midland Ave., Kearny NJ 07032. Produces three-act plays for "regional theater located in New Jersey, 20 minutes from New York City. Cast is professional. The audience is best described as a general theater audience composed of suburbanites, generally with a higher education and with wide interests. Age range is from late teens through middle age." Wants "general" plays. "Approach should be for a 100-seat house, with a theme and structure acceptable and understood by a general suburbanite audience which is deserting New York theater because of general themes and prices there. Structure should be a full evening's entertainment. Authors should be engaged in proposing a positive statement about people or society. We prefer small cast shows, 10 or under, with little or no set changes, minimum props and effects." Recent productions include *Who's Afraid of Virginia Woolf?* (Albee) and *South Pacific* (Rodgers & Hammerstein). Produces about 15 plays a year; "no originals in the last 3 years." Rights to be arranged, "especially if future productions based on our premiere staging, or if future production is direct result thereof." Pays set fee of $25 to $100, depending on author and play. Query first with synopsis only. Reports "in 1 day for some; if we are seriously considering production, up to 3 months." Enclose S.A.S.E. for reply to queries.

HARWICH JUNIOR THEATRE, Box 168, West Harwich MA 02671. Produces two-act and three-act plays; semiprofessional productions in winter theatre or summer children's theatre. Children's plays are 1½ hours in length; any size and age cast. Winter plays are full length with small casts. Drama, comedy, musicals, adaptations. Any structure which may be considered in play form. No happenings. Nothing controversial. Recent productions include *The Welfare Family* (Hancock) and *The Drunkard* (Herrod). Produces 13 plays a year; 6 children's plays and 7 adult. "We expect the playwright to obtain his own copyright." Pays an average of $10 to $15 per performance for children's plays; average of $15 to $20 for adult plays. Send complete script. Reports in March. Enclose S.A.S.E. for return of submissions.

HEDGEROW THEATRE, Moylan PA 19065. Producer: David Ralphe. Produces two-act and three-act plays for a "52-week repertory." Audience is public, 43% student. Limited production capabilities." Produces about 8 plays a year. "We purchase only performance rights." Pays "percentage of gross to be negotiated." Send synopsis or complete script. Reports in 30 days. Enclose S.A.S.E. for return of submissions.

HIGH TOR SUMMER THEATRE, Ashby West Rd., Fitchburg MA 01420. Produces three-act plays "performed during a summer season by professional and amateur performers in a resident company. Public audience of varying ages, education, and interests. Interested in all kinds of plays which might be suitable for our particular setup. No X-rated plays. Our theater is an arena stage, holding between 120 and 140 people. We sometimes perform end stage, i.e., three sides. our repertoire is extremely varied." Recent productions include *Not By Bed Alone* (Feydeau), *The Miracle Worker* (Gibson), *The Prime of Miss Jean Brodie* (Allen). Produces about 8 plays a year. "Royalties are negotiable because of our nonprofit educational setup." Percentage offered will vary, according to author and nature of script. Send complete script only. Enclose S.A.S.E. for return of submissions.

CHARLES HOLLERITH, JR., 18 W. 55th St., New York NY10019. Will look at any type of play he feels is well-written and has merit, including original plays and musicals. Dramatists Guild minimum royalties. Submit through agent only.

HONOLULU THEATRE FOR YOUTH, P.O. Box 3257, Honolulu HI 96801. Managing Director: Mrs. Lorraine Dove. Produces plays of "1 hour without intermission. Plays are produced "in Honolulu in various theater buildings; also, an annual tour in theater buildings on Neighbor Islands, state of Hawaii. Casts are amateur with professional direction and production; adult actors, with children as needed. Plays are produced for school children, grades 2 through 12, individual plays directed to specific age groups; also public performances." Interested in "historical (especially American) plays, plays about Pacific countries and Pacific legends, and Asian legends and Asian history. Plays must have strong character with whom young people can identify, with stress on action rather than exposition, but not at the expense of reality (i.e., not slapstick). Plays should be reasonably simple technically and use primarily adult characters. Fairy tales (especially mod versions) are at the bottom of the priority list, as are elaborate musicals requiring large orchestras. Casts up to 15, preferably. Technical requirements should be reasonably simple, as sets have to be built at one place and trucked to the theater." Recent productions include *The Lark, The Miracle Worker, Legend of Sleepy Hollow.* Produces 6 plays a year. Royalty fee is based on number of performances. Query first with synopsis only. Reports in 1 to 2 months. Enclose S.A.S.E. for reply to queries.

WILLIAM E. HUNT, 801 West End Ave., New York NY10025. Interested in reading scripts for stock production, off-Broadway and even Broadway production. "Small cast, youth-oriented, meaningful, technically adventuresome; serious, funny, far-out. Must be about people first, ideas second. No political or social tracts." Pays royalties on production. Off Broadway, 5%; on Broadway, 5%, 7½% and 10%, based on gross. Reports in "a few weeks." Enclose S.A.S.E. for return of submissions.

ROBERT LEWIS KARLIN, Oregon Ridge Dinner Theatre, Box 304, Cockeysville MD 21030. Produces two-act and three-act plays for "professional equity dinner theater which runs 50 weeks a year. Average suburban audience; average age, 37 to 45; middle class, racially integrated. We produce only comedies—no subject taboo except race or drugs. No 'black' comedies, please, and only satire that is not biting or political. Satires on marriage, generation gap, and loose women acceptable. Multiscene acts okay. All scene changes must be accomplished during intermissions. Cast limitations: 5 to 8 adults, balanced. All youngsters must be 12 or over." Recent productions include "Broadway comedies (hit or flop) produced in the past 20 years." Produces about 20 plays a year. Royalty payment "negotiated." Send complete script only. Enclose S.A.S.E. for return of submissions.

FRANK KENLEY, Box 1, Hartford OH 44424. For public, general summer theatre audience. Plays performed at Star Theatre of Flint, Whiting Auditorium, Flint MI 48502. Three-act plays, comedies, comedy-drama, musicals, situation comedies, generally light, summer theatre or potential Broadway material. Cast should not exceed 15. Produces about 10 plays a year. Pays standard royalty percentage. Send complete script only. Enclose S.A.S.E. for return of submissions.

LAKEWOOD MUSICAL PLAYHOUSE, 277 W. 22nd St., New York NY10011. Producer: Robert Buchanan. Produces two-act plays for "professional summer theater in Pennsylvania. The audience is varied; middle-aged. Interested in only musicals with any theme. Use whatever approach works. Have only done Broadway successes, but am somewhat secure enough now to do new shows." Produces 10 or 11 plays a year. Pays "about $500." Send synopsis or complete script. Enclose S.A.S.E. for return of submissions.

FRANKLYN LENTHALL, Boothbay Playhouse, Boothbay ME 04537. Produces two-act and three-act plays for "summer theater with professional union actors. Public audience; very sophisticated." Interested in "comedy, but not limited to that. The playwright should just write the play as he sees it, wants it. We do not place limitations. No obscenity for obscenity's sake. I personally consider nudity on the stage a bore. The fewer sets the better." Recent productions include *The Rules of the Game* (Pirandello), *Design for Living* (Coward) and *The Chinese Prime Minister* (Bagnold). Produces 9 plays a year. "Our minimum varies from $100 to $300-plus, depending on the quality of the play, reputation of playwright, etc. Standard contract: 4% weekly gross up to $5,000." Query first with synopsis only. "Deadline on new scripts is April 1." Enclose S.A.S.E. for reply to queries.

MAX LIEBMAN, 130 W. 56th St., New York NY10019. Producer of TV and stage shows. Pays according to Dramatists Guild contract. Enclose S.A.S.E. for return of submissions.

GUY S. LITTLE, JR., Little Theater-On-The-Square, Sullivan IL 61951. Wants original comedies and dramas for two or three acts. Pays royalty on production—standard 4%, 5%, etc. Enclose S.A.S.E. for return of submissions.

LORETTO-HILTON CENTER REPERTORY THEATRE, 130 Edgar Road, St. Louis MO 63119. Managing Director: David Frank. Looks at original plays; full-length, suitable for wide audiences. Payment on 5% royalty basis. Query first with synopsis. Enclose S.A.S.E. for reply to queries.

METROPOLITAN THEATRE GUILD, INC., Box 4973, Panorama City CA 91402. Managing Director: David Rodich. "All scripts will be read and considered for production and publication. As a matter of fact, this group prefers new plays over previously produced or published ones because part of its purpose is to expose the public to new dramatic literature and help talented young playwrights become known. Productions are designed to showcase performers, directors, and writers before the Hollywood entertainment industry. All types and lengths are read and considered. However, full-length plays, especially comedies, with simple sets and small casts, are preferred. This is an educational organization as well as a play production group producing professional showcase productions. If a young playwright wants advice regarding his writing, proper play script form, how to secure copyrights, etc., an experienced playwright will answer his letter at no charge." Send complete script with synopsis. Enclose S.A.S.E. for return of submissions.

MUSE, INC., THEATRE OF ORIGINALS, Box 5510, Cleveland OH 44101. "We prefer full-length plays. Plays will be produced in our own theater. Casts are amateur, but carefully selected. Plays should have general appeal. We prefer to avoid the wildly avant-garde at this time. Subjects are completely open, as long as they have general appeal. We particularly like theatrical pieces, with plenty of drama, and reasonable settings. Musicals are welcome, as long as they are scored for piano. Two- and three-act plays, musical or otherwise, have the best chance here. Our one-act plays are done as trios, perhaps twice a year, so the market is limited. Elaborate settings, multiple settings, huge casts, etc., have little chance. We have no fly room, and not a huge amount of wing room. Once again, one-set, reasonably sized casts have the best chance here." Recent productions include *You Look Just Like a Rich Jewish Lady* (Halas) and *Earthly and Heavenly Bodies* (Disch). Produces about 12 plays a year. Pays $100 for the use of the play script. "All rights remain with the author. We prefer unproduced plays, but will look at those that have had showcase or college production." Send synopsis or complete script. Enclose S.A.S.E. for return of submissions.

MUSIC FAIR ENTERPRISES, INC., 1 Bala Ave., Bala Cynwyd PA 19004 or 32 East 57 St., New York NY 10022. Attention: Mr. Lee Guber or Mr. Shelly Gross. Produces two-act or three-act plays "either in our own chain of summer stock theaters or on Broadway. General audience. All kinds, but will read works only from professional authors. No amateur work." A recent production is *Inquest* (Freed). Pay "to be negotiated according to terms of Authors Guild." Send complete script only. Enclose S.A.S.E. for return of submissions.

NEW HERITAGE REPERTORY THEATRE, INC., 43 East 125th St. New York NY 10035. One-act and two-act plays dealing with the black life style in America. Any style. Professional cast as well as amateur and sometimes "others." People from Harlem, college students and "whoever" as audience. Send complete script only. Reports in 4 to 5 weeks. Produces 2 plays a year. "Payment by negotiation." Recently produced titles include *Long Black Block* (Furman) and *Madam Odum* (Rivers). Enclose S.A.S.E. for return of submission.

OFFICE FOR ADVANCED DRAMA RESEARCH, 3526 Humboldt Ave. S., Minneapolis MN 55408. Director: Arthur H. Ballet. "The Office for Advanced Drama Research, operating with a grant from the Rockefeller Foundation, concentrates its entire attention on playwrights, who are invited to submit unproduced scripts for consideration. The Office each year reads hundreds of scripts; of these a number are selected and submitted to cooperating theatres for consideration. If a theatre agrees that rehearsal and production facilities should be made available to the playwright, the Office in essence underwrites limited facilities for the theatre and the playwright. For the most part these are professional or semiprofessional companies, but a limited number of educational and community theatres are included. The University of Minnesota, uniquely recognizing its responsibility to the art of the theatre as it long has recognized its responsibilities to the sciences, utilizes this facility for a laboratory where the artist can work his play, try a new idea, form, or style without great financial and personal risk as an artist. The O.A.D.R. is not dedicated to or limited to a particular kind of drama or theatre. The O.A.D.R. does not work with previously produced plays, with adaptations, or with musicals. The playwright agrees to make every effort to be available to the producing theatre before and during the rehearsal period, clearly understanding that the O.A.D.R. involvement is in behalf of the playwright and that that involvement presupposes substantial in-residence availability during the rehearsal period." For complete details of the terms and conditions of the program, write for brochure and enclose S.A.S.E.

OLD LOG THEATER, Box 250, Excelsior MN 55331. Producer: Don Stolz. Produces two-act and three-act plays for "a professional cast. Public audiences, usually adult. Interested in contemporary comedies. Small number of sets. Cast not too large." Recent productions include *Gingerbread Lady, Best of Friends* and *How the Other Half Lives*. Produces about 14 plays a year. Payment by Dramatists Guild agreement. Send complete script only. Enclose S.A.S.E. for return of submissions.

GUY PALMERTON, 210 West 55th St., New York NY10019. Wants original comedies, perhaps comedy dramas. Presents outstanding Broadway and film stars in major productions plus occasional tryout on summer theatre tours with stars and all pro companies. Enclose S.A.S.E. for return of submissions.

JOSEPH PAPP, New York Shakespeare Festival Public Theater, 425 Lafayette St., New York NY 10003. "Interested in plays and musicals with contemporary relevance, but no restrictions as to style, historical period, traditional or experimental form, etc." Recent productions include *That Championship Season* (Miller), *Wedding Band* (Childress) and *The Orphan* (Rabe). Produces plays at the Public Theatre (housing six theatres) and at the Delacorte Theatre (Central Park). Pays according to standard play option and production agreements. Advance varies. Reports in 4 to 6 weeks. Enclose S.A.S.E. for return of submissions.

PATRICIAN ARTS, 101 Colonial Manor Rd., Irwin PA 15642. Produces three-act plays for "semiprofessional summer theater. Audience is middle age with middle American tastes. They do not like anything controversial. Interested in good comedies (3 acts). Nothing avant-garde. We prefer one-set shows with limited casts." Produces 12 plays a year "and we like to do several originals" and have produced 10 original shows in 5 years. Usually pays 5% or $100 a week. Send complete script only. Reports in 1 month to 6 weeks. Enclose S.A.S.E. for return of submissions.

PIED PIPER THEATRE, P.O. Box 3725, Wilmington NC 28401. Producer: Doug Swink. Produces one-act plays "about 45 minutes to an hour in length. Our plays are presented in a large proscenium theater, with the Board of Education busing the students there. The cast is amateur, composed mostly of mothers who are available. The plays are attended by kindergarten, first, second, and third grades of all schools in our county and surrounding areas. Plays should be ones with a lesson to be learned. We desire it to be musical, lively and colorful. No goody-goody plays." Recent production is *Alice in Wonderland* (Stone). Produces about 1 play a year. Pays "$100 to $150 for all performances (7 to 10), and permission to copy music to send to schools for children to learn so they can sing along with actors during the play." Send complete script only. Reports in 3 weeks. Enclose S.A.S.E. for return of submissions.

PITTSBURGH PLAYHOUSE, Craft Ave. at Hamlet St., Pittsburgh PA 15213. Wants original adult, full-length dramas. Pays royalty of $25 to $50 per performance. Recent new work produced: *Alfred, the Great* (Horovitz). Send mss to Director. Enclose S.A.S.E. for return of submissions.

PRODUCING MANAGERS CO., 330 W. 45th St., New York NY10036. Wants original plays, preferably submitted through an agent. Offers standard Dramatists Guild arrangement. Reports in 1 month. Enclose S.A.S.E. for return of submissions.

REPERTORY THEATER OF LINCOLN CENTER, 150 West 65th St., New York NY10023. Produces plays at Lincoln Center with professional cast. "Public audience, average ages, 30 to 45; high education level, predominantly professional occupations. Subject matter is open, but literate, intelligent writing required. Not interested in musicals. Small casts preferred." Produces 10 to 12 plays a year. Rights "negotiable." Pay "negotiable." Send complete script only. Reports in 6 to 8 weeks. Enclose S.A.S.E. for return of submissions.

ROCHESTER COMMUNITY PLAYERS, INC., 820 Clinton Ave. S., Rochester NY 14620. Artistic Director: Harriet Warren. Plays produced "during the Rochester Playhouse's 12-month season, including teen summer program, mainstage, children's theater, and social service series." Audience is of 3 types: "general public; teen/youth, social problem plays; and children's theater." Wants "interesting plays for any of the above 3 groups. Also will accept new musical scripts. Will especially be looking for scripts that can be mounted on an open stage without technical problems." Recent productions include *The Last Sweet Days of Isaac.* Produces about 14 plays a year. Pay "varies; generally maintain the $50 to $25 agreement." Send complete script only. "Scripts that interest the staff are then reviewed by committee. We cannot promise the prompt return of script." Enclose S.A.S.E. for return of submissions.

STEFAN RUDNICKI, University of Rochester Drama Center, c/o Morey 411, University of Rochester, Rochester NY 14627. Plays produced for "summer theater, classroom, readers theater, and workshop productions (large and small scale). Casts will include students and professionals. For a university audience; some community orientation." Interested in "anything, but especially American themes, the American Indian included. Also interested in new translations. Avoid rigidness of thought or structure." Recent productions include the premiere English language production of *Operetta* (Gombrowicz) and a reader's theatre performance of *Vincent and Liza,* an original play written in workshop by students and Anthony Scully. Produces 15 plays a year; 8 to 10 are one-act plays. Pays "amateur royalty, (a flat fee of $35 to $50 for the first performance and $15 to $35 for each subsequent performance, usually paid to author's agent)." Send synopsis or complete script. Reports in 2 months. Enclose S.A.S.E. for return of submissions.

ANNIE RUSSELL THEATRE, Rollins College, Winter Park FL 32789. "For public, professional, somewhat conservative, hard core, senior citizens who like the classics, but we are trying to broaden their horizons." Amateur, educational theatre. Three-act plays. "Good plays of any kind." Does not copyright plays. "We don't want plays with overt sex, nudity or the most recently popular four-letter words; otherwise, fairly free." Recently produced plays included *The Petrified Forest* and *The Time of Your Life.* Produces 12 to 14 plays a year. Travel expenses and fee up to $1,000. Query first with synopsis only. Enclose S.A.S.E.

S.R.O. STRAW HAT THEATRE, U.N.C.-W., Wilmington NC 28401. Producer: Doug W. Swink. Produces "1½- to 2-hour plays with 1 intermission. During the summer, between June and August, we produce 8 plays. All of our actors are amateurs. Some of them are local residents; others (about 6) come from out of town. Our summer audience has no limits at all. When we announce the plays, each carries with it a recommendation as to its appeal: 'all ages,' 'family,' 'adult entertainment.' We want only good plays, and ones that will afford our actors a good selection of roles and ones that are worthy of witnessing. We prefer a lighthearted comedy with a message. No nudity and vulgarity for the sake of nudity and vulgarity. In the summer, we operate in 2 theaters, one very small (actually a classroom) and the other a large proscenium theater." Send complete script only. Reports in 3 weeks. Enclose S.A.S.E. for return of submissions.

ST. BARTHOLOMEW'S COMMUNITY CLUB, 109 East 50th St., New York NY 10022. Drama Director: Joe Sutherin. Produces one-act and two-act plays. Produces comedy, musicals, tragedy, drama. Interested in plays concerned with "overpopulation, ecology, and environment problems." Looks for "clarity of message. I am unable to produce plays with abusive language, and there would be trouble with certain topics, such as abortion, anti-religion, etc. I would be able to pay very little to the author unless he considers a New York mounting worthwhile. I have no budget money for new material, but if something was good enough, I might give a box office percentage." Send complete script. Reports in 1 to 3 months. Enclose S.A.S.E. for return of submissions.

DORE SCHARY, 641 Lexington Ave., New York NY 10022. Now prepared to consider material.

ARTHUR ALAN SEIDELMAN, L.S.V. Productions, Ltd., c/o S. Edward Katz, 250 W. 57th St., Suite 301, New York NY 10019. Currently interested only in material (plays, novels, screenplays) for feature films. "Nothing cheap, vulgar or sensational." Audience is the general public. No limitations on subject or theme." Recent productions include *Brothers.* Produces about 3 or 4 plays a year. "We purchase all production and allied rights." Outright sale for fee and percentage. Send complete script. Reports in 2 months. Enclose S.A.S.E. for return of submissions.

STAGE/WEST, 1511 Memorial Ave., West Springfield MA 01089. Producer: Stephen E. Hays. Resident equity. Looks at new plays with emphasis on contemporary problems. Budget requires small cast plays, but grants can be obtained to do larger cast plays. Payment is 4% of gross. Prefers synopsis. Enclose S.A.S.E.

STARLIGHT CABARET THEATRE, Wm. F. Miller, Executive Producer, 1413 Bates Ave., Springfield IL 62704. For middle aged audience that prefers light, risque comedy or farce. Typical dinner-theatre fare. Indoor summer theatre, professional, non-Equity company. Three-act plays, omnibus of three 1-act plays, such as *Plaza Suite.* "Small cast, simple production. No taboos except plays must be in good taste. No homo themes or black problem plays. Plays should have lead roles for mature actor and actress. Buys first performance rights only. No one-acts, dramas, tragedies or problem plays. Stage is really a band stand, 20x11 feet. Entrances downstage and right and left, low ceiling, limited lighting. Cast limited to 3 to 6 people. Recently produced plays include *the Only Game in Town, Barefoot in the Park* and *The Perfect Setup.* Produces 5 plays each summer, weekend performances. "We pay flat rate of $100 for 6 performances, $150 for 9 performances and $200 for 12 performances. We pay less for untried plays not previously produced." Send complete script only. Reports in 30 days. Enclose S.A.S.E. for return of submissions.

ROBERT L. STEELE ASSOCIATES, 40 East 52nd St., New York NY 10022. Produces plays of one, two, or three acts, for larger city audiences. Subject matter open. Broadway, off-Broadway, professional cast. "Well-written, well-constructed plays with a beginning, middle and ending. We are more interested in conventional 3-act plays. Structure is very important; developed characters. We prefer not to accept one-act plays unless three 1-act plays are offered at the same time. Unless it is a musical, we prefer a smaller cast, less than 10 is reasonable. We option for a limited time if play is to be reworked." Pays Dramatists Guild terms. Send synopsis or complete script. Reports in 8 to 10 weeks. Recent productions include *Any Resemblance to Persons* (Caplin), *Stag Movie* and *Six.* Enclose S.A.S.E. for return of submissions.

HENRY SWANSON, Arrow Rock Lyceum, Arrow Rock MO 65320. Produces plays of "any length for professional theater. We have an urban professional theater audience. We want plays of all kinds. No poorly written, trite plays. Other than that, we will look at anything." Pay is "individually negotiated." Send complete script only. Reports in 2 to 3 months. Enclose S.A.S.E. for return of submissions.

JOSEPH W. TALAROWSKI, State University of New York, Department of Theater, Brockport NY 14420. Produces two-act and three-act plays in a fine arts theater on the Brockport campus. "Cast is amateur, student. Audience is chiefly college students and faculty. No specific theme is sought for plays. Plays should be full-length, previously unproduced; straight, musical, or children's theater. No one-act plays. Moderate costuming would help." Produces 6 to 7 plays a year. Does not copyright plays. Pays "cost of production and promotion." Send complete script only. "Plays must be submitted prior to March 15. Selection is made by May 1." Enclose S.A.S.E. for return of submissions.

TEN PENNY PLAYERS, INC., 799 Greenwich St., New York NY 10014. Executive Director: Barbara Fisher Perry. Produces children's plays; "60 minutes maximum; that's about 40 full dialog script pages. Performed by equity performers only in theaters, museums, the streets. For children 2½ to adolescent age in New York City primarily. Plays should be small character productions; realistic children-oriented situations and dialog. We want only to see plays by those who have a realistic understanding of the needs and language of today's children. We want only plays that reach up to the level of our audience, rather than those that put our children down because they are children. We are not interested in ye olde traditional fairy tales, folk tales, etc. Cast limited to 5. Much as we would like to encourage amateurs, we really are only interested in the work of professionals with solid theater backgrounds. All plays are copyrighted in the author's name. We purchase rights to New York City productions for a period of 5 years, New York state productions for a period of 3 years. We pay a fee plus $10 each performance. This is negotiated, depending on our budget, length of play, amount of reworking we have to do." Send complete ms only. Reports in 2 to 4 weeks. Enclose S.A.S.E. for return of submissions.

THEATRE AMERICANA, P.O. Box 245, Altadena CA 91001. Attn: Playreading Committee. Full-length dramas, comedies or musicals by American authors, appropriate for presentation by a community theater. Produces three-act plays; limited playing time, 1½ to 2 hours. "No pornography. We value new approaches but cannot produce the obscene." Musicals should include piano arrangements. Plays with a Christmas theme or setting are welcomed. Looks for audience appeal; originality; excellence of characterization. No royalties can be paid, but the 4 original plays produced each year are eligible to compete for the $300 C. Brooks Fry Award. Enclose S.A.S.E. for return of submissions.

DONALD E. THOMSON, 54 Prospect Dr., Great Falls MT 59405. Produces two-act and three-act plays "in a summer repertory theater with about 20 performers. The audience is of all ages, mainly tourists; wide educational backgrounds and a variety of interests." Interested in "musicals, light entertainment. Our audience is fairly conservative, so many modern topics may not be suitable; i.e., nudity. The stage is small, and at present we have a fairly limited budget." Produces about 4 plays a year. Does not copyright plays. Pays "about $50 to $100 per show." Send synopsis or complete script. Enclose S.A.S.E. ·

TOBY THEATRE INCORPORATED, 1821 Fifth St., Rapid City SD 57701. For a middle American audience, very catholic tastes. Good solid story construction is a must. Generally prefer comedies, musicals, light dramas. Minority theatre (American Indian) is extremely solicited by theatre management, public audience. All plays produced at Toby Theatre use a mixed cast of professional and semi-professional actors. Two-act and three-act plays, and revue material (if a complete evening). "Old-fashioned melodramas (8 characters); three acts, good solid stories, characters, and theme. Generally we do not care for 'message' plays unless they are extremely entertaining as well. Emphasis on identifiable characters, situations, and structures." Will copyright plays. Buys American rights if play is producible in other markets. "We want no plays with war or violence in the theme. No dated indictments of political figures. Prefer small casts (10 maximum), stage size is 24x16 feet. Recent productions include *Your Place or Mine* and *The Gross National Product.* Produces 20 plays per year. Payment is negotiable. Send complete script only. Reports in approximately 3 weeks; sometimes longer if production is being considered. Enclose S.A.S.E. for return of submissions.

ROBERT K. TROIE, 28 Greenwich Ave., New York NY 10011. Produces two-act and three-act plays, revues, and rock or traditional musicals. "The plays will be performed by a professional cast at the Thomas Playhouse, South Casco, Maine. Any subject or theme. The approach is up to the playwright. We have a small stage, minimal sets, and a cast of no more than 10 persons." A recent production is *Decades.* Produces 4 plays each summer. Pays $100 to $150 for 10 performances. Send complete script. Reports September through May. Enclose S.A.S.E. for return of submissions.

RICHARD TYLER, 544 Brompton Place, Chicago IL 60657. Produces plays for "community theater and a summer theater; amateur and semiprofessional." Plays for "public and private audiences; mostly adults at college level. No limitations" in subject matter, approach, cast, or staging. Operas and musicals accepted. Recent productions include *Anything Goes.* Produces 3 to 10 plays a year. No payment for community theater. For summer theater, pays $15 per performance to $50 to $100 per week. Query first with synopsis only. Enclose S.A.S.E. for reply to queries.

W.P.A. THEATRE, 333 Bowery Ave., New York NY. Interested in all types of plays, more in the experimental and "now" than in what is usually considered Broadway fare; will look at originals. "Ours is a very workable space, thrust, environmental and round." Cast of 20 characters or under. Produces 15 to 20 plays a year from freelancers and playwrights-in-residence. "If ms is accepted, a two-year contract is signed with the playwright. 5% to 10% for 2 years only." Submit entire ms. Reports in 6 months. Enclose S.A.S.E. for return of submissions.

MAURICE WATSON, Afro-American Theatre Workshop, Brooklyn College, Bedford and Ave. H, Brooklyn NY 11210. Wants plays from black or Puerto Rican playwrights and dealing with black and Puerto Rican people. Looks at originals; prefers a synopsis. No limitations, but preferably an all black cast. Pays token amount of $100 if play is chosen for production. Reports in 3 to 5 weeks. Enclose S.A.S.E. for return of submissions.

WAYSIDE THEATRE, c/o Gerald Slavet, Middletown VA 22645. Looks at original plays for small cast. Produces one-act, two-act, and three-act plays; comedy, musicals, tragedy, drama and one-act children's plays. Pays royalties on production. Query first with synopsis. Reports "as soon as possible." Enclose S.A.S.E.

ARTHUR WHITELAW, Ritz Theater, 219 W. 48th St., New York NY 10036. Producer's Agent: L. Arnold Weissberger. Wants original musicals and comedies. "I will only accept scripts through known agents. All others will be returned unread."

RONALD A. WILLIS, University Theater, University of Kansas, Lawrence KS 66044. Produces plays for the university theater and for the classroom. "No length requirements." Audience is "university students and university community." Subjects, themes, approach are open. "We prefer low budget staging requirements." Recent productions include: *The Kiss* (Joler) and *Poor Baby* (Willis). Produces 11 to 12 plays a year. Does not copyright plays. Pays $25 to $50 for a "5-night run mainstage to about $100 for a 10-night run experimental stage for originals." Send synopsis or complete script. Reports "mid-May yearly for following September-through-May season." Enclose S.A.S.E. for return of submissions.

LEE R. YOPP, Bucks County Playhouse, New Hope PA 18938. Produces three-act plays: comedy, musicals, tragedy, drama. Payment "varies." Send complete script. Reports in 1 month. Enclose S.A.S.E. for return of submissions.

Play Publishers

The markets for the playwright's work are several: play publishers, whose names and addresses follow; play producers, listed in the Play Producers section; television producers, and motion picture producers. Film producers, like television producers, will not look at scripts submitted directly by the writer. They must be submitted through recognized literary agents. A list of these agents appears in the Authors' Agents section.

Publications which do not primarily publish plays but occasionally may publish dramatic material in some form are listed in the Juvenile and Literary and Little categories in the Consumer Magazines section. The playwright should also check the Book Publishers for additional play markets.

AMURU PRESS, INC., 161 Madison Ave., #2A, New York NY 10016. Editors: Jeremy Randolph, Georgia C. Nicholas, Ray Manieson. "Plays will be published and produced for black theater, theaters in general (all audiences), and will be performed by amateur and professional casts. We are interested in plays from our black writers in the United States and in all other countries covered by copyright law, and accept plays which have a defined 'direction' in the social, political, economic, and religious subject and topical theme. The playwright should observe the total effects of a stage production: structured with a clear and direct continuity of subject matter, a simplified but well-developed plot; it should be written in perspective for future presentation; it should entail depth which has been well thought out from research, experience, or creativity; the play must have a strong story line, tight continuity, and a suspense factor leading to a major climax. We expect works to embody the immense intellectual spectrum of black life. No plays entailing long speeches or long quotes from other writers' works. We invite comedy, allegory, satire, farce, musicals, poetic drama. Plays may involve any number of characters, props, sets, etc., but make sure that each character is definite, and that the play is designed economically." Offers "standard royalty rates." Playwright must "enclose detailed background of your writing career and future ambitions and include a 2x2 b&w photo." Reports in 2 weeks. Enclose S.A.S.E. for return of submissions.

ART CRAFT PLAY COMPANY, 233 Dows Building, P.O. Box 1058, Cedar Rapids IA 52406. Editor: J. Vincent Heuer. Interested in produced and unproduced three-act plays for high school production. Limited playing time: 1¾ to 2 hours. "Must be comedy or mystery with high moral standard; 10 to 20 characters (more female than male parts); on interior setting." Pays $500 and up; royalty or cash payment. Purchases amateur rights. Send synopsis with complete script. Reports in 2 weeks. Enclose S.A.S.E. for return of submissions.

BAKER'S PLAYS, 100 Chauncy St., Boston MA 02111. Editor: Edna M. Cahill. Caters especially to schools, colleges, churches, women's clubs, etc. Wants "plays or entertainment material; anything dealing with the dramatic form for the most part scaled to the amateur market." Submit complete ms. Reports promptly. Enclose S.A.S.E. for return of submissions.

CONTEMPORARY DRAMA SERVICE, Box 457, Downers Grove IL 60515. Editor: Arthur L. Zapel, Jr. "Interested in one-act plays, documentary dramas, adaptations, and church liturgies. Subject matter should be of interest and concern to school-age audience, from junior high through college. Treatment of material should make classroom presentation easy. Current affairs and social dilemmas of special interest. Currently interested in women's lib, abortion, ecology. Plays must present both sides of issue. Presentations for religious holidays Christmas, Purim, Shabuoth, and Easter accepted. Simple structure, not dependent on props and complicated staging. Novelty drama such as puppet-theater, skits, and monologues also considered. Particularly interested in good comedy material. We look most for unique style in staging ideas as well as action. We see drama as a means of communication through participation. Not interested in 3-act 'message plays' or traditional theater fare. We prefer realistic dialog written artfully. A 30-page script is maximum for us. Prefer about 6 in cast." Accepts over 20 plays a year from freelancers. Buys all rights. Pays 10% royalty "up to agreed amount." Send complete script with short synopsis and author's production notes. Reports in "about 1 month." Enclose S.A.S.E. for return of submissions.

DODD, MEAD AND COMPANY, 79 Madison Ave., New York NY 10016. Executive Editor: Allen T. Klots, Jr. Only interested in "playwrights after professional production, who promise to contribute to the literature of the theater." Royalty negotiated. Buys book rights only. Reports in about 4 weeks. Enclose S.A.S.E. for return of submissions.

THE DRAMATIC PUBLISHING CO., 86 East Randolph St., Chicago IL 60601. Editors: Sherman L. Sergel and Christopher Sergel, Jr. Uses one- and three-act plays and musicals for high schools, colleges, children's theater, church and community theater groups, comedy, drama or musicals. "Quality is more important than qubject matter." Recent productions include *Flowers for Algernon* and *Diary of Adam and Eve.* Publishes about 50 new plays a year. Pays percentage of performance royalties; twice a year on royalty contract; otherwise, outright purchase at agreed price. Submit complete script. Will consider photocopied submissions "if legible." Reports in 3 to 6 weeks. Enclose S.A.S.E. for return of submissions.

DRAMATISTS PLAY SERVICE, INC., 440 Park Ave. S., New York NY 10016. Executive Director: F. Andrew Leslie. Primarily interested in plays from Broadway and off-Broadway. Rarely able to offer publication for unproduced plays. "Our organization is concerned exclusively with the handling of amateur leasing rights for the plays listed in our catalog"

ELDRIDGE PUBLISHING COMPANY, P.O. Drawer 209, Franklin OH 45005. Editor: Kay Myerly. Wants good three-act and one-act plays. Publishes comedy, drama, high school plays, seasonal plays. Special day, church, and school entertainments for all ages and all occasions. Unusual plots, snappy dialog, good curtains. "All settings must be kept at a minimum. We do not accept anything on a controversial theme. Writers should bear in mind that short dialog is much better than a long, drawnout speech." Accepts 15 to 20 plays a year from freelancers. Payment on acceptance. "Payment varies with well-known authors and the type of script." Query first. Reports "as soon as possible; during our busy season it might take longer than 90 days." Enclose S.A.S.E. for reply to queries.

SAMUEL FRENCH, 25 W. 45th St., New York NY 10036. Editors: William Talbot and Jack Walsh. Willing at all times to read mss of books concerning the theater, as well as mss of plays. Wants plays that are "original, imaginative. Interested in character. No motion picture scenarios, verse plays, single-shot TV plays, Biblical plays, or children's plays on subjects already published." Accepts 10 to 15 mss a year from freelancers. No reading fee. In addition to publishing plays, also acts as agents in the placement of plays for Broadway production, and of program series for television production. Payment on royalty basis. Send complete script. Reports in 6 to 8 weeks. Enclose S.A.S.E. for return of submissions.

THE HEUER PUBLISHING COMPANY, 232-234 Dows Bldg., Cedar Rapids IA 52406. Editor: Edward I. Heuer. Wants 3-act comedy and mystery plays suitable for high school production. "One interior setting; 12 to 18 characters." Pays $500 to $1,000 for three-act play. Pays on acceptance. Query first with synopsis. Buys amateur rights. Reports "promptly." Enclose S.A.S.E. for reply to queries.

THE INSTRUCTOR PUBLICATIONS, INC., *Instructor Magazine,* Dansville NY 14437. Editor: Dr. Ernest Hilton. Will consider any type play suitable for presentation in elementary schools by children from 4 to 14. Most are from 10 to 25 minutes playing time, but occasionally interested in longer productions. Limited music—melody of one or two songs. Interested especially in dramatic material that offers opportunities for creativity—ideas for play frameworks on which children can build. Subject matter should reflect the serious nature of education today, and the current interests of children. Fairies and fantasy are temporarily out of favor. Assembly program suggestions and seasonal plays welcomed. Freelance writers outside the educational field should consult qualified persons in regard to educational value of script before submitting. Payments range from $20 to $50. Submit seasonal material at least 5 to 6 months in advance. Buys all publication rights. Reprinting in books is subject to company's approval. Reports in 2 weeks. Enclose S.A.S.E. for return of submissions.

DAVID McKAY COMPANY, INC., 750 Third Ave., New York NY 10017. Publishes 1, 2, and 3-act plays. "Majority of plays are produced for high school audiences, church audiences, and summer amateur productions. We have a high rate of local productions being put on by small theater groups and civic groups. One part of our audience is for children, roughly ages 6 to 14. Plays about clowns, magic, etc. We also have a selection of religious plays, mostly dealing with aspects of the Crucifiction, and several tragedies dealing with figures in religious history. Any play that is interesting, and deals with subjects people can relate to. The plays can be of varied interests, and should be entertaining enough for children. Subjects to be avoided could be things like drugs, violence, and sex. No specific format, as long as the play works. We will not publish any plays that are in bad taste. Anything that will lose the attention of the audience, and might possibly turn them against the play, will probably not be considered. No limitations in cast, props, or stage. The plays should not be too elaborate; something that an amateur group can produce without too much trouble regarding the sets and costumes. A recent production is *The Night of January 16th,* a courtroom drama proved to be very successful. Payment for the play is based upon the play itself." Send synopsis or complete script. Reports usually in 3 to 5 weeks. Enclose S.A.S.E. for return of submissions.

PERFORMANCE PUBLISHING, 978 N. Maclean Ave., Elgin IL 60120. Editor: Virginia Butler. "We are extremely interested in seeing any play suitable for production by amateurs. We are particularly interested in plays (or even television scripts) that would be of interest to the high school market. We supply plays to all nonprofessional theater groups in the U.S. and Canada: 50% high school; 15% children's theater; 35% college, community stock, and church theater groups. We're more anxious to work with new writers because we have a great need to develop new writers." Uses some Christmas plays. "Plays should be 15 minutes to 2½ hours playing time. The rates we pay are consistent with everybody in each of 3 basic categories: original plays, dramatizations (which command half the percentage of original plays), and Broadway plays, in which the percentage is controlled by the Dramatists Guild basic contract." Enclose S.A.S.E. for return of submissions.

PIONEER DRAMA SERVICE, 2172 S. Colorado Blvd., Denver CO 80222. Editor and Publisher: Shubert Fendrich. "Our main needs now are for children's theater plays (plays that have been produced by adults for children), about an hour in length, and old-fashioned melodrama. We also buy a very few outstanding one-act plays. We are interested only in plays that have been successfully produced on the amateur or professional stage." Does not want to see "unproduced plays, one-acts with more than one set, plays which are largely male in cast." Accepts a maximum of 10 plays a year from freelancers. "We either select plays on a basis of outright purchase or pay a royalty of 10% of copy sales and 50% of production royalties and resale rights." Buys all rights. Reports in 1 to 2 months. Enclose S.A.S.E. for return of submissions.

PLAYS, The Drama Magazine for Young People, 8 Arlington Street, Boston MA 02116. Publishes approximately 90 one-act plays each season. Interested in buying good plays to be performed by young people of all age groups—junior and senior high, middle grades, lower grades. In addition to comedies, farces, melodramas, mysteries and dramas, can use plays for holidays and other special occasions, such as Book Week, National Education Week. Adaptations of classic stories and fables, historical plays, plays about other lands, puppet plays, plays for an all-girl or all-boy cast, folk tales, fairy tales, creative dramatics, plays dramatizing factual information and on such concepts as good government, importance of voting, involvement and participation as citizens, and plays for conservation, ecology or human rights programs are needed. Prefers one scene; when more than one is necessary, changes should be simple. Mss should follow the general style of *Plays*. Stage directions should not be typed in capital letters or underlined. Every play ms should include: a list of characters, an indication of time, a description of setting; an "At Rise," describing what is taking place on stage as curtain rises; production notes, indicating the number of characters and the playing time, describing the costumes, properties, setting and special lighting effects, if any. Playwrights should not use incorrect grammar or dialect. Characters with physical defects, speech impediments should not be included. Desired lengths for mss are: Junior and Senior high—20 to 25 double-spaced ms pages (25 to 30 minutes playing time). Middle Grades—12 to 15 pages (15 to 20 minutes playing time). Lower Grades—6 to 10 pages (8 to 15 minutes playing time). Pays "good rates on acceptance." Reports in 3 to 4 weeks. Enclose S.A.S.E. for return of submissions.

PROSCENIUM PRESS, P.O. Box 361, Newark DE 19711. Editor: Robert Hogan. "We publish plays and books related to drama. Most of our books are paperbacks. We publish a Lost Play series which prints notable plays that have never been published, a short play series, an Irish play series, a series of adaptations such as Mary Manning's adaptation of Frank O'Connor's novel *The Saint and Mary Kate*, and we have recently brought out the first volume in a Contemporary Drama series." Publishes about 6 books of plays a year. Offers standard 10% royalty contract. Submit complete script in conventional format. Rights purchased vary; usually buys serial, anthology and translation rights. Reports in 1 month. Enclose S.A.S.E. for return of submissions.

Syndicates

Syndicates sell editorial copy to publishers on a commission basis, with the author receiving 40 to 60 percent of the gross proceeds. Some syndicates, however, pay the writer a salary or a minimum guarantee. Writers of top syndicated columns may earn $50,000 or more per year. The aspiring syndicate writer must first make sure his work won't be competing in an already flooded field. Second, he must select a syndicate which will properly promote his material. The larger syndicates, of course, usually have better promotional facilities. (A list of syndicates which includes all the titles of the columns and features they handle appears in the *Editor and Publisher Syndicate Directory*, published at 850 Third Avenue, New York NY 10022. $3.) It's best to query the syndicate editor first, enclosing a half-dozen sample columns or feature ideas and a stamped addressed envelope. Some writers self-syndicate their own material. The writer here earns 100% of the proceeds but also bears the expense of soliciting the clients, reproducing and mailing the features, billing, etc. See the chapter "How To Syndicate Your Own Column" in the Writer's Digest book *The Creative Writer*.

AMERICAN FEATURES SYNDICATE, 964 Third Ave., New York NY 10022. Editor: David Mark. Copyrights material. Will consider photocopied submissions. Reporting time "varies." Enclose S.A.S.E. for return of submissions.
Nonfiction: Travel and true adventure. Buys single features and article series. Does not contract for columns. Length: 1,000 to 5,000 words. Pays $100 to $750. Usual outlets are newspapers and regional magazines, including some trade publications.

AP NEWSFEATURES, 50 Rockefeller Plaza, New York NY 10020. General Editor: Dan Perkes. Enclose S.A.S.E. for return of submissions.
Nonfiction, Photos, Fillers, and Puzzles: Buys article series or column ideas "dealing with areas of science, social issues that can be expanded into book form. Do not usually buy single features." Length: 600 to 1,000 words. Pays minimum $25.

ARTISTS AND WRITERS SYNDICATE, 918 Sixteenth St., N.W., Suite 302, Washington DC 20006. Editor: Philip W. Steitz. Supplies material to metropolitan daily newspapers. Does not copyright material. Cartoons, comic strips and newspaper columns. Will consider photocopied submissions. Reports in 4 weeks. Enclose S.A.S.E. for return of submissions.
Nonfiction: "Freelance material that could be used in a daily newspaper column that we are now developing for children." Length: "no minimum or maximum. Payments vary."

AUTHENTICATED NEWS INTERNATIONAL, ANI, 170 Fifth Avenue, New York NY 10010. Editor: Jesse J. Seigel. Supplies material to newspapers, magazines, and house organs in the United States, Canada, South America, and overseas countries. Buys exclusive and nonexclusive rights. Reports in 3 months. Enclose S.A.S.E. for return of submissions.
Nonfiction, Humor, and Photos: Can use photo news, photo features, photo stories of human interest, travel, animals, science, medical, religious, children, industry, architecture, construction, education, art and handicraft, teenage activities and hobbies. Prefers 8x10 b&w glossies, color transparencies, 4x5 prints, 2¼x2¼, 35mm color. Requires model release where necessary. Pays 50% royalty.

AUTO NEWS SYNDICATE, 8530 Canfield Dr., Dearborn MI 48127. Editor: Don O'Reilly. Reports "within a few days." Enclose S.A.S.E. for return of submissions. **Nonfiction and Photos:** Syndicates articles, photos on automotive subjects and motor sports. Pays 50% royalty, no flat fees.

BLACK PRESS SERVICE, 166 Madison Ave., New York NY 10016. Editor: Roy Thompson. Supplies material to "newspapers throughout the world." Buys all rights. Will handle copyrighted material. Buys "thousands" of features a year from freelancers. Reports "as soon as possible." Enclose S.A.S.E. for return of submissions.
Nonfiction and Photos: "Hard news stories, features, and photos concerning black people. We do purchase single features of particular interest to black people. We do not provide standing columns." Material must be "hard news, regular journalistic style." Photos should be b&w glossies. Word length open. Rate of payment by arrangement.

CANADA WIDE FEATURE SERVICE, 245 St. James W., Montreal 126, Que., Canada. Photo Editor: Tom Pigeon. Supplies material "for editorial purposes, public relations advertisements, etc. We do not buy outright but accept on consignment."
Photos: "Color slides of cities, countryside, social problems (pollution, poverty, etc.), sports, leisure activities-industry, communications, general stock." B&w glossies, color transparencies. "We give 60% commission."

CANADIAN SCENE, Suite 305, 2 College St., Toronto, Ont., Canada. M5G 1K3. Editor: Miss Ruth Gordon. Query first. Submit seasonal material 3 months in advance. Reports in 1 week. Enclose S.A.S.E. for reply to queries.
Nonfiction: "Canadian Scene is a voluntary information service. Its purpose is to provide written and pictorial material to democratic, foreign language publications in Canada. The material is chosen with a view to directing readers to an understanding of Canadian political affairs, foreign relations, social customs, industrial progress, culture, history, and institutions. In a 700-word article, the writer can submit almost any subject on Canada, providing it leaves the newcomer with a better knowledge of Canada. It should be written in a simple, tightly knit, straightforward style." Length: 500 to 1,000 words. Pays 3¢ a word.

CHICAGO TRIBUNE-NEW YORK NEWS SYNDICATE, INC., 220 East 42nd St., New York NY 10017. Editor: Thomas B. Dorsey. Supplies material to Sunday supplements and newspapers in North America and abroad. Buys "worldwide rights, where possible; must have North American rights to be interested." Will consider photocopied submissions "if clean and clear." Submit "at least 6 samples of any submission for continuing feature, plus statement of philosophy for column." Enclose S.A.S.E. for return of submissions.
Nonfiction, Photos, and Puzzles: "Political, women's, humor, sports, health, food, furnishings, fashion columns. We're looking for short, topical series on social, psychological, news-oriented subjects—6 to 12 parts, 7,500 to 15,000 words; topical and humor columns. Must be extremely well-written. No single features unless highly exclusive and topical." Buys article series. Recently bought in-depth interviews with Bob Hope, Charles Boyer; series on "Roberto Clemente, The Real Godfather" and "Should You Push Your Child Into Learning?". Contracts for columns. "Anything fresh and original is considered. Must be extremely well-written and provide a new idea or a very different approach to what's in field now. No bad carbon copies of columns already on market." Length: "whatever the writer is comfortable with and works for the subject." Pay "varies, depending on market. Usual 50-50 split on contractual material." Photos purchased with features. Wants "top grade b&w glossies and/or original color transparencies."

COLLEGE PRESS SERVICE, 1452 Pennsylvania Ave., Denver CO 80203. Supplies material to 350 college newspapers. Does not copyright material. Offers material for one-time use "for reproduction by our subscribers." Buys 50 to 75 features a year from freelancers. Will consider photocopied submissions. Reports in 3 weeks. Enclose S.A.S.E. for return of submissions.
Nonfiction and Photos: "Features of national angle that are of interest to a college

audience. Coverage supplied by CPS can be divided into 6 major categories: events and activities on individual campuses; curricular and educational reform and other campus trends; conferences and activities of national education and student groups: governmental activity and programs affecting higher education and students; general national and international affairs; analysis and opinion articles." Buys single features. Does not buy article series. Contracts for columns, "but not often." Does not want "articles on speeches by famous people." Length: "usually less than 6 pages double-spaced." Pays $5 to $15—"we are nonprofit." Captioned photos purchased with features. "Not fussy about size, but clarity important."

CRISWELL PREDICTS NEWSPAPER SYNDICATE, 6620 Selma Avenue, TV-Bldg.-ONE, Hollywood CA 90028. Editor: Jeron King Criswell. Buys all rights. Will handle copyrighted material. Buys about 50 features a year from freelancers. Query first. Reports in 1 week. Enclose S.A.S.E. for reply to queries.
Nonfiction: Buys very specialized material dealing with predictions, past and present. Length: open. Pays 10¢ a word.

CRUX NEWS SERVICE, Shickshinny PA 18655. Editor: Thourot Pichel. Does not copyright material. Buys "very few" features a year from freelancers. Will consider photocopied submissions. Enclose S.A.S.E. for return of submissions.
Nonfiction: "History and political only." Buys single features. Does not buy article series or columns. Pays "nominal standard."

CURIOUS FACTS FEATURES, 514 Deerfield Road, Lebanon OH 45036. Editor: Donald Whitacre. Buys all rights. Reports in 2 weeks. Enclose S.A.S.E. for return of submissions.
Nonfiction: Uses "oddities" of all types including strange animals, strange laws, people, firsts, etc. Length: 50 to 100 words. Pays $10 to $15.

DETJEN PHILATELIC NEWS SERVICE, Salt Point Turnpike, Clinton Corners NY 12514. Editor: Gustav Detjen, Jr. Does not copyright material. Reports in 2 weeks. Enclose S.A.S.E. for return of submissions.
Nonfiction: Looking for anything that concerns postage stamps, stamp collecting, history of postage stamps and collecting. Occasionally buys single features and column ideas. Length: 250 to 500 words. Pays $5 to $30.

DISPATCH NEWS SERVICE INTERNATIONAL, INC., 1826 R St., N.W., Washington DC 20009. Editor: Richard Berliner. Supplies material to major dailies, weekly publications and college newspaper. "Most regular users are the large dailies such as *Newsday, San Francisco Chronicle* and others." Buys worldwide rights for one-time use. Purchases 100 to 150 features a year from freelancers. Suggests query first. Will not consider photocopied submissions. Reports in 1 week. Enclose S.A.S.E. for reply to queries.
Nonfiction and Photos: "Investigative reports, both from U.S. and abroad which either relate to the U.S. and its people, government, or foreign policy actions—or in the case of files from abroad (particularly interested in files from Asia, Latin America, and Africa) which relate to the people, problems and cultures of foreign lands so as to build a meaningful and educational communication link between this country and the other countries. Have no use for polemics. Want the writers to have a fine, critical eye for truth; ability to analyze and ferret out his/her facts. We buy single features, but would stress that we're also interested in going beyond the single feature to get a continued coverage of an area of particular topic. The basic need of the single feature is that it *not* be a filler or fluff article. To use a feature from a writer we have never dealt with before requires that the documentation be impeccable, the credibility not open to question, and that it be a sure seller. Prefer not to see human interest articles that are so localized, so syrupy, that the interest is only for a home-town paper. Length: single features, 440 to 1,200 words; articles, 1,000 words per part." Pays $20 to $150. "Freelance contributors currently receive a flat $20, payable upon distribution, for articles distributed to the commercial dailies but used in the other markets. Freelancers also receive 50% of money paid by commercial papers for a particular article. (The flat rate of $10 and $20 comes from the income derived from papers on contract.) Payment from magazine articles is split 80/20 for

the writer and the service respectively." Photos purchased with features. B&w preferred; 1 negative and 1 print (or contact sheet) for each photo.

EDITORIAL CONSULTANT SERVICE, P.O. Box 120, Babylon NY 11702. Director: Art Ingoglia. Buys all rights. Pays on acceptance. Handles copyrighted material "on occasion." Query first. Reports in 2 to 3 weeks. Enclose S.A.S.E. for reply to queries.
Nonfiction: Freelance material welcome for business press, newspapers, top magazines. Column ideas accepted for automotive column "Let's Talk About Your Car." General features accepted after writer has been assigned by editor. Payment on percentage basis of 50%.

EDITORIAL SUPPLY HOUSE INC., 210 E. 35 St., New York NY 10016. Editor: Christopher Watson. Buys first rights. Buys more than 100 features a year from freelancers. Reports in 2 to 4 weeks. Enclose S.A.S.E. for return of submissions.
Nonfiction, Fiction, and Humor: Erotic fiction, unusual articles, and satire. Single features. For columns: sexually oriented material, erotic book reviews, stag movie reviews. Seldom buys article series. Single feature lengths: 2,500 words. Columns: 1,500 words. Pays $50 to $75 for fiction. Outlets for material have been *Rogue, Swank, Dapper, Topper,* and *Swingle.*
Photos: Purchased without features. Prefer contacts first for consideration.

ENTERPRISE SCIENCE NEWS, 230 Park Ave., New York NY 10017. Editor: David Hendin. Buys all rights. Pays on acceptance. Query first. Reports in 2 to 4 weeks. Enclose S.A.S.E. for reply to queries.
Nonfiction: "We only buy from professional science-medical writers." Wants feature-type newspaper stories on scientific subjects of current interest. The science should be interesting and applicable to the reader. Must be clear, concise, accurate and objective. Stories with good art receive preference. Length: 700 to 1,200 words. Pays $30 to $500, "depending on author, length and type of story, quality of writing, whether commissioned or not, etc."
Photos: Buys with features or with captions only. Color or b&w. Rates vary.

GENERAL FEATURES CORPORATION, Times Mirror Square, Los Angeles CA 90053. Chief Editor: Patrick McHugh. Buys newspaper syndication rights. Reports in 2 weeks. Enclose S.A.S.E. for return of submissions.
Nonfiction: Buys columns. Interested in fresh and original features of a continuing nature. Contract arrangements are made in payment for material.

GLANZER NEWS SERVICE, P.O. Box 42, Adelaide St. Station, Toronto, Ontario, Canada. Editor: Phil Glanzer. Editorial correspondents and representatives in Canada for a number of American weekly and monthly publications. Also takes care of the editorial requirements of a number of Canadian publications. Buys all rights. Does not accept much freelance material. Enclose S.A.E. and International Reply Coupons for return of submissions.
Nonfiction: Can use some articles on credit and collections; also on the Small Claims Court. Length: 1,500 words. Pays $50 to $75; $100 to $125 for articles on assignment.

GLOBE PHOTOS, INC., 404 Park Ave., S., New York NY 10016. Editor: Dave Wilson. Supplies photojournalism material to magazines, newspapers, and advertising agencies. "We do not purchase material. We act only as agents for freelance photographers and photographer/writers on a 50/50 commission basis. We report sales on the month following payment from the purchaser. We require a steady flow of photo features with text and captions, b&w and color; all sizes from 35mm up."

GOOD NEWS FROM EVERYWHERE, Box 296, South Laguna CA 92677. Editor: Hubbard Keavy. "Weekly column syndicated by Los Angeles Times to approximately 50 newspapers." Buys 520 clippings a year from freelancers. Will consider photocopied submissions. "Clippings cannot be returned."
Nonfiction: "We are reporting the good news—anything that shows people going beyond normal duties to perform good or unusual deeds for others. We want the kind of stories that cause readers to say, 'Well, there is some good news after all.' We

want stories of man's compassion and concern; stories of the extraordinary things ordinary people do for their neighbors; stories of the pursuit of constructive adventure. We do not want wire service or other syndicated material." Pays $5 a clipping.

DAVE GOODWIN & ASSOCIATES, P.O. Box 6094, Surfside FL 33154. Editor: Dave Goodwin. Buys first rights. Will handle copyrighted material. Buys about 35 features a year from freelancers. No query required. Reports in 2 weeks. Enclose S.A.S.E. for return of submissions.

Nonfiction: "Money-saving information for consumers: how to save on home expenses; auto, medical, drug, insurance, boat, business items, etc." Buys single features "but prefer series." Buys column ideas. Material should be "brief, pithy, practical. We prefer meaty subject matter to lofty prose." Typical column is "Insurance for Consumers." Length: 50 to 500 words. Pays "50% on publication, or $3 per piece minimum and 10¢ per word maximum."

GREENWICH FEATURES, INC., Time-Life Bldg., New York NY 10020. Executive Editor: George F. Foley. Buys syndicate and book rights. Reports in 10 days. Enclose S.A.S.E. for return of submissions.

Nonfiction: "Name features, books, current events features, youth-oriented material. We are interested in bylined 5- to 10-part features on special subjects by experts or well-researched documentaries on all subjects." Payment negotiable.

HEAVENLY COMICS, 1316 E. 6th, Tulsa OK 74120. Editor: Ruth Davis. Buys all rights. Reports in 2 weeks. Enclose S.A.S.E. for return of submissions.

Poetry: Wants "poetry with a religious, humorous quality. Must be professional quality and have good rhythm. We pay flat rate or percentage as applicable."

HOLLYWOOD INFORMER SYNDICATE, P.O. Box 3049, Hollywood CA 90028. Editor: John Austin. Buys first serial rights for one-time use. Handles copyrighted material. Usual outlets are Australia, England, Japan, Germany, U.S.A. Buys about 50 features a year from freelancers. Reports in 6 weeks. Enclose S.A.S.E. for return of submissions.

Nonfiction and Photos: "Mainly 'show biz' oriented material, and offbeat human interest. New medical discoveries; personality features on new show business and TV faces, not written from 'clips.' Photojournalism pieces for Europe." A recent example of a single feature is "Marilyn Monroe Was Murdered." Single feature length: 750 to 800 words. Also buys articles series such as photo features on exotic dancers for European magazines or offbeat series on famous murders. "Good market in Europe for photographers." Length: 4 to 6 parts, 1,500 words. Photos: 6x9 or 8x10 glossies. Captions required. Pays $20 to $150 and up for series.

INFORMATION PRESS SERVICE, Key Colony Beach FL 33051. Editor: Frederick G. Philcox. Buys first publication rights. Pays on publication. No query required. No bylines used, since material is rewritten before submitted to clients. Enclose S.A.S.E. for return of submissions.

Nonfiction and Photos: Articles and travel photos of interest to the general magazine reader. Especially interested in consumer-oriented articles, exposes, war adventure tales slanted toward the men's adventure line (*a la Stag, Man's World*), health and how-to-save-money tips. Length: 1,500 to 3,000 words. Pays $25 to $250.

Fiction: Not interested in fiction except for mysteries in the style currently being used in Alfred Hitchcock-type magazines. Plot should have a twist ending. Length: maximum 7,500 words.

INTERCITY NEWS SERVICE, 103 Park Ave., New York NY 10017. Editor: Edgar W. Nassauer. Query first; "only queries of 50 words or less. If queries are to be returned, sender must enclose return postage."

Nonfiction: "Newspaper features on business and financial topics. All material is staff-written unless specifically assigned. Do not send prepared articles. Pay rate by negotiation on each special assignment."

INTERMEDIA NEWS AND FEATURE SERVICE, 229 Seventh Ave., New York NY 10011. Editor: Charles B. Yulish. Query first with feature proposals for possible placement. Enclose S.A.S.E. for reply to queries.

Nonfiction: Single features dealing with consumer entertainment and interpretive news reporting of current national and international subjects and events. Length: 500 words maximum. Pays flat fee according to the piece.

INTERNATIONAL NEWSFEATURE SYNDICATE, 1310 Lindahl Ct., San Jose CA 95120. Editor: Ed Dunckelmann. Supplies material to newspapers. Buys first newspaper rights. "No unsolicited submissions. Send only credentials and credits for our files." Reports in 30 days. Enclose S.A.S.E. for reply to queries.
Nonfiction: "We will maintain a file of responsible accredited environmental and consumer writers for possible assignment in their local area for our 'Ecology Line' column. Writers must be able to do complete job, not merely cry panic. Any preconceived opinions or bias is immediate cause for nonconsideration. No unsolicited features or series. Length will be assigned." Pay open.

JEWISH TELEGRAPHIC AGENCY, 660 First Ave., New York NY 10016. Editor: Murray Zuckoff. Enclose S.A.S.E. for return of submissions.
Nonfiction: Buys Jewish news and features. Interested in news features dealing with aspects of Jewish life. Length: 800 to 1,200 words. Pays $20.

KEISTER ADVERTISING SERVICE, INC., Strasburg VA 22657. Buys all rights. Will handle copyrighted material. Buys about 50 features a year from freelancers. Query first. Reports in 2 to 8 weeks. Enclose S.A.S.E. for reply to queries.
Nonfiction: Religious and inspirational texts "with human interest angle to attract the unchurched." Length: 150 to 200 words. Pays $15 to $20 per single feature.

KING FEATURES SYNDICATE, 235 E. 45th St., New York NY 10017. Supplies material to newspapers. Submit new features to Neal Freeman, Vice President and Editor. Submit photos to Louis Messolonghites, Assistant to the Editor. Enclose S.A.S.E. for return of submissions.
Nonfiction and Photos: "Topical nonfiction, 'service' material, leisure activities." Buys single features and article series. Contracts for columns. Length: 500 to 750 words. Pays in commission percentage.

LOS ANGELES TIMES SYNDICATE, Times Mirror Square, Los Angeles CA 90053. Chief Editor: Patrick McHugh. Buys newspaper syndication rights. Reports in 2 weeks. Enclose S.A.S.E. for return of submissions.
Nonfiction: Buys columns. Interested in fresh and original features of a continuing nature. Syndicates the Art Buchwald, Joseph Alsop columns. Contract arrangements are made in payment for material.

MEL MARTIN ENTERPRISES, P.O. Box 22505, Houston TX 77027. Editor: Melbourne M. Martin, Jr. Buys exclusive publication rights and right to assign. Reports in 1 month. Enclose S.A.S.E. for return of submissions.
Nonfiction: Interested in automotive, boating, adventure, investments, business, conservative political columns and articles. Does not, as a general rule, buy single features, but will consider "one shots." Pays up to 40% of selling price.

MARTIN'S INTERNATIONAL NEWSREEL, P.O. Box 8688, Columbus OH 43215. Editor: M.W. Martin. Supplies material to "consumer, trade, and professional magazines here and abroad." Does not copyright material. "Material is protected by the copyrights of our clients. Rights vary from one-time U.S. rights to all rights worldwide. We can handle only professional presentations." Will not consider photocopied submissions. Reports in 2 weeks. Enclose S.A.S.E. for return of submissions.
Nonfiction and Photos: "Captioned photos suitable for 'Martin's International Newsreel,' a captioned photo feature. Also, featurettes with photos suitable for the same title. Interest areas: science, medicine, technology, and limited human interest. We sell our pictorials to top magazines in this country, as well as to many leading publications abroad. We can always use good pictorials, but we are unable to work with new talent. Our need is only for established professionals." Does not buy article series or column ideas. "No religion, fashion, food, or politics. No local interest material. National or international interest only." Length: "best length is 300 to 500 words, if with one photo; 800 to 1,200 words if several photos. Nothing over

1,200 words." Uses "captioned photos, b&w only, 5x7 or larger. Best size is 8x10 glossy. Featurettes may contain color; all sizes of transparencies. Correspondents average $12 per captioned photo per use. Featurettes average $25 to $75, depending on length."

McNAUGHT SYNDICATE, INC., 60 E. 42 St., New York NY 10017. Editor: Anne Rickey. Buys about 4 features a year fron freelancers. Will consider photocopied submissions. Reports in 4 weeks. Enclose S.A.S.E. for return of submissions.
Nonfiction and Humor: Puzzles, cartoons, comic strips, political and medical columns. Contracts for columns: Washington editorial, medical, and humor. Columns are 500 words in length. Pays $25 for accepted material for panel, "This Funny World." Newspapers are usual outlet for material.

MID-CONTINENT FEATURE SYNDICATE, Box 1662, Pittsburgh PA 15230. Editorial Chairman: Charles L. Conover. Supplies material to "600 small and medium-sized daily newspapers." Buys North American rights. Pays on acceptance. Reports in 5 days. Enclose S.A.S.E. for return of submissions.
Nonfiction: Book reviews, serialized books, fashion series, urban redevelopment series, pollution control articles, memoirs, world movie (not Hollywood) material. Purchases single books for serialization; buys features in minimum six-article form in areas of current events, education, women's interest, cookbook materials. Wants "materials for syndicated columns being distributed: food, fashion, drama, business (2 columns), humor, book review (3 columns), Washington news, and special metals technical review. Our contracts with syndicated writers and artists call for the usual 50/50 division of net proceeds, after production and distribution expenses. Materials bought on a spot basis are on standard per word or per panel rates, depending on the stature of the writer or artist, and going from 5¢ a word upward."

NATIONAL CATHOLIC NEWS SERVICE, 1312 Massachusetts Ave., N.W., Washington DC 20005. Editor: A.E.P. Wall. "Individual judgments are made" as to copyrighting material. "We are served by a number of stringers as well as freelancers. We provide a daily service and have a fairly constant market. Inquiries are welcomed, but they should be both brief and precise. Too many inquiries are coy and/or vague. Will consider photocopied submissions." Reports in 2 to 3 weeks. Enclose S.A.S.E. for reply to queries.
Nonfiction: Short news and feature items of religious or social interest, particularly items with a Catholic thrust. Buys single features and articles series. Feature examples: Buddhists in Hawaii, religious life today in the Soviet Union, development of new teaching techniques in U.S. Catholic diocese; social-ethnic implications of the presidential election. Series examples: programs to provide alternatives to abortion for unwed pregnant women; changing attitudes toward activist programs among U.S. Protestants. Contracts for columns: "This is a highly competitive market and we are extremely selective. Our columns range from labor concerns to the liturgy." Length for single features: no minimum, maximum of 800 words. Article series: maximum of 3 parts, about 700 words each. Columns: open in length; generally, the shorter the better. Generally pays a maximum of 5¢ a word for news and feature copy. "We market primarily to more than 100 Catholic weekly newspapers. We also serve foreign Catholic agencies and U.S. Catholic weekly newspapers."
Photos: Purchased with or without features. Captions required. News and feature photos of interest to Catholic periodicals. "We operate a photo service that mails to clients four times a week." Pays from $5 to $15 for each photo, depending on quality and originality.

NATIONAL FEATURES SYNDICATE, 1052-A National Press Bldg., Washington DC 20004. Editor: Fred Rosenblatt. Reports in 1 week or less. Enclose S.A.S.E. for return of submissions.
Nonfiction: Inside stories of politics and economics of health industry and no-fault and malpractice insurance. Buys singles as well as column ideas.

NATIONAL NEWSPAPER SYNDICATE, 20 N. Wacker Drive, Chicago IL 60606. Editor: Thomas Hirsh. Buys all rights. Reports in 3 weeks. Enclose S.A.S.E. for return of submissions.
Nonfiction: Buys only columns and comic strips on continuous basis, daily or

weekly; no series or short run features. No general commentary; columns on specific subject areas only.

NC NEWS SERVICE, U.S. Catholic Conference, 1312 Massachusetts Ave. N.W., Washington DC 20005. Director: A.E.P. Wall. Serves a circulation of 4,000,000 plus. Supplies material to "more than 200 publications." Buys all rights. Will handle copyrighted material. Buys over 1,000 features a year from freelancers. Query first. Reports in 2 weeks. Enclose S.A.S.E. for reply to queries.
Nonfiction and Humor: News and features on religious and allied subjects, now broadly interpreted to include all current news. Occasional Christmas and Easter materials. "Our audience is Catholic, so the material should have some orientation to this special audience but not a pious approach. We reflect the Church's concern for social issues." Buys single features and column ideas. Length: 850 words maximum. Payment "depends on material and ranges up to 5¢ a word. We pay more for exclusive stories of special interest."
Photos: Purchased with mss or with captions only. B&w glossies. Religious photo features preferred, but good, natural (unposed) features of all types considered. Photo Editor: Thomas Lorsung.

NEWS FLASH INTERNATIONAL INC., 508 Atlanta Ave., North Massapequa NY 11758. Editor: Jackson B. Pokress. Supplies material to Observer/Tribune newspapers and Champion sports publications. "Contact editor prior to submission to allow for space if article is newsworthy." Will consider photocopied submissions. Enclose S.A.S.E. for reply to queries.
Nonfiction: Material on "sports action—all sports (football, baseball, boxing, wrestling, etc)." Buys single features, such as "profiles on athletes, sports action concentrating on a single player, current trend of women in sports." Does not contract for columns. Pay "depends on assignment."
Photos: Purchased on assignment; captions required. Uses "good quality 8x10 b&w glossies; good choice of angles and lenses." Pay "depends on assignment."

NEWSCO PRESS FEATURES, INC., P.O. Box 91, Blairsville PA 15717. Editor: William H. Thomas. Supplies material to newspapers. Buys "world rights, all media, unless specifically agreed otherwise." Buys about 100 features a year from freelancers. Query first to William H. Thomas, 253 E. 62nd St., New York NY 10021. "Send features to Blairsville address." Will consider photocopied submissions. Reports in 2 to 4 weeks. Enclose S.A.S.E. for return of submissions and reply to queries.
Nonfiction, Fillers, and Puzzles: Wants "articles on timely sports, famous sports personalities, local unusual sports copy of national interest." Buys single features, such as "The Way It Was" ("sports nostalgia by Red Barber") and "Tennis: the Romance is Gone" ("a comparison of tennis as it was and is today by former amateur tennis veteran Andrew Stern"). Buys articles series on "almost any subject suitable for family newspapers. We prefer a 3-part or 6-part series, with each installment running 750 to 1,000 words." Contracts for columns. "Columns on almost any subject will be considered. Presently have mostly columns on sports themes. Also, 'Man to Man,' a fashion column distributed on a once-a-week basis; 'Sportsword Puzzle,' a crossword puzzle for both weekly and once-a-month publication; and 'New Products' column. No travel articles, please." Length: maximum 2,000 words. Pays $25 to $150, "more for special assignments."
Photos: Purchased with features, without features, and on assignment. Captions required. Wants "b&w only, top quality, exclusive. 8x10's or 5x7's preferred." Pays $5 to $35.

NEWSPAPER ENTERPRISE ASSOCIATION, 230 Park Ave., New York NY 10017. Executive Editor: Robert J. Cochnar. Supplies material to "more than 600 daily newspapers." Buys world rights. Will handle copyrighted material. Buys 50 to 75 features a year from freelancers. Query first; send samples. Reports in 2 weeks. Enclose S.A.S.E. for reply to queries.
Nonfiction and Photos: "Science-oriented material; investigative reports; good ideas well-executed. We seldom purchase single features. We are interested in well-researched series on topics of particular interest to general audiences. We contract for columns and distribute material on practically all subjects. Do not want to see

any Ann Landers type columns or humor columns." Length: 600 to 900 words. Pays $15 to $500. "We are launching a new service for Sunday Newspapers and supplements and expect to purchase at least 12 nonfiction articles which should run about 1,500 to 2,500 words. For these, we expect to pay up to $2,500." 7x9 or 8x10 b&w glossies purchased with or without features; captions required.

NORTH AMERICAN NEWSPAPER ALLIANCE, 220 E. 42nd St., New York NY 10017. Editor: Sheldon Engelmayer. Supplies material to leading U.S. and Canadian newspapers, also to South America, Europe, Asia and Africa. Buys Newspaper syndication rights. Reports in 2 weeks. Enclose S.A.S.E. for return of submissions.
Nonfiction and Photos: In the market for background, interpretive and news features. The news element must be strong and purchases are generally made only from experienced, working newspapermen. Wants timely news features of national interest that do not duplicate press association coverage but add to it, interpret it, etc. Wants first-class nonfiction suitable for feature development. The story must be aimed at newspapers, must be self-explanatory, factual and well condensed. It must add measurably to the public's information or understanding of the subject, or be genuinely entertaining. Broad general interest is the key to success here. Rarely buys columns. Looking for good one-shots and good series of 2 to 7 articles. Where opinions are given, the author should advise, for publication, his qualifications to comment on specialized subjects. The news must be exclusive to be considered at all. Length: 800 words maximum. Rate varies depending on length and news value. Minimum rate $25, but will go considerably higher for promotable copy. Buys 8x10 glossy photos when needed to illustrate story. Pays $5 to $10.

NUMISMATIC INFORMATION SERVICE, Rossway Rd., Pleasant Valley NY 12569. Editor: Barbara White. Buys all rights and reprint rights. Reports in 1 week. Enclose S.A.S.E. for return of submissions.
Nonfiction: Looking for material relative to coin collecting and the hobby of numismatics in general. Buys single features as well as column ideas. Length: 500 words maximum. Pays $5 per column per week.

OCCULT NEWS SERVICE, 240 Main St., Danbury CT 06810. Editor: R.C.H. Parker. Supplies material to occult and metaphysical magazines, newsletters, and newspapers. Buys all rights. Handles copyrighted material "with releases furnished." Query first "on large items." Submit photos to Gilles Rousseau. Reports in 4 weeks. Enclose S.A.S.E. for return of submissions or reply to queries.
Nonfiction, Humor, Fiction, Photos, Fillers, and Poetry: "All slanted to occult, metaphysics, mind development, personal awareness and spiritual development. We want news stories, interviews with photos. We are interested in single features which are confirmed interviews with individuals having psychic experiences or unusual experiences. All reports are subject to a full check. We have ESP and general occult columns. We need one for younger people. Be precise when preparing material for us. Check facts and terms." Length: 1,500 words maximum. Pays $5 to $50—"commission of 50% on each sale."

OCEANIC PRESS SERVICE, 4717 Laurel Canyon Blvd., North Hollywood CA 91607. Editor: J. Taylor. "We serve the entire free world and will only look at material which is of global interest from Finland to India. Material has to be published in the U.S.A. first and in one of the well-known magazines." Buys outright or pays 50/50 syndicate rate for serialization; 20% on foreign book and TV sales. Buys, if possible, U.S. second rights and world rights. Buys 300 to 400 features for reprint from freelancers each year. Reports in 1 month. Enclose S.A.S.E. for return of submissions.
Nonfiction: Considers only published columns for foreign markets; ESP columns, Solve a Crime, 2 Minute Mystery, Test Yourself, illustrated tests, etc. Occasionally buys single features, if they're very outstanding and concern worldwide known personalities.
Photos: Outdoors, sports, underwater picture stories; color transparencies (but not singles).
Fiction: Wants published books for serialization and syndication for U.S. and foreign markets. Prefers love novels, war books, science fiction, mysteries, psychologi-

cal novels. Motion picture rights to published works only; paperback rights for abroad. Also TV screen plays.

PUBLISHERS-HALL SYNDICATE, 401 N. Wabash Ave., Chicago IL 60611. Editor: Richard Sherry. Supplies material to newspapers. Buys all rights. Reports in 3 to 4 weeks. Enclose S.A.S.E. for return of submissions.
Nonfiction: Article series "only on highly promotable topics by pros with top credentials." No single features. Contracts for columns. Syndicates columns such as Ann Landers, Sylvia Porter, Joseph Kraft, and Erma Bombeck. Interested in columns on "service, do-it-yourself, commentary." Length: 750 words maximum. Pay varies according to newspaper sales.

PUNGENT PRAYER, P.O. Box 77, Ellsworth IL 61737. Editor: Rev. Phil E. Pierce. Supplies material to newspapers. "Copyright registration optional with author." Buys second and third reprint rights, if specified. Buys 25 to 50 features a year from freelancers. Will consider photocopied submissions. Reports in 2 weeks. Enclose S.A.S.E. for return of submissions.
Nonfiction and Poetry: "Prayers and prayer stories only. Colorful prayers. Prayers that are different—salty, earthy, or humorous, with pathos or social concern, related to everyday life or life crises. Prayer-poems acceptable if colorful, especially those concerning church and patriotic holidays and major events. No ordinary prayers. We welcome true stories of answered prayers with verification." Maximum length: 350 words or 40 lines. Pays $2 to $7.

QUEEN CITY PUBLISHERS, 6541 South Pontiac Court, Englewood CO 80110. Editor: Jack Parish. Supplies material to weekly newspapers. Buys about 25 features a year from freelancers. Will not consider photocopied submissions. Reports "3 weeks ahead of deadline." Enclose S.A.S.E. for return of submissions.
Fillers and Puzzles: "Items of most interest to weekly editors." Handles a horoscope and women's interest column. Length: "should not exceed 14 inches in depth." Pays 40% commission.

SANDY RAINES FEATURES, 409 Wabash Avenue, Belleville IL 62221. Editor: Sandy Raines. Generally buys all world rights, but not as an ironclad rule. Prices and contracts will vary accordingly. Generally reports in less than 2 weeks. Enclose S.A.S.E. for return of submissions.
Nonfiction: Wants writers who can furnish features with photos on entertainment personalities, short crime, wholesome sex, oddities (with photos). Length: 500 to 1,000 words. Pays $25 to $100.

REGISTER AND TRIBUNE SYNDICATE, 715 Locust St., Des Moines IA 50304. President: Dennis R. Allen. Supplies material to newspapers. Buys all rights. Buys about 10 features a year from freelancers. Reports in 4 to 6 weeks. Enclose S.A.S.E. for return of submissions.
Nonfiction and Photos: Does not buy single features. Buys 6- to 12-article series "on current topics such as ecology and bicycles (safety and maintenance). We prefer not to see puzzles. Writers are overworking nostalgia features." Syndicates features like "The Family Circus," "The Better Half," "The Alumnae," Dr. Walter C. Alvarez, Dr. S. I. Hayakawa and others. Length: 50 to 1,000 words. Payment in royalty commission. 8x10 glossies purchased with features; captions optional.

RELIGIOUS NEWS SERVICE, 43 W. 57th St., New York NY 10019. Editor: Lillian R. Block. Supplies material to "secular press, religious press of all denominations, radio and TV stations." Enclose S.A.S.E. for return of submissions.
Nonfiction and Photos: "Good news stories on important newsworthy developments. Religious news." Will buy single features "if they have news pegs. Most of our article series are produced by our own staff." Length: 200 to 1,000 words. Pays 2¢ a word. Photos purchased with and without features and on assignment; captions required. Uses b&w glossies, preferably 8x10. Pays $5 minimum.

BP SINGER FEATURES, INC., 3164 West Tyler Ave., Anaheim CA 92801. Editor: Jane Sherrod. Supplies *France Soir, Der Stern, National Enquirer,* and others.Does not copyright material. Will handle copyrighted material. Send tearsheets

or books. "Prefer camera-ready copy." Reports in 2 weeks. "If accepted for syndication, we report monthly on sales only." Enclose S.A.S.E. for return of submissions.
Nonfiction, Fiction, Puzzles, and Books: "Books for serialization (romance, mystery, biography, war, health, success, gothic); particularly fiction for women's magazines and good mystery novels." Buys single features, such as interviews with famous people (for example, "Why Robert Young Quit Drinking" and "Interview With Ali McGraw." Buys article series, books in serial form such as *Jackie O.* Contracts for illustrated puzzles. "Successful with us are Solve-a-Crime, 2-minute mysteries, horoscopes, and Can-You-Fix-It?" Does not want to see "crossword puzzles or articles on ecology, local events; no sex fiction." Length: "no limit"; 500 words minimum. Pays 50% commission.
Photos: Purchased with features and on assignment; captions required. "Prefer 4x5 transparencies or jacket covers, greeting cards, posters of racing cars in action, romantic art, movie and TV stars." Pays $20 to $100 each, "depending on topic."

SOCCER ASSOCIATES, P.O. Box 634, New Rochelle NY 10802. Editor: Irma Ganz Miller. Buys all rights. Query first. Reports at once. Enclose S.A.S.E. for reply to queries.
Nonfiction and Photos: Buys very little. Currently syndicating "Soccer Shots" and special soccer coverage. Pays $25 to $100.

TEENAGE CORNER, INC., 4800 Ellinda Circle, N.W., Canton OH 44709. Editor: David J. Lavin. Buys no rights. Reports in 1 month. Enclose S.A.S.E. for return of submissions.
Nonfiction: Buys material on teenage problems and situations. Length: 300 to 500 words. Pays $5 to $10.

TRANS WORLD COMMUNICATIONS, INC., 166 Madison Ave., New York NY 10016. Editor: Jay Levy. Writer must have tape recorder. Buys all rights. Enclose S.A.S.E. for return of submissions.
Nonfiction: Worldwide audio news service. Seeks freelance correspondents around the world. Buys news and feature interviews. Length: "no more than ½ hour." Pays "approximately $10 per 3 minutes of tape used."

TRANSWORLD FEATURE SYNDICATE, INC., 141 E. 44th St., New York NY 10017. International Manager: Mary Taylor Schilling. North American Sales Manager: Elsa H. Zion. Supplies material to "magazine and newspaper publishers all over the world." Does not copyright material. Reports "quarterly." Enclose S.A.S.E. for return of submissions.
Nonfiction, Photos, and Puzzles: Wants "magazine features, pictures on personalities, and current events." Pays 40% to 50% commission. Photos purchased on assignment; captions required.

TRANS-WORLD NEWS SERVICE, Division of International Press Service. Mail address: P.O. Box 2801, Washington DC 20013. Office: 923 National Press Bldg., Washington DC 20004. Editor: Dr. E. Rothkirch. Buys first rights; reprint rights negotiated. Buys about 400 to 500 features a year from freelancers. Will consider photocopied submissions. Usually reports in 2 weeks to 2 months, depending on material. Enclose S.A.S.E. for return of submissions.
Nonfiction, Fillers, and Humor: General. Buys single features and article series; travel, industrial development abroad. Looking for new entertainment columns, women's columns, etc. Lengths are 600 to 2,200 words. Pays $5 to $100 for material. Outlets are weekly U.S. papers, and overseas English language papers, plus companion foreign language papers.
Photos: Purchased with features, or on assignment. Captions required. B&w 5x7 or 8x10 glossy.

U-B NEWSPAPER SYNDICATE, 15155 Saticoy St., Van Nuys CA 91405. Editor: Steve Ellingson. Supplies material to "leading newspapers in all cities." Buys all rights. Will handle copyrighted material. Query first. Reports "immediately." Enclose S.A.S.E. for reply to queries.
Nonfiction and Photos: Syndicates detailed do-it-yourself articles. Length: 200 to 400 words. Pays $100 to $500.

UNITED FEATURE SYNDICATE, INC. 220 E. 42nd St., New York NY 10017. Managing Editor: James L. Freeman. Supplies material to "newspapers throughout the world." Buys all rights. Will handle copyrighted material. Buys 25 to 40 features a year from freelancers. Query first with outline of series. Reports in 2 weeks to 3 months. Enclose S.A.S.E. for reply to queries.
Nonfiction and Puzzles: Buys article series. "3 to 6 parts; human interest, how-to, personalities in the news, etc." Does not handle single features. Contracts for columns. Current columnists include Marquis Childs, Jack Anderson, Henry J. Taylor, Barbara Gibbons, Marya Mannes, and William S. White. Does not want to see material on "ecology or cooking." Length: 500 to 1,000 words. Pays 50% commission.

UNITED OVERSEAS PRESS, 663 Fifth Ave., New York NY 10022. Editor: Liselle Brent. Enclose S.A.S.E. for return of submissions.
Nonfiction, Humor, Fiction, and Photos: Photos purchased with features. Captions required. Pays 50% of fee.

UNITED PRESS INTERNATIONAL (UPI), 220 E. 42nd St., New York NY 10017. Editor: H.L. Stevenson. "Features and columns are usually staff-written. We sometimes approach prominent personalities and authorities—such as a statesman or a doctor—to write for us. We do employ some freelance stringers, who supply us with local spot news. Professional writers interested in becoming stringers for UPI should query first."

U.S. NEWS SERVICE, Suite 862, National Press Building, Washington DC 20004. Bureau Chief: Walter Fisk. Buys all rights. May handle copyrighted material. May not return rejected material. Enclose S.A.S.E. for return of submissions.
Nonfiction, Humor, Fiction, Photos, Fillers, and Poetry: Buys single features and column ideas. Length varies. Payment varies. 8x10 single weight glossies purchased with features, without features, and on assignment. Captions required.

UNIVERSAL PRESS SYNDICATE, 475 Fifth Avenue, New York NY 10017. Editor: James F. Andrews. Buys syndication rights. Reports normally in 4 weeks. Enclose S.A.S.E. for return of submissions.
Nonfiction: Looking for features—columns for daily and weekly newspapers. "Any material suitable for syndication in daily newspapers." Payment varies according to contract.

UNIVERSAL SCIENCE NEWS, 314 W. Commerce, Tomball TX 77375. Editor: William J. Cromie. Supplies material to "60 U.S. and Canadian newspapers and about 20 foreign magazines and news agencies." Buys first rights. Will handle copyrighted material. Buys 100 to 125 features a year from freelancers. Query first. Artists should submit samples. Photographers should submit contact sheets. Enclose S.A.S.E. for reply to queries and all other correspondence.
Nonfiction and Photos: "Science-oriented news and timely features. Articles that describe new developments in the field of science. Those that sum up or give a comprehensive overlook of a science subject in the news. Background material on science stories in the news. Science angles of stories in the news." Buys single features and series. Does not buy column ideas. Writer should use "news magazine or newspaper style." Length: 300 to 1,800 words; "occasionally more." Pays $100 to $200 for "usual articles under 2,500 words. More on special assignments, newsbreaks, or series."

UNIVERSAL TRADE PRESS SYNDICATE, 37-20 Ferry Heights, Fair Lawn NJ 07410. Editor: Leon D. Gruberg. Buys first trade paper rights only. Query first. Enclose S.A.S.E. for reply to queries.
Nonfiction: Buys merchandising features in all fields; knitwear merchandising at the retail level; features on knitting mill operations. Length: 1,250 words. Pays 65%.

DOUGLAS WHITING, LIMITED, 930 De Courcelle St., Montreal 207, Que., Canada. Editor: D.P. Whiting. Supplies material to "all major dailies in Canada and many in the United States." Buys all newspaper rights. No query required. Reports in 4 to 6 weeks. Enclose S.A.S.E. for return of submissions.
Nonfiction: Science panels, contest promotions, puzzle features and feature col-

umns. "The freelancer should look for ideas and content that are unique. Too much of the sample material received by us is very similar to established syndicated features. Bear in mind, too, that we are a Canadian syndicate. Most of the material received is too American." Does not buy single features. Length: 150 to 250 words, daily columns; 700 to 1,000 words, weekly columns. "Usually author's share is 40% of net after production costs are deducted. Costs do not include our sales calls and promotion material."

WOMEN'S NEWS SERVICE (a division of North American Newspaper Alliance), 220 E. 42nd St., New York NY 10017. Editor: Sid Goldberg. Buys all rights. Will handle copyrighted material. Buys about 300 features a year from freelancers. No query required. Reports in 2 weeks. Enclose S.A.S.E. for return of submissions.
Nonfiction and Fillers: Buys background, interpretive and news features of interest to women. News element must be strong. Looking for good, sprightly news features that do not duplicate press association coverage, but add to it, interpret it, etc. Family problems, feminism, consumerism, female careers, abortion reform, women's rights, etc. Prefers single features. Rarely takes on a new column. Also looking for good series ideas. Make sure it has a news peg or relates to a current trend." Length: 300 to 1,500 words; 500 to 700 words, single features. Pays "$25 minimum, may go considerably higher for block-busters, series." Also buys fillers (30 to 150 words) of interest to women. Pays $5 to $15.

WORLD UNION PRESS, 507 Fifth Ave., New York NY 10017. New York Editor: David Horowitz. Associate Editors: Wolf Pasmanik; Dr. M. I. Salomon. United Nations Bureau: Room 373, Press, United Nations, New York NY 10017. Israeli Editor: Moshe Ben Shachar. Pays flat fees. Enclose S.A.S.E. for return of submissions.
Nonfiction: Full UN coverage, general news items, features, books, theater, poems.

ZODIAC NEWS SERVICE, 950 Howard St., San Francisco CA 94103. Editor: Jon Newhall. Supplies material to FM stations across the U.S. "We only require exclusive rights for 72 hours." Buys about 1,000 features a year from freelancers. "We purchase 3 each day. Please mail in material (typed) and include phone number for additional information." Will consider photocopied submissions. "If we accept an item for use, it is sent out within 48 hours." Enclose S.A.S.E. for return of submissions.
Nonfiction: "We want exclusive, short news stories suitable for radio reporting. Our audience is young, disenchanted with the establishment. All news stories must be national, not regional or local in interest. Features must be short. We have done radio features (150 to 200 words at most) on ecology problems such as Black Mesa and the Big Sky development, on war protests, on drugs, on rock musicals, on bizarre, offbeat human interest anecdotes and results of psychological studies." Does not buy article series or column features. Length: 200 words "at most, but the shorter, the better." Pays $7.50.

Writers' Clubs

These clubs are local or regional nonprofit social or professional groups. They are listed geographically by state, then club name within the state. Writers are requested to enclose a self-addressed stamped envelope when writing any club about membership, meeting times, etc.

Alabama

ALABAMA STATE POETRY SOCIETY. Contact Carl P. Morton, President, 1732 Shades View Lane, Birmingham AL 35216.

Arizona

ARIZONA STATE POETRY SOCIETY. Contact Jean Humphrey Chaillie, 4549 East Montecito, Phoenix AZ 85018.

Arkansas

ARKANSAS PIONEER BRANCH, NATIONAL LEAGUE OF AMERICAN PEN WOMEN. Contact Mrs. Swann Kohler, 819 N. Arthur, Little Rock AR 72205.

AUTHORS, COMPOSERS AND ARTISTS' SOCIETY. Contact Peggy Vining, Counselor, 6817 Gingerbread Lane, Little Rock AR 72204.

POETS' ROUNDTABLE OF ARKANSAS. Contact Roberta E. Allen, 6604 Kenwood Rd., Little Rock AR 72207.

California

THE CALIFORNIA WRITERS' CLUB. Contact Mrs. Dorothy Benson, Secretary, 2214 Derby St., Berkeley CA 94705.

CALIFORNIA WRITERS GUILD. Contact Dorothy-Marie Davis, Secretary, 2624 G North Lake Ave., Altadena CA 91001.

CHRISTIAN WRITERS' LEAGUE. Contact Jean Hogan Dudley, 4211 Olds Road, Oxnard CA 93030.

DALY CITY CREATIVE WRITERS' GROUP. Contact Margaret O. Richardson, President, 243 Lakeshire Dr., Daly City CA 94015.

ENTERTAINMENT INDUSTRY EXPLORERS. Contact Ken Eisenberger, P.O. Box 69191, Los Angeles CA 90069.

THE FICTIONAIRES. Contact Armand Hanson, 2725 Dayna, Santa Ana CA 92701.

THE GEORGE FREITAG WRITERS' SEMINAR. Contact Jewell Swertfeger, P.O. Box 826, Colton CA 92324.

INLAND WRITERS WORKSHOP. Contact Ed Rimbaugh, 1051 Western Ave., Colton CA 92324.

MOUNTAIN-VALLEY WRITERS. Contact Pat Wolff, Secretary, 18140 Hawthorne, Bloomington CA 92316.

NORTHERN CALIFORNIA CARTOON & HUMOR ASSOC. Contact Walt Miller, Secretary, 609 29th Ave., San Mateo CA 94403, or Glenn R. Bernhardt, President, P.O. Box 3772, Carmel CA 93921.

RIVERSIDE WRITER'S CLUB. Contact Margaret Arensberg, President, 3993 Larchwood Pl., Riverside CA 92506.

SAN DIEGO PROFESSIONAL WRITERS WORKSHOP. Contact Chet Cunningham, 8431 Beaver Lake, Dr., San Diego CA 92119.

SOUTHWEST MANUSCRIPTERS. Contact Audrey Ruika, 280 Via Linda Vista, Redondo Beach CA 90277.

SURFWRITERS. Contact Ms. LaVada Weir, 905 Calle Miramar, Redondo Beach CA 90277.

WRITERS' CLUB OF SANTA BARBARA. Contact Donna Dalton, 3333 Padaro Lane, Carpinteria CA 93013.

WRITERS' CLUB OF WHITTIER, INC. Contact Jeanne Bergstrom, 9844 S. Grovedale Dr., Whittier CA 90603.

WRITERS' GUILD OF DOWNEY. Contact Bob McGrath, 17909 San Gabriel Ave., Cerritos CA 90701.

Colorado

WE WRITE OF COLORADO. Contact Joan Domning, 8506 Quay Dr., Arvada CO 80002.

Connecticut

SPEAK OUT LITERARY ASSOCIATION. Contact Agnes D'Ottavio, Box 1211, Stamford CT 06901.

District Of Columbia

WRITERS LEAGUE OF WASHINGTON. Contact Mrs. Helen B. Thompson, 6110 Broad Branch Rd. N.W., Washington DC 20015.

Illinois

KANKAKEE AREA WRITER'S CLUB. Contact Mildred N. McAnally, 54 Emery Dr., Bourbonnais IL 60914.

OFF-CAMPUS WRITERS' WORKSHOP. Contact Jane Howard, 851 Warrington Rd., Deerfield IL 60015.

WRITER'S STUDIO. Contact David R. Collins, President, 3724 15th Ave., Moline IL 61265.

Indiana

POETS' STUDY CLUB OF TERRE HAUTE. Contact Mrs. Louise Nelson, President, 302 N. 3rd St., Marshall IL 62441.

SOUTH BEND WRITER'S CLUB. Contact Virginia T. Columbus, President, 1075 Riverside Drive, South Bend IN 46616.

STORY-A-MONTH CLUB. Contact: Mrs. Ellyn Kern, 46 N. Sheridan Ave., Indianapolis IN 46219.

Iowa

JASPER COUNTY WRITERS, INC. Contact Olin C. Bissell, 1320 North 4th Ave. West, Newton IA 50208.

Kansas

WICHITA LINE WOMEN. Contact Mrs. Jacquelyn Terral Andrews, 2350 Alameda Pl., Wichita KS 67211.

Kentucky

KENTUCKY STATE POETRY SOCIETY. Contact Fran Cornett, Membership Chairman, 1754 Algonquin Pkwy., Louisville KY 40210.

LOUISVILLE WRITERS CLUB. Contact Mrs. Jane Westbrook, 2800 Cleveland Blvd., Louisville KY 40206.

Massachusetts

AGNES CARR WRITERS' CLUB. Contact Mrs. S.C. Traegde, 84 Central St., Stoneham MA 02180.

AUTHORS WORKSHOP OF BOSTON. Contact Mrs. S.C. Traegde, 84 Central St., Stoneham MA 02180.

THE MANUSCRIPT CLUB OF BOSTON. Contact Katherine Saunders, President, 76 Lincoln St., Norwood MA 02062.

PIONEER VALLEY SCRIPTORS. Contact Merrie Hagopian, 116 Meadowbrook Rd., E. Longmeadow MA 01028.

Michigan

ANN ARBOR CHRISTIAN WRITERS CLUB. Contact Mrs. Lee F. Smith, 1839 Shirley Lane, Ann Arbor MI 48105.

DETROIT WOMEN WRITERS. Contact Mrs. Bettie Cannon, President, 2707 Comfort Dr., West Bloomfield MI 48033.

JUVENILE WRITERS WORKSHOP. Contact Mrs. Irene S. Miner, 17869 North Shore Estates, Spring Lake MI 49456.

POETRY SOCIETY OF MICHIGAN. Contact Mrs. S. Geneva Page, President, 256 Burr St., Battle Creek MI 49015.

UPPER PENINSULA WRITERS. Contact Ms. Moira Reynolds, 225 E. Michigan, Marquette MI 49855.

Minnesota

MINNEAPOLIS WRITERS' WORKSHOP. Contact Grace Riger, President, 3148 Holmes Ave., Minneapolis MN 55408.

MINNESOTA CHRISTIAN WRITER'S GUILD. Contact Nancy Pike, Publicity Chairman, 6901 Oakland Ave., S., Richfield MN 55623.

Missouri

MISSOURI WRITERS' GUILD. Contact Joseph F. Callahan, President, 1016 W. Truman, Independence MO 64050.

NATIONAL LEAGUE OF AMERICAN PENWOMEN, ST. LOUIS BRANCH. Contact Mrs. Edward M. Mason, 8410 Madeline Dr., St. Louis MO 63114.

ST. LOUIS WRITERS' GUILD. Contact Antonio Betancourt, 426 Flora Place, St. Louis MO 63110.

Nebraska

NEBRASKA WRITERS GUILD. Contact Mrs. Royce N. Kent, President, 4865 Wirt St., Omaha NE 68104.

New Hampshire

MANCHESTER AREA WRITERS' WORKSHOP. Contact Leroy Fromer, Jewish Community Center, 698 Beech St., Manchester NH 03104.

POETRY SOCIETY OF NEW HAMPSHIRE, INC. Contact Mr. Leighton Bryne, Treasurer, P.O. Box 525, Concord NH 03301.

New Jersey

NEW JERSEY POETRY SOCIETY, INC. Contact Howard Reeves, Public Relations Vice-President, R.D. 2, Box 33, Boonton NJ 07005.

WRITERS' WORKSHOP. Contact Mrs. Sylvia Dichner Weiss, Wynbrook West J-6, E. Windsor Township NJ 08520.

New Mexico

FARMINGTON WRITERS ASSOCIATION. Contact Mrs. I. K. Holliday, P.O. Box 1760, Farmington NM 87401.

ROSWELL WRITERS GUILD. Contact Lois Reader, 1104 Avenida Del Sumbre, Roswell NM 88201.

New York

ASSOCIATION OF PROFESSIONAL WOMEN WRITERS. Contact Isabel K. Hobba, 6007 Lockport Road, Niagara Falls NY 14305.

BROOKLYN CONTEST AND FILLER WRITING CLUB. Contact Selma Glasser, 241 Dahill Rd., Brooklyn NY 11218.

HARLEM WRITERS GUILD. Contact Rosa Guy, P.O. Box 845, Ansonia Station, New York NY 10023.

Ohio

GEEBURG LITERARY AND CHOWDER SOCIETY (Youngstown area). Contact Mrs. Maureen Creager, 106 E. Main St., Canfield OH 44406 or Mrs. Frances Esson, 160 Northview Dr., Canfield OH 44406.

LORAIN COUNTY WRITERS CLUB. Contact Wilbur Karl, President, 1001 East Ave., Elyria OH 44035.

OHIO AMATEUR PRESS GUILD. Contact William Earl Boys, 5255 Fenway Pl., Columbus Oh 43214 or Robert W. Hill, 3804 Severn Rd., Cleveland Heights OH 44118.

VERSE WRITERS GUILD OF OHIO. Contact Ray E. Buckingham, President, 285 N. Sandusky St., Apt. 15, Delaware OH 43015.

Oklahoma

OKLAHOMA WRITERS FEDERATION. Contact Ernestine Gravley, Ph.D., 1225 Sherry Lane, Shawnee OK 74801.

STILLWATER WRITERS. Contact Florence French, Corresponding Secretary, 513 South Knoblock, Stillwater OK 74074.

WRITERS' GROUP OF CUSHING. Contact Mazie Cox Read, President, South Kings Highway, Cushing OK 74023.

Pennsylvania

LEHIGH VALLEY WRITERS' GUILD. Contact Mrs. Paul Guth, President, 1420 Gordon St., Allentown PA 18102.

Rhode Island

BLACKSTONE VALLEY WRITERS GUILD. Contact Mrs. June Morse, P.O. Box 384, Greenville RI 02828.

RHODE ISLAND WRITERS' GUILD. Contact Muriel E. Eddy, President, 139 Colfax St., Providence RI 02905.

Texas

ABILENE WRITERS GUILD. Contact Juanita Zachry, 502 E. N. 16th, Abilene TX 79601.

BEAUMONT POETRY SOCIETY. Contact Violette Newton, Councillor, 3230 Ashwood Ln., Beaumont TX 77703.

THE EL PASO WRITERS' LEAGUE. Contact Ralph Voigt, President, 3712 San Mateo, El Paso TX 79902.

HOUSE OF POETRY, INC. Contact James J. Brophy, 3611 Oak Lawn Ave., Dallas TX 75219.

POETRY SOCIETY OF SAN ANTONIO. Contact Mrs. Stella Woodall, President, 3915 S.W. Military Dr., San Antonio TX 78211.

SOUTH PLAINS WRITERS ASSOCIATION. Contact Mrs. Etta Lynch, 5101 41st St., Lubbock TX 79414.

Vermont

LEAGUE OF VERMONT WRITERS. Contact R.P.T. Jutson, Director of Publicity, Pittsfield VT 05762.

Virginia

POETS TAPE EXCHANGE. Contact Frances Brandon Neighbours, Director, 116 Twin Oak Dr., Lynchburg VA 24502.

Washington

SEATTLE FREE LANCES. Contact Martha King, 15405 S.E. 25th, Bellevue WA 98007.

TACOMA WRITER'S CLUB. Contact Mrs. Hugo Smith, Secretary, 3806 E. 104th St., Tacoma WA 98466.

West Virginia

HUNTINGTON POETRY GUILD. Contact Edith Hite McElfresh, President, P.O. Box 1315, Huntington WV 25715.

MORGANTOWN POETRY SOCIETY. Contact Kimberly Dunham, Publicity Chairman, 673 Bellaire Dr., Morgantown WV 26505.

WEST VIRGINIA POETRY SOCIETY. Contact Mrs. Walter Pratt, President, 1625 Oak St., Parkersburg WV 26101.

Writers' Colonies

Freelance writers who remember that James Jones was one of the outstanding "alumni" of the late Lowney Handy's writers' colony in Illinois, often ask the editors of *Writer's Digest* if there are any writers' colonies still active today.

Since Huntington Hartford sold his California estate where writers were formerly welcomed, there are, to our knowledge, only four writers colonies currently in existence. They're listed below, with appropriate details. Probably the closest climate to a writers' colony available elsewhere in the U.S. are the numerous writers' conferences held each year for anywhere from one day to two weeks. A list of these conferences appears annually in the May issue of *Writer's Digest*.

THE MacDOWELL COLONY, 1083 Fifth Ave., New York NY 10028.

MILDRED I. REID WRITERS' COLONY, Contoocook NH 03229.

VIRGINIA CENTER FOR THE CREATIVE ARTS, Box 3720, Charlottesville VA 22903.

YADDO, Curtis Harnack, Executive Director, Saratoga Springs NY 12866.

Writers' Organizations

The national associations for writers listed below usually require that potential members have attained a professional status before applying. Local or regional writers' clubs which are more social in nature are listed in the Writer's Clubs section. You can also learn about meetings of such groups through your newspaper. If you wish to start a club of your own, consult the booklet How To Start/Run a Writer's Club (Writer's Digest, 50¢).

ACADEMY OF AMERICAN POETS, 1078 Madison Ave., New York NY 10028. Established in 1934. President: Mrs. Hugh Bullock. The purpose of The Academy of American Poets is "to encourage, stimulate, and foster the production of American poetry by providing fellowships for poets of proven merit, by granting scholarships, awards, and prizes for poetic achievement, and by such other means as the Board of Directors with the approval of the Board of Chancellors may from time to time devise and determine. The Academy annually awards a fellowship of $10,000 for distinguished poetic achievement. It also annually purchases 1,000 copies of the winning Lamont Poetry Selection for a manuscript of poetry by an American poet who has had no published book of poetry. The manuscript is to be entered by a publisher of poetry. The Academy annually offers $100 prizes in 63 colleges and universities for the best poems by graduates or undergraduates."

AMERICAN ACADEMY OF ARTS AND LETTERS, 633 West 155th St., New York NY 10032. Established in 1904. The American Academy of Arts and Letters, an honor society of artists, writers, and composers, was created as a section of the National Institute of Arts and Letters and is limited to 50 members chosen from the Institute. Noted foreign artists, writers, and composers are elected to the Academy and Institute as honorary members. Exhibitions of works of art, books, and mss are held during the year and awards and honors, for which application may not be made, are conferred at an annual ceremonial. Publications include *Yearbook*, *Proceedings*, and catalog of exhibitions.

AMERICAN AUTO RACING WRITERS AND BROADCASTERS ASSOCIATION, 922 N. Pass Ave., Burbank CA 91505. Established in 1955. Executive Secretary: Ms. Dusty Brandel. "This organization bands together a group of writers and broadcasters who cover auto racing throughout the United States. It aims primarily to improve the relationship between the press and the promoters, sanctioning bodies, sponsors, and participants in the sport. Members receive a numbered identification card, a working credential, monthly bulletins, and are allowed to enter the yearly writing contest that pays some $3,000 in prize money." Dues: $5 annually, full members; $25 annually, associate members.

THE AMERICAN GUILD OF AUTHORS AND COMPOSERS, 50 West 57th St., New York NY 10019. Established in 1931. Executive Director: Lewis M. Bachman. President: Ervin Drake. The organization was formed to provide better royalty contracts from music publishers. For songwriters who have their works covered by the AGAC contract, the Guild has obtained these advantages: 1) a 50% minimum on recording, transcription, and motion picture synchronization royalties prevails; 2) foreign royalties for the writer are now a minimum of 50% of the publisher's foreign income; 3) the writer's song is returned if it is not exploited in a specific way within 1 year; 4) the right to keep any advances on a song prevails. AGAC does not do several things: it does not secure a collaborator or someone to make a musical setting for a poem; it does not criticize, comment, or pass judgment on the merits of a work; it does not assist in the placing of songs with publishers, record manufacturers, etc. The Guild offers a copyright renewal service in which members are notified when their song copyright renewals are due. The Guild has approximately 3,000 song-writer members and it deals with about 1,000 music publishers who have signed a basic agreement in which they are authorized to use the AGAC standard contract. AGAC collects royalties and audits for its members, regardless of the type of contract, and charges 5% commission (but not exceeding $1,400 in 1 year). A regular member is a songwriter who has had at least 1 song published or recorded by a recognized company. The dues he pays are based on the size and activity of his catalog. Associate members are songwriters who have not yet published. Dues: $20 annually, associate members; $37.50 to $250 annually, members.

AMERICAN MEDICAL WRITERS ASSOCIATION, 9650 Rockville Pike, Bethesda MD 21609.

AMERICAN SOCIETY OF COMPOSERS, AUTHORS AND PUBLISHERS (ASCAP), One Lincoln Plaza, New York, NY 10023. Director of Public Relations: Walter Wager. "A clearing house for performing rights in music, ASCAP licenses the right to perform in public for profit in the United States the copyrighted musical works of its members and the members of affiliated societies in more than 30 countries. It is an unincorporated, nonprofit society of writers and publishers, has no treasury, and regularly distributes all revenues above operating expenses to its members. Any composer or lyricist of a copyrighted musical work may join if he or she has had at least 1 musical work 'regularly published.' Associate membership is open to any writer who has had 1 work copyrighted." Annual dues: $10 for writers, $50 for publishers.

THE ARMED FORCES WRITERS LEAGUE, INC., George Washington Station, Alexandria VA 23305. Established in 1954. Executive Director: Lieutenant Commander Ray S. Ewing, SC, USN, Ret. This group was founded as a mutual self-help organization for military writers needing technical assistance. Membership is now open to any U.S. citizen interested in the Armed Forces and the national defense of the U.S. "Help Write America Right" is its motto. About 1,200 members and 18 branches in the U.S. and overseas exist in its regular and professional divisions. The league offers manuscript criticism services, writing contests, technical bulletins and the services of an agent in New York City for a fee plus the usual 10% commission, and a short story correspondence course. Dues: $8 annually.

ASMP—THE SOCIETY OF PHOTOGRAPHERS IN COMMUNICATIONS 60 East 42nd St., New York NY 10017. Executive Secretary: Suzanne MacDonald. Established "to promote and further the interests of established workers in their profession," ASMP has a membership of over 800 professional photographers. It publishes minimum rate standards and definitions of rights; acts as a clearing house for photographic information on markets, rates, and business practices of magazines, advertising agencies, publishers and electronic media; works for copyright law revision; offers legal advice to members concerning questions of rights, ethics, and payments; and offers other useful services to members. Membership categories include Sustaining, General, Associate, and Student.

THE ASSOCIATED BUSINESS WRITERS OF AMERICA, P. O. Box 135, Monmouth Junction NJ 08852. Executive Secretary: Hazel Palmer. All members are skilled in one or more facets of business writing (advertising copy, public relations, ghost writing, books, reports, business and technical magazines, etc.). Members are full-time writers; associates may hold other jobs. ABWA publishes an annual directory profiling writers who are "editor-approved." Free lists of ABWA members and other information about ABWA are mailed to employers of business writers: business and industrial firms, advertising and public relations agencies, editors of business magazines and house organs. "Realistic rates and fair treatment" are sought by ABWA members. ABWA does not place mss for its members. The ABWA may apply third person pressure when an impasse occurs between editor and writer. A monthly bulletin is published for members. Dues: $30 annually.

AUTHORS GUILD, 234 W. 44th St., New York NY 10036. Established in 1912. Executive Secretary: Peter Heggis. The basic functions and purposes of The Authors Guild, a corporate member of the Authors League, are: "(a) To act and speak with the collective power and voice of all American freelance writers in matters of joint professional and business concern; (b) To keep informed on market tendencies and practices, with emphasis on new markets just developing, and to keep its members informed; (c) To advise members on individual professional and business problems so far as possible." Those eligible for membership include "any author who shall have had a book published by a reputable American publisher within 7 years prior to his application; any author who shall have had 3 works, fiction or nonfiction, published by a magazine or magazines of general circulation, either national or local, within 18 months prior to his application; or any author whose professional standing, in the opinion of the Membership Committee, shall entitle him to membership whether or not he shall have had work published as defined above." Annual dues: $30.

AUTHORS LEAGUE OF AMERICA, INC., 234 West 44th St., New York NY 10036. Established in 1912. Executive Secretary: Mills Ten Eyck, Jr. The Authors League membership is restricted to authors and dramatists who are members of the Authors Guild, Inc., and the Dramatists Guild, Inc. Matters of joint concern to authors and dramatists, such as copyright and freedom of expression, are in the province of the League; other matters, such as contract terms and subsidiary rights, are in the province of the guilds.

AVIATION/SPACE WRITERS ASSOCIATION, 101 Greenwood Ave., Jenkintown PA 19046. Established in 1938. President: C.W. Borklund. Founded "to establish and maintain high standards of quality and veracity in gathering, writing, editing, and disseminating aeronautical information." The AWA numbers 930 members who work for newspapers, press services, TV, radio, or other media and specialize in writing about aviation or space. The organization offers several annual awards for aviation or space writing or reporting. Regional meetings are held frequently and an annual meeting and news conference is held in May or June. Dues: $10, initiation fee; $20, annual dues.

BROADCAST MUSIC, INC., 90 W. 57 St., New York NY 10019. Established in 1940. Public Relations Vice President: Russell Sanjek. A major performing rights collecting agency for song writers and composers, BMI today numbers over 35,000 affiliated writers and publishers and is the largest licensing organization in the world. BMI licenses broadcasting stations, night clubs, etc., at specific fees for the right to use the BMI music catalog. This agency has reciprocal agreements with 32 other performing rights licensing societies around the world.

CONSTRUCTION WRITERS ASSOCIATION, 202 Homer Building, Washington DC 20005. Established in 1958. "The Construction Writers Association was organized by a group of editors who saw need for an association that would lend prestige and professional status to writers and public relations people representing and reporting upon the world's biggest business, the construction industry. CWA is the only such organization for construction industry journalists and PR specialists. Its membership is international in scope. Any person principally engaged in writing or editing material pertaining to the construction industry for any regularly published periodical of general circulation is eligible for membership. Any public information or public relations specialist who represents an organization or agency the existence of which depends in whole or in part on the construction industry is also eligible. Through frequent meetings and communications from its secretary-treasurer, CWA offers its members a forum for the interchange of information, ideas and methods for improving the quality of reporting, editing and public relations in the construction field. It also provides contact between the membership and newsmaking officials in government, contracting firms, equipment manufacturers and distributors, consulting firms, and other construction trade and professional groups. Members may compete for the Robert F. Boger award for journalistic achievement. Only CWA members are eligible. Also, to compete for the Silver Hardhat award for outstanding writing or editing that has served to advance understanding of the construction industry and its objectives." Publishes *CWA Newsletter*. Annual dues: $20.

COUNCIL FOR THE ADVANCEMENT OF SCIENCE WRITING, INC., Kimgarten Rd., Chester Springs PA 19425. President: Pierre C. Fraley. "The purpose of the CASW is to increase both the quality and quantity of the coverage of science, medicine, and health, the environment, technology, the social sciences, etc., in all the mass media." A five-day briefing on new horizons in science is held every November, and other programs are held throughout the year. "The Council for the Advancement of Science Writing is not a membership organization. The 20 'members' of the Council actually make up the Board of Directors, and there are no other members."

DOG WRITERS' ASSOCIATION OF AMERICA, INC., 3 Blythewood Rd., Doylestown PA 18901. President: John T. Marvin. The Association aims to provide a medium for "the exchange of ideas, methods, and professional courtesies among its members." Membership is limited to salaried writers, editors, and publishers of dog magazines. annual dues: $10.

DRAMATISTS GUILD, INC., 234 W. 44th St., New York NY 10036. Established in 1912. Executive Secretary: David E. LeVine. Active membership in the Dramatists Guild, a member corporation of the Authors League, is open to "any playwright or composer who has had a production of his work on Broadway (or, as of 1969, off Broadway). Associate membership is open to anyone who has written or is engaged in writing dramatic or dramatico-musical works for the theater, by vote of the membership committee." Annual dues: $20, active; $10, associate, "plus percentages of royalties from certain production rights."

EDUCATION WRITERS ASSOCIATION, P. O. Box 1289, Bloomington IN 47401. Established in 1947. Executive Director: G.K. Hodenfield. "The Education Writers Association is a professional organization for those chiefly engaged in transmitting information about education—at the elementary, secondary, and college levels—to the general public. Its goals are to provide its members with timely and pertinent new ideas, to keep them informed about controversies in the field of education, and to enlarge the scope of their interest in education. Active membership is open to those who cover education news for newspapers, magazines of general circulation, and radio/TV stations. Associate membership is open to writers for special education publications not of general circulation, and other persons closely connected with education writing or with a genuine interest in education and education writing. Group memberships are open to nonprofit educational institutions and organizations. The EWA in 1965 formed the National Council for the Advancement of Education Writing (NCAEW), registered with the Bureau of Internal Revenue as a nonprofit educational organization, to solicit and administer grants from philanthropic foundations. The NCAEW conducts an annual awards contest in education writing, publishes and distributes 'deep background' papers on vital educational issues, sponsors an internship program for young journalists with an interest in education writing, and—when funds are available—sponsors foreign and domestic travel grants for education writers. All EWA members are kept thoroughly informed of NCAEW programs and projects through *The Education Reporter* and by special mailings when necessary. The EWA also sponsors an annual seminar at which members can listen to, and question, leaders in education who are both expert and newsworthy; have new techniques demonstrated; visit outstanding educational institutions on field trips, and discuss their own ideas and particular problems among themselves." Annual dues: $10, active members; $25, associate members; $100, institutional/organizational members.

MOTOR SPORTS PRESS ASSOCIATION, c/o Ed Dunckelmann, 1310 Lindahl Court, San Jose CA 95120. Established "for the advancement of editorial skills, ability, and coverage of auto and auto racing activities; for the interchange of ideas and information; to provide an authoritative platform, credentials, annual awards, and recognition to the motor sports press. To be a board member, one must be an editor or an auto-racing columnist or broadcaster for a newspaper, TV, or radio. The industry and the public who are interested in autos and/or auto racing are eligible for membership." Annual dues: $12.

MUSIC CRITICS ASSOCIATION, INC., c/o Irving Lowens, President, Washington Star-News, Washington DC 20003. Treasurer: Byron Belt. The purposes of the Association are "to act as an educational medium for the promotion of high standards of music criticism in the press in America, to hold meetings where self-criticism and exchange of ideas will promote educational opportunities, and to increase the general interest in music in the growing culture of the Americas. Membership is open to persons who regularly cover musical events in the cities of America." Publishes newsletter *Critics Criteria*. Annual dues: $15.

MYSTERY WRITERS OF AMERICA, INC., 105 E. 19th St., New York NY 10003. Established in 1944. Executive Secretary: Gloria Amoury. "Gregarious ghouls" is how former MWA president Howard Haycraft described the 600 members of this organization, "dedicated to the proposition that the detective story is the noblest sport of man." Membership ranks include active members, who have made at least 1 sale in mystery, crime, or suspense writing, and associate members, who are either novices to the mystery writing field or nonwriters allied to the field—editors, publishers, etc. The MWA has directed its efforts to raise the stature of the mystery story: it annually awards the "Edgar" (Allan Poe statuette) to writers for the best mystery literature in various categories; it annually publishes an anthology containing work of its members. The Society maintains a reference library on poisons, police procedures, etc., and often invites an expert to meetings to discuss some aspect of crime or mystery. The Society publishes a news bulletin, *The Third Degree*, for members and offers free advice to members on book contracts, agents, and other areas of interest to the mystery writer. With international mystery clubs, the MWA is working to secure adherence to the international copyright law. Five chapters of the MWA have been established: New York, Chicago, San Francisco, Los Angeles, and Boston. Annual dues: $30 for U.S. members, $8 for Canadian and overseas members.

THE NATIONAL ACADEMY OF TELEVISION ARTS AND SCIENCES, 291 South La Cienega Blvd., Beverly Hills CA 90211. President: Robert F. Lewine. A nonprofit membership organization of professionals working in the television industry, the Academy presents annual Emmy Awards for achievements in television. Active members must have worked actively and creatively in television for at least 2 years. Membership activities include forums on related topics, workshops, and seminars. Chapters are located in Chicago, Cleveland, Columbus (Ohio), Hollywood, New York, Phoenix, San Diego, St. Louis, San Francisco, Seattle, Washington DC. Dues: $15 to $30 annually, according to chapter.

NATIONAL ASSOCIATION OF EDUCATIONAL BROADCASTERS, 1346 Connecticut Ave., N.W., Washington DC 20036. Established in 1925. President: William G. Harley "NAEB is an association designed to serve the professional needs and interests of educational radio and television. Its membership includes more than 400 noncommercial radio and television stations; 3,500 individual members; more than 200 schools, universities, related associations, broadcasting services, commercial stations, and industrial firms; production centers, and instructional television fixed service systems. NAEB serves as a clearing house for cooperative action among the members of the organization." Its publications include a semimonthly newsletter, an annual directory of educational telecommunications, and a bimonthly journal, *Educational Broadcasting Review*. Annual dues: $30.

NATIONAL ASSOCIATION OF GAGWRITERS, Box 835, Grand Central Station, New York NY 10017. Executive Director: George Q. Lewis. Members in this 600-member organization are primarily caption writers for cartoons and comedy writers for performers. The Association holds open-house meetings in New York where gagwriters try out comedy routines and closed-house workshop sessions for the writing of comedy. The Gagwriters Round Table hosts famous comics, who exchange ideas with writers. The Gagwriters Comedy Workshop showcases members' material. Members and nonmembers may compete for the title "Gagwriter of the Month" by submitting 50 original jokes on 50 different subjects. "Gagwriter of the Month" winners are chosen for the All-American Comedy Writing Team. "We maintain a telephone comedy corps to answer questions from members and potential members. Call 201-229-9472 before noon. In local chapters, members learn the rudiments of comedy development through experience and exposure." The organization publishes the *Humor Exchange Newsletter* for members of its Humor Exchange Network. Dues: $25.

NATIONAL ASSOCIATION OF SCIENCE WRITERS, INC., Box H, Sea Cliff NJ 11579. Established in 1934. Administrative Secretary: Rosemary Arctander. This organization was established to "foster the dissemination of accurate information regarding science through all media normally devoted to informing the public. In pursuit of this goal, NASW conducts a varied program to increase the flow of news from scientists, to improve the quality of its presentation, and to communicate its meaning and importance to the reading public. About one-third of all NASW members—writers, editors, or producers—work directly in preparing material that goes straight to the layman. Other members convey the news of science indirectly. They are professors in colleges of journalism, writers and editors for specialized publications that are not distributed generally, or information officers who supervise the release of news from scientists in universities, government, industry, and foundations. The organization maintains liaison with policy-making groups that may influence the flow of science news. It is a member society of the American Association for the Advancement of Science (Section T), and is represented on pertinent AAAS committees. Two NASW committees provide special help for members. The Vocational Committee offers a job placement service, matching members seeking jobs with organizations seeking qualified science writers. The Free Lance Committee deals with the special problems of members who freelance, either on a full-time or moonlighting basis. Anyone who is actively engaged in the dissemination of science information, and has two years or more experience in this field, is eligible to apply. There are several classes of membership. Active members must be principally engaged in reporting science through media that reach the public directly: newspapers, mass-circulation magazines, "trade" books, radio, television and films. Associate members report science through special media: limited-circulation publications and announcements from organizations such as universities, research laboratories, foundations and science-oriented corporations. Affiliated membership is limited to those who have been active or associate members but are no longer primarily engaged in the reporting of science. Lifetime membership is extended to members after they have belonged to NASW for 25 years. Honorary membership is awarded by NASW to outstanding persons who have notably aided the objectives of the association." Publishes a quarterly newsletter and clipsheet. Annual dues: $20.

NATIONAL FREE LANCE PHOTOGRAPHERS ASSOCIATION, 4 E. State St., Doylestown PA 18901. Founded in 1962. Purpose of this organization is "to bring together all those interested in photography and provide them with the backing, support and benefits of an internationally recognized organization. Members include studios, labs, retail stores, camera repair stations, photographic manufacturers and dealers, schools, clubs, amateurs and professionals. We publish newsletters which contain valuable information and advice, as well as news of members and activities in the field of photography. We hold national and international exhibits and conduct discussions on problems common to the membership." Plan One Membership: $18 annually. Plan Two Membership: $24. Associate Member: $14. Student Member: $10.

NATIONAL INSTITUTE OF ARTS AND LETTERS, 633 West 155th St., New York NY 10032. Established in 1898. Executive Director: Margaret M. Mills. Founded for the purpose of furthering literature and fine arts in the United States, the Institute has three departments: art, literature, and music. Membership is limited to 250 American citizens. In order to establish cultural ties with other countries, the Institute and the American Academy of Arts and Letters, a section of the Institute, elect 75 foreign artists, writers, and composers as honorary members. The Institute holds exhibitions of works of art, books, and mss during the year. It inducts members and confers awards, for which application may not be made, at an annual ceremonial. Publications include *Yearbook*, *Proceedings*, and catalogs of exhibitions.

NATIONAL LEAGUE OF AMERICAN PEN WOMEN, INC., 1300 17th St., N.W., Washington DC 20036. Established in 1897. "Professionally qualified women engaged in creating and promoting letters, art, and music" are eligible for membership in the National League of American Pen Women, Inc., whose purpose is "to bring together for their mutual professional and financial benefit women engaged in the creative work of pen, pencil, or brush." It does so "by promotion and protection of literary, artistic, and music production, by promotion and protection of freedom of the press, and by publication of *The Pen Woman*." Women interested in membership must qualify professionally and be presented for membership and endorsed by two active members in good standing in the League. The League holds branch, state, and national meetings. Dues: Initiation fee $25. Annual branch dues plus $10 national dues. For further information, write to national president at address given above.

NATIONAL PRESS CLUB, National Press Bldg., 529 14th St., N.W., Washington DC 20004. Executive Secretary: Miss E. R. Schaefer. Initiation fee: $25 to $125. Annual dues: $30 to $220, depending on membership status.

NATIONAL TURF WRITERS ASSOCIATION, Pennsylvania Bldg., Suite 1038, 425 13th St. N.W., Washington DC 20004. Secretary-Treasurer: Tony Chamblin. The purposes of this organization are "to promote, foster, and encourage closer relationships among its members, improved working conditions, better understanding between its members and the governing powers of thoroughbred racing, and the development of throughbred racing and breeding. Membership is limited to newspaper or magazine writers who regularly cover thoroughbred racing, sports editors of newspapers which regularly print throughbred racing news and results, and sports columnists who write columns on thoroughbred racing. Ineligible are handicappers who do not write racing stories or columns for their papers, desk men who do not cover thoroughbred racing at the tracks, radio and TV sportscasters, racetrack officials, and photographers. There are 3 classifications of membership: regular, associate, and honorary." Dues: $10, regular membership; $20, associate membership.

NATIONAL WRITERS CLUB, INC., 1365 Logan, Suite 100, Denver CO 80203. Established in 1937. Executive Director: David Raffelock. "Founded for the purpose of informing, aiding and protecting freelance writers worldwide. Members receive authoritative answers to questions about writing and personal help on any writing problem. NWC monitors all services offered to writers and reports on them. Intercession is offered whenever a member needs help in getting an editorial report or payment for an accepted or published ms. A continuing project is encouraging writers to achieve professional standards and to market material intelligently. The club's Standard of Practice and Code of Ethics has been widely accepted by educational institutions, editors, and writers. An extensive specialized library of books and courses on writing is maintained as are collections. NWC does not act as a literary agent, critic, or teacher of writing (except, in the latter case, for members only), but it does issue annual reports on recommended agents, literary agents, literary services, and home study courses in writing. An annual Creative Writing Workshop is held each autumn. Associate membership is available to anyone seriously interested in writing. Qualifications for professional membership are publication of a book by a recognized book publisher; or sales of at least three stories or articles to national or regional magazines; or a television, stage, or motion picture play professionally produced. Among the regular publications are *Authorship*, quarterly newsletter, *Flash Market News* and *Inside Facts About Writing*, issued bimonthly, and *Show Window* and *The Professional Bulletin*, annuals. Various reports on viable subjects are available, as are surveys of all market groups." Annual dues: $15, associate membership; $20, professional membership

OUTDOOR WRITERS ASSOCIATION OF AMERICA, INC., 4141 W. Bradley Rd., Milwaukee WI 53209. Established in 1927. Executive Director: Edwin W. Hanson. A nonprofit professional and educational organization comprised of newspaper and magazine writers, editors, photographers, broadcasters, and lecturers engaged in the dissemination of information on outdoor sports such as hunting, boating, fishing, camping, etc., and on the conservation of natural resources. Its objectives are "providing a means of cross-communication among specialists in this field, promoting craft improvement, obtaining fair treatment from media, and increasing general public knowledge of the outdoors. Among other subjects, the membership deals extensively in current environmental issues." The week-long annual conference, usually held in June, combines craft skill courses and examination of conservation issues. The association maintains a university-level scholarship program for students, conducts youth training programs, and has an information liaison system with firms and associations in the outdoor and conservation fields. Publications include *Outdoors Unlimited*, a monthly newsletter, an annually revised *Directory of Outdoor Writers*, and the *Outdoor Writers Instruction Manual*. The association requires that each member annually have published a specified quantity of paid material. Sponsorship by an active member of the OWAA is required for membership applicants. Dues: $25, initiation fee; $25, annual fee.

P.E.N., American Center, 156 Fifth Ave., New York NY 10010. Established in 1921. Executive Secretary: Mrs. Kirsten Michalski. A world association of poets, playwrights, essayists, editors, and novelists, the purpose of P.E.N. is "to promote and maintain friendship and intellectual cooperation among men and women of letters in all countries, in the interests of literature, the exchange of ideas, freedom of expression, and good will." P.E.N. has 82 centers in Europe, Asia, Africa, Australia, and the Americas. The association annually awards a prize for the best translation into English published in the United States. Publications include *List of Grants and Awards Available to American Writers*, *Lists of Grants and Awards Available to Foreign Writers*, *The World of Translation*, *A History of the First 50 Years*, and a quarterly journal *The American Pen*. "Membership is open to all qualified writers, translators, and editors who subscribe to the aims of International P.E.N." To qualify for membership, an applicant must have "acknowledged achievement in the literary field, which is generally interpreted as the publication by a recognized publisher of 2 books of literary merit. Membership is by invitation of the Admission Committee after nomination by a P.E.N. member."

PEN AND BRUSH CLUB, 16 E. 10th St., New York NY 10003. Established in 1893. President: Mrs. Harriet M. Hagerty. "The Pen and Brush Club is a club of professional women, writers, painters, graphic artists, sculptors, and craftsmen, with a resident membership limited to 350 active members in these fields. Exhibits are held in the galleries of the clubhouse by painters, sculptors, graphic artists, and craftsmen. A monthly bulletin keeps members informed of programs and exhibits and gives personal news of members and their achievements. Through its nonresident membership, Pen and Brush reaches into almost every state of the Union, and even abroad."

POETRY SOCIETY OF AMERICA, 15 Gramercy Park, New York NY 10003. Executive Secretary: Charles A. Wagner. The oldest and largest group working for an appreciation of poetry and for wider recognition of the work of living American poets, the Society has a membership of traditionalists and experimentalists. It is the parent organization of many regional groups, but dissociates itself from the activities of those groups which bestow honors "without critical discrimination." An applicant for membership must either be a recognized poet or submit 5 poems for consideration by the Governing Board.

SCIENCE FICTION WRITERS OF AMERICA, Rt. 3, Hartford City IN 47348. Contact: Robert Coulson, Secretary. "Membership in SFWA is limited to professional writers. We have about 400 on our list now, including virtually all of the established science fiction writers in the country and as many of the newcomers as we have been able to reach. Our purposes are to inform writers of matters of professional benefit, to serve as an intermediary in disputes of a professional nature, and to act as a central clearing house for information on science fiction and science fiction writers. We publish a bimonthly journal, the *SFWA Bulletin*. Subscriptions are available to nonmembers at $8 per year from George Zebrowski, Box 122, Westview Station, Binghamton NY 13905. The journal is free to members. In addition, there is a correspondence supplement, the *SFWA Forum*, available to members only, and professional pamphlets are issued occasionally. Each year the membership is polled on its preferences for the outstanding science fiction stories of the year; the authors of the winning stories receive trophies known as Nebulas. Active membership is open only to writers who have had science fiction short stories or books professionally published in the United States or who have had science fiction screenplays, telecasts, or radio scripts performed. We have 2 categories of membership: active and associate. Publication of a novel confers 5 years of eligibility for active membership; of a short story or novelette, 3 years; release of a screenplay, 2 years; performance of a telecast or radio script, 1 year. Those writers whose credentials have expired may remain as associate members, who may not hold office or vote in SFWA elections." Dues: $12.50 annually.

SIGMA DELTA CHI, 35 E. Wacker Dr., Chicago IL 60601. Established in 1909. Executive Officer: Russell E. Hurst. Sigma Delta Chi "is dedicated to the highest ideals in journalism" and sees itself as comparable to those professional organizations serving the fields of medicine and the law. Its membership extends horizontally to include persons engaged in the communication of fact and opinion by all media (newspaper, radio-television, magazines), and vertically to include in its purposes and fellowship all ranks of journalists. Professional membership is by invitation, following nomination by a chapter and election by the National Board of Directors. Undergraduate membership is by invitation, following election by a student chapter. Directors supervise the 11 Regions of Sigma Delta Chi, located throughout the nation. Sigma Delta Chi publishes *The Quill*, the magazine for journalists, and conducts the annual SDX Distinguished Service Awards Contest, which recognizes superior journalistic performance in the following categories: newspaper, magazine, radio and television reporting; public service in newspaper, magazine, radio and television journalism; newspaper, radio and television editorials; foreign correspondence; Washington correspondence; news photography; editorial cartooning, and research about journalism. A separate contest for college students annually recognizes outstanding performance in newspaper, magazine and broadcast journalism. The Society confers the honor of Fellow of Sigma Delta Chi annually on three persons adjudged to have made notable contributions to the profession, and confers the Wells Memorial Key annually on the member adjudged to have served the Society in the most outstanding manner. Dues: $15 annually.

SOCIETY FOR TECHNICAL COMMUNICATION, 1010 Vermont Ave., N.W., Suite 421, Washington DC 20005. Established in 1953. Executive Director: Curtis T. Youngblood. Dedicated to the advancement of the theory and practice of technical communication in all media, the STC aims primarily for the education, improvement, and advancement of its members. Actively involved in training programs in the field of technical communication, the Society has established 4 grades of membership based on experience and interest in technical communication. Dues: $5, enrollment fee; $20, annual dues. Membership includes subscription to a quarterly journal, *Technical Communication*, and a newsletter, *Intercom*, and assignment to one of 50 chapters. Chapters conduct autonomous programs. STC sponsors an annual conference and provides services and information to membership.

SOCIETY OF AMERICAN SOCIAL SCRIBES, c/o The Plain Dealer, 1801 Superior Ave., Cleveland OH 44114. Secretary: Mary Strassmeyer. "The Society of American Social Scribes is a nonprofit organization dedicated to serving the interest of the reading public, to promote unbiased, objective reporting of social events and to promote journalistic freedom of movement. It endeavors to upgrade the professional integrity and skill of its members to work to increase the pleasures of the reading public, to support all legitimate efforts toward developing the education of its members, and to help its members offer greater service to their readers. Membership is limited to those regularly engaged as salaried society editors or devoting a substantial or regular part of their time to society coverage and the balance to other strictly editorial work. Society writers on daily newspapers with circulations of

200,000 or more and magazine writers and authors of books on the subject are also eligible for membership." Annual dues: $15.

SOCIETY OF AMERICAN TRAVEL WRITERS, 1146 Sixteenth St., N.W., Washington DC 20036. Established in 1956. President: Alfred S. Borcover. The Society of American Travel Writers is "dedicated to serving the interest of the traveling public, to promote international understanding and good will, and to further promote unbiased, objective reporting of information on travel topics." The Society presently has a membership of approximately 600 persons. Frequency of regional chapter meetings varies; an annual membership meeting is held in the fall. Active membership is limited "to those regularly engaged as salaried travel editors, writers, broadcasters, or photographers actively assigned to diversified travel coverage by a recognized medium or devoting a substantial or regular part of their time to such travel coverage to satisfy the Board of Directors; or to those who are employed as freelancers in any of the above areas with a sufficient steady volume of published work about travel to satisfy the Board. Associate membership is limited to persons regularly engaged in public relations or publicity within the travel industry to an extent that will satisfy the Board of Directors. All applicants must be sponsored by 2 active members with whom they are personally acquainted." Dues: $50 initiation fee for active members, $100 initiation fee for associate members; $35 annual dues for active members, $75 annual dues for associate members.

SOCIETY OF CHILDREN'S BOOK WRITERS, P.O. Box 827, Laguna Beach CA 92652. Established in 1968. President: Stephen Mooser. "The Society is an organization strictly for writers, editors, and others interested in and allied with the children's book field. It publishes a bimonthly bulletin and a yearly magazine. Full membership is open to anyone who has published a children's story or book in the past 6 years. Associate membership is open to anyone with an interest in children's literature, whether or not they have published." Annual dues: $20.

SOCIETY OF CONFESSION WRITERS, P. O. Box 33, Adams NE 68301. President: Ernest C. Clement. "The purposes of the organization are to establish a procedure for the dissemination of professionally pertinent information among its members, to act as a whole on behalf of its members in matters of mutual professional interest, and to improve the professional standing of writers of confession fiction. Active members must have sold not less than 12 confession stories in the 12 months prior to the date of application for membership; thereafter, they may not have sold less than 12 confession stories during the 12 months prior to any annual meeting of the Society. Associate members must have sold not less than 3 confession stories during the 12 months prior to the date of the application for membership; thereafter, they may not have sold less than 3 confession stories during the 12 months prior to the annual meeting of the Society. Probationary members are those interested in the writing and selling of confessions, but who do not qualify for associate or active membership. Probationary memberships are for one year only and may not be renewed. Annual dues: $20. The annual meeting is held during the month of August.

SOCIETY OF MAGAZINE WRITERS, INC., 123 W. 43rd St., New York NY 10036. Established in 1948. President: David R. Zimmerman. Among the benefits which the SMW offers its members are the following: "a confidential monthly SMW Newsletter; a continuing rate survey, in which members report anonymously each month on their articles sold and the prices, and comment on the promptness of payment and experience with the editor; eligibility for grants up to $1,000 each to support writing of articles and books on significant subjects; discount buying service; magazine subscription at a fraction of the newsstand price; representation in Congressional hearings on matters that concern professional nonfiction writers; use of air-conditioned SMW office; opportunity to have work incorporated into SMW books; referral service for jobs and assignments; a confidential loan fund; listing in the annual SMW Directory; assistance and mediation services in conflicts with editors over pay and other issues; a voice, among colleagues, in a professional field." Dues: $25, initiation fee; $50, annual dues for residents of New York City and environs; $35, annual dues for those residing 200 or more miles from New York City.

UNITED STATES BASKETBALL WRITERS ASSOCIATION, c/o *Indianapolis Star*, 1425 E. Banta Rd., Indianapolis IN 46227. Contact: Ray Marquette. "The United States Basketball Writers Association is composed of 600 to 650 newspapermen and sports information directors on college, high school, and professional levels. Our dues are $5 a year and include 5 issues of *The Tipoff* as well as entry in writing contest and brochure (college) judging."

UNITED STATES SKI WRITERS ASSOCIATION, c/o Peninsula Newspapers, Inc., 2066 Potomac Way, San Mateo CA 94403. President: Hal Roberts. The purposes of this association are "to foster a strong relationship among ski writers throughout the United States as well as in foreign counties, to exchange ideas and views with ski writers from various sections of the United States, to encourage high standards in ski journalism in reporting and writing ski news, and to do such things as membership may from time to time direct which will work toward the betterment of skiing. The association consists of the following regions: Eastern, Midwest, Rocky Mountain, Intermountain, Southern California, Northern California and Nevada, and Pacific Northwest. Active membership is open to fulltime employees of newspapers who write at least 2 articles a week for the same newspaper or the equivalent thereof during the ski season, persons who maintain ownership or a position of editorial staff capacity on a publication which carries ski news on a regular monthly basis during the ski season, any radio personnel directly associated with live or taped production of a daily or biweekly program of at least 5 minutes duration for the complete run of the ski season, any television personnel associated with the production of at least 8 programs in a ski season of no less than 2 minutes duration devoted to the reporting of ski news or the filming of special events in skiing, or photographers who demonstrate active participation in skiing by photographing skiing and whose work is regularly published in any skiing media." Annual dues: $10.

WASHINGTON PRESS CLUB, Suite 505, National Press Building, 14th and F Sts., N.W., Washington DC 20004.

WESTERN WRITERS OF AMERICA, INC., 1505 W. "D" St., North Platte NE 69101. Contact: Nellie Yost. Writers eligible for membership in this organization are not restricted in their residence, "so long as their work, whether it be fiction, history, adult, or juvenile, book-length or short material, movie or TV scripts, has the scene laid west of the Missouri River." WWA annually bestows the Spur Awards in 7 categories for writing excellence.

WOMEN IN COMMUNICATIONS, INC., (formerly Theta Sigma Phi Inc.) National Headquarters, 8305-A Shoal Creek Blvd., Austin TX 78758. Established in 1909 as Theta Sigma Phi. President: Fran Harris. A professional society for women in journalism and communications, the purposes are "to work for a free and responsible press, to unite women engaged in all fields of communications, to recognize distinguished achievements of women in these fields, to maintain high professional standards, and to encourage members to greater individual effort." The organization provides its members with a job placement service, professional workshops, seminars, and career conferences. Nationally an annual research grant is given to members for graduate study or independent research. Women in Communications has professional chapters in 79 cities, student chapters in 81 universities where there is a school or department of journalism, and 7,000 active members *Matrix* is its official magazine. Dues: $20, annual national dues for professional members, $32, application fee.

WRITERS GUILD OF AMERICA, Writers Guild of America, East, 1212 Avenue of the Americas, New York NY 10036; Writers Guild of America, West, 8955 Beverly Blvd., Los Angeles CA 90048. "The Writers Guild is a labor organization representing all screen, television, and radio writers. It bargains for pay scales and working conditions on behalf of its members. It is made up of Writers Guild of America, East, with offices in New York City, and Writers Guild of America, West, with offices in Los Angeles. The Mississippi River is the dividing line for administrative jurisdiction between the branches. The administration of the two branches is carried out under the supervision of an executive director for each organization." Intiation fee: $200. Dues: $6.25 per quarter (East) or $10 per quarter (West) and 1% of gross earnings as a writer in WGA fields of jurisdicition.

FOREIGN MARKETS

The magazines and book publishers in this list have all indicated their willingness to receive original submissions from U.S. and Canadian freelance writers. If they wish to see material to reprint or publish anew in their country, their listings say this. Bear in mind that, if not interested in your idea, the foreign editor may not reply to your query.

The postage charges to send your query letters and mss airmail to most foreign countries (excluding Mexico, Caribbean countries, and Central and South America) are 21c per half ounce. Book mss may be mailed as "Printed Matter" at a lower rate—check with your local post office for the exact amounts.

Be sure to enclose International Postal Reply Coupons with submissions to foreign markets for safe return of your ms. Reporting times given by these foreign markets apply only to submissions which have enclosed sufficient reply coupons for an airmail reply. You can buy these coupons at your local post office. The selling price for reply coupons in the United States is 22c each; the redemption value in the U.S. is 15c each. One of these coupons is exchangeable in any other country for a stamp or stamps representing the international postage on a single-rate surface-mailed letter. Details on the amount of return postage necessary from individual foreign countries to the U.S. for book mss, etc., is available from Director, Classification and Special Services Division, Bureau of Operations, Washington, D.C. 20267.

Consumer Magazines

ADAM, 142 Clarence St., Sydney, N.S.W., Australia 2000. For a "general audience, but probably mainly men in the 18 to 35 group." Monthly. Circulation: 42,000. Rights negotiable. Buys 100 mss a year. Pays on acceptance. Will send a sample copy to a writer for 35¢. Reports "within a month." Enclose S.A.E. and International Reply Coupons for return of submissions.
Nonfiction and Fiction: Uses "action fiction, factual adventure, historical." Buys personal experience, humorous, and historical articles. Also buys mystery, science fiction, adventure, and humorous fiction. Nonfiction length: 2,000 to 3,500 words; Fiction length: 2,000 to 4,000 words. Payment negotiable.

AIRFIX MAGAZINE, 9 Ely Place, London EC1N 6SQ, England. Editor: Bruce R. B. Quarrie. Established in 1960. Monthly. Circulation: 47,500. Copyrighted. Payment on publication. Will send sample copy to writer on request. Will consider material previously published in U.S. or Canada offered for first time publication in England. Submission of previously published material may be made by the publisher or his representative or by author direct, if he can also supply a letter from the previous publisher authorizing UK publication. Will consider unpublished material offered for first time use. Submissions of unpublished material may be made directly by the author. Query first or submit complete ms. Enclose S.A.E. and International Reply Coupons with all correspondence.
Nonfiction and Photos: "*Airfix* deals with all aspects of scale modelling, primarily based on plastic construction kits. It includes model conversion and 'scratch building' instruction articles alongside technical reference features on aircraft, tanks, ships, etc., their service history, colour schemes, armament, serial codes, etc., plus reviews of new kits and books of interest to modellers." Will consider the following material previously published in U.S. or Canada: "Any article dealing with aviation or military history, specific aircraft or vehicles, marking and camouflage schemes, unit serial codes, etc. The publication is basically directed at scale mod-

ellers and this should be borne in mind, but an article need not be specifically on modelling a piece of equipment. Should be readable English but note form is acceptable on unit code listings. Preferred length for a single article is 800 to 1,200 words plus illustrations, but ideas for series considered." Will consider the following unpublished material: "Anything on the Air Force, Army Air Force, Naval Air Force, Marine, and Army aircraft (including helicopters and hovercraft), tanks, self-propelled guns, armoured cars, etc.; technical descriptions with scale drawings and photographs; service histories with photographs; marking scheme and camouflage descriptions with photographs and black and white line illustrations. Similarly for Canadian military forces. Main emphasis on WW2. Any style as long as grammatical. Length of single articles: approximately 800 to 1,200 words." Pays 6 pounds per published page "whether all text, all illustrations, or a combination of both. Average payment on an illustrated 800-word article would be approximately 12 pounds; on 1,000 words, 15 to 18 pounds; on 1,200 words, 18 to 24 pounds."

AMATEUR PHOTOGRAPHER, 161 Fleet St., London, E.C. 4, England. Editor: R.H. Mason. Published weekly for amateur photographers. Pays on publication. Buys British reproduction rights. Will send a sample copy to a writer for $1. Reports in 5 to 10 days. Include S.A.E. and International Reply Coupons.
Nonfiction and Photos: Buys "central photo features." Length: 1,000 to 3,000 words. Pays 7.50 pounds per page if accompanied by b&w photos, 10 pounds if accompanied by color photos.

AMATEUR WINEMAKER, North Croye, The Avenue, Andover, Hants, England. Editor: Mr. C.J.J. Berry. For "persons from all walks of life interested in home winemaking and brewing." Monthly. Circulation: 34,000. Pays on publication. Enclose S.A.E. and International Reply Coupons for return of submissions.
Nonfiction: "Articles allied to home winemaking and brewing." Length: 500 to 1,500 words. Payment "by arrangement."

AMBIT, 17 Priory Gardens, London, N.6., England. Editor: Dr. Martin Bax. Published for those interested in the arts. Pays on publication. Reports within three months. Buys serial rights. Include S.A.E. and International Reply Coupons.
Nonfiction, Fiction, and Poetry: All critical material is commissioned. Query on feature articles. Also buys some original drawings, preferably line, some halftone. Buys short stories. Length: 5,000 words maximum. Buys some poetry. Payment in sterling, by arrangement; "about $2.50 a page."

ANGLO-WELSH REVIEW, Deffrobani, Maescelyn, Brecon, Wales. Editor: Roland Mathias. Established in 1949. 3 times a year. Circulation: 1,500. Copyrighted. Will rarely consider material previously published in U.S. or Canada. Will send a copy to a writer for $1.50. Submit complete ms. Enclose S.A.E. and International Reply Coupons for return of submissions.
Nonfiction, Fiction: "Literary criticism of Welsh authors or writers with Welsh connections. Historical articles with a Welsh content or significance. Stories of high literary quality." Length: 5,000 words maximum. Pays $5 to $20 for poems; $20 to $60 for articles.

ANIMALS, 21 & 22 Great Castle St., London, W.1., England. Editor: Nigel Sitwell. For "all ages, social groups, fairly well-educated, unified by interest in wildlife and natural history." Monthly. Circulation: 40,000. Buys first rights. Pays on publication. Will send a free sample copy to a writer on request. Query first. Submit seasonal material 3 months in advance. Reports in 4 to 8 weeks. Enclose S.A.E. and International Reply Coupons for return of submissions.
Nonfiction: Buys how-to, personal experience, travel articles, zoological/biological research; anything, in fact, concerning wildlife and conservation of wildlife. Also buys exposes and photo features. Does not want articles on "domestic animals, hunting, etc." Length: 500 to 3,500 words. Pays minimum $25 per 1,000 words.
Photos: Purchased with mss; with captions only. Buys b&w glossies, color transparencies, 35mm color. Buys one-time rights. Pays $7.20 for b&w, $25 for color.

ANNABEL, D.C. Thomson & Co. Ltd., 80 Kingsway East, Dundee, Scotland. Editor: Mr. Scott Smith. Established in 1966. Monthly. Circulation: 155,000. Will send free sample copy on request. Aimed at the modern woman with wide interests. Buys first British serial rights. Pays on acceptance. Will consider material previously published in U.S. or Canada offered for first publication in Britain or unpublished material. Enclose S.A.E. and International Reply Coupons.

Nonfiction: Wants personal experience stories, biographical articles of well-known personalities, articles on fashion, cookery, knitting. Interested in "good human stories simply told. There is wide coverage of the traditional subjects (fashion, beauty, etc.), but we seek to inform and entertain readers on a wide range of material slanted to the family woman." Length: 500 to 2,500 words. All payments are by mutual agreement between editor and writer with a minimum of $50.

Fiction: Wants emotional, romantic short stories of 1,000 to 3,000 words. Pays $50 minimum.

Fillers: Uses short humor and puzzles.

ANTIQUE COLLECTING, S. Church St., Woodbridge, Suffolk, England. Editor: John J. Steel. For antique collectors and dealers. Established in 1966. Monthly. Copyrighted. Payment on acceptance. Will send sample copy to writer on request. Query first. Reports in 4 weeks. Enclose S.A.E. and International Reply Coupons.

Nonfiction and Photos: Interested in articles on 19th Century collectable subjects. Author should "outline the subject and proposed treatment." Length: open. Pays 18 pounds per 1,000 words. Photos are purchased with ms.

ART AND ARTISTS, Artillery Mansions, 75, Victoria Street, London, SW1H OH2. Editor: Colin Naylor. For art dealers, students, artists interested in all aspects of fine art. Issues "occasional special numbers on art fairs and on specialized aspects of the subject." Buys first rights. Buys 100 to 120 mss a year. Will send a free sample copy to a writer on request. Query first. Submit seasonal material 2 months in advance. Returns rejected material "as soon as possible." Enclose S.A.E. and International Reply Coupons for return of submissions.

Nonfiction and Photos: Subject matter is "international coverage of art world, avant-garde and traditional art movements as well as in-depth specialist features." Uses "art subjects, reviews of exhibitions, features on artists and art movements." Buys interviews, profiles, and think pieces. Length: 300 to 2,000 words. Buys photos with mss; payment is negotiable.

THE ARTIST, 33 Warwick Sq., London, S.W.1., England. Editors: Peter Garrard and Frederic Taubes. For "amateur, student, and professional painters." Monthly. Circulation: 25,000. Buys first rights. Buys about 60 mss a year. Pays on publication. Will send a sample copy to a writer for 75¢. Query first with synopsis. Submit seasonal material 6 months in advance. Reports in 1 month. Enclose S.A.E. and International Reply Coupons for return of submissions.

Nonfiction and Photos: Uses "instructional articles for artists, illustrated by own work." Buys how-to and personal experience articles, "all on aspects of painting, drawing, and sculpture." Does not want to see articles on flower painting. Length: 1,500 to 2,500 words; "can be in series of 3 articles of this length." Pays $24 per 1,000 words. Buys photos with mss.

ARTS OF ASIA, Room 1002, Metropole Bldg., Peking Rd., Kowloon, Hong Kong. Editor: Tuyet Nguyet. For "the collector, student of arts, investor, and anyone wishing a wider knowledge of Asia." Established in 1971. Bimonthly. Circulation: 10,000. Copyrighted. Will send sample copy to writer for $1.50. Will consider unpublished material submitted directly by the author. Query first or submit complete ms. Enclose S.A.E. and International Reply Coupons.

Nonfiction and Photos: "Articles by experts in their own fields on various aspects of Asian arts. This type of article mainly derived from curators or serious collectors. Exhibition reviews. These should be illustrated. Exhibitions should be of outstanding interest (e.g., Japanese art at the British Museum, etc.)" Length: 2,000 words minimum. Payment varies proportionately with length. Pays $100 for articles of 2,000 to 3,000 words "including at least 10 to 12 illustrations which should be mainly black and white. Colour material should be of exceptional quality."

THE ARYAN PATH, Theosophy Hall, 40 New Marine Lines, Bombay 400020. (London office: 62 Queen's Gardens W2 3AH). Editor: Sophia Wadia. For the "general educated reader. Serious but not academic." Established in 1930. Monthly except July and August; 10 issues a year. Copyrighted. "First publication rights acceptable; author obtaining subsequent copyright; we reserve right to reprint in later issue." Payment on acceptance. Will send sample copy by sea-mail on request. Will consider unpublished material submitted directly by the author and offered for first time use. Query first or submit complete ms. Enclose S.A.E. and International Reply Coupons.

Nonfiction: "Aims at comparative study of eastern and western ideas in religion, philosophy, social and environmental problems and literature. Untechnical but serious style preferred. Must be of interest and intelligible to eastern and western readers and convey a philosophical or mystical perspective." Length: 1,800 to 2,500 words. Payment "by arrangement, from 2 pounds to 3 pounds per 1,000 words."

ASHORE AND AFLOAT, Agnes Weston House, 32 Western Parade, Southsea, Hants, PO5 3JE England. Editor: John Bentliff. Bimonthly for those interested in naval affairs and nautical matters. Will send sample copy on request. Normally reports within seven days. Buys first British serial rights. Pays on publication. Enclose S.A.E. and International Reply Coupons. All mss must be typed, double-spaced with wide left margin. Should have front cover sheet showing the title of the article or story, the name or pen name of the author, the approximate length of the ms and the name and address of the author shown separately. Title and name of author should also be shown on the first page only of the ms.

Nonfiction. Articles on naval affairs and maritime subjects. Seasonal articles on the Christian faith. Style should be simple and straightforward. Taboos are references to gambling, drunkenness, and the use of bad language. To 1,000 words. Pays $3 to $4 per 1,000 words.

Photos: Purchased with mss. Pays $1.

Fiction: Stories of interest to naval personnel and others interested in the sea. Style: for light reading. Taboos same as for nonfiction. Length: 1,000 words. Pays $3 to $4.

Fillers: Short humor.

AUSTRALASIAN POST, 62 Flinders Lane, Melbourne 3000, Australia. Editor: Jack Hughes. For persons "somewhere in the middle of high brows and low brows." Established in 1930. Weekly. Circulation: 280,000. Not copyrighted. Will consider material previously published in U.S. or Canada offered for first publication in Australia. Enclose S.A.E. and International Reply Coupons for return of submissions.

Nonfiction and Photos: "A weekly, factual, general interest magazine aimed at a male market, but concocted in such a way that women would find much of interest. We prefer illustrated stories that would have broad interest to Australians. Articles should be brash, dramatic, popular, boldly illustrated, down-to-earth, urgent. No profiles, no history." Length: about 1,000 words. Pays $30 "for approximately 500 to 1,000 words." Pays $15 minimum for photos.

AUSTRALIAN HOME BEAUTIFUL, 61-73 Flinders Lane, Melbourne, Victoria, Australia. Editor: A.J. Hitchin. Published for homemakers. Payment by arrangement on acceptance, high by Australian standards "but finds much material unacceptable as being too U.S.-orientated." Reports promptly. Usually buys one-time Australian magazine rights only. Include S.A.E. and International Reply Coupons.

Nonfiction: Buys articles on decoration, room settings, gardens, do-it-yourself, etc.

Photos: Buys photo material—singles, series, illustrated articles, b&w and color.

AUSTRALIAN PHOTOGRAPHY, Box 4689 GPO, 381 Pitt St., Sydney, N.S.W., Australia 2001. Editor: Bradford West. Monthly. Will send sample copy on request. For photographers, both amateur and professional. Pays on publication. Enclose S.A.E. and International Reply Coupons.

Nonfiction and Photos: Reports on new or different techniques illustrated with appropriate photos. How-to-do-it articles. Pays $8 to $12 Australian per page for b&w; 10 to $25 Australian for color.

BLACKWOOD'S MAGAZINE, 32 Thistle Street, Edinburgh, Scotland, U.K. Editor: Douglas Blackwood. For "middle-aged, highly educated audience interested in quality literature." Monthly. Circulation: 14,000. Buys first rights. Buys 120 mss a

year. Pays on publication. Will send a sample copy to a writer for 25¢. "Writers are asked to submit material only when they have studied the magazine." Submit seasonal material 3 months in advance. Reports "immediately." Enclose S.A.E. and International Reply Coupons for return of submissions.
Nonfiction, Fiction, and Poetry: Buys "short stories, articles, poetry—all of a high standard. *Blackwood's* is the oldest monthly magazine in the U.K., and its idiom is unique." Buys personal experience and travel articles. Also buys humorous, historical, and adventure fiction. Length: 3,000 to 9,000 words. Uses traditional, contemporary, and light verse. Length: open. Payment is "according to merit. Basic rate: 8 pounds per 1,000 words for the first 3,000 words; 5 pounds per thousand thereafter."

BOOKS AND BOOKMEN, Artillery Mansions, 75 Victoria Street, London, SW1H OH2, England. Editor: Frank Granville Barker. For "adults interested in literary subjects." Monthly. Buys first rights. Pays on publication. Will send a free sample copy to a writer on request. Query first. Submit seasonal material 2 months in advance. Reports "usually as soon as possible." Enclose S.A.E. and International Reply Coupons for return of submissions.
Nonfiction: Buys "reviews of books (fiction, biography, social studies, etc.)." Payment "by prior arrangement only."

CARITAS, Granada, Stillorgan, Dublin, Ireland. Editor: Rev. Brother Flavian Keane, O.H. Established in 1935. Quarterly. Circulation: 60,000. Copyrighted. Will consider material previously published in U.S. or Canada offered for first publication in Ireland. Will send a sample copy to a writer on request. Submit complete ms. Will consider photocopied submissions. Enclose S.A.E. and International Reply Coupons for return of submissions.
Nonfiction: "A magazine of Christian concern. Interested in medical, social, Christian concern, and health subjects." Length: 750 to 1,500 words. Pays 10 pounds (about $25).

CATHOLIC GAZETTE, 114 West Heath Rd., London, NW3 7TX, England. Editor: Rev. B. Howling. For "priests and religious—the 'thinking' Catholic in Britain." Special September "Home Mission Sunday" issue. Monthly. Circulation: about 8,000. Copyrighted. Enclose S.A.E. and International Reply Coupons for return of submissions.
Nonfiction: Publication is concerned with "Roman Catholic Church life and theology in England and Wales." Buys "articles on theological aspects of the Church, scripture, liturgy, religious life; articles on aspects of the life and development of the Church, with particular reference to England and Wales. Short, interesting articles are preferred to longer ones. 'Viewpoint' is a regular feature reflecting ideas and experiments in the life and apostolate of the Church, with special reference to the Catholic Church/Christian Churches in England and Wales." Length: 1,500 to 4,000 words. Pays 2 pounds to 6 pounds.

CATHOLIC STANDARD, 11 Talbot St., Dublin 1, Ireland. Editor: John Feeney. For "average middle class readership with average to high intelligence." Established in 1938. Weekly. Circulation: 22,000. Not copyrighted. Will consider material previously published in U.S. or Canada offered for first publication in Ireland. Will consider photocopied submissions. Enclose S.A.E. and International Reply Coupons for return of submissions.
Nonfiction: "A religious periodical devoted to news comment and views on religious and social topics. The purpose is to inform and move readers with social and moral awareness. We require articles of social and religious problems treated from a Christian point of view aimed at a readership of average to high intelligence. Emphasis should be on the Christian point of view. The articles should be structured in a logical order to make a moral point and built around examples from life." Length: 500 to 1,000 words. Pays $20 to $70.

CHALLENGE, Revenue Buildings, Chapel Road, Worthing, Sussex, England. Editor: Derek Sangster. An interdenominational Gospel monthly in tabloid newspaper form which is distributed through Evangelical churches and Christian groups in Britain; however, most readers have no church connection. Circulation:

215,066. Include S.A.E. and International Reply Coupons.
Nonfiction: Buys stories "with strong British connection on what the Lord is doing in the world today. This is an evangelical paper which brings news of Christ. Stories might concern missionary adventure, lives transformed by the power of Christ, sickness cured and so on. Style should be that of the British press." Features should be between 300 and 700 words. Pays $10 for main features.
Photos: B&w only; strong human and dramatic interest preferred. Pays commercial rates for agency photos.

CHIC, In the Asian Manner, 404 Asian House, 1 Hennessy Road, Hong Kong. Editor: Mrs. Blanche D. Gallardo. General interest women's magazine edited for the 20 to 45 age group of Asian women belonging to upper-income levels. Established in 1971. Published every two months. Circulation: 20,000 in Asia. Copyrighted. Will send sample copy to writer on request. Will consider material previously published in U.S. or Canada submitted directly by author. Will consider unpublished material submitted directly by author. Query first or submit complete ms. Enclose S.A.E. and International Reply Coupons for return of submissions or reply to queries.
Nonfiction and Photos: Interested in the following material (previously published in the U.S. or Canada, or unpublished): Stories on outstanding Asian personalities, male or female, in any line of work, living either in Canada or the U.S. whose work have received nationwide, or worldwide recognition. "The stress is on the achiever personality, or the pioneer, although I can't see why the occasional unconventional 'nut' who has done or is doing something interesting won't make good copy as well. The idea is to show the Asians back home what their expatriate countrymen are up to abroad. We would also be interested in women's lib type features relevant to the conditions in this part of the world. Lengths of 2,500 to 3,000 words would be ideal. Articles and stories of medical interest, again as they relate to Asia and the people in this part of the world. 1,500 to 2,000 words depending on importance of subject matter. A review of latest books of particular interest to women which are shortly expected to make their appearance in the Asian bookshops with listing of countries where books will be made available, although I suppose it will be quite impossible to pin down various prices that will apply. 2,000 words for reviews. Horoscope feature especially geared to women. Especially interested in a horoscope column based on the Chinese Zodiac. We prefer to keep the writing style light and entertaining, but informative and meaty. Basic rates are as follows: $20 for simple research, backgrounders in question and answer form; $25 for articles of 1,500 to 2,000 words; $35 for major feature stories of 2,500 to 3,000 words; $25 each for color transparencies and $10 each for b&w prints."

COMMANDO, D.C. Thomson & Co., Ltd., Albert Square, Dundee, Scotland. Eight issues per month. Copyrighted. Will consider unpublished material offered for first time use only. Will send a sample copy to a writer on request. Query first "with synopsis, please, of about 1,500 words." Enclose S.A.E. and International Reply Coupons for return of submissions.
Fiction: "Scripts for picture stories for boys of 10 to 15. World War II. British characters principally—Army, Navy, or Air Force. Length: approximately 140 pix. Payment by arrangement."

CONTEMPORARY REVIEW, 37 Union Street, London, S.E.1., England. Editor: Rosalind Wade. For a "very intelligent lay audience; we have subscribers all over the world." Established in 1866. Monthly. Pays on publication. Query first. "Study journal; a query is desirable as to whether or not a particular subject has been covered recently. We are not interested in previously published material." Submit "topical material" 5 weeks in advance. Reports "within a week or so." Enclose S.A.E. and International Reply Coupons for reply to queries.
Nonfiction, Fiction, and Poetry: "We are completely 'independent' although 'liberal' in origin. We can provide a platform for a very wide range of ideas. Our circulation is greater in the U.S.A. than in England. Freshness of approach and some new and authoritative information is essential. Only material written with authority can be considered." Buys interviews, profiles, and personal experience articles on "the arts, history, home and international politics, domestic subjects, theology, etc." Occasionally buys "short stories and poems of the highest literary merit." Length:

1,500 to 3,000 words for articles; 4,000 words maximum for fiction. Pays 2 pounds 50 shillings per 1,000 words.

THE COUNTRYMAN, Sheep St., Burford, Oxford, OX8 4LH England. Editor: Crispin Gill. Established in 1927. Quarterly. Circulation: 60,000. Copyrighted. Will consider unpublished material offered for first time use only. Will send a sample copy to a writer for 45 pence. Query first or submit complete ms. Enclose S.A.E. and International Reply Coupons for return of submissions or reply to queries.
Nonfiction: "Rural life and interests; factual and down to earth. No 'townee' sentimentalizing about the countryside." Length: 2,000 words maximum. Pays 10 pounds per 1,000 words, or more on merit.

THE CRITICAL QUARTERLY, The University, Manchester, England. Editors: Prof. C.B. Cox and Mr. A.E. Dyson. For teachers, school and college students. Established in 1959. Quarterly. Circulation: 5,000. Copyrighted. Will send sample copy to writer for $1. Will consider unpublished material offered for first time use in England. Submission of unpublished material may be made directly by author. Submit complete ms. Enclose S.A.E. and International Reply Coupons for return of submissions.
Nonfiction: Will consider the following unpublished material: Scholarly essays about British, European, and American literature of the 20th century. One bibliographical issue each spring. New poetry, general articles on pre-1900 British literature. Literary criticism of highest standard. Length: 500 to 6,000 words. Pays in 5 to 10 offprints.

THE CROSS, Mount Argus, Dublin 6, Ireland. Editor: Father Brian D'Arcy, C.P. For "the average Catholic family—young and old interests catered for." Monthly. Circulation: 25,000. Buys British and Irish rights. Pays on publication. Will send a free sample copy to a writer on request. Enclose S.A.E. and International Reply Coupons for return of submissions.
Nonfiction and Photos: Buys "articles of general and Catholic interest; articles that would suit the young and old in the average Catholic family." Length: 1,000 to 1,500 words. Pays 3 to 5 pounds. Purchases photos with mss.

CURRENT, 140 Kensington Church St., London W8 England. Editor: Lorna Low. For teenagers learning English as foreign language. Established 1968. Monthly. Circulation: 53,000. Copyrighted. Pays on publication. Will send sample copy to writer on request. Will consider material previously published in U.S. or Canada, offered for first publication in United Kingdom. Submission of previously published material for consideration may be made directly by author. Enclose S.A.E. and International Reply Coupons for return of submissions.
Nonfiction and Fiction: Will consider the following material previously published in U.S. or Canada: Articles, short stories, features about life in Canada and especially in U.S. of interest to teenagers in Europe. Simple, straightforward, journalistic style. Length: 700 to 1,300 words. Pays 2 pounds per 100 words.

DANCE AND DANCERS, Artillery Mansions, 75 Victoria Street, London, SW1H OH2, England. Editor: Peter Williams. For "dancers, students, dance lovers of all ages interested in all aspects of dance in the theatre." Monthly. Buys first rights. Will send a free sample copy to a writer on request. Query first. Submit seasonal material 2 months in advance. Reports "as soon as possible." Enclose S.A.E. and International Reply Coupons for reply to queries.
Nonfiction and Photos: Wants "in-depth coverage of current productions; special emphasis on new creations with experts reviewing production, dancing, and music; regular interviews with important personalities in every branch of the field." Payment negotiable. Buys b&w glossy photos.

DRIVE MAGAZINE, Berkeley Square House, Berkeley Square, London, W1X 5PD, England. Editor: Paul M. Bradwell. Quarterly. Circulation: 4½ million. Buys all rights. Buys about 40 mss a year. Pays on acceptance. Will send a sample copy to a writer on request. "It is essential that any would-be contributors familiarize themselves with the magazine." Query first, submitting an outline of the idea. Reports in 2 to 3 weeks. Enclose S.A.E. and International Reply Coupons for reply to queries.

Nonfiction: "As a magazine which circulates to all the members of the British Automobile Association, it is concerned especially with leisure, travel, environment, and motoring. *Drive* insists, particularly for its major features, on detailed, accurate research which throws a new and significant light on matters of public interest, particularly directed at motoring. Material should preferably, but not necessarily, be consumer-oriented." Buys how-to's, personal experience articles, profiles, inspirational articles, coverage of successful business operations, historical and think pieces, new product articles, travel articles, and coverage of merchandising techniques. Length: 2,000 words. Pays average of $250, negotiable upwards.
Photos: Color transparencies, 35mm color. Payment "on agreement with individual."

ECOLOGIST, 73 Molesworth St., Wadebridge, Cornwall PL27 7DS, United Kingdom. Editor: Edward Goldsmith. For a general audience, especially students and academics educated to university standard. Established in 1970. Monthly. Circulation: 14,000. Copyrighted. Pays on publication. Will send sample copy to writer on request. Query first. Enclose S.A.E. and International Reply Coupons for reply to queries and return of submissions.
Nonfiction and Photos: Publishes material about environment, resources, human ecology. "Avoid jargon and, so far as possible, technicalities. Aim for high literary quality. We are interested in general articles on the environmental crisis or pollution, and especially in articles covering the future of resources, energy and anthropology." Length: 500 to 4,000 words. Pays 10 pounds per 1,000 words. Plate or half-plate b&w prints are purchased with accompanying mss or on assignment. Captions required. Pays for photos by arrangement.

EDITIONS AGENTZIA, BP 50, 75.222 Paris Cedex 05, France. Collective Editorship. Will send sample copy for $2. For avant-garde readers. Buys all rights. Pays on publication. Include S.A.E. and International Reply Coupons.
Fiction and Photos: Works on visual and concrete literature, underground, happenings, events, intermedia. Texts in French, English, German, Italian.

ENCOUNTER, 59 St. Martin's Lane, London, WC2N 4JS, England. Editors: Anthony Thwaite and Melvin J. Lasky. Pays on publication. Buys first English language serial rights. Rejected mss returned in about one month, provided International Reply Coupons are enclosed.
Nonfiction, Fiction, and Poetry: Uses reportage, literary criticism, sociology; high literary standard and interest. Study of the magazine, which is available in the United States, is urged. Pays about $22 per 1,000 words. Also buys short stories and poetry.

FABULOUS 208, P.O. Box 21, Tower House, 8-14 Southampton St., London WC2E 9QX England. Editor: Betty Hale: For girls between the age of 13 and 16 who are bright and intelligent, interested in their own lives and problems and relationships with people in the outside world, particularly with their relationships with their parents. They are also interested in careers, holidays, fashions, and very especially boys and pop stars. Established in 1964. Weekly. Circulation: 300,000. Copyrighted. Pays on acceptance. Will send sample copy to writer for 50¢. Query first. Enclose S.A.E. and International Reply Coupons for reply to queries or return of submissions.
Nonfiction and Fiction: Specially written short stories of about 2,500 words. "Commissioned features on subjects like careers, human relationships; emotional and helpful articles. Anyone wishing to write for this magazine should first read it and study it, otherwise they may be wasting their time. I think *Fabulous* is rather more serious in its approach to its contents. Everything in the magazine is very wholesome and we never accept things which are permissive nor do we refer to drugs." Length: 750 to 2,000 words. Pays 15 to 25 pounds. For serials of 1,500 to 3,500 words, payment is 25 to 40 pounds, or by arrangement in exceptional circumstances. Fiction Dept. Editor: Fid Backhouse. Photos are purchased with accompanying mss. Photo Dept. Editor: Josie Higgs.

THE FIELD, 8 Stratton St., London, England. Editor: Wilson Stephens. Weekly. Sometimes buys first British serial rights only. Pays on publication. Include S.A.E. and International Reply Coupons.
Nonfiction: "Factual accounts on fishing, shooting, hunting, countryside, natural history." Minimum and maximum rates of payment are "at editor's discretion."

FILM MAKING, Wessex House, 26 Station Rd., Cambridge, CB1 2LB, England. Editor: Russell Roworth. Established in 1963. Monthly. Circulation: 26,000. Copyrighted. Will consider unpublished material offered for first time use only. Will send a sample copy to a writer on request. Enclose S.A.E. and International Reply Coupons for return of submissions.
Nonfiction: "Amateur and semi-pro techniques on film making; practical ideas, sound features." Length: 2,000 to 3,000 words. Pays "approximately 25 pounds for 3,000 words."

FILMS AND FILMING, Artillery Mansions, 75, Victoria Street, London, SW1H, OH2, England. Editor: Robin Bean. For "those with a serious interest in all aspects of films." Special Cannes Film Festival issue (June). Monthly. Buys all rights. Will send a sample copy to a writer on request. Query first. Reports "as soon as possible." Enclose S.A.E. and International Reply Coupons for reply to queries.
Nonfiction: Wants "in-depth coverage." Buys "reviews plus features on directors, actors, particular genre and picture spreads, sections on documentary, film music, animation." Payment negotiable.

GAMEKEEPER AND COUNTRYSIDE, c/o Gilbertson and Page Ltd., Tamworth Rd., Hertford, Hertfordshire, England. Editor: Anthony Clarkson. For sportsmen, naturalists, countrymen, and would-be countrymen. Established 1897. Monthly. Not usually copyrighted. Pays on publication. Will send sample copy to writer in certain circumstances. Submit only complete ms for nonfiction. Query first or submit complete ms for other material. Enclose S.A.E. and International Reply Coupons for reply to query or return of submission.
Nonfiction, Fiction and Photos: "All subjects connected with country life, country occupations, sports (field sports, not games). Straightforward approach. Material must be authoritative." Informational, how-to, personal experience, profile, humor, historical, think pieces, personal opinion, new product, and technical articles. Humorous fiction is also considered. Length: 200 to 2,000 words. Pays about 5 pounds for 800 words. B&w photos are purchased with accompanying manuscripts, captions required. Pays 1 to 3 pounds.

GARDEN NEWS, E.M.A.P. Oundle Rd., Woodston, Peterborough PE2 9QR England. Editor: Frank Ward. For private gardeners. Established in 1957. Weekly. Circulation: 100,000. Not copyrighted. Pays on publication. Will send sample copy to writer for postage. Will consider material previously published in U.S. or Canada, offered for first publication in England. Submission of previously published material may be made directly by the author. Will consider unpublished material offered for first time use. Submission of unpublished material may be made directly by the author. Submit complete ms. Enclose S.A.E. and International Reply Coupons for return of submission.
Nonfiction: Will consider the following material (previously published in U.S. or Canada, or unpublished): "Any material connected in some way with private gardening and professional horticulture. Illustration essential. Our purpose is to advise horitculturally and entertain with national and international news. Style is chatty. We consider people as interesting as the plants they grow." Pays 7 pounds per 1,000 words minimum.

THE GEOGRAPHICAL MAGAZINE, New Science Publications, 128 Long Acre, London WC2E 9QH, England. Editor: Derek Weber. Query first. Enclose S.A.E. and International. Reply Coupons.
Nonfiction and Photos: Uses informative, readable, well-illustrated, authentic articles, 1,500 to 2,500 words in length, dealing with the interpretation of modern geography in all its aspects: "cartography, conservation, hydrology, meteorology, communications, urbanization and the Third World, economic developments, geographical background to social and political organizations. Man's control and

management of the enviroment in which he lives, works and plays. News and re-views regarding significant events in geographical research and publications. Travel guide is a geographical approach to world travel and tourism. Photographs must be of very high quality." Preliminary letter prior to submitting material is recommended. Pays$ $40 per 1,000 words. Pays $30 for color photos, $10 for b&w.

GOLF MONTHLY, 113 St. Vincent St., Glasgow, Scotland. Editor: Percy Huggins. Monthly. Circulation; 8,500. Will send sample copy on request. Include S.A.E. and International Reply Coupons. Aimed at golfers. Buys all rights. Pays on publication.
Nonfiction: Can use nonfiction on golf topics and personalities, no word length limitations. Payment rates to be negotiated.
Photos: Purchased with mss or with captions only.
Fiction: About golf. Length: 2,500 words maximum.

GOOD HOUSEKEEPING, Chestergate House, Vauxhall Bridge Road, London S.W.1, England. Editor: Laurie Purden. Monthly aimed at the intelligent, lively married woman. Emphasis on food, family matters, furnishing and home management—material almost always provided by the magazine's own staff and domestically qualified Institute writers. Usually buys first British serial rights. Reports as soon as possible—"usually within a month; if not, soon after." Include S.A.E. and International Reply Coupons.
Nonfiction: Strong general features of topical/controversial interest (medical, psychological, social, etc.) and profiles of well-known or exceptionally interesting people—usually commissioned, but ideas and second rights considered. Pays "average 25 to 80 pounds. We have no set rate and never pay per word." Length: 600 to 2,000 words.
Fiction: "We buy only 1 or 2 stories per issue, so they must be good. Wide range of subjects accepted, always providing there is genuine emotional involvement. But stories with a domestic background should either reflect British way of life or be capable of realistic anglicization." Length: 1,500 to 4,500 words. Pays 35 to 100 pounds.
Fillers: Fillers and light, humorous articles, maximum 900 words, accepted on a nonsolicited basis. Pays $8 to $25 pounds.

GOOD MOTORING, 2 Ellis St., Sloane St., London SW1X 9AN, England. Editor: Richard Howell. For experienced motorists. Established in 1935. Monthly. Circulation: 101,000. Copyrighted. Pays on publication. Will send sample copy to writer for 20 pounds. Query first. Enclose S.A.E. and International Reply Coupons for reply to query.
Nonfiction and Photos: Any motoring subject, touring in Europe, general motoring news. Length: 500 to 1,500 words. Pays 4 to 12 pounds. 8x6 b&w photos are purchased with accompanying mss; captions required. Pays 2 pounds per photo.

HERS, IPC Magazines, Ltd., 30-32 Southampton St. London, WC2E 9QX, England. Editor: Miss Katherine Walker. Address submissions to the American office: Philip Fleet, IPC Magazines, Ltd., 300 E. 42nd St., New York NY 10017. Established in 1965. For "predominantly young married women, 18 to 25, with modest incomes and domestic interests, desirous of emotional excitement." Monthly. Circulation: 250,000. Rights purchased vary with author and material. Buys all rights; or first serial rights." Buys about 100 mss a year. Pays on acceptance. Will send a sample copy to a writer on request. Submit through New York office of IPC Magazines, Ltd. Reports in 1 month. Enclose S.A.E. and International Reply Coupons for return of submissions.
Fiction: Confession stories. "Interested in drama, emotion and credibility—not in sensational sex. Current need is for "real life stories. Each story should deal with a problem women would instinctively sympathize with and the narrator of the story should come to terms with her problem in a thoroughly realistic way. Great care should be taken that stories are psychologically valid and realistic in physical details; story should be warm and draw readers into the emotions it's dealing with and be quick moving and exciting. We do not publish sensational or deliberately sexy material." Length: 2,000 words minimum. Pays "about 10 pounds per 1,000 words."

HI-FI NEWS & RECORD REVIEW, Link House, Dingwall Ave., Croydon, CR9 2TA, England. Editor: John Crabbe. For a "lay to specialist audience." Established in 1956. Monthly. Circulation: 64,000. Copyrighted. Will consider material previously published in the U.S. or Canada offered for first publication in U.K. Will send a sample copy to a writer on request. Will not consider photocopied submissions. Enclose S.A.E. and International Reply Coupons for return of submissions.
Nonfiction: "Specialist magazine dealing with records, tapes, musical and audio matters over a wide range." Length: 1,000 to 3,000 words. Pays $25 per 1,000 words.

HISTORY TODAY, 388/389 Strand, London WC2R, OLT, England. Editors: Peter Quennell and Alan Hodge. Published for the general reader and students of history. Buys first serial rights. Pays on publication. Include S.A.E. and International Reply Coupons.
Nonfiction: Uses articles on any historical subject. All writers are specialists in history. Wants articles about 3,000 to 4,000 words, with suggestions for illustrations. Pays 25 or 30 pounds per text.
Photos: Buys b&w photos. Pays maximum of 6 pounds.

HOMES OVERSEAS, 10 East Rd. London, N. 1, England. Editor: M.A. Furnell. For home owners. Bimonthly. Circulation: 11,000. Buys U.K. rights. Pays on publication. Will send a sample copy to a writer for 30¢. Query first. Reports "by return mail." Enclose S.A.E. and International Reply Coupons for reply to queries.
Nonfiction and Photos: Buys "articles about homes for sale in all parts of the world; buying a house abroad; also information on living costs, local facilities, and attractions." Recent articles include "Taxation on Residents of Portugal" and "The Island of La Palma, Canary Islands." Length: 1,000 words. Pays $15 per 1,000 words. Photos purchased with mss.

INSIGHT MAGAZINE, 118 Windham Rd., Bournemouth, Hampshire BH1 4RD, England. Editor: Deric R. James. "Audience from all walks of life—professional people, retired people, artists, students, doctors, clergy, etc." Quarterly. Circulation: 500. Buys first rights. Pays on publication. Will send a sample copy to a writer on request. No query required. Submit seasonal material 3 months in advance. Reports in 3 months. Enclose S.A.E. and International Reply Coupons for return of submissions.
Nonfiction and Photos: "Any aspect of occultism, ceremonial magic, etc. The writer should always send a photo or sketch pertaining to his thesis. We also publish articles on black magic. No comparative and eastern religions material or paraphysical subjects, healing, etc." Buys personal experience articles, interviews, spot news, photo articles. Length: 1,000 to 3,000 words. Pays 50 pence to 2 pounds. Photos purchased with ms. Payment to be negotiated.

INTERNATIONAL CONSUMER, International Organization of Consumers Unions, 9 Emmastraat, The Hague, Netherlands. Editor: John Calascione. Established in 1962. Quarterly. Circulation: 1,000. Not copyrighted. Pays on publication. Will send sample copy to writer on request. Will consider material previously published in U.S. or Canada, offered for first publication in Netherlands. Submission of previously published material may be made directly by author, through an agent, or by the publisher or his representative. Will consider unpublished material. Submission of unpublished material may be made directly by the author or through agent. Query first or submit complete ms. Enclose S.A.E. and International Reply Coupons for reply to query or return of submission.
Nonfiction: Interested in the following material (previously published in U.S. or Canada, or unpublished): Articles on consumer protection; activities of consumer groups and/or government consumer agencies; consumer education; case studies/exposes of commercial or other practices contrary to consumer interest. Feature article structure: international and professional class readership. Length: 2,000 to 3,000 words. Pays $30 to $60 per 2,000 words.

IRISH NURSING NEWS, 91 Lower Baggot St., Dublin 2, Ireland. Editor: Rev. Br. Finian Gallagher, O.H. For nursing personnel. Established in 1922. Quarterly. Circulation: 1,500. Not copyrighted. Pays on publication. Will send sample copy to writer on request. Will consider material previously published in U.S. or Canada, offered for first publication in Ireland. Submission of previously published material may be made directly by author, through an agent or by publisher or his representative. Will consider unpublished material. Submission of unpublished material may be made directly by the author. Submit complete ms. Enclose S.A.E. and International Reply Coupons for return of submission.

Nonfiction: Interested in the following material: (previously published in U.S. or Canada, or unpublished): Articles about professional nursing, medical; nursing, ethical nursing, aimed at all branches of nursing. Length: 600 to 900 words. Pays approximately 2 pounds.

ISRAEL MAGAZINE, 88 Hahashmoniam St., Tel Aviv, Israel. Editor: Nahum Sirotsky. Managing Editor: Dianne Nicholson Lawes. For "United States residents interested in Israel. They are of all age groups and levels of education." Monthly. Buys all rights. Buys approximately 200 mss per year. Pays on publication. Will send sample copy to writer for $1. Query first; "assignments usually will be made only on the basis of proven, published writing ability." Submit seasonal material 8 months in advance. Reports "soon." Enclose S.A.E. and International Reply Coupons for return of submissions.

Nonfiction: "Articles must deal with some aspect of Israel, Jewish affairs, or Judaism. We accept a wide range of articles on the subjects of politics, society, youth, personalities, religion, nature, culture, etc. We are an independent publication and interested in projecting various viewpoints within our format of presenting a well-rounded magazine. Printing and surface postal schedules demand that all articles be written to withstand a lapse of 8 months between submission and publication. Prospective writers are asked to please study a copy of the magazine before attempting to write an article for us. We receive too many articles dealing with personal experiences in Israel. These are rarely used. Certain articles are tied into religious or national holidays. Also, we run tourist articles during the peak season. Our regular features are staff-written; and most articles come from people living in Israel." Buys interviews, profiles, inspirational and think pieces, humor, coverage of successful business operations, photo features, travel articles. Length: 2,000 words preferred; 5,000 words maximum. Payment in the U.S. can be made in dollars, at the official rate of exchange from Israeli pounds into dollars. Fees vary and are not according to word count. $100 to $150; "sometimes less, sometimes more, depending on ms." Allowance is made for unusual expenses or research. Photos: "Most photos are supplied by our staff. Others are purchased for one-time events." Buys b&w glossies, color transparencies with mss. Payment open.

Fiction: "We publish short stories which are set in Israel. All subjects will be considered."

Poetry: Also considered according to the general format policy.

JEWISH TELEGRAPH, Levi House, Bury Old Road, Manchester, M8 6HB, England. Editor: Frank Harris. For "Jewish families." Special issues for Jewish New Year and Passover. Weekly. Circulation: 10,000. Pays on publication. Will send a sample copy to a writer on request. Submit seasonal material 2 to 3 weeks in advance. Reports "immediately." Enclose S.A.E. and International Reply Coupons for return of submissions.

Nonfiction and Fiction: Looks for "Jewish essence." Wants news and articles of Jewish humor, personal experience and historical articles, interviews, profiles, spot news, and photo features. Also buys humorous, religious, and contemporary problem fiction. Length: open. Pays 2 pounds 80 pence minimum.

KARATE AND ORIENTAL ARTS, 638 Fulham Rd., London, S.W. 6, England. Editor: Paul H. Crompton. Established in 1966. Bimonthly. Circulation: 5,000. Copyrighted. Will consider material previously published in U.S. or Canada offered for first publication in U.K. Will send a sample copy to a writer for $1. Query first. Enclose S.A.E. and International Reply Coupons for reply to queries.

Nonfiction and Photos: Articles on "judo, karate, aikido, kendo, wrestling, weapon training, physical fitness, body development, kinetic studies, oriental medicine, art. Edited to inform people interested in these subjects of the current affairs and studies in their field; also, historical interest. Must be illustrated." Length: maximum 3,000 words. Pays $6.50 per 1,000 words for previously published material and $7.50 per 1,000 words for unpublished material.

KENT LIFE, New Hythe Lane, Larkfield, Kent, England. Editor: Robert Song-hurst. For "county level (i.e., nobility, professional, middle class)." Monthly. Circulation: 15,000. Rights negotiable. Pays on acceptance. Will send a free sample copy to a writer on request. Type name and address in block capitals on mss. Reports "within 10 days." Enclose S.A.E. and International Reply Coupons for return of submissions.

Nonfiction: Uses "material connected with the county of Kent only, i.e., historical, country, old houses, folklore, industry, ships, modern aspects of Kent. Avoid race, religion, pornography. Material should be aimed at the cultured reader and must be connected with Kent. Always glad to consider the 'Kent through American eyes' type of article, or similar, whether flattering or otherwise." Length: 1,000 to 1,200 words. Payment "varies, but seldom exceeds 6 pounds."

Photos: "The majority of pictures are taken by staff photographers. However, I am always glad to consider unusual b&w pictures. Suggested subjects to avoid: Canterbury Cathedral, and Rochester and Dover Castles. Very fine buildings, but photographed to death." Buys photos with mss and occasionally with captions only. Pays 1 pound per picture.

cFi tion and Poetry: "Must be connected with Kent. Avoid religion or race." Little fiction used. Length: 1,000 to 1,200 words for fiction; 20 to 30 lines for poetry. Pays 1 pound for poetry.

LANCASHIRE LIFE, Whitethorn Press, Thomson House, Withy Grove, Manchester, United Kingdom M60 4BL. Editor: William Amos. For a general audience, sharing an interest in their region. Established in 1947. Monthly. Circulation: 16,000. Copyrighted. Pays on publication. Will send sample copy to writer for $1. Query first. Enclose S.A.E. and International Reply Coupons for reply to query.

Nonfiction, Fiction, Poetry, and Photos: "Articles (historical, topographical, personality), stories, poems, all specifically concerned with Lancashire. Avoid cliches, study magazine first and use double-spacing." Informational, personal experience, interview, profile, humor, historical, nostalgia. Length: 500 to 3,000 words. Pays 3 to 25 pounds. Mainstream fiction with a Lancashire setting. Length: 500 to 2,000 words. Pays 5 to 15 pounds. Traditional form poetry of 4 to 40 lines. Pays 3 to 5 pounds. B&w and 2¼ square color photos purchased with accompanying manuscripts or on assignment. Captions required. Payment by negotiation.

LONDON MYSTERY, 268/270 Vauxhall Bridge Road, London, S.W. 1, England. Editor: Major Norman Kark. Established in 1950. Quarterly. Copyrighted. Will consider unpublished material offered for first time use only. Will send a sample copy to a writer for 60¢. Submit complete ms. Enclose S.A.E. and International Reply Coupons for return of submissions.

Nonfiction and Fiction: "Whodunits; crime, mystery and detective stories; fact and fiction." Length: 1,500 to 2,000 words. Payment "by offer."

LOOK AND LISTEN, Artillery Mansions, 75, Victoria Street, London, SW1H OH2 England. Editor: Robin Bean. For general audience. Enclose S.A.E. and International Reply Coupons for return of submissions.

Nonfiction: General subject matter: "covers radio and TV."

LOOK EAST, Sixth Floor, Thaniya Bldg., Silom Rd., Bangkok, Thailand. Editor: Satish Sehgal. For a general, travel oriented, audience. Established in 1970. Monthly. Circulation: 5,000. Will send sample copy to writer on request. Will consider material previously published in U.S. or Canada, offered for first publication in Southeast Asia. Submission of previously published material may be made directly by author, through an agent, or by publisher or his representative. Will consider unpublished material. Submission of unpublished material may be made directly by the author. Query first. Enclose S.A.E. and International Reply Coupons for reply to queries.

Nonfiction and Photos: Will consider the following material previously published in U.S. or Canada: "Articles on people, places, festivals, and humor. Articles should be entertaining, informative (although not necessarily scholarly) and apolitical. Our articles average 2,000 to 3,000 words in length, but we also accept longer pieces for serialized publication." Payment between $25 to $50 per article. Will consider unpublished material also. Pays $100 per article for unpublished material.

MAN JUNIOR, 142 Clarence St., Sydney, N.S.W., Australia 2000. For "young men in the 18 to 25 age group." Monthly. Circulation: 36,000. Rights negotiable. Buys 120 mss a year. Pays on acceptance. Will send a sample copy to a writer for 40¢. Reports "within a month." Enclose S.A.E. and International Reply Coupons for return of submissions.
Nonfiction, Fiction, and Photos: Uses "factual adventure, action fiction." Buys personal experience articles and nonfiction humor. Also buys science fiction, mystery, adventure, and humorous stories. Length: 2,000 to 3,000 words for nonfiction; 2,000 to 3,500 words for fiction. Photos purchased with mss. Payment negotiable.

MAYFAIR, 95 A Chancery Lane, London WC2A 1DZ, England. Editor: Kenneth Bound. For a male audience. Established in 1966. Monthly. Circulation: 100,000. Pays on acceptance. Will send sample copy to writer for $1. Will consider material previously published in U.S. or Canada, offered for first publication in United Kingdom. Submission of previously published material may be made directly by the author or through an agent. Will consider unpublished material offered for first time use. Submission of unpublished material may be made directly by author or through an agent. Query first. Enclose S.A.E. and International Reply Coupons for reply to query and return of submissions.
Nonfiction, Fiction, and Photos: Interested in the following material (previously published in U.S. or Canada, or unpublished): "Male orientated features, humor, mainly with erotic appeal. Not show business material. *Playboy* format providing entertainment for men." Length: open. Pays 20 to 200 pounds. Also interested in sets of color transparencies of glamour material or male orientated interest.

MEANJIN QUARTERLY, University of Melbourne, Parkville, Victoria 3052, Australia. Editor: C.B. Christesen, O.B.E. Pays on acceptance. Buys first Australian serial rights. Reports in one month. Include S.A.E. and International Reply Coupons.
Nonfiction, Fiction, and Poetry: Publishes top quality literary criticism (contemporary, mainly) and essays of general cultural/intellectual interest; 2,500 to 4,000 words. Emphasis on high, professional quality. Publishes short stories and quality poetry. Pays $40 to $100 according to quality. Verse is usually bought at a flat fee of $5 to $10 per poem.

THE MODERN CHURCHMAN, Caynham Vicarage, Ludlow, Calop, England. Editor: W.H.C. Frend. Established in 1911. Quarterly. Circulation: 1,300. Not copyrighted. Will consider material previously published in U.S. or Canada offered for first publication in U.K. Will send a sample copy to a writer on request. Query first or submit complete ms. Enclose S.A.E. and International Reply Coupons for return of submissions or reply to queries.
Nonfiction: "Church and theological subjects of high academic standards." Length: 2,000 to 6,000 words. Pays 3 pounds.

MODERN MOTOR, 15 Boundary St., Rushcutters Bay, Sydney, New South Wales, Australia. Editor: Rob Luck. For a motoring oriented audience, ages 13 through 70. Established in 1956. Monthly. Circulation: 70,000. Copyrighted. Buys full Australian rights. Pays on publication. Will send sample copy to writer on request (surface mail, unless payment for airmail included with request). Query first. Enclose S.A.E. and International Reply Coupons for reply to query.
Nonfiction: "Accent is on hard news. However, we are interested in hard-hitting features that show variety in motoring around the world. No travel articles. Our style is pure news—fast, race news, presentation, packed with fact and good info. We are not interested in flowery prose, but we welcome good 'color' writing." Informational and spot news. Length: 1,000 to 3,000 words. Pays A$20 per 1,000 words. (May be increased substantially for world first news, or scoops.)
Photos: B&w 6x8 photos are purchased with or without accompanying mss and on assignment. Captions required. Pays A$5 each. Transparencies or good reflective art purchased for $10 each. "We prefer photos with a high emphasis on action."
Fillers: Newsbreaks and jokes. Length: 50 to 200 words. Pays A$5 to $A20.

MON TRICOT, 41 bvd des Capucines, Paris 2e, France. Editor: Pascal Bourguignon. Established in 1932. Quarterly. Circulation: 200,000. Buys all rights. Pays on publication. Will send a sample copy to a writer on request. Write for copy of guide-

lines for writers. Submit complete ms. Submit seasonal material 3 months in advance of issue date. Enclose S.A.E. and International Reply Coupons for return of submissions.
Nonfiction: Articles on "knitting, crochet works, all needlecraft. Creative hand-knitting and crochet models; fashions and needlecrafts; knitting hints." Buys personal experience articles. Length: "short texts." Payment to be negotiated.

MOTOR BOAT AND YACHTING, Dorset House, Stamford St., London SE1, England. Editor: Dick Hewitt. For people interested in motor boating, from large motor yachts in the luxury class to small boats with outboards. Established in 1904. Every two weeks. Circulation: 33,500. Copyrighted. Pays on publication. Query first or submit complete ms. Enclose S.A.E. and International Reply Coupons for reply to query or return of submission.
Nonfiction and Photos: Accounts of cruises; technical and informative features on boating subjects. Powerboat racing and inland waterway information. Length: 2,500 words maximum. Standard rate of payment is 10.50 pounds per 1,000 words. Photos purchased with accompanying mss or without mss. Captions required. B&w and color. Pays from 2.10 pounds to 6.30 pounds.

MOVIE MAKER, 13-35 Bridge St., Hemel Hempstead, Hertfordshire, England. Editor: Tony Rose. For "amateur film makers and fringe professionals." Monthly. Circulation: 30,000. Buys U.K. serial rights. Pays on publication. Will send a sample copy to a writer for $1. Query "advisable but not obligatory." Reports "within 3 weeks." Enclose S.A.E. and International Reply Coupons for return of submissions or reply to queries.
Nonfiction and Photos: Buys "articles on all aspects of movie making—must be based on the writer's own expereince and preferably be illustrated." Length: 2,000 words maximum. Pays 5 pounds per page. 8x10 glossy photos purchased with mss. Buys transparencies for cover use. Pays 15 to 75 pounds.

MUSIC AND MUSICIANS, Artillery Mansions, 75, Victoria Street, London, SW1H OHZ, England. Editor: Tom Sutcliffe. For "professionals in the musical fields of publishing, performance, recording, instrument making, etc., and the general musical public." Monthly. Buys first rights. Pays on publication. Will send a sample copy to a writer on request. Query first. Submit seasonal material 2 months in advance. Reports "as soon as possible." Enclose S.A.E. and International Reply Coupons for reply to queries.
Nonfiction and Photos: Uses "news, features, musical extracts, and reviews. The publication covers a very wide musical field." Length: 600 to 2,000 words. Buys b&w glossy photos.

MY WEEKLY, 80 Kingsway East, Dundee, Scotland. Editor: Maurice F. Paterson. For women of all ages. Established in 1913. Weekly. Circulation: 850,000. Copyrighted. Pays on acceptance. Will send sample copy to a writer on request. Submit only complete ms. Enclose S.A.E. and International Reply Coupons for return of submissions.
Nonfiction and Fiction: Interested in fiction and nonfiction which appeals to women. "Make material of real interest. Use a warm, personal approach." Personal experience, interview, humor, and travel. Nonfiction length: 750 to 1,500 words. Pays 10 to 20 pounds. Mystery, adventure, humorous and romantic fiction. Serialized novels. Fiction length: 1,000 to 5,000 words. Pays 12 to 30 pounds.

THE NAUTICAL MAGAZINE, 52 Darnley St., Glasgow, G41 2SG, Scotland. Editor: R. Ingram-Brown. For "the seafaring profession." Monthly. Circulation: 3,500. Buys all rights. Pays on publication. Will send a sample copy to a writer on request. Enclose S.A.E. and International Reply Coupons for return of submissions.
Nonfiction: Articles of interest to merchant navy; astronomical; navigational. Length: 2,000 words. Pays 2 pounds per 500 words on publication.

THE NEW BEACON, Royal National Institute for the Blind, 224 Great Portland Street, London, W1N 6AA, England. Editor: Donald Bell. For "those interested in blind welfare." Monthly. Circulation: 3,700. Buys no rights. Pays on publication.

Reports "immediately." Enclose S.A.E. and International Reply Coupons for return of submissions

Nonfiction, Photos, and Poetry: Buys authoritative articles on all aspects of blind welfare throughout the world and causes and prevention of blindness, news items (home and overseas)." Also buys "original material (prose and verse) by blind authors." Pays 2 pounds 10 pence per 1,000 words. Length: 900 to 5,000 words. Buys photos separately, "rarely" with articles. Payment negotiable.

NEW HUMANIST (formerly *Humanist*) 88 Islington High St., London N. 1., England. Editor: Christopher Macy. For "humanists and rationalists; broad age spread, mostly with higher education, broad interests." Monthly. Circulation: 5,000. Buys first rights. Buys about 50 mss a year. Pays on publication. Will send sample copy to writer on request. No query required. Submit seasonal material 6 weeks in advance. Reports in 6 weeks. Enclose S.A.E. and International Reply Coupons for return of submissions.

Nonfiction and Photos: Publishes "examinations of current or historic problems from a rationalist (bias-free) standpoint." Style should be "serious, popular, critical, balanced, with well-constructed arguments. We don't want arguments by clergymen on the evils of the permissive society." Buys personal experience and historical articles, interviews, profiles, think pieces, exposes. Length: 1,100 to 2,400 words. Pays 11 to 24 pounds. Pays 3 to 5 pounds for b&w glossies purchased with mss.

Poetry: Buys contemporary poetry. Length: 30 lines maximum. Pays 3 pounds to 5 pounds.

Fillers: Buys clippings and short humor. Pays 2 to 5 pounds.

NEW JUNIOR CHURCH PAPER, St. Mary's House, 125 Herne Hill, London SE24, England. Editor: Mrs. Mary Thompson. A church paper for boys and girls ages 7 through 11; a religious paper that aims to give teaching and enjoyment to children. Established in 1948. Monthly. Circulation: 25,000. Copyrighted. Pays on publication. Will consider material previously published in U.S. or Canada, offered for first publication in United Kingdom. Submission of previously published material may be made directly by author, through an agent, or by the publisher or his representative. Will consider unpublished material offered for first time use. Submission of unpublished material may be made directly by author. Submit complete ms. Enclose S.A.E. and International Reply Coupons for return of submission.

Nonfiction and Fiction: Interested in the following material (previously published in U.S. or Canada, or unpublished): "Short exciting stories for children ages 7 through 11. Stories should have some point or purpose. Prayers, puzzles and crafts are also considered. A series of stories, strips or features would be considered. Length: about 1,000 words. Pays minimum 3 pounds; 5 pounds or more for series.

19, IPC Magazines Ltd., Tower House, Southampton St., London WC2E 9QX, England. Editor: Margaret Koumi. For independent, modern, working class girls aged 17 through 25, mostly interested in fashion, beauty, travel and boyfriends. Established in 1969. Monthly. Circulation: 200,000. Copyrighted. Pays on publication. Query first for nonfiction. Submit only complete ms for fiction. Enclose S.A.E. and International Reply Coupons for reply to query and return of submission.

Nonfiction and Fiction: "Articles and fiction on social problems; social/sexual education. Anything to do with young people today. Short stories should have a plot, a deep relationship but not necessarily a happy ending. We never commission until we know a writer. A writer should contact us giving ideas and outlining the article in question. We don't want anything concerning women's lib, travel, and sexual problems." Informational, how-to, personal experience, interview, profile, inspirational, humor, historical, think articles, expose, nostalgia, and new product. Length: 1,250 to 3,250 words. Pays 30 to 100 pounds. Nonfiction Dept. Editor: Margaret Koumi. Fiction, experimental, fantasy, humorous, romance, and serialized novels. Length: 1,250 to 3,250 words. Pays 30 to 100 pounds. Fiction Dept. Editor: Mrs. Ann Totterdell.

OASIS MAGAZINE, 12 Stevenage Road, London SW6 6ES, England. Editor: Ian Robinson. Established in 1969. Tri-annually. Circulation: 1,000. Payment only in copies. Will send sample copy to writer for $1. Will consider unpublished material offered for first time use in United Kingdom. Submission of unpublished material

may be made directly by the author. Enclose S.A.E. and International Reply Coupons for return of submission.
Nonfiction, Fiction, and Poetry: Will consider the following unpublished material: poetry, prose fiction, articles, criticism, essays, letters, reviews, and graphics. No maximum or minimum length; any structure, style, or approach. Only literary quality. Pays only in copies.

ORBIS, Hub Publications Ltd., Youlgrave, Bakewell, Derbyshire, England. Editor: Robin Gregory. For "academic institutions and professional readers." Established in 1969. Quarterly. Circulation: 3,000. Not copyrighted. Pays on publication. Will send a sample copy to a writer for $1. Query first or submit complete ms. Reports "usually in 1 month." Enclose S.A.E. and International Reply Coupons for return of submissions or reply to queries.
Nonfiction: Uses unpublished material offered for first time use. "Intelligent, readable articles about writers, poets, etc. High academic standards, but must be suitable for the nonspecialist reader. No special length requirements. Payment is small and submissions by members of the International Poetry Society receive preference."

ORIENTATIONS, News Building, 633 King's Rd., North Point, Hong Kong. Editor: Juan T. Gatbonton. Established in 1970. Monthly. Circulation: 22,000. Copyrighted. Pays on publication. Will send sample copy to writer on request. Will consider unpublished material offered for first time use. Submission of unpublished material may be made directly by the author. Query first. Enclose S.A.E. and International Reply Coupons for reply to query or return of submission.
Nonfiction: Will consider the following unpublished material: Articles and photographic essays on travel in Asia and the Pacific. History, culture and art of Asia and the Pacific. Pays $50 to $150 for articles, depending on length. Pays $20 to $25 for color transparencies.

OUTPOSTS, 72 Burwood Rd., Walton-on-Thames, Surrey, England. Editor: Howard Sergeant. Established in 1943. Quarterly. Circulation: 1,500. Copyrighted. Buys first rights. Will consider unpublished material offered for first-time use only. Will send a sample copy to a writer for $1.25. Will consider photocopied submissions. Enclose S.A.E. and International Reply Coupons for return of submissions.
Poetry: "Poetry only." Length: "no longer than 80 lines preferred." Pays about $1 per page.

PAKISTAN PICTORIAL, Adil Chambers, Sadar, Rawalpindi, Pakistan. Editor: S. Amjad Ali. Published by the Government of Pakistan Ministry of Information and Broadcasting. Established in 1973. Bimonthly. Not copyrighted. Payment on acceptance. Will send sample copy on request. Submissions of unpublished material may be made directly by the author. Query first. Enclose S.A.E. and International Reply Coupons for reply to query.
Nonfiction and Photos: Will consider unpublished material "seeking to present a picture of the life of Pakistan in words and photographs. People at work in different fields, making an honest living and also helping the country to move forward. People at work and play, labour and recreation. Farmers, fishermen, mill workers, office workers, teachers, doctors, and so on. The style should be descriptive, lively and imaginative." Length: 1,500 to 2,000 words. Pays "about $20 to $25."

PETFISH MONTHLY, 554 Garratt Lane, London, SW17 0NY, England. Editor: Anthony Evans. Established in 1966. Monthly. Copyrighted. Will consider unpublished material offered for first time use only. Will send a sample copy to a writer for 4 International Reply Coupons. Enclose S.A.E. and International Reply coupons for return of submissions.
Nonfiction: "Technical and practical articles on aquarium fishes and aquarium and pond fishkeeping. Payment by arrangement."

PHP, PHP Institute, Inc., W.D. Section, P.O. Box 157, World Trade Center Bldg., Shiba Hamamatsu-cho, Minato-ku, Tokyo 105, Japan. Editor: Mr. Ken Iwai. Established in 1970. Monthly. Circulation: 50,000. Will send a sample copy to a writer

on request. Buys first rights. Enclose S.A.E. and International Reply Coupons for
return of submissions.

Nonfiction and Fiction: "A general interest magazine devoted to the better understanding and enjoyment of human life on all levels. We are seeking articles from writers with varied experiences, backgrounds, nationalities, and opinions. Though the theme or approach is left to the choice of the writer, the magazine consists of articles in the following categories: helpful thoughts for living based on personal experiences; travel sketches; essays accompanying a photograph bringing out the beauty in nature and in the works of man; quizzes and puzzles, humorous and witty sayings, funny stories, science fiction." Length: 200 to 1,000 words. Pays $20 to $70.

PLAYS AND PLAYERS, Artillery Mansions, 75, Victoria Street, London, SW1H OHZ, England. Editor: Peter Ansorge. For "the general theater-going public of all ages, students and professionals." Monthly. Buys first rights. Will send a sample copy to a writer on request. Query first. Reports "as soon as possible." Enclose S.A.E. and International Reply Coupons for reply to queries.

Nonfiction and Photos: Uses "reviews, feature reviews of new productions, plus features on directors, actors, etc., and regular complete text of play; also coverage of TV and radio drama plus regional, European, and New York newsletters." Wants in-depth coverage. Buys b&w glossy photos. Payment negotiable.

POETRY AUSTRALIA, 350 Lyons Rd., Five Dock, N.S.W., Australia 2046. Editor: Grace Perry. Quarterly. Circulation: 2,000. Copyrighted. Sample copies free when available. Reports in two to four weeks. Pays on acceptance. Special issues include one overseas issue each year; other special issues announced. Deadlines are two months before publication. Editor suggests prospective contributors study journal first. Enclose S.A.E. and International Reply Coupons for ms return.

Nonfiction: Pays $10 per page for poetry criticism.

Poetry: Contributors may need to read several issues to get the "flavor," since some special issues may not present the whole picture.

THE POLITICAL QUARTERLY, 48 Lanchester Road, London, N6 4TA, England. Editors: William A. Robson and Bernard Crick. For "political scientists, politicians, officials, and general intelligent readers." Quarterly. Buys all rights. Pays on publication. Will send a sample copy to a writer for $2. Reports "usually within 4 weeks." Enclose S.A.E. and International Reply Coupons pons for return of submissions.

Nonfiction: Wants "articles discussing political, social, or international questions or problems. The style must be appropriate for a highly educated audience, but we want lucidity, an absence of jargon, closely argued statements, rather than an abundance of footnotes. Study the periodical before submitting your article, and be sure that the length, style, and subject are appropriate." Length: 4,000 words. Pays 5 pounds per 1,000 words published.

PRACTICAL HOUSEHOLDER, Fleetway House, Farringdon St., London EC4A 4AD, Great Britain. Editor: Denis Gray. For couples owning, buying, or renting their homes and interested in improving them, as regards decoration, extensions, building furniture, loft conversions, etc. Established in 1955. Monthly. Circulation: 200,000. Copyrighted. Pays on publication. Will send sample copy to writer on request. Query first or submit complete ms. Enclose S.A.E. and International Reply Coupons for reply to query or return of submission.

Nonfiction and Photos: "Illustrated prose articles on every aspect of houses and their improvement and maintenance, plus occasional features on gardens, greenhouses, and garages. Special interests and personality stories also welcomed. Use a strictly practical approach; simple, informal language. The entire tone of the magazine is colloquial and chatty. Accurate, comprehensible rendering of facts is more important than any lyrical literacy. We are hoping to make the magazine a little more international, so articles from outside the United Kingdom especially welcome. Spring issues: garden ponds, swimming pools. November issue: heating. December: toys and lighting. No rigid length of articles, but 5,000 words maximum. Payment varies, but usually not under 20 pounds." Nonfiction Dept. Editor: Peter Herring. Photos are purchased with or without accompanying mss. Captions required. Halfplate or whole plate; prefer glossy. 2¼" square transparencies and 35mm color considered. Payment negotiated. Photo Dept. Editor: Alan Mitchell.

PRACTICAL WIRELESS, IPC Magazines Ltd., Fleetway House, Farringdon St., London EC4A 4AD, England. Editor: Morris A. Colwell. For constructors and users of radio, audio, TV, electronics equipment. Established in 1933. Monthly. Circulation: 100,000. Copyrighted. Pays on publication. Will send sample copy to writer for 0.50 pounds. Query first or submit complete ms for topical stories on radio communication techniques, space applications. Submit only complete ms for full do-it-yourself constructional projects in detail. Enclose S.A.E. and International Reply Coupons for reply to query or return of submission.
Nonfiction and Photos: "Technical do-it-yourself projects on radio, audio, TV, electronics equipment, using components readily available in the United Kingdom. Also occasional features on communications, including space electronics. Especially interested in significant breakthrough in new communications techniques." Length: 1,000 to 5,000 words. Pays 8 to 18 pounds per 1,000 words plus photos. Photos purchased with accompanying ms; captions required. B&w specifications: 5x3½ inches minimum. Payment according to subject.

PREDICTION, Link House, Dingwall Ave., Croydon, CR9 2TA, England. Editor: Philip Pond. Established in 1936. Monthly. Copyrighted. Will consider material previously published in U.S. or Canada for first publication in U.K. Will send a sample copy to a writer on request. Submit complete ms. Enclose S.A.E. and International Reply Coupons for return of submissions.
Nonfiction: "Concerned with all aspects of the occult." Length: 1,000 to 1,700 words. Payment to be negotiated.

PUNCH, 23 Tudor St., London EC4, England. Editor: William Davis. For quite young, more liberal type of businessman, well educated. Established in 1841. Weekly. Circulation: 100,000. Copyrighted. Payment at end of month of publication. "Will expect writer to be curious enough to buy or steal sample copy." Will send editorial guidelines sheet to writer on request. Query first or submit complete ms. Enclose S.A.E. and International Reply Coupons for reply to query or return of submission.
Nonfiction and Fiction: "Topical humor, politics, fashionable but irritating subjects. Inside information. Anything that deflates pretension. Frivolous, stylish, informed, unobscurantist, funny and about 1,200 words long, though we also print pieces of as little as 1,190. Brilliant humor on seasonal topics is always welcome, although almost impossible to find." Informational, personal experience, humor, expose, and book reviews. Humorous fiction. Length: "937 to about 1,425 words." Pays 20 to about 100 pounds.
Poetry and Fillers: Light verse of not less than four lines. Parodies and very funny, long epics. "Payment on whim." Filler Dept. Editor: David Taylor. "Unbelievable provincial cuttings." Length: open. Pays 1 pound.

QUADRANT, Box C344, Clarence St. Post Office, Sydney, N.S.W., Australia 2000. Editors: Peter Coleman and James McAuley. For "professionals, academics, students, and the general intelligent public." Established in 1956. Bimonthly. Circulation: 4,000. Not copyrighted. Will consider material previously published in U.S. or Canada offered for first publication in Australia. Will send a sample copy to a writer on request. Submit complete ms. Enclose S.A.E. and International Reply Coupons for return of submissions.
Nonfiction, Fiction, and Poetry: "Short stories, poetry, articles, on politics, history, social thought, arts, literary criticism. Material is written in simple, no jargon English." Pays "about $50 an article."

THE RADIO CONSTRUCTOR, 57 Maida Vale, W9 1SN, England. Editor: J.H. Burrows. For persons "interested in radio and electronics; somewhat technically minded; all ages, classes, and nationalities." Monthly. Circulation: 25,000. Buys all rights. Buys about 150 mss a year. Pays on publication. Query first. Reports in 6 weeks. Enclose S.A.E. and International Reply Coupons for reply to queries.
Nonfiction: "Articles about electronics—transistor techniques, radio equipment, recording equipment, television, intercoms, amplifiers, aerials, etc." Length: 1,000

to 5,000 words; "usually not longer than 3,000 words, with diagrams." Pays 5
pounds per 1,000 words; "extra for diagrams."

RECORDS AND RECORDING, Artillery Mansions, 75, Victoria Street, London,
S.W.1., England. Editor: Trevor Richardson. For "record collectors, music lovers,
and professionals." Special issues are Audio Fair (October) and Sonex (April).
Buys first rights. Pays on publication. Will send a sample copy to a writer on
request. Query first. Enclose S.A.E. and International Reply Coupons for reply to
queries.
Nonfiction: Uses "material covering every aspect of classical music on record, plus
rock, jazz, and folk and a substantial audio section; reviews and features on important artists in the field and events in the record world." Buys b&w glossy photos and
color transparencies. Payment negotiable.

RED LETTER, D.C. Thomson & Co., Ltd., Albert Square, Dundee, DD1 9QJ,
Scotland. For women. Weekly. Copyrighted. Will consider material previously
published in U.S. or Canada offered for first publication in U.K. Will send a sample
copy to a writer on request. Submit complete ms. Will consider photocopied submissions. Enclose S.A.E. and International Reply Coupons for return of submissions.
Nonfiction and Fiction: "Romantic stories and short features of interest to ordinary
housewives. Stories should be written about ordinary people and should be written
with good feeling." Length: 1,500 to 4,000 words. Payment "on merit."

RHODESIAN WOMAN, P.O. Box U.A. 439 Union Ave., Salisbury, Rhodesia. Editor: Mrs. J.L. Fubbs. For "women generally, whether career women or homemakers. Age group: 20 to 45." Established in 1972. Monthly. Circulation: 80,000. Copyrighted. Will consider material previously published in U.S. or Canada offered for
first publication in Rhodesia. Payment made 60 days after publication. Will send a
sample copy to a writer for $1. Enclose S.A.E. and International Reply Coupons for
return of submissions.
Nonfiction and Fiction: "The magazine consists of articles, short stories, and homecrafts such as crocheting, sewing and knitting. We have beauty, fashion, gardening,
'mothercare,' book and film reviews and a page for children. We aim to inform, to
entertain, educate and generally assist the housewife. We would like informative
articles, humorous articles and fiction." Length: 600 to 5,000 words. Pays $5 to $50.
"No mss will be returned unless correct postage is enclosed."

SAMPHIRE, New Poetry, 45 Westfields, Catshill, Bromsgrove, Worcs., England.
Editors: Michael Butler and Kemble Williams. Established in 1968. Quarterly. Circulation: 700. Copyrighted. Pays on publication. Will send sample copy to writer
for $1 and postage. Will consider unpublished material offered for first time use.
Submission of unpublished material may be made directly by the author. Query
first for prose. Submit complete ms for poetry. Enclose S.A.E. and International
Reply Coupons for reply to query or return of submission.
Poetry: "Normally only new work is published. Exceptions might be made. Reviews of poetry, criticism and occasional prose pieces. It is necessary to study the
magazine before contributing anything other than poetry." Pays 1 pound per poem
and 1 free copy of the magazine.

SCRIP, 67 Hady Crescent, Chesterfield, Derbyshire, England S41 OEB. Editor:
David Holliday. For heterogeneous audience, interested in good poetry. Established in 1962. Quarterly. Circulation: 350. Copyrighted. Pays on publication. Pays
in complimentary copies only. Will send sample copy to writer on request. Will consider material previously published in U.S. or Canada, offered for first publication
in Great Britain. Submission of previously published material may be made
directly by the author. Will consider unpublished material offered for first time use.
Submission of unpublished material may be made directly by the author. Submit
complete ms. Enclose S.A.E. and International Reply Coupons for return of submission.
Poetry: Interested in the following material (previously published in U.S. or Canada, or unpublished): "Poems, most styles, preferably short. Not chopped waffle.
Good poetry on any subject in almost any style." Pays 2 complimentary copies.

SEA ANGLER, 21 Church Walk, Peterborough PE1 2TS England. Editor: Ted Lamb. For sport sea fishermen of all ages. Established in 1972. Monthly. Circulation: 30,000. Not copyrighted. Will send sample copy to writer on request. Will consider material previously published in U.S. or Canada, offered for first publication in Great Britain. Submission of previously published material may be made directly by author or by the publisher or his representative. Will consider unpublished material offered for first time use. Submission of unpublished material may be made directly by the author. Enclose S.A.E. and International Reply Coupons for return of submissions.
Nonfiction: Interested in the following material (previously published in U.S. or Canada, or unpublished): General articles on sea angling and the people involved, with photos if possible. Length: 750 to 1,500 words. Payment for previously published material is "variable, according to merit." Payment for unpublished material is 10.50 pounds per 1,000 words.

SEA SPRAY, P.O. Box 793, Auckland, New Zealand. Editor: Mr. David Pardon. Monthly. Circulation: 14,000. Will send a free sample copy, surface mail, on request. Aimed at yachting and boating enthusiasts. Reports promptly. Buys New Zealand and Australian rights. Pays on publication. Wherever possible, use English terms and spelling (colour, favour, etc.); U.S. terminology and spelling, however, can be corrected during editing if necessary. Deadlines are on the 26th of the month, two months preceding publication dates on the first. Enclose S.A.E. and International Reply Coupons for return of submissions.
Nonfiction and Photos: Wants articles and b&w photos of general interest to audience. Subject matter must be related to yachting and/or power boating. Use plain, easy-to-read English; technical details when necessary. Take into account that import restrictions limit the range of marine products, equipment, etc., available to New Zealand yachtsmen and boat owners. Definitely no politics and no "slant" toward a particular company or product. Articles should be from 500 to 3,000 words; size of captioned, glossy b&w prints may vary with 8x6 a good average. Pays approximately NZ$15 per 1,000 words and approximately NZ$2.50 per published photo.

SEACRAFT, 142 Clarence St. Sydney, N.S.W., Australia 2000. Editor: Paul Hopkins. For "all interested in sailing, power boats, and boating in general." Monthly. Circulation: 15,000. Rights negotiable. Buys 150 mss a year. Pays on acceptance. Will send a sample copy to a writer for 50¢. Reports "within a month." Enclose S.A.E. and International Reply Coupons for return of submissions.
Nonfiction: Buys "technical and general articles on all forms of boating; also some factual cruising and sea adventure stories." Buys how-to and personal experience articles, profiles, and coverage of new boating products. Length: 1,500 to 3,000 words. Pays A.$10 per 1,000 words "if up to standards. If an article is interesting but poorly written, payment is reduced."

SECOND AEON, 3 Maplewood Court, Maplewood Ave., Handaf North, Cardiff CF4 2NB, Wales. Editor: Peter Finch. Established in 1966. Quarterly. Circulation: 2,000. Not copyrighted. Payment in copies. Will send sample copy to writer for $1.50. Will consider unpublished material offered for first time use. Submission of unpublished material may be made directly by the author. Query first or submit complete ms. Enclose S.A.E. and International Reply Coupons for reply to query or return of submission.
Poetry: Will consider the following unpublished material: Poetry in all forms and styles. Payment in copies.

SOUND & PICTURE TAPE RECORDING, 2-6 High St., Haverhill, England CB9 8AY. Editor: Douglas Brown. For hobbyists practicing creative tape recording of all kinds. Established in 1957. Monthly. Circulation: 20,000. Copyrighted. Pays on publication. Will send sample copy to writer on request. Query first. Enclose S.A.E. and International Reply Coupons for reply to query or return of submission.
Nonfiction: "Feature articles of practical value reporting on author's experiences, news of new developments and products. Simple, direct, succinct, factual approach. Especially interested in home experience of video recording." Informational, how-

to, personal experience, interview, travel, new product and technical articles. Length: 800 to 2,000 words. Pays 10 pounds per 1,000 words.

SPORTS CAR WORLD, 142 Clarence St., Sydney, N.S.W., Australia 2000. Editor: M. Nicholes. For "sports car enthusiasts, generally in the 18 to 35 age group." Monthly. Circulation: 18,500. Rights negotiable. Buys 150 mss a year. Pays on acceptance. Will send a sample copy to a writer for 40¢. Enclose S.A.E. and International Reply Coupons for return of submissions.
Nonfiction: Wants "factual material on sports and performance cars, car racing, and mechanics." Buys how-to articles, profiles, and coverage of new products in the car field. Length: 1,500 to 3,000 words. Pays A$30 to A$70.

STAMP COLLECTING, 42 Maiden Lane, WC2E 7LL, England. Editor: Kenneth F. Chapman. For "general and advanced stamp collectors of all adult ages." Special Christmas issue (early December), Exhibition issue (March), and "occasional special issues devoted to philately of one single country." Weekly. Circulation: 30,000. Not copyrighted. Buys 100 mss a year. Pays on publication. Will send a sample copy to a writer on request. Submit seasonal material 2 months in advance. Returns rejected material "usually within 2 weeks." Acknowledges acceptance of material "usually within 1 month." Enclose S.A.E. and International Reply Coupons for return of submissions.
Nonfiction and Photos: Uses "articles with technical philatelic bias on stamps, postal history, and philatelic subjects generally. Authors must be familiar with philatelic outlook. No room for 'waffle' articles suited to nonphilatelic journals. Articles on how good stamp collecting is educationally, historically, and geographically are not wanted." Buys personal experience and historical articles and humor. Length: 1,000 to 3,000 words, "unless for serial publication by arrangement." Pays an average of 4 pounds per 1,000 words. Buys b&w glossy photos with mss.

STAMP MAGAZINE, Link House, Dingwall Ave., Croydon, CR9 2TA, England. Editor: Richard West. For "persons of all ages, all walks of life, with hobby interests." Monthly. Circulation: 40,000. Buys first rights. Buys 20 to 30 mss a year. Pays on acceptance. Query first. Submit seasonal material 6 weeks in advance. Enclose S.A.E. and International Reply Coupons for return of submissions.
Nonfiction and Photos: "Postal history, semitechnical articles on postage stamps, etc. Writers should study the magazine, since our outlook varies with the subject. Background stories, such as the story behind a stamp design, new issues of a stamp, etc." Length: 100 to 2,000 words. Pays 1 to 15 pounds. B&w glossies purchased with mss; with captions only. Payment by arrangement.

STAMP MONTHLY, Stanley Gibbons Magazines, Inc., Drury House, Russell St., London, W.C. 2, England. Editor: Russell Bennett. For stamp collectors. Buys first British and American rights or second rights if first publication was limited. Pays on acceptance. Reports immediately. Enclose S.A.E. and International Reply Coupons.
Nonfiction: Articles on all philatelic subjects: general articles, 1,500 to 2,500 words; philatelic studies, maximum 3,000 words; humorous shorts, 300 to 500 words. Pays $6 to $15 per 1,000 words, depending on content.

STAND, 58 Queens Rd., Newcastle on Tyne, NE2 2PR, 22PR, England. Editors: Jon Silkin, Lorna Tracy, Ed Brunner. Established in 1952. Quarterly. Circulation: 4,200. Copyrighted. Will consider unpublished material offered for first time use only. Will send a sample copy to a writer for $1. Submit complete ms. Enclose S.A.E. and International Reply Coupons for return of submissions.
Fiction and Poetry: Publishes fiction and poetry. Length: 10,000 words maximum for fiction. Pays $10 a poem "and upwards"; pays $10 per 1,000 words for prose.

STAR, D.C. Thomson & Co., Ltd., Albert Square, Dundee, Scotland. Biweekly. Copyrighted. Will consider unpublished material offered for first time use only. Query first "with synopsis of about 1,500 words." Will send a sample copy to a writer on request. Enclose S.A.E. and International Reply Coupons for reply to queries.

Fiction: "Scripts for love stories in pictures; fiction only. Payment by arrangement." Averages 55 pounds.

THE STATESMAN, 260-C, Commercial Area, P.E.C.H.S., Karachi, Pakistan. Editor: M. Owais. For "highly educated sections of our society, those particularly interested in nonsensational journalism and having an inclination towards literature." One special issue every December. Weekly. Buys first rights, "second rights in some cases." Buys about 150 mss a year. Pays on publication. Will send a sample copy to a writer on request. Query first. Submit seasonal material "at least" 1 month in advance. Returns rejected material "in 14 days at the latest." Acknowledges acceptance of material "within 10 days." Enclose S.A.E. and International Reply Coupons for reply to queries.
Nonfiction: "Literary, social, and nonpolitical articles alone are considered from writers who are not specially commissioned regular contributors." Writers should have "absolute objectivity and thoroughness." Buys personal experience and inspirational articles, profiles, and think pieces. Length: 800 to 1,200 words. Pays 50 rupees minimum, "but in other cases according to the merit of the article and the standing and prestige of the writer."

SUNDAY MAIL, Campbell St., Bowen Hills, Brisbane, Queensland, 4006, Australia. Editor: H.G. Turner. Established in 1916. Weekly. Circulation: 350,000. Will consider material previously published in U.S. or Canada offered for first publication in Australia. Will not consider photocopied submissions. Enclose S.A.E. and International Reply Coupons for return of submissions.
Nonfiction: Articles of general interest. This is a Sunday newspaper with a free color magazine. Length: about 1,200 words. Pays "on merit."

TEMPO, 295 Regent St., London W1A 1BR, England. Editor: David Drew. Established in 1939. Quarterly. Copyrighted. Pays on publication. Will consider unpublished material offered for first time use. Submission of unpublished material may be made directly by the author. Query first. Enclose S.A.E. and International Reply Coupons for reply to query.
Nonfiction: Will consider the following unpublished material: Literate and professional studies of any significant aspect of 20th Century music. Only original critical work, competently organized and clearly expressed, can be considered. Preferred length: 3,500 words (with minimum necessary music examples) up to 5,000 words in exceptional cases. Payment "open to negotiation."

TREES, 18 Lye Mead, Winford, Bristol, Somerset, BS18 8AV, England. Editor: Mr. Robin J. Gurney. For "members of the Society of Men of the Trees. (This international society, founded in 1922, is concerned essentially with trees, their place in the ecological pattern, and their amenity value.)" 3 times a year. Circulation: 7,500. Not copyrighted. Pays on publication. Will send a sample copy to a writer on request; must enclose International Reply Coupons for postage. "As a number of mss are submitted by Society Members who do not require a fee, freelancers are asked to state that they are such when sending mss, etc." Reports "by return mail." Enclose S.A.E. and International Reply Coupons for return of submissions.
Nonfiction: Buys articles on trees: "amenity, forestry, simple technical; conservation, especially including tree planting/preservation; historic trees, famous trees. Articles illustrated with good b&w photos stand best chance of acceptance." Length: 500 to 1,500 words. Pays "by arrangement, at valuation, generally 2 to 4 pounds per 1,000 words."
Photos: May be purchased with mss, with captions only. Subject matter should be "trees, or others if supporting text." Buys b&w glossy prints, 35mm color, and "larger color transparencies and prints." Pays 1.50 pounds for b&w, 5.25 pounds for color.
Fillers: Buys newsbreaks. Length: 100 to 150 words. No payment.

TROUT AND SALMON, 21 Church Walk, Peterborough, PE1 2TW, England. Editor: Jack Thorndike. Established in 1955. Monthly. Circulation: 35,000. Will send sample copy to writer on request. Will consider unpublished material offered for first time use. Submission of unpublished material may be made directly by the

author. Query first. Enclose S.A.E. and International Reply Coupons for reply to query and return of submission.
Nonfiction: Will consider the following unpublished material: "Practical aspects of rod and line fishing with fly or lure for salmon, sea trout, brown and rainbow trout. Articles must not exceed 1,500 words." Pays minimum of 8.40 pounds per 1,000 words.

TV TIMES, Dudley Bldg., 630 George St., Sydney, N.S.W., Australia 2000. Editor: Christopher Day. TV magazine and program guide. Weekly. Circulation: 278,000. Buys Australian rights. Buys about 150 mss a year. Pays commissioned features on approval; submitted features on publication. Will send a sample copy to a writer on request. Reports "almost immediately." Enclose S.A.E. and International Reply Coupons for return of submissions.
Nonfiction and Photos: Uses newsy stories and features about television series personalities; also features on trends in television and television series. "Thoughtful, penetrating profiles of TV performers. We are not a fan magazine in the accepted sense of the word." Length: 500 to 1,200 words. Pays "up to and about $100." Color transparencies purchased with mss. Pays $5 to $25.

VOYAGER, 63 Shrewsbury Lane, Shooters Hill, London, SE18 3JJ, England. Editor: Dennis Winston. The in-flight magazine of British Midland Airways. Readers are in transit between Britain and the U.S.A., points in Europe and some other destinations. All ages, reasonably affluent, well educated, varied interests. Established in 1973. Published three times a year. Circulation: 100,000. Copyrighted. Pays on publication, "occasionally earlier." Will send sample copy to writer for $2. Query first or submit complete ms. Enclose S.A.E. and International Reply Coupons for reply to query and return of submission.
Nonfiction: "Informative, well-researched, fairly sophisticated and/or humorous material designed to entertain and/or inform people travelling to places outside the U.K., often to places they have not visited before. Nontechnical approach and absolute accuracy are essential. Topical subjects we'd like to see articles about are budget holidays in the U.S., Canada, the Caribbean and Europe. The food and drink, sport, art, business in these areas. Occcasional need for seasonable travel articles; for example, skating, but should be submitted at least 6 months before relevant season commences." Informational, personal experience, interview, profile, humor, photo, travel, and successful business operations articles. Length: 800 to 2,500 words. Pays $50 to $100. "English Spoke Here," examples of crazy English seen abroad (for example, hotels, restaurant menus, guidebooks). Anything from one line upwards. Give source. Pays $2.40 per item printed.
Photos: Purchased with or without accompanying mss; captions required. Payment depends on size, minimum $5 for b&w.
Fillers: Puzzles, all types. Maximum 100 words. Pays $10 to $20.

WATER SKIER, 52 High Street, Broadstairs, Kent, England. Editor: Tony Reader. For "water skiers, old and young." Special Boat Show issue (January). Monthly. Circulation: 5,000. Buys all rights. Buys 30 mss a year. Pays on publication. Will send a sample copy to a writer for $1. Submit seasonal material 6 weeks in advance. Reports in 1 month. Enclose S.A.E. and International Reply Coupons for return of submissions.
Nonfiction and Photos: Wants "only water skiing copy; i.e., news, equipment, boats, competition, competitors, etc." Buys how-to, personal experience, and humor articles; profiles; spot news; exposes; new product coverage; and photo and travel features. Length: 500 to 3,000 words. Pays $10 to $45. Buys b&w glossy photos with mss, with captions only.

WHEELS, 142 Clarence St., Sydney, N.S.W., Australia 2000. Editor: P. Robinson. For "motorists generally." Monthly. Circulation: 58,000. Rights negotiable. Buys 100 mss a year. Pays on acceptance. Will send a sample copy for 50¢. Reports "within a month." Enclose S.A.E. and International Reply Coupons for return of submissions.
Nonfiction: Uses "all types of motoring material." Buys how-to articles, profiles, and coverage of new products of motoring interest. Length: 1,500 to 3,000 words. Pays $30 to $75.

WINE MAGAZINE, Southbank House, Black Prince Rd., Lambeth, London, S.E.1, England. Editor: K.C. Bourke. For "wine and food lovers; sophisticated mostly, but some beginners. All members of the International Wine and Food Society receive this magazine." Bimonthly. Circulation: 40,000. Rights vary. Buys about 50 mss a year. Pays on publication. Will send a sample copy to a writer on request. Query first; "sometimes no query is required if the material is original and good." Submit seasonal material 3 to 4 months in advance. Reports "as soon as there has been time to consider it." Enclose S.A.E. and International Reply Coupons for reply to queries.
Nonfiction: Articles on "wine, food, travel. Should be entertaining but have a hard core of interest or fact. Read a few copies of *Wine Magazine* to learn our approach." Does not want coverage of "memorable single meals, vague travel stories, all superlatives and no facts." Buys personal experience and travel features. Length: 500 to 5,000 words. Pays approximately 10 to 26 pounds.
Photos: Purchased with mss; with captions only. Should "feature wine, food, entertaining, travel." Buys b&w glossies for interior use, color transparencies and 35mm color for cover use. Payment varies.

WOMAN & HOME, 40 Long Acre, London WC2E 9QB, England. Editor: Angela Wyatt. For women. Established in 1926. Monthly. Circulation: 700,000. Pays on acceptance. Will send sample copy to writer on request. Will consider material previously published in U.S. or Canada, offered for first publication in Great Britain. Submission of previously published material may be made directly by the author, through an agent, or by the publisher or his representative. Will consider unpublished material offered for first time use. Submission of unpublished material may be made directly by the author or through agent. Submit complete ms. Enclose S.A.E. and International Reply Coupons for return of submission.
Nonfiction and Fiction: Will consider the following material (previously published in U.S. or Canada, or unpublished): Biographical articles on celebrities and articles on topical subjects of interest to women. Cookery, fashion, beauty and homemaking. Fiction of general appeal to women, with a strong romantic theme, a contemporary background. Short stories approximately 3,000 to 5,000 words. Serials, approximately 50,000 words. Payment negotiated with authors.

WOMAN'S DAY, 57 Regent St., Chippendale, Sydney, N.S.W., Australia. Editor: Mrs. Joan Reeder. For women. Established in 1954. Weekly. Circulation: over 550,000. Copyrighted. Buys first Australian rights. Will consider material previously published in U.S. or Canada offered for first publication in Australia and New Zealand. Will send a sample copy to a writer on request. Will consider photocopied submissions. Enclose S.A.E. and International Reply Coupons for return of submissions.
Nonfiction: "A newsy, topical magazine, mainly but not exclusively for women, which covers basic service items (food, fashion, etc.). Interested in general women's interest articles which are, therefore, topical and newsy." Length: 1,000 to 2,000 words; "usually around 1,000 words." Payment "subject to negotiation; usually $50 per 1,000 words."

WOMAN'S WAY, P.O. Box 320, Botanic Rd., Glasnevin, Dublin 9, Ireland. Editor: Caroline Mitchell. For "women of all ages and income groups." Weekly. Circulation: 90,000. Buys 500 to 600 mss a year. Pays on publication. Will send a sample copy to a writer on request. Will consider submissions of published or unpublished material directly from the author. Submit seasonal material 3 months in advance. Enclose S.A.E. and International Reply Coupons for return of submissions.
Fiction and Nonfiction: Short stories, prepared and synopsized serials (divided into 5 or 6 installments; popular biographies. Length: 3,000 words (short stories); 30,000 words (serials). Pays 3 to 20 pounds per 1,000 words.

THE WORD, "Glena," Rock Road, Booterstown, Dublin, Ireland. Editor: Brother Paul, S.V.D. For "the sort of people who read *Time* magazine." Monthly. Circulation: 150,000. Not copyrighted. Buys about 50 mss a year. Pays on acceptance. Will send a sample copy to a writer on request. Query first with samples of published articles. Submit seasonal material at least 6 months in advance. Enclose S.A.E. and International Reply Coupons for reply to queries.

Nonfiction and Photos: "Articles of general interest which can be illustrated with photos. Ours is a pictorial magazine. Hobbies, ruins, and 'passing interest' subjects are currently overworked." Buys interviews, profiles, historical articles, exposes, photo pieces, and travel articles. Length: 500 to 2,000 words. Pays an average of $20 per 1,000 words. B&w glossies, color transparencies, and 35mm color purchased with mss. Pays $5 for b&w, $20 for color.

WORKSHOP NEW POETRY, 2 Culham Ct., Granville Rd., London, N4 4JB, England. Editor: Norman Hidden. Established in 1967. Bimonthly. Will consider unpublished material offered for first time use only. Will send a sample copy to a writer for $1. Query first. Will consider photocopied submissions. Enclose S.A.E. and International Reply Coupons for return of submissions.
Poetry: "A leading U.K. poetry magazine. Only the highest quality material will be considered." Length: "under 40 lines." Payment "by arrangement."

Trade, Technical, and Professional Journals

ACCOUNTANCY, The Journal of the Institute of Chartered Accountants in England and Wales, 56-66 Goswell Rd., London, E.C.1, England. Editor: Geoffrey Holmes. Monthly. Buys first serial rights. Pays on publication. Reports by return mail. Submissions of previously published material may be made directly by the author, through an agent or by the publisher or his representative. Enclose S.A.E. and International Reply Coupons for return of submissions or reply to query. Query first or submit complete ms.
Nonfiction: "Articles of interest to accountants in industry and commerce, on accounting, finance, management, tax, investment and business machines, particularly from a Canadian standpoint." Pays 10 pounds per 1,000 words.

ACCOUNTING & BUSINESS RESEARCH, 56-66 Goswell Road, London, E.C.1, England. Editor: Walter Taplin. For "accountants, economists, businessmen interested in accounting research." Quarterly. Circulation: 3,000. Buys first rights. Buys 40 mss a year. Pays on publication. Will send a sample copy to a writer on request. Reports "by return mail." Enclose S.A.E. and International Reply Coupons for return of submissions.
Nonfiction: "Only high level professional articles of a research nature on accounting and finance." Length: 1,000 to 20,000 words. Pays 5 to 100 pounds.

THE AERO FIELD, Sutton Coldfield, Warwickshire, B73 6BJ England. Editor: N. C. Baldwin. Usually buys no rights because of different copyright laws in U.S. and England. Enclose S.A.E. and International Reply Coupons for return of submissions.
Nonfiction: Buys articles of interest to aerophilatelists (stamp collectors and postal historians interested in airmails). Length: 500 to 2,000 words depending upon subject matter. "Rates of payment subject to negotiation."

ANGLO-AMERICAN LAW REVIEW, Little London, Chichester, Sussex, England. Editors: G. W. Keeton, Keith Devlin, D. Murray. For "lawyers on both sides of the Atlantic." Established in 1972. Will consider unpublished material only. Query first. Enclose S.A.E. and International Reply Coupons for reply to queries.
Nonfiction: Material of interest to American and European lawyers. Pays 1 pound per page.

ART & CRAFT IN EDUCATION, Montague House, Russell Square, London, W.C.1, England. Editor: Henry Pluckrose. For "teachers in training; teachers of nursery, primary, secondary, and art school age levels; art school students, etc." Monthly. Circulation: 21,000. Buys first rights. Buys 10 to 12 mss a year. Pays on publication. Will send a sample copy to a writer on request. Submit seasonal material 3 months in advance. Reports "immediately." Enclose S.A.E. and International Reply Coupons for return of submissions.

Nonfiction: Publishes articles on "how art and craft can be integrated into the school curriculum, how art and craft can help a child's understanding of other subjects—art in history, geography, mathematics, etc. New ideas, new materials, etc. The more straightforward the better. Simple articles giving materials required, method of construction, similar extensions of the idea, and further uses for it." Buys how-to and new product articles. Length: 700 words. Pays 5 to 12 pounds.

Photos: Buys photos with mss; with captions only. Buys b&w glossies and/or color transparencies with clear contrasts. Photos must show "details of manufacture and of finished articles." Pays 1 to 8 pounds. Dept. Editor: Julia Hagedorn.

AUDIO VISUAL P.O. Box 109, Croydon, CR9 1QH, England. Editor: Stanley W. Bowler Hon. FRPS. Established in 1972. Monthly. Circulation: 21,000. For teachers, industrialists, training executives; all users and makers of factual media. Buys first serial rights. Enclose S.A.E. and International Reply Coupons for return of submissions.

Nonfiction and Photos: Buys articles on use of audio-visual media in education, training, business. Length: 1,000 to 2,500 words. Pays $18 per 1,000 words minimum. Buys b&w photos only.

AUTOMOTIVE DESIGN ENGINEERING, Mercury House, Waterloo Rd., London, SE1 8UL, England. Editor: Don Goodsell. For "qualified design engineers in the automotive industry." Established in 1962. Monthly. Special issues include Farm Machinery and Mobile Construc-Plant Design (quarterly). Circulation: 7,000. Buys all rights. Pays on publication. Will send a sample copy to a writer on request. Submit seasonal material 2 months in advance. Reports in 1 month. Enclose S.A.E. and International Reply Coupons for return of submissions.

Nonfiction and Photos: Buys "design digests of automotive products and equipment, educational articles on automotive design techniques." Buys how-to, new product, and "design philosophy" articles. Does not want "descriptions of production and service equipment." Send short synopsis first, as this will obviate waste of effort in writing on a subject we have already covered. Photos purchased with mss. "Contains up to 50% line drawings combined with accompanying article." Length and payment "depend solely on quality."

BAKING INDUSTRIES JOURNAL, P.O. Box 109, Davis House, 69/77 High St., Croydon, CR9 1QH, England. Editor: Frank Jeffares. Established in 1949. Monthly. Buys only unpublished material offered for first time use. Query first or submit complete ms. Will send a sample copy to a writer on request. Enclose S.A.E. and International Reply coupons for return of submissions or reply to queries.

Nonfiction and Photos: "Technical or management articles aimed at upper management brackets in the large scale sectors of the baking industry, i.e., bread, biscuits, or cake production on automatic plants. The journal is read by chairmen, vice-chairmen, production, and sales directors and managing directors. Emphasis is on modern or new production techniques or management techniques. New machinery details especially welcome. Ms preferably authenticated by baking company concerned, where applicable." Length: 1,000 to 4,000 words. Pays "approximately $24 per 1,100 words." B&w photos purchased with ms.

BETTER BUSINESS, 360 Dominion Road, Auckland, New Zealand. Editor: David Pardon. For "professional men and women, business managers, company directors, accountants, advertising agencies, etc." Monthly. Circulation: 21,900. Buys New Zealand rights only. Buys 40 mss a year. Pays on publication. Will send a sample copy to a writer on request. No query required. Submit seasonal material 2 months in advance. Reports "within 7 to 10 days." Enclose S.A.E. and International Reply Coupons for return of submissions.

Nonfiction and Photos: "Articles about commercial, industrial, or technical developments, management subjects, production methods, marketing; anything of interest or value to New Zealand businessmen, professional men (doctors, scientists, etc.). Must relate to the New Zealand scene or have some value to New Zealand business. Anything that might bear on New Zealand trade relations with other countries, imports, exports, etc., of particular value." Buys coverage of successful business operations, new products, and merchandising techniques. Length: 2,000 words maximum. Pays NZ$25 to NZ$40. Buys b&w photos with mss; pays NZ$2.50 to NZ$5.

BRITISH JOURNAL OF CHIROPODY, 300 Bramhall Lane South, Bramhall, Stockport, Cheshire, SK7 3DJ, England. Editor: J.C. Dagnall. "Serves the British profession of chiropody primarily, with consideration of a worldwide readership of podiatrists and podologists." Established in 1933. Monthly. Copyrighted. Will send a sample copy to a writer for $1. Submit complete ms. Enclose S.A.E. and International Reply coupons for return of submissions.
Nonfiction: "Deals with the disorders, and their treatment, of the human foot; covers orthopaedics, dermatology, medicine, and surgery pertaining to the foot; footwear; history of footcare; national systems of health care; professional organization. Style: 'potted' magazine form, but professional tone. Editorial purpose: the promotion of foot health and the development of international cooperation between the professionals involved in this aim. Material should be authoritative but easily read. The emphasis is on treatment of aspects of a subject in depth. Payment is by arrangement, but it is purely nominal by U.S. standards. This is an outlet for the medical writer who wishes to propogate his ideas and methods. Certain articles can be accepted without payment. 'Letters to the Editor' offers an outlet for views on subjects covered (controversy welcomed)." Length: 500 words. Book reviews are also used.

BRITISH PRINTER, 30 Old Burlington St., London W1X 2AE, England. Editor: Roy Brewer. For commercial printers and printing technologists. Established in 1888. Monthly. Circulation: 12,800. Copyrighted. Pays on acceptance. Will consider material previously published in U.S. or Canada, offered for first publication in Europe. Submission of previously published material may be made directly by the author, through an agent, or by the publisher or his representative. Will consider unpublished material offered for first time use. Submission of unpublished material may be made directly by the author. Query first or submit complete ms. Enclose S.A.E. and International Reply Coupons for return of submissions or reply to queries.
Nonfiction: Will consider the following material previously published in U.S. or Canada: "The author should read *British Printer* and understand its purpose and editorial syle. He should also have a technical and, if possible, practical knowledge of printing or allied subjects. No PR promises and no long, boring historical pieces. BP is read by busy professionals." Pays 20 pounds per 1,000 words. Will consider the following unpublished material: "Basically technical. All articles must be of direct, practical value to commercial printers and printing technologists." Pays 20 pounds per 1,000 words.

BROADCAST (formerly *Television Mail*), 111A Wardour St., London W1, Great Britain. Editor: Rod Allen. For program executives, television and radio station management, advertising agencies, commercial and independent program companies and industry service companies. Established in 1959. Weekly. Copyrighted. Pays on publication. Will send sample copy to writer on request. Will consider material previously published in U.S. or Canada, offered for first publication in Europe. Submission of previously published material may be made directly by author, through an agent, or by publisher or his representative. Will consider unpublished material offered for first time use. Submission of unpublished material may be made directly by author. Query first. Enclose S.A.E. and International Reply Coupons for response to query.
Nonfiction: Will consider the following material (previously published in U.S. or Canada, or unpublished): Articles dealing with non-showbiz aspects of broadcasting and broadcast advertising. Noncommissioned outside contributions are only occasionally accepted. Articles should be no longer than 1,500 words except by prior arrangement. Pays 5 to 10 pounds per 1,000 words.

BROKERS' CHRONICLE, Association of Insurance Brokers, Craven House, 121 Kingsway, London, WC2B 6PO, England. Editor: A.S.E. Trayford. For "insurance brokers—medium and small, in provinces (i.e., outside London metropolis)." Established in 1966. Monthly. Circulation: 2,500. Buys all rights. Will consider material previously published in U.S. or Canada offered for first publication in England. Buys 30 mss a year. Pays on acceptance. Submit seasonal material 2 months in advance. Reports in 2 weeks. Enclose S.A.E. and International Reply Coupons for return of submissions.

Nonfiction and Photos: Buys "articles with a bearing on insurance, unit trusts, property trusts, intermediaries; slanted toward our members." Length: 1,000 to 2,000 words. Pays 15 pounds per 1,000 words for previously published material and "up to 25 pounds" per 1,000 words for unpublished material. Buys photos "if applicable to article."

BUILDING, The Builder House, 4 Catherine St., Aldwych, London, WC2B 5JN, England. Editor: Anthony R. Davis. For "all members of the building team (architects, surveyors, engineers, contractors, clients)." Established in 1842. Weekly. Circulation: 25,000. Copyrighted. Will consider material previously published in the U.S. or Canada, offered for first publication in England. Query first. Enclose S.A.E. and International Reply Coupons for reply to queries.

Nonfiction: "Articles dealing with recent building, planning, and civil engineering projects; recent developments in architectural design, component technology, and building technique. Should be illustrated and written for a professional audience." Length: 2,000 words. Payment "by arrangement."

CARPETS & TEXTILES, Bowling Green Lane, London, E.C. 1, England. Editor: Jean Sheridan. For "mainly retailers of carpets and household textiles, plus wholesalers, contract houses, manufacturers, and designers." 10 times a year. Payment "follows publication; 2 or 3 weeks." Will send a sample copy to a writer on request. Query first. Will consider photocopied submissions. Enclose S.A.E. and International Reply Coupons for reply to queries.

Nonfiction and Photos: "Must deal directly with carpets, textiles, and methods of distributing them. Every feature must be judged against the question, 'Does this help the retailer make more money or improve his business?' The publication deals with long term trends, assessment of events in the industry, retail managements, selling-out problems. No items of no use to the U.K. retailer, such as overseas merchandise he cannot import, etc." Buys how-to's, interviews, profiles, coverage of successful business operations, new product articles, photo articles, and articles on merchandising techniques. Length: 500 to 2,000 words. "Most pay rates are negotiated and thus have no recognized maximum or minimum. Uncommissioned copy which appears of interest is usually paid for at 2 pounds, 10 pence, per 100 words used." Photos purchased with mss; with captions only.

CONCRETE, 52 Grosvenor Gardens, London, SW1W OAQ, England. Editor: R.J. Barfoot. Established in 1967. Monthly. Circulation: 12,000. Copyrighted. Considers unpublished material offered for first-time use only. Will send a sample copy to a writer on request. Will consider photocopied submissions. Submit complete ms. Enclose S.A.E. and International Reply Coupons for return of submissions.

Nonfiction and Photos: "Articles of any type, either human or technical, but hung on the hook of concrete as a material. As a specialist journal, *Concrete* features technical articles which are deliberately practical rather than esoteric. As a source of information about the Concrete Society, the journal presents discussion, conference, and personality features with countrywide news in a lively and visually attractive fashion." Length: 500 to 2,000 words. Payment varies, "from a basic 10 pounds per 1,000 words. Such factors as the author's status, news value, type of illustrations, etc., are all taken into account."

CONTROL & INSTRUMENTATION, 30 Calderwood St., Woolwich, London SE18 6QH England. Editor: William Gledhill. For "mainly systems engineers from all sectors of industry who are engaged in control and instrumentation technology." Established in 1969. Monthly. Circulation: 15,000. Will consider unpublished material offered for first-time use only. Will send a sample copy to a writer on request. Enclose S.A.E. and International Reply Coupons for return of submissions.

Nonfiction and Photos: "The policy of the journal is to provide the readership with information which is confined to the technologies of control, instrumentation and measurement, and is of practical use and not of just academic interest. Each article should represent current technology and, where applicable, forecast future development. Any article should have as broad an appeal as possible for the readership." Length: 2- or 3-page articles. The maximum size of a 3-page article is 2,500 words together with about 5 illustrations." Pays maximum 10 pounds per 1,000 words.

THE CRIMINOLOGIST, 9, Old Bailey, London, E.C.4., England. Editor: Nigel Morland. For professionals and students interested in police affairs, criminology, forensic science, the law, penology, etc. Quarterly. Will send a sample copy to a writer for $1.70. Query first with outline. Enclose S.A.E. and International Reply Coupons for reply to queries.
Nonfiction and Photos: Considers articles of very high standards, authoritatively written and factually sound, informative and sober, and not in a popular or sensational style. All material must have attached list of references or sources (title of source, author or editor, town of publication, date, and, if a periodical, page number, issue number, and volume). Articles from police officials, experts, etc., are welcomed. Buys photos with mss. Length: 2,000 to 5,000 words. Payment negotiable.

DAIRY FARMER, Fenton House, Wharfedale Road, Ipswich, IP1 4LG, Suffolk, England. Editor: Donald Gomery. For "commercial dairy farmers." Established in 1929. Monthly. Circulation: 16,000. Will consider material previously published in U.S. or Canada, offered for first publication in the United Kingdom. Pays on publication. Will send a sample copy to a writer on request. Query first or submit complete ms. Submit seasonal material 6 weeks in advance. Reports "immediately on receipt." Enclose S.A.E. and International Reply Coupons for return of submissions or reply to queries.
Nonfiction: Buys "previously published articles dealing with dairy farm management techniques that are also suitable for application to U.S. dairy farming systems. Articles cover the on-the-farm production of milk, new farming methods, new equipment, farm stories, and management techniques." Length: 1,000 to 2,500 words. Pays minimum 12 pounds per 1,000 words; "maximum by negotiation."
Photos: "Illustrations required only to back up feature articles." Buys b&w glossies with mss; with captions only. Pays 25 shillings minimum, per photo, "maximum by negotiation."

DATA SYSTEMS, Mercury House, Embankment Press Ltd., Hutton House, Hutton St., London EC4, England. Editor: Michael Blee. For business data processing executives and personnel. Established in 1958. Monthly. Circulation: 7,278. Buys all rights. Will not consider previously published material. Submit complete ms. Enclose S.A.E. and International Reply Coupons for return of submissions.
Nonfiction: Buys management-orientated articles on developments in electronic data processing and automation, case histories, semi-technical "state-of-the art" articles. Length: 1,000 to 3,000 words. Pays 16 pounds per 1,000 words minimum, on publication.

DIPLOMATIC BOOKSHELF AND REVIEW, 44-46 South Ealing Road, Ealing, London, W.5., England. Editor: A. H. Thrower. For the Diplomatic Corps, governmental institutions, universities, and colleges. Established in 1966. Monthly. Enclose S.A.E. and International Reply Coupons for return of submissions.
Nonfiction: Buys "book reviews, articles on diplomacy and international relations." Length: about 150 words. Payment negotiable.

DISPLAY INTERNATIONAL, 167 High Holborn, London, WC1V 6PH, England. Editor: Hazel Thompson. Monthly. Circulation: 18,800. Buys all rights. Will consider material previously published in U.S. or Canada, offered for first publication in Britain. Pays on publication. Will send a sample copy to a writer on request. Reports "as soon as possible." Enclose S.A.E. and International Reply Coupons for return of submissions.
Nonfiction and Photos: Buys news items and articles. Length: 500 to 1,500 words. Payment negotiable, usually $24 to $85. Buys photos with mss and with captions only. Subjects should be "window displays, exhibition displays, new stores and shops (exterior and interior), shopping centres, all forms of visual merchandising

and commercial presentation. Names of architects, display managers, and designers are desired."

ELECTRICAL REVIEW, Dorset House, Stamford St., London SE1 9LU, England. Editor: R.F. Masters. For electrical and electronics engineers, mainly at professional and managerial level. Weekly. Pays on publication. Will send sample copy to writer on request. Will send editorial quidelines sheet to writer on request. Query first. Enclose S.A.E. and International Reply Coupons for reply to queries.
Nonfiction and Photos: "Technical articles on subjects appertaining to heavy electrical engineering industry; business and news concerning current trends in the electrical industry, research and development, new methods of application in the electrical industry; new products." Length: 500 to 2,000 words. Pays "average 15 pounds per 1,000 words." Photos are purchased with or without accompanying ms. Captions required.

ELECTRONIC COMPONENTS, United Trade Press, Ltd., 42-43 Gerrard St., London, W1V 7LP, England. Editor: R.G. Atterbury. Copyrighted. Will consider material previously published in the U.S. or Canada offered for first publication in England. Query first. Enclose S.A.E. and International Reply coupons for return of submissions.
Nonfiction: "Articles or news items concerned with electronic components: their application, testing, and reliability aspects. Features on component testing and materials used in their manufacture will also be considered." Length: 1,000 to 3,000 words. Pays 12 pounds per 1,000 words "or page equivalent."

ELECTRONICS AUSTRALIA, Box 157, Beaconsfield, N.S.W., Australia 2015. Editor: Mr. J. Rowe. For "the Australian electronic industry and radio amateurs and hobbyists." Established in 1939. Monthly. Circulation: 48,000. Copyrighted. Will consider material previously published in U.S. or Canada offered for first publication in Australia. Will send a sample copy to a writer on request. Query first or submit complete ms. Enclose S.A.E. and International Reply coupons for return of submissions.
Nonfiction: "Electronics or electronics-oriented science subjects written for engineers, technicians, and hobbyists (not necessarily all 3, but at least for 1 readership group). Mainly news, industry analysis, and technical theory articles. We look for accuracy and clear explanation." Length: about 2,000 words. Pays "approximately $18 per published page, but depends on quality."

THE FLORIST, 120 Lower Ham Road, Kingston-upon-Thames, Surrey, England. Executive Editor: Jayne Foster. For professional retail florists. Special issues: Christmas, Mother's Day, Anniversaries. Monthly. Buys all rights. Pays on publication. Will send a sample copy to a writer on request. Submit seasonal material at least 2 months in advance. Reports "by return mail." Enclose S.A.E. and International Reply Coupons for return of submissions.
Nonfiction and Photos: Buys articles on "retailing—all aspects—and profitability and technique of design" in floristry. Length: 500 to 1,000 words. Pays 5 to 25 pounds per 1,000 words. Pays 2 to 10 pounds for b&w photos purchased with mss.
Fillers: Buys puzzles and jokes, "nonreligious, nonpolitical." Pays 2½ pence per line.

FOOD MANUFACTURE, 30 Calderwood St., London SE18 6QH, England. Editor: Anthony Woollen. For "technical management in food manufacturing industry." Monthly. Circulation: 6,650. Buys first rights. Pays on publication. Will send a free sample copy to a writer on request. Query first with synopsis and suggestions. Reports "immediately." Enclose S.A.E. and International Reply Coupons for reply to queries.
Nonfiction: "Most articles are commissioned, but good freelance copy within our field is acceptable." Buys "review articles on technical developments in food processing; descriptions of new food factories, processing machines, processes, and packaging techniques and materials. Brevity and readability are essential. Facts must be 100% accurate. We do not cover catering, distribution, or retailing." Buys how-to articles and coverage of new products and successful business operations.

Length: 500 to 2,500 words. Pays about $30 per 1,000 words. Photos: Buys original b&w photos. Pays $3.

FREELANCE WRITING AND PHOTOGRAPHY, Forestry Chambers, 67 Bridge St., Manchester, M3 3BQ, England. Editor: Arthur Waite. For "freelance writers and photographers of all ages, 18 to 70." Established in 1965. Quarterly. Circulation: 3,500. Buys first British rights. Buys about 150 mss a year. Pays on acceptance. Will send a sample copy to a writer for 40 cents. Submit seasonal material 4 months in advance. Reports "immediately." Enclose S.A.E. and International Reply coupons for return of submissions.
Nonfiction and Photos: "Articles that assist the freelance writer or photographer to produce salable work. Interviews with successful writers. Market information of what editors want to buy. Photographs that have sold to a number of periodicals are wanted. State total earning of photographs and the periodical that used the picture." Length: 1,200 words maximum. Pays $10 per 1,000 words.

FREIGHT MANAGEMENT, IPC Transport Press, Dorset House, Stamford St., London, S.E. 1, England. Editor: Norman N. Tilsley. For "shippers—people with cargoes to be moved, whose job function at the managerial level has an influence on physical distribution; circulation in U.K. only." Established in 1965. Monthly. Circulation: 20,000. Will consider previously unpublished material only. Will send a sample copy to a writer on request. Query first. Enclose S.A.E. and International Reply Coupons for reply to queries.
Nonfiction: "Concerning all methods of freight transport—land, rail, sea, air, and containerization." Length: 2,000 words maximum. Pays 15 pounds per 1,000 words.

GARDENERS CHRONICLE/HORTICULTURAL TRADE JOURNAL, Haymarket Publishing Ltd., 5 Winsley St., London, W1A 2HG, England. Editor: Geoffrey Bateman. For "professional horticulturalists, from land worker to company directors employed on ornamental plant production and marketing; parksmen employed in city and country parks; landscape architects, botanic garden staffs, and lecturers in colleges." Established in 1841. Weekly. Circulation: 12,000. Buys all rights. Buys about 50 mss a year. Pays on publication. Will send a sample copy to a writer on request. Write for copy of guidelines for writers. Query first or submit complete ms. Will consider photocopied submissions. Submit seasonal material 1 month in advance. Reports in 1 month. Enclose S.A.E. and International Reply Coupons for return of submissions or reply to queries.
Nonfiction: "Factual material on ornamental plant production and marketing; landscape design; research on plant production; new species and varieties of seed and ornamental plants. Take a reasonably serious approach, bearing in mind that your are writing for professionals with some knowledge of their subject. We do not want amateur gardening articles." Interested in articles on research into Dutch elm disease, modern management techniques, including financial management. Buys informational articles, personal experience articles, interviews, coverage of successful business operations, new product articles, coverage of merchandising techniques, and technical articles. Length: "open; good long articles will be published as series." Pays "up to 12 pounds per 1,000 words."
Photos: Purchased with or without mss; captions required. For b&w glossies, pays 1.50 pounds.

GEM TRADER, 29, Ludgate Hill, London, EC4M 7BQ, England. Editor: Richard Lambert. For dealers catering to the rockhound market. Established in 1972. Every two months. Circulation: 2,000. Not copyrighted. Pays on publication. Will send sample copy to writer on request. Will consider material previously published in U.S. or Canada, offered for first publication in Great Britain. Submission of previously published material may be made directly by the author, through an agent, or by the publisher or his representative. Will consider unpublished material. Submission of unpublished material may be made directly by the author or through agent. Query first or submit complete ms. Enclose S.A.E. and International Reply Coupons for return of submissions or reply to queries.
Nonfiction: Will consider the following material previously published in U.S. or Canada: News stories up to about 800 words on new mineral finds and other matter

of interest to dealers in the lapidary and mineralogical field. Pays 1 guinea to 6 guineas. Will consider the following unpublished material: News stories of interest to dealers, from paragraphs to about 800 words. Pays 1 guinea to 10 guineas.

THE GROWER, 49 Doughty St., London, WC1N 2LP, England. Editor: John Bloom. For "commercial growers, seeds salesmen, and manufacturers of all equipment for commercial growers, markets men, universities, research stations, students, etc." Weekly. Circulation: 11,000. Will consider material previously published in the U.S. or Canada offered for first publication in U.K. Pays in "month following publication." Will send a sample copy to a writer for $2. Query first. Reports "as soon as possible." Enclose S.A.E. and International Reply Coupons for reply to queries.
Nonfiction, Photos, and Fillers: Buys "many mss, but mostly from experts in the field of horticulture." Uses "technical articles and news items of current research, marketing techniques, packaging, transport, weather, methods and culture of growing, etc." Articles should be "short, direct, simply written." Buys how-to and personal experience articles, interviews, spot news, photo features, and coverage of successful business operations, new products, and merchandising techniques. Also buys newsbreaks. Length: 1,500 words for articles; 500 words for news. Pays 10.50 pounds per 1,000 words. Buys b&w glossy photos with mss, with captions only. Payment "variable."

INDEX, P.O. Box 109, Davis House, 69/77 High St., Croydon, CR9 1QH, Surrey, England. Editor: Ray Knight. For "executives and end-users of office equipment— the buyer/specifier." Established in 1967. Monthly. Circulation: 60,000. Copyrighted. Will consider material previously published in U.S. or Canada offered for first publication in U.K. Will send a sample copy to a writer "for postage fee." Submit complete ms. Enclose S.A.E. and International Reply Coupons for return of submissions.
Nonfiction: For published pieces, is interested in "articles concerning applications of business equipment and systems aimed at the end-user." For unpublished pieces, is interested in "case histories on equipment applications, news of office products and systems." Length: maximum 1,000 words for case histories; maximum 2,000 words for features and surveys. Pays 15 pounds per 1,000 words. Photos purchased with ms.

INDUSTRIAL ADVERTISING AND MARKETING, 110 Fleet St., London, E.C.4., England. Editor: Bill Price. For industrial marketing men. Quarterly. Circulation: 2,000. Buys first U.K. rights. Submit complete ms. Enclose S.A.E. and International Reply Coupons for return of submissions.
Nonfiction: Wants case histories on successful marketing operations of industrial products (as opposed to domestic products) or any section of industrial marketing (i.e., advertising, selling, design, etc.). Articles should show British industrial companies how their American counterparts set about marketing. Also buys articles on good or bad marketing by British companies in the U.S. Writers should be aware of th. difference between industrial (i.e., capital goods, services for industry, raw materials) and domestic products (vacuum cleaners, motor cars, detergents) when producing a marketing article. Length: 4,000 words maximum. Pays minimum of 15 pounds.

INDUSTRIAL DIAMOND REVIEW, 7 Rolls Buildings, Fetter Lane, London, EC4A 1HX, England. Editor: Paul Daniel. Established in 1941. Monthly. Circulation: 3,700. Not copyrighted. Will consider unpublished material offered for first time use only. Will send a sample copy to a writer on request. Query first or submit complete ms. Enclose S.A.E. and International Reply Coupons.
Nonfiction: "Articles on industrial diamonds (basic and applied research), diamond tooling, machines for use with diamond tools, case histories on applications of diamond tooling." Length: 600 to 6,000 words. Pays 10.50 pounds per 1,000 words.

INDUSTRIAL FINISHING & SURFACE COATING, 157 Hagden Lane, Watford, Herts, WD1 8LW, England. Editor: J.B. Ward. For a "technical and management audience." Monthly. Circulation: 6,850. Not copyrighted. Pays on publication. Will

send a sample copy to a writer on request. Submit seasonal material 1 month in advance. Reports in 2 weeks. Enclose S.A.E. and International Reply Coupons for return of submissions.
Nonfiction: "Technical articles which are end-use oriented. We do special coverage of marine wood finishing, marine coating, powder coating and plating on plastic." Length: 1,000 to 3,000 words. Pays $19 per 1,000 words.

INDUSTRIAL SAFETY, United Trade Press Ltd., 42 Gerrard St., London, W1V 7LP, England. Editor: Mrs. Margaret Hamilton. For "professional safety officers, factory inspectors, and other safety specialists. Also, management and manufacturers of protective clothing, equipment, and devices such as machine guards." Established in 1955. Monthly. Circulation: 10,000. Copyrighted. Will consider unpublished material offered for the first time only. Will send a sample copy to a writer on request. Query first. Enclose S.A.E. and International Reply coupons for reply to queries.
Nonfiction: "Articles on occupational health and safety. An original article on some aspect of U.S. or Canadian industrial safety which is new and may be of interest to safety professionals in the U.K." is sometimes bought. Length: about 1,000 words. Pays 10.50 pounds per 1,000 words, "or by arrangement with author."

INSURANCE BROKERS MONTHLY, 9 Market St., Stourbridge, Worcs, England. Editor: John Sadler. Established in 1950. Monthly. Circulation: 7,750. Copyrighted. Will consider only published material offered for first-time use. Will send a sample copy to a writer for 35 pence. Enclose S.A.E. and International Reply coupons for return of submissions.
Nonfiction: "Limited use of insurance and financial articles only." Length: 1,500 to 2,500 words. Pays 4.20 pounds per 1,000 words, "except sometimes higher for exceptional material."

JOURNAL OF PARK AND RECREATION ADMINISTRATION, Institute of Park and Recreation Administration, Lower Basildon, Reading, Berks, RG8 9NE, England. Managing Editor: Kenneth L. Morgan. For "a professional membership." Established in 1926. Monthly. Not copyrighted. Will consider material published in U.S. or Canada offered for first publication in the United Kingdom. Will send a sample copy to a writer on request. Will consider photocopied submissions. Author should submit directly. Query first. Enclose S.A.E. and International Reply Coupons.
Nonfiction: "Parks, recreation, leisure, conservation; material dealing with parks and recreation in North America." Length: 600 to 1,000 words. Pays 5 to 10 pounds per 1,000 words.

JOURNAL OF THE ROYAL UNITED SERVICES INSTITUTE FOR DEFENSE STUDIES, Whitehall, London, SW1A 2ET, England. Editor: Brigadier R.G.S. Bidwell. O.B.E. members or RUSI—both civilian and service. Quarterly.
Nonfiction: Considers original material in the field of defense studies including contemporary strategy, weapon technology and international affairs relating to defense. Accepts original material only. Rates adjustable: 4 to 5 pounds per 1,000 words.

JUSTICE OF THE PEACE, Little London, Chichester, Sussex, England. Editor: Barry Rose. Established in 1837. Copyrighted. Pays on publication. Will send sample copy to writer on request. Will consider unpublished material offered for first time use. Submission of unpublished material may be made directly by author. Enclose S.A.E. and International Reply Coupons for return of submissions.
Nonfiction: Will consider unpublished articles on law, criminology, police science. Preferred length: 1,500 words. Maximum length: 3,500 words. Pays 2 pounds per column minimum.

LOCAL GOVERNMENT REVIEW, Little London, Chichester, Sussex, England. Editor: Barry Rose. Established in 1837. Weekly. Circulation: 2,000. Copyrighted. Will consider unpublished material for first time use only. Will send a sample copy to a writer on request. Query first or submit complete ms. Enclose S.A.E. and International Reply Coupons for return of submissions or reply to queries.

Nonfiction: "Deals with municipal law and with local government generally." Pays 10 pounds for 1,500 words.

MANUFACTURING CLOTHIER, 42 Gerrard St., London, WlV 7LP England. Editor: Basil Wardman. Established in 1946. Monthly. Circulation: 5,500. Copyrighted. Will consider unpublished material for first use only. Will send a sample copy to a writer on request. Enclose S.A.E. and International Reply Coupons for return of submissions.
Nonfiction: "Features on the factory production of men's and boys' clothing, including methods, machinery, personnel, management, budgeting aspects. Articles will be considered only from writers working in the industry and in the country concerned." Length: 800 to 2,000 words; larger features serialized. Pays $25 to $30 per 1,000 words.

MARKETING, Haymarket Publishing, S. Winsley St., London WlA 2H6, England. Editor: Michael Rines. Established in 1925. Monthly. Circulation: 18,000. Copyrighted. Will send sample copy to writer on request. Will consider unpublished material offered for first time use. Submission of unpublished material may be made directly by the author. Query first. Enclose S.A.E. and International Reply Coupons for reply to query or return of submission.
Nonfiction: Interested in unpublished "articles on marketing of around 3,000 words or more. Generally with a practical approach, or if there is a good story, or case of a firm's experience but only when written by an outsider other than a PR man." Pays up to 60 pounds.

MEAT, IPC Consumer Industries Press, 161/166 Fleet St., London, EC4P 4AA, England. Editor: John Michael. Audience: retail butchers and meat manufacturers, buyers, slaughterers. Established in 1928. Monthly. Circulation: 10,000. Not copyrighted. Will consider material previously published in the U.S. or Canada offered for first publication in Europe. Will send a sample copy to a writer on request. Query first or submit complete ms. Will consider photocopied submissions. Enclose S.A.E. and International Reply Coupons for reply to queries and return of submissions.
Nonfiction: For previously published material, wants "short articles relating to meat exports/imports and trade in meat affecting Europe." Also wants "news stories relating to trade or international supplies of meat. We prefer short (250 words) stories in standard American journalese. Obviously, time elements are not important." Pays $1 a column inch (about 1¢ a word).

MINE AND QUARRY, 42 Grays Inn Road, London, WC1X 8LR, England. Editor: David Buntain. Established in 1926. For mining engineers, quarry operators, machinery manufacturers, and mineral processing engineers. Buys no rights; considers simultaneous submissions. Payment on publication. Will consider material previously published in the U.S. or Canada offered for first publication in U.K. Submit complete ms. Enclose S.A.E. and International Reply Coupons for return of submissions.
Nonfiction and Photos: Buys practical or research articles pertaining to the technical side of the mining industry. "Technical articles on advanced mining and quarrying practice, research, or development. Coverage of complete extractive minerals industry from initial prospecting to final preparation for the market." Length: 5,000 words maximum. Pays about $10 per 1,000 words. Buys b&w photos only.

NEW SCIENTIST, 128 Long Acre, London, W.C. 2, England. Editor: Dr. Bernard Dixon. For "scientists and nonscientists." Established in 1956. Weekly. Circulation: 72,000. Copyrighted. Will consider material previously published in the U.S. or Canada for first publication in the U.K. Will send a sample copy to an author on request. Query first or submit complete ms. Will consider photocopied submissions. Enclose S.A.E. and International Reply Coupons for reply to queries or return of submissions.
Nonfiction: "This is a weekly magazine of news, comment, and review of science and technology and their social implications, written in nonspecialist language." Interested in previously published material on "science, technology, and their social, political, and economic implications." Length: about 2,000 words. For unpub-

lished material, interested in articles on "research and development, scientists as people, the wide relation of science to society, etc." Length: "about 2,000 words for features." Pays a minimum rate of 15 pounds per 1,000 words.

OEM DESIGN, Broadwall House, Broadwall, London, SE1 9PN, England. Editor: Bob Hersee. Established in 1971. Monthly. Circulation: 24,000. Copyrighted. Will consider unpublished material offered for first time use only. Will send a sample copy to a writer on request. Submit complete ms. Enclose S.A.E. and International Reply Coupons for return of submissions.
Nonfiction and Photos: "Articles of practical value to designers of engineering products." Length: about 2,500 words maximum. Pays "about 7 pounds per page published. 1 page averages about 600 words plus illustrations."

PARKS & SPORTS GROUNDS, Armour House, Bridge Street, Guildford, Surrey, Great Britain. Editor: D. Colbeck. For park directors, local authority and private sports club groundsmen, education authority playing fields officers. Established in 1955. Monthly. Circulation: 4,000. Copyrighted. Pays on publication. Will send sample copy to writer on request. Will consider material previously published in U.S. or Canada, offered for first publication in United Kingdom. Submission of previously published material may be made directly by author. Will consider unpublished material offered for first time use. Submission of unpublished material may be made directly by the author. Enclose S.A.E. and International Reply Coupons for return of submission.
Nonfiction: Interested in the following material (previously published in U.S. or Canada, or unpublished): All aspects of turf care, maintenance and management. All aspects of outdoor recreation for local authority parks directors and their staff. Local authority and sports club groundsmen, education authority playing fields officers. Pays 10 to 20 pounds per 1,000 words.

PIG FARMING, Fenton House, Wharfedale Road, Ipswich, IP1 4LE, Suffolk, England. Editor: B. T. Hogley. For "pig producers of all ages all over the world." Six supplements a year: Pig Health, Pig Housing, Pig Management, Pig Feeding, Pig Breeding, National Pig Fair (held in Britain). Established in 1953. Monthly. Circulation: 21,500. Buys all rights. Buys 10 to 12 mss a year. Pays on publication. Will send a free sample copy to a writer on request, "if he can show he really knows something about pigs." Query first. Submit seasonal or special material 2 months in advance. Reports "immediately." Enclose S.A.E. and International Reply Coupons for reply to queries.
Nonfiction: Buys articles on "modern methods of pig management. Too many articles submitted are hackneyed—no reference book is a substitute for first-hand knowledge of pig production. The style should be as simple as possible." Buys how-to and personal experience articles and coverage of successful business operations and new products. Length: 500 to 2,000 words. Pays 10 pounds per 1,000 words, "contributors with specialized knowledge may be paid double this rate."
Photos: Buys b&w glossies with mss; with captions only. Buys first rights. Pays 1 to 1½ pounds.
Fiction: Buys humorous fiction "very occasionally." Length: 750 to 1,500 words. Pays 10 pounds per 1,000 words.

POULTRY INTERNATIONAL, Watt Publishing Co., Mt. Morris IL 60154. Editorial address: Woodley House, Hill Brow, Liss, Hampshire, England. Editor: Anthony Phelps. Controlled circulation to "worldwide audience outside the Americas. Recipients must qualify as producers (minimum 3,000 layers and/or 40,000 broilers annually and/or 3,000 turkeys annually); allied occupations accepted." Circulation: 12,000. "Query essential." Buys all rights. Payment on acceptance. Will send free sample copy to writer on request. Reports on submissions in 10 days. Enclose S.A.E. for reply to queries.
Nonfiction: Business and technical information related to poultry production, processing, marketing. Emphasizes Europe but uses articles about almost any part of the world outside the Americas. Wants analytical articles, not straight news or general descriptive articles. Length: up to 1,000 to 1,500 words; "the shorter, the better." Pays $35 to $95 depending on content and quality.
Photos: Glossies purchased with mss as package. No size requirements.

PULSE, Morgan-Grampian House, 30 Calderwood Street, London, England SE18 6QH. Editor: Peter Head. For general medical practitioners. Established in 1962. Weekly. Circulation: 38,000. Copyrighted. Pays on publication. Will send sample copy to writer on request. Query first. Enclose S.A.E. and International Reply Coupons for response to query.
Nonfiction: "Medico-political and leisure material. Of interest to British doctors, using British English. In-depth treatment of pertinent issues." Interview, profile, and think articles. Length: 1,200 to 2,500 words. Pays 15 to 30 pounds. Photos purchased with accompanying mss; captions required. 10x8 b&w preferred.

THE QUEEN'S HIGHWAY, 25 Lower Belgrave Street, London, SW1W 0LS, England. Editor: Ian S. Menzies. For "a cross-section of all those interested in roads and road construction in Great Britain—British highway engineers and executives and their families." Established in 1931. Semiannual. Circulation: 4,000. Buys all rights. Will consider material previously published in the U.S. or Canada offered for first publication in Great Britain. Buys 12 mss a year. Pays on acceptance. Will send a sample copy to a writer on request. Submit seasonal material "as early as possible, but in any case at least 4 months before" publication. Reports "within a month." Enclose S.A.E. and International Reply Coupons for return of submissions.
Nonfiction and Photos: "We have a very small market for U.S. originated items since *The Queen's Highway* circulates mainly in the United Kingdom and is intended to reflect British road construction practice and the British scene at leisure-time." Buys "illustrated technical articles on asphalt road construction, showing unusual features or specifically U.S. and Canadian features. Also, general articles or features on highways in the U.S. or Canada, particularly reportage on Pan-American and trans-Canada highways. Interesting, 'way out' angles on highways, features on the interrelationship of highways and the environment." Length: open. Pays 7 pounds per page. Buys photos with mss; pays 2½ pounds per photo.

REFRIGERATION AND AIR CONDITIONING, Davis House, 69-77 High St., Croydon, CR9 1QH, England. Editor: Terence A. O'Gorman. For engineers, contractors, consultants, marketing personnel and users. Established in 1898. Monthly. Circulation: 5,000. Buys first British rights. Query first with synopsis. Enclose S.A.E. and International Reply Coupons for reply to queries.
Nonfiction, Photos, and Fillers: Buys technical and commercial features. "covering any aspect of refrigeration and air conditioning which has relevance in the United Kingdom and Europe. The approach to technical articles should not be too heavy, as readership includes apprentices and service engineers as well as very highly qualified people. At the same time, too basic an approach would not be welcomed." Length: 2,000 words minimum; 3,000 words preferred. Buys news items for fillers. Payment negotiable. Buys b&w photos.

SELLING TODAY, U.C.T.A., Bexton Lane, Knutsford, Cheshire, England. Editor: Andrew Lincoln. For "salesmen and sales managers." Monthly. Circulation: 30,000. Buys all rights. Buys 25 mss a year. Pays on publication. Will send a sample copy to a writer on request. Returns rejected material "immediately." Reports acceptance of material in 1 month. Enclose S.A.E. and International Reply Coupons for return of submissions.
Nonfiction and Photos: Buys "articles on selling, marketing, and allied subjects. Must have sales angle." Seeks "general interest news" and motoring material. Does not want to see "psychological themes." Buys personal experience articles, interviews, profiles, humor, photo features, coverage of successful business operations, and articles on new products and merchandising techniques. Length: 750 to 2,000 words. Pays 5 to 20 pounds. Buys b&w glossies with mss.

SERVICE STATION, 178-202 Great Portland St., London W1N 6NH, England. Editor: Mark A. Siggers. For people engaged in operating retail motor trade outlets; most are executives with buying influence. Established in 1925. Monthly. Circulation: 23,000. Not copyrighted. Will send sample copy to writer on request. Will consider material previously published in U.S. or Canada, offered for first publication in Great Britain. Submission of previously published material may be made directly by author, through an agent, or by the publisher or his representative. Will consider unpublished material offered for first time use. Submission of unpublished material may be made directly by the author. Query first. Enclose S.A.E. and International Reply Coupons for response to query.

Nonfiction: Will consider the following material previously published in U.S. or Canada: "Features and news of specific interest to British service station, garage, repair shop and tire shop operators. Preferably 1,500 words long. Emphasis on trade association and relevant political developments." Pays 12.50 to 20 pounds for 1,000 words; "more by agreement." Will consider the following unpublished material: Exclusive news stories about oil companies, motor manufacturers and North American trade associations. Pays by arrangement, but never less than 15 pounds per 1,000 words.

SHIP & BOAT INTERNATIONAL, Saracen's Head Buildings, 36-37 Cock Lane, London, EC1A 9BY, England. Editor. Kenneth D. Troup. For "naval architects, shipbuilders, owners, consultants, engineers, equipment manufacturers." Monthly. Circulation: 5,000. Buys all rights. Buys 20 mss a year. Pays on publication. Will send a sample copy to a writer on request. Query first. Submit seasonal material 2 months in advance. Reports "immediately." Enclose S.A.E. and International Reply Coupons for reply to queries.
Nonfiction: Buys "strictly technical articles on ship design and construction." Does not want to see "anything with a personal angle." Buys coverage of successful business operations and new products. Length: 300 to 2,000 words. Pays 10½ pounds per 1,000 words.

SHOPFITTING INTERNATIONAL, Blandford Publications, Ltd., 167 High Holborn, London WC1V 6PH, Great Britain. Editor: Martin Staheli. Monthly. Circulation: 19,000. Payment on publication. Will send free sample copy to writer on request. Enclose S.A.E. and International Reply Coupons for return of submissions.
Nonfiction and Photos: Buys news items and features. Subject should be the fitting out of new shops, departmental stores, hotels (public areas only); banks, prestige showrooms, night clubs, restaurants; the materials and techniques used for the fitting-out of the above; new shopfitting equipment. Uses photos. Captions required. Payment negotiable.

SPECIAL EDUCATION, 12 Park Crescent, London, W1N 4EQ, England. Editor: Mrs. Margaret Peter. "The majority of readers are teachers but the journal is read by other professional workers (university and college lecturers, therapists of various kinds, medical personnel, psychologists and social workers, administrators) who are interested in special education and handicapped children." Established in 1965. Quarterly. Will send a sample copy to a writer on request. Will not consider photocopied submissions. Include a carbon copy and information on author's professional duties. Enclose S.A.E. and International Reply Coupons for return of submissions.
Nonfiction: "The aim of *Special Education* is to provide articles on special education and handicapped children which will keep readers informed of practical and theoretical developments not only in education but in the many other aspects of the education and welfare of the handicapped. While we hope that articles will lead students and others to further related reading, their main function is to give readers an adequate introduction to a topic which they may not have an opportunity to pursue further. References should therefore be selective and mainly easily accessible ones. It is important, therefore, that articles of a more technical nature (e.g., psychology, medical, research reviews) should, whenever possible, avoid unnecessary technicalities or ensure that necessary technical terms or expressions are made clear to nonspecialists by the context or by the provision of brief additional explanations or examples." Length: 1,750 to 3,750 words. Pays 5 guineas.

SWIMMING POOL REVIEW, Armour House, Bridge St., Guildford, Surrey, England. Editor: D. Colbeck. For "swimming pool superintendents (municipal authorities), education authorities, holiday camps, hotels, private pool owners." Established in 1960. Quarterly. Circulation: 6,000. Copyrighted. Will consider material previously published in the U.S. or Canada offered for first publication in the United Kingdom. Will send a sample copy to a writer on request. Author should submit material directly. Enclose S.A.E. and International Reply Coupons for return of submissions.

Nonfiction: "Aims to cover the design, construction, and maintenance and management of all types of indoor and outdoor swimming pools in the U.K. and abroad, including privately owned pools." Interested in articles on "design, construction, and management of indoor recreational facilities, emphasizing swimming pools." Length: 1,500 to 2,500 words. Pays 10 to 20 pounds per 1,000 words.

TABLEWARE INTERNATIONAL, 17 John Adam Street, London, W.C.2., England. Editor: E. M. G. Gibbins. For executives. Special issues on "Blackpool Gifts Fair, Atlantic City Fair, Hanover Fair, Paris SIFE Exhibition, Frankfurt Fair, Harrogate Fair, etc." Monthly. Circulation: 5,000. Buys first rights. Buys 40 mss a year. Pays on publication. Will send a sample copy to a writer on request. Query first. Submit seasonal material 3 months in advance. Reports "as soon as possible." Enclose S.A.E. and International Reply Coupons for reply to queries.
Nonfiction: Buys "features of interest to pottery, glass, chinaware shops and stores." Buys articles on successful business operations and merchandising; "sometimes" buys historical articles. Length: 1,000 to 1,500 words. Pays 15 to 25 pounds per 1,000 words.

TOURISM INTERNATIONAL, 154 Cromwell Rd., London SW7, England. Editor: John Seeking. For people concerned professionally with international tourism. Established in 1973. Every two weeks. Circulation: 500. Not copyrighted. Pays on publication. Will consider material previously published in U.S. or Canada, offered for first publication in England. Will consider unpublished material offered for first time use. Submission of unpublished material may be made directly by the author. Query first or submit complete ms. Enclose S.A.E. and International Reply Coupons for response to query or return of submission.
Nonfiction: Will consider the following material previously published in U.S. or Canada: "Management-orientated features between 500 and 2,500 words concerning the tourism industry and aimed at tourism experts." Pays minimum $75, maximum $125 per 1,000. Will consider the following unpublished material: "Most features will be either a case study on a specific situation or a survey on a specific problem." Pays $75 to $125 per 1,000 words.

WATER POWER, Dorset House, Stamford St., London, SE1 9LU, England. Editor: Julian Fox. For "international engineers involved in hydroelectric developments." Established in 1947. Monthly. Circulation: 3,000. Copyrighted. Will consider unpublished material offered for first-time use only. Will send a sample copy to a writer on request. Query first or submit complete ms.
Nonfiction: "Fully technical material on new hydro stations, equipment, construction techniques, etc." Length: 4,000 to 5,000 words. Pays "approximately $40 per 1,000 words for articles in excess of 4,000 words; depends on type and value of material."

WORLD TOBACCO, 17-19 John Adam St., London, W.C.2., England. Editor: Michael F. Barford. For specialist readers in major tobacco manufacturing and distribution businesses and monopolies in 171 countries. Established in 1962. Quarterly. Circulation: 3,375. Buys all rights. Pays on or before publication. Query first with writer's technical credentials in tobacco. Reports "promptly."
Nonfiction and Photos: Wants tobacco market analyses and articles on distribution methods, manufacturing technology, promotional methods in cigarette selling, with preference for contributions about the less sophisticated countries of the world. Also buys short notes on new brands of tobacco products and new machinery for the tobacco industry, the former excluding the U.S.A., Canada, and much of western Europe. Length: 1,200 to 1,500 words. Pays 5 cents to 7½ cents per word. Buys b&w photos with mss and captioned only.
Fillers: Buys material for these regular columns: New Brands and Packs; New Machinery and Equipment; News, Views, Trends; Marketing Impact.

THE WRITER, 124 New Bond St., London W1A 46J, England. Editor: H. Johnson. For freelance writers. Established in 1921. Monthly. Copyrighted. Buys first serial rights. Payment on publication. Will send sample copy to writer on request, but airmail postage must be enclosed with request. Submit complete ms. Enclose S.A.E. and International Reply Coupons for return of submissions.

Nonfiction: "Articles giving really practical information or advice to freelance writers. Must have positive approach. Interviews with well-known and successful writers." Does not want to see personal success stories or humorous pieces on rejection slips. Length: 300 to 1,500 words. Pays 1 to 10 pounds.

WRITING, 4 Union Place, Fowey, Cornwall PL23M 1BY, England. Editor: Sean Dorman. For writers, theatre directors and actors. Established in 1959. Published two times a year. Circulation: 1,000. Pays on publication. Will send sample copy to writer for $1. Submit only complete ms. Enclose S.A.E. and International Reply Coupons for return of submission.
Nonfiction and Poetry: Articles of 300 to 350 words of interest to authors and journalists. Use a literary style. Pays $2.50 for 300- to 350-word articles. Poems, 8 to 20 lines, of literary quality, any style, are also considered.

Book Publishers

ADLARD COLES LTD., 3 Upper James St., London, W1R 4BP, England. Editor: Keiren Phelan. Publishes hardcover originals and reprints. Will consider only previously unpublished material from U.S. and Canadian authors or their representatives. Payment "by negotiation." Offers standard book contract. Advance varies. Published 20 titles last year. Will send a catalog to a writer on request. Submit query first or outline and sample chapters. Unsolicited material returned unread. Enclose S.A.E. and International Reply Coupons for reply to all correspondence.
Nonfiction: "Adlard Coles is the largest and best respected publisher of sailing books in the world. The company publishes many Anglo/North American editions covering yacht designs and construction, racing, seamanship, historical books, and superior narratives, and is always sympathetic to new ideas. We'd like to consider any books on the sea and sailing. Must be authoritative and potentially leading works in their specialized subjects or branches of sailing and the sea." Length: 25,000 words minimum.

GEORGE ALLEN & UNWIN LTD., 40 Museum St., London, WC1A 1LU, England. Established in 1914. Publishes hardcover and paperback originals; publishes reprints "rarely." Will consider material previously published in U.S. or Canada offered for first publication in U.K. and the rest of the world. Payment is negotiated; "each book is treated on its own merits." Published 250 to 300 books last year. Will send a catalog to a writer on request, "but we only welcome necessary requests." Submission of previously published material may be made by author, his agent, or original publisher. Query first, submit outline and sample chapters, or submit complete ms. Enclose S.A.E. and International Reply Coupons with ms.
General Nonfiction: "Any good nonfiction, whether popular or academic. Especially books of high quality and originality."

J.A. ALLEN & CO., LTD., 1 Lower Grosvenor Place, London, SW1W 0EL, England. Established in 1926. Publishes hardcover originals and reprints. Will consider material previously published in U.S. or Canada. Offers 10% royalty contract on previously unpublished books; offers 5% to 10% royalty on published retail price for material previously published in U.S. or Canada. Published 12 titles last year. Submission may be made by the author, his agent, or original publisher. Query first or submit complete ms for previously unpublished material. Enclose S.A.E. and International Reply Coupons for return of submissions.
Nonfiction: "Publications relating to the horse and equestrianism and allied activities such as racing and breeding, riding, schooling, driving, polo, snow jumping, etc."

AQUARIAN PUBLISHING CO. (LONDON) LTD., Denington Estate, Wellingborough, Northants NN8 2RQ, England. Established in 1968. Publishes hardcover and paperback originals and reprints. Will consider material previously published in U.S. or Canada offered for first publication in U.K. Offers 10% royalty contract for hardcover originals and 8% royalty contract for paperback originals. Will send a catalog to a writer on request. Submission may be made directly by au-author, his agent, or original publisher. Submit complete ms for original nonfiction. Address communications to "The Editor." Enclose S.A.E. and International Reply Coupons with ms.

Nonfiction: "Publishers of books on astrology, magic, witchcraft, palmistry, and other occult subjects."

BERNARDS PUBLISHERS LTD., The Grampians, Western Gate, Shepherds Bush Rd., London, W6 7NF, England. Editor: Mr. B. Babani. Established in 1942. Publishes paperback originals and reprints. Will consider material previously published in U.S. or Canada offered for first publication in Great Britain. Offers royalties of "5% on invoice value or outright purchase, by arrangement." Published 37 titles last year. Submission may be made by the author, his agent, or original publisher. Submit complete ms for unpublished material. Enclose S.A.E. and International Reply Coupons with ms.

Nonfiction: "Specialty house in radio-electronics, slanted to popular market. Publish do-it-yourself radio and electronic handbooks, practical construction data, etc. Any interesting D.I.Y. material in other fields also considered. Any length."

BLACKIE & SON, LTD., Wester Cleddens Rd., Bishopbriggs, Glasgow, G64 2NZ, Scotland. Established in 1809. Publishes hardcover originals and reprints. Will consider material previously published in U.S. or Canada offered for first publication in U.K. Royalty is "negotiated" for previously published material; offers royalty contract of 7½% for British rights and 10% for world rights for unpublished books. Published 180 titles last year. Will send a catalog to a writer on request. Submission may be made by the author, his agent, or original publisher. For unpublished material, query first for nonfiction and submit complete ms for fiction. Enclose S.A.E. and International Reply Coupons for reply to query or return of submissions.

Juveniles and Textbooks: "Material suitable to a U.K. audience. We are well-known in U.K. as publishers of a wide range of books, from picture books for young children to textbooks for all levels of school from Infant upwards. Also equally engaged in scientific and technical book publishing at University and Technical College level. One of the best known educational publishers in Britain."

JOHN JONES CARDIFF LTD., 41 Wochaber St., Cardiff CF2 3LS, England. Editor: John Idris Jones. Established in 1968. Publishes hardcover and paperback originals and reprints. Published 4 books last year. Will consider material previously published in U.S. or Canada, offered for first publication in United Kingdom. Submission of previously published material may be made directly by author, through an agent, or by the publisher or his representative. Will consider unpublished material offered for first time publication. Submission of unpublished material may be made directly by the author or through agent. Query first or submit complete ms. Enclose S.A.E. and International Reply Coupons for response to query or return of submission.

Sports: Will consider the following previously published material: "Sports, short, factual handbooks on leisure-interest sports. Usually pays a percentage to the original publishers; author's percentage subject to negotiation." Will consider the following published material: "We're very small, but growing. Mostly sports for an international market, especially Australia, New Zealand and South Africa." Pays 10% royalty to author.

CASSELL & CO. LTD., 35 Red Lion Square, London, W.C. 1, England. Editor: Kenneth Parker. Established in 1848. Publishes hardcover and paperback originals and reprints. Will consider material previously published in U.S. or Canada offered for first publication in U.K. Royalty contract to be arranged. Published about 140 titles last year. Will send a catalog to a writer on request. Submission may be made by the author, his agent, or the original publisher. Enclose S.A.E. and International Reply Coupons for return of submissions.

General: "General books, memoirs, biographies, fiction, music, juvenile nonfiction, dictionaries, reference books, commercial, technical, etc. No verse, short stories, plays. We have a distinguished list of authors. Royalty terms vary from book to book."

CENTAUR PRESS LTD., (including Linden Press), Fontwell, Arundel, Sussex, England. Editor: Jon Wynne-Tyson. Publishes hardcover and paperback originals and reprints. Published 6 titles last year. Will send a catalog to a writer on request. Query first. Reports in 1 week. "We do not invite unsolicited mss, nearly all the books we publish being commissioned from ideas we have had ourselves. If we receive a letter from an author we reply at once, usually with a catalog saying whether we would be likely to be interested."

W. & R. CHAMBERS LTD., 11 Thistle St., Edinburgh, EH2 1DG, Scotland. Editor: A.S. Chambers. Publishes hardcover originals and translations. Offers standard royalty contract. Published 25 titles last year. Will send a catalog to a writer on request. Query first with sample chapter. Reports in 6 weeks. Enclose International Reply Coupons for return postage with ms.
General Nonfiction, Juveniles, Reference, Technical, Medical, Scientific and Textbooks: Current leading title is *Paul and Fritzi's Year: Spring, Summer, Autumn, Winter.* General Nonfiction and Juveniles; T.C. Collocott, Reference; I. Gould, Technical, Medical, Scientific, and Textbooks. Reference books, educational books and full-colour picture books for young children.

DAVID & CHARLES, South Devon House, Newton Abbot, Devon, England. Editorial Director: Mrs. Pamela Thomas. Established in 1961. Publishes hardcover and paperback originals and reprints. Will consider material previously published in U.S. or Canada offered for first publication in U.K. Royalties negotiated for previously published material; "royalty rates normally start at about 10%" for unpublished materials. Advance varies. Published about 300 titles last year. Will send a catalog to a writer on request. Submission may be made by the author, his agent, or original publisher. Query first with outline and sample chapters for unpublished material. Enclose S.A.E. and International Reply Coupons.
Nonfiction: "Both general and academic books on a wide range of subjects. We are particularly interested in books which bridge gaps between laymen and specialists—for example, a biology book on sperm whales that is intelligible to secondary school students and would still be useful to nonspecialist biologists in the marine field. Main lines of development nowadays are natural history, astronomy, science and technology in both the academic and general field. We regard ourselves very much as an international publishing house; a high proportion of the books that we originate over here are published in the U.S. by American publishers. We certainly distribute in Canada and occasionally we publish Canadian editions as well, though most often an American publisher takes the Canadian market when he buys rights. We like books to be international, particularly when we think in terms of importing them from U.S. publishers. We also sell a good deal to Australia and South Africa, and, of course, there are translation rights as well. We're on the lookout for really top trade books which will sell widely to the general public. We do a lot of heavily illustrated books with popular flavor."
Juveniles: "A recent development here is that we are moving into children's books for the '10 plus' age group, both fiction and nonfiction, though we don't see our output here rising to more than a dozen books or so in any one year for the present."
Education: "We are increasing the strength of our education list, but authors do need to be familiar with U.K. and Commonwealth curricula."

DRUMMOND PRESS, 64 Murray Place, Stirling, Scotland. Editor: John Birkbeck. Established in 1848. Publishes hardcover and paperback originals and anthologies. Contract arranged "by mutual agreement between author and publisher." Will consider material published in U.S. or Canada offered for first publication in Great Britain as submitted by the publisher or his representative. Published "8 books and many tracts" last year. Will send a catalog to a writer on request. Send complete ms. Reports in 1 to 2 weeks. Enclose International Reply Coupons for return of submissions.
Religion and Philosophy: "Religious publisher—tracts, sermons, pamphlets dealing with specific human problems, sermons, doctrine, illustrations and quotations, anecdotes. Material should be short, succinct, simple, specific."

EDITIONS PIERRE BELFOND, 3 bis, passage de la Petite-Boucherie, 75006 Paris, France. Editor: Sylvie Messinger. Established in 1966. Publishes hardcover and paperback originals and hardcover reprints. Published 40 books last year. Will send catalog to writer on request. Submit outline and sample chapters for nonfiction. Submit complete manuscript for fiction. Enclose S.A.E. and International Reply Coupons for return of submission.
General Fiction and General Nonfiction: "Our special reputation in U.S. comes from the publication of some bestsellers and from our youngness and dynamism." Fiction, new writers, nonfiction, modern history, from 200 to 500 pages. Royalty arrangement for material previously published in the U.S. or Canada is 8, 10, 12, and 14 percent. Royalty arrangement for unpublished books submitted for first time publication is 10, 12 and 14 percent.

PAUL ELEK LIMITED, 54-8 Caledonian Road, London N1 9RN, England, Editor: Moira L. Johnston. Publishes hardcover originals and reprints. Average advance is $250 to $300, but often higher. Royalties are considered separately for each case. Published 40 books last year. Will consider photocopied submissions. Enclose S.A.E. and International Reply Coupons for response to queries or return of submissions.
General Nonfiction: "Art monographs, academic text, high quality illustrations; general nonfiction with academic slant; biography and history; economics and managment studies; literature; scientific; 'Life and Leisure' series; 'Plays of the Year' series. Writers should bear in mind an international audience. We prefer illustrated books. Recent titles include *The Conquest of the Air*, and illustrated history of flight and *Grand Trunk Road*, an account of walk from Khyber Pass to Calcutta. We're planning a new archaeology series."

FEMINA BOOKS LTD., 1-A Montagu Mews North, London, W.1, England. Editor: Mrs. C. Whitaker. Established in 1966. Publishes hardcover and paperback originals and reprints. Will consider material previously published in U.S. or Canada offered for first publication in U.K. "Royalties usually start at 10%; an advance is paid against royalties." Published 3 titles last year. Will send a catalog to a writer on request. Submission may be made by the author, his agent, or the original publisher. Enclose S.A.E. and International Reply Coupons with ms.
Fiction and Nonfiction: "All books published by this company have to have a definite angle on women in general or a woman in particular." Length: 50,000 to 100,000 words.

FOCAL PRESS LTD., 31 Fitzroy Square, London, W1P 6BH, England. Editor: A. Kraszna-Krausz. Established in 1938. Publishes hardcover and paperback originals only. Offers "standard U.K. publishers royalty agreement based on U.K. selling price." Published 52 titles last year. Will send a catalog to a writer on request. Submit outline and sample chapters. Enclose S.A.E. and International Reply Coupons
Nonfiction: "Publishers of the most comprehensive range of books on photography and motion picture techniques, sound and image recording, television and graphic arts: levels ranging from the popular to the scientific. The material should be structured into chapters in logical sequence, approach and emphasis suited to proposed readers; style direct without being colloquial; and, above all, technically accurate and up-to-date." Length: 80,000 to 100,000 words.

G.T. FOULIS & CO., LTD., 50-A Bell St., Henley-on-Thames, Oxfordshire, England. Editor: John Hassell. Established in 1926. Publishes hardcover and paperback originals and reprints. Will consider material previously published in U.S. or Canada offered for first publication in U.K. Payment for previously published material "always negotiable according to the book"; for unpublished books, offers "10% royalty on U.K. selling price of book." Published 20 titles last year. Will send a catalog to a writer on request. Submission may be made by the author, his agent, or original publisher. Submit complete ms for unpublished material. Enclose S.A.E. and International Reply Coupons with ms.
Nonfiction: "A small, well-established independent house specializing in motoring, aviation, general nonfiction, scientific and technical. Especially well-known for its traditionally strong motoring list. Interested in mss on motor sport, motor engineering, aviation, general adult nonfiction, biography. Length is immaterial to us."

GOWER PRESS LTD., Epping, Essex, England. Editorial Director: Andrew Buckley. Publishes hardcover originals. Offers choice of royalty or fee. Advances depend on author's reputation and nature of the book. Fee ranges from $500 to $5,000, depending on the project. Published 65 titles last year. Will send a catalog to a writer on request. Send complete ms or send query with outline and sample chapter. Reports in 2 weeks. Enclose International Reply Coupons for return postage with ms or query.

Reference and Business and Professional: Publishes "management, industrial, and economic information: books, reports, studies, surveys, directories, reference works, and professional work tools for general and specialized industrial markets, e.g., financial and economic, marketing, manufacturing, distribution, administration, etc. Treatment of information is factual, practical, technique-oriented, well-illustrated. A variety of formats are used to suit the information and the market." Current titles are *Director's Guide to U.S.A., Japanese Markets Review, European Financial Analysis* and *Industrial Expansion in Western Europe.*

Textbooks: "Graduate level business, economics for world market."

GRANADA PUBLISHING, 3 Upper James St., Golden Square, London, W1R 4BP, England. Editorial Director, Paperback: A.S. Mehta. For information concerning Hardback Division, contact Michael Dempsey. Publishes paperback originals and reprints. Will consider material previously published in U.S. or Canada offered for first publication in U.K. Royalty contract "varies." Published about 130 titles last year. Submission made by author, his agent, or original publisher. For unpublished material, query first for fiction and children's books; query first with outline and sample chapters for nonfiction. Enclose S.A.E. and International Reply Coupons for response to queries.

General: "General fiction, nonfiction suitable for paperback audience. The paperback division of Granada Publishing consists of 4 imprints: Panther, Mayflower, Dragon, and Paladin. The distinctions are subtle, but material submitted will be routed to the most likely editor."

GEORGE G. HARRAP & CO., LTD., 182-4 High Holborn, London, W.C. 1, England. Editor: Peter Sommer. Established in 1902. Publishes hardcover and paperback originals and reprints. Will consider material previously published in U.S. or Canada offered for first publication in U.K. Royalty "negotiable, but usually not less than 10% of domestic published price." Published 120 titles last year. Submission may be made by the author, his agent, or original publisher. For unpublished material, query first for fiction; submit outline and sample chapters for nonfiction. "In certain instances, books are commissioned jointly by trade and educational editors." Enclose S.A.E. and International Reply Coupons.

General: "Full-length adult and juvenile fiction and nonfiction aimed at middle- to high-brow audience" wanted for previously published material. "We have a catholic taste." Length: 45,000 to 85,000 words.

Textbooks: "Leading modern language textbook publishing house in U.K., with world-famous dictionaries. 60% educational and college."

HART-DAVIS MAC GIBBON, LTD., 3 Upper James St., London, W.C. 1, England. Managing Director: J.C. Reynolds. Established in 1946. Publishes hardcover originals and reprints. Will consider material previously published in U.S. or Canada offered for first publication in U.K. "Normal royalties are 10% to 15% on a rising scale." Will send a catalog to a writer on request. Submit outline and sample chapters or complete ms for nonfiction; submit complete ms for fiction. Enclose S.A.E. and International Reply Coupons.

General: "Archaeology, biography, children's books, fiction, history, politics, sociology, science, travel and adventure. All high standards only."

INTER-AMERICAN UNIVERSITY PRESS (formerly Editorial de la Universidad), P.O. Box 1239, Hato Rey PR 00919. Editor: John Zebrowski. Publishes hardcover and paperback originals. Royalty schedule; 50% on all subsidiary rights. Advance is negotiable according to author and subject. Send query or complete ms for nonfiction; send query first for fiction of novel length; send complete ms for short fiction. Send 2 copies of ms. Reports in 10 to 12 weeks.

General: Will consider mss in all areas for science, philosophy, the arts, history, political science, and general nonfiction. "Preference given to Puerto Rican, Caribbean, Latin American or inter-American orientation." Word length is "flexible."

DERIC ROBERT JAMES, 118 Windham Road, Bournemouth, Hampshire, England. Editor: Deric Robert James. Publishes paperback originals. Established in 1967. Published 4 books last year. Will send catalog to writer on request. Will consider unpublished material offered for first time publication. Submission of unpublished material may be made directly by the author. Query first, submit outline and sample chapters, or submit complete ms for nonfiction. Royalty payment by arrangment.
Nonfiction, Occult: "We consider only nonfiction general articles on all topics of occultism, especially cults and societies and ceremonial magic. Must be accompanied by photograph or sketch to illustrate same. Ceremonial magic and witchcraft. Not first hand accounts but general in style. Length: 10,000 words maximum."

KOTHARI PUBLICATIONS, Jute House, 12 India Exchange Place, Calcutta, 1, India. Editor: Ing. H. Kothari. Send outline. Enclose International Reply Coupons.
Reference, Technical, Scientific, and Business and Professional: Publishes "mainly reference works."

MACDONALD AND CO. PUBLISHERS, LTD., Technical and Scientific Dept., 49/50 Poland St., London, W1A 2LG, England. Editor: W. John Redman. Established in 1938. Publishes hardcover originals and reprints. Will consider material (especially computer books) previously published in U.S. or Canada offered for first publication in U.K. For previously published material, "we usually buy bulk sheets or bound copy with price inclusive of royalty from American publishers." Pays royalties of 10% of published price for unpublished material. Published 40 titles last year. Will send a catalog to a writer on request. Submissions may be made by author, author's agent or original publisher. Enclose S.A.E. and International Reply Coupons with ms.
Scientific and Technical: "Subjects: computers (programming and science), mathematics, physics, chemistry. Emphasis is on textbook learning. The audience is undergraduate and post-graduate students and academic staff. Length is unimportant. The department is quite small, but has a good reputation for books on all aspects of computers. Almost all of our books are aimed at the university and college market."

MACDONALD & EVANS, 8 John St., London, W.C. 1, England. Managing Director: G.B. Davis. Established in 1908. Publishes hardcover and paperback originals and reprints. Will consider material previously published in U.S. or Canada offered for first publication in U.K. Offers royalty payment "according to title, author, market, and format. Sometimes 7½% flat; 10% flat (paperback)." Published 50 titles last year. Will send a catalog to a writer on request. Submission may be made by the author or the original publisher. Submit outline and sample chapters for unpublished material. Enclose S.A.E. and International Reply Coupons.
Textbooks: Commerce, management, professional studies; geography, geology; movement and movement notation; technical and scientific. Level: final years at high school, university, technical colleges. Length: 10,000 to 250,000 words. "Most titles are commissioned. Length would be stated in the contract."

FREDERICK MULLER LTD., 110 Fleet St., London, EC4A 2AP, England. Editor: Paul Barnett. Established in 1934. Publishes hardcover and paperback originals and hardcover reprints. Will consider material previously published in U.S. or Canada offered for first publication "in U.K. publishers' traditional market but prefer world rights." Royalty contract "depends on the book." Published 60 titles last year. Submission may be made by the author, his agent, or the original publisher. Enclose S.A.E. and International Reply Coupons with ms.
Nonfiction: "Science and technology, militaria, sociology, the occult. Basically interested in books for specialist markets rather than for the general reader, although the latter are occasionally considered. We are gaining a reputation for first rate books for collectors, books on the occult, and in the field of anthropology."
Juveniles: "Juvenile nonfiction, particularly for young children and backward readers. Length: open. Our children's books have always had a high reputation."

NAUTICAL PUBLISHING CO. LTD., Nautical House, Lymington, Hampshire, SO4 9BA, England. Editors. Erroll Bruce, Richard Creagh-Osborne, Peter Johnson, Adlard Coles. Established in 1967. Publishes hardcover originals and reprints. Will consider material previously published in U.S. or Canada offered for first publication in U.K. Royalty for previously published material "negotiated, but normally 10% royalty on English home sales"; for unpublished material, royalty "dependent on authority of author and the status of his previous books, but about 10% royalty for English home sales." Published 13 titles last year. Will send a catalog to a writer on request. Submission may be made by the author or the original publisher. For unpublished material, query first with outline and sample chapters. Enclose S.A.E. and International Reply Coupons with ms.
Nonfiction: "All types of nautical books with international significance, particularly yachting books by authors of proven international achievement in their subject. Nautical is a specialized house, owned by partners who themselves take part in international competitive yachting and also its honorary administration. Each has written successful books of his own."

OUTPOSTS PUBLICATIONS, 72 Burwood Rd., Walton-on-Thames, Surrey, England. Editor: Howard Sergeant. Established in 1943. Publishes hardcover and paperback originals. Royalties "by arrangement." Published 60 titles last year. Enclose S.A.E. and International Reply Coupons with ms.
Poetry: "Collections of poetry by individual poets."

STANLEY PAUL & COMPANY LIMITED, 3, Fitzroy Square, London W1P 6JD, England. Editor: R.B. Bloomfield. Publishes hardcover and paperback originals and reprints. Advance: 350 pounds. Royalties: 10%, 12½%, 15%. Published 40 books last year. Will send catalog to writer on request. Submit outline and sample chapters for all material. Will consider photocopied submissions.
Sport and Leisure: "Biographies and instructional books. Ms should be readable, in practical language, comprehensive and not jargonistic. Instructional, do-it-yourself and hobbies. Practical and technical subjects should be made readable and comprehensive without becoming over-simplified." Biography, cookbooks, humor, reference, self-help and how-to, and sports, hobbies, recreation and pets are subjects also considered. Length: 30,000 to 100,000 words. Recent titles include *Practical Golf* (Jacobs), and *Creative Flower Arrangement* (Taylor).

PELHAM BOOKS LTD., 52 Bedford Square, London, WC1B 3EF, England. Editor and Managing Director: William Luscombe. Established in 1963. Publishes hardcover originals and reprints. Will consider material previously published in U.S. or Canada offered for first publication in British Commonwealth. "Royalties subject to negotiation, depending on material." Published 90 titles last year. Will send a catalog to a writer on request. Submission may be made by the author ("if he controls British rights"), his agent, or original publisher. For unpublished material, query first with outline and sample chapters. Enclose S.A.E. and International Reply Coupons.
Nonfiction: For previously published material, wants material on "sports, hobbies, crafts, recreational books. Must have general interest, not solely U.S. interest. For ages 14 to 90. and up. Length: about 50,000 words with illustrations." For unpublished material, interested in "encyclopedias, practical books on sports and hobbies, autobiographies by leading sportsmen and sportswomen, books about the countryside and natural history, and books on crafts and of practical use in and around the home. Length: about 50,000 words with illustrations."

THOMAS REED PUBLICATIONS, LTD., 36-37 Cock Lane, Snow Hill, London, EC1A 9BY, England. Editor: Kenneth D. Troup. Publishes hardcover and paperback originals. Offers standard royalty contract. Submit outline and sample chapter. Enclose S.A.E. and International Reply Coupons.
Nonfiction: "Marine only."

RIDER AND COMPANY, Hutchinson Publishing Group, Ltd., 3 Fitzroy Square, London, W1P 6JD, England. Editor: Daniel Brostoff. Publishes hardcover and paperback originals and reprints. Offers 10% royalty contract. Published 6 books last year. Query first with outline and sample chapters. Enclose S.A.E. and International Reply Coupons.

Nonfiction: "Subjects: meditation, mysticism, Hinduism (including yoga), Buddhism, and other aspects of Oriental religion and philosophy. We aim to produce works of vigor and quality for 2 broad groups of people: absolute beginners in the quest for increased self-awareness who need some guidance in selecting the most suitable path, and advanced students who require critical commentaries and translations of original texts. In both cases, the writers need to be accomplished in a spiritual sense and have a masterly command of the subject matter. The ability to explain complex matters cogently and concisely is a prerequisite." Length: 50,000 to 90,000 words. Recent titles include *Buddhism, an Outline of Its Teaching and Schools* (Schumann), *Free of Life: Introduction to the Cabala* (Haleir), *The Other Universe* (Sinclair).

BARRY ROSE PUBLISHERS, Little London, Chichester, Sussex, England. Editor: Barry Rose. Publishes hardcover and paperback originals. Pays 10% "ordinarily," but if joint authorship, pays 12%. Advance negotiable. Published 21 books last year. Will send catalog to writer on request. Query first or submit outline and sample chapters. Will consider photocopied submissions. Reports in 6 weeks. Enclose S.A.E. and International Reply Coupons.

General Nonfiction: "We publish books on law and local government; sometimes legal history and legal and local government humor. Audience would be almost entirely professional lawyers, administrators, and treasurers. Always interested in short (14,000 words maximum) booklets describing various aspects of crime, punishment, law, and local government. Also publish longer length books." Recent titles include: *Criminal Jurisdiction of Magistrates* (Harris) and *Local Authorities' Powers of Purchase* (Wisdom).

SEVENSEAS PUBLISHING PTY., LTD., 5-7 Tory St., Wellington, New Zealand. Editor: Murdoch Riley. Publishes hardcover and paperback originals. Offers standard royalty contract; "have done subsidy publishing." Published 4 titles last year. Query first with outline and sample chapter. Reports "as soon as considered." Enclose International Reply Coupons for return postage. "We return mss by sea to overseas addresses unless postage for return mail is forwarded."

Fiction and Nonfiction: Publishes "books on the South Pacific, craft, music." Length: 10,000 words minimum; no maximum. Recent titles include: *Fiji, I Love You Full Speed* and *Primitive Art of the New Zealand Maori.*

SOUVENIR PRESS, LTD., 95 Mortimer St., London, W1N 8HP, England. Executive Director: Ernest Hecht. Publishes hardcover and paperback originals, translations, and anthologies. Offers standard royalty contract. Published 35 titles last year. Will send a catalog to a writer on request. Send complete ms. Enclose International Reply Coupons for return postage with mss.

General: Publishes books "on all subjects with the emphasis on books suitable for bestseller promotion. Especially interested in nonfiction documentaries."

TEXTILE TRADE PRESS, 11 Albert Square, Manchester, M2 5HD, England. Established in 1966. Publishes hardcover and paperback originals. Royalty contract "negotiable." Royalty or fee or lower fee with royalty after agreed volume of sales. Published 3 titles last year. Will send a catalog to a writer on request. Enclose S.A.E. and International Reply Coupons with ms.

Nonfiction: "Anything relating to textiles, fibres, marketing thereof, etc. Textile Trade Press concentrates entirely on technical and marketing mss concerning the textile industry in all its aspects. It is a small, specialized, and highly individualized organization." Length: 50,000 words minimum.

THORSONS PUBLISHERS LTD., Denington Estate, Wellingborough, Northants, NN8 2RQ England. Established in 1930. Publishes hardcover and paperback originals and reprints. Will consider material previously published in U.S. or Canada offered for first publication in England. Payment to be negotiated for published material; for unpublished material, offers "10% royalty for hardcovers, 8% royalty for paperbacks." Published about 80 titles last year. Submission may be made by the author, his agent, or original publisher. For unpublished material, submit com-

plete ms. Enclose S.A.E. and International Reply Coupons with ms.
General Nonfiction. "We are publishers of books on general subjects—nonfiction only. We are interested in mss on health, dietetics, herbalism, psychology and self-improvement, yoga, hypnotism, and acupuncture."

TRANSWORLD PUBLISHERS LTD. (A Subsidiary of Bantam Books Inc.), Cavendish House, 57/59 Uxbridge Road, London W.5, England. Editor: Michael R. Legat. Publishes paperback originals and reprints. Established in 1950. Pays 7½% of published price on U.K. sales; 6% of published price on other sales. Query first. Enclose S.A.E. and International Reply Coupons for response to query.
General Fiction and Nonfiction: "Popular fiction and nonfiction for the entertainment market. High quality essential; no pornography. Not less than 35,000 words."

TRITON PUBLISHING CO. LTD., 1-A Montagu Mews North, London, W.1, England. Editor: Mrs. C. Whitaker. Established in 1963. Publishes hardcover originals and reprints. Will consider material previously published in U.S. or Canada offered for first publication in U.K. and British Commonwealth. "Royalties usually start at 10%; we offer an advance against royalties." Published 6 titles last year. Will send a catalog to a writer on request. Enclose S.A.E. and International Reply Coupons with ms.
General: "General fiction of high quality and nonfiction of general interest (biographies, etc.) Length: 50,000 to 100,000 words."

TURNSTONE BOOKS, 37 Upper Addison Gardens, London, W14 8AJ, England. Editor: Alick Bartholomew. Publishes hardcover and paperback originals and reprints. Established in 1971. Offers "standard British scale of royalties: 10% of list to 2,500 copies, 12½% on next 3,000 copies, and 15% thereafter. First list of 4 books appeared in 1972." Publishes 20 books a year. Will send a catalog to a writer on request. Query first with outline and sample chapter. Follow Chicago *Manual of Style*. Enclose S.A.E. and International Reply Coupons with query.
Nonfiction: "Popular, informative books for the general market in the areas of metaphysics, cosmology, prehistory, healing, parapsychology. Emphasis on originality, integrity, and controversiality, with high standard of writing and international interest." Length: 60,000 to 120,000 words.

CHARLES E. TUTTLE CO., INC., 2-6, Suido 1-chome, Bunkyo-ku, Tokyo 112, Japan. President: Charles E. Tuttle. Publishes hardcover and paperback originals and reprints. Offers 10% basic royalty, with advance.
General Nonfiction: "We are especially interested in books on the Asian area and books on any aspects of collecting; anything from buttons through Chinese bronzes, toy soldiers, etc."

VALLENTINE, MITCHELL & CO. LTD., 67 Great Russell St., London, WC1B 3BT, England. Editor-in-Chief: Jeremy Robson. Publishes hardcover and paperback originals, reprints, translations, anthologies. Offers standard royalty contract. Published 30 titles last year. Will send a catalog to a writer on request. Send query with outline and sample chapter or complete ms. Reports in 4 to 6 weeks. Enclose International Reply Coupons for return postage.
General Fiction, General Nonfiction, History and Biography: "General publishers, biography, history. Specialists in books of Jewish interest." Current titles include *The Champagne Spy* (Lotz), *One More River* (Banks).

VISION PRESS LTD., 157 Knightsbridge, London, SW1X 7PA, England. Editor: Miss Norma O'Lea. Established in 1946. Publishes hardcover originals and reprints. Will consider material previously published in U.S. or Canada offered for first publication in the U.K. and British Commonwealth. For previously published material, "we normally buy sheets from U.S. publishers inclusive of royalties"; for unpublished books, offers average 10% royalties "with advance rarely given, and then only minimal." Published 14 titles last year. Will send a catalog to a writer on request. Enclose S.A.E. and International Reply Coupons with ms.
Nonfiction: "We are a small nonfiction publisher with a reputation for publishing well-produced, interesting titles with specialist appeal. We do not want books on specifically American subjects. Books with a wide appeal to students and well-in-

formed lay readership are welcomed." Is interested in unpublished books on "art, education, film, history, literary criticism, music, philosophy, psychology, religion, science, and theater."

Syndicates

GRAHAM & HEATHER FISHER LTD., 29 Forest Drive, Keston, Kent, England BR2 6EE. "We place material in Britain, Europe and the British Commonwealth, selling it to top magazines in each country." Pays 50% though "we sometimes pay on acceptance for shorter articles. Payment for these is $75 to $150." Submit query with brief outline. "We prefer articles that have already sold in U.S. or Canada, but will also consider original material if subject is right." Enclose S.A.E. and International Reply Coupons for reply to query.
General Nonfiction: "Most of the magazines are aimed at women and it follows that so is the material we seek; celebrity life stories, celebrity interviews, stories of physical and emotional adventure involving women; in fact, almost any popular-type article which might appeal to the young marrieds or unmarrieds. But not articles about cooking, beauty, interior decoration, or other similar subjects which magazines prefer written by their own staffs." Length: one-shots, 1,000 to 4,000 words. Series, 3,000 to 3,500 words per part.

INTERNATIONAL NEWS SERVICE LTD., Central Post Office Box 1651, Tokyo, Japan. Editor: Miss Hiroko Nishigaki. Buys one-time production rights in Japan only. Buys about 250 to 300 features a year from freelancers.
Nonfiction and Photos: "Color transparency for record jacket, poster, calendar, cover, and editorial. By-line features of international interests." Layout in color of Steve McQueen's home and color layouts of Elvis Presley are examples of single features handled recently. "Interested in article series about secret of Kennedy's family, inside report of White House, or how-to sex articles. Photos are purchased with features, with or without captions." 4x5, 6x6, and 35mm specifications. Usual outlets for material syndicated: posters, own cover, magazine, commercial, and advertisement. Pays 30% commission.

MAHARAJAH FEATURES PRIVATE LTD., 5/226 Sion Road East, Bombay-22; India. Editor: Mrs. Janaki Swamy. Supplies material to "major journals in Europe, British Commonwealth, India, and southeast Asia." Buys all rights. Query first— "summary advisable." Returns rejected material in 2 weeks "by surface mail." Enclose S.A.E. and International Reply Coupons for reply to queries.
Nonfiction: "Features of general interest, especially pertaining to India. It is essential that the features do not become dated or obsolete. We will buy single features on interesting places, monuments, historical events, and exotic subjects. Subjects like 'how rich were the maharajahs' or 'they wanted to build another Taj Mahal.' Crisp style; exotic, interesting subjects." Length: 1,000 to 1,500 words. "Should be accompanied by 1 or 2 photos. Uses b&w glossies, color transparencies, color prints." Payment "depends on the articles—usually 50% commission or outright purchase."

A Glossary of Publishing Terms

(and other expressions used in this directory).

All rights—author gives the publisher complete rights for any use of his material and forfeits any further use of that same material by himself.

Assignment—editor asks a writer to do a specific article for which he usually names a price for the completed manuscript.

B&W—abbreviation for black and white photograph.

Bimonthly—every two months. See also semimonthly.

Biweekly—every two weeks.

Blue-pencilling—editing a manuscript.

Caption—originally a title or headline over a picture but now a description of the subject matter of a photograph, including names of people where appropriate. Also called cutline.

Chapbook—a small booklet, usually paperback, of poetry, ballads or tales.

Chicago Manual of Style—a format for the typing of manuscripts as established by the University of Chicago Press (Chicago, 60637, revised 12th edition, $10).

Clean copy—free of errors, cross-outs, wrinkles, smudges.

Clippings—of news items of possible interest to trade magazine editors.

Column inch—all the type contained in one inch of a newspaper column.

Comp copy—means complimentary copy.

Contributors' copies—copies of the issues of a magazine in which an author's work appears.

Copy editing—editing the manuscript for grammar, punctuation and printing style as opposed to subject content.

Copyright—under the present law is for 28 years with one renewal for 28 years. Since 1962, Congress has been considering revising the Copyright Law and has been automatically extending any copyrights which might have expired since 1962.

Correspondent—writer away from the home office of a newspaper or magazine who regularly provides it with copy.

Epigram—a short, witty, sometimes paradoxical saying.

Fair use—a provision of the Copyright Law that says short passages from copyrighted material may be used without infringing on the owner's rights. There are no set number of words. A good rule of thumb: "Does my use of this copyrighted material impair the market value of the original?"

Feature—an article, usually with human interest, giving the reader background information on the news. Also used by magazines to indicate a lead article or distinctive department.

Filler—a short item used by an editor to "fill" out a newspaper column or a page in a magazine. It could be a timeless news item, a joke, an anecdote, some light verse or short humor, a puzzle, etc.

First North American serial rights—the right to first publish an article, story or poem in a copyrighted newspaper or magazine in the U.S. or Canada.

Formula story—familiar theme treated in a predictable plot structure—such as boy meets girl, boy loses girl, boy gets girl.

Gagline—the caption for a cartoon, or the cover teaser line and the punchline on the inside of a studio greeting card.

Ghostwriter—a writer who puts into literary form, an article, speech, story or book based on another person's ideas or knowledge.

Glossy—a black and white photograph with a shiny surface as opposed to one with a non-shiny matte finish.

Gothic novel—one in which the central character is usually a beautiful young girl, the setting is an old mansion or castle; there is a handsome hero and a real menace, either natural or supernatural.

Honorarium—a token payment. It may be a very small amount of money, or simply a byline and copies of the publication in which your material appears.

Horizontal publication—usually a trade magazine, published for readers in a specific job function in a variety of industries. For example, *Purchasing Magazine.* (See also vertical publication.)

House organ—a company publication: internal—for employees only; external for customers, stockholders, etc., or a combination publication to serve both purposes.

Illustrations—may be photographs, old engravings, artwork. Usually paid for separately from the manuscript. See also "package sale."

International Postal Reply Coupons—can be purchased at your local post office and enclosed with your letter or manuscript to a foreign publisher to cover his postage cost when replying.

Invasion of privacy—cause for suits against some writers who have written about persons (even though truthfully) without their consent.

Kill fee—a portion of the agreed-on price for a complete article that was assigned but which was subsequently cancelled.

Libel—a false accusation; or any published statement or presentation that tends to expose another to public contempt, ridicule, etc. Defenses are truth; fair comment on a matter of public interest; and privileged communication—such as a report of legal proceedings or a client's communication to his lawyer.

Little magazines—publications of limited circulation, usually on literary or political subject matter.

MLA Style Sheet—a format for the typing of manuscripts established by the Modern Language Association (62 Fifth Ave., New York NY 10011, 2nd edition $1.25).

Model release—a paper signed by the subject of a photograph (or his guardian, if a juvenile) giving the photographer permission to use the photograph, editorially or for advertising purposes or for some specific purpose as stated.

Ms—abbreviation for manuscript.

Mss—abbreviation for more than one manuscript.

Multiple submissions—some editors of non-overlapping circulation magazines, such as religious publications, are willing to look at manuscripts which have also been submitted to other editors at the same time. See individual listings for which editors these are. No multiple submissions should be made to larger markets paying good prices for original material, unless it is a query on a highly topical article requiring an immediate response and that fact is so stated in your letter.

Newsbreak—a newsworthy event or item. For example, a clipping about the opening of a new shoe store in a town might be a newsbreak of interest to a trade journal in the shoe industry. Some editors also use the word to mean funny typographical errors.

Novelette—a short novel, or a long short story; 7,000 to 15,000 words approximately.

Offprint—reprints of a published article, story, poem.

Offset—type of printing in which copy and illustrations are photographed and plates made, from which printing is done; as opposed to letterpress printing directly from type metal and engravings of illustrations.

On assignment—the editor asks you to do a specific article for which he pays an agreed-on rate.

On speculation—the editor is willing to look at an article or story manuscript but does not promise to buy it, until he reads it.

One-time rights—is a phrase used by some publications, especially newspapers, to indicate that after they use the story, the writer is free to resell it elsewhere, outside their circulation area, after they've published it. It is not the same as "first rights" since they may be buying one-time rights to a story that has already appeared in some other publication outside their area.

Outline—of a book is usually a one-page summary of its contents; often in the form of chapter headings with a descriptive sentence or two under each one to show the scope of the book.

Package sale—the editor wants to buy manuscript and photos as a "package" and pay for them in one check.

Page rate—some magazines pay for material at a fixed rate per published page, rather than so much per word.

Payment on acceptance—the editor sends you a check for your article, story or poem as soon as he reads it and decides to publish it.

Payment on publication—the editor decides to buy your material but doesn't send you a check until he publishes it.

Pen name—the use of a name other than your legal name on articles, stories, or books where you wish to remain anonymous. Simply notify your post office and bank that you are using the name so that you'll properly receive mail and/or checks in that name.

Photo story—a feature in which the emphasis is on the photographs rather than any accompanying written material.

Photocopied submissions—are acceptable to some editors instead of the author's sending his original manuscript. See also multiple submissions.

Piracy—infringement of copyright.

Pix—an abbreviation for the plural of photo.

Plagiarism—passing off as one's own, the expression of ideas, words of another.

Primary sources—of research are original letters and documents, as opposed to published articles, books, etc.

Pseudonym—see pen name.

Public domain—material which was either never copyrighted or whose copyright term has run out.

Publication not copyrighted—publication of an author's work in such a publication places it in the public domain, and it cannot subsequently be copyrighted. Poets especially should watch this point if they hope to republish their work elsewhere.

Query—a letter of inquiry to an editor eliciting his interest in an article you want to write.

Qualified freelancer—a professional writer who has published work in the specific field in which the editor is seeking material.

Reporting times—the number of days, weeks, etc., it takes an editor to report back to the author on his query or manuscript.

Reprint rights—the right to reprint an article, story, poem that originally appeared in another publication.

Retention rights—you agree to let a magazine hold your article or story or poem for a length of time to see if they can find space to publish it. Since this keeps you from selling it elsewhere (and they might subsequently decide to return it), we don't advocate this practice.

Round-up article—comments from, or interviews with, a number of celebrities or experts on a single theme.

Royalties, standard hardcover book—10% of the retail price on the first 5,000 copies sold; 12½% on the next 5,000, and 15% thereafter.

Royalties, standard mass paperback book—4 to 8% of the retail price on the first 150,000 copies sold.

Runover—the copy in the back of a magazine continued from a story or article featured in the main editorial section.

S.A.E.—self-addressed envelope.

S.A.S.E.—self-addressed, stamped envelope.

Sample copies—will be sent free to writers by some editors; others require sample copy price and/or postage. See individual listings.

Second serial rights—publication in a newspaper or magazine after the material has already appeared elsewhere. Usually used to refer to the sale of a part of a book to a newspaper or magazine after the book has been published, whether or not there was any first serial publication.

Semimonthly—twice a month.

Semiweekly—twice a week.

Serial—published periodically, such as a newspaper or magazine.

Shelter books—magazines that concentrate on home decoration.

Short-short story—is usually from 500 to 2,000 words.

Short story—averages 2,000 to 3,500 words.

Simultaneous submissions—submissions of the same article, story or poem to smaller magazines with non-competing circulations and whose editors have agreed to accept same.

Slides—usually called transparencies by editors looking for color photographs.

Speculation—the editor agrees to look at the author's manuscript but doesn't promise to buy it until he reads it.

Special 4th class rate—manuscripts—can be used by writers submitting articles, stories, books to publishers. Rate is 14¢ for first pound, 7¢ each additional pound with an extra 8¢ if first class letter is enclosed. (These are rates for mailing in U.S. Consult Post Office for Special Foreign Rates.) Be sure to add "Return Postage Guaranteed" on your outside envelope; otherwise Post Office is not obliged to return to you if for some reason package is undeliverable.

Stringer—a writer who submits material to a magazine or newspaper from a specific geographical location.

Subsidiary rights—all those rights, other than book publishing rights included in a book contract—such as paperback, book club, movie rights, etc.

Subsidy publisher—a book publisher who charges the author for the cost to typeset and print his book, the jacket, etc., as opposed to a royalty publisher which pays the author.

Syndication rights—a book publisher may sell the rights to a newspaper syndicate to print a book in installments in one or more newspapers.

Tabloids—newspaper format publication on about half the size of the regular newspaper page. A group of publications in this format on major newsstands, such as *National Enquirer*.

Tagline—an editorial comment on a filler, such as those in *The New Yorker*. In some contexts, it is also used to mean a descriptive phrase associated with a certain person, such as newscaster John Cameron Swayze's "Glad we could get together . . ."

Tearsheet—pages from a magazine or newspaper containing your printed story or article or poem.

Think piece—a magazine article that has an intellectual, philosophical, provocative approach to its subject.

Topical—very timely, of current news interest.

Transparencies—positive color slides; not color prints.

Uncopyrighted publication—such as most newspapers or small poetry and literary magazines. Publication of an author's work in such publications puts it in the public domain.

Unsolicited manuscripts—a story or article or poem or book that an editor did not specifically ask to see, as opposed to one he did write the author and ask for.

Vanity publisher—same as subsidy publisher. One who publishes books for an author who pays the production cost himself.

Vertical publication—a publication for all the people in a variety of job functions within the same industry, such as *Aviation Week and Space Technology* or *Hospitals*.

Vignette—a brief scene offering the reader a flash of illumination about a character as opposed to a more formal story with a beginning, middle and end.

INDEX